Computers and End-User Software with BASIC

THIRD EDITION

Computers and End-User Software with BASIC

Thomas H. Athey
California State Polytechnic University at Pomona

John C. Day
Ohio University

Robert W. Zmud
Florida State University

HarperCollins*Publishers*

Sponsoring Editor: Rick Williamson
Development Editor: Trish Nealon
Project Coordination: Business Media Resources/Melanie Field
Text and Cover Design: John Edeen
Text Art: Winston Sin
Photo Research: Judy Mason
Production: Michael Weinstein
Composition: Terri Wright, Richard Palmer, and Winston Sin
Printer and Binder: R.R. Donnelley & Sons, Company
Cover Printer: The Lehigh Press, Inc.

For permission to use copyrighted material, grateful acknowledgment is made to the copyright holders on pp. R-2, which are hereby made part of this copyright page.

Computers and End-User Software with BASIC, Third Edition

Library of Congress Cataloging-in-Publication Data

Athey, Thomas H.
Computers and End-User Software with BASIC/Thomas H. Athey, John Day, Robert W. Zmud. — 3rd ed.
p. cm.
Includes bibliographical references and index.
1. Electronic digital computers. 2. Microcomputers. 3. Application software. 4. BASIC (Computer program language) I. Day, John C. (John Charles), 1956 II. Zmud, Robert W., 1946- . III. Title.
QA76.5.A7786 1991 90-20489
004. 16 — dc20 CIP

ISBN 0-673-46421-0 (student edition)
ISBN 0-673-46510-1 (teacher edition)

91 92 93 94 9 8 7 6 5 4 3 2 1

Brief Contents

Contents

Preface

Today educators are finding it increasingly easy to convince students they should learn about computers. Indeed, the demand for this knowledge is growing almost as fast as the number of computer products and applications. It is less easy to decide what—or how—to teach these students. Many textbooks focus on the "what"—computers and information systems in and of themselves. We call this the "computer literacy" approach and we feel that it neglects the "why"—the reasons we use computers.

We wanted to write a book that was different. All of us feel a strong conviction that today's students need *computing literacy*, the ability to use the computer as a tool to enrich their personal and professional lives. As computers become more common, the likelihood increases that students will need to understand and use computers in their careers, even if they do not become computer professionals. Like many employees, they may someday find themselves on a steering committee charged with developing or evaluating a computer application.

Our goal in this book is to help students become informed consumers of computer technology and information systems. This goal is expressed in four major ways:

- *Emphasis on end-user computing*. Recent technological advances in producing high-powered, but inexpensive, microcomputers have combined with increased availability of low-cost, but powerful, software packages to usher in the era of end-user computing. The *end-user*, usually a business professional, interacts directly with the computer through the use of commercial software packages to develop his or her own computerized applications. In Part IV, "End-User Software," we examine word processing, electronic spreadsheets, database management systems, graphics, and data communication packages. Our emphasis is not on the keystrokes required for specific packages, but rather on giving the student an understanding of the important features of each type of software. We illustrate these points by using practical examples and showing screens from popular software packages. Additionally, there is a separate chapter that provides students with a framework for understanding the importance of decision support and expert systems in today's business.
- *Role of end-users in CIS development*. It is important for students to understand that as business professionals they will also need to work with CIS professionals in developing important business applications that affect many functional areas. In Part III, "Computer Information System Development," we discuss the complementary roles of end-user computing and what we call *CIS computing*. The traditional topics of systems development, file and database systems, and program development and languages are discussed from the perspective of what the end-user needs to know to be an effective project team member.

- *Integration of technology and its applications.* We also made a commitment to focus on applications and to explain how technology affects our use of computers. Thus, every major discussion of technology is illustrated by an application. This deliberate integration can be seen in "Special Feature: A Systems Approach to Selecting a Microcomputer," which shows students how to apply systems development techniques to their own computer-selection decisions.

- *Understandable depth.* Each topic is approached with the goal of giving students the information they need to be able to understand the ways computers and information systems can be used to improve our lives. This does not mean, however, that we avoid technical detail or ignore recent advances. As required by today's computing environment, we explain the workings of the most recent technological advances. We are also careful to show students what these technologies mean to the users of computers and information systems.

We also developed some recurring features to help us meet our goal:

- *A "Computers at Work" feature* at the close of each chapter excerpts an article from a business or computer magazine that shows the varied, real-world uses of computers or presents an advanced issue related to the content of the chapter.

- *Full-color illustrations* explain and clarify both technical processes and business procedures. Color photographs of computer applications are most useful when integrated within the text rather than grouped in isolated collages. Thus, the text features a functional, as well as attractive, illustration program interwoven with the text.

In addition, we have provided a number of study aids to reinforce important text concepts, including chapter outlines, bold-faced key terms, detailed chapter summaries with key terms reviewed in context, expanded end-of-chapter review questions with both multiple choice and true-false questions. Our text is also offered in two versions: one with appendices introducing popular software packages, and one without these appendices.

The Third Edition

In a field that is changing as rapidly as computer information systems, keeping abreast of current developments is critically important. Thus, discussions of technology are completely updated in the second edition. New "Computers at Work" articles are included and exhibits have been updated. Coverage in Part IV, "End-User Software," has been expanded to include discussions of the Macintosh computer and related software. The special feature "Careers in Computing" includes the latest information on the types of careers available to CIS professionals or business professionals in the computing field.

Although 30 to 40 percent of the book has been updated or changed, it maintains the technical accuracy, clarity of explanation and the helpfulness of exhibits that was so well received in the first two editions. Further, the level of discussion has been simplified somewhat, without sacrificing the quality of the discussion.

The Supplement Program

The introductory computer course in a business program is no longer a theory course. Most schools have microcomputer laboratories in which students can gain hands-on experience through computer exercises that use practical applications. *Computers and End-user Software* is accompanied by a full range of supplements to meet the needs of both instructors and students. These ancillary materials include both innovative software teaching aids and outstanding text-related materials.

Textbook Support Materials

A full complement of traditional supplements accompany this book:

- The *Instructor's Manual* provides an overview and summary of each text chapter, lecture outlines, ideas for lecture and discussion, and answers to in-text review questions.
- The *Test File* contains approximately twenty-five true/false and sixty multiple-choice items for each chapter. These same questions are available through the HarperTest classroom management software.

The HarperTest program is a computerized test generator that allows instructors to create and edit exams flexibly and easily. HarperTest operates on any IBM PC or compatible microcomputer with 512K of memory. It features an extensive Item Bank of test questions keyed to the text. Questions from the Item Bank may be fully edited using the program, or instructors may create their own Item Bank of test questions. Instructors may also assign up to nine criteria to each question in an Item Bank and then select items for their exams by matching any combination of those criteria using the program's search feature. Tests may be saved in ASCII format and may be edited and reformatted using many popular word processing programs. Printing options allow instructors to customize the order of the test questions and the amount of work space for each item. HarperTest is compatible with the HP LaserJet printer and many other popular printers. It is available to adopters free of charge.

- To enhance classroom lectures, a package of full-color, professional prepared *Overhead Transparencies* are provided to adopters.
- The *Study Guide* includes chapter summaries, detailed annotated chapter outlines, drill sections made up of fill-in-the-blank, matching, short-answer, and essay questions, and practice tests.

Software Package Instruction

- *Up & Running with DOS, WordPerfect, Lotus 1-2-3 and dBASE IV*, by Thomas W. Warrner and D. Michael Werner of InfoSource, Inc., is a step-by-step, hands-on guide to these four software packages. It provides the basic commands, functions, and menu procedures to enable students to use the software quickly and with a minimum of frustration. This software guide can be packaged with the text for students who need an overview of these software packages.

- *Using DOS*, by Thomas W. Warrner and D. Michael Werner, features step-by-step command procedures for introductory and advanced users of DOS. This guide can be packaged with the text for students who need an in-depth knowledge of DOS commands and structures. A demonstration diskette is available with the guide.

- *Using Lotus 1-2-3*, by D. Michael Werner and Thomas W. Warrner, contains introductory and advanced material on Lotus 1-2-3. A demonstration diskette that illustrates the key features and functions of the program, as well as prebuilt student work files, is available to users of the guide.

- *Using WordPerfect*, by Thomas W. Warrner and D. Michael Werner, is a detailed guide to this word processing package. This text is also offered with a demonstration diskette and prebuilt student work files, so that the student does not have to master keyboarding before understanding the software.

- *Using dBASE IV*, by D. Michael Werner and Thomas W. Warrner, contains introductory and advanced material on the latest version of this powerful database package. It comes with a demonstration diskette and can be packaged with the textbook.

Software Tutorials and BASIC Programming Instruction

Computers and End-User Software, Third Edition, is available in two versions: one with software tutorials and a BASIC appendix and one without. In the larger version, the four tutorial appendices provide an introduction to DOS 3.3, WordPerfect 5.1, Lotus 2.2, and dBASE IV. Each appendix is designed as a keystroke guide to these specific packages and will help students practice the concepts introduced in the text chapters covering microcomputer operating systems, word processing, electronic spreadsheets, and databases.

At the introductory level, the BASIC appendix provides examples of control structures common to all programming languages through its emphasis on structured programming and design. Its exercises gradually build in difficulty up to the presentation of a complete, short program. This important material has been totally rewritten for this edition by John Day.

Acknowledgments

To Our Publisher and Families

It is a rare experience for authors to work with a team of professionals who are committed to excellence in everything they do. We were privileged to become part of the HarperCollins team. We thank Rick Williamson, acquisitions editor in Computer Information Systems, Trisha Nealon, developmental editor, and Melanie Field, who managed the project through Business Media Resources.

But, most important, we had the understanding and support of our families: Nancy Athey and children Tim, Jay, and Carol; Ruth Day and children Elizabeth, Sam, and Jonathan; and Jo Anne Zmud and children Danny and Jana. Their contributions were invaluable.

To Our Colleagues

We owe a special debt to the many colleagues who reviewed our manuscript and gave us valuable feedback. Special thanks must go to Kate Kaiser, University of Wisconsin at Milwaukee, for her contribution to the special feature on selecting a microcomputer; to Robert F. Zant for his excellent technical comments; and to James Wynne and Fred Scott for their insightful comments on content. To all our reviewers, who critically reviewed significant portions of the manuscript, we extend our gratitude.

Reviewers of the Third Edition

Ernest Bourgeois	Castleton State College
David Callaghan	Bentley College
Jeff Frates	Los Medanos College
Franca Giacomelli	Humber College
Christine Grossman	Schenectady County Community College
Judith Gurka	University of Colorado at Denver
Hank Hartman	Iowa State University
Rebecca Hartman	Iowa State University
Shohreh Hashemi	University of Houston, Downtown
Russell Holingsworth	Tarrant County Community College
Ray Johnston	Coastal Carolina Community College
Richard Kerns	East Carolina State University
Dennis Lundgren	McHenry County College
John Mead	Santa Barbara City College
Mike Michaelson	Palomar College
Douglas Myers	Des Moines Area Community College
Carl Penziul	Corning Community College
Ernie Rilke	William Rainey Harper College
Evelyn Seils	Ulster County Community College
Steven Silva	DeVry Institute, Phoenix

Linda Simmons	Cardinal Stritch College
Jan Truscott	San Joaquin Delta College

Reviewers of Previous Editions

James Adair	Bentley College
Virginia Bender	William Rainey Harper College
Richard Bernardin	Cape Cod Community College
Kathy Blicharz	Pima Community College
James Buxton	Tidewater Community College
Frank E. Cable	Pennsylvania State University
David R. Callaghan	Bentley College
Mary J. Culnan	American University
Branston DiBrell	Metropolitan State College
Richard Fleming	North Lake College
M. H. Goldberg	Pace University
Thomas M. Harris	Ball State University
Jean Margaret Hynes	University of Illinois at Chicago
Peter L. Irwin	Richland College
Durward P. Jackson	California State University, Los Angeles
Richard Kapperman	El Camino College
James Kasum	University of Wisconsin, Milwaukee
Richard Kerns	East Carolina University
James Kho	California State University, Sacramento
Lyle Langlois	Glendale Community College
Jeffrey L. Mock	Diablo Valley College
Patrick Olson	California State University, Pomona
Christopher W. Pidgeon	California State Polytechnic University
Janet Pipkin	University of South Florida
Leonard Presby	William Patterson College
Herbert F. Rebhun	University of Houston, Downtown
Brian Reithal	West Texas State University
Tom Richard	Bemidji State University
Leonard C. Schwab	California State University, Hayward
Fred Scott	Broward Community College
Sumit Sircar	The University of Texas at Arlington
Vince Skudrna	Baruch College (CUNY)
Glenn Smith	James Madison University
Janet C. Smith	University of Tennessee, Chattanooga
Bob Tesch	Northeast Louisiana University
Nai-kuan Tsao	Wayne State University
Michael Wolfe	The University of Texas at Austin
James Wynne	Virginia Commonwealth University
Robert F. Zant	North Texas State University

Thomas H. Athey
John Day
Robert W. Zmud

PART I

The Information Society

CHAPTER 1

Welcome to the Information Society

We live in an age in which computers now outnumber the people living on Earth. This fact may scare people who do not understand what computers are, what they do, or how they do it. The sheer number of computers now in use is a bit surprising, even for those of us who have been working with and around computers for more than twenty years. The overpowering fact is that we are seeing just the beginning of a surge in the use of computers. How will they all be used? How will their use affect people, businesses, and society? And, perhaps most importantly, how might computers affect you and your career?

While no text can fully answer all of these questions, this text can give you the information you need to understand and deal effectively with the growing predominance of computers in your personal and professional life. In Part I we will introduce you to the information society and give an overview of key concepts that will be covered in detail in later chapters. In this chapter, you will begin by learning to do the following:

1. Define the term *information society* and explain its meaning within the world of work
2. Define the term *computing literacy* and describe its five levels
3. Define the term *information system* and describe the three basic elements that make up an information system
4. List and describe the four stages of the i*nformation processing cycle*

Computing Literacy in an Information Society

Are you aware that our society has been transformed from an industrial society into an information society? In fact, in this **information society,** the collection, processing, and distribution of information have actually replaced the manufacture of goods as the primary source of wealth and work.

For most of the twentieth century, economic growth has been fueled by "heavy" manufacturing industries, such as the steel and auto industries. These industries transformed basic raw materials such as iron, coal, and oil into a wide range of products for markets across the world. But since the 1960s, a transformation has been taking place in our economy. Today, more than half of all economic activity in the United States involves the processing of knowledge or facts, or *information*, rather than physical goods. This proportion continues to increase over time (see Exhibit 1.1).

A major factor behind the growth of this information society is the amazing developments that have occurred in the field of computers. **Computers** are electronic devices that process information. A key aspect

Exhibit 1.1

The Transformation to an Information Society

Important turning points occurred around 1880, when less than 50 percent of the work force was in agriculture; around 1920, when over 50 percent of workers were in industry; and around 1980, when over 50 percent of all workers were classified as "information" workers.

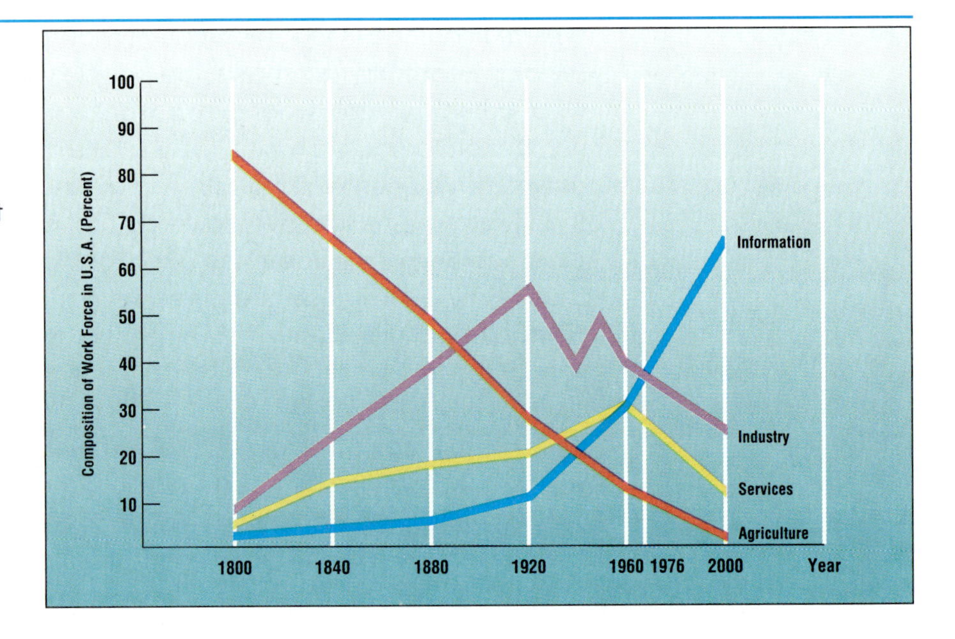

of today's computers is that they can process information in all of its forms—words, numbers, voice, and pictures. As Appendix A shows, many years of effort went into the development of this fast, reliable, and relatively inexpensive way to process information using electricity instead of human labor.

Throughout the 1980s, the fastest growing segment of the computer industry involved *personal computers*, or computers meant to be used by an

Exhibit 1.2

The Emergence of the Personal Computer

The microcomputer became a viable personal computer around 1980 and within four years the total dollar value of its shipments exceeded all shipment values of all other-sized computers. It will be a dominant force in the 1990s.

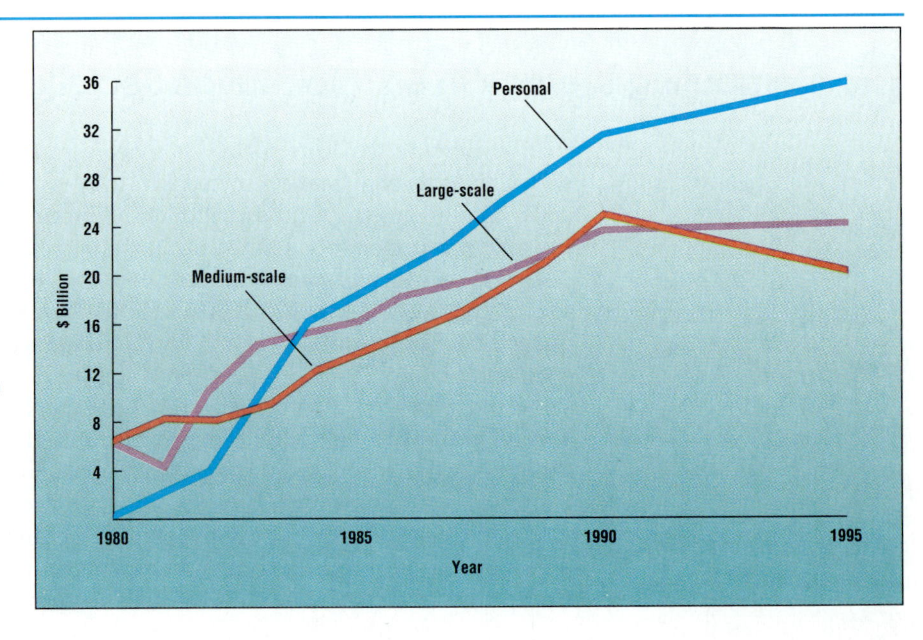

Exhibit 1.3

Personal Computers

individual (see Exhibit 1.2). Another term for these computers is *microcomputers,* a reference to the microchips that enable these computers to function.

By bringing the computer down in scale, personal computer manufacturers allowed people to hold it and prod it and play with it. As a result, it is common to find people without formal training in computers improving their professional and personal lives by using personal computers. Some of these people might even say the computer has "liberated" them from much of their work's monotony and tedium (see Exhibit 1.3).

Another major impact of the computer involves its role in creating the information society. The economies of many nations are becoming increasingly dependent on the processing of information. The need to create, collect, store, and dispense this information has launched many new industries. Consulting firms, public and private information services, and research organizations represent just a few examples. Older industries have been affected as well. For example, insurance and banking are, first and foremost, information processing businesses. Insurance companies process vast amounts of customer and claim information, and banks process vast amounts of data describing the financial transactions of their customers. Even in government and the more traditional manufacturing, retail, and service industries, the movement of information is fast becoming the lifeblood of business and management. As a consequence, industries directly supporting information processing, such as communications, transportation, and office equipment manufacture and sales, are growing.

Computing, Not Computer, Literacy

What impact does the information society have on you? It primarily affects the career options open to you. Exhibit 1.1 showed that in 1976, white-collar workers outnumbered blue-collar workers for the first time. Today, "information occupations" represent over 60 percent of the American work force. **Information workers** are professional employees who collect and process data that, combined with their own expertise, judgment, and creativity, can be used to create and communicate information. Information workers include salespeople, lawyers, bankers, teachers, librarians, secretaries, accountants, stockbrokers, managers, engineers, and computer programmers. The typical information worker is constantly sifting through mail, memos, magazines, technical documents, reports, and books and preparing memos, letters, reports, and presentations as part of his or her job. Although information workers were around long before computers, computers are having a major impact on improving the workers' productivity.

What does the information worker have to do with you? Not only are you likely to find yourself in an information occupation, but the odds favor your working with computers in that occupation. Because computers will probably play an important part in your career, Part V of this book discusses in detail the information society and its impact on people and work.

You are probably already aware of the key role computers play in today's work world. The news media routinely run stories about computers and the need to educate people so that they can fill meaningful and productive roles in an information society. Computers are found in educational institutions, computer camps, computer magazines, on *Sesame Street*—the list goes on and on (see Exhibit 1.4). In the business world, computer training has become a major industry.

Some debate exists regarding the type of computer education, or **computer literacy,** people need to function in an information society. Is it important for everyone to become a computer expert? More directly, what do you need to learn to benefit from computers? The answer depends on how you intend to use computers.

Computer professionals certainly need to understand how computers work. Few computer users, however, really need to understand all the technology behind today's computers. Fortunately, you can take advantage of most of the computer's capabilities without knowing how electrical circuits function or how to program. (Programming is the process of developing the instructions or programs that direct a computer in its information processing.) On the other hand, you may find computer

Exhibit 1.4

The Growing Need for Computing Literacy

technology interesting and computer programming fun; and learning these skills may even be useful in your career.

What most computer users need is an understanding of what computers can do and an ability to feel comfortable when using a computer. You need to develop the same sense of command and confidence toward computers that you have toward automobiles. Although you do not need to be an engineer to drive a car, you do need to know the "rules of the road" and to feel at ease while driving. **Computing literacy** is the ability to use the computer as a tool to enrich your personal and professional life. Computing literacy—not computer literacy—should be the educational goal for most students.

Exhibit 1.5

The Staircase of Computing Literacy

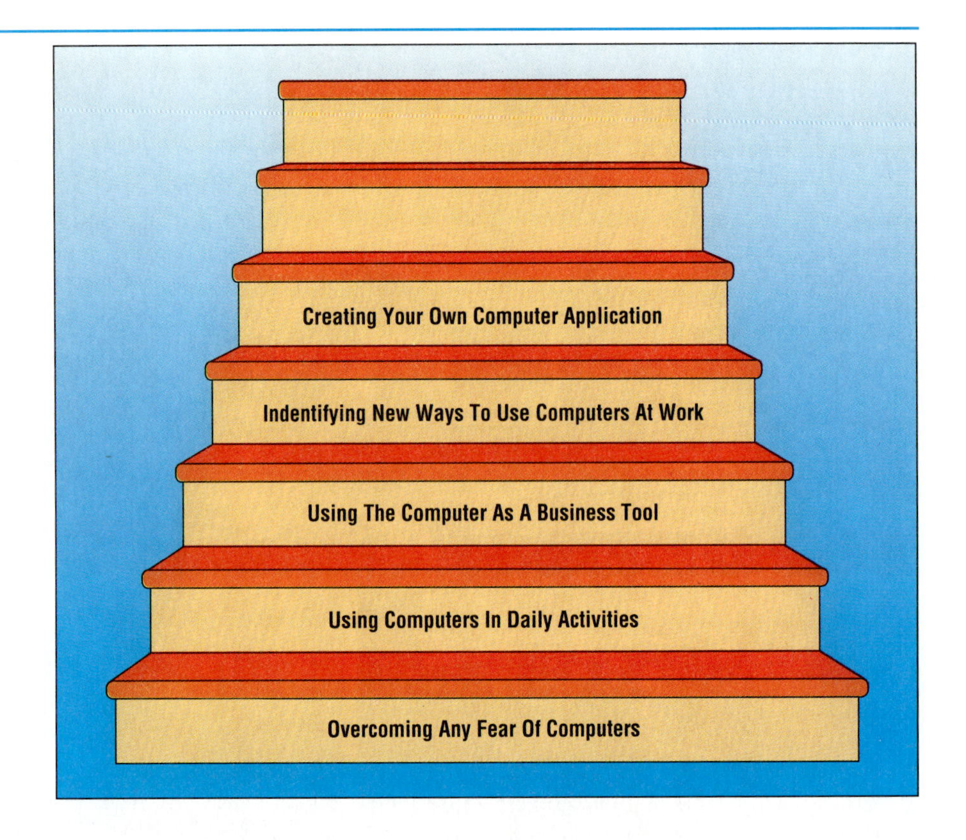

Computing literacy can be divided into different levels (see Exhibit 1.5). These levels reflect the fact that people differ in their involvement with computers. As this involvement grows, a deeper and broader understanding of computers is needed. The following five levels of computing literacy also indicate the variety of ways you are likely to become involved with computers:

1. *You develop an understanding of the basic roles that computers serve in an information society well enough to overcome any fear of computer use.* The computer will affect even those people who never come into physical contact with it. A person with a true fear of computers probably won't be able to cope in such a world. This first level of computing literacy must be acquired by all members of an information society.
2. *You become comfortable with the use of computers as machines.* This level involves the use of computers in everyday tasks that have been automated. Examples include banking, shopping, health care, and education tasks, as well as information search tasks in libraries and government agencies. People without this second level of computing literacy will find they cannot take advantage of many of the services and conveniences of an information society.
3. *You develop a willingness and an ability to use computers as tools to support routine business activities.* This level includes using the

computer for typing and clerical tasks and other tasks involved in the collection, storage, and retrieval of information. An inability to reach this third level of computing literacy will exclude an applicant from many kinds of jobs.

4. *You understand the strengths and weaknesses of computers, as well as the tasks being performed with computer support, so that you can identify new ways of improving work performance.* Business and professional success is increasingly being tied to the innovative use of computers. Employees not acquiring this fourth level of computing literacy may be bypassed for promotions and other professional rewards.
5. *You design a computer application by specifying what the computer is to do and how it will do it, and you perhaps do some of the programming as well.* Although these activities have traditionally been performed by computer specialists, computer technology has advanced to the point that many employees are developing their own computer applications.

What is fascinating about this list is that none of these literacy levels requires a detailed knowledge of the inner workings of computers, although professional information workers need to have some conceptual understanding of what makes computer systems work. Only the people who go on to become computer professionals will need to attain higher levels of computing literacy.

You can begin to develop your computing literacy in very little time, particularly with today's personal computers. Personal computer hardware and software are fairly easy to understand and are simple to use, and they can provide immediate practical benefits to anyone willing to learn about them. But before beginning, you need to recognize that simply reading about computer use and computer technology will not move you up many of the levels of computing literacy. Just as in playing tennis or any other sport, you must actually use computers if you wish to gain any kind of familiarity with them. Computing literacy can be achieved only through practice. Computing literacy is a participation sport! Acquiring computing literacy requires both an investment of your time and a willingness to make mistakes and learn from them. As you'll see, though, learning to use computers need not be all hard work.

This text will start you on your progress up the ladder of computing literacy. How far you go and what you do with this knowledge, however, depends on your willingness to experience computer technology on a firsthand basis. As a first step, the remaining sections of this chapter take a closer look at both computers and computing.

What a Computer Information System Is

The primary purpose of this text is to study the computer not as an end itself, but rather as a means to an end—its productive use in business. When

Exhibit 1.6

Basic Computer System Hardware

A computer system is generally composed of the computer itself and peripheral devices which are used for input, output, and storage of data and information.

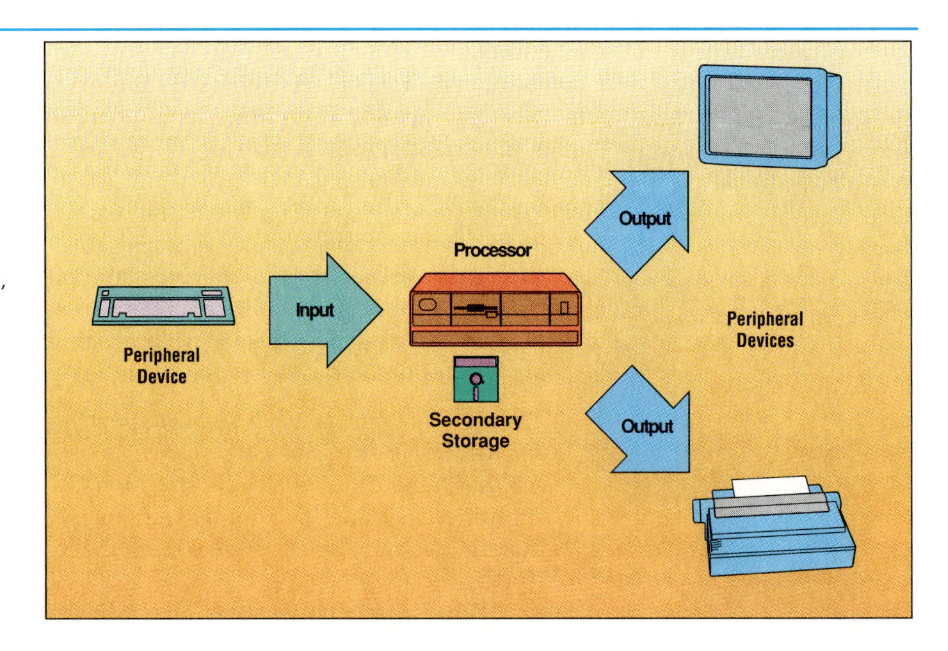

a computer system serves a practical use in a business, the application is termed a **computer information system (CIS).** A computer information system processes data to produce information. The term **data** refers to symbols used to represent a fact, event, or thing. **Information** refers to the meaning given to a set of data that has been processed.

Computer information systems are actually made up of four components: hardware, software, data, and people. People both build and use information systems. Parts IV and V of this text focus on these "people" roles. The rest of this section discusses ways in which hardware, software, data, and people interact.

Hardware

When most people refer to the computer, they usually are referring to what is more properly called a computer system. A **computer system** is composed of computer hardware and software. **Computer hardware** refers to the physical devices that can be used to enter, process, store and retrieve, and deliver data and information. As shown in Exhibit 1.6, the **computer** itself is where all the processing operations take place. **Peripherals** are devices added to the computer and used for input, storage, or the display of information. Examples of input devices are the keyboard, where data can be keyed into the computer and the mouse, which can be used to select functions displayed on a computer screen. Output devices include the printer, which can be used to display information on paper, and the plotter, which can be used to produce detailed graphics. The display screen can be used to see what data is being entered into the computer and also for displaying the results of computer processing (see Exhibit 1.7).

INPUT

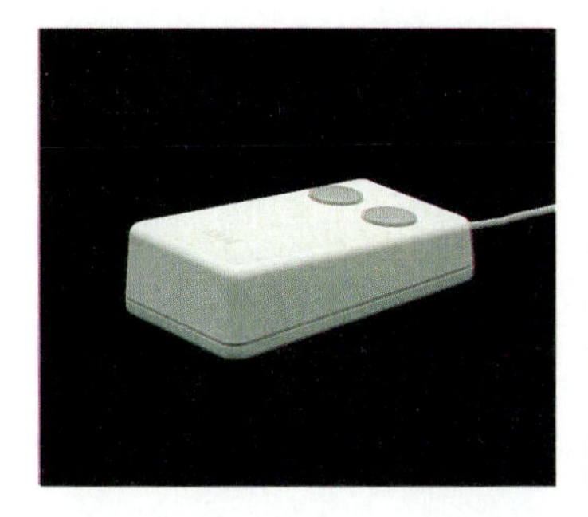

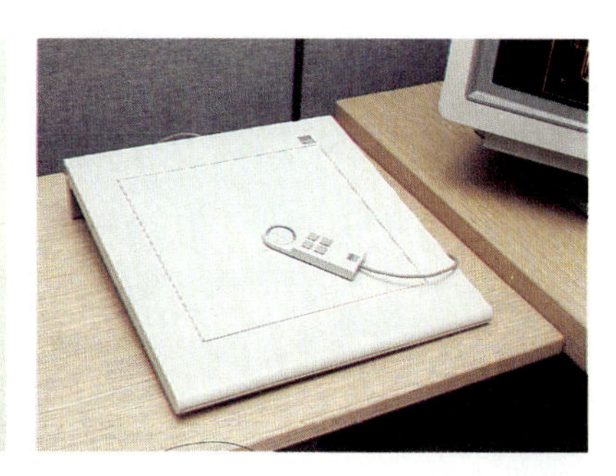

OUTPUT

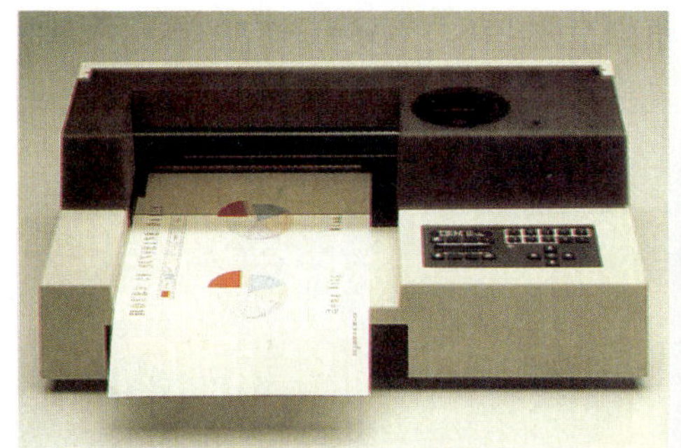
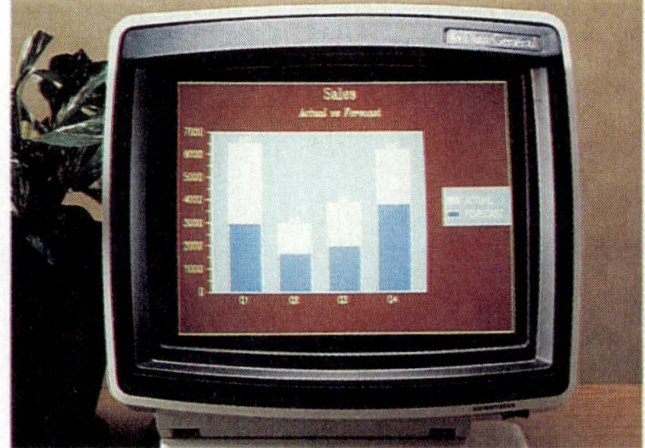

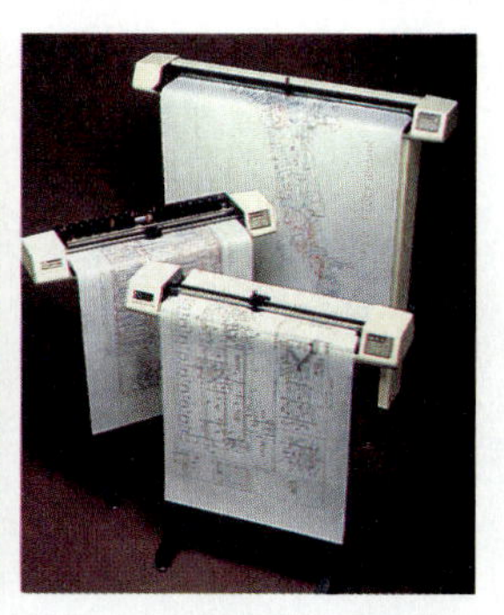

STORAGE

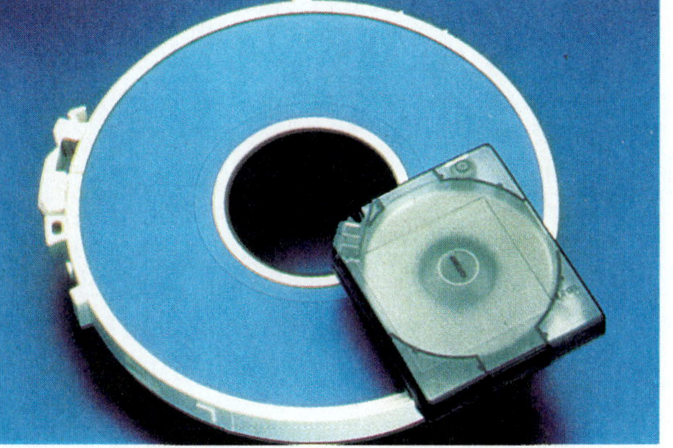

Exhibit 1.7

Computer Peripheral Devices

Secondary storage devices are used to provide permanent storage of data and information that is kept in computer-readable form. Furthermore, data can be retrieved from secondary storage; thus, these devices can be used as an input medium. Two of the more common secondary storage devices are magnetic disks and magnetic tape. Floppy diskettes are a form of disk commonly used with personal computers. The tape units shown in Exhibit 1.7 are reels of magnetic tape, which are often used with larger computer systems.

Exhibit 1.8

A Wide Range of Computer Applications

Software

Computer hardware by itself is useless. Hardware must be directed in its information processing role by software. **Software** is a collection of instructions, written in a computing language, that is used to direct the computer to accomplish specific tasks. The instructions are called programs. There are three major types of software: application, end-user, and systems software.

Application software is the general term for programs that have been written, usually by computer professionals, to perform specific user-oriented tasks. These tasks can range from doing payroll and customer billing to playing chess or aiding in air traffic control applications (see Exhibit 1.8).

End-user software is composed of prebuilt programs, called packages, which are available to help information workers design their own computer-based applications. An example of end-user software, shown in Exhibit 1.9, includes packages that allow creation of documents, calculation of budgets, retrieval of lists of customers by region of the country, and graphing of sales data to depict critical trends.

Exhibit 1.9

End-User Software Packages

One of the driving forces behind the surge in the use of personal computers is the ready availability of end-user software packages.

Operating systems software are sets of programs that have been written by computer specialists to ease the task of working with the computer system itself. The operating system acts as an interface between application or end-user software and the computer (see Exhibit 1.10). This allows end-users and computer professionals to concentrate more on the information processing problem that needs to be solved and less on the details of the computer. Chapter 11, "Microcomputer Operating Systems," gives you the background necessary to interact with the operating system. For a deeper understanding of operating systems, refer to Appendix B, "Mainframe Operating System Concepts."

Data

Data serve as the raw material for a computer system. The goal of the creators of an information system is to use hardware and software to manipulate data to create information to meet the needs of the user. Data are entered, processed, stored and retrieved, and delivered as information. An information system without data would be like a car without fuel.

People

People, most simply, breathe life into an information system. People play two major roles in computer-based information systems: that of information system user and that of information system creator.

The **user role** involves people that use computer-based information systems to aid them in carrying out their jobs. Almost all data used by

Exhibit 1.10

The Three Major Types of Software

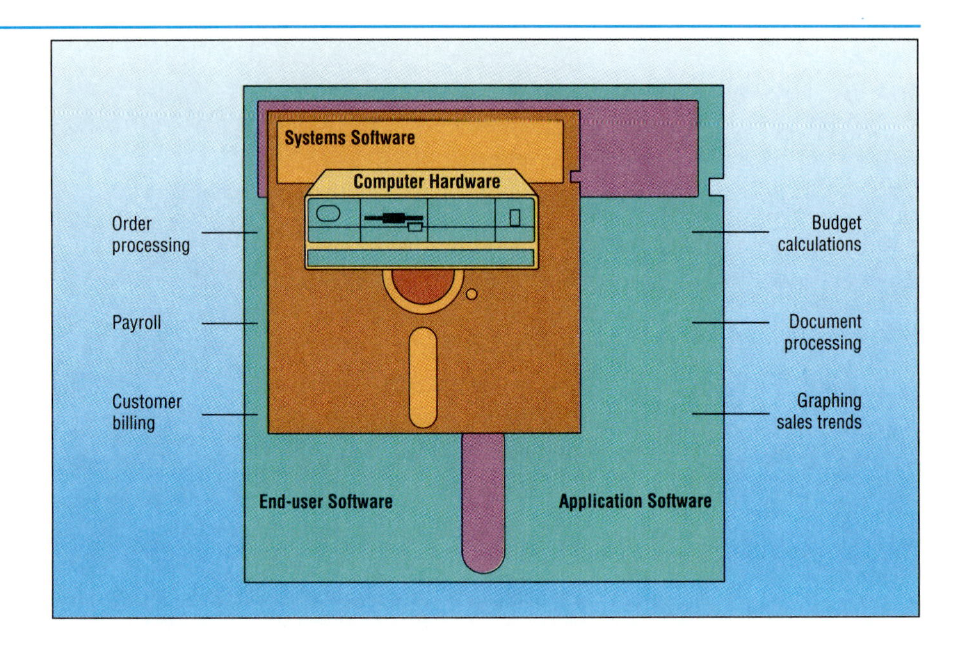

information systems must be entered into the computer system by people. Most information system outputs are displayed for a business professional, who then makes use of the information. Without these users, there would be no data to process and no reason to create or use information systems.

The **creator role** involves those people who develop computer-based information systems. Before the advent of microcomputers, the creation and enhancement of computer-based information systems was primarily the responsibility of computer professionals who wrote application software. These computer professionals needed to work in concert with the business professionals who had detailed knowledge of the information needs of particular functional areas of business. With the development of end-user software and microcomputers, information professionals have taken on more of a creator role for certain types of information system development, with computer specialists playing more of a support role.

What a Computer Does

On the surface, computers may seem to have mysterious and limitless powers. The computer applications pictured in Exhibit 1.8 include some of the sophisticated uses of computers. With these or any other computer applications, however, the computer is merely processing data to produce information. When people process information, they receive data from the environment, interpret that data by comparing it to data already stored, and, if necessary, produce a response. Consider what happens when you approach a red stop light in a car. You receive (input) data concerning the color of the light. You retrieve stored information that you have concerning

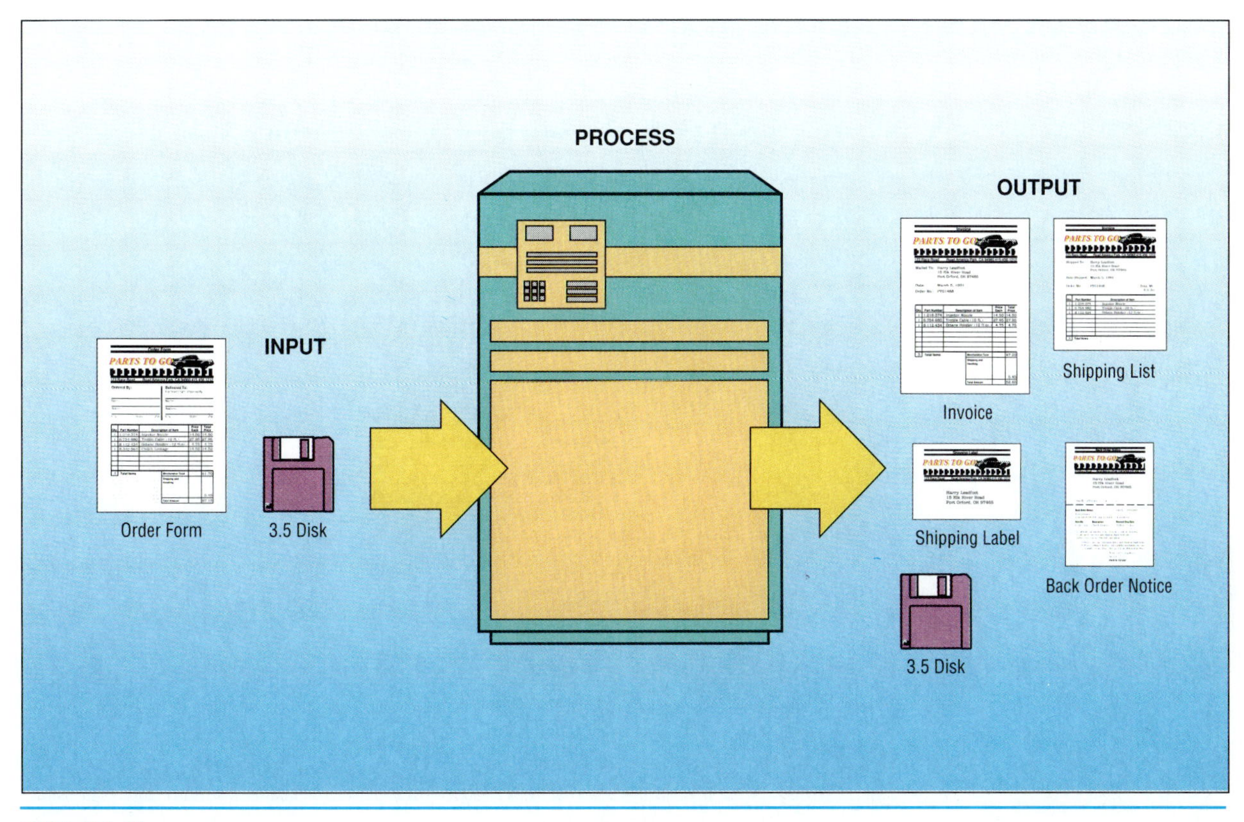

Exhibit 1.11

The Computer Information Processing Cycle

In a mail-order firm an order is entered into the computer processor and product information is retrieved from secondary storage. Processing operations calculate the total cost of the order. An invoice, a packing list, a shipping label, and possibly a back-order note are printed by the computer.

the meaning of the red light. Based on your interpretation of the signal, you produce a response: you apply the brake.

The stages of input, processing, storage and retrieval, and output are exactly what a computer does when it processes information. They are referred to as the computer **information processing cycle.** Exhibit 1.11 portrays these stages for a relatively simple business information processing task, the processing of a customer order by a mail-order autoparts firm. You will see this example throughout the rest of this chapter.

Inputs Data

Both people and computers take in data. We, for example, capture data through our senses of sight, hearing, touch, smell, and taste. Most people, however, do not realize that our sensory organs are much more sophisticated than are a computer system's input devices. Much of the data we capture is in its original form. The computer is not so flexible. It must have data prepared in special ways and must be instructed, through a program, to look for and collect these data. The computer then translates the data into a pattern of electrical signals it can process. We will discuss this series of activities in greater detail in Part II of this text.

Exhibit 1.12

Auto Parts Order Form

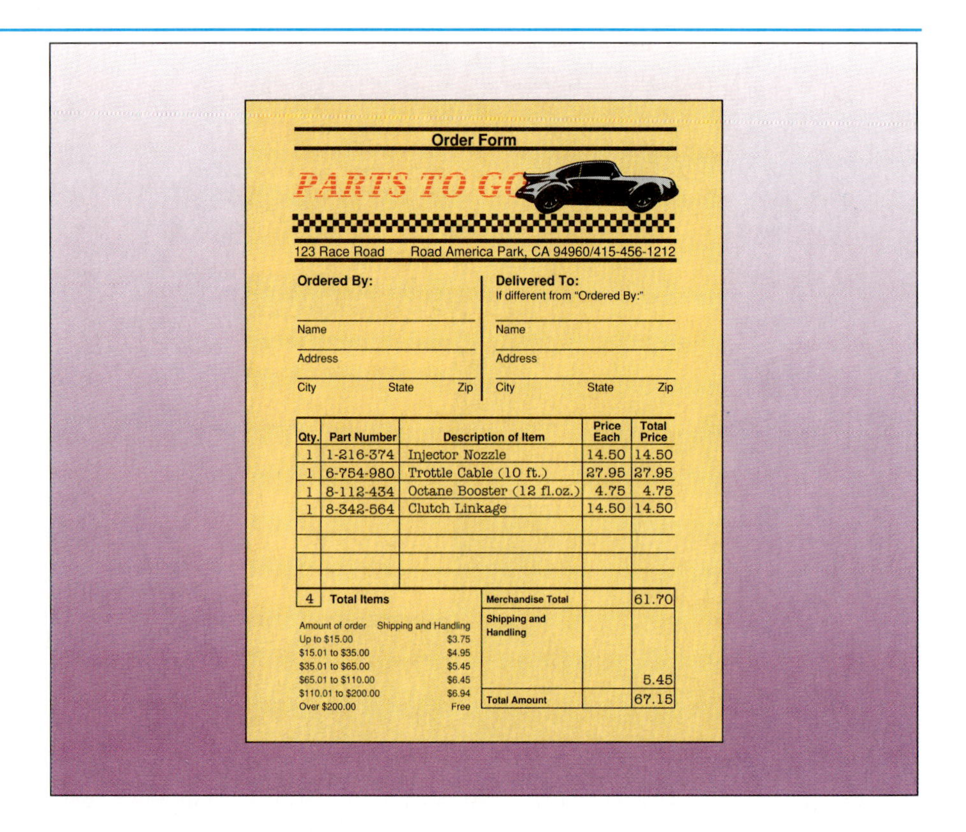

Order Form

PARTS TO GO

123 Race Road Road America Park, CA 94960/415-456-1212

Ordered By:

Name

Address

City State Zip

Delivered To:
If different from "Ordered By:"

Name

Address

City State Zip

Qty.	Part Number	Description of Item	Price Each	Total Price
1	1-216-374	Injector Nozzle	14.50	14.50
1	6-754-980	Trottle Cable (10 ft.)	27.95	27.95
1	8-112-434	Octane Booster (12 fl.oz.)	4.75	4.75
1	8-342-564	Clutch Linkage	14.50	14.50

4 Total Items

Amount of order	Shipping and Handling
Up to $15.00	$3.75
$15.01 to $35.00	$4.95
$35.01 to $65.00	$5.45
$65.01 to $110.00	$6.45
$110.01 to $200.00	$6.94
Over $200.00	Free

Merchandise Total	61.70
Shipping and Handling	5.45
Total Amount	67.15

The parts order form has been enlarged in Exhibit 1.12. To process the order, the computer will need to do the following:

1. Read the customer name and address
2. Read the quantity, part number, description, unit price, and total cost, of each part being ordered
3. Read the total cost of the order

Notice in Exhibit 1.12 that this set of input data includes both letters and numbers. Both are easily captured by computers. However, it is unlikely that the computer will be able to enter this data directly from the order form. Instead, a clerk will prepare the data for entry, perhaps using a computer terminal.

Once the order data are organized and entered in a form that the computer can handle, termed a **computer-readable form,** the data can be captured and processed in a fraction of the time it would take a person to read the data items.

While this speed may be of little benefit when processing a single part order, the benefit is significant when thousands of orders are processed each day. Not only can all these orders be processed in a short period of time, but the cost of processing the orders is far less than if they were processed by hand. Furthermore, it is unlikely that the computer will make any errors in processing the data. People, in contrast, are prone to typing mistakes and mathematical errors. Finally, once the order data have been entered into the computer, they become available for further computer-based information processing. The advantages of this will become clearer as the remaining stages of the information processing cycle are discussed.

Processes Data

Both people and computers process data. People, in fact, possess some very sophisticated information processing capabilities. Our ability to work with incomplete sets of data and to generalize meanings across sets of data is very powerful. Most important, however, is our ability to create. When we are faced with a new problem, we are often able to arrive at a solution by piecing together prior experiences, sketchy facts, and "human intuition."

Computers, on the other hand, have extremely limited data processing capabilities. They are limited to two rather basic processing operations:

> *Computers perform simple **arithmetic operations,** such as addition, subtraction, multiplication, and division.*
>
> *Computers perform simple **logic operations,** such as comparing the values of two numbers or determining whether two words contain the same letters.*

Furthermore, computers must be directed in a step-by-step fashion to perform these operations.

Given these limitations, why should we use computers? The computer's speed and reliability prove to be key factors. The speed of today's computer systems enables them to process vast amounts of data very quickly. As a result, the overall cost of processing large sets of data is far less than it would be if people did the data processing. Some tasks, such as processing today's U.S. Census, would be virtually impossible to complete without the processing power of computer systems.

The fact that computer systems can perform only very simple arithmetic and logic data processing operations turns out to be a fairly minor limitation. Computer programs can be developed to handle just about any information processing task. The limit to what can be done with computer systems lies not in the computer, but rather in our skill in using the computer's capabilities.

The data processing operations required in processing the auto parts order described in Exhibit 1.11 are fairly simple. In fact, most of the resulting information is the same data that were entered into the computer: customer name and address; part identification numbers and descriptions; quantities and prices; and total cost of an order. As a double check, the computer will probably calculate the total price charged the customer.

The process becomes a bit more complex when a part is out of stock. In these cases, the applications program will direct the information

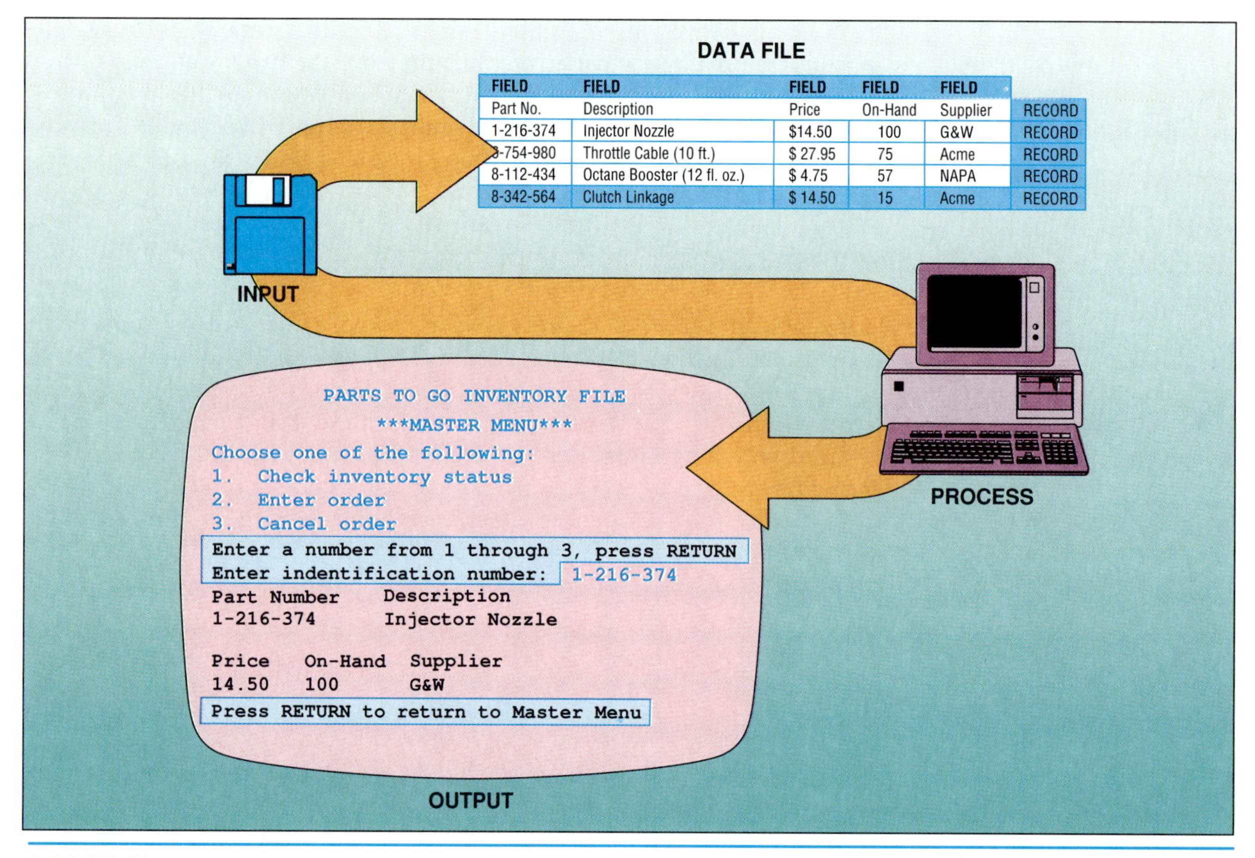

Exhibit 1.13

Auto Parts Data File

Organizing the auto parts file in a systematic manner makes it fairly easy for the information system to locate the record for a particular part. Once located, the data stored in this data record can be retrieved for use in processing an auto part order.

system to perform two additional tasks. First, the computer system will recalculate the amount due. Second, the computer system will print a back-order notice to be sent to the customer. Producing this back-order notice is easy, since much of the information remains the same whenever the notice is used. What changes from notice to notice are data items that come directly from the order form: the customer's name and address and the identification numbers, descriptions and prices of the out-of-parts.

Stores and Retrieves Data and Information

Both people and computers store and then retrieve data and information. Your mind, in fact, can hold more data than the largest of today's computers. The "data" stored in your memory include your past experiences, facts and concepts that you have learned, and ideas that you have developed. Our ability to retrieve data from our memories also turns out to be far more sophisticated than that available with computer systems.

Why, then, are computers used so extensively in storing data and information? The answer comes back to the computer's speed and reliability. If information is stored in an organized manner within a computer, it can be retrieved quickly and accurately when it is needed. "Organizing" a set of data means storing it in a way that fits the data retrieval operations to be performed. Also, the cost of storing a large quantity of data within a computer system has become much less than the cost of storing these same data in file cabinets.

In the parts order example, data are retrieved from a data file. A **data file** refers to an organized set of related data items. In this case, data describing all the parts offered by the mail-order firm are kept in a part file (see Exhibit 1.13). All the data for a particular part are stored in a data record within this file. Each of the data items that describes a feature of a part is termed a data field.

When the data file is organized in this way, retrieving the record for a particular part becomes easy—just search through the part file until a match is found between the identification number of the part being ordered and the "identification number" field of a particular record. When a match occurs, the correct data record, or part in this case, has been found.

Notice that the operations to be performed in processing a parts order may be affected by this retrieved information. What if no match was found in the part file for an ordered part? Or, what if a match is found, but the part's description or price do not agree with what is on the parts order? In such cases, it may be best to return the order form to the customer with a polite form letter—generated by the information system.

Outputs Information

Both people and computers communicate information. People, however, are much more versatile than computers in expressing their information. For example, we have developed sophisticated abilities to transmit quite different messages with only slight changes in the information being communicated. Have you ever said one thing while indicating just the opposite through your tone or facial expression? Computers simply do not have the versatility or the sophistication that people have when communicating.

What computers provide, not surprisingly, is the ability to produce information quickly, accurately, and inexpensively. An obvious benefit is the ability to process the large number of outputs, such as the shipping lists, shipping labels, and back-order notices needed by the mail-order auto parts company in processing thousands of parts orders each month. A more detailed view of these outputs is illustrated in Exhibit 1.14. It is common, as shown here, to find that a few input data items "trigger" a number of information system outputs.

Another benefit of computer-based information processing is the ability to easily vary the form of an information output. Exhibit 1.15, for example, shows the same information in three different forms—table, graph, and chart. Each form might be useful for different situations. In

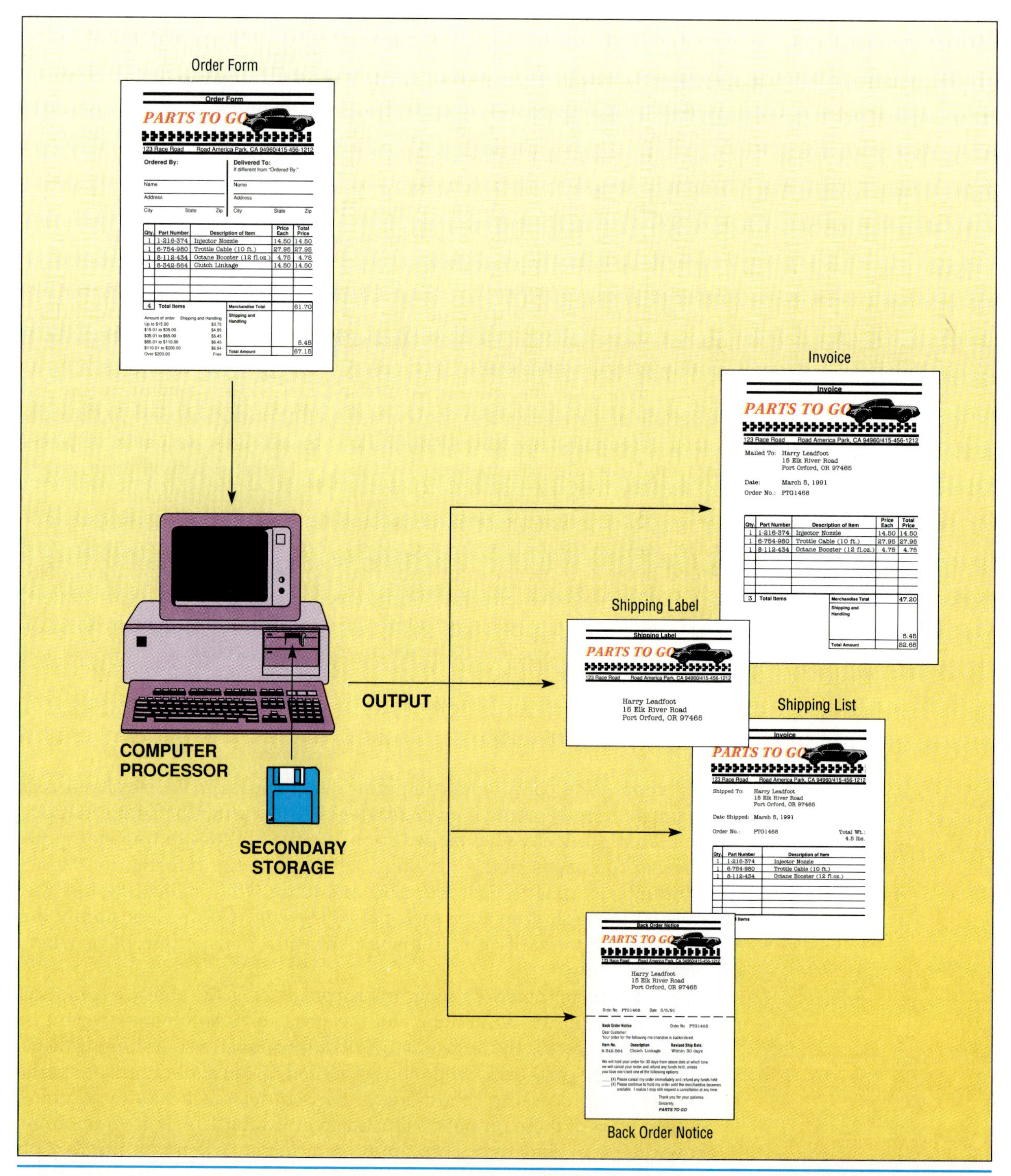

Exhibit 1.14

Computer Information System Outputs

By capturing data from an order form, an information system can produce much of the paperwork necessary for handling a customer's parts order.

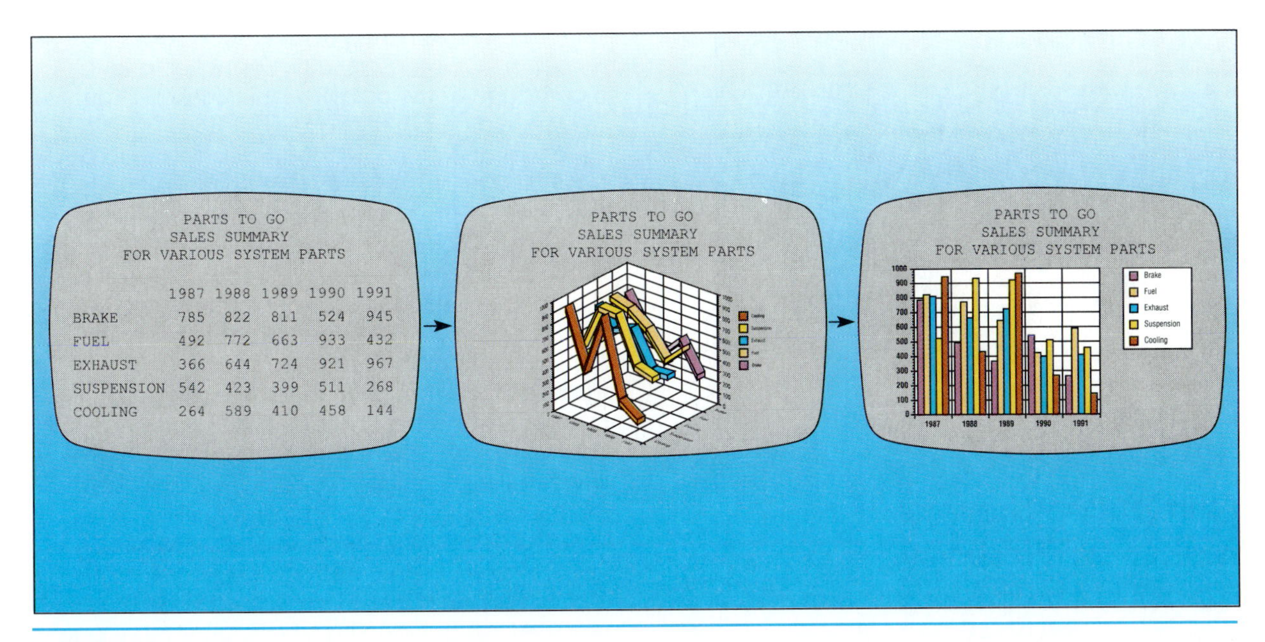

Exhibit 1.15

Flexibility in Displaying Information

The same information can appear in different forms on a computer system. Information outputs can thus be tailored to meet the information user's needs.

producing these "user-oriented" outputs, each information item is translated from the electrical signals used to represent it within the computer to the symbols used to print it on paper.

Summarizing the Computer's Basic Capabilities

What, then, can a computer do?

1. Both numbers and text can be entered into a computer. These data items can then be stored within a data file to be available for retrieval as needed.
2. New data items or information can be created by performing arithmetic operations on data or by changing or rearranging text.
3. Data or information previously stored within the computer can be retrieved for processing or displayed as output.
4. Information produced by earlier input, processing, and storage and retrieval operations can be displayed on the screen or as printed output in tabular or graphical form.

The real advantage of computer-based information processing, however, is that these operations can be performed more quickly, more reliably, and less expensively when done by a computer rather than by people. You will begin to learn in Chapter 2 how to spot situations in which these advantages are likely to arise.

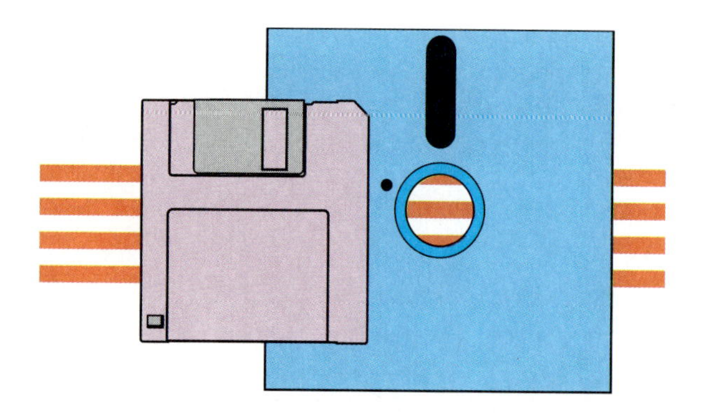

Computers At Work

Computing Literacy Makes a Difference

Four years ago, Robert Baird bought his first computer, an IBM PC AT. The 11-year veteran commodities broker, working out of Paine Webber's San Diego office, needs a computer to do calculations too complicated to do by hand.

"Basically, I was a computer illiterate," Baird says of his first foray into personal computing.

Yet today Baird is managing money with the help of one of the most sophisticated applications made for brokers, one that involves satellite feeds, complex Elliott waves (a mathematical formula that tracks patterns in prices), and the nearest thing to real-time market tracking yet.

How did this self-avowed computer illiterate come near the leading edge of PC technology? It all started two years ago, when Baird spent $890 of his own money for a copy of Trading Techniques' G.E.T. (Gann-Elliott Trader) and $1,200 to install a satellite dish on the roof of his downtown San Diego office building. An additional $600 bought him commodities market software modules to interact with the basic G.E.T. program: S&P 500, U.S. Treasury Bonds, Swiss Franc and Japanese Yen, and the NYFE (New York Futures Exchange).

Today, Baird relies on G.E.T. for position and day trading. A data feed from Future Source (a service of Commodities Communications Corp., Chicago) supplies daily high/low/close data on the commodities markets. This decision-making program automatically advises Baird when to go long (buy) or short (sell) on commodities.

Baird is constantly looking for even faster, more profitable ways to track and trade commodities. So, when Trading Techniques, a Barberton, Ohio-based software maker, a few months ago came out with J.E.T. (Joseph-Elliott Trader), a program that allows intraday trading, Baird was one of the first customers on line to pay the $2,950 quarterly lease. He also picked up the 386 computer to run the program, and began paying the $600-plus monthly fee to add another Future Source on-line market feed that updates each market's condition in 5-minute intervals.

Based on the Future Source data feed and the various algorithms resident in J.E.T. (similar to those in G.E.T., though refined), the program graphically displays as many as 400 bars of up-to-the-minute high/low/change information on the commodities selected. It beeps a warning when there is an up or down change in market conditions, beeps again to indicate a market "watch" when trends start showing a buy or sell probability, then beeps and flashes when the program has decided it's time to go short or long on a particular commodity.

The advisories of J.E.T., backed up by G.E.T.'s daily analyses, provide Baird with a high probability of success. They also allow him to consistently outperform the markets he trades in. Baird says that he's been "enormously successful," posting profits for his customers and commissions for himself, "just by doing what it (J.E.T.) says."

Cutting-edge technology often leads to big profits. Baird cites an account he manages: Starting with $35,000 equity, profits were a staggering $28,000 within two months. He says that using J.E.T.'s advice, most accounts with similar equity will average between $5,000 and $10,000 in profits a month.

J.E.T. builds in a degree of market slippage between the time an order is placed and executed, but usually there is none, says Baird. He attributes that to the program's ability to swiftly analyze market turning points, combined with its near-real-time tracking of the various commodities exchanges. "Let's face it," says Baird, "a computer is able to figure things out a hell of a lot quicker than I can."

Though it is available, Baird uses no brokerage-issue technology from Paine Webber. Anything that a brokerage firm would offer would be too general for his specialized work in commodities, he says. Furthermore, since there are no regulations that require posting commodities transactions (as is the case with stocks), Baird says he has no use for the record-keeping ability of a computer. "I just make sure that my customer statements match the tickets I have on a daily basis, and that takes about 10 or 15 minutes," he says. "It would take as much time or more to do them with a computer."

All Baird needs now is the next version of J.E.T., maybe an even faster computer, and perhaps "1-minute rather the 5-minute market updates" to keep himself—and his customers—on the leading edge of profit making.

Summary and Key Terms

In an **information society,** the collection, processing, and distribution of information are the primary sources of wealth and work. A major factor behind the growth of the information society is the progress in the field of computers. **Computers** are electronic devices that process information.

Information workers are those professional employees who collect and process data that, when combined with their expertise, judgment, and creativity, can be used to create and communicate information. Today, information workers represent over 60 percent of the American work force.

More and more, the information workers using computer information systems are business and computer professionals. These professionals are learning to be both users and creators of computer information systems. The **user role** includes those people who use a computer information system to aid them in carrying out their jobs. The **creator role** involves those people who develop computer information systems.

In the future, most workers will probably work in "information careers," using computers. Some debate exists about the type of computer education, or **computer literacy,** people need to function in an information society. Computer professionals need to understand computer technology and how to write computer programs. Most people, however, need **computing literacy,** the ability to use the computer as a tool to enrich their personal and professional lives. Exhibit 1.6 shows five levels of computing literacy.

A **computer system** is composed of computer hardware and software. **Computer hardware** refers to the physical devices that can be used to enter, process, store and retrieve, and deliver data and information. When a computer system serves a practical use in a business, the application is termed a **computer information system.** A computer information system processes data to produce information. **Data** refers to symbols used to represent a fact, event, or thing. **Information** refers to the meaning given to a set of data that has been processed. **Peripherals** are devices added to the computer and used to input, store, or display information. **Secondary storage devices** are used to provide permanent storage of data and information that is kept in computer-readable form.

Software is a collection of instructions written in a computing language, called a program, used to direct the computer to accomplish specific tasks. There are three major types of computer software. **Application software** is the general term for programs that have been written, usually by computer professionals, to perform specific user-oriented tasks. **End-user software** is software composed of prebuilt programs, called packages, that are available to aid an information worker in designing his or her own computer-based application. **Systems software** is a set of programs that has been written by computer specialists to ease the task of working with the computer hardware itself.

Computers transform data into information through an **information processing cycle** made up of input, processing, storage and retrieval, and output stages. A computer can only accept data in a **computer-readable** form. In processing data, computers need programming instructions to perform simple **arithmetic** and **logic operations.** Computers are used to process data because they are reliable and fast.

For storage and retrieval, data must be organized into **data files,** which are collections of records composed of data fields. For output, the computer is able to display data and information on a computer screen or print it in a tabular or graphical form. The real advantage of computer-based information processing is that these operations can be performed more quickly, more reliably, and less expensively when done by a computer rather than by a person or many people.

Review Questions

1. What is the difference between data and information?
2. Identify and discuss four ways in which the computer has had an impact on your life.
3. Identify and describe an "information business" that you have read or heard about recently.
4. List and briefly describe the five levels of computer literacy.
5. Differentiate between hardware and software. Which is more important to computer users? Explain your answer.
6. Identify the four basic types of computer hardware and briefly describe their functions.
7. Differentiate between application, end-user, and system software.
8. Explain the difference between the user and creator roles in a computer-based information system.
9. Briefly describe the steps in the computer information processing cycle.
10. Evaluate the following statement: "The computer is overrated—it is not as creative as a human being, cannot accept as wide a range of inputs, cannot store as much data, and is not as flexible in presenting the results of its efforts."

T F **11.** The terms *computer literacy* and *computing literacy* are synonymous.

T F **12.** In order to achieve true computing literacy, it is necessary for one to become proficient in programming.

T F **13.** The term *hardware* is broad enough to encompass both the computer's electromechanical devices and the programs that direct their operation.

T F **14.** Information systems are composed of hardware, software, data and people.

T F **15.** Secondary storage devices maintain stored data in computer-readable form.

T F **16.** The display screen is unique among input/output devices in that it is capable of performing both input and output functions.

T F **17.** The problem of losing data, information, and programs due to power outages can be solved by utilizing secondary storage devices.

T F **18.** Application software is used to coordinate the flow of data, information, and programs within a computer system.

T F **19.** Compared to a human being, a computer is a "dumb" machine that happens to offer superior speed and reliability.

T F **20.** The fact that the computer is capable of performing only a few basic processing operations is a major limitation.

21. _____ Modern America is *best* described as a(n):

a. production society
b. marketing society
c. affluent society
d. information society

22. _____ The electronic and electromechanical parts of the computer are collectively termed:

a. software
b. hardware
c. a computer system
d. an information system

23. _____ The set of hardware and software used as a single unit is most properly referred to as a(n):
   a. computer
   b. information system
   c. application
   d. computer system

24. _____ When a computer system is employed to serve a practical use in a business setting, it is termed a:
   a. computer information system
   b. software system
   c. hardware system
   d. computer system

25. _____ The symbols used to represent facts, events, or things are called:
   a. information
   b. data
   c. code.
   d. input

26. _____ The meaning given to a set of data that has been processed is referred to as:
   a. logic
   b. a program
   c. information
   d. an application

27. _____ Those devices added to a computer system to provide input, storage, or the display of information are called:
   a. peripherals
   b. software
   c. hardware
   d. secondary storage devices

28. _____ Which of the following parts of a computer system are used to provide permanent storage of data and information in a computer-readable form?
   a. peripherals
   b. programs
   c. applications
   d. secondary storage devices

29. _____ Those programs that perform specific user-oriented tasks are called:
   a. application software
   b. dedicated software
   c. specialized software
   d. systems software

30. _____ The computer can perform which of the following basic processing operations:
   a. arithmetic operations
   b. formatting
   c. intelligent operations
   d. creative operations

CHAPTER 2

Computers in Business

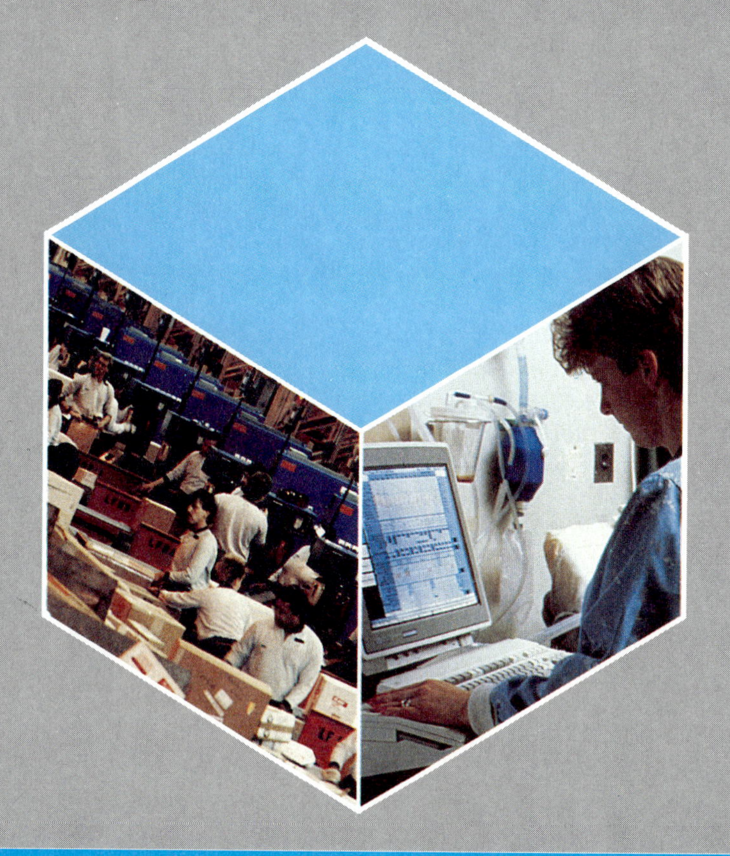

Growth of Business Computer Use
Advances in Computer Systems
Influence of End-User Computing
Gaining a Competitive Edge with Computers

The Expansion of End-User Computing
Business
Politics
Education
Art and Entertainment
Science and Medicine
Communication

Information Needs of Business
What Doing Business Involves
How a Business Uses Computers
How Information Systems Interact
Information Systems Between Businesses

Computers at Work
A Copy Writer's Journey into the Age of PCs

Summary and Key Terms

Review Questions

Business firms today are greatly expanding their use of computers. Many have recognized that innovative uses of the computer's information processing capabilities can provide them with an edge on their competitors. An ability to spot situations where computers can be used in business is becoming extremely valuable, and this chapter will help you to develop that skill. You will learn to do the following:

1. Explain some of the factors involved in the increase in business computer use
2. List and discuss five ways that a business can gain a competitive edge by using computers
3. List some of the areas of society where end-user computing is growing
4. Describe what a business does
5. List the three major types of computer information systems, and describe how they are related

Growth of Business Computer Use

As Exhibit 2.1 shows, the use of computers in business of all sizes has grown rapidly over the last ten years. Many firms would simply not exist today without the use of a wide variety of computers and information systems. There are three reasons for this growth. First, advances in microelectronics have increased the power and reduced the cost of business computing. Second, the explosive growth of personal computing has increased the computer literacy of employees, and the end-user orientation of microcomputers and their software has allowed more users to become creators of information systems. Finally, as competition among companies continues to increase, a company's gaining a competitive advantage often depends on its ability to use computers efficiently and innovatively.

Advances in Computer Systems

Stated simply, today's hardware provides more capability for less money. For example, a microcomputer can be purchased today for less than $2000. In terms of processor speed and primary memory, this personal computer is more powerful than the System/360 series computer system offered by IBM in the 1960s. Yet, the price of a System/360 computer at that time was over $1 million. In addition, System/360 computer systems also required a large, costly computer staff. Consequently, only large, wealthy corporations could justify computer use. As hardware prices have dropped, however, more and more businesses are able to afford a computer system (see Exhibit 2.2). In addition, pressure from users to be able to connect computer hardware

Exhibit 2.1

The Growth of Business Computing

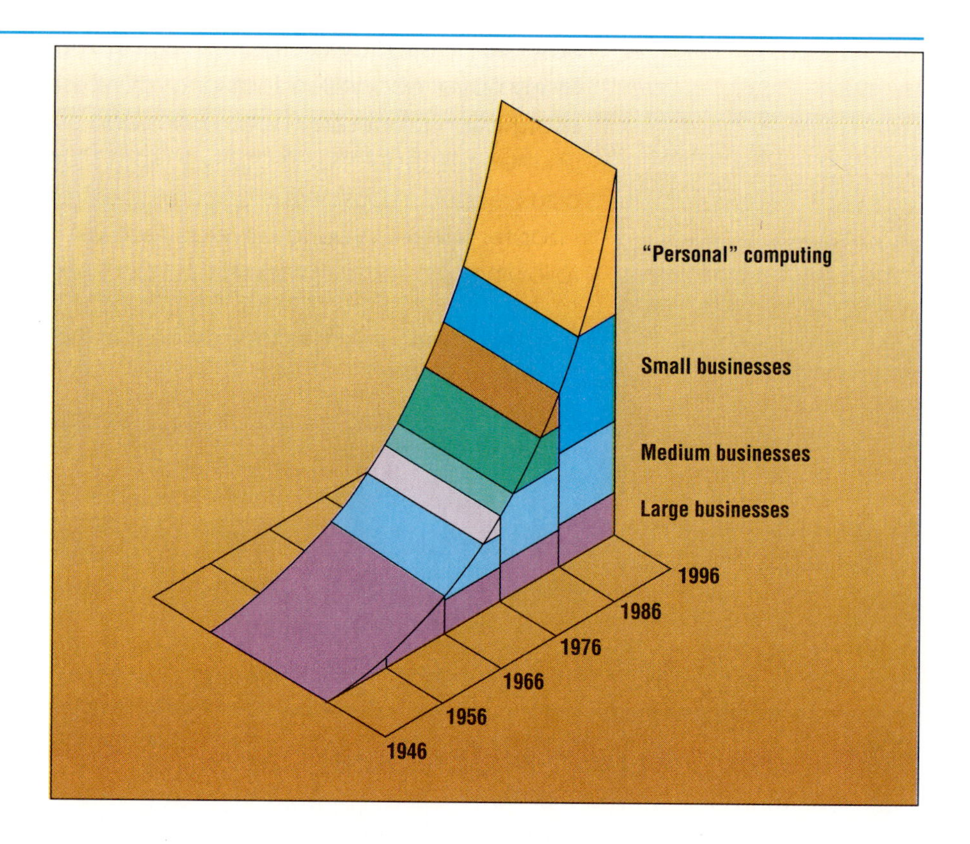

from different vendors has led the industry into producing compatible computers. This allows users to purchase hardware from a number of vendors; the increased competition in the marketplace in turn keeps costs down.

Although hardware advances prompted this surge in business computing, software is now the driving force. Hardware provides a tool for solving business problems, but software puts this tool to use. Why has software become such a key factor in today's world of business computing?

The growing number of businesses owning computer systems has created a thriving market for software packages that perform standard business applications. And, as more specialized software packages become available, even more businesses become convinced that they can benefit from computer use.

The attraction of "ready-made" software packages is easy to understand. When you take a trip, you don't draw your own map, because you can buy very good maps at low prices. The same reasoning applies to standard business software. Why should a firm develop its own programs when it can buy them from a software company, which spreads the development cost over a large sales volume?

Improvements in today's hardware allow programmers to develop software that is far more powerful and far simpler to use than software developed only a decade ago. Sophisticated and easy-to-use business software requires large amounts of primary memory and secondary storage

Exhibit 2.2

PC Penetration in Small Businesses

As hardware prices drop and power increases, more and more smaller businesses are able to afford a computer system.

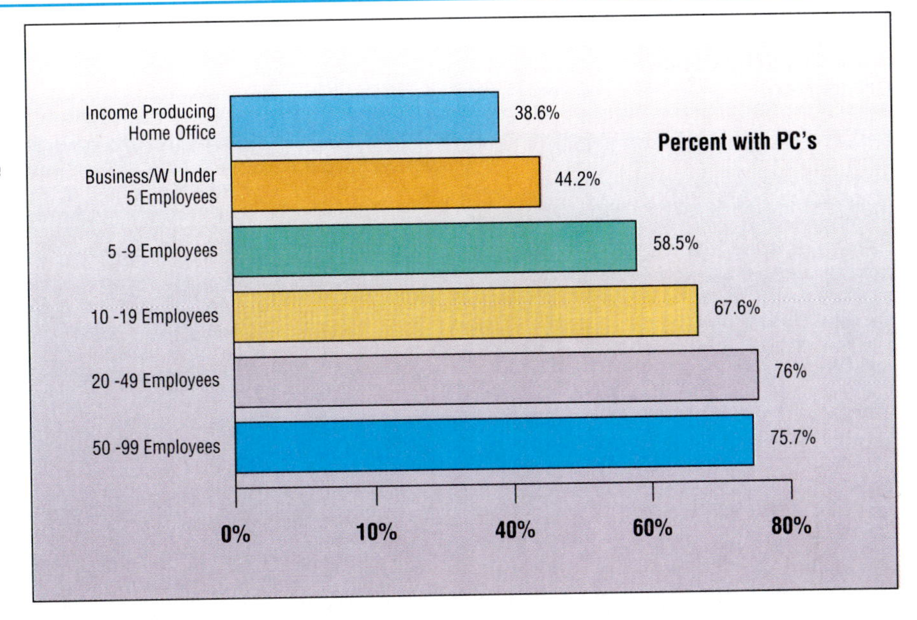

as well as fast processing and data retrieval speeds. Much of the success of today's popular microcomputer software packages can be traced to the fact that the software packages are very efficient and convenient to use. Also, with the compatibility of hardware, a software package can be run on computers supplied by many different vendors.

The result of these advances in information systems is a growing spiral of computer use. As hardware becomes more advanced and less expensive, more businesses use computers. With more computer systems in place, the cost of sophisticated, easy-to-use software decreases, prompting even more business computing (see Exhibit 2.3).

Influence of End-User Computing

Advances in computers' capabilities and ease of use have led to the emergence of a new style of computing known as *end-user computing*.

In the past, the complexity of large computer systems made the creation of information systems a task that was performed only by specially trained computer experts. There was a clear distinction between the users and the creators of an information system. Business professionals—such as managers, financial analysts, market researchers, and accountants—use information to carry out business functions; they are not required to be computer experts. Computer professionals have the technical understanding of computer systems and knowledge of business functions. **CIS computing** is the development of computer information systems in which the user role is assumed primarily by the business professional and the creator role is assumed primarily by the computer professional. This type of computing will be discussed in detail in Chapter 7, "Systems Development."

Exhibit 2.3

Increases in Business Computing

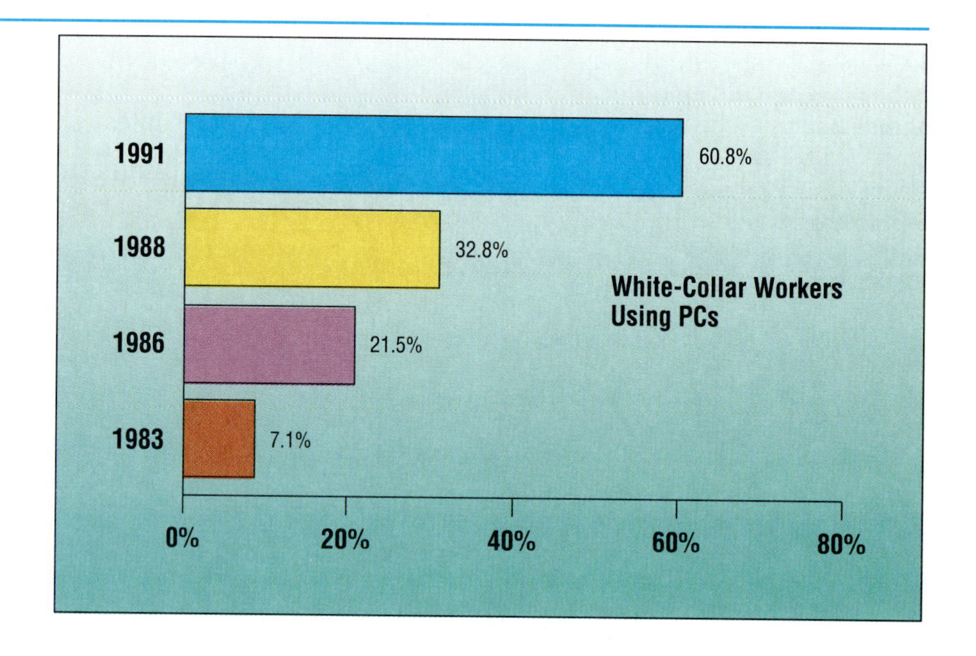

In contrast, **end-user computing** is the development of computer information systems in which both the user and creator roles are assumed primarily by the business professional. End-user computing has grown because of the wide availability of powerful, easy-to-use software packages for microcomputers.

There are software packages designed for a wide variety of information processing tasks. *Word processors* allow users to create, edit, store, and print "electronic" documents. *Electronic spreadsheets* allow users to work with tables of numbers. A user can enter, edit, store, and print numeric data as well as produce graphs. *Graphics programs* allow users to create graphs based on numbers and also transform the microcomputer screen into an electronic drawing board on which diagrams and pictures can be created. *Database management systems* allow users to store data in an electronic filing cabinet and later retrieve that data to produce reports. *Communications software* allows a user to connect a microcomputer to other computers and exchange information. The features of all these software products are discussed more fully in *Part IV* "End-User Software."

As Exhibit 2.4 illustrates, projections for the future indicate that end-user computing based on these types of software packages will continue to grow. As this trend continues, increasing numbers of business professionals will become creators of information systems in addition to maintaining their more traditional role as users of information.

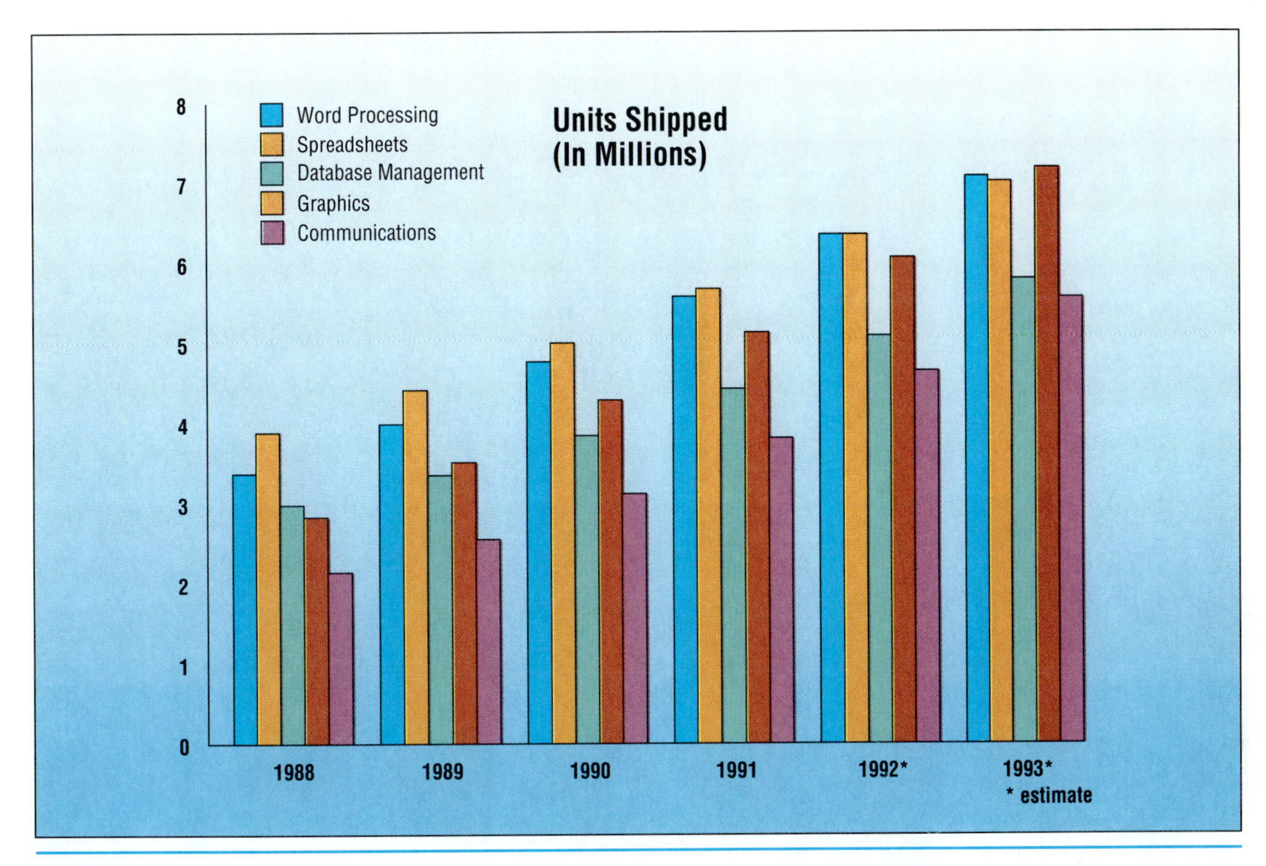

Exhibit 2.4

Growth in Microcomputer Software Sales

Gaining a Competitive Edge with Computers

Information systems are becoming important weapons in the battles being fought in today's highly competitive marketplace. If a business's managers are knowledgeable about computers and information systems, they may be able to introduce new information systems that can give them significant advantages over their competitors.

There are five basic strategies for gaining a competitive edge through computers:

- Become the *low cost producer* in a market
- Introduce *new products and services*
- Impose *high switching costs* on customers to prevent them from moving to a competitor
- Introduce *barriers* that prevent new competitors from entering your market
- Provide *high-quality management information* so that better decisions can

Exhibit 2.5

Computers and Information Systems Used in Business

Federal Express and other air express companies depend heavily on computers and information systems for business success.

Air express companies, such as Federal Express (see Exhibit 2.5), provide good examples for illustrating these five strategies. Automatic sorting systems eliminate the high costs of manual labor, which is important if a firm strives to be the low-cost producer in the industry. Computerized tracking systems provide new services, such as guaranteeing the exact status of a package within thirty minutes. By providing high-volume customers with a microcomputer and software to manage mailroom activities, an air express company can provide strong incentives that "lock-in" the customer. The huge investment in computers and information systems required to be competitive in the air express industry limits the number of active competitors. Finally, many services that air express companies offer, such as guaranteed delivery before 10:00 a.m., are expensive to provide. Should a new service be provided? Should a firm react to a new service being offered by a competitor? Information systems developed to provide management with the answers to questions such as these can be extremely valuable for helping managers make better decisions.

As you can see, effective use of computer technology is helping companies gain an edge over their competitors. In the future, a company's ability to remain competitive will be determined by its ability to use technology effectively. The next section offers some examples of how computers are being used both in business and in other parts of our society.

The Expansion of End-User Computing

With the birth of end-user computing, business professionals are able to create their own information systems and in the process redefine the nature of their work. The personal computer has changed how businesses are run, redefined the role of workers, and changed the way we communicate. This revolution has affected many parts of our society and our personal lives as well (see Exhibit 2.6). This section illustrates some of the innovative ways that personal computers are being applied in business, politics, education, art and entertainment, science and medicine, and communication.

Exhibit 2.6

The Location of Installed PCs

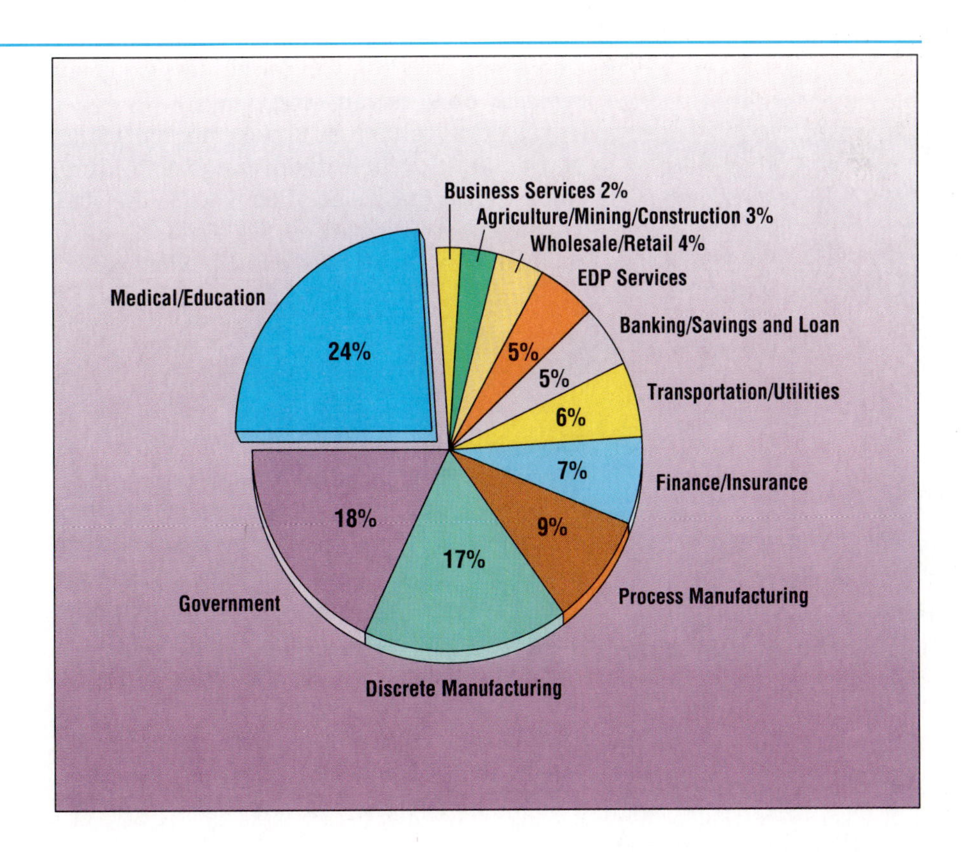

Business

Many companies are redefining the customer-salesperson relationship by arming their sales staff with laptop personal computers. By linking these computers to a main computer in the office, sales representatives can get up-to-the-minute inventory and pricing information. Orders can be placed and verified electronically. With the power of the personal computer, sales reps can also perform analyses on pricing, to help customers determine the most cost-effective products to buy. Orders can be printed and given to the customer immediately, which helps reduce later disputes about what was ordered. These applications of personal computers not only help reduce business costs, they also redefine the salesperson's job by allowing them more time to discuss new products and market trends with the customer.

Realtors are making long-distance house hunting simpler by offering computerized data bases that substitute for the usual guided tours. Using the database buyers can view digital images of house exteriors and interiors while listening to a voice-over narration. The database also contains information about room dimensions, school systems, and property taxes.

Personal computers equipped with laser printers and specialized software have created a new form of publishing known as desktop publishing. When marketing products, companies can quickly design brochures and promotional materials on a computer capable of desktop publishing, rather than relying on the traditional method of creating layouts on paper and going through typesetting and paste-up procedures. Desktop publishing is not only faster but less expensive for many of the design jobs typically done within a company.

On Wall Street, brokers are replacing older terminals with personal computers that help them monitor trading, look for trends, and order trades. With these electronic links to the stock exchange and commodities markets, brokers can obtain almost real-time access and use complex mathematical analyses to make buying and selling decisions.

Politics

The application of personal computers in the election process has gone far beyond just electronically counting votes. Some of the most successful campaign managers are using personal computers to help coordinate direct-mail fund raising. Computerized lists of contributors are used to target donors with particular political interests.

A personal computer can maintain a list of phone numbers for polling voters and help campaign managers target precincts that need more attention. Schedules for candidate appearances, financial records, and information about opponents can be maintained. Voter statistics such as location, sex, age, and political party can be stored. Efforts of campaign workers and volunteers can be coordinated.

Software capable of electronically storing maps and attaching data to locations on those maps can be used to combine geographic data with voting history to more efficiently target a door-to-door campaign. Following the 1990 census, mapping software will play a vital role in political redistricting to ensure that each electoral district is equal.

Education

The most common use of personal computers in the educational environment takes place in computer labs, where students study the computer itself in the context of an information systems course. Today, computers are also being viewed as vehicles for innovative ways of teaching and learning. Computers are now being applied to the tasks of accelerating and enhancing the learning process.

The marriage of interactive computer technology and videodisc images can be used to present material and to test students' comprehension through practice exercises and simulations. Business schools are developing simulated companies in which students can apply concepts learned in classes and textbooks to near real-life situations (see Exhibit 2.7).

Art and Entertainment

Artists are using personal computers to generate and manipulate experimental images. Sculptors, for example, can use personal computers to

Exhibit 2.7

Computers Are Redefining the Teaching and Learning Process

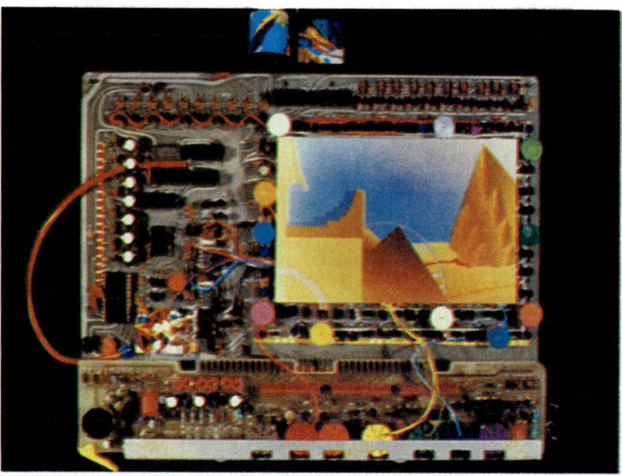

Exhibit 2.8

Computer Art
These are two examples of computer generated art from the New York City SIGGRAPH show.

create models and experiment with variations before committing to an actual physical piece. The Fine Arts Museum of Long Island recently created a permanent exhibit of computer art, in which visitors can view art and also use computers to experiment with their own images (see Exhibit 2.8).

Personal computers have reinvented the concept of entertainment. Improvements in personal computer graphics and speed have allowed sophisticated games to be created. In 1988 a short film called *Tin Toy* became the first computer generated film to win an Academy Award. LucasFilm's Industrial Light and Magic division makes extensive use of personal computers to control camera movements for special effects sequences in movies such as those in the *Star Wars* series. With a Musical Instrument Digital Interface (MIDI), personal computers can be used to control synthesizers to produce music.

Science and Medicine

Personal computer applications in science and medicine are also beginning to appear (see Exhibit 2.9). The highly sophisticated diagnostic equipment in modern hospitals relies heavily on computerization. For example, CT (computed tomography) uses X-ray images analyzed by computer to produce a detailed series of images representing cuts or sections through the body. Magnetic Resonance Imaging (MRI) uses magnetic fields and radio waves to create electronic pulses that can be amplified and analyzed by computer to produce images of the spinal cord and brain.

Personal computers help neurosurgeons locate within a millimeter the area of the brain needing surgery. Computer data bases can help doctors understand diseases and determine who is at risk. For example, a personal computer was used to discover the genealogical links in ovarian cancer and can be used to determine others who will be at risk for the disease.

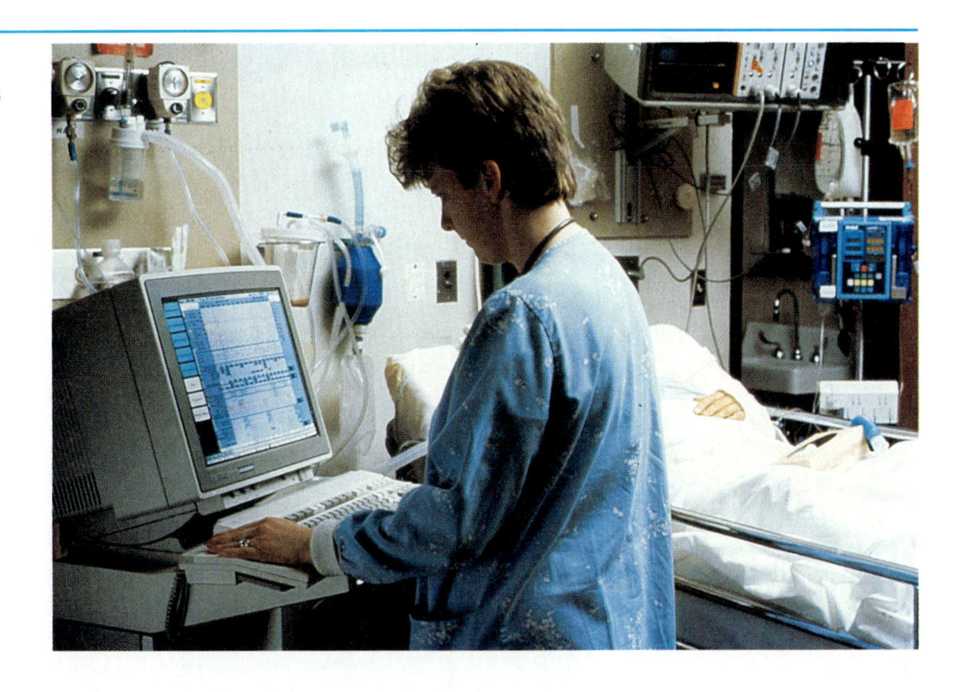

Exhibit 2.9

Application of Computers to Medicine

Personal computers are also being used in the fight against AIDS. Researchers can compare the AIDS virus to genetically engineered viruses in hopes of finding a way to create a vaccine.

Communication

Computers are changing the way we communicate. FAX machines allow documents to be sent from coast to coast in fifteen seconds. FAX machines were used to send information into and out of China during the June 1989 incident in Tiananmen Square. By electronically linking with the office, employees are able to work at home.

The quality of written communication has improved through the wide availability of word processors and desktop publishing software. Electronic bulletin boards and electronic mail allow information to be exchanged more freely and easily.

Cooperative processing systems, such as Prodigy, are making a wide variety of electronic services and information available to personal computer users. These systems link the power of mainframes, the speed of minicomputers, and the versatility of personal computers to provide these services, with low processing and access times. For example, Prodigy users can display on their PC screens a map of the country showing local and national weather conditions (see Exhibit 2.10).

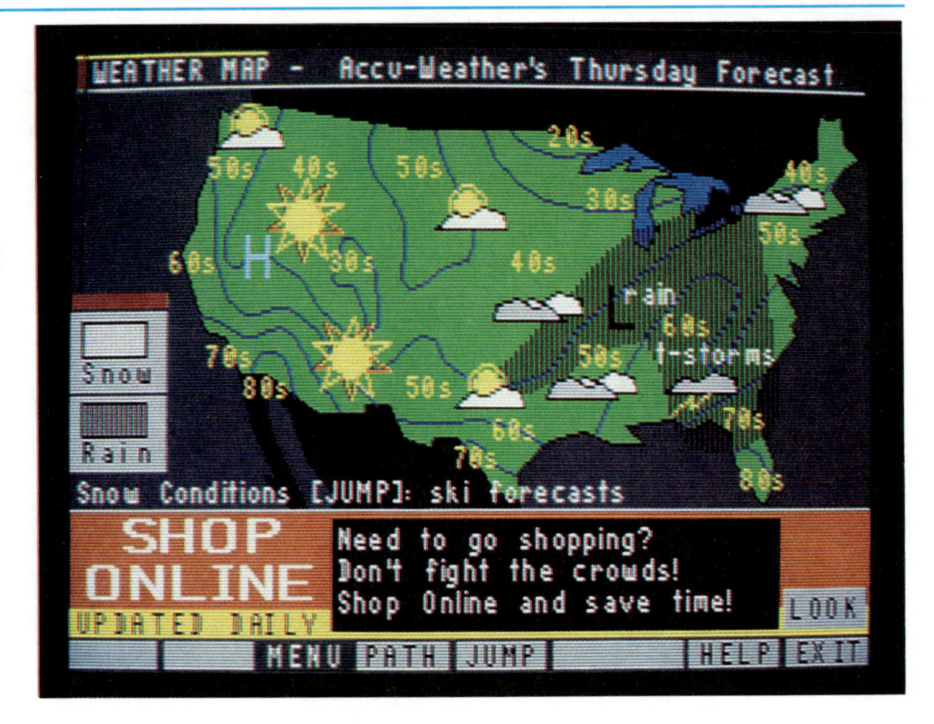

Exhibit 2.10

Personal Computers Change the Way We Communicate

A daily weather report and on-line shopping are just two of the features a Prodigy subscriber can call up on their PC.

Information Needs of Business

Although end-user computing has had an impact on many aspects of our society, the most prevalent use of computers is still within the area of business. This section presents a brief introduction to the various functions within business and a more detailed look at the types of information systems used in business.

What Doing Business Involves

Before looking at the types of information systems used in business, let's briefly review the major functional areas within business.

Buying and Selling

Among the most important aspects of business operations are, of course, buying and selling. **Buying** is the determination of which goods are needed and from which suppliers they should be purchased. You might be surprised to learn that businesses' buying behaviors are very similar to your own behaviors as a consumer. For example, a business must do the following:

- Assess needs (How many units are needed?)

- Set purchasing priorities (Is quick delivery more important than low price?)
- Evaluate the goods offered by suppliers (Is the higher quality of product A worth its higher price?)
- Make the purchase
- Receive the purchased goods
- Examine the quality of the received goods
- Pay for the purchase

The other side of the coin is business **selling.** Deciding what products to offer and creating a demand for those products is the general responsibility of marketing; selling and delivering goods is the responsibility of sales. For example, a business must do the following:

- Decide what goods it will offer to others
- Create a demand for its products
- Maintain a sufficient inventory of its products to meet customer demand
- Accept customer orders
- Process customer orders
- Deliver the goods the customers ordered
- Bill the customers
- Receive and process customer payments

Often the items purchased by a company are parts that are the raw materials for creating the products that are sold. **Manufacturing** is the making and assembling of parts into finished goods.

The activities of buying, manufacturing, and selling are the obvious aspects of doing business that occur to most of us. What might not be so obvious, however, is the crucial link between buying and manufacturing and between manufacturing and selling. This link is provided by **inventory,** a supply of goods held in reserve. As seen in Exhibit 2.11, inventory acts as a buffer between a business's manufacturing, buying, and selling activities. Without this buffer, manufacturing, buying, and selling would have to be perfectly coordinated. Imagine how difficult that would be! Monitoring inventory is important, particularly because inventory is a major business expense. Too little inventory means the company runs the risk of being unable to fill important customer orders. Too much inventory means that company money is tied up in unneeded products stored in a warehouse.

Exhibit 2.11

The Linking Role of Inventory

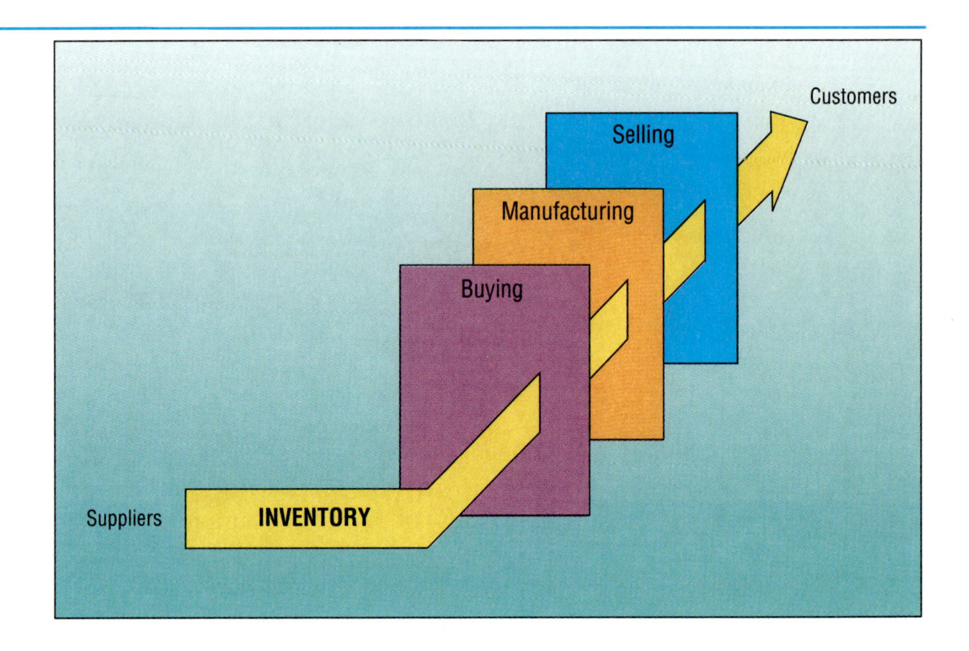

Accounting

Most business activities involve the exchange of valuable resources. The financial aspects of these exchanges must be accurately and promptly handled and reported. This is the responsibility of the **accounting** function. These financial accounts are kept in a **general ledger system,** which is used to produce business financial statements such as the income statement and balance sheet (see Exhibit 2.12). Similar to inventory, the general ledger system serves as a financial link between the different parts of a business (see Exhibit 2.13).

Office Work

Do you want an "office" job? *Office* is a term people use every day. It's no wonder—a majority of the labor force works in offices. Even people who do not have office jobs spend a great deal of their time in offices. What types of work do office jobs entail? There is surprising variety of answers to this question.

The **office** is commonly seen as those parts of a business that handle the paperwork associated with coordinating and controlling a business. Most of this paperwork falls into one of three categories:

- Various sets of administrative records, such as payroll, personnel, and equipment records
- General management activities, such as planning, budgeting, evaluating employee and department performances, and evaluating major investment decisions
- General office work that occurs throughout all businesses, such as typing, document copying, and company mail

Exhibit 2.12

Two Primary Types of Accounting Information Reports

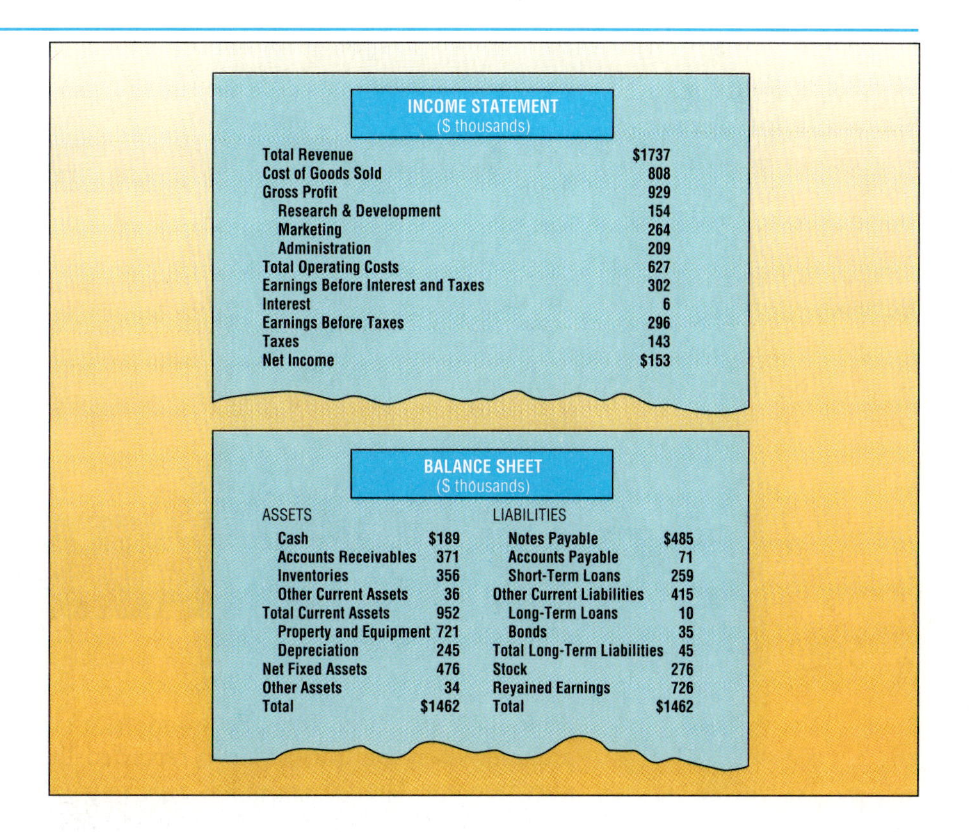

INCOME STATEMENT
($ thousands)

Total Revenue	$1737
Cost of Goods Sold	808
Gross Profit	929
Research & Development	154
Marketing	264
Administration	209
Total Operating Costs	627
Earnings Before Interest and Taxes	302
Interest	6
Earnings Before Taxes	296
Taxes	143
Net Income	$153

BALANCE SHEET
($ thousands)

ASSETS		LIABILITIES	
Cash	$189	Notes Payable	$485
Accounts Receivables	371	Accounts Payable	71
Inventories	356	Short-Term Loans	259
Other Current Assets	36	Other Current Liabilities	415
Total Current Assets	952	Long-Term Loans	10
Property and Equipment	721	Bonds	35
Depreciation	245	Total Long-Term Liabilities	45
Net Fixed Assets	476	Stock	276
Other Assets	34	Reyained Earnings	726
Total	$1462	Total	$1462

How a Business Uses Computers

The preceding simplified description of what a business does may give you some idea of the vast amount of data involved in everyday business activities. Computer information systems provide a fast and accurate way of handling and controlling these data. However, computers can also be a powerful tool for the managers responsible for setting and meeting the goals of a business. An information system used for managerial support is called a **management information system,** or **MIS.**

There are three categories of management information systems: transaction processing systems, information reporting systems, and decision support systems. Each type of information system serves a distinct information processing role. Brief discussions of these three types of information systems are given here. Chapter 6, "Management Information Systems," covers these systems in more depth.

Transaction Processing Systems

A transaction is a single business event, such as making a sale, taking an item out of inventory, or paying a bill. **Transaction processing systems** are used to record, process, and manage data. Historically, the earliest and still one of the heaviest users of business information systems is the accounting function.

Exhibit 2.14 illustrates the standard inputs and outputs normally associated with a transaction processing system. The input data describe a

Exhibit 2.13

The Linking Role of the General Ledger System

The general ledger system tracks the cash inflows and outflows associated with a business's buying, manufacturing, and selling activities.

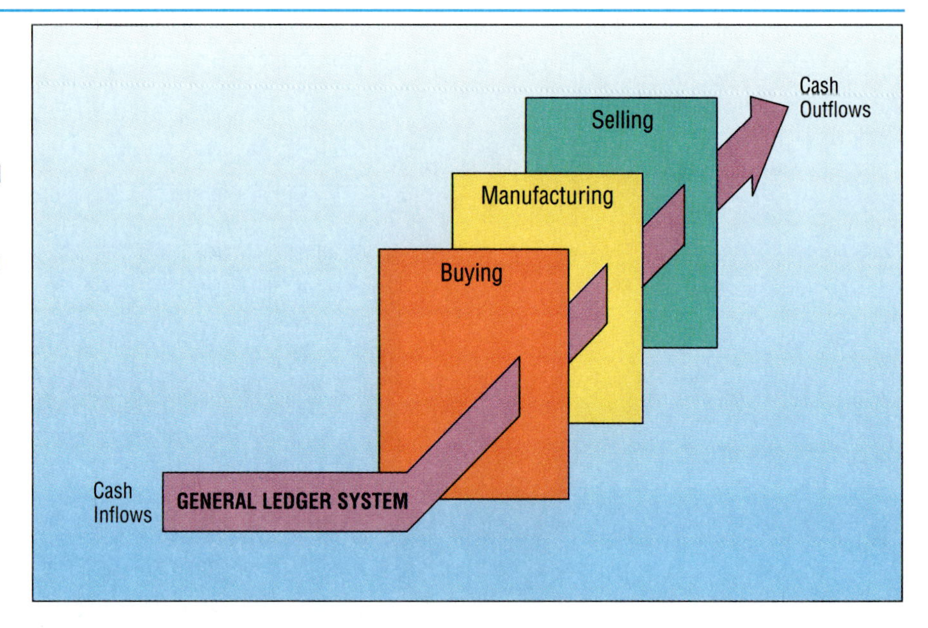

business transaction. Take, for example, a supply order. The supplies are ordered. Then the transaction is recorded in secondary storage—an open purchase file. The firm now has a permanent record that it ordered these supplies on this date. Then a business document, in this case a purchase order, is printed. Usually, in processing transactions, data also need to be retrieved from other data files. To print a purchase order, for example, the

Exhibit 2.14

A Transaction Processing System

Transaction processing systems support the day-to-day activities of a business. Here, business purchases are processed and recorded.

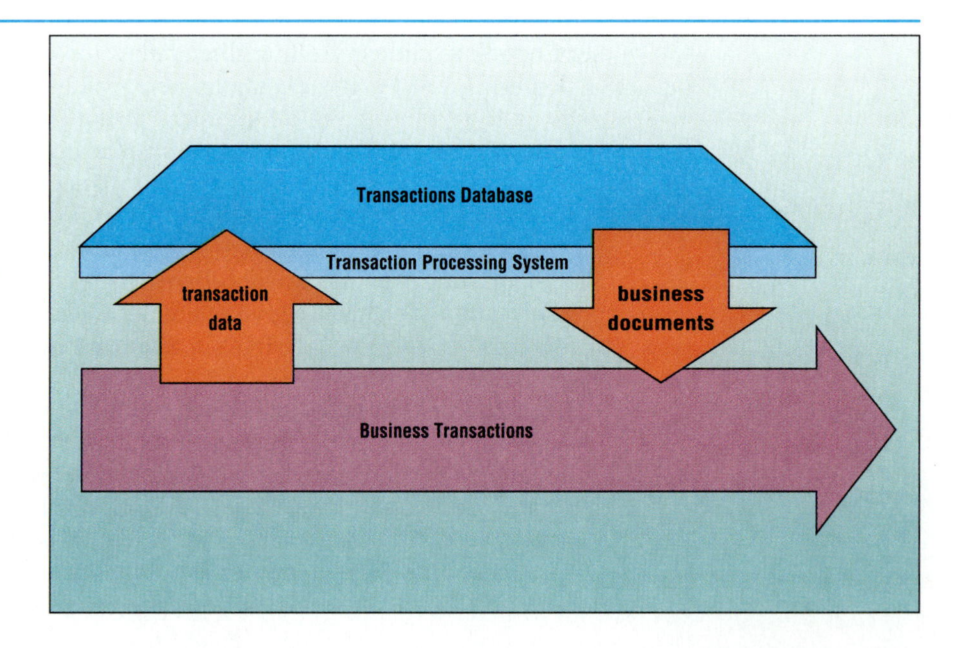

computer may need to read the supplier's name and address from a supplier file.

A key point to note is that transaction processing systems build and maintain data files that provide a detailed description of a firm's business activities. The term *database* is often used when referring to such a computerized pool of business data.

Information Reporting Systems

While transaction processing systems help a business to carry out its day-to-day activities, they do not provide much support to mid- and upper-level managers. To do their jobs well, these managers need more general types of information—what should be done, what was done, and how well it was done. The data available in transaction processing systems are just too detailed, and thus not very useful, for most managers. **Information reporting systems** "massage" these raw data to produce summary reports that are useful to managers.

For example, a sales manager is generally not interested in knowing how many wrenches Joe Smith sold to the Acme Company on April 15, or how much Joe spent on a business lunch that day. What the sales manager needs to know are answers to questions such as:

Has Joe Smith met his sales quota yet?

Is the overall sales goal for wrenches on schedule?

Are the department's travel expenses within budget?

To answer questions such as these, previously stored data about sales and travel transactions need to be analyzed and presented in a summary report to the sales manager at regular intervals. Information reports such as this help managers keep abreast of important issues.

Exhibit 2.15 illustrates the inputs and outputs that are found in an information reporting system. Raw data are retrieved from data files, transformed into meaningful information, and distributed in the form of management reports. The information produced for one report may also be stored in the database. Then this "information" can become the "data" for yet another management report.

Decision Support Systems

Although information reporting systems can keep managers apprised of the general well-being of their departments, this type of information system is often not particularly helpful when a manager must make a specific decision. Of more help in this situation is the **decision support system,** which allows managers to produce information tailored to a specific decision in an ad hoc fashion. The phrase *ad hoc* here means that the need for a specific collection of information need not have been anticipated.

Exhibit 2.15

An Information Reporting System

Information reporting systems provide managers with the information they need to keep a business performing at an efficient level.

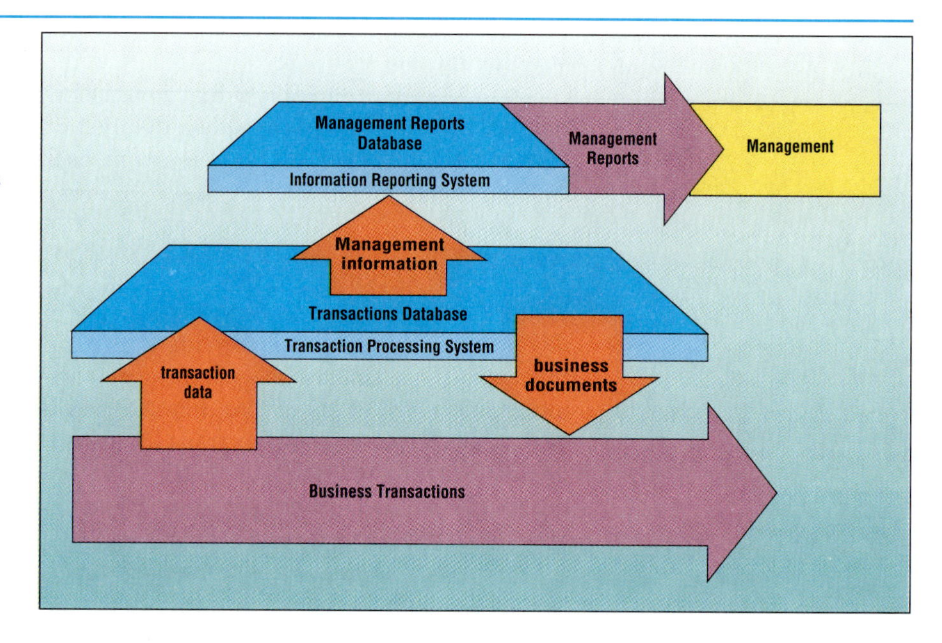

Consider, for example, a plant manager who receives the following urgent request from a senior executive:

> *How long would it take to manufacture and deliver a rush order to a new customer? If we can meet the customer's request, what impact will this have on producing regular orders scheduled for completion in the next two weeks?*

How useful are the following reports: a weekly status report on inventory levels (three days old), a monthly sales forecast (two weeks old), and a daily status report on all customer orders (twelve hours old)? Although each of these reports provides the plant manager with some picture of how well the plant is operating, they are not much help in answering the executive's question.

What the plant manager needs is some way to pull together current data on inventory levels, manufacturing operations, and order priorities so that he or she can determine whether it would be possible to rearrange manufacturing schedules for this rush order. Decision support systems provide this type of ad hoc information reporting. Further, the plant manager could use a decision support system to forecast the impact of the rush job on manufacturing during the next month.

Exhibit 2.16 illustrates the inputs and outputs normally found within a decision support system. A manager can directly interact with this information system to indicate which data are needed and what processing operations are to be performed. The decision support system then retrieves the requested data from the decision database, sets up the needed processing operation, processes the data, and produces the results. The manager can easily rerun the decision support system using different scenarios.

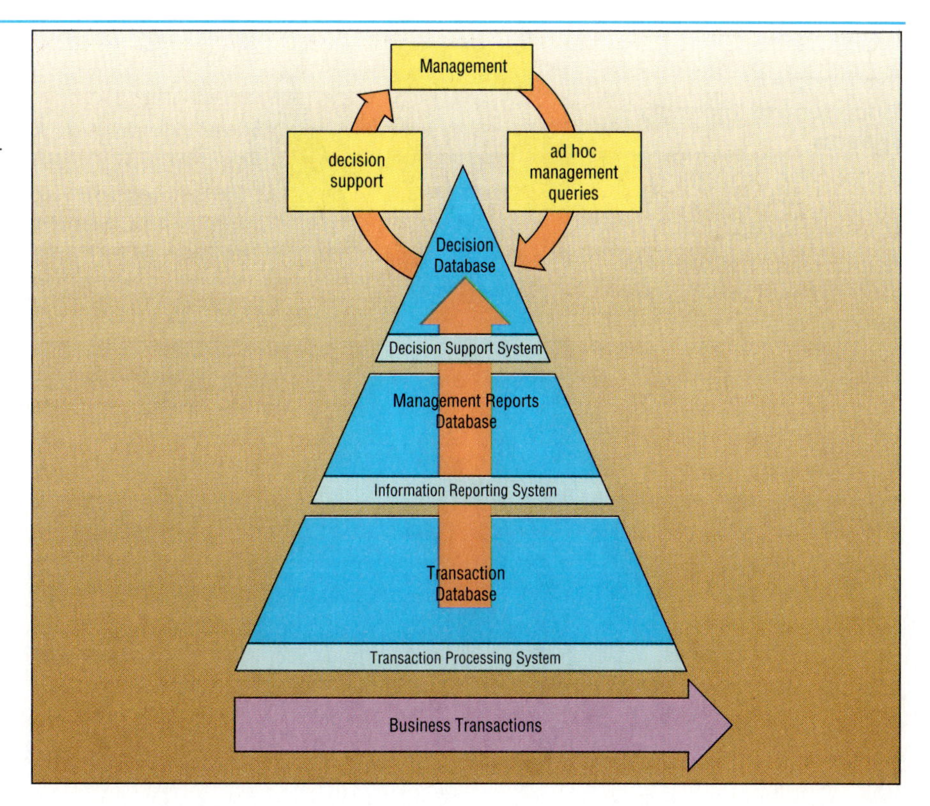

Exhibit 2.16

A Decision Support System

Decision support systems allow managers to interact with an information system, define ad hoc information reports, and do "what-if" planning.

How Information Systems Interact

Transaction processing systems, information reporting systems, and decision support systems fill three levels of business computing needs (see Exhibit 2.17). These levels reflect two ideas:

- Information systems at higher levels make use of data stored by information systems at lower levels. Information reporting systems "feed off" transaction processing systems, and decision support systems feed off both transaction processing systems and information reporting systems.
- Information systems at higher levels tend to serve higher business needs. Recall that transaction processing systems primarily support a firm's day-to-day activities. Information reporting systems are chiefly used by the managers responsible for making sure these day-to-day activities can be performed and are being performed well. Managers responsible for a firm's major business decisions depend upon decision support systems for vital information to give them a broad picture—backed up by and based upon specific details.

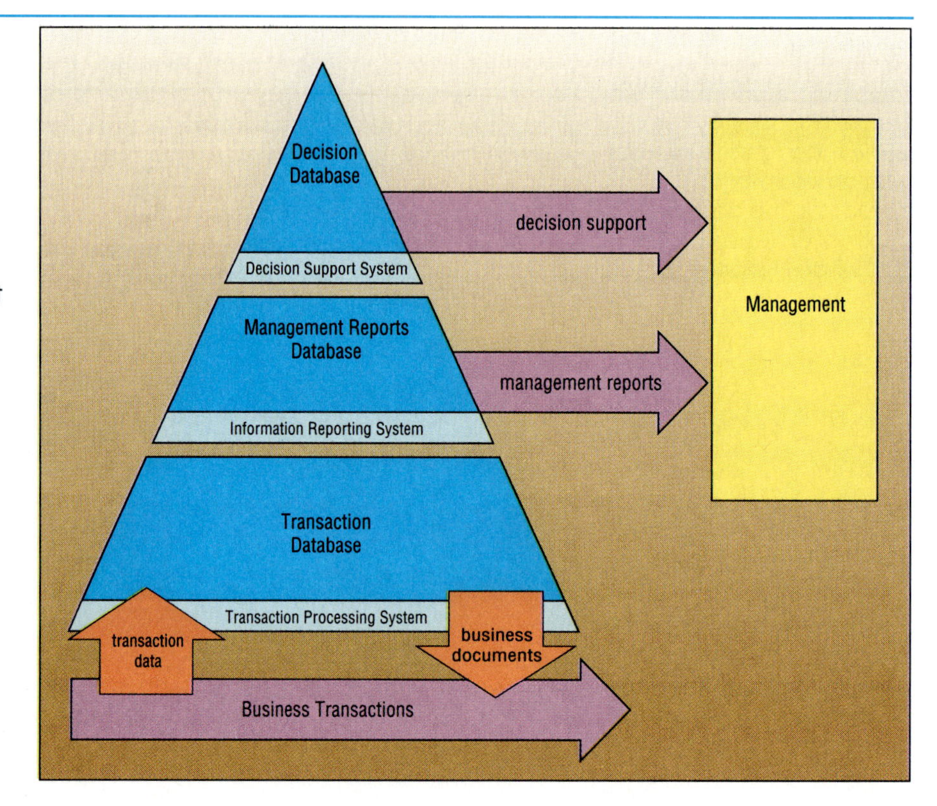

Exhibit 2.17

The Triangle of Management Information Systems

Transaction processing systems, information reporting systems, and decision support systems tend to serve three distinct levels of business computing.

Did you notice that the discussion shifted from talking about information systems that support business activities to information systems that support individual managers in a business? This dual nature of many business information systems emphasizes the key role that people play in an effective information system.

Information Systems Between Businesses

Businesses increasingly are using information systems to form electronic links among themselves, their suppliers, and their customers. Exhibit 2.18 illustrates this using the example of an automobile manufacturer. When a customer orders a particular model and color of car, the dealer types the order into a terminal in his or her showroom (1). Computer information systems then order parts (2), schedule shipments from suppliers (3), order the assembly line to interrupt its routine to make the special order (4), and track the car along the way (5). Not only do such electronic linkages help speed goods to market, but they also lower a business's costs.

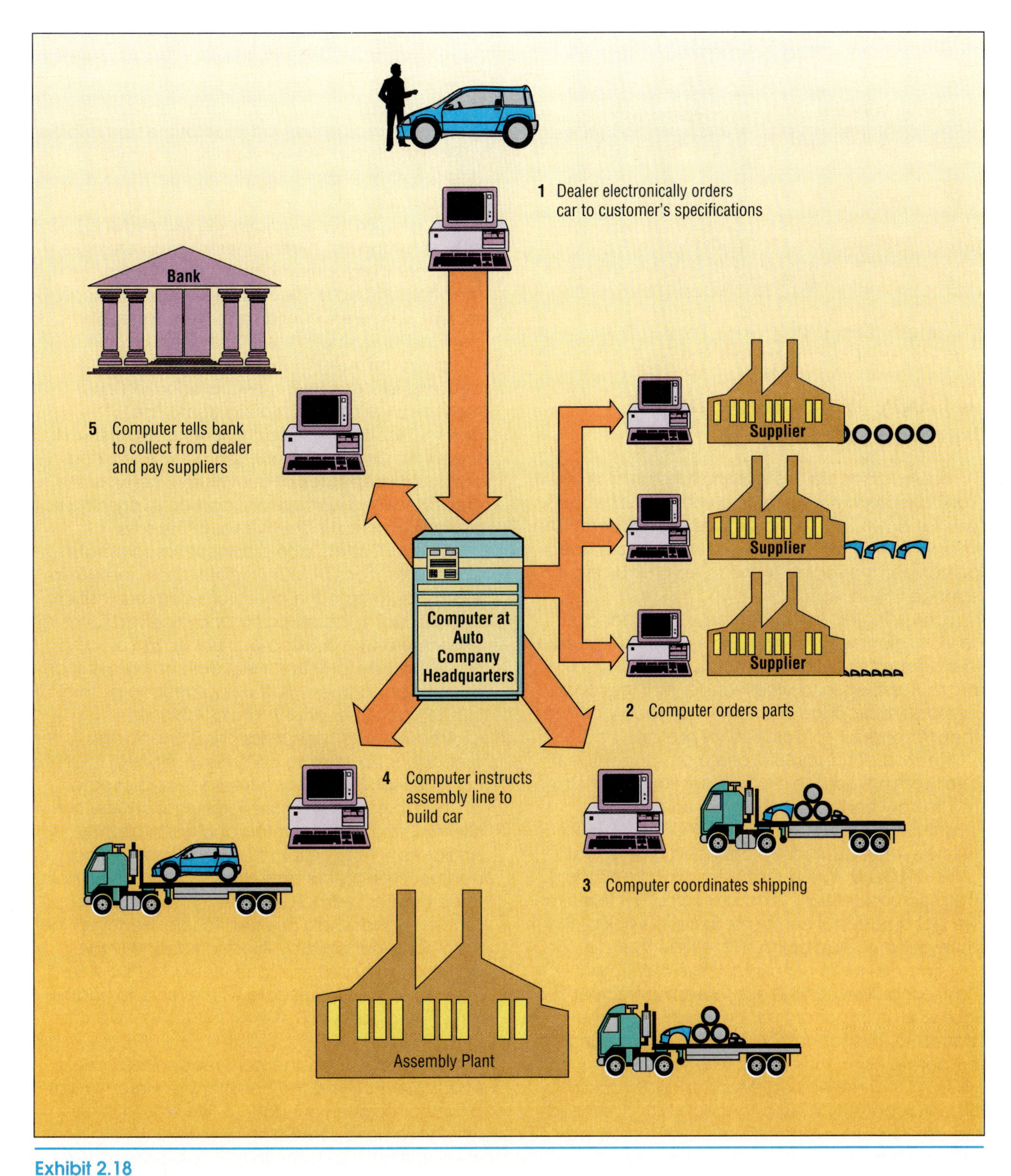

Exhibit 2.18

How an Automaker's Electronic Links with Other Businesses Help Build Cars

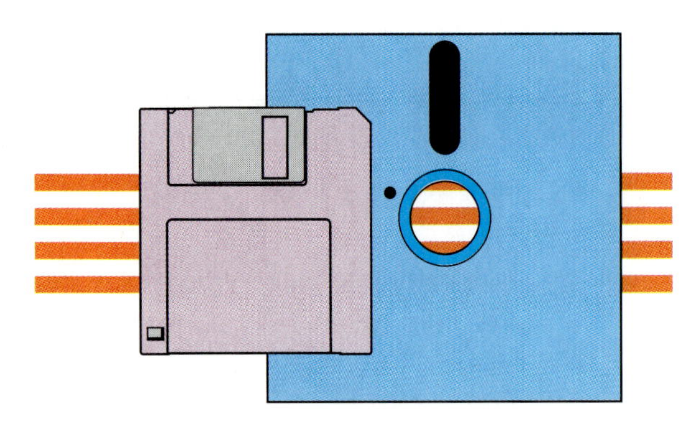

Computers at Work

A Copy Writer's Journey Into the Age of PCs

When Joe Lane started working for Mutual of New York, a laptop was something you formed when you sat down, and a mouse was just a rodent. The year was 1958, and computers were still confined primarily to the realms of the research lab and the science fiction story.

Lane's first job at the insurance and financial services giant was writing sales promotion literature in a department that churned out the many brochures, fliers, and prospectuses that insurance companies produce in volume. His typed work was then farmed out to a service for printing.

For most of his career, Lane did his job without ever coming close to a computer keyboard. He made slow and steady progress at MONY, eventually supervising a staff of four production workers. Then his work life changed dramatically.

"In 1983, I was responsible for print production of all corporate work," Lane explains. "At that time we got a personal computer to keep track of the many jobs we had going all the time that we contracted out to our printers. We monitored costs, deadlines, and specs." Keeping track of jobs was an important first step, but then Lane started to think about the 40 people specializing in corporate communications who worked at MONY's four major sites—Manhattan, Syracuse, N.Y., Purchase, N.Y., and Teaneck, N.J. "I realized we could make substantial improvements if we worked in a coordinated way," Lane recalls.

Lane started his PC experiment with an Apple II. He took several college courses on using it and programming with it. "I realized that we couldn't hook Apples to the mainframe network," Lane says. "By that time, I realized there was potential for end-user computing and that we needed structure so that using desktops wouldn't be a haphazard affair. Because Syracuse and the main office had to be in constant contact, I knew that I had to have desktops that connected with a mainframe as well as to each other."

By late 1984, Lane was turning his interest in PCs into a new job at MONY. "There was a very large group of MIS people who were interested in mainframes, and a small office systems unit, real PC experts, who were available to me," Lane recalls. "I decided to work with the office systems unit."

Lane continued to experiment with PCs. He became less involved in print production and more involved in automating corporate communications. "I thought, if we could network the writers and the production people together, we could keep track of our volume, network the creative writers with editors, and do everything in a timely and cost-effective way," he says.

Michael Cohen, vice president for corporate communications at MONY, gave Lane free rein in 1985 to automate the corporate communications department. Lane asked for and received funds to experiment with desktop publishing and used his natural affinity for PCs to help train others. He soon had the department staff doing desktop publishing using PageMaker and Ventura Publisher.

Among those Lane helped is Salina Wilson, manager of corporate communications at MONY's Purchase location. "I had to produce a directory of PPOs (preferred provider organizations) for our clients, listing which doctors and hospitals they could use," Wilson explains. "An outside vendor had been doing this at an astronomical cost and three months behind deadline. I explained the problems and what I needed to Joe. He set up the system, we cut costs by 75 percent, and I have camera-ready pages in one week. Joe's a wizard. He's able to communicate with everyone and he never intimidates you. He just makes you want to use a PC."

MONY's top management recognized Lane's efforts. He received the company's "Hero Award," a top honor given annually to five or six officers who have done something unusual or extraordinary that benefits the company. In 1986 MONY made him manager of electronic publishing and relocated him to the Syracuse office, where the company's computer center is based.

Lane, who is 53, retired from MONY this past June. As manager of electronic publishing, his job was significantly different from anything he envisioned when he started with MONY 31 years ago. "My staff and I did everything to support end users," he says. "We were the problem solvers. We taught them how to do their jobs better. If anyone had told me when I started my career I'd be working full-time in a computer environment, I wouldn't have known what they were talking about."

Summary and Key Terms

The use of computer systems by business is increasing at a rapid rate. Three major forces behind this growth are the remarkable advances in computer technology, explosive growth in end-user computing, and the growing need for companies to use computer technology in innovative ways to remain competitive.

Today's computer hardware provides continually greater information processing capabilities for less money. Although hardware originally prompted the surge in business computing, advances in computer software are now the driving force. This is due to the ready availability of powerful and easy-to-use business software packages.

The primary role business and CIS professionals play in the development and use of computer information systems depends on the type of information system under consideration. **CIS computing** is the development of computer information systems in which the user's role is assumed by the business professional and the creator's role is assumed by the CIS professional. **End-user computing** is the development of computer information systems in which both the user and creator roles are assumed primarily by the business professional.

Information systems are becoming important weapons in the battles being fought in today's highly competitive marketplace. The five basic strategies businesses use to gain a competitive edge through computers include becoming the low cost producer in a market, introducing new products and services, imposing high switching costs on customers, introducing barriers to prevent new competitors from entering the market, and making better decisions with the aid of high-quality management information.

The expansion of end-user computing is affecting all aspects of our society. Personal computing is changing how businesses are run, redefining the roles of workers, and changing the way we communicate.

Businesses create goods and services and then buy and sell them. Coordinating and controlling these functions requires a great deal of information. **Buying** is the determination of which goods are needed and from which suppliers these should be purchased. **Manufacturing** is the making and assembling of parts into finished goods. **Selling** is the sale and delivery of goods and services.

All these activities require careful coordination and planning and are linked through **inventory,** which is a supply of goods held in reserve. These business functions are further linked through the **general ledger,** which is used to produce financial statements. The **accounting** function is responsible for accurately and promptly handling and reporting the financial exchange of resources between businesses. **Offices** are those parts of an organization that handle the paperwork associated with coordinate and control, which keeps a business going.

The three categories of **management information systems** (MIS) are transaction processing systems, information reporting systems, and decision support systems. **Transaction processing systems** are used to record, process, and manage data. **Information reporting systems** massage these raw data to produce summary reports. **Decision support systems** allow managers to produce information tailored to a specific decision in an ad hoc fashion.

Review Questions

1. Briefly list and discuss the activities required in the buying and selling process. How can the computer be applied?
2. How can a computer be used in the office?
3. Describe the three categories of management information systems.
4. What are the two major roles that are required in the development of computer information systems? What role would business professionals assume?
5. What is the difference between CIS computing and end-user computing?
6. What are some of the fundamental tools used in end-user computing? Which ones have you heard about before?
7. Talk with friends or relatives to determine which end-user computing tools they have used and what they think are the advantages and disadvantages of those tools.
8. Find a newspaper or magazine article that shows the ways business is using information systems to electronically exchange orders or services.
9. What are some of the college classes that you would recommend a business professional take so that he or she could become an effective member of a computer information system development project?

T F **10.** End-user computing is the development of computer information systems in which both the user and creator roles are primarily used by the business professional.

T F **11.** CIS computing is the development of computer information systems in which both the user and creator roles are assumed primarily by the computer professional.

T F **12.** One method of gaining competitive advantage in which computers are useful is in the increasing a business's ability to create new products and services.

T F **13.** Information systems that are used for managerial support are called management information systems.

T F **14.** A transaction is the development of a computer information system by a business professional.

T F **15.** A transaction processing system is used to record, process, and manage data.

T F **16.** An information reporting system works with raw data to produce summary reports that are useful to managers.

T F **17.** Decision support systems are used to link transaction processing systems to information reporting systems.

T F **18.** Inventory is a supply of goods held in reserve that provides a crucial link between manufacturing, buying, and selling.

T F **19.** A general ledger system is used primarily in the manufacturing process.

20. _____ Which is not a strategy for gaining competitive advantage?

a. becoming a low cost producer
b. charging a higher price when costs go down
c. creating new products and services
d. creating barriers to new competitors

21. _____ An information system that is used to combine raw data to produce summary reports that are useful to managers is:

a. a transaction processing system
b. an information reporting system
c. a decision support system
d. a management information system

22. _____ An information system that records, processes, and manages data is:

a. a transaction processing system
b. an information reporting system
c. a decision support system
d. a management information system

23. _____ An information system that allows managers to produce information tailored to answer an ad hoc question is:

a. a transaction processing system
b. an information reporting system
c. a decision support system
d. a management information system

24. _____ __________ acts as a buffer between a business's manufacturing, buying, and selling activities:

a. A general ledger
b. An office
c. An inventory
d. A management information

PART II

Computer Hardware Technology

CHAPTER 3

Computers, Small and Large

Every day, computers perform valuable functions in the workplace and the home. They are a popular source of entertainment for both children and adults. Clearly, computers are becoming an important part of modern society. Yet many people interact with computers without learning how they actually work, and thus they are missing an exciting and valuable part of the computing experience.

This chapter introduces you to the workings of the central processing unit, the computer's "brain." This knowledge can be useful in many ways. First, it can take the mystery out of the way a computer works. Too often, people think computers are capable of magic. In this chapter, you'll learn how and where the so-called magic happens. Second, understanding how a computer works can help you evaluate the relative merits of various computer models. This knowledge will be critical if you are faced with the responsibility of either choosing a computer for a specific business application or responding to the proposal of a systems analyst. This chapter concludes with a section on evaluating the relative power of computers (Part III of this book discusses the process of systems analysis and design). In this chapter, you will learn to do the following:

1. Describe the problem-solving process used in creating instructions for the computer and explain why this process is necessary
2. Describe the architecture of the central processing unit and explain the function of each part
3. Define the technology used for the major functions in microcomputers
4. Explain three primary means of classifying computers
5. Define and explain the two criteria used to determine computer power
6. Describe the effect of computer evolution on price and performance

The Problem-Solving Process

The reason computers are becoming so widely used in business, in government, at school, and even at home is that they help users solve problems. To learn how computers do this, you first need to understand the general problem-solving process. Then you will see some of the criteria for using computers to solve problems.

Much of the time, problem solving requires that you come up with a step-by-step procedure that leads to the desired result. This process is quite common in everyday life. Assume, for example, you are having

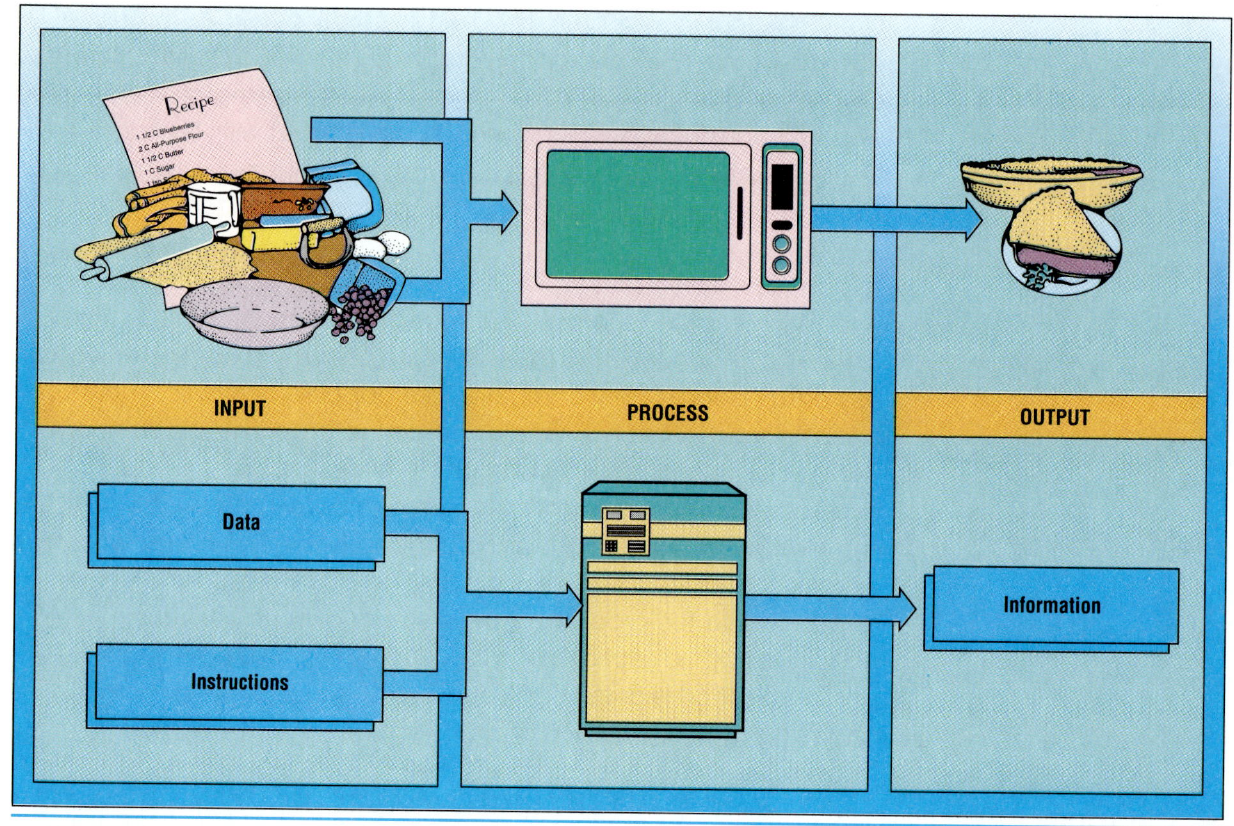

Exhibit 3.1

The Problem-Solving Process

A computer's problem-solving process is analogous to the procedures involved in baking a pie. Data or ingredients are input and processed according to a computer program or recipe. The outcome within the case of computers is information, which satisfies a need as a baked pie does.

friends over to your home, and you want to bake a pecan pie to offer them. The general procedure for solving this problem is listed in a recipe, which is made up of a list of ingredients and a list of instructions.

First, you need to get the ingredients: pecans, corn syrup, eggs, a pastry shell, and so on. Second, you need to follow the step-by-step procedure for preparing these ingredients and baking the pie. Step 1 is to cream the butter and sugar until light. Step 2 is to beat the eggs with a fork. In later steps, the pie is placed in the oven and baked for 35 to 40 minutes at 425 degrees. The result of this procedure is a baked pecan pie.

The major aspects of this problem-solving method are the input, process, and output functions. The input is a recipe and ingredients. The oven performs the process of transforming the raw ingredients into a baked pie. The baked pecan pie itself is the output and the desired solution to the problem (see Exhibit 3.1).

This example is similar to how problem solving works with a computer. Computer instructions, or programs, function like the recipe, and the data are the ingredients. The computer is used to process the data according to the program instructions, and it produces the desired output. The computer output could be a management report of sales activities, payroll checks, or a patient's medical record.

There are several key differences between the baking analogy and actual computer processing. One difference is that the oven is a rather simple single-purpose machine. Computers, on the other hand, are general-purpose machines that can be instructed to perform a variety of tasks, such as generating musical output, controlling traffic lights, and even playing chess. The second difference is that, although recipes contain step-by-step procedures, they would not be specific enough to direct a computer.

For example, a recipe assumes you have or will get the ingredients and utensils needed to perform each instruction. Furthermore, some of the instructions require interpretation. You are told to "cream butter and sugar until light," but how light is "light"? And when, for example, is the pie really baked to perfection? The suggested period of 35 to 40 minutes is just a general guideline. The instructions in recipes leave gaps that must be filled by experience and interpretation. Computers can neither learn nor interpret.

To process information, the computer needs very specific instructions that state explicitly what is to be done. There is no room for vagueness. Like a mathematical formula, the step-by-step instructions given a computer must make no assumptions and must lead to the same result every time. Precise instructions for solving a particular type of problem are called **algorithms.** Algorithms are used as the basis of computer programs or software.

To see how this concept is applied, consider the simple payroll example in Exhibit 3.2. John Avery worked 40 hours last week, and he gets

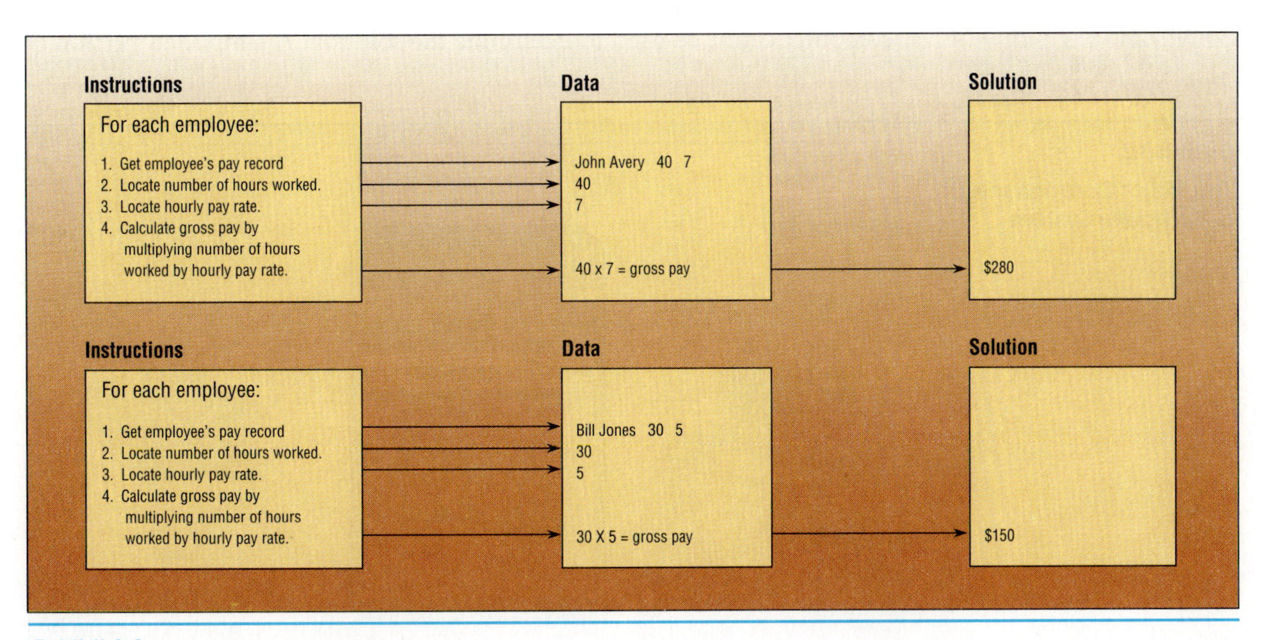

Exhibit 3.2

The Payroll Problem-Solving Process

paid $7 per hour. What is his gross pay? Even without your calculator, you know that the answer is $280. But how did you figure this out? More importantly, what instructions would a computer need to execute in order to calculate the gross pay for all employees of this company? Keep in mind that the computer cannot do anything beyond your instructions. The step-by-step instructions might be the following:

For each employee

1. Get employee's pay record.
2. Locate number of hours worked.
3. Locate hourly pay rate.
4. Calculate gross pay by multiplying number of hours worked by hourly pay rate.

This set of instructions would be an algorithm for calculating gross pay. The problem-solving process would be to apply these instructions to a set of data. In John Avery's case, the resulting solution would be $280.

This procedure would work equally well for determining the gross pay of any employee. You would simply need to change the data (employee name, hours worked, and pay rate) and reapply the algorithm. For example, Bill Jones worked 30 hours and gets paid $5 per hour. Thus, his gross pay is calculated to be $150.

Let's take the payroll problem-solving steps and see how a computer could be used to determine the solution. A simplified version of

Exhibit 3.3

The Major Components of a Computer System

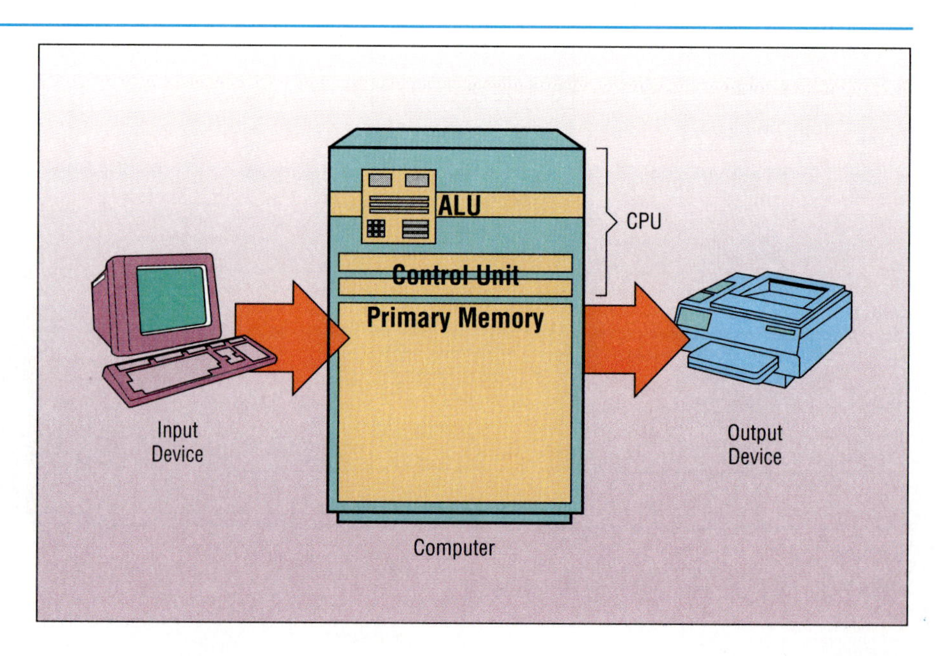

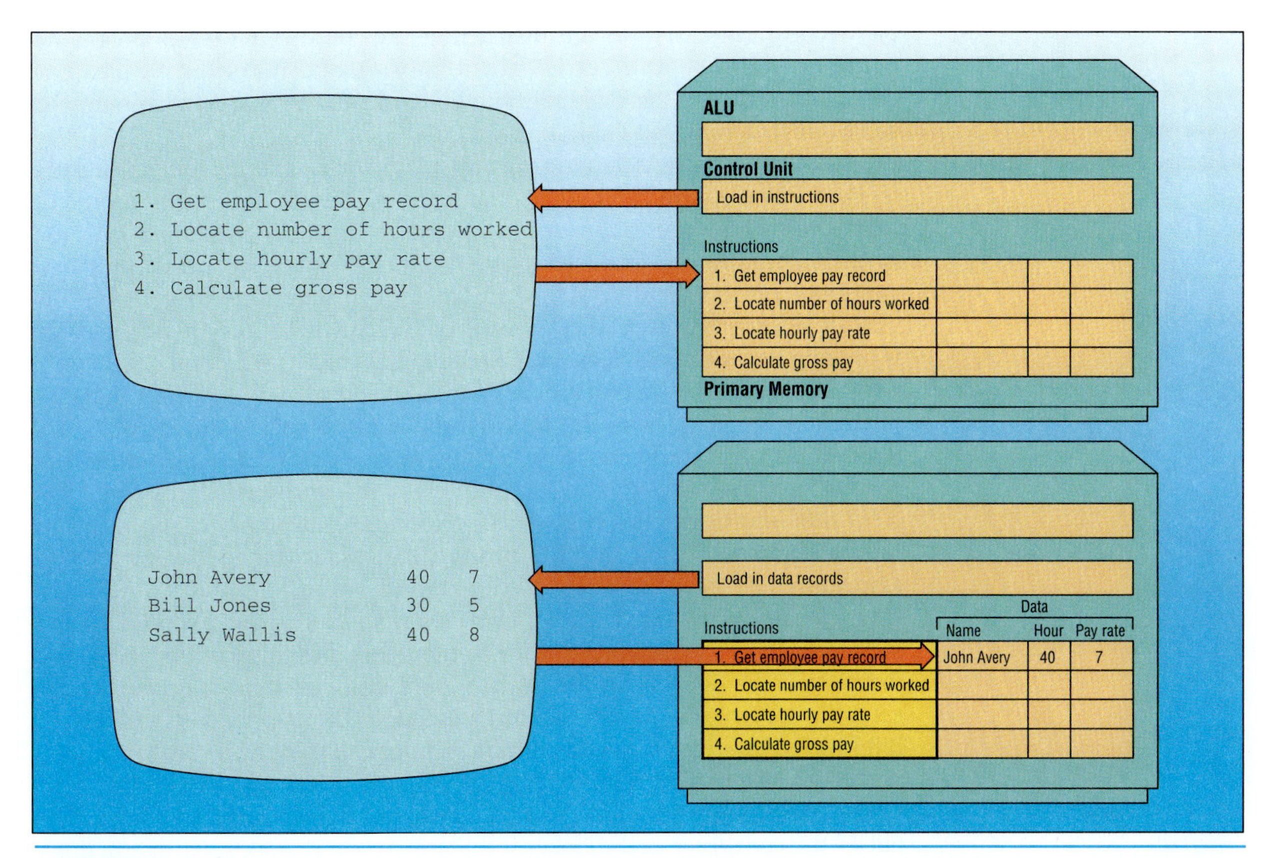

Exhibit 3.4

Loading Instructions and Data into Primary Memory

(a) In using a computer system to solve a problem, the first step is to enter, or load, instructions into primary memory.

(b) Once the appropriate instructions have been loaded, the data records are loaded into primary memory.

the computer system will be used, so as to highlight the main concepts and not be overloaded with complex details at this point.

The major components of a computer system are the input and output devices, primary memory, and the central processing unit. **Primary memory** is where the computer stores all instructions and data it is actively processing. The **central processing unit (CPU)** is the "brain" of the computer responsible for carrying out all computations and manipulations the computer is instructed to carry out. The CPU contains the control unit and the arithmetic-logic unit. The **control unit** determines which instruction the CPU will execute and retrieves the necessary data from primary memory. The **arithmetic-logic unit (ALU)** is the part of the computer that actually carries out the instructions. The CPU and primary memory are housed in the computer (see Exhibit 3.3).

The first step in using a computer system to solve a problem is to enter or *load* the appropriate instructions into primary memory. As you can see in Exhibit 3.4, the control unit shows which events are being processed. The red arrows indicate the sequence of steps being carried out. After the instructions are loaded (see Exhibit 3.4a), the data records are loaded into primary memory (see Exhibit 3.4b).

This process instructs a part of the control unit to go to primary memory and select the first instruction, which in this case is "Get employee pay record." To carry out this instruction, the control unit sends a signal to primary memory and retrieves the pay record for John Avery. The completion of this task signals the control unit to start processing the second instruction (see Exhibit 3.5a).

The second instruction in memory is "Locate number of hours worked." The control unit copies the value of "hours" from the record for John Avery and places that value (40) in the arithmetic-logic unit for later use in the calculation of gross pay (see Exhibit 3.5b). The control unit then continues on to execute the next instruction in sequence. Instruction 3 is "Locate hourly pay rate." John Avery is paid $7 per hour. A copy of this value is put into the arithmetic-logic unit by the control unit (see Exhibit 3.5c).

The fourth instruction is "Calculate gross pay." Recall that the formula to be used was the following: "Multiply the number of hours worked by the hourly pay rate." Thus, to carry out this instruction, the control unit sends a signal of "multiply" to the arithmetic-logic unit. The ALU then multiplies the two values it contains (40 times 7). The result of the calculation is 280. At this point all instructions of the gross pay algorithm have been carried out (see Exhibit 3.5d).

One additional major point that needs to be covered is the statement, "For each employee," in the gross pay algorithm. After the instructions have been carried out for one employee, this statement would reset the control unit to cycle through the algorithm for the next employee, Bill Jones. This cycling would continue until all employee records had been processed (see Exhibit 3.5e).

The algorithm didn't state a way to get the information, Gross Pay, out of the computer and display it for use. To do this, several instructions would have to be added to the algorithm. These instructions would include storing the result of the ALU calculation in primary memory as Gross Pay, and associating it with the employee name, John Avery. For convenience, however, these steps will be omitted. Therefore, only a final instruction ordering the printing of the employee name and gross pay amount is added (scc Exhibit 3.5f).

Although this payroll problem is very straightforward and the complex workings of the computer have been greatly simplified, it is nonetheless helpful in understanding the following key points about computer processing:

1. Instructions, in the form of an algorithm, must provide a step-by-step procedure leading to the desired result.
2. Instructions and data must be loaded into the computer's primary memory to be processed.
3. The control unit sequences the events within the computer system according to the instructions of the program.
4. All calculations and logic comparisons take place in the arithmetic logic unit of the CPU.

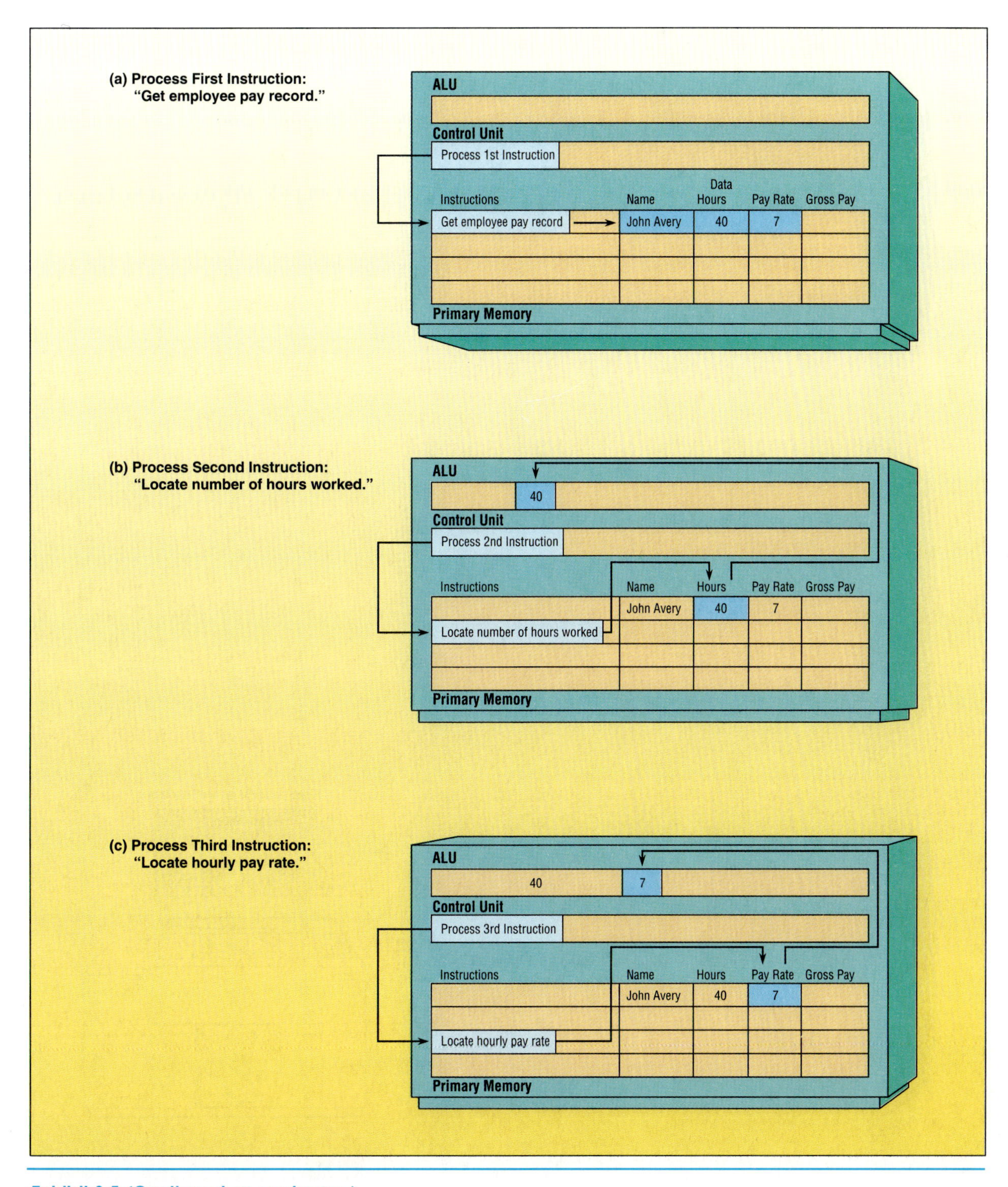

Exhibit 3.5 **(Continued on next page)**

Computer Problem-Solving Process

(a) Process First Instruction: "Get employee pay record."
(b) Process Second Instruction: "Locate number of hours worked."
(c) Process Third Instruction: "Locate hourly pay rate."

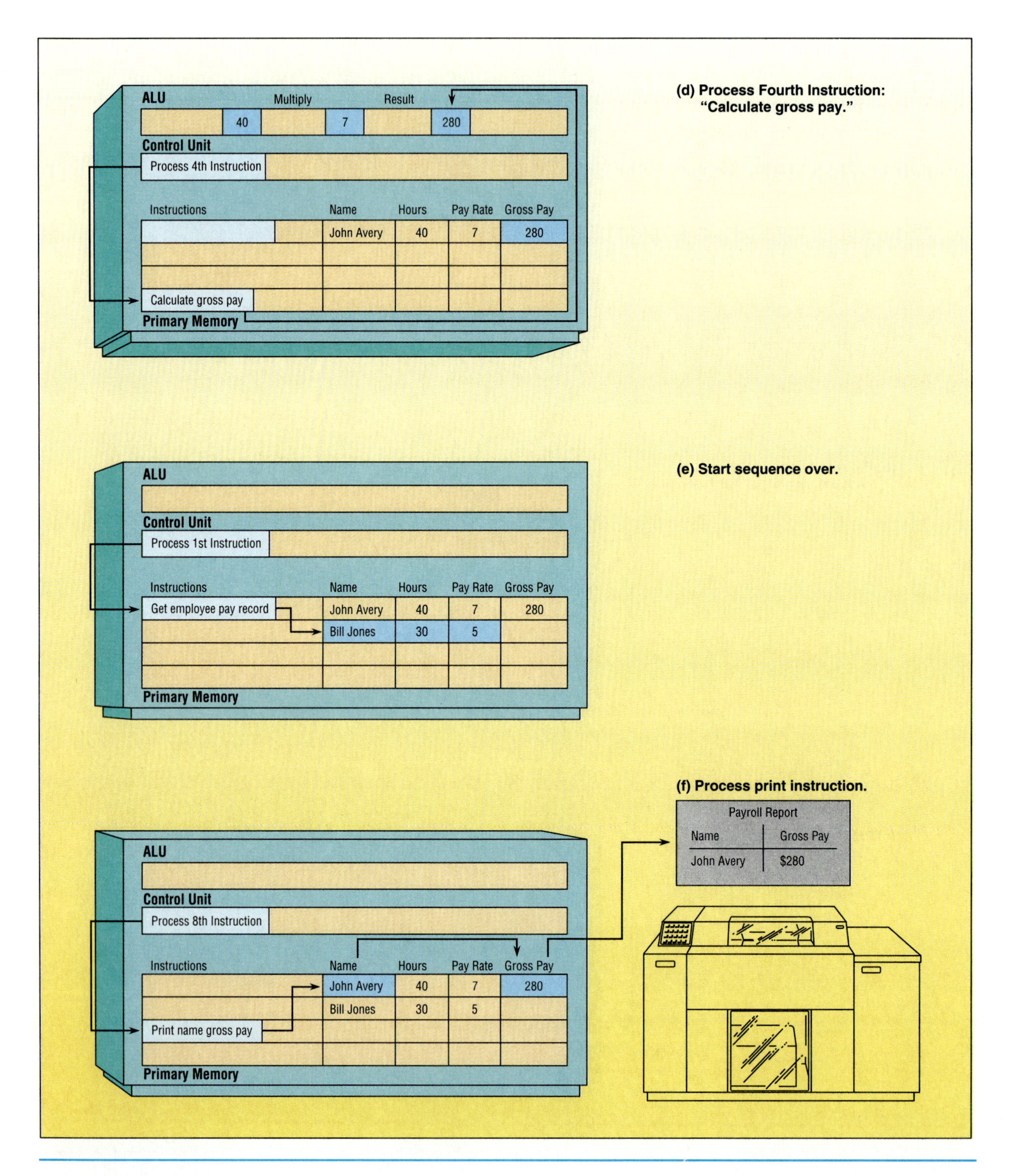

Exhibit 3.5 (Continued)
(d) Process Fourth Instruction: "Calculate gross pay."
(e) Start sequence over.
(f) Process print instruction.

5. The set of instructions within the algorithm is applied to one case and then recycled as necessary.
6. To see the results of computer processing, the solution must be displayed by means of an output device (printer or monitor screen).

What has been described here is the **von Neumann architecture,** in which digital computers use program instructions stored in primary memory to sequence computer actions. For the most part, the smallest and the largest computers work in this same fundamental way.

Coding Data for Computer Use

Although computers are very complex electronic devices, they work on a very simple principle. Data can be represented by two states. For example, an electrical current is either flowing or not flowing; a particle is either magnetized or it isn't; a voltage is either high or low. These two "on/off" or "high/low" states are the basis for everything the computer does. Thus, all computer problems, such as payroll calculations, word processing, and graphics, must be broken down to this fundamental level. That is, all data, program instructions, and arithmetic-logic operations must be represented in the binary system of 1s and 0s. To see how this works, let's start by discussing what a binary number system is, and how data and instructions are coded for computer use.

The Binary Number System

A **number system** is simply a way of representing numbers. The system we commonly use is the base 10 or decimal system. In base 10, there are ten symbols, 0 through 9. Numbers higher than 9 are represented through the use of place values, each of which is represented by a digit. For example, the number 185 is made up of three digits and could also be represented as shown in Exhibit 3.6. In the notation 10n, 10 represents base 10 and the exponent *n* indicates the place value. Any number with an exponent of zero equals 1. Because they are familiar to us, we usually don't bother to break decimal numbers down to their place values. This knowledge is useful, however, when dealing with number systems with bases other than base 10.

In the binary or base 2 system, the symbols used are limited to 1 and 0, which correspond to the two-state nature of computer systems. Higher numbers are shown by using place values. For example, the binary number 10111001 is equivalent to 185 in the decimal system. Each place value is called a binary digit or **bit.** A bit is the smallest possible piece of data.

Any decimal number can be converted to its binary equivalent and vice versa. Also, other number systems such as base 8 (octal) and base 16 (hexidecimal) have value when working with computer systems.

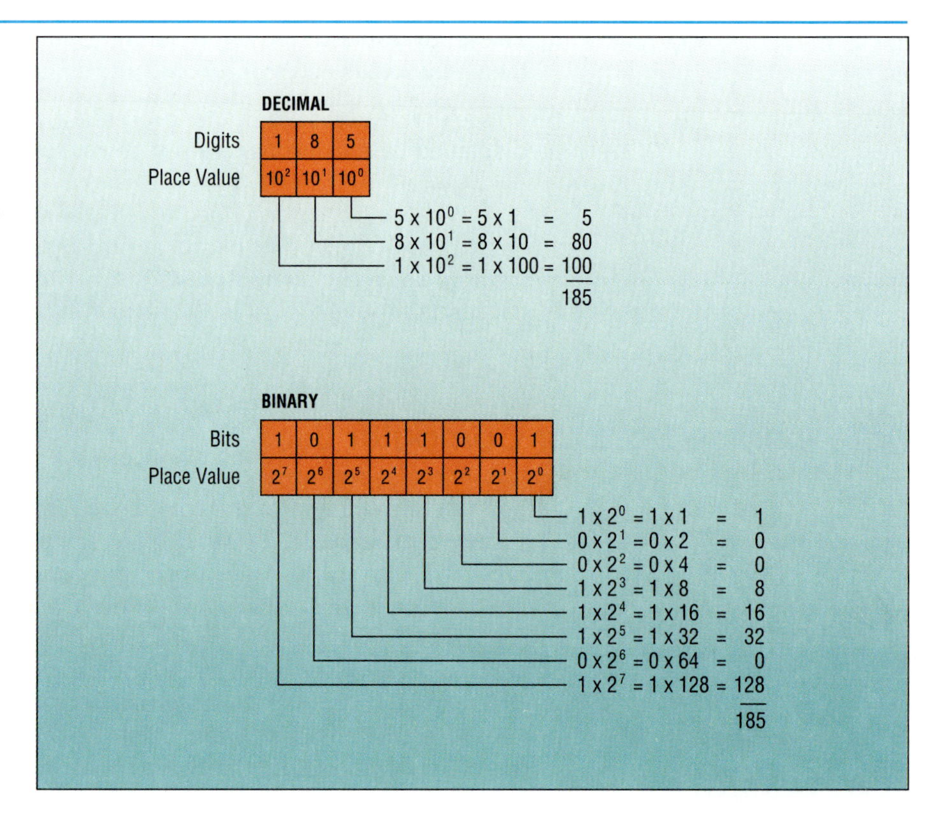

Exhibit 3.6

Number Systems

The decimal system uses ten symbols. In the binary or base 2 system, the symbols used are limited to 1 and 0, which correspond to the two-state nature of computer systems.

Data Encoding Schemes

How are letters, such as A or j, or special characters, for example, $ or !, represented in computer systems? What about numbers used as characters in ZIP codes, phone numbers, or mechanical part numbers? A modification to the pure binary number system has been developed for encoding letters, special characters, and numbers.

Two popular coding schemes are the Extended Binary Coded Decimal Interchange Code (EBCDIC) and the American Standard Code for Information Interchange (ASCII). IBM developed EBCDIC, and uses it, as do several other computer manufacturers, on its large mainframe computers. ASCII was developed by the American National Standards Institute, and it is used on almost all microcomputers, including IBM's, and on many minicomputers and large computers as well. Software is available to translate from one code to the other.

For our purposes, the importance of these codes is that each letter, special character, and number is given a unique code made up of a fixed number of bits. For example, in the EBCDIC system the digit 1 would be coded as 1111 0001, the uppercase letter *J* would be 1101 0001, and the special character $ is 0101 1011 (see Exhibit 3.7). (Note that the ASCII codes are different.)

The combination of bits that represents a character is called a **byte.** An 8-bit coding scheme allows up to 256 unique symbols to be defined.

Exhibit 3.7

Selected EBCDIC and ASCII-8 Binary Codes

EBCDIC

Uppercase Alpha		Lowercase Alpha		Special Characters		Numeric	
A	11000001	a	10000001	!	01011010	0	11110000
B	11000010	b	10000010	"	01111111	1	11110001
C	11000011	c	10000011	#	01111011	2	11110010
D	11000100	d	10000100	$	01011011	3	11110011
E	11000101	e	10000101	%	01101100	4	11110100
F	11000110	f	10000110	&	01010000	5	11110101
G	11000111	g	10000111	(	01001101	6	11110110
H	11001000	h	10001000	)	01011101	7	11110111
I	11001001	i	10001001	*	0101100	8	11111000
J	11010001	j	10010001	+	01001110	9	11111001

ASCII-8

Uppercase Alpha		Lowercase Alpha		Special Characters		Numeric	
A	10100001	a	11100001	!	01000001	0	01010000
B	10100010	b	11100010	"	01000010	1	01010001
C	10100011	c	11100011	#	01000011	2	01010010
D	10100100	d	11100100	$	01000100	3	01010011
E	10100101	e	11100101	%	01000101	4	01010100
F	10100110	f	11100110	&	01000110	5	01010101
G	10100111	g	11100111	(	01001000	6	01010110
H	10101000	h	11101000	)	01001001	7	01010111
I	10101001	i	11101001	*	01001010	8	01011000
J	10101010	j	11101010	+	01001011	9	01011001

This is more than enough to represent all ten digits, the lower- and uppercase letters, and a variety of special characters, graphic symbols, and data communication codes.

An important aspect of these coding schemes is the change they make in the way numbers are represented. Under normal circumstances, base 2 would require 4 bits—1111—to represent the decimal number 15. In a similar way, base 2 would require 8 bits—10111001—to represent the decimal number 185. The problem is that base 2 requires a different number of bits to represent different decimal numbers. Both EBCDIC and ASCII avoid this problem by converting each digit individually. Thus, the decimal number 15 would be encoded in EBCDIC as 2 bytes of 8 bits each, 1111 0001 (the 1) and 1111 0101 (the 5).

Microcomputer Architecture

If you took the case off a computer, you might think you were looking at a science fiction city, with clusters of low buildings connected by superhighways. In fact, the engineers who design modern computers often play the role of architects in planning the layout and design of these computer "cities." The microcomputer system in Exhibit 3.8 is typical of what you might see the next time you go to a computer store or visit a computer lab. And what you have learned thus far has given you a good foundation for understanding what it all means.

Semiconductor Chip Technology

The basic building block of the computer system is the semiconductor chip. These chips are composed of anywhere from several thousand to hundreds of thousands of transistors.

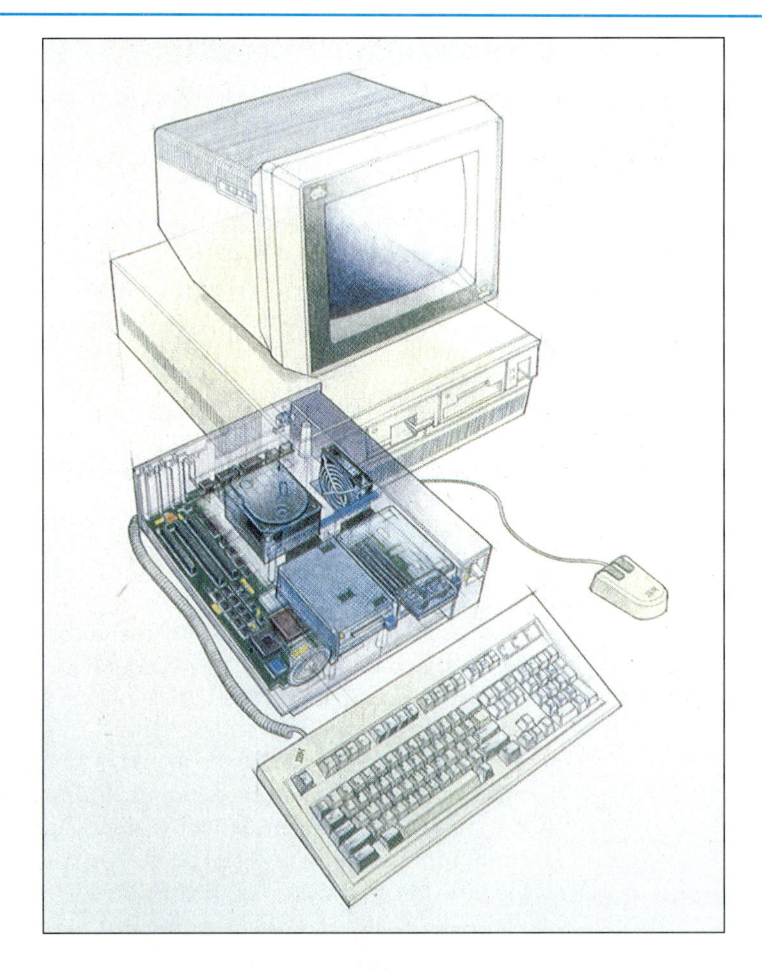

Exhibit 3.8

Inside the Microcomputer

Many components, chips, boards, and peripherals are necessary to build a microcomputer.

Transistors are electronic components that function as semiconductors. A transistor is made up of silicon (a product of sand, which since it is nonconducting acts as an insulator) that has been injected with small amounts of conducting materials. The result is a **semiconductor,** a solid-state device that can be made to conduct or inhibit the flow of electricity, depending on conditions. Thus, a transistor can be made to represent a 1 (conductor) or a 0 (insulator). The transistor is highly reliable, requires little power, and can be manufactured very inexpensively. In addition, unlike vacuum tubes, which required air-conditioned environments to function, transistors give off very little heat.

Individual transistors can be combined to encode and store information, or to carry out arithmetic or logic operations. Semiconductor chips are used for the CPU, for primary memory, and for the interface devices between various hardware components.

As shown in Exhibit 3.9, collections of chips are mounted on printed circuit boards so as to perform particular functions, such as connecting a printer or disk drive to the microcomputer. The largest circuit board, called the **motherboard,** generally contains the central processing unit. Other boards are used to adapt the microcomputer to a particular user's needs. Add-on boards for increasing primary memory or connecting a graphics monitor can be plugged into **expansion slots,** built-in brackets for holding additional circuit boards. With this overview in mind, let's study the major parts in more detail.

Primary Memory Chips

In the explanation of how a computer could be used to process employee gross pay, you saw the importance of using primary memory as a storage area. The two main types of memory chips used in primary memory are called RAM and ROM.

RAM stands for **random access memory,** which means that program instructions and data can be written into this form of primary

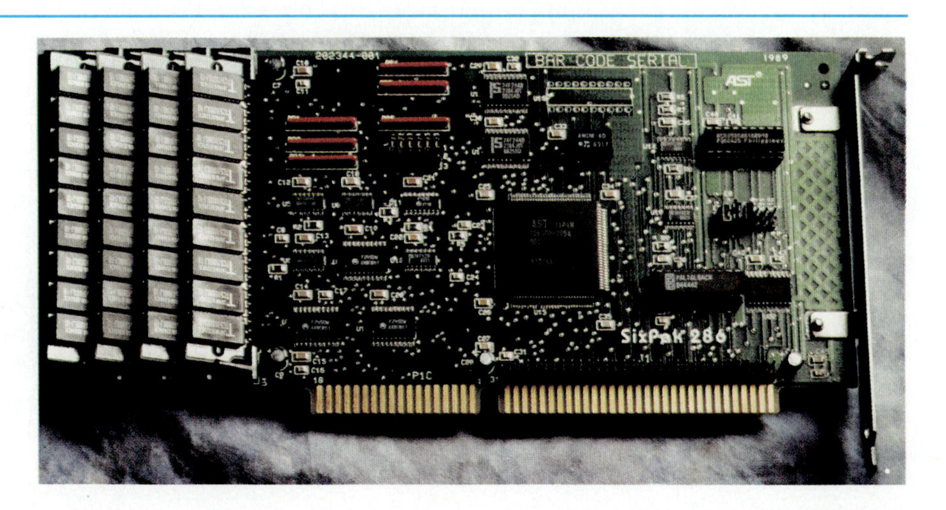

Exhibit 3.9

Enhancement Boards

Chips that provide for increased memory, a faster clock, a different CPU, and even software are conveniently packaged on a board that can be easily inserted into one of the expansion slots in the back of the microcomputer to enhance its performance.

memory as needed. These instructions or data can also be read out of memory as needed and transferred to the CPU for processing. Thus, RAM is sometimes referred to as **read/write memory**.

On the other hand, **read only memory**, or **ROM**, can only be used to read data or instructions that have been permanently loaded onto the chip. Nothing can be written into this memory by the computer user. It is common, for example, to put portions of the operating system and sometimes software language such as BASIC in ROM. This makes the operating system software readily available to translate programming instructions and still protects it from users who might accidentally order the computer to write over this valuable information. Software that is stored in ROM hardware is called **firmware.**

RAM primary memory is used for temporary storage of users' program instructions and data. Primary memory size is specified in the number of bytes that can be stored. For example, a computer that has 256K of RAM memory would have about 256,000 bytes. K and kilo are abbreviations for kilobyte, or 2^{10}, or 1024 bytes.

The types of RAM memory chips most commonly used today have one major disadvantage: whenever electric power is turned off, the contents of RAM are lost. This is known as **volatile** RAM. To keep memory loss from happening during temporary power outages, a backup power supply must be used. ROM uses a different storage technology, which is nonvolatile and thus is not affected by power problems. However, ROM's major advantage—its ability to protect valuable information by storing it permanently—can be a disadvantage when that information needs to be changed. However, certain types of ROM chips, such as EPROM, have been developed that can be modified through programming.

Microprocessor Chips

You have seen that the key element of the computer is the central processor unit. A CPU that has been implemented on a single silicon chip is called a **microprocessor**. This chip would contain the control unit and the arithmetic-logic unit at a minimum. In more advanced designs, the chip could also include RAM, ROM, and other support devices.

Microprocessor chips use many different internal designs, and the chips vary in appearance and capability. For example, microprocessors differ in the type of transistor technology used, the range of instructions they are capable of executing, the speed of their machine cycles, and their physical packaging. The most popular microprocessors are from INTEL and Motorola. As shown in Exhibit 3.10, the early IBM PC uses the 8088 and the Apple Macintosh Plus uses the 68000. Two examples of the newest generation of microprocessor chips from INTEL are the 80386 and the 80486, which are used in various models of the IBM Personal System/2 microcomputers and comparable computers from other vendors. The Motorola 68030 chip is used in the Apple Macintosh IIx and the NeXT microcomputer. A major indicator of **computing power** is the

Exhibit 3.10

Popular Microprocessor Chips

The INTEL 80486 computer chip.

Microprocessor Chip	Date Introduced	Manufacturer	MIPS	Microcomputer Using This Chip
8088	1981	INTEL	.3	IBM PC/XT HP150
68000	1984	Motorola	.5	Apple Mac Plus
80286	1984	INTEL	2	IBM PC/AT AST 286 IBM PS/2 Model 50
80386	1987	INTEL	5	Compaq DeskPro 386 IBM PS/2 Model 80
68030	1989	Motorola	5	Apple Mac IIx NeXT
80486	1990	INTEL	15	Compaq 486 Advanced Logic Research 486

number of instructions that can be processed in a given time period, commonly measured in millions of instructions per second or **MIPS**. The newest chips have made significant jumps in computing power.

Support Units

To perform its tasks, the control unit needs the support of a variety of devices. One support device is a clock, which plays an important part in the computer's performance. Each event in a computer needs to be sequenced, and many things need to be going on simultaneously. To orchestrate this process and ensure its precision, the control unit needs to set a certain beat. This beat is established by the timing signal of the **clock** and is measured in megahertz (MHz), or millions of cycles per second. Typical microcomputer clock measurements which you will come across are 12, 20, and 33 MHz. Therefore, with a 35 MHz clock, events could be sequenced 33 million times per second!

If you looked inside a microcomputer, you could see sets of tiny lines connecting the various chips. These electronic highways, called **buses,** are used to send electrical signals between functional units, such as between primary memory and the CPU and to and from peripherals. **Interface devices** are needed to coordinate the flow of data between the computer and peripheral devices. Because of the highly variant characteristics of peripherals such as a keyboard, mouse, printer, video display, or hard disk, frequently a separate interface is needed for each peripheral.

This section has used the microcomputer as an example of the technology used in the CPU, primary memory, and support devices. As you will learn later in this chapter, large computers and small computers work in the same fundamental way.

Understanding Computer Classification

In this chapter you have gained a conceptual understanding of how computer systems work and some of the technology they use. But it is also important for you to learn about the power, capability, and prices of different classes of computer systems. In the Special Feature, "Selecting a Microcomputer," you will learn how to use this knowledge and become familiar with some other important factors in selecting computer systems to match users' needs.

The primary ways in which computers differ are in terms of flexibility, purpose, and power. **General-purpose computer systems** are extremely flexible, in that they can be programmed at different times to perform significantly different tasks. These computers can be used to do accounting, then word processing or graphics, and later even music composition. In contrast are the special-purpose or **embedded computer systems,** which have been designed to do one task very efficiently. Video games and digital watches are examples of dedicated, nonprogrammable computer systems.

A second classification scheme is based on whether the computer has been designed for use in scientific work, such as weather forecasting, medical imaging, and nuclear research, which are all highly mathematical. These applications are called **scientific computing** and require a computer system that can perform arithmetic operations rapidly and accurately. Such computers are sometimes called number crunchers. In contrast, **business computing** involves calculating and printing payroll checks, retrieving medical records, processing text, and producing selected and sorted mailings. These activities use relatively simple mathematics for any calculations, but place a heavy demand on the quick retrieval of records from secondary storage, or, in other words, on efficient input and output operations.

Computing Power

A third classification is based on computing power. This text discusses four of the major classes: the micro-, the mini-, the mainframe, and the supercomputer. One measure of *computing power* is the number of instructions that can be processed in a given time period, commonly measured in millions of instructions per second, or MIPS. Exhibit 3.11 shows an example from each of the major classes of computing power.

In practice, this means that the more powerful the computer, the more complex the applications it can be programmed to handle and/or the more users it can serve at the same time. Thus, there is a direct relationship between power and performance. For example, microcomputers often are used as personal computers in the home or in the office for word processing, spreadsheet analysis, or business graphics applications. Generally, they can be used by only one person at a time. Microcomputer systems generally cost less than $3000.

Minicomputers can be used to do accounting applications such as payroll, accounts receivable, and income statements for small- and medium-sized businesses. They can also be used for processing orders and for inventory control. Minicomputers generally can support ten to thirty users at one time, and cost between $5000 and $100,000.

Mainframe or maxicomputers have been the mainstay of business, government, and education for most of the history of computers. These large computer systems can usually be found in special air-conditioned rooms at the data processing centers of large corporations. Mainframes are used by airlines to support their reservation systems. Government agencies use mainframe systems for processing the records of millions of people. Imagine the data processing demands of the Social Security Administration, the Department of Motor Vehicles, or the Internal Revenue Service. Colleges often use a mainframe to provide hundreds of terminals for use by students, while handling the administrative tasks of servicing 20,000 students. Mainframes vary in cost from $500,000 to $10 million.

Supercomputers are the most powerful computers available today. These computers are the true number crunchers and have been designed for use in scientific work. They are also used to produce the graphic designs for special effects movies. The manipulation of mathematical formulas that describe geometric shapes gives the illusion of movement to these computer-generated images. Supercomputers cost over $5 million.

Actually, classifying computers into performance categories is not so straightforward. Tremendous advances in technology have meant that computer users can buy more computing power for less money. This, in turn, has blurred the boundaries between traditional classifications. Furthermore, superminicomputers such as DEC VAX and the supermicro have been introduced within the last five to ten years. A supermicro is a microcomputer, such as the Compaq 486, that uses an advanced microprocessor chip and is capable of supporting several users—at a price under $10,000.

Exhibit 3.11

Class of Computing Power

The four major classes of computing power discussed in this text are the micro- (top left), the mini- (bottom left), the mainframe (bottom right), and the supercomputer (top right).

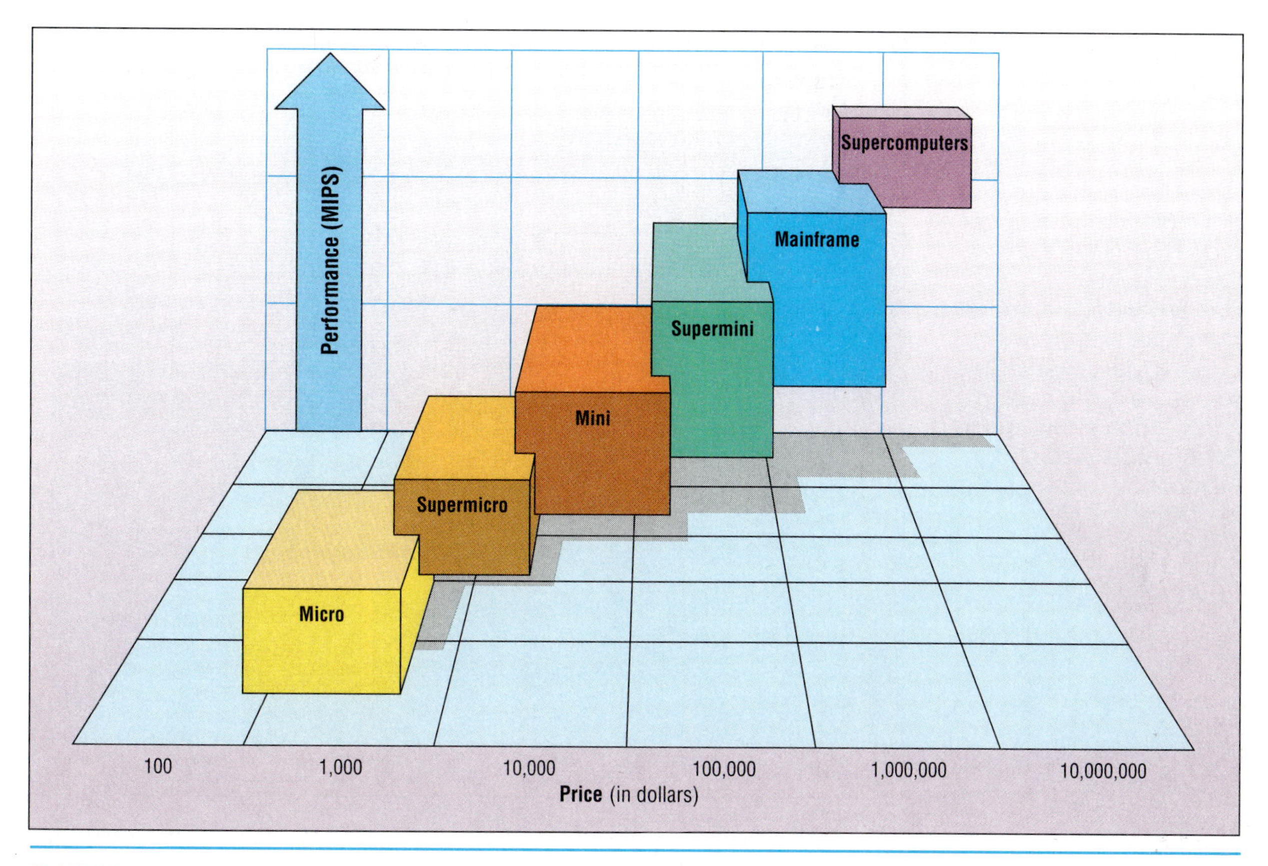

Exhibit 3.12

Computer Classification

The main indication of computing power is MIPS. With increased performance comes an increase in selling price of the various categories of computer systems.

Exhibit 3.12 reflects these new classifications and shows the overall relationship between increased performance and increased price of the computer system. In the highly competitive world of computing, marketing forces tend to equate value with price. Therefore, selling price is a reasonably good indicator of computing power, particularly if one looks at prices by order of magnitude (that is, powers of 10 such as $100, $1000, $10,000, and so on). Although the purchase price for each computer category shows a general upward trend as performance increases, there is some overlap between classifications. This overlap reflects the fact that the overall worth of a computer system is affected by computing power and such factors as the availability of software and maintenance, as well as the marketing strategy of the manufacturer.

Evolutionary Path

Because computer performance increases every year and prices drop even faster, an indirect indication of computing price versus performance is the date the computer was designed. The computer evolution traced in Exhibit 3.13 shows the effect of this interesting progression. The red line shows vertical comparison, and the green line shows horizontal comparison.

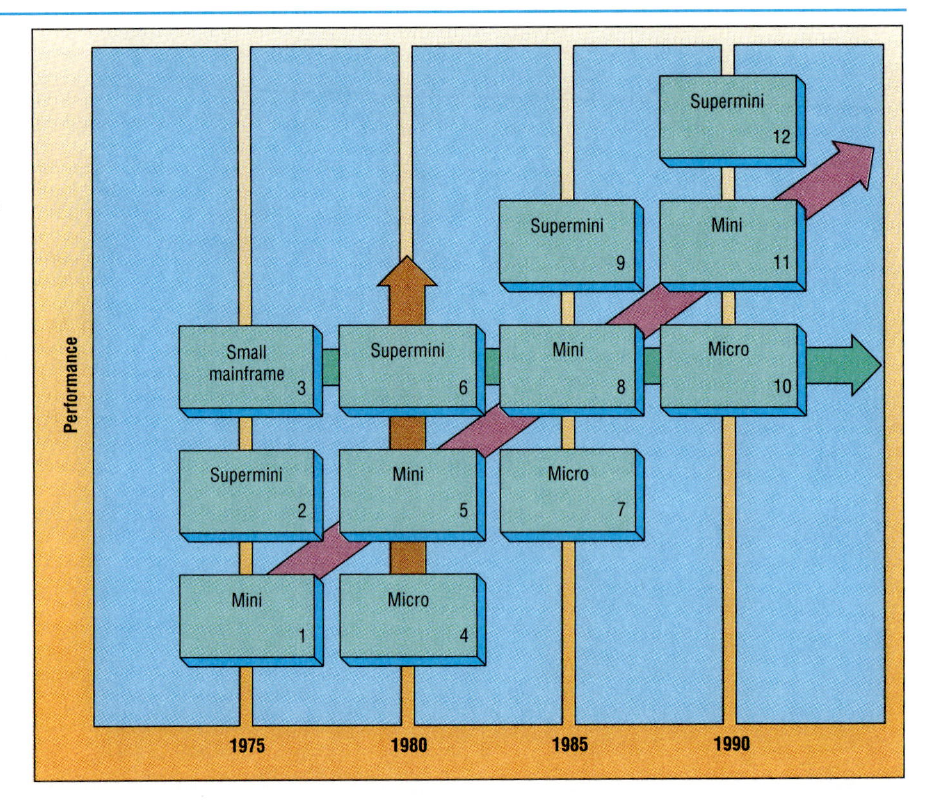

Exhibit 3.13

The Evolution of Computing Power

For any given year, the larger computer systems have greater performance than the smaller systems. For any level of performance, the smaller computer systems will equal larger systems sometime in the near future. Each classification of computer systems increases in relative power over time.

For any given year, the larger computer systems have greater computer performance than smaller computer systems. Thus for the year 1980, performance for the supermini (6) was greater than that of the minicomputer (5), which in turn was greater than the microcomputer (4). For any level of performance, the smaller computer system will equal a larger computer system sometime in the near future. Thus the performance of the small mainframe in 1975 (3) was equaled by the supermini around 1980 (6), by the mini around 1985 (8), and by the micro around 1990 (10).

Another dimension is shown by the purple diagonal line. It shows that each classification of computer system increases in relative power over time. Therefore, a computer's classification is relative to both other computer system classifications and a particular time frame. One of the conclusions that can be drawn is that the inexpensive microcomputer of tomorrow will have the power of the expensive superminicomputer of today.

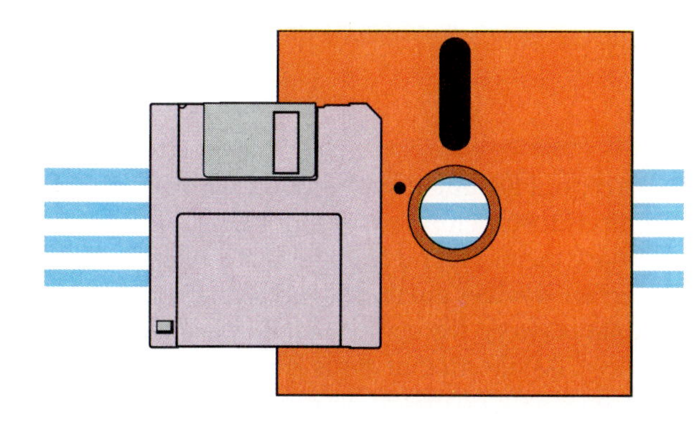

Computers at Work

Will NeXT Computer Change the Way Computing Is Done?

"When I saw the machine, I saw the possibility of a whole new set of applications that you could do on no other computer."

STEP BACK in time to 1984—an eon ago in the personal computer industry. Steve Jobs, then 29, was chairman of Apple Computer and still a good friend of John Sculley, his hand-picked CEO. That year the two launched a cute little machine called the Macintosh with an instantly famous television commercial bashing Apple's archrival IBM as a monolithic, sinister Big Brother.

Fast-forward to the present. Cast out of Apple in 1985 by Sculley, Jobs started a new company, NeXT Inc., that was finally to begin shipping his latest creation in mid-September. Jobs claims that the NeXT computer, a starkly elegant black cube with a powerful array of up-to-the-minute goodies, could transform the PC business as thoroughly as the Macintosh has.

Guess who is Jobs's biggest believer this time? None other than Big Bad Blue. IBM was so impressed by NeXT's distinctive software and three-dimensional look on the screen that it agreed to pay tens of millions for the right to offer them on a new line of high-powered computer workstations that it will introduce in a few months. In effect IBM could be selling NeXT clones, although Big Blue—more cloned against than cloning—would cringe at the term.

Even before he sold a single NeXT computer to the general public, Jobs is once again trying to realign and redefine the industry he helped create. He intends to break the software barrier that usually holds back new computers by persuading software companies to write programs that will distinguish the machine from its competition. So far, more than 70 have signed on.

Jobs has other powerful supporters. He has lined up Businessland Inc., the premier seller of personal computers to big corporations, as NeXT's exclusive U.S. distributor. He has persuaded Japan's Canon Inc., which will handle distribution in Asia, to invest $100 million in the company.

He is signaling his lofty intentions in an ad campaign that Jobs calls "pretty cool." His ad proclaims: IN THE 90S WE'LL PROBABLY SEE ONLY 10 REAL BREAKTHROUGHS IN COMPUTERS. HERE ARE SEVEN OF THEM. The copy ticks off a septuplet of flashy features, including a massive optical disk drive whose CD-like disks hold 300 times more data than a normal floppy disk.

The NeXT computer has an oversize, high-resolution monitor and an optional $3,495 laser printer that produces finer work than standard PC printers. Especially after color becomes available, it will be a natural for editing and laying out professional-looking books, newsletters, even magazines.

Still more intriguing is a feature called voice annotation. With a click of the NeXT mouse, an editor can pick up a microphone to record comments about the document he is working on. When he's done, the computer marks the document to alert future readers that a question or a comment has been recorded. They can play back the editor's remarks with another simple click of the mouse. Some PCs can be modified to do this, but at a cost of hundreds, sometimes thousands of dollars. On NeXT, voice annotation is standard equipment.

Summary and Key Terms

To process information, a computer needs very specific instructions that explicitly state what is to be done. Special step-by-step instructions that lead to the same result every time are called **algorithms.** They are used as the basis for computer programs.

The smallest and largest computers use the **von Neumann architecture,** in which program instructions are stored in primary memory to sequence computer actions.

The computer processor unit is made up of a CPU and primary memory. The **CPU** contains the arithmetic-logic unit (ALU) and a control unit. The **ALU** is where all arithmetic and logic operations are performed. The **control unit** is used to sequence computer events, such as moving data between primary memory and the CPU or between input/output devices and primary memory, according to program instructions. **Primary memory** is used to hold data and program instructions.

A **number system** is simply a way of representing numbers. The number system commonly used is the base 10 or decimal system.

In the binary or base 2 system, the symbols used are limited to 1 and 0, which correspond to the binary nature of computer systems. Higher numbers are shown by using place values. Each place value is called a binary digit or **bit.**

A modification to the pure binary number system has been developed for encoding letters, special characters, and numbers. Two of the more popular coding schemes are the EBCDIC and ASCII. The combination of bits referring to a complete character is called a **byte.**

A basic building block of modern computer circuitry is the semiconductor chip. These chips are composed of thousands of **transistors,** which are electronic components that function as semiconductors. A **semiconductor** is a solid-state device that can be made to conduct electricity under certain conditions and act as an insulator, inhibiting electrical flow, at other times.

Individual transistors can be combined to encode and store information, or they can be used to carry out arithmetic or logic operations. Semiconductor chips are used for the CPU, for primary memory, and for interface devices. **Interface devices** are used to coordinate the flow of data between the computer and peripheral devices. A collection of chips is mounted on printed circuit boards to perform particular functions. The largest circuit board, called the **motherboard,** generally contains the central processing unit. Add-on boards for increasing primary memory or connecting a graphics monitor can be plugged into **expansion slots,** built-in brackets for holding additional circuit boards.

Primary memory chips are designated as RAM or ROM. **RAM** stands for **random access memory,** which means that instructions or data can be read from this memory or written to it. Thus, RAM is sometimes referred to as **read/write memory.** The RAM chips most commonly used today are **volatile,** meaning that the contents will be lost when the electrical power is turned off.

ROM, or **read only memory,** can only be used to read permanently loaded instructions or data. It is common, for example, to put a part of the operating system in ROM. Software that is stored in ROM hardware is called **firmware.** ROM uses storage technology that is nonvolatile, and thus is not affected by loss of power.

A CPU that has been implemented on a single silicon chip is called a **microprocessor.** Microprocessor chips use many different internal designs, and the chips vary in appearance and capability.

Several devices are used to support the microprocessor. One is the **clock,** which is used by the control unit to establish the precise timing for sequencing of computer events. **Buses** are electronic highways that are used to send electrical signals between functional units.

General-purpose computers are systems that can be programmed at different times to perform significantly different tasks. In contrast are special-purpose or **embedded computers.** These systems are designed and configured to do one task very efficiently.

Scientific computing is used for applications that require arithmetic operations to be performed rapidly and accurately. **Business computing** is used for applications that place heavy demands on efficient input and output operations.

Computers differ in their **computing power.** This can be measured in a number of ways. One such way is **MIPS**, which is a measure of millions of instructions per second.

Review Questions

1. How do computer algorithms differ from general instructions you use in everyday life?
2. What is the CPU? What are its major components? Where is the CPU housed?
3. Briefly describe the components and functions of the control unit.
4. Describe how the smallest and largest computers work using the von Neumann architecture.
5. Briefly explain the binary system and describe its role in the operation of the computer. Convert 01000110 (binary) to its decimal equivalent.
6. How can letters, special characters, and numbers be encoded into binary code?
7. What is a semiconductor? Why is it important to the operation of the computer?
8. Compare RAM and ROM.
9. What is a microprocessor? How is the computer's microprocessor related to the computer's power?
10. Describe how different classes of computers differ.

T F **11.** The problem-solving process used by computers is completely different from that utilized by human problem solvers.

T F **12.** Unlike human problem solvers, the computer does not require highly specific instructions.

T F **13.** The program counter is used to identify the next instruction to be processed by the computer.

T F **14.** Only the largest of modern computers utilize the von Neumann architecture.

T F **15.** Both EBCDIC and ASCII convert each digit individually.

T F **16.** The smallest piece of information that can be manipulated by a computer is called a bit.

T F **17.** The combination of bits that represents a character is called a byte.

T F **18.** Essentially, a transistor is a type of semiconductor.

T F **19.** The greatest disadvantage associated with RAM stems from the volatile nature of this type of storage.

T F **20.** MIPS is a major measure of a computer's power.

21. _____ The precise instructions used by the computer are called:

a. anonyms
b. algorithms
c. algonyms
d. software

22. _____ Which of the following is *not* one of the major components of a computer system?

a. input and output devices
b. primary memory
c. software
d. central processing unit

23. _____ All calculations and logic comparisons take place in the computer's:

a. ALU unit
b. control unit
c. primary memory unit
d. algorithm unit

24. _____ Regardless of size, most computers are constructed according to the _____ architecture.

a. CPU
b. Van Cliburn
c. ALU
d. von Neumann

25. _____ The number of instructions that can be processed in a given time period is indicative of the computer's:

a. computing power
b. cost
c. size
d. format

26. _____ The smallest piece of information that can be manipulated by a computer is called a:
a. byte
b. megabyte
c. bit
d. megabit

27. _____ The combination of bits referring to a complete character is called a:
a. bit
b. megabit
c. megabyte
d. byte

28. _____ The basic building block of a microcomputer system is the:
a. interface device
b. semiconductor chip
c. motherboard
d. expansion slot

29. _____ When instructions are read into the computer they are stored in:
a. RAM
b. ROM
c. peripheral devices
d. firmware

30. _____ Which of the following is the major disadvantage of RAM memory chips?
a. the cost
b. the difficulty in writing in new information
c. the fact that they are volatile
d. the difficulty in removing them from the computer

CHAPTER 4

Input and Output Devices

Every year the Internal Revenue Service processes the federal income tax returns of about 100 million Americans. How should the data from those returns be entered into a computer system? A supermarket serves hundreds of customers each day. How should the buying transactions be recorded and the thousands of items sold be accounted for? A small business pays its employees twice a month. When and how should the data from the employees' time sheets be entered into the computer for processing? Each semester colleges need to update student records to reflect the classes taken and the grades received. In what form should the course grades be collected, how should they be processed, and in what form should the results be displayed?

These are examples of the kinds of data processing tasks facing organizations every day. In each case, data input is a major factor. For certain government agencies, retail operations, and industries such as insurance and medicine, the cost of entering data into a computer system is estimated as one-third or more of the total data processing budget.

In this chapter we will concentrate on the fundamental devices that are used to collect data, enter it into a computer system for further processing, and output the results.

You will learn to do the following:

1. Explain the major ways input and output devices can be classified
2. Describe the methods that have been used to automate the collection of data at its source
3. Describe the way people communicate with computers and understand how this communication is progressing to a more natural human approach
4. Define the three primary factors that differentiate the technologies used with printers

Classifying Input and Output Devices

To help you understand how the input and output functions work with computer systems think about an automatic teller machine (ATM). Exhibit 4.1 shows a typical ATM device. Suppose you wanted to withdraw $80 from your checking account. First you would enter your bankcard into the lower

Exhibit 4.1
Typical ATM Device

right-hand slot. The computer system would read the magnetic strip that is encoded with your account identification number. The ATM would then request on the viewscreen that you enter your password. You would use the numeric keypad to enter your unique combination of letters and/or digits.

If this were all acceptable, the next message from the ATM would be to select the action you want taken. In this case, you would select the function key representing CASH WITHDRAWAL and then the function key to specify CHECKING ACCOUNT. You would use the keypad to type in 80.00 and after verification would press the ENTER key. The ATM would dispense the $80 and return your bankcard and a receipt of the transaction.

This typical ATM transaction can be used to understand the basic classification of input devices. The two major types of entries into a computer system are data and functions. **Data** are letters and/or digits that are used singularly or in combination to represent events or facts. **Functions** are instructions used to specify an action for the computer system to take.

In our ATM example, data was represented by the account identification number, password, and the amount of the cash withdrawal.

Functions that were selected included the CASH WITHDRAWAL and CHECKING ACCOUNT keys. Other functions available might include ACCOUNT BALANCE, TRANSFER, and CREDIT ACCOUNT.

Another major approach to classifying input devices involves how the data and functions are entered into the computer system. The major distinction is key entry versus keyless entry. In **key entry** someone must enter data or functions into the computer system by pressing keys on a keypad or keyboard. In the ATM example the numeric keypad was used to enter the password and the amount of desired cash withdrawal. The function keypad was used to select the appropriate functions.

Keyless entry is the entry of data into the computer system or the selection of functions by means other than keying. In the ATM example the magnetic strip on the bankcard was used by the computer system to read the account identification number. You did not have to key in this data. The basic ATM used in the example only allowed you to select functions by pressing specific keys. Other ATMs have screens that show the functions, which can be selected by touching the screen at the correct function box. With advances in voice recognition techniques, you may soon be able to select functions by just speaking the words "Cash withdrawal from checking account."

Computer output can be classified in several different ways. **Hard copy,** such as paper printouts, provides the user with a permanent record. **Soft copy** output, such as the visual display on a terminal or computer voice output, provides a temporary record. In the ATM example the screen was used for describing what steps should be taken next—for example, to enter your password or the amount of money you wish to withdraw. It is also used for displaying output information, such as the balance owed in your credit card account. These are examples of soft copy output. An example of hard copy output is the small paper receipt that displays the transaction just processed. In the cash withdrawal example the cash itself can also be considered a hard copy output.

Information presented in the form of letters, numbers, and special characters is termed **alphanumeric.** In contrast, **graphics** are pictures or graphs depicting information. ATMs at this stage of development produce only alphanumeric computer output. A graphic of your daily account balance over the last week is probably more than you want to know!

This chapter will first explore the variety of input devices currently available that are used with computer-based information systems. Then the technology and devices available for displaying the printed information will be covered.

Human-Computer Interface

The **human-computer interface,** often called the man-machine interface, refers to the basic problem that arises when people have to communicate with machines. What is best and most comfortable for an individual is not always the most efficient use of the machine.

Exhibit 4.2

Variety of Keyboard Designs

Keyboard designs reflect the nature of users and their purposes. Shown (clockwise from top left) are keyboards used in food service, bookkeeping, and graphic design.

When any technology is new, it is costly and awkward to use. Moreover, at that beginning stage, people are forced to adapt to the machine in order to perform their tasks. As the technology reaches a certain level of maturity, it can then be cost-effectively designed to meet its users' needs more efficiently and conveniently.

For much of the history of computing, people have been limited to using some form of keyboard as the primary way to enter data or give commands to the computer. At first, this was through keypunch machines. Now computer terminals, both special function and general purpose, with a variety of types of keyboards, are the primary data entry devices. Alternate ways of entering data, including touchscreens, mice, and voice, have emerged as more natural ways for humans to interact with computers.

Keyboards

Keyboard designs reflect the purpose they serve and the nature of their users. Note that, in the collection of keyboards shown in Exhibit 4.2, there are significant differences in the number, placement, and function of the keys.

For example, the point-of-sale cash register, at the top left, used at McDonald's, has keys bearing the names of McDonald's products. *Big Mac* appears on one key and *Reg Fries* on another. The clerk presses the key once for each time the particular item is requested. In other words, for an order of two cheeseburgers, the cheeseburger key is pressed twice. The microprocessor inside the cash register is programmed to retrieve from memory the current price of that item, which is then used to automatically calculate the cost of the order. This keyboard simplifies the data entry process because the employee doesn't have to know either product codes or prices. Results are totaled quickly and accurately.

Shown in the lower two photos is the keyboard typically used with general-purpose computers. The main body of this **QWERTY** keyboard (which refers to the five keys in the top left-hand corner of the typewriter keyboard) is very similar to the keyboard arrangement of a standard typewriter.

Until ten years ago, the standard keyboard was sufficient for keying in data or entering programming instructions in various computer languages. However, as computer systems became more interactive, ordinary users, not computer experts, needed to be able to select functions from a menu. What was needed was an enhanced keyboard, to simplify word processing, spreadsheet analysis, and data queries.

A **numeric keypad,** a set of numeric keys similar to those on a calculator keyboard, was added to the regular typewriter keyboard. These keys allowed faster entry of numeric data. (Recall that, on a standard typewriter keyboard, numbers are in the top row.) **Arrow keys** were added to facilitate the movement of the cursor. **Function keys** were added to provide a way to command certain common tasks in one step, rather than requiring several keystrokes to accomplish the same thing. For example, a function key could be defined for activities such as HELP, PRINT, GRAPH, and END. An example of such a keyboard is shown in Exhibit 4.3.

Even though the enhanced keyboard can be more efficient, it still has several important drawbacks for people using the computer interactively. Many people who don't know how to type feel uncomfortable with a keyboard system. And there are those who don't want to use a keyboard—regardless of its convenient design. Some executives consider keyboarding to be clerical work and are concerned about loss of status. Using a keyboard is also slow and often requires that you split your attention between the screen and the keyboard to find special keys.

Alternatives to the Keyboard

There are several alternatives to the keyboard that allow a user to point to options or functions on the screen. The screen displays windows that contain the names of functions or a menu of options. Selections are made by the user touching a light pen to a specific area on the screen. The light pen's contacting the screen causes a change in electrical potential, which

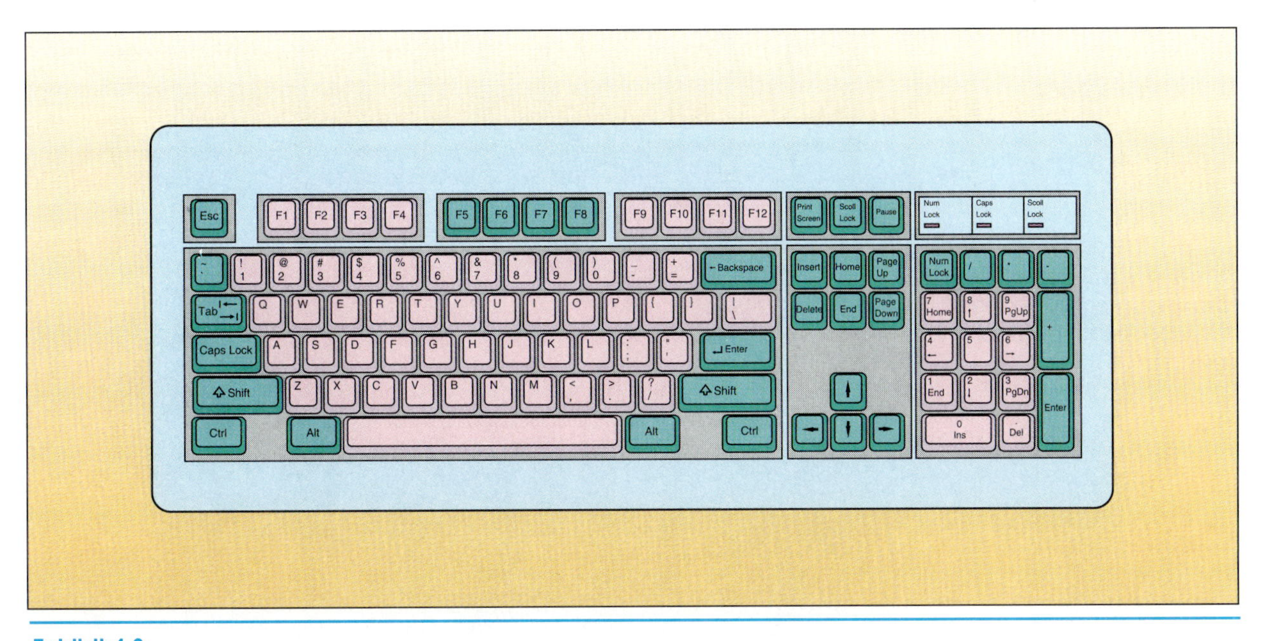

Exhibit 4.3

The Enhanced Keyboard

signals the computer to perform specific actions. A similar method allows the user to interact with the computer through the touch of a finger.

All the interface methods discussed so far have used words, such as LOAD,DISPLAY, and EXIT, for the functions to be performed. The next advancement in making the human-computer interface more natural is the use of **icons.** Icons are graphic symbols for functions. There are symbols for new document creation, application tools, and documents in computer storage, among others.

In 1984, Apple Computer introduced several microcomputers; the one having the greatest impact was the Macintosh, which used the icon approach. Apple's concept in developing the Macintosh was to make the screen layout resemble a desk top and thus allow the user to function as he or she normally would at a desk. That is, the user would select documents from the file folders, use a calculator to do arithmetic, write letters and file them, and throw away waste in the trash can.

With the Macintosh, the user selects functions by moving the cursor over the icon. The movement of the cursor is controlled with a hand-sized box called a **mouse.** As the mouse moves around the desk top, the cursor moves correspondingly on the screen. For example, if the mouse moves to the left, the cursor moves to the left on the screen. To select an item, the user simply positions the cursor on it and pushes a button on the top of the mouse (see Exhibit 4.4).

We have discussed the keyboard and pointing devices that are used with text or icons as ways of interacting with the computer. The dominant technology is the keyboard, and most experts believe it will continue to be so for the foreseeable future because pointing devices don't do away with the keyboard; they are a complementary input means, primarily useful for

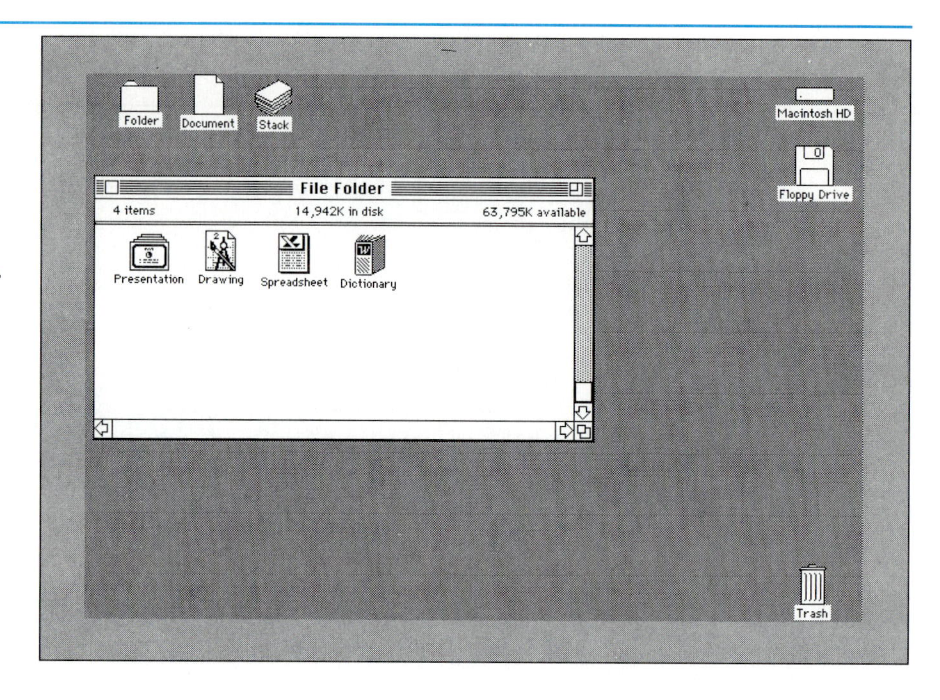

Exhibit 4.4

The Icon Interface

Apple's Macintosh screen layout resembles a desk top. Moving the mouse around the desk top causes the cursor to move accordingly on the screen. Clicking the mouse selects the icon that the cursor rests on.

selecting functions. Any applications requiring substantial data or text input are generally done with the keyboard.

Source Data Automation Devices

Keying data can be a slow, error-prone, and time-consuming process, especially if there are large volumes of data to be entered. **Source data automation (SDA)** is a form of keyless data entry that captures the data from its original source. Three common types of technology used in SDA are optical, magnetic, and voice recognition systems.

Optical Recognition

Source data automation devices that use light images to read data are classified as **optical recognition** machines. The many types of optical recognition machines differ significantly in the complexity of data that they can interpret.

Mark-Sense

One of the simplest optical recognition techniques used in SDA is mark-sense. A **mark-sense** machine is a reader that has been programmed to scan for marks in specific locations on source documents containing rows of bubbles or circles. This reader can distinguish only between dark, a space that's been filled in, and light, a space left blank. This technology is often used in college course registration and college and graduate school admission tests. The Educational Testing Service, one of the biggest users of these forms, uses mark-sense to score tests such as the Scholastic Aptitude Test (SAT).

Bar Codes

The use of **bar codes** represents a fairly low level of optical complexity. You have probably seen bar codes on many things, from grocery items to paperback books. Although about a dozen bar coding standards are in use, they all work on a similar coding principle. Numbers and letters are encoded by different combinations of bar widths and different widths of space between bars. For example, in the Universal Product Code (UPC) used in retail operations, bar widths are thin, medium, and thick, and the spacings between the bars are narrow, medium, or wide (see Exhibit 4.5).

Supermarket applications account for about one-half of the market for bar-code readers. Before the use of bar-code labels, supermarket checkers had to identify the item, read the price sticker, and then key in the item description and its price. This complete process can now be handled in one step, as a clerk passes the item across a bar-code reader. In addition to speeding up the checkout process, the scanner is 10,000 times less prone to error than is a clerk keying in the data. Furthermore, the cost of adding bar codes to packages or canned goods is minimal, since it can be done as part of the manufacturing process.

Manufacturing and distribution account for the remaining half of the bar-code market. Railroads use trackside scanners to read the bar codes on the sides of passing cars. Traffic management applications such as train-yard scheduling and track switching are performed based on this information. Raw materials and parts in factories are laser-etched or labeled with bar codes. Scanner devices can then track these items as they move on conveyor belts. United Parcel Service uses gate-controlled conveyor belts to automatically sort bar-coded packages by destination.

OCR Fonts

While bar codes are adequate for product identification, they would require too much space in many of the paper-based transactions in industries such as banking and utilities. Therefore, special **optical character fonts** such as OCR-A and OCR-B have been developed for printing machine-readable data on credit card slips, utility bills, insurance forms, and airline tickets.

Retailers such as Sears Roebuck and J. C. Penney use OCR wands to read merchandise tags coded in OCR-A font. This information is passed directly to a point-of-sale (POS) cash register, which processes the data to complete the sales transaction. The information on the sale amount and the merchandise sold can later be transferred to a central computer system for updating inventory and sales records and developing management reports.

Interleaved 2 of 5
Standard Density

05945

Exhibit 4.5

Industry Standard Bar Codes

Bar codes have become the most widely used method of identifying product codes in commercial, factory, service, and government applications. Data are represented by varying bar widths and spacing between bars.

Exhibit 4.6
Digital Scanner

Digital Scanners

One of the latest additions to optical recognition machines is the **digital scanner.** It is used to capture digital images of a paper document. Digital scanners can be used to scan graphical images, such as artwork, graphics, or photos, to be later incorporated, for example, in desktop publishing applications (see Exhibit 4.6).

More expensive scanners recognize a much wider variety of characters than would be found with most OCR machines. These scanners are being used for the processing of documents that have already been printed. Through digital scanning, this information can be stored electronically and later modified by word processing software.

Magnetic Recognition

One of the earliest uses of character recognition machines was **magnetic ink character recognition (MICR).** MICR has been used since the 1950s in the banking industry as the standard method for processing checks. Checks are preprinted with the bank identification and customer account numbers encoded in MICR characters (see Exhibit 4.7). After a check is presented for payment, the first bank to receive the check will encode the amount of money specified using a MICR enscriber.

Batches of checks are processed by the MICR reader-sorter unit. Data from the checks are read and transferred to magnetic tape or directly entered into the CPU for processing. (Daily updating of customer checking account balances is done in this manner.) Checks are then sorted for further routing to other banks, the Federal Reserve Bank, or the customer's account file.

Exhibit 4.7

Magnetic Ink Characters Shown on a Sample Check

Since the 1950s, the banking industry has used Magnetic Ink Character Recognition (MICR) as the standard method for processing checks.

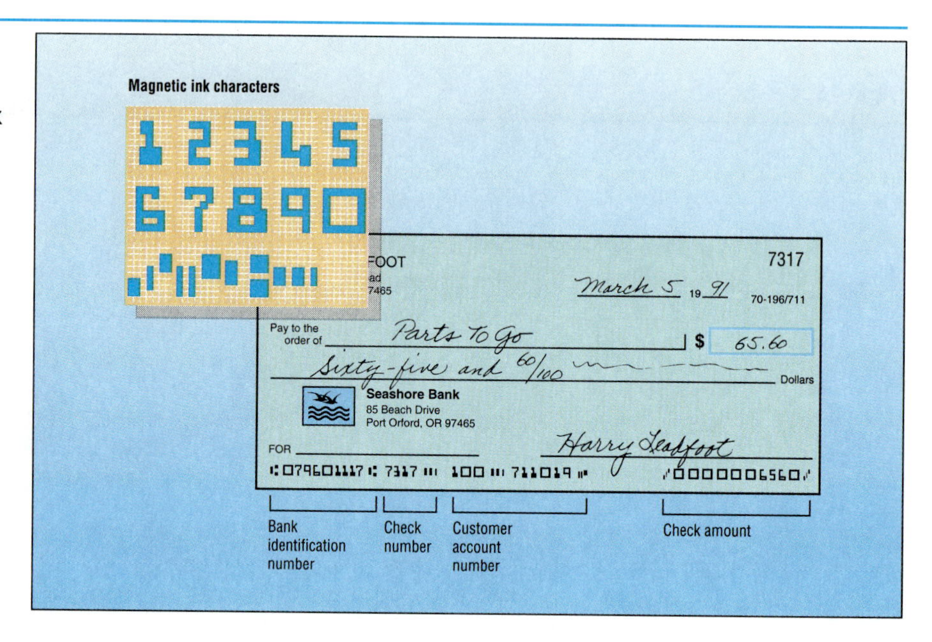

Recognition Equipment, Inc., has developed a system that optically and magnetically reads checks. The account numbers are still used for sorting checks, but, in addition, a digitized image of the check is created. The customer's monthly bank statement contains images of the canceled checks rather than the checks themselves.

For MICR to be a true form of source data automation, checks would have to be read directly by a machine. Unfortunately, handwritten check amounts can't consistently be accurately read by OCR machines. Therefore, the amount has to be keyed in. This, of course, is a costly and time-consuming process, given the tremendous number of checks written each year (over 100 billion checks in the United States alone). Once the check amount has been keyed in, however, machines can be used to automatically read and process the check data in the remaining stages.

Another form of magnetic recognition is the **magnetic strip.** As in the ATM example earlier, this strip is used on bank cards as a means of account identification.

Voice Recognition

One of the newer technologies for automating source data entry is voice recognition. For example, quality control inspectors are now able to speak into a microphone and specify the defects that need to be corrected on specific parts on the assembly line. This frees the inspector from the task of writing information on a form or typing it into a computer terminal. Voice recognition is a more natural, direct, and expedient source of data input.

In **voice recognition** systems, a microphone converts the spoken word into electrical signals. The signal patterns are processed to extract a set of identifying features, which are then compared to a set of voice templates stored in machine memory. The templates form the vocabulary of words the machine can recognize.

A technological obstacle to voice recognition devices is the consistency of the sound of spoken word and its correspondence to the stored template. An individual will say the same word differently at different times, depending on his or her energy level, mood, and health. Colds and allergies, for example, can change voice quality. Even more variation occurs when different speakers say the same word. Physiology, age, sex, and geographic origin all contribute to this variability.

To surmount this obstacle, speaker-dependent voice recognition systems have been developed. In this case, a specific individual "trains" the voice recognition machine by speaking a word a number of times. The resulting signal patterns are averaged, and a template is developed for the word. This process is repeated for each word that is to be recognized (see Exhibit 4.8).

Computer Output Devices

Useless. That's what even the most sophisticated computer would be if it couldn't present data in a form that people could understand. For some users printed output is adequate—others prefer graphic displays or even voice output. Historically, printed output was the only means of showing results of computer processing. Although paper remains the primary medium for computer output, a variety of alternative means to communicate information has emerged. In the rest of this chapter we will discuss the technology and capabilities of visual display, print and film, and synthesized speech devices.

Visual Display

Visual display of information is one of the most effective means for communicating the results of computer processing. The primary technologies for producing and displaying the images on the terminal screen are the cathode-ray tube and the flat-panel.

Cathode-Ray Tube Displays

For many years, the primary technology used to create a visual image on the terminal screen has been the **cathode-ray tube (CRT).** In fact, this technology has become so dominant that computer terminals are often called CRTs. CRTs, like television picture tubes, electronically paint characters on a screen. Inside the tube, an electronic "gun" shoots a beam of electrons upon the back of the phosphor-coated glass face of the screen. The movement of the beam creates images on the face of the screen.

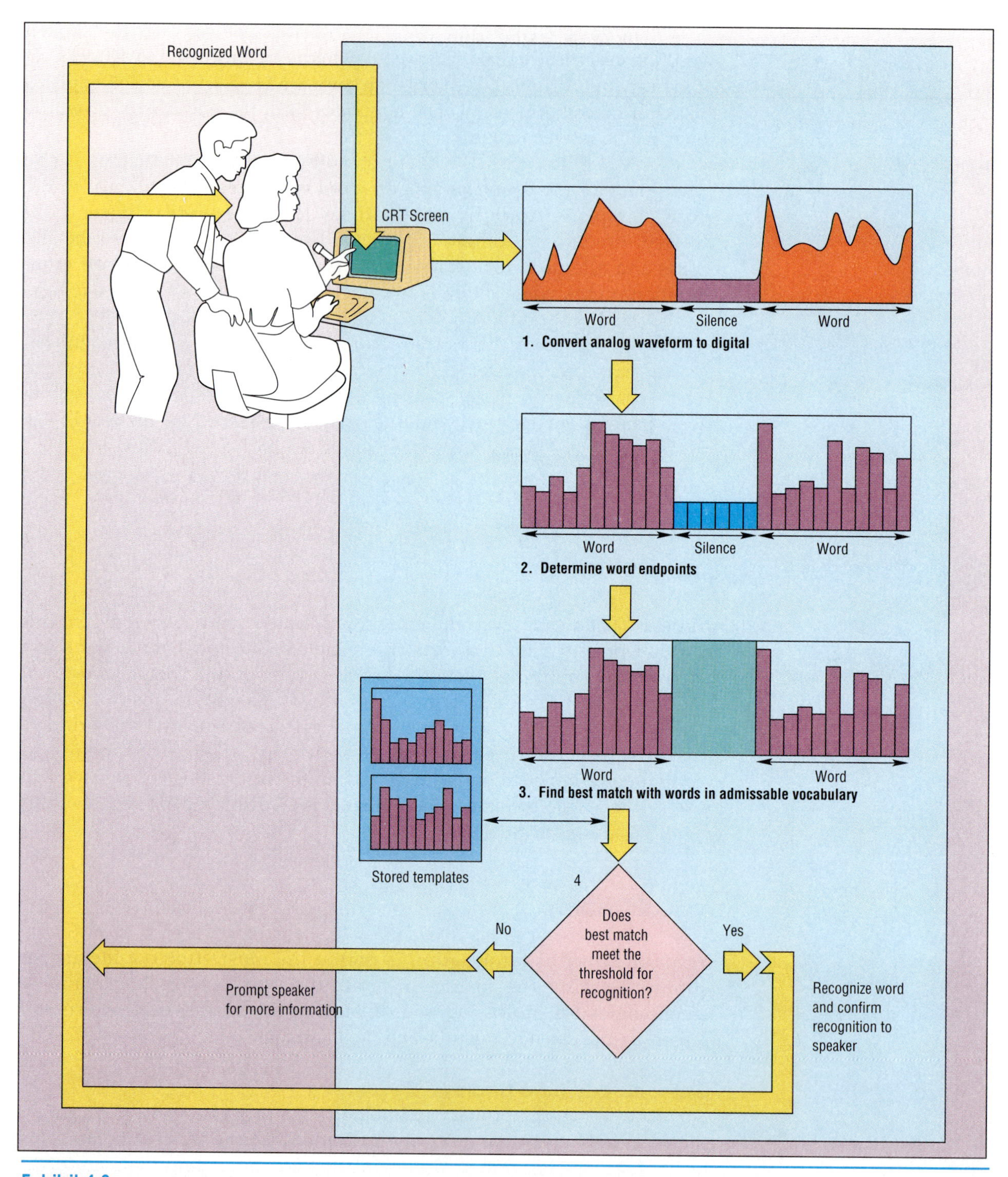

Exhibit 4.8

The Voice Recognition Process

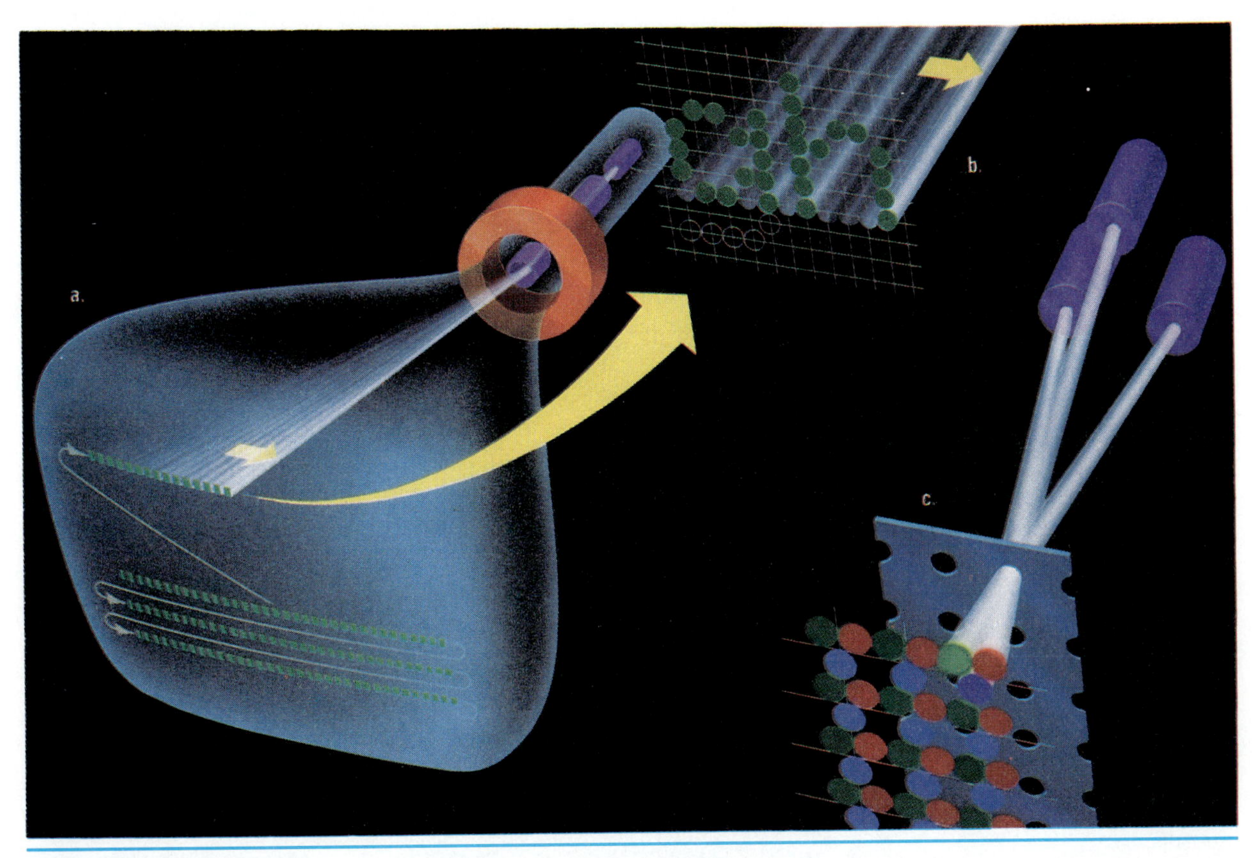

Exhibit 4.9

Raster Scan Process in CRTs

(a) A beam of electrons sweeps across a CRT horizontally in raster scan.

(b) Pixels are selectively turned on to form characters.

(c) Red, green, and blue are the three primary colors that are "electronically" mixed to produce other colors of the spectrum. Different combinations of the RGB electron guns create different colors by "firing" on triads of phosphor dots.

In a CRT using **raster scan,** a beam of electrons sweeps back and forth horizontally across the screen. As the beam moves across the screen, the electrical current is increased or decreased to create brighter (on) or darker (off) points. These points are **pixels,** or picture elements. This sequence is continued for each line of the screen (see Exhibit 4.9).

The color of the phosphor coating on the glass face of the screen determines whether the characters displayed are green, amber, or another color. As the beam of electrons passes across the screen, the phosphors emit light instantaneously and then decay (go dark) quickly. This means that an image must be constantly *refreshed*. Typically, the whole screen is repainted at least thirty times per second. The advantage of the fast decay rate is that screen displays can be changed rapidly. The disadvantage is that, to the viewer's eye, the display may seem to flicker slightly.

CRTs are used in monochrome and color monitors. **Monochrome monitors** display one color, such as green or amber, on a black background or black on a white background (see Exhibit 4.10). Each pixel is represented by a green or amber phosphor dot. A single electron gun directs the beam to each dot .

Color monitors use a triad, or trio, of dots to form a pixel. The three phosphor dots are red, green, and blue in color. **RGB** (red, green, and blue)

Exhibit 4.10

Monochrome and Color Monitors

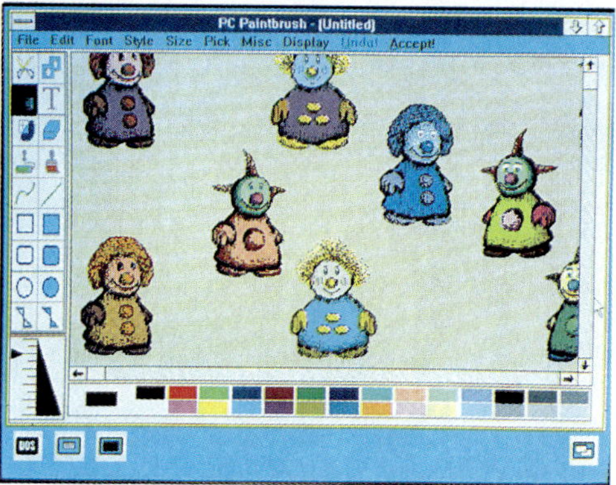

monitors use three electronic guns—one for each color. These three primary colors can be "electronically" mixed to produce many colors.

Another major factor affecting display screens is the number of addressable locations on the screen being used. In a **bit-map** or **dot-addressable display,** each individual pixel is addressable. Only blocks of pixels can be addressed or manipulated in **character-addressable displays.** The major advantage of the character-addressable approach is that it requires much less memory capacity. The number of locations is specified by the number of characters that can be displayed on a row and the number of rows on the screen. Typically, CRT screens can display 80 characters per row and have 24 or 25 rows. **Resolution** is a measure of the number of pixels that can be addressed on the screen.

Flat-Panel Displays

A new technology is emerging to challenge the CRT as the primary means of displaying alphanumeric and graphical images—the flat-panel display. Plasma and liquid crystal are two of the primary technologies used with it.

The CRT has several disadvantages. One is that the screen-painting approach has a strobe effect. The flicker causes many people who use a computer for hours at a time to develop eye fatigue. Second, the shooting of electrons against the phosphors causes radiation, as well as light, to be given off. Studies seem to indicate that the levels of radiation are too low to be dangerous, but many people are still concerned. Third, displays using CRTs have a large *footprint,* a reference to the amount of desk space occupied by the terminal. The culprit is the electronic gun. For a typical CRT with a 12-inch display screen, the gun measures approximately six inches long from front to back. To accommodate the gun, most CRTs are about a foot deep and weigh as much as a 12-inch TV. The flat-panel display, a possible successor to the CRT, does not have these disadvantages.

The flat-panel display shown in Exhibit 4.11 is a computer terminal using plasma technology. The display is only 3 inches thick, is lightweight, and has a resolution rivaling that of a photograph. Here is how the plasma display works. An ionized gas (plasma) is held between two glass plates. A set of horizontal wires is embedded in one of the glass plates, and a set of vertical wires is embedded in the other plate. These wires form a grid or matrix in which each intersection is a pixel. A particular pixel is turned on by the current traveling through the appropriate horizontal and vertical wires. The current at the intersection excites the plasma—a neon-argon gas mixture—between the plates, and this produces orange light at that pixel. **Flat-panel displays** create a screen image by illuminating discrete dots to display alphanumeric data, graphics, and video images.

The high resolution and steadiness of flat-panel displays yield high-quality results. CRTs using raster scan to refresh the screen sometimes produce images with a wavy quality. In contrast, plasma display images are

Exhibit 4.11

A Flat-Panel Plasma Display

Glowing neon-argon gas produces a high-resolution, flicker-free image.

stable, with each pixel emitting a steady glow until it is turned off. Though the plasma flat-panel display technology has many exciting advantages, these displays cost more than CRTs. This expensive price tag will slow market penetration.

To meet the needs of people who want to use their computers in the office, at home, and on business trips, the portable computer was developed. The Toshiba TI000SE is a truly portable, lightweight full-power computer with a full-size screen. This briefcase-size computer weighs 6 pounds and has a flat-panel display using the liquid crystal display (LCD) technology (see Exhibit 4.12). You may be familiar with LCD technology since it is used in a variety of products, including pocket calculators and digital watches. A thin layer of liquid crystal molecules is put between two sheets of glass and separated into little squares. When a voltage is applied to the liquid crystal in an individual cell or square, the normally clear material will turn opaque and block light reflected from behind it. The result is a black square. The display screen is thus a pixel grid, which can be controlled so that characters can be shown by patterns of dots.

The major advantages of an LCD computer screen are that it doesn't give off radiation and it has no flicker. It also has a very low power requirement, so it can run off a small battery pack for many hours before recharging is necessary. The POQET PC is another example of a laptop computer. This computer system weighs 1 pound, and it can be folded and put into your coat pocket!

Exhibit 4.12

Portable and Laptop Computers

The Toshiba T1000SE is a truly portable computer that is lightweight and small enough to fit into a briefcase. It has the same computer capabilities as the larger desktop personal computers.

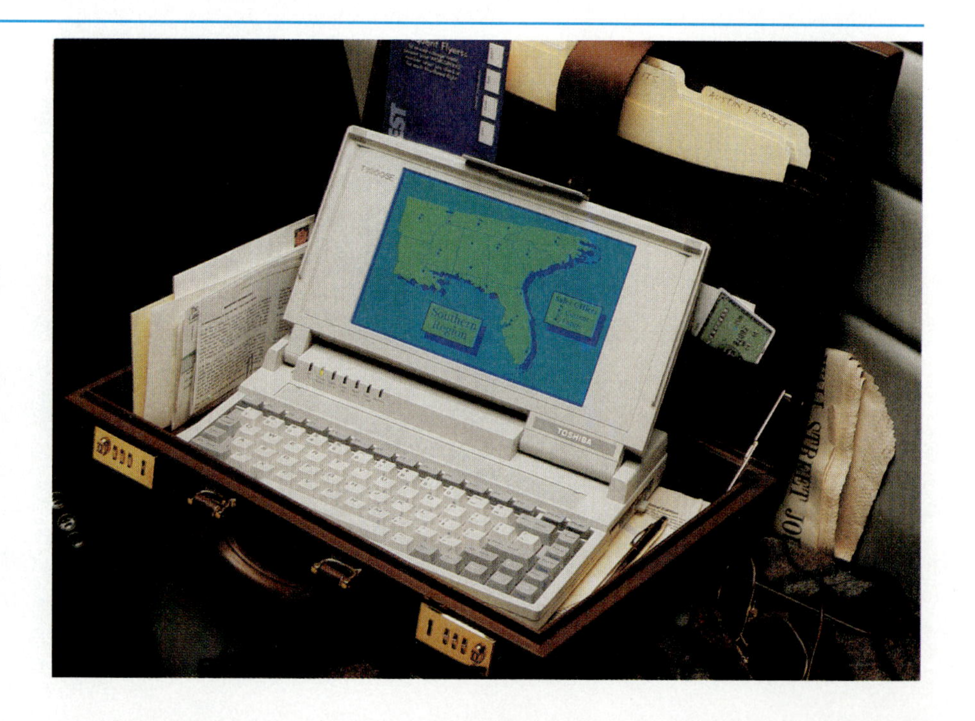

Print and Film

The ATM example showed the need for some form of output that could be read by a person and would serve as a permanent record. The number and type of output forms used to communicate results will vary from situation to situation, of course, but paper has traditionally been the dominant form of output. In spite of all the talk about the concept of the "paperless office," it appears that paper will continue to be the major medium for communication and documentation.

Historically, it is also true that alphanumeric data has been the primary information output. Thus, the computer printer, with its capability to print alphanumeric data on paper, has been the predominant means of generating hard copy output. More recently, the need for graphical displays has changed the type of printers that are in demand and has also encouraged the development of plotters. Filmed output, such as microfilm and microfiche, is attractive as a computer output medium because of its lower storage cost and reduced space requirements compared to those for paper.

In this first section, we will discuss the technology for computer printers used primarily to print alphanumeric data. In the next section, printers and plotters used mainly for printing graphics will be described. Keep in mind that, generally, output devices that can print graphics can also print alphanumeric data. However, not all devices that print alphanumeric data can print graphics.

Alphanumeric Printers

The computer printer industry has not yet settled on a limited number of ways to print alphanumeric information. Rather, a dozen or so technologies are being used today. These technologies differ in three basic ways: the way in which characters are formed, the way in which characters are transferred to paper or other medium, and the number of characters printed at any one time.

Character Formation

There are three methods for forming a character: fully formed, dot-matrix, and image. The old manual typewriters and the newer electric ones both use the **fully formed character** approach. Both the striker arms on the manual style and the "golf ball" typing element on the electric model have permanently shaped, or *fully formed,* characters. The electric typewriter is more versatile, in that different type fonts are available on different typing elements.

In computer printers, the fully formed character approach has been implemented by using either a golf ball, daisy-wheel, thimble, band, belt, or chain as the print mechanism (see Exhibit 4.13). In a daisy-wheel printer, each "petal" contains an embossed character. The wheel is rotated until the appropriate character is in place, and then a hammer presses the character against a ribbon, which transfers an impression onto the paper. A variation, in which the petals appear to be folded back, is called a thimble.

The dot-matrix approach has become the most widely used character formation method in computer printers. In **dot-matrix** printers,

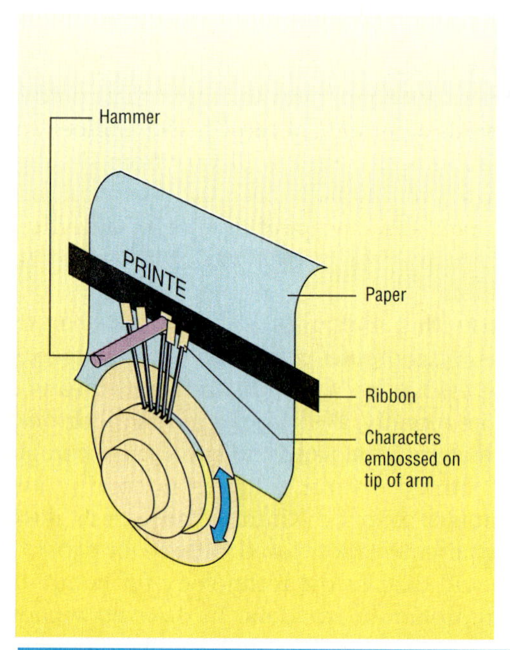

Exhibit 4.13

Fully Formed Character Printing Mechanisms

Photo shows thimble mechanism (left), golf-ball mechanism (right), and the daisy-wheel (top and bottom).

characters are formed by a pattern of dots. In a 5 times 7 dot-matrix, the 5 refers to the number of horizontal dots, and the 7 refers to the number of vertical dots. Selective pins are activated to form characters, as shown with the letter *T* (see Exhibit 4.14).

The third way to form a character is by image. The dot-matrix approach uses a fixed block pattern of dots, such as 9 times 18 or 18 times 36, for each character. **Image processing** differs in that it generates characters through a raster scan type of approach, in which selected dots are "turned on" on a line-by-line basis. When all lines have been scanned, the resulting image will show the characters in their appropriate positions. This method is used by laser printers; we will discuss that particular technology later.

Character Transfer

Characters can be transferred by either an impact or nonimpact method. The **impact** method of character transfer is widely used with computer printers. It works much like a typewriter, in that an impression-making element pushes a ribbon against paper. This transfers an ink impression onto the paper in the color of the ribbon. Daisy-wheel and thimble printers use this approach, as do belt, band, and chain printers. There is variation in whether the ribbon, paper, or fully formed character is struck first.

At one time, the impact method was limited to fully formed characters. But dot-matrix impact printers now make wide use of the impact method. Dot-matrix printers that form characters using columns of "dot hammers" are classified as impact printers.

The other major approach to character transfer is **nonimpact.** No physical hammering is used with this method. The character is transferred

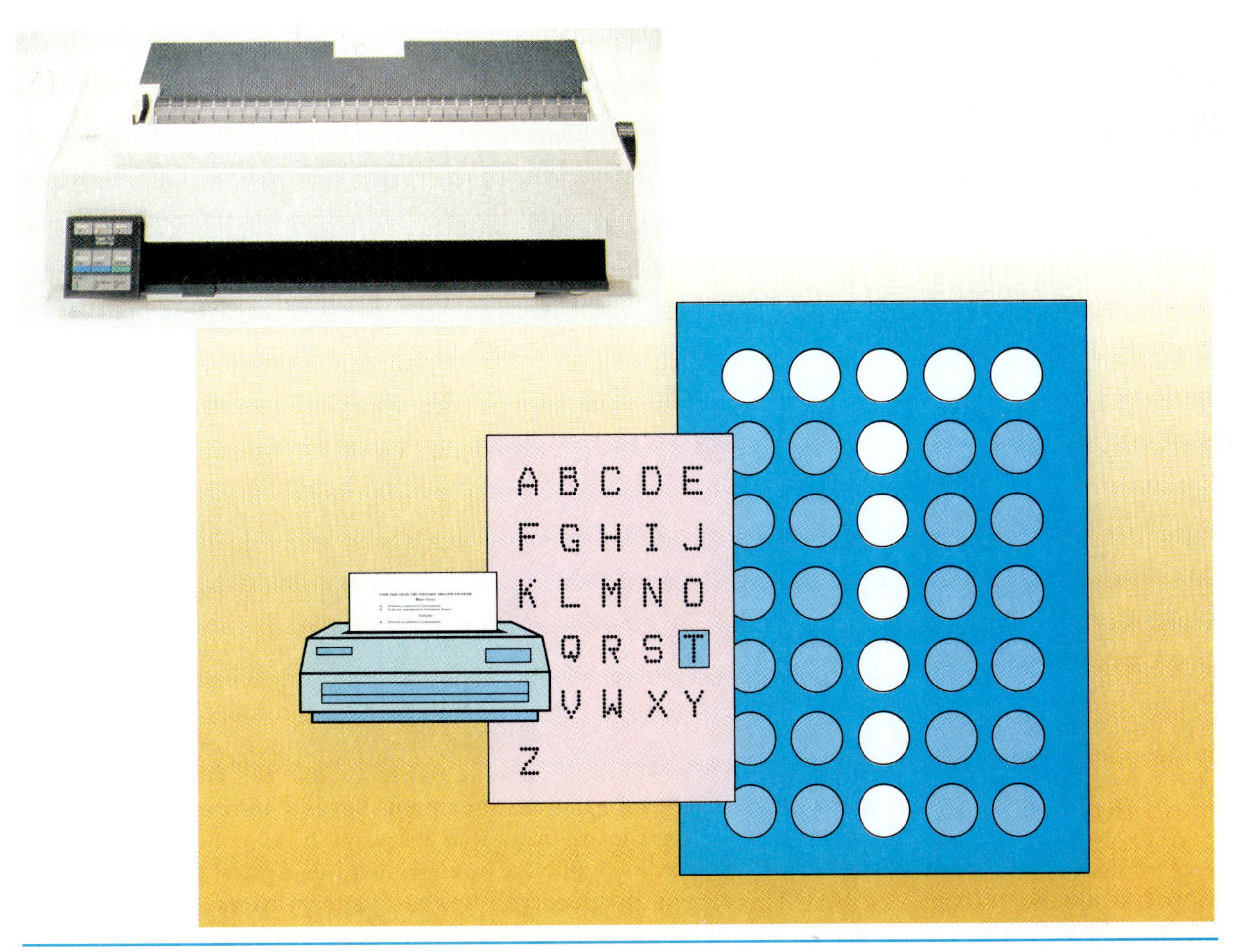

Exhibit 4.14

Dot-Matrix Computer Printing

to the paper by means of heat, electrostatic charge, magnetism, or ink applied to selected parts of the paper. The nonimpact technique can be used with either the dot-matrix or image method of character formation. An application of this concept is shown with thermal and electrostatic dot-matrix printers. Each method forms characters on specially treated paper. Thermal printers use heated printheads to burn dots onto heat-sensitive paper. Electrostatic printers use electrically charged printheads to melt away dots in thin aluminum-coated paper.

Characters Printed at a Time

Most of the inexpensive printers print one character at a time. Thus, a line of text is generated as with a typewriter. **Character printers** move the printhead from left to right, line by line. This is a relatively slow process, however. A modification used in many printers is bidirectional printing, or printing left to right and then right to left. This saves the time it takes the printhead to return from the end of one line to the beginning of the next one.

A faster method is **line-at-a-time printing.** Instead of having the printhead move back and forth as in character printing, multiple print

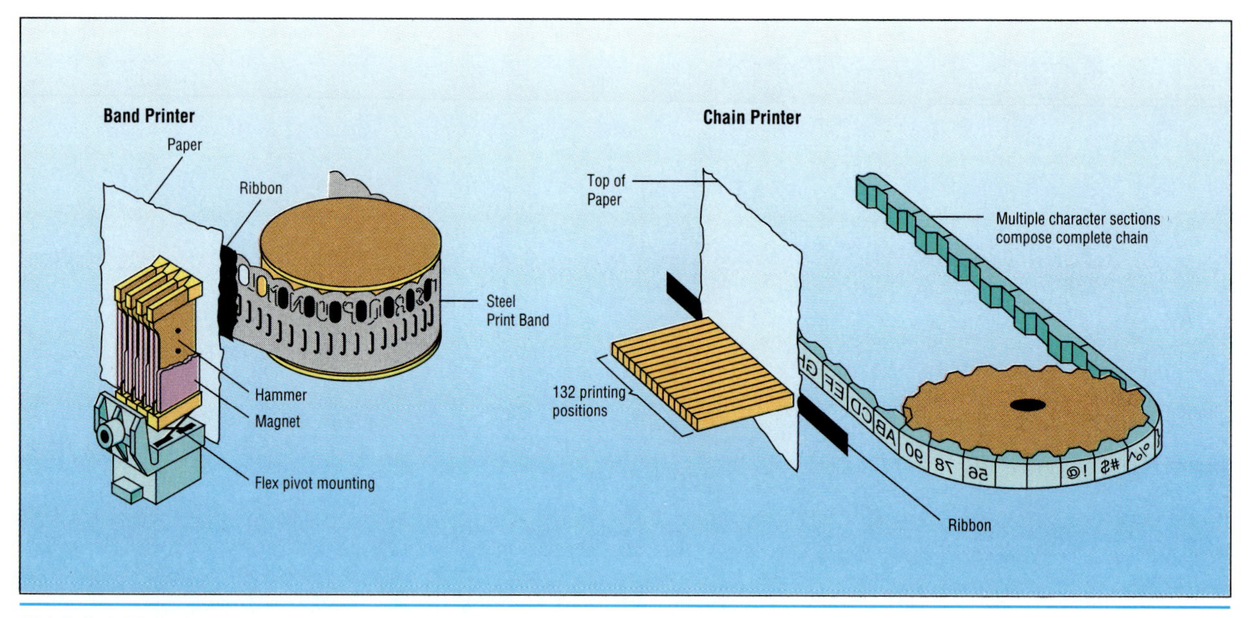

Exhibit 4.15

Line Impact Printers

Band printers use a hammer to strike the paper against the ribbon and the fully formed character. The embossed characters are on a band that rotates horizontally. Chain printers use multiple hammers that are each released when the correct character slugs contained on the rotating chain are in the proper print position.

hammers are used by line printers. For example, one type of chain printer has 132 print hammers. A chain of characters rotates past the print hammers at a very high speed. When the proper character is in front of a hammer, it releases and strikes the paper against the ribbon, and then against the chain. Since the chain contains several 48-character sections, multiple characters can be printed at the same time. On one pass of the chain, the complete line will have been printed (see Exhibit 4.15).

The very high-speed printers are **page printers.** Typical of this process is the electrophotographic approach used with laser printers. Laser printers use a combination of raster scan and xerographic copy machine technologies. The raster scan approach is used to trace an image of an entire page onto a photosensitive drum. The drum is rotated and the image, a pattern of charges, is transferred to a plain sheet of paper by attracting toner that is fused on by heat.

A summary of the key approaches to printing characters is given in Exhibit 4.16. The character formation options are fully formed, dot-matrix, or image. Characters, once formed, can be transferred by an impact or nonimpact method. The number of characters to be transferred in one operation can range from a single character to an entire line and even to a complete page.

Current printer technology consists of combinations of these three key aspects of printing characters. At present, state-of-the-art image formation is always nonimpact and is used with page printers. Fully formed characters are always used with impact technology, which is characteristic of character and line printers. The dot-matrix approach is the most flexible. It can be used with either impact or nonimpact technology and is suitable for either character or line printing.

Exhibit 4.16

Key Printer Approaches

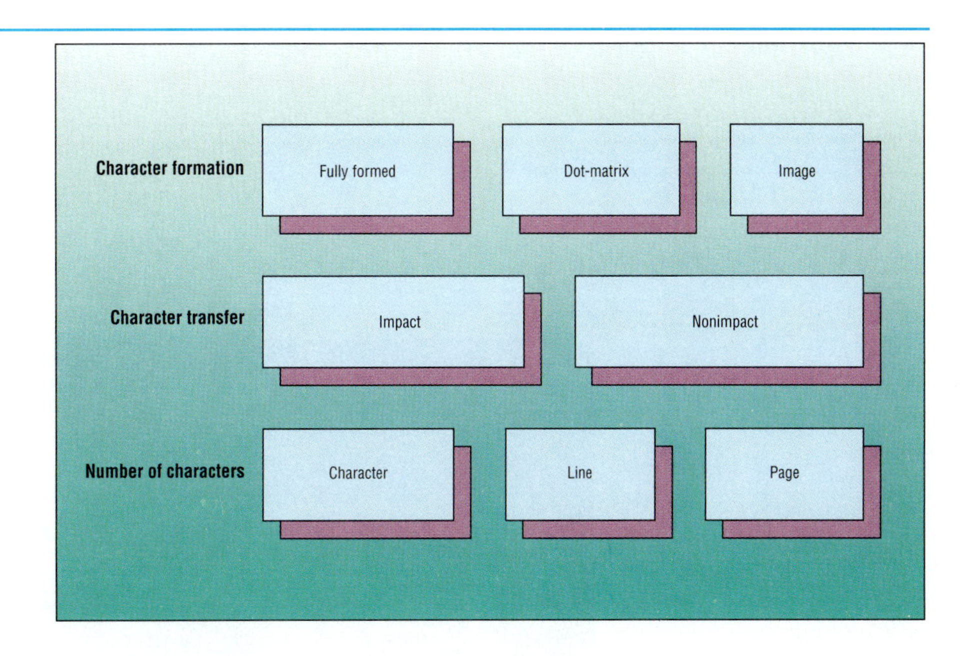

Graphics Printers and Plotters

The growing popularity of graphics displays has been accompanied by an increasing need for hard copies of the graphics. Fortunately, the low-cost text and graphics dot-matrix printers used with personal computers can print business graphics such as bar graphs and pie charts.

Ink-jet technology is being used to generate higher quality images. Fine-nozzle jets spray individual ink drops at the paper. By using multiple-nozzles, several colors of ink can be printed at one time. This form of dot-matrix projection is useful for printing text and graphics. The nonimpact process is also used for printing on packages or odd-shaped objects. Flexibility in printing, color, and high resolution make this technology useful in a variety of areas, including engineering and business.

Very expensive laser printers offer the best quality in hard copy graphics. Because they make use of the raster-scan method, higher resolution is possible. This form of image processing is so good that it is being used as the base technology for electronic publishing (see Exhibit 4.17). For example, banking and insurance industries and governmental agencies conduct many of their activities using a multitude of preprinted forms. Previously, in-house printing departments had to run off thousands of copies of each form and store them for later use. Now, the computer is being used to operate laser printers, which produce each form as it is needed and fill in the appropriate data as part of the output process. Recent breakthroughs in inexpensive laser printers have made possible desktop publishing. This will be explored further in Part IV, "End-User Software."

Plotters are output devices that are specialized to produce graphics.

The Adventure Begins

Chapter 1

The Adventure Begins

This trip really began in September last year when Gerry won first
prize in a raffle at the fashion show which Rush-Presbyterian-St.
Luke's Medical Center holds every year. The prize was two round
trip tickets to Hong Kong on United Airlines, and te
Hong Kong Hyatt Hotel. Analyzing our good fortune,
that we wanted to do more than spend ten days in H
return, but at the same time, United, having just gotten
equipment from Pan American, had not yet received
to other destinations or between points in the Far Eas

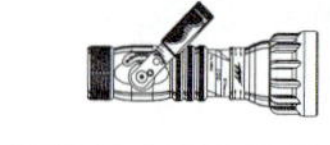

Figure 1-1 This picture has very little to do with this story.
want to place a more appropriate picture in this frame.

On February 10th, United acquired this authority, a
11th Debbie began putting our trip together. We left
and returned on March 26th. We entered seven cou
over 25,000 miles on four airlines, made over 500

Exhibit 4.17

The Hewlett-Packard Desktop Laser Printer and Printed Sample

can only be programmed to move right, left, up, down, or diagonally. Curves are drawn as a series of very short lines. The quality of the output is a direct function of the fineness of the lines, the type of pen tips used, and the number of color pens available. This low-cost approach can give surprisingly high-resolution graphics. Note in Exhibit 4.18 the complex drawings produced by the plotters.

Plotters come in a wide variety of sizes, ranging from small desktop models to enormous devices that can be used to draw full-scale airplane designs. The two basic types of plotters are flat-bed and drum. Flat-bed plotters move the pens along the X and Y axes according to software instructions. The material being printed on is flat and stationary. With drum plotters, the pen moves perpendicularly to the direction of the rotating drum, which can move the paper backward and forward. The major advantage of the drum plotter is that the length of the paper roll allows very long printouts, which are useful for scientific work such as seismic tracings and other applications.

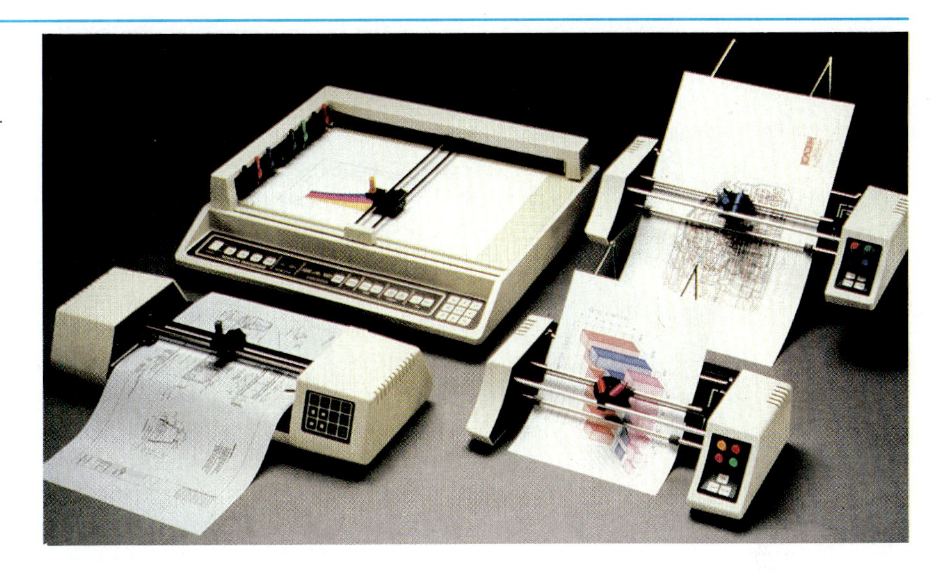

Exhibit 4.18

Graphics Plotters

Plotters can produce high-resolution graphics at low cost. Computer plotters are used in a variety of applications.

Computer Output Microform

One of the options for producing hard copy output of data or graphical images is **computer output microform (COM).** This is a technique in which a microphotographic copy of information is recorded on a microform, such as a microfilm reel or a microfiche card. With some systems, the computer data are first recorded on magnetic tape. The tape is later used as input to a COM machine, which reads the data and produces a microform copy of the information. In other systems, the computer can directly transfer data to the COM machine.

COM is especially useful in those situations in which certain computer records stored on magnetic tape or disk are no longer active, but need to be referenced occasionally or kept to meet a legal requirement. Examples include the medical and financial records of patients after they have left a hospital, the transcript records of students after they have graduated from college, and old insurance claims. To store this type of data on computer disk or tape would cost approximately twenty times more than storing it on microfilm. The other option has been to store computer printouts of inactive data. But printouts cost ten times as much to produce, and take up fifty times more physical space than microfilm. These cost relationships also affect how active data is stored and retrieved.

Speech Synthesis Devices

In a growing number of applications it is advantageous to have the computer communicate information by output that has human voice characteristics. **Speech synthesizers** are devices that enable computers to transform electronic data into voice output.

DECtalk, by Digital Equipment Corporation, is a voice synthesis machine that can generate natural-sounding voice output. DECtalk is a self-contained unit that receives text output from a computer system. Instead of printing the text, DECtalk speaks it through a speaker or over a telephone line. Voices of male or female adults or children can be used, and the speaking rate can be varied.

Voice synthesis systems such as DECtalk have many applications. One example is computer-aided instruction systems that allow a student to both see and hear the information that is displayed on the video screen. This reinforcement can make the instruction clearer and the system more pleasant to use. An example of another use for this system is to allow people to use their telephones to consult computer files. For example, a sales representative could get immediate inventory information during a customer meeting; a lawyer could check records in an office file during a break in court proceedings; an investor could get up-to-the-minute quotes from stock brokerage firms. Clearly, a voice synthesis system can be a useful tool for professionals in a variety of work situations.

Voice synthesis systems are also being used to aid the visually impaired. OCR systems have been combined with voice systems to create reading machines. The OCR scans the text in a book or report and transmits it to a computer system, where it is processed. The output is synthesized speech.

Computers at Work

The Ultimate Interface

A small group of visionaries would like you to get into computing—literally.

At a handful of corporate and university research labs across the country, hardware and software engineers are teaming up with urban planners, psychologists, and other "soft science" experts to develop a suite of technologies known as "artificial reality," "virtual reality," or "virtual worlds."

Broadly stated, their goal is to develop new ways of working with computers that are far more intuitive and powerful than today's common metaphor of the two-dimensional desktop. They are developing systems in which computer users rely on special equipment, including goggles, gloves, and even entire suits to manipulate objects and otherwise work and play in a virtual world, a world that, depending on the specific application, may or may not resemble what most of us think of as reality.

While these developers still face fundamental problems in bringing virtual technology into widespread use, their efforts have already found several niche markets. And, they say, virtual reality's potential is so great that it will not only find applications in business environments but in entertainment, the arts, and a host of consumer applications as well.

Computer interfaces have been receiving an enormous amount of attention as people try to find ways to use the machines to boost productivity aside from automating tedious processes, such as filing records. But most interface developments have been only slight improvements to the desktop setup, which uses a mouse or other point-and-click device to manipulate icons, invented at Xerox Corp.'s Palo Alto Research Center in the '70s and popularized by Apple Computer Inc. in the '80s.

Most researchers in virtual-worlds technology say their aim to give users a genuine three-dimensional interface; they want to eliminate the barrier between human and machine with technologies that make it difficult to tell where the user leaves off and the machine begins.

To date many experts in the field admit that no one has come up with the appropriate metaphor for 3-D computing—that is, a method for performing various tasks that is intuitive and consistent. As Eric Lyons, chief technologist at Autodesk Inc. in Sausalito, Calif., says, "Most people who have used a desktop or window environment know how to discard a file or move a window even if they haven't used that particular system before. But there's no metaphor for working in 3-D. We need to bridge that gap."

Lyons says that while devising a suitable metaphor is critical, development is not completely hamstrung in its absence. "We can't rely on a brainstorm," he says. "We have to plug away from the left side of the brain."

The effort is worth it, he adds, because the productivity gains and ease of use of virtual-worlds technology over the desktop metaphor will be at least as great as those achieved when the latter replaced the one-dimensional command-line interface.

The theory is that users will get far more out of computers because they will interact with the machines in a completely natural way. The desktop metaphor may be relatively easy for people to learn, but a fair amount of training is still required. With virtual worlds, researchers are interested in minimizing training and concentrating on the psychological aspect of how people approach computing, an area which has been ignored in the past. With virtual technology, "You can't dictate to the user 'Learn these rules and that's how you use the machine,'" says William Bricken of the Washington Technology Center's Human Interface Technology Laboratory in Seattle.

Thus, Bricken says, one challenge in advancing virtual reality will be to "pay attention to all the human interface questions we've been ignoring."

Virtual reality was born in the military, specifically from efforts to design a "virtual cockpit" that would free pilots from the constraints of actual reality by giving them a representation of reality inside a special helmet. Today the proponents of virtual reality not only see uses for the technology in the military and the workplace, but also in nearly all situations involving human-computer interaction—and even some that don't.

Substantial progress has already been made in some areas: in entertainment, for example, with arcade-style games in which the participant is immersed in a computer-generated world; in new approaches to architecture, with systems that allow clients to "walk through" 3-D computer simulations of buildings and recommend changes before construction begins, or even make the changes themselves by pushing walls back; in medicine, with new prosthetic devices that allow even the most severely handicapped people to participate in a variety of activities.

More distant applications are also promising. Consider "televirtuality," in which a videoconference could entail far more than seeing the image of the person you're talking to. Instead, you might see yourself and others together in a simulated environment, all touring the workings of a new aircraft that you're designing.

In fact, despite the lack of a dominant metaphor for computing in a virtual world, the barriers to widespread adoption of the technology are as much economic as technical. "For people with a lot of money to spend, we've got an elegant product right now," says Lyons of Autodesk. "But we want to continue development and hit the (price-performance) curve at the optimum point."

Summary and Key Terms

The foundation of computer processing is data. Much effort is expended in entering data into the computer and ensuring their accuracy. **Data** are the letters and/or digits that are used singularly or in combination to represent events or facts. **Functions** are instructions used to specify an action for the computer system to take.

Input devices can be classified as to how these data and functions are entered into the computer system. **Key entry** is the entry of data or functions into the computer by means of pressing keys on a keypad or keyboard. In contrast is **keyless entry,** which is the entry of data into the computer or the selection of functions by means other than keying.

Computer terminals are the predominant data entry device. The **human-computer interface** refers to the means of interaction between a human being and the machine.

Keyboards are the primary means through which humans interact with computers. Keyboard designs differ significantly in terms of the number, placement, and function of the keys. A typical keyboard used with general-purpose terminals is very similar to the **QWERTY** keyboard arrangement of a standard typewriter.

To simplify word processing, spreadsheet analysis, and data queries, users needed an enhanced keyboard. To the typewriter keyboard has been added a **numeric keypad,** which is quicker for entering numeric data than the top row of the typewriter keyboard. **Arrow keys** were incorporated to facilitate movement of the cursor. **Function keys** were added to provide a way to command certain common tasks in one step, rather than requiring several keystrokes to accomplish the same thing.

Pointing devices are a complementary input means, primarily useful for selecting functions. A recent advancement that makes the human-computer interface more natural is the use of **icons.** These are graphic symbols for functions such as selecting documents, using a calculator, filing letters, and removing unwanted data. These functions are selected by the movement of the cursor, which is controlled with a hand-sized box called a **mouse.**

Source data automation (SDA) is a form of keyless data entry that captures the data from its original source. These special machines read data directly from the source document and convert it to computer-readable form.

SDA devices that use light images to read data are classified as **optical recognition** machines. Examples include **mark-sense, bar codes, OCR fonts,** and **digital scanners.** Magnetic recognition devices use magnetic patterns to read data. **Magnetic ink character recognition (MICR)** devices and **magnetic strips** are examples. In **voice recognition** systems, the electrical signal pattern of spoken words is compared to that of the stored voice template's vocabulary.

Computer output can be classified in several different ways. **Hard copy** output, such as paper printouts, provides the user with a permanent record. **Soft copy** output, such as the visual display on a terminal or computer voice output, provide a temporary record. Information that is presented in the form of letters, numbers, and special characters is **alphanumeric.** In contrast, **graphics** are pictures or graphs depicting information.

Cathode-ray tubes (CRTs), like television picture tubes, electronically paint characters on a screen. In the **raster scan** process, a beam of electrons sweeps back and forth horizontally across the screen. **Resolution** is a measure of the number of **pixels** or picture elements that can be addressed on the screen.

CRTs are used in monochrome and color monitors. **Monochrome monitors** display one color such as green or amber on a black background. **Color monitors** use a triad or trio of dots to form a pixel of various colors while RGB monitors use three electronic guns to electronically mix the three primary colors.

If each individual pixel is addressable, this is known as a **bit-map** or **dot-addressable display.** When only blocks of pixels can be addressed or manipulated in displays, this is known as **character-addressable display.**

Flat-panel displays create a screen image by illuminating a pattern of discrete dots. The high resolution and steady image of flat-panel displays yield high-quality results.

Printer technologies differ in three basic ways: **character formation, character transfer** (to paper or another medium), and **number of characters printed at a time.** Character formation options are **fully formed, dot-matrix, and image.** Characters, once formed, can be transferred by an **impact** or **nonimpact** method. The number of characters to be transferred at a time can range from one character to an entire line or a complete page.

Business graphics use multifunction dot-matrix impact printers, as well as printers using nonimpact thermal, ink-jet, and laser technology to provide hard copies of screen graphics.

Plotters are output devices that are specialized to produce graphics. Plotters come in a wide variety of sizes, ranging from small desktop models to enormous devices used to draw full-scale airplane designs.

Computer output microform (COM) is a microphotographic copy of information recorded on a microform such as a microfilm reel or a microfiche card.

Speech synthesizers are devices enabling computers to transform electronic data into voice output.

Review Questions

1. What advantages and disadvantages are offered by key entry and keyless entry devices?
2. Why are some input devices better for selecting functions than for data entry?
3. How can bar-code systems benefit organizations?
4. Explain why the MICR system currently used by the banking industry is not a true SDA system.
5. Briefly explain the advantages offered by a voice recognition system. What technological problems must still be overcome in order to fully utilize such a system?

6. How is communication with computers becoming more natural for people?
7. Briefly describe the basic classifications of computer output.
8. How does a CRT display work? What is meant by the term *raster scan?* What is *resolution,* and why is it important?
9. Compare flat-panel displays and CRT displays. What advantages does the flat-panel display offer?
10. Briefly summarize the text's conclusions regarding current printer technology. Which of the current printer technologies is the most flexible?

T F **11.** Source data automation refers to several techniques that allow the computer to "capture" data directly.

T F **12.** Optical character recognition machines use light images to read data.

T F **13.** The most advanced MICR devices are capable of "reading" the entire face of a check.

T F **14.** Speaker-dependent voice recognition systems utilize an "averaged" recognition template created by having the user verbalize the same word a number of times.

T F **15.** An RGB monitor utilizes three electron guns to achieve a sharper video image than is possible with a composite video monitor.

T F **16.** The bidirectional printer offers the fastest printing speed currently available.

17. _____ Peter Myers is preparing to run his firm's computerized payroll. For this purpose, Peter must first collect payroll time sheets. The time sheets serve as:

a. punched cards
b. source documents
c. status reports
d. special media

18. _____ A mark-sense reader is a basic type of:

a. verifier
b. dumb terminal
c. source data automation device
d. punched-card reader

19. _____ Source data recognition devices that use light images to read data are called:

a. magnetic character readers
b. light pens
c. optical character recognition devices
d. imagers

20. _____ Graphic symbols that are used to represent computer functions are called:

a. picto-graphs
b. function-grams
c. icons
d. displays

21. _____ William Carson selects computer functions by using a special device that moves the cursor across the screen until it points at the icon representing the desired operation. William is using a(n):

a. electronic point
b. mouse
c. OCR wand
d. arrow key

22. _____ The picture elements embedded in the CRT screen are called:

a. dot elements
b. photons
c. phonemes
d. pixels

23. _____ Output devices that are specialized to produce graphics are called:

a. imagers
b. drafting devices
c. plotters
d. graphers

CHAPTER 5

Secondary Storage

Chapter 3 included a simple payroll application in which both program instructions and data were entered through the keyboard of a CRT. This approach is fine for programs that are going to be run only once or very infrequently. But in real payroll applications, the instructions for calculating and deducting taxes and insurance premiums would make the program longer and more complicated, and an employer may have hundreds of employees to pay weekly. Entering the necessary program instructions and data via a keyboard each pay period would be a waste of time and money and would increase the chance of error.

In applications such as these, it makes more sense to store both the payroll program and employee pay records in secondary storage, such as on magnetic tape or disk. When the time came to run the payroll program, the computer instructions and master data for each employee would be read into primary memory from secondary storage. A payroll clerk would have to key in only those changes to the payroll records that had occurred since the last run. For example, an operator might have to key in the number of hours an employee worked in the latest pay period.

As computers have progressed from merely processing business transactions to more interactive tasks, such as information reporting, decision support, and computer-aided design, corresponding developments in storage media have been required. Different forms of data are also being processed now. Historically, data have been primarily alphanumeric. The 1970s saw the additional need for text processing, the 1980s added graphics, and the 1990s will require video. Different storage devices and media are emerging to handle these diverse needs. In this chapter you will learn to do the following:

1. Explain the major ways secondary storage devices are classified
2. Describe available magnetic disk technologies and compare their capabilities and limitations
3. Identify the unique characteristics of optical disks
4. Identify the types of magnetic tape units that are used with large computers and personal computers

Classifying Computer Storage

This chapter will discuss the characteristics of storage devices, such as magnetic disks, optical disks, and magnetic tape. To understand the advantages and disadvantages of these media, you have to think about them in terms of an organization's needs in data processing.

Organizations process data in the computer in one of two ways. The first way is to record and process a single event as it happens. This immediate processing is called **transaction processing,** where the word *transaction* refers to a specific event. The second way is to process a batch of similar transactions as a group. This is called **batch processing.** Each is appropriate for certain situations.

For example, in the reservation systems of airlines and hotels, the inventory of available flight seats or hotel rooms must reflect the current situation in an accurate and timely fashion. Therefore, each flight or room request (a transaction) needs to be processed immediately. In this case, transaction processing is the appropriate mode.

In contrast is a business that pays its employees twice a month. Data from the time cards can be entered a day or so before the paychecks are due. Since all employees are paid on the same day, it is most efficient to process these payroll transactions as a group. Thus, for this task batch processing is most appropriate.

Since computers are being used more and more for interactive transaction processing applications, direct-access storage devices are becoming the dominant storage medium. But sequential-access media have an important role to play as well—for batch processing applications and inexpensive offline storage. The following discussion of sequential-access media centers on magnetic tape, but it is important to note that disk storage can also be used in this way. Computer storage can be divided into three basic categories: volatile versus nonvolatile, sequential versus direct access, and fixed versus removable.

Volatile Versus Nonvolatile Storage

To be processed, computer programs and data have to be loaded into primary memory. But current primary memory technology has several major problems. One is that read/write primary memory such as RAM can only be used for temporary storage of information, since it is **volatile.** That is, when power to the computer is cut off, the information in RAM is lost. In contrast, secondary storage is **nonvolatile.** Tapes and disks use magnetic recording techniques that retain the data when the power is shut off.

A second problem is primary memory's limited storage capacity. Often, the complete program and all the data records needed cannot fit into primary memory at one time. This limitation can be overcome, in part, by the use of secondary storage.

Sequential-Access Versus Direct-Access Storage

The limitations of primary memory—that it is volatile and has limited capacity—are two of the reasons secondary or auxiliary storage is needed. The particular type of secondary storage medium that is most appropriate depends on whether batch processing or transaction processing applications are being run. These two approaches differ significantly in the way they access specific data in secondary storage. Batch processing usually uses sequential access; transaction processing requires direct access.

To understand the terms *sequential access* and *direct access*, imagine that you are playing recorded music on an audio cassette player and on a jukebox. Songs are recorded on audio cassette tapes sequentially. In other words, if you want to play song number four, you must first pass or play songs one, two, and three. This method is called **sequential access.** In contrast, a jukebox lets you select any song from a list. By pushing a couple of buttons, you have direct access to your song without having to pass or play any other songs. This method is called **direct,** or **random access.**

Magnetic tape, such as that in an audio cassette, is the most widely used strictly sequential-access storage medium. To access a specific data record on magnetic tape, each record must be checked in sequence, up to the desired one. Thus, to find Sally Wallis's record in an alphabetized file, the magnetic tape unit would have to first check records for John Avery and Bill Jones. Imagine the search time that would be required if Sally's record were number 1000. Clearly, sequential access holds a distinct disadvantage for a user interested only in specific records. However, if it is necessary to process almost all the records on the tape anyway, the lack of sequential-access capability would not be a limitation (see Exhibit 5.1).

Magnetic tape is ideal for batch processing applications such as a weekly payroll, monthly inventory status report, monthly accounts receivable billing, or for quarterly income statements. All of these programs are run rather infrequently, and when they are run almost all data records are processed to produce the required output. Individual records do not have to be located directly. Since almost all records in the file will be affected, they can be processed in their existing sequence, or they can be sorted beforehand to produce the desired output.

Magnetic disk is the most popular direct-access secondary storage medium. Data are recorded on the disk in concentric circles. A read/write head is used to directly locate the place where the data record is to be read or written, in much the same way you can move the tone arm of a phonograph player to a particular song on a record album.

One instance in which direct access is essential is for transaction-processing applications, such as airline reservations. Assume you call XYZ Airline to find out what flights are available between Chicago and Los Angeles on a specific date. The computer needs to be able to directly locate the records for only those particular flights from among thousands of records about flight schedules for XYZ Airline.

With disk storage, direct access to specific records is readily available. Since there is no way to anticipate exactly which records will be needed when, or in what order, direct access is crucial. In most interactive applications, the ability to respond quickly to inquiries and to update records immediately as change occurs is also essential. For example, in an airline reservation system it is important not only to confirm flight information, but also to change the record for the number of open seats left on the Los Angeles–Chicago flight so that it accurately reflects the available seats.

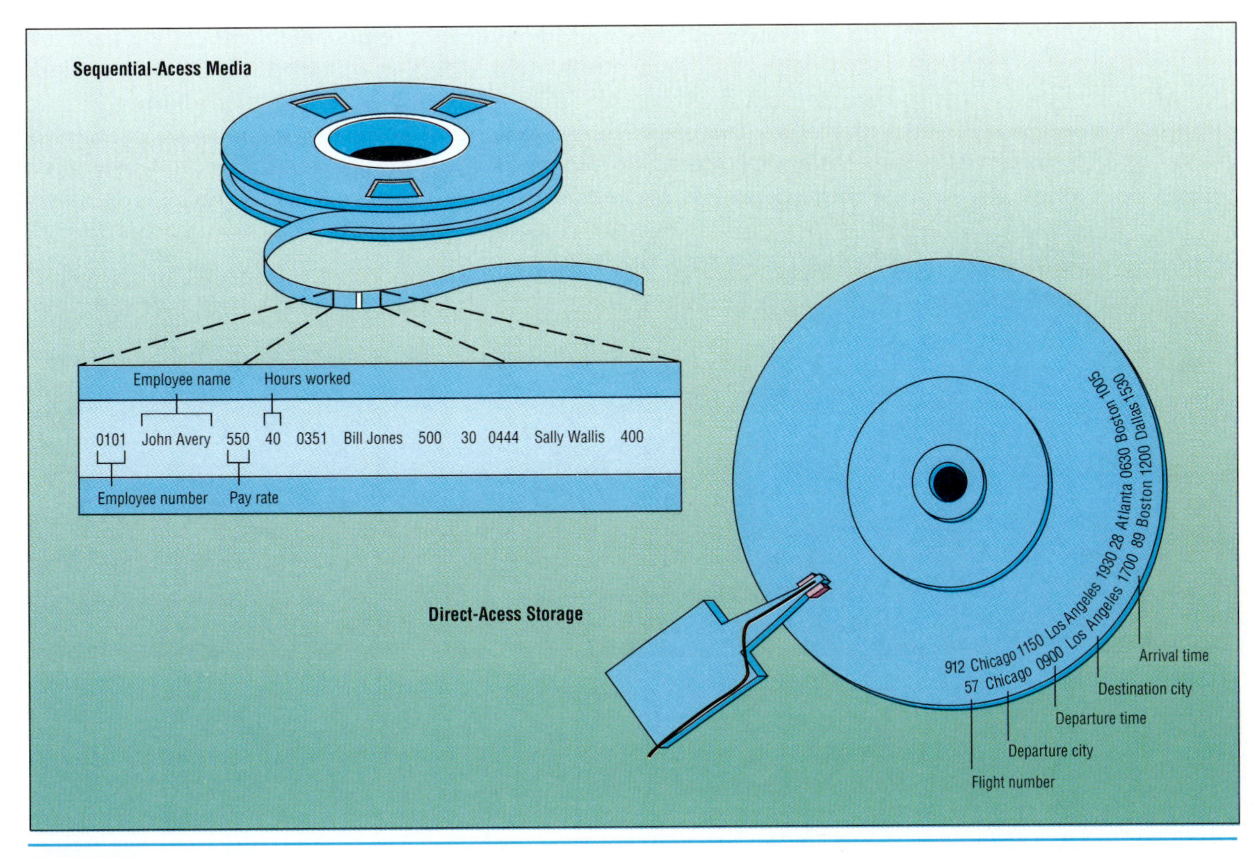

Exhibit 5.1

Sequential-Access Versus Direct-Access Storage

Sequential-access media require that each record preceding the desired record be checked. Direct-access media allow the desired record to be located directly.

You will learn more about how data access and data organization work in Chapter 8, "File and Database Management." The important point to note here is that the access characteristics of the storage medium need to effectively meet the needs of the specific application. In general, batch processing applications are most efficient using a sequential-access storage medium, and interactive processing applications are most efficient using a direct-access storage medium.

Fixed Versus Removable Storage

A third important variable of storage media is whether they are removable or fixed. **Removable media,** such as magnetic tape and many disk systems, allow the user to swap one set of data for another. This gives almost unlimited secondary storage capacity. In addition, this characteristic allows the storage media to be used as a backup. A **backup** is a duplicate set of computer-readable data that is used only when the original data is damaged, lost, or destroyed. When needed, a backup of computer-readable data can be connected online and used either directly or to reconstruct the destroyed information.

One of the major disadvantages of removable media is that they can be damaged by fingerprints, dust, or being dropped. Thus, they are less reliable than fixed media. In contrast, **fixed media** cannot be touched or removed by the user. For example, fixed hard disk systems are often used as secondary storage systems providing high reliability and extensive storage capacity. Generally these high-precision systems have their read/write heads and disk platters sealed in contaminant-free environments (see Exhibit 5.2).

Direct-Access Storage Devices

The medium that has clearly come to dominate the secondary storage market is the magnetic disk. This situation primarily reflects the current prevalence of transaction processing. With batch processing, the sequential record storage on magnetic tape was fine. However, transaction processing requires that the user have direct access to any given record, and this is exactly what disks allow. Disks also offer the flexibility of doing traditional sequential processing, if desired.

One direct-access secondary storage device, the optical disk, is emerging as an important secondary storage medium. It is attractive because of its very large storage capacity and its ability to store high-quality video images.

Magnetic Disks

There are two basic forms of magnetic disks—hard and floppy. **Hard disks** are rigid aluminum platters coated with a magnetic oxide. They come in a variety of sizes and have a wide range of storage capacity. They can be further categorized in terms of being fixed or removable. **Diskettes** (also called floppy disks) are made of a flexible Mylar plastic coated with magnetic oxide. These diskettes also come in several physical sizes, but all are designed to be removable.

The variety of disks available will be discussed shortly. First, though, it is important to understand how disks store and gain access to data.

The disk itself is sometimes compared to a phonograph record, but there is a major difference. The disk has a series of invisible concentric circles called **tracks.** Note that this differs from a phonograph record, which has a single, visible groove that spirals toward the center of the record. Disk tracks are invisible, since they are simply composed of magnetically encoded data.

Along each track, data are encoded in the form of magnetic bit patterns. A read/write head is used to sense the magnetic direction of each bit or to change magnetic patterns in the appropriate place on a specific

Exhibit 5.2

Fixed and Removable Storage Media

Removable media allow almost unlimited storage capacity, as one set of data can be swapped for another. Fixed secondary storage media offer higher reliability and extensive storage capacity without operator intervention.

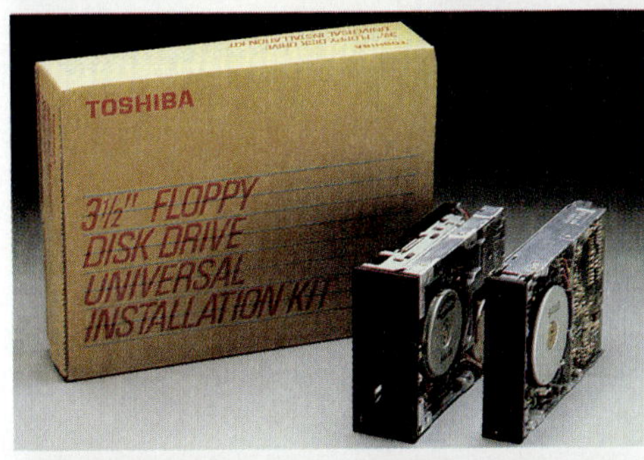

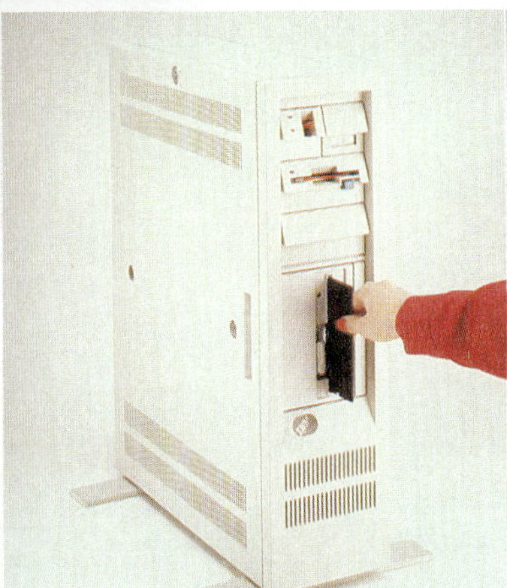

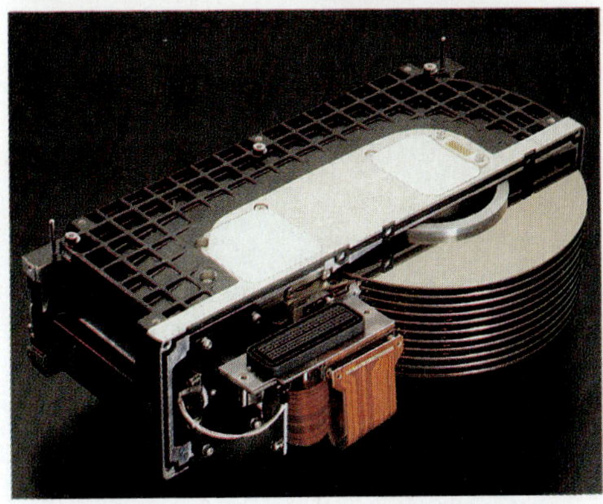

track. The magnetic bit pattern for the letter *K*, using an 8-bit ASCII code, is shown in Exhibit 5.3. To read or write data, one or more disk platters are mounted on a spindle, which rotates at a fixed speed. For hard disk systems, this is commonly 3600 revolutions per minute (rpm), whereas floppy disk systems spin at around 400 rpm.

Exhibit 5.3

Encoding Data on a Magnetic Disk

Along each invisible concentric track, data are encoded in the form of magnetic bit patterns.

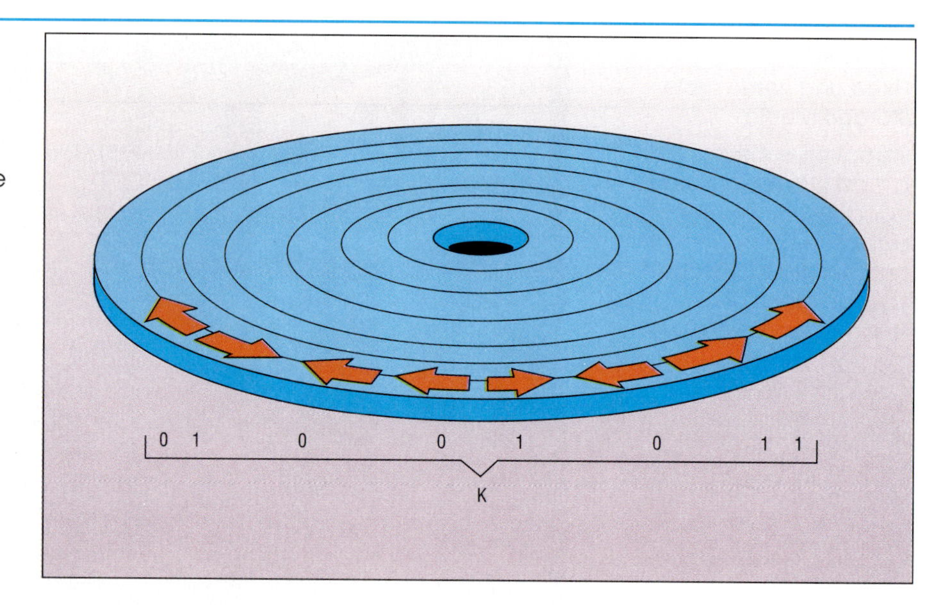

The storage capacity of a disk is a function of the number of tracks per surface, the bit density, and the number of recording surfaces (see Exhibit 5.4). The number of tracks per surface is determined by the physical size of the disk and the technology used to record the data. Platter size is commonly either 14 inches, 8 inches or 5-1/4 inches in diameter for large-capacity hard disk systems, and is primarily 5-1/4 inches or 3-1/2 inches in diameter for diskette systems (see Exhibit 5.5). The number of tracks on a surface can range from 40 to 80 on smaller diskettes to 200 to 800 on larger

Exhibit 5.4

Disk Storage Capacity Factors

The storage capacity of disks is a function of the number of tracks per surface, the bit density, and the number of recording surfaces.

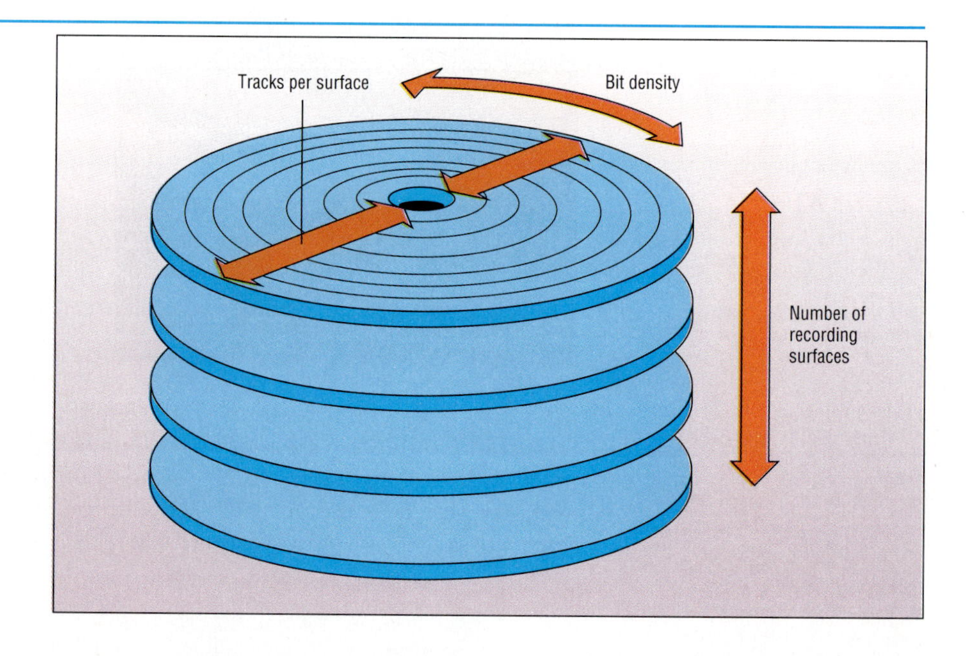

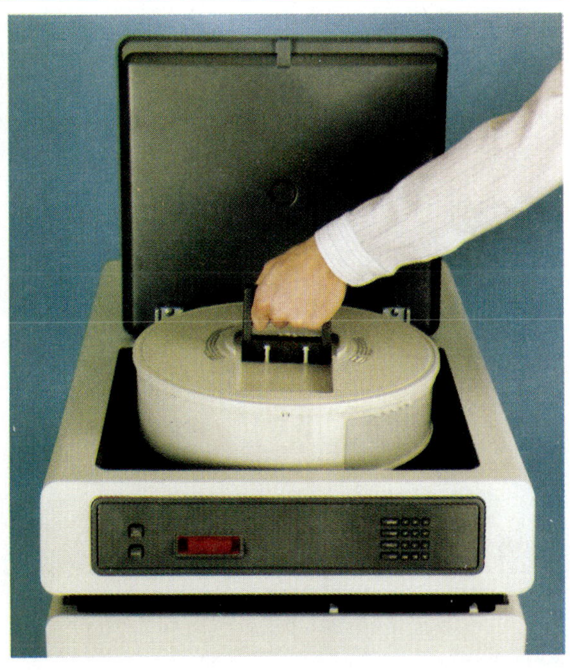

Exhibit 5.5

Disk Platter Sizes

Disk platters come in a variety of sizes. The smallest is 3 1/2 inches in diameter (left) and the largest is 14 inches in diameter (right).

disks. The trend is to pack more and more data onto smaller and smaller disks.

Bit density is measured in terms of the number of bits per inch (bpi). The bpi measure ranges from 2000 in diskette systems to, commonly, 12,000 in hard disks. These measurements correspond to 250 and 1500 characters per inch. The latest technology uses a thin layer of magnetic metal film, as opposed to iron-oxide particles used previously, to record bit densities of 24,000 bpi. The metal film allows a greater, more uniform concentration of magnetic particles.

Overall, disk storage capacity ranges from less than 1 megabyte on the smaller diskette systems used with microcomputers up to several gigabytes on mainframe computers. A *gigabyte* is 1 billion bytes, or 1000 megabytes. About 500 typewritten pages can be recorded in a megabyte of storage. While at first glance it may be hard to imagine what people would do with a gigabyte of storage, the reality is that disk storage demand is growing at a rate of 20 to 30 percent per year, and there seems to be no end in sight. Even now, only a small percentage of the data used daily in commercial, educational, and government organizations is stored on computer disks. Most is still on paper, stored in crowded file cabinets.

The number of platters used with disk systems ranges from one on microcomputer diskettes to nineteen on large-capacity hard disks on mainframe computers. Sometimes only one side of a single platter is used to record data. More frequently, both sides of a platter are used. In any case, the storage capacity of a disk is directly related to the number of recording surfaces.

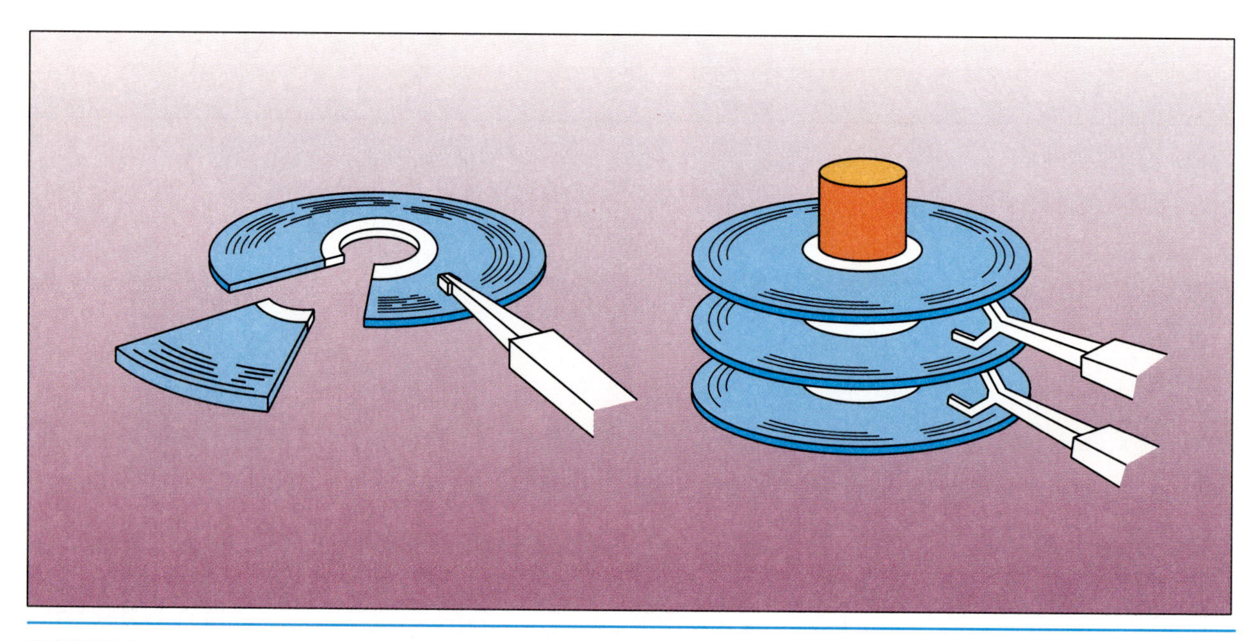

Exhibit 5.6

Data Organization Methods on Disk

Two ways of organizing data on disks are the sector and cylinder methods. With the sector method, the disk surface is logically divided into sectors or horizontal sections. Data are located by surface number, sector, and track number. The cylinder method is based on a vertical plane. The collection of all Track 30s, for example, would comprise Cylinder 30. Data are located by cylinder and surface number.

To read or write data, a read/write head must be positioned over the appropriate track. For single platter systems, an *actuator,* which contains the read/write head, swings in and out over the disk surface to locate the correct track. Once the read/write head is positioned, the disk rotates beneath the read/write head until the needed data record is found. For multiple-platter disk systems, a set of access arms is used. The access arms move in and out to position the read/write heads over the appropriate tracks. Generally, each access arm has two read/write heads—one for the surface above, and one for the surface below.

The two basic ways of organizing data on the disk are the sector and cylinder methods (see Exhibit 5.6). With the **sector method,** the disk surface is logically divided into sectors (like slices of pie). Often, there are eight or more sectors on a surface. Data are located by their surface number, sector, and track number.

The **cylinder** method is based on a vertical plane. For example, in a multiple-platter disk system, each recording surface would contain a Track 30. The collection of all Track 30s would be considered Cylinder 30. When data are recorded with the cylinder method, the data in a file are recorded on Track 30 of Surface 1 and continued on Track 30 of Surfaces 2, 3, 4, and so on, until all data are recorded or the cylinder is filled. In the latter case, an additional cylinder would then be used. The advantage of this approach is that once the first record is located, the access arm does not have to be repositioned to read sequential records. This reduces the time needed to retrieve data.

The speed at which data can be found and retrieved is a function of access time. **Access time** is the amount of time elapsed from the point of requesting data until the data are retrieved. With disks, access time is a function of the time required to position the read/write head over the desired track plus the time it takes for the requested data to rotate under the read/write head. Once the data is located, they can quickly be transferred into primary memory. Overall, the access time for floppy disk systems is around 250 milliseconds, whereas hard disk systems can access data in 25 milliseconds.

Hard Disks

The largest capacity magnetic disks have been the hard disk systems. They come in three standard sizes: 14-inch, 8-inch, and 5-1/4-inch. Mainframes tend to use 14-inch disks with a storage capacity of several gigabytes. These disk systems cost under $100,000. Superminicomputer applications generally do not need that much online capacity. More typical of this group are 8-inch fixed disks with several hundred megabytes of storage, for around $10,000.

To attain high storage capacities and quick access rates, the read/write head needs to be very close to the surface of the disk. When the disk is at rest, the read/write head rests on the disk surface. As the disk starts to spin, the read/write head takes off like an airplane and flies a fraction of an inch above the disk surface. Because the strength of the magnetic field diminishes quickly as the distance above the surface increases, the closer the read/write head is to the disk, the more tightly packed (and weaker) the data can be. The greatest storage capacities are gained when the head is as close as possible to the surface without touching it.

This distance is so close that any kind of dust or foreign matter can make the disk head crash (see Exhibit 5.7). A head crash causes the disk head to scratch the disk surface, resulting in loss of the data stored in those

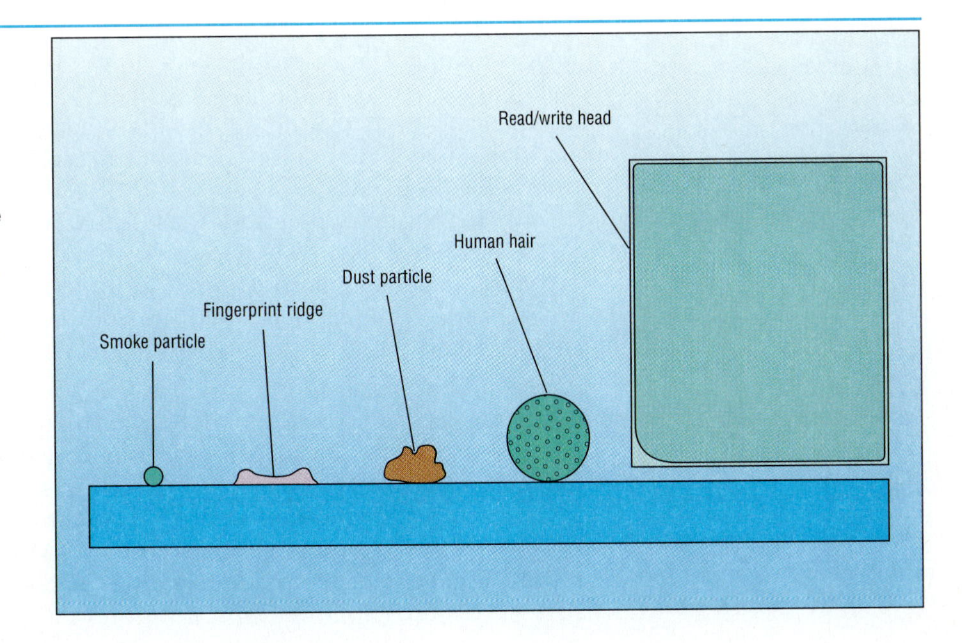

Exhibit 5.7

Potential Causes of Disk Head Crashes

To attain high storage capacities and quick access rates, only minute distances between the read/write head and the surface of the disk are possible. Dust or hair can cause the disk head to scratch the disk surface, resulting in the loss of data stored in those areas. Winchester technology helps to prevent this by hermetically sealing the disks.

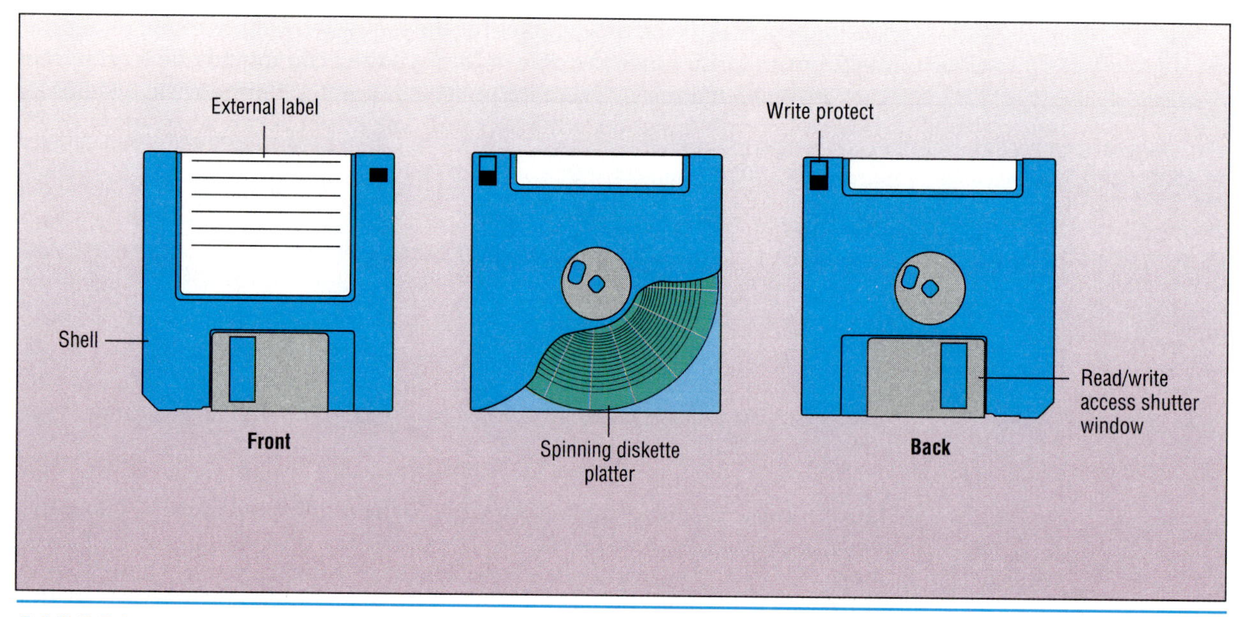

Exhibit 5.8

The 3 1/2-Inch Diskette in Its Protective Cover

areas. To cope with the need for dust-free environments, **Winchester technology** is used. Basically, this technology seals the disk inside a hermetic (airtight) container. This approach has greatly increased the reliability of hard disk systems. The major disadvantage has been that Winchester disks were not removable. However, some removable Winchester disks have recently been developed.

A **disk pack** is a multiplatter hard disk that can be loaded onto, and later removed from, a disk drive. These packs are very useful for data that aren't needed online at all times. A single-platter removable disk is called a **disk cartridge.** Disk cartridges are often used with minicomputers, for loading programs, and for use as backup storage. The major disadvantage of removable disks that do not use the Winchester technology is that they are very susceptible to damage from fingerprints and dust particles and from being dropped.

For business applications, mini- and microcomputers primarily use 5-1/4-inch Winchester disks. However, the newer 3-1/2-inch Winchester is becoming more and more popular. In professional microcomputers, a 40 Mbyte hard disk has become quite common as part of the standard configuration.

Diskettes

Diskettes, or floppy disks, are used primarily with microcomputers. The most popular size of diskette is 5-1/4 inches in diameter. It is made of Mylar plastic and is coated with a thin layer of metallic oxide particles. Diskettes vary in capacity from 100K to 2 Mbytes. The latest trend is toward smaller diameter diskettes called microfloppies or *microdiskettes.*

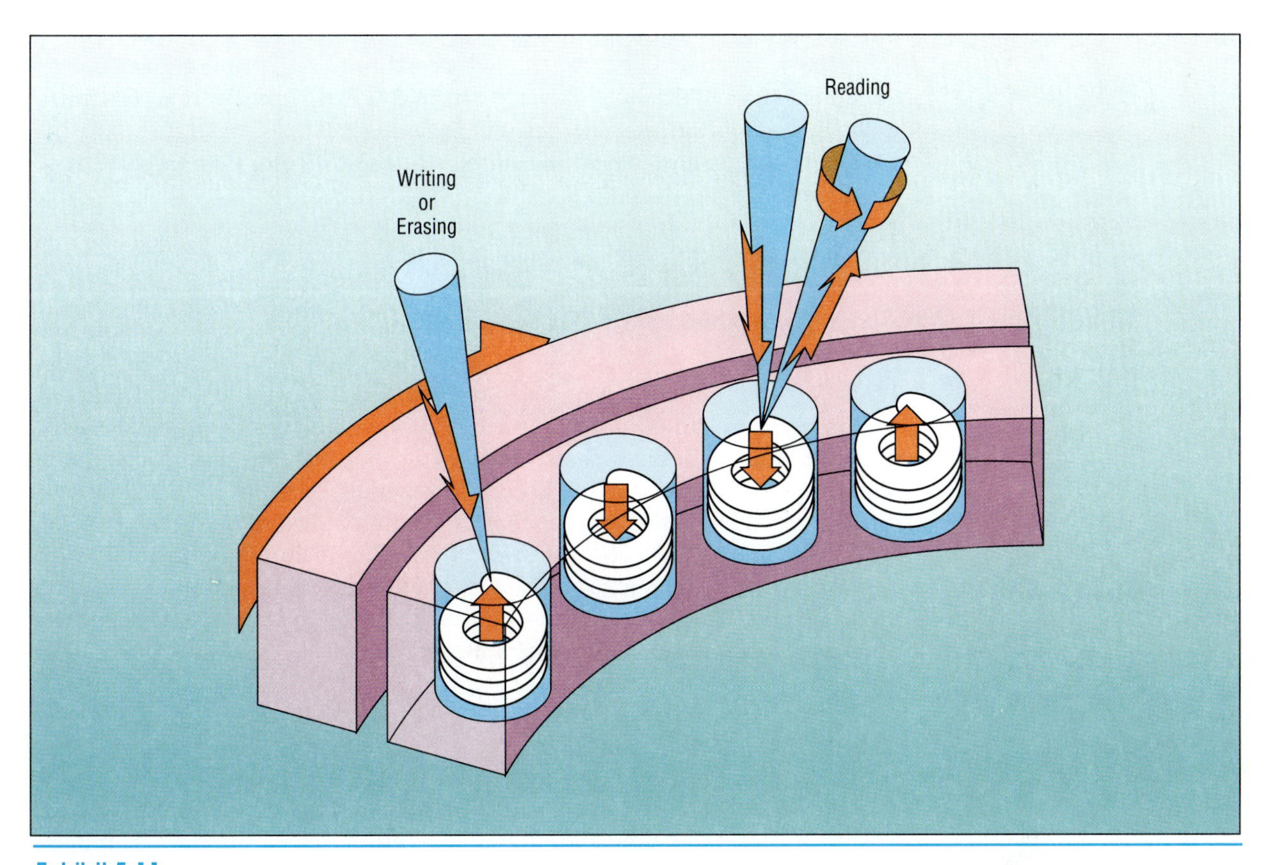

Exhibit 5.11

How Erasable Disk Storage Works

Erasable optical disk storage uses a combination of optical and magnetic properties to provide read/write and erase capabilities.

them freely, without lessening the disk's readability. Optical disks also don't wear out as diskettes do. To summarize, the optical disk is removable, has high storage capacity, and is very reliable.

Optical disks have another very important attribute—the ability to store high-quality video images and sound. These video images are far superior to the graphical images possible with magnetic media.

Digitized patterns of the images and sounds are stored in frames. A typical optical disk has 54,000 frames, which can be used to store anything from screen images to a complete 30-minute audio-video presentation. Each frame of an optical disk can be directly addressed.

Less expensive optical disk systems called **CDROM** (compact discs with read-only memory) are also available. As with the compact disc used in your stereo, CDROMs can only be read (played), and the data cannot be added to or erased.

Even as a read-only device, optical disks have great potential as a medium for archiving important records and documents for long-term storage. Organizations are often required by law to store documents from ten to twenty years, and sometimes even longer. To date, much of the archiving has been done on microfilm or microfiche, but overall, this micrographics approach has never really taken off. It is too expensive, labor intensive, and awkward. Edward Rothchild, publisher of *Optical Memory Newsletter*, predicts that optical disk systems will make film-based document storage obsolete. Lower costs and greatly improved access times will be the important advantages. But the real target of optical disk systems are the paper documents in the office, which still comprise 95 percent of document storage.

Sequential-Access Storage Devices

Thus far this chapter has primarily discussed the many different technologies and media used in direct-access devices. This section will consider storage devices that can provide sequential access. A magnetic disk can be considered to be both a sequential-access and a direct-access device. You will see the benefits that can be derived from this combination.

Most of this section will center on the technology and common applications of magnetic tape storage, beginning with the reel-to-reel tape units used with large computers and then covering the newer cartridge tape units used with micro- and mainframe computers.

Magnetic Disks

The previous section spent much time discussing the characteristics of magnetic disks and how they have become the predominant secondary storage medium. This dominance is a product of organizations' need for direct access to selected data. But in addition to direct access magnetic disks offer organizations the ability to process data sequentially. Thus, magnetic disks are used to meet both the direct-access needs of transaction processing and the sequential-access needs of batch processing. And whereas any direct-access media could also provide sequential access, none does it as well as a magnetic disk when flexibility, access times, and cost are considered.

Magnetic Tape

Magnetic tape is available primarily in two forms—reel-to-reel and cartridge. All magnetic tapes work in a similar fashion; an example is audio cassettes, with which you are probably familiar. A thin plastic tape coated with magnetic material is passed over a read/write head, which either creates or senses a magnetic pattern of bits. Data tapes can be written over, and the tape itself can be reused many times. Tapes are portable, compact, and relatively inexpensive. However, they are vulnerable to dust, breakage, and stretching. Further, they can only be used for sequential access.

To understand how data are stored on magnetic tape, imagine that a piece of tape has been divided into parallel lanes or tracks that run its

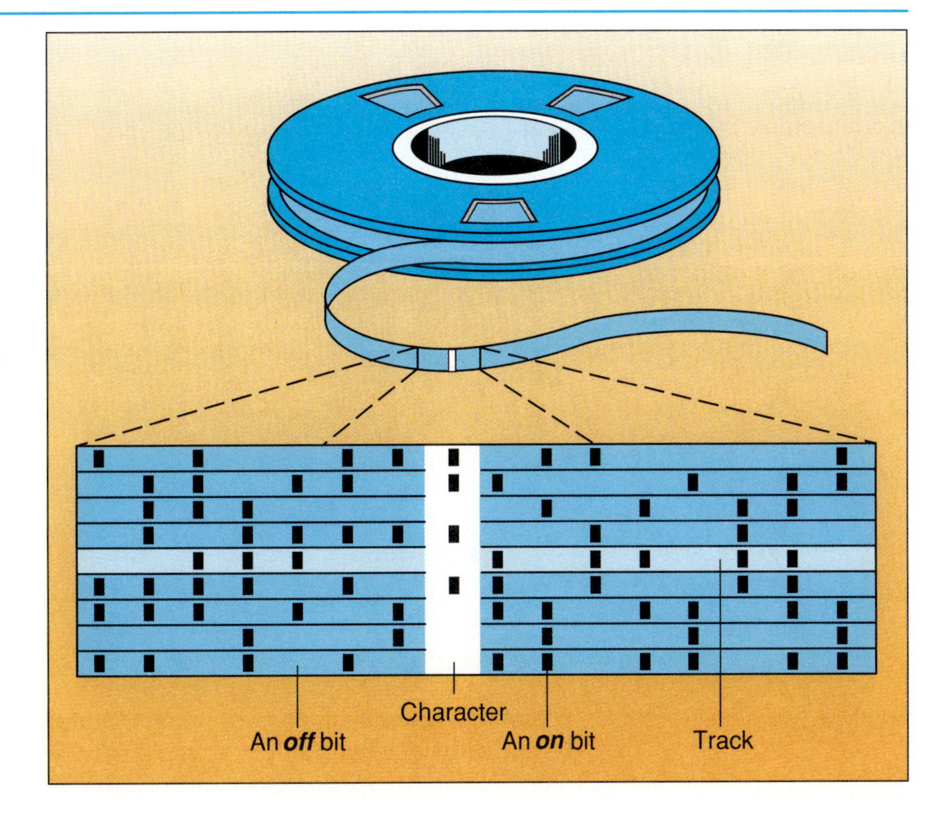

Exhibit 5.12

Encoding Data on Magnetic Tape

Characters on magnetic tape are recorded by bit patterns on a column of tracks. The most common coding scheme is the 8-bit EBCDIC. A ninth track is reserved for a parity bit, used in checking for errors.

length. Within each track, a magnetic spot represents a 1, and no magnetic spot represents a 0. A column of tracks, each containing a byte, represents a single character. Most magnetic tapes are recorded using an 8-bit coding scheme like EBCDIC. A ninth track is reserved for a parity bit. The **parity bit** is used to check for errors that might have occurred during transmission (see Exhibit 5.12). This bit will either be a 0 or 1, depending on the method used. In an even parity system, the sum of the bits should be an even number. With odd parity, the sum of the bits should be an odd number. The wrong sum will cause an error message to be generated. Although the parity bit scheme cannot catch all errors, its ability to catch most transmission errors has made it a standard feature of magnetic tape.

The storage capacity of a tape is determined by the number of bits per inch that can be recorded on the length of the tape. The majority of tape drives record at either 800 or 1600 bpi. For tape, a character or byte is represented by a vertical column of bits, so the terms *bits per inch* or *bytes per inch* are interchangeable in measuring density. The standard reel-to-reel tape width is 1/2 inch wide. A 2400 foot reel recorded at 1600 bpi gives a potential storage capacity of 35 Mbytes. The very high performance tapes can be recorded at 6250 bpi, yielding a capacity of 100 Mbytes. Exhibit 5.13 shows a typical magnetic tape reel unit and the newer tape cartridge unit.

Because it is a sequential-access device, magnetic tape is subject to limitations that direct-access devices do not share. One of these limitations

Exhibit 5.13

Magnetic Tape Units

The smaller tape unit is made possible by the recent development of the compact 4-inch by 5-inch tape cartridge, which holds twenty percent more data than the standard 10 1/2-inch reel.

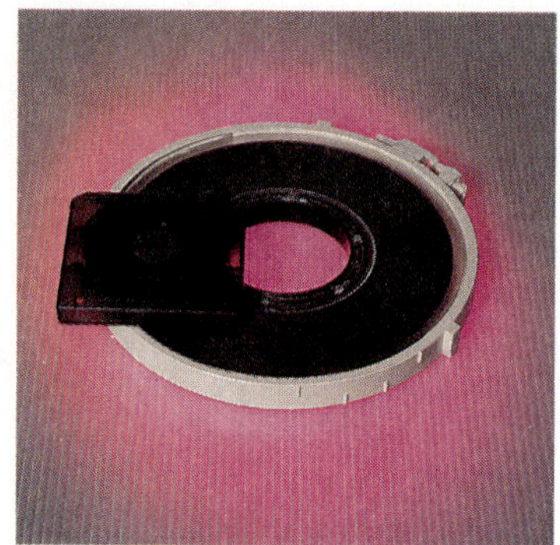

is that the contents of a record on tape cannot be changed, nor can records be added or deleted. Rather, a whole new set of records has to be written onto a different tape in the sequence desired. This process will be discussed in Chapter 8, "File and DataBase Management." For now, it is important to recognize that the direct-access read and write capability of the disk has made it much more attractive than magnetic tape for most roles in the era of interactive processing.

Since computers do fail, disk systems do crash, and files are inadvertently deleted, it is prudent to have a backup copy of data and

Exhibit 5.14

Backup Tape Cartridge

Data cartridge tapes can be used as a high-speed backup alternative to the diskette. These tape units can store 60 megabytes of data and transfer it in ten minutes.

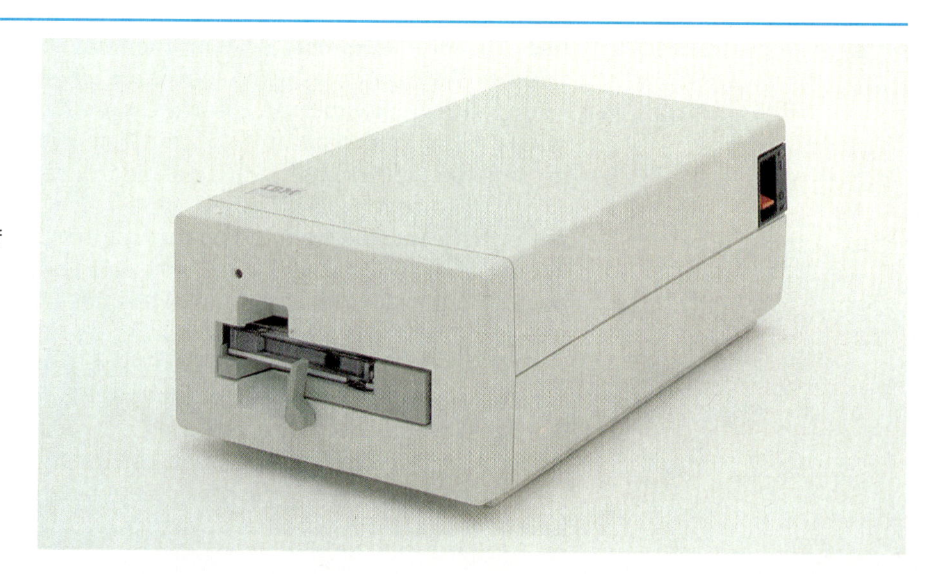

programs. This is one role that magnetic tape performs well and at a low cost. Programs and data on disk are often backed up by dumping them onto magnetic tape. *Dumping* means moving all the files, intact, from disk to tape. Backing up is a function that makes good use of the sequential nature of tape. If the backup copy is later needed to reconstruct data lost from a disk, the programs and data are loaded from tape onto disk for processing.

However, expensive magnetic tape units aren't a practical backup alternative for many minicomputers or most microcomputer systems. Smaller computer systems such as these are generally strictly disk-based and use diskettes backups. However, since a diskette can hold only a megabyte or so, thirty diskettes would be needed to back up a 30 Mbyte Winchester hard disk. This approach is expensive, awkward, and slow.

Magnetic tape vendors have developed the 1/4-inch-wide data cartridge as a backup alternative to the diskette. Very small, inexpensive, and convenient, these units can store up to 100 megabytes, and can transfer this amount of data in ten minutes (see Exhibit 5.14).

For the larger mainframe computer systems, the 3480 cartridge tape units are becoming the new industry standard. For storage requirements that do not require the quick response of disk units, but need access to a massive amount of data, there are *mass storage systems* such as StorageTek's Automated Cartridge System. This system can store 6000 cartridge tapes—250 gigabytes of storage! The data from any of the tape units can be brought online robotically in seconds (see Exhibit 5.15).

Exhibit 5.15

Mass Storage System

With this cartridge system, current manual tape operations can be automated, resulting in dramatically improved performance, costs, and floor-space efficiency. This cartridge–based unit can store up to 6000 cartridges. Data from any sixteen storage tape units can be brought online robotically with a mount time of about ten seconds.

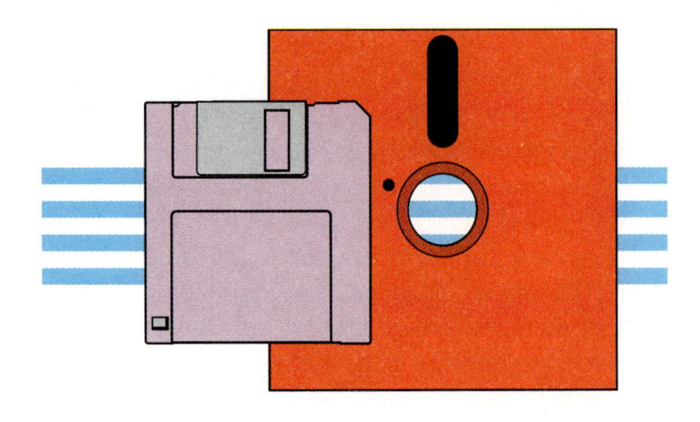

Computers at Work

Multimedia Gets Down to Business

Multimedia moved a few steps closer toward acceptance in the business workplace last week when several companies demonstrated multimedia products at Macworld Expo.

While Apple Computer announced no new multimedia products of its own, the company showcased the products of six "information providers."

Datapro, Harvard University, ABC News Interactive, public broadcast station WGBH, *Newsweek* magazine, and Warner Audio demonstrated how Hypercard can be used as an access tool to retrieve graphic and video images from a laser disc or sound from a CD player. Most companies plan to release products within two months.

"Today we are seeing the dream of multimedia turning into product reality on the Macintosh," said Apple CEO John Sculley in his keynote address.

Harvard University's Three Mile Island—A Crisis Management Game is an interactive simulation that brings the school's case-study method to the computer. Students are placed in the role of the public relations manager at the Metropolitan Edison Utility company during the 1979 crisis. The package—the first of a series the school plans to produce—shows how interactive media can be used to train managers in such complex fields as crisis management, negotiations, and government relations.

For example, in the game the Hypercard front end informs the students of new developments and asks them how to respond. Responses determine how the next phase of the simulation will proceed. The laser disc contains ABC News footage of the crisis, as well as commentary from several management experts.

ABC News Interactive and *Newsweek* both showed how a multimedia format can add excitement to the presentation of current-events information to children. Both projects combine archival video and still-photo images on laser disc taken from recent events as well as commentary from reporters, historic information, and explanations.

ABC has three intreactive titles and plans to add nine more over the next 12 months.

While much of the work with interactive multimedia technology is being directed at the K-12 market, independent suppliers believe that multimedia will soon find a role in business.

"You will see business applications of this technology within three to five months," said Arthur F. Scotten, president of Orange Micro Inc., which is selling the Personal Vision digitizing card and an NTSC-to-RGB converter.

Already, corporations such as Boeing and Domino's Pizza are building test projects using the Personal Vision system for training workers in such areas as aircraft repair and pizza making. In addition, software publishers such as Acius and Aldus are working on incorporating hooks for digitized video images in their software, Scotten said.

Apple is encouraging traditional Mac developers as well as its new partners in the information business to use multimedia technology to create new, different applications. Rather than just see a CD ROM-based dictionary, vendors will have an opportunity to add information through video images and sound, said Jean-Louis Gassee, president of Apple Products.

Apple is working with developers and companies that have an idea of how to better present information, rather than with well-known publishers who might just duplicate their paper-based products electronically, Gassee said.

As part of its multimedia campaign, Apple last week announced the Media Control Architecture, a suite of protocols and device drivers for use in creating multimedia applications.

Summary and Key Terms

You have seen that, for computer programs and data to be processed, they have to be put into primary memory. Read/write primary memory such as RAM can only be used for temporary storage of information, since it is **volatile.** That is, when the computer is turned off, the information in RAM is lost. In contrast, secondary storage is **nonvolatile.** Tapes or disks use magnetic recording techniques that retain the data when power to the computer is turned off.

Which type of secondary storage medium is most appropriate? It depends on the types of programs that are being run, and whether they require sequential or direct access to the data records. With **sequential-access** media, you must check each record key, in sequence, for all the preceding records in order to gain access to the desired one. With **direct,** or **random access,** you can directly reach the data record desired.

The medium that has come to clearly dominate the secondary storage market is the magnetic disk. This is primarily a reflection of the move from batch to transaction processing. With **batch processing,** sequentially accessing records on magnetic tape was efficient. However, **transaction processing** requires direct access to a specific record; this is what disks allow. Disks offer the additional flexibility of doing sequential processing, if it is required.

A third important variable of storage media is whether they are **removable** or **fixed.** Removable media, such as magnetic tape and many disk systems, allow the user to swap one set of data for another and can be used to create a duplicate set of data or a **backup**. However, removable media are generally susceptible to fingerprints, dust, and being dropped, and thus have lower reliability than fixed media. When there is a need for high reliability and extensive storage capacity, fixed hard disk systems are used for secondary storage systems. Generally, these high-precision systems use the **Winchester technology,** in which the read/write heads and disk platters are sealed in an environment free from contaminants.

There are two basic forms of magnetic disks: hard disks and floppy disks, or **diskettes**. Magnetic disks are divided into a series of concentric circles or **tracks. Hard disks** are rigid aluminum platters coated with a magnetic oxide. They come in a variety of sizes and have a wide range of storage capacities. They can be further categorized in terms of being fixed or removable. A major disadvantage of Winchester hard disks has been that they could not be removed. **Disk packs** and **disk cartridges** are examples of removable hard disk. However, removable Winchester disks have recently been developed to overcome this limitation.

The storage capacity of a disk is a function of the number of tracks per surface, the **bit density,** and the number of recording surfaces. The speed with which data can be found and retrieved is a function of access time. **Access time** is the amount of time it takes from the point of requesting data until the data are retrieved. Data are organized on disks using either the **sector method** or the **cylinder method.**

Diskettes, or floppy disks, are made of a flexible Mylar plastic coated with a thin layer of metallic oxide particles. These diskettes also come in several physical sizes; all of which are designed to be removable.

A disk cartridge called the **Bernoulli Box** offers the removability and convenience of floppy diskettes, but with the much greater storage capacities typical of hard disks.

Optical disks used laser technology to provide very high storage capacities. **Erasable optical disk systems** use a combination of light energy and magnetic fields to store data and to provide read/write and erase capabilities. The compact optical disk or **CDROM** is emerging as an important direct-access read-only secondary storage medium. It is attractive because of its large storage capacity and its ability to store high-quality video images.

Magnetic tapes are thin plastic tapes coated with magnetic material. They come in two forms: reel-to-reel and cartridge. All magnetic tapes work in a similar fashion; audio cassettes are one example. The storage capacity of a tape is determined by the number of bits per inch that can be recorded and the length of the tape. Most tapes use an 8-bit coding scheme with a ninth track used for a **parity bit** for error checking.

Review Questions

1. What are the two major disadvantages of primary memory? How are these limitations most frequently overcome?
2. Compare sequential and direct access. Under what conditions would direct access be most needed?
3. What are the major advantages and disadvantages of removable media?
4. Name several media that are removable and provide direct access.
5. What factors influence the storage capacity of a disk?
6. Compare the two basic methods of organizing data on a disk.
7. Briefly describe the components of access time as applied to disks. Assuming that a firm requires the fastest possible access times, would diskettes or hard disks be more likely to be used?
8. What are erasable optical disks? What advantages do such storage systems have? How are data recorded on optical disks?
9. What determines the actual storage capacity of magnetic tape? What are the advantages of the new cartridge tape units used with mainframe computers?
10. What is backup? Why is it important? What are two major disadvantages of using a floppy disk as a backup medium?

T F **11.** The recent movement from batch to transaction processing led to the greater use of sequential-access storage devices.

T F **12.** One of the major advantages of RAM is it is nonvolatile.

T F **13.** Magnetic disks are the foremost direct-access secondary storage medium.

T F **14.** With hard disk systems that use Winchester technology, the platters are commonly removable.

T F **15.** The storage capacity of disk systems is a function of tracks per surface and the bit density.

T F **16.** Access time is the amount of time elapsed from the time of requesting data until the data are retrieved.

T F **17.** Optical disk systems used with microcomputers today are strictly read-only.

T F **18.** The advent of transaction processing and magnetic disks has made magnetic tapes completely obsolete.

T F **19.** Optical disks can only store video images.

T F **20.** The primary backup storage medium used with microcomputers is floppy disks.

21. _____ If the data contained in primary memory is lost when the computer is shut off, that memory is called:

a. nonvolatile c. random access
b. volatile d. removable

22. _____ The primary access method used for printing out college grades at the end of the semester is:

a. direct access c. random access
b. sequential access d. fixed access

23. _____ Optical disks can store which of the following types of information?

a. data c. video
b. audio d. all of the above

24. _____ Floppy disks come in which of the following physical sizes?

a. 2-inch c. 13-inch
b. 4-1/4-inch d. none of the above

25. _____ Which of the following media for a given physical size would have the most storage capacity?

a. magnetic tape c. optical disk
b. floppy disk d. hard magnetic disk

PART III

Computer Information System Development

CHAPTER 6

Management Information Systems

Managers are finding that good management information systems can greatly improve their decision-making capabilities and thus improve their business's performance.

Operating managers make use of transaction processing systems that record and track the events that make up the daily activities of a business. Middle managers tend to rely on information reporting systems that summarize data collected and stored by transaction processing systems. Senior managers require decision support systems that allow them to access and transform data to aid in making decisions. Together these three types of information systems are combined to create the overall management information system for the business.

In this chapter you will learn how to do the following:

1. Describe what a management information system is
2. List the three levels of management, explain their business roles, and describe their information needs
3. Explain what an MIS architecture is and why it is important to a firm's overall MIS design
4. Explain what an MIS master plan is, what its components are, and why it is important to a firm's overall MIS design
5. Describe the information systems life cycle
6. Explain what a feasibility study is used for and its three major aspects

Computer Support of Management

To help you understand how computers can be used to support managerial functions, imagine a small retail computer store called CompuStore, founded in 1983 when the world of microcomputers was still young. CompuStore, in fact, was the first store in the state to sell microcomputers to businesses rather than hobbyists.

Many of CompuStore's early customers were surprised to find that the store owners did not use computers in managing their business. Their management information came from accounting records, paper files of purchase orders and sales receipts, and lots of memos.

All this has changed. CompuStore today is a major retail chain with eight locations, annual revenues of over $15 million, and close to 100 employees. On average, the chain carries more than 200 hardware components, at least 400 software packages, and a variety of supplies and publications. Rather than only dealing with "walk-in" customers,

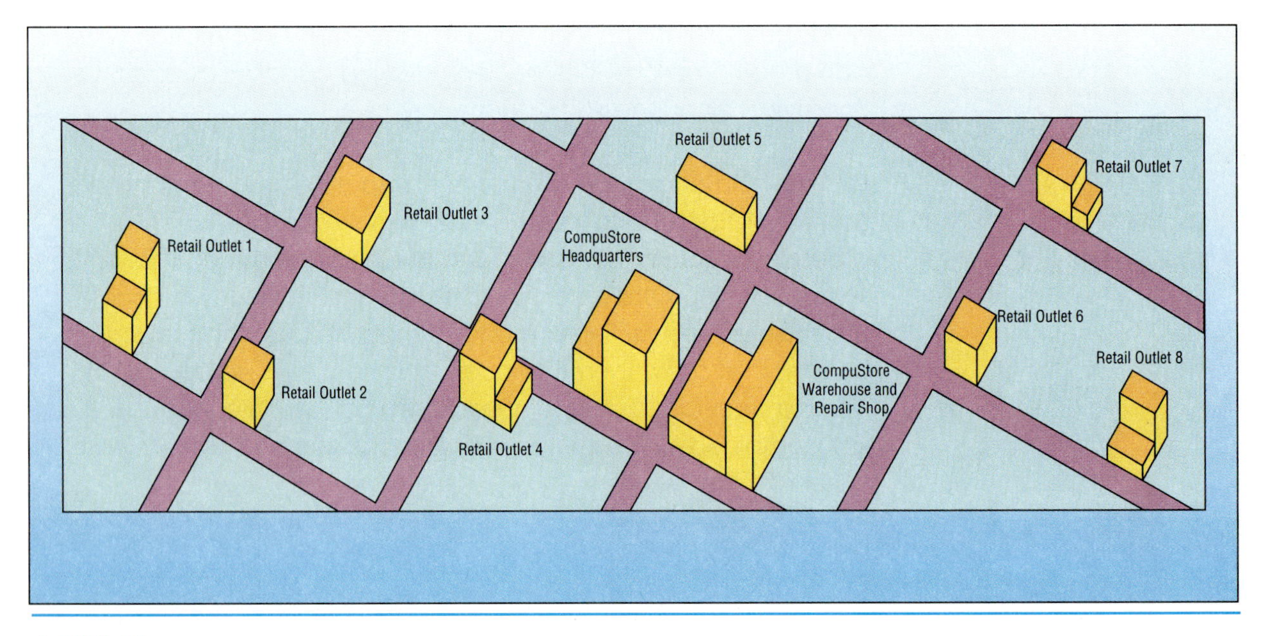

Exhibit 6.1

Compustore's Current Facilities

CompuStore has grown from a one-store business in 1983 to an eight-store chain today. The growth has made it more difficult for managers throughout the firm to fully grasp all of CompuStore's business activities.

CompuStore now handles many corporate accounts. In contrast to 1983, when it dealt with 15 suppliers, CompuStore now orders products from over 100 suppliers. Exhibit 6.1 depicts CompuStore's current facilities.

Most of the firm's employees are specialists. They include accountants, bookkeepers, a financial analyst, a marketing manager, a marketing analyst, an advertising manager, salespeople, a general manager, an office manager, store managers, secretaries, inventory clerks, buyers, purchasing clerks, computer technicians, a systems analyst, and a programmer.

While all this specialization has played a part in CompuStore's success, none of the firm's managers now has a complete grasp of the business. Without computer support, managers would have to track down the employees who had the needed information—or at least knew where to find it. If this took too much time, a manager would have to act without the information. But when managers act without a good grasp of the situation, the result is often unsatisfactory. Important facts are ignored or forgotten, and mistakes occur.

Information systems that provide managers with information enabling them to perform their jobs quicker, better, or both, are called **management information systems,** or **MIS** for short.

The Role of MIS in a Business

The obvious role that management information systems play in any business is to provide managers with the information they need to carry out their own duties. For example, a monthly report summarizing profits on a store-by-store basis could be used to assess growth patterns and determine which retail outlets might be having problems. A weekly report that analyzes the firm's cash position could be used to assess whether loans need to be arranged for the business. A weekly report listing the fastest selling items at each retail location could provide the firm's buyers with information about which product lines to concentrate on.

A less obvious role that management information systems play is to provide a means by which managers can coordinate the activities of different parts of a business. For example, CompuStore lost over $80,000 in 1987 because it failed to take advantage of volume discounts offered by some suppliers. If the firm's buyers could have been provided with monthly sales volumes for specific products broken down by supplier, these discounts might have been realized. Coordinating sales activities with buyer activities could result in better purchasing decisions.

Thus, there are two major roles of MIS in a business:

- Providing managers with information that enables them to carry out their own assigned duties, and
- Providing managers with information that enables them to better coordinate business activities

Management information systems cover a wide range of computer support for managers because of the variety of management positions that exist.

Levels of Business Management

One way of looking at different management positions is shown in Exhibit 6.2. **Operating managers** (or *operations managers)* make sure that a business's day-to-day activities are performed. They direct and oversee workers, and they solve any immediate problems that arise. **Middle managers** make sure that business objectives are achieved. They make certain that operating managers are given enough resources (people, money, facilities, and supplies), they direct and oversee the work of operating managers, and they identify and react to major problems and opportunities. **Senior managers** make sure that the business will, over time, be successful. They decide on the type of customers to be served and the type of products to be offered, they provide the resources necessary for long-term success, and they decide how the business should be organized.

These three levels of business management have quite different information needs. As a result, an MIS designed for one level is unlikely to meet the needs of the other two. Managers' information needs vary in five basic ways:

- A need for *detailed* or *summarized* information
- A need for *more* or *less current* information
- A need for *past, present*, or *future* information

Exhibit 6.2

Three Levels of Management

Sequential-access media require that each record preceding the desired record be checked. Most management positions fit one of three categories. Operating managers make sure day-to-day activities are performed. Middle managers make sure business objectives are achieved. Senior managers make sure the business continues to be successful over time.

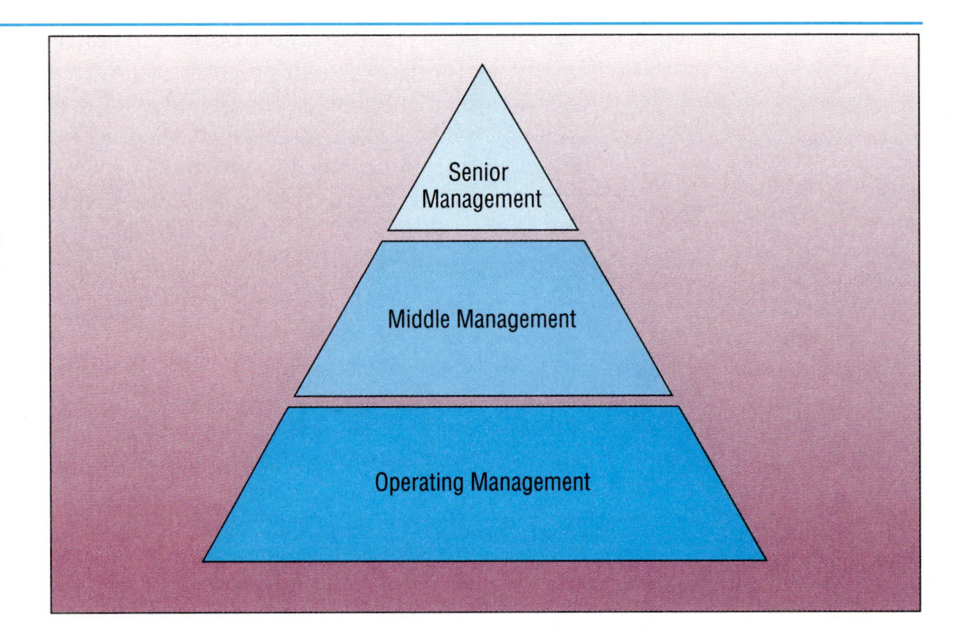

- A need for a *narrow* or *broad range* of information
- A need for *internal* or *external* information

Operating Management

A store manager at CompuStore must manage the store's employees, keep track of daily sales receipts, keep track of products kept on the sales floor and in the stockroom, make sure that customer orders arrive on time, schedule store maintenance, and coordinate with the firm's advertising, warehouse, and repair shop staffs. These are the types of duties characteristic of an operations manager.

An operations manager needs information to track events as they occur. Such information tends to be detailed and current, is concerned with the present, and focuses rather narrowly on the internal activities of a business. Exhibit 6.3 summarizes these information needs.

Middle Management

The duty of CompuStore's marketing manager is to see that the firm's sales goals are met. The marketing manager must set sales targets and then work with the marketing staff, the buyers, and the store managers to see that these sales targets are met.

The marketing manager must have a good grasp of sales trends at each of the retail outlets, sales trends for each of the product lines, the extent to which the firm's marketing and advertising strategies are working, any problems in the warehouse or the repair shop that might be hurting sales, national sales trends, and sales trends for CompuStore's main competitors. In short, a general picture of sales potential along with a fairly detailed understanding of actual sales relative to sales targets is required. Such

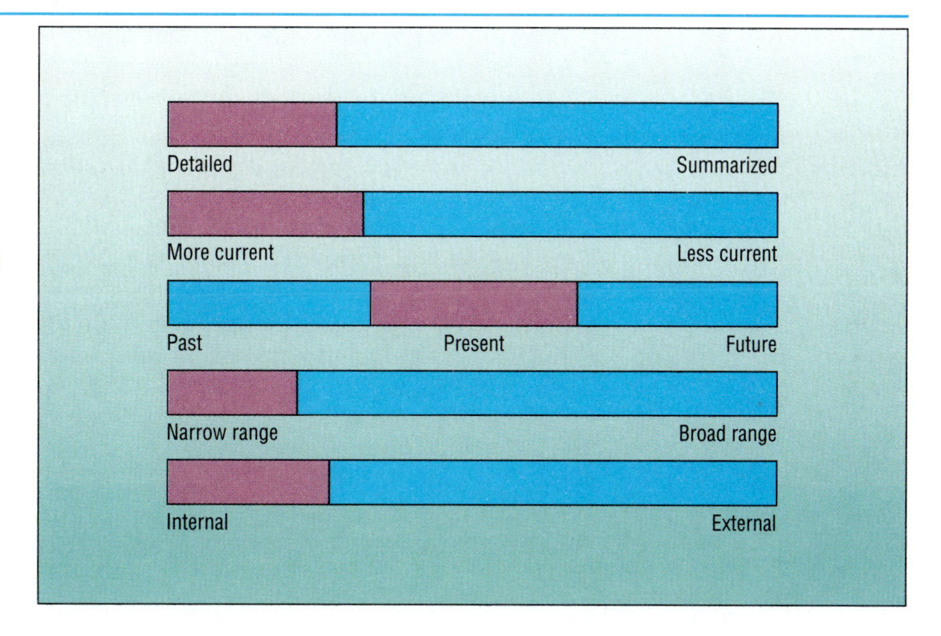

Exhibit 6.3

Information Needs of Operating Managers

Operating managers (purple) need information that is detailed, current, concerned with the present, and focused on a narrow set of internal business activities.

information tends to be categorized by product and collected by time period so that trends can be observed. Exhibit 6.4 summarizes these information needs.

Senior Management

Senior managers are more concerned about whether the overall business is making a profit and how the business compares to its competitors. For

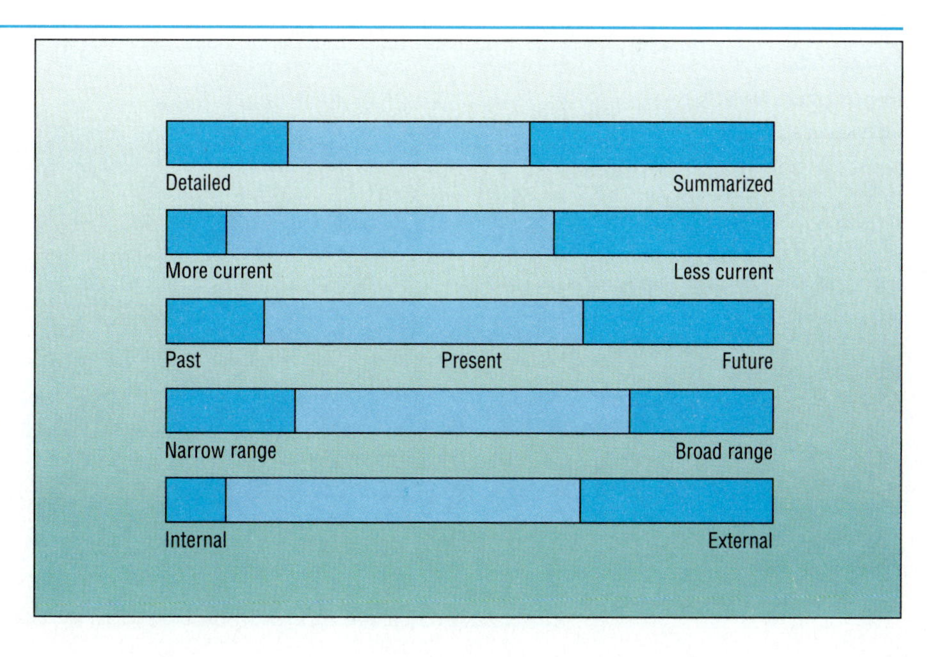

Exhibit 6.4

Information Needs of Middle Managers

Middle managers (turquoise) need information that is condensed, fairly current, and that compares the present with the recent past, and that covers a broad range of internal business activities but only a narrow range of external business activities.

example, the vice president of marketing is responsible for identifying exactly who CompuStore's customers are and what types of microcomputer products they are most likely to buy. She also sets CompuStore's sales strategies and targets.

The vice president of marketing needs to know how well CompuStore's sales are doing relative to its sales targets and in comparison to its major competitors. And it is equally important for her to follow nationwide microcomputer sales trends, to keep up with new technical developments, and to understand the general level of business activity in and around CompuStore's sales region. In order to deal with such a broad range of internal and external information, information is needed that is very summarized and collected over fairly long periods of time, covering the past and future as well as the present. Exhibit 6.5 summarizes these information needs.

Management Support Provided by Business Information Systems

Three types of business information systems were introduced and described in Chapter 2: transaction processing systems, information reporting systems, and decision support systems. Each type produces useful management information. Generally, operating managers tend to make more use of transaction processing systems, middle managers tend to make more use of information reporting systems, and senior managers tend to make more use of decision support systems (see Exhibit 6.6). This is due to the nature of the information typically produced with each type of information system.

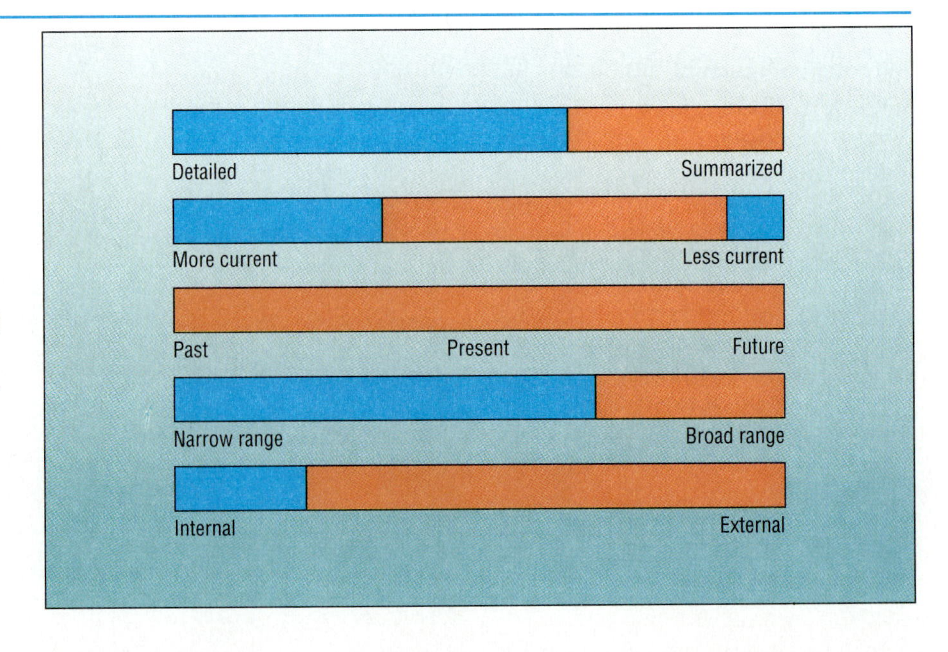

Exhibit 6.5

Information Needs of Senior Managers

Senior managers (orange) need very summarized information that is collected over long time periods; that covers the past, present, and future; and that includes a broad range of internal and external business activities.

Exhibit 6.6

Information Systems Usage Across the Three Levels of Management

Each type of business information system can be used to produce management information. Generally, operating managers make more use of transaction processing systems, middle managers make more use of information reporting systems, and senior managers make more use of decision support systems.

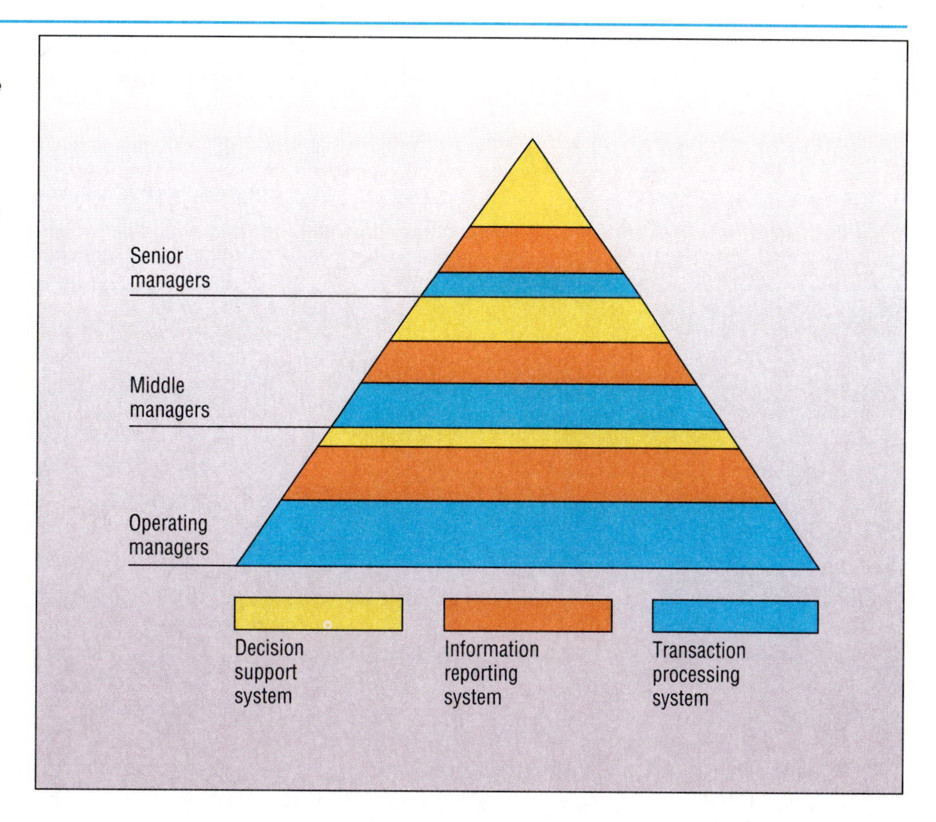

Transaction Processing Systems

Transaction processing systems record, process, store, and release data describing the daily activities of a business. The management information produced by transaction processing systems usually takes the form of a listing of transactions, or business events, that have recently occurred or are scheduled to occur.

Consider a transaction processing system that captures daily sales activities at CompuStore's retail outlets. Three main sales activities are involved: customers ask for items that are in stock and then purchase them, customers ask for items that are not in stock and place future orders, and customers ask for items that are not in stock and then leave without making a purchase or placing an order. This last sales activity is called a lost sale.

Operations managers, middle managers, and senior managers could all make good use of outputs from the transaction information system. A store manager, given a listing of orders due to be delivered the next day, could make sure that the ordered products were at the store. If some deliveries were delayed, the manager could then call the customers, tell them about the delays, and inform them of the new delivery dates. The marketing manager would be very interested in a listing of all lost sales over $100. With this information, product sales volumes could be forecast better. Also, as lost sales are often a symptom of larger troubles, a growing problem

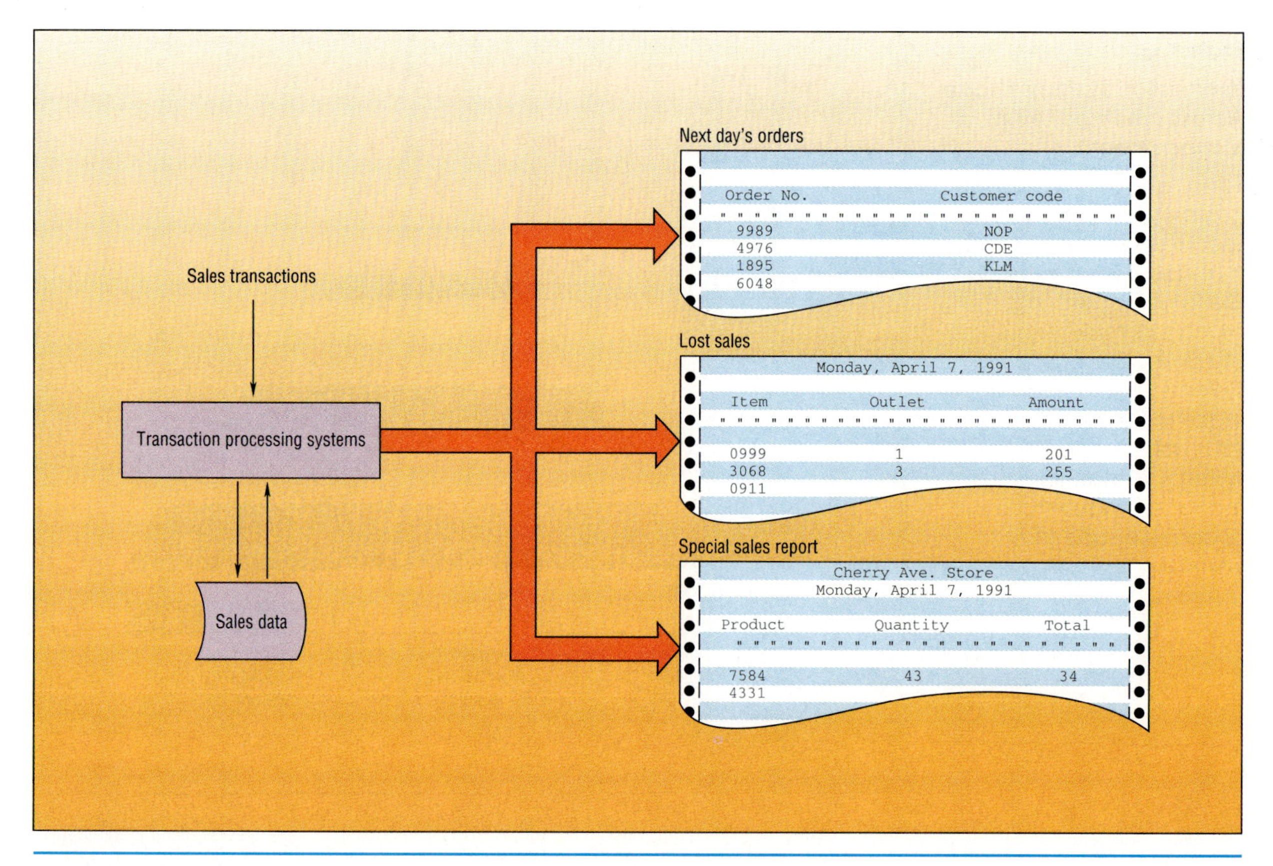

Exhibit 6.7

A Sales Tracking Transaction Processing System

Managers at all levels of CompuStore can use outputs from a transaction processing system that tracks sales activities at retail outlets.

could be spotted before it got out of hand. The vice president of marketing would be very interested in the impact on CompuStore's sales whenever competitors opened up new retail stores. With this information it could be determined whether or not CompuStore was losing sales to a competitor.

Transaction processing systems serve one other key MIS role. Most of the data in a firm's database are captured by transaction processing systems. This database is then accessed by information reporting systems and decision support systems to produce still more management information. Exhibit 6.7 illustrates how the three transaction listings described above might be produced.

Information Reporting Systems

Information reporting systems retrieve data from a firm's database to produce prespecified management reports. Usually the information output is quite different from the data that were initially captured. It is summarized, sorted, and otherwise transformed to produce reports that enable managers to monitor business activities, spot problems and opportunities, and analyze specific issues.

Three types of reports can be produced. **Periodic reports** are generated at regular intervals: daily, weekly, monthly, quarterly, or annually. What "triggers" the release of the report is the elapse of the

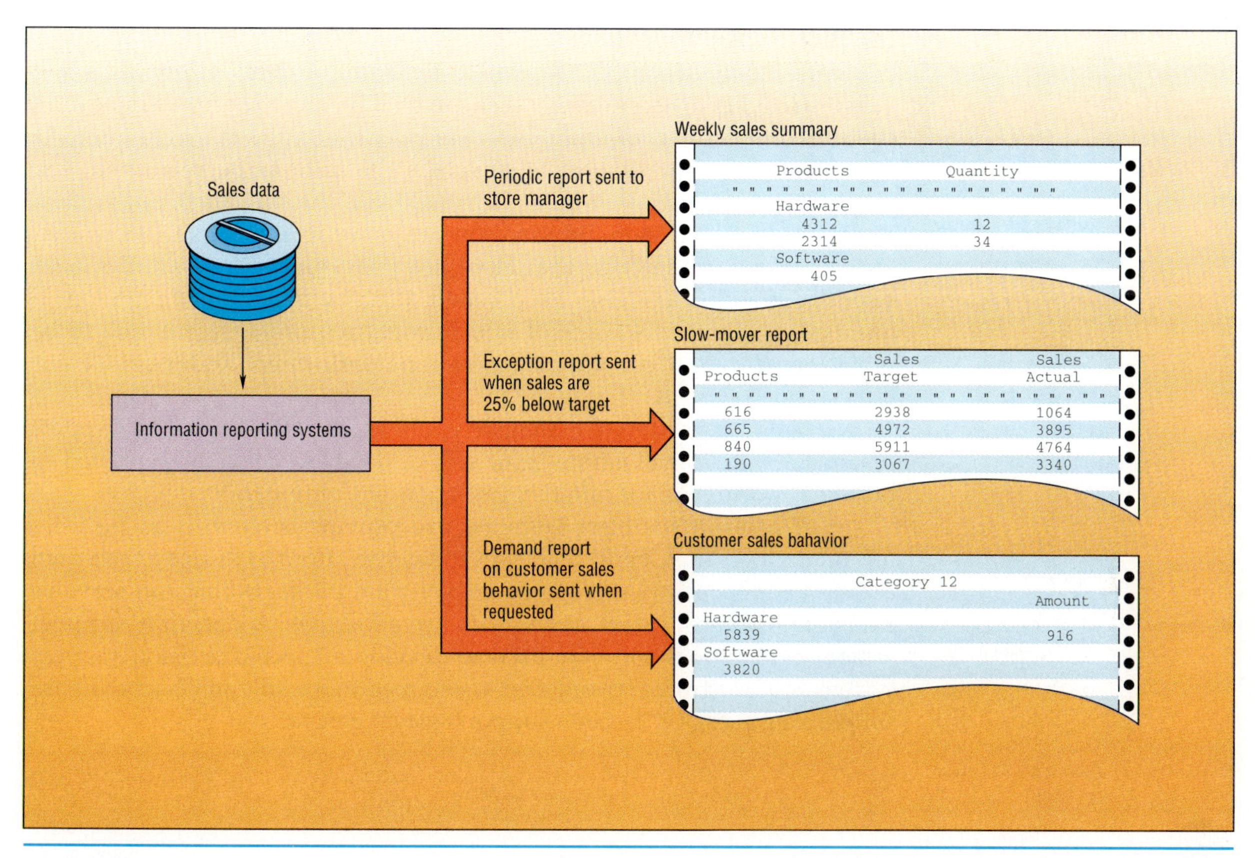

Exhibit 6.8

A Sales Information Reporting System

Managers at all levels at CompuStore can have prespecified reports produced from data retrieved from the firm's database.

specified time period. A store manager, for example, might get a weekly report that summarizes sales of specific hardware and software products at the store. This information could be used to place weekly and monthly product orders.

Exception reports are generated only when an "exception" occurs, usually a missed business target. What actually triggers the report are processing rules that detect an exception. The marketing manager might receive a special report whenever sales for any of the firm's hardware or software product lines are 25 percent under the forecast sales target.

Demand reports are generated only when asked for by a manager. This typically occurs when a manager wishes to analyze a particular issue in more depth. What triggers the report is the request for the report. Exhibit 6.8 illustrates these three types of reports.

A key aspect of these types of information reporting systems is that the reports are **prespecified**. As these reports are carefully designed and programmed, they can be produced very efficiently. It often takes long periods of time, however, to develop these information systems. Furthermore, managers often wish to make changes in the reports they receive. For example, the marketing manager may wish to receive exception reports when sales are 25 percent over the forecast sales targets. Modifying a report requires that one or more programs be revised. Revising programs, as you will see in Chapters 7, 8, and 9, can be difficult and time consuming.

Decision Support Systems

In contrast to prespecified information reporting systems, are systems that allow managers to access and transform data on an *ad hoc* basis. Instead of specifying his or her information needs in advance, the manager interacts with the computer system to describe the data to be retrieved, the processing operations to be performed, and the output form. With a decision support system, information can be provided for situations that arise only occasionally or that have not previously occurred. Decision support systems are also used when a manager wishes to try out a number of alternatives, each of which might require different data to be retrieved, different processing operations performed, and/or different information released.

All CompuStore's managers could make use of decision support systems. Exhibit 6.9 illustrates how sets of database items are retrieved to produce information for different managers at CompuStore.

Decision support systems are powerful as well as flexible information systems. Few businesses today can afford to develop their own decision support software. However, software packages that can serve as decision support system generators are available. A **decision support system generator** is software used to develop a specific decision support system. The electronic spreadsheets described more fully in Chapter 13 are simple examples of a decision support system generator.

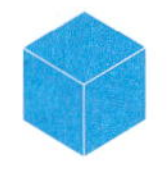

Designing a Business's Overall MIS

A business's MIS needs to serve all the firm's managers. For this to occur, the firm's database must contain a broad range of data items. If information systems are developed on a piecemeal basis, such a database will not exist. Data will tend to be haphazardly collected as specific requests for MIS support are made.

This piecemeal approach to MIS design can be avoided. Each information system being developed needs to be viewed in relation to all other information systems: those already in use, those currently under development, and those planned for future development.

Computer hardware that will support present and planned information systems must be acquired. Further, the hardware should be expandable to meet future growth.

The MIS Architecture

So far, the MIS discussions in this chapter have focused on information output and on the importance of a firm's database. It is easy to forget that other information processing activities, such as data entry and data processing, must also take place. It is also easy to overlook the fact that

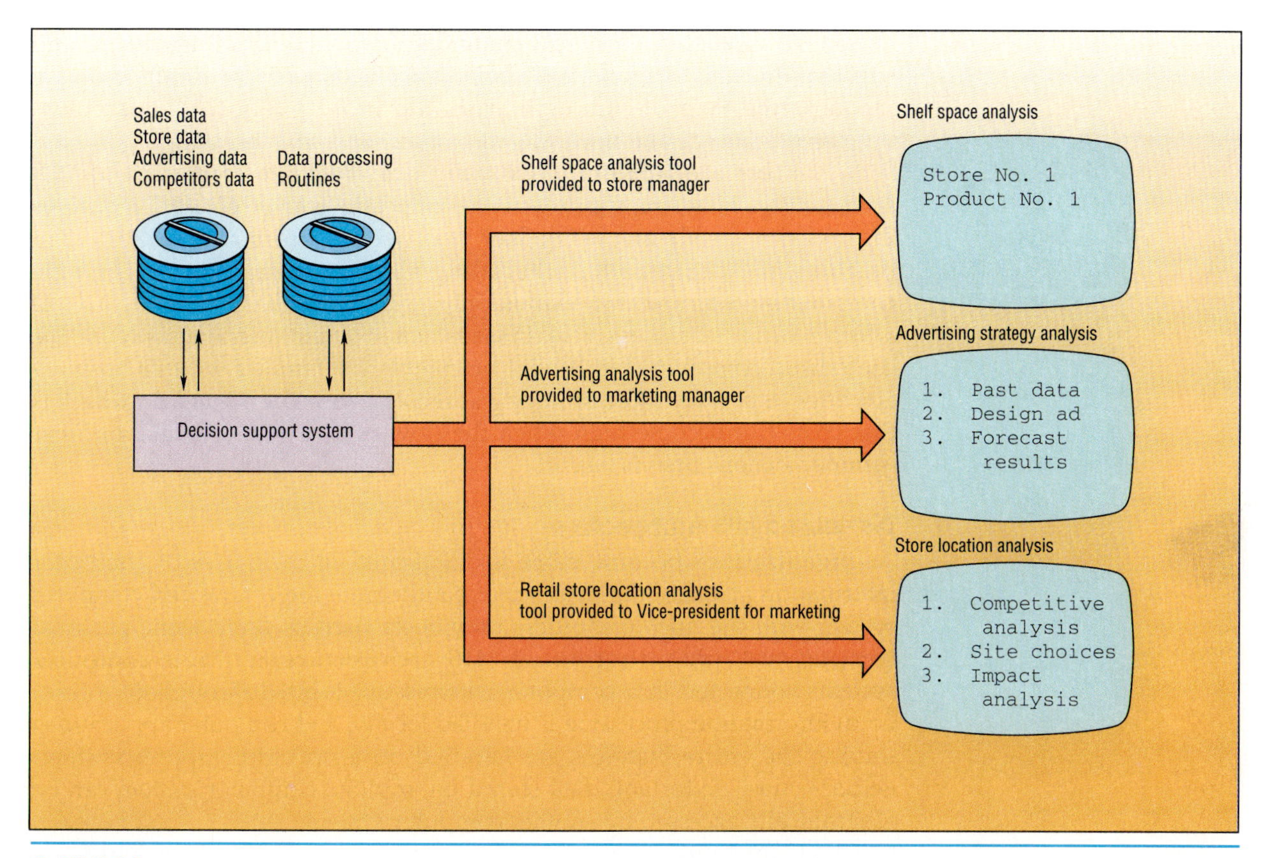

Exhibit 6.9

Sales Decision Support System

Managers at all levels at CompuStore can interact with a decision support system to produce information to make better decisions.

where these information processing activities take place can affect managers' ability to retrieve needed information, as well as the cost of the information systems. **MIS architecture** refers to where data entry, processing, storage and retrieval, and output actually occur.

Centralized MIS Architecture

With a **centralized MIS architecture**, all data processing, data storage, and retrieval are performed on a central-host computer system. Entry and output of data can occur either at the central facility or at other locations via terminals connected to the central computer system through communications lines.

In 1985, CompuStore's MIS architecture was centralized. At that time the firm consisted of three retail outlets and a headquarters building holding the central office, a warehouse, and a repair shop. A larger centralized computer located at the headquarters building was the firm's only computer system. Each retail store had a CRT that was linked through telephone lines to this central computer system (see Exhibit 6.10).

A centralized MIS architecture offers a number of advantages over other forms. A firm can usually employ a more specialized computer staff and more sophisticated hardware and software. With all hardware and software located at one site, it is less likely that hardware or software incompatibility problems will arise and more likely that data entry, processing, storage and retrieval, and output will be integrated.

There are, however, two main drawbacks to a centralized MIS architecture. First, managers at remote locations may not feel that their information needs are being met very well. Data may be delayed in reaching the central site, scheduling conflicts can occur on a single computer system, and information outputs may take some time to arrive at a firm's various business sites. Dissatisfaction might also arise because the centralized computer staff cannot be completely familiar with all business activities, especially those occurring at remote sites. The second drawback is that costs can become high when the flow of data and information over communications lines is heavy.

Distributed MIS Architecture

As organizations become more sophisticated in their uses of computer information systems, the need arises to integrate the centralized computer system with the microcomputers previously used as stand-alone personal computers. With a **distributed MIS architecture,** multiple computer systems connected in a computer network are located throughout a firm. Local information processing is handled locally, and computer applications serving the entire business are handled on a central computer system. Perhaps most important, data stored on any one computer system can be electronically accessed by another computer system.

CompuStore today has eight retail locations along with the headquarters office and the warehouse/repair shop building. A new minicomputer is located at the warehouse/repair shop, microcomputers are

Exhibit 6.10

A Centralized MIS Architecture

In 1985, CompuStore used a centralized MIS architecture. Note that all processing and storage occurs on the central minicomputer system, but that some entry and display of data can occur via terminals located at the retail outlets.

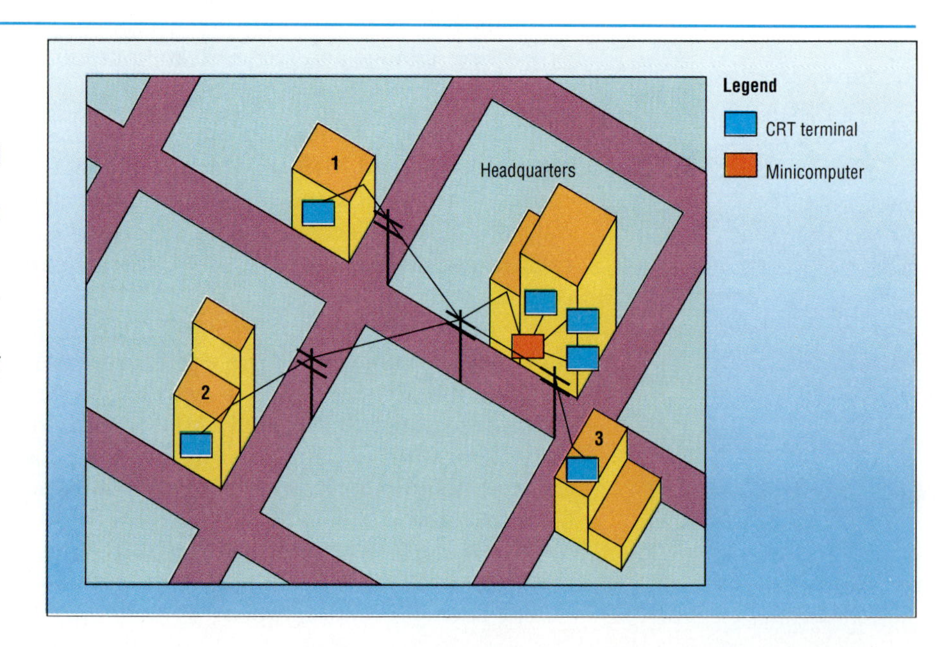

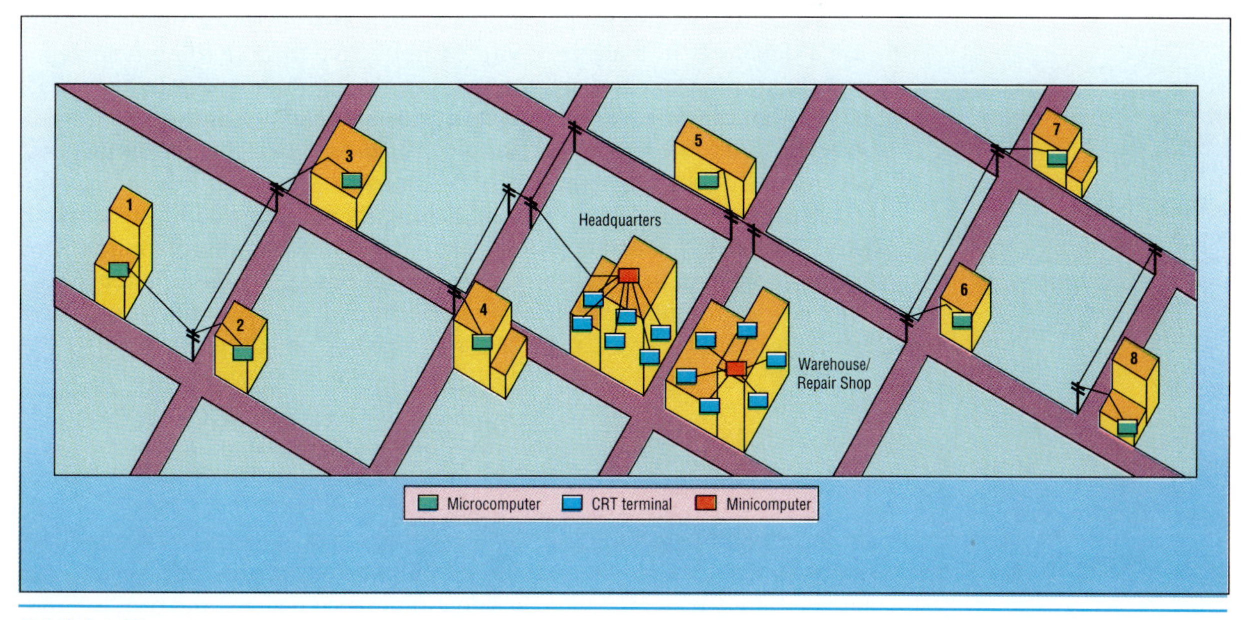

Exhibit 6.11

A Distributed MIS Architecture

Today, CompuStore uses a distributed architecture. Note that all the firm's computer systems are linked so that each can access the data, peripheral devices, and software of the others.

used at each retail location, and seven microcomputers are used at the firm's headquarters. As the firm's computer systems are now linked, terminals are no longer used except at the warehouse/repair shop. Exhibit 6.11 shows this architecture.

A distributed MIS architecture offers the advantages of both the centralized and decentralized architectures, plus some additional advantages. Managers throughout the firm now have access to the data, peripheral devices, and software kept on any of a business's computer systems.

However, all these advantages of a distributed MIS architecture do have a cost. Developing and maintaining the MIS architecture requires a good deal of technical expertise, a lot of MIS planning and coordination, and the active involvement of all managers.

The MIS Master Plan

An **MIS master plan** consists of descriptions of a business's current information systems, as well as descriptions of and a development schedule for information systems to be developed in the near future. These descriptions should include the purpose and users of each information system, the data files being manipulated, linkages with other information systems, and the information system's current status. *Status* here refers to whether an information system is currently in use, being modified, under development, or planned for future development.

Putting together such a plan offers three major benefits. First, money can be saved. An MIS project proposed by one manager may be seen as similar to one already being used by another manager, or the data needed for a new MIS project may be recognized as already available in the firm's database. It is clearly more cost-effective to take full advantage of existing information systems than to operate redundant systems. Second, a master plan can uncover ways to link information systems through the data being entered, stored, and released. With linked information systems, business activities can more easily be coordinated. When two information systems are developed in isolation, linking them later can be very difficult. Third, when they are able to have an overview of the information systems in use and those that will be developed, managers have a better idea of what new computer hardware must be acquired to support these activities. Exhibit 6.12 shows an example MIS master plan for CompuStore.

The Information Systems Life Cycle

All information systems initially start as an idea in someone's mind. For example, the idea for CompuStore's purchasing information system was initially raised when the vice president of finance realized the firm lost over $80,000 in 1987 because of poor purchasing decisions. This idea was then transformed into a working information system that meets the business need that triggered the idea in the first place.

The complete set of activities that produce, enhance, and later phase out a computer information system is known as the **systems life cycle.** The term *life cycle* suggests the creation, or birth, of an information system through the systems development activities. The new information system then matures into a practical business tool with use and continued improvements. When the information system no longer serves its business purpose, it is phased out. Well-designed information systems may be in place in major organizations for more than twenty years. Poorly thought-out information systems die in the development stage or soon after implementation.

The two major processes within the systems life cycle are systems development and systems maintenance. **Systems development** consists of the analysis, design, acquisition, and implementation of a computer information system. As shown in Exhibit 6.13, about one third of all development efforts of the CIS professional staff is devoted to producing new computer information systems. **Systems maintenance** covers the efforts taken to ensure that an existing information system either continues to meet

Exhibit 6.12

MIS Master Plan

The word *batch* refers to the batch processing of transactions and *online* refers to immediate transaction processing.

Present	Next Year	In Two Years
Accounting systems		Accounting (online)
Inventory (batch)	Inventory (online)	
Purchasing (batch)		Purchasing (online)
Billing (batch)		
Sales analysis (internal)	Sales analysis (internal and external)	
	Advertising reports	Advertising analysis

Exhibit 6.13

Percentage of CIS Time Spent on New and Enhanced Systems Development

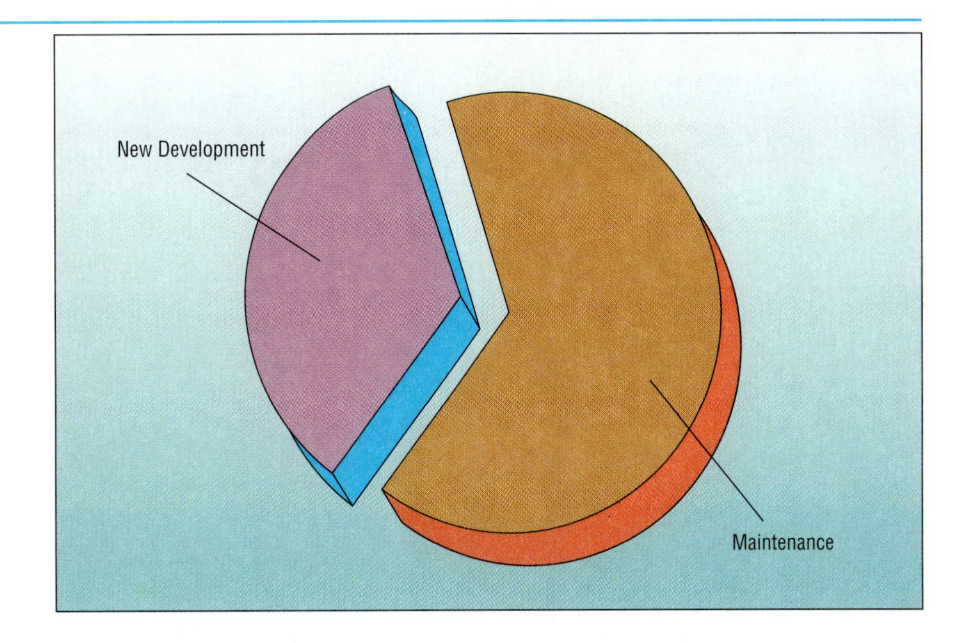

business needs or is phased out. The great majority of CIS professionals are involved in making improvements on existing computer information systems. Enhancements to computer information systems require the same development activities of analysis, design, acquisition, and implementation; the difference is that one does not have to start from scratch but rather works within an existing framework. The overall concept is analogous to building a new home versus being in the remodeling business.

The Systems Development Process

Shown in Exhibit 6.14 are the major stages of systems development, which include feasibility study, systems analysis, systems design, systems acquisition, and systems implementation. The purpose of the feasibility study is to determine if an information system should be developed. This analysis examines the information system proposal from three perspectives:

- *Technical:* Can the information system be developed?
- *Operational:* If developed, will the information system be used?
- *Economic:* Can the business afford the information system?

The final decision is based on expected benefits and costs. The next section of this chapter demonstrates how a feasibility study is performed. For now, recognize that a go/no-go decision is made at the end of the study. A system development project is started *only* for those proposals that merit further consideration.

Exhibit 6.14

Relative Time Spent in Each Systems Development Stage

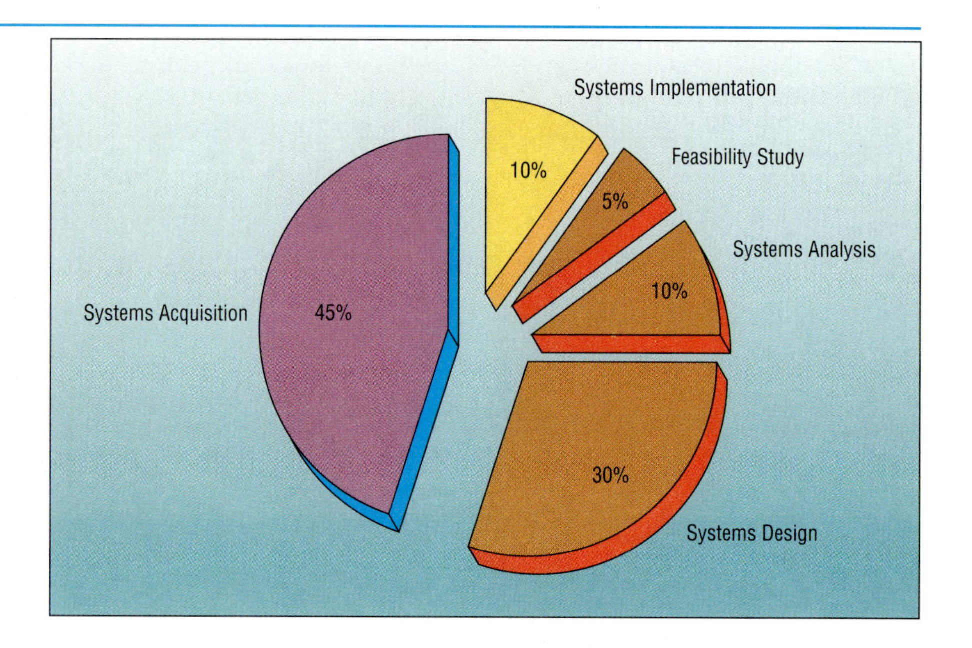

Thus, the first stage in the actual system development process is systems analysis. The purpose of this phase is to specify the information needs of the business in more detail and to establish the information relationships between the functional activities. In a typical systems development project requiring about ten months of total effort, one month—or 10 percent of the development time—would be devoted to systems analysis.

In systems design the emphasis is to determine the best combination of computer hardware and software to meet the information requirements specified in the systems analysis stage. In the example ten-month project, 30 percent of the time allotted—or about three months—would be devoted to the design effort.

Clearly, the most time spent in the systems development process is in systems acquisition. It is here that the actual programming is done or the appropriate software package selected. When custom programs have to be developed, this stage can take upwards of 45 percent of the development effort, depending on the complexity of the programming required and the experience of the CIS staff. Conversely, time often can be reduced when existing software packages can be used.

The information system is introduced into a business during systems implementation. 10 percent of the development effort in this stage is spent carefully testing and anticipating problems involving the use of the information system, in training, and in developing an appropriate conversion strategy. The other chapters in Part III of this book will treat specifically the development process and the tools used in CIS computing.

Systems Maintenance

Building a business information system is like trying to hit a moving target. Businesses constantly change. Computer technology constantly changes. The systems maintenance stage of the information systems life cycle consists of the efforts taken to ensure that an information system continues to meet business needs. Two basic activities are involved: identifying the need to change the information system and making appropriate changes. These activities are repeated throughout the life of an information system.

Most firms use two strategies to identify desired information system changes. First, suggestions for business-related changes are gathered from users. Second, suggestions for technology-related changes are offered by the systems analyst.

If the systems analyst has established a good working relationship with users, the users should feel comfortable telling the systems analyst about their information system problems and ideas for improving it. These conversations can occur spontaneously or during scheduled meetings. Some of the questions to be raised include

- Have the business activities changed in any way?
- Are the business activities supported by the information system going smoothly?
- Are the information system's objectives being achieved?
- Is the information system being used?
- Are users satisfied with the information they are receiving or with their access to the information system?

If systems analysts are expected to identify ways to technically improve a firm's information systems, they must be given ample time to study the performance of those information systems. Measures of information system performance can be very helpful in evaluating performance. Examples of these measures include CPU processing time for batch applications and response time for interactive applications.

Systems maintenance projects are actually systems development projects. Most times these projects are small. Some, however, can be quite large. All the activities discussed in systems development are likely to be performed during the systems maintenance stage.

The obvious difference between developing an information system initially and maintaining that information system is that the information system already exists. If you are asked to change an existing information system, you must work with an existing design. This can lead to two types of problems. First, you may find it difficult to understand the existing design. It is sometimes hard to understand your *own* software design, especially if you haven't looked at it recently. Likewise it can seem impossible at times to understand someone else's software design. While this problem will always exist, it can be lessened if CIS professionals follow structured design principles and carefully document their systems development projects.

Second, you may find it difficult to determine how to change the existing design. If the initial software design did not anticipate the change, it can be extremely hard to implement the change. Again, this problem will always exist, but it can be lessened if the structured design principles are followed and all likely future changes are clearly described in the requirements specification.

As more changes are made to an information system, it becomes increasingly harder to make subsequent changes. An initially "clean" design has become a very "messy" design. Sometimes it is better to completely rebuild, rather than change, the existing information system. Recognizing this point is another important skill for a systems analyst.

The Feasibility Study

Two major questions need to be addressed in the decision to computerize a business task. First, do the information processing characteristics of the task—such as large volumes of data to be processed, need to perform a large number of complex calculations, need for accuracy and speed, and so on—match the information processing strengths of a computer system? Second, do the benefits of computer use outweigh the costs? Answering the first question provides a quick means of identifying likely computer applications. A yes answer here, however, is not a guarantee that a firm should computerize the task. Business investments need to produce economic benefits. If the rule isn't followed, a business won't be around for very long! Decisions to computerize should only follow yes answers to both questions.

To get the answer to these important questions a feasibility study is performed. The main purpose of a **feasibility study,** also called a **systems survey** or a **preliminary investigation,** is to determine whether an information system should be developed or not. The three major parts of a feasibility study are to develop a graphic model of the business area, analyze the tasks involved, and weigh the expected costs of developing a computer information system against the probable resulting benefits.

Graphic Model of the Business System

One of the very first things that the business and CIS professionals need to do is work together to develop a graphic model or representation of the main avenues of information flow within and external to the business. Shown in Exhibit 6.15 is such a model of CompuStore. It is composed of four main processes: marketing, warehousing, sales, and accounting. Notice that specific inputs and outputs are labeled on the flow lines that connect various parts of the model. Arrows point in the direction of the flow. In these initial drawings both materials and information flows are shown.

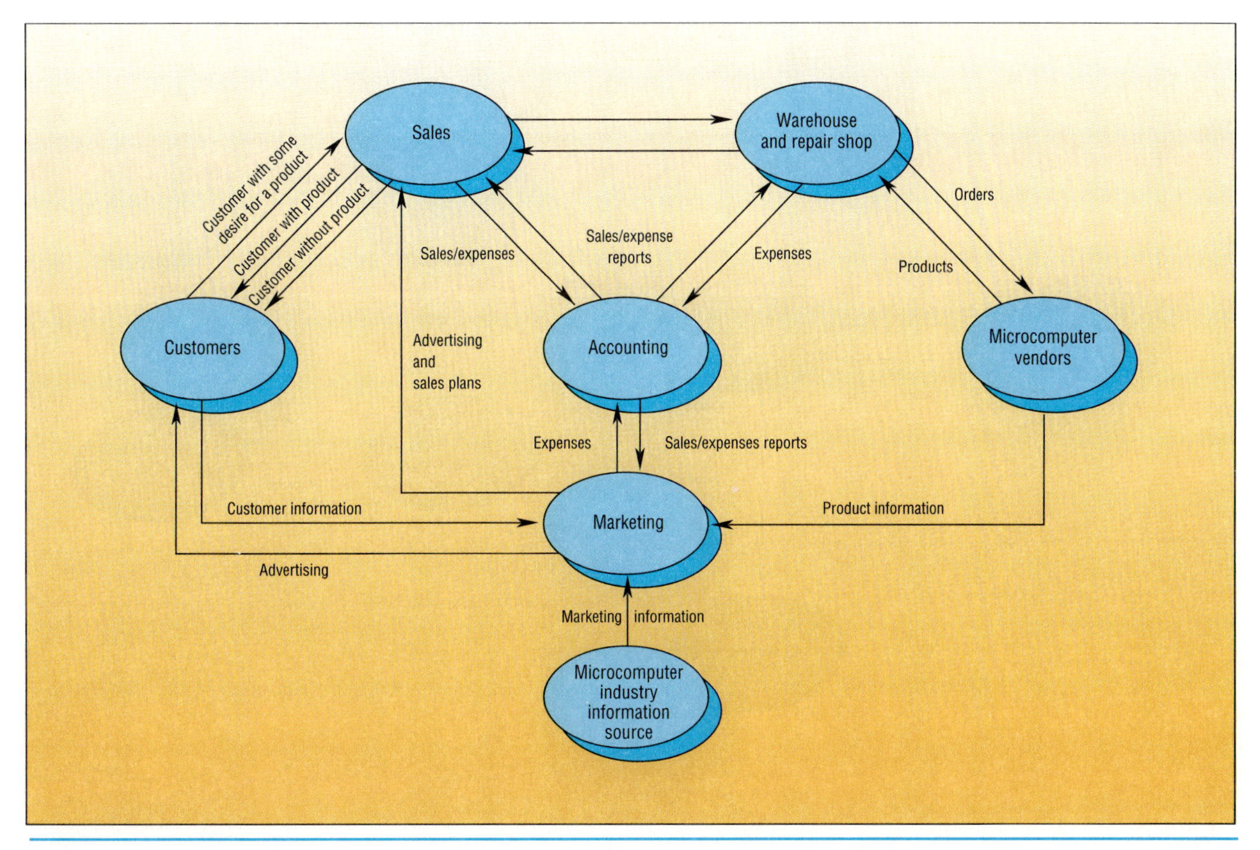

Exhibit 6.15

An Overall Graphic Model of CompuStore

Once this overall graphic model of CompuStore was understood, then a lower level diagram would be developed that represented the *scope* or area of study. Take the sales function as an example. Shown in Exhibit 6.16 are the key subactivities within sales. Three main operations take place at each store: customer sales, store inventory, and store accounting. Customer sales involves the direct customer contact that produces sales. Store inventory refers to maintaining appropriate product stock levels at the retail outlet. Store accounting tracks the store's sales and expense data.

Analyzing the Tasks

The graphic model of the business and the lower-level diagrams of the particular functions within the scope of the study should provide a way to examine the flow of information between functional areas. Now this knowledge must be analyzed to decide which tasks would lend themselves to computerization (see Exhibit 6.17).

Input

A task in which a large amount of data needs to be entered is usually a good candidate for computerization. Entry of large amounts of data by computer

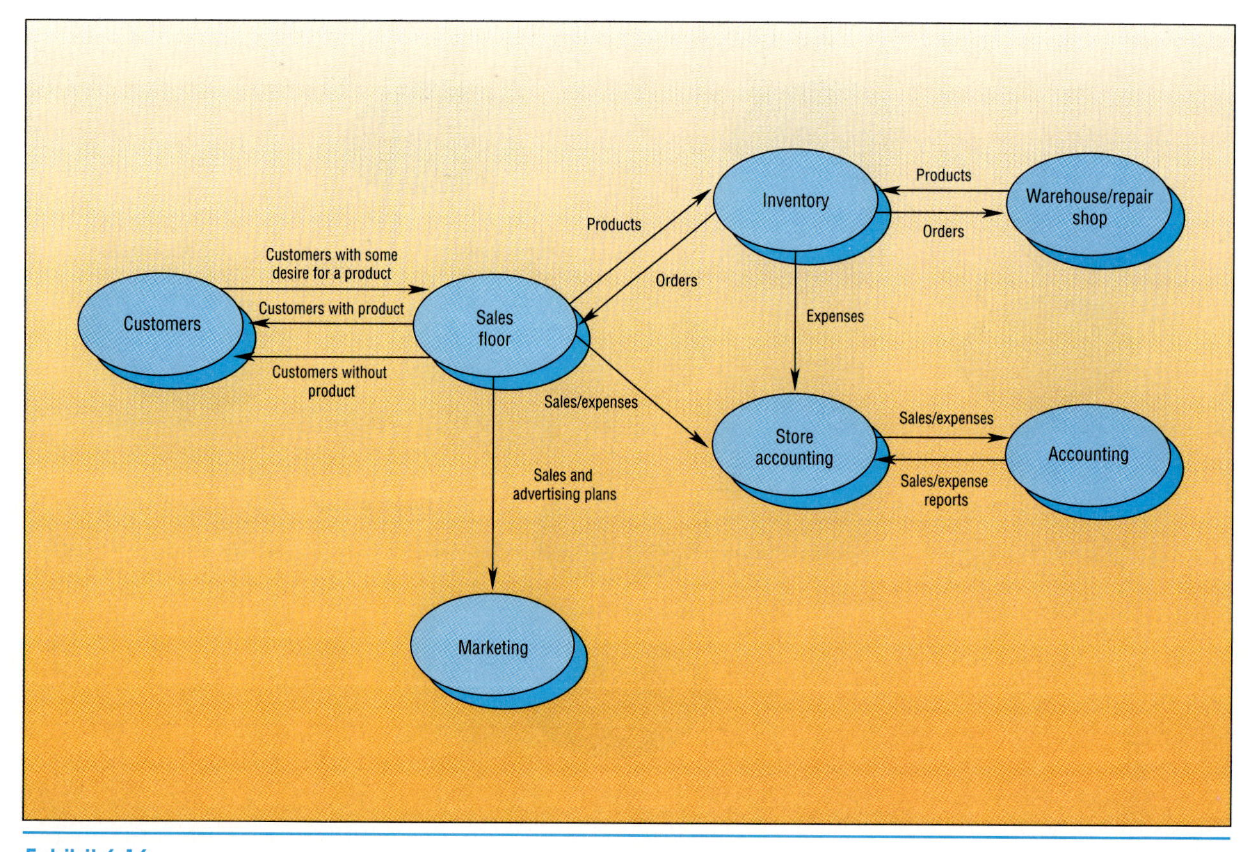

Exhibit 6.16

A Graphic Model of CompuStore's Sales Function

will probably cost less per data item, and data entry will certainly be completed much more quickly. Computerized data input, however, requires special equipment and the data must be in computer-readable form. If only a small amount of data needs to be entered, it might be best to do so manually. A factory needing to enter the number of hours worked for each of 3500 workers is sure to benefit from putting its payroll on a computer. A factory with 15 employees may not.

Processing

The computer is well suited for tasks that involve many complex calculations. In planning each day's work, for example, a factory supervisor might have to determine the best way to process eighty orders for six different products through three or four manufacturing steps. Figuring out the best schedule by hand would be a very time-consuming task. Performing this task with a computer would seem a far better solution.

A scheduling program, however, must first exist before it can perform this task on a computer. Can the factory supervisor list all the decisions he or she makes in putting together a daily work schedule? Are all these steps clearly defined, are they somewhat ambiguous, or do they vary? Without a clear set of processing rules, it will be difficult for a programmer

	YES	NO
Input: Does a *large volume* of data need to be entered? Is the data *already stored* in a computer system? Can the data be easily converted to a *computer-readable form*?		
Processing: Do a *large number* of calculations need to be performed? Do *complex calculations* need to be performed? Can a *clear set of rules* be stated that define the processing operations to be performed? Will these rules *remain fixed* for the foreseeable future? Are these processing operations performed on a *frequent basis*?		
Storage and Retrieval: Does a *large volume* of data need to be stored? Does stored data need to be *retrieved frequently*?		
Output: Does a *large volume* of data need to be printed?		
Overall Task Needs: Is *accuracy* important? Is *speed* important? Are *current data* needed?		

Exhibit 6.17

Checklist: Task Characteristics Favorable to Computerization

to develop the needed program. Even if a clear set of rules can be defined for the scheduling task, it might take a long time and cost a great deal of money to develop the program.

Storage and Retrieval

If a large amount of data needs to be stored, such as the classes and grades of all the students at the local college, it will probably be less expensive to store the data in a computer system than in filing cabinets. If only a small amount of data needs to be stored, however, such as warranty information on three company cars, it makes little sense to computerize. But what about storing an amount of information in between these two examples? The answer may depend on how often the data items need to be retrieved. Consider the following two situations:

- A purchasing clerk must refer to a list of 1500 supplier names and addresses one day each month in order to mail out about fifteen purchase orders.
- Another purchasing clerk must constantly refer to another list of 1500 supplier names and addresses in mailing out about sixty purchase orders per day.

In the first case, computer use is probably not needed. In the second case, it would be extremely helpful.

Output

As with data input, a task that requires a large amount of data output is a good candidate for automation. Preparing 3500 paychecks by hand would take a great deal of time, but could be done quickly and inexpensively by a computer. But typing fifteen paychecks would probably cost less than printing the checks on a computer.

Overall Task Needs

This final set of issues can be critical in successfully computerizing a task—the accuracy, speed, and currentness of information processing. Accuracy and speed are a computer's primary advantages. Whenever accuracy or speed is important, computer use should be considered. The need for high levels of accuracy in financial records is one reason accounting applications are usually one of the first information systems used in most businesses. The speed with which travel agents need information makes accessing airline schedules an extremely important computer application for travel agencies.

The speed of computers can also result in very current data files. If it is crucial that information outputs are up-to-date, then computer use might be very appropriate. When an important customer demands to know when an order is to be delivered, a salesperson would naturally want access to the most current data possible from the manufacturer.

Weighing the Benefits and Costs

Assigning dollar values to information system benefits and costs can often be difficult. To perform these calculations, you will need to know far more about computer hardware and software than this text has presented so far. This section briefly introduces the major categories of these benefits and costs (see Exhibit 6.18).

Benefits

There are four categories of information system benefits. With some proposed computer applications, only one of the categories may apply. With other applications, all may appear.

The most common information system benefit occurs when *costs are reduced* with computer use. The costs normally affected are labor costs, equipment costs, and materials costs. An inventory control application, for example, may have the following impacts:

- Inventory clerks no longer need to work overtime.
- Two, rather than three, warehouses are needed.
- The amount of inventory kept in stock is reduced by 40 percent.

Another common information system benefit is that computer use *avoids some future costs*. Again, labor, equipment, and supply costs are

Exhibit 6.18

Benefit and Cost Categories

Benefits	Costs
Reducing Costs labor equipment materials	**Hardware** purchase installation maintenance
Avoiding Future Costs labor equipment materials	**Software** development purchase maintenance
Products or Services improvements new	**People** training use
Management Information improvements new	**Operations** data preparation overhead

typically involved. By replacing an old accounts receivable information system with one using newer technology, the following benefits might arise:

- Clerks in the accounting department can handle increased work loads without working overtime.
- The cost of the computer equipment needed to process these customer payments is cut in half.
- The cost of office supplies is reduced by 20 percent.

A less common, but very important, benefit is realized when the information system allows a firm to offer its customers *new products and services* or *improved products and services*. Examples of these benefits include

- *New product:* A savings and loan institution offers its customers a combination savings and checking account, in which savings are automatically transferred into the checking account when the checking account balance is low.
- *New service:* A bank offers its business customers the service of managing the excess cash in these customers' checking accounts.
- *Improved product:* An information system helps an automobile manufacturer turn out engines with fewer defects.
- *Improved service:* A mail-order firm reduces the time it takes to process a customer's order.

The final category of information system benefits, *management information*, is common, but often very difficult to quantify. A new marketing information system, for example, may provide the marketing staff with customer surveys that previously were not available, as well as more current sales information on competitors' products.

Costs

There are four categories of information system costs: hardware, software, people, and operating expenses. All four cost categories usually apply to all information systems.

The most obvious cost category involves *hardware* costs. The cost of new hardware, such as terminals and microcomputers, is a major factor in estimating the cost of a proposed information system. Hardware costs also include installation and maintenance costs. **Hardware maintenance** refers to the technical work involved in repairing or servicing equipment.

Another cost category that is usually considered is *software* costs. New information systems always require investment in computer programs. Software costs include the price of a software package, the labor costs involved with any software development, and software maintenance costs. **Software maintenance** involves fixing software errors and keeping the information system up-to-date.

A third cost category, and one often overlooked, is *people* costs. Computer use may take employees away from other tasks they need to perform, particularly when an information system is first introduced. Also, all computer users require training if they are to make good use of an information system.

The final set of information system costs are those directly associated with the day-to-day operation of an information system. Data input often requires that data first be placed in computer-readable form and then entered into a computer system. Also, the overhead costs and any supplies involved with input, processing, storage and retrieval, and output activities must also be considered as part of an information system's costs.

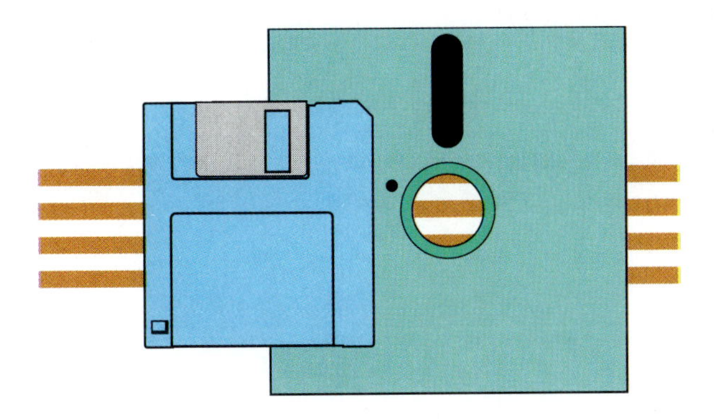

Computers at Work

Quaker Oats Builds Decision-Support System to Gain Marketing Edge

Several large company acquisitions, the establishment of several new sales forces and the introduction of diverse products recently led the Quaker Oats Co. to develop a new marketing decision-support system (DSS).

Designed with its user community's preference for a personal computer environment iin mind, and as an outgrowth of a decision to redevelop its basic data processing systems, Quaker Oats' "Mikey" DSS was born.

Currently, Mikey gives several hundred Quaker Oats users at corporate headquarters and sales offices throughout the country on-line access and ad hoc query capabilities for large corporate marketing databases. The majority of users at headquarters work on IBM PS/2s and connect to the mainframe via an AT&T ISN (Integrated Systems Network). The sales offices and other remote branches also predominantly use PS/2s and connect to the mainframe over phone lines utilizing a dial-back security system.

The DSS is a distributed application utilizing a PS/2-based user interface as the means for gaining quick and easy access to complex mainframe databases. The system has become Quaker's central coordinating facility for the creation and distribution of marketing plans, production requirements and financial estimates.

The system got its name from a Quaker Oats TV commercial in which a finicky young boy named Mikey tries Life cereal and likes it.

"It's sort of like our marketing users. They didn't like anything before. But we gave them the Mikey system, and they like that okay," reported Alan D. Mitchell, decision-support systems supervisor for the firm's marketing information department, in Chicago.

Mitchell said that the DSS was developed because the company decided to change its mainframe vendor, from the former Burroughs Corp. to IBM Corp.

"We did have an existing DSS system on the Burroughs mainframe, which used line-by-line input. We could have transferred that to the IBM mainframe." But this "was an old system, and we didn't want to move that to a new platform," he said.

After the company evaluated several applications development tools, it chose pcExpress and Express MDB, from Information Resources Inc., of Chicago, to build its DSS. Quaker Oats developed the system in the first six months of 1988, and it was implemented that July 1, on time and under budget.

The company's main objective, said Mitchell, was to develop a system that was easy to use—to save on training time—and had an integrated planning and reporting database.

Currently, Mikey's application modules include business review reporting, market planning, ad hoc reporting, general information and utilities. The business review reporting module shows standard reports based on the company's historical sales and comparisons with competitors. Although Mikey has only 10 standard reports, they can be generated for an extensive range of market, brand, time and measure selections or time aggregations.

The company uses the market planning module—which includes such data as package weight, cases, the cost of the product to the company, the prices of the items and advertising budgets—to review its marketing performance. Should one category, for example, package weight, be changed, the system automatically changes the other relevant components.

The ad hoc reporting module allows marketing users to look at data and create their own brand or market aggregates and to store and retrieve entire report selections.

Mikey offers a help section that explains basic calculations and explicates a report to users. The system is also entirely menu-driven, with pop-up selections for staffers who cannot type.

The utilities modules allows users to set up printer control codes and database maintenance and to pass data, such as planning information, to other systems throughout the company.

Mikey uses database administrator (DBA) utilities because the company's databases are very large and complex. Quaker, said Mitchell, has several thousand products and five different sales forces.

The system also provides a communications link enabling users to get in touch with the mainframe. The only thing required of users wishing to access the mainframe is an ID and password.

Summary and Key Terms

Management information systems are information systems that provide managers with information that enables them to perform their jobs quicker, better, or both. Management information systems perform two main business roles: they provide managers with information needed to carry out their own duties, and they provide managers with information needed to coordinate business activities.

There are three main levels of management. **Operating managers** make sure that day-to-day activities are performed. **Middle managers** make sure that business objectives are achieved. **Senior managers** make sure that the business continues to be successful over time.

These three levels of management tend to have different information needs. Information can be detailed or summarized; more or less current; focused on the past, present, or future; narrow or broad in scope; and internal or external.

Operating managers tend to need information that is detailed, current, concerned with the present, and focused on a narrow set of internal business activities.

Middle managers tend to need information that is less detailed but fairly current, that compares the present with the recent past, and that covers a broad range of internal business activities but only a narrow range of external business activities.

Senior managers need very summarized information collected over a long time period; that covers the past, present, and future; and that covers a broad range of internal and external business activities.

Transaction processing systems produce listings of business events that have recently occurred or are scheduled to occur. They also capture most of the data placed in a firm's database.

Information reporting systems retrieve data from a database and produce **prespecified** management reports. These reports can be produced on a **periodic** basis, when **exceptions** occur, and on **demand.**

Managers obtain the information they need by interacting with the decision support system to describe the data to be retrieved from a database, the processing operations to be performed, and the form of the information being released. Software packages that can serve as **decision support system generators** are available today.

An MIS master plan serves two major purposes: it enables managers to take full advantage of a firm's existing information systems, and it promotes efforts to link a firm's information systems.

MIS architecture refers to the physical locations where data entry, processing, storage and retrieval, and output take place. By employing an appropriate MIS architecture, one can improve access to a firm's information systems and reduce the cost of these systems.

Two of the basic MIS architectures include a centralized form and a distributed form. A **centralized MIS architecture** is best when most of a business's activities occur at the same site. A **distributed MIS architecture** is best when a business's activities are located at multiple sites and require tight coordination.

An **MIS master plan** lists all a business's current information systems as well as those that are planned for future development. This plan includes descriptions of each information system and a schedule for developing future information systems.

The complete set of activities that produce, enhance, and later phase out a computer information system is the **systems life cycle.** The two major processes of the systems life cycle are systems development and systems maintenance. **Systems development** consists of the analysis, design, acquisition, and implementation of a computer information system. The majority of CIS staff time is concerned with **systems maintenance,** which comprises efforts taken to ensure that an existing information system continues to meet business needs or is phased out.

The main purpose of a **feasibility study,** also called a **systems survey** or a **preliminary investigation,** is to determine whether an information system should be developed or not. This analysis examines the information system proposal from three perspectives. Technically, can the information system be developed? Operationally, if developed, will the information system be used? And economically, can the business afford the information system?

Benefits come when present costs can be reduced or future costs avoided. Further benefits could arise from new or improved products or services that the information system could render. Costs of the information system would include those associated with hardware, software, people, and operating expenses. **Hardware maintenance** refers to the technical work involved in repairing or servicing equipment. **Software maintenance** involves fixing software errors and keeping the information system up to date.

Review Questions

1. What are the two major roles of MIS in business?
2. Relate the five characteristics of information to the three levels of business management.
3. Briefly describe the differences between periodic, exception, and demand reports.
4. How does a decision support system differ from an information reporting system?
5. Describe how a company's MIS architecture might evolve from the initial stages to meeting more integrated information needs.
6. The Alpha Corporation is considering the creation of an MIS. Why should it formulate an MIS plan?
7. Why is more effort of the CIS staff devoted to systems maintenance than new system development? Is this good or bad?
8. Why might feasibility studies be used more with new information system proposals than in the modification of existing ones?
9. Why is it desirable to develop a graphic view of the overall flow of both internal and external business information?
10. As computer hardware becomes more powerful and much less expensive, shouldn't all tasks be computerized?

T F **11.** Management information systems cannot be used to coordinate business activities.

T F **12.** There is no difference in the types of information needs of operations, middle, and senior managers.

T F **13.** A transaction processing system captures most of the data in a firm's database.

T F **14.** Decision support systems are designed to produce information when the information needs have not been specified in advance.

T F **15.** *Centralized* and *distributed* describe types of MIS architecture.

T F **16.** Efforts directed toward ensuring that an existing information system continues to meet business needs or is phased out are known as systems development.

T F **17.** The process of determining if a task is suitable for computerization and whether the information system can be afforded is known as a feasibility study.

T F **18.** Information reporting and decision support systems are largely based on the data captured by transaction processing systems.

T F **19.** With a distributed MIS architecture, a firm can usually employ a more specialized computer staff and more sophisticated hardware and software.

T F **20.** An MIS master plan consists of only descriptions of current information systems.

21. _____ Which is not one of the three types of reports that can be generated with an information reporting system?
a. period reports
b. exception reports
c. *ad hoc* reports
d. demand reports

22. _____ Which is not one of the three levels of business management?
a. middle managers
b. executive managers
c. operating managers
d. senior managers

23. _____ Which is not one of the three types of business information systems?
a. transactions processing systems
b. information reporting systems
c. periodic reporting systems
d. decision support systems

24. _____ Which of the following is not one of the five basic ways that information needs of managers differ?
a. accurate versus inaccurate
b. narrow versus broad
c. detailed versus summarized
d. internal versus external

25. _____ Which is not one of the three perspectives used when examining the information system proposal during a feasibility system?
a. technical
b. operational
c. economic
d. functional

CHAPTER 7

Systems Development

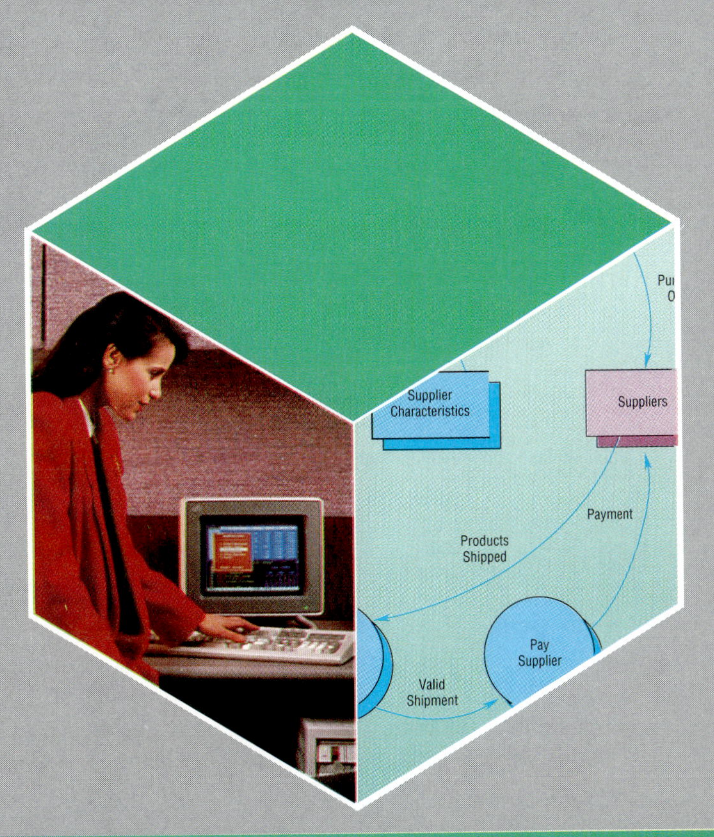

System development efforts are critical to the modernization of an organization's computer information systems. Systems development projects are not always complex and difficult, but even if they are smaller in scope and less complex, success is not assured. Because of the amount of money being spent on these efforts in organizations today, it is very important that business and CIS professionals have the most current information on how to make these projects successful.

In this chapter, you will learn to do the following:

1. Describe the major activities within each of the systems development phases
2. Describe the role of users and CIS professionals in each of the systems development phases
3. Explain why the choice between custom-designed and prewritten software is an important part of the systems acquisition phase

Systems Analysis

A feasibility study is usually performed first, to establish the technical, operational, and economic costs and benefits of developing a new or enhanced computer information system. As a result of the feasibility study, a project could be rejected either because it is not practicable or because other projects have a higher priority. Usually however, such projects are either approved as originally stated or are reduced in scope to make them more manageable.

Project Management

After it has been decided that a development effort is worthwhile, a development project team is put together, a time table for systems development is decided on, and the development cost is estimated.

The **project development team** consists of a group of CIS professionals and users that is charged with analyzing, designing, acquiring, and implementing an information system. Exhibit 7.1 shows the composition of a typical project team and who each team member reports to. The users are represented by a manager and a clerk from the purchasing department. The creators, from the CIS department, include a systems designer and a programmer. In this case the project manager is a CIS professional. It is becoming more common, however, for business professionals to assume leadership roles in systems development projects.

Exhibit 7.1

Composition of a Typical Project Team

The development of important computer information systems in business today is a joint effort of people from the user department and CIS professionals.

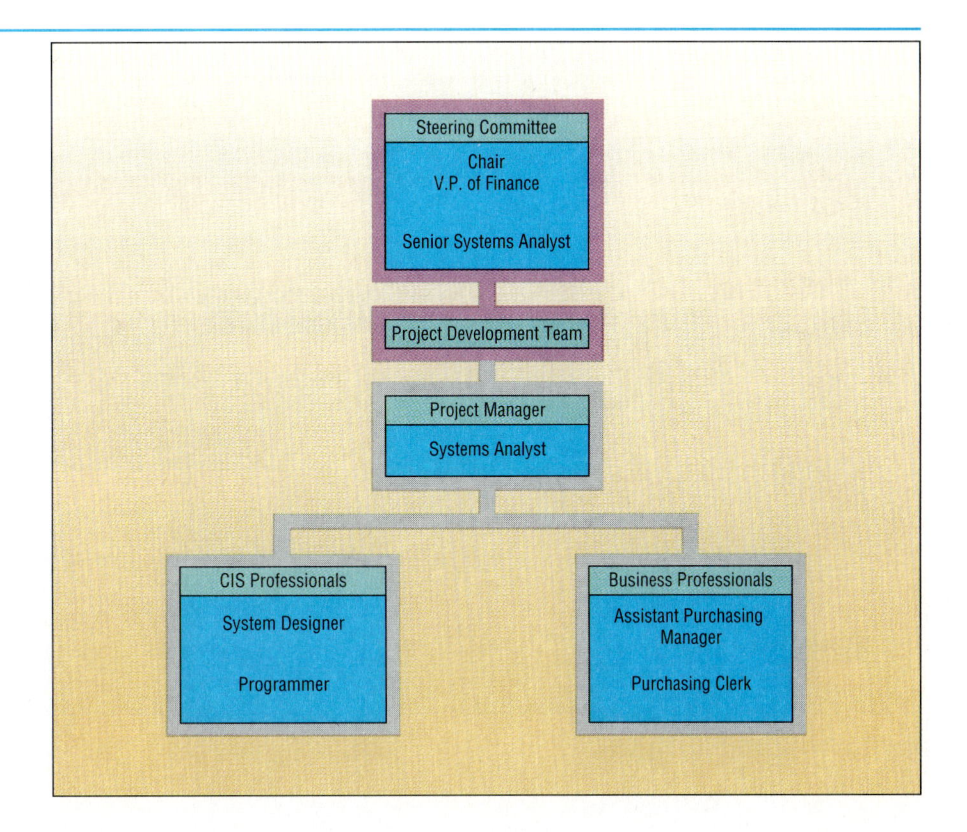

The project team reports to a **steering committee** that is composed of senior-level business and CIS professionals. The purpose of the steering committee is to give overall guidance to the project development team about the business purpose of the project, assist in providing resources such as personnel and financial support, and ensure that actions are taken to keep the project proceeding on schedule and within the determined budget.

The steering committee is almost always chaired by a senior manager representing the users—such as the vice president of finance—who has a vested interest in seeing that the project is successful and helps the company solve a business problem. To supplement the business orientation of the steering committee, there is generally a senior CIS professional who can provide broad technical knowledge and has the respect of the business leaders. As you will see, it is critical that business users and CIS professionals be able to work together effectively if successful information systems are to be developed.

The steering committee uses **project management tools,** such as the Gantt and cost-tracking charts shown in Exhibit 7.2, to measure how well the project is going. The **Gantt chart** is a project management tool that compares the actual versus estimated time needed to complete each major activity. The **cost-tracking graph** is a project management tool used to track the actual cost versus estimated cost of the project.

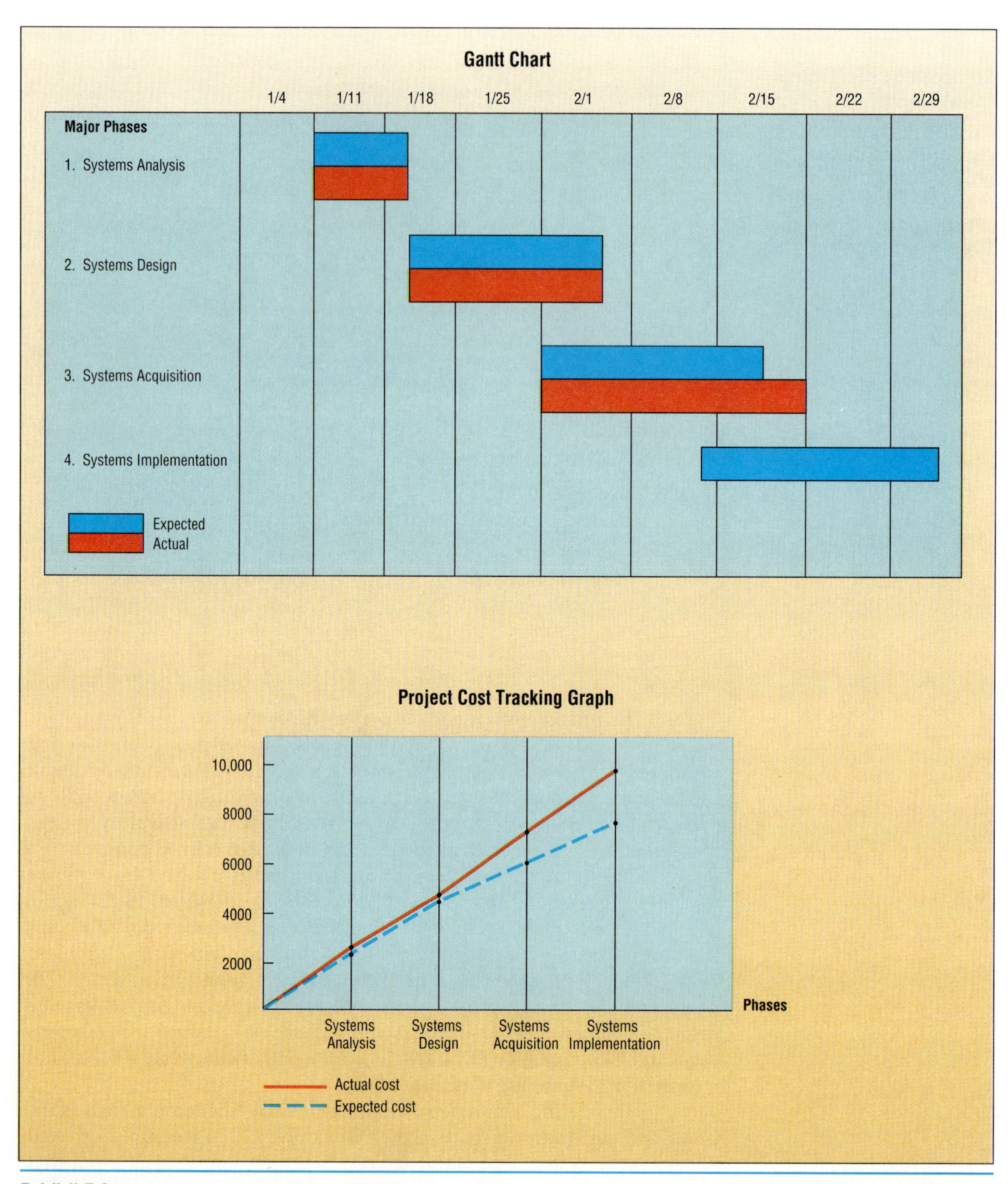

Exhibit 7.2

Project Management Tools

Project Definition

One of the first tasks of the project development team during systems analysis is to finalize the project definition that was initiated in the feasibility study. As shown in Exhibit 7.3 the **project definition** is a statement of the overall purpose of the project and the scope of its activity. It is important that the steering committee and the project development team agree on the validity of this statement.

Project definition is critical because, along with the cost and time schedule, it establishes what will constitute a *successful* project. For the proposed purchasing information system to be a success it must (1) reduce the cost of purchased goods, (2) reduce the size of the product inventory, and (3) reduce the number of lost sales due to out-of-stock items.

Notice that these success factors are stated in business terms. It is a major responsibility of the users and CIS professionals on the project team and steering committee to constantly assess what is being done in terms of these project goals. For a project to be successful, not only must the project goals be met, but the computer information system has to be developed on schedule and within budget. Thus, business and CIS professionals need to make ongoing comparisons of how much tasks cost and how much time they take versus what was originally planned and approved.

Exhibit 7.3
Project Definition Statement

```
                PROJECT DEFINITION

SYSTEM:   The proposed Purchasing Information System

PURPOSE:  This information system is being developed
          for three main reasons: (1) to reduce the
          cost of purchased goods, (2) to reduce
          the size of the product inventory, and
          (3) to reduce the number of lost sales
          attributed to being "stocked-out" of a
          popular product.

SCOPE:    This information system supports
          purchasing clerks in ordering products,
          printing purchase orders, and providing
          the purchasing manager with monthly reports
          on the quality of the firm's purchasing
          decisions.  Two data files -- a supplier
          file and a product inventory file -- are
          maintained by the information system.
```

Information System Requirements

Once the project definition has been clarified and approved, the next major activity in systems analysis is to specify the information needs of the business in more detail and establish the relationships among the functional activities. The primary way to show these information relationships is through the use of a data flow diagram (see Exhibit 7.4). A **data flow diagram (DFD)** is a graphic view of the flow of data between processes, data files, and external organizations.

The example feasibility study used a high-level graphic model of the flow of information and material in the business and then looked in more detail at specific functional areas within the scope of the project. The purpose of the DFD is to refine this view by going into even further detail and limiting the graphing to the "computer-related" flow of data. Further, it is used to reflect not just the current flow but also the changes that will be necessary to meet the new information requirements.

As shown in Exhibit 7.4, a DFD is composed of processes, shown as bubbles or circles; data files, shown as rectangles open on the right side; data flows, shown as arrows; and external organizations, shown as boxes. Let's see how this all works.

Several of the major processes or functions that a purchasing system must perform are *Prepare Product Order*, *Receive Shipment*, and *Pay Supplier*. To accomplish these tasks requires that data from one or more sources be gathered and manipulated to produce the required information. The process *Prepare Product Order* takes the selected product supplier information plus the addresses of the selected suppliers to produce a purchase order.

The source of information that triggers this whole purchasing process is the product sales data from *Retail Stores*. The destination of one of the outputs of the purchasing system is *Suppliers*, who receive purchase orders. The data files are used to store data to be retrieved at a later time. In this example *Product Inventory* and *Supplier Characteristics* are data files.

The data flows show the information that travels between processes, data files, and/or external organizations. For example, the *Select Products to Order* process requires information on the current inventory status of products. This information is drawn from the *Product Inventory* file. With this data the desired versus the actual inventory level of each product can be compared. The result of that comparison yields the amount of each product to be ordered.

To complete the specification of information requirements, the procedures needed to carry out each process must be delineated. Using a decision table is one way to specify rules or procedures that accomplish a specific task. Other ways include describing the procedures in structured English or pseudocode. These procedures will be explained in Chapter 9, "Program Development."

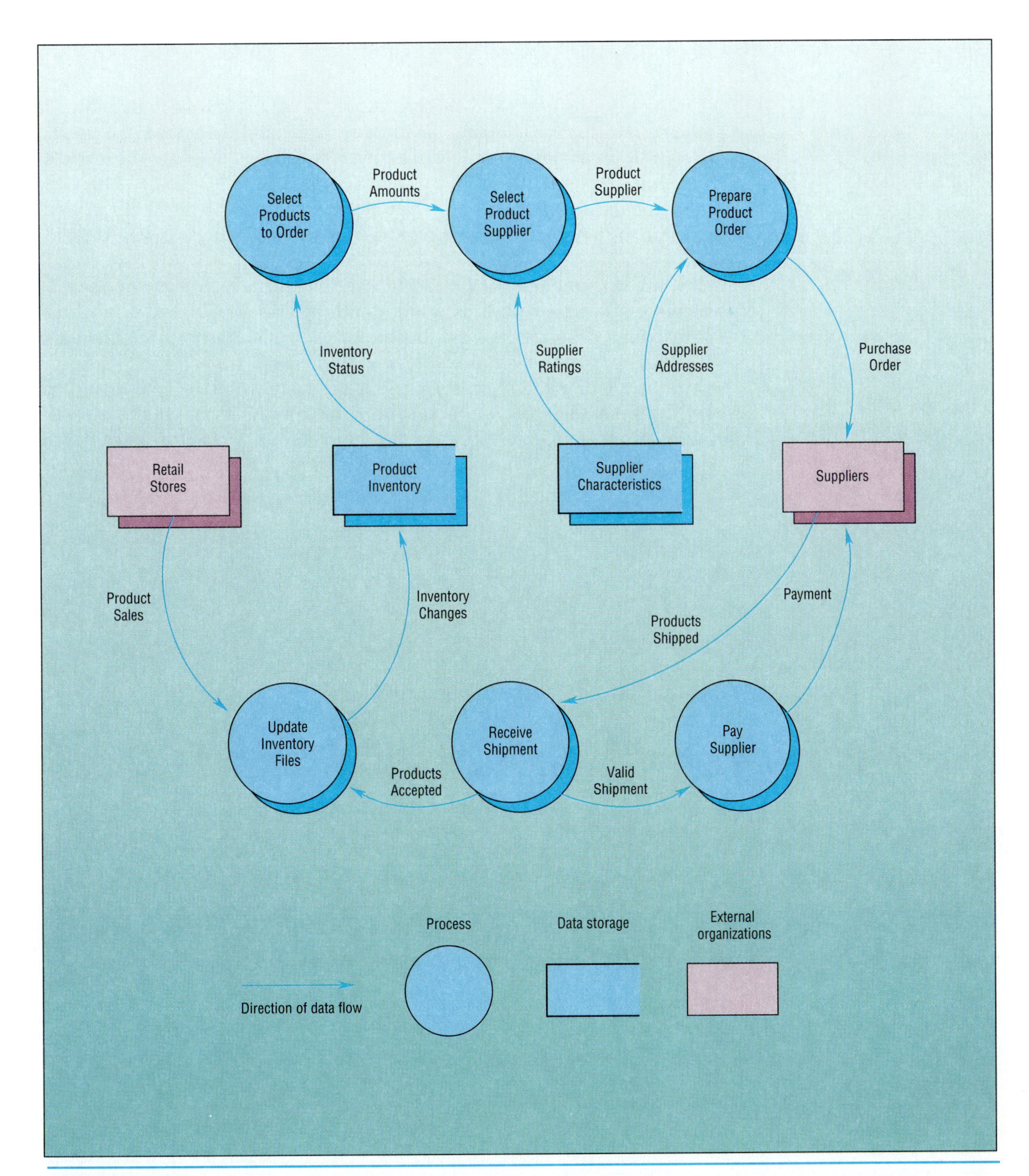

Exhibit 7.4

Data Flow Diagram

The data flow diagram is used as a primary way to show the relationships and flow of information a business system must support.

User and CIS Professional Roles

What roles do the users and CIS professionals play in the systems analysis phase of information systems development? Exhibit 7.5 shows the users' critical role in systems analysis. The users are the business professionals who know the business, the way it operates, and its goals. The CIS professionals generally do not. The major functions of the users in this phase are to state the information requirements and changes to be made, to work with the CIS professionals by answering their questions and providing documents that are being used in the present system, and to review the systems analysis diagrams developed by the CIS professionals to see that they describe how the business area functions and the changes needed to meet the new information requirements.

The CIS professionals are primarily responsible for documenting how the present information system functions in terms of the inputs, outputs, functions, data files, and procedures, and most importantly, for creating the changes to the data flows, data files, or processes that will be

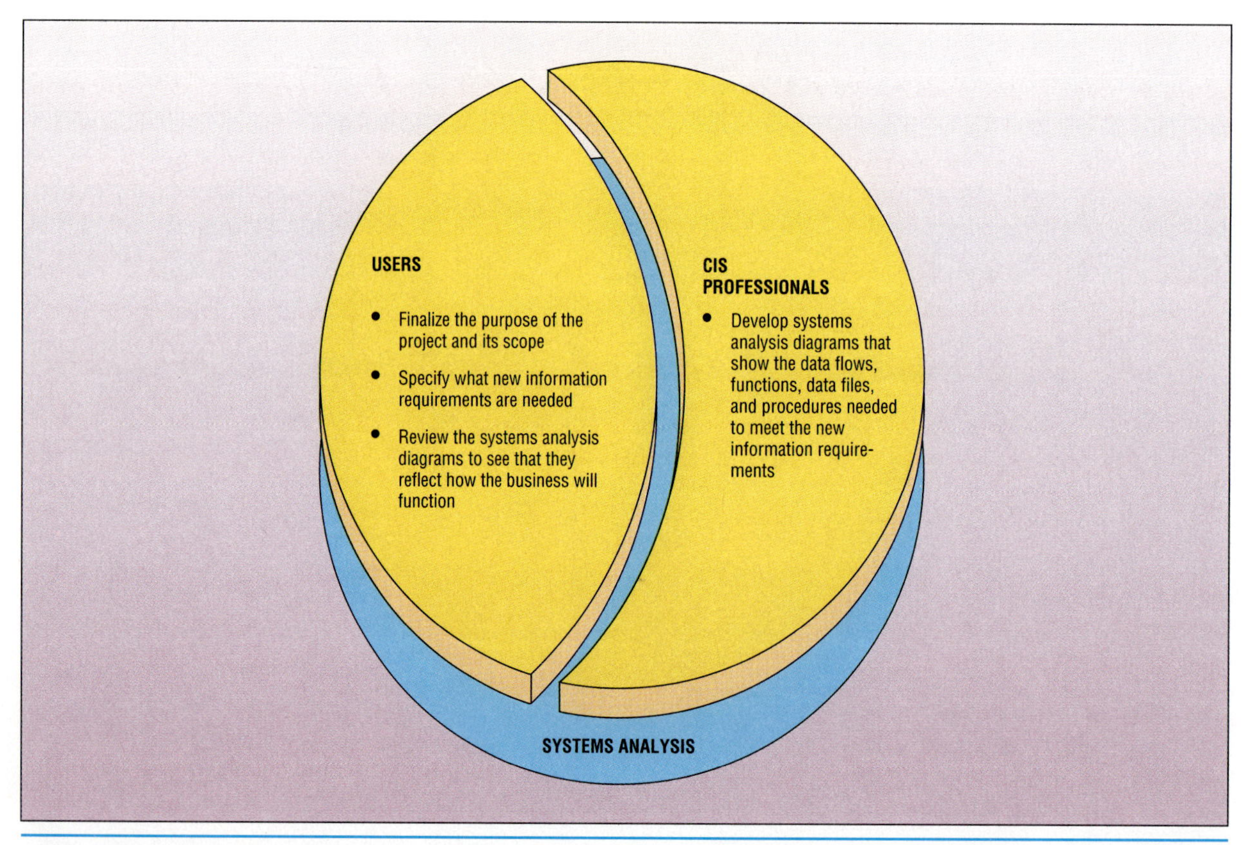

Exhibit 7.5

User and CIS Professional Roles in the Systems Analysis Phase

needed to meet the new information requirements. The CIS professionals use data flow diagrams and process descriptions in the systems analysis diagrams to present the existing system and proposed changes. The business and CIS professionals work together to finalize the purpose of the project and its scope.

Systems Design

The systems design stage of systems development produces a physical design of the information system being developed. The physical design describes the hardware, software, and operating procedures that should enable the information system's conceptual or logical design to become a reality.

While technical knowledge is important in systems design, the human touch cannot be overlooked. What is needed is a workable design; a design that fits the task, fits the firm, and fits the people. And the design shouldn't become out of date next year.

There are three things designers need to be concerned with. First, they must use appropriate computer technology. The information needs described in the requirements specification must be met, but the designers must also be sure that the design is affordable, compatible with existing equipment and the abilities of the users, and that it makes use of up-to-date technology. Second, the new design shouldn't unnecessarily upset the firm or its employees. The goal is to maximize positive changes—changes that improve business operations or people's jobs—while at the same time minimizing the disruption of business operations and the work environment. Third, the design needs to be able to grow with the business. Increases in work volumes, in staffing, or in the product line should be able to be handled easily, as should changes in computer hardware.

If the systems design meets these three objectives in the physical design of an information system, a successful information system should follow. To accomplish these objectives, one doesn't have to be a technical expert. What is needed is a knowledge of the basic technical alternatives, some sense of current hardware and software trends, and most importantly, a good understanding of the business and the information system's users. This need to constantly address both technical and people issues is precisely what makes the systems analyst's job such a challenging and rewarding career.

The major design activities undertaken during the systems design phase concern outputs, inputs, processes, and testing procedures.

Output Design

Information systems produce three types of outputs. Two of these have been discussed in detail in earlier chapters: business documents and management reports. The third type of output can be thought of as an electronic document, a business transaction sent from one computer system to another; for example, purchase orders that are transmitted directly from an organization's computer to its suppliers' computers. This electronic purchase order could reduce paperwork and improve the accuracy and speed of the purchasing process.

The data for these outputs were described in detail during systems analysis. What, then, takes place in **output design**? First, the information system's purpose and benefits are reviewed and a decision is made as to whether the outputs are relevant. Are the data and information complete? Has anything been overlooked? Are all data and information needed? Are data and information being produced in a timely fashion? Can outputs be produced less frequently and still be effective?

Second, documents and reports are examined to determine if the format of data and information can be improved. Are the data readable? Can tabular information be replaced with charts or graphs? Can color be used to clarify a document or enhance a report? (See Exhibit 7.6)

Third, the accessibility of documents, reports, and the information system to users must be considered. Will access be difficult or inconvenient? If so, users may stay away from the information system. Will hard copy output be needed or will a computer screen image be sufficient? Might users wish to access the information system immediately after looking at a document or a report? Notice the common theme that runs through each of these considerations—an attention to "people issues."

Fourth, any new hardware and software that will be needed must be described in terms of its information processing characteristics and costs.

Exhibit 7.6

Output Design

This CRT screen layout form shows a screen display that would aid the purchasing director in selecting a supplier for a particular product. The numbered columns across the top and the numbered rows down the left side of the form show precisely where information will appear on the CRT screen. More and more, output is designed on the computer screen itself.

CRT LAYOUT FORM

PROGRAM NAME ____ PROGRAM IDENTIFICATION ____

PROGRAMMER ____ DATE ____ PAGE ____ OF ____

PRODUCT NUMBER: XXXX

PRODUCT DESCRIPTION: XXXXXXXXXXXXXXXXXXXXXXXXX

SUPPLIER NUMBER	NAME	PRICE	DISCOUNT	ON-TIME DELIVERY	REJECTION RATE
XXXX	XXXXXXXXXXXXXXXXXXXXX	$XXXX.XX	XXX.X %	XXX.X %	XXX.X %
XXXX	XXXXXXXXXXXXXXXXXXXXX	$XXXX.XX	XXX.X %	XXX.X %	XXX.X %
XXXX	XXXXXXXXXXXXXXXXXXXXX	$XXXX.XX	XXX.X %	XXX.X %	XXX.X %
XXXX	XXXXXXXXXXXXXXXXXXXXX	$XXXX.XX	XXX.X %	XXX.X %	XXX.X %
XXXX	XXXXXXXXXXXXXXXXXXXXX	$XXXX.XX	XXX.X %	XXX.X %	XXX.X %

DETAILS:

Input Design

Input design is concerned with the procedures followed in entering data into an information system. As with output design, the first task of the designer is to make sure that the input items specified in the logical design are complete and relevant. Are all the inputs present that are required to produce each output? Are all inputs being used to produce outputs? Once this has been done, three design issues remain: selection of a dialogue style, selection of a data entry procedure, and the design of the forms.

Dialogue Design

Dialogue refers to the interactive "conversations" between an information system and a user. Usually, this interaction takes place so that the user can select an information processing action or enter data for processing or storage. For example, a purchasing clerk engages in both these types of interaction with a purchasing information system. He triggers the actions to be performed, such as listing the current status of an inventory item and printing a purchase order, and he enters data, such as the name of the selected supplier and the quantity to be ordered.

The three most common dialogue styles are commands, menus, and prompts. These styles vary in the flexibility provided users and in the demands placed on users.

With the **command dialogue style**, each information system action is represented by a command. Because the user actively directs the computer information system's actions, this style provides users the most flexibility. However, the user has to remember the commands in order to use the information system. This can be difficult, especially when a large number of commands are available.

Commands vary in their form. Abbreviations, single words, and phrases are all used. Exhibit 7.7 illustrates the two extremes, abbreviations and phrases. Abbreviations require fewer keystrokes, but they are often hard to remember. Phrases tend to be easier to remember, but keying a long series of characters can be slow and tedious.

Exhibit 7.7

Input Design: Command Dialogue

The command dialogue style can vary in form. Abbreviations are easy to use, but hard to understand and remember. Phrases are easier to understand and remember, but can be inconvenient.

Abbreviations	Phrases
LSTS	LIST SUPPLIERS
LSTI	LIST INVENTORY ITEMS
FCSTS	FORECAST SALES
DSPS	DISPLAY SUPPLIER INFORMATION
DSPP	DISPLAY PRODUCT INFORMATION
PREPO	PREPARE PURCHASE ORDER
PRIPO	PRINT PURCHASE ORDER

With the **menu dialogue style**, the information system lists a series of actions and the user selects an action from this list. Often, menu options may lead to other submenus until the action sought by a user is reached. Exhibit 7.8 illustrates the main menu from the purchasing information system.

With menus, the software limits the user's choice of action. Another disadvantage is that it may take the user a long time to reach the desired action by going through a series of menus. On the other hand, menus are easy to use; an inexperienced user can quickly begin to use an information system. There is no command list to be learned, and the menus inform users of the information system's basic capabilities.

The final dialogue style uses **prompts**—simple instructions or questions posed to a user by the information system. If the prompts used are clear, they require minimal effort on the part of users. However, users do lose considerable flexibility—the software dictates the sequence in which actions are taken. Exhibit 7.9 illustrates how prompts might be used with the purchasing information system.

Data Entry Design

Data entry design refers to the manner in which data are initially entered into an information system. The important issues center on whether data will be keyed in or whether some type of keyless device will be used. The following are important questions to be answered before design is begun: How much data has to be entered? In what form is the source data; is it computer-readable? How quickly must this data be read into the computer system? The various data entry approaches can have a large effect on data

Exhibit 7.8

Input Design: Menu Dialogue

This main menu is the purchasing clerk's "entrance" into the purchasing information system. To select a supplier, the number 3 would be entered.

```
Purchasing Information System
         Main Menu

1. Select items to order
2. Select products
3. Select suppliers
4. Prepare purchase order
5. Print purchase order

Select desired menu choice:
```

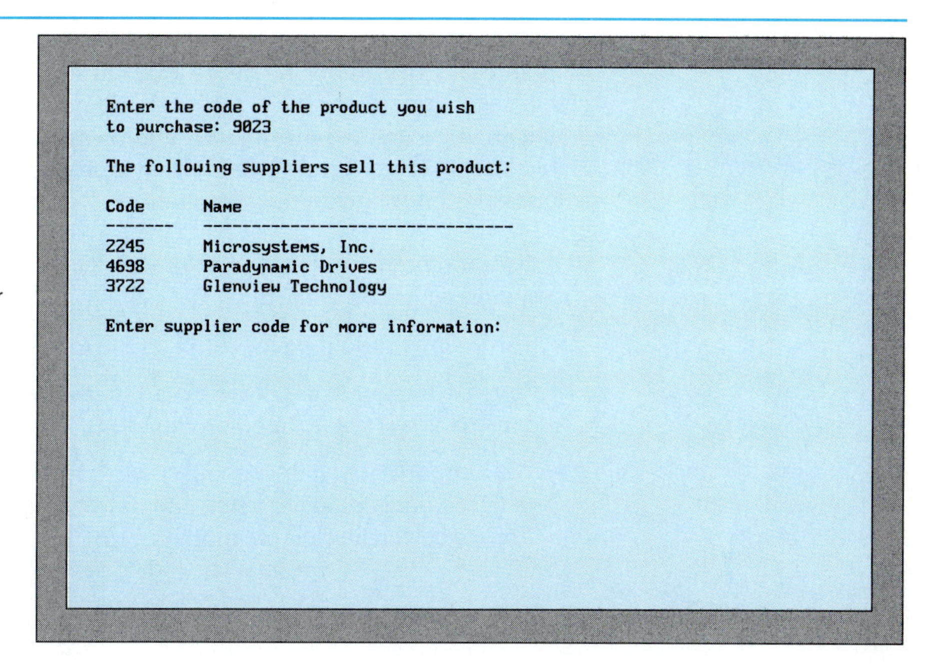

Exhibit 7.9

Input Design: Prompt Dialogue

This computer screen appears when 3 is selected on the purchasing information system's main menu. First appears a prompt to enter the code number of the product to be purchased. This response produces a list of suppliers that sell the product. To obtain information about a particular supplier, the supplier's code would be entered.

that enter an information system, on the impact an information system has on business operations, and on an information system's cost.

Two key characteristics of data are integrity and currentness. *Data integrity*, or accuracy, is achieved in one of two ways: either by preventing errors or by detecting and then correcting them. Errors can be prevented by eliminating steps in data entry procedures, by simplifying data entry procedures, or by training the people who perform data entry tasks. The computer itself can be used to detect the accuracy of the data being entered—a process referred to as **edit checking**. For example, the computer can be programmed to reject any numeric product ID containing characters other than digits. The computer might also perform a *range check*, verifying that certain data values fall within a prespecified range. For example, the quantity ordered of any product should never be zero or negative. The maximum number of 999 might be set, with larger orders requiring management approval.

Data currentness, or timeliness, is achieved by data being entered as soon as it is practical to do so. The important issue is the timeliness of information, not the currentness of data. If an information system produces monthly reports, it is not necessary to enter data as soon as they are captured. Entering data an hour, a day, a week, or even two weeks after they have been captured might be fine.

Data entry can be very disruptive. Procedures that require employees to fill out forms or use a keyboard can take people away from their normal jobs. Not only does this interrupt their work, but it causes them to be careless as they enter data. As a result, automated data entry is almost always preferred. When employees must perform data entry tasks, it is important that these tasks be similar as their normal work duties.

Forms Design

Businesses use many forms to track their day-to-day activities. Large businesses use thousands of forms. When a business form captures data that are to be entered into an information system, the form is called a **source document**. Fewer errors occur when well-designed forms are used. Good forms design follows a few simple rules:

- It should be easy to read or enter data on a form. A lot of white space should be left on the form.
- Instructions should be included on the form.
- Prerecording all data known ahead of time will reduce the amount of data needing to be entered on the form.
- Most important, the data being collected should be *necessary*. Some collected data are never used, and data collected on one form have often already been collected on another form.

Process Design

Most computer-generated business documents and management reports are produced from stored data. These data are transformed into outputs by programs. File design and software design are the main components of process design.

File Design

File design includes the determination of what data items are needed and the subsequent design of the data's organization or structure. Adding new data items to an information system's data files late in the development cycle is often very costly in time and effort. As you will see in the next chapter, one of the main benefits of database management systems is the ease with which data files can be changed or corrected.

The method of updating or changing values of particular data items is an important file design consideration. Organizing the data so that they can be accessed efficiently and limiting data access to authorized individuals are also concerns of the system designer. Data design is an important topic covered in Chapter 8, "File and Database Management."

Software Design

In software design, the programs that handle the various information processing activities are first described and then linked. In preparing a software design, the designer must make sure that all required information system outputs will be produced. A software design that will be easy to maintain is also a necessity.

Because software design is a major factor in information systems development, this process and the tools it requires are discussed in Chapter 9, "Program Development." This chapter concentrates on those considerations that are especially important when acquiring a prewritten software package and examines the development of custom programs.

Testing Procedures Design

Information systems testing takes place in the systems acquisition and systems implementation stages. During systems acquisition, software packages that have been purchased and programs that have been written are tested to make sure they perform as required. During systems implementation, all the hardware and software components are joined and tested to make sure the complete information system performs as required.

If testing procedures are not designed prior to acquisition and implementation, business pressure to get the information system up and running can force a hurried, incomplete set of testing procedures. The time taken to design a good set of testing procedures during the design stage is well worth it. Many headaches might be avoided, such as software failures (called crashes) and angry users.

The key to a good set of testing procedures is the test data that will be used. Some of this test data is artificial and some is live. Artificial test data, created just for testing, usually assess how the software would react to extreme or unusual situations. Live test data are taken from existing business records and usually assess how the software would handle day-to-day situations. The best sets of test data seem to be built when systems analysts and users work together to create them.

User and CIS Professional Roles

The systems design phase of systems development is an important one for both the user and CIS professional. Reconfiguring a poor design after a system is developed is very costly and time consuming.

In systems design, the user continues to work closely with the CIS professional, but in this phase, as compared to systems analysis, the user's role is more reactive. For example, the user reviews input screens to make sure appropriate dialogue is used and that data edit checks are accurate. Further, the user should check that the dialogue progresses in a natural way and that edit checks are made at the appropriate time. The user must also ensure that the output reports contain the information he or she needs, and that it is displayed in the most appropriate way. The user should step through the input screens to ensure ease in entering data and selecting functions.

The CIS professionals are the primary creators in the systems design phase. They take the information requirements specified in the systems analysis phase and design the computer system that will provide this information. More specifically, as shown in Exhibit 7.10, the creators must design a set of outputs to include reports and displays that will show the required information.

In addition to these considerations, the CIS professionals must decide on a structure so that the data can be accessed and maintained easily. The procedures for testing the design in the systems implementation phase begin at this point.

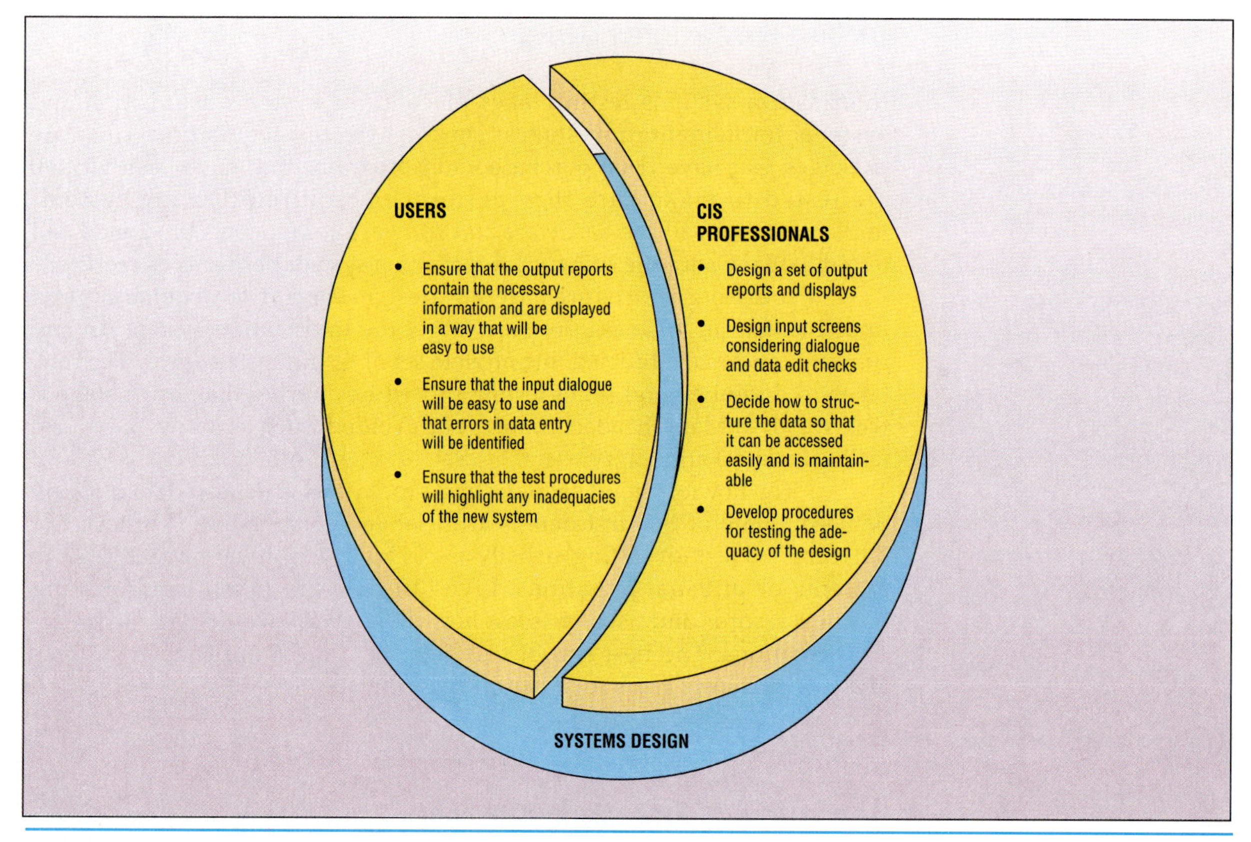

Exhibit 7.10

User and CIS Professional Roles in the Systems Design Phase

Systems Acquisition

During the systems acquisition phase of systems development, the option arises whether to purchase new software packages or to develop customized software. This decision is critical in this phase, as the result could make or break the project. This section concentrates on this decision and what then needs to be done to arrive at the solution.

The Make-Versus-Buy Software Decision

Generally, it is better to acquire a prewritten software package than to develop custom software. The software package usually will cost less, be immediately available for use, contain few errors, and be of high quality overall. Two other benefits are also important. First, the software vendor will be making ongoing improvements to the package. These new versions of the software normally are made available to existing customers for a nominal cost. Second, businesses that buy most of their software do not need a large programming staff.

The main drawback to software packages is that they don't meet every business's information needs. Software vendors develop generalized packages that can be sold to a large number of firms. If a particular business has unique needs, it may not be able to find a suitable package.

There are other disadvantages to software packages. If a software package needs modification, the work must usually be done by the software vendor. The fees charged depend on the amount and complexity of the modifications, but they are usually high. If the package is modified by someone else, the vendor may refuse to support the program. This means the vendor will no longer be responsible for any errors that arise. A risky situation to be in!

Another option does exist. Business procedures can be changed to fit the software package. This option should be viewed with caution, however. In some cases such a change might improve business operations. But in other cases there may be very good reasons for existing business procedures. In either case, systems implementation costs will increase if workers need to be trained in new procedures.

Purchasing Packaged Software

One of the more difficult tasks in the systems acquisition phase is to find out what software packages are available for use on what computers. Fortunately, there are technical surveys, such as the *ICP Software Directory*, that list information about various software packages, including which computers the package will run on, the package price, and the software vendor. Exhibit 7.11 gives relevant information on purchase order software packages found in the *ICP Directory*.

If the initial screening of software vendors indicates that existing software packages are suitable, then a process needs to be set in place to choose and purchase an appropriate package. The following process is typical:

1. The key performance factors of the software package are identified. Most often, these factors will parallel the output, input, and processing designs that have been documented. The forecast of likely information system changes are particularly important. No one wants to solve today's problem with tomorrow's headache!
2. The criteria to be used in selecting a package are identified. In addition to the software's meeting key performance factors, it is important that the software vendor's track record and financial stability be considered, as well as the support the vendor can provide.
3. A formal statement that describes these selection criteria is prepared. This document is often referred to as a **Request for Proposal** or **RFP**.

PROCUREMENT MANAGEMENT

Hardware Supported: IBM 370, 30XX Series, 43XX Series, 9370 Series

Operating Systems: SSX/VSE, DOS/VSE, OS/VS1, MVS, VM

Narrative: The Procurement Management system provides accurate inventory valuation, product costing and variance analysis. It creates purchase requisitions automatically or manually, with automatic conversion to purchase orders. The system prints requisitions, purchase orders and material move tickets. It reports status of requisitions, purchase orders and, material receipts. Inquiring and reporting are by requisition, purchase order, receiving lot, part or vendor number and by buyer and expeditor. The receiving function tracks material from time of receipt to inspection, dispositioning, stock, rework, return-to-vendor or to specify work order. It posts to general ledger, work-in-process subsidary ledger and transaction register, as required. Early/overshipment analysis at time of receipt maintains cash flow and inventory at planned levels. It maintains price variance by standard to purchase order cost, and purchase order cost to vendor invoice. A version of Procurement Management designed for public service organizations is available with the Xerox Public Service System.

Contact Data
Ron Rich
Marketing Services
Xerox Computer Services
5310 Beethoven Street
Los Angeles, CA 90066
Tele. 213-306-4000

Pricing
$11,250.00—
$45,000.00
Graduated
LICENSE

P18757

PSI/3000

Hardware Supported: Hewlett-Packard 3000

Operating Systems: MPE

Languages: COBOL

Numbers of Clients/Users: 7

Narrative: Computers PSI/3000, Purchasing Stores Inventory system is designed to fully automate the MRO, (maintainance repairs and operations) environment with three fully integrated modules: Purchasing, Material Management and Financial Control. PSI/3000 takes advantage of advanced materials management techniques which use historical demand and usage, lead times and service levels to accurately order MRO items and services. Whether a single site or multiple sites, PSI/3000 will shrink costs and widen profit margins by efficiently servicing material requirements.

Contact Data
Susan Baust
Sales Coordinator
SATCOM
4521 Professional Circle
Virginia Beach, VA 23455
Tele. 800-472-8266 or
800-499-9803

Pricing
PRICE UPON
REQUEST

P33554

PURCHASE ORDER (PO)

Hardware Supported: DEC VAX

Operating Systems: VMS

Languages: COBOL, DIBOL, C Language

Narrative: Purchase Order allows entry of purchase orders, retrieving vendor and products information automatically. Partial invoicing and receiving is accommodated with a scolling region from thta allows unlimited PO-lines. Interfaces include Accounts Payable, Inventory Control, General Ledger, Order Entry, and Job Cost. Extensive documentation and 90-day Full Service Support is provided with the software.

Contact Data
Sales Department
Compu-Share, Inc.
5214 68th Street
Lubbock, TX 79424
Tele. 800-794-1400

Pricing
PRICE UPON
REQUEST

P32578

Exhibit 7.11

Reference Information on Available Software Packages

When vendors know the "rules of the game," the whole process goes more smoothly.

4. Vendors are identified and given RFPs. Identification of vendors is one of the hardest tasks in purchasing a software package. There are thousands of potential sources of software packages. They include software vendors, hardware vendors, mail-order houses, computer retailers, and consulting firms. Some consulting services even exist to help other firms locate suitable software packages.

5. Vendors who have suitable packages are helped in preparing proposals. Vendors often need more information about a business and its software needs than is included in the RFP. This is particularly true when a package must be modified.

6. The vendors' bids are evaluated and a software package chosen. An **evaluation matrix** is very useful in comparing vendor proposals. Exhibit 7.12 shows an evaluation matrix used to select a new payroll and fringe benefits software package. Each of these three packages is rated on a 1-to-10 scale, where a 1 means the package is barely acceptable and a 10 means the package is superior. These ratings can be arrived at by reading vendors' proposals, by studying documentation, and by talking with other firms that have used each package.

Exhibit 7.12

Software Package Evaluation

An evaluation matrix is a useful tool for comparing software packages or hardware devices. The "weights" shown are the analyst's opinion of the importance of the five selection criteria. Each package rating is multiplied by these weights. Summing up the adjusted ratings results in an overall rating for each package. The overall benefit score is then compared to the cost of the package to make the selection.

Software Packages	(Weight)	#1	#2	#3
Selection Criteria				
Payroll functions	3	8	6	10
Fringe benefit functions	2	7	9	7
Growth capability	2	3	10	10
Vendor reputation	2	7	9	10
Training provided	1	10	8	8
Overall Benefit Score		68	82	92
Cost		$3000	$8500	$7000

7. A contract with the vendor is negotiated. This is a critical task. The contract should protect the business if a vendor fails to produce what was promised. **Acceptance tests**, or tests that check key performance factors, should be written into the contract. Penalty payments should also be placed in the contract to cover instances in which software is delivered late or fails to perform as expected.

Depending on the situation, such a formal purchasing process may not be necessary. Even so, it is always important to define performance factors and other important selection criteria. Choosing the wrong software package is the most common "computer mistake" being made today.

Purchasing Hardware

The physical design includes descriptions of all the new hardware to be acquired. Decisions about these hardware purchases should be delayed until it is known how software will be acquired. As much as is possible, the software should drive the acquisition decisions. One of the main reasons for the success of the IBM PC was all the business software developed for it. However, there are exceptions to this rule. If the application is to be run on an existing computer system, only software packages available on that computer system would be considered. At other times, however, software and hardware are purchased as complete systems from vendors known as *systems houses*. Once the hardware to be acquired is identified, a process similar to that given for purchasing software is followed.

Developing Customized Software

Two choices exist when software is customized. A firm can contract the software development project to a consulting firm, or it can have the software developed by its own programmers.

Contract programming has a number of advantages. If a consulting firm has experience in a certain area, its programmers can develop a high-quality information system. They may even do it faster and at less expense than if it were done in-house. Contract programming, however, can be expensive. If a business has its own staff of programmers, it usually is less expensive to have software developed in-house. Details of program development are discussed in Chapter 9.

User and CIS Professional Roles

In the systems acquisition phase of information system development, the critical decision is whether to make or to buy a software package. The user and CIS professional work together in making the decision and also in acting on the choice (see Exhibit 7.13).

The user participates fully in the make-versus-buy decision and examines the reasons for a particular choice. If the user decides to purchase a software package, he or she will attend demonstrations given by the vendor and assess the package's usefulness. Further, since a purchase of a software package often implies a long-term relationship with a vendor, the user will determine how amicable this relationship would be. The user plays the key role in deciding which vendor's software package to acquire. If the decision is made to develop the software, then the user has little more to do until the programs are developed and ready to be tested.

The CIS professional will work closely with the user and provide him or her with a cost-benefit analysis of both software purchase and custom development. If the decision is made to buy the software package, the creators then develop an RFP and select suitable vendors. From the vendor responses, the CIS professional develops an evaluation matrix, and the user and CIS professional work together to evaluate the choices. The user often asks the CIS professional for a recommendation; after discussion the user makes a decision. Usually it is the CIS professional's task to purchase the software package and the hardware. If the decision is made to custom develop the software, the CIS professional is involved in designing the programs, coding the programs, and testing that the programs are free of errors.

Systems Implementation

The systems implementation stage has two main objectives: (1) to install the information system so that its benefits can be achieved and (2) to accomplish the installation in a manner that disrupts normal operations as little as possible. Three activities are performed to reach these objectives: systems testing, training, and conversion. Systems implementation differs from the other systems development stages in that its activities are not performed in sequence. Most often, they occur simultaneously.

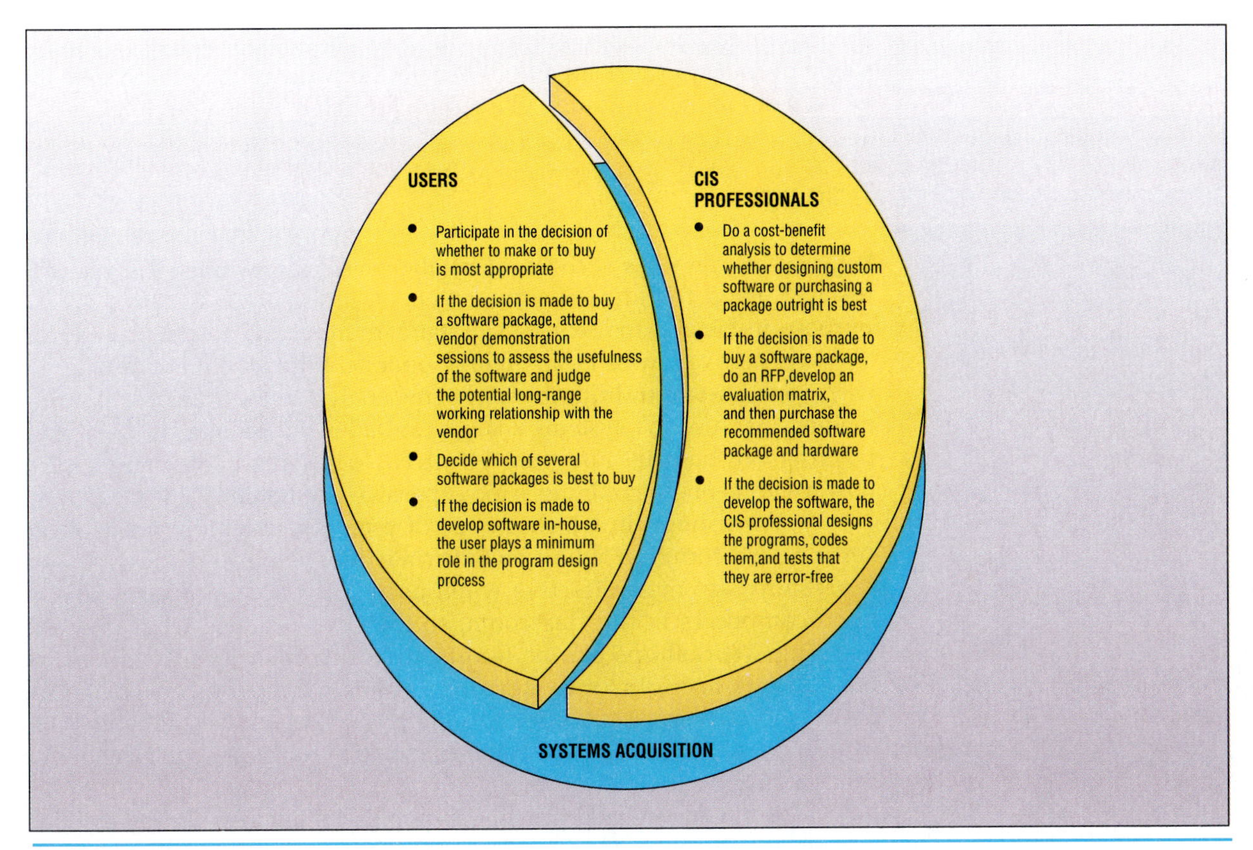

Exhibit 7.13

User and CIS Professional Roles in the Systems Acquisition Phase

Systems Testing

The testing done in systems acquisition has three components. First, tests are performed to make sure all the parts work correctly once they are joined. Second, tests are performed to make sure that any electronic links with other information systems work as expected. Third, tests are performed to make sure that all the "people links" work. That is, that user input and output procedures function as planned.

Two systems testing methods commonly used in checking these people links are structured walkthroughs and pilot studies. **Structured walkthroughs** are reviews by users and CIS professionals who are not members of the project team, that evaluate the usefulness and appropriateness of the system design. These reviews are used throughout the systems development effort. In systems testing they can be used by the users as step-by-step guides through the input and output procedures, thus helping them decide whether the developed system meets the information requirements specified in the systems analysis phase.

Pilot studies simulate how a system will work by testing its usefulness and accuracy under controlled conditions. Either just a part of the system is put in operation or the entire system is introduced into a single division of the company. When all the snags in the new system are worked out in the pilot study, the rest of the system is then put in place.

Training

Before users can work with an information system, they must learn how to use it. A good training program covers an information system's overall purpose, its benefits to users, and all standard input and output procedures.

There are three basic training options. When there are only a few users, **one-on-one training** by a systems analyst is the standard training method. Because the systems analyst can tailor the training to each user, training can be brief and very effective. When there are many users, however, one-on-one training is too expensive (see Exhibit 7.14).

Workshops, in which groups of users are trained in a classroom setting, are common when an information system has many users. Workshops are most effective when users have access to terminals or microcomputers in the classroom, so they can practice what they are learning. Workshops can be taught by a firm's in-house staff or by consultants brought in to develop the training program. When an information system uses a popular software package, it is usually possible to send users to workshops developed and run by the package's vendor or by a consultant.

A training method growing in popularity involves computer-aided instruction, or CAI. In CAI, a software program is developed that instructs users through an interactive dialogue. A major benefit of CAI training is that it is self-paced. Trainees can select the topics to be covered, the sequence in which topics are covered, and the pace at which training takes place.

Exhibit 7.14

Training the Users

One-on-one training is often the best way to learn a system. Such training can provide the human touch and ease the transition to a new way of doing business.

Conversion

The purpose of most information system projects is to improve the manner in which a set of business activities is handled. The purchasing information system, for example, automates the preparation of purchase orders, which were formerly written or typed by hand. The term **conversion** refers to the manner in which a business converts from the "old way" of doing business to a "new way."

Conversion involves two steps. In the first step, existing data files must be changed to fit the new information system. Thus, when a change is made from a manual system to a computer-based system, paper files need to be converted to computer-readable media—which can be very time-consuming. In the second step, the new information system is physically introduced into the work place.

The aim of all conversion efforts is to introduce the new information system quickly and smoothly. The problem is, it is virtually impossible to develop an error-free information system. Errors lead to mistakes and failures, and these disrupt business operation. Also, as information systems increase in size and complexity, the number of errors that are not caught before conversion increases.

Direct conversion means switching immediately from the old system to the new system. The advantage of direct conversion is that people can start working with the new system right away. The risk, particularly with complex systems, is that everything may not work correctly right from the start.

With **parallel conversion** the old and the new systems are run together for a while. This way, results from the old system can be used to verify the accuracy of the output of the new system. Also, if the new system fails, the old system will still be there to use. The only major problem with this parallel approach is that it increases the workloads, which in turn causes costs to rise.

A direct conversion is fine when the new information system is simple or when information system failures won't disrupt business operations. When an information system's failure might be disruptive, other conversion strategies should be used. The parallel strategy is one option. Another alternative is known as a phased conversion, in which the conversion is broken into smaller steps, or *phases*. Each phase can then be implemented either directly or in parallel.

User and CIS Professional Roles

In the systems implementation phase, the user's role is very important. The user's aim is to successfully implement into the organization the information system that has been designed and tested. Thus, the user's first step is to accept the information system from the CIS professionals only after it is shown to work as advertised. Usually, the user will then assume responsibility for

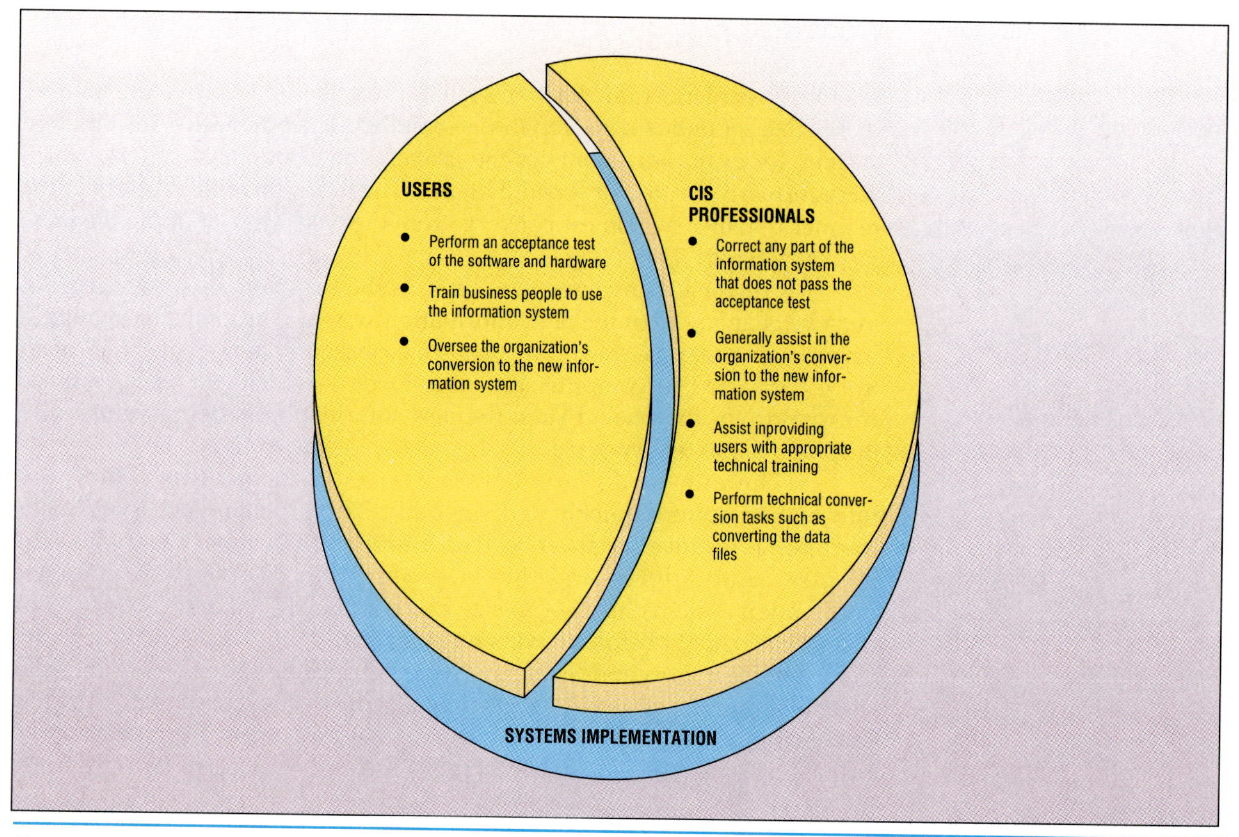

Exhibit 7.15

User and CIS Professional Roles in the Systems Implementation Phase

training the business people to use the new information system and for making the overall transition a successful one (see Exhibit 7.15).

The role of the CIS professional in this phase is to correct any part of the system that does not pass the acceptance test. Once the system has been successfully tested, the CIS professional works to assist the user in integrating the information system in the organization. Part of the CIS professional's task could include providing technical training and converting any manual files into the appropriate computer formats.

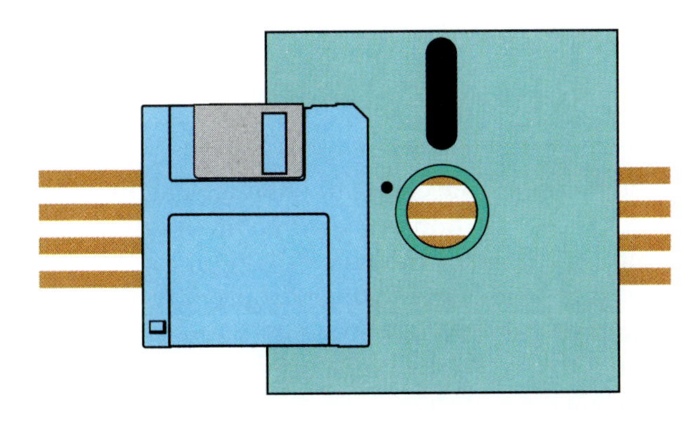

Computers at Work

The Software Prototype

One of the most difficult and error-prone parts of a system's development project is requirements analysis. This is the process of finding out what a customer wants from a system and writing this down in a document called the system specification.

Requirements analysis is difficult for several reasons. First, there is a cultural difference between the software developer and the customer. The former is often skilled in the latest development methods, but may have a scant knowledge of an application area. The customer will know the application area in minute detail, but will have, at best, an outdated view of the capabilities of software systems.

The second problem occurs inside the system specification. Normally, developers use natural language to write this document. Now, natural language is excellent for creating literary works of art. Poems and books are often prized for the subtlety and ambiguity of their text. Unfortunately, this makes it a poor choice of medium for specifications, which must be precise. Errors in interpretation of a system specification can cause projects to go over budget, software to be delivered late or produce useless software that misses the user's requirements. There are many documented instances where misinterpretation of a system specification by a software developer has led to the cancellation of million dollar projects. I have heard many stories from developers who, while demonstrating a system during acceptance testing, have had the customer turn to them and say, "This is not the system I want! If only you had shown it to me earlier!" This phrase is the key to software prototyping.

Software prototyping is the process of developing an early version of a system which can be shown to the customer before system specification. When the prototype has been agreed, it can be signed off by the customer and used as a reference point during development. The last five years have seen the emergence of many tools for quick development of prototypes.

The most widespread type of prototyping language is the fourth generation language. Commercial DP departments use these to manipulate large data files. A fourth generation language contains facilities for defining transaction screens (as used by bank clerks and air line reservation staff), for generating reports and for accessing complex databases. There are now hundreds of fourth generation languages and they are gradually replacing the ageing COBOL language for commercial data processing applications.

One powerful method of prototyping is called "specification execution"—the developer actually runs a compiled version of the system specification document. The developer produces the specification as normal. It is then processed by a special-purpose tool which translates the specification into a computer program. This program may then be executed. The important advantage of this technique is that it requires little work from the developer, once he has completed the specification. There is another aspect of a computer system which requires prototyping: the human-computer interface (aka Man Machine Interface or MMI). Many fourth generation languages have facilities which let the user design his own input and output screens. The definition of such screens often requires only a few minutes' effort. There are now tools capable of processing descriptions of the interactions between a user and a computer system. Working from these descriptions, the tools can generate a prototype MMI. Prototyping is based on the strong notion of producing software that meets the needs of users. It heralds a new way of treating the customer, by placing him firmly within the software development project.

Summary and Key Terms

Generally, after a feasibility study has shown that a development effort is worthwhile, the project development team is put together, a time table is agreed to, and a development cost is estimated. The **steering committee** is a group composed of senior-level business and CIS professionals, formed to give overall guidance to the project development team concerning the business purpose of the project, to assist in providing resources, and to keep track of progress.

The steering committee uses **project management tools** such as Gantt and cost-tracking charts to measure how well the project is going. The **Gantt chart** is a project management tool that shows the actual versus estimated time taken to complete each major activity. The **cost-tracking graph** is a project management tool used to track the actual versus estimated cost of the project.

The **project development team** is a group of CIS professionals and users that is charged with analyzing, designing, acquiring, and implementing an information system to accomplish the project definition. The **project definition** is a statement of the overall purpose of the project and the scope of its activity. Project definition is critical because it establishes, along with the cost and time schedule, what a successful project will be.

Once the project definition has been clarified and agreed to, the next major activity in systems analysis is to specify the information needs of the business in more detail. The primary way to show information relationships is through the use of **data flow diagrams (DFD)**, which are graphic views of the flow of data between processes, data files, and external organizations.

The major activities that take place during systems design involve outputs, inputs, processes, and testing procedures. **Output design** is the design of the reports and displays to show required information in a useful way. **Input design** is the design of input dialogue and data edit checks. **Dialogues** refer to the interactive "conversations" between the information system and its users. The **command dialogue style** triggers each action of the information system with a command. The **menu dialogue style** lists a series of actions from which the user selects. **Prompts** are simple instructions or questions posed to the user by the information system.

Data entry design refers to the manner in which data are initially entered into the information system. *Data integrity* or accuracy is achieved either by error prevention or by error detection and correction. **Edit checking** is a means to detect the accuracy of the data being entered. **Data currentness** refers to the timeliness of the data being entered. **Source documents** are business forms that capture data that will be entered into the information system.

During the systems acquisition phase, the hardware and software packages are purchased or customized software is developed. A **Request for Proposal (RFP)** is a formal statement of a company's information needs and the criteria to be used for selection. This RFP is sent to potential vendors. An **evaluation matrix** is used to select the best of several vendor alternatives. **Acceptance tests** are ways to check on key performance factors of information systems.

Systems implementation is concerned with system testing, training, and conversion. Systems tests are ways to check the information system itself, external electronic links to other systems, and people links. The people links can be tested by using structured walkthroughs and pilot studies. **Structured walkthroughs** are reviews by users and CIS professionals who are not members of the particular project development team, as to the usefulness and correctness of the system design. A **pilot study** is a controlled test of the new information system.

In **one-on-one training**, the systems analyst trains the user in an individual, hands-on manner. When many individuals need to be trained, the use of **workshops** as a means of training a group of users in a classroom setting is more cost effective. Software programs can be developed to instruct users through an interactive dialogue in the **computer-aided instruction** method.

Conversion refers to the manner in which a business converts from the "old" way of doing business to a "new" way. The conversion can be a **direct conversion** in which the switch from the old system to the new system is immediate or a **parallel conversion** in which both systems are run together for awhile.

The role of users and CIS professionals varies during the different phases of the system development effort. The user's role in the systems analysis and implementation phases is to establish what information the system will need to provide and then check that the developed system accomplishes these goals. During systems acquisition the user must be concerned with the make-versus-buy decision and choosing the best vendor package. If the decision is to make it in-house or custom-develop the software, the user plays a smaller role in the systems acquisition phase. The CIS professional's role in systems development is to analyze the needs of the users, document the existing and new information relationships, design the system, recommend whether the company should make or buy, and help implement the new information system.

Review Questions

1. Describe the composition of a typical steering committee and project development team.
2. What are two of the project management tools used by the steering committee? How do they differ?
3. Describe the ways to determine whether a developed information system is a success.
4. How are information requirements specified?
5. Briefly describe the important aspects of evaluating an output design.
6. Compare the three most common dialogue styles used in computer systems.
7. Compare the advantages and disadvantages of making versus buying software.
8. What are the three ways to convert from the old system to the new?
9. Explain the role of users in the four phases of systems development.
10. Explain the role of CIS professionals in the four phases of systems development.

T F **11.** Steering committees for information systems projects are generally composed of high-ranking business managers and staff professionals.

T F **12.** The scope of a project is part of the project definition statement.

T F **13.** Output design is the design of the reports and displays used to show the required information in a useful way.

T F **14.** Menu dialogue style limits a user's choice of action while command dialogue style can be more difficult to learn.

T F **15.** One of the best ways to achieve data integrity is to prevent data entry errors from entering the system.

T F **16.** A Request for Proposal (RFP) is sent to vendors as a formal statement of a company's information needs and criteria to be used for selection.

T F **17.** Acceptance tests are ways that users can check computer system performance against the information requirements.

T F **18.** Training of users in the methods and software of a new computer system is a minor consideration given the high level of computer literacy today.

T F **19.** Users have a minor role to play in the development of information systems, once they have specified what their information needs are.

T F **20.** Information systems are generally developed by a team of business and CIS professionals.

21. _____ Systems development includes which of the following phases?

a. systems analysis
b. systems analysis and design
c. systems acquisition and implementation
d. all of the above

22. _____ Conversion from the old system to the new way by running both new and old systems is called:

a. direct conversion
b. parallel conversion
c. phased conversion
d. intermittent conversion

23. _____ Users as business professionals have the primary responsibility for checking that the developed system accomplishes the stated information needs during which phase?

a. systems analysis
b. systems design
c. systems acquisition
d. systems implementation

24. _____ The primary project management tool used to show the actual versus estimated time taken to complete each activity is:

a. cost-tracking graph
b. Gantt chart
c. precedence chart
d. time management chart

25. _____ A means of comparing various vendors' computer solutions to arrive at the best proposal is called:

a. RFP
b. cost-performance analysis
c. evaluation matrix
d. payback method

CHAPTER 8

File and Database Management

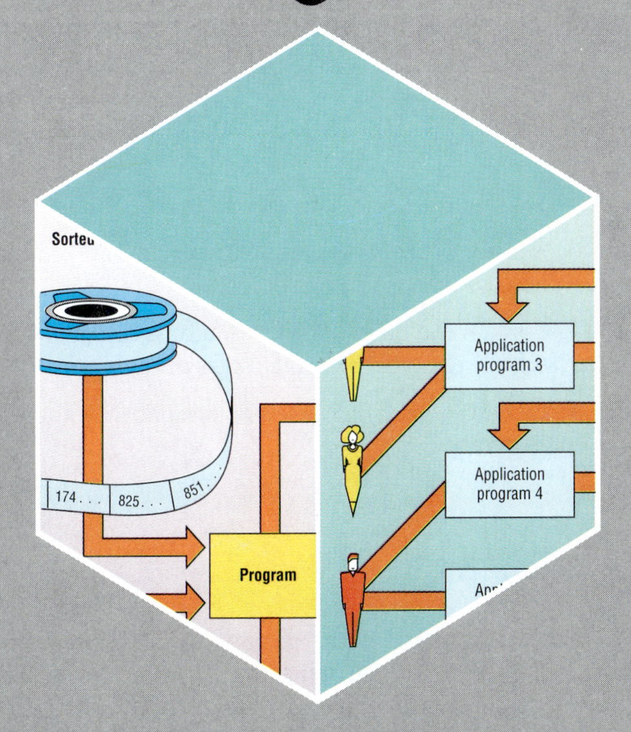

So far, this book has discussed computer hardware and the important roles played by application and operating software. Today, however, information is being used in a seemingly endless variety of ways, from telephone lists to criminal records to sophisticated medical applications. Actually, it is only recently that organizations have begun to appreciate the importance of data and the ability to retrieve data easily to provide information. As much an asset as plant and equipment, skilled employees, and money, carefully managed data is essential.

In this chapter you will learn to do the following:

1. Explain the basic parts of a file
2. Specify the three ways files can be organized and describe how they are accessed
3. Explain the three primary database organization models and the advantages and disadvantages of each
4. List the four criteria used to compare file and database management systems

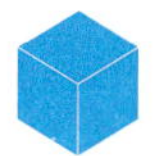

Traditional File Systems

Information systems are designed to store, maintain, and retrieve data from files to develop information to meet users' needs. The way data are organized within files often determines how efficiently the data can be retrieved to produce information. This section looks at basic file concepts, three common ways data are organized within a file, and how data are shared among files. The next section contrasts the traditional file system approach with the database management approach, which is designed to share data between different data files and provide easier ways to update and retrieve data.

Basic File Concepts

A familiar example—a phone book—is helpful for showing the basic concepts of data organization and how they affect the way a user can access data to answer questions.

In Exhibit 8.1, a portion of a college phone directory shows the various components of a file. A collection of related characters forms a **field.** Employee name and the phone extension are examples of fields. The combination of values in all the fields for a given employee is called a **record.** A **file** is a collection of records. In this particular case, the telephone directory file contains the records of all the faculty and staff members of a college.

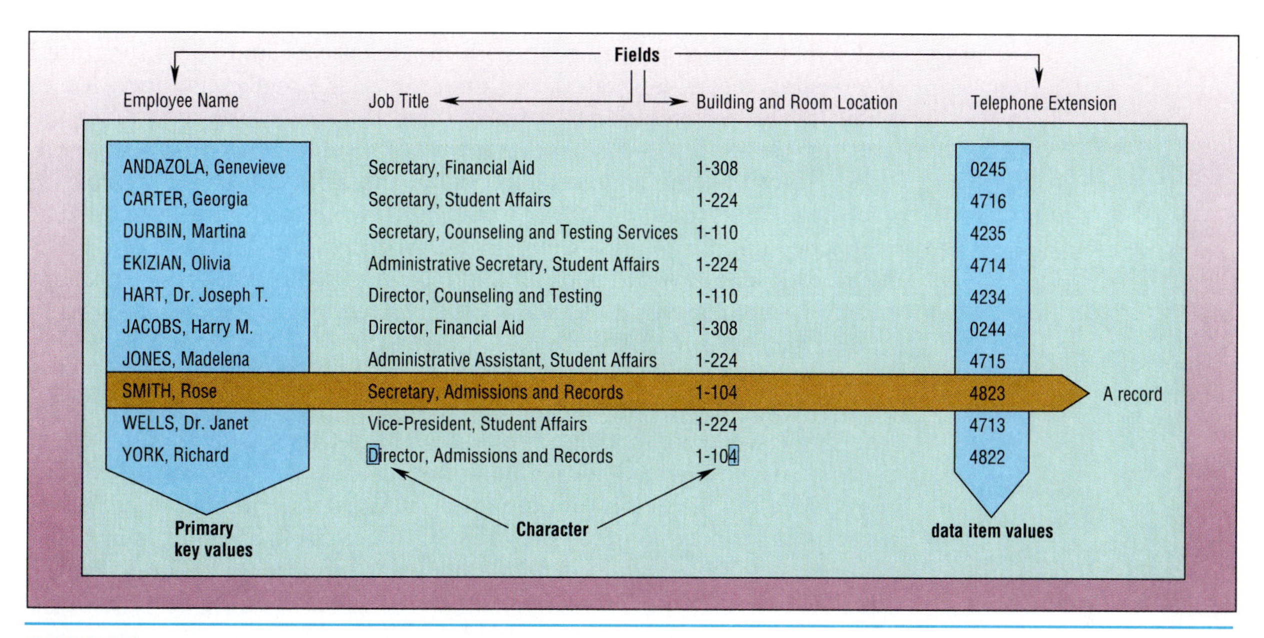

Exhibit 8.1

A File Made Up of Records Sequentially Ordered by Primary Key

When data are stored in a file, it is helpful to have a field that can be used to uniquely identify the records. This field is known as the **primary key** for the file. Each record in the file must contain a different value in this primary key field. For example, if the employee name field in the phone directory is designated as the primary key, no two employees may have exactly the same name. Since names are not always unique, organizations often have to use an employee number or social security number as the primary key, to ensure that each record will have a unique value in the primary key field.

A university would need many other files to conduct its daily business. There would be separate files for student grades, for courses offered, for personnel information, for payroll, and so on. An integrated collection of files is called a **database.** The special characteristics necessary to make a database more than just a group of files are discussed later in the chapter.

The way in which data are arranged is called **data organization.** This term refers to data items within a record, records within a file, and files within a database.

File Organizations

This section examines the various ways a file can be organized and accessed and how this affects the updating and retrieval of data. Data records have most commonly been organized in business applications into three types of files: sequential, indexed, and relative. The data records within a file can be accessed in sequence or, when means provide for it, directly by specific record. With *sequential access*, records must be retrieved from the file in the order they were stored, starting with the first record and continuing until the desired record is located. With *direct access*, a method is provided to allow the desired record to be retrieved directly—records above it in the file are undisturbed. Exhibit 8.2 shows the major combinations possible.

Not all combinations of sequential and direct access are possible on each type of secondary storage device. In Chapter 5 you learned that magnetic tape can provide only sequential access capability. On the other hand, disks can provide both direct access and sequential access. Let's go through several examples to show how different organizations are used to update and retrieve files.

Sequential File Organization

The simplest file organization is the **sequential file organization** in which records are sequenced by primary key values. To the payroll record introduced in Chapter 1, an employee identification number is added to serve as the primary key (see Exhibit 8.3). To process the weekly payroll, the first record in the payroll file on the magnetic tape would be located (0101 John Avery 550 40). This employee data would then be read into the computer. The pay rate data would be multiplied by the hours worked, and the gross pay determined. Then the next record would be read (0351 Bill Jones 500 30), and so on. The records are being accessed sequentially. Sequential files are used primarily with batch processing applications, where most or all of the records on the file are needed each time the application is run.

Some types of sequential file organization do not allow data records to be updated unless the entire file is copied. For example, a record cannot be added within a sequential file recorded on magnetic tape since adding a record would require all following records to "move down by one." Thus,

Exhibit 8.2

Possible Combinations for Accessing Different File Organizations

File Organization

Access	Sequential	Indexed	Relative
Sequential			
Direct			

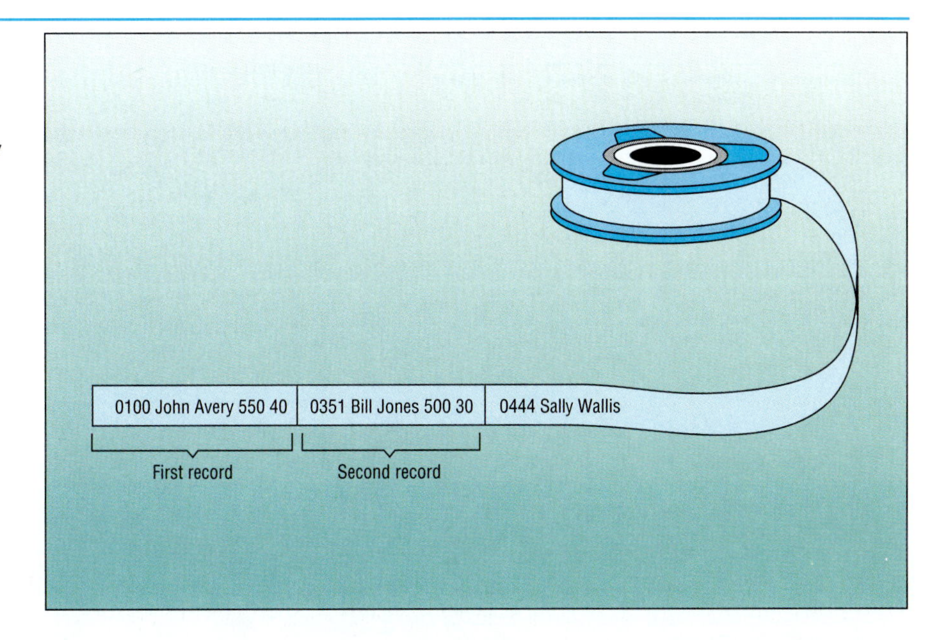

Exhibit 8.3

Sequential File Organization

Data can be located only by reading records sequentially.

the most practical approach for the updating of files on tape is to rewrite all the records onto a new tape while the appropriate changes are made.

To envision how this would work, assume the changes shown in Exhibit 8.4 happened since the present payroll file was last updated. The present collection of payroll records is considered to be the old payroll master file. The transaction file includes all the changes that have taken place since the last update. These changes must be applied to the old master file to produce a new (current) payroll master file.

To process these changes, the first step would be to sort each file into like order. The sort could be based on a primary key such as employee identification number. Then the first record in the transaction file would be read in and the key number noted. Next, the first record of the old master file would be read in and its key noted.

If there wasn't a match, the record from the old master file would be recorded in the new master file. When a match of key numbers did occur, a change such as a pay rate adjustment would be made and written in the new file. A need to delete a record would result in that record not being written in the new file. A new record would be added to the new master file in the appropriate sequence. The new master payroll file could then be used to process inquiries and develop payroll reports.

Indexed File Organization

Another approach to file organization is called **indexed file organization**. Like sequential file organization, this type of file is organized in sequence by key, but it also has an index that specifies the correspondence between the key value and the disk location of the record. The index key shows the highest key value associated with a record held on a particular track. This approach is analogous to the alphabetical listing of a phone directory,

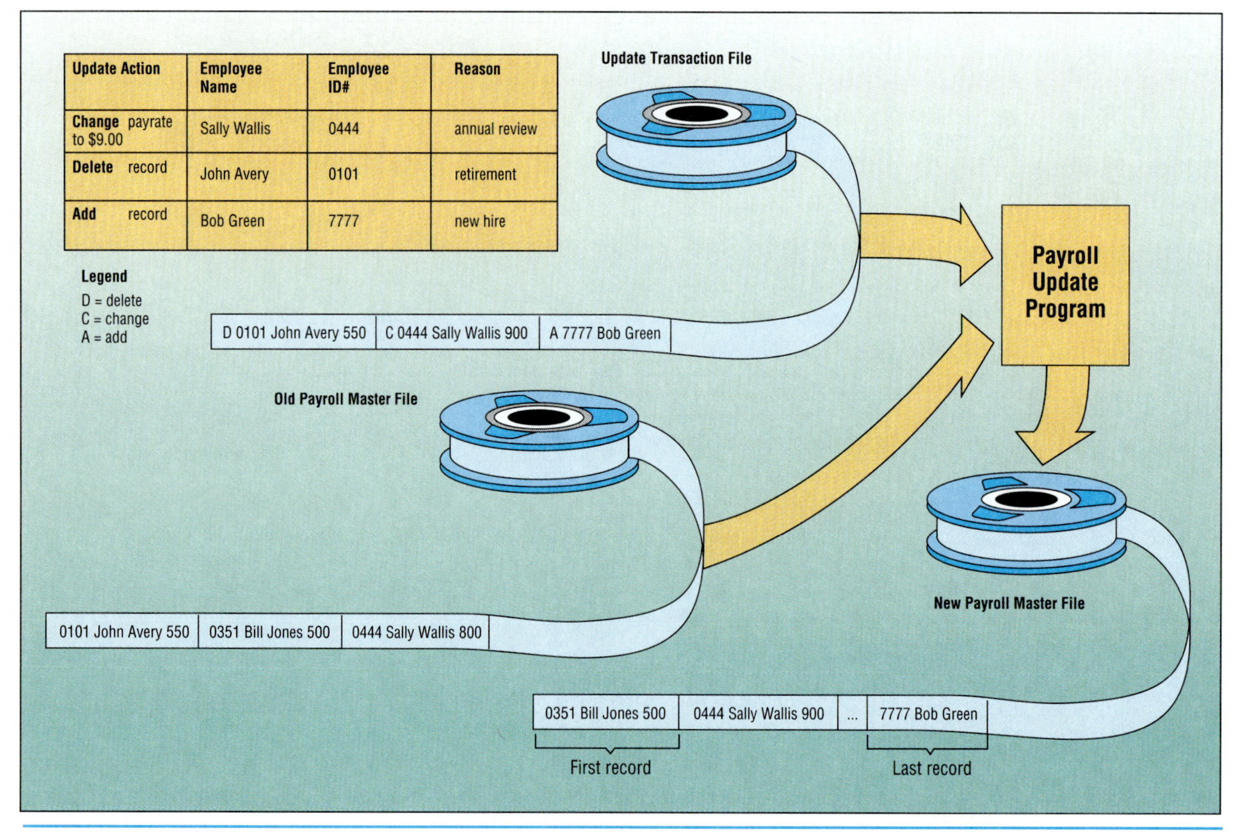

Exhibit 8.4

Master File Updating Process

An update transaction file would contain all the changes that have taken place since the last update. The present collection of payroll records is the old payroll master file. Each file would need to be sorted on the primary key Employee ID. By comparing the records on each tape file, a new payroll master file would be produced that incorporated the latest changes.

where the top of a page includes an index of the first and last entries appearing on that page.

In data retrieval from an indexed sequential file, either a specific record is located directly through the use of the index, or the records are read sequentially. This flexibility enables both transaction and batch processing to be handled efficiently. Exhibit 8.5 illustrates this process. For example, to answer a query by a counselor as to what grades Jerry Berry (student number 106) received last semester, a direct-access approach would be used. The index would first be searched by student identification number and the appropriate track located. Then the records within that track would be searched sequentially until record 106 was found.

To update the student files at the end of the semester, a sequential-access approach would be used since almost all records would be affected. Therefore, a search starting with the first record on track 1, would locate the record for the student with number 101. Then, each record would be read in sequence (106, 119), with a check made for matches with student numbers on a sorted transaction file of updated grades.

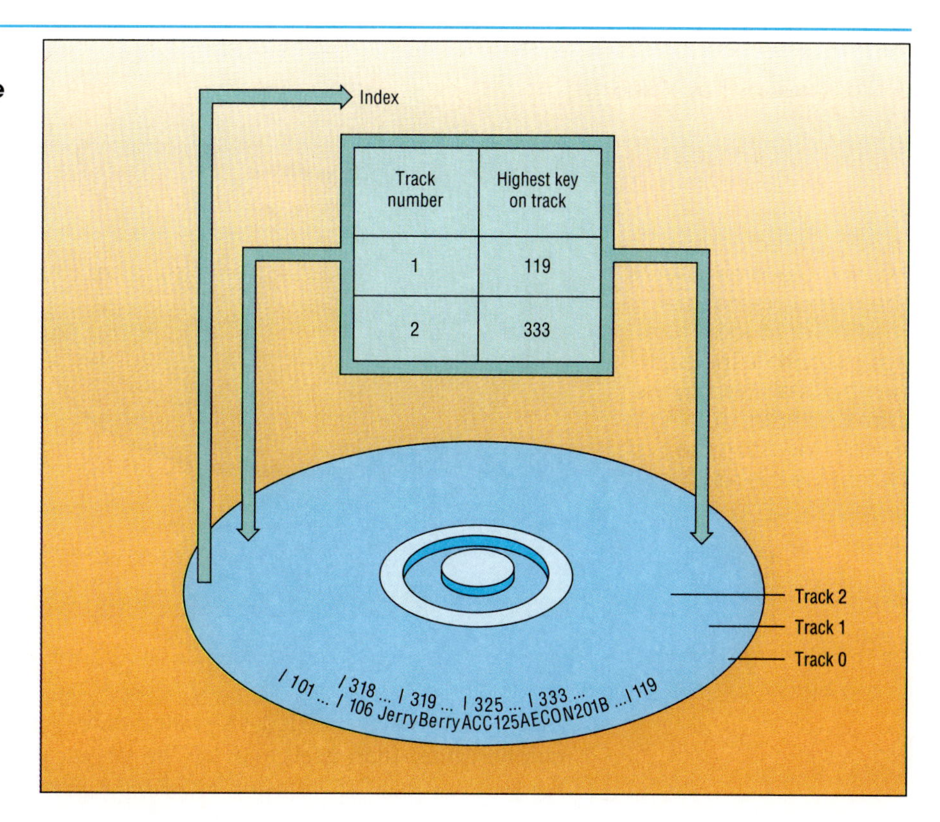

Exhibit 8.5

An Indexed Sequential File of Student Grades

Data can be retrieved from an indexed sequential file by locating a record through the use of an index or by reading records sequentially.

Relative File Organization

Relative file organization arranges records by key, but does not use an index. The key value is used to directly calculate the relative record number (first, tenth, twenty-first, and so on) for storing the record. One of the disadvantages of large indexed files is the amount of time needed to search the many indexes to find the appropriate disk address. Relative organization files are used for applications that require direct access and rapid response time, such as hotel or airline reservation systems.

To see how this works, assume in an inventory example that a three-digit part number is the key identifier. At most fifty types of parts are stocked during the year. If a disk address were allocated for each possible part number, much disk space would be wasted. Instead of 1000 storage locations (000 through 999), only fifty are really needed. The problem, then, is how to use the three-digit part number as a key to identify which of the fifty disk addresses should be placed in the data record. Computer scientists have developed mathematical formulas called *hashing algorithms* to randomize this allocation.

One allocation approach used is the division/remainder method (see Exhibit 8.6). In the current example, the part number identifier would be divided by the largest prime number less than the maximum number of

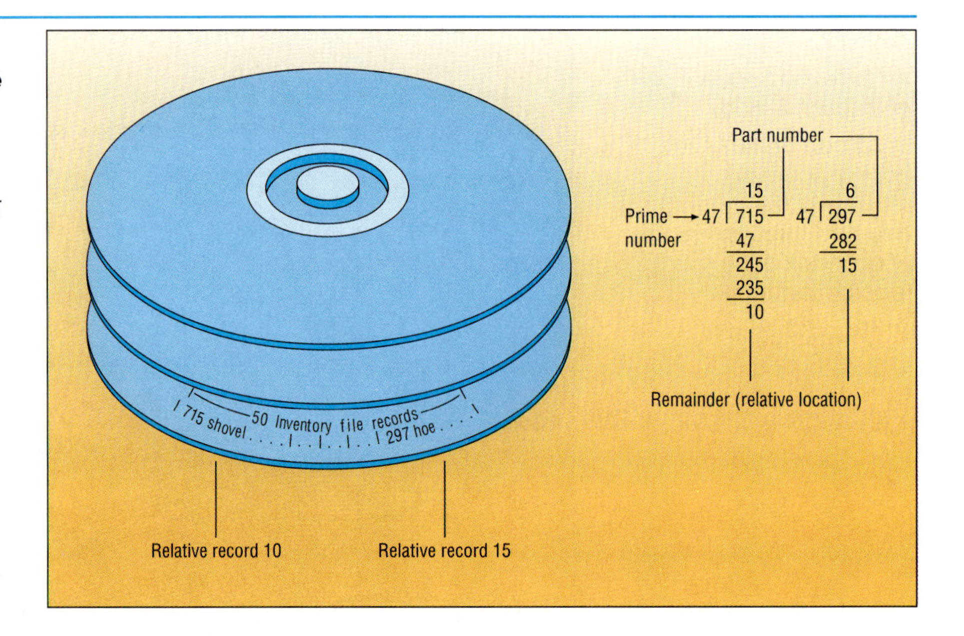

Exhibit 8.6

A File Stored by Key Value Calculation

The key value is used to calculate directly the relative record number for storing a record. The hashing algorithm used is the division/remainder method of randomizing this allocation. The part number is divided by the prime number, yielding a remainder that is used to determine the relative record location.

records that will be needed. (A *prime number* is a number not divisible by any number other than itself and 1.) The largest prime number below 50 is 47. For part number 715, division by prime number 47 yields a remainder of 10. This record would be placed in the inventory file in the tenth record space. Part number 297 would be in the fifteenth space. Occasionally, this division/remainder method will yield the same remainder for different key values. This is known as a *collision* and the two records that have collided are known as *synonyms*. In such instances, the second of these records to be stored is generally placed in the next available storage location.

To update a relative file is conceptually quite easy. To modify a record on the disk, the record is located by division of the key by the largest prime number. The resulting remainder is used to determine the relative record location. That record is then read into primary memory, the appropriate data elements are changed, and the complete record is written back to the same location. If a record is to be added, the relative address is calculated and the new record is placed in that space in the file—if no synonym record has already been recorded there.

You have seen that files are organized in three primary ways—sequential, indexed, and relative files. Each approach has its own strengths and weaknesses. The processing requirements of the application determine which file design is best. The primary criterion for determining file design is whether the application is to be used in a batch or transaction processing. Batch processing generally uses sequential access. Transaction processing requires direct access, which can be handled by either relative or index files. Index file organization is a composite approach that can be used when both sequential and direct processing of a file are necessary for different applications.

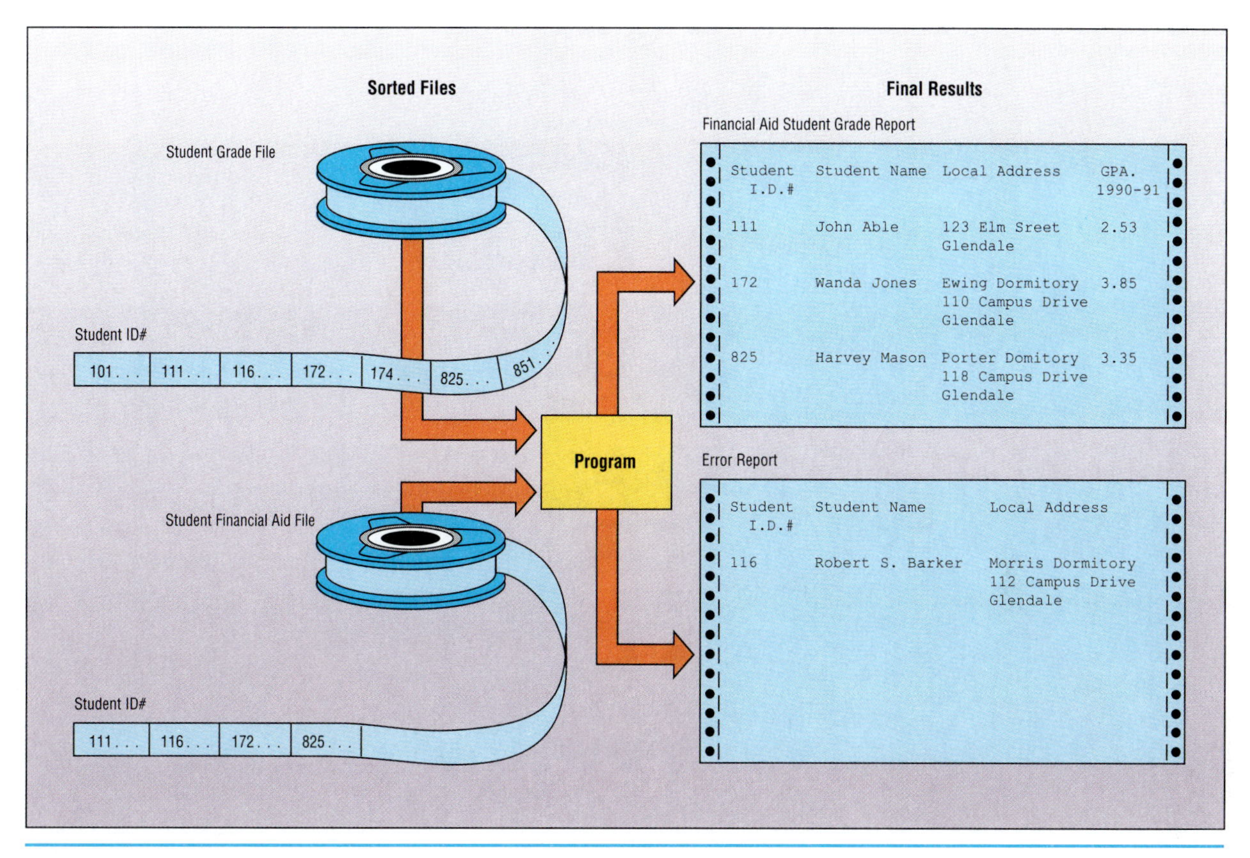

Exhibit 8.7

Sort/Merge Approach to Answering a Query

To answer a query that requires data stored in two separate files necessitates that the tape files be sorted first. The information is then merged based on key value.

Sharing Files

So far, the different ways a file can be organized and accessed have been discussed. File organization affects the accessibility of data for retrieval and updating purposes. Thus far, it has been assumed that all the information needed for a particular program can be obtained by searching a specific file, but that isn't always true. What happens, for instance, if some additional data items in another file are needed to answer a user's question?

Often, data that are needed for a given application are already in a file previously developed for a different application. Sometimes data items contained in separate files may need to be combined to produce the necessary reports.

One way to combine data from different sources is to use a sort/merge routine. Suppose the financial aid department of a college had a requirement that each student receiving financial aid had to have a grade point average of at least a 2.00 for the year. They have asked that a program be written to make this check (see Exhibit 8.7).

Financial aid files exist containing the following information: student name, identification number, local address, parents' annual income, and so on. There are also student grade files, which the data processing department updates each semester. They contain each student's identification number, name, classes taken, grades earned, and so on.

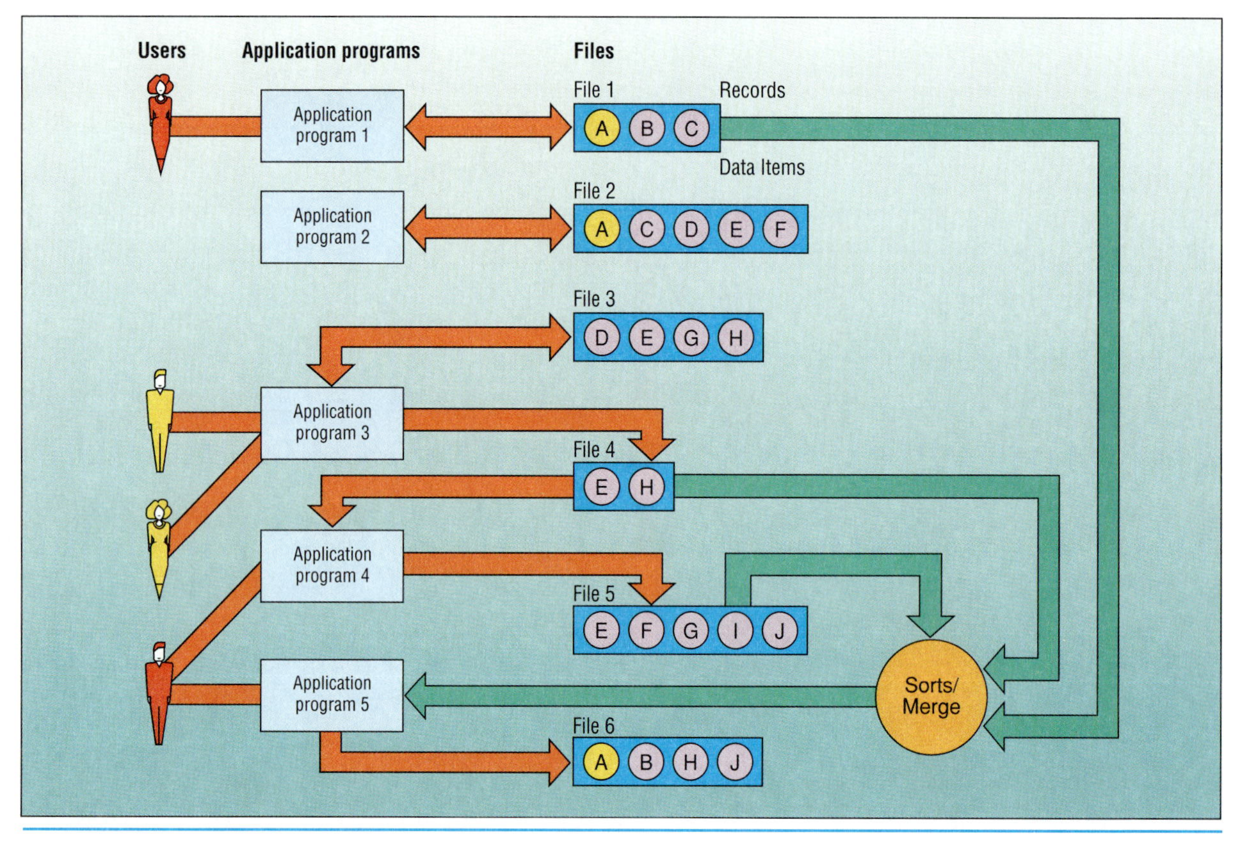

Exhibit 8.8

Inadequacy of File-Based Systems

A system without a database has much data redundancy, program overlap, and inflexibility.

So, the information needed is already available in computer-readable form, though it is contained on separate tapes or disk packs. The financial aid file would first have to be sorted by student identification number, to match the sequence of the student grade file. Then, since only a percentage of students receive financial aid, a matching process would have to be initiated. Where the student ID numbers match on both files, the data items needed from the record in each file would be processed. The result would be shown on the Financial Aid Student Grade Report. If any students listed in the financial aid file were not listed in the student grade file, an error list would have to be generated.

Thus, the **sort/merge** method is a way of combining selected data items from several files to produce needed information. It is a common approach used in organizations that don't have the use of a database. Exhibit 8.8 shows a generalization of this concept. The organization has many users who need information to accomplish their jobs. The data processing department has written programs with which users can produce accounting reports (Application Program 1), information on sales analysis (Application Program 2), and so on. Ordinarily, an application program is written to produce each particular report and sometimes separate data files are created to hold the data for each application. This results in an

Data Items	Order from Customer	Customer File	Warehouse Order	Warehouse Ticket	Invoice	Weekly Total Shipment Report	Weekly Item Shipment Report	Year-to-Date Shipment Report	Year-to-Date Item Report	Item File	Weekly Item Inventory Report	Inventory File	Branch File	Monthly Branch Summary	Year-to-Date Sales Report	Item On-Order Report	Total On-Order Report	Monthly Customer Report	Customer Payment	Accounts Receivable	Overdue Accounts	Overdue Notices
Customer Number	●	●	●		●													●	●	●	●	●
Customer Order Number	●		●		●														●	●	●	●
Itcm Number	●		●	●	●		●		●	●	●	●				●		●				●
Item Type and Size	●		●	●	●		●		●	●	●	●				●		●				●
Corporate Order Number			●	●	●		●											●		●	●	
Invoice Number					●														●	●	●	●
Branch Office Number	●				●								●	●	●		●	●		●	●	●
Customer Name	●	●			●									●				●	●	●	●	●
Item Name	●		●	●	●		●		●	●	●	●		●	●			●				●
Date of Invoice					●															●	●	●
Quantity Ordered	●		●	●	●				●		●	●				●		●				●
Quantity Shipped				●	●	●	●	●										●		●	●	●
Quantity Out of Stock				●	●	●	●	●	●		●							●				
Shipping Instructions			●	●	●																	
Code for Shipping			●	●	●																	
Customer Address		●			●																	
Branch Office Name	●	●			●								●	●	●		●	●				●
Branch Office Address	●				●								●									●
Price					●	●	●	●	●	●									●	●	●	●
Invoice Line Value					●															●	●	●
Discount Rate					●					●										●	●	●
Invoice Line Discount					●																	●
C.O.D. or Credit Code	●	●			●													●				●
Weekly Total of Item Shipped						●	●	●	●		●											
Weekly Value of Item Shipped						●	●	●	●													

Files, Reports, and Documents

Exhibit 8.9

Implications of Data Redundancy

Multiple input documents contain the same data items as those in various data files used to produce reports. A concern is that when updating data held in several different files, all copies of a data item are changed. Also, it is unclear whether data items with the same name used in different contexts mean exactly the same thing.

abundance of files that contain many of the same data items, resulting in much **data redundancy.** For example, data item A is used in three different files.

Exhibit 8.9 shows a typical list of organizational reports and the data items contained in each report. The sort/merge method is the primary way that relationships among these files have been handled. There are several distinct disadvantages to this approach, however. First, creating files with sort/merge requires a significant amount of computer resources and time to accomplish. Second, when updating data held in several different files, care must be taken to change all copies of a data item. Last, even if a needed data item is in an existing file, it is not always clear that the data element has the desired meaning in that file or is in the required format. For example, does "price" refer to the retail price of an item, the wholesale price, or the discounted price given to special customers?

Database Management Systems

The development of **database management systems (DBMS)**, in the late 1960s for large computers and the early 1980s for microcomputers, has provided significant help in sharing and managing corporate data. The primary function of the DBMS is to enable users to establish the structure of the database itself, which organizes data to be used in many different applications. Secondly, the DBMS facilitates initial loading of the data into the database and enables the user to easily update the database. A third function is to provide an easy way for managers and staff personnel who are not computer experts, as well as programmers, to retrieve selected data items. Lastly, a DBMS must provide means for managing and protecting this organizational data, which generally is to be shared among a large number of users.

Logical Versus Physical Views

The concept of a database has emerged to provide users with a generally more effective way of sharing organizational data. It is a uniform way of managing data as a critical organization resource. Conceptually, a **database** is an integrated collection of data items that can be retrieved in any combination necessary to produce needed information. Programmers can, for example, write application programs to directly extract data and develop overdue notices or weekly inventory reports. Users, themselves, can make inquiries of the data by using English-like statements in a database query language (see Exhibit 8.10). In contrast to the database concept, file systems do not provide an integrated way of accessing, linking, or managing the data in a collection of files.

A major purpose of the DBMS is to divide the accessing of data into logical and physical concerns. The logical question refers to *what* data are needed to answer a variety of questions users might have. *How* those data should actually be positioned on the disk or be accessed is the physical question.

To accomplish this division, there must be a separation between the logic of the programs and queries and the physical placement and retrieval of the data on secondary storage devices. The significance of this separation is this: (1) users now have a much easier way to visualize and use shared data and (2) changes to the logic of programs and/or the structure of shared data can be made without one affecting the other.

Let's examine how this works. The logical description of the organization of the complete database is referred to as a **schema**. A schema includes the names of the data items and specifies the relationship among them. A description of a particular subset of the total database that can be useful in answering a user's specific question is called a **subschema**. Each subschema is also called a **user's view**. In Exhibit 8.11, User 1 is using data items C, D, E, M, and N, and User 3 views the database to be composed of data items F, G, K, L, M, and N. The concept of a user's view allows each

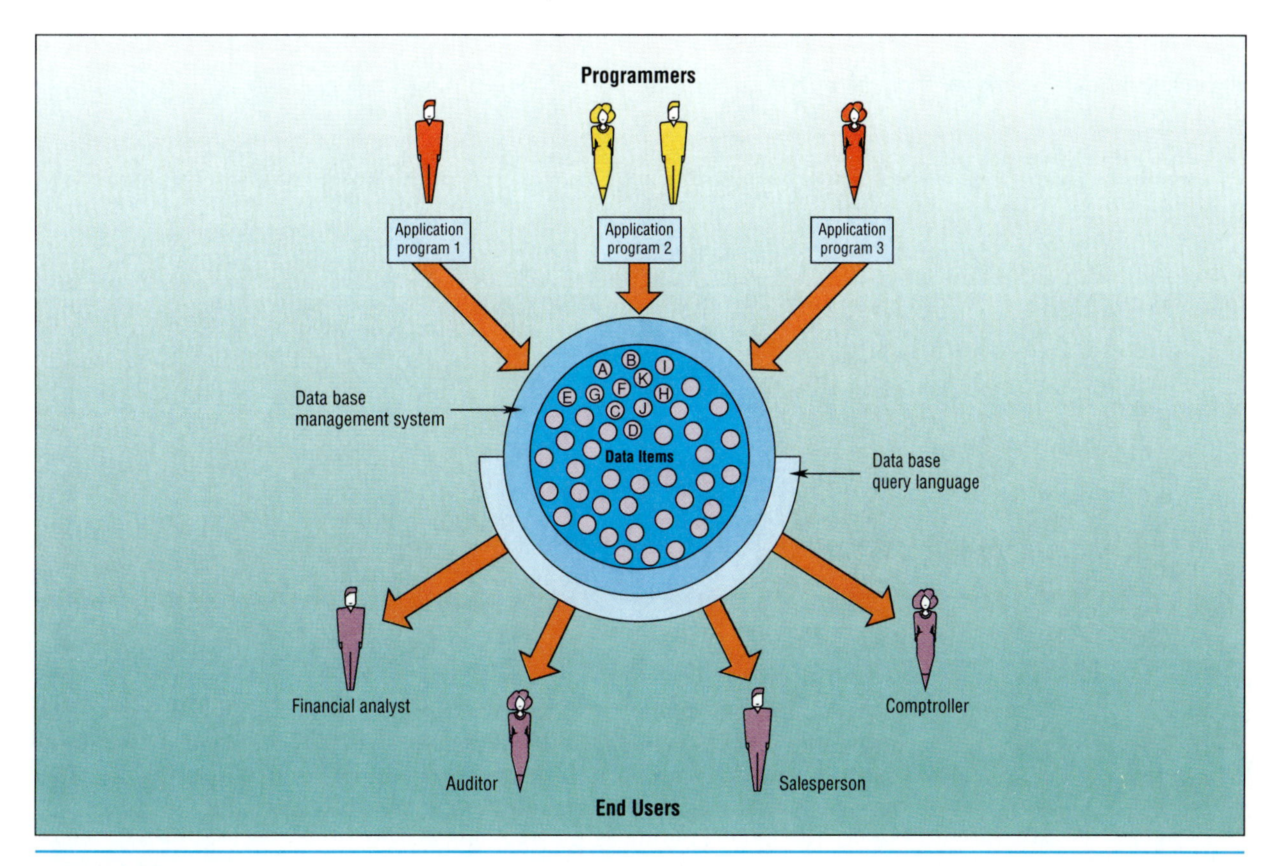

Exhibit 8.10

A Conceptual View of a Database System

The database management system provides programmers and users with access to data items. The database query language helps users retrieve data items without having to write a program.

user to be concerned only with the data of interest to him or her. From a security standpoint, a user's view can be implemented to keep unauthorized users from gaining access to specific data.

With a file system, a programmer has to specify the next record that is needed. For example, a program to determine gross pay would be designed to request retrieval of the next employee's pay record. After the record had been retrieved and put in primary memory, the application program instructions would take the data items needed with the pay record—pay rate and hours worked—and perform the multiplication.

This approach requires that the size of the record and the number and order of data items be known and specified in the program. This is a **program data dependent** situation. The implication of this dependency is that if one of the fields within the employee record were to change, such as ZIP codes increasing from five to nine digits, all programs using this particular file would have to be rewritten to accommodate the change in record length. This is true even for those programs that do not use ZIP codes, but use other data items in that record.

With a DBMS, the application program simply requests the specific data items that are needed, rather than the complete record. The data management software takes the logical request for pay rate and hours worked and issues the commands necessary to physically place those data

Exhibit 8.11

Specifying Users' Views

A database can be defined to accommodate specific users' views and as a means for limiting users' access to specific data.

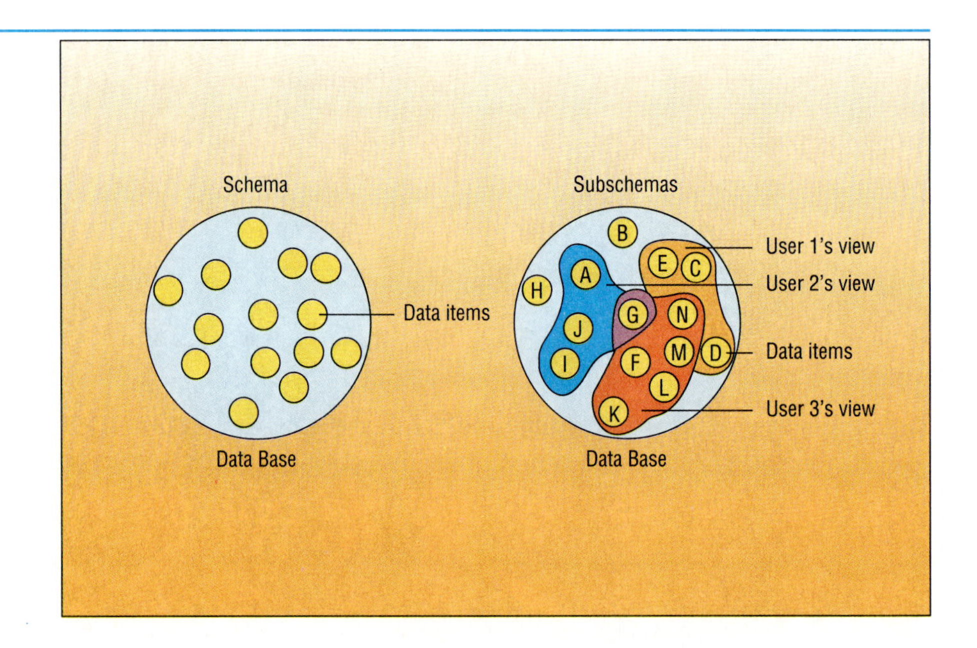

items in primary memory. The net result is that, with the DBMS, this payroll program would not be affected by an increase in ZIP code length within the payroll record. **Program data independence** means that changes in either programs or data can be made without significantly affecting the other.

Database Organization Models

Just as there are different ways of organizing records within a file, there are different ways of organizing files within a database. As an example, let's look at a simplified database of students at the local college, what courses they took for one semester, and the instructors for the course.

In the **hierarchical database model,** data is organized in a top-down manner. In Exhibit 8.12 the record of a student is the main or root record and it contains his or her personal identification number (PIN), name, address, and phone number. For each student record, there is an explicit link that associates it with specific lower level records in other files. This record shows what courses a student has taken, and another lower level record indicates the particular instructor associated with each course.

A characteristic of the hierarchical data model is that it supports **one-to-many** relationships. This means that each higher level record, called a parent, can be associated with one or more lower level records, called children. For example, the higher level student record can be linked to one or more courses. But each course (child) can only be associated with one student record (parent).

How would this database model be used to answer the query, "Who was Mike Masters' instructor in English 101?" The DBMS would search the student records to first find the record of Mike Masters. Given

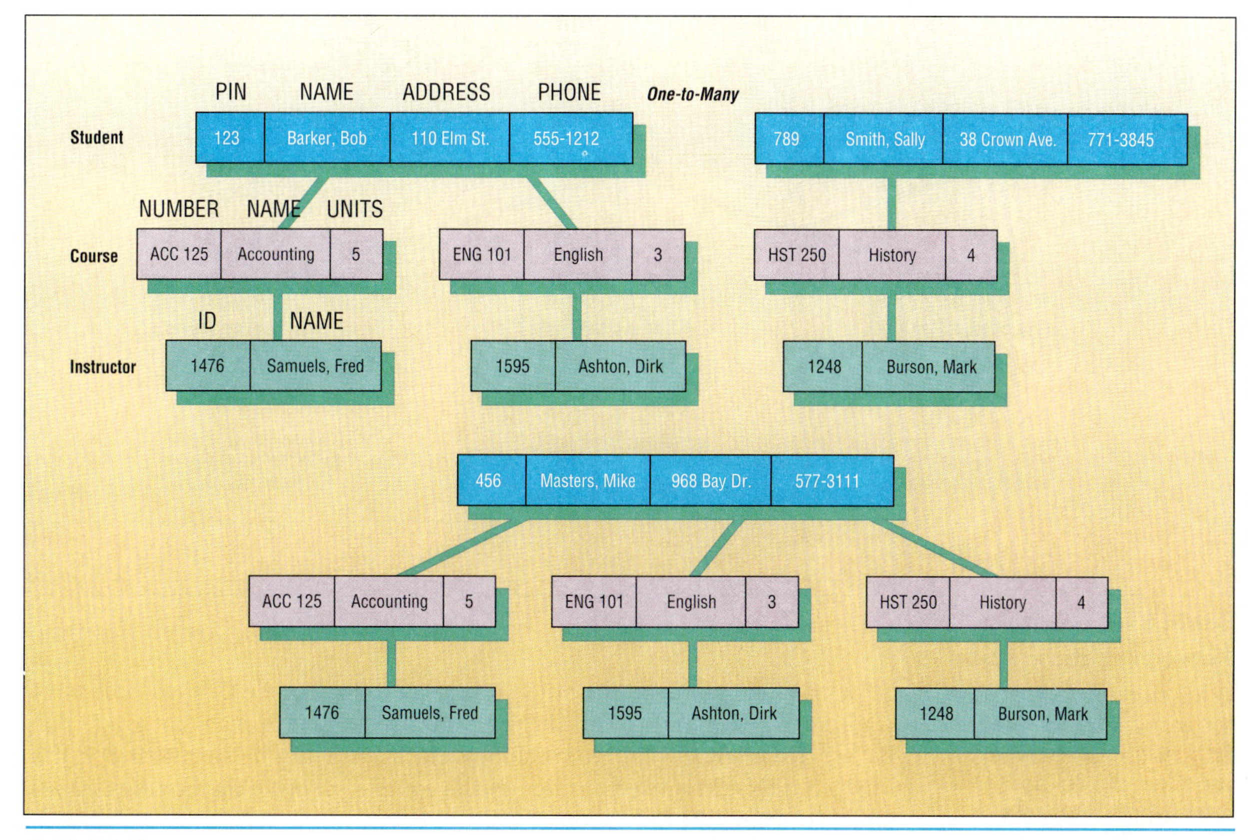

Exhibit 8.12

Hierarchical Database Model

In this hierarchical database the student record is the main record. It is explicitly linked to the course or courses the student has taken and the course records are linked to the instructor for the course. This forms a hierarchy of associations that form a one-to-many relationship among parent and child records.

that record, it would follow the explicit links to the course records associated with Mike Masters. In this case there are three. It would select the English 101 record and follow the associated link that shows that the instructor was Dirk Ashton.

A different way of structuring this same data is the **network database model** (see Exhibit 8.13). This is a **many-to-many** data model. As before, the student records (parents) are associated with one or more courses (children). Note, however, that each course now has explicit links that associate it with one or more student records. Thus we can explicitly see through the links that History 250 was taken by both Mike Masters and Sally Smith. In contrast, note in the hierarchical model, to answer this same question, all student records would have to be searched to see where HST 250 was an explicit link.

A third representation is the **relational database model** (see Exhibit 8.14). It is based on the presentation of data in the form of tables or relations. In this example, there is a table containing information on all courses offered, a table containing all student records, and a table on instruction. In each table the horizontal rows are records, and data items are shown in the columns. There are no parent and child relationships nor explicit links. Rather, there are implicit associations between records in different tables created by the duplication of the primary key of one table in another table.

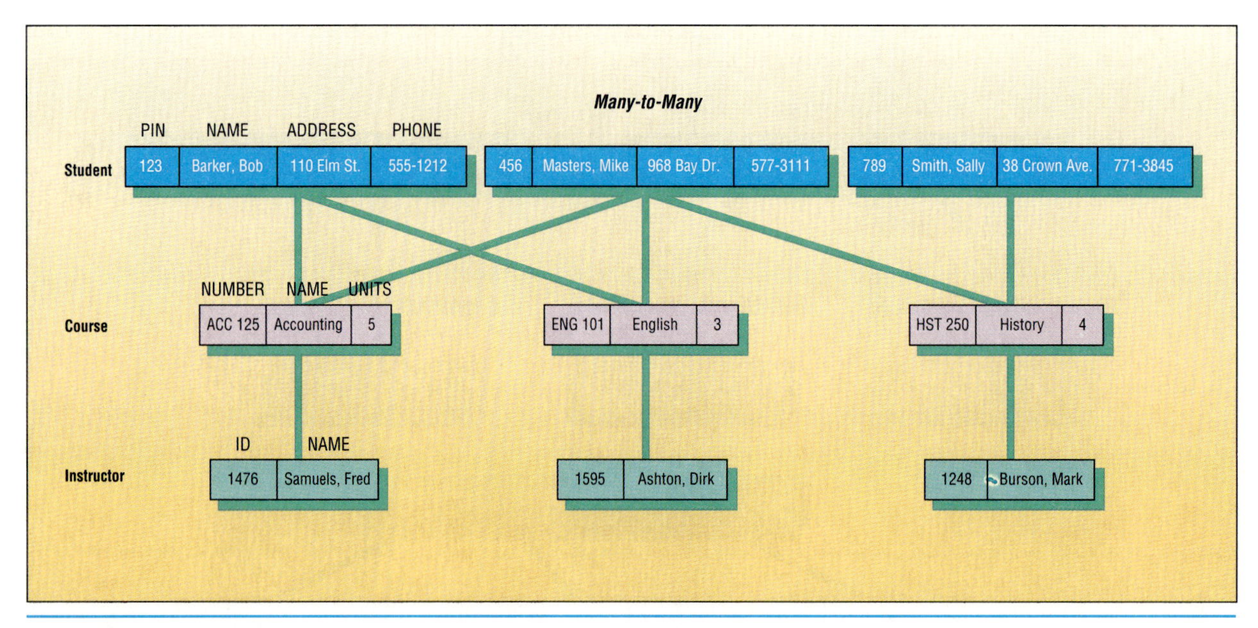

Exhibit 8.13

Network Database Model

In this network database, the same student, course, and instructor records are used but are linked somewhat differently. More flexibility is attained by allowing a record to have many superior records and many subordinate ones. This makes it readily apparent that the three students took English 101 last semester.

For example, records in the Student table and the Course-Grades table have common PIN numbers. This duplication can be used to see what grade Bob Barker got in ACC 125. From the Student table it can be seen that Bob has PIN 123. PIN 123 is used to identify the courses taken in the Course-Grades table. For ACC 125 Bob received a *B*.

Although a simplified example has been used here, it is important to understand the implication: generally, data can be shown in the three equivalent forms. Why have three database models? Each has its particular strengths and weaknesses, which need to be matched to the database requirements of an organization. The major advantages of the hierarchical and network models are economy and speed. In general, these models, in comparison to the relational model, have less data redundancy and allow faster access to the information. However, these database models are complex to update, since all affected links must be reconfigured.

The major advantage of the relational model is that any combination of data in the database can be easily retrieved. Links between data records (tables) can be established by users' commands as the need arises. This great flexibility allows the relational database to be easily configured to answer new and unanticipated questions. In contrast, the hierarchical and network models require that the links be built into the design of the database. Programs must follow established paths to find information. These paths or links are designed to quickly answer the typical questions that will be asked, but retrieval may be slow for questions that require accesses not supported by the built-in links.

Relational models are generally slower to access data in fairly large databases. To speed up access to data, relational models often use indexes for the most common search paths.

Course

NUMBER	NAME	UNITS
ACC 125	Accounting	5
ENG 101	English	3
HST 250	History	4

Student

PIN	NAME	ADDRESS	PHONE
123	Barker, Bob	110 Elm St.	555-1212
456	Masters, Mike	968 Bay Dr.	577-3111
789	Smith, Sally	38 Crown Ave.	711-3845

Course - Grades

PIN	COURSE	GRADE
123	ACC 125	B
123	ENG 101	C
456	ACC 125	B
456	ENG 101	A
456	HST 250	A
789	HST 250	D

Exhibit 8.14

Relational Database Model

In the relational model, records are arranged in tables. There are neither predetermined links nor superior-subordinate relationships. Rather, records in various tables can be associated by using commands. This results in greater flexibility in looking at the database in different ways.

In historical terms, the hierarchical and network models were developed first. They have been the major types used on mainframe computers. The relational database model is a recent development used extensively on microcomputers, and is finding more and more applications on mini- and mainframe computers.

In looking at the diagrams of the three models, you probably felt most comfortable with the relational model. Your preference would probably be even stronger if there were thousands of entries, rather than the small number shown. We are used to seeing data in tables.

A trend is appearing that takes advantage of the ability to distinguish logical from physical structures of data. Since users are more comfortable with relational tables, the DBMS provides a relational look to the user. Internally, however, the DBMS translates the relational commands into a hierarchical or network model for structuring and retrieving the data from secondary storage. This dual approach maximizes the strengths of both humans and computers.

Database Administration

When important corporate data and computer resources are going to be shared among users with diverse interests, much time and thought must go toward balancing the often conflicting objectives of meeting user needs and making efficient use of computer systems. The **Database Administrator (DBA)** plays a key role in this effort. The DBA is the person acting as the keeper of the database. Some organizations have more than one DBA. The DBA ensures the effectiveness of data retrieval and the accuracy and confidentiality of data and also keeps the physical database running efficiently. As you might imagine, the DBA needs both technical and political skills to accommodate multiple users of a shared database.

There are several important features that a DBMS should have to aid the database administrator. The creation and maintenance of the database structure is fundamental to the management of the DBMS. The complete description of the database is contained in a data dictionary. The **data dictionary** is a collection of all the specifications of the data elements, records, and relationships that exist in the database. In addition, schemas, subschemas, and programs are described in the data dictionary.

Since the data are being shared, it is important to determine who will be allowed access to any given data item and to establish modification rights. Exhibit 8.15 shows a set of **authorization rules** that specifically state who is allowed to do what with the various data records. For example, Sally Smith is authorized only to read the order record. She can't modify it, nor can she add or delete data items within the record. In contrast, the application program PGM OEI04J can make insertions to the order record. This is true so long as the amount is less than $500,000. The payroll supervisor is the only one who can delete an employee record, and then only for hourly workers—not salaried employees. The payroll supervisor is also the only one who can grant the various actions (insert, delete, modify) to the records of payroll personnel. The critical point is that a user is allowed to perform only a limited set of authorized actions, based on his or her password.

Support for auditing a database is an important part of a DBMS in which data are particularly sensitive or where possibilities for fraud exist. An **audit log** is a file in which data on all operations performed by users of the database are chronologically recorded. A typical entry in the audit log

Exhibit 8.15

Authorization Rules for Accessing and Modifying a Database

Authorization Rules for Accessing and Modifying a Database

Subject	Object	Action	Constraint
PGM OE104J	ORDER Record	Insert	Amount less than $500,000
Sally Smith	ORDER Record	Read	None
Payroll Dept	EMPLOYEE Record	Read	Hourly workers
Payroll Dept	EMPLOYEE Record	Modify	Hourly workers
Payroll Dept	EMPLOYEE Record	Insert	Hourly workers
Payroll Supv	EMPLOYEE Record	Delete	Hourly workers
Payroll Supv	Read Permission of EMPLOYEE Records	Grant	To payroll personnel only

would include the following information for each transaction: the terminal used, the log-in code used; the date and time; the database, record, and field affected; and the old and new value of the data item. With an audit trail, the changing status of the database can be tracked. Events can be reconstructed and suspicious outcomes can be traced. The use of audit logs in the detection of fraud and embezzlement is one of the major responsibilities of EDP auditors.

The sharing of data means that many applications will depend on the same data. This means that data integrity becomes even more critical when DBMS are used. Problems can be created by hardware and software errors—for example, a disk crashes, or a programmer writes a program containing bugs that introduce errors into the database. DBMS systems have been designed to recover from these kinds of failures. The most straightforward strategy is for the DBA to periodically make a backup copy of the database and keep a log of all transactions that occur from that time until the next backup copy is made. If the computer system were to fail, the transactions could then be reapplied against the backup copy of the database to restore it to its state prior to the error.

The DBA is concerned with monitoring DBMS performance and with evaluating potential changes to the design of the database to make it more responsive to users' needs. Any database structure when it is first designed and implemented, gives its users a quick response. But a database has to evolve to reflect the changing nature of the demands generated by an organization. New data items are added, additional security measures are taken, and more users need to access the database. These changes usually cause the DBMS to become overloaded and slow down unless preventive measures are taken.

The DBA uses performance monitors that are a combination of hardware and software. These monitors generate statistics on the utilization of database resources as well as the CPU, primary memory, input/output channels, and secondary storage units. From this, specific data bottlenecks can be identified. Solutions may range from modifying the scheduling of applications so that certain jobs are run during slow periods, to increasing I/O speeds, to allocating more primary memory to the DBMS, and even to getting a more powerful computer system.

File Versus Database Management Systems

Now that some of the characteristics of file and database systems have been explored, let's see how these systems compare on several major criteria: data, cost, risk, and personnel.

One of the major strengths of a DBMS is that it provides much greater access to organizational data through the use of host and query languages. The database allows a significant reduction in data redundancy and provides for standard definition of data items and for control of the modification of records. This results in greater data integrity. The DBMS

	File Systems	Database Management Systems
Data		
Access	limited	extensive
Redundancy	much	significant reduction
Integrity	little	great
Program	dependent	independent
Cost		
Data Management Software	less expensive	very expensive
Computer Hardware	less powerful computer	more powerful computer
Risk		
Failures	low	medium
Security	low	medium
Conversion	low	high
Personnel		
Computer Experts	programmers	programmer, DBA, technical specialist
Users	departmental	user groups

Exhibit 8.16

A Comparison of File Systems and Database Management Systems

also provides for the separation of logical and physical concerns, which leads to program data independence (see Exhibit 8.16).

In contrast, with the use of a file system, there is much data redundancy. Access to data in several files is awkward and time-consuming. Further, there is little assurance that the same data items in different files are defined similarly or have been kept updated. This results in a lack of data integrity. Programs and data are dependent, meaning that a change in either can cause changes to be required in the other.

Database management systems have some significant disadvantages, however. The sophisticated DBMS software designed to run on mainframe computers costs hundreds of thousands of dollars—substantially more than the cost for file systems software. Generally, organizations considering purchasing a DBMS of this sophistication will have to move to a more powerful model of computer. This upgrade is necessary in order to accommodate the large amount of primary memory the DBMS itself will occupy, as well as to ensure a quick response time to users' requests to compensate for the greater amount of time required to process the DBMS.

The biggest drawback of a DBMS, however, is the conversion effort required to move from a file-based system to a database system. First the database must be designed—which entails forming a committee representing the potential users. The committee members work together to establish the critical data items, their definitions, and the access privileges. A specialist must be hired to function as the database administrator, and technical experts must be brought in for the DBMS software itself. Programmers and end-users must be trained in how to use the new DBMS.

In contrast, file systems have been used in organizations for years, and most programmers know how to use them. No lengthy coordination effort among many diverse user groups across the company is necessary. Rather, programmers can continue to work with users to develop programs that will meet their departmental information needs.

Its strengths of centralization of the data and the ease of retrieval also lead to one of the main drawbacks of a DBMS. The all-eggs-in-one-basket approach increases a company's vulnerability to failures of the database system itself. All the application programs and user requests using the DBMS cannot function until the system is corrected. Further, the centralization of data offers a wealth of well-organized company data to an intruder, if he or she can penetrate the security system. The great overlap and chaos of individual file systems act as a form of protection in this sense.

In summary, the major trade-off in deciding to use a DBMS rather than a file system is whether the benefits of greater access to more accurate and timely corporate data are worth the considerably higher costs of a more powerful computer system, expensive data management software, greater numbers of specialized personnel, the higher risk associated with conversion efforts, and the more widespread impact of temporary failures of the DBMS system. Overall experience has been for companies to work toward using a DBMS as the foundation of their corporate data needs. This trend will continue to strengthen as new advances are made in improving the ease of interaction with the DBMS and as database recovery and security protection schemes are improved.

The foregoing comparison is primarily relevant in the case of organizations that have a need to share an extensive amount of corporate data. In these situations, medium- to large-size database management systems make sense. But another trend is for a microcomputer DBMS, costing from several hundred dollars to $2000, to be used where there is a need to share a limited amount of data. These systems could be used in small companies or in divisions or departments of large companies. Chapter 14, "Microcomputer Databases," will show how these DBMS work.

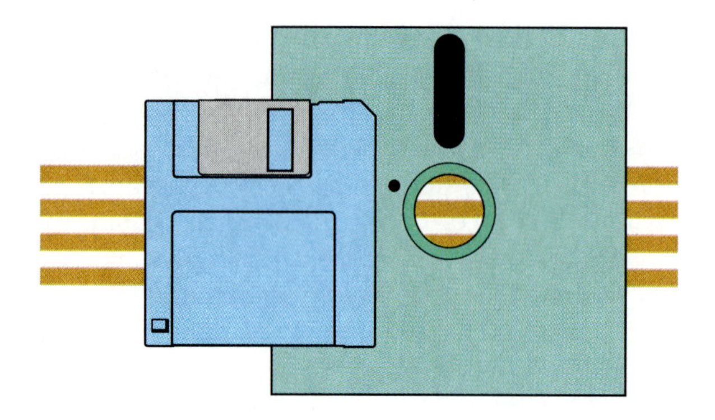

Computers at Work

United Technologies Puts Insurance Costs On-line

United Technologies Corp. had a lot of valuable information it could not use. Locked away in volumes of books were claims data and other insurance-related records dating back to 1976. This was the corporate insurance database.

Insurance records tell a company more than just how big a check it is going to have to make out to its insurance company. These records enable a company to negotiate more favorable premiums with insurance companies and also are used to make crucial decisions that could make or break certain lines of business.

These decisions, not lightly made, were not being served by UTC's hard-copy insurance records. The corporation required active measurement and independent analysis of how the claims affected lines of manufacturing ranging from elevators to air conditioners to jet engines.

UTC at first attacked its problem by developing an on-line insurance database using Lotus 1-2-3. When it was clear that Lotus was not designed to be a major repository of information for a Fortune 500 corporation, UTC developed its Risk Research & Reporting (R3) system—a full-fledged relational database, largely built with Oracle—which revolutionized the operations of UTC's risk management group.

Now, for instance, a trend analysis of insurance outlays helps determine where UTC should hire or fire workers or close a plant. Insurance payment reports can be used to spot patterns of product liability which help determine whether it is worthwhile to manufacture a given product.

John Polakovic, director of risk management, came aboard on July 1, 1986, as a part of a new group charged with taking control of UTC's property and casualty insurance purchasing. The risk management group, which also included MIS and a full-time in-house insurance actuary, set about putting insurance records to work for UTC. Polakovic quickly found the hard-copy data wholly inadequate for the task. "It was useless as a management tool," he said. The data could not be manipulated, details were lacking and the historical information was poor. The latest records were three months old.

In the risk management group, MIS was represented by David Chzaszcz (pronounced "Shah-zee"), director of corporate information systems. Chzaszcz decided in the summer of 1987 to bring MIS resources to bear on the problem. With the assistance of Oracle Corp. of Belmont, Calif., UTC developed a relational database.

Almost all insurance companies store their records on electronic media. A large proportion of these have relational databases to generate flexible and timely reports for their own purposes. "The insurance companies gear their systems for generating internal reports first," Chzaszcz observed. "Reports to comply with government statutes come second, and customer reports are at the very bottom of the list."

The R3 system liberated UTC from depending upon reports which trickled down from its insurance companies. Oracle permitted a tape-to-tape capability by which UTC acquired raw data records from its insurers' systems and fed it into R3. With R3, the UTC actuary had a lot of flexibility in putting information into whatever format he wanted. "That put us in an enviable position," Chzaszcz said. "We had our own statistical information with which we can present our version of what our insurance costs should be."

The relational grouping characteristics of R3 are almost endless. The actuary is able to cluster information into similar forecast groups. For example, insurance statistics relating to machine operations or high-tech assembly businesses can be analyzed independently.

"Information can be broken down in finer detail than the insurance companies can, or are likely to, give you," said Chzaszcz, adding that R3 provides state-of-the-art loss detail. The actuary can report on who is causing what accidents and how much the accidents are costing. He can generate reports on the frequency of claims and their severity: He can detail how much minor workmen's compensation claims are costing as opposed to claims for serious back injuries, for example.

Armed with this information, UTC now insures different parts of the diverse corporation with different insurance companies, with those whose policies provide the most cost effective coverage.

Hidden costs have been uncovered. According to Chzaszcz, because of the R3, the risk management group can report to senior management with real dollar savings. The exact figure is something of a state secret because, as Chzaszcz put it, "we want to keep our cards close to the vest." However, he did indicate that the system cost about two years' worth of outside actuarial service and that in 1990, its third year, R3 will have more than paid for itself.

Summary and Key Terms

In an information system, data are organized into files. A collection of related characters forms a **field.** An occurrence of all fields is called a **record.** A **file** is a collection of similar types of records. A **primary key** is a data item that has a unique value that can be used to identify a single record. An integrated collection of files is called a **database.** Different **data organizations** affect how the efficiency of accessing or locating specific data records and what types of questions can be easily answered.

The simplest file organization is **sequential file organization**, in which records are sequenced by primary key and are accessed in sequence. Another approach to file organization is called **indexed file organization.** Indexed files are organized in logical sequence by key and have an index that shows the correspondence between the key value and the disk location of the record. **Relative file organization** arranges records relative to a key. This key value is used to directly calculate the disk address of a record.

In information systems based on files, sharing data between files requires the use of the **sort/merge** method to match records in the two files as they are processed. This approach can lead to an abundance of files. Although different files support different applications, there is much duplication of data items or **data redundancy.**

The concept of a database has emerged to provide a more effective way of sharing organizational data. In fact, it is a more uniform way of managing data as a critical organizational resource. Conceptually, a **database** is an integrated collection of data items, which can be retrieved in any combination necessary to produce needed information. In contrast, a file system provides no integrated way of accessing, linking, or managing the data contained in a collection of files.

A major purpose of the **database management system (DBMS)** is to divide the accessing of data into logical and physical concerns. The logical question is concerned with which particular data are needed to answer a variety of questions users might have.

Exactly how the data should actually reside on the disk or be accessed is the physical question. A DBMS allows programs and data to be more independent. **Program data independence** means that changes in either programs or data can be made without significantly affecting the other. In contrast, the use of a file system makes for **program data dependence.**

The logical description of the organization of the complete database is called its **schema.** The description of a subset of the total database that is useful in answering a user's particular question is called a **subschema.** Each subschema is also called a **user's view.**

The three major models for database organization are hierarchical, network, and relational. In a **hierarchical database structure,** the relationship among records is always **one-to-many.** Each parent, or higher-level record, can have one or more children, but each child, or lower-level record, can have only one parent. **Network database structure** allows **many-to-many** relationships among parent and children records. Also, it allows a record to be a child in more than one relationship. The third database model is the relational model and is based on presenting data in the form of tables or relations. The **relational database structure** shows relationships among records by linking tables together as needed.

The keeper of the database is called the **database administrator (DBA).** The DBA ensures the effectiveness of data retrieval, the accuracy and confidentiality of data, and keeps the physical database running efficiently. The creation and maintenance of the database structure is fundamental to management of the DBMS. A **data dictionary** is used to identify the data elements, records, and relationships that exist in the database. In addition, schemas, subschemas, and programs are identified in the data dictionary.

Authorization rules specifically state who is allowed to access the various data records. Another security protection used is the **audit log,** in which data on all operations performed by users of the database are chronologically recorded.

Greater access to corporate data by programmers and end-users, reduction of data redundancy, and program data independence are the major advantages of the DBMS, compared to file systems. However, the DBMS also has some significant advantages. For example, the sophisticated DBMS software designed to run on the larger computers can cost hundreds of thousands of dollars.

Also, organizations considering acquiring a sophisticated DBMS may have to move to a more powerful model of computer. The biggest drawback, however, is the conversion effort required to move from a file-based system to a database system.

Review Questions

1. Briefly identify the three basic types of data organization. What are the advantages of each?
2. Briefly describe the sequential file approach. What problems are associated with this method?
3. Explain how an index file system works. What disadvantages are associated with this method?
4. How is a relative file system organized? What advantages are offered by this approach?
5. What ways are available to share data using file systems?
6. Briefly define database. What logical and physical questions must be answered?
7. What are the three major models used in the organization of a database? How many of these models can the typical database use?
8. The Bartlett Corporation desires to create a database system that will provide the greatest possible flexibility. Which of the three database models would you recommend? Defend your position.
9. What features should a DBMS have in order to aid the database administrator?
10. Briefly discuss the advantages and disadvantages of a DBMS versus file systems.

T F **11.** A file is a collection of records made up of fields.

T F **12.** Direct access occurs when a single record can be retrieved from a file without the records preceding it being read.

T F **13.** The indexed file organization allows sequential access but not direct access.

T F **14.** In a relative access file organization, the position of a record in the file is determined by applying a hashing algorithm to the key value in the record.

T F **15.** A sort/merge utility is a method of combining selected data from several files.

T F **16.** A schema is a logical description of the organization of the database.

T F **17.** Program data independence is characteristic of traditional file systems.

T F **18.** In the hierarchical database model, data is presented in the form of tables.

T F **19.** The network database model is organized in a top-down manner which supports only one-to-many relationships.

T F **20.** Authorization rules specifically state who is allowed to do what with the various data records in a database.

21. _____ Which is not a common file organization?

a. hierarchical
b. sequential
c. relative
d. indexed sequential

22. _____ Which is not one of the three database models?

a. relative
b. hierarchical
c. network
d. relational

23. _____ What are the two common ways to access information in a file?

a. logical and physical
b. sequential and direct
c. dependent and independent
d. relative and indexed

24. _____ The database model in which data are presented in the form of a table is:

a. hierarchical
b. network
c. relative
d. relational

25. _____ The file organization that uses a hashing algorithm to locate records within a file is:

a. relative
b. sequential
c. network
d. indexed sequential

CHAPTER 9

Program Development

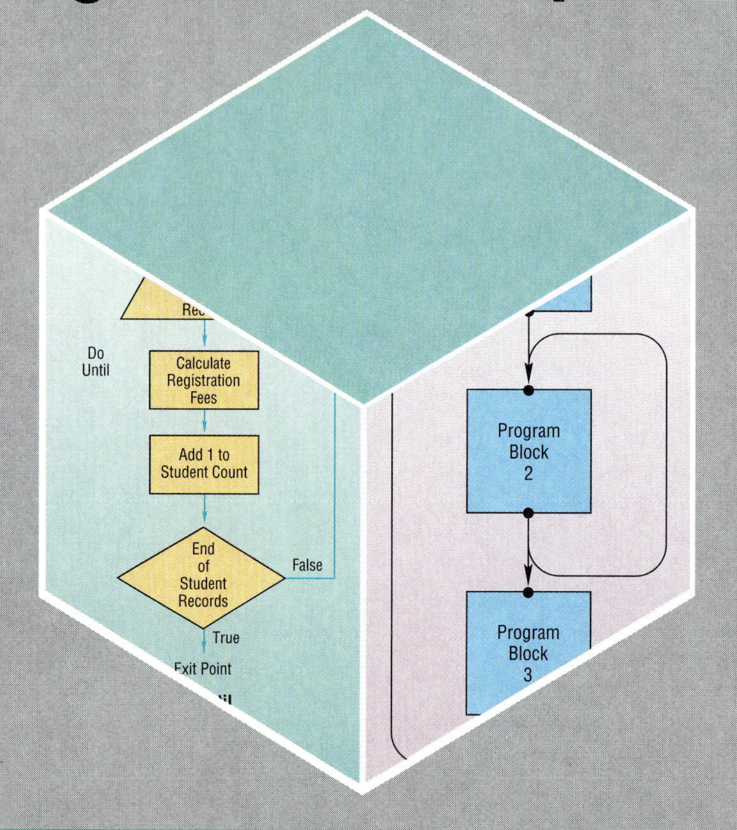

Without programs, computers would be useless collections of electronic parts. Every activity that a computer performs is in response to an instruction from the program. Programs control every phase of the information processing cycle from input, processing, storage, and retrieval of data to the output of information. As you learned in Chapter 7, "Systems Development," systems development is the process of designing an information system to satisfy a business need. One of the goals of the systems design stage of this process is to produce specifications for the programs that will control the processing of data to produce information. This chapter presents a more detailed look at the steps involved in producing the programs that breathe life into an information system.

In this chapter, you will learn to do the following:

1. Describe the two main goals in business programming and explain how they are achieved
2. List the three types of activities that take place during the program development process
3. Describe how top-down design is applied in program development
4. Describe how flowcharts and pseudocode are used in program module development
5. Explain the relationship between program design and program coding
6. Describe the purpose of program testing and the two types of test data

It is important to realize that every interaction a user has with a computer is under the control of a program. All common types of end-user software, from word processors to electronic spreadsheets to databases, are simply a program or set of programs. Whatever the software package, the computer is only capable of responding to requests in ways designated in the program.

Program Development Process

In the systems development life cycle, the systems acquisition phase is concerned with acquiring application software that solves a business problem. If acquiring a software package is not the best choice, then developing customized programs is an alternative.

The acquisition of either an existing software package or a customized package is dependent on the program specifications derived from the systems analysis and design phases. *Program specifications* are guidelines indicating the production goals of an information system (see

Exhibit 9.1). Specifications include the major functions and the required outputs, inputs, and data file organization.

Meeting these specifications is the role of program development. **Program development** establishes correct step-by-step procedures that will instruct a computer system to produce the desired results and be easily modified to accommodate future changes in specifications. The main goals in business programming are to develop programs that are correct and maintainable. A **correct program** completely and accurately performs the information processing activities stated in the program specifications. A **maintainable program** can be changed easily by the same or another programmer.

Creating a program that is both correct and maintainable can be achieved by following a simple rule: programs should be written so they are easily understood by people. Why? First, readable code makes it easier to resume work on a program that hasn't been worked on for a few days. Second, if programs are intelligibly written, others can understand the program and offer their assistance. Third, a readable program is far easier for another programmer to modify in the future. The techniques discussed in this chapter are all geared toward developing correct and maintainable programs.

The **program development process** involves the three distinct activities of program design, coding, and testing. The purpose of program

Exhibit 9.1

Program Specifications for the Book Fair Project

```
PROGRAM SPECIFICATIONS FOR BOOK FAIR PROJECT

Project:      Book Sales and Purchase Analysis Program
Purpose:      This program is to support the sales of
                 books at the Book Fair by simulating the
                 action of our cash register.
              It should do the following major tasks:
                 A.  Process each customer's purchase and
                        print a customer receipt.
                 B.  Collect data from each purchase
                        transaction and print a management
                        summary report at the end of the day.

Input Data:   Purchase price and identification number of
                 each book
Data File:    Customer purchase data

Output        CRT display of input for each customer
Information:     transaction and totals for the cashier
              Printed customer receipt
              Management summary report of all purchase
                 transactions
```

design is to develop a "road map" to meet the program specifications. The translation of the program design into a computer program using a programming language is called program coding. Testing checks the correctness of a program's design and code.

Most people think of program development as primarily the coding of the program. Actually, program coding should account for the smallest amount of the total effort put into program development. Exhibit 9.2 shows the typical percentage of time that good programmers spend on each of the programming activities. Far more time is spent on both designing and testing than on coding.

The program development process includes the features associated with many problem-solving activities. An organized and methodical approach will usually yield greater dividends than a haphazard one. The approach discussed here is called structured programming. **Structured programming** uses particular design methods to develop solutions to programming problems. It includes the use of top-down design, module logic, and control-structure methods, which are discussed in the next section of this chapter. Following this approach leads to correct and maintainable programs.

It is important to understand that once a program has been designed, coded, tested, and put into use, it will not remain static. Just as the business world is dynamic and ever-changing, information systems must also change in response to changing business needs. Thus, although a program has been carefully designed to meet a business need, it will often need to be changed over time if it is to continue to meet that need. The process of **program maintenance** involves the changing of existing programs to keep them up to date and useful. Given the large number of programs currently in place in information systems, it is more common for a programmer to be involved in

Exhibit 9.2

Time Allocation of Programming Activities

Good programmers actually spend very little time coding their programs. Much more time is spent designing programs and checking designs and codes.

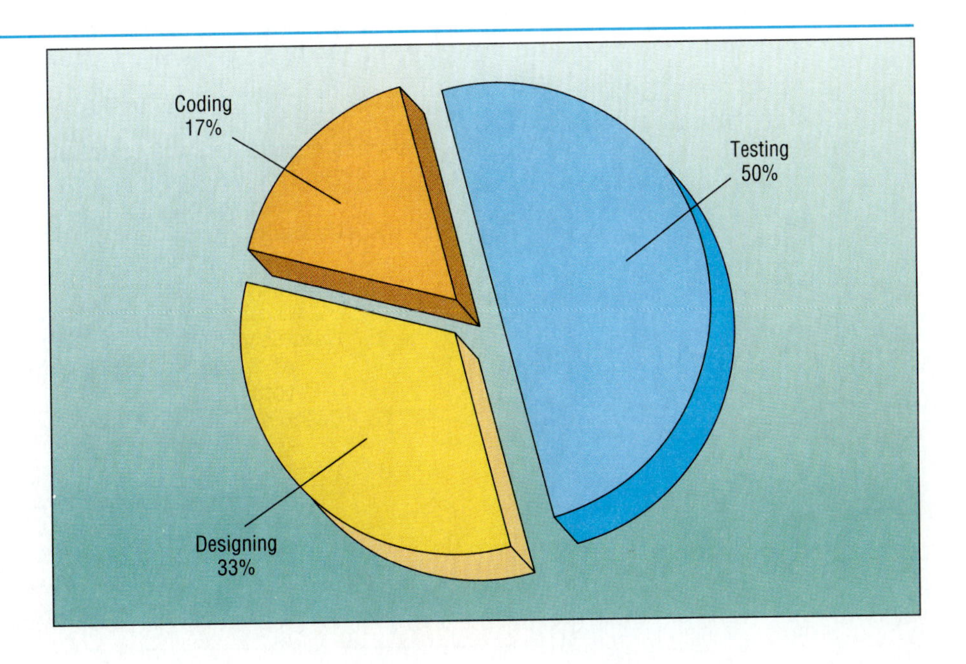

the maintenance of existing programs than in the creation of new programs. Some estimates indicate that as much as 80 percent of the programming staff in large companies is devoted to maintaining existing programs, and only 20 percent is devoted to the creation of new information systems. This is why the use of structured programming as a method to make programs easier to maintain is so important.

Program Design

Program specifications are an outcome of the systems design phase and are the point from which the programmer starts work. Program specifications are a business-oriented overview of the project that specifies what is to be done, rather than the way it is to be accomplished.

What is to be gained from the program specifications document? It becomes a method of communication among the systems designer, programmer, and other interested parties such as the user and review teams. It encourages understanding of the problem, its scope, and its expected solution. It provides the standard by which the performance of the finished program will be measured.

For programming purposes, this high-level document needs to become more specific. This can be accomplished through **step-wise refinement**, in which general statements are broken down into lower level specifics. The major tasks for the book fair project (introduced in Exhibit 9.1)

Exhibit 9.3

Step-Wise Refinement of Customer Transaction Processing Task

BOOK FAIR SALES AND PURCHASE ANALYSIS PROGRAM

Major Tasks

A. Process a customer's transaction.
B. Print the Management Summary Report.

Subtasks

A. Process customer's transaction.
   1. Display the individual book purchases of each customer.
   2. Calculate and display the customer's total book purchases.
   3. Provide a 20 percent discount for customers who are store employees.
   4. Calculate and display the state sales tax at 6 percent of the customer's purchase total.
   5. Calculate and display the final customer purchase total.
   6. Print a customer's receipt on the printer. The receipt will contain the information specified in items 1 through 5 above.
   7. For each purchase, collect data and price on each book, if discount was granted, and total currency collected.

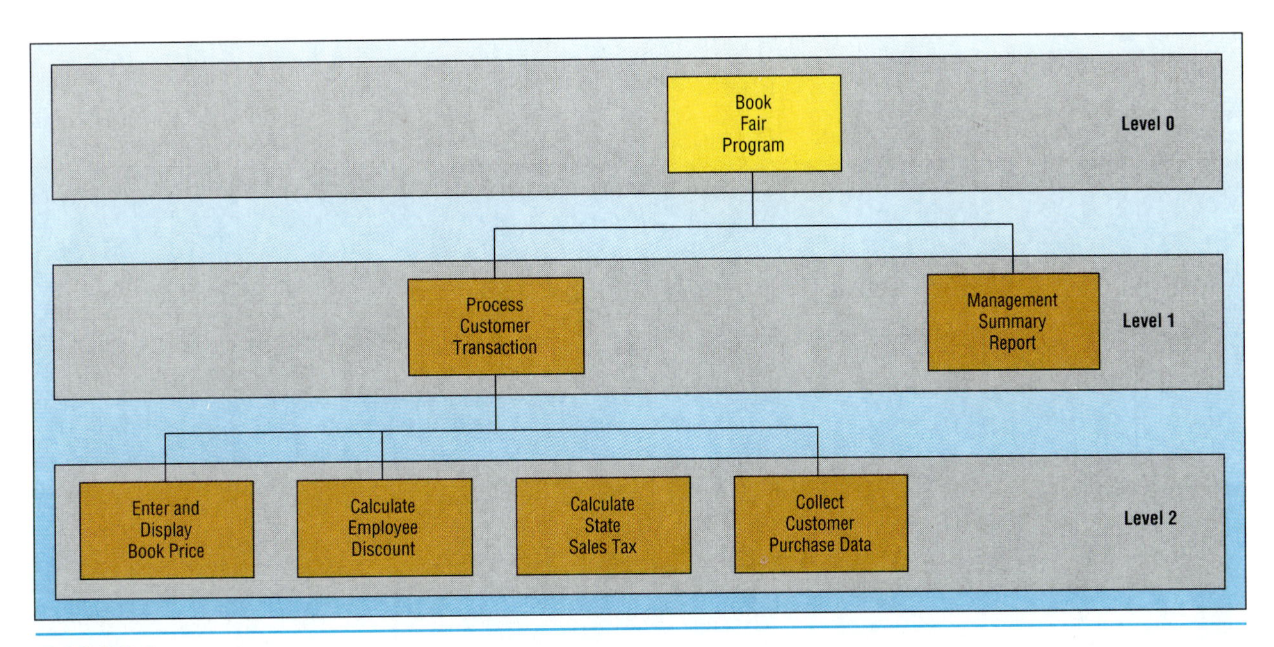

Exhibit 9.4

The Structure Chart for the Book Fair Program

A structure chart shows the overall organization of the program design and the hierarchy of program modules.

are to process a customer transaction and print a management summary report of all transactions for a given time period. Processing in this case means a customer transaction is broken down into seven specific subtasks (see Exhibit 9.3). Further detail could also be developed for the data file and output information.

Top-Down Design

Structured programming uses top-down design to take the overall problem and break it down into smaller problems that are more easily understood and solved. The program design for the overall problem is shown through a structure chart; each of the subproblems are called modules.

Structure charts are used to represent the overall organization of a program design using a hierarchical structure of program modules (see Exhibit 9.4). The purpose of the structure chart is to show how the parts of a program design make up the whole program and further define the relationship among the modules—their levels and their superior and subordinate modules.

The structure chart fosters communication among the programmer, designer, user, and other interested parties. It has many of the attributes of a table of contents since it shows major headings and subheadings. It has been compared to a company's organization chart because it has a similar look.

Each of the boxes in a structure chart is referred to as a **module**. A structure chart has only one module at its top level. This level is referred to as level 0 and is used to state the purpose of the total program. Level 1 modules are used to specify the major parts of the program specified in the

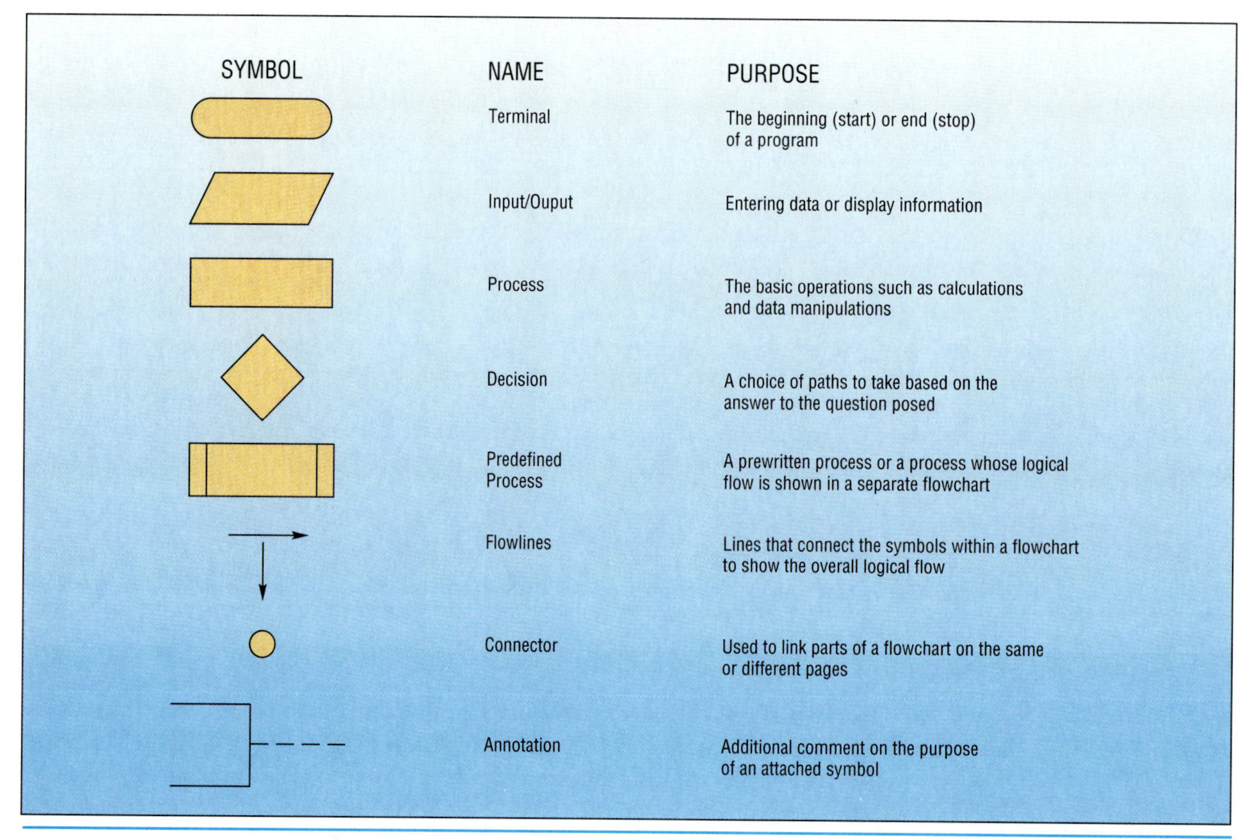

SYMBOL	NAME	PURPOSE
	Terminal	The beginning (start) or end (stop) of a program
	Input/Ouput	Entering data or display information
	Process	The basic operations such as calculations and data manipulations
	Decision	A choice of paths to take based on the answer to the question posed
	Predefined Process	A prewritten process or a process whose logical flow is shown in a separate flowchart
	Flowlines	Lines that connect the symbols within a flowchart to show the overall logical flow
	Connector	Used to link parts of a flowchart on the same or different pages
	Annotation	Additional comment on the purpose of an attached symbol

Exhibit 9.5

Standard Flowchart Symbols

level 0 module. The book fair program has two major tasks: processing customer transactions and printing the management summary report.

In Exhibit 9.4, the processing of customer transactions can be seen in further detail in the level 2 modules, which are subordinate to the level 1 Process Customer Transaction module. These level 2 tasks include the subtasks of entering and displaying the price of the book and selecting the employee discount rate.

Notice that the Management Summary Report module is not broken into lower level modules. In this case the program designer felt that further refinement was unnecessary since this report involved very simple calculations and logic and consisted mostly of averages and final totals.

Module Design

The creative part of program design is the decision of how to subdivide tasks and to what level modules should be broken down. The lowest level modules should be single-purpose functions that can be used as building blocks in higher level tasks. Ultimately, the overall design must be translated into a series of specific steps that when followed leads to the desired information system. A series of exact steps to accomplish the specific task of a module is called an **algorithm.** All programming tasks can be broken down into fundamental building blocks known as **control structures**. Two of the tools used in describing the step-by-step processing logic for a module are flowcharts and pseudocode.

Flowcharts

Flowcharts represent a program's processing flow by showing the operations to be performed, the order in which they are performed, and the conditions that affect this order. Exhibit 9.5 shows the standardized symbols used in flowcharts. As shown in Exhibit 9.6, these symbols are connected by flow lines to present step-by-step procedures. Let's see how the concepts of program flowcharts can be used for calculating the employees' discount (in the book fair program).

The annotation symbol at the upper right of Exhibit 9.6 states the purpose of the flowchart. The oval terminal symbol indicates where to look for the start of the programming flow. The diamond symbol shows that there are two possible paths, depending on whether or not the person buying the book is a store employee. If the person is a store employee then the flow proceeds to set the discount rate at 20 percent. If the person is not a store employee then the discount rate is zero.

Following either flowline leads to the connector; the process rectangle that follows indicates the customer's purchase amount is to be reduced by the appropriate discount. Once this is done, the output

Exhibit 9.6

Flowchart for Calculating Employee Discount

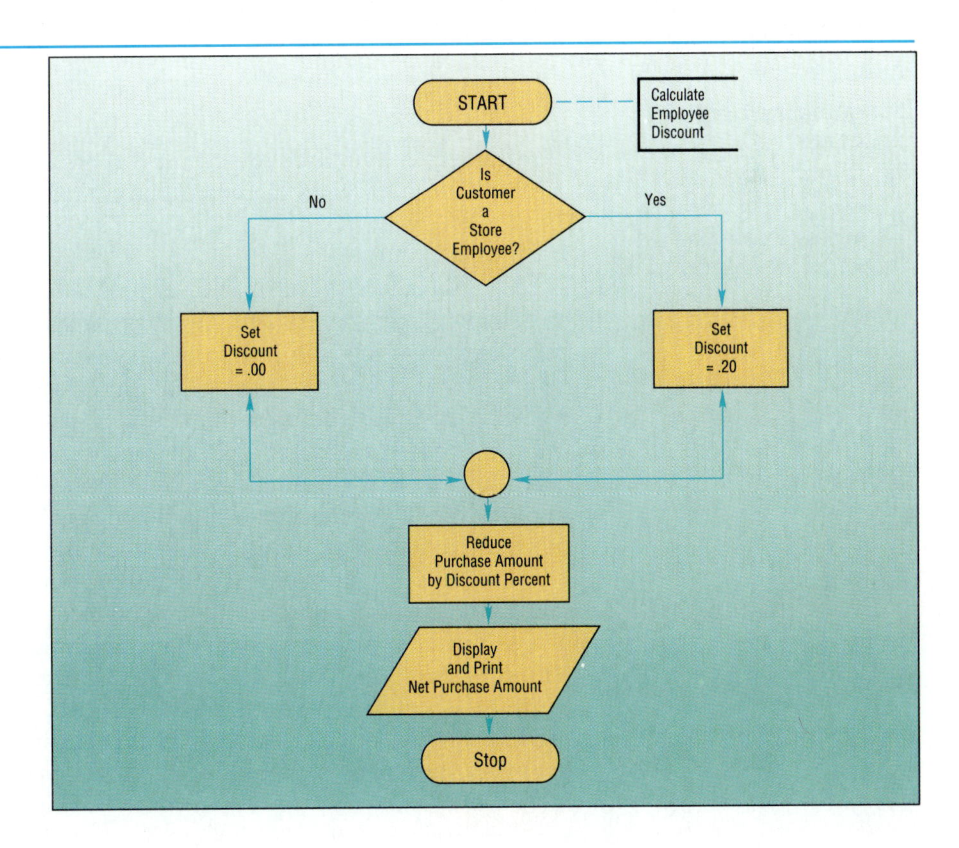

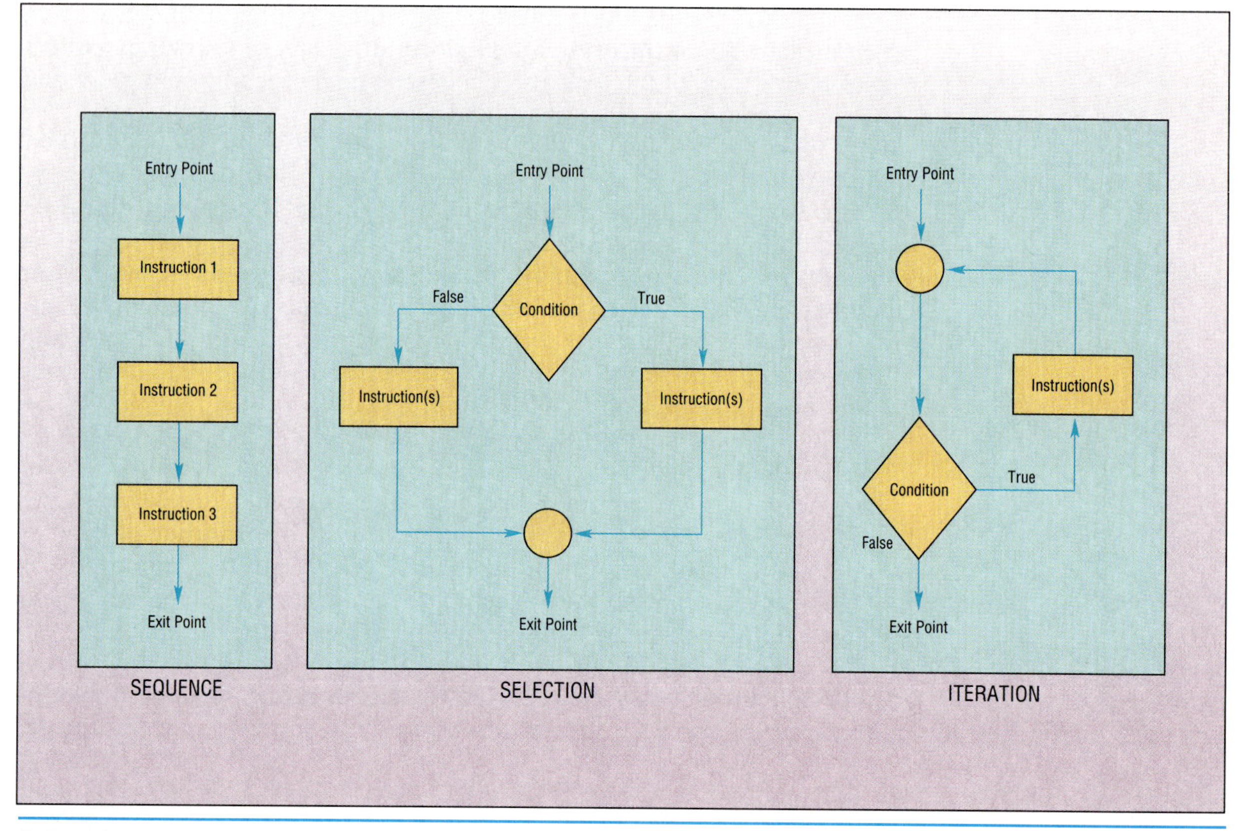

Exhibit 9.7

Fundamental Control Structures

The three control structures for use in all structured programs are sequence, selection, and iteration.

parallelogram symbol shows that the results should be displayed and printed. The oval symbol indicates the end of the flowchart.

Control Structures

A very important part of structured programming is the concept of control structures. Many years ago, two mathematicians, Bohm and Jacopini, published an article in a prestigious computer science journal proving that all programs could be designed using only three fundamental building blocks, or control structures.

A **control structure** is a method of controlling the order of execution of the programming statements within a program. The group of statements being controlled is called a **block**. The three control structures or patterns are sequence, selection, and iteration, or loop (see Exhibit 9.7).

The **sequence control structure** is a series of statements in a block that are executed in order from top to bottom. Exhibit 9.8 shows an example of a sequence control structure that calculates registration fees for college students. First the student identification number, student name, and number of credits taken are entered into the program. Second, the registration fees are calculated. Third, the results are displayed as output. For every student these same steps will be executed in this order.

Exhibit 9.8

Sequence Control Structure

All statements within the block are executed in order each time the block is entered.

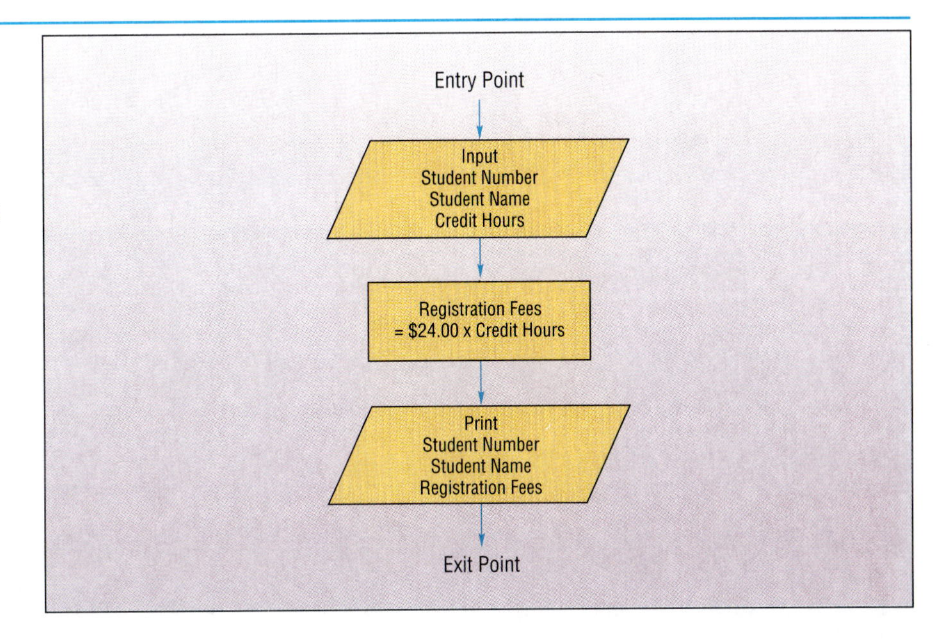

In programming languages, the sequence control structure is represented by the actual positioning of the instructions (or statements) within the program. Normally, the instructions within a program are processed from top to bottom. The selection and iteration control structures provide ways to interrupt this normal top-to-bottom flow within the program.

The **selection control structure** is a block of statements that are executed differently depending on whether a decision statement is true or false. In Exhibit 9.9 the total fees for a student registering at college depends on whether he or she will be living in a dorm. If the student wants on-campus residency (the condition is true), then fees for the dorm and meals should be added to the total registration fees; otherwise (the condition is false) no dorm or meal fees are to be included, because the student is living off campus.

This particular form of selection structure is called IF. . .THEN. A variation is the IF. . .THEN. . .ELSE, also shown in Exhibit 9.9. Here the selection control structure shows a block that adds one-half or the entire health service fee to the student's registration fees, depending on whether the student is taking twelve units or more.

The **iteration control structure** is a block of statements that are repeated a number of times, depending on certain conditions. You can see in Exhibit 9.10 why iteration is also called a **loop structure**. There are two forms of looping, depending on whether the conditions are pretested or post-tested.

The loop structures shown in Exhibit 9.10 on page 225 are used to calculate the registration fees for each student until all student records have been processed. Because the DO WHILE is a pretest loop, the first student's record is read before the loop begins since the first question asked is if there

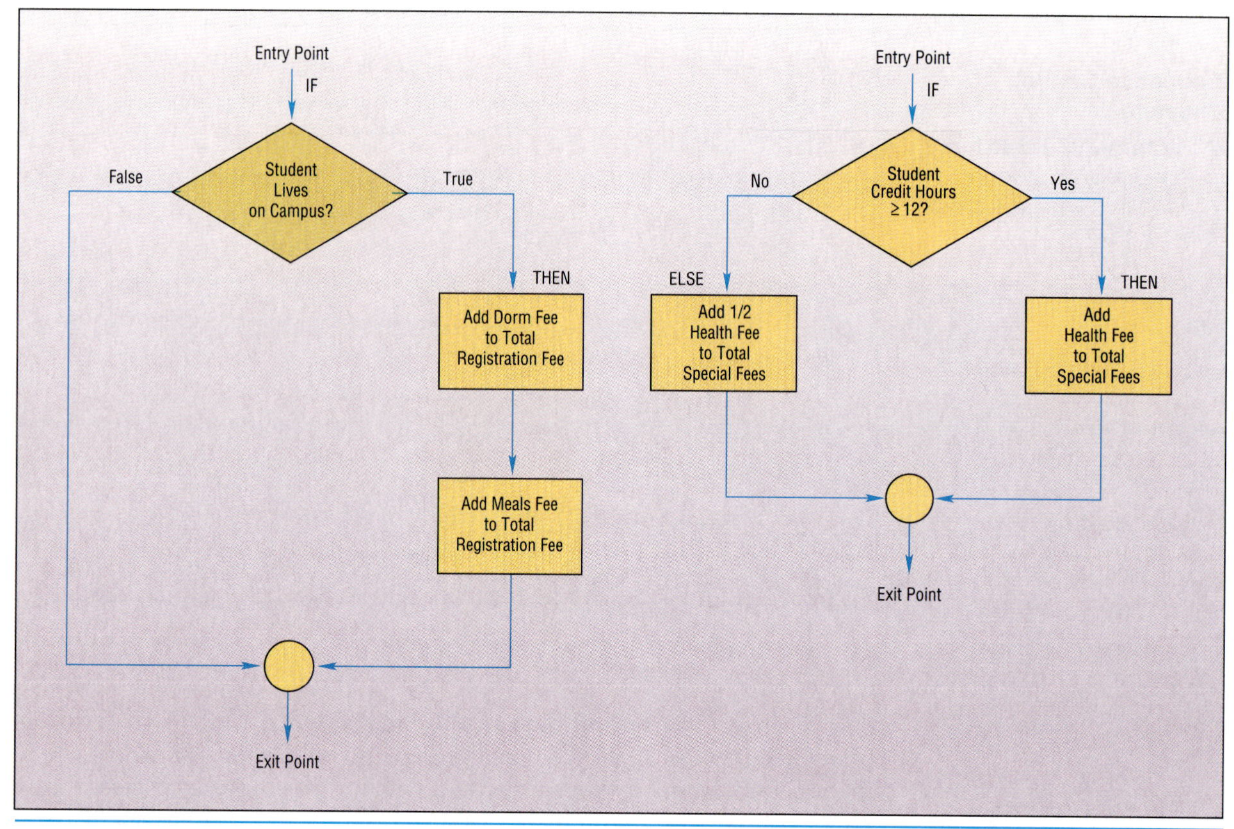

Exhibit 9.9

Selection Control Structures

Shown are two forms of the selection control structure: IF...THEN and IF...THEN...ELSE. Each block of statements is executed differently depending on whether the answer to the IF statement is yes or no.

are any more student records. If there are, the fees are calculated and the next student record is read. When all student records have been processed, this block is exited.

The DO UNTIL is a post-test loop. After each student's fee has been calculated, the question asked is if this completes the student records to be processed. If the answer is false, then the next student record is read and the fee is determined. Otherwise, the loop is exited. The major difference between these two forms of loop structures is that the DO UNTIL block is always executed at least once because the condition (decision diamond) is a post-test, whereas the DO WHILE condition is a pretest, and the whole process could be skipped.

A program flowchart can consist of any or all of these blocks, depending on the nature of the program. Additionally, one control structure may be used inside another. This is commonly referred to as *nesting*. For instance, a loop construct may contain a selection construct, which in turn may have a sequence construct.

There are some general rules for program design using control structures. These rules concern what is known as **single-entry, single-exit processing**, in which each block has one entry point and one exit point. Exhibit 9.11 on page 226 shows an example of well-structured and poorly structured ways of controlling the overall processing of a program.

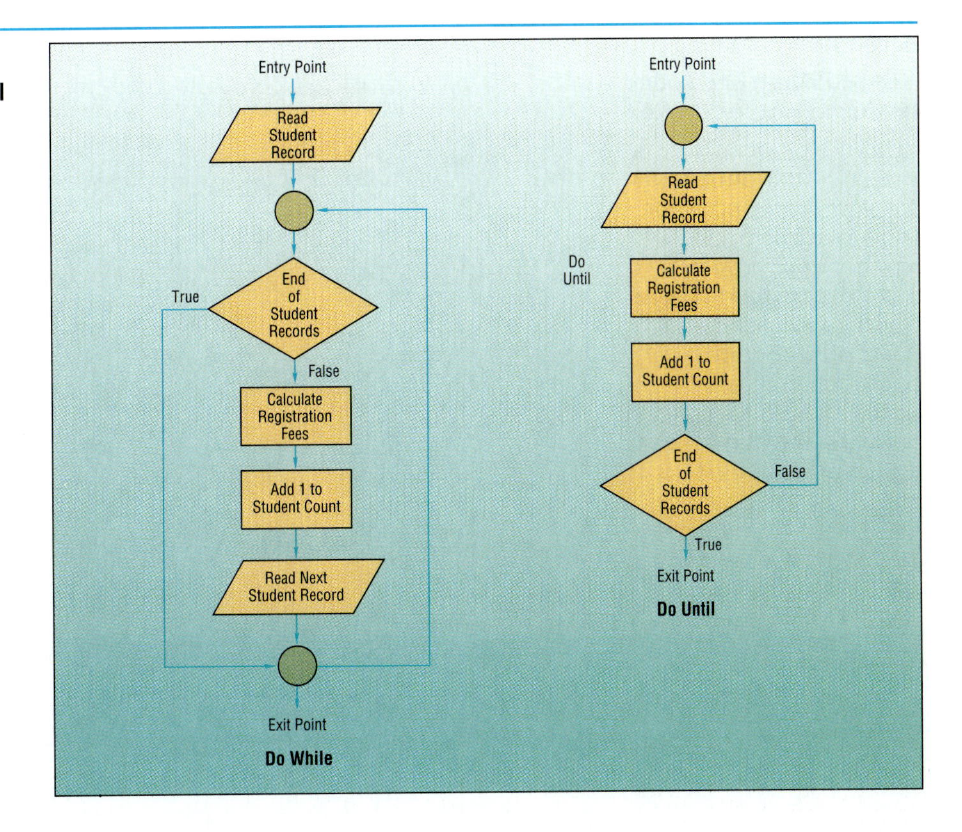

Exhibit 9.10

Iterative (Looping) Control Structures

Shown are two forms of the iterative control structure. The block of statements is repeated while the condition is true (DO WHILE) or until the condition is true (DO UNTIL).

The poorly structured approach is shown on the left. Programs written in this way are known as **spaghetti code** since the flow of the program goes any which way and individual blocks have multiple entry and exit points. In a much more complex program that has hundreds, perhaps thousands of blocks, it would be almost impossible, or at least very time consuming, to decipher the program. In contrast, the design approach on the right shows the well-structured way, in which entry and exit points for each block are restricted. Consequently, the purpose of each block becomes clearer, as does the relationship between blocks.

Pseudocode

It is very common for those planning a program to first write out the underlying logic using English statements before diving into the intricacies of a particular programming language. **Pseudocode** uses English-like keywords to describe the logic of a program using control structures.

Some of the key words used in pseudocode for entering data are INPUT, READ, ENTER, and GET. To indicate a calculation, the keywords COMPUTE, CALCULATE, FIND, and DETERMINE can be used. For displaying results, keywords such as DISPLAY, OUTPUT, PRINT, and WRITE are used.

Exhibit 9.11

Well-Structured and Poorly Structured Program Design

To create an easy-to-maintain program, each program block should be single-purpose and the flow between blocks should be limited to single points of entry and exit. The spaghetti code approach on the left would be hard to maintain because any changes to a program block would affect changes in many other blocks throughout the program.

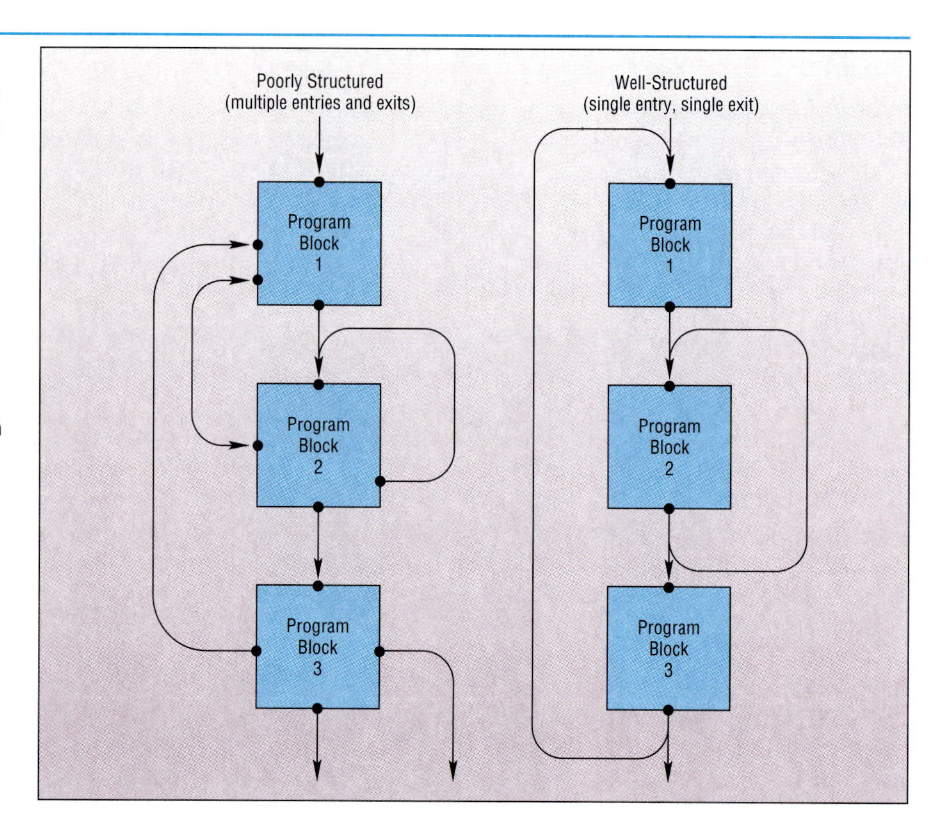

To show the selection control structure in pseudocode, the IF. . . THEN. . .ELSE. . .END IF key words are used, and indentation is used to mark the start and finish of a particular block of statements. Also, the DO WHILE. . .END DO and DO UNTIL. . .END DO key words are used for looping iterative structures (see Exhibit 9.12).

The particular keywords used in pseudocode will vary depending on the programming language that will ultimately be used in program coding. Often keywords similar to the keywords of the programming language are used. This saves time when the programmer goes from program design to coding.

Exhibit 9.13 shows how pseudocode could be applied to a payroll problem in which the amount of the paycheck is dependent on the number of hours an employee worked; hours over forty are paid at time and a half. Since there are many employees to pay, the iterative control structure is used, as shown by the DO UNTIL. . .END DO block.

The key decision concerning the employee's total pay is whether he or she worked overtime. Selection control is shown by the IF. . .END IF block. The THEN is used to calculate pay for the true condition, in which hours worked is greater than forty. ELSE shows the false condition. The processing of the paycheck is shown by the BEGIN. . .END sequence block. In addition to the control structures, other key words are shown, such as READ employee pay record, COMPUTE overtime hours, and PRINT total pay.

Exhibit 9.12

Common Keywords Used in Pseudocode

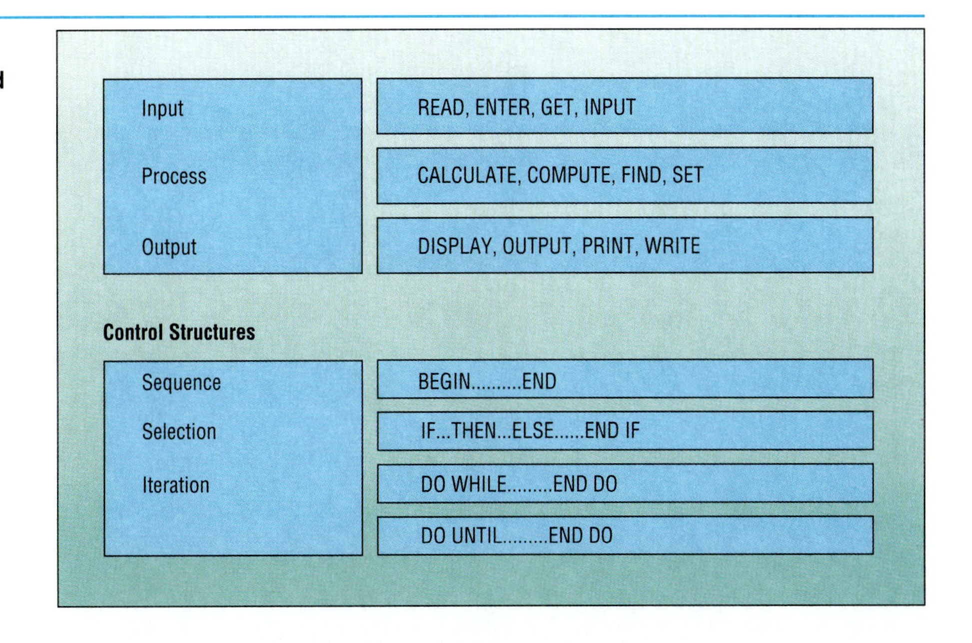

Exhibit 9.13 also shows the problem as it would appear as a flowchart. The two module design tools have many similarities, however, the flowchart gives a better visual picture of the logical flow of a complex program, whereas pseudocode is often easier to code from since it is written in programming language-like statements. Many organizations establish one approach or the other as their standard. Because of the closeness of pseudocode to the programming language used in coding the program, pseudocode is generally becoming more popular than flowcharts.

Once a program design is complete, before actual coding begins, the design should be thoroughly reviewed to make sure it meets all the original specifications. Interactions with the ultimate users of the program can also be important at this stage to ensure that the program will meet their needs. In general, any errors or omissions in the design are best caught as early as possible. Once coding begins it becomes very expensive and time-consuming to make changes.

Program Coding

Once the design phase is finished and a complete set of flowcharts or pseudocode statements has been developed and reviewed, it is time to start coding this logic into the appropriate programming language. Chapter 10, "Programming Languages," introduces the characteristics of the most popular programming languages and discusses the advantages and disadvantages of each.

This section concentrates on the purpose of coding and shows how the control structures and processing steps are translated into the

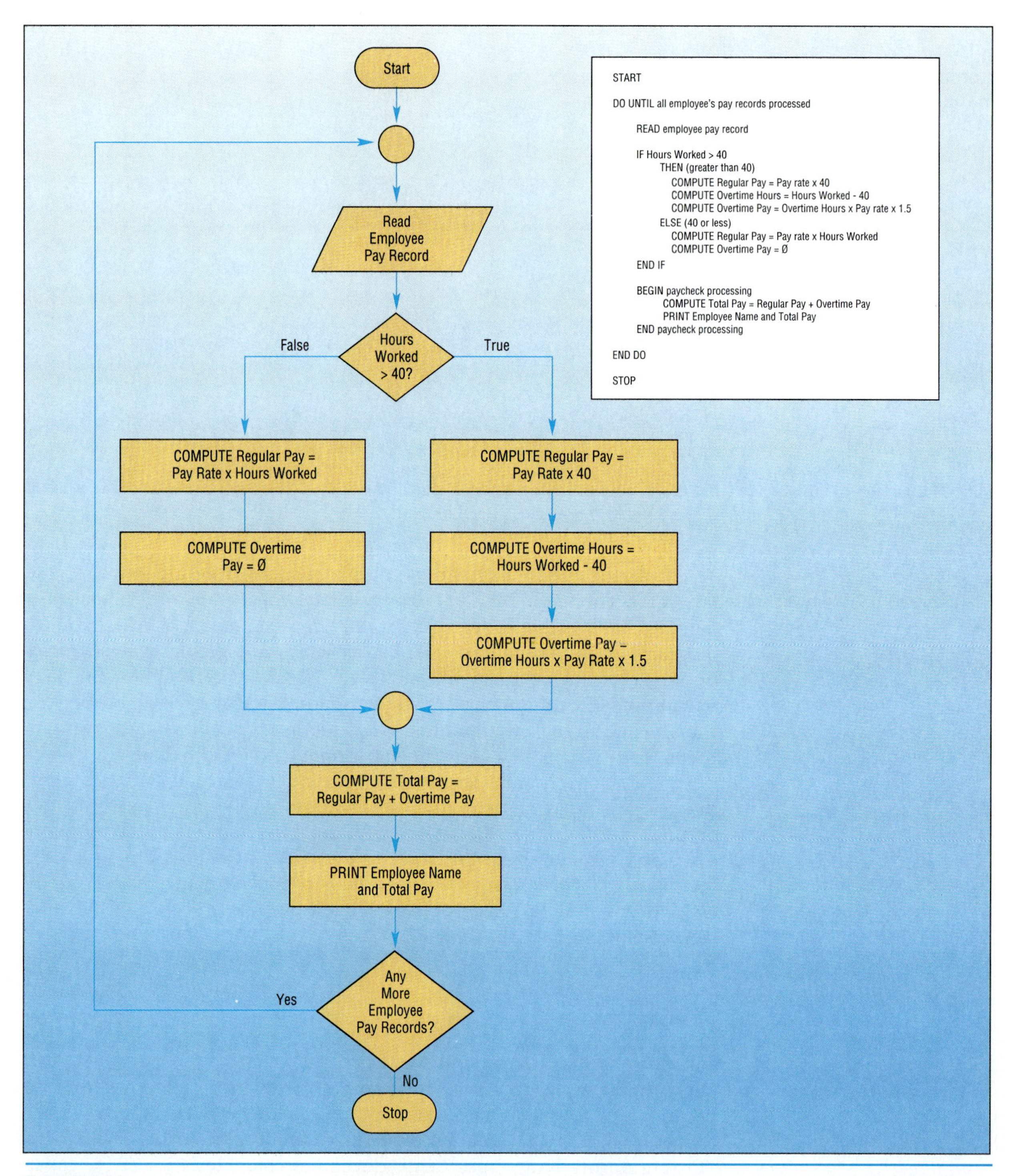

Exhibit 9.13

Equivalent Pseudocode Statements and Flowchart

By looking at the two diagrams, you can see the close correspondence between them. In actual practice these initial diagrams would have to be refined to check for the end of the employee pay records (i.e. end-of-file) and reset the overtime pay to zero after each read statement.

Exhibit 9.14

Microsoft's QuickBASIC Language Version of Payroll Problem

Translating from pseudocode or flowchart to most programming languages is relatively easy.

```
DO

        READ Empl.Name$, Hrs.Wrked

        IF Hrs.Wrked > 40.0 THEN
                Ovtm.Hrs = Hrs.Wrked - 40.0
                Reg.Pay = Pay.Rate * 40.0
                Ovtm.Pay = Ovtm.Hrs * Pay.Rate * 1.5
          ELSE
                Reg.Pay = Pay.Rate * Hrs.Wrked
                Ovtm.Pay = 0
         END IF

         Total.Pay = Reg.Pay + Ovtm.Pay
         PRINT Empl.Name$, Total.Pay

LOOP UNTIL Empl.Name$ = "Last"
```

programming language. Each programming language has a particular set of instructions or commands that can be used to accomplish specific tasks such as reading in data, making calculations, or displaying information.

A programming language has very specific rules that govern its use, such as the spelling of commands or instructions, where they must be placed, the structure of the instructions, the punctuation needed, and many other items. These rules constitute the **syntax** of the language and must be followed exactly; otherwise the computer will not be able to follow the instructions.

Structured program design emphasizes the development of the overall design through the use of a structure chart showing the hierarchy of modules. The lowest level modules are designed to perform a single task, the processing logic of which could either be flowcharted or written out in pseudocode. **Program coding** is the translation of the overall program design and specific module logic into a particular programming language.

As you saw earlier, the coding operation should take about half as much time as the design effort. In most cases, the coding of the design into the selected programming language is a relatively straightforward activity. Exhibit 9.14 displays the payroll problem coded in a particular version of the popular programming language BASIC. Compare the closeness of the pseudocode version of Exhibit 9.13 with the BASIC statements.

The newer programming languages have specific commands directly designed to implement control structures, and thus the translation is easy. Versions of older programming languages, developed prior to the concept of control structures, can be somewhat inflexible, making the conversion more difficult since several commands are necessary to implement a control structure. Exhibit 9.15 shows the program design for the book fair project and the way it would be coded in the BASIC

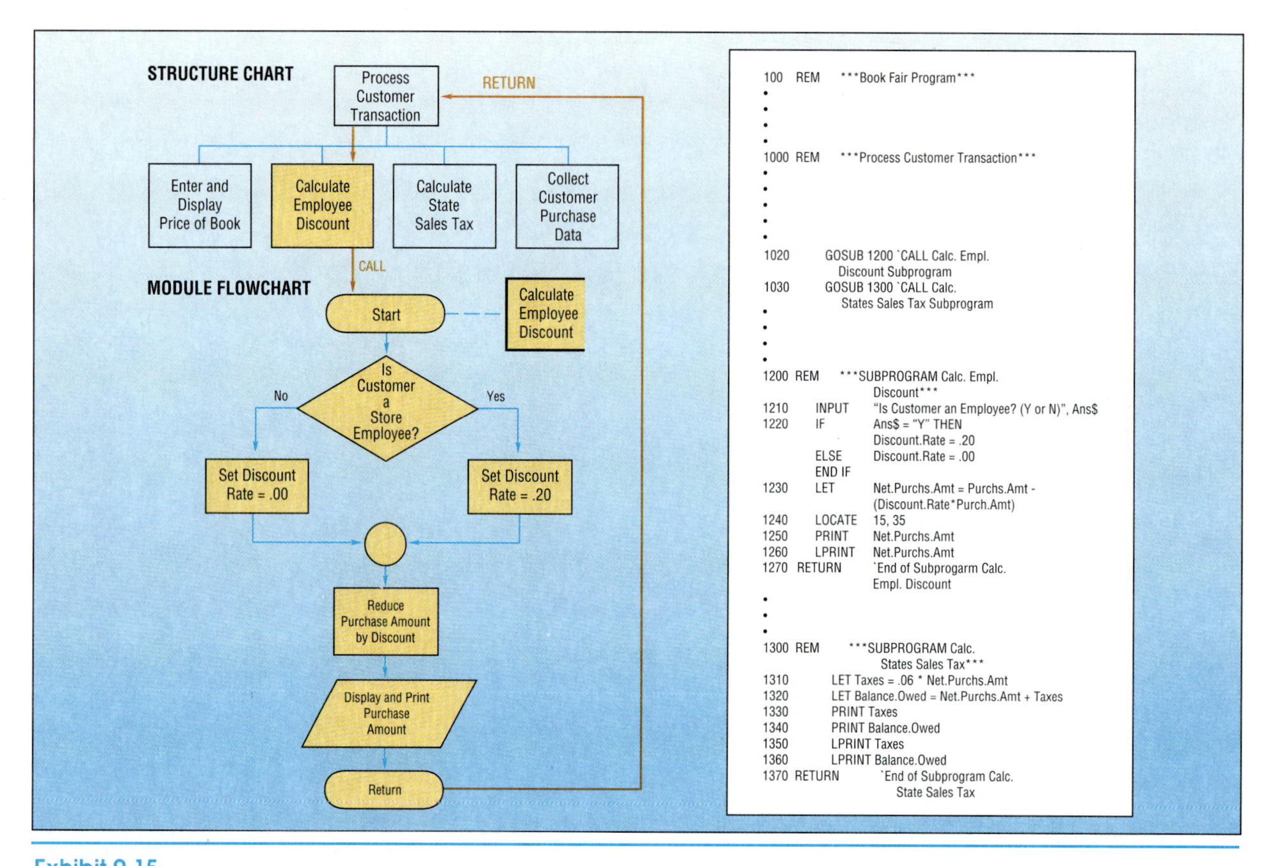

Exhibit 9.15

The Relationship Between Program Design and Program Coding

programming language. Although the details of this program are beyond what is needed here, it is important as a user that you understand what the programmer is trying to accomplish through the programming language.

The structure chart shows the overall program design for processing customer transactions and the modules for calculating employee discounts, state sales tax, and so on. The arrow between the higher and lower level modules indicates that the Calculate Employee Discount procedure can be called whenever it is needed. The module flowchart shows the step-by-step procedures that would be processed to calculate the appropriate discount. The resulting value would then be returned to the main module.

Let's look at the program listing and see how this design is coded. There are several important points to understand. Program commands such as INPUT, PRINT, IF. . .THEN. . .ELSE, and REM are displayed in capital letters. Each line of the program is numbered for easy reference. The REM command stands for remarks and is used to define for the reader of the program listing the purpose of a particular block of code.

In the programming language, modules are written as **subprograms** or single-purpose functions. These subprograms are **called**, or **invoked**, into action as needed from a higher level program or module.

At line 1000 the program for processing customer transactions begins. At line 1020 a call is made to the subprogram at line 1200 that is used to calculate the employee discount.

The GOSUB command indicates a jump to the subprogram specified by line number. At line 1200 the code for the subprogram corresponding to the module flowchart is listed. Note that at line 1270 there is a RETURN command that returns the value of the subprogram calculation to the main program.

An important and often under-emphasized part of coding a program is the documentation of the program. **Program documentation** is the inclusion of text material within the program itself that explains the purpose and design of the program to anyone reading it. As was illustrated by the REM statements in Exhibit 9.15, all programming languages allow the programmer to place notes within the program to document the program. Such comments can speed up the program maintenance task by helping the programmer making the modifications to understand what the program was originally designed to do and the specific steps used to accomplish that task.

Whereas early programming languages restricted the length of variable names, newer programming languages are allowing much longer ones so that programmers can use meaningful variable names. For example, earlier versions of BASIC would have required a statement like LET B = N + T rather than the statement LET BALANCE.OWED = NET.PURCHS.AMT + TAXES, which is permissible in current versions of BASIC. These more meaningful variable names enable a reader to understand what the programming is doing by simply reading the lines of the program. Programming languages that can be understood simply by being read are commonly called **self-documenting.**

Many companies have strict rules about the types of comments and variable names that must be included within programs to help ensure that program maintenance is as efficient as possible.

Program Testing

Program testing is an activity undertaken to ensure that the program meets the program specifications and performs as expected. It is a major responsibility of the programmer to conduct the testing process and often takes up 50 percent of the time allocated to program development.

Much time should be spent on testing because program failures can cause immense inconvenience or even damage, both to the users of the program and to the reputation and credibility of the information system department. For example, it is easy to see that programs written for a hospital unit that monitors patients' vital signs could in fact cause death if not written correctly. There have been several such lawsuits based on programmers' "malpractice."

Payroll programs intended to incorporate new tax laws, if incorrectly written, could inconvenience employees greatly, perhaps resulting in action from the Internal Revenue Service. Direct deposit programs enable an employee's paycheck to be electronically deposited in his or her bank. What if the program deposits the check to the wrong financial institution or sends the wrong amount? What if the software written to determine grade-point averages miscalculated or incorrectly recorded the courses taken? The consequences of errors in most of the programs you encounter will not be as dramatic as those just discussed, but be aware that the cost of fixing errors increases significantly after a program is in production, compared to its testing stage.

There are three broad categories of programming errors: syntax errors, run-time errors, and logic errors. **Syntax errors** are violations of the grammatical rules of the programming language; they generally cause the program not to run. Syntax errors can be caused by misspelled keywords, omitted punctuation marks, or by incorrectly placed punctuation marks. For example, if line 1250 in the sample book fair program were written as PRUNT Net.Puchs.Amt, this would be considered a syntax error since the keyword PRINT was misspelled as PRUNT. This type of error plagues beginning programmers since they are unfamiliar with the language's rules. As students become more comfortable with the language, however, the incidence of syntax errors is greatly reduced and those that do occur are easily discovered and fixed. Eventually, as programs increase in complexity and difficulty, logic errors become the main concern.

Run-time errors are errors that occur when data are processed by the program. The program statements are syntactically correct, but the program contains a request to manipulate data in an improper way, such as dividing a number by zero or placing character data into a numeric variable. For example, if a program contained a statement such as LET Avg. Salary = Total.Salary/No.of.Emp and the number of employees was zero, this program would generate an error when it was run, causing the program to crash.

Logic errors are those actions that cause a program to produce incorrect results. They occur when the program design is faulty. The program is syntactically correct and runs without crashing, but incorrect results are generated. Logic errors are the hardest to detect and correct. One can never be sure that a program is without logic errors; thus a thorough testing of the program's logic is very important.

An example of a logic error would occur if the book fair program set the employee discount rate at .02 rather than .20. The program would still run but all the orders involving employees would be based on the 2 percent discount rather than on the correct 20 percent discount rate.

Syntax errors are detected automatically (but not corrected) in the most popular high-level programming languages such as BASIC, COBOL, and Pascal. Special operating system software, such as a compiler or translator, reviews the program to be run and indicates the type and location of syntax errors. The programmer then can review these errors and make the necessary grammatical corrections. Run-time errors are more difficult—the correct detail must be processed to uncover the error.

Unfortunately, software that detects logic errors does not exist. Errors in logic can only be found by running the program using test data and seeing if the correct results are produced. The overall process of finding errors and correcting them is called **debugging.** Corrected programs can then be put into operational use (see Exhibit 9.16).

Test data is used to determine the point or points at which the program does not function according to program specifications. Representative and artificial are the two major types of data used for testing.

Representative test data is data that would normally be processed when the program is operational. Representative data can be gathered by taking samples of actual data used over several time periods for the task being programmed. For example, in testing a program that calculates the mortgage payment on house loans, data from various sized loans made during the past two months could be used and the program results compared with manual calculations.

Artificial test data is data developed to ensure that each path of the program is exercised and to see how the program handles unusual conditions. For example, in the book fair example, test data would be developed to ensure that both employee and nonemployee discount paths were checked for those people that bought several books at one time. Test data for unusual conditions would be developed to see what the program would do when erroneous data was entered, such as the price of the book being –$4.00, or what would happen if the clerk accidentally hit the wrong keys and the price of the book was stated to be $400.00. What if the value RE.00 was entered instead of 43.00?

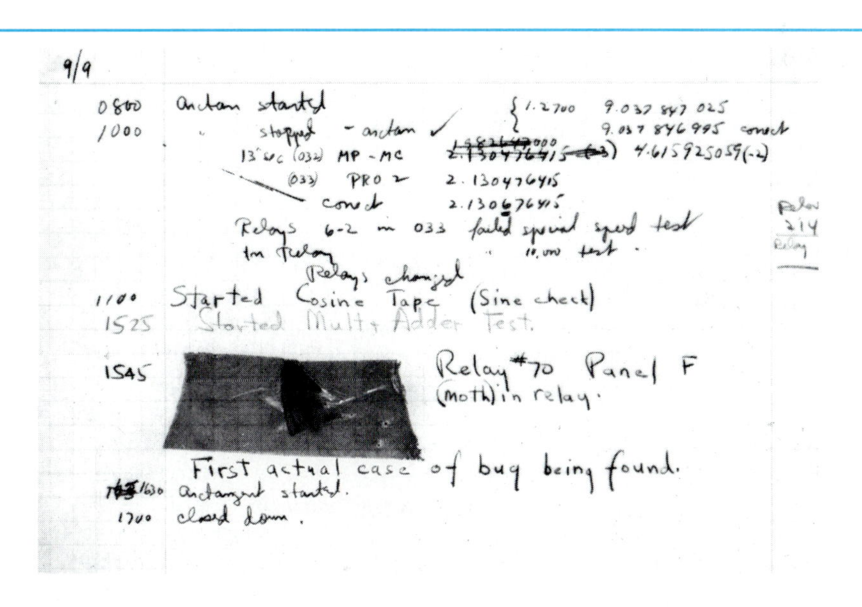

Exhibit 9.16

The First Program Bug

Back in the early days of computers, naval officer Grace Hopper was stymied as to why the Mark II computer stopped running. Review of the program revealed no errors. Looking inside the computer, however, she discovered a moth in a relay switch. This page from the original log book shows the moth that was found and taped into the logbook. Thereafter, getting the computer running became known as "debugging" the program.

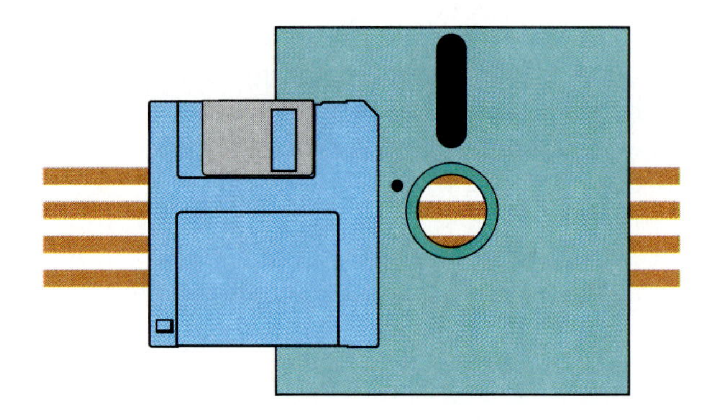

Computers at Work

A Master Programmer

By 1966 Hungarian-born Charles Simonyi had not only completed high school but also his first compiler. With the experience gained from writing the compiler, he was able to obtain employment at A/S Regnecentralen in Copenhagen, Denmark. In 1968 Simonyi left Denmark to study in the United States at the University of California at Berkeley, where he received his bachelor of science degree in 1972, and his doctorate degree from Stanford University in 1977.

Simonyi has worked at the UC Berkeley Computer Center, the Berkeley Computer Corporation, the ILLIAC 4 Project, Xerox PARC, and since 1981, Microsoft Corporation. At Microsoft, Charles organized the Application Software Group, which as produced Multiplan, Microsoft Word, Microsoft Excel, and other popular application products.

INTERVIEWER: Is programming a technique or a skill?

SIMONYI: What is programming? People argue about it all the time. Some people call it a *science,* some people call it an *art,* some people call it a *skill* or *trade.* I think it has aspects of all three. We like to pretend that it has a lot of art in it, but we know it has a lot of science.

There is a lot of science in programming, and at the same time it is somewhat of a trade. In fact, for many people, programming is a complex skill, very much like toolmaking, that requires a lot of care. I think if you take a healthy dose of all three (science, art, and skill), you can get some very exciting results.

INTERVIEWER: What is the part of programming that you consider to be art? Is it designing the user interface?

SIMONYI: I think that there is certainly an aesthetic aspect to programs, not only in the design, but even in the appearance, of the user interface. The artistic limitations of programmers come to light when you look at some ugly screens. Otherwise, computer programming is an art just as high-energy physics is an art.

INTERVIEWER: What do you perceive as aesthetically beautiful or pleasing in either the listing or the structure of the algorithms when you look at a particular program?

SIMONYI: I think the listing gives the same sort of pleasure that you get from a clean home. You can just tell with a glance if things are messy—if garbage and unwashed dishes are lying about—or if things are really clean. It may not mean much. Just because a house is clean, it might still be a den of iniquity! But it is an important first impression and it does say something about the program. I'll bet you that from ten feet away I can tell if a program is bad. I might not guarantee that it is *good,* but if it looks bad from ten feet, I can guarantee you that it wasn't written with care. And if it wasn't written with care, it's probably not beautiful in the logical sense.

INTERVIEWER: Let's talk about the process you go through in creating programs. Is there a process you can apply to all programs?

SIMONYI: Sure. If we're talking strictly about programming, then let's assume I already know what I want to do. If I don't, then there is some aspect of the process that is common to all problem solving: What am I trying to do? What is the goal?

INTERVIEWER: When you shift gears and actually start programming, what do you do first?

SIMONYI: The first step in programming is imagining. Just making it crystal clear in my mind what is going to happen. In this initial stage, I use paper and pencil. I just doodle. I don't write code. I might draw a few boxes or a few arrows, but it's just mostly doodles, because the real picture is in my mind. I like to imagine the structures that are being maintained, the structures that represent the reality I want to code.

Once I have the structure fairly firm and clear in my mind, then I write the code. I sit down at my terminal—or with a piece of paper in the old days—and write it. It's fairly easy. I just write the different transformations and I know what the results should be. The code for the most part writes itself, but it's the data structures I maintain that are the key. They come first and I keep them in my mind throughout the entire process.

Summary and Key Terms

Program development is the development of correct step-by-step procedures that will enable a computer system to produce the desired results and yet be easily modifiable in order to accommodate future changes in specifications. The main goals in business programming involve developing programs that are correct and maintainable. A **correct program** completely and accurately performs the information activities as specified in the system design. A **maintainable program** can easily be changed at some future time by the same or another programmer.

The **program development process** involves the three distinct activities of program design, coding, and testing. Program coding should take the least amount of time, with testing often taking up to 50 percent of the phase activity. **Structured programming** is the use of top-down design, module logic, and control structures.

Structured design is particularly important during **program maintenance**, when the program is modified as business needs change. Program specifications are guidelines for what is to be produced in an information system: the major functions and the required outputs, inputs, and data file organizations. **Step-wise refinement** is used to break general statements into lower level specifics. Top-down design is used to show the overall problem as a structure chart and each of the subproblems as modules. **Structure charts** visually show the overall organization of a program design as a hierarchical structure of program modules. Each box in the structure chart is referred to as a **module.**

The series of steps used to accomplish the specific task of a module is called an **algorithm.** Two of the tools used to describe a module's algorithm are flowcharts and pseudocode. **Flowcharts** portray a program's processing flow by showing the operations to be performed, the order in which they are performed, and the conditions that affect this order. **Pseudocode** uses English-like words to describe the logic of a program module.

A very important part of the development of structured programming is the control structures of sequence, selections, and iteration, or looping. A **control structure** is a method for controlling the order of execution of the programming statements within a program. The group of statements controlled by the construct is described as a **block.**

The **sequence control structure** is a series of statements in a block that are executed in order from top to bottom. The **selection control structure** is a block of statements that are executed differently depending on whether a decision statement is true or false. The **iterative** or **looping control structure** is a block of statements that are repeated depending on certain conditions.

Some general rules for using control structures in program design include **single-entry, single-exit processing**, in which each block has one entry and one exit point. Programs written based on this rule are considered to have a good design. Those that have multiple entry and exit points are known as **spaghetti code** and are poorly designed.

Program coding is the translation of the overall program design and specific module logic into a particular programming language. Each programming language has its own rules for how statements are written, known as the **syntax** of the language. With the newer programming languages that contain control structures, the translation is relatively straightforward. Older versions of certain languages make the conversion more difficult. In programming languages, modules are written as **subprograms** or single-purpose functions. The subprograms are **called** or **invoked** into action as needed from a higher level program or module. In-line **program documentation** should be used to guide the reader of the program listing, explaining the purpose of a particular block of code and showing the overall flow of the program. Meaningful variable names also help users understand a program by making it **self documenting**.

Program testing is the activity undertaken to ensure that a program meets the program specifications and performs as expected. **Syntax errors** are violations of the grammatical rules of the programming language and generally cause the program not to run. **Run-time errors** occur when data are processed; they cause the program to crash. **Logic errors** are those actions that cause a program to give incorrect results. Logic errors are detected by good testing data, whereas syntax errors are exposed by the computer's translating software. The overall process of finding errors and correcting them is called **debugging**.

Test data are used to determine where the program behaves according to program specifications and where it does not. **Representative test data** are data that would normally be processed when the program is operational. **Artificial test data** are data developed to ensure that each path of the program is exercised and to see how the program handles unusual conditions.

Review Questions

1. At what point in the systems development life cycle are programs written? Why?
2. Identify and briefly discuss the two major goals of business programming.
3. Describe the three major activities that comprise program development. Why should coding take the least amount of time?
4. How is the overall program design displayed? What is the purpose of modules?
5. What two tools are available for module design? What are several advantages and disadvantages of each?
6. Explain the purpose of control structures in programming. Describe each of the fundamental control structures.
7. What is the difference between spaghetti code and structured code?
8. What is program coding and how does it relate to program design? What is the purpose of subprograms?
9. What is the purpose of program testing? Why should so much time be allocated to it?
10. What are the two different types of test data? When would each be used?

T F 11. Structured programming uses particular design methods, including top-down design, module logic, and control structures.

T F 12. Structure charts are used to show every detail of a single module in the overall organization of the program.

T F 13. An algorithm is a specific set of steps designed to accomplish the specific task of a module.

T F 14. Flowcharts are used to visually show the overall organization of a program design as a hierarchical structure of program modules.

T F 15. The selection control structure is a series of statements in a block that are executed in order from top to bottom.

T F 16. The iteration control structure is a block of statements that are repeated a number of times depending on certain conditions.

T F 17. A well-structured program uses control structures that follow the general rule of single-entry, single-exit processing.

T F 18. Pseudocode is a programming language that was developed for end-users so that real programs would not need to be written.

T F 19. Program coding is the translation of the overall program design and specific module logic into a particular programming language.

T F **20.** Program testing refers to the process of showing users the statements in the program to see if they like them.

21. _____ Which of the following is not a control structure?

a. sequence
b. iteration
c. algorithm
d. selection

22. _____ Which term refers to the support of meaningful variable names in a program to make the program statements themselves more readable?

a. self-documenting code
b. variable-enhancing code
c. iterative processing
d. logical code

23. _____ Which is not one of the major types of errors that occur in programs?

a. logic error
b. syntax error
c. test error
d. run-time error

24. _____ Which is not one of the three types of activities that take place during the program development process?

a. design
b. coding
c. debugging
d. testing

25. _____ What term refers to an English-like set of keywords that describes the logic of a program using control structures?

a. flowchart
b. algorithm
c. syntax language
d. pseudocode

CHAPTER 10

Programming Languages

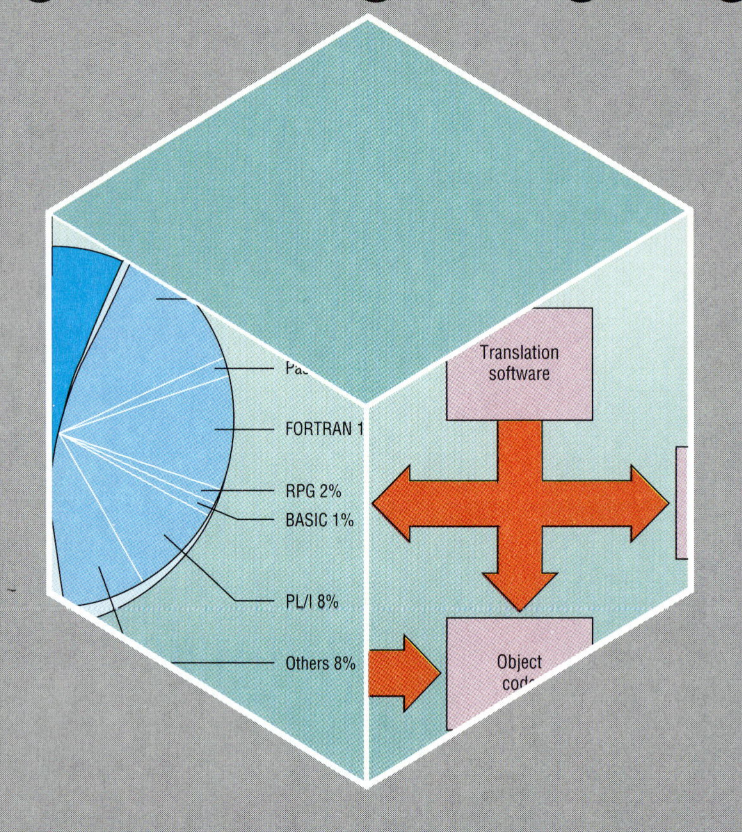

As you have already seen, programs are the core of an information system. For a program design to be implemented, it must be coded in a language "understood" by the computer system on which the program is to be executed. Now you will be introduced to programming languages—the means by which a programmer communicates a program design to a computer system.

In this chapter, you will learn to do the following:

1. Describe the differences among the three levels of programming languages
2. List and explain eight features useful in comparing programming languages
3. List some of the most popular programming languages and discuss their strengths and weaknesses
4. Describe some of the programming languages of the future
5. List six factors important in selecting a programming language

Programming Language Levels

The fundamental language for every computer is a set of electrical impulses, or sequences of "0s" and "1s." The circuitry of most CPUs allows only a limited set of processing operations, which are directed by program instructions in **machine language,** or 0 and 1 form. A program must be in machine language form to direct the CPU in processing a set of data.

The first electronic computers were actually coded in machine language, a very tedious chore. Programmers not only had to be hardware experts, they had to think like a computer as well. Steps were soon taken to develop people-oriented programming languages, alleviating the need to code in machine language today.

Three levels of programming languages are in common use: **assembly languages, high-level languages,** and **very high-level languages.** Assembly languages were developed in the early 1950s, high-level languages in the mid-1950s, and very high-level languages in the mid-1970s. Each higher level of language makes coding a little easier.

As most programs are not coded in machine language, they are translated into machine language by systems software (see Exhibit 10.1). The initial version of a program is called the **source code** and the machine language version is called the **object code.** Listings of the source code and source code errors are usually produced along with the object code. These error listings are very important in debugging a program.

With assembly languages, an **assembler** performs the translation. With high-level languages, the translation is performed by a compiler or interpreter. A **compiler** translates the entire program source code into object

Exhibit 10.1

Program Translation

Systems software translates a program's source code into its object code. Programmers create the source code. The object code is the machine language version of the program used to direct the CPU's operation.

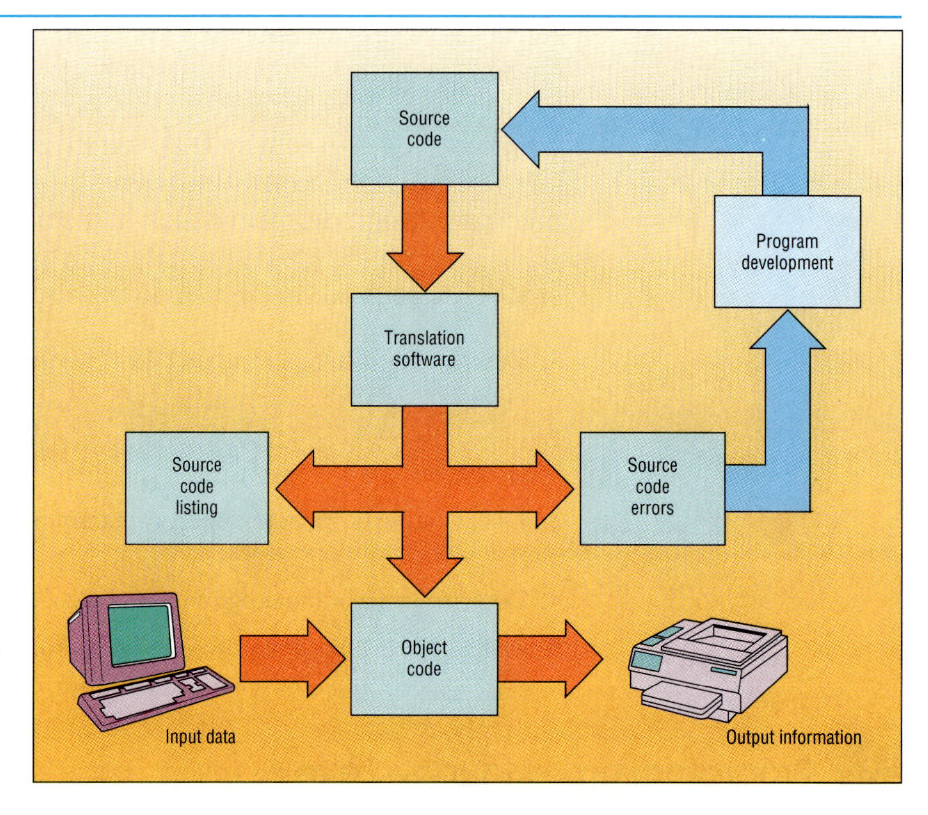

code, but does not execute the object code. Normally, compilers produce very efficient object code. An **interpreter** translates a program, one statement at a time, and executes each statement before translating the next. Since this way programmers can follow the execution of their programs step by step, interpreters can be very helpful when debugging a program. Executing a program through an interpreter, however, is slower than with a compiler. A compiled instruction might take a few microseconds to execute; the same instruction might require thousands of microseconds to execute through an interpreter. No specific name has been given to the translation software associated with very high-level languages.

With long programs, translation of a source code into object code can take a fairly long time. Consequently, a program's source and object codes are both stored in secondary storage. The object code can then be retrieved and executed without source code having to be translated. The source code can be retrieved from storage in case the program needs to be revised.

Assembly Languages

Assembly languages were developed to relieve the tedium and reduce the errors of machine language programming. They can be a fairly readable form of machine language—primary memory locations, CPU registers, and

Exhibit 10.2

An Assembly Language Program

Using an assembly language requires the programmer to keep track of primary memory locations, CPU registers, and the movement of characters between them to conduct specific arithmetic and logic operations. This example program written in the IBM PC assembly language prints "HELLO" on a CRT screen.

Line number	Program statements
100	MOV BX,108
101	MOV CX,5
102	MOV DL,[BX]
103	MOV AH,6
104	INT 21
105	INC BX
106	LOOP 106
107	NOP
108	48,45,4C,4C,4F

CPU processing operations are represented by abbreviated names rather than 0s and 1s. However, each assembly language statement still translates into a specific machine language instruction.

The assembly language program shown in Exhibit 10.2 was written for the IBM PC and prints the word "HELLO" on a CRT screen. Someone who knows assembly languages might see this, but it is not obvious to a user or a programmer of high-level languages.

The characteristics of assembly languages are such that they allow very efficient programs to be written, which generally run very fast. However, coding in an assembly language requires attention to the smallest detail. Further, assemblers provide very little error protection compared with compilers and interpreters. Just about everything coded, whether correct or incorrect, will be executed.

In addition, since assembly language deals directly with a CPU and primary memory, an assembly language program written for one CPU cannot be run on a computer using a different CPU. Thus, assembly language programs are not portable between computers with different CPUs.

The relatively free-form nature of assembly-level programming doesn't encourage the programmer to follow structured programming practices. Producing a program in an assembly language requires more time than do high-level languages, and when the program is complete, adjustments and changes will be difficult to make.

From this discussion you can see why most programming is conducted in high-level languages. However, assembly-language programming is still needed in those applications requiring quick execution of programs.

High-Level Languages

High-level languages consist of sets of predefined commands, which are combined according to a tightly specified syntax. The processing commands made available to programmers are most often oriented toward a certain type of information processing. Most high-level languages were designed to be very efficient with a specific type of information processing need. Yet these commands are general enough that they can be used with almost any information processing problem. The syntax is a set of rules, similar to rules of grammar, that programmers must follow in coding the commands.

In high-level languages, the disadvantages of assembly language programming are overcome in the following ways:

- As the programming language commands are problem-oriented rather than machine-oriented, the programmer can concentrate on solving information processing problems. This also makes it easier to run the same program on computers with different CPUs since the commands do not need to be different.
- Most programming language commands translate into multiple machine language instructions. The translation software actually handles many of the hardware and systems software details involved with information processing.
- Although having translation software handle some processing details lessens the programmer's control over the computer system, it also reduces the chance that the programmer will use a hardware device or systems software feature incorrectly. The translation software also locates syntax errors.
- The requirement that programmers follow a strict syntax can result in program code that is quite easy to understand—if the syntax encourages good programming practices.

As a result of these characteristics, program coding usually proceeds much faster with high-level languages than with assembly languages. Some specific high-level programming languages most often used in business computing are covered later in this chapter.

Coding in a high-level language is certainly easier than coding in assembly language. Much training, however, is still required for a person to become proficient in a high-level programming language. Furthermore, it takes a long time to code a set of commands that completely describes how the required information processing tasks are to be handled.

Very High-Level Languages

Very high-level languages, also called *fourth-generation languages*, differ from high-level languages in two major ways. First, the translation software performs most of the details involved with handling information processing tasks. Second, the commands are such that the programmer need only specify what tasks are to be performed, rather than how they are to be performed. Stated simply, they provide a comfortable degree of information processing support.

Very high-level programming languages are easy to use and require little training. Both users and computer specialists can develop application software with these programming languages. Very high-level languages are examined in more detail in Part IV of this book, in the discussion of end-user software.

To reap the benefits of very high-level programming languages, the programmer gives up a lot of control over how information processing tasks are handled. A very high-level language is tailored to a rather narrow set of information processing tasks. As long as the problem being worked on fits with this set of information processing capabilities, coding proceeds quickly and smoothly. When the information processing capabilities are not appropriate to a problem, coding can be difficult, if not impossible.

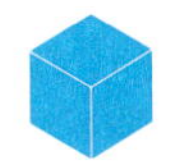

Programming Language Features

Hundreds of programming languages have been developed across all three language levels. Some were successful and are in common use today; many others have not been so successful. What makes some programming languages more successful than others? More important, what should you look for in a programming language?

Every programming language is designed to achieve certain goals. These goals can be thought of as the *design features* of the language. The more successful languages are those whose design features are found useful by a large number of programmers. Although many features have been incorporated, there are eight that are particularly helpful in comparing the strengths and weaknesses of different programming languages.

General-Purpose Programming Languages

General-purpose programming languages provide a set of processing capabilities that can be applied to most information processing problems. Special-purpose programming languages focus on a particular type of information processing problem. Although it is easier to handle any processing task with a programming language designed for the task, that language might not be very helpful in other situations.

For example, it can be difficult to produce high-quality graphic displays with most general-purpose programming languages, but such displays can be produced quite easily with a graphics-oriented programming language. However, it would be difficult, if not impossible, to develop even a relatively simple payroll program with a specialized graphics programming language.

Assembly language is the most general-purpose of the language levels. A skilled assembly language programmer can handle any type of processing task. The commands available with most high-level languages are flexible enough that these languages can also handle most processing tasks. Very high-level languages, however, use quite specialized commands.

Hardware Control

Programming languages that give a programmer extensive **hardware control** provide commands that operate directly on primary memory, CPU registers, secondary storage devices, input devices, and output devices. With such capabilities, a programmer can improve an information system's performance by using a computer's hardware and systems software features.

The speed with which an information system's users enter data and retrieve information through a CRT can be increased if the programmer can directly manipulate a primary memory region used by a computer's operating system to represent the CRT's display screen. However, a programmer has to know a lot about the computer's hardware to "build" a display screen in this fashion. Also, program development is likely to take longer than when a programming language's translation software is used to control how data and information are sent to and from a CRT.

On the other hand, since programmers work at the "level of the machine" with assembly language, it gives them extensive control of the computer system's hardware devices and systems software. Some high-level languages also provide commands that access some hardware devices and systems software components. Very high-level languages "hide" all these technical details.

Interactive Programming

With **interactive programming languages,** the programmer directly interacts with a computer during program development. This interaction is achieved by using an interpreter rather than a compiler to translate source code into object code. The immediate feedback that results is useful in locating and correcting both syntax and logic errors.

The main disadvantages of interactive, or interpreted, languages are that they execute more slowly than compiled languages and they can be an inefficient way to handle large volumes of data. Also, the temptation to hurry a program design so that coding can begin is hard to resist with an interactive programming language.

Control Structures

Program designs possessing a clear, logical structure result in programs that take less development time, have fewer errors, and are easier to maintain. Programming languages offering **sophisticated control structures** that follow the structured programming concepts of program design produce a code that is easy to understand.

Most of the newer high-level languages provide very sophisticated control structures. As very high-level languages do not depict logical processing flows, they have little need for sophisticated control structures.

Data Structures

Programming becomes much easier when the programmer can work with data types and structures that naturally fit the processing tasks being performed. It could be hard to set up a table of data and then retrieve values from it if the programming language lacked this data structure. Programming languages with more **sophisticated data structures** enable programmers to work with many data types and structures.

Most of the newer high-level programming languages also provide for sophisticated data structures. The very high-level programming languages usually provide a small set of data structures that are very useful for the processing tasks being handled.

Nonprocedural Commands

Nonprocedural commands allow programmers to describe *what* processing is to occur, rather than requiring them to detail *how* processing is to occur. Programmers "paint pictures" of display screens, records in data files, and reports. Translation software provides the detailed processing operations.

When a language's commands match the processing to be performed, it is generally easier and quicker to develop business applications with nonprocedural programming languages. The only programming languages that use many nonprocedural commands are the very high-level languages.

Easy-to-Use Languages

In programming, an **easy-to-use language** is always preferred to one that is not. Easy-to-use programming languages allow programmers to develop simple programs very quickly. Such languages provide very readable programs. As a general rule, the programming languages that are easy to use have an English-like syntax and a small number of commands.

The very high-level languages are specifically designed to be easy to use. Some of the high-level languages are also fairly easy to use.

Standardization

Each computer system's object code is unique. Translation software must thus be developed specifically for each computer system. A programming language's syntax rules and commands may or may not be similar across the versions developed for different computer systems. When versions for different systems are the same, the language is said to be **standardized.**

Programming language standardization may occur officially or unofficially. In the United States, the American National Standards Institute

(ANSI) sets official computer standards. Unofficial standards are set when a particular version becomes so popular that most other vendors copy it.

The advantage of standardized programming languages is that the source code is similar across its different versions. As a result, it is fairly easy to execute a program written for one computer system on another computer system—the source code is simply processed by translation software developed for the second computer system. When this occurs, the program is said to be *"portable."*

A number of the high-level programming languages have officially been standardized, and most of them, to some extent at least, have unofficial standard versions. Very high-level languages are too new for a standardization effort to have taken place. However, the market success of certain software packages, such as Lotus 1-2-3, is beginning to create some unofficial standards. As an assembly language's commands represent the CPU's processing circuitry for a particular computer, this level of language cannot be standardized.

Comparing the Language Levels

Exhibit 10.3 rates the three language levels on these eight language features. This comparison should provide some insight into when the various levels should be used.

Exhibit 10.3

Language Level Comparison

The strengths and weaknesses of the three programming language levels become apparent when they are compared across the eight language features.

	Assembly Language	High-Level Language	Very High-Level Language
General-purpose programming			
Hardware control			
Interactive programming			
Control structures sophistication			
Data structures sophistication			
Nonprocedural commands			
Easy-to-use language			
Standardization			

Note: [dark blue] means that the language level usually exhibits the feature.
[light blue] means that the language level sometimes or partially exhibits the feature.

When high efficiency is critical, the power and flexibility of assembly languages are very attractive. As a result, most systems software is partially written in assembly language.

The portability and maintainability of programs written in high-level languages make this language level attractive for developing the information systems that handle a business's day-to-day activities. Also, some high-level languages provide programmers with a great deal of power and flexibility. These factors, combined with the fact that high-level languages are fairly easy to use, has resulted in this language level's increasing use in systems software development.

Since very high-level languages are so easy to use, many business applications are now being developed at this language level. Most of these programming languages, however, can only be applied to a narrow range of problems and are not portable. As a result, very high-level languages are being used primarily to develop relatively small, management-oriented applications.

Most business information systems have been developed using high-level languages. How exactly does one select among the various high-level languages? The next two sections should enable you to make such decisions. First, the six most popular high-level programming languages are described; then decision criteria commonly used in choosing among these six languages are discussed.

Survey of Popular High-Level Languages

Exhibit 10.4 shows the approximate proportions of business information systems written in assembly language and each of the six most popular high-level programming languages. COBOL remains the programming language for most business information systems.

In this section, the eight language features will be used to compare the strengths and weaknesses of five of these high-level languages. Then these strengths and weaknesses will be illustrated by showing how each language handles a typical business information processing problem.

The task is to produce a CRT display screen using an item inventory file. Two steps are required. First, the user is prompted to enter an item number. Second, all the inventory status information is displayed (see Exhibit 10.5). For more information on these programming languages and the people associated with their development, see Appendix A, "The History of the Computer."

FORTRAN

FORTRAN, which stands for FORmula TRANslation, was developed by IBM and came into general use in 1956. Its designers' main goals were to provide an easier way of writing scientific and engineering programs, to simplify the processing of large quantities of numeric data, and to produce efficient object codes.

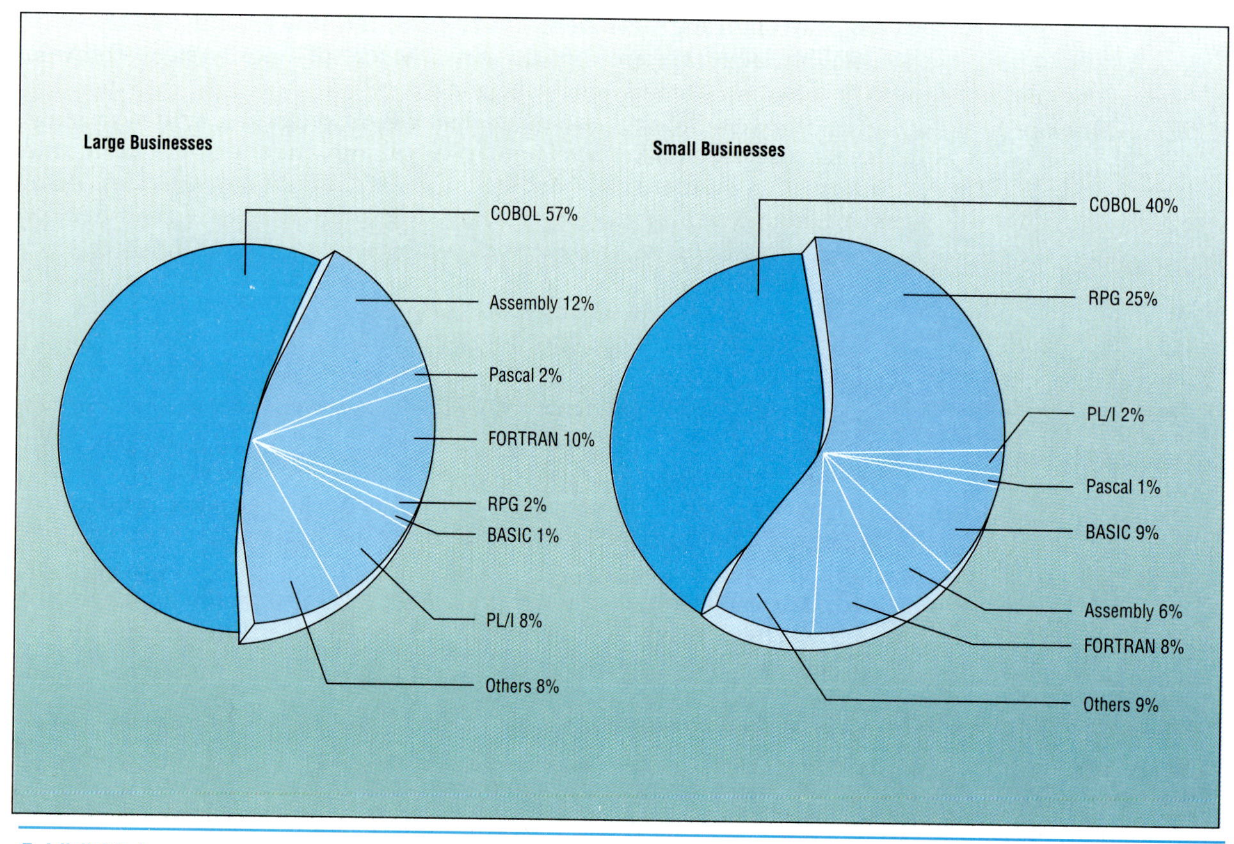

Exhibit 10.4

High-Level Program Language Use in Business

The six programming languages discussed in this chapter account for most of the business information systems in use today.

Strengths

Almost any type of mathematical or business problem can be solved with FORTRAN. While only a few data structures are provided, they include the data structures most commonly used for scientific and engineering problem solving. Because FORTRAN is made up of a few English-like commands, it is relatively easy to learn. Since FORTRAN has been standardized, it is possible to develop quite portable programs by limiting oneself to these official standards.

Weaknesses

Although FORTRAN can be used for almost any type of information processing task, input and output processing, as well as the handling of alphanumeric data, can be cumbersome, inflexible, and slow. As a result, few business applications are written in FORTRAN. Early versions of the language did not provide very sophisticated control structures. However, FORTRAN 77, the latest standard, does provide some structured programming logical flow patterns. Finally, even though FORTRAN is easy to learn, its syntax rules are complex. It is easy to make errors when keying in programs or choosing names for a program's variables that cause the program not to execute or, worse, to result in execution errors.

Exhibit 10.5

Programming Task for Language Comparison

In each of the high-level languages surveyed, a program will be written to extract data from the item inventory file (a) and display it as shown on the screen (b).

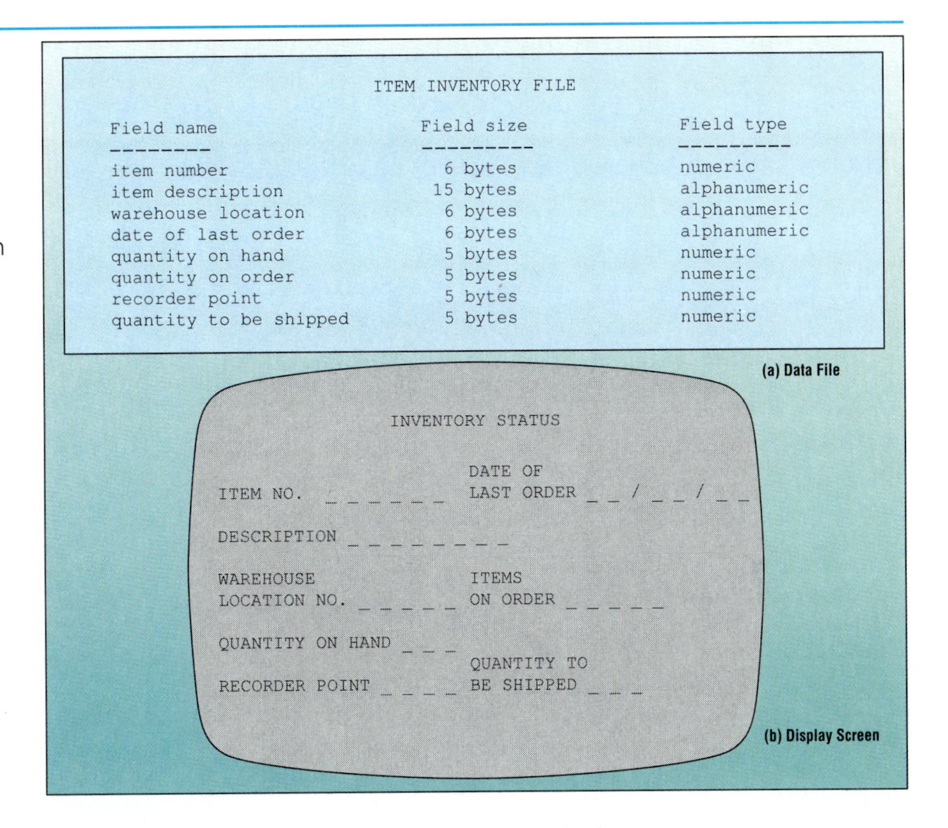

(a) Data File

(b) Display Screen

An Example

Exhibit 10.6 lists the FORTRAN program that produced the screen display shown in Exhibit 10. 5. Although the program is short and the processing flow relatively clear, it can be difficult to see how data are moved from the item inventory file to the CRT screen. The key is knowing that FORMAT statements indicate how data are stored, printed, or displayed. Thus, the READ statement on line 950 retrieves one data record from the file using FORMAT 1080. The other FORMAT statements along with the PRINT statements display prompts, messages, or headings on the screen.

One reason it is difficult to understand a FORTRAN program is the syntax rules used in naming the program's variables. ITEM is easy to understand, but what is IWHLC or IQTSH? Since you already know what this program is doing, you might correctly guess that these refer to "warehouse location" and "quantity to be shipped." Most FORTRAN programs require extensive internal documentation to be truly readable.

COBOL

COBOL, which stands for COmmon Business-Oriented Language, came into general use in 1960 as the result of a Department of Defense initiative to create a business-oriented programming language that would produce portable and easily maintained programs. COBOL is an extremely

```
C          FORTRAN PROGRAM
C          SCREEN INQUIRY
           INTEGER MO,DA,YR
           CHARACTER ANS*1
           REAL ITEMNO
    900  OPEN(UNIT=9,FILE='INV.DAT',ACCESS='SEQUENTIAL',STATUS='OLD')         {open file}
           PRINT 1010                                                          {print screen headings}
   1010  FORMAT(27X,'INVENTORY STATUS INQUIRY')
           PRINT 1020
   1020  FORMAT ('$',25X,'ENTER ITEM NO.?')                                    {prompt for an item}
           READ *,ITEMNO
           PRINT 1040
   1040  FORMAT(33X,'FINISHED GOODS')
           PRINT 1050
   1050  FORMAT(32X,'INVENTORY STATUS')
    950  READ(UNIT=9,FMT=1080,END=960)ITEM,DESC,IWHLC,IDLMO,IDLDA,IDLYR        {read...until (match on
                  item)}
       $   IONHND,IFGOR,IROPT,IQTSH
   1080  FORMAT(I6,A15,I6,3I2,4I5)
           IF (ITEMNO .EQ. ITEM) THEN
              PRINT 1085
              PRINT 1090,ITEM,IDLMO,IDLDA,IDLYR
              PRINT 1100,DESC                                                  {display item
              PRINT 1110                                                       information}
              PRINT 1120,IWHLC
              PRINT 1130,IONHND
              PRINT 1140,IFGOR
              PRINT 1150,IROPT
              PRINT 1160,IQTSH
           ELSE
           ENDIF
           GO TO 950
    960  PRINT 1170
           READ *,ANS
           IF (ANS .EQ. 'Y') THEN                                              {repeat....until(no
                                                                               more items)}
              CLOSE (UNIT=9)                                                   {close file}
              GO TO 900
           ELSE
           ENDIF
   1085  FORMAT(47X,'DATE OF')
   1090  FORMAT(4X,'ITEM NO.',2X,I6,27X,'LAST ORDER',2X,I2,'/',I2,'/',I2)
   1100  FORMAT(/4X,'DESCRIPTION',2X,15A)
   1110  FORMAT(/4X,'WAREHOUSE')
   1120  FORMAT(4X,'LOCATION NO.',2X,I6)
   1130  FPR,AT(/4X,'QUANTITY ON-HAND',2X,I5,20X,'FINISHED GOODS')
   1140  FORMAT(47X,'ON ORDER',2X,I5)
   1150  FORMAT(/4X,'RE-ORDER POINT',2X,I5,22X,'QUANTITY TO BE')
   1160  FORMAT(47X,'SHIPPED',2X,I5)
   1170  FORMAT('$','DO YOU WISH TO SELECT ANOTHER ITEM (Y OR N?')
```

Exhibit 10.6

A FORTRAN Program for Displaying Information from the Item Inventory File on a CRT Screen

This program is written in FORTRAN 77 on a Digital Equipment Corporation VAX minicomputer.

successful programming language—more than half of today's business information systems are written in it.

Strengths

COBOL is very good at what it does—processing large data files and performing repetitive data processing tasks such as payroll and customer billing. This is largely due to the way COBOL handles business-oriented data structures such as records, files, and tables. Also, COBOL's wordy, English-like syntax can produce codes that are fairly easy for managers, as well as computer professionals, to understand. Finally, perhaps more than any other higher-level programming language, COBOL's different versions generally do conform to the official standards for the language.

Weaknesses

Although COBOL is very good at many business computing tasks, other types of processing tasks can be quite awkward. Complex mathematical operations, for example, are very difficult to perform in COBOL. COBOL's wordy syntax can also lead to problems. It is easy to develop a simple COBOL program, but it can take a long time to write complex programs. Also, if programmers are not careful, the syntax can become confusing to anyone but an experienced COBOL programmer.

An Example

Exhibit 10.7 lists a COBOL program that handles the item inventory file task. At first glance, a COBOL program can appear very imposing. With a little explanation, however, the program's parts should begin to make sense.

All COBOL programs have four major divisions. An identification division (lines 1 and 2) is used to identify the purpose and author of the program. An environment division (lines 3 through 9) describes any needed hardware devices. The data division (lines 10 through 85) lays out all the data structures that will be used. Here the data file (lines 12 through 25) and various screen displays (lines 31 through 85) are described in great detail. Finally, a procedure division (lines 86 through 104) provides the program's processing. The readability of the procedure division and the great detail of the data division are the major reasons COBOL programs can be relatively easy to maintain.

BASIC

BASIC, which stands for Beginner's All-purpose Symbolic Instruction Code, was developed by John Kemeny and Thomas Kurtz of Dartmouth College and made available for general use in 1964. The design goals emphasized by Kemeny and Kurtz reflected their desire to develop an interactive programming language that would be easy for students to learn and use.

Strengths

BASIC is a "Jack of all trades" language, able to handle just about any processing task, but excelling at few. Its strength lies in the ease with which it can be learned and used. It has only a few commands, the purposes of which are self-evident, and it handles many programming details for the programmer. As intended by Kemeny and Kurtz, BASIC is a very popular language for teaching people how to program. Also the relatively small size of BASIC compilers and interpreters has resulted in BASIC's becoming the universal microcomputer programming language.

```
 1    IDENTIFICATION DIVISION.
 2    PROGRAM-ID.
 3    ENVIRONMENT DIVISION.
 4    INPUT-OUTPUT SECTION.
 5    FILE-CONTROL.
 6           SELECT MASTER-FILE ASSIGN TO DISK
 7           ACCESS MODE IS RANDOM
 8           ORGANIZATION IS INDEXED
 9           RECORD KEY IS ITEM-NO.
10    DATA DIVISON.
11    FILE SECTION.
12    FD MASTER-FILE
13           LABEL RECORDS ARE STANDARD
14           VALUE OF FILE-ID IS "INPUT.DAT"
15    01 MASTER-REC.
16           02 ITEM-NO                         PIC 9(6).
17           02 DESCRIPTION                     PIC X(15).
18           02 WHSE-NO                         PIC 9(6).
19           02 ON-HAND                         PIC 9(6).
20           02 RE-ORDERPT                      PIC 9(6).
21           02 ITEM                            PIC 9(6).
22           02 QT-SHIP                         PIC 9(5).
23           02 MONTH                           PIC 99.
24           02 DAY                             PIC 99.
25           02 YEAR                            PIC 99.
26    WORKING-STORAGE SECTION.
27    01 WORK-AREAS.
28           02 ITEM-NO2                        PIC 9(6).
29           02 ANS                             PIC X.
30    LINKAGE SECTION.
31    SCREEN SECTION.
32    01 INQUIRY-SCREEN.
33           02 BLANK SCREEN.
34           02 REVERSE-VIDEO
35                LINE 3 COLUMN 36
36                VALUE "STATUS INQUIRY".
37           02 LINE 7 COLUMN 5 VALUE "Item No".
38           02 LINE 7 COLUMN 14                PIC 9(6)
39                                              USING ITEM NO.
40           02 LINE 9 COLUMN 19                PIC X(15)
41                                              USING DESCRIPTION.
42           02 LINE 9 COLUMN 5                 VALUE "Description".
43           02 LINE 11 COLUMN 5                VALUE "Warehouse".
44           02 LINE 12 COLUMN 19               PIC 9(6)
45                                              USING WHSE-NO.
46           02 LINE 12 COLUMN 5                VALUE "Location No".
47           02 LINE 14 COLUMN 23               PIC 9(6)
48                                              USING ON-HAND.
49           02 LINE 14 COLUMN 5                VALUE "Quantity On-Hand".
50           02 LINE 16 COLUMN 20               PIC 9(6)
51                                              USING RE-ORDERPT.
52           02 LINE 16 COLUMN 5                VALUE "Re-order Point".
53           02 LINE 7 COLUMN 50                VALUE "Date of".
54           02 LINE 8 COLUMN 50                VALUE "Last Order".
55           02 LINE 8 COLUMN 65                PIC 99
56                                              USING MONTH.
57           02 LINE 8 COLUMN 67                VALUE "/".
58           02 LINE 8 COLUMN 68                PIC 99
59                                              USING DAY.
60           02 LINE 8 COLUMN 70                VALUE "/".
61           02 LINE 8 COLUMN 71                PIC 99
62                                              USING YEAR.
63           02 LINE 10 COLUMN 50               VALUE "Items".
64           02 LINE 11 COLUMN 50               VALUE "On Order".
65           02 LINE 11 COLUMN 65               PIC 9(6)
66                                              USING ITEM.
67           02 LINE 15 COLUMN 50               VALUE "Quantity to be".
```

```
68          02 LINE 16 COLUMN 50               VALUE "Shipped".
69          02 LINE 16 COLUMN 65               PIC 9(5)
70                                             USING QT-SHIP.
71      01 ASK-SCREEN.
72          02 LINE 24 COLUMN 30
73                                             VALUE "More Item Inquires <Y/N>".
74          02 LINE 24 COLUMN 56               PIC X TO ANS.
75      01 ERROR-SCREEN.
76          02 BLANK SCREEN.
77          02 LINE 12 COLUMN 32
78                                             VALUE "Cannot locate by item no".
79          02 LINE 12 COLUMN 58               PIC 9(6)
80                                             USING ITEM-NO.
81      01 ITEM-SCREEN.
82          02 BLANK SCREEN.
83          02 LINE 12 COLUMN 30
84                                             VALUE "Input ITEM-NO <999999> TO EXIT>".
85          02 LINE 12 COLUMN 61               PIC 9(6) TO ITEM-NO.
86      PROCEDURE DIVISION.
87      CALC-RTN.
88          OPEN INPUT MASTER-FILE.                           {open file}
89          DISPLAY ITEM-SCREEN.
90          ACCEPT ITEM-SCREEN.
91          IF ITEM-NO=999999 CLOSE MASTER-FILE
92              STOP RUN.
93          READ MASTER-FILE INVALID KEY CLOSE MASTER-FILE    {read...until(match on item)}
94              PERFORM ERROR-RTN.
95          DISPLAY INQUIRY-SCREEN.                           {print item information}
96              DISPLAY ASK-SCREEN.
97              ACCEPT ASK-SCREEN.                            {enter item}
98          IF ANS IS EQUAL TO "Y" CLOSE MASTER-FILE          {repeat...until (no more items)}
99              GO TO CALC-RTN.
100         CLOSE MASTER-FILE.                                {close file}
101         STOP RUN.
102     ERROR-RTN.
103         DISPLAY ERROR-SCREEN.
104         STOP RUN.
```

Exhibit 10.7

A COBOL Program for Displaying Information from the Item Inventory File on a CRT Screen

This program is written in IBM COBOL on an IBM PC.

Weaknesses

BASIC's greatest weakness lies in its limited control and data structures. This weakness, combined with a limited set of syntax rules for naming variables, can result in program code that is extremely hard to understand. It is easy not to practice good programming practices in BASIC! Another of BASIC's weaknesses is that the official ANSI standard for BASIC is so limited that almost every version of the language includes additions to the standard. As a result, BASIC programs are not that portable, despite the many computer systems that have BASIC compilers and interpreters. These weaknesses are being overcome in many newer versions of the language.

An Example

Exhibit 10.8 shows a BASIC program for the item inventory file task. BASIC's strengths and weaknesses are clearly seen. The program makes use

```
 10   REM BASIC PROGRAM
 20   REM
 30   CLS:SCREEN 2:KEY OFF
 40   LINE (1,1)-(620,200),,B
 50   LOCATE 5,23:PRINT "ITEM STATUS INQUIRY"                   {print screen headings}
 60   LOCATE 6,23:PRINT "——————————"
 70   LOCATE 10,13:INPUT "ENTER ITEM NUMBER      ";XXXX          {prompt for an item}
 80   OPEN "INV.DAT" FOR INPUT AS #1                            {open file}
 90   INPUT #1,ITEM,DESC$,WLNO,DORD,ONHD,FGOR,REPT,QSH          {read...until(match on item)}
100   IF XXXX=ITEM THEN 130
110   IF EOF(1) THEN 370
120   GOTO 90
130   CLS:SCREEN 2:KEY OFF
140   LINE (1,1)-(620,200),,B
150   LOCATE 4,31:PRINT "INVENTORY STATUS"
160   LOCATE 5,31:PRINT "————————"
170   LOCATE 7,7:PRINT USING "ITEM NUMBER:       ######";ITEM
180   LOCATE 10,7:PRINT USING "DESCRIPTION:       \                \";DESC$
190   LOCATE 13,7:PRINT "WAREHOUSE"
200   LOCATE 14,7:PRINT USING "LOCATION NO:       ######";WLNO
210   LOCATE 17,7:PRINT "QUANTITY"
220   LOCATE 18,7:PRINT USING "ON-HAND:           #####";OHND      {display item information}
230   LOCATE 21,7:PRINT "RE-ORDER"
240   LOCATE 22,7:PRINT USING "POINT:  #####";REPT
250   LOCATE 17,50:PRINT "ITEMS"
260   LOCATE 18,50:PRINT USING "ON ORDER:        #####";FGOR
270   LOCATE 21,50:PRINT "QUANTITY TO"
280   LOCATE 22,50:PRINT USING "BE SHIPPED:      ######";QSH
290   LOCATE 10,50:PRINT "DATE OF"
300   LOCATE 11,50:PRINT USING "LAST ORDER:      ######";DORD
310   LOCATE 24,13:INPUT "WOULD YOU LIKE TO INQUIRE ABOUT A DIFFERENT ITEM";ANS$
320   IF ANS$="N" OR ANS$="NO" THEN 420
330   IF ANS$="Y" OR ANS$="YES" THEN 340 ELSE 310               {repeat ... until (no more items)}
340   CLOSE #1                                                  {close file}
350   GOTO 30
360   END
370   LOCATE 23,25:PRINT "ITEM NUMBER NOT FOUND"
380   LOCATE 24,14:INPUT "DO YOU WISH TO SELECT ANOTHER ITEM(Y OR N)":ANS$
390   IF ANS$="N" OR ANS$="NO" THEN 420
400   IF ANS$="Y" OR ANS$= "YES" THEN 410 ELSE 380
410   CLOSE #1:GOTO 30
420   CLS:LINE (1,1)-(620,200),,B
430   END
```

Exhibit 10.8

A BASIC Program for Displaying Information from the Item Inventory File on a CRT Screen

This program is written in IBM Microsoft BASIC on an IBM PC.

of very few commands and is quite short. However, it is initially difficult to follow even this simple program's logical flow.

The key to understanding the program lies in knowing that the LOCATE command displays messages and information on a CRT screen. Lines 30 through 70 initialize the CRT screen and prompt the user for an item. Line 150 retrieves a record from the item inventory file. Line 100 tests the retrieved record to determine if it contains the desired inventory item. Lines 150 through 300 display the retrieved information on the CRT screen.

RPG

RPG, which stands for Report Program Generator, was developed by IBM and made available for general use in 1964. IBM's aim in developing the language was to ease the effort required of small businesses in switching their data processing from punched card equipment to electronic computers. As a result, the goals of RPG's designers were to produce a language that duplicated punched card data processing procedures and could be learned easily by people without any prior programming experience.

Strengths

RPG's greatest strength lies in the ease with which it can be learned by people who know very little about computers or programming. "Programs" are coded by filling out forms to specify the layout of data files, input records, reports, and CRT screen displays, as well as processing operations. As a result, RPG provides good data structures for standard business computing applications such as payroll and customer billing.

Weaknesses

The "form filling" nature of RPG coding does have its disadvantages. Although some current versions of the language go beyond the language's original purposes, many versions are still quite inflexible. To a large degree, this inflexibility arises out of the very limited set of control structures made available for directing processing operations. Also, whereas coding via forms does away with much of the need for professional programmers, RPG's source code is very difficult for someone who knows little about RPG to understand.

An Example

Exhibit 10.9 shows some of the forms used in the RPG program that handles the item inventory file task. The "program" simply consists of filled-out forms. The I form defines input records from the item inventory file. The S and D forms define the various CRT screen images used with the program. Finally, the C form defines the processing logic that ties everything together.

Pascal

Pascal, named for the French inventor of the mechanical calculator, was developed by Niklaus Wirth, a Swiss computer science professor. It was made available for general use in 1971. Professor Wirth's design goal was to develop a language for teaching structured programming concepts. He wanted a programming language that would provide a powerful set of information processing capabilities but still be easy to learn. Pascal is used in most computer science curricula because it is easy to learn and emphasizes structured programming.

RPG INPUT SPECIFICATIONS

```
I
SCRNFILENS    01    1 C0    2 C1
 * FORMAT-SCRN01
                                        1   20RECID
                                        3   80SITEM
          NS  02    1 C0    2 C2
 * FORMAT-SCRN02
          NS  99                        1   20RECID
INVNMASTNS    03
                                        1   60IITEM
                                        7  120ILORDR
                                       13   27 IDESC
```

System/36 Display Format Specifications

Display Control Specification

```
S
00010S SCRN01   0124      44                                   AG
```

Field Definition Specification

```
D
00020D RECID    020102Y  YN          Y     Y      C01
00030D          160232Y                 Y         COMPUSTORE
00040D          240328Y                 Y         CINVENTORY STATUS INQUIRY
00050D Y
00060D          190510Y                 Y         CENTER ITEM NUMBER?
00070D IITEM     60530Y  YN    ZY          Y
00080D          602410Y                 Y         CCMD 7 FOR EOJ : PRESS EX
00090D NTER TO VIEW DATA : CMD 1 FOR RESTART
```

RPG CALCULATION SPECIFICATIONS

```
C
C*******************************
C*          MAINLINE           *
C*******************************
C                     SETOF                     98
C     KG              SETON                     LR
C     KG              SETOF                     0102
C     KG              GOTO ENDM
C     KA              SETON                     99
C     KA              SETOF                     010298
C     KA              GOTO ENDM
C**
C     01              EXSR SCR01
C     02              EXSR SCR02
C**
C           ENDM      TAG
C*******************************
C*        SCREEN 01            *
C*******************************
CSR         SCR01     BEGSR
C           SITEM     CHAININVNMAST             98
C                     Z-ADDILORDR    SLORDR  60
C                     MOVE IDESC     SDESC  15
C                     Z-ADDILOCAT    SLOCAT  60
C                     Z-ADDIQUANT    SQUANT  50
```

Exhibit 10.9

Some of the Forms Used in an RPG Program

This program is written in RPG II for an IBM System 36 minicomputer.

Strengths

Pascal's greatest strength is the sophistication of its control structures and data structures. Programmers are encouraged to follow structured programming concepts through the language's commands and syntax. As a result, Pascal code usually possesses a very clear, logical structure. In addition to providing many standard data structures, Pascal allows programmers to define new data structures to be used in their programs. Also, like BASIC, Pascal uses relatively few commands. As a result, one can write simple programs with very little training. Finally, Pascal's popularity as a teaching language has made it widely available.

Weaknesses

Although Pascal was designed to serve as a general-purpose programming language, its relatively weak input, output, and file-handling capabilities have limited its use for business computing. Pascal's highly structured but terse syntax can also prove a liability at times. It can be difficult to understand a program's processing flow if the program has not been well documented.

An Example

Exhibit 10.10 lists a Pascal program that handles the inventory file inquiry task. Pascal's "bookkeeping" demands and terse, but strict, syntax result in a code that is difficult to understand unless you understand the Pascal language. All data structures must be very carefully described. Lines 3 through 33 define the different data structures used in the program. Pascal "hides" many of the details for processing inputs and outputs from the programmer (see lines 35 through 43 and lines 60 through 76). Although this makes it easier for the programmer to concentrate on a program's logical structure, it makes it harder to learn and follow Pascal code. This program's actual processing operations occur in lines 53 through 91. If you ignore the statements that link retrieved data items to previously defined data structures (lines 65 through 72) and those involved with displaying these data on the CRT screen (lines 73 through 89), you can see just how concise Pascal code can be.

Some New Languages

New programming languages are still being designed. Three recently developed languages have gained a lot of support throughout the computer industry. It is too early to know if Ada, Modula-2, or C will attain the success of FORTRAN, COBOL, or BASIC, but the future of these languages looks bright.

Ada

Like COBOL, the development of **Ada** was supported by the Department of Defense for use in building large, reliable, and efficient military software. The major goals of Ada's designers were to provide programmers with sophisticated control and data structures and to provide commands that

```
 1    PROGRAM inventory:
 2
 3    TYPE
 4           key_t = ARRAY[1..256] of CHAR;
 5           rec_t = ARRAY[1..2048] of CHAR;
 6           ctrl_rec = RECORD
 7                c_1:ARRAY[1..4] of INTEGER;
 8                rec_size : INTEGER;
 9                c_2 : INTEGER;
10                key_size : INTEGER;
11                END;
12    index_record = RECORD
13                disk : CHAR;
14                filename : ARRAY[1..8] of CHAR;
15                return_code : INTEGER;
16                res_: INTEGER;
17                ctl : ^ctrl_rec;
18                reserved : ARRAY[1..196] of CHAR;
19                END;
20
21    VAR
22           key : key_t;
23           rec : rec_t;
24           cmd : CHAR;
25           ir : index_record;
26           tem_d : ARRAY[1..2048] of CHAR;
27           description : ARRAY[1..15] of CHAR;
28           last_order : ARRAY[1..8] of CHAR;
29           whse_loc : ARRAY[1..7] of CHAR;
30           quan_on_hand : ARRAY[1..5] of CHAR;
31           on_order : ARRAY[1..5] of CHAR;
32           reorder_point : ARRAY[1..5] of CHAR;
33           quan_ship : ARRAY[1..5] of CHAR;
34
35    PROCEDURE INDEX0 (command : CHAR;
36                    var key : key_t;
37                    var rec : rec_t;
38                    var ir  : index_record );extern;
39
40    PROCEDURE INDEX1 (command : CHAR;
41                    var key : key_t;
42                    var rec : rec_t;
43                    var ir  : index_record );extern;
44
45    BEGIN
46    ir := ' ';
47    cmd := '0';
48    WRITE('Disk: ');
49    READLN(ir.disk);
50    WRITE('File: ');
51    READLN(ir.filename);                          {open file}
52    INDEX0(cmd,key,rec,ir);
53    REPEAT                                        {repeat...until(no more items)}
54                key :=' ';
55                rec :=' ';
56                cmd :='R';
57                WRITE('Next Item: ');              {prompt for an item}
58                READLN(key);                       {read...until(match on item)}
59                key :=UPCASE(key);
60                INDEX0(cmd,key,rec,ir);
61                IF (ir.return_code <> 0) THEN
62                    BEGIN
63                    WRITELN('Error: ',ir.return_code);
64                    END;
65                tem_d := copy(rec, ir.ctl^.key_size + 1,ir.ctl^.rec_size - ir.ctl^.key_size);
66                last_order := copy(tem_d,1,15);
```

```
67              description := copy(tem_d,16,8);      {display item information}
68              whse_loc := copy(tem_d,24,7);
69              quan_on_hand := copy(tem_d,31,5);
70              on-order := copy(tem_d,36,5);
71              reorder_point := copy(tem_d,41,5);
72              quan_ship := copy(tem_c,46,5);
73              WRITELN('                             Inventory Status');
74              WRITELN;
75              WRITELN;
76              WRITELN(' Item No: ',copy(rec, 1,ir.ctl^.key_size),'           Date of');
77              WRITELN('                             Last Order: ',last_order);
78              WRITELN(' Description: ', description);
79              WRITELN;
80              WRITELN(' Warehouse');
81              WRITELN(' Location: ',whse_loc);
82              WRITELN;
83              WRITELN(' Quantity On Hand: ',quan_on_hand,'      Items');
84              WRITELN('                                      On Order: ',on_order);
85              WRITELN;
86              WRITELN(' Re-order Point: ',reorder_point,'                  Quantity to be');
87              WRITELN('                                      Shipped: ',quan_ship);
88              WRITELN;
89              WRITELN;
90      UNTIL (key = 'END');
91      END.
```

Exhibit 10.10

A Pascal Program for Displaying Information from the Item Inventory File on a CRT Screen

This program is written in JRT Pascal for a Zenith Z-100 microcomputer.

directly operated on hardware devices. These design features have resulted in Ada's being a very complex but powerful programming language,.

Currently, Ada is primarily used to develop information systems that control and direct military weapons systems. Its strengths suggest that it will also be a very good language for nonmilitary computer applications demanding very high levels of efficiency and reliability. Likely applications include air traffic control, hospital patient monitoring, manufacturing control, and electronic banking.

Modula-2

Niklaus Wirth, Pascal's developer, designed **Modula-2** to improve Pascal. Modula-2 corrects Pascal's limitations and adds some new features. Wirth's main aim was to rewrite Pascal so it could serve as an applications software development tool as well as a teaching tool. Some key enhancements to Pascal include the capabilities to better handle business data processing tasks, to directly control hardware, and to improve program modularity. As Modula-2 becomes better known and more widely available, it may very well become a successful programming language for business computing.

C

Bell Laboratories developed the **C** language to use in building systems software. C was created by combining some features of assembly languages and high-level languages. It produces very efficient programs that are easy to maintain.

C combines the advantages of assembly and high-level languages. It offers programmers extensive control of a computer system's hardware devices, provides some very sophisticated control and data structures, but remains a very concise language. These strengths lead directly to C's major weakness: skilled programmers are needed to develop, or even to understand, C programs. As a result, C might best be described as an "industrial strength" programming language. Even though it allows programmers to do tricky and powerful things, it does not have many of the "safety net" features built into languages such as Pascal and Modula-2. Still, C increasingly seems to be the language of choice for many serious professional programmers.

Today C is primarily used to develop systems software for minicomputers and microcomputers. However, some business applications are also beginning to be developed in C.

Selecting a High-Level Programming Language

As you saw in the previous sections of this chapter, there is a wide variety of programming languages available. You also learned some of the strengths and weaknesses of each language and saw examples of how each language could be used to accomplish a particular inventory control task.

The question now is how to select the programming language that will best fit a specific project. Factors to be considered are

- ***The nature of the program.*** Business programming covers a wide variety of processing tasks. Many business programs emphasize file processing, but programs in applications such as sales forecasting are very similar to scientific or engineering programs. Selecting a language designed to handle the type of information processing being performed can both ease program development efforts and result in better computer applications.
- ***The performance objectives of the program.*** Program performance objectives vary a lot more than you might initially think. Efficiency is extremely important for programs that run continuously and require fast response times, such as programs used in airline reservation systems. Efficiency, however, is not that important with programs that are seldom used or for which response time is not crucial. An example might be a firm's quarterly financial report.
- ***The availability of a language.*** A programming language cannot be used if it is not compatible with your computer system. Similarly, it would be far more difficult to develop a program in a new programming language than in a language you already know. Even though a programming language might be ideal in terms of the proposed program's nature and performance objectives, it might be impossible or infeasible to use that language.

- ***The portability of a language.*** If a program were developed in a language with no official standard or in a nonstandard version of a standardized language, it might have to be changed before it could be run on a different computer system or even on a different operating system with the same computer system. You should consider whether any equipment or systems software changes are planned for the future. Will the program be used on more than one computer system?
- ***Program development needs.*** Business needs often place limits on the amount of money or time available for a programming project, as well as on the skill level of the programmers assigned to the project. When money, time, or programmer expertise is lacking, then programming languages that are easy to use become very attractive.
- Program maintenance needs. If frequent modifications are expected, a programmer unfamiliar with a program must be able to understand its processing flow. Programming languages that are English-like, that separate data descriptions from processing operations, and that support structured programming concepts, are generally easier to understand than languages that lack those features.

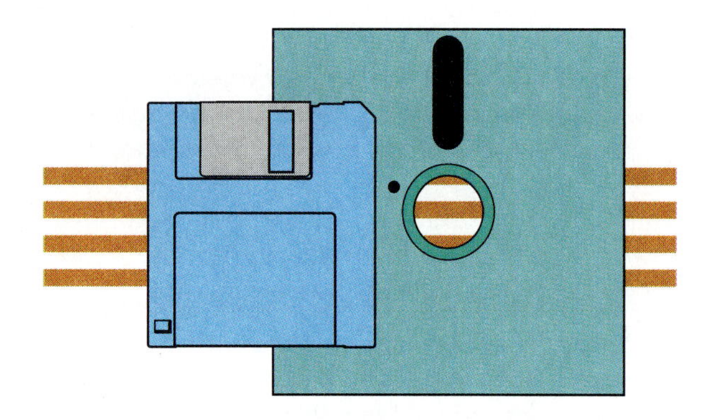

Computers at Work

A Different Orientation

"Object-oriented programming is not the weapon, it's the war," says Stepstone's Cox, who compares the coming change in software development to the Industrial Revolution.

Object-orientation is a step removed from the structured languages and programming techniques of the last decade, as represented by Pascal and C, and two steps removed from unstructured third-generation languages, such as Cobol and Fortran. In fact, some developers see it as revolutionary. "Object-oriented programming is not the weapon, it's the war," says Cox, who compares the coming change in software development to the Industrial Revolution.

Object-orientation uses radical software programming techniques, such as encapsulation, a way to bundle data and methods together to form objects that can act by themselves or interact with other objects; polymorphism, which allows an object to represent a generic action, such as executing a drawing before being given specific instructions; and inheritance, the ability to pass on attributes from one object to another. The primary advantages offered by object-oriented programming are security, development speed, and re-usability of code.

Totally Transparent

Philippe Kahn, president and CEO of Borland International, the Scotts Valley, Calif.-based software vendor, calls object-orientation "the next level of abstraction" in the development of software technology. Ultimately, object-orientation, says Kahn, "should become totally transparent to the user."

The first step on the road to software abstraction is to provide tools and systems that make the object-oriented technology, and Borland is busy marketing such products as Turbo Pascal 5.5 (also known as Turbo Pascal with Objects), which it began shipping last year. Kahn claims to have shipped more than 150,000 copies of the product.

Turbo Pascal with Objects is an example of a "hybrid language"—based on a structured language but incorporating concepts and techniques of object-orientation.

Another hybrid language, one that is becoming a *de facto* standard in the object-oriented marketplace, is C + + from AT&T. C + + is an extension of the C language that AT&T licenses to developers and independent software vendors. Both Borland and Microsoft Corp. of Redmond, Wash., will deliver versions of C + + soon.

What makes a hybrid language attractive is the ability to leverage the experience of a programmer without having to relearn another system from the ground up. "C + + is a good pragmatic environment for developers," says Chris Stone, president of the Object Management Group (OMG) in Westboro, Mass.

Efforts are underway to integrate object-oriented technology with traditional, unstructured methods. For example, the Codasyl Committee is considering recommendations from companies such as Hewlett-Packard Co. on ways to integrate object techniques into standard Cobol.

Yet there are still critical issues in the object-oriented marketplace that need to be addressed. One is standards. Because of the inherent modularity of the object-oriented environment, the possibility of interoperability in heterogenous environments is strong. For that promise to be realized, however, standards for objects and object-oriented languages must be established, and several vendors are now thinking about cooperative efforts such as OMG to standardize object formats.

Another issue is extravagant promotion. In the face of an object-oriented explosion, says Stewart Chapin, group product manager for the languages group at Microsoft, "We're dangerously close to being over-hyped on the object stuff." He and others emphasize that the real benefits of object-oriented programming are three to five years away.

Summary and Key Terms

Programming languages are the means by which a programmer communicates a program design to a computer system. Three levels of programming languages are in common use: assembly languages, high-level languages, and very high-level languages.

Since most programs are not coded in the 0 and 1 form of **machine language**, they must translate into machine language by systems software. The initial version of a program is called the **source code**; the translated version is called the **object code.** With assembly languages, an **assembler** performs this translation. With high-level languages, **compilers** and **interpreters** perform the translation.

Assembly languages, which were developed to relieve the tedium and reduce the errors of machine language programs, are essentially a more readable form of machine language. **High-level languages** have more powerful commands that are "problem-oriented" rather than "machine-oriented" and that translate into multiple machine language instructions. **Very high-level languages** consist of even more powerful commands that enable programmers to specify what processing tasks are to be performed, rather than how the tasks are to be performed.

Every programming language is designed to achieve certain goals. The design features of the language reflect these goals. Eight design features are particularly useful in comparing the strengths and weaknesses of different programming languages: the extent to which the language is (1) **general-purpose**, (2) provides for **hardware control**, (3) is **interactive**, (4) provides **sophisticated control structures** and (5) **sophisticated data structures**, (6) is **nonprocedural**, (7) is **easy to use,** and (8) is **standardized**.

The five most popular high-level languages used for business programming are FORTRAN, COBOL, BASIC, RPG, and Pascal. **FORTRAN** is primarily used for scientific and engineering problem solving. **COBOL** is a business-oriented language that is well suited for processing large data files and handling repetitive data processing operations. **BASIC** is a general purpose programming language that is very easy to learn and to use. **RPG** is an easy-to-learn, business-oriented language that is well suited to repetitive data processing operations. **Pascal** is a general-purpose programming language that offers very sophisticated control and data structures.

Three new high-level languages that are likely to be successful are **Ada, Modula-2,** and **C.**

Six factors should be considered in selecting a programming language for a particular programming project: the nature and performance objectives of the program, the availability and portability of the language, and program development and maintenance needs.

Review Questions

1. Briefly describe the three levels of programming languages in use today.
2. Explain the difference between source code and object code.
3. How does the term *portable* apply to high-level languages?
4. What is meant by the interactive feature of a programming language?
5. Discuss the advantages offered by sophisticated control structures.
6. Under what conditions are assembly, high-level, and very high-level programming languages each most likely to be used?

7. Which language would be best to use for a program to handle payroll and customer billing operations? Why?
8. Why is BASIC called a "Jack of all trades" language? What advantages and disadvantages does it offer?
9. Briefly discuss the three "new" languages described in the text.
10. What factors should be considered when selecting a high-level language?

T F 11. A compiler translates a program, one statement at a time, and executes the statement before translating the next statement.

T F 12. Assembly language is a fairly readable form of machine language in which primary memory locations, CPU registers, and CPU processing operations are represented by abbreviated names.

T F 13. Syntax is a set of rules, similar to rules of grammar, that the programmer follows in coding commands.

T F 14. All programming languages are equally good for all types of information processing problems.

T F 15. Nonprocedural commands allow programmers to describe what processing is to occur, rather than requiring them to detail how processing is to occur.

T F 16. A portable programming language is one in which the source code can be translated and executed on different computers.

T F 17. The FORTRAN programming language was developed to provide an easier way of writing scientific and engineering programs.

T F 18. The BASIC programming language is called the "Jack of all trades" because it is the best programming language for every type of information processing problem.

T F 19. The COBOL programming language is the most popular programming language for business-oriented information processing.

T F 20. The Pascal programming language was developed to teach structured programming techniques.

21. _____ Which of the following is not one of the three programming language levels?
a assembly c. high-level
b. interpreted d. very high-level

22. _____ Which of the following translates an entire program's source code into object code but does not execute the object code?
a. interpreter c. compiler
b. translator d. assembler

23. _____ Which programming language was designed as a business-oriented programming language that would produce portable and easily maintained programs?
a. COBOL c. RPG
b. FORTRAN d. Pascal

24. _____ Which of the following is not one of the newer programming languages that is gaining support in the computer industry?
a. C c. Ada
b. Modula-2 d. RPG

25. _____ Which programming language was based on punched card processing and was designed to be easily learned by people without any prior programming experience?
a. RPG c. Pascal
b. FORTRAN d. COBOL

PART IV

End User-Software

CHAPTER 11

Microcomputer Operating Systems

As explained in Parts I, II, and III of this textbook, a computer is directed by a series of program instructions. **System software** is a series of programs that has been written to act as an interface between application programs, which have as their focus the needs of end-users, and the computer itself. These are programs that perform such functions as starting up the computer, displaying information on the computer's screen, and retrieving and storing information on secondary storage devices. The system software first interprets and then carries out the commands necessary to run an application program. This intermediary role allows users to be less concerned with the inner details of computer operations and provides for more efficient use of computer resources.

This chapter concentrates on the operating system—the foundation of system software—and microcomputer operating systems in particular. You will learn to do the following:

1. Explain the different roles operating software and support software play
2. Describe the primary ways operating systems can differ
3. Identify which brands of operating systems are becoming predominant for use with microcomputers
4. Understand some of the commands used with microcomputer operating systems
5. Identify some of the advanced features associated with a microcomputer operating system

The Role of System Software

When an application program is used, the user relies on the system software to interface with the computer hardware. The user can then concentrate on creating his or her application.

System Software Functions

System software is generally composed of an operating system, language translators and utilities, data management routines, and data communication systems. The overall function of the **operating system** (OS) is to control the activities of the computer system. It serves as the traffic cop, directing and managing computer events. To do this, the OS has a set of programs called a **supervisor** (also called an executive or monitor). The supervisor handles the overall management of the many jobs and tasks being conducted by the computer system. First, the supervisor selects the application program to be run, based on pre-defined rules. Once an application is running, the supervisor is concerned with making the computer resources, such as the CPU, primary memory, input/output devices, and support software, available in an efficient way.

To enable efficient use of the computer system, the operating system must perform a variety of tasks. In large computer systems, the OS measures performance in terms of the number of jobs that have been processed, the resources that are being under utilized, and those that are creating bottlenecks. In order to account for computer use when users are billed for access to the system, the OS provides information on who is using the system, for how long, and what resources and data are used. This type of information can also be valuable for security purposes, to prevent accidental or purposeful abuse of computer systems and data resources.

Although high-level languages allow programmers to write programs more easily, computers only understand machine language instructions. Thus, an OS must be supplemented by **language translators.** These are programs that translate the English-like program instructions of a high-level language such as BASIC or COBOL into the binary code of machine language. **Utilities** are programs that have been written to accomplish common tasks such as sorting records and copying disk files on magnetic tape for backup. Operating systems enable programmers to increase their productivity by using utilities directly or by incorporating these utilities into application programs rather than writing their own programs for these tasks.

Data management routines can be used to create new files; make additions, deletions, and alterations to files; reorganize or merge existing files; and extract data selected by user inquiries. Data management options and procedures are discussed in Chapter 8, "File and Database Management."

In the execution of computer programs, data must be transferred between primary memory and peripherals. This involves the use of data paths, interfaces with many different types of input and output devices, and often the movement of data over long distances through telephone networks and other telecommunication links. These types of data communication functions are discussed in more detail in Chapter 16, "Microcomputer Data Communications." Exhibit 11.1 shows the varied roles of system software.

How Operating Systems Differ

This chapter concentrates on the operating system. As a potential user of computer systems, it is important that you recognize the vital role the OS plays in effective computer systems. Many people consider the operating system to be what gives the computer hardware its "personality." That is, different operating systems will make the same computer appear different

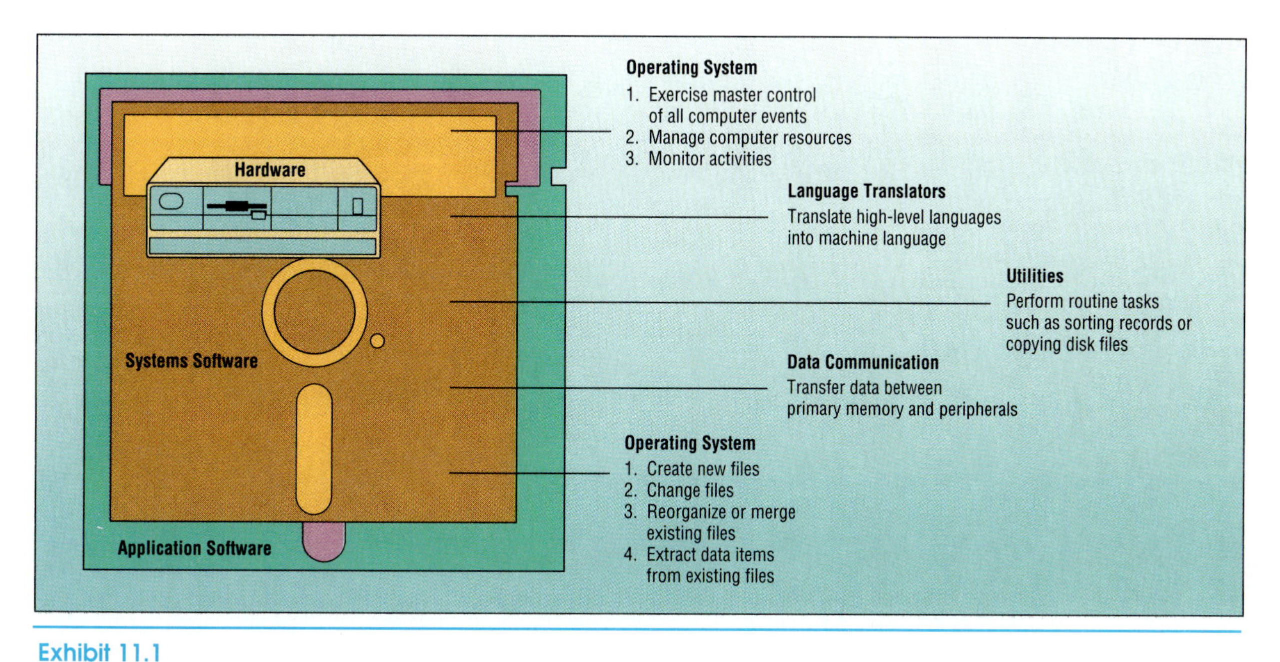

Exhibit 11.1

Varying Roles of System Software

to different users. For example, ease of interaction with the computer system and the degree of efficiency with which various applications programs run are two aspects that can vary depending on the OS.

To be able to distinguish among operating systems, a user must ask several questions. First, was the OS designed to be used primarily with batch or interactive processing jobs? The initial function of operating systems was to facilitate the running of a series of programs, one after another. An OS that performs this type of sequential processing of jobs is called a **batch-oriented operating system.** In a batch-oriented operating system, a user sends a program and data to be processed to the computer. The computer then processes the program using the data provided and sends back the results. In contrast, some operating systems have been designed to handle conversational responses, in which a programmer or end-user interacts with the program while it is running. These types of operating systems are **interactive-oriented.** The user can provide data to the program and receive information back from the program as it is running. Most operating systems today can accommodate both batch and interactive processing. However, it does make a difference in efficiency if the OS was designed primarily for one approach and adapted to handle the other type of processing.

Second, is the OS designed to be a single or multiuser system? Most microcomputer systems today are used as personal computers. That is, they serve only a *single user* at any one time. However, certain other operating systems can be used with some microcomputers to allow them to serve *multiple users* at any one time. Multiuser operating systems designed for microcomputer and small minicomputer systems generally accommodate from two to sixteen users, depending on the system. The larger, more powerful computer systems, when combined with more sophisticated

Exhibit 11.2

Operating Systems

Operating systems can be designed to accommodate hundreds of users or a single user.

multiuser operating systems, allow the computer to be shared by hundreds of users at the same time (see Exhibit 11.2).

In most microcomputer operating systems, a user can run only one end-user application at a time. If the user were running a spreadsheet program and wanted to switch to a word processing program, the user would have to exit from one program and load the other. When the word processing program is loaded, it replaces the spreadsheet program in primary memory.

With recent improvements in the capacity of microcomputers, however, operating systems are able to execute more than one application concurrently. This OS feature is known as **multitasking** (see Exhibit 11.3). Thus, in a multitasking OS, a user could have both a spreadsheet and a word processing program running concurrently. While the spreadsheet was printing a file, the user could switch to the word processor instead of waiting for the spreadsheet to finish its task. The task the user is currently operating is typically referred to as the **foreground task.** The task that is not currently interacting with the user is called the **background task.** It is important to realize that when the user leaves a task in the background to switch to another task in the foreground, the background task continues to execute and carries out any operations it was performing when the user left.

A final important question is whether the OS has been designed for use on a specific computer model or on a variety of computer systems. Historically, computer manufacturers have developed their own operating systems. This allowed the vendor to tailor the OS to the specific hardware characteristics of a particular computer in order to optimize its performance. This type of OS is **computer-specific.** An example of a microcomputer operating system written by a computer manufacturer and not licensed to run on any other manufacturer's computers is the Macintosh

Exhibit 11.3

Multitasking

Multitasking operating systems allow a user to work concurrently on several different tasks.

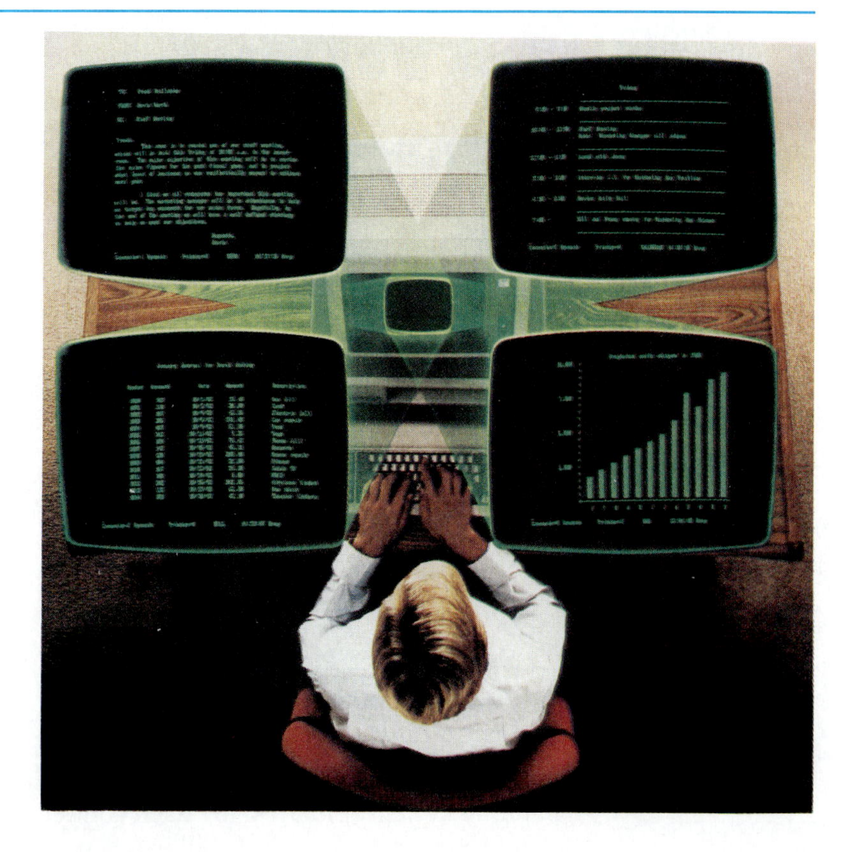

operating system; it is designed to run on Apple's Macintosh family of microcomputers only.

The major disadvantage of these proprietary operating systems is that application software written to run on a computer using a particular OS cannot, in general, be used on another computer model. When software written for one computer will not run on a different computer, the two machines are said to be incompatible. This greatly limits the user's flexibility in changing computer models or upgrading to a more powerful computer system, since existing application software is not transferrable without extensive rewriting.

The introduction of the IBM 360 computers in the mid-1960s developed the concept of a **family of computers,** a series of computer models based on the same computer architecture. A single OS was designed to accommodate users of the least powerful 360 models up through those owning the most powerful versions. The standard interface meant users could acquire more powerful computer models in the series and still have their original application software be compatible.

In the case of the IBM 360, the OS was usable across a family of computers, all based on the same computer architecture and made by the same computer manufacturer. A variation of this is seen with the microcomputer. Here, operating systems have been written by third-party vendors, not computer manufacturers, for use not only on IBM systems, such

Exhibit 11.4

IBM PS/2 Family of Computers

The PS/2, IBM's latest family of personal computers, can run on a DOS or an OS/2 operating system.

as the new PS/2 line (see Exhibit 11.4) but also on *clones*—computers with very similar architecture. For example, Microsoft has written the MS-DOS operating system primarily for microcomputers based on the Intel 8088 microprocessor (although it will also run on the Intel 80286 and 80386 microprocessors as well). Any microcomputer based on any of these microprocessors can use the MS-DOS operating system. This trend is making it much easier for third-party software houses to develop application software packages that will run on several different computers, and thus, users are not so limited to a particular computer model.

However, one must be cautious. Although most application software interacts with the computer hardware through the operating system, some software vendors write application programs containing instructions that bypass the operating system layer and interact directly with the computer hardware. This approach is sometimes used to increase the speed and efficiency of the application program, but can cause problems for users who try to run the application program on another computer model. For example, programs of this type originally written for the IBM PC would not run on the computers of other manufacturers, even though the two computers were considered compatible since they were both based on the same microprocessor and both used the MS-DOS operating system.

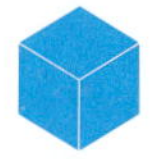

Microcomputer Operating Systems

Historically, operating systems for microcomputers have been developed in a different way from those for large mainframe computer systems. One

Macintosh Plus

Macintosh SE

Macintosh II

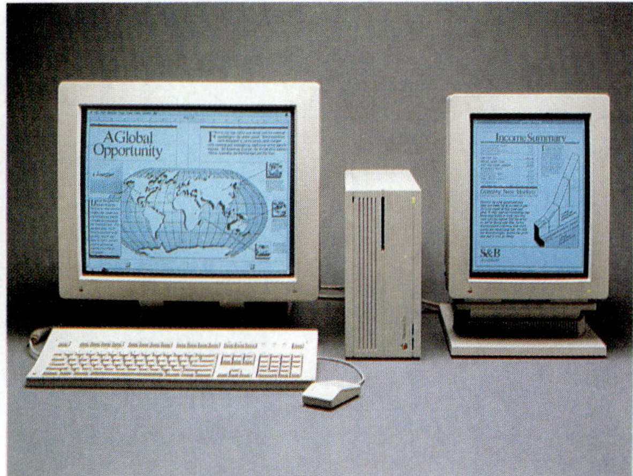

Macintosh FX

Exhibit 11.5

Macintosh Computers

The Macintosh operating system is a graphical operating system that runs on the Macintosh family of computers.

difference has been the move into interactive systems. Most micro- and minicomputers have avoided strictly batch-oriented operating systems.

The major difference, however, has been the public orientation of most microcomputer operating systems, as opposed to the proprietary single-vendor orientation of microcomputer and mainframe computer operating systems. (A notable exception would be the Macintosh operating system, which is discussed later. See Exhibit 11.5, above.) For the larger computer systems, an operating system is generally developed by the manufacturer for use with its own computers only. Thus, there is an OS for use with IBM minicomputers only, a different OS for use with DEC minicomputers only, and so on. Developing the OS in this way allowed each computer manufacturer to tailor its OS to its own computer system's characteristics.

However, because manufacturers would not readily divulge detailed information on the internal workings of their operating systems, third-party hardware and software vendors couldn't easily design their

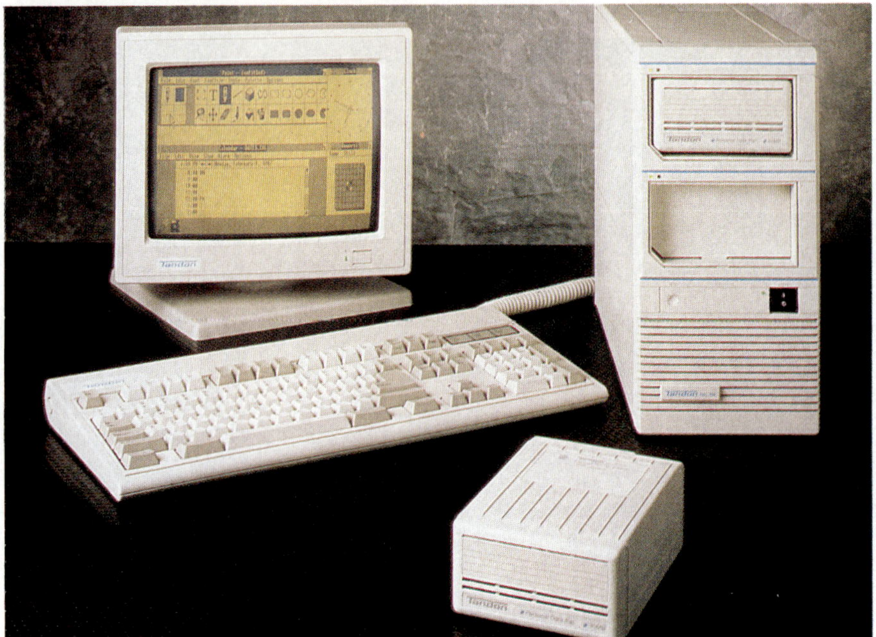

Exhibit 11.6

IBM PC and Compatibles

The microcomputers by Compaq and Tandy are IBM PC-compatible.

offerings to "plug into" these computer systems. The net result was that users were forced to select peripheral equipment and application software from a single manufacturer (see Exhibit 11.6).

With microcomputers, the orientation leaned toward unbundling the facets of hardware, software, training, financing, and even maintenance. Often, a user will buy a microcomputer manufactured by one vendor and disks from another vendor. The OS will come from someone else, and the word processing or decision support software from still other independent vendors. Thus, microcomputers are sold somewhat like stereo equipment—a system's components can each be produced by a different vendor. Unfortunately, there isn't yet a standard way to connect a microcomputer's hardware and software, as there is with stereos.

De Facto Standard Operating Systems

Although an official committee has not specified standards for operating systems, several de facto standards have evolved. A **de facto standard** is one that vendors informally accept, generally because it has come to dominate a market segment.

For microcomputers with 8-bit processors, the OS developed by Digital Research called CP/M (Control Program for Microcomputers) became one of the first de facto standard operating systems. CP/M-80 was developed initially in 1974 as a single-user interactive system; it could process only one task at a time.

In 1984 this operating system was used on 100 different brands of microcomputers by more than 500,000 users. Over five hundred independent software vendors were making their products compatible with CP/M. But this effort faded substantially after the IBM PC entered the personal-computer market.

For 16-bit microprocessors, the IBM PC very quickly became a dominant force. The OS that IBM chose was the operating system developed by Microsoft (see the Computers at Work segment at the end of this chapter). The IBM PC version is called PC-DOS (Personal Computer Disk-Based Operating System), and is a variation of MS-DOS (Microsoft Disk-Based Operating System) sold by Microsoft to computer vendors other than IBM.

MS-DOS is designed for the 8086 and 8088 16-bit microprocessors, which are used in the IBM PC and other IBM compatible computers. This is a single-user interactive system that cannot do tasks concurrently. In 1987, 75 percent of all personal computers sold used Microsoft's operating system.

Because of its popularity and due to rapid advances in the capabilities of microcomputers, there are actually many versions of MS-DOS in existence. As microcomputers have improved, Microsoft has altered MS-DOS to take advantage of those improvements. The later releases of MS-DOS are fully compatible with earlier versions. Thus, files and applications written for an earlier version of MS-DOS can still be used with the later versions. A problem occurs, however, when a user takes a file or application that was created with a later version of MS-DOS and tries to run it using an earlier version of MS-DOS.

For those users who would like a multiuser environment for the IBM PC or some other 16-bit microcomputer, the Oasis-16 operating system has been developed. It is possible to have 32 concurrent users with this OS.

In the 32-bit microprocessor world, it is not clear yet what the dominant OS will be. In fact, there may be three operating systems aimed at different market segments. The UNIX operating system developed by AT&T has been touted to be the OS for this market. But it has not dominated the marketplace as expected because there are multiple versions, which reduces compatibility of applications written in different versions. There is, however, a current attempt to unify UNIX which, if successful, could significantly increase its popularity. Some versions of UNIX are on the DEC microVAX, Compaq Deskpro 386, Tandy 3000 personal computers, and the SUN workstation. These UNIX-type operating systems are multiuser time-sharing systems.

Apple's Macintosh Operating System was initially based on the Motorola 68000 chip and more recently the 32-bit 68020 and 68030 microprocessor chips. The Macintosh OS is a single-user system that does multitasking. Because of the Macintosh's success, its operating system is important, but the possibility of it becoming dominant in the 32-bit world is small. Not that it isn't a good OS, but so far Apple has chosen not to license it for use by other computer vendors.

The other major player in the 32-bit OS world is Operating System/2, which is aimed primarily at the IBM Personal System/2 models, which use INTEL's 80386 microprocessor. There are versions of OS/2 made by IBM and by Microsoft. This operating system offers significantly more advanced features than MS-DOS, including multitasking, the ability to address larger amounts of RAM, a presentation manager that allows a Macintosh-type user interface, and the ability to connect personal computers in a local-area network.

User Interfaces

Command-Line Interface

The MS-DOS operating system is an example of an operating system with a **command-line interface**. To instruct this type of OS to carry out a task, the user must type the commands using the keyboard. The user must remember the name of the command and enter it perfectly for the OS to understand what is to be done. Examples of commands can be found later in this chapter.

Graphical Interface

In contrast, with the command-line interface, an OS with a **graphical interface** presents the user with pictures, called **icons**, which represent the various components (such as files, disk drives, and application programs) that the user needs to interact with. Using a mouse in addition to the keyboard, a user can point to these objects and activate pull-down menus found under the words at the top of the screen (see Exhibit 11.7). When a pull-down menu is selected, the menu appears and the mouse is used to make selections from the menu to perform various functions. A pull-down menu will often include sub-menus and some operations will require input from the user at the keyboard.

In addition, when the user "opens" an icon, an OS with a graphical interface will create a window on the screen (see Exhibit 11.7). The **window** is used to represent a currently open file or currently executing application. Thus, when an icon representing a disk is opened, a window is created and the contents of the disk are represented by icons within this window. The user can manipulate the window on the screen by using the mouse to reposition the window, change the size of the window, and move the contents within the window. In a multitasking OS such as that of the Macintosh, several windows can be open on the screen at one time. The

Exhibit 11.7

The Macintosh OS Graphical Interface

In a graphical interface, the objects the user deals with are represented as icons, and pull-down menus are used to pick the operation to be performed on the icons.

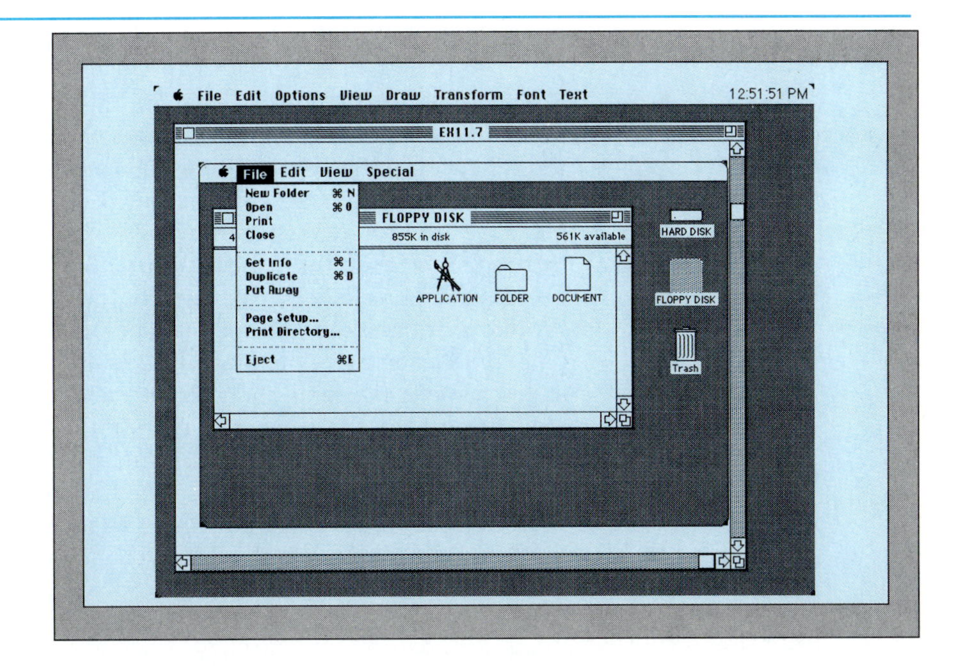

mouse can be used to pick which window to interact with and that window will become the foreground task while all other windows become background tasks.

Software known as a **shell** is available to create a menu-driven interface for an OS that has a command-line interface. For example, a shell may present the user with a set of menus. The shell translates the user's menu choices to build an MS-DOS command, which is then sent to MS-DOS for execution. Thus, MS-DOS still receives commands as it normally would, but the user does not have to type them.

There are also programs available that allow a normally singletasking operating system such as MS-DOS to be used on computers based on the Intel 80386 chip, which supports a multitasking environment. These applications typically use a graphical interface, including windows and pull-down menus that are manipulated with a mouse.

With the availability of products such as shells that transform the user interface, it becomes difficult to make a clear distinction between a command-line and a graphical OS. The classification of operating systems as command-line and graphical may be better thought of as a continuum, with some operating systems being more graphical than others. This distinction between interfaces can be applied to other categories of end-user software. For example, some word processors interact with the user via commands, others present the user with menus. The same is true with spreadsheets, databases, and the other end-user software products discussed in Part IV of this text.

Files and Disk Drives

When using a microcomputer operating system, an end-user should be aware of the way files are named in the OS, the way the OS is used to start the microcomputer, the way the OS can be tailored to a user's specific needs, and the way the user interacts with the OS.

The OS allows a user to work with data stored in a **file**, a collection of related information. A file can contain a document from a word processor, a spreadsheet, or even a program. The OS provides commands for information about and maintenance of the file. In MS-DOS, and most other microcomputer operating systems, a file is given a two-part name: an eight-character file name and a three-character file type, or extension. These two parts are joined by a period to form the complete file specification. For example, a document might be named LETTER.DOC. The file name is LETTER and the file type is DOC. The file type typically is used to indicate what the file is used for. A document might have a DOC (for document) or TXT (for text) extension, and a spreadsheet could have a WKS (for worksheet) extension.

Most early microcomputers had two disk drives, enabling users to work with files on two different diskettes at the same time. Exhibit 11.8 shows a microcomputer with two disk drives. The two drives are usually labeled A and B, although some microcomputers, such as the Apple IIe, use numbers as labels. It is now becoming common to find microcomputers with hard disk drives. Typically the hard disk drive is referred to as drive C. One disk drive on the microcomputer is always designated as the default disk drive. The microcomputer will automatically look for the OS files on this designated drive. When there is a hard disk, *it* is typically the default drive. When only floppy disk drives are available, the drive labeled A is typically the default.

Exhibit 11.8

A Microcomputer with Two Floppy Disk Drives

After the OS is found on the default drive, the microcomputer loads it into primary memory. The OS then takes over the system and interacts with the user. This process of loading the OS into primary memory from the diskette in the default drive is known as **booting** the microcomputer.

The user can manipulate files on any of a microcomputer's disk drives. When a command deals with a file on one of the disk drives other than the default drive, the name of the file must be preceded by the letter of that drive. Thus, if the LETTER.DOC file is on the disk in drive B, the file is identified as B:LETTER.DOC. If the file is in drive A, A:LETTER.DOC is used.

Having one of the disk drives designated as a default allows the user to omit the drive letter in front of a file name when that file is on the disk in the default drive. The default drive is also important when a software package such as a word processor, a spreadsheet, or a database is being used. When two drives are available, the software is often placed in the default drive so that the OS can find the files containing the software programs without having to decide which drive contains those files.

Operating System Files

The operating system usually consists of a small group of files with a special file type, such as COM or CMD (for *command*). There are also sometimes "hidden" files that are part of the OS. These files cannot be manipulated by the user, but are used by the microcomputer to configure the keyboard and other parts of the computer so that they work with the system. The computer can be booted with any diskette containing those files.

In MS-DOS an end-user can also create a special configuration file called CONFIG.SYS. This configuration file can contain commands that alter MS-DOS as it is loaded into memory. Using this file, a user can control parameters used in MS-DOS such as the maximum number of files that can be open simultaneously, the number of disk buffers, and the definition of devices such as virtual disks and input/output devices. Many of the newer programs for microcomputers, such as WordPerfect and dBASE IV, must use a CONFIG.SYS file to alter the MS-DOS environment before they can run. Thus, the end-user must be aware of the need for that file when those software products are installed on his or her microcomputer.

Prompts

Once the OS is loaded into primary memory, there are a group of commands available to the user for maintaining diskettes and manipulating files. When the microcomputer is waiting for the user to indicate which command is to be executed, a **prompt** is displayed on the screen. In the MS-DOS operating system, the prompt is A>. This prompt indicates which disk drive is the default (A, in this case) and that the user can type any OS command on the line following the prompt. Thus, when MS-DOS is busy executing an instruction, the prompt will not be displayed on the screen.

When the task is finished, the prompt will reappear to let the user know that MS-DOS is ready to process commands again.

In a command-line OS such as MS-DOS, the ENTER, or RETURN, key on the keyboard is pressed when the user is finished typing the command to let the OS know that it should begin executing the command. If the user makes a mistake when typing a command, the BACKSPACE key can be used to erase the error and the correct command can be retyped. The OS will not begin executing the command until the user presses the RETURN key.

Commands

Microcomputer OS commands allow the user to perform many different operations both on a disk and on the files stored on the disk. The same types of commands are available in all microcomputer operating systems, but the method used to enter the commands differs depending on the extent to which the OS is graphically oriented. In the following discussion of OS commands, the examples involve the MS-DOS since it is currently the most popular OS and its nongraphic interface shows the commands clearly. A detailed discussion of MS-DOS commands can be found in Appendix C.

Commands for Maintaining Disks

A microcomputer OS typically provides a group of commands that allow the user to maintain floppy diskettes. These include commands for preparing new diskettes for use by the OS, providing information about the storage space on the diskette, and listing the contents of the diskette.

Preparing New Diskettes

Before a file can be placed on a new floppy diskette, the diskette must be formatted for use by the OS. A command is used to initialize a diskette by dividing it up into sectors and tracks and creating a directory that keeps track of the names of all files and their exact locations on the diskette.

An example of the FORMAT command for MS-DOS is shown in Exhibit 11.9. Following the word FORMAT, the user types the letter of the drive containing the diskette to be initialized. The user can also have the OS perform additional tasks during formatting. In this case, the /S (read *slash S*) option has been specified. This tells the OS to transfer the OS files, needed to boot the computer, onto the blank diskette after the disk has been formatted. Different operating systems will have different parameters for the FORMAT command.

After the user enters the FORMAT command and strikes a key, the OS formats the disk and then shows the user how much space is on the disk and how much is used by the system. In addition, if any unusable spots exist

Exhibit 11.9

The FORMAT Command in MS-DOS

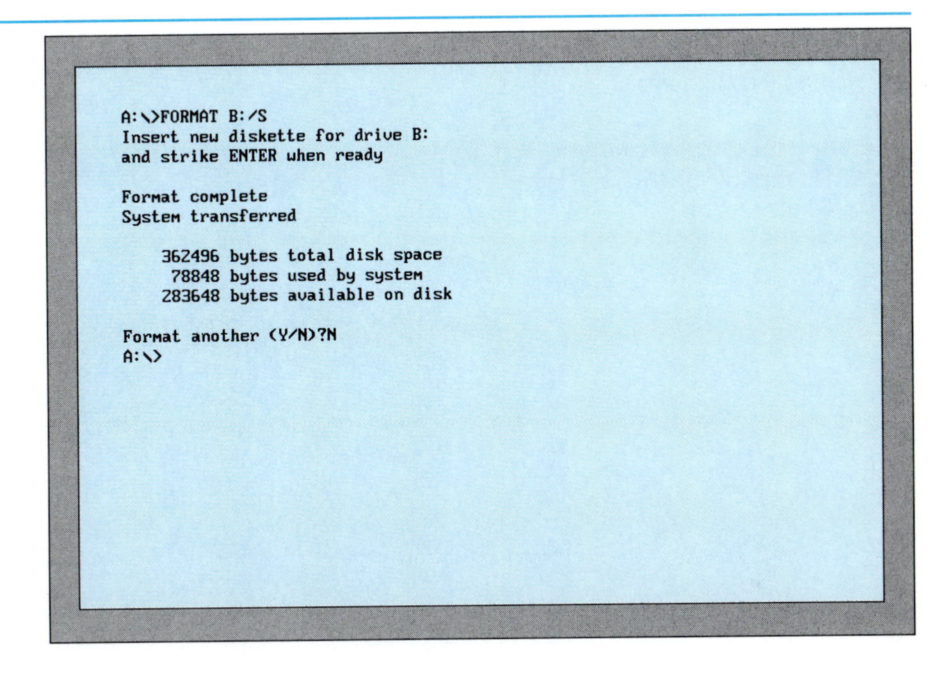

on the disk, the FORMAT command will mark them and tell the user how many bytes are usable. At the end of the FORMAT command the user has the option of immediately formatting another disk or stopping the format process. A slightly more complex but similar disk preparation procedure is used with new hard disk drives that are to be used with MS-DOS.

Displaying Storage Information

A floppy diskette is capable of holding only a certain number of files. At some point the diskette will become full and will not hold any additional files. A user can find out how full a disk is by using a command such as the MS-DOS CHKDSK (check disk) command.

Directory Commands

All microcomputer operating systems include commands that let the user view the contents of a disk. In MS-DOS the DIR command can be used to display a list of the files and additional information such as the size of the file and when it was last modified (see Exhibit 11.10).

Commands for Manipulating Files

In addition to providing the user with commands for manipulating a disk as a whole, a microcomputer OS also gives the user control over individual files. There is typically a group of basic commands for file manipulation, which provide capabilities for displaying a file on the screen, erasing a file, renaming a file, copying a file, and printing a file. All operating systems, including those for minicomputers and mainframes, provide the user with

Exhibit 11.10

Displaying the Contents of Disks

The MS-DOS DIR command is used to display the files on a diskette. In this example the contents of the diskette in drive B are displayed.

```
A:\>DIR B:

 Volume in drive B has no label
 Directory of  B:\

COMMAND  COM    25308   2-02-88  12:00a
PROGRAM  BAS     8128   8-25-88  11:11a
INCOME   WKS     1629   7-19-89   1:23a
LETTER   DOC     2319  10-26-90   2:44p
RESUME   TXT     2213  10-25-90   9:41a
BACKUP   COM    30280   2-09-88  12:00a
        6 File(s)    236544 bytes free

A:\>
```

these same types of functions. Exhibit 11.11 shows corresponding commands in the MS-DOS, CP/M, and UNIX microcomputer operating systems as well as the VMS-OS for DEC minicomputers and the CMS-OS for IBM mainframe computers.

Displaying a File

A user can display the contents of a file on the screen by using a command such as the MS-DOS TYPE command. This command will work only with files that contain text. Certain files, such as spreadsheet files, are stored in special formats. When they are typed on the screen they are typically unreadable.

Erasing a File

A user often finds that certain files on a diskette are no longer needed. An OS provides a command that allows a user to delete a file from a diskette's directory. This command is commonly called ERASE (or sometimes DEL). It can be used to delete a single file, a group of files with a common file name or file type, or all the files on a disk.

Renaming a File

An OS also allows users to change the name of files on diskettes. This command is usually RENAME. Following the name of the command, the user types the old name of the file and then the new name for the file. If the file is not on a diskette in the default drive, the letter of the drive must precede the file name.

Exhibit 11.11

Basic Operating System Functions and Commands

	OS				
OS FUNCTION	**MS-DOS**	**CP/M**	**UNIX**	**VMS**	**CMS**
List Files in Directory	DIR	CAT	ls	DIR	LISTFILE
Display File on Screen	TYPE	TYPE	cat	TYPE	TYPE
Erase	ERASE or DEL	ERA	rm	DELETE	ERASE
Rename File	RENAME	REN	mv	RENAME	RENAME
Copy File	COPY	PIP	cp	COPY	COPYFILE
Print File	PRINT	PIP	lp	PRINT	PRINT

Copying a File

An OS allows a user to copy files from one diskette onto another or make another copy on the same diskette. The command is usually called COPY. The most common use of this command is in transferring files between diskettes. It is important to realize that copying a file does not destroy the original file; instead, the OS duplicates the original file.

The COPY command can be used to copy a single file, a group of files, or all the files on a diskette. The MS-DOS OS also includes a command called DISKCOPY, which can be used to copy an entire diskette. With the DISKCOPY command, the diskette onto which the original diskette is being copied does not even need to be formatted. The DISKCOPY command will automatically prepare the new diskette before copying the files from the original.

Printing a File

Some operating systems have a PRINT command, which is similar to the TYPE command, except that the contents of the file go to a printer attached to the microcomputer rather than to the screen. The same constraints on typing files exist for printing. Files stored in special formats, such as spreadsheet files, cannot be printed by the OS. (The software that works with these files has a PRINT command within it that handles output to a printer.)

Advanced OS Features

The OS commands discussed so far represent the most basic features of a microcomputer OS. There are often additional features included in an OS that give an end-user more complete control over the files on diskettes and the microcomputer itself.

Editors

Most of the files on a diskette are used in conjunction with some type of software such as word processors, spreadsheets, or databases. When a user wants to alter the contents of one of these files, he or she simply uses the functions built into that software.

Occasionally, however, users want to create files that are not associated with any particular software product. (The startup files discussed in the next section are an example of this.) An OS will usually contain a program, called an **editor**, that can be used to create and edit such files. An editor is similar to a word processor and allows the user to enter information into a file or change its contents. Editors, however, do not contain as many features as word processors. Many editors are referred to as line editors; word processors are usually full-screen editors since the user can view and work on an entire screen of data at one time. A line editor allows a user to work on only one line of a file at a time. A full-screen editor allows a user to move through the file with the arrow keys on the keyboard. The MS-DOS OS comes with an editor called EDLIN, which is an example of a line editor.

Subdirectories

When disks contain a large number of files, it can become difficult for a user to locate a file. This is a common problem with even the smallest hard disks, which have storage space greater than thirty floppy diskettes combined. A disk always contains a single **root directory**, but most operating systems allow users to divide a disk into multiple directories. Exhibit 11.12 shows the structure of a disk with **subdirectories.** Note the way directories form a tree structure, similar to a business's organizational chart, with one directory at the top and many levels of subdirectories below. Below the ROOT directory are subdirectories for word processing files (WP), spreadsheet files (SPREAD), and database files (DATABASE). The WP directory has two subdirectories of its own, one for letters (LETTER) and one for memos (MEMO). The OS will provide the user with commands to create and delete subdirectories and to move from one subdirectory to another.

When subdirectories are used, the user must specify which subdirectory contains the file as well as which disk. For example, a file called LETTER.DOC in the LETTER subdirectory of a hard disk drive would be specified as C:\WP\LETTER \LETTER.DOC. The user is specifying that the OS could find this file by first going to the WP subdirectory and then to the LETTER subdirectory below that.

Startup Files

Most operating systems allow the user to place a special file, called a **startup file**, on a diskette. This file is given a special name and contains certain OS commands that the user wants to have executed whenever the computer is booted with that diskette. During the booting of the computer, the OS is loaded and looks at the diskette to see if it can find this special file. If the file

Exhibit 11.12

An Example Subdirectory Structure

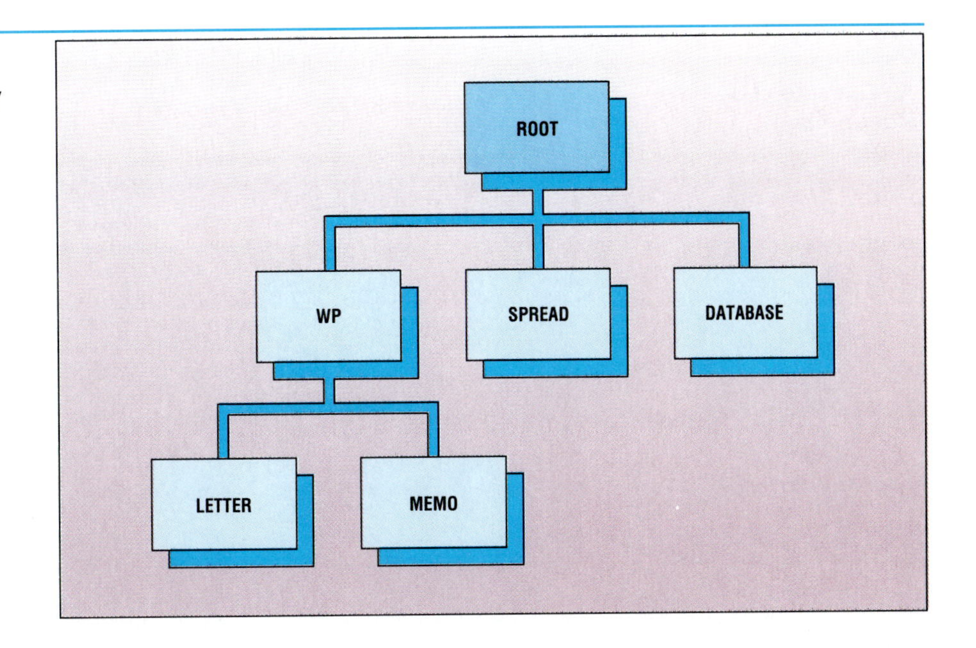

exists, the OS executes its commands before giving the user the prompt to indicate that the OS is ready.

In MS-DOS, this file is called AUTOEXEC.BAT. In other operating systems it may have another name. A diskette containing software, such as a word processing program, will often have a startup file that runs the software program. A user simply puts the diskette in the default drive, boots the computer, and the startup file puts the user directly into the word processing program. This allows a user who knows nothing about the OS to use the software; it also reduces the number of keystrokes needed to get into an application program.

A user can create a startup file or alter its contents with an editor. The startup file can be tailored to perform any OS command the user needs executed when that diskette is used to boot the computer. Exhibit 11.13 shows an example of a startup file. Note how this file simply contains OS commands that the user could have entered individually.

Hard Disks and Backup

Floppy diskettes are particularly vulnerable to damage. It is easy for the exposed magnetic surfaces to be smudged with fingerprints, for example. Because of the fragile nature of floppy diskettes, and the value of the data stored on them, making backup copies of diskettes is an extremely important part of using a microcomputer and one that is often overlooked.

Hard disks give users greater speed and more storage space, but they are also vulnerable. Because even the smallest hard disk can store the equivalent of more than thirty floppy diskettes, a failure can be extremely

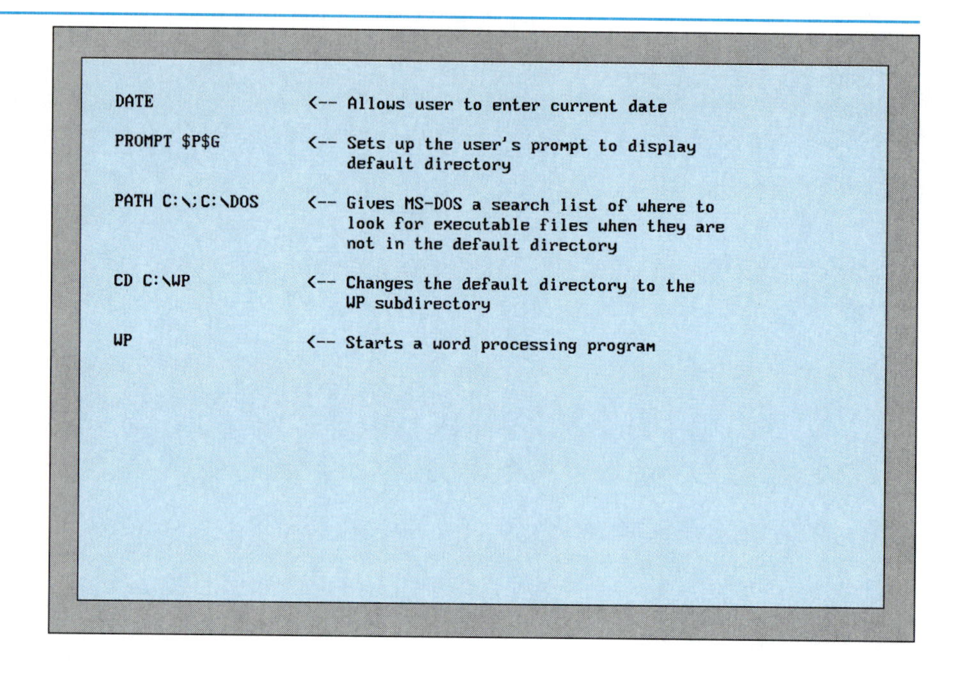

```
DATE              <-- Allows user to enter current date

PROMPT $P$G       <-- Sets up the user's prompt to display
                      default directory

PATH C:\;C:\DOS   <-- Gives MS-DOS a search list of where to
                      look for executable files when they are
                      not in the default directory

CD C:\WP          <-- Changes the default directory to the
                      WP subdirectory

WP                <-- Starts a word processing program
```

Exhibit 11.13

An Example of a Startup File

costly. This increased storage capacity makes it more difficult to make backup copies because the contents have to be copied to so many diskettes. Recent developments in tape cassette backup systems have eased this problem. Also, some operating systems now include a backup facility designed to transfer the contents of a hard disk to floppy diskettes or a tape drive.

Some of the capabilities of a backup facility include the ability to transfer (or back up) hard disk files onto floppy diskettes, transfer (or restore) the files from floppy diskettes to the hard disk, compare hard-disk files to files on backup diskettes, and list the files on a backup diskette.

When hard-disk files are backed up on floppy diskettes, the user has certain options about which files will be transferred. A hard disk is typically referenced as if it were a third floppy disk drive. In Exhibit 11.14 the hard disk has been designated as C.

Exhibit 11.14 shows the MS-DOS BACKUP command being used to transfer only the files on the hard disk with the extension WKS to a floppy diskette in drive B. The /M is an optional keyword that tells MS-DOS that only files that have been changed since the last backup should be transferred to the diskette. Other options include /S, to back up any subdirectory files in addition to the files specified; /A, to add the files to any files already on the backup disk; and /D, to back up files that have changed on or after a specified date. In front of the file name, the user must specify the path the OS must use to find this file, first going to the WP subdirectory and then to the LETTER subdirectory below that.

Exhibit 11.14 also shows the RESTORE command, which will retrieve files with a WKS extension from the backup diskette in drive B and copy them to the hard disk. A single file, a group of related files, or all the files on the backup diskette can be retrieved using this RESTORE command.

Exhibit 11.14
Backup Options

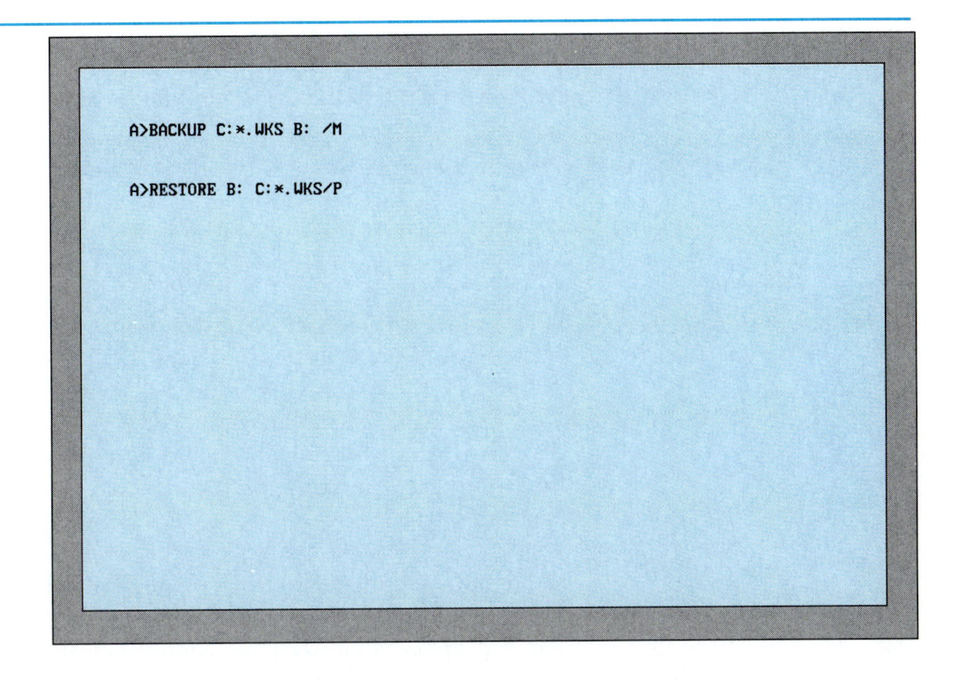

The Macintosh Operating System

Perhaps the most well-known example of an operating system with a graphical user interface is the Macintosh operating system. In the preceding discussion of the MS-DOS operating system, you were introduced to the types of functions provided by an operating system, such as the ability to work with disk directories and subdirectories and manipulate files. Although the interface used in the Macintosh OS is different from the interface used in MS-DOS, the types of functions available are very similar.

For example, in the Macintosh OS, the naming of files (typically called documents in the Macintosh OS) is more flexible. A file name can be up to thirty-one characters and, unlike MS-DOS, blanks can be used within the name of a file. There are no file extensions; instead, the type of icon is different for different files.

Even though a command line is not used in the Macintosh OS, the concept of using a prompt to let the user know when the OS is ready for the user to provide input still applies. In the Macintosh OS the display of the mouse pointer on the screen changes to a symbol that looks like a wristwatch to let the user know when the OS is busy. When the OS is waiting for the user to do something, the mouse pointer appears as an arrow on the screen.

In the Macintosh OS, commands are selected with the mouse pointer. When the user has selected the desired command, a button on the mouse is pressed to execute the command, in much the same way as the ENTER key is pressed to execute a command in MS-DOS.

The file manipulation operations discussed previously for MS-DOS can also be accomplished in a graphical operating system like the Macintosh OS. For example, copying is accomplished by selecting the icon of the file or disk to be copied and holding the mouse button down while pulling a copy of the icon off the original icon. This copy is then pulled to the icon representing the destination for the file or disk. Even though this procedure is quite different from that used in a command-line OS like MS-DOS, the point to appreciate is that all operating systems provide the same types of functions.

In the Macintosh OS the contents of a disk can be viewed by opening the icon representing that disk. The resulting window shows icons that represent the contents of the disk (see Exhibit 11.15).

In contrast to entering a command to instruct MS-DOS to erase a file, a user of the Macintosh OS simply uses the mouse to point to and select the icon representing the file and then pulls that icon to the trash can icon (see Exhibit 11.16).

In the Macintosh OS, the equivalent of a subdirectory is a folder. In the window representing the contents of a disk, a user can create a folder and place files inside the folder. When the folder is opened, another window appears, showing the contents of the folder. Sub-subdirectories can be created within a folder by simply creating another folder within the original folder. The user can move from one folder to another using the mouse, and files can be copied and moved from one folder to another with the mouse as well. Overall, it is important to realize that although different operating systems use different interfaces, the kinds of functions they provide are similar.

Exhibit 11.15

Opening the Icon

In the Macintosh OS the contents of a disk are displayed as icons in a window when the icon representing the disk is opened.

Exhibit 11.16

Interacting with Command-Line and Graphical Interfaces

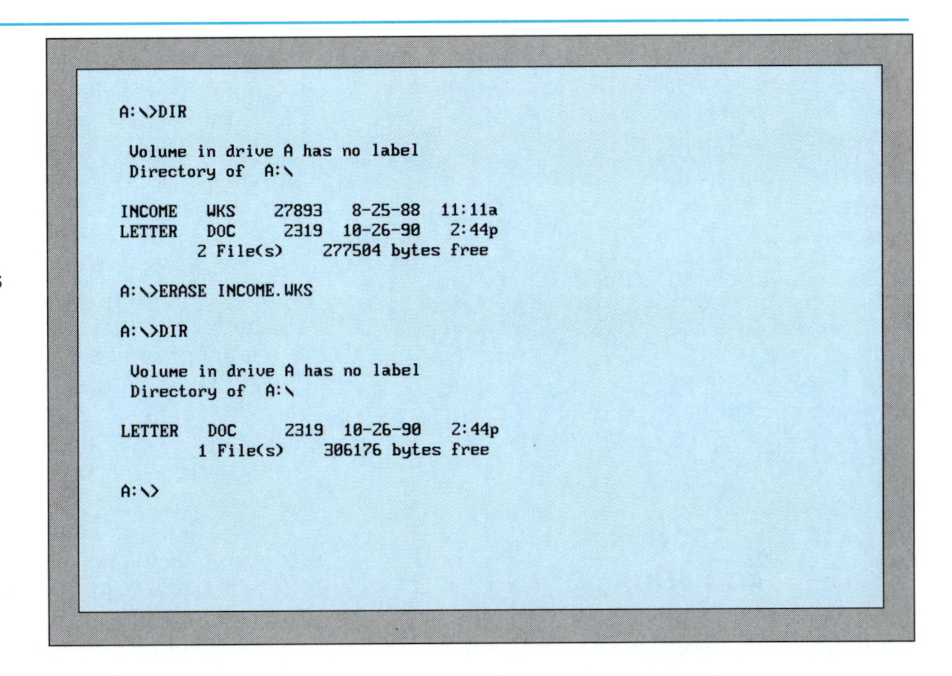

(a) In an OS with a command-line interface, the user must enter commands to display files and erase them.

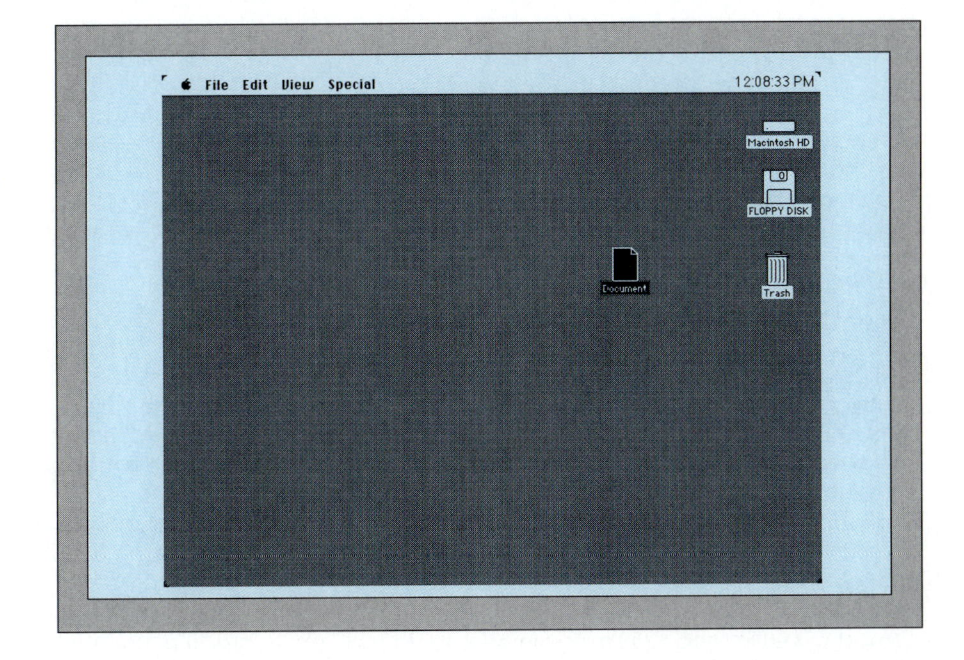

(b) In an OS with a graphical interface, the user erases a file by selecting the icon representing the file and pulling that icon on top of the icon representing the trashcan.

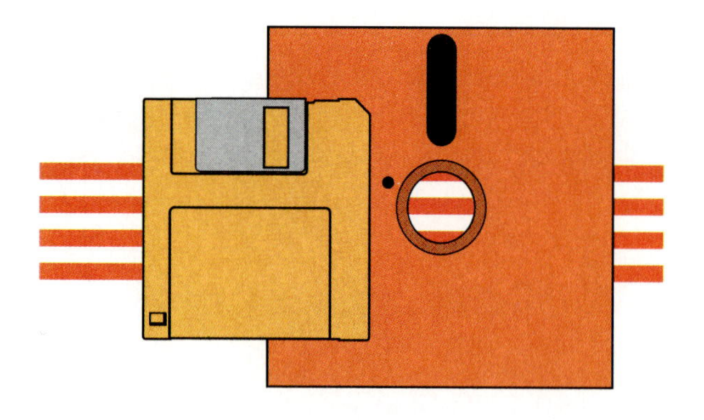

Computers at Work

A Computer Jock's $550-Million Jackpot

Superlatives are always hard to prove, but apparently no one ever made more money at an earlier age than William H. Gates III. Chief executive and a cofounder of Microsoft, a suburban Seattle software company, Gates changed the way American business works by creating some of the most widely used personal computer software. He would much rather discuss that than his fortune. But for 1989 the preeminent fact about Bill Gates is that, at age 32 (and looking 20), he took Microsoft public and held on to shares that at last count were worth around $550 million.

The essence of Microsoft's business is its close dealings with personal computer manufacturers, particularly IBM, which license Gates's software and relicense it to those who buy their machines. About 40 percent of the 23 million personal computers used in business run Microsoft's computer languages, according to InfoCorp, a California market research company; half use the company's operating-system software for controlling basic computer functions. Such products will account for roughly half the company's estimated $280 million in sales for the fiscal year ending next June; the rest comes from software for such applications as word processing.

Gates describes himself as a hands-on manager with a passion for excellence. "I give people a hard time," he says. Then he falls into his own brand of computerspeak. "When they come to meetings they'd better be ready to respond to my questions in real time and at high bandwidth." Gates often applies his intensity and intelligence to subjects beyond computers—the law, for example. But he is also known as an avid party person and something of a lady's man.

Gates started writing programs for computers at 14. His first computer job was finding the bugs in a new Digital Equipment machine. As long as there were bugs, the company that was buying the computer could delay paying for it. His compensation: free time on the computer. Gates's horizons expanded in January 1975, when *Popular Electronics* ran a cover story on the Altair, the first personal computer to come to market. That inspired Gates, a Harvard freshman, to write a version of the Basic computer language that would run on PCs and to drop out of school to sell it. The first five customers went bankrupt, but within 18 months Gates and Microsoft's other founder, Paul Allen, a friend from high school and a University of Washington dropout, had landed contracts with Apple, Commodore, and Radio Shack.

A competitor's mistake led Microsoft to glory. In late 1980 a team from IBM, looking for an operating system to run its forthcoming PC, visited Digital Research Inc., a tiny California company that was selling the industry's first standard system. The head of Digital Research was not around, but the company's lawyer was. He recoiled at the intimidating nondisclosure agreement IBM insisted he sign before opening talks. So the blue suits from Armonk turned to Gates, who gladly accepted the business. Never having written an operating system, he spent $50,000 to buy one quite similar to Digital Research's. Then he reworked and polished it into a system called PC-DOS. Today most IBM PCs and clones of those widely popular machines use Microsoft's program.

Gates says he is proudest of conceiving ideas that will make personal computers easier to use and to program. His most urgent project: an advanced PC-DOS that will enable software to catch up with recent advances in personal computer hardware. Says David Norman, chief executive of computer retailer Businessland: "Bill Gates is the key to the advancement of the entire industry."

Ask if it is too late for other software entrepreneurs to cash in, and Gates's killer instinct comes out. "There are great opportunities for storing mixed information—data, images, voice, and music—on optical disks and for using artificial intelligence to make computers friendlier," he says. "But you'd better try to make me and the rest of the industry look dumb. Whatever big opportunities I see are sure to show up in Microsoft's products."

Summary and Key Terms

System software is a series of programs written to simplify the interface between the user and the computer hardware. System software is generally composed of an **operating system**, **language translators** and **utilities**, data management routines, and data communication systems.

The overall purpose of the operating system is to control the activities of the computer system. It serves as the traffic cop or **supervisor**, directing and managing computer events.

There are several major design factors that can be used to distinguish among operating systems. Was the OS designed to be used primarily with **batch** or **interactive** processing jobs? Was it designed to accommodate single or multiple users? Was the OS designed to do **multitasking**, allowing the OS to process one application running as a **foreground task** and other applications running as **background tasks?** Is the OS **computer-specific** or is it designed to run on a **family of computers?**

A major difference between operating systems designed for microcomputers and those for mainframe and mini-computers is a public, rather than a proprietary, orientation. This unbundled approach has led to a variety of choices of operating system for use on a given microcomputer. Operating systems can also be adapted for use on different microcomputers.

Although no official committee has specified industry standards, several de facto standards for microcomputer operating systems have developed. A **de facto standard** is one that vendors informally accept, generally because it has come to dominate a market segment of the business. For the 8-bit microcomputer, it is the CP/M operating system; for the 16-bit micro, it is MS-DOS; and for the 32-bit micro, UNIX and OS/2 appear to be the dominant operating systems on IBM compatible computers. The Macintosh OS is the only operating system for the Macintosh family of computers.

The interface between a user and the OS is either command-line or menu-driven. A **command-line interface** requires the user to type commands. A **graphical interface** represents the objects that the OS deals with as **icons**, or pictures reflecting a function or object. The user interacts with these icons, using a mouse pointer to select icons, activate pull-down menus, and work with **windows** displaying the contents of icons. A **shell** is a piece of software used to create a menu-driven interface for an OS.

Microcomputer operating systems are designed to function with two disk drives (and/or sometimes a hard disk), one of which is labeled as the default drive. When the computer is **booted** it looks for the OS on the disk in the default drive and loads it into the primary memory of the computer. The OS typically consists of a small group of command files, some of which may be hidden from the user. Any disk containing these files can be used to boot the computer. An OS will interact with the user via a **prompt,** which is simply a way for the operating system to let the user know when it is ready to receive instructions.

The OS provides many commands that enable the user to maintain disks and the files on those disks. The user interacts with data in the form of **files**, which are simply a collection of related information. Files are typically given two names: a file name and a file type. The file type usually indicates what the file is used for.

In MS-DOS, the FORMAT command lets a user prepare a blank diskette for use by the operating system. CHKDSK gives the user information about the use of a diskette's storage space. A directory command provides a list of the files on a disk. The TYPE command allows a user to display the contents of a file on the screen. The ERASE command deletes a file from a diskette. RENAME lets a user change the name of a file. The COPY command lets a user make copies of a file on the same diskette or a second diskette. The PRINT command transfers the contents of a file to a printer connected to the microcomputer.

An OS often includes advanced features such

as an **editor**, which helps a user create and modify files. Line editors allow the user to work with a file one line at a time while full-screen editors allow the user to interact with an entire screen of data at once. An OS allows a user to create a special **startup file** containing OS commands that are to be executed whenever the computer is booted from the diskette containing that file. An OS can create **subdirectories** below a **root directory**, and the user can then work with a hierarchy of directories. A microcomputer with a hard disk can often take advantage of backup commands in an OS, which allow backup copies of the hard disk to be made.

Review Questions

1. Briefly describe the functions of the operating system.
2. Explain the major factors that are used to distinguish among operating systems.
3. Explain the term *multitasking.*
4. Explain what *booting* a microcomputer means.
5. Explain how a prompt is used when a user interacts with the operating system.
6. Explain what a startup file is and how it is used.
7. What is an editor?
8. What is a subdirectory?
9. What does the term *de facto standard* mean?
10. What is the difference between batch and interactive processing?

T F **11.** A series of computer models that have a similar architecture and can all run the same OS is called a family of computers.

T F **12.** A de facto standard is an unofficial standard that vendors tend to follow because of its popularity.

T F **13.** An OS with a command-line interface allows the user to build commands by choosing options from menus.

T F **14.** A shell is a program that alters the interface of an OS.

T F **15.** The default drive on a microcomputer is the drive that has the most free storage space.

T F **16.** A graphical OS, such as the Macintosh OS, does not allow the user to perform the same types of operations (such as copying, renaming, erasing, and printing) as a command-line OS, such as MS-DOS.

T F **17.** Folders in the Macintosh OS are equivalent to subdirectories in MS-DOS.

T F **18.** A startup file is a special file that the OS executes when the computer is booted.

T F **19.** Backup commands are not important to users of microcomputers with hard disk drives.

T F **20.** In MS-DOS diskettes do not have to be prepared by the OS before they can be used to store files.

21. _____ Which item in the following list is not considered a part of system software?

a. operating system
b. language translator
c. application programs
d. utilities

22. _____ A(n) __________-oriented OS receives programs and data, processes them one at a time, and sends the results back.

a. multitasking
b. batch
c. interactive
d. object

23. _____ A(n) __________ OS allows the user to run more than one application program at the same time.

a. batch
b. multitasking
c. interactive
d. flexible

24. _____ In a multitasking OS, the application the user is currently interacting with is known as the:

a. background task
b. interactive task
c. foreground task
d. operational task

25. _____ Which of the following is part of an OS with a graphical interface?

a. icon
b. window
c. pull-down menu
d. all of the above

26. _____ The process of starting a microcomputer by loading the OS files into primary memory is known as __________ the microcomputer.

a. booting c. initializing
b. starting d. formatting

27. _____ All operating systems use a(n) __________ to signal to the user when it is ready to receive instructions.

a. flag c. prompt
b. pointer d. indicator

28. _____ The command for preparing diskettes in MS-DOS is:

a. PREPARE c. EDIT
b. INITIALIZE d. FORMAT

29. _____ The MS-DOS command for copying the contents of an entire disk to an unformatted disk is:

a. COPY c. DISKCOPY
b. REPLICATE d. DUPLICATE

30. _____ Which of the following is not an OS command for manipulating files?

a. ERASE c. COPY
b. RENAME d. LOAD

CHAPTER 12

Word Processing

Word processors can be used by employees at all levels of a business. Clerks use them to improve productivity when handling documents needed in daily operations; managers and executives use them to prepare reports and memos.

If you make a mistake when using a typewriter, the error has to be erased from the paper. If new words or lines need to be added, the entire document has to be retyped. In contrast, a word processor allows you to store text electronically rather than typing it directly on paper. You can make any changes in the electronic version of the document and commit it to paper after all editing and revision is complete. And even after a document is printed, it is quite simple to make changes and then have the word processor print a new copy.

With a word processing system, a user can almost instantly print a document using a few simple commands. If multiple documents are needed, perhaps for letters sent in mass mailings, a single document can be created and the word processor will create the copies, each of which is an original with a different addressee. (With a typewriter each copy would have to be typed individually.)

This discussion of word processors covers five basic functions that all word processors provide: document creation, editing, formatting, printing, and handling. Some advanced features included in word processors are also examined: spelling checkers, thesaurus programs, style checkers, and mail merge programs.

In this chapter you will learn to do the following:

1. Explain how a document is created
2. Describe how the contents of a document can be changed
3. Recognize how word processors format documents
4. Understand how word processors handle documents
5. Evaluate and compare various word processing programs

Creating a Document

A **document** is a collection of text and special symbols used to convey a message to the reader. It can take on many forms, such as memos, letters, and reports. A user enters the text into the computer, which stores the electronic document in a separate file on a floppy diskette or a hard disk.

When a document is created, it is given a name so that the user can identify it when he or she wants to use it. In order for the user to use the document, it must be in the primary memory of the computer.

Most word processors do not ask the user to assign a name to a newly created document until it is saved. Other word processors ask the user to name a document first, and, if that name does not refer to an existing document, the word processor assumes the user wants to create a new document under that name.

After a new document has been created, the user can begin to enter text. Some word processors allow the user to begin entering text immediately. Alternatively, the user may be required to select what is called an *edit mode* before text can be entered.

Document Editing

Once the word processor is in edit mode, the user can type text on the screen. As long as the document remains in primary memory, the user can "move around" the document to look over what has been entered and correct any mistakes that have been made.

The Cursor

A cursor on the screen indicates the user's current position in the document. Typically the **cursor** is an underscore (_) or a rectangle (▭) about the size of one character. The user moves through the electronic document by repositioning the cursor at the desired position within the document. Exhibit 12.1 shows a document in the WordPerfect word processor. The document in Exhibit 12.1 is used throughout this chapter to demonstrate the various features of word processors. Note that the cursor is on the *M* in *Mr.* at the top of the document.

Moving the Cursor

At the most basic level, documents are simply collections of characters (letters, numbers, and special symbols). These characters are grouped into words, which are grouped into lines. All word processors allow movement in any direction, one character at a time. Many word processors use arrow keys on the keyboard. Other word processors still require the user to hold down the control key while pressing one of the letter keys to move the cursor.

In addition to moving through a document one character at a time, many word processors allow movements of a word at a time, a line at a time, and even a screen at a time. There are also special combinations of keys that permit the user to move the cursor immediately to the top or

Exhibit 12.1

The Example Letter as It Appears in the Word Perfect Word Processor

```
Mr. William Williams
123 Cherry Street
Appleton, OH 44444

Dear Mr. Williams:

I would like to apply for your position as a microcomputer
specialist.  I feel that I have many skills which are appropriate
for this job.

     1.  I have worked with microcomputer operating systems.

     2.  I am an expert user of word processors, electronic
     spreadsheets, graphics, databases, and data communications.

     3.  I am well motivated and eager to learn.

I believe that I can be an asset to your organization and I look
forward to hearing from you soon.

                                   Sincerely,

                                   Sam Samuels

                                                    Doc 1 Pg 1 Ln 1" Pos 1"
```

bottom of the document. Exhibit 12.2 shows the movement functions implemented in the PFS: First Choice word processor. Word processors like PFS: First Choice take advantage of many of the special keys on a microcomputer's keyboard to execute such cursor movement functions (see Exhibit 12.3 on page 299).

Word Wrap

It's very frustrating to be typing a document on a typewriter and suddenly realize you have typed off the side of the page. To alleviate this problem, word processors have a feature known as **word wrap**, so that, at the end of a line, the user does not have to press the RETURN or ENTER key to move down to the next line. Instead, he or she simply continues typing, and when a word is typed that goes beyond the right margin, the word processor automatically takes that word and moves it, and the cursor, down to the next line. In essence, the word that is too long for the current line "wraps" around to the beginning of the next line. The only time the RETURN key needs to be used is when a line ends short of the right margin.

In the letter in Exhibit 12.1, the lines at the top and bottom are examples of short lines where the RETURN key has to be pressed. Thus, after the user types *Mr. William Williams,* the RETURN key must be pressed so the cursor will move down to the beginning of the next line, for the address. In the body of the letter, however, the user begins typing and doesn't press RETURN until a paragraph ends. A blank line is created by pressing RETURN at the beginning of the line.

Exhibit 12.2

The Movement Functions in the PFS: First Choice Word Processor

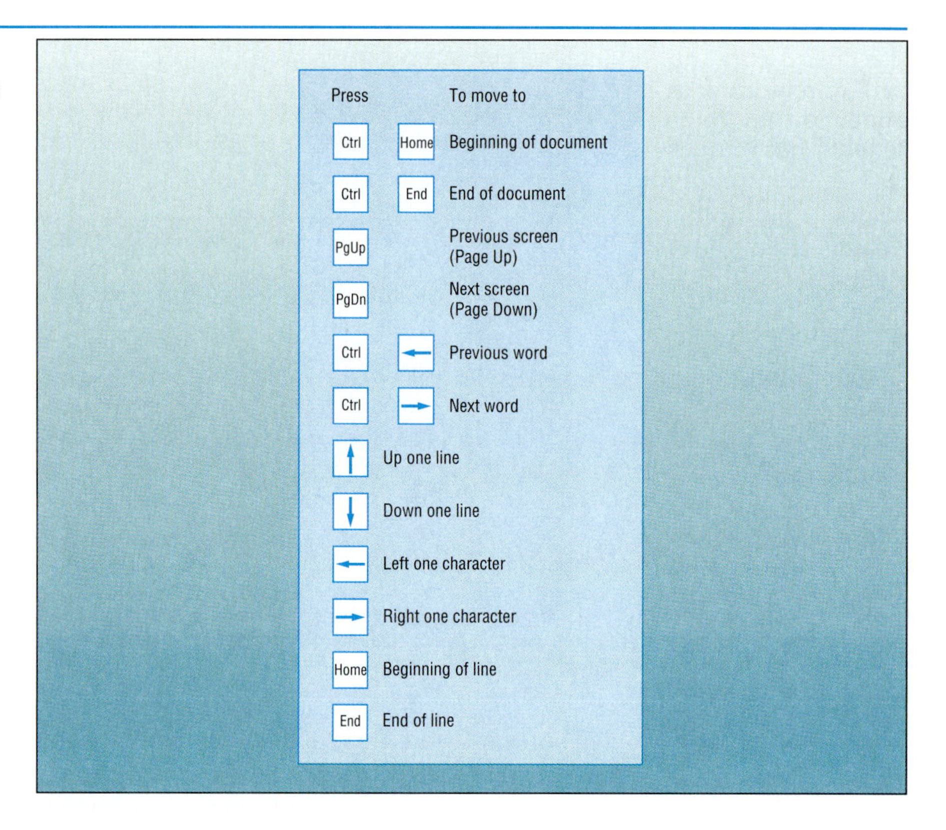

Revising a Document

When creating a document with a word processor, the user initially only has to worry about getting all the words on the screen in the correct order, along with the blank lines necessary to separate paragraphs and other items. Special spacing, such as indenting, can be accomplished when the document is formatted. Once a letter is typed in, the user can edit it and fix any mistakes that have been made. Exhibit 12.4 on page 300 shows what the letter looks like after it has been typed into the computer. Note that some mistakes have been made and should be corrected before the document is printed. Although these mistakes are relatively minor, they would necessitate retyping if a typewriter were being used. On a computer, the extra characters can be removed, the gaps closed up, and the misplaced item moved quickly and easily prior to printing the letter.

Typeover Mode

When a document's contents need revision, there are two typing modes that can be used to correct and modify text. The first one is known as **typeover mode**. Word processors that operate in this mode allow the user to position the cursor on a word and type new characters over the characters that are already in the document. Thus, the new characters replace existing characters.

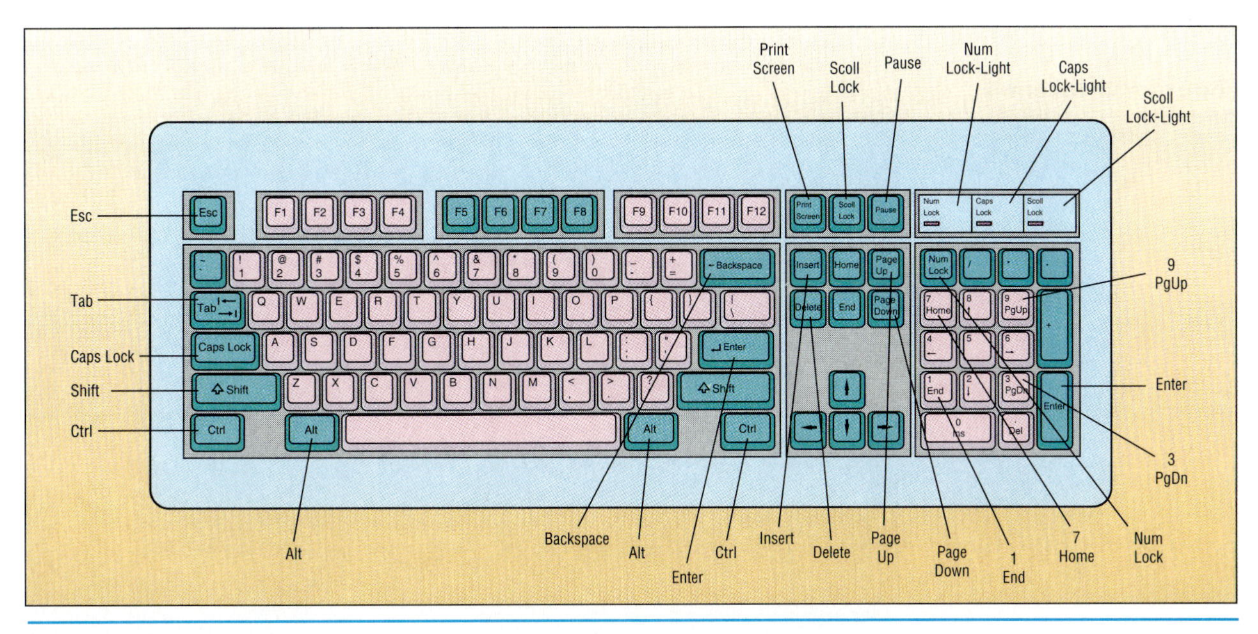

Exhibit 12.3

The Keyboard of an IBM PS/2

Word processors usually use the arrow keys and the PGUP, PGDN, HOME, and END keys when implementing movement functions. The CTRL key and the twelve function keys (F1 through F12) are sometimes used in movement functions. The backspace and DEL keys are used for revising a document.

In order to fix a mistake such as the misspelling of *Cherry* on the second line of the example letter, the user would position the cursor on the letter *a* and type *e*. In typeover mode, the *e* replaces the *a*.

A mistake such as the spelling of *Dear* as *Der* in line five cannot be corrected with the typeover mode. If the user moves to the *r* in *Der* and "corrects" it, the *r* would be changed to *a*, but there would be no room for the *r* after the *a* because the space between *Dear* and *Mr.* is still needed. What the user needs to do is insert an *a* between the *e* and the *r*. This requires a second typing mode.

Insert Mode

The **insert mode** creates space so that a letter or word can be inserted in its proper position. First the cursor is positioned over a character. Then a new character is typed and appears to the left of the cursor, and the characters to the right of (and under) the cursor move to the right. In the example letter, the user can put the cursor on the *r* in *Der* and type an *a*. In insert mode, the *r* and everything to the right of it is pushed to the right one space as the *a* is inserted between the *e* and the *r*. In this mode the text that is already in the document is not destroyed; it gets pushed to the right and down.

Deleting Text

There are varying levels of deletion, just as there are varying levels of movement throughout a document. At the most basic level, there is the elimination of a single character—the cursor is moved to the character and a key is pressed or a delete command issued. In the example letter, the cursor would be positioned on the extra *p* in the word *apply* and the delete function used.

Exhibit 12.4

The Example Letter with Mistakes

```
Mr. William Williams
123 Charry Street
Appleton, OH 44444

Der Mr. Williams:

I have would like to appply for your position as a microcomputer
specialist.  I feel that I have many skills which are appropriate
for this job.

     1.  I have worked with microcomputer operating systems.

     3.  I am well motivated and eager to learn.

     2.  I am an expert user of word processors, electronic
     spreadsheets, graphics, databases, and data communications.

I believe that I can be an asset to your organization and I look
forward to hearing from you soon.

                                    Sincerely,
                                    Sincerely,

                                    Sam Samuels
                                              Doc 1 Pg 1 Ln 1" Pos 1"
```

Another character deletion mechanism often provided by word processors is the BACKSPACE key. This special key is helpful if the user notices a mistake while typing. The user simply backs up over the mistake, deleting it as the cursor moves backward, and then types in the correct characters. In the example letter, the extra *p* could be removed by positioning the cursor on either of the last two *p*'s or the letter *l* and using the backspace key. If the cursor were positioned on the first *p* the letter *a* would be deleted, since the backspace key deletes the letter to the left of the cursor.

If a user wants to delete entire words or lines at one time, either a key press or a command can be used. Even entire blocks of text can be deleted with a single command.

In the example, the word *have* in the first line of the body of the letter could be removed by positioning the cursor on the *h* and using the word delete function to take out that entire word. The line delete function could be used to delete the extra line (with the word *Sincerely* on it) at the bottom of the document. As with the word delete function, the cursor is positioned at the beginning of the line to be deleted before the line delete command is used. Exhibit 12.5 illustrates these levels of deletion.

Another important feature related to deleting text is the **undelete** function. With the ability to delete whole lines and blocks of text with a single command comes the risk of making costly mistakes by deleting the wrong thing—or you might change your mind. The more advanced word processors do not immediately destroy deleted text; instead, the deleted text is stored in designated memory locations that are used as temporary holding places (usually called *buffers*). If you did not really want to delete the text, you could issue an undelete command, which will go to this buffer and bring back the deleted text (see Exhibit 12.6 on page 302). Typically the

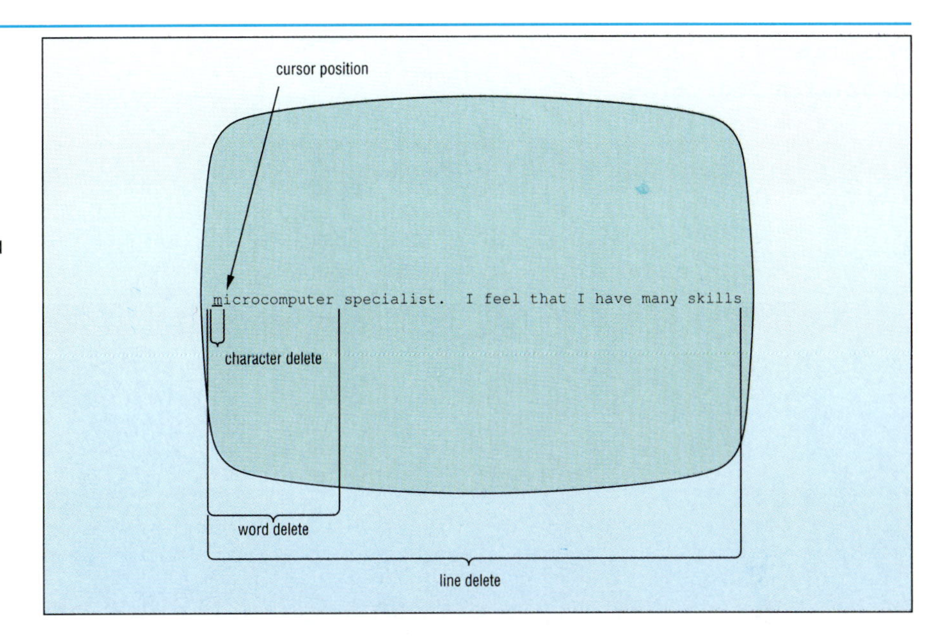

Exhibit 12.5

Delete Functions

Word processors give the user various levels of deletion. The effects of character, word, and line deletes are illustrated on a line from the example letter.

buffer holds only the last character or group of characters deleted. When another deletion is performed, the most recently deleted information replaces the information placed in the buffer previously.

Block Moves and Deletes

When entering large amounts of text, a user may find that a group of words would work better in a different location in the document. Rather than making the user delete the words where they are and retype them in the new place, most word processors provide a way to move sections of text. These sections are commonly referred to as blocks. A **block** is simply a group of characters. It can be as small as a single character or can include several words, lines, paragraphs, or pages of the document.

Word processors allow users to delete entire sections in the same way. For example, a user might want to remove several paragraphs from the document. Instead of deleting these paragraphs a word or a line at a time, the user can specify that they be treated as a block of text.

Typically, word processors provide a command that allows the user to specify the location of a block by marking its beginning and end. As the block is specified, the word processor usually highlights the block so the user can see exactly what text is included. Exhibit 12.7 on page 303 shows the sample letter with item 3 highlighted as a block.

Once a block is highlighted, a user can control it as a single unit of text. The entire block can be deleted, or the appearance of the text in the block can be changed in a variety of ways. But perhaps the most important advantage of being able to group text into a block is the option to change its location within the document. This process is referred to as a **block move.**

Exhibit 12.6
Undelete Function

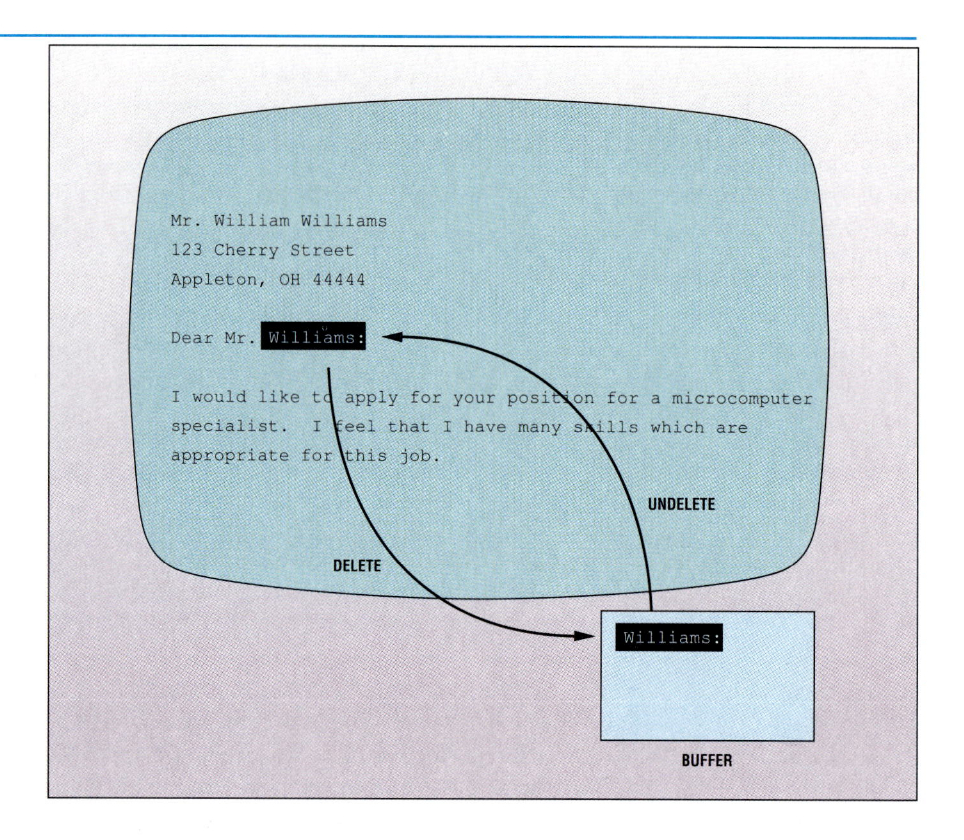

In a block move, the user first highlights the block and then issues a move command. The bottom of the screen in Exhibit 12.7 shows the options for the move command in WordPerfect. Once the move command is issued, it is removed from the document and placed into a buffer.

In the example, item 3 has been typed in the wrong place and needs to be moved to follow item 2. Rather than deleting item 3 and retyping it in the correct location, a user can mark it as a block, place the block in the buffer (sometimes referred to as "cutting" the block), move the cursor down to the blank line below item 2, and put the block back into the text at that location (sometimes referred to as "pasting" the block back in). Exhibit 12.8 shows how the document looks after the letter has been corrected.

Searching

Another common function provided by most word processors is the ability to search for a particular group of characters or words in a document. Most SEARCH commands ask what the user wants to find. If the word *expert* was supplied, the SEARCH command would look through the document for the next occurrence of that word and place the cursor there. Usually this search takes place from the current cursor position down through the document

Exhibit 12.7

Moving a Block of Text

The block of text to be moved is highlighted during the block move command in WordPerfect. Once the block is marked, the user issues a move command to place the marked block into a buffer. When moving the block to the buffer, the user can specify whether to remove (move) the block from the text or make a copy of it (copy). The text can also be placed in another file or it can be deleted entirely.

```
     3.  I am well motivated and eager to learn.

     2.  I am an expert user of word processors, electronic
     spreadsheets, graphics, databases, and data communications.

I believe that I can be an asset to your organization and I look
forward to hearing from you soon.

                              Sincerely,

                              Sam Samuels

1 Move; 2 Copy; 3 Delete; 4 Append: 0
```

Exhibit 12.8

The Completed Example Letter

```
Mr. William Williams
123 Cherry Street
Appleton, OH 44444

Dear Mr. Williams:

I would like to apply for your position as a microcomputer
specialist.  I feel that I have many skills which are appropriate
for this job.

     1.  I have worked with microcomputer operating systems.

     2.  I am an expert user of word processors, electronic
     spreadsheets, graphics, databases, and data communications.

     3.  I am well motivated and eager to learn.

I believe that I can be an asset to your organization and I look
forward to hearing from you soon.

                              Sincerely,

                              Sam Samuels

                                        Doc 1 Pg 1 Ln 1" Pos 1"
```

(toward the end). If the word is above the current position in the document (nearer the beginning), the SEARCH command may fail to find it. Thus, a common practice is to first move to the top of the document before issuing a SEARCH command, so that the entire document will be scanned. Some word processors, however, will also search backward through the document.

An available option is the substitution of a special wildcard character for parts of the string of characters being searched for. For example, in some word processors a user can specify *ex** as the string to search for, the word processor will locate the first string that begins with *ex*. The * indicates that the user doesn't care what characters follow the *ex*.

Also associated with the search function is a feature known as **search and replace**. In search and replace the user specifies two strings: a string to search for and a string to replace it with once it is located. When the search string is located, the user can decide if it is to be replaced. In addition to a normal search and replace, there is also a **global search and replace**, in which each occurrence of the search string throughout the document is replaced. Thus, all the misspellings of *received* as *recieved* throughout a manuscript can be corrected with a single command.

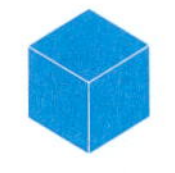

Document Formatting

Once all the words have been entered into the document, there are a group of commands that can be used to affect the document's overall appearance. These are usually referred to as **formatting commands.** Formatting commands can be broken into three rough categories: character formats, line formats, and page formats.

Character Formats

Character formats affect the way the characters in the text look. These formatting options allow a user to change the appearance of text using

Exhibit 12.9

Character Formats

Character formats include options for changing the appearance of text, applying different type styles to the text, and changing the size or pitch of the characters.

Character Formats

In this paragraph, each word associated with a text appearance feature is printed with that feature: (e.g., **bold** super script, sub script, *italics*, shadow, and ~~strikeout~~). Some further additions to the list are double underlining and single underlining. You may also choose not to underline spaces.

In this paragraph, each word associated with a different font or type style is printed with that font (e.g., Courier, Helvetica Palatino, New Century Schoolbook, and Times Roman).

Print sizes include small, normal, large, and VERY LARGE sizes of print options such as boldfacing, underlining, and italics, among others. Another feature related to character appearance is the ability to change the typeface of characters. Some common typefaces include Courier, Helvetica, and Times Roman. Finally, the size of characters (commonly referred to as their point size) can also be altered with most word processors. Alternatively, by choosing a font, with some word processors, all three types of character formatting can be determined at once. A font is a particular size of a typeface and has the attribute of being bold, roman, or italic, for example. Exhibit 12.9 shows a paragraph that illustrates some common character formatting.

Line Formats

Line formatting options affect the way lines on the page are built. These options include right and left margins, spacing between lines, tabs and indents, and alignment (and justification) of text. Exhibit 12.10 illustrates some of these formatting options.

Margins

All word processors include the ability to set right and left margins independently. A common method of specifying margins uses a special

Exhibit 12.10

Line Formatting Options

Common line formatting options include the ability to determine the type and position of tabs, indent text from the right and left margins, and align a block of text to the left, right, or center.

Tabs can be used to position characters anywhere on a line and to line those characters up to the left, right, or centered over the tab position. Tabs can also be used to line numbers up on the decimal place.

Left Tab	Center Tab	Right Tab	125.00 Decim.al

This text is indented from the left margin using an indent command. Notice how the indenting will continue until the ENTER key is pressed.

This text is indented from both left and right. Note that the text is indented from both margins according to the tab settings.

Various text alignments can be accomplished with most word processors:

Text can be flush left

Text can be centered

Text can be flush right

feature called a ruler. A **ruler** is a line that runs across the computer screen, on which the user can indicate the positioning of various formatting elements, such as the right and left margins and the positions for tabs and indents (see below). Rulers often show numbers or markers that indicate the position of every fifth or tenth character across the line. Exhibit 12.11 shows a ruler in the PFS: First Choice word processor. Rulers can be inserted into a document as often as needed. Thus, the settings for right and left margins can be changed several times on a single page.

Line Spacing

Word processors also allow the user to determine the spacing between lines in the document. Normally documents are initially created single spaced, but with a simple command the user can set up a double spaced (every other line) or triple spaced (every third line) line format. When the line spacing is changed, the additional blank lines are automatically inserted in the document and the word wrap automatically moves the cursor to the appropriate line when the end of a line is reached. Some word processors actually show the line spacing on the screen; in others the line spacing doesn't take effect until the document is printed.

Tabs and Indenting

Word processors typically allow users to specify the positioning of tab stops, which can be used to construct tables and other documents requiring precise alignment of columns of text and numbers. Like margins the locations of these tabs are typically specified using some sort of ruler that lets the user see exactly where the tabs are being placed. There are several types of tabs, which allows the user to achieve different types of text alignments (see Exhibit 12.10). Once the user sets up the position and type of tabs, the tab key can be used to position text accordingly.

Exhibit 12.11

Setting Margins with a Ruler

The PFS: First Choice word processor uses a ruler to set margins in the document. When the rule line is edited, the user can enter a (on the line to represent the position of the left margin. A) represents the right margin and a T represents a position for a tab.

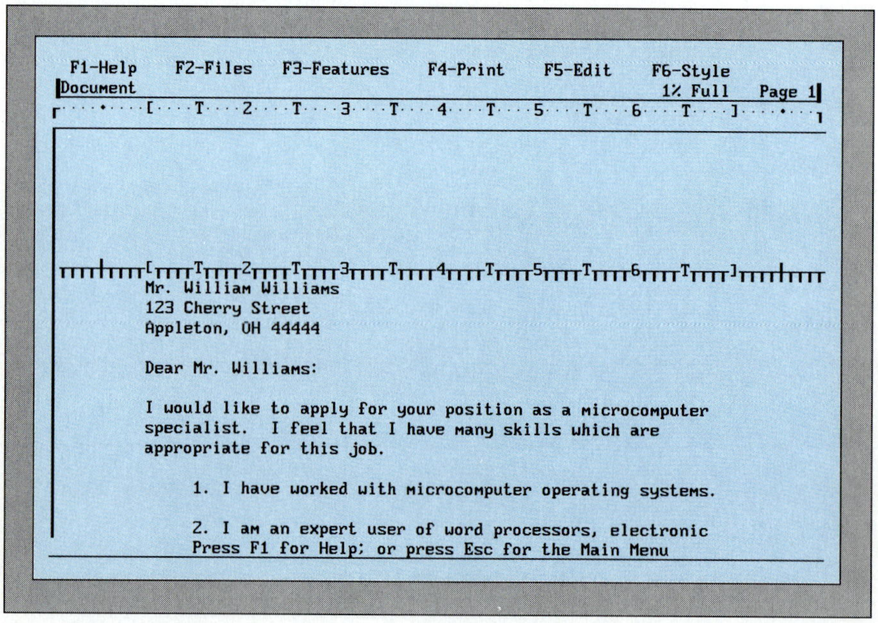

```
F1-Help   F2-Files   F3-Features   F4-Print   F5-Edit   F6-Style
Document                                           1% Full   Page 1

        Mr. William Williams
        123 Cherry Street
        Appleton, OH 44444

        Dear Mr. Williams:

        I would like to apply for your position as a microcomputer
        specialist.  I feel that I have many skills which are
        appropriate for this job.

             1. I have worked with microcomputer operating systems.

             2. I am an expert user of word processors, electronic
             Press F1 for Help; or press Esc for the Main Menu
```

Indents are used to bring a block of text in from the left margin or from both the right and left margin at the same time (see Exhibit 12.10). The numbered items in the example letter shown at the beginning of this chapter are examples of indented text. Some word processors simply use the position of tab stops to determine how far an indent will bring the text in from the margin. Others use a special symbol on a ruler to indicate the position for indenting.

Once indenting takes effect, it typically continues until a hard return is reached (where the user has pressed the ENTER key), such as the end of a paragraph. With this approach, the user must reissue the indent command at the beginning of each paragraph that is to be indented. Some word processors use separate commands to indicate where an indent is to begin and where it is to end. With this approach indenting can continue through several paragraphs until the user indicates that indenting is to stop.

Alignment of Text

A final line formatting option involves the position of a block of text in relation to the right and left margins. Exhibit 12.11 illustrates the alignment of a block of text with the left margin, the right margin, and centered between the right and left margins. If the right or left margin is changed the aligned text will be automatically repositioned in the new margin settings.

Another alignment option common in word processors is known as justification. **Justification** is the alignment of text with the margins such that the edges of the text are straight and parallel. Typical examples of justified text can be found in newspapers—or in this textbook. As you may have noticed, justification is accomplished by inserting extra space between characters or words, so that the last character on a line is even with the margin. Some word processors show the justification on the screen; others only justify the printed text.

Page Formats

Page formats include options that affect all the pages in the document. Common page formatting options include those determining top and bottom margins and page number position and options to set up headers and footers and multiple columns.

In addition to allowing the user to determine left and right margins, word processors provide commands for setting top and bottom margins. In contrast to right and left margins, top and bottom margins always affect an entire page. Thus, setting the top or bottom margin must be done at the beginning of a page and will continue in effect until the setting is changed on another page.

In a typical document there will be ten characters per inch and six lines per inch. To achieve a standard one-inch margin around all four sides of the page, left and right margins would be set at ten characters and the top and bottom margins would be six lines each. Exhibit 12.12 illustrates the common margin dimensions used in many word processors.

A page formatting feature closely related to top and bottom margins is the capability of adding headers and footers to the document. A header is simply a line of text that appears in the top margin of every page; likewise, a footer is a line of text that appears in the bottom margin. Headers or footers can be created on any page and typically take effect for all subsequent pages in the document unless the user cancels them.

Page numbering can also be determined by the user. Typically the user can control what number to begin with, and can determine the placement of the page number on the screen. Like headers and footers, page numbers appear in the top or bottom margin. The user can specify the placement of the page number as left or right aligned or centered between the right and left margins.

A final page formatting feature is that of creating multiple columns of text on a single page, similar to the way a newspaper is constructed. When a column format is chosen, the user can often determine how many columns there are to be and how much space is to be left between them.

Exhibit 12.12

Typical Margin Measurements for a Microcomputer Printer

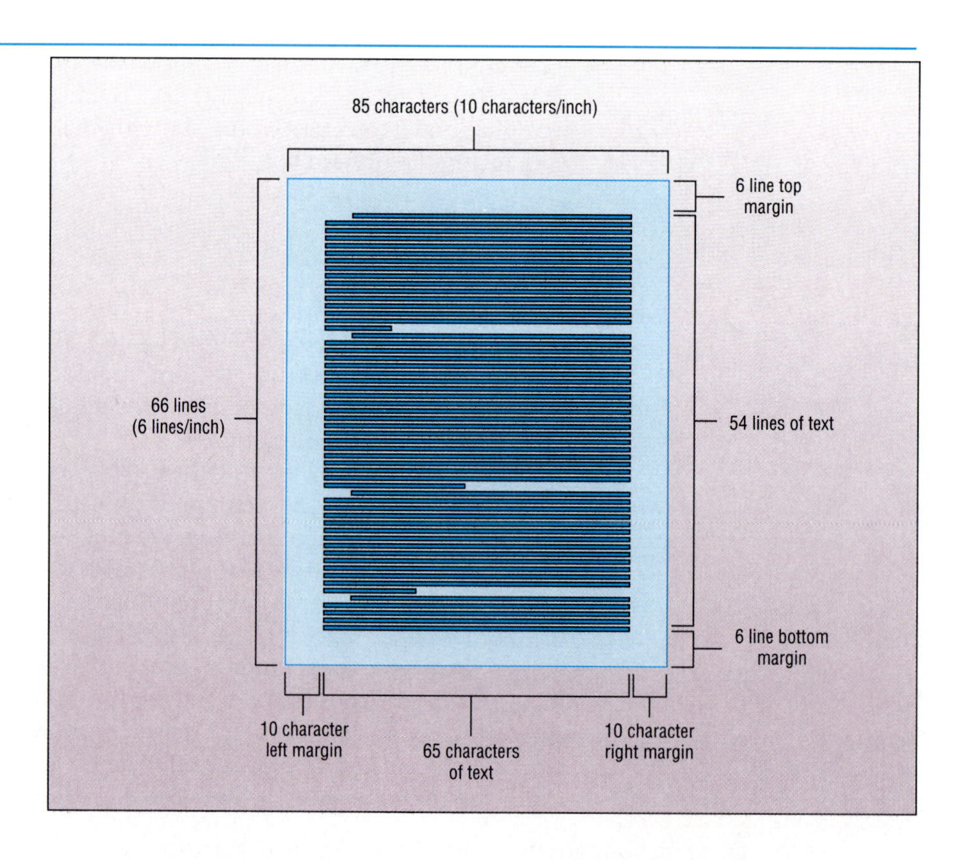

Formatting Methods

There are two major ways that word processors deal with formatting. Some word processors do not do any formatting on the screen, but wait until the document is to be printed before putting it into its final form. These types of word processors commonly use what are known as embedded commands to do formatting. Unlike the text of the document itself, the **embedded command** is a message to the word processor that tells it how to format the document. The command is entered in such a way that it is identified as an embedded command, either by the use of a special symbol (such as a beginning period) or by its position in the document (such as on a line by itself). The word processor will look for these indications that the characters are not to be treated like others in the document but are rather to be interpreted as a command. Thus, an embedded command may appear on the screen as part of the document, but does not appear in the document that is printed.

Exhibit 12.13 shows how the example letter looks in the WordStar word processor, which uses embedded commands for formatting. For example, the .MT6 at the top instructs WordStar to create a top margin of six lines when the document is printed.

The second way of formatting is to format a document on the screen as it is entered, so that the user can see exactly what will appear on paper when the document is printed. This kind of formatting is performed as the document is edited. Then, when it is printed, it will be reproduced on paper in essentially the same format as it appeared on the screen. A word processor that does the formatting on the screen is often said to be WYSIWYG (pronounced wizzy-wig) which stands for *What You See Is What*

Exhibit 12.13

Embedded Command

The WordStar word processor uses embedded commands to do some of the formatting of a document when it is printed. The .MT6 sets a top margin of 6 lines. The .MB6 embedded command sets a 6-line bottom margin. .PL66 sets the page length at 66 lines, and .OP suppresses page numbering.

```
  A:LETTER              L00001  C01 Insert
                 N O N - D O C U M E N T   E D I T   M E N U
    CURSOR        SCROLL          ERASE       OTHER                 MENUS
 ^E up          ^W up           ^G char    ^J help               ^K block & save
 ^X down        ^Z down         ^T word    ^I tab                ^P print controls
 ^S left        ^R up screen    ^Y line    ^V turn insert off    ^Q quick functions
 ^D right       ^C down        Del char    ^O set tab width     Esc shorthand
 ^A word left      screen       ^U unerase ^N split the line
 ^F word right                  ^B top bit ^L find/replace again
.MT6                                                                            <
.MB6                                                                            <
.PL66                                                                           <
.OP                                                                             <
Mr. William Williams                                                            <
123 Cherry Street                                                               <
Appleton, OH   44444                                                            <
                                                                                <
January 1, 1989                                                                 <
                                                                                <
Dear Mr. Williams:                                                              ^
                                                                                ^
                                                                                ^
 Display Center  ChkRest ChkWord Del Blk HideBlk MoveBlk CopyBlk Beg Blk End Blk
1Help   2Undo   3Undrlin4Bold   5DelLine6DelWord7Align  8Ruler  9Save & 0Done
```

Exhibit 12.14

Microsoft Word Screen (Macintosh)

A screen from the Macintosh version of Microsoft Word. This word processor displays text on the screen exactly as it will be printed.

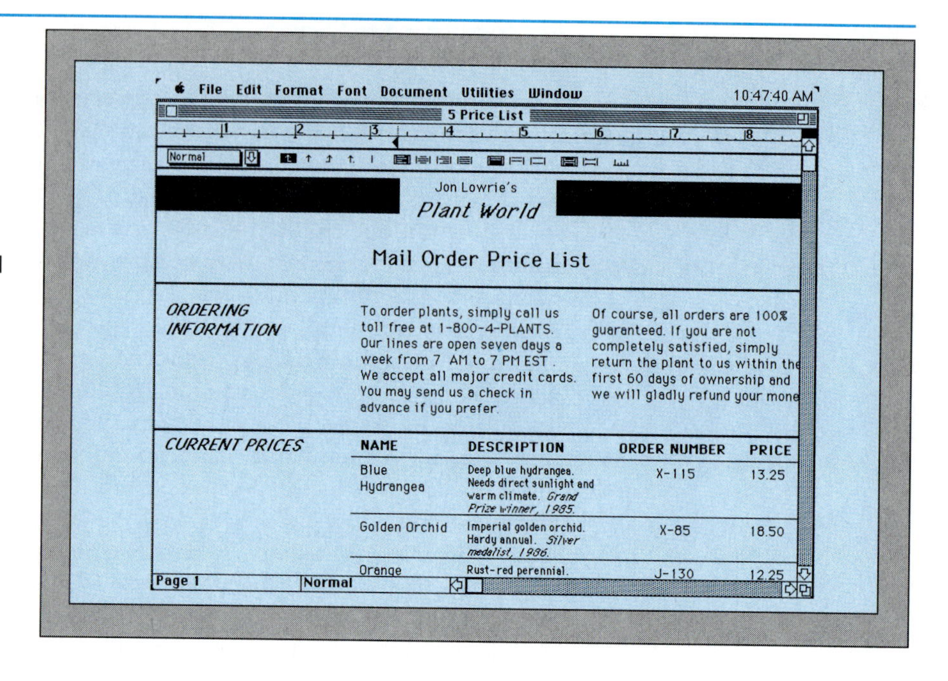

You Get. Exhibit 12.14 shows an example of a word processor that displays the document on the screen exactly as it will be printed.

Document Printing

As mentioned earlier, some of the formatting commands may be part of the printing process. When a user instructs the word processor to print a document, he or she can specify how the document is to be printed. A user typically has control over such things as the margins used during printing, the number of copies to be printed, how the pages will be numbered, and the line spacing (single, double, and so on). Most word processors will let the user print just selected pages or sometimes even a single block of text.

Once the user has determined the formatting of the document and any other special settings related to the printing of the document, a simple command transfers the contents of the document to a printer. With a typewriter, making revisions and retyping a document can be very time-consuming. With a word processor a document can be retyped easily with the use of a simple print command. Thus, word processors free a user from worrying about making a costly change and let the user concentrate on creating the best possible document.

Most advanced word processors provide a preview facility that allows the user to see a copy of the document on the screen exactly as it will look when it is printed. This feature is particularly useful in word processors that don't normally show the results of all formatting commands until the document is printed.

Exhibit 12.15

Preview Facility

The preview facility in the Macintosh version of Microsoft Word shows the user an image of how the document will look when it is printed.

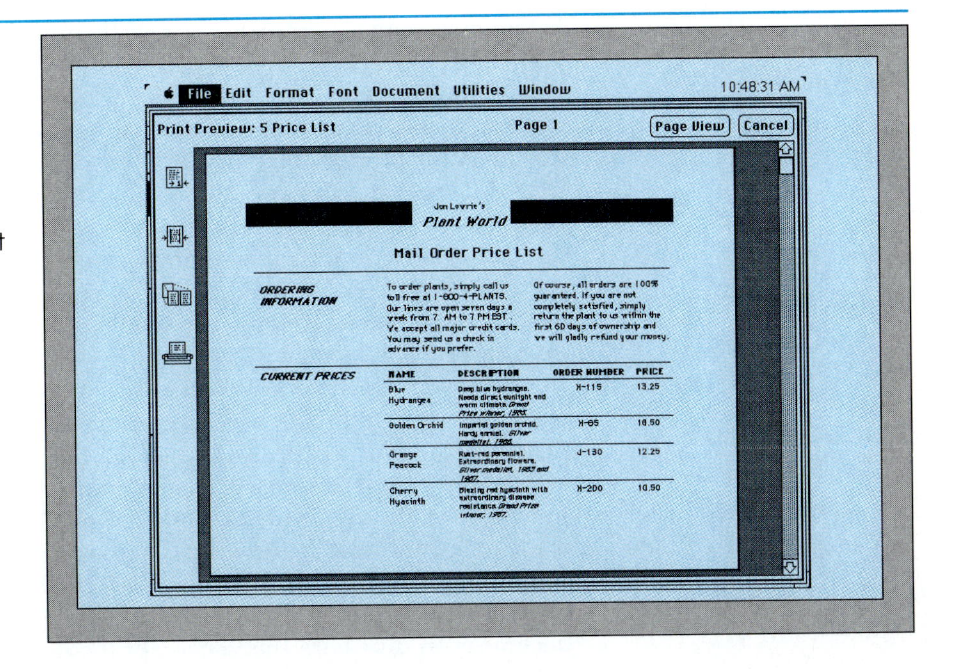

Exhibit 12.15 shows the preview facility of Microsoft Word. Notice that to get an image of the entire page on the screen, some of the detail of the text must be sacrificed. The intent of this preview is to show a general image of how the page will look when printed rather than an exact reproduction of every detail.

Document Management

The primary job of word processors is to produce documents. These documents can be as small as a simple one-paragraph memo and as large as a book. Regardless of its size, the document is the unit of storage in word processors. Word processors usually store each document in a separate file on a diskette.

One of the major functions that a word processor must support is the management of the documents it stores. Word processors respond to commands that allow creation of new documents, saving of documents on disks, retrieval of documents from floppy diskettes or hard disks, listing of available documents, and deletion, copying, and renaming of documents.

The two functions used most often are probably the save and retrieve commands. Because word processors, like most humans, can work on only one thing at a time, only one document can be actively processed in the microcomputer at once. Other documents must be stored in permanent form on disks. Whenever a document is being worked on, it must be moved into the primary memory of the microcomputer so that the word processor can work on it. When that document is finished, it must be put back on disk before exiting the word processor. If the old document is not saved in a permanent form on the disk, it will be lost. Thus, documents are constantly being moved in and out of primary memory using RETRIEVE and SAVE commands. Some word processors allow a user to hold more than one document in primary memory. The user can still only work on one at a time, however, and eventually all documents must be saved on a disk before the microcomputer is turned off.

When a document is retrieved, word processors make a copy of the document that is on disk and place that copy into primary memory for the user to work on. As changes are made, the copy of the document rather than the original document is actually being altered.

Word processors typically offer a user three ways of ending an editing session. First, the user has an option (usually called QUIT) which instructs the word processor to destroy the copy of the document in primary memory and, thus, leave the original document intact on the disk. In this option the user is instructing the word processor to forget all changes made to the document since the editing session began.

A second option (usually called UPDATE, REPLACE, or REVISE) allows the user to instruct the word processor to replace the original document on disk with the version of the document in primary memory. Often the original version of the document is destroyed during this process and the copy of the document in primary memory is stored on the disk under the same name as the original.

Some word processors use a slightly different version of this second option in which the original document is not destroyed. Instead, it is placed in a separate file with the original document name but a special extension (BAK for backup is a common extension). Thus, if the original document was called ORIGINAL.DOC, the copy in primary memory would be placed on the disk under ORIGINAL.DOC and a new file called ORIGINAL.BAK would be created for the storage of the original version. This gives the user another level of protection against accidentally destroying an original document. If the user decides the old version of the document is needed again, it is always available on the disk in the file with the BAK extension.

The third option available in word processors that use copies of an original document is the option commonly referred to as *saving*. When the copy is to be moved to a disk for permanent storage, the user can instruct the word processor to store that file under a different name than the name of the original document. This way the copy gets stored and the original is left intact. When this third option is used, the user must give a name for the file under which the document in primary memory is to be stored. Some word processors do not separate this third option from the second. Instead, the user must always supply a name of a file under which the copy of the document is to be stored. If the user wants to update the original document, the file name is the same as that under which the original is stored. If the file name is different, then a new file is created with the copy in it, and the original is left intact under the old name, Exhibit 12.16 illustrates the retrieval of a file and the three options a user has when ending a session.

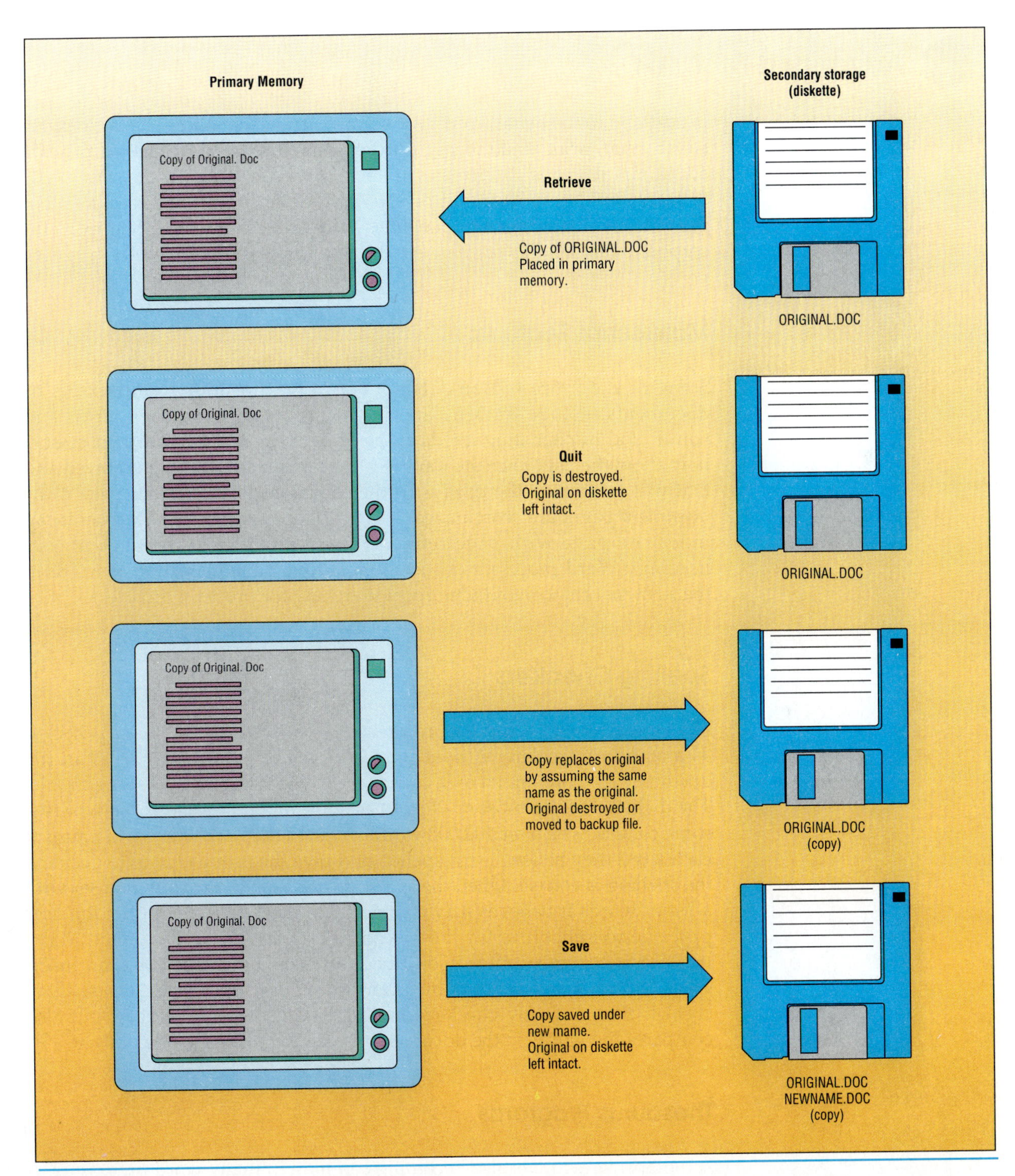

Exhibit 12.16

Retrieving and Saving a Document in a Word Processor That Works with Copies of Original Documents

Advanced Features

In addition to the usual word-processing features that allow a user to create, edit, format, print, and manage documents, many word processors provide additional features to increase the user's productivity. In the past, these features could only be found on the more expensive word processors, but recently even the least expensive word processors have begun to incorporate them.

Manuscript Features

Some of the more tedious elements of creating long manuscripts or documents include tracking and placing footnotes, indexing terms and names, and hyphenating words at the ends of lines. Many word processors now allow the user to create footnotes that are automatically numbered and that will remain on the page with the corresponding reference even if the document pages are reorganized. It is possible to automatically generate an index complete with page references and a table of contents that lists headings. Word processors also feature automatic hyphenation of words at the right margin to avoid time spent searching for proper word breaks.

Spelling Checkers

Even the most inexpensive word processors now include a spelling checker as a standard feature. A **spelling checker** compares each word in the document to words in its own dictionary to see if the word is recognizable. The dictionaries for most spelling checkers contain at least 50,000 words—some contain well over 100,000 words. Most spelling checkers will pause at each word they believe is misspelled and give the user a chance to decide if the spelling is correct. Often the spelling checker will provide the user with a list of words it believes may contain the correct spelling and let the user pick one to substitute for the misspelled word in the document. Many spelling checkers support user dictionaries in which the user can insert special words that are not in the standard spelling dictionary. The spelling checker then not only checks words against its own dictionary, but also compares the words in the document to words in the user's dictionary.

Thesaurus Programs

A thesaurus feature is also becoming common in many word processors. A **thesaurus** contains synonyms for words. The user can highlight a word in the document and invoke the thesaurus program. The thesaurus then produces a list of synonyms for the word and the user can choose to replace the word in the document with a word in the list.

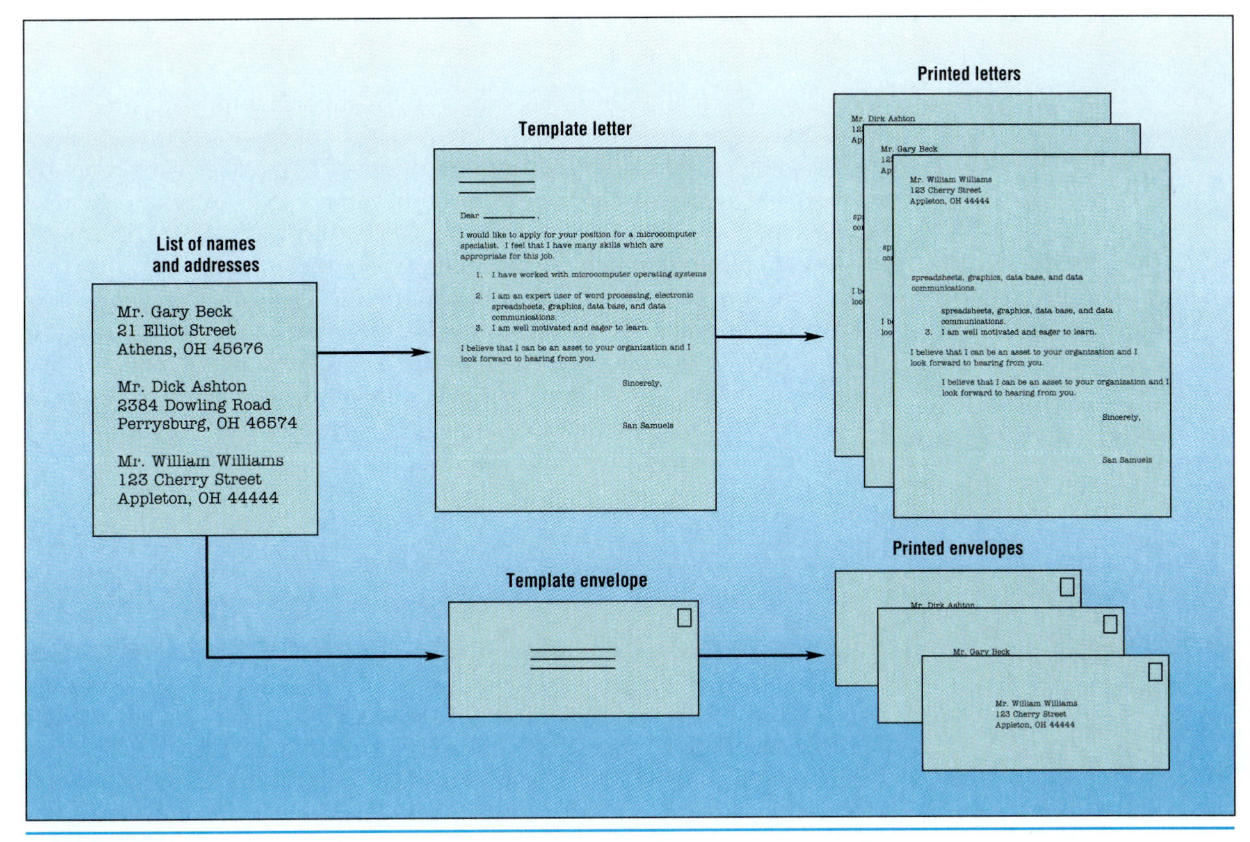

Exhibit 12.17

Mail-Merge Facility

With a mail-merge facility, a user creates a list of names and addresses and a template document containing some missing information corresponding to the names and addresses in the list. The mail-merge facility can combine the information in the list with the template to generate a series of letters and envelopes.

Mail-Merge Facilities

Another important advanced feature in word processors is a mail-merge feature. **Mail merge** allows a user to create a document with certain pieces of information left out. For example, a form letter can be created with a special symbol replacing the name in the greeting at the beginning of the letter. In addition to the document file, the user creates a file of names to be substituted for the special symbol in the greeting of the letter. When the document is printed, the word processor puts the first name from the list into the greeting and prints the letter. Then a second copy of the letter is printed using the second name in the list, and so on. Thus, the information left out of the document is added as the document is printed, to create a group of form letters. Exhibit 12.17 shows how a mail-merge facility can use a list of names and addresses to generate a series of letters and envelopes automatically.

Macros

A final feature that is becoming increasingly important in word processors is the ability to create macros. A **macro** is a set of keystrokes that are often used together. Instead of entering the series of keystrokes each time, the user creates a macro containing those keystrokes. Then when the user wants to perform the function accomplished by those keystrokes, the macro is executed rather than the user pressing keys one at a time.

An important component of a macro facility is the incorporation of a learn mode. Initially the user activates the learn mode, which tells the word processor to begin recording all the keystrokes and commands that the user executes. All this information is stored as a macro, and the user can then have the word processor repeat the sequence of keystrokes by activating the macro.

Choosing a Word Processor

Now that you have seen what word processors can do, you should be able to evaluate any word processor with respect to the features it supports and how it accomplishes them. Exhibit 12.18 shows the results of a recent survey of 1000 users showing the advanced word processing features they believed were important. Exhibit 12.19 shows some of the features of popular word processing packages for IBM compatible and Macintosh computers.

Exhibit 12.18

Rating Word Processing Features

A survey of 1000 users shows the percentage of users that thought each word processing feature was important.

Feature	Percentage
Mail-merge	45.5%
Spell checker	86.7%
Thesaurus	61.5%
Macros	51.3%
Table of contents generation	47.5%
Index generation	41.2%
Footnoting	41.8%

IBM Compatible Computers

Feature	Microsoft Word 5.0	WordPerfect 5.0	DisplayWrite 5/2 Composer
Double Underlining	Y	Y	Y
Insert and overtype modes	Y	Y	Y
Ruler line can be suppressed	Y	Y	N
Undelete capability	Y	Y	Y
Forward and backward search	Y	Y	Y
Number of printers supported	275	450	60
Prints block of text	N	Y	N
Creates backup file	Y	Y	Y
Words in spell dictionary	130,000	130,000	100,000
Footnotes	Y	Y	Y
Table of contents	Y	Y	Y
Indexing	Y	Y	Y
Maximum columns	22	24	12
Macros	Y	Y	Y

Macintosh Computers

Feature	Microsoft Word 4.0	MacWrite II 1.0	WordPerfect 1.0.2
Maximum open documents	22	7	Y
Macros	Y	N	Y
Mail merge	Y	Y	Y
Indexing	Y	N	Y
Table of contents	Y	N	Y
Footnotes	Y	Y	Y
Spelling checker	Y	Y	Y
User spell dictionary	Y	Y	Y
Thesaurus	Y	Y	Y
Preview before printing	Y	Y	Y
Maximum columns	22	10	24

Exhibit 12.19

A Comparison of Word Processor Features for IBM Compatible and Macintosh Computers

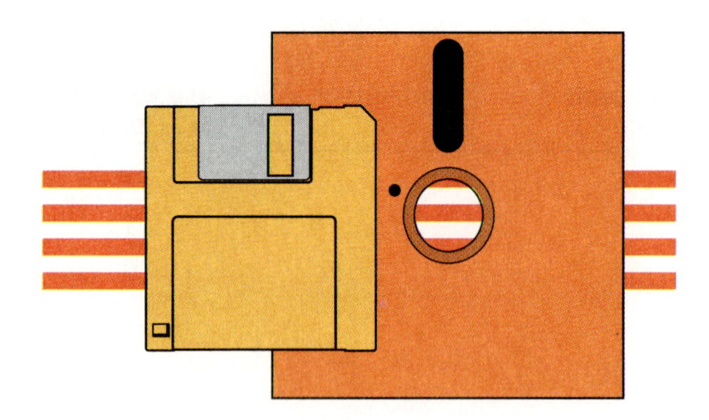

Computers at Work

Programs Help Corporate Writers in Matters of Style

Building consistency across reams of corporate documentation is one of the most difficult tasks a corporate publications department faces. Good writing, like art, often varies tremendously from writer to writer.

PCs and word-processing software have eased the pain of putting out the corporate newsletter, but they haven't done much to promote consistency. Fortunately, grammar- and style-checking software is providing some relief to corporations trying to set style guidelines.

Two style-checking packages currently on the market are the $95 RightWriter from RightSoft Inc. of Sarasota, Florida, and the $89 Grammatik II, from Reference Software of San Francisco. Both products check documents for errors in grammar, style and usage.

Customized Dictionary

Grammatik II contains a phrase dictionary, against which it compares documents.

The phrase dictionary can be customized to reflect a particular corporation's style guidelines, explained Toni Delacorte, a spokeswoman for Reference Software.

RightWriter contains an expert system with a rule base and a dictionary, against which it checks documents for grammar weaknesses, said Ted Beesley, RightSoft's director of national sales.

Grammatik II is being used across a variety of documentation groups at Hewlett-Packard Co., according to Bob Silvey, HP's communications coordinator for corporate documentation support.

"We recommend beginning writers use it to help them become more aware of their writing style," he said.

"I'm writing a style guide for the whole company and that will become a standard for all HP English-language documentation groups," explained Mr. Silvey. The company is currently evaluating the possibility of setting up customized phrase dictionaries within Grammatik II to accompany the HP style guide," he said.

"RightWriter also is being used in many large corporations to ensure correct grammar and usage in documentation," said RightSoft's Mr. Beesley.

"In fact, one federal agency has been running congressional documentation through RightWriter to check style and usage before the documents are sent on to the Congress for approval," he said.

Large accounting firms must also produce enormous quantities of documentation. For instance, Laventhol & Horwath, of Philadelphia, has included a customized version of Grammatik II with its NAAD (National Accounting and Auditing Department) Style Manual, according to Sherri Downes-Johnson, director of computer assisted auditing for Laventhol and Horwath.

Both RightSoft and Reference Software are working on new versions of their products.

The new version will have much more intelligence and will be able to parse sentences and check them more thoroughly for things like verb and noun agreement. It will also allow users to edit their documents while still within Grammatik.

Summary and Key Terms

Word processors deal with **documents** stored on floppy diskettes and hard disks. When a document is retrieved, a copy of that document is placed in primary memory and the user works on that copy.

The contents of a document are changed by editing that document. The word processor allows the user to move a **cursor** around in the document with various movement commands.

When the user begins entering text into a document, the words automatically wrap to the next line when they go beyond the right margin. This is known as **word wrap.**

Word processors usually support both a **typeover mode**, in which characters can be replaced by typing new characters over them, and an **insert mode**, in which new characters are always inserted in front of the cursor and old characters are pushed to the right.

Word processors give users various deletion capabilities, with which a character, word, line, or block of text can be deleted. A **block** is simply a group of characters. It can be as small as a single character or can include several words, lines, paragraphs, or pages of a document. When text is deleted, it is often temporarily stored in a buffer. An **undelete** function can be used to move the deleted text from the buffer back into the document to reverse deletion.

Text can be moved around in the document by using a **block move** feature. Generally, in a block move, the beginning and end of the text to be moved are marked, the text is removed from the document, the user moves the cursor to the new location, and the block is placed back into the text.

Word processors allow users to search through the document for specific words or phrases. A **search and replace** option allows the user to replace a string when it is found. This can be done for a single occurrence of the string or for every occurrence of the string in the document **(global search and replace)**.

Document **formatting commands** can be used to change the appearance of the document. There are separate commands for character, line, and page formatting.

Character formatting involves changing the appearance (boldfacing, underlining, italics), type style, and size of the characters.

Line formats use commands that let the user set the left and right margins, control line spacing, set up tabs and indentations, and determine the alignment of text with the right and left margins. Specification of right and left margins and tabs is often done using a **ruler**. Common alignment options include left and right alignment and centering of text between the margins and the **justification** of text, which causes the first and last characters on each line to align.

Page formats involve the specification of top and bottom margins, setting up headers and footers, determining page number positions, and creating multiple columns.

Document formatting is accomplished in some word processors with **embedded commands.** These commands are used by the word processor to format the document at the time of printing.

Other word processors actually format the document on the screen so that the user can see exactly how it will look at the time of printing.

Documents are put on paper by using a print command. Most word processors provide a command that will let the user preview the printed document on the screen before actually committing it to paper.

When a user ends an editing session there are three possible options. One option ends the session by destroying the copy of the document in primary memory and leaving the original document on disk unchanged. The REPLACE option puts the copy in the place of the original document on disk. The original document is either destroyed or "moved" to a backup file. The SAVE option lets the user put the copy on disk under a name different from the original.

Advanced features incorporated into many word processors include special features helpful with long documents or manuscripts: **spelling checkers, thesaurus programs, mail-merge facilities,** and **macros.**

Review Questions

1. Explain the difference among the QUIT, REPLACE, and SAVE options for ending an editing session with a word processor.
2. What is the difference between typeover and insert?
3. What is word wrap?
4. Explain how a block move is accomplished.
5. How is the search function in a word processor used?
6. Explain how an undelete is accomplished.
7. What is a spelling checker?
8. What is a ruler? How is it used in indenting text?
9. Explain justification.
10. What is an embedded command?

T F **11.** A ruler can be used to set top and bottom margins in the document.

T F **12.** Word wrap is the feature that lets the user type text and automatically have words that go beyond the right margin move to the next line.

T F **13.** In the insert mode the user can type new characters over the top of the existing characters in the document to replace them.

T F **14.** Commands that allow the user to change the appearance of the document are called formatting commands.

T F **15.** A font refers to the way words are lined up with the right and left margins.

T F **16.** Justification is the process in which the validity of the text is verified.

T F **17.** Indents can be used to bring a block of text in from the left margin but can never be used to bring text in from the right margin as well.

T F **18.** An embedded command is a command stored in a macro.

T F **19.** Mail-merge refers to a feature in which a letter is automatically formatted for mailing.

T F **20.** Spelling checkers sometimes allow the user to create a personal dictionary containing special words the spelling checker does not have in its own dictionary.

21. _____ Word processors typically have a feature that causes words that go beyond the right margin to automatically move to the next line. This is known as:

a. justification c. word wrap
b. alignment d. formatting

22. _____ During the editing process, sometimes the user can type new characters on top of the existing characters to replace them. This is called:

a. typeover mode c. replace mode
b. insert mode d. overwrite mode

23. _____ Accidentally deleted text can be placed back into a document using this feature:

a. retrieve command c. the oops button
b. fetch command d. undelete command

24. _____ The process of moving a group of text from one location in the document to another is called:

a. block move c. buffering text
b. search and move d. text relocate

25. _____ The combination of a typeface (Courier, Helvetica, and so on), size, and appearance (bold, italic) of characters in a document is known as:

a. pitch c. appearance
b. alignment d. font

26. _____ A common method of specifying the positions of right and left margins and tabs is to use a:

a. ruler c. indent
b. margin d. format

27. _____ This feature refers to the alignment of characters at the ends of lines:

a. alignment c. indenting
b. justification d. centering

28. _____ This is a word processing facility that lets a user combine a list of information with a document to create form letters:

a. macro
b. mail merge
c. style checker
d. thesaurus

29. _____ The feature that would let you automatically exchange every occurrence of a word in the document with another word is called:

a. search and replace
b. justification
c. search and destroy
d. global search and replace

30. _____ A feature that allows a user to record a series of keystrokes and play them back later is called a:

a. macro
b. merger
c. block
d. mail merge

CHAPTER 13

Electronic Spreadsheets

Spreadsheets make up the second major category of microcomputer software. Spreadsheets are particularly helpful in financial and accounting applications in which large numbers of figures and formulas must be organized to ensure accuracy. Applications that require reports, such as income statements, balance sheets, and budgets, would use spreadsheet programs. The reports are laid out in columns and rows to create cells. Many of these cells contain labels or headings that give general information about groups of entries. Other cells contain data about the company, and some contain figures derived from values appearing in other cells on the spreadsheet.

In this chapter you will learn to do the following:

1. Identify the various components of a spreadsheet
2. Understand how labels and numbers are entered into a spreadsheet
3. Learn how formulas are entered and copied
4. Learn the various options for editing a spreadsheet
5. Understand how a spreadsheet is formatted
6. Identify the types of commands used in a spreadsheet

Interacting with a Spreadsheet

The electronic spreadsheet, like its paper ancestor, is simply a large grid of cells that is created by the intersection of columns and rows. Electronic spreadsheets, however, hold many more cells than would be practical on a sheet of paper; the largest ones today contain as many as 32,000 columns and 32,000 rows, giving a user over one billion cells to work with. There are, of course, practical limitations to using this many cells—including the memory size of the microcomputer running the spreadsheet and the ability of a user to keep track of so many cells. Most users can get by with less than a thousand cells for most applications.

Naturally, thousands of cells cannot be placed on a computer screen at one time. Approximately twenty rows and eight columns of most spreadsheets can appear on a screen at one time. The columns are usually labeled with letters of the alphabet. (Notable exceptions include MultiPlan, which uses numbers, and PFS: First Choice, which uses C1, C2, C3, and so on). Since there are only twenty-six letters, columns from 27 on are labeled AA, AB, AC, and so on. The rows are usually labeled with numbers. Each cell in the spreadsheet is referred to by its *address*, which is a combination of the letter of the column and the number of the row that the cell is in. Cell addresses include A1, AC87, and BB2045. Typically the column letter comes first, followed by the row number. Exhibit 13.1 displays the Lotus 1-2-3 electronic spreadsheet.

Movement Functions

When you are using a spreadsheet, your current location, sometimes known as the *active cell,* will always be represented by the **current cell pointer.** In Exhibit 13.1 the current cell pointer is the rectangular highlight shown in cell A1. This current cell pointer can be moved one cell at a time in any direction by using the arrow keys on the numeric keypad portion of the keyboard. There are varying degrees of movement through a spreadsheet, just as there are through the text in a word processor. Usually the PGUP and PGDN keys move the spreadsheet up and down a full screen (about twenty rows). TAB key using the SHIFT key with the TAB key move the screen right and left about eight columns at a time.

In addition, spreadsheets include a jump feature, which allows the user to specify an address of a cell and jump to the part of the spreadsheet containing that cell, making it the current cell. One particular jump common to most spreadsheets uses the HOME key. By pressing this key, you can jump immediately to cell A1, which is considered the "home" location in the spreadsheet. More advanced spreadsheets give more complex movement functions, but the ones discussed are typical of most electronic spreadsheets. Some newer spreadsheets even allow a mouse to be used to move the current cell pointer.

Exhibit 13.1

The Lotus 1-2-3 Electronic Spreadsheet

The Lotus 1-2-3 Spreadsheet is the most popular spreadsheet on the market to date.

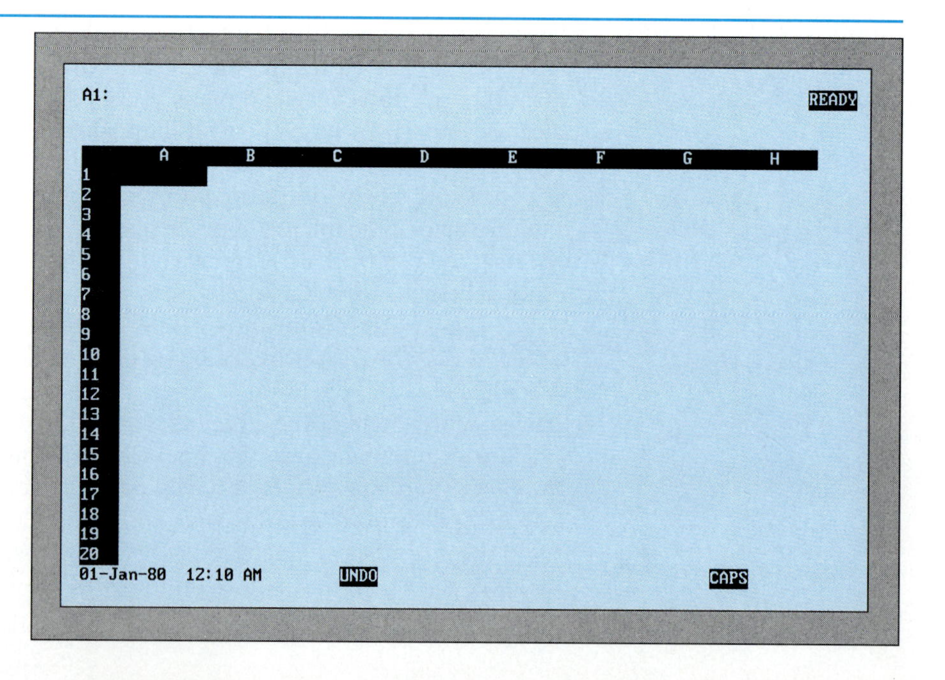

Windows

When interacting with a spreadsheet, the end-user must think of the screen as a **window** through which the spreadsheet is viewed. For example, Exhibit 13.1 represents a window that shows the top left corner of the spreadsheet. There are additional columns to the right and additional rows at the bottom that cannot be seen.

To see the columns farther to the right, the user can move the current cell pointer to the right until it moves past the right edge of the window. This causes new columns to appear at the right as others disappear at the left. In other words, the window has been shifted to the right so new columns can be seen. Rows that are below the edge of the window can be revealed using a similar process. The process of shifting the window in any direction is known as **scrolling.**

Creating a Spreadsheet

A spreadsheet is created by entering data into the cells. This section examines the different types of data that can be entered. For purposes of illustration, the example spreadsheet in Exhibit 13.2 is used. It shows a break-even analysis.

The Control Panel

In Exhibit 13.2 there are four lines at the bottom of the screen known as the **control panel.** Some spreadsheets have a control panel at the top of the screen (Lotus 1-2-3, for example) and others put part of the control panel at the top and part at the bottom (Quattro, for example).

Regardless of where it is placed, the control panel serves several functions. The control panel typically displays status information about the current cell. For example, the first line of the control panel in Exhibit 13.2 displays the address of the current cell (D9) and the current contents of the cell (the formula + D5 + D6 + D7). A second function of the control panel is to provide an area where the user can enter information that is to be placed in the current cell. In Exhibit 13.2, the third line of the control panel is used for this purpose. The user can type and edit information on this line in preparation for entering it into the spreadsheet. A final function of the control panel is to display menus and messages to the user while the user is issuing spreadsheet commands. A common approach is to display a list of options in the control panel and let the user make a choice by highlighting the option he or she wants.

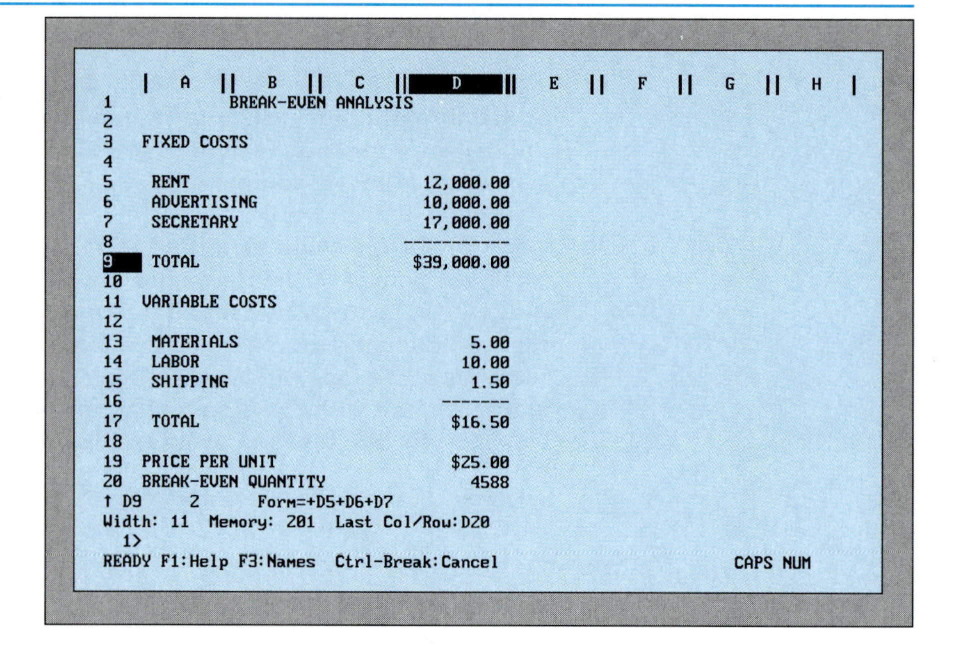

Exhibit 13.2

The Break-Even Analysis Shown in the SUPERCALC4 Spreadsheet

The control panel is the group of four lines shown below line 20.

Labels, Numbers, and Formulas

Any entry in a cell on the spreadsheet must be one of the following: a label, a number, or a formula. A **formula** is a combination of cell addresses and numbers joined by mathematical symbols (+, -, *, and /). In Exhibit 13.2, cell A3 contains the label FIXED COSTS. An example of a cell containing a number is cell D5, which contains the number 12000.00. However, notice the comma in the display (12,000). Special characters like commas and dollar signs are added to numbers with format commands (discussed later in this chapter).

Note this important concept in spreadsheets: the information *displayed* in the cell on the spreadsheet is not always the same as what is actually *stored* in that cell. The number 12000.00 is stored in cell D5 but on the spreadsheet cell D5 displays 12,000.00. Differences between what is displayed and what is stored also occur in formulas. For example, cell D9 contains the formula + D5 + D6 + D7. This formula instructs the spreadsheet to add the contents of cells D5, D6, and D7 together and display the result. Thus, when + D5 + D6 + D7 is stored in cell D9, the number $39,000.00 is displayed in cell D9 on the spreadsheet.

The only way to tell what is actually stored in a particular cell on a spreadsheet is to move the current cell pointer to that cell and look at the control panel (see Exhibit 13.2), which displays the actual contents of the cell.

Entering Labels and Numbers

When the user wishes to enter something into a cell on the spreadsheet, he or she must first place the current cell pointer on that cell. As indicated earlier, the letters or numbers the user types appear on a line in the control panel. When the user presses the RETURN key, the information is placed in the current cell.

Some spreadsheets allow the user to make entries directly into the current cell (PFS: First Choice, for example) or display the data being typed in the control panel and the current cell simultaneously (Excel, for example). This way a user can see exactly what the entry will look like in the spreadsheet.

Spreadsheets determine whether an entry is to be a label or a number by looking at the first character typed on the entry line. Some spreadsheets treat every entry that begins with a letter as a label. Others require the use of a special label-prefix character (usually a double quotation mark) to indicate that an entry is to be treated as a label. If the first character of an entry is a number or a decimal point, the spreadsheet treats that entry as a number.

Entering Formulas

Like a label or a number, a formula is typed into the control panel and then entered into the current cell by pressing the RETURN key. A formula contains numbers and cell addresses connected by mathematical symbols. The most common symbols include addition (+), subtraction (–), multiplication (*), division (/), and exponentiation (** or ∧). A formula may contain numbers only, cell addresses only, or a mixture of both. For example, a call may contain the formula 18/3. The result of this calculation, 6, will be displayed on the screen in the cell in which this formula is stored. The simplest formula involving a cell address is one that simply sets one cell equal to another. If cell A10 contains the number 56 and the formula + A10 is entered into cell F34, then the value 56 will be displayed in cell F34. A formula in a cell indicates that the cell in which the formula is stored is equal to the result of the calculation. Thus, + A10, stored in cell F34, essentially says F34 = + A10. When a formula begins with a cell address, the first character must be a symbol so that the spreadsheet will treat the entry as a formula rather than a label. In most spreadsheets, the first character in a formula is a plus sign. Some spreadsheets (such as Excel) use an equal sign.

Formulas can, of course, be much more complicated than the ones used in these examples. For example, cell D20 on the example spreadsheet in Exhibit 13.3 contains the formula +D9/(D19–D17). (See the control panel at the bottom of the screen.) In other words, cell D20 is equal to +D9/(D19–D17). The use of parentheses in this formula brings up an important concept in constructing formulas, known as **precedence,** which means that computers perform mathematical operations in a particular order when a calculation is made. First, any exponentiations are performed, followed by any multiplications and divisions, and then all additions and

Exhibit 13.3

The Break-Even Analysis in Quattro

The formula in the current cell of the spreadsheet (D20) is displayed in the control panel at the bottom of the screen. This formula illustrates the use of parentheses to control the order of the mathematical operations.

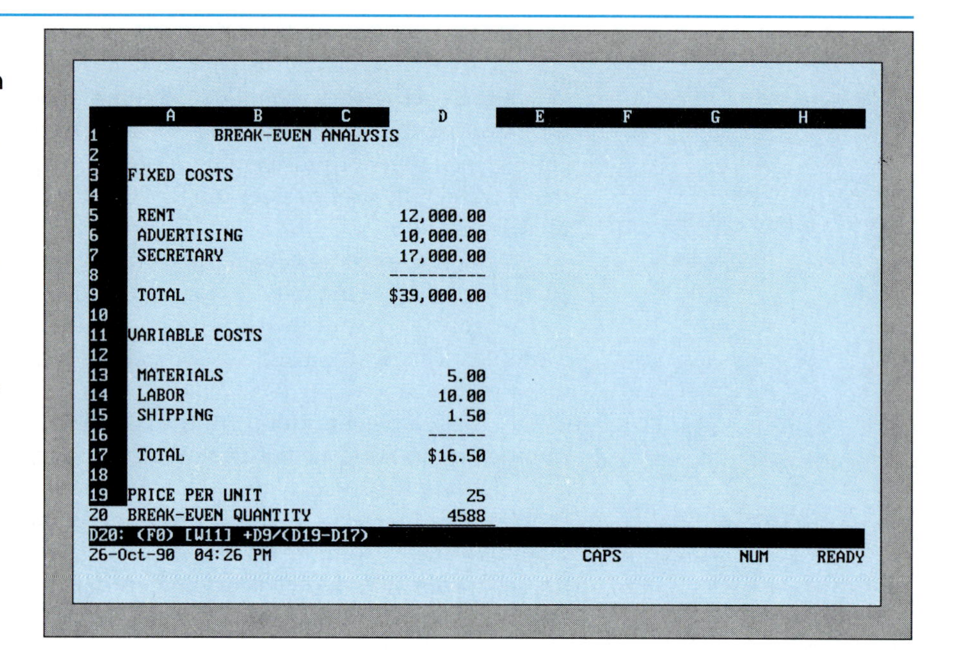

subtractions are performed. Operations at the same level are performed in order from left to right.

Consider the example without the parentheses: + D9/D19 – D17. Under the normal rules of precedence, the division of D9 by D19 would be performed first, since divisions are performed before subtractions. Thus, 39,000 is divided by 25, yielding 1560. Then D17 will be subtracted from that (1560–16.50) which is 15435. This is not the correct answer, because the break-even quantity is calculated by first finding the difference between the total variable costs (D17) and the selling price (D19) and then dividing the fixed costs by that difference. Thus, the spreadsheet needs to calculate the difference between D19 and D17 first and then do the division. When the normal precedence of operations will not do the job, it can be overridden by putting the calculations to be performed first inside parentheses, as was done in cell D20 of Exhibit 13.3.

Automatic Recalculation

When a formula involves cell addresses, a change in a cell referenced in a formula causes the result to be recalculated. The formula + D9/(D19 – D17) currently displays 4588 in the cell in which it is stored, which is the breakeven quantity rounded to the nearest whole number. If the entry in cell D19 was changed from 25 to 30, the number displayed in cell D20 would automatically be updated to 2889. It is as if the spreadsheet is constantly monitoring all the formulas so that a change in a cell that affects the answer to a formula automatically causes the results of that formula to be

Exhibit 13.4

The Break-Even Analysis After a Calculation

When the entry in D5 is changed to 10,000 the results of the formula in cells D9 and D20 are automatically recalculated.

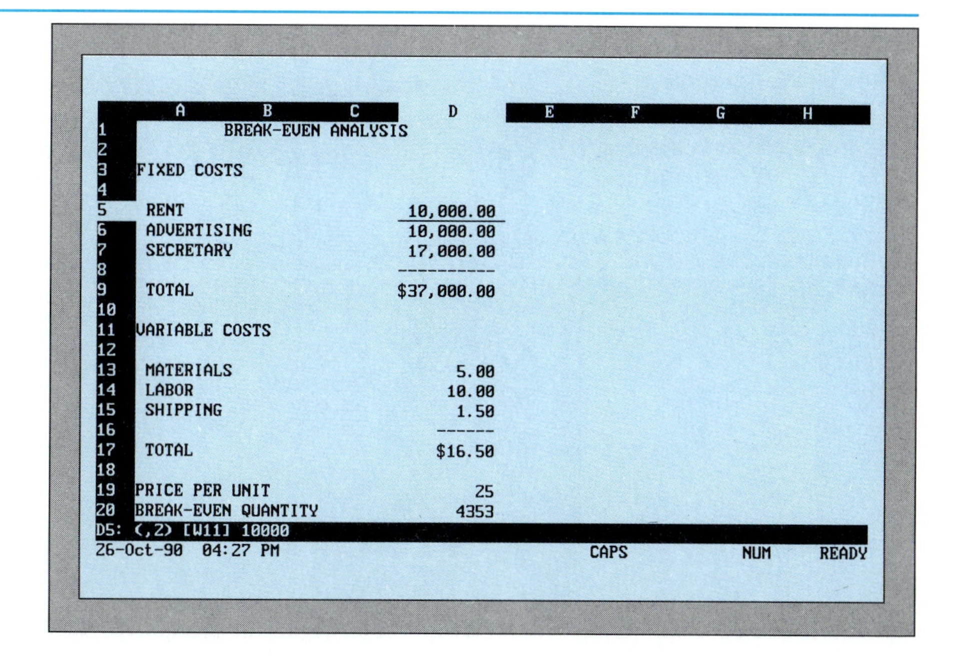

recalculated and updated on the screen. Sometimes a change in a single cell can cause a ripple effect throughout the spreadsheet. For example, Exhibit 13.4 shows the example spreadsheet after the entry in cell D5 is changed from 12000 to 10000. This change causes the total for the fixed costs in cell D9 to change to 37000. Cell D9 is, in turn, used in the formula in cell D20, so that the formula is recalculated and the result changed to 4353.

No matter how complex the formula, if any of the cells referenced in that formula change, the result is automatically recalculated and the new result is displayed. This automatic recalculation feature makes a spreadsheet extremely useful to managers who want to perform a "what-if" analysis. A manager can see how an increase in rent by 1000 dollars will affect the break-even point by simply increasing the rent entry by 1000. The effect on the break-even quantity of a decrease in labor costs coupled with a simultaneous increase in shipping costs, can be determined by simply changing the two entries and watching the spreadsheet do the recalculation.

It is possible to turn off the recalculation feature on most spreadsheets. When automatic recalculation is suppressed, the spreadsheet waits until the user presses a certain key (the F9 key in Lotus 1-2-3, for example) before doing a recalculation.

In the older spreadsheet packages, a recalculation involves checking every cell on the spreadsheet that contains a formula. And this recalculation takes place every time an entry is made on the spreadsheet, in the event that entry would require a change in the result of a formula. With large spreadsheet applications this process can become very time consuming and ultimately slow down the data-entry process. More recent spreadsheets, such as Excel, are programmed to recalculate only those cells containing a formula that is affected by changes in other cells.

Exhibit 13.5

Personnel File Spreadsheet in VP-Planner

All of the numbers in the RAISE, NEW SALARY, and YEARLY TAX columns are the end results of formulas.

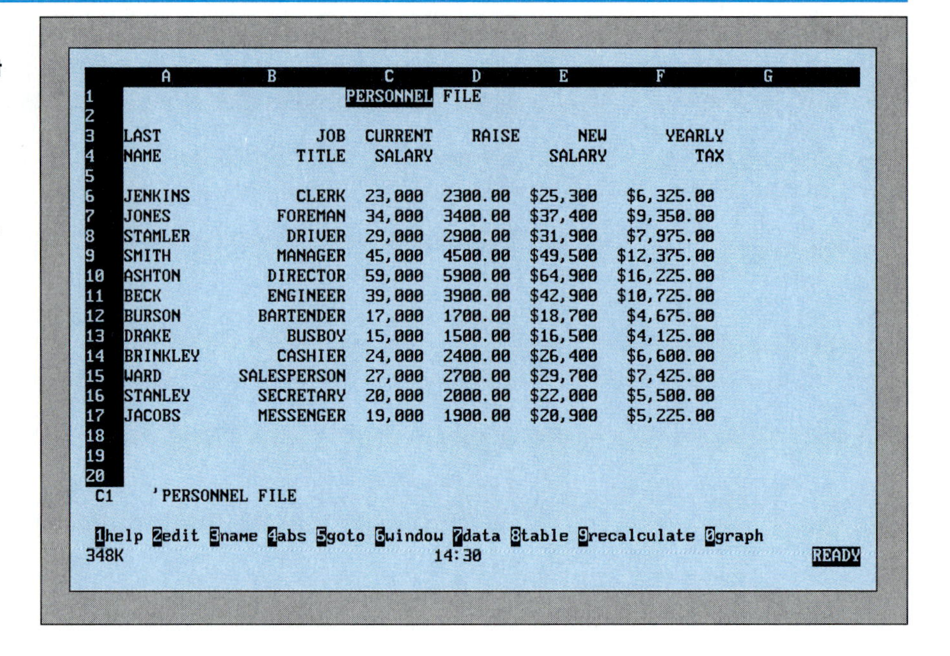

PERSONNEL FILE

	A	B	C	D	E	F	G
1			PERSONNEL	FILE			
2							
3	LAST	JOB	CURRENT	RAISE	NEW	YEARLY	
4	NAME	TITLE	SALARY		SALARY	TAX	
5							
6	JENKINS	CLERK	23,000	2300.00	$25,300	$6,325.00	
7	JONES	FOREMAN	34,000	3400.00	$37,400	$9,350.00	
8	STAMLER	DRIVER	29,000	2900.00	$31,900	$7,975.00	
9	SMITH	MANAGER	45,000	4500.00	$49,500	$12,375.00	
10	ASHTON	DIRECTOR	59,000	5900.00	$64,900	$16,225.00	
11	BECK	ENGINEER	39,000	3900.00	$42,900	$10,725.00	
12	BURSON	BARTENDER	17,000	1700.00	$18,700	$4,675.00	
13	DRAKE	BUSBOY	15,000	1500.00	$16,500	$4,125.00	
14	BRINKLEY	CASHIER	24,000	2400.00	$26,400	$6,600.00	
15	WARD	SALESPERSON	27,000	2700.00	$29,700	$7,425.00	
16	STANLEY	SECRETARY	20,000	2000.00	$22,000	$5,500.00	
17	JACOBS	MESSENGER	19,000	1900.00	$20,900	$5,225.00	
18							
19							
20							

C1 'PERSONNEL FILE

1help 2edit 3name 4abs 5goto 6window 7data 8table 9recalculate 0graph

348K 14:30 READY

Copying Formulas

Since spreadsheets are capable of constantly recalculating the results of formulas, users typically use formulas on a spreadsheet whenever possible. In this way, errors are reduced since the spreadsheet rather than the user is performing the calculations. Also, what-if analyses can be performed easily.

A relatively simple spreadsheet can require the entry of a large number of formulas. For example, in Exhibit 13.5 all the numbers in the RAISE, NEW SALARY, and YEARLY TAX columns are the results of formulas. This means that thirty-six formulas would have to be keyed in, and to avoid any errors the user would have to be sure that all the cell addresses in every formula were correct. Exhibit 13.6 shows the sample spreadsheet with the thirty-six formulas displayed in the cells where the results of those formulas would normally appear. Observe that the formulas within a column are all similar. For example, the formulas in the RAISE column all multiply the number in the cell to the left by 0.1 (that is, a 10-percent raise across-the-board). Spreadsheets are able to take advantage of this similarity by allowing a user to enter a formula only once and then copy the formula to other cells that require one of similar form. This approach is more efficient and reduces errors.

When a formula is entered into a cell, a spreadsheet program interprets that formula in a special way. Take, for example, the formula + C6 + D6 in cell E6 of Exhibit 13.6. In performing this calculation, the formula treats the addresses C6 and D6 as relative distances from the cell (E6) in which the formula is stored. Thus, C6 is two cells to the left and D6 is one cell to the left of the location of the formula. The formula is, therefore, read by the spreadsheet as "add the entry in the cell that is two cells to the left to

Exhibit 13.6

The Personnel File Formulas

Note how the formulas displayed in each column are similar to one another.

	A	B	C	D	E	F	G
1			PERSONNEL FILE				
2							
3	LAST	JOB	CURRENT	RAISE	NEW	YEARLY	
4	NAME	TITLE	SALARY		SALARY	TAX	
5							
6	JENKINS	CLERK	23,000	.1*C6	+C6+D6	+E6*.25	
7	JONES	FOREMAN	34,000	.1*C7	+C7+D7	+E7*.25	
8	STAMLER	DRIVER	29,000	.1*C8	+C8+D8	+E8*.25	
9	SMITH	MANAGER	45,000	.1*C9	+C9+D9	+E9*.25	
10	ASHTON	DIRECTOR	59,000	.1*C10	+C10+D10	+E10*.25	
11	BECK	ENGINEER	39,000	.1*C11	+C11+D11	+E11*.25	
12	BURSON	BARTENDER	17,000	.1*C12	+C12+D12	+E12*.25	
13	DRAKE	BUSBOY	15,000	.1*C13	+C13+D13	+E13*.25	
14	BRINKLEY	CASHIER	24,000	.1*C14	+C14+D14	+E14*.25	
15	WARD	SALESPERSON	27,000	.1*C15	+C15+D15	+E15*.25	
16	STANLEY	SECRETARY	20,000	.1*C16	+C16+D16	+E16*.25	
17	JACOBS	MESSENGER	19,000	.1*C17	+C17+D17	+E17*.25	
18							
19							
20							

A1

1help 2edit 3name 4abs 5goto 6window 7data 8table 9recalculate 0graph

348K 14:31 READY

the entry that is one cell to the left." All cell addresses in the formula are interpreted as *relative distances* from the location of the formula rather than as *actual locations.*

Since the cell addresses in a formula are stored internally by the spreadsheet as relative distances from the formula, if the formula is copied to a different cell, the actual cell addresses in the formula are altered. In other words, if the formula in cell E6 is copied into cell E7, the formula becomes + C7 + D7. This occurs because the cell that is two cells to the left of the formula is now C7, and the cell that is one cell to the left is now D7. This translation of the relative addresses in the formula into the new cell addresses is known as **adjustment.**

Thus, the formula in E6 appears as + C6 + D6; and when that formula is copied into E7, it appears as + C7 + D7. As far as the spreadsheet is concerned, both cells contain the same formula because the addresses in both formulas are the same relative to where the formula is located. The first address is always two cells to the left of the formula and the second address is always one cell to the left. This adjustment of formulas will occur automatically when copies of formulas are made and placed into other cells.

When formulas in a group have the same relative description, as in the last three columns of Exhibit 13.6, a user can enter a formula once and then copy it to the other cells requiring the same type of formula. The spreadsheet will automatically adjust the formula in each cell, thus saving the user a considerable number of keystrokes and cutting down the possibility of errors. This copying command is probably one of the most powerful features of spreadsheet programs.

When using a command to copy a formula, the user must first enter the formula into a cell of the spreadsheet. The copy command then asks the

Exhibit 13.7

Some Examples of Ranges

A range can be a single cell, a column or row, or a block of cells. In each case, the range is specified by giving a beginning and ending cell address.

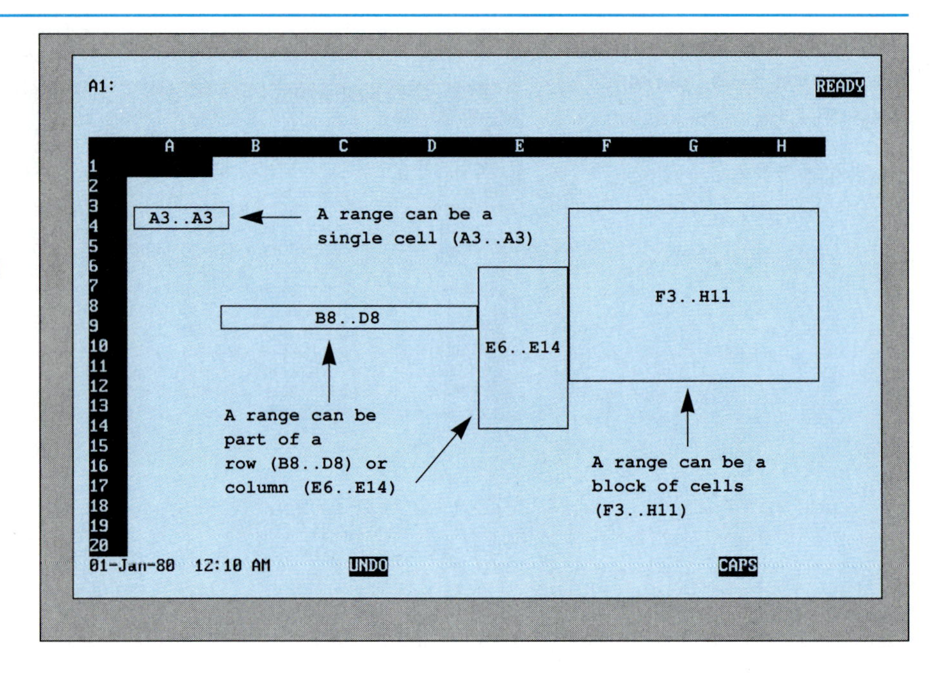

user for the address of the cell (or group of cells) containing the formula to be copied and the address of the cell (or group of cells) in which the copies are to be placed. Whenever a group of cells needs to be specified, a user must create a range.

In spreadsheets it is necessary to understand the concept of a range before seeing how commands are used. A **range** is simply a continuous group of cells. It can be used in commands when the user wishes to perform an operation on many cells rather than just one. A range can be as small as a single cell or as large as the entire spreadsheet. A range can be a row or a column; or it can be part of a row or part of a column. It can be a block of cells (several columns and rows). All ranges must be identified by a beginning and an ending cell address, separated by some special character (usually periods or a colon). Exhibit 13.7 shows some examples of valid ranges.

In the spreadsheet in Exhibit 13.8a, the user would enter a formula in the top of each of the three columns requiring formulas. A copy command could then be used to fill in the rest of each column with copies of the formula in the cell at the top of each column. Exhibit 13.8b shows how the Lotus 1-2-3 copy command could be used to fill in the formulas in the RAISE column.

Absolute Cell Addresses

Occasionally the adjustment of cell addresses that occurs when a formula is copied will not be appropriate. Exhibit 13.9a on page 334 shows an alternative method for computing the raises for employees in the personnel

Exhibit 13.8

The Copy Command

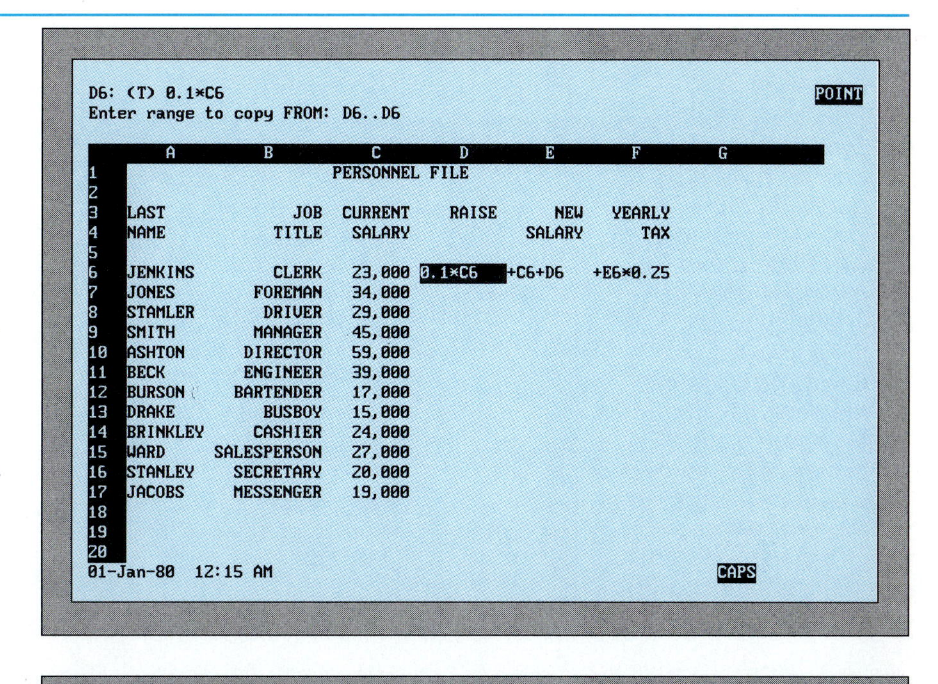

(a) After the user has entered a formula in the cell at the top of the RAISE column, a copy command can be used to fill in the rest of the cells in the column. In Lotus 1-2-3, the copy command first asks the user for the range where the formula to be copied is located. In this case, the range is a single cell—D6 . . D6.

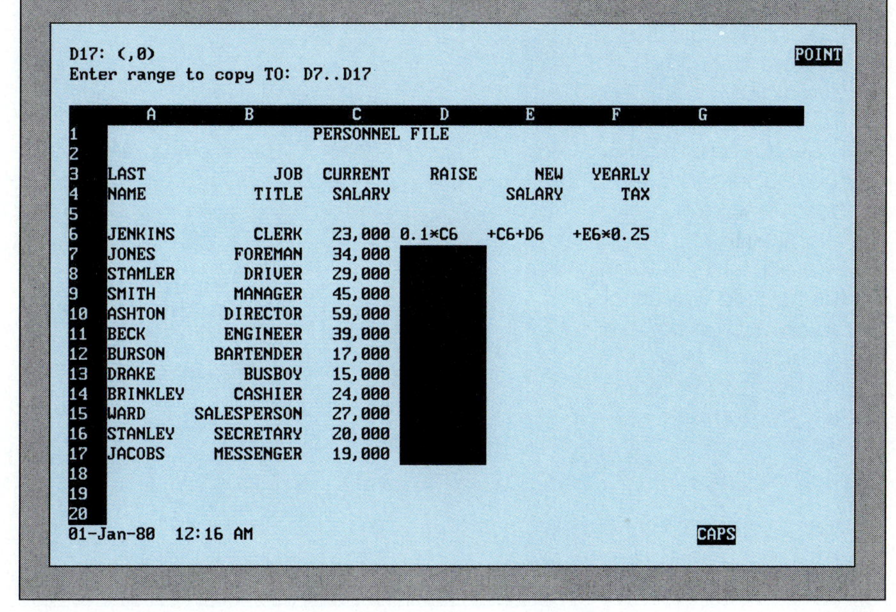

(b) Once the range where the formula is located has been specified, the user must then enter the range that indicates where copies of the formula are to be placed. In this case, the second range is D7 . . D17.

spreadsheet. In this example, the percentage for the raise was placed in cell D4 and the formula to compute raises for each employee multiplies the employee's salary by that percentage. Normally, a formula would be placed in the first cell of the raise column and then copied down the rest of the column. The exhibit illustrates that the method of adjusting all cell references to remain the same relative distance from the location of the formula would be inappropriate in this case. If the percentage for the raise

Exhibit 13.9

Using Absolute Cell Addresses in a Formula

(a) Sometimes the normal adjustment of cell addresses during the copying of the formula will not be appropriate. Here the reference to cell D4 in the formula must always be D4 for all the copies of the formula in the RAISE column. If the formula shown in D6 is copied, the spreadsheet will change the reference to D4 automatically.

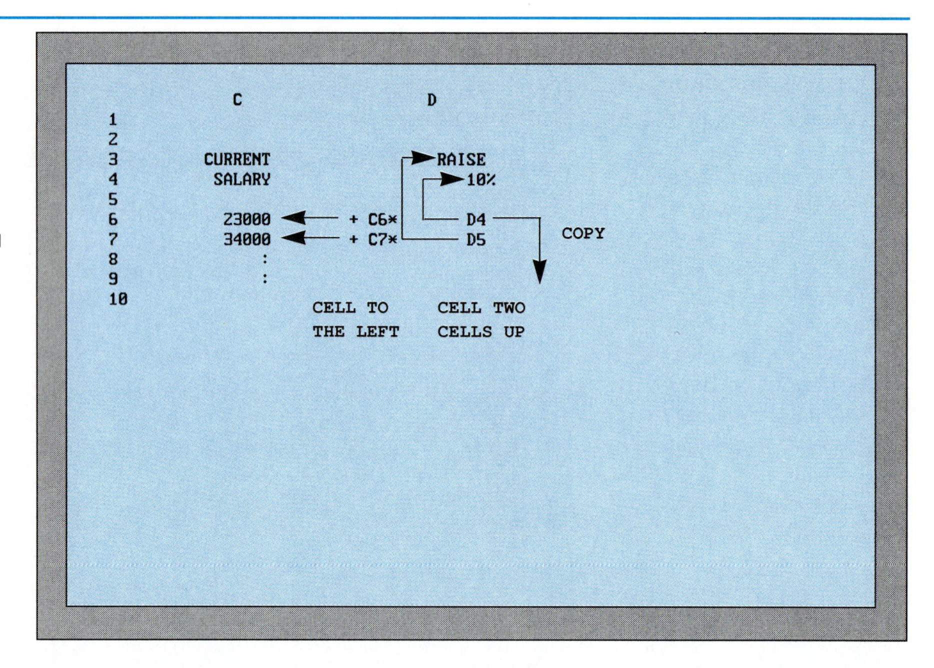

(b) To tell the spreadsheet that it is not to adjust a cell reference in a formula as it is copied, most spreadsheets allow the user to mark a cell address as absolute. In this example the reference to cell D4 in the formula was made absolute by placing a dollar sign in front of the column letter and the row number.

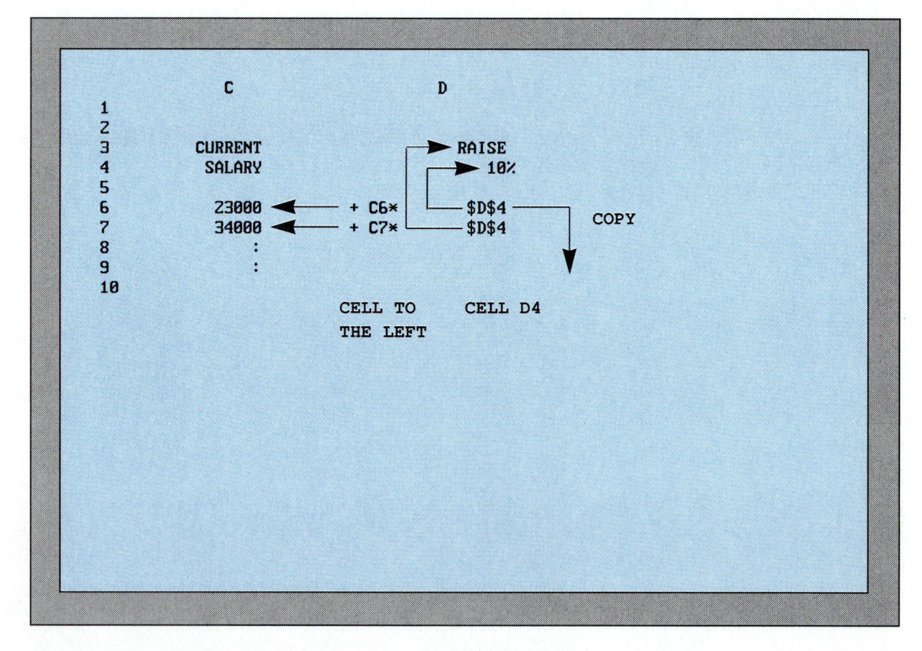

for each employee is always found in cell D4, the reference to cell D4 in the formula must be D4 for all the copies of the formula in the RAISE column. If the formula shown in D6 is copied, the reference to D4 should not change.

To tell the spreadsheet not to adjust a cell reference in a formula as it is copied, most spreadsheets allow the user to mark a cell address with a special symbol. This creates what is known as an **absolute cell address**. In Exhibit 13.9b, the reference to cell D4 in the formula was made absolute by placing a dollar sign in front of the column letter and the row number. When this formula is copied down the column, the first address, referring to the employee's salary, will be adjusted (as it should be), but the reference to cell D4 will remain constant. Thus, to fully understand how to make copies of spreadsheet formulas, the user must be aware of when and how to use absolute addresses as well as how to use the copy command itself.

Built-in Functions

Spreadsheets provide functions that perform operations that would otherwise require complex formulas. For example, the + D5 + D6 + D7 formula in cell D9 of the break-even analysis was used to add, or sum up, the contents of three cells. Note that these cells are also the range D5 . . D7 (D5 to D7). Spreadsheets have a built-in function, called SUM, which will sum up contents of all the cells in range. Thus, SUM(D5 . . D7) could have been used to do the same thing as the formula + D5 + D6 + D7. The advantage of the sum function is that it can be used to add up the contents of cells in a range of any size. Thus, if you wanted to sum the first 100 cells in column D, you could use SUM (D1 . . D100). This is clearly much more efficient than writing a formula with 100 cell addresses separated by plus signs.

Exhibit 13.10 shows the break-even analysis with the SUM function used to total the variable costs (see the control panel at the bottom). Note how there is an @ in front of the word SUM. Remember, in many spreadsheets, if an entry begins with a letter, it is treated as a label. Thus, if the user entered SUM(D13 . . D15) it would become a label instead of a formula. To avoid this problem, built-in functions typically begin with a special character such as @. Other spreadsheets require a label prefix in

Exhibit 13.10

The Break-Even Analysis in the Quattro Spreadsheet

The @SUM function in cell D17 is visible in the control panel at the bottom of the spreadsheet. This function is used to add up the contents of all the cells in the range D13 . . D15.

```
        A         B         C         D          E         F         G         H
1                BREAK-EVEN ANALYSIS
2
3   FIXED COSTS
4
5    RENT                          12,000.00
6    ADVERTISING                   10,000.00
7    SECRETARY                     17,000.00
8                                  ---------
9    TOTAL                        $39,000.00
10
11  VARIABLE COSTS
12
13   MATERIALS                          5.00
14   LABOR                             10.00
15   SHIPPING                           1.50
16                                    ------
17   TOTAL                            $16.50
18
19  PRICE PER UNIT                        25
20  BREAK-EVEN QUANTITY                 4588
D17: (C2) [W11] @SUM(D13..D15)
26-Oct-90  04:27 PM                                                          READY
```

Exhibit 13.11

Some of the Built-in Functions Available in Lotus 1-2-3 and VP-Planner

MATHEMATICAL FUNCTIONS	
@SQRT(X)	square root
@ABS(X)	absolute value
@LOG(X)	log base 10
@PI	pi
@SIN(X)	sine
@COS(X)	cosine
@TAN(X)	tangent

FINANCIAL FUNCTIONS	
@NPV(x,range)	net present value
@PMT(principal,interest,term)	monthly payment
@FV(payment,interest,term)	future value
@PV(payment,interest,term)	present value

STATISTICAL FUNCTIONS	
@SUM(range)	total value
@AVG(range)	average
@MIN(range)	minimum
@MAX(range)	maximum
@STD(range)	standard deviation

front of all labels so that formulas can start with the letter in a cell address or the letter that begins a function name.

Spreadsheets provide many different types of built-in functions, for calculations that are mathematical, financial, and statistical. Exhibit 13.11 shows some of the functions provided by most spreadsheets. More advanced spreadsheets provide functions for manipulating dates, time, and text. Functions are also available to look up values in tables and selectively perform different calculations based on a logical condition.

Editing a Spreadsheet

Once entries have been made in the cells of the spreadsheet, the user still has a great deal of control over how the spreadsheet is arranged. The contents of any cell can be changed, new columns and rows can be added, and entries can be moved from one cell to another.

The simplest form of editing is to replace a cell's contents with something else. If a second entry is made in a cell that already contains an entry, the new entry replaces the existing one.

Most spreadsheets provide an edit command or key, which lets the user pull the contents out of the current cell and put them back on a line in the control panel where they can be altered. Once the entry has been changed, the user can press RETURN, and the entry will be placed back in the current cell. This is particularly useful when there is a minor mistake in a long label; typing the whole label over would be inefficient.

When an entry is in the control panel, a spreadsheet will allow editing of that entry by deletion and addition of characters. Usually the right and left arrow keys can be used to move the cursor across the line. Sometimes the HOME and END keys can be used to jump to the beginning or end of the entry. Some spreadsheets will not permit the user to type over any characters that are already in the entry, which forces the user to specifically delete any character that isn't wanted. Other spreadsheets have both an insert and a typeover mode, just like some word processors.

A user can create new cells on a spreadsheet by inserting a new column or row. For example, if a user needs some additional cells to the left of column A, a command can be used to instruct the spreadsheet to create a new column A. When this column is inserted, the entries in the old column A and all the entries in the columns to the right are shifted one column to the right (see Exhibit 13.12).

The same thing can be done with rows. If a new row 11 is inserted, the old row 11 and all the rows below it will be moved down one row.

Columns and rows can also be deleted using a command. When a column is deleted, all the entries to the right of that column are shifted to the left to fill in the gap. When a row is deleted, all the entries below that row are shifted up.

It is important to note that when columns or rows are added, some of the numbers and formulas may be shifted into different cells. Spreadsheets can adjust all formulas so that their relative locations to the cell addresses they contain are preserved. This occurs automatically whenever the location of a formula is altered by the insertion or deletion of a column or row. The adjustment allows the formula to remain correct when columns and rows are inserted or deleted, so long as a cell used in the calculation is not deleted.

The user can also move an entry from one cell to another, using a special move command. The user must supply the address of the cell to be

Exhibit 13.12

Inserting a Column

When column A is inserted, the contents of the spreadsheet are shifted to the right.

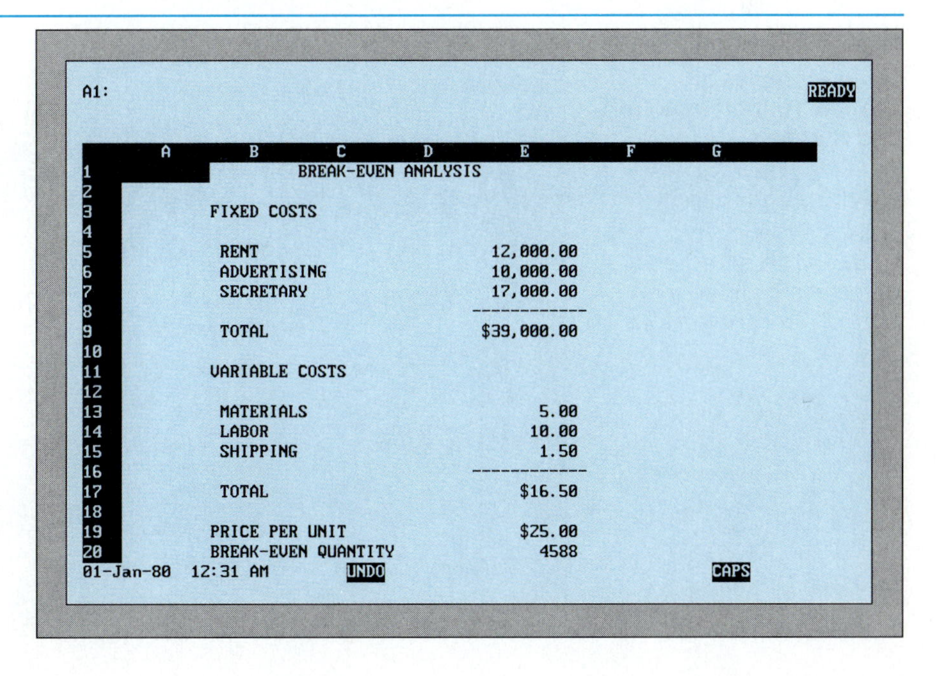

moved and the new address to which the entry will be moved. However, if a number used in a formula is moved, an error would occur since the location of the cell relative to the location of the formula is changed. Thus, the move command is most useful in rearranging headings and must be used with great care when numbers and formulas are involved.

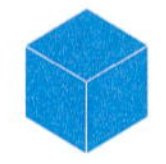

Formatting a Spreadsheet

Formatting is the process of altering the way in which numbers and labels are displayed on the spreadsheet itself. Labels can be moved within a cell to line them up any way the user desires. Once a number has been entered into a cell, its appearance can be altered by adding special characters like dollar signs and commas. The widths of columns can be altered to control the spacing of information on the spreadsheet.

The formatting of labels is typically accomplished in one of two ways. Some spreadsheets provide different label prefixes that can do the formatting. Others give the user control over label formatting in the form of a command. Some spreadsheets use both methods.

Basically, the types of label formatting include left-justified, right-justified, centered, and repeating. Exhibit 13.13 shows examples of these types of formatting. The repeating prefix repeats the entry across a cell. In this exhibit, the repeating text entry is displayed in the control panel and the cell on the spreadsheet shows how the entry is repeated all the way across the cell.

Some spreadsheets give the user control over the positioning of a number in a cell, just as can be done with labels. Usually right- and left-

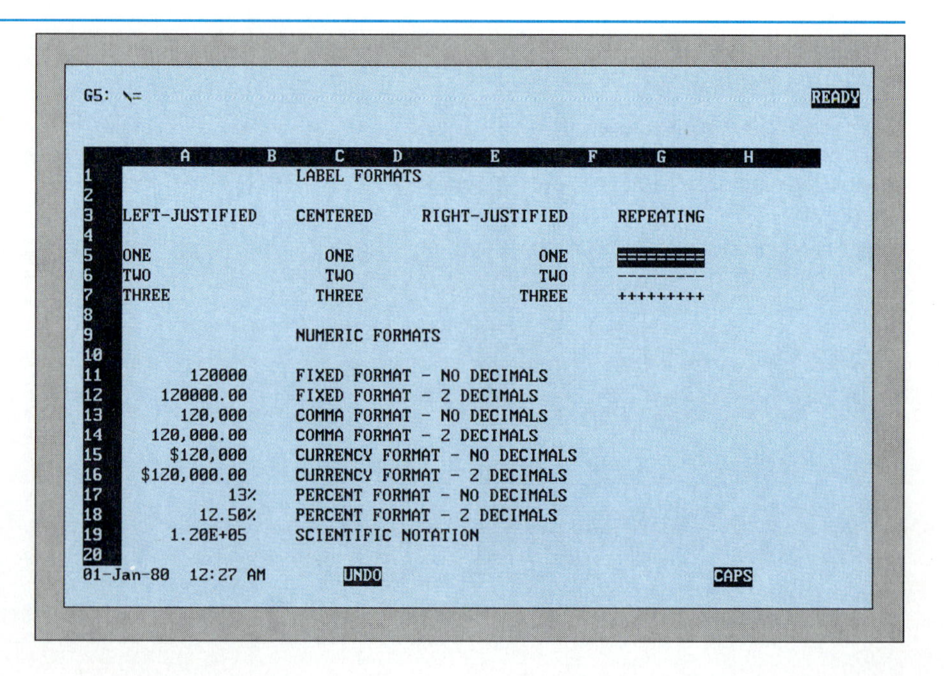

Exhibit 13.13

Some Examples of Different Formats for Labels and Numbers

Note how the repeating text character \ in G5 causes the entry that follows to be repeated across the cell. See the control panel at the top.

justification options are available. Other spreadsheets force all numbers to be right-justified in order to make the decimal places line up better and to make it easier to read the numbers without making an error.

Many more format variations exist for numbers than for labels. Spreadsheets give various levels of control over the number of decimal places displayed. Dollar signs and commas between thousands can also be displayed. Some spreadsheets offer a percent format and scientific notation. The types of formats available and the amount of control possible vary widely among the different spreadsheet programs. Exhibit 13.13 also shows some of these numeric formats.

It is important to realize that the size of a cell shown on the screen does not limit the size of the entry that can be placed in that cell. In most spreadsheets, each cell can hold up to 256 characters, regardless of how big it looks on the screen. Its size on the screen is simply the *display width.*

The user can alter the display width of a cell on the screen only by altering the width of an entire column. In order to keep things lined up, the spreadsheet programs do not allow the width of individual cells to be changed. The width of any column can be set from 1 to 256 by using a column-width command. Spreadsheets have a special way of dealing with entries that are too long to fit in the display width of a cell. If an entry is a label, characters that do not fit in the cell overflow into the cells to the right, as long as those adjacent cells are empty. If they are not empty, the label will be truncated.

Numbers that are too large to be displayed in a cell are treated differently. When a number is too long, it would not be good to truncate it and display only the part that fits, because the user might think the entire number is being shown. Therefore, when a number is too large, the cell will usually be filled with asterisks (*) to indicate that the cell is occupied but the number is too big to be displayed (sometimes < is used). This often occurs when a number is formatted, because several formats add extra characters to the number. The user's only option for displaying the entire number, is to widen the column enough that the number can be displayed.

In addition to altering column widths, recent spreadsheets (such as Excel) also allow users to alter row height for even finer control over spreadsheet spacing. In addition, these more recent spreadsheets offer the user many more formatting options with which to manipulate the appearance, typeface, and size of the text, as can be done in the more advanced word processors (see Exhibit 13.14).

Spreadsheet Commands

As indicated earlier, certain functions can be accomplished using commands. In spreadsheets, commands are used to format entries, change the layout of the spreadsheet, print spreadsheets, and work with spreadsheet files. The user tells the spreadsheet when a command is to be entered by typing a special character (usually a slash) in the first position on the entry line. When the slash (/) is typed, the spreadsheet enters the command mode and shows the user menus of commands from which to choose.

Exhibit 13.14

Varying Labels and Numbers

In the Macintosh version of Microsoft Excel the user has control over the appearance, typeface, and size of the labels and numbers displayed on the spreadsheet.

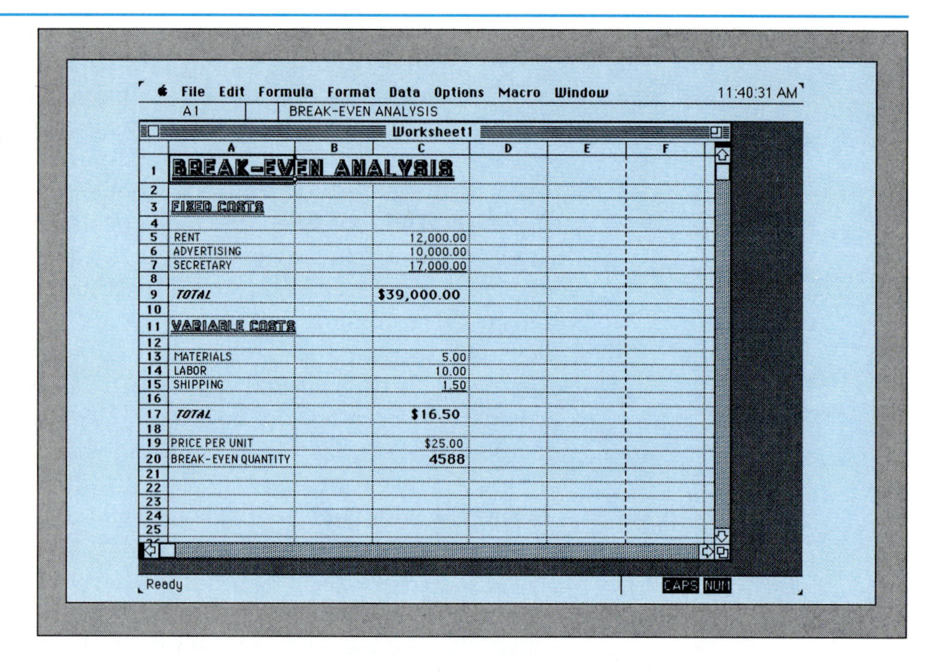

Exhibit 13.15

The SUPERCALC4 Command Menu

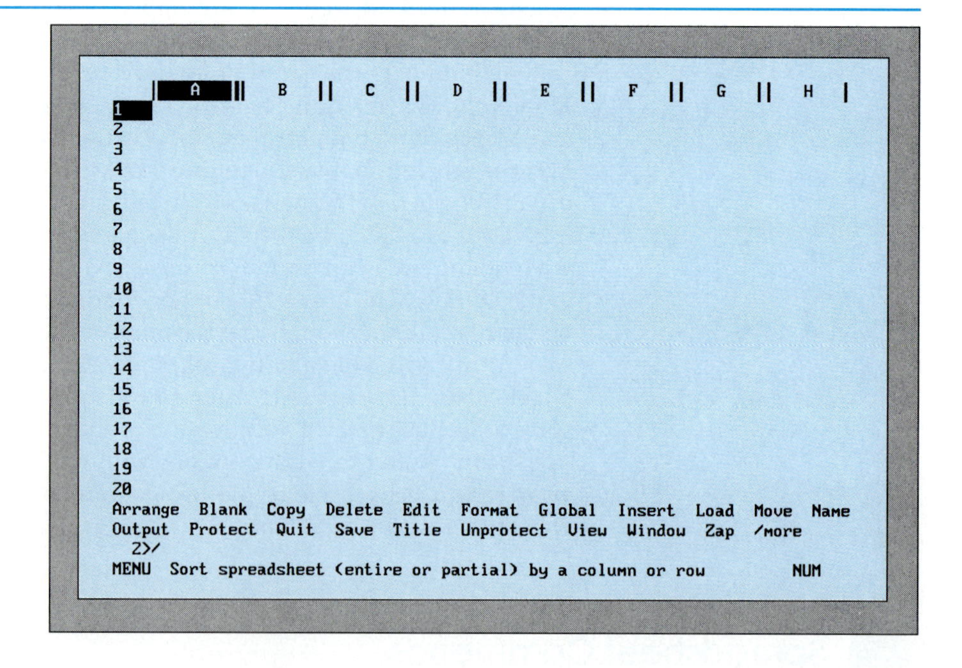

In most spreadsheets, the menu of commands appears in the control panel (see Exhibit 13.15). The user can choose an option in the menu by moving the highlight with the arrow keys and pressing RETURN to select the highlighted choice. A choice can also be selected by typing the first letter of the option.

As options are chosen, a submenu usually appears that allows the user to enter the detailed information needed to complete the command. As the user goes deeper into the hierarchy of menus, the possibility of an incorrect choice being made increases. Spreadsheets usually allow a user to back up through the various menus by hitting a certain key (such as the ESC key) to return to the preceding menu.

Spreadsheets that run on the Macintosh and some newer spreadsheets for IBM-compatible computers (such as Excel) give the user pull-down menus that can be activated with a mouse. As with all spreadsheet menus, these pull-down menus will sometimes lead to submenus, in which the user may need to enter text from the keyboard, such as when naming a file.

The HELP Facility

Spreadsheet programs provide a special help key (F1 in most spreadsheets) that can be pressed at any time to get information about using the spreadsheet. Some spreadsheets contain very complex help facilities that allow the user to choose among screens that cover almost every aspect of spreadsheet use. Exhibit 13.16 shows the Lotus 1-2-3 help screen, in which the user can choose among various topics for which help is available.

An important feature of the help facility is that it is sensitive to what the user was doing before he or she asked for help. For example, if the user was making an entry, the help facility will provide information about how entries can be made. If the user was issuing a print command, the help facility will provide information about the way the print command works.

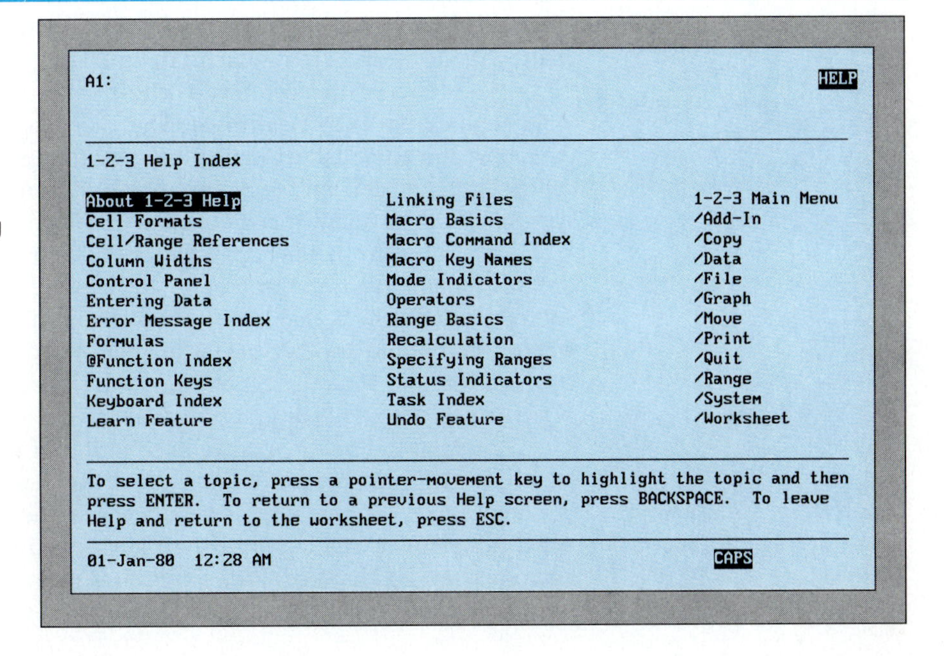

Exhibit 13.16

The Lotus 1-2-3 Help Facility

In the Lotus 1-2-3 Help facility, a user can get information about any aspect of creating or using a spreadsheet.

When the help facility is entered, the spreadsheet disappears, so that the help screens can be shown. The work the user was doing on the spreadsheet remains in memory, so that when the help facility is terminated, the user is returned to the exact place he or she was before the help key was used.

Global Commands Versus Range Commands

Most spreadsheets make some type of distinction between **global commands** and **range commands**. This distinction has to do with the amount of the spreadsheet affected by the commands. For example, spreadsheets have a global format command and a range format command. Global formats affect all the cells in the spreadsheet. A user can set the global format for numbers to a currency format with two decimal places. Conversely, if a user only wanted to change the format of only the numbers in a few cells, a range format command can be used. The user specifies the range over which that format takes effect.

Other global commands can set the column width for all columns and choose an alignment for all labels. It is important to realize that a global format cannot override a range format. Thus, if the display width of column C is set to 13, a subsequent global column-width setting of 12 will not affect column C. The same thing occurs with numeric and label formats. Those set with a range command are unchanged by subsequent global commands.

Printing and Saving

Once a spreadsheet has been created, it can be printed on paper at any time. As with word processors, a single command causes the spreadsheet to be printed. Thus, making a mistake is not costly, since the information is stored in electronic form, which can be easily corrected and reprinted.

In the print command, the user must specify the range that represents what is to be printed. The user has complete control over how much of the spreadsheet is run off. As little as one cell or as much as the entire spreadsheet can be printed; the only limitation is that the part to be printed must be a valid range of cells.

Print commands give a choice of destinations for a document. It can be sent either to a printer or to a file. The advantage of sending the document to a file is that this file is in electronic form, and can therefore be incorporated into another file such as a word processing document. Thus, a user can send a spreadsheet to a file, then use a word processor to pull the spreadsheet into a document so it can be used as a table or figure.

Once the range and the destination of the file have been specified, the user also has various options about the printing of the range. It can be printed as it is displayed on the screen, or the actual contents of the cells (including formulas) can be listed. Headers and footers can be specified, margins can be changed, and sometimes even the borders (column letters and row numbers) can be included on the printout. Exhibit 13.17 shows

Exhibit 13.17

An Example of the Printed Break-Even Analysis Spreadsheet

```
                  BREAK-EVEN ANALYSIS

FIXED COSTS

   RENT                                  $12,000.00
   ADVERTISING                            10,000.00
   SECRETARY                              17,000.00
                                         ----------
TOTAL                                    $39,000.00

VARIABLE COSTS

   MATERIALS                                $ 5.00
   LABOR                                     10.00
   SHIPPING                                   1.50
                                            ------
TOTAL                                       $16.50

PRICE PER UNIT                              $25.00
BREAK-EVEN QUANTITY                           4588
```

how the break-even spreadsheet looks when it is printed, using A1 . . D20 as the range.

Saving and retrieving a spreadsheet also involves a spreadsheet command. The program asks for the name of the file to be used. Normally files are assumed to be on drive B, but this can be overridden by specifying the drive letter along with the file name. File extensions are usually omitted because each spreadsheet program has a default extension it uses.

When a spreadsheet is saved for the first time, it is simply put into the file named. Some spreadsheets have options during the save command about saving just the values on the screen or saving all the contents of the spreadsheet, including values and formulas.

When a spreadsheet is altered, the user has a choice of saving the new version of the spreadsheet under the original name or under a new name. Usually, the user specifies a file name under both circumstances, and, if the name given is the same as the name of a file already on the disk, the spreadsheet asks if the new version is to replace the old one.

When a file is retrieved, a copy of the spreadsheet is placed in primary memory, where it can be worked on. As with word processors, this leaves the original spreadsheet intact on the disk. Therefore a user can make changes on the spreadsheet in memory but not change the original; or a user might retrieve a spreadsheet just to get a look at it and then go on to something else without having to save it. Normally, when a file is retrieved, any spreadsheet currently in memory is destroyed when a new spreadsheet is brought in. There are, however, different ways of retrieving a file. A user can copy all, or part, of a spreadsheet in a disk file into the current spreadsheet without destroying the current spreadsheet. When two spreadsheets are combined in this way, the user indicates where the two are to be merged.

Templates

When spreadsheets are used in business, there may be a large number of similar spreadsheets among the various divisions and departments in the company. A **template** that has the headings and formulas already filled in can be created so that the user only has to put in the numbers to have a completed spreadsheet. A manager can use such a template to create an application without having to design all the details of the spreadsheet. In addition, once the template is completed, the manager can use it to do what-if analyses of data in the resulting spreadsheet.

Almost any spreadsheet can be used as a template by leaving blank any entries a user will complete. Exhibit 13.18 shows a template constructed from the break-even analysis. The entries for fixed costs, variable costs, and price per unit have been left blank. The formulas for totaling the fixed and variable costs and the break-even formula are entered but the cells display zero, since the cells used in the formulas are blank. A user can retrieve this spreadsheet and type in the missing entries. The cells with formulas in them will automatically be recalculated so that, when the user finishes entering numbers, the spreadsheet will be finished.

Two additional spreadsheet features that can be important when designing a template are hiding and protecting cells on the spreadsheet. Many spreadsheets allow the user to give a cell a special hidden format, which will suppress the display of the cell contents on the spreadsheet. However, the contents of the cell can still be seen in the control panel when the hidden cell is made the current cell on the spreadsheet. Some spreadsheets allow an entire column to be hidden. Hidden cells and columns allow the designer to place intermediate calculations in cells but

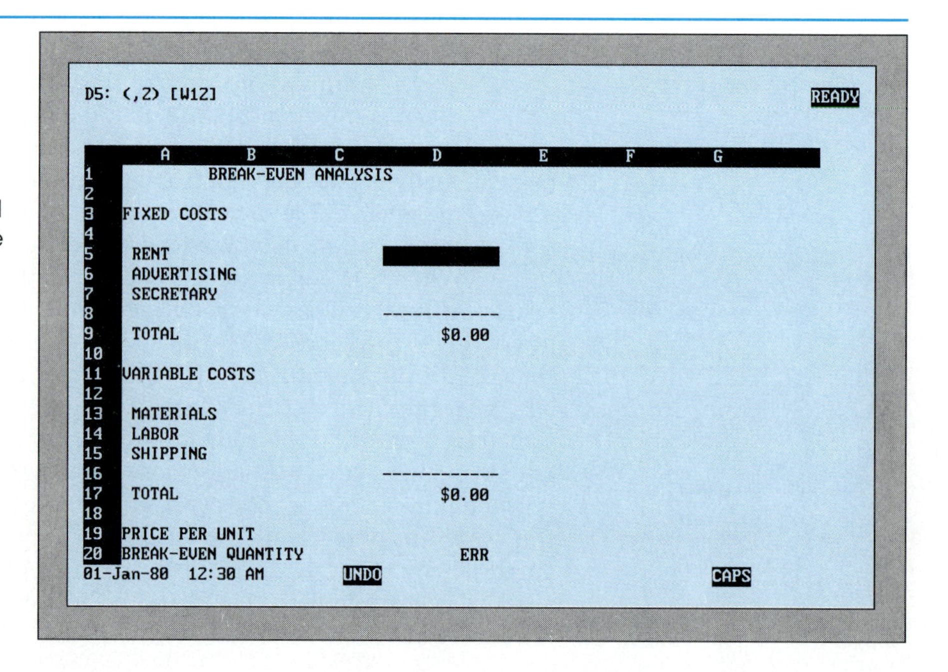

Exhibit 13.18

A Template for the Break-Even Analysis

Zeroes are displayed in cells containing formulas. The user enters all the fixed and variable costs and the price to finish the spreadsheet.

not display them to the user. This can create a cleaner-looking spreadsheet and reduce the likelihood of accidental tampering with a cell.

To further reduce the possibility of accidental or intentional tampering with the contents of a cell, spreadsheets also allow cells to be designated as protected. Typically a command (such as the RANGE, PROTECT command in Lotus 1-2-3) is used to protect a cell. When a cell is protected, no new entries can be made in that cell until another command is used to "unprotect" it.

Macros

Although templates are useful because they reduce design time and minimize the data the user must enter to create a spreadsheet, the user must still know something about the spreadsheet in order to use it effectively. The creation of a spreadsheet can be simplified even more by creating **keyboard macros,** which are cells on the spreadsheet (or sometimes separate files) containing keystrokes that are used to perform spreadsheet functions. A keyboard macro contains symbols that emulate the keystrokes used when carrying out a particular spreadsheet function. It also contains commands of its own that obtain data from the user, show the user menus from which to make choices, and control the execution of the macro itself. A macro is given a name and can be executed by pressing a single key. In many ways, a macro is like a program that works with the spreadsheet; like a program, it is not something that the casual user will be able to write.

As with macros in word processors, however, macro facilities in spreadsheets often include a learn mode. When this learn mode is activated, the spreadsheet records as a macro all the keystrokes the user issues to accomplish a task.

Choosing an Electronic Spreadsheet

Exhibit 13.19 compares some of the features that may be important to an end-user when selecting an electronic spreadsheet for IBM compatible and Macintosh computers.

For spreadsheet packages that run on IBM compatible computers, this exhibit shows whether the spreadsheet requires a PC with a hard disk drive. The maximum size of a spreadsheet is shown in terms of columns and rows, and the largest entry that can fit into a single cell is indicated. In the area of user interfaces, the exhibit indicates if a mouse can be used and if the spreadsheet uses pull-down menus. In the area of macros, the exhibit shows which spreadsheets have a learn mode for the creation of macros and if macros can be stored in files external to the spreadsheet file. Finally, the table indicates which spreadsheet packages provide a minimal recalculation feature to speed the data entry process.

For spreadsheet packages that run on the Macintosh family of computers, the exhibit compares the three most popular spreadsheets in terms of size (rows and columns) and the number of built-in functions

IBM Compatible Spreadsheets

	Excel 2.1	Lotus 3.0	Quattro 1.0	Supercalc5 5.0	VP-Planner Plus 2.0
Hard disk required	Y	Y	N	Y	N
Maximum rows	16384	8192	8192	9999	9999
Maximum columns	256	256	256	255	256
Max characters/cell	255	256	255	340	254
Mouse support	Y	Y	N	N	N
Minimal recalculation	Y	Y	Y	Y	Y
Learn mode	Y	Y	Y	Y	Y
External macros	Y	Y	N	Y	Y
Pull-down menus	Y	N	Y	N	N

Macintosh Spreadsheets

	Full Impact 1.1	Wingz 1.0	Excel 2.2
Maximum rows	2048	32000	16000
Maximum columns	256	32000	256
Background recalculation	N	Y	Y
Built-in functions	89	146	129
Cell notes	Y	Y	Y

Exhibit 13.19

A Comparison of Spreadsheet Features for IBM Compatible and Macintosh Computers

provided. In addition, the use of background recalculation is indicated, which is another method of speeding data entry similar to minimal recalculation. The exhibit also indicates which packages allow the user to associate a block of text with a cell (a cell note), which can be used to provide a user of the spreadsheet with an explanation of the contents of a cell.

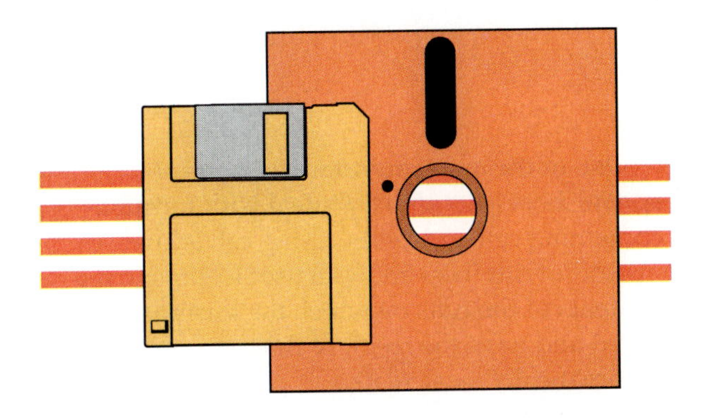

Computers at Work

Where 1-2-3 Makes Deals in a Hurry

One year ago, Jim Lynch left the campus of Yale University with a freshly minted MBA. Today he spends a good part of his workday at an IBM PC AT, intently tapping his way through *1-2-3* worksheets.

Lynch is just one of 200 young analysts and associates who work in open office spaces spread across eight floors at the Manhattan headquarters of Bankers Trust Co. As part of the Corporate Finance department, their job is to analyze the details of financial proposals for the bank's corporate clients. And the Lotus spreadsheet program is how they do it. "We work our kids awfully hard in *1-2-3*," says Henry Ford, a vice president in the Merchant Banking group.

As is the case in many corporations, the power of the computerized spreadsheet has changed the way Bankers Trust does business. "It has made the business more complex," says Ford. "We analyze a lot more structures." And therein, some in the department say, lies a concern. Sometimes, says Ford, "we suffer from analysis paralysis."

It's hard to say which came first, *1-2-3* or the growing complexity of corporate deals. But without computerized spreadsheets, it might not be possible to cope effectively with today's alphabet soup of high-finance arrangements.

Let's Make a Deal

The analyst turns to a spreadsheet "deal" template. When considering an acquisition, for example, he or she cranks in the figures from a company's balance and income statements, as well as such key data as capital expenditures and growth projections. One type of output is key financial ratios, such as receivables turnover, current ratio, and asset coverage. Another is a projection of future performance. If the results look promising, the analyst starts to tailor the worksheet to reflect the proposed deal.

Some deals are large and complex, involving tens or even hundreds of investors. An analyst uses *1-2-3* to assign portions of the proposed investment to the "players" that the senior staff has identified. Inevitably, such a deal is restructured to accommodate new players, changing priorities, or revised economic assumptions. With a spreadsheet, an analyst can come up with a new deal in less than 24 hours.

Speed and Complexity

The bank's ability to analyze many different scenarios quickly is important to clients. Howard Riker, an analyst who specializes in real estate capital markets, notes that the investment market is highly competitive. "You must cover all the different cases," he says, "in order not to get burned."

Among the bank's analysts, there is immense respect for *1-2-3* as a tool. There are also some reservations, however. Many analysts echo Henry Ford's concern over the possibility of "paralysis," noting that *1-2-3* makes it easy to get lost in formulas and numbers and to lose sight of the deal. "Too much analysis," says Riker, "clouds the fact that a building is a building and an investment is an investment."

Jim Lynch agrees that it's easy to "get lost in a model." Lots of analysis, he says, "can still be done effectively on the back of an envelope."

Like many *1-2-3* users, the bank's analysts realize that there are technical limits to what the program can do well. There is some dissatisfaction with recalculation speeds. The limitations of the program's graphical output long ago led to reliance on *Freelance*, a powerful graphics program. As for database operations, Ken Abbott, vice president of research and analytics in the Money Market Economics group, says, "You have to move to *dBase* at around 1,000 records." Some people also use *Paradox*, a stand-alone, multiuser database program from Borland International.

Summary and Key Terms

A spreadsheet is a grid of columns and rows, forming cells that contain labels and numbers.

The active location on the spreadsheet is usually highlighted by the **current cell pointer.** This pointer can be moved in any direction with arrow keys.

Only a fraction of a spreadsheet can be seen at one time. This **window** of cells can be moved **(scrolled)** to reveal columns and rows not being displayed. A user can also move through the spreadsheet a screen at a time in any direction and can use special keys to jump immediately to a specified cell on the spreadsheet.

Most of the activity involved in creating a spreadsheet takes place in the **control panel.** The control panel gives the user information about the current cell and provides an area where entries are typed before being placed into the spreadsheet itself. When something is displayed in this area, the user can edit that entry until it is correct.

The control panel is also used to display messages to the user during commands.

Both labels and numbers can be entered into cells. Labels are usually preceded by a label prefix, which indicates how the label is to be placed in the cell containing that label. A spreadsheet can also contain **formulas**, which are numbers and cell addresses joined by mathematical symbols to designate calculations to be performed.

In a spreadsheet, there is a difference between what is stored in a cell and what is displayed on the spreadsheet. For example, formulas are stored in cells, but the result of the calculation is what is displayed on the spreadsheet.

A formula is entered in the same way as a label or number. When mathematical symbols are used, there is a specific order in which the calculations will be performed. This is known as **precedence.** Normally exponentiation is performed first and is followed by multiplication and division and finally addition and subtraction. This order can be altered by enclosing the parts of the calculation that are to be performed first in parentheses.

One of the most important features of a spreadsheet is its ability to deal with formulas containing cell addresses. Using cell addresses instead of numbers allows a user to change the contents of the cells on which the formula is based and have the result of the formula automatically recalculated.

The process of entering formulas can be made more efficient by using a copy command. A spreadsheet interprets cell addresses in a formula as relative distances from the cell containing the formula. When a formula is copied to a new cell, those addresses change so that they represent the cells that are the same relative distances from the new formula as the cells in the original formula. This is known as **adjustment.**

The copy command requires the user to specify a range indicating the location of the formula or formulas to be copied and a range that indicates where the copies of the formula are to be placed.

A **range** is any continuous group of cells that can be specified by a beginning and ending cell address.

Often a formula will contain cell addresses that should not be adjusted when the formula is copied. Typically, a user can mark these cell addresses to make them **absolute cell addresses,** which instructs the spreadsheet not to adjust that cell address as the formula is copied.

Spreadsheets provide built-in functions such as the sum function, which can add the numbers in a range of cells.

Spreadsheets also have an edit function, which allows the user to move an entry from the spreadsheet back onto the entry line for further editing.

Rows and columns can be inserted and deleted from the spreadsheet, and entries can be moved from one cell to another.

Formatting is the process of altering the appearance of entries on the spreadsheet. Labels can be formatted to be left- or right-justified, centered, or repeated. Numbers can be formatted with various numbers of decimal places, commas, and dollar signs. There are also percent formats and scientific notation available.

A cell can contain entries up to 256 characters long. The size of the cell shown on the spreadsheet is only the display size—it does not reflect the actual size of the cell. The display width of any column on the spreadsheet can be changed by the user.

Spreadsheet commands allow a user to perform tasks involving the spreadsheet as a whole or involving parts of the spreadsheet. When the command mode is entered, a user receives a menu from which choices can be made.

A special help key can provide a user with more information about commands.

A distinction is made between **global commands** and **range commands.** Global commands affect the entire spreadsheet. Range commands affect only cells in a specified range. A global command cannot override a setting made by a range command.

The contents of a spreadsheet can be printed to a disk file or to a printer. Any range on the spreadsheet can be printed. The user has options about setting margins, headers and footers, and the way the contents of the spreadsheet will be printed.

When a spreadsheet is saved, it can be stored in a new file, or it can replace a spreadsheet in an existing file. When a spreadsheet is retrieved, a copy of the spreadsheet is placed in primary memory. A user can also retrieve all, or part, of a spreadsheet and merge it with a spreadsheet already in memory.

A **template** is a partially completed spreadsheet in which many of the entries are already made. A user can retrieve this spreadsheet and complete it to produce a finished application. The cell protection feature of spreadsheets is useful in designing a template in which all the cells the user should not alter are protected. Hidden cells can also be used on a template to hide columns or cells containing information the user does not have to see.

Keyboard macros are cells or files that contain spreadsheet commands. A macro can be executed simply by pressing a single key; all the spreadsheet functions in the macro will then be carried out. Newer spreadsheets also include a learn mode for macros, in which the keystrokes performed by the user are recorded as a macro.

Review Questions

1. List some problems in other courses you have taken that could be solved by using electronic spreadsheets.
2. Give an example of how the contents of a cell can differ from the display of that cell in a spreadsheet.
3. Explain how a spreadsheet interprets cell addresses as relative distances from the location of the formula.
4. Explain how the copy command works and what the two ranges specified in that command are for.
5. Describe the spreadsheet's control panel. Tell what the control panel is used for.
6. Explain how a manager can use the automatic recalculation feature of a spreadsheet to perform a what-if analysis.
7. List some of the built-in functions of spreadsheets.
8. What is the difference between global and range commands?
9. What type of formatting can be done to numbers and labels on a spreadsheet?
10. Explain what an absolute cell address is and why it is needed.

T F **11.** A range is a continuous group of cells.

T F **12.** A global command can override a range command.

T F **13.** An absolute cell address is one that changes as the formula is copied.

T F **14.** Adjustment refers to the process of changing the appearance of a label or number.

T F **15.** Automatic recalculation can never be turned off in a spreadsheet program.

T F **16.** Once information is entered into the columns on a spreadsheet, new columns cannot be inserted into the spreadsheet without destroying the formulas.

T F **17.** The control panel is the area where the user interacts with the spreadsheet during data entry and when issuing commands.

T F **18.** If a column or row in the spreadsheet moves off the screen, the data in that area will be lost.

T F **19.** A label-prefix character is used to affect the alignment of a text entry in a cell.

T F **20.** Once an entry is placed in a cell, it can never be brought back to the control panel for further editing.

21. _____ A highlight on the spreadsheet screen that indicates the user's position on the spreadsheet is called the:

a. window c. range
b. current cell pointer d. scroll bar

22. _____ The process of moving the window on the screen to reveal unseen columns and rows is known as:

a. scrolling c. formatting
b. copying d. previewing

23. _____ The area on the top or bottom of the screen where data is entered and information is displayed to the user is called the:

a. range c. control panel
b. current cell pointer d. template

24. _____ The spreadsheet feature that continuously updates cells containing formulas so that they always display the correct results is known as:

a. adjustment c. automatic recalculation
b. copying d. scrolling

25. _____ The spreadsheet feature that allows the cell addresses in formulas to automatically change as the formula is copied is called:

a. scrolling c. absolute addressing
b. copying d. adjustment

26. _____ Which is not a valid range?

a. C4 through C10 c. A1
b. A10 through C10 d. C10 and A5

27. _____ When a user marks a cell address in a formula so it will not be changed during the copying of the formula, the user has created:
   a. a range
   b. an absolute address
   c. a relative address
   d. a formula

28. _____ A __________ is a partially completed spreadsheet already containing many formulas and formatting. It is designed to allow the user to enter some data to complete a spreadsheet without having to design it.
   a. template
   b. macro
   c. range
   d. control panel

29. _____ Which of the following is not something that can be entered into a cell on the spreadsheet?
   a. number
   b. formula
   c. label
   d. command

30. _____ A series of keystrokes stored in a cell that can be executed with a single command to accomplish a common task is a:
   a. template
   b. range
   c. control panel
   d. macro

CHAPTER 14

Microcomputer Database Programs

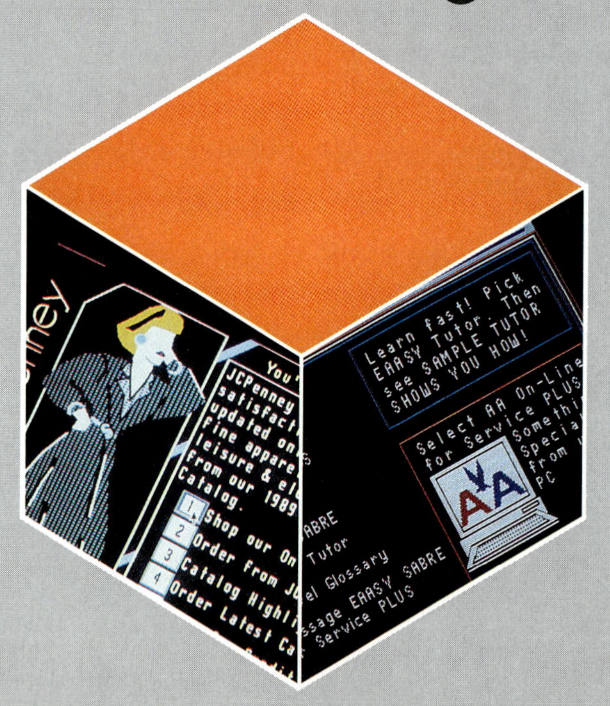

Just as word processors are replacing typewriters and electronic spreadsheets are replacing paper and calculators, the microcomputer database is replacing the filing cabinet of the office. Databases are collections of data that are organized for easy retrieval in decision-making situations. When data are retrieved from a microcomputer database, selected pieces can be sorted into the order most useful to the end-user. This chapter looks at the range of features provided by microcomputer database programs and explores how these programs are used to store, maintain, and retrieve data.

In this chapter you will learn to do the following:

1. Understand how a database is designed
2. Explain the difference between file managers and relational database programs
3. Describe some of the features used in creating a database
4. List some of the features important in the retrieval of data
5. Understand some of the advanced features of database programs

Database Design

Before examining the features of microcomputer database programs, it is important to understand some of the concepts involved in organizing data. In a database, data are typically stored in **tables**. The data within a table are organized into various **columns**, which represent the different types of information being stored. For example, Exhibit 14.1 shows a table containing student data. The columns in this table include the ID number, last name, first name, campus address, and campus phone for each student. Each line in this table represents the data for a particular student. This collection of the data in all the columns for one student represents a **row** in

Exhibit 14.1
A Table Containing Student Information

ID NUMBER	LAST NAME	FIRST NAME	CAMPUS ADDRESS	CAMPUS PHONE
111111	GRANT	GREG	LINCOLN HALL	555-4534
222222	SPADE	STEVE	COPELAND HALL	555-3454
333333	JONES	JANE	BOYD HALL	555-3433
444444	DRAKE	DREW	BOYD HALL	555-5965
555555	SMITH	SALLY	BYERS HALL	555-4845

Exhibit 14.2

A Table Containing Course Information

COURSE CODE	COURSE NAME	CREDIT HOURS
MIS100	INTRODUCTION	5.0
MIS200		
	PROGRAMMING I	4.0
MIS250	COMMUNICATIONS	4.0
MIS300	Database	4.0

the table. When a database is created, a user must describe to the database program the tables that are to be created and the rows and columns to be contained within them.

Exhibit 14.2 shows a table of data listing courses that students can take. Like the student table, this table contains rows that are divided into columns. Exhibit 14.3 shows a third table that represents the transcript for each student and shows the courses each student took and the grade he or she received in those courses. Notice that this third table contains the same student numbers as the student table and the same course numbers as the course table.

These tables illustrate another important feature of database programs: the ability to relate data in one table to data in another table. Using the three tables in the exhibits, a user might want to find a specific student in the student table and then go to the transcript table to find all the courses taken by that particular student. Furthermore, having found the courses in the transcript table, the user might want to know the number of credit hours associated with each course, which can be found in the course table. Allowing users to obtain information in this fashion requires the data in one table to be related to data in another. This group of related tables is known as a database. Thus, a **database** is a group of tables containing data that are related. A database must not only store the data itself but must also relate the data across tables.

Exhibit 14.3

A Table Using Both Student and Course Information

Note how the student IDs match the ID numbers in the student table and the course IDs match the course codes in the course table.

STUDENT ID	COURSE ID	GRADE
111111	MIS100	C
111111	MIS200	B
333333	MIS100	C+
333333	MIS200	A
333333	MIS250	A-
444444	MIS100	B+
444444	MIS200	B
444444	MIS300	A
444444	MIS400	A-

When a database is designed, the designer must determine the tables to be created and the columns in each table. Typically, the data that are stored in a table have something in common. For example, the data in the student table are all related to students; the data in the course table are all related to courses; and the data in the transcript table all represent courses completed by students. During database design, all the data to be stored must be separated into groups of common data that will then be placed in tables. The formalized process used in database design to group data is called **normalization.** This process is too complex for the scope of this text and is typically only performed by trained database specialists. It is, however, critical to appreciate the importance of a good design. A poorly designed database can lead to data validity problems if data cannot be updated properly. Also, users may not be able to retrieve the data they require from a poorly designed database.

File Managers Versus Relational Database Programs

The ability to represent relationships among data in different tables is a major distinguishing feature of microcomputer database programs. Many software products that are referred to as database programs do not allow users to relate data across tables. These programs allow databases to contain only a single table and are more appropriately labeled **file managers** (often also called *flat-file databases* or *list-managers).* Since these products cannot represent the relationships among data in different tables, these products are not true database programs. Database programs that do allow data to be related across tables are commonly called **relational database programs.**

Although file managers do not allow tables (or files) to be related, they do offer many of the other capabilities of relational database programs. The ability to relate tables is not always required by end-users, so file management programs are quite popular since they are simpler to use than true databases, and they are adequate for the needs of most end-users. End-users working with sophisticated applications requiring the relation of data across tables must use the more powerful relational database programs. This chapter uses illustrations from both file management and relational database programs. Due to the convergence of many of the capabilities of these programs the term *database program* will be used throughout the chapter to represent both file managers and relational database programs. Features unique to relational database programs will be emphasized when they are discussed.

Creating a Database

The unit of storage in all database programs is a table (or file). Thus, the primary task in the creation of a database is to define the tables to be used. Exhibit 14.4 shows a database containing two tables: a PRODUCT table (top), and a SUPPLIER table (bottom). The last column in the PRODUCT table is a number for a supplier, which matches the number of a supplier in the SUPPLIER table. Assuming that the database has been carefully designed, using a database program to create a database simply involves naming the tables and specifying the names of columns within the tables and the type of data they are to hold. A final step in some programs is the specification of key columns within each table.

Since a database is actually a group of related tables, some relational database programs (such as dBASE IV and R:BASE FOR DOS) allow the user to create a name for the database itself and to specify which tables are contained within the database. Since file managers cannot relate tables to create a database, they do not support this feature. The database in Exhibit 14.4 might be called PURCHASE, because the

THE PRODUCT TABLE

PRODUCT CODE	PRODUCT DESCRIPTION	PRODUCT GROUP	STOCK QUANTITY	PRODUCT PRICE	PRODUCT SUPPLIER
12111	KEYBOARD	COMPUTER	200	125.00	111
12222	TURNTABLE	STEREO	45	175.95	222
12333	HARD DISK	COMPUTER	320	350.00	111
12444	SPEAKER	STEREO	345	59.90	333
12555	RECEIVER	STEREO	100	150.00	222
12666	ANTENNA	TELEVISION	35	15.89	444
12777	COLOR TV	TELEVISION	10	259.00	444
12888	DISK DRIVE	COMPUTER	125	204.00	222
12999	MONITOR	COMPUTER	36	235.00	111
12112	NEEDLE	STEREO	340	7.95	333
12113	B & W TV	TELEVISION	359	175.00	333

THE SUPPLIER TABLE

SUPPLIER ID	SUPPLIER NAME	SUPPLIER PHONE
111	HERBST ELEC.	555-2543
222	P & W ELEC.	555-4389
333	HIGH VOLTAGE	555-5489
444	IMACO	555-4783

Exhibit 14.4
The Tables in the PURCHASE Database

data will be used to show the products that can be purchased from various suppliers. The tables included in this database can be named PRODUCT and SUPPLIER.

All database programs allow the user to define data at the level of the table. When a table is defined, the user must determine what columns to create, the maximum length of each column, and the type of data to be contained in each column.

Defining Tables and Columns

Exhibit 14.5 shows a screen from the R:BASE FOR DOS program in which the PRODUCT table is being defined. Exhibit 14.6 shows how the Paradox relational database program is used to specify the columns in the SUPPLIER table. There are two basic types of data stored in a database: numeric and alphanumeric. The user typically must decide if a column is to be designated as numeric or alphanumeric because the database program does not store numeric and alphanumeric data in the same way. Usually a column must be designated as numeric if the user wants to be able to perform mathematical operations, such as totals and subtotals, on the data in the column. Often numeric data is divided into integer (no decimal places) and decimal (or currency) data types.

In Exhibit 14.5 the product code column is alphanumeric, even though the data in Exhibit 14.4 suggest that the codes for the products are five-digit numbers. This is an instance in which, although the data are numbers, the column is designated as text because the user does not need to perform calculations with the numbers. In this example, there would be no need to produce a total of all the product codes. On the other hand, the

Exhibit 14.5

Defining the Columns in the PRODUCT Table Using RBASE FOR DOS

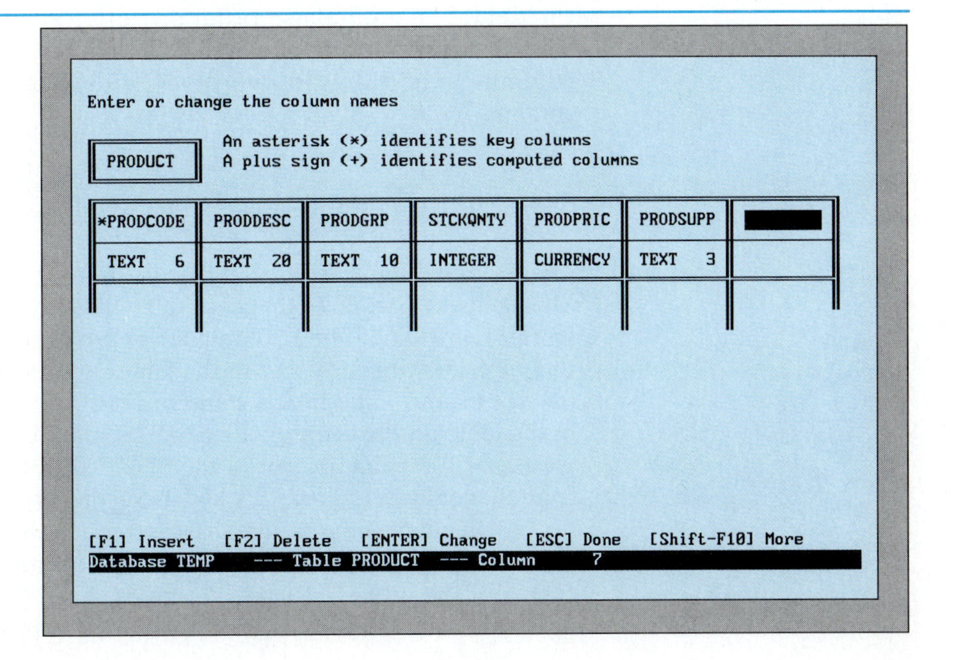

Exhibit 14.6

Creating the SUPPLIER Table in Paradox

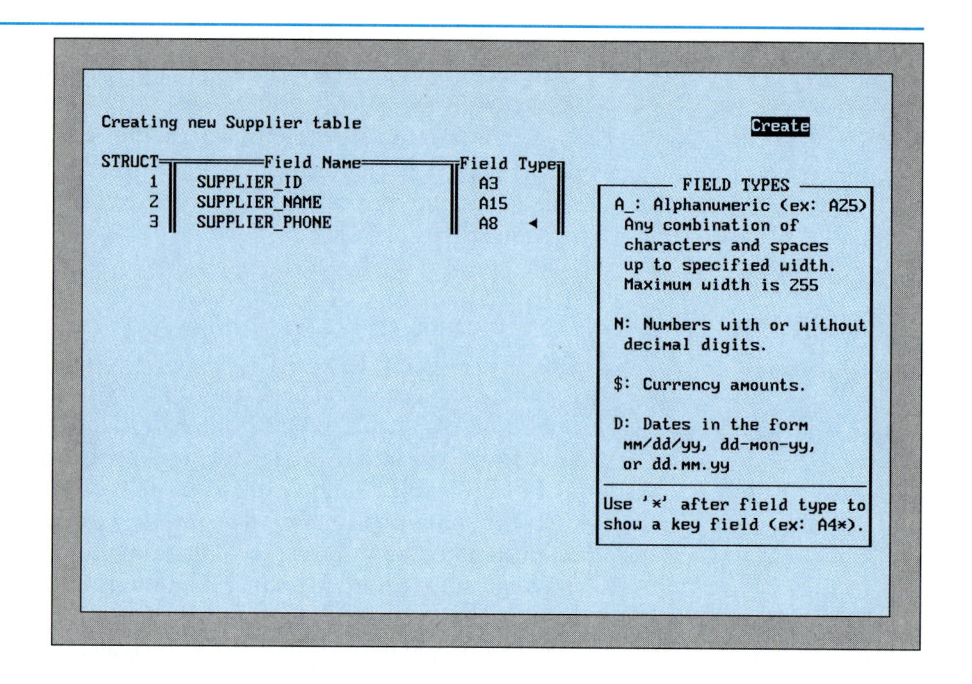

column that contains prices of products is declared as numeric since it is likely that a user would need the total of a group of product prices.

In many database programs, the user can make further distinctions among various types of numeric data. A common classification of numeric data is to distinguish between columns that allow decimal places and those that do not. An **integer column** is a numeric column that does not allow the storage of decimal places. A **decimal column** does allow decimal places in the data. Some database programs offer even more types of numeric columns. For example, R:BASE FOR DOS offers date, time, and currency columns in addition to two types of decimal columns and an integer column.

Specifying Key Columns

The relational database model discussed in Chapter 8, "File and Database Management," requires that each table have rows that are unique. In other words, there should be a column (or group of columns) that can be used to uniquely identify each row in the table. No two rows are allowed to have the exact same value in this column. This is referred to as the **primary key** of the table. In the example PURCHASE database, the supplier ID column would be the primary key in the SUPPLIER table and the product code column would be the primary key in the PRODUCT table.

In practice, most database programs for microcomputers do not require users to designate a primary key column, but do allow one to be created if the user so desires. Programs that allow primary keys offer the user some advantages. For example, using a primary key in the Paradox database program automatically prevents the user from entering two rows with the same data in the primary key column. Thus, if a product 12111 were already in the PRODUCT table, Paradox would not let the user create a second product with a code of 12111. This ensures that when a user retrieves the data for product 12111 the data returned are for the one and only product 12111.

When a column is designated as a primary key, the database program will sometimes create an index for that column. An **index** is a sorted list of all the values that appear in the column. The database program can use this list to facilitate very fast retrieval of a row from the database when the user gives the program a specific value from that column to look for. The index functions in much the same way as an index for a book. The reader goes to the index to locate a topic and the index tells the reader where to go in the book to find information on that topic. A primary key index is a sorted list of all the values in the primary key column. When the value desired is found in the list, the index tells the database program where to find the row in the table with that value in the primary key column.

Thus, if the product code column is designated as the primary key in the PRODUCT table, the user can request a search for a particular product code. The database program would then use the index to quickly look up the location of that product in the table and retrieve it. This type of retrieval is much faster than for a non-key column. If the user asked for a search for a product with a description of COLOR TV, the database would have to go to the table and begin retrieving rows from the top of the table until the desired row was found. This process of scanning through the rows in the table from top to bottom is much slower than a retrieval using an index.

In many database programs, the user can create an index for any column in a table. For example, dBASE IV does not use a primary key column for each table, but rather allows the user to create an index for any column in the table. Exhibit 14.7 illustrates how an index can be created for the product code column and shows how the index can then be used to retrieve a specific product.

Indexing Versus Sorting

Database programs are primarily used to store and retrieve data as quickly and efficiently as possible. Organizing the data that is stored can improve the ease with which the user can retrieve the data needed to make meaningful decisions. Two common methods of organizing stored data in a microcomputer database are to create an index and to sort the rows in the database table.

It is important to realize that creating an index does not alter the order of the rows in the table. Typically, when data are entered into the table, the rows are stored in the order in which they were entered. Thus, the row at the top of the table is the first row entered and the row at the bottom of the table is the last one. An index is a sorted list of all the values in the key column. Thus, if a user retrieves rows from the table using the index, it will

Exhibit 14.7

Creating an Index for the Product Code Column

In dBASE IV, the INDEX command creates an index for the product code column called PRODINDEX. A subsequent FIND statement with a value for product code 12777 will locate that record. The DISPLAY command shows the located record on the screen.

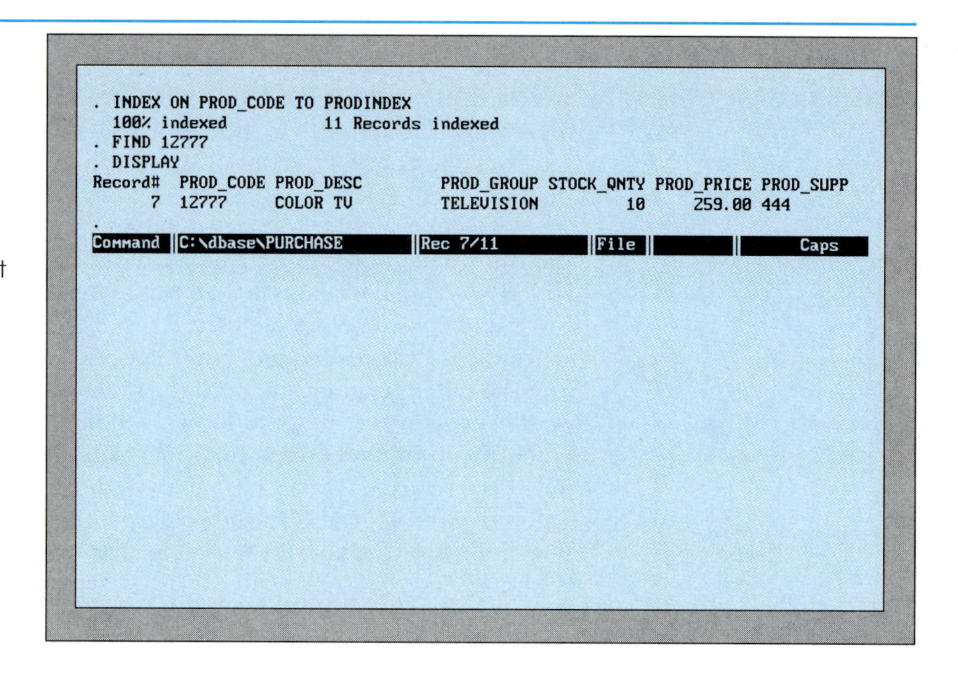

appear as if the rows are stored in order by the value in the key column. This ordering of the rows in the index represents a *logical* arrangement of the data. Physically, the rows are still stored in the order in which they were entered, but to the user (that is, logically) the rows appear as if they were stored in order by the indexed column (see Exhibit 14.8). If a table has several indexes, the single physical ordering of the rows can appear in many different logical orders, depending on which index is being used.

Many database programs allow the data in a table to be rearranged physically by sorting the rows. **Sorting** actually changes the order of the rows in the table. Typically, sorting is accomplished by the creation of a second table that duplicates the structure of the table being sorted. The rows are then moved into the new table according to their value in the column on which the sort is based. The rows in the new table are physically stored in sorted order (see Exhibit 14.9 on page 362). Some database programs allow sorting within the original table, eliminating the need for the creation of a second table.

When rows are sorted, a user can typically specify whether the sort is to be ascending or descending. In an **ascending sort,** rows are arranged starting with the row with the smallest value in the key column and ending with the row with the largest value in that column. A **descending sort** arranges the rows from largest to smallest. When rows are sorted using a column with text data, the letter *A* is considered to be the smallest value and *Z* is the largest.

Database programs also allow sorting on more than one column at a time. In this situation, the user must determine which column is to be the most important for ordering the rows. This column is used to create the **primary sort order** (not to be confused with a primary key). Any additional

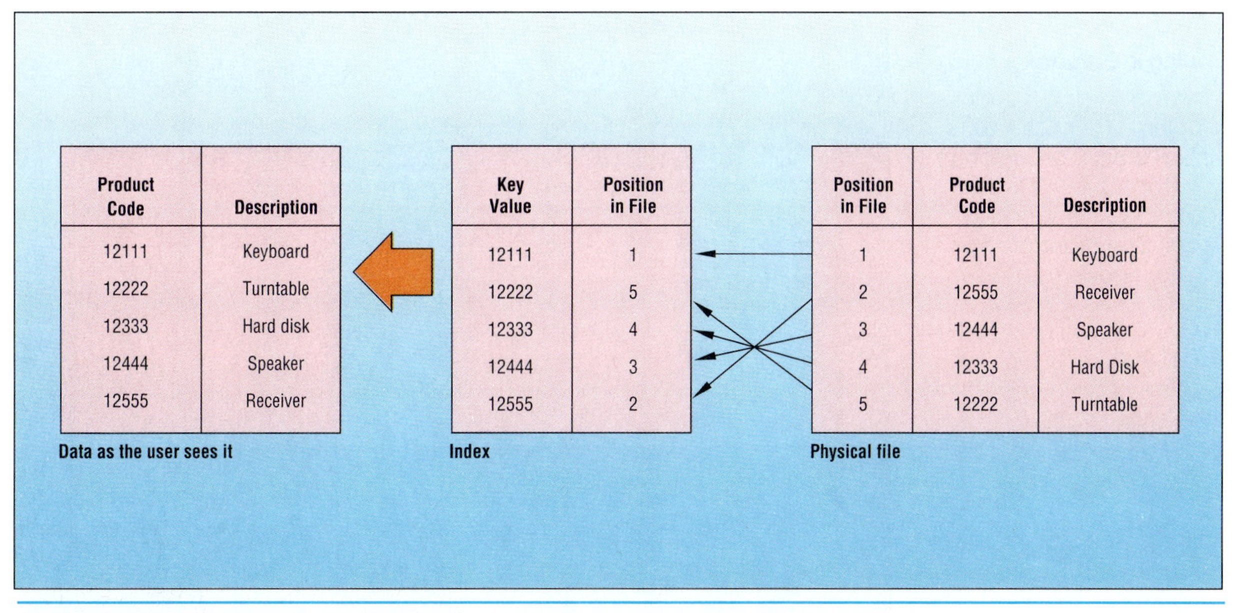

Exhibit 14.8

Ordering of Rows Using an Index

The rows are stored in the order in which they were entered, but to the user they will appear to be sorted by the value in the indexed columns.

columns used in the sort are used as "tie-breakers" for determining the positioning of rows that have the same value in the column used for the primary sort.

A common example of a multiple sort is a phone book. First, all rows are sorted by last name (primary sort order). If two rows have the same last name, this primary sort order cannot determine their precise position in the table. The **secondary sort order** (first name) is then used to determine the order of any rows that cannot be positioned using the primary sort order alone. Thus, a secondary sort order does not change the order determined by the primary sort order, but rather specifies an order for any rows that have the same value in the column used to determine the primary sort order (see Exhibit 14.10 on page 363).

Entering and Modifying Data

Once the database and its tables have been defined, the user must enter data into the table. And after the data have been entered, the database program must provide the user with the capability of changing the data in the tables.

Many database programs have a special entry mode that is used to add rows to a table. The database program prompts the user for values for each column in a row one at a time. When the row is complete, the user can verify the correctness of the row and give the database program approval to place the row in the table. Another common approach is to show the user a screen with areas in which data can be typed for each column (see Exhibit 14.11 on page 364). The user can move among the columns, editing the data as often as desired. The user can also enter a group of rows at one time.

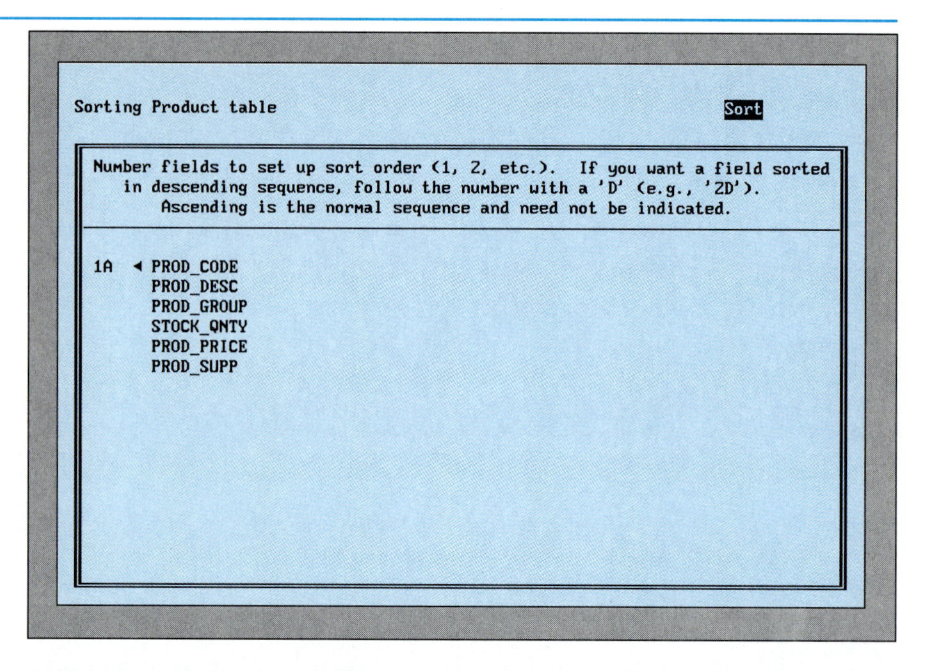

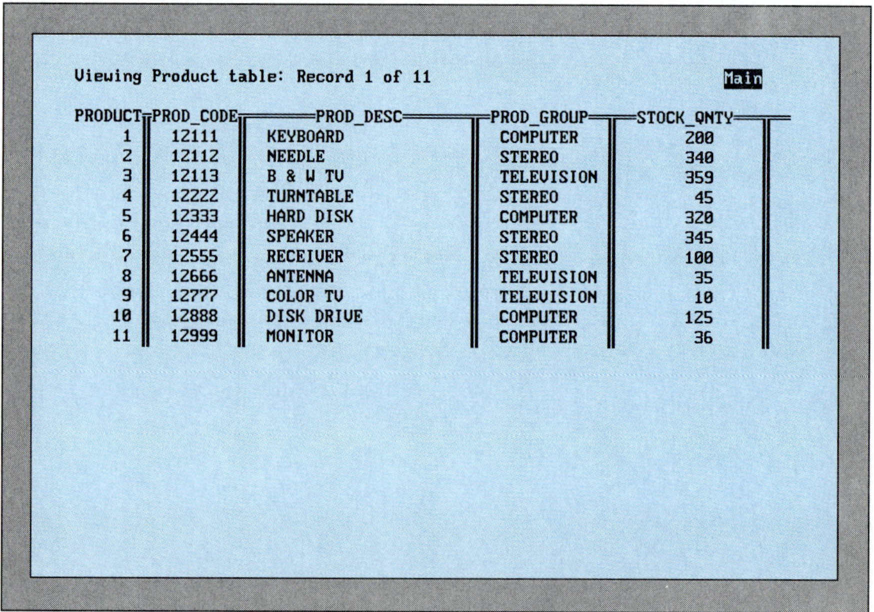
Viewing Product table: Record 1 of 11 Main

PRODUCT	PROD_CODE	PROD_DESC	PROD_GROUP	STOCK_QNTY
1	12111	KEYBOARD	COMPUTER	200
2	12112	NEEDLE	STEREO	340
3	12113	B & W TV	TELEVISION	359
4	12222	TURNTABLE	STEREO	45
5	12333	HARD DISK	COMPUTER	320
6	12444	SPEAKER	STEREO	345
7	12555	RECEIVER	STEREO	100
8	12666	ANTENNA	TELEVISION	35
9	12777	COLOR TV	TELEVISION	10
10	12888	DISK DRIVE	COMPUTER	125
11	12999	MONITOR	COMPUTER	36

Exhibit 14.9

Sorting in Paradox

In Paradox, a user chooses a column (or columns) to use as a basis on which to sort (top). The PRODUCT table rows are sorted in ascending order of product code (bottom).

A final option used for entry of data into a database table is to allow the user to take data from an ordinary text file and load it into the database table. This approach can be much faster, especially if the text table is already in existence. However, the text table must be carefully constructed, and the arrangement of the data in the text file must conform to certain rules, so that the database program will be able to put the data into the correct columns in the database table.

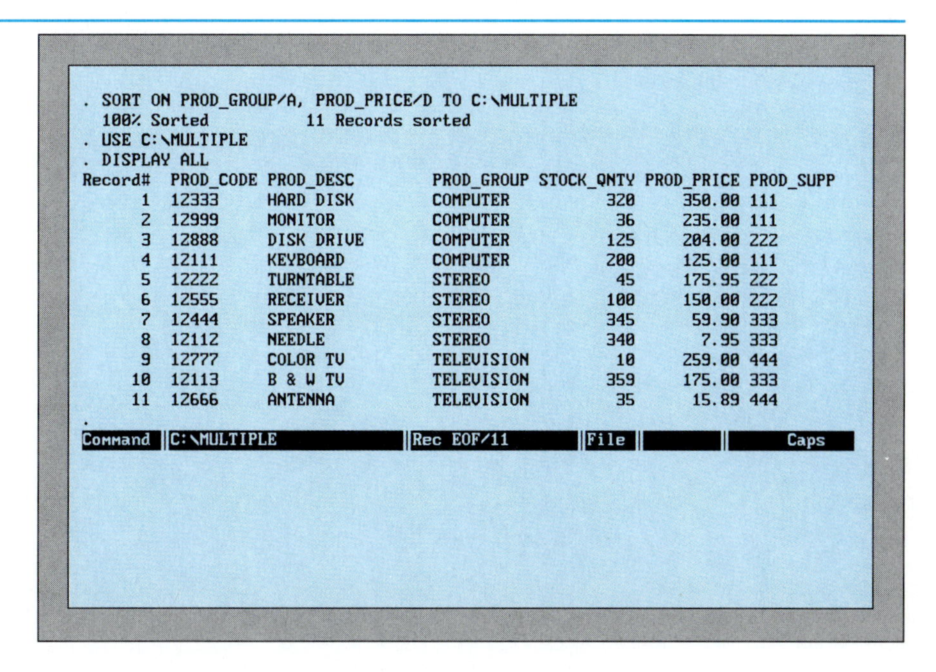

```
. SORT ON PROD_GROUP/A, PROD_PRICE/D TO C:\MULTIPLE
  100% Sorted           11 Records sorted
. USE C:\MULTIPLE
. DISPLAY ALL
Record#  PROD_CODE PROD_DESC        PROD_GROUP STOCK_QNTY PROD_PRICE PROD_SUPP
      1  12333     HARD DISK        COMPUTER          320     350.00 111
      2  12999     MONITOR          COMPUTER           36     235.00 111
      3  12888     DISK DRIVE       COMPUTER          125     204.00 222
      4  12111     KEYBOARD         COMPUTER          200     125.00 111
      5  12222     TURNTABLE        STEREO             45     175.95 222
      6  12555     RECEIVER         STEREO            100     150.00 222
      7  12444     SPEAKER          STEREO            345      59.90 333
      8  12112     NEEDLE           STEREO            340       7.95 333
      9  12777     COLOR TV         TELEVISION         10     259.00 444
     10  12113     B & W TV         TELEVISION        359     175.00 333
     11  12666     ANTENNA          TELEVISION         35      15.89 444
.
Command  C:\MULTIPLE              Rec EOF/11       File                Caps
```

Exhibit 14.10

Multiple Sort in dBASE IV

The SORT Command orders rows by product group (primary order) in ascending order and on product price (secondary order) in descending order. The USE command makes the MULTIPLE file containing the sort result the current database file and the DISPLAY command shows the data. Note how the secondary order sorts only rows with the same value in the column used for the primary sort.

Since valuable data are often stored in a database, the integrity (or correctness) of the stored data becomes very important. Thus, a database program provides commands that allow the user to maintain the data. The user can *insert* new rows, *update* the values in the columns, and *delete* unwanted rows. In order to update and delete specific rows, the database program must allow the user to retrieve specific rows from the database. This is usually accomplished by requiring the user to supply the record's primary key value or the value for an indexed column.

When data are scattered across related tables, maintaining the integrity of the data as they are changed is much more difficult with a file manager than with a relational database program. For example, in the PURCHASE database, if a user wanted to delete supplier 111 from the SUPPLIER table an integrity problem would arise if all the references to supplier 111 were not also removed in the product supplier column in the PRODUCT table. Ensuring that the supplier numbers in the PRODUCT and SUPPLIER tables are kept valid is much easier in a relational database program than in a file management program since file managers cannot closely relate tables.

Retrieving Data

As discussed, database programs are designed to store and retrieve data. Data must be retrieved in a way that will produce information useful in making decisions. To make the information as meaningful as possible, data must be focused and organized. This section discusses database programs

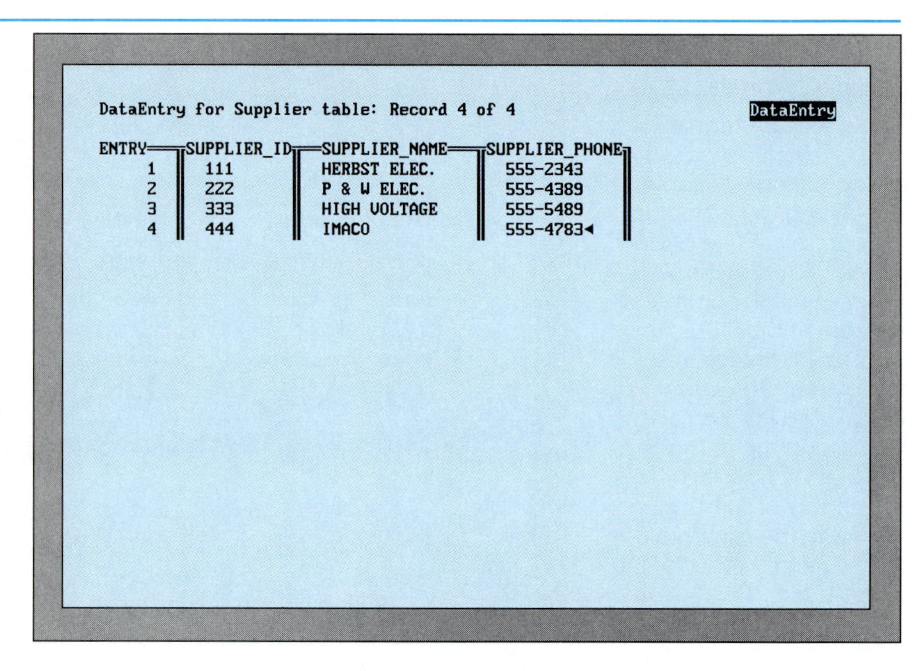

DataEntry for Supplier table: Record 4 of 4 DataEntry

ENTRY	SUPPLIER_ID	SUPPLIER_NAME	SUPPLIER_PHONE
1	111	HERBST ELEC.	555-2343
2	222	P & W ELEC.	555-4389
3	333	HIGH VOLTAGE	555-5489
4	444	IMACO	555-4783◄

Exhibit 14.11

Entering and Modifying Data in Paradox

In Paradox, a user can enter an entire screen of data at one time and press a key to send all the data to the table at once. While the data are being entered, the user is free to move through the data and make any necessary corrections before sending the data to the table.

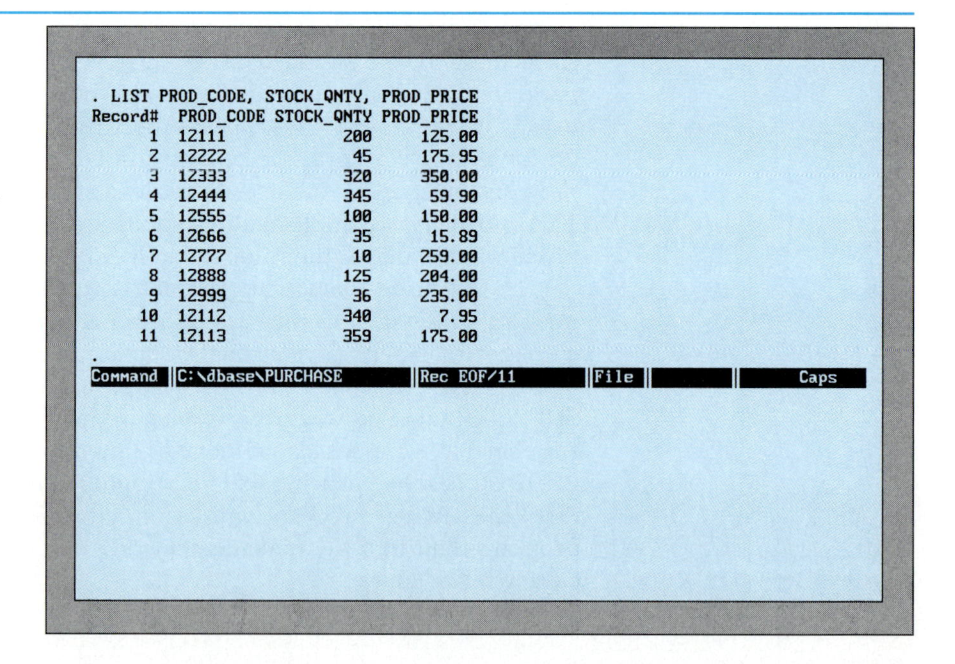

. LIST PROD_CODE, STOCK_QNTY, PROD_PRICE

Record#	PROD_CODE	STOCK_QNTY	PROD_PRICE
1	12111	200	125.00
2	12222	45	175.95
3	12333	320	350.00
4	12444	345	59.90
5	12555	100	150.00
6	12666	35	15.89
7	12777	10	259.00
8	12888	125	204.00
9	12999	36	235.00
10	12112	340	7.95
11	12113	359	175.00

.

Command | C:\dbase\PURCHASE | Rec EOF/11 | File | | Caps

Exhibit 14.12

Retrieving Data in a Database Program

In dBASE IV, the LIST command projects a subject of the columns for all of the rows in the database.

that can extract a subset of rows from a database (showing only the columns needed), link tables together, and perform certain calculations on the data retrieved. These features are designed to help the end-user retrieve the exact data needed.

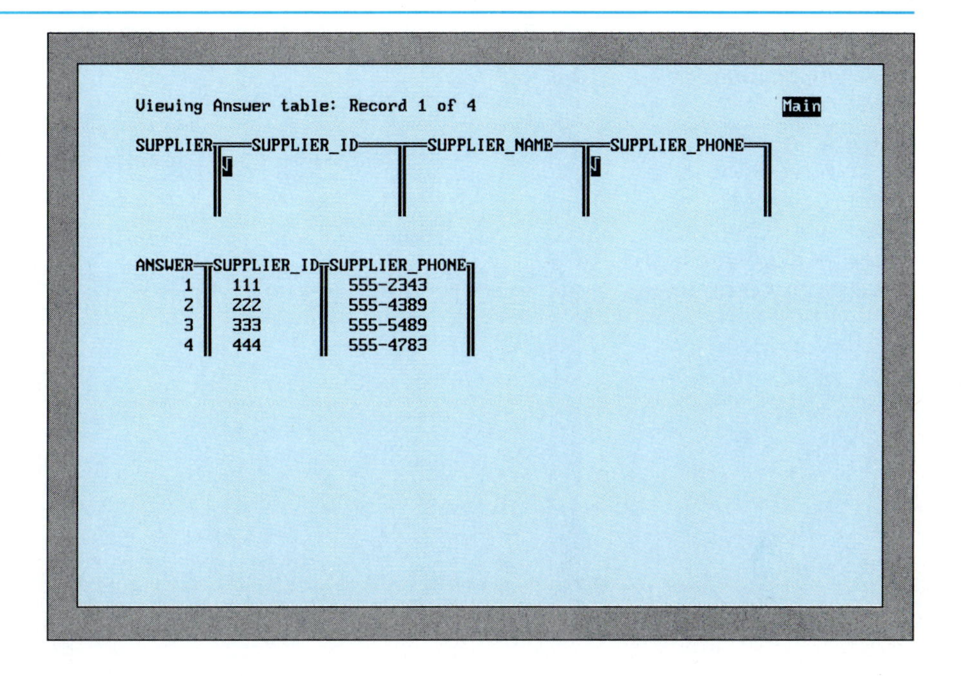

Viewing Answer table: Record 1 of 4
Main
SUPPLIER SUPPLIER_ID SUPPLIER_NAME SUPPLIER_PHONE
ANSWER SUPPLIER_ID SUPPLIER_PHONE
1 111 555-2343
2 222 555-4389
3 333 555-5489
4 444 555-4783

Exhibit 14.13

Marking and Displaying Columns in Paradox

A user marks the columns desired and Paradox displays the results below.

Projecting Columns

Projecting is the extraction of a column subset from the database. When data are retrieved, a user typically needs only a few of the columns from the database. A database program allows a user to project only the columns needed for a report. Exhibit 14.12 shows a projection in the dBASE IV database program. When a user requests a projection, the database program must be told which columns the user wants. In Exhibit 14.12, the columns desired are listed in the command that initiates the projection. Another common approach is to display a screen of all the columns in the database table and ask the user to mark the desired columns (see Exhibit 14.13).

Selecting Rows

In addition to projecting a column subset from the database, a user will often need a subset of the rows as well. **Selecting** is the process of retrieving a subset of the rows from the database.

When selecting rows, the user must construct a criterion that gives the basis of the selection. A **criterion** is a comparison of the data in the database to a rule supplied by the user. For example, Exhibit 14.14 shows a DISPLAY command in dBASE IV that uses a criterion of STOCK_QNTY > 100. This criterion selects rows in which the value in the stock quantity column is greater than 100. This comparison involves a numeric column, but it is also possible to use a character column. For example, PROD_GROUP = "COMPUTER" would select rows with COMPUTER in the product group column (see Exhibit 14.15a).

Exhibit 14.14

DISPLAY Command in dBASE IV

In dBASE IV, the DISPLAY command can be used to perform a selection of rows in which the stock quantity field contained a value greater than 100.

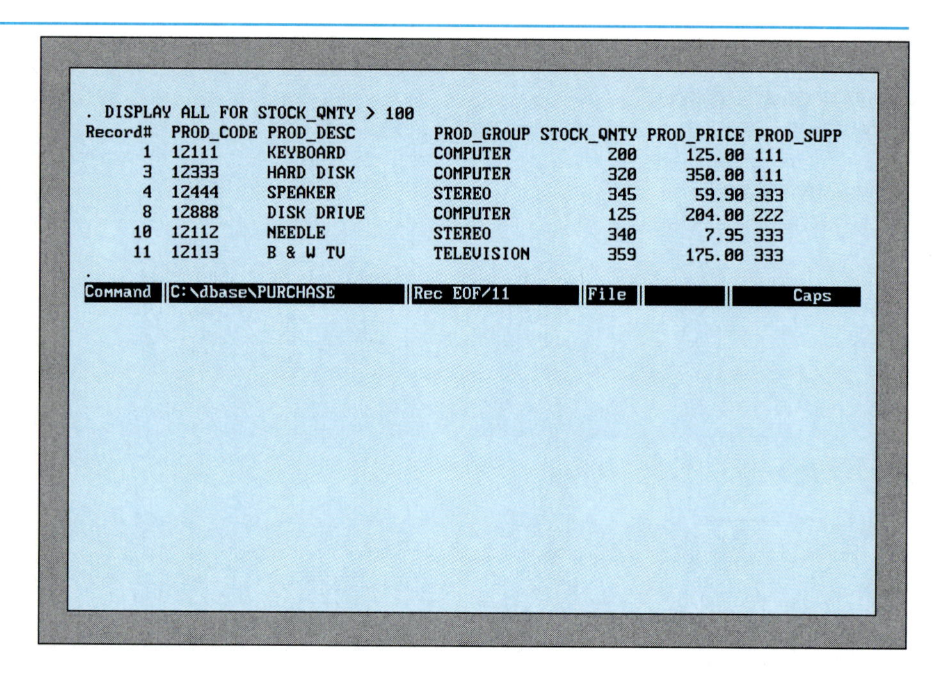

When constructing a criterion, possible comparisons include *less than, not equal to, greater than or equal to,* and *less than or equal to* in addition to the *greater than* and *equal to* comparisons already illustrated. Simple criteria can also be joined together using the logical operators AND and OR. For example, Exhibit 14.15b shows a criterion that joins the criteria used in Exhibits 14.14 and 14.15a with an AND relationship. When two single criteria are joined with the AND logical operator, both criteria must be satisfied for a row to be selected. If the two criteria in Exhibit 14.15b had been joined by an OR operator, the results would have been different (see Exhibit 14.15c). When criteria are joined with an OR, a row is selected if it meets *either* of the two criteria.

In many database programs, the process of specifying columns to be projected and rows to be selected is done with a single command. For example, the SELECT command in R:BASE FOR DOS is used both to specify columns to be projected and as a criterion to be used to select rows (see Exhibit 14.16). Another approach is shown by Paradox, which uses the Query-by-Example (QBE) method (see Exhibit 14.17 on pge 368). In QBE the user works with a grid that looks like the table. In this grid the user marks the columns to be projected and can enter a criterion in any columns to be used to select rows. In this way the user is building an example of what the desired rows should look like.

Joining

The main advantage of relational database programs is their ability to merge data from several tables into a single report. The process of linking

Exhibit 14.15

Three Criteria Used in Selecting Rows in dBASE IV

(a) When the criterion involves a character column, enclose the value to be searched for in quotation marks.

(b) AND operator: a row must have both a quantity greater than 100 and be in the COMPUTER product group.

(c) OR operator: a row is selected if the value in the product group column is COMPUTER or the value in the stock quantity column is greater than 100, or both.

```
. DISPLAY ALL FOR PROD_GROUP = "COMPUTER"
Record#  PROD_CODE PROD_DESC          PROD_GROUP STOCK_QNTY PROD_PRICE PROD_SUPP
      1  12111     KEYBOARD           COMPUTER          200     125.00 111
      3  12333     HARD DISK          COMPUTER          320     350.00 111
      8  12888     DISK DRIVE         COMPUTER          125     204.00 222
      9  12999     MONITOR            COMPUTER           36     235.00 111

. DISPLAY ALL FOR STOCK_QNTY > 100 .AND. PROD_GROUP = "COMPUTER"
Record#  PROD_CODE PROD_DESC          PROD_GROUP STOCK_QNTY PROD_PRICE PROD_SUPP
      1  12111     KEYBOARD           COMPUTER          200     125.00 111
      3  12333     HARD DISK          COMPUTER          320     350.00 111
      8  12888     DISK DRIVE         COMPUTER          125     204.00 222

. DISPLAY ALL FOR STOCK_QNTY > 100 .OR. PROD_GROUP = "COMPUTER"
Record#  PROD_CODE PROD_DESC          PROD_GROUP STOCK_QNTY PROD_PRICE PROD_SUPP
      1  12111     KEYBOARD           COMPUTER          200     125.00 111
      3  12333     HARD DISK          COMPUTER          320     350.00 111
      4  12444     SPEAKER            STEREO            345      59.90 333
      8  12888     DISK DRIVE         COMPUTER          125     204.00 222
      9  12999     MONITOR            COMPUTER           36     235.00 111
     10  12112     NEEDLE             STEREO            340       7.95 333
     11  12113     B & W TV           TELEVISION        359     175.00 333
.
Command ||C:\dbase\PURCHASE          ||Rec EOF/11          ||File ||        ||   Caps
```

Exhibit 14.16

The SELECT Command in R:BASE FOR DOS

This SELECT command projects the product code, description, and price columns and selects only rows with a value greater than 200 in the price column.

```
. DISPLAY ALL FOR PROD_GROUP = "COMPUTER"
Record#  PROD_CODE PROD_DESC          PROD_GROUP STOCK_QNTY PROD_PRICE PROD_SUPP
      1  12111     KEYBOARD           COMPUTER          200     125.00 111
      3  12333     HARD DISK          COMPUTER          320     350.00 111
      8  12888     DISK DRIVE         COMPUTER          125     204.00 222
      9  12999     MONITOR            COMPUTER           36     235.00 111

. DISPLAY ALL FOR STOCK_QNTY > 100 .AND. PROD_GROUP = "COMPUTER"
Record#  PROD_CODE PROD_DESC          PROD_GROUP STOCK_QNTY PROD_PRICE PROD_SUPP
      1  12111     KEYBOARD           COMPUTER          200     125.00 111
      3  12333     HARD DISK          COMPUTER          320     350.00 111
      8  12888     DISK DRIVE         COMPUTER          125     204.00 222

. DISPLAY ALL FOR STOCK_QNTY > 100 .OR. PROD_GROUP = "COMPUTER"
Record#  PROD_CODE PROD_DESC          PROD_GROUP STOCK_QNTY PROD_PRICE PROD_SUPP
      1  12111     KEYBOARD           COMPUTER          200     125.00 111
      3  12333     HARD DISK          COMPUTER          320     350.00 111
      4  12444     SPEAKER            STEREO            345      59.90 333
      8  12888     DISK DRIVE         COMPUTER          125     204.00 222
      9  12999     MONITOR            COMPUTER           36     235.00 111
     10  12112     NEEDLE             STEREO            340       7.95 333
     11  12113     B & W TV           TELEVISION        359     175.00 333
.
Command ||C:\dbase\PURCHASE          ||Rec EOF/11          ||File ||        ||   Caps
```

tables so a report can contain information from more than one table is called **joining.** When performing a join it is critical that the tables have a common column that can be used as a basis for merging the rows. In the PURCHASE database the PRODUCT table contains a column of supplier numbers in which the values match the supplier ID numbers in the

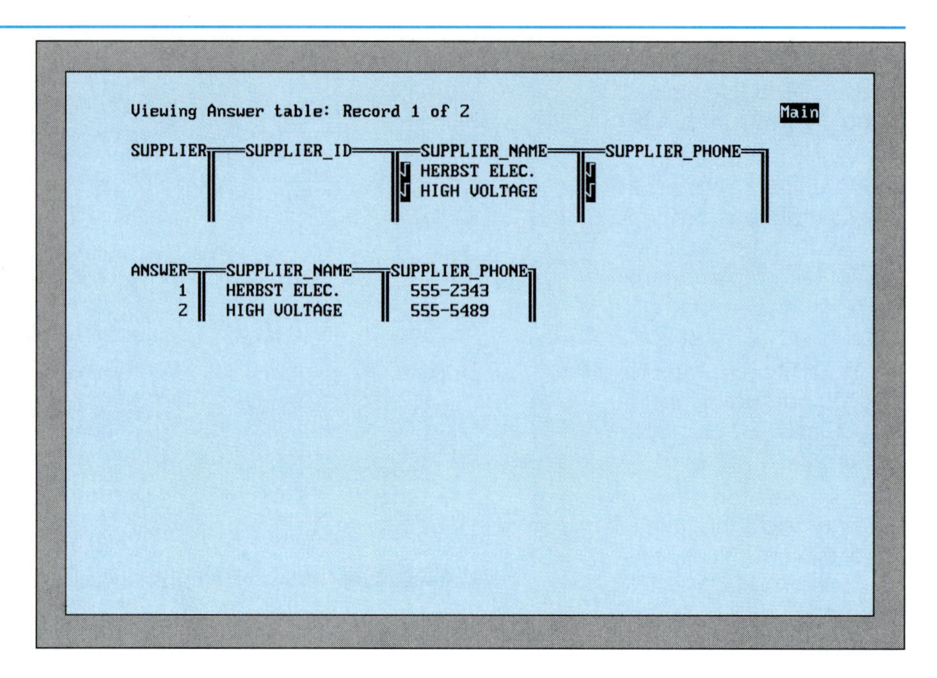

Exhibit 14.17

Query-by-Example Method in Paradox

The user marks the columns to be projected and in any column may build a criterion to be used as a basis for selection. In this example the criterion selects rows where the supplier name is Herbst Elec. or High Voltage. The results are shown below the query form.

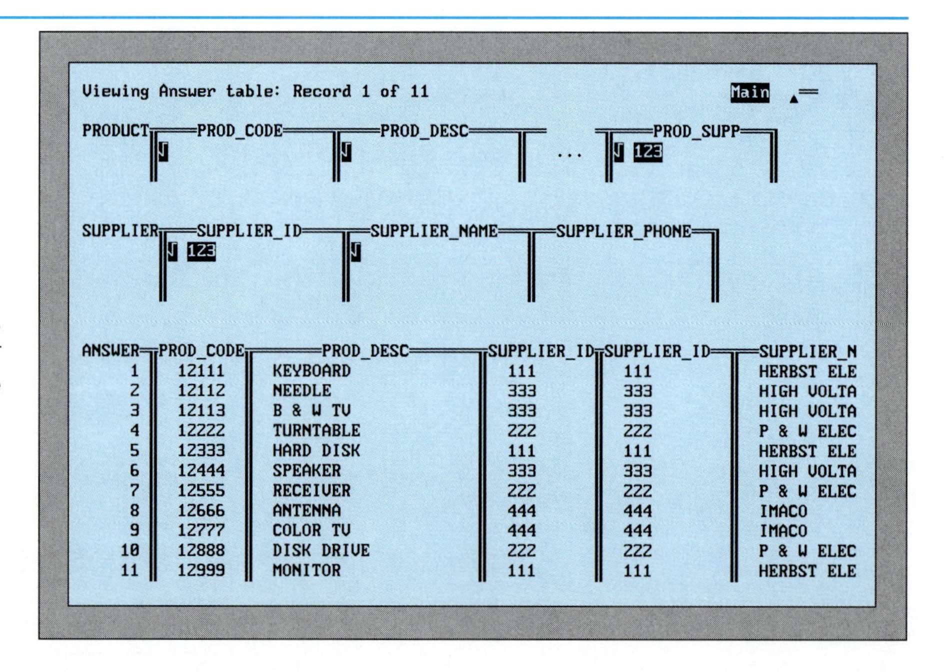

Exhibit 14.18

The JOIN Command in Paradox

A join is specified by putting the same value in two fields in different tables. The actual value placed in the two fields can be anything. This instructs Paradox to merge records from the PRODUCT and SUPPLIER tables where the values in these two fields are the same.

SUPPLIER table. When the two tables are joined, rows with matching values in these two columns can be linked together (see Exhibit 14.18).

Note how the common column in the two tables does not have the same name. Some database programs require the common columns used in a join operation to have the exact same name in both tables. Even in

Exhibit 14.19

Commands for Linking Tables in R:BASE FOR DOS

(a) Note how supplier numbers 333 and 444 in the PRODUCT table do not have corresponding records in the SUPPLIER table. In the SUPPLIER table, note that the numbers 555 and 666 do not have corresponding values in the PRODUCT table.

```
R>SELECT ALL FROM PRODUCT
 PRODCODE PRODDESC         SUPP_ID
 -------- ---------------- --------
 12111    KEYBOARD         111
 12222    TURNTABLE        222
 12333    HARD DISK        111
 12444    SPEAKER          333
 12555    RECEIVER         444
R>
R>SELECT ALL FROM SUPPLIER
 SUPP_ID  SUPPNAME
 -------- ----------------
 111      HERBST
 222      P & W
 555      GE
 666      WATTS
R>
```

(b) The UNION command combines the two tables and displays all the rows from both tables regardless of whether each row has a matching value in the other table.

```
R>UNION PRODUCT WITH SUPPLIER  FORMING RESULT
 Successful union operation, 7 rows generated
R>SELECT ALL FROM RESULT
 PRODCODE PRODDESC         SUPP_ID  SUPPNAME
 -------- ---------------- -------- ----------------
 12111    KEYBOARD         111      HERBST
 12222    TURNTABLE        222      P & W
 12333    HARD DISK        111      HERBST
 12444    SPEAKER          333      -0-
 12555    RECEIVER         444      -0-
 -0-      -0-              555      GE
 -0-      -0-              666      WATTS
R>
```

database programs that allow the name to be different, the user must take care that the two columns match in terms of length and data type. Thus, if the supplier numbers were alphanumeric in the PRODUCT table and numeric in the SUPPLIER table, the join operation would not be able to match values across the two tables.

The join illustrated in Exhibit 14.19 displays only those rows in the PRODUCT table that have a matching row in the SUPPLIER table.

(c) The SUBTRACT command lists rows in the table that do not have corresponding values in the other table. Since SUPPLIER was subtracted from PRODUCT, this example lists all rows from the PRODUCT table that did not have matching records in the SUPPLIER table.

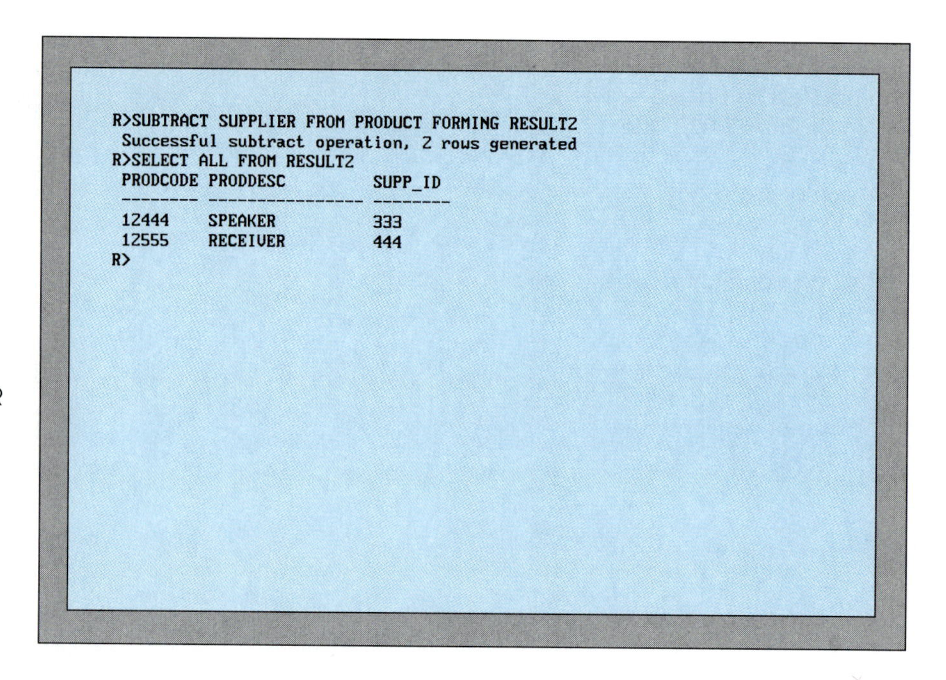

Sometimes rows in one table will not have corresponding rows in the other. Some database programs provide different methods of linking tables with unmatched rows. For example, Exhibit 14.19a shows new PRODUCT and SUPPLIER tables. Note how some of the supplier numbers in the PRODUCT table do not match the supplier numbers in the SUPPLIER table. Also, there are suppliers in the SUPPLIER table whose numbers do not appear in the PRODUCT table, and vice versa. The R:BASE FOR DOS database program allows the user to link these two tables in several ways. Exhibit 14.19b illustrates the UNION command, in which all the data from both tables are displayed and rows are matched whenever possible. Exhibit 14.19c shows the SUBTRACT command, which displays only the rows in the PRODUCT table that do not have corresponding rows in the SUPPLIER table. It is also possible to *subtract* the PRODUCT table from the SUPPLIER table. This would show the rows in the SUPPLIER table that did not have corresponding rows in the PRODUCT table.

Performing Calculations

A final database feature used in retrieving data is the capability to perform calculations. It is often desirable to have summary statistics produced for certain columns of a report. Common statistical functions include minimum, maximum, total, count, and average. Usually any or all of these functions can be used on any column that contains numeric data. For example, a database program can be instructed to produce an average and a total for the product price column (see Exhibit 14.20).

Exhibit 14.20

Summary Statistics and Calculated Columns in PFS: First Choice

The average and totals are summary statistics involving the price and value columns. The data in the value column are calculated by multplying the corresponding data in the quantity and the price columns.

REPORT OF INVENTORY VALUE

CODE	DESCRIPTION	GROUP	QUANTITY	PRICE	VALUE
12111	KEYBOARD	COMPUTER	200	125.00	25,000.00
12112	NEEDLE	STEREO	340	7.95	2,703.00
12113	B & W TV	TELEVISION	359	175.00	62,825.00
12222	TURNTABLE	STEREO	45	175.95	7,917.75
12333	HARD DISK	COMPUTER	320	350.00	112,000.00
12444	SPEAKER	STEREO	345	59.90	20,665.50
12555	RECEIVER	STEREO	100	150.00	15,000.00
12666	ANTENNA	TELEVISION	35	15.89	556.15
12777	COLOR TV	TELEVISION	10	359.00	3,590.00
12888	DISK DRIVE	COMPUTER	125	204.00	25,500.00
12999	MONITOR	COMPUTER	36	235.00	8,460.00
			Average:	168.88	
			Total:	1,857.69	284,217.40

Esc-Cancel There is more to print ↵ to continue

A second type of calculation involves the creation of new columns from other columns. For example, if the total value of the inventory on hand is needed, the stock quantity would be multiplied by the product price to get a total value for each product. Then these values would be summed to get the total value of inventory. On this report, the code, description, group, quantity, and price for each product came from the product database, and the value column was calculated when the report was created by multiplying the quantity and price for each product.

Advanced Database Program Features

Microcomputer database programs include many features that can make the creating, updating, and retrieval of data easier and more efficient. This section examines some of these features and how they are used.

Data Dictionary Features

The core of any database program is the **data dictionary,** which holds the definitions of all of the columns in the database. At a minimum, it supports the definition of column names, lengths, and data types. Some database programs have a more advanced data dictionary that lets a user determine how the data are stored to prevent some of the errors that may be made during data entry.

The user can sometimes specify the maximum and minimum values that can be entered in a numeric column. Also the user does not specify a value for a specified column when a row is being inserted, the database program can be instructed to automatically fill in that cell with a *default value,* a value that is specified in the data dictionary.

Some data dictionaries have a *query* capability, which lets a user get information about the database from the data dictionary. In dBASE IV, for example, the DISPLAY STRUCTURE command will display the current definitions of the columns in the database (see Exhibit 14.21).

Some data dictionaries also provide *password protection,* so that only certain users are able to see what is in the data dictionary. Any user can still enter and retrieve data from the database, but only a user with the appropriate password can change the actual structure of the database. Some databases also enable protection of additional sets of data. In this way, not every user has access to all the data in the database, but only to selected data. Different types of access can also be defined for a specific set of data. Some users may be able only to retrieve information from the database, not alter the values in the columns. Other types of access might include the ability to change column values in the database, add new rows to the database, or delete rows from the database.

There may be occasions when a database's structure is no longer appropriate because some aspect of the data has changed. Perhaps a new column needs to be added to the database or an existing column's length or data type needs to be changed. For example, a column containing a five-character ZIP code might need to be lengthened to accommodate the ZIP-plus-four ZIP code.

When a column needs to be lengthened or added to a database already containing data, the data must be rearranged. This rearrangement cannot be accomplished directly by many database programs. In such

Exhibit 14.21

The DISPLAY STRUCTURE Command in dBASE IV

In dBASE IV, the user can access information about a database from the data dictionary by using the DISPLAY STRUCTURE command.

```
. DISPLAY STRUCTURE
Structure for database: C:\DBASE\PURCHASE.DBF
Number of data records:       11
Date of last update   : 01/01/80
Field  Field Name  Type       Width    Dec    Index
    1  PROD_CODE   Character      6               N
    2  PROD_DESC   Character     16               N
    3  PROD_GROUP  Character     10               N
    4  STOCK_QNTY  Numeric        4               N
    5  PROD_PRICE  Numeric        7      2        N
    6  PROD_SUPP   Character      3               N
** Total **                      47
.
Command ||C:\dbase\PURCHASE     ||Rec 11/11       ||File ||    ||      Caps
```

situations, the database program requires the user to create a new database with the correct structure and then copy the data from the old database into the new one.

Forms

Many microcomputer database programs allow the user to create customized forms that can be used when working with the data in the database. Once a form is created, it can be used to enter data, edit data already stored, and display data on the screen (see Exhibit 14.22). With a form-design facility, the user has control over how the data will be shown on the screen, rather than being forced to see the data the way the database program was designed to show it.

Report Generators

Most database programs include a feature designed to help the user produce reports. A **report generator** is a facility with which the user can precisely describe the way data selected for a report are displayed. Often a report generator will have default settings so that the user can produce a quick report without having to go through a detailed specification process. Such a report will be formatted according to defaults, producing reports in a standard format. For more complex reports that do require specialized formatting, the user can control the exact appearance of the report using the report generator.

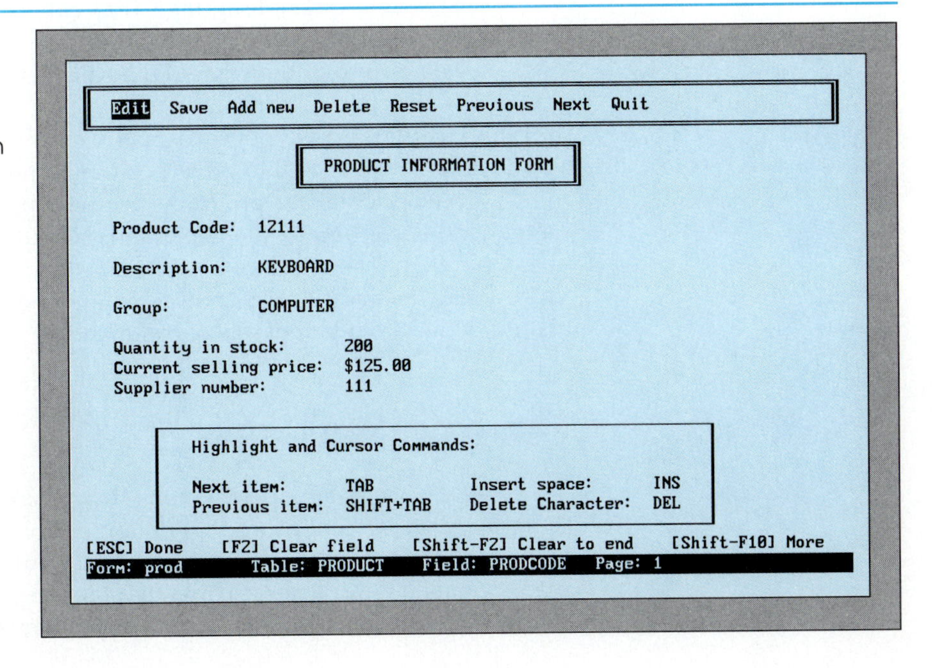

Exhibit 14.22

A Form Created in R:BASE FOR DOS

This form shows information displayed from the example PRODUCT table during an editing operation.

Report generators include options for specifying a title for the report, setting up headers and footers to appear on each page of the report, paginating the document, and even automatically printing the current date and time on the report when it is generated. When columns are shown on the report, the user can control the order in which the columns appear, specify a heading for each column of the report, and precisely define how the data will be shown in the column. For example, the use of decimal places, commas, and a dollar sign can be specified for numeric data. Special date formats may also be available.

When the data are placed in the report, a report generator will allow the user to determine the order in which the rows appear. Rows can be sorted or grouped together by common values in specified columns. Calculations can also be done at the time of the report. Totals and subtotals can be specified, and calculated columns can be created from other columns, even when those columns used in the calculation do not actually appear on the report itself. Exhibit 14.23a shows a report specification in Paradox, and Exhibit 14.23b shows the resulting report.

Structured Query Language (SQL)

In 1985, the American National Standards Institute (ANSI) announced **Structured Query Language (SQL)** as the standard language to be used with relational database programs. By design, SQL is also portable across a wide range of different computer manufacturers' hardware and operating systems at the mainframe, mini-, and microcomputer level. These two factors, combined with the emerging importance of relational database programs, will likely have a profound effect on how end-users and programmers interact with database programs.

SQL is a query language that can be used to create database structures, perform data manipulation, and ensure data integrity.

For example, the CREATE TABLE command in SQL is used to create the structure of a database table. There are UPDATE, DELETE, and INSERT commands for entering and maintaining data. The SELECT command in SQL is used to project columns and select rows.

Newer database programs are incorporating SQL into their user interfaces. For example, the commands in R:BASE FOR DOS are directly based on SQL. The interface of dBASE IV also includes SQL commands in addition to the traditional dBASE commands, and the user can switch freely between the two different sets of commands.

Database Programming

Normally, when database operations such as creating a database structure, entering data, or producing reports are performed, the user must enter a series of commands, one at a time. The user must know the exact syntax of each command and enter it correctly. An inexperienced user who doesn't know the commands will have difficulty interacting with the database. To

Exhibit 14.23

A Report Specification and the Resulting Report

(a) In Paradox, the user creates a structure for the report on this screen. Here the user can set up headings, group rows, position columns on the report, and set up summary calculations.

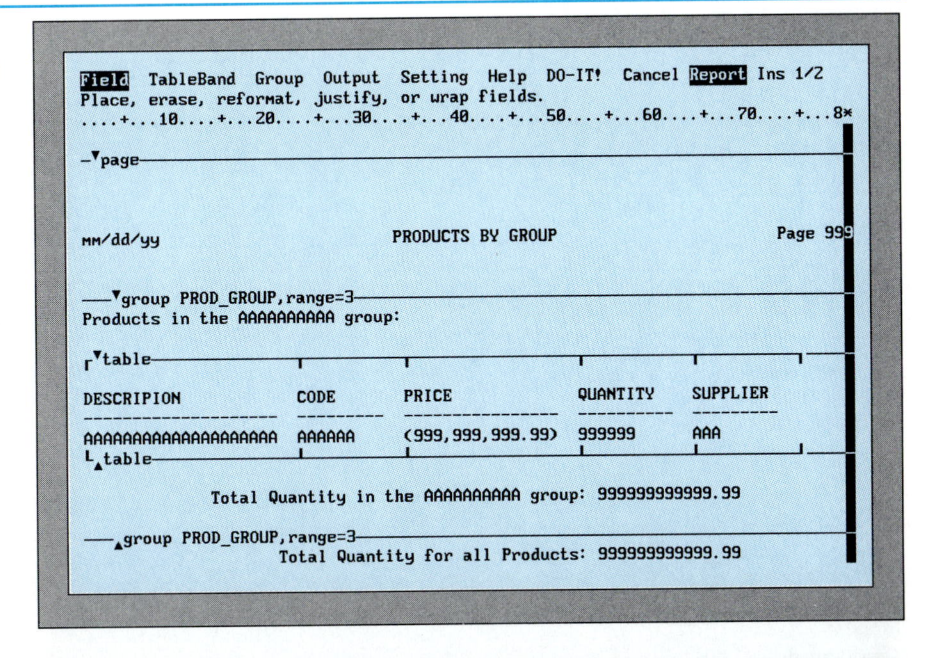

(b) The report that results from the report specifications.

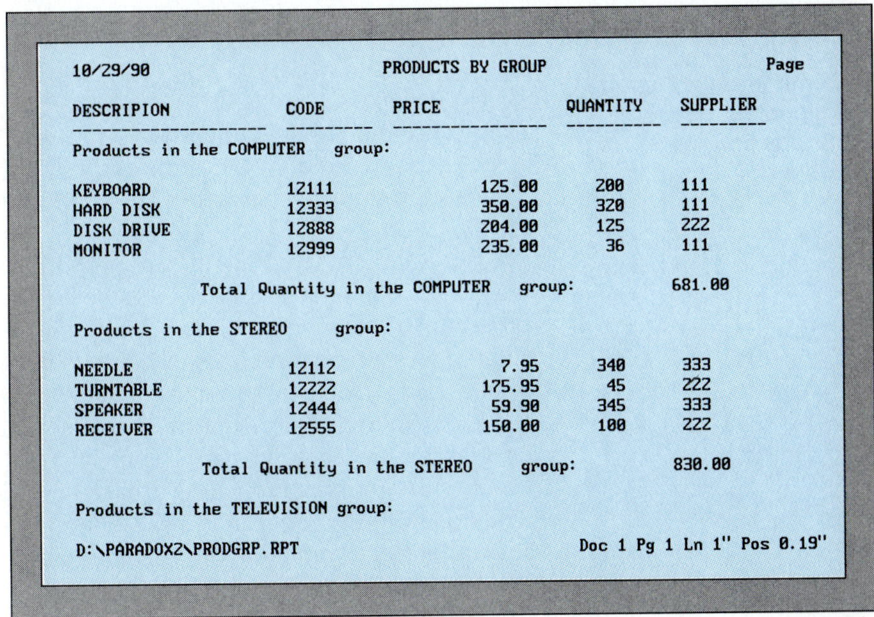

overcome this problem, a program already containing the commands necessary to perform a certain task can be written by an experienced user who is familiar with programming. The program (sometimes called a macro or a script) can be set up to prompt any user for the information needed to build the commands. In this way, an inexperienced end-user can use the database without having to understand how the database commands work. Not only can the procedural commands for data retrieval be used in these

Relational Database Programs Features	Paradox 3.0	R:BASE FOR DOS	dBASE IV	Team-up
Rows per table	2 billion	Disk space	1 billion	4 billion
Columns per row	225	400	255	1000
Characters per column	255	4092	255	1900
Passwords	Y	Y	Y	Y
SQL	N	Y	Y	N

File Managers Features	PC-File:DB	Professional File	Q & A	Reflex
Rows per table	1 billion	59000	16 million	65520
Columns per row	70	3200	2182	250
Characters per column	5000	1760	1678	254
Column types				
Text	Y	Y	Y	Y
Numeric	Y	Y	Y	Y
Date	Y	Y	Y	Y
Time	N	Y	Y	N
Integer	N	Y	N	Y
Money	N	Y	Y	N
Calculated	Y	Y	Y	Y

Exhibit 14.24

A Comparison of Current Relational Database Programs and File Managers

programs, but other commands, such as those to create the database structure and modify the data, may also be included. Thus, in some database programs, the user can automate most of the tasks performed with the database.

Another advantage of programming certain database functions is the automation of tasks that need to be done at regular intervals. Without a program, the commands necessary to produce a particular report have to be entered every time a report is needed. With a program, a single command can be used to run a program that produces the report.

Although only expert end-users would be able to write database programs, some database products (such as R:BASE FOR DOS) provide users with application facilities that allow them to develop applications without writing a program. In these facilities, users can build menus and attach database commands to menu choices. The application facility then builds the program automatically.

Backup and Recovery Features

When important data are stored in a database, the ability to keep those data safe from accidental loss is crucial. In microcomputer database programs, backup and recovery features are often lacking. They are, however, no less important for data stored on a microcomputer than for data stored on a mainframe computer. Some of the more advanced microcomputer database programs, such as R:BASE FOR DOS, have specialized backup and recovery commands. For example, in R:BASE FOR DOS, a user can issue a simple command to back up not only the tables containing the data, but also any files used to store the structure of the database. An obvious, but often overlooked, backup procedure is to keep one or more duplicate copies of diskettes containing the database tables. If the original is ever damaged, a backup copy can take its place.

Deleting a row is often a simple procedure, and accidental deletion may occur easily. Some database programs do not actually erase the information in a deleted row, but rather simply mark that row as deleted so that it is not printed on reports. If a row has been unintentionally deleted, the process can be reversed simply by removing the mark.

Choosing a Database Program

There is a large number of database products for microcomputers. At the upper end are the expensive, full-featured products, such as R:BASE FOR DOS and Paradox, used primarily in business. There are also many inexpensive database products, such as PC-File:DB. The more expensive products often provide advanced features such as query and programming languages, report generators, and integrity and security features.

Exhibit 14.24 compares some current relational database programs and file managers. For the relational database programs, the exhibit shows the maximum rows per table, columns per row, and characters per column allowed in each product. Also indicated is whether the database program supports the user of passwords and includes an SQL interface. For file managers, the exhibit again indicates the maximum rows per table, columns per row, and characters per column allowed in each product. In addition, the support of various data types is shown.

Exhibit 14.25 compares four relational database packages for the Macintosh family of computers. This exhibit shows the maximum number of rows per table and columns per row. The ability to create columns that will store pictures and set up ranges of values or default values for a column are also indicated. The number of columns in a database that can be indexed and the ability to assign passwords to the database are also shown.

Double Features	FoxBASE+ dBASE Mac	4th Helix	Mac	Dimension
Rows per table	unlimited	unlimited	10 billion	16 million
Columns per row	32,001	unlimited	unlimited	500,000
Picture data type	Y	Y	Y	Y
Range testing	Y	Y	Y	Y
Default values	Y	Y	Y	Y
Indexed columns	1	unlimited	unlimited	32,000
Database password	Y	Y	N	Y

Exhibit 14.25

A Comparison of Four Relational Database Packages for the Macintosh

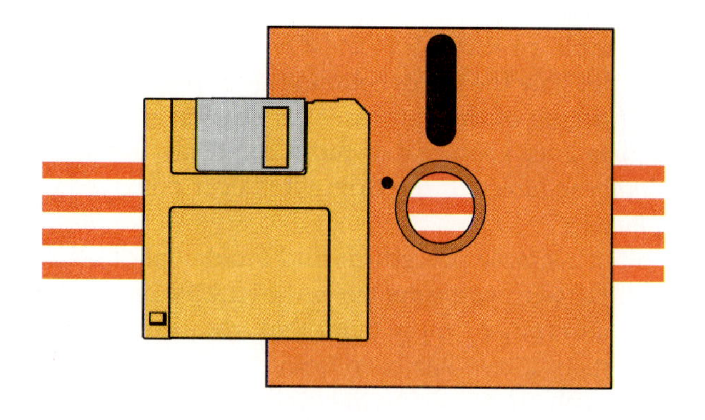

Computers at Work

Smile—You're on Corporate Camera

Combined with typed records of an employee's background and history with the company, these photographic records provided the focus for management-review meetings in the past.

Picture a corporate boardroom. A dozen executives are gathered to review the performance of their company's top managers. One executive asks about the progress of a recently promoted product manager, whose face she cannot recall. At the front of the room, an oversized television monitor lights up with the employee's picture and resume. The executive suddenly remembers a terrific presentation this employee gave in a tense meeting about a new product line. She proposes that the group consider him for the position of division manager.

In these days of decentralization and diversification, the personnel procedures at mammoth corporations tend to be anything but personal. Many middle and upper-level managers rarely have day-to-day contact with the top executives who make decisions about their performance and career futures. And executives are often required to review the performance of people who they have never actually seen on the job.

At the high-management level, decisions about who gets promoted, moved during a reorganization or assigned to a special project are critical. Prolonged discussions about employees who, to the reviewers, are just names on resumes or out-of-date photos are the standard at many companies. To offset the negative aspects and enhance executive review of upper-level managers, some major corporations are using picture databases of employees.

E, I. du Pont de Nemours & Co., a chemical company in Wilmington, Del., and United Technologies Corp. (UTC), an aerospace firm in Hartford, Conn., are using PCs to bring modern technology and human recognition to the boardroom.

Faces To Remember

"Our people are scattered over different states and even countries," explained Gary Thomas, a management-resources consultant in du Pont's Petrochemicals Department. A video-database system helps the executive remember what he knows about employees by putting faces with the resumes, Mr. Thomas said.

"We try to tie a picture to the job," elaborated Jim Beardsley, manager of executive-resources planning at UTC. Mr. Beardsley, working with George Glaser, manager of human resources in the data-processing department, started development of UTC's video database two-and-a-half years ago.

"One of the reasons for doing it was a desire on the part of the chairman to start to share an understanding of the top positions and who is in those positions," Mr. Glaser said.

Using photographs of employees during the review process is not a new idea. Du Pont has used 35mm slides, and UTC has used black-and-white photos of employees in the management-review process for years. Combined with typed records of an employee's background and history with the company, these photographic records provided the focus for management-review meetings in the past.

Du Pont found the slide-carousel system limited, however, because it didn't allow executives to move easily from employee to employee during a discussion. Any deviation from the order of the slides meant clicking back through the entire circle of slides. For UTC, it meant shuffling through piles of papers, and photos to find information on the employee in question.

The paper element presented problems for both organizations. Updates to an employee's record required retyping of the whole resume for use in executive-review meetings. There were no floppy-disk files to simply update.

"We went to this because we were looking for a way to be more efficient in the review process," Mr. Thomas commented.

In addition, both companies acknowledged that their roles in high-tech manufacturing warranted a high-tech approach to a business problem. "I think our executives value the improvement that (the system) allows in reviews," Mr. Thomas said.

Before a management-review meeting, Mr. Thomas downloads employee images and resume information to his PC from the company mainframe. He then takes the floppy disk of information, along with the PC, to the meeting.

The meeting centers on two 26-inch Sony television monitors, one for the employee's picture, and the other for his or her resume file. A third standard-size monitor, seen only by the PC operator, flashes a list of employee names, which are easily accessed by cursor selection.

Mr. Thomas praises the presentation value of the system, while pointing out its unobtrusiveness. By having the picture and the data on separate monitors, he said, "the picture doesn't get cluttered, and it lets us blow up the (data) so it's readable. We may present this to 30 people at a time, for instance." And, he added, "the computer and the operator are sort of out of the way."

An executive has only to mention an employee's name for the operator to call up his or her photo on the screen.

"It keeps the mechanics of the meeting from getting in the way" of the review process, Mr. Thomas said. This way, an executive can follow his or her train of thought, rather than the alphabetical order of the presentation.

UTC, which also uses PicturePower and runs on a Compaq, presents what George Glaser likes to call a "photo album" of 300 management employees.

Mr. Glaser opted for a single-screen approach in the meeting room, projecting such information as the employee's title and organizational affiliation onto a Sony RGB projection screen.

Between meetings, employee data resides on an IBM System/36. With the portable PC, Mr. Glaser pointed out, "we're not tied to a home base." Both Mr. Glaser and Mr. Beardsley stress the usefulness of a flexible video system to a company as diversified as UTC, which owns such aerospace concerns as Pratt & Whitney Aircraft, Sikorsky Aircraft (a helicopter manufacturer), Norden Systems Inc. (a radar manufacturer) and Hamilton Standard, to name a few.

"It gives (the executives) the benefit of recognition," Mr. Beardsley pointed out. "We have an annual meeting of the top 400 executives at UTC. We'd like for the very top tier of management to recognize some individuals. Later, when these people are at a (review) meeting, they recognize the individual on the screen. It personalizes the process."

While bringing a human face to a business procedure can, indeed, personalize it, there is some concern in the business community that video reviewing might de-emphasize the need for face-to-face contact in the decision-making process.

"In the process of selecting people, regardless of whether it's for a new job inside your company or a promotion of a special project, the advantage of talking with a candidate in person is clear," said Ben Borne, president of Ben Borne & Associates, a management consultancy in Chicago. "It's what the human-resource pros would call the ability to observe frequent, repetitive behavior.

"I see nothing wrong with it as long as it's a step in the process," he said.

Both UTC and du Pont see it as just that. "The purpose of these meetings is not to make an actual selection at that point in time," Jim Beardsley pointed out. "It's for recognition, particularly at that level. The performance of the person is the actual basis of selection."

"All a picture does for you is help you connect (facts and people) in your mind," Mr. Thomas pointed out. "It helps you pull into focus all those years of experience.

"Our job in personnel," he added, "is to ensure that the top managers have an environment in which to make personnel decisions and focus on real issues."

Summary and Key Terms

A database is designed to store and retrieve data to satisfy the needs of end-users. Data are stored in **tables**, which are in turn made up of **rows** containing individual **columns** that represent the different types of information being stored.

A **database** is a group of related tables. When a database is designed, a **normalization** process is used to group data into tables in which the data within a table are closely related.

Microcomputer database programs can be separated into table managers and relational database programs. **File managers** are able to deal only with single-table databases. **Relational database programs** are capable of linking tables together to create multi-table databases.

When a database is created, a user defines the columns to be stored within each table. When columns are defined, the user must name the column, specify a width, and indicate the type of data that is to be stored in the column. The data type is typically either text or numeric. Some database programs subdivide numeric data into integer and decimal data. **Integer data** contain no decimal values; **decimal data** allow decimal values to appear in the number.

Some database programs allow the user to specify a **primary key** column for a table. A primary key ensures that no duplicate values will be placed in that column and often creates an index for retrieval. An **index** is a sorted list of all the values in the primary key column. The index is used to support direct retrieval of rows based on primary key value. The index also causes the rows in the table to be displayed as sorted by primary key value, even though the rows are physically stored in the order in which they were inserted.

Some database programs also allow the sorting of rows. In a **sort,** rows are physically reordered by moving them to a second table and inserting them in order by primary key value. The user can specify a **descending sort** or an **ascending sort.** In addition, the user can sort by more than one column at a time. The first sort column creates a **primary sort order**, and other columns create a **secondary sort order**, which determines the order of any rows that have the same value in the column used for the primary sort order.

When entering data the user is typically prompted to fill in the columns one at a time. A form can also be used to enter rows. Once stored in the table, the columns in the rows can be updated, new rows can be inserted, and unwanted rows can be deleted.

Data retrieval is the second major purpose of database programs. When data are retrieved, a user can perform a **projection**, which causes a subset of the columns in the table to be retrieved. Further filtering of the data can be accomplished with a **selection**, in which a subset of the rows is chosen for retrieval. Selection requires the construction of a criterion. A **criterion** is a comparison of values in the database to a value supplied by the user. Criteria involve comparisons such as equal to, not equal to, greater than, and less than. Any rows that satisfy the criterion are selected for retrieval. A single criterion can also be joined with another to construct multiple criteria using the AND or OR logical operators. In an AND relationship both parts of the criteria must be true to select a row, whereas in an OR relationship a row is selected if either one of the criteria is true.

A third command used in retrieving rows is the **join** operation. A join merges two tables together using a common column. This requires that there be a column that is the same in both tables.

When producing a report, a user can perform a number of calculations. Summary statistics, such as totals and averages, can be computed for the rows that are retrieved. New columns can be created by manipulating existing columns mathematically.

In addition to those used in data retrieval, a database program contains many features that make interaction with the database more efficient. The **data dictionary** may allow maximum, minimum, and default values for columns.

Sometimes the user can display information about the entries in the data dictionary. Some data dictionaries are password protected and allow the tables of the database to be assigned various levels of protection.

A database program may provide features that allow a user to change the structure of the database. This usually involves creating a new database and transferring the data from the old structure to the new.

Some database programs allow users to create customized forms for entering, editing, and displaying data.

Report generators are similar to query facilities, in that the information retrieved is formatted for printing rather than displayed on the screen. The user can make margin settings, create headings, and obtain totals and subtotals for the report.

An important developing standard is the **Structured Query Language (SQL)**, which provides commands for creating databases, editing data, and retrieving data. Many new database programs are incorporating SQL commands.

A database program may include a programming language, which can be used to automate the process of creating the database, entering data, and retrieving information. There are usually commands, similar to those in traditional programming languages, that allow the user to construct a program that can make decisions, perform loops, and get data from the end-user when the program is running.

Backup and recovery features are often lacking in microcomputer database management systems. A good practice is to keep backup copies of database tables on diskettes. In addition, some database management systems allow the user to recover an accidentally deleted row. In these systems, the row is not actually deleted; the program simply marks it as unused. This allows the row to be unmarked if it is accidentally deleted.

Review Questions

1. What is a data type and what are the differences among the three most common data types?
2. Explain the difference between sorting and indexing. What are the advantages of each?
3. When would projecting and selecting be used to retrieve data? Give examples.
4. What is a criterion? Give an example of a simple criterion and a multiple criterion.
5. Explain the difference between the AND and OR logical operators.
6. What is the difference between a primary and a secondary sort order?
7. Describe some of the calculations that can be performed when a report is produced with a database management system.
8. What is one of the advantages of having the capability of programming a database?
9. Explain how a form is used in some database programs.
10. What is SQL and why is it important?

T F **11.** Columns defined with a decimal data type cannot contain decimal values.

T F **12.** A primary key is a column that can be used to uniquely identify each row in the table.

T F **13.** Creating an index for a column causes the rows in the table to actually change their positions within the table.

T F **14.** A secondary sort order takes over when rows have the same value in the column used in the primary sort order.

T F **15.** Projecting is the process of retrieving a subset of the rows in the table.

T F **16.** A criterion is a true/false comparison used as a basis for determining which rows from the table will be selected for printing.

T F **17.** In a join it is not necessary for the common column in the two tables being joined to have the same data type.

T F **18.** A data dictionary will often allow a user to set up minimum and maximum values and default values for a column.

T F **19.** SQL is a language that is currently being proposed as a standard language to be used in all database programs.

T F **20.** File managers and relational database programs are the same.

21. _____ The formalized process for designing the tables included in a database is called:

a. normalization c. description
b. determination d. design

22. _____ The data type that stores numeric data without any decimal places is:

a. decimal c. integer
b. whole d. text

23. _____ A special column in a table that is used to uniquely identify each row is called:

a. primary key c. secondary key
b. primary sort d. secondary sort

24. _____ A sorted list of values that is used to speed up retrieval of data is called:

a. data type c. criterion
b. form d. index

25. _____ The process of retrieving a subset of the columns from a table is called:

a. selection c. projection
b. sorting d. indexing

26. _____ The process of retrieving a subset of the rows from a table called:

a. selection c. projection
b. sorting d. indexing

27. _____ When specifying which rows to retrieve, the values in a column in the database are compared using a rule supplied by a user. This rule is called:

a. a criterion c. a sort order
b. an index d. a projection

28. _____ Merging data from two tables using a common column is known as a:

a. criterion c. projection
b. join d. selection

29. _____ The definitions of the columns and data types used in the database are stored in the:

a. data dictionary c. table
b. index d. default value

30. _____ The emerging standard language that is to be used in all database programs is:

a. DOS c. STC
b. SAS d. SQL

CHAPTER 15

Graphics

Everyone has heard that a picture is worth a thousand words. It may also be worth a thousand numbers. Graphics can be used to condense large amounts of data into a simple picture that emphasizes the relationship among the various pieces of data. Graphics software allows an end-user to store and display numeric data in the form of a picture or to create simple drawings using lines and geometric shapes.

This chapter looks at four categories of software that involve graphics. These types of software can be used by end-users to create and display information graphically. Typically, graphics software is used to display numeric data in the form of a chart or graph, but it also can be used to create pictures that are not numerically oriented. Charting programs are used to produce graphs for charting and displaying numeric data. Drawing and painting programs are used to create pictures that are not numerically oriented. Presentation managers can be used to display previously created graphs and pictures in a sequence determined by the end-user. A final application of graphics is known as desktop publishing, in which an end-user can merge graphics with text to create professional-looking publications.

In this chapter you will learn to do the following:

1. Understand the similarities and differences among pie, bar, and line graphs
2. Understand the differences between spreadsheet and dedicated charting programs
3. List some of the features that are important when choosing a charting program
4. Describe some of the features of drawing and painting programs
5. Identify some of the features of presentation managers
6. Explain the role of desktop publishing software and list some of the features included in these programs

Charting Programs

Charting programs are used to present numeric data in the form of a chart or graph. It is important to remember that graphs are typically used to help a viewer understand the relationship among groups of numbers. An end-user must create a graph that shows that relationship as clearly as possible.

Because a charting program is used to display numbers in graphic form, it is often incorporated as part of a spreadsheet program. Since spreadsheets already deal with numbers, it makes sense to have charting capabilities integrated into the spreadsheet program itself. A charting program that is incorporated into spreadsheet programs is referred to as an **integrated** or **spreadsheet** charting program. There are also many charting packages that are separate programs. These are referred to as **stand-alone** or **dedicated** charting programs, because they can be used without any associated spreadsheet program and are designed to do only charts and graphs. Because the functioning of these two types of charting software is slightly different, spreadsheet and dedicated charting programs are discussed separately.

Spreadsheet Charting Programs

Most of the more powerful spreadsheet programs on the market today include some sort of charting capability. Thus the numbers in the spreadsheet can be graphed on the screen without the user having to leave the spreadsheet program. The advantage of producing graphs directly from the numbers in the spreadsheet is that, if the numbers on the spreadsheet change, the graph is automatically updated without any intervention on the part of the user. Just as spreadsheets automatically recalculate the results of a formula, the graph is automatically adjusted every time a number in the graph is changed.

Spreadsheets that include charting capabilities provide a command or menu option that can be used to create the specifications for a chart. In general, the graphics command will provide options for selecting the type of graph to produce, specifying the data to be graphed, labeling the various parts of the graph, and customizing the graph to create the appearance desired.

Exhibit 15.1 shows a menu from the Quattro spreadsheet, which illustrates some of the common graph types available in spreadsheet programs. Many of the graph types are similar enough in structure that the user can simply go to a menu and change the graph type after the graph has been created. In this way, the user can see what graph type is best for displaying the data.

In addition to choosing a graph type, the user must specify the groups of data to be used as the basis of the graph. A block or group of data is typically referred to as a *series* in the graph. Since the data to be graphed is stored in cells on the spreadsheet, the specification of data is usually accomplished by telling the spreadsheet which cells contain the data for each series. In most spreadsheets the series data correspond to a *range*, or continuous group, of cells in the spreadsheet. Exhibit 15.2 shows a screen from a spreadsheet on which the user is specifying a series to be graphed. After the series data are chosen, the basic structure of the graph is complete and the user can place titles on the graph and label its various parts.

Spreadsheet charting programs typically provide an option that allows the user to display the graph on the microcomputer screen at any

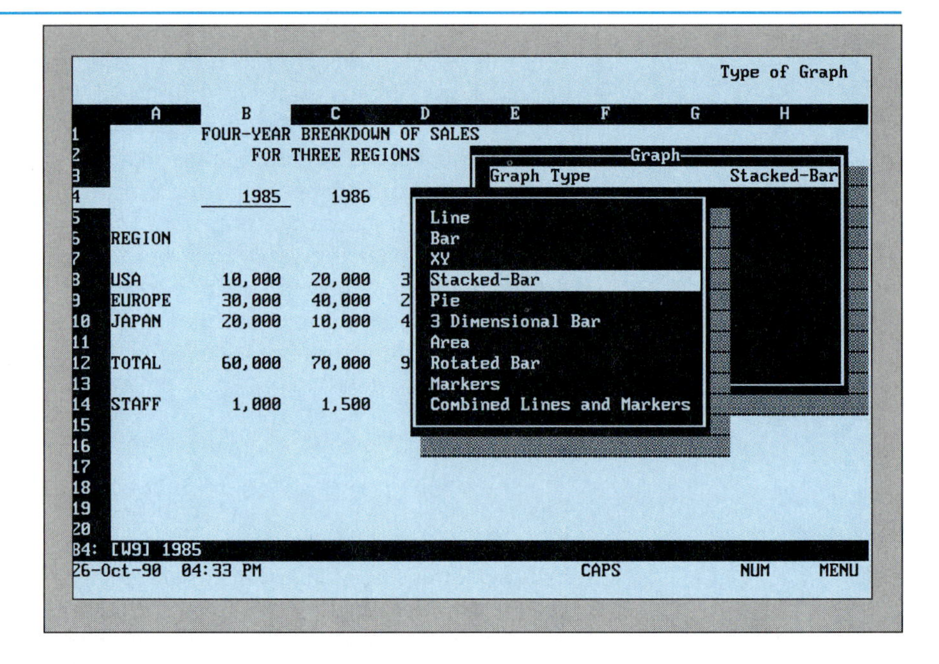

Exhibit 15.1

A Quattro Spreadsheet Menu

With the Quattro GRAPH command a user can choose from ten different types of graphs.

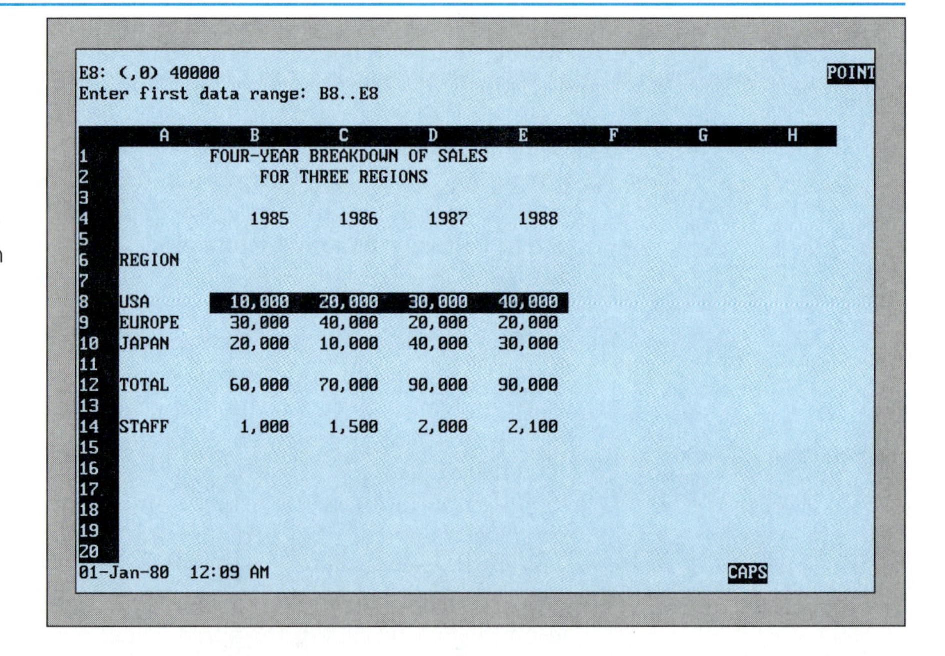

Exhibit 15.2

A Lotus Spreadsheet Containing Sales Figures for Three Regions Across Four Years

When a graph is created in a spreadsheet, the user must indicate the location of each series to be used in the graph. In this example, a user is specifying the location of the first series or data range to be included in the graph.

point in the graph-creation process. If the user's microcomputer is capable of displaying graphics on the screen, the user can preview the graph and see the effect of various options on the graph's appearance. The appearance of the graph can be altered by shading various areas and changing the sizes of some parts of the graph. However, this process of customization depends on the type of graph being produced. Using the preview feature, a user can get the exact appearance desired before printing the graph on paper.

The spreadsheet in Exhibit 15.2 contains the data used in later exhibits to illustrate some common types of graphs produced with spreadsheet charting programs. This spreadsheet shows sales data for three regions (USA, Europe, and Japan) across four years (1985 through 1988). At the bottom, the total sales and the number of employees in the company are shown. This data will be used to illustrate four of the most common types of graphs: a pie chart, a bar graph, a line graph, and an XY graph.

The Pie Chart

Exhibit 15.3 shows an example of a pie chart. **Pie charts** are a simple form of graph used to show how values compare across a single category. The exhibit shows the sales for three regions in a single year (1988). In 1988, the sales figures were 40,000 in the USA, 20,000 in Europe, and 30,000 in Japan. The pie chart shows how much each region contributed to the total sales in 1988 in percentage terms. In 1988 the total sales were 90,000. The size of the slices in the pie indicates how much each region contributed to that total sales figure. As you can see, the slice corresponding to the USA is largest, since that region accounted for 44.44 percent of the sales; Japan accounted for 33.33 percent, and Europe only 22.22 percent. Note that, when all of the slices of the pie are added together, the result is approximately 100 percent.

When a pie chart is created in a spreadsheet, the user must specify the range of data to use to construct the pie. The range for this pie chart would be the three sales figures in the 1988 column of the sample spreadsheet. In a pie chart, the user is limited to a single series, since the pie can be sliced only one way. Thus, if the user wanted to compare the sales of the three regions across more than one year, a pie chart could not be used.

Exhibit 15.3

A Pie Chart Generated by the Macintosh Excel Spreadsheet

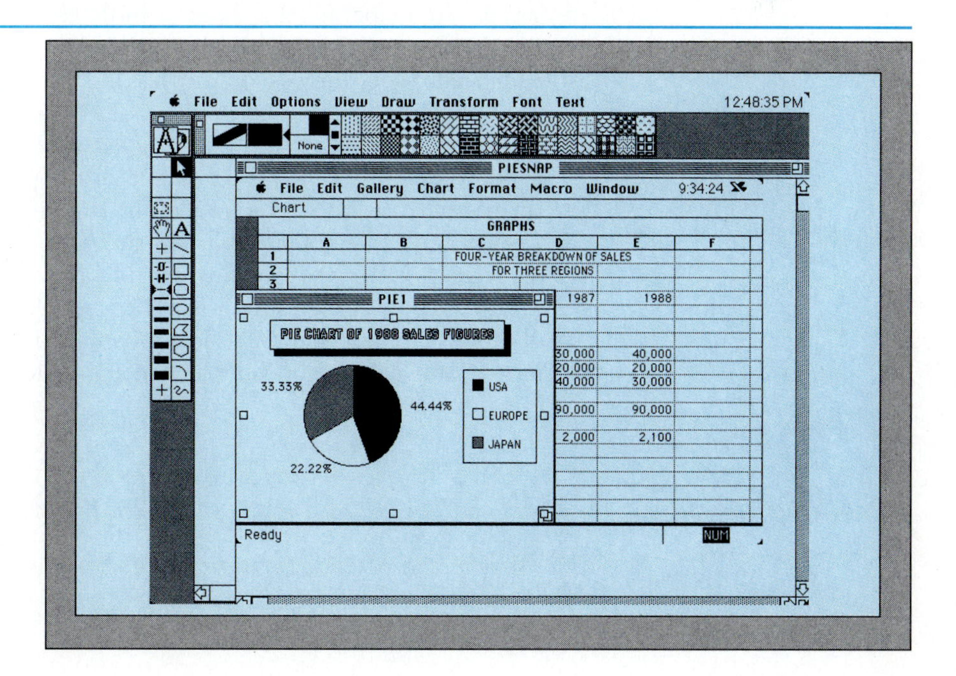

Exhibit 15.4

An Exploding Pie Chart Created in the Quattro Spreadsheet

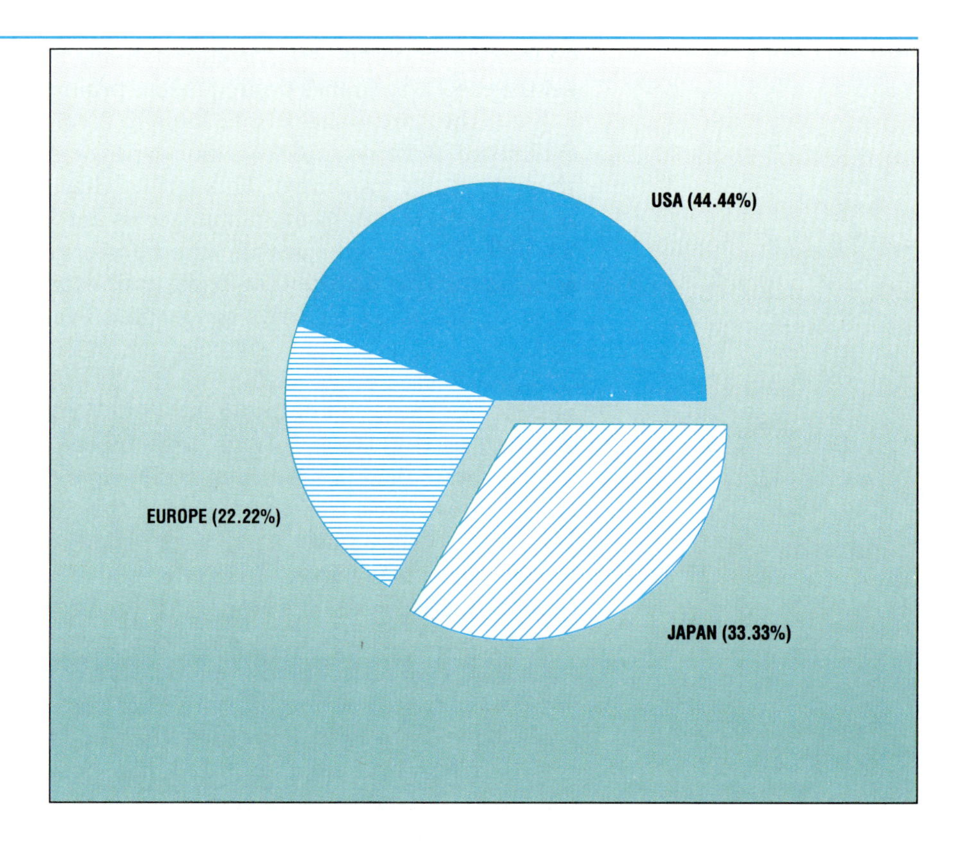

When labeling a pie chart, the user can typically specify a title and subtitle for the graph and can also label the various slices in the pie. The user types in a label for the slices or indicates a range of cells that contain the labels for the slices. In addition to labeling the slices with words, some spreadsheets allow the user to display the value of each slice either as the actual data used to construct the slices or as percentages.

A customizing option often used with pie charts is the ability to "explode" one or more slices. In an **exploding pie chart**, one or more slices of the pie can be pulled away from the rest to emphasize the data represented by that slice. Exhibit 15.4 shows an example of an exploded pie chart with the slice representing the sales in Japan pulled away for emphasis. Another customizing option available with pie charts is the ability to specify the color or shading pattern used for each slice of the pie. Other options include choosing a type style and size for the various labels on the graph.

The Bar Graph

Exhibit 15.5 shows an example of a **bar graph** created in the Lotus 1-2-3 spreadsheet showing the sales data. In a bar graph, the vertical line of numbers at the left side is known as the ***y*-axis**. The *y*-axis usually shows the measurement scale for the numbers being graphed. In the exhibit, the *y*-axis shows sales figures, since the numbers being graphed all represent

Exhibit 15.5

A Bar Graph Created in Lotus 1-2-3

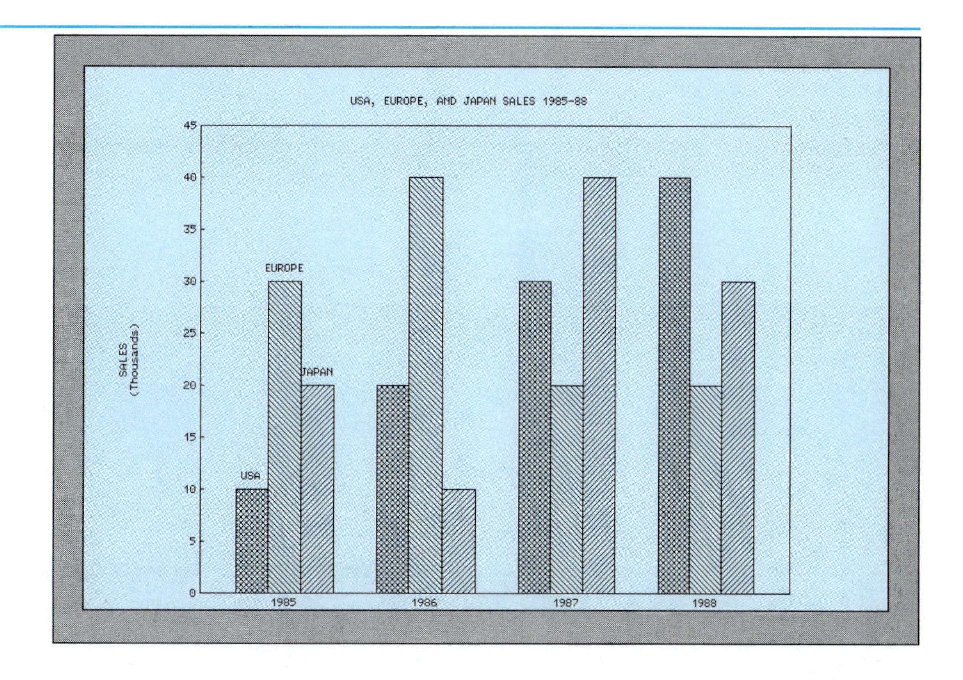

sales. The height of each bar in the graph corresponds to the number on the *y*-axis that represents the amount of sales. The line of numbers across the bottom of the graph makes up the ***x*-axis**. The *x*-axis always represents values for a category across which a comparison is being made. In the exhibit, the values for the year category were used to create the *x*-axis. The bars represent the sales figures for each of the various years. The region category could have also been used for the *x*-axis.

When there is a second category to be graphed, as occurs here, values for that second category are represented by different kinds of bars. Exhibit 15.5 shows a bar graph with three types of bars represented by different colors. Each bar color represents a value in the region category. If the data for only one region were graphed, there would be only one bar over each year on the *x*-axis. However, since sales figures for three regions are shown, there are three bars over each year on the *x*-axis.

When a bar graph is created in a spreadsheet program, the bars of the same color or shading pattern represent the values for a series. Thus, the bar graph in Exhibit 15.5 would require the specification of three different series. There would be a series to represent the sales in the USA across four years, a series for Europe, and a series for Japan. As you can see, the number of series needed is the same as the number of values in the second category being graphed.

In addition to the series used to represent the bars, a bar graph requires a separate series be used to label the *x*-axis. Exhibit 15.6 shows a spreadsheet in which the user is specifying a range of cells to serve as labels for the *x*-axis of the graph. In this exhibit, the four cells containing the years that label the four columns are being used as the labels for the *x*-axis. As shown in Exhibit 15.5, each axis, as well as the graph itself, has labels.

Exhibit 15.6

Specification of X-Axis Labels in the Quattro Spreadsheet

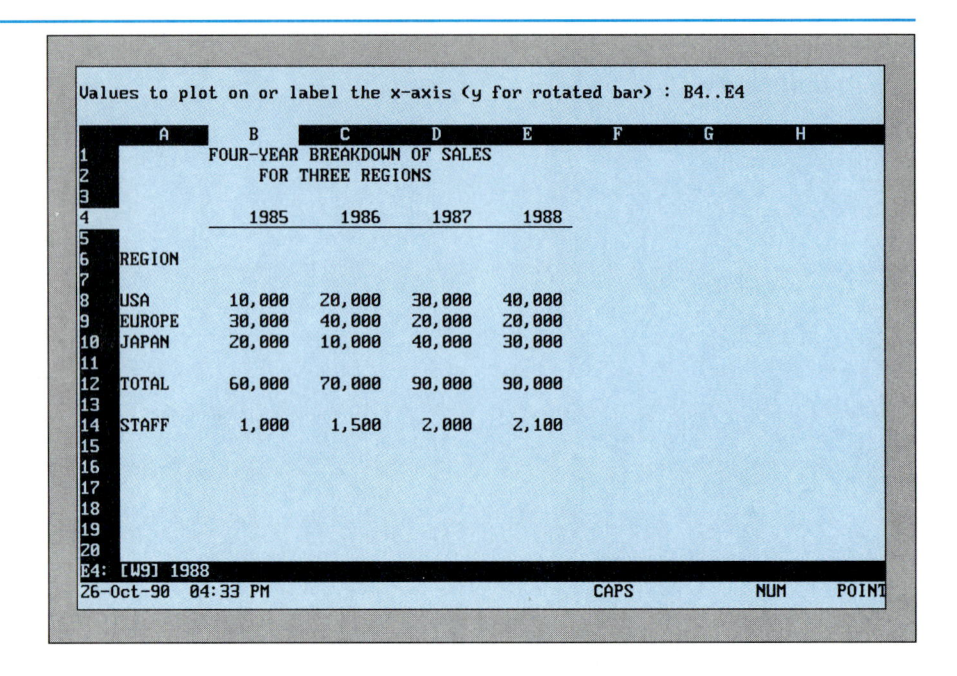

Within the graph in Exhibit 15.5 are labels used to identify the three bars. These **data labels** are used to identify the values for the second category being graphed (in this case, the region).

Various points on each axis are labeled, in addition to the label for the entire axis itself. For example, the *y*-axis has the points for 0, 10,000, 20,000, 30,000, and 40,000. Spreadsheet charting programs typically determine the data values shown on the *y*-axis automatically, using the maximum and minimum values in the data being graphed. Many programs also give the user the option of manually determining the values displayed on an axis through a process known as **scaling.** In addition to scaling the *y*-axis, customizing options for bar graphs include the ability to specify the shading pattern or color of the bars and to change the type style and size of various labels.

Other variations on the bar graph include stacked bar and horizontal bar graphs. Particular spreadsheet programs may support either or both of these variations. In the stacked bar graph, one bar is shown at each point on the *x*-axis (see Exhibit 15.7a). The height of each bar in the exhibit represents the total sales for all three regions in a particular year. The bar is then divided to show the relative contributions of each region to the total sales in that year, similar to the way a pie graph is divided. Thus, in the bar for 1985, you can see that most of the sales for that year came from Europe, since that region takes up most of the bar for 1985.

In the horizontal bar graph, the measurement scale for the numbers being graphed is on the *x*-axis, and one of the categories is on the *y*-axis (see Exhibit 15.7b). The bars extend horizontally from the *y*-axis.

The Line Graph

Like bar graphs, **line graphs** can be used to compare values across one or two categories. However, instead of bars being used to represent each

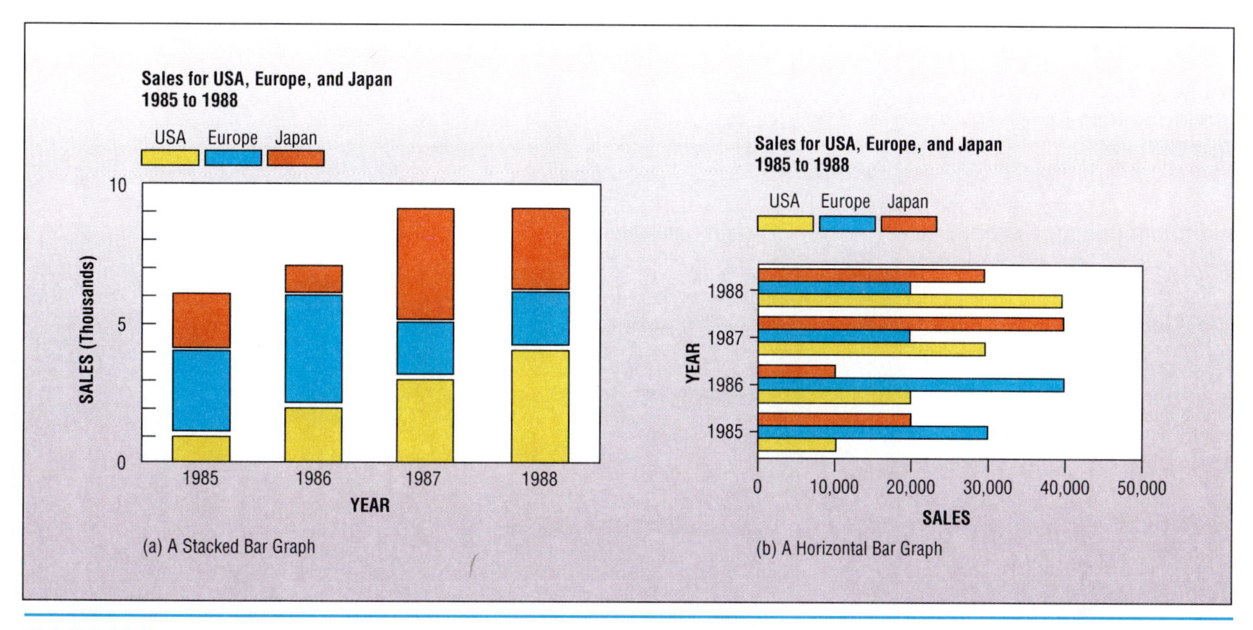

Exhibit 15.7

Bar Graphs Created in the TWIN Spreadsheet

A Stacked Bar Graph and a Horizontal Bar Graph.

number in a series, a point is placed on the graph in the appropriate position. A line is then drawn to connect the points. When a second category is graphed, the values in the second category are represented by a different line. Exhibit 15.8 shows a line graph of the sales data for the three regions from 1985 to 1988. The points on each line are in the same positions as the tops of the bars in the bar graph (see Exhibit 15.5), since the same data are represented in both graphs. The series needed to create the sample line graph are the same as that for the bar graph. Exhibit 15.8 also shows the use of a **legend** to identify the lines corresponding to the three regions. A legend performs the same function as a data label. The other labels for a line graph are similar to those for a bar graph. Some common customizing options include the ability to scale the y-axis, alter the type style and size of labels, and determine the symbols used on the graph to represent the points in each series.

The XY Graph

Exhibit 15.9 shows an example of an XY graph that compares the total sales of a company across four years to the number of employees in the company across the same four years. From this graph, a user can see that the relationship between sales and staff is one in which staff and sales increase together. Although an XY graph looks very similar to a line graph, the way the values are plotted is not the same. In an XY graph, a minimum of two series are specified. These two series are used to construct the x- and y-axes. The values used to label both the x- and y-axes are determined from the data in the two series. Points on the graph represent a value on the x-axis that corresponds to a value on the y-axis. Thus, the number of employees in a given year is matched with the total sales figure for that same year to produce a point on the graph. Titles and customizing options for XY graphs are typically similar to those for line graphs, an addition being the ability to scale both the x-axis and the y-axis.

Exhibit 15.8

A Line Graph Created by the Macintosh Excel Spreadsheet

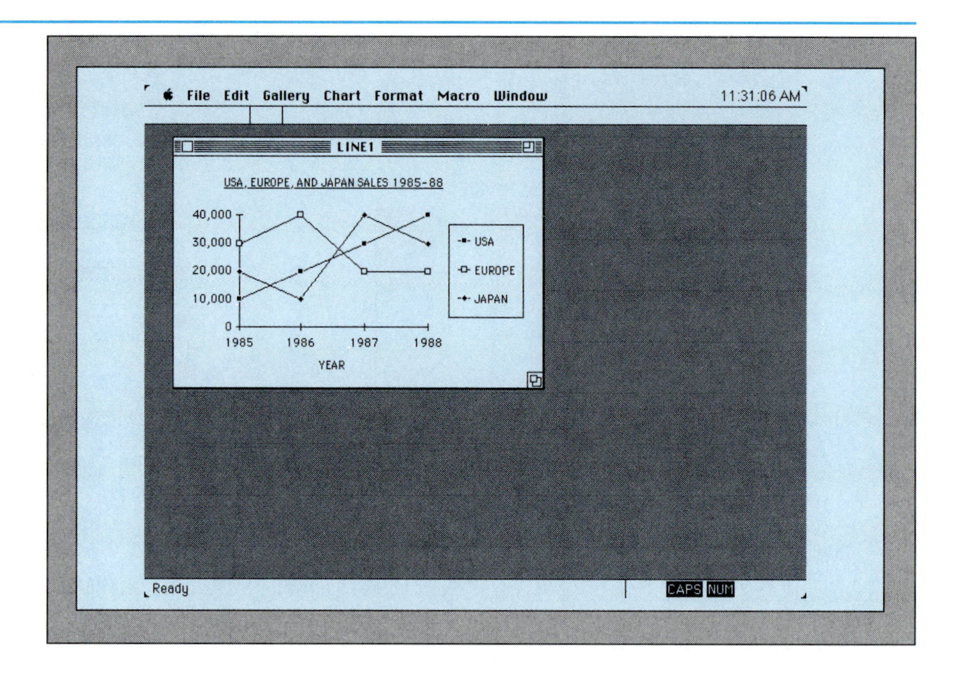

Exhibit 15.9

An XY Graph Created in the SUPERCALC4 Spreadsheet

The graph shows the relationship between total sales and staff increase.

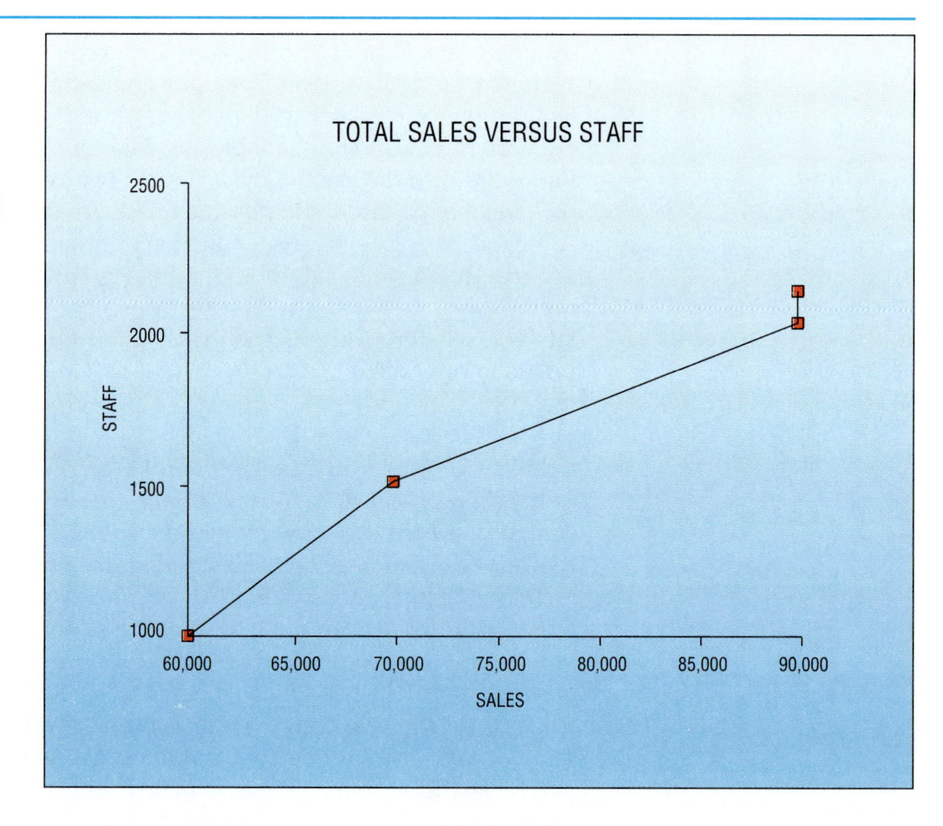

Dedicated Charting Programs

Although spreadsheet charting programs have undergone many improvements recently, the quality and flexibility of those programs still cannot match that of the better dedicated charting programs. A dedicated charting program (sometimes known as a *presentation graphics* program) is specifically designed to produce professional quality graphics for use in presentations and publications. Spreadsheet charting programs are best suited for analytical use when the user is attempting to summarize and understand particular data.

Dedicated charting programs typically offer many more graph types and more control over those graphs (see Exhibit 15.10). Graphs can be stylized by adding arrows, circles, and other shapes in any place the user desires. Although they contain more options than spreadsheet charting programs, dedicated charting programs are designed to be very simple to use. Typically, default settings are provided that allow the user to create standard graphs very quickly. The defaults can also be overridden to give the user more precise control over the graph. For example, the user can control the placement of text within the graph, the size of the text, and the type style of the text. The user can manually control the *x*- and *y*-axes. A variety of shadings or colors can be used to emphasize parts of the graph. Dedicated charting programs also include three-dimensional graph styles, in which the user can rotate the perspective of the graph to almost any angle (see Exhibit 15.11).

Dedicated charting programs also include the ability to import data from a wide variety of sources. Data can be drawn from ASCII (text) files, and from files created by spreadsheets, word processors, and database programs. Some of the newer programs can be linked with spreadsheet files, and the user can draw the current information from the spreadsheet at any time to create a graph.

Selecting a Charting Program

Exhibit 15.12 lists some of the common dedicated charting programs available for IBM compatible computers and some of the features that might be important to users. The majority of charting programs currently on the market allow the user to create the standard pie, bar, and line graphs. It may also be important to the user to have a graphics package capable of producing types of graphs beyond the basic types included in most packages. The chart shows which packages can create two special types of graphs that might be important to a user: the *stacked bar* and *exploding pie.*

The exhibit also indicates whether the program supports true three dimensional graphs with *x*-, *y*-, and *z*-axes. The number of data points for a line on the graph and the number of lines per graph are also shown. The number of different patterns available for shading parts of the graph, the ability to create text on the graph with a text editor, and the ability to rotate text are also indicated.

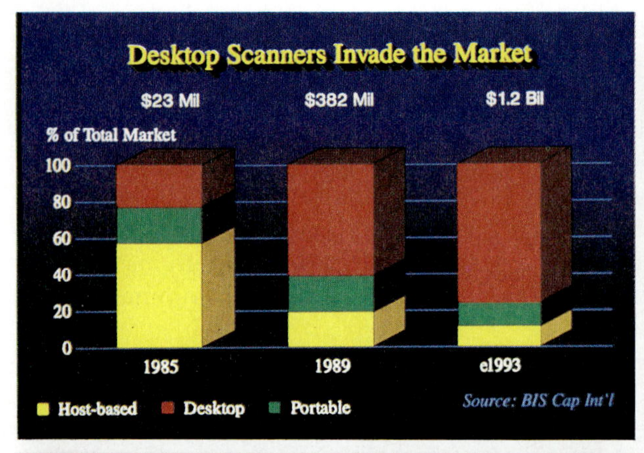

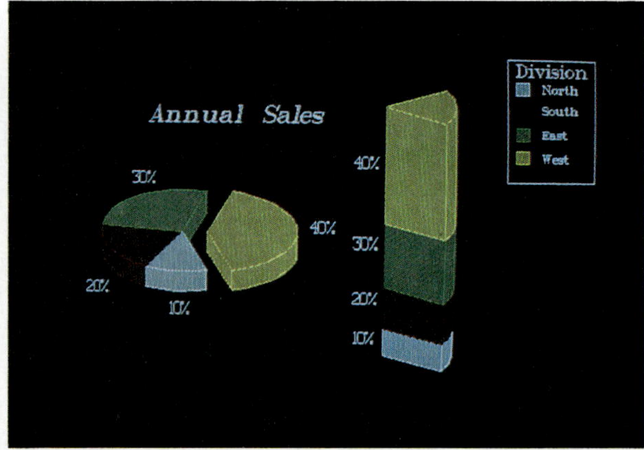

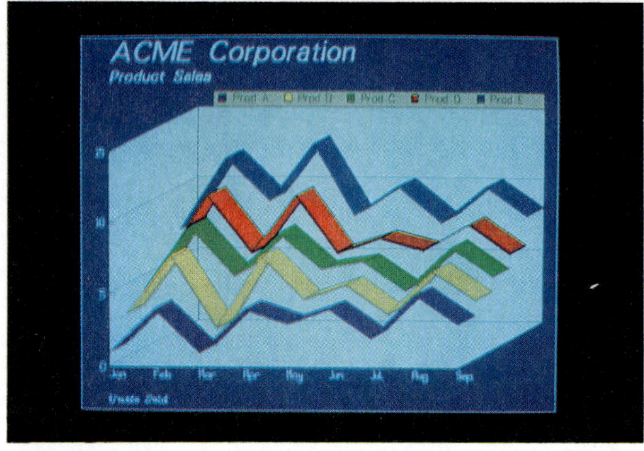

Exhibit 15.10

Graphs Produced by a Dedicated Charting Program

Designing Graphs

Perhaps the most common problems users have with graphics are determining what kind of graph to use and knowing how to design an effective graph. The kind of information being graphed and the intent of the graph affect the type of graph you might choose. Each type of graph works best with a certain type of data. A pie chart is typically used when you wish to show how much the various parts contribute to the whole. Thus, if you want to show the extent to which five divisions of a company contribute to the total sales, a pie chart is a good choice. Remember that a pie chart can only be used when there is a single series of data to be graphed.

A bar graph is best used to display differences among individual items or times. It is particularly useful in emphasizing differences in size or amount since the sizes of the bars reflect the relative sizes of the data. Typically, the *x*-axis of a bar graph shows specific values or points in time, rather than a continuous series of values.

When a continuous series of values is needed on the *x*-axis, a line graph is a better choice than a bar graph. Line graphs are particularly well suited for graphs that are intended to show patterns or trends over time. For example, a line graph could be used to display the growth in sales across time for three companies.

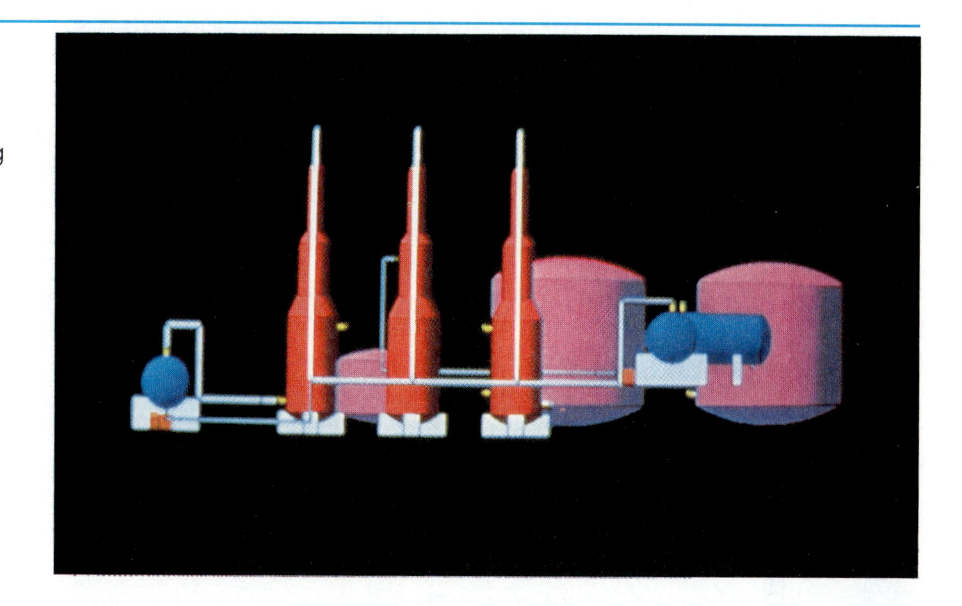

Exhibit 15.11

Three-Dimensional Graphing Options

Some dedicated charting programs, such as Perspective Jr., give the user extensive three-dimensional graphing options.

An XY graph is useful for showing the ways two variables relate to one another. For example, illustrating the relationship between length of employment and salary would be a good application for an XY graph.

Guidelines for Creating Graphs

Even though you may not be a trained graphic artist, it is easy to produce high-quality graphs and charts with the right software and a few simple guidelines. When creating graphs it is important to keep in mind the intended use of the graph. What is the intended audience and what point are you trying to make with your graph? Construct the graph so that it is as simple as possible while still conveying the message. For example, consider the amount of data you are going to plot on the graph. Too much data could make the graph cluttered—the audience may miss your point. Also

	.	Graphics	Freelance	Presents
Stacked bar	Y	Y	Y	Y
Exploding pie	Y	Y	Y	N
3-D charts	Y	N	Y	N
Points per line	4.2 mil	240	500	20
Lines per graph	4.2 mil	8	6	4
Fill patterns	40	12	15	16
Text editor	Y	Y	N	Y
Text rotation	Y	N	Y	N

Exhibit 15.12

A Comparison of Four Dedicated Graphics Packages for IBM Compatible Computers

consider carefully the amount and placement of text in the graph. Use labels to clarify the data but don't clutter the graph unnecessarily.

Because of the power of graphics in persuading a viewer, the graphics user must be careful not to present data in a misleading way. Sometimes graphs are purposely distorted to give the casual viewer the wrong impression. For example, the graph in Exhibit 15.13a shows a graph of sales increases over six years. The data in this graph indicate a modest increase in sales over the period. The graph in Exhibit 15.13b shows exactly the same data. In this graph the user has scaled the *y*-axis so that it does not show the value of zero at the bottom. This way a casual viewer might look at this graph and get the impression that there has been a major increase in sales when the increase is really not that impressive. Thus, the user must be careful not to accidentally mislead the viewer, and viewers should carefully analyze the graph being presented.

Drawing and Painting Programs

Drawing and painting programs are typically used for creating images, as opposed to graphing numbers. They turn a microcomputer into an electronic drawing board on which a user can liven up a graph or create a picture. The arrow keys on the keyboard or special input devices, such as a joystick or mouse, are used to move a cursor on the screen to create a drawing. The user can call up certain common shapes (such as squares and circles), change the size of those objects, and move them around on the screen. Objects can be erased, shaded, rotated, inverted, stretched, and magnified. Text can be placed anywhere on the screen in different sizes and styles. These programs are designed so that in a matter of minutes a user can create simple pictures, save them permanently on disk, and print them out. Many drawing and painting programs include libraries of previously created images, often called "clip-art," that a user can retrieve and include in a drawing.

A **drawing** program is designed to work primarily with geometric shapes such as lines, arcs, circles, squares, and rectangles. Horizontal and vertical rulers are available to precisely control the placement of objects on the screen. Exhibit 15.14 shows a screen from the MacDraw II program for Macintosh computers. The tools available to the user include tools for pointing, inputting text, and creating different lines and shapes. Drawings that are larger than the screen can be created and accessed through the use of the scroll bars on the bottom and right of the screen.

The pull-down menus in drawing programs include options for saving the drawing, cutting and pasting parts of the drawing, shading objects, specifying the directions of lines, controlling the rulers, and manipulating any text on the screen.

In a drawing program, objects such as circles and squares are treated as individual units than can be moved, shaded, or resized. In contrast, **painting programs** work with bit-mapped images rather than lines and objects. A bit-mapped image is treated as a pattern of pixels or

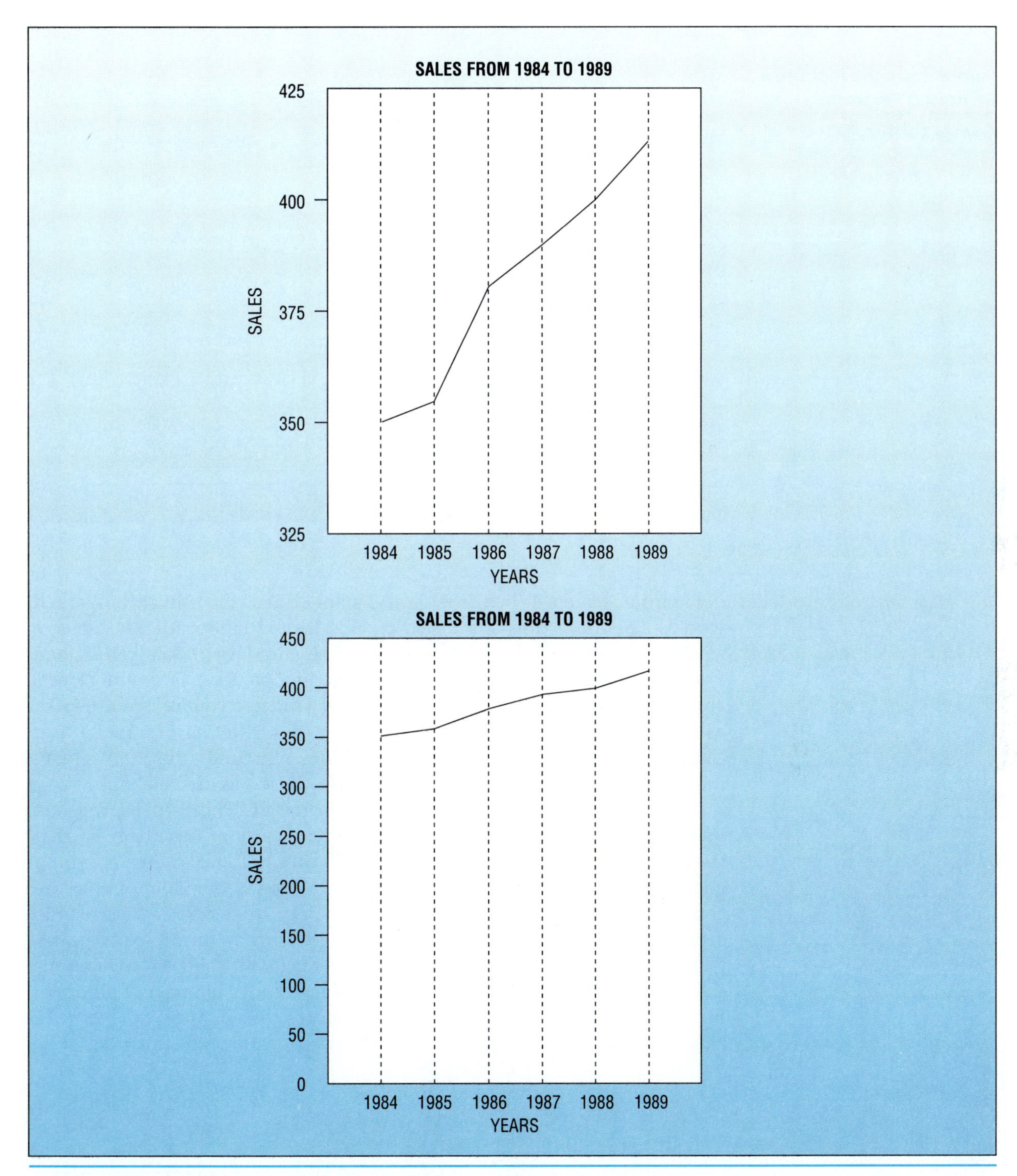

Exhibit 15.13

Two Quattro Graphs Displaying the Same Data

(a) This graph shows company sales over a six-year period. Note the relatively modest increase in sales.

(b) When the y-axis is scaled, this Quattro graph seems to indicate a major increase in sales although the data is the same as in Exhibit 15.13a.

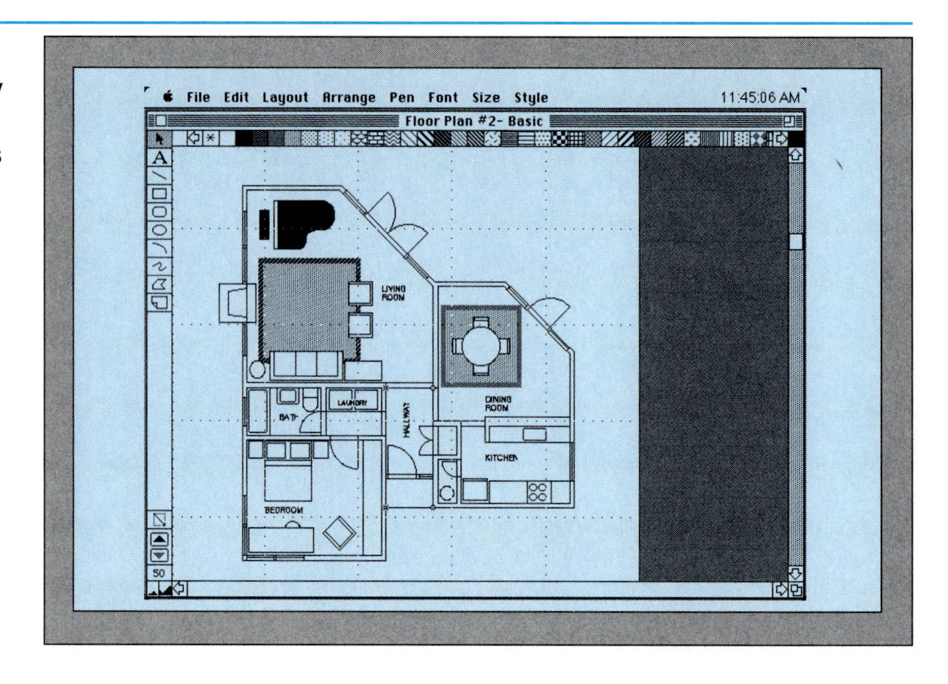

Exhibit 15.14

Screen From the MacDraw II Drawing Program

A drawing program allows a user to work precisely with geometric shapes and text.

dots on the screen. When these images are edited, they must be worked with as a series of dots since each pixel is treated independently. Thus, a square drawn with a paint program is actually a group of dots, rather than a single unit as it is in a drawing program. In a painting program, objects are not treated as individual units. In other words, a square is not treated as a single unit but as a series of dots. Thus, in a painting program a user can erase part of a square, whereas in a drawing program the entire square must be erased since drawing programs treat objects as discrete units.

Exhibit 15.15 shows a screen from the PC Paintbrush program. Painting programs include tools for selecting parts of the image so that they can be manipulated. There are also tools for creating common geometric shapes such as circles and squares. Various shading options are controlled by tools that allow the user to "spray" dots across the screen to create a pattern much like that produced with a can of spray paint. Additional tools are available to control the thickness of lines drawn on the screen, erase parts of the image, and shade parts of the image. Pull-down menus allow the user to save images, control the characteristics of text, choose a shading pattern, and change the size of parts of the image.

Presentation Managers

A third category of graphics software is designed to use a microcomputer to display a series of previously created graphs and drawings. Presentation managers use a microcomputer monitor to display a series of screens as a

Exhibit 15.15

A Screen From the PC Paintbrush Program

In a painting program, the entire screen is treated as a grid of thousands of dots that are either light or dark.

slide show, with various types of transitions available between the screens that make up the presentation. With presentation managers, such as those included in packages like PC Storyboard, Freelance, SlideWrite Plus, and Harvard Graphics, the user starts with a series of screens that have been saved in files. In order to create these files, presentation managers typically contain a component that allows a user to take a "snapshot" of a screen and save it in a file. Because of their similarity to cameras, these components are often called screen capture programs or cameras. The screen capture program is started by the user and remains active in the RAM of the computer. The user can then access other software, such as a spreadsheet or graphics program. To save a screen image, the user presses a special key sequence to have the screen capture program store the current contents of the screen in a special file. Thus, anything that can be displayed on the screen can be captured in a file.

Once the screens needed for a presentation have been saved in files on a disk, the user can use a story editor program to create a sequence of screens to be displayed. In the story editor, the user simply names the screens within the file or files that have been saved on disk. The order in which the screens are named determines the order in which they will be displayed (see Exhibit 15.16).

The user can also pick a transition to be used from one screen to the next. Just as the screen capture program is similar to a camera, the types of transitions available are similar to those used in motion pictures. The user can have a new picture replace an existing picture by pushing the old one off the screen in any of four directions. Or the old picture can split in the middle and the two halves move off horizontally or vertically to reveal the new one. The new picture can *explode* from the center and move

Exhibit 15.16

The Story Editor in the IBM Storyboard Presentation Manager

The Picture Name column shows the names of files containing previously captured screens. The Method column indicates the type of transition to be used when moving from one picture to the next.

PC STORYBOARD Story Editor
Edit the Story

Story Name D:TEMP

Label	Picture Name or Command	Display picture using:				Then wait for	Set Color		Area
		Method	Dir	Line	Time		Pal	Back	
	INTRO	CRUSH	UP	CYN	FAST	KEY	LCMW	BLK	FULL
	INT1	DIAGONAL	OUT-V	WHT	4	KEY	GRY	BLK	FULL
	INT2	REPLACE	IN-V	BACK	20	KEY	LCMW	IWHT	FULL
	INT2A	SPLIT	LEFT	MAG	60	40	CMW	LYEL	FULL
	CHART1	EXPLODE	RIGHT	BACK	40	60	LCMW	LMAG	FULL
	INT2B	FADE	DOWN	CYN	10	12	CMW	LRED	FULL
	INT3	WEAVE	OUT-H	BACK	7	7	LGRY	LCYN	FULL
	INT4	STRIPES	IN-H	BACK	5	30	LGRY	IWHT	FULL

FUNCTION KEYS F3 Step Story F6 Save Story F8 Select Story
F1 Help F4 Run Story sF6 Save & Quit sF8 Quit (NO Save)
F2 Editing Keys F5 View Picture F7 Print Story F9/10 Rotate
CAP NUM

out over the old one in all four directions. A *crush* is the opposite of exploding—the new picture comes from the outside and moves over the old one toward the center in all four directions. In *diagonal transition*, the new picture starts in one corner and moves diagonally to cover the old picture. A *fade* makes the existing picture fade out as the new one fades in.

Once the sequence of pictures and the transitions have been specified, the presentation description is saved on disk, along with the files containing the screens used in the presentation. The user can then run the presentation and have all the screens displayed in the order specified using the chosen transitions.

Desktop Publishing

Desktop publishing is the design and production of sophisticated documents that combine text and graphics using a personal computer and laser printer. Typical desktop publishing applications include newsletters, business correspondence, invoices, forms, marketing brochures, product descriptions, management presentations, and instructional materials for class handouts, and technical manuals (see Exhibit 15.17).

Desktop publishing enables an office worker to create a high-quality document with a relatively small investment in training and equipment. This is done by using page composition software, which allows an end-user to set up a page design and select from various type sizes and styles and different graphic icons. To be most effective, the desktop publishing system must have a what-you-see-is-what-you-get (WYSIWYG)

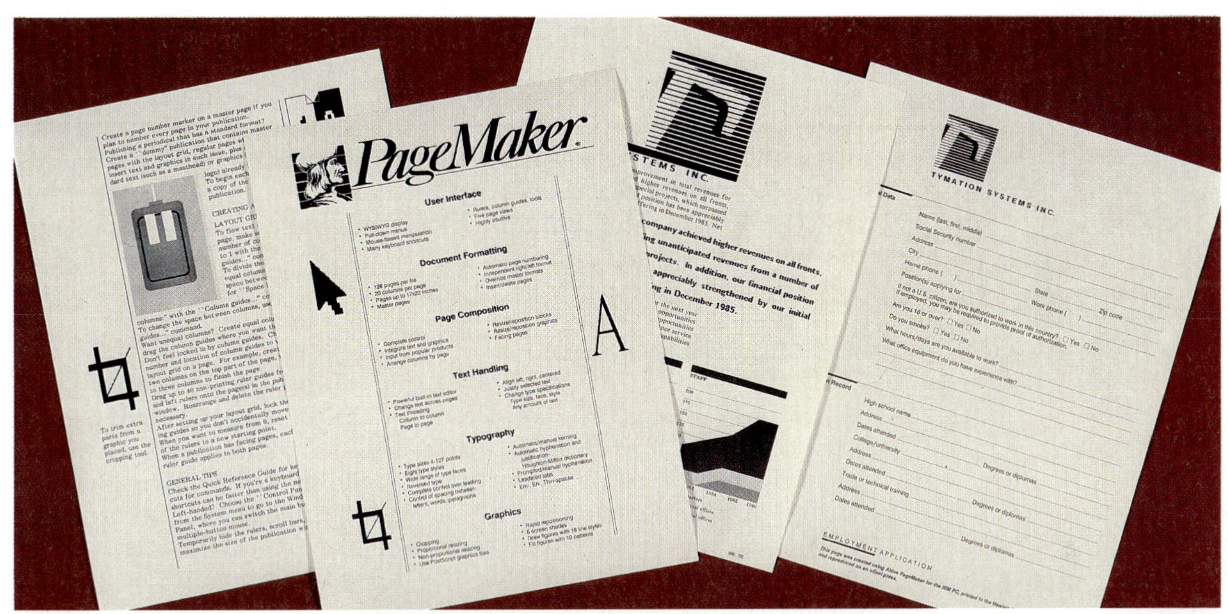

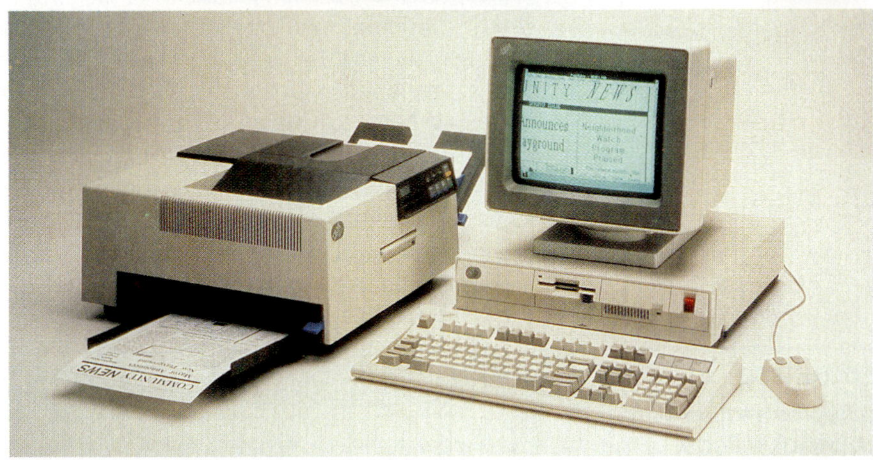

Exhibit 15.17

Desktop Publishing

Using a personal computer, page composition software, and a laser printer, you can easily design and print informative publications at your desk.

presentation. The ability to see the results of the design on the screen when type and layout are changed is what makes these systems so efficient and easy to use.

The idea of desktop publishing is to keep the work of production as close to the document's writer and designer as possible. Substantial savings in time and costs can result from the elimination of the communication that was previously required when multiple people were involved in the production of a document. Errors are also reduced since the transitional steps between manuscript and typesetting and pasteup have been streamlined. Most importantly, changes to the document are easily accommodated.

Desktop publishing is generally regarded as beginning with the introduction of the small laser printer in 1985. Laser printers were important to the success of desktop publishing because previously there was no low-cost device that could produce output of similar quality to that of typesetting machines.

The early commercial success of the market is due to Apple Computer Corporation, which combined the Macintosh computer, a laser printer, and the page-layout software. Desktop publishing was a natural for the Macintosh concept and it initially captured some 80 percent of this market, before desktop publishing became available on IBM PCs and compatibles.

Creating Publications

Exhibit 15.18 shows the layout of the PageMaker page composition program. When a user creates a publication, the master page icons at the bottom are used to specify the general characteristics of the pages. Both left and right master page icons can be used for publications that are to be printed like a book, with left and right facing pages. The user selects one of these master icons using a pointing device, such as a mouse. The user can then specify the types of units to be used in the measurements of the page (inches, spaces, centimeters) as well as page size, number of pages, margins, and the use of facing pages. Once the basic layout is specified, the user is presented with a blank page meeting those specifications.

When creating a publication, the user can take advantage of many special features that make it easy to lay out a page. As shown in Exhibit 15.18, rulers can be used to determine page height and column positioning; icons representing all of the pages in the publication appear at the bottom to aid in the selection of the page to be displayed; and various pull-down menus can be used to issue commands.

Exhibit 15.18

A Representation of the PageMaker Page Composition Program

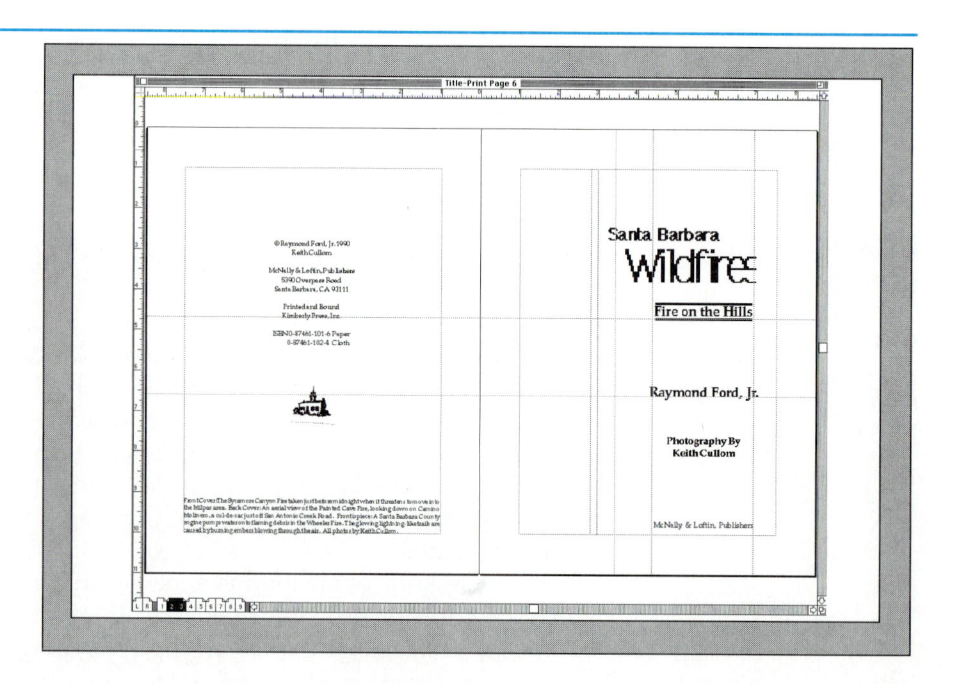

Manipulating Text

The user can enter text from the keyboard or can import it from word processors such as WordPerfect and WordStar. Text on a page can be highlighted using the mouse pointer, and the characteristics of the highlighted text can be adjusted by the user. With the proper equipment, PageMaker gives the user over 100 combinations of typefaces, sizes (ranging from 4 to 127 points), and type styles, such as bold, underline, italic, superscript, and subscript. Text can be automatically hyphenated using a dictionary of hyphenations, or the user can be prompted to indicate the position of the hyphen.

Manipulating Graphics

The toolbox in Exhibit 15.18 provides features that allow the user to create simple graphics using lines, text, and geometric shapes. As with illustration graphics programs, users can specify line thickness, shade objects, position objects, and alter the size of objects. More importantly, PageMaker allows the user to import graphics from other graphics programs, such as Harvard Graphics, Lotus Freelance, and others. Graphics can be placed anywhere on the page and adjusted to fit as they are imported.

Page Layout

When building a page, the user can divide the page into columns, set up headers and footers, control page numbering, and wrap text around graphics. While a page is being constructed, the user can place blocks of text or graphics in the pasteboard area of the screen (see Exhibit 15.18). These text blocks and graphics can be pasted onto any page and sized to fit. Perhaps the most important aspect of PageMaker, and all other page composition programs, is that the user sees the page formatted on the screen the way it will be printed. To accomplish this, these programs require microcomputers capable of displaying graphics on the screen.

The pages shown in Exhibit 15.17 illustrate how text and graphics can be combined in a single document. Both illustrations and number-based graphs can be placed within the text. The text itself is displayed in many different sizes and styles in multiple columns. With desktop publishing and the other types of graphics programs discussed in this chapter, the end-user can produce professional-quality charts and graphs without a highly trained graphic-arts staff.

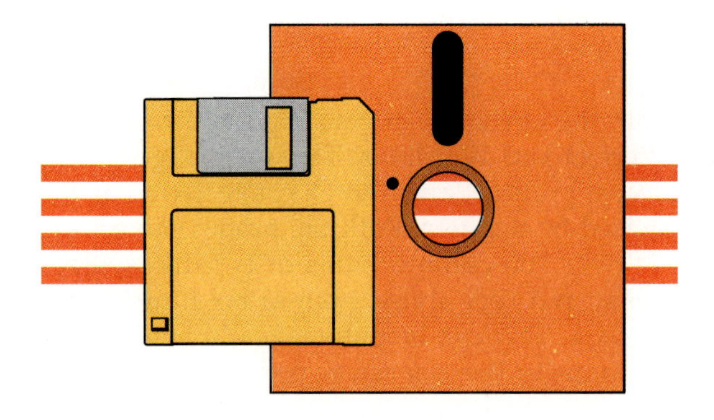

Computers at Work

The Package Puzzle: Word-Processor or Page-Layout Software?

The line between high-end word processors and page-layout software continues to blur, as word processors take on more features once considered the domain of dedicated page-layout packages.

Many users are surprised to find that their word processor now supports many of the features they used to look at a page-layout package to provide: winding columns, graphics support and advanced font support.

The increasing similarities between these types of software now makes it more difficult for corporate buyers and users to determine which package will best meet their publishing needs.

The problem can be approached from several different angles—starting with the origins of the software itself. As WordPerfect Corp. Executive Vice President Pete Peterson pointed out, the word processor has evolved form the typewriter, while the page-layout package is a direct descendant of the paste-up board.

From this fundamental difference, the decision is fairly straightforward: Use a word processor if the work to be done involves mainly text, but use a desktop-publishing package for projects that emphasize visual aspects or consist mainly of graphical items. Unfortunately, most choices aren't so simple. Other questions must be answered before deciding which genre of software provides an optimal mix of features, compatibility and ease of use.

Considering Particular Needs

One question to consider is what the user intends to do with the software. At this level, particular needs often translate into specific requirements for a package.

For instance, if the project is a newsletter for distribution outside the company, the software of choice is a page-layout product. Xerox Corp.'s Ventura Publisher and Aldus Corp.'s PageMaker offer features that are not yet found in even the high-end word-processing products. For the high-quality newsletter, the capacity to do color separations, registration and crop marks still lie firmly in the desktop-publishing camp.

"If you want to produce a relatively small number of pages for high-quality distribution—such as advertising, flyers, poster art, billboards—then desktop publishing may be the way to go," said Garrett Hayes, a micro manager at First Interstate Bancorp in Los Angeles.

In addition, desktop-publishing programs are still the only place to find support for process and spot (Pantone) color. The need to use color makes the decision fairly simple, because word processors produce only black and white output.

On the other hand, internal newsletters or other publications not intended for outside circulation can often be done quite nicely with a high-end word processor. Such documents do not need to be typeset and often lack color or high-quality graphics.

Surprisingly, the length of a document does not always dictate the type of software required. Both Ventura Publisher and Lotus Development Corp.'s Manuscript offer superb support for technical manuals and software documentation by offering extensive style sheets and global format settings.

The next step in choosing between a word processor and desktop publisher is to find out which of the two has the features that are most critical to the task.

For example, users who need to produce high-quality equations—perhaps for software documentation or complex financial reports—would consider Ventura Publisher or Lotus Manuscript because of their outstanding support for scientific and mathematical symbols.

Also, if the user often creates financial reports—Lotus calls it "financial publishing"—the product should have links into spreadsheets or graphics packages. If this feature is important, users can consider Lotus Manuscript for providing hot links into the Lotus spreadsheet family or Microsoft Word for links to Lotus 1-2-3 or to Excel.

A third consideration is the environment in which the user is most accustomed to working. Differing working styles might suggest one type of product over another.

For instance,some people find it easier to work in a what-you-see-is-what-you-get (WYSIWYG) environment, while others contend that document composition and content are best done first, followed by formatting and appearance.

On the subject of placing appearance over content, one microcomputer manager for a large West Coast financial company joked: "Ninety percent of desktop publishing consists of putting bow ribbons on horse manure."

But for those who need WYSIWYG, desktop publishers are the way to go. Both Ventura and PageMaker use graphical environments to display text and graphics almost exactly as they will appear on the printed page.

For those who prefer text-based programs, high-end word processors are the ones to consider. Most of them feature a WYSIWYG page preview with graphics and correctly sized text fonts.

Users will also want to look at the following key features as they consider whether to purchase a desktop-publishing package or word processor. Both types of software already support most of these features to some extent.

Does the product support multiple typefaces? Are the typefaces easy to use? Many products will print out a test file that shows off the font support.

Beware of Terminology

Does the package offer advanced control over sophisticated typographic features such as kerning, leading and preferred spacing? Buyers should be careful with terms here; several vendors use different terms in similar contexts. What one vendor calls "snaking columns," another calls "winding columns," and a third calls "newspaper columns."

How many different ways can the software measure distances? Many packages offer measurements in inches, lines, picas, centimeters or points.

Does the package offer support for style sheets, a method of consistently formatting a newsletter or report? Some desktop publishers can even directly import text and style sheets form word-processing programs, preserving not only formatting commands such as indents and spacing but also font information and global styles.

Also, how easy is the product to learn and use? For users not familiar with the concepts of page-layout software, the learning curve can be prohibitively steep. Getting up to speed in Ventura, for example, might take the better part of a week. On the other hand, someone already using WordPerfect 5.0 would only have to learn how to access the advanced features.

Also, many high-end products offer similar or identical interfaces to other products within that vendor's family of software. Microsoft Word looks like Microsoft Multiplan, which looks like Microsoft Chart.

Finally, desktop-publishing packages usually cost more than high-end word processors; companies can save a considerable sum by buying word processors with graphics features instead of desktop publishers with text-handling features.

The choice between a high-end word processor and a desktop publisher isn't easy, but the right decision could go a long way toward saving money and still having a package that gets the job done.

Summary and Key Terms

Graphics software can be used to display numeric information in the form of a graph. There are four categories of software involved in the creation and use of graphics: charting programs, drawing and painting programs, presentation managers, and desktop publishing software.

Charting programs display numeric data graphically. Charting programs can be separated into software integrated into a spreadsheet (**spreadsheet charting programs**) and software that functions independent of any spreadsheet (**dedicated charting programs**). Spreadsheet charting programs can take advantage of the spreadsheet's ability to recalculate numeric results and update the graph as the numbers change.

Common types of graphs include pie charts, bar graphs, line graphs, and XY graphs. **Pie charts** are used to compare values across one category as percentages of the whole. Each value in the category is represented as a slice of the pie, where the size of the slice indicates the percentage. An **exploding pie chart** lets the user pull one or more of the slices away from the pie for emphasis.

A **bar graph** is used to show how data differ across one or two categories. Values in one category are shown on the ***x*-axis** with a bar above each value. The height of the bar indicates a value on the ***y*-axis,** which represents the measurement scale for the numbers being graphed. If a second category is graphed, it is represented by multiple bars over each value on the *x*-axis. Bar graphs also usually include titles for the graph and for each axis. **Data labels** can also be used within the graph to label the various bars. The user can manually set the points shown on each axis through the use of a **scaling** feature. Variations of the bar graph include stacked-bar and horizontal-bar graphs.

Line graphs are similar to bar graphs, except that data are graphed as a group of points joined by a line. In both line and bar graphs, a **legend** can be used to identify the lines or bars.

An **XY graph** is used to show the relationship between two variables. The *x*- and *y*-axes each show the value of a variable. Points are placed on the graph by pairing a value on the *x*-axis with a value on the *y*-axis.

Certain types of graphs are best suited for displaying certain types of information. Pie charts are used to show the way parts relate to the whole. Bar graphs are best for showing differences in relative quantities, and line graphs are useful for displaying trends over time. XY graphs are used to show the relationship between two variables. When creating a graph, it is important to keep the graph as simple as possible while still delivering the intended message. Care must be taken when constructing and viewing a graph to avoid a misinterpretation of the meaning of the graph, particularly when the *y*-axis has been scaled.

Dedicated charting programs typically have more options than those that are part of a spreadsheet package. Default settings can be used to create a graph quickly, or they can be overridden to allow the user more flexibility. The user has control over the placement of text within the graph, over the size of the text, and over the style of that text. Data from a number of sources such as spreadsheets, word processors, and databases can be used as input for a dedicated charting program.

Drawing and painting programs allow the end-user to create free-form pictures by drawing or painting images on the screen. These programs let the user draw objects, move them around, shade them, and manipulate their shapes. These images can be printed or stored on disk for future use. A **drawing program** allows a user to precisely position geometric shapes. These shapes are treated as units that can be moved and shaded. A **painting program** creates an image made up of tiny dots (a **bit-mapped image**). A drawing is created by making some of these dots dark instead of light. Objects created in a painting program are actually treated as a collection of dots. Thus, the dots making up a square in a painted image can be manipulated individually.

Presentation managers allow users to place graphic images in a sequence and determine transitions between them. These programs also include software that allows the user to capture a picture of a screen in a file for use in a presentation. Once a presentation is defined, the user can call it up, and the images listed in the presentation are displayed using the selected transitions.

Desktop publishing software involves the incorporation of graphics into text to create professional-quality publications. Desktop publishing uses page layout software to position text and graphics on a page and to select different text styles and sizes. This software, combined with a laser printer capable of producing high-quality output, allows a user with little training to produce high-quality publications, such as user manuals and newsletters.

Review Questions

1. List some of the common types of graphs that can be produced with graphics software.
2. Compare graphics software incorporated in a spreadsheet program to stand-alone graphics software.
3. Explain how a pie chart is used to graph data.
4. When would a stacked bar graph be a more appropriate choice for displaying numerical data?
5. What are the similarities and differences between a bar graph and a line graph?
6. Explain the difference between drawing and painting programs.
7. Explain the function of the screen capture software in a presentation manager.
8. What are the three components responsible for the popularity of desktop publishing?
9. What is the role of page-layout software in desktop publishing?

T F **10.** A bar graph can only be used to compare values for a single category.

T F **11.** In an exploding pie graph, one or more of the slices of the pie are pulled away for emphasis.

T F **12.** A legend is the part of the graph that lists the assumptions that went into making the graph.

T F **13.** Scaling is a process that allows the user to determine how many bars will appear in the graph.

T F **14.** Presentation managers allow the user to create a sequence of previously created graphics to create a presentation.

T F **15.** A drawing program treats the objects created as a series of dots on the screen.

T F **16.** A painting program treats each geometric shape on the screen as an individual unit.

T F **17.** In a desktop publishing package, the user combines text with graphics to create publications such as newsletters.

T F **18.** An XY graph is used to show the relationship between two variables.

T F **19.** Data labels are the labels that appear below the x-axis.

20. _____ A graph that is used to compare various values of a single category as percentages of a whole is a:

a. line graph | c. XY graph
b. bar graph | d. pie chart

21. _____ The line across the bottom of a line or bar graph used to show various values for a category across which a comparison is made is called the:

a. x-axis | c. legend
b. y-axis | d. a-axis

22. _____ The graph used to show how two variables are related is the:

a. line graph | c. bar graph
b. XY graph | d. pie chart

23. _____ An area on the graph that is used to help identify the various symbols on a graph is called the:

a. legend | c. y-axis
b. x-axis | d. data label

24. _____ The graph type best used to show trends over time is the:

a. bar graph | c. XY graph
b. pie chart | d. line graph

25. _____ A program that lets the user create images that are treated as groups of dots on the screen is:

a. drawing program | c. painting program
b. dedicated charting program | d. presentation manager

26. _____ A graphics program that allows the user to create a series of previously created graphic images on the screen of a computer is a:

a. drawing program | c. painting program
b. dedicated charting manager | d. presentation program

27. _____ Software that allows a user to combine text with graphics to create documents such as newsletters is called a:
a. desktop publishing program
b. presentation manager
c. dedicated charting program
d. integrated charting program

28. _____ A type of pie chart that allows the user to pull one of the slices of the pie away from the pie for emphasis is called a:
a. emphasized pie chart
b. separated pie chart
c. imploded pie chart
d. exploding pie chart

29. _____ A special type of bar graph that uses bars that are divided to show how much each value of a category contributes to the whole is the:
a. stacked bar graph
b. percentage bar graph
c. 3-D bar graph
d. horizontal bar graph

CHAPTER 16

Microcomputer Data Communications

This chapter discusses the hardware and software needed for a microcomputer to send data to other devices such as printers and other computers. These devices may be directly attached to the microcomputer or remotely located in another building or even another part of the country. In this chapter you will learn to do the following:

1. Understand the different methods of transmitting data to peripheral devices attached to a microcomputer
2. Describe the difference between analog and digital signals and how a modem can translate signals from one type to another
3. List the three major functions performed by communication support software
4. Describe the three types of communication applications for which microcomputers are commonly used
5. Understand what a local-area network is and the functions it serves

Data Communication

The movement of data from one device to another is called **data communication.** The types of communication hardware and support software that are necessary to move that data depend primarily on the distance involved. To move data within the computer itself, or to and from peripherals within a radius of a hundred feet, the only hardware needed is a set of comparatively simple cables, and the only software needed is the standard operating system.

If the peripherals are several miles away, or across the country, a telecommunication network, such as the phone system of AT&T, must be used to move data. **Telecommunication** refers to the transmission of data over long distances. This task requires extensive communication hardware and communication software. However, data communication doesn't always occur over long distances. Recently, many organizations have realized the advantages of communicating data between microcomputers and shared peripherals within an office building. Such computer systems, called **local-area networks,** require a moderate amount of communication hardware and software. To develop an understanding of what sending and receiving data involves, let's look at the hardware and software required for these three types of data communication.

Communication with Peripheral Devices

A typical microcomputer system is attached to several peripheral devices that are used for input and output. Data is transmitted to and from devices such as monitors, disk drives, and printers. The connection of these devices to the microcomputer is usually accomplished using special kinds of cables (see Exhibit 16.1).

A printer cable links the CPU and the printer; similarly, most microcomputer systems also have a disk cable and a monitor cable. Let's look a little more closely at these cables.

The CPU uses digital signals to communicate 1s and 0s. Typically, high voltage represents a 1 and low voltage represents a 0. These data bits can be sent down the cable in a **serial** fashion, which means that one bit is sent after the other. Alternatively, data can be transmitted in a **parallel** fashion, in which the eight bits that represent a character are sent simultaneously on eight separate data paths. A cable containing eight separate wires is a common cable for a parallel data path. The outlet where the cable is plugged into the computer is called an **input/output (I/O) port.** The number of devices that can be connected to a computer is a function of the number of I/O ports.

Serial and parallel connections require different types of I/O ports. Typically, a microcomputer will contain both serial and parallel ports. For

Exhibit 16.1

Connecting Cables

Special cables are used as transmission media to send and receive data between the computer and its input and output devices.

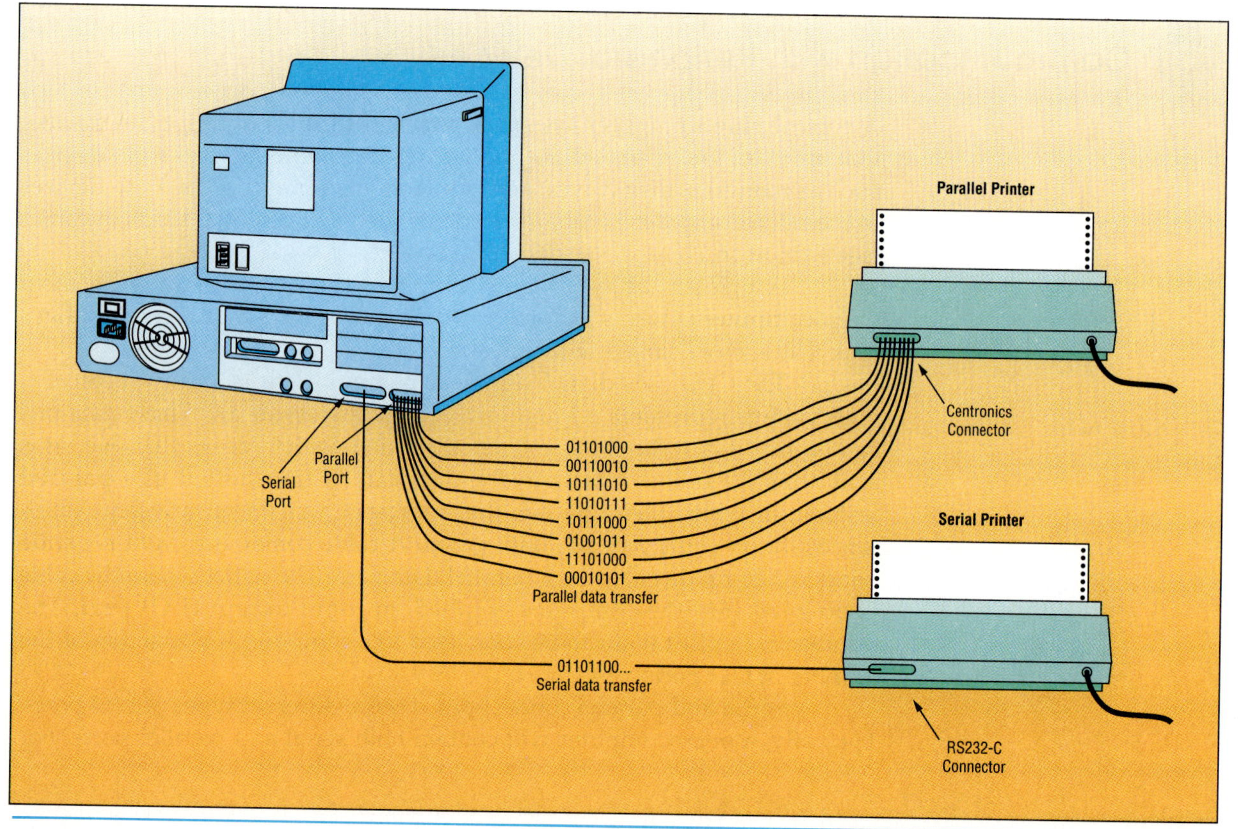

Exhibit 16.2

Serial and Parallel Data Transfer

In serial data transfer, the eight bits that make up a character are sent along a single data path one after the other. In parallel data transfer, all eight bits are sent down eight data paths simultaneously.

serial data transfer, the de facto standard is the RS232-C (recommended standard number 232, version C). It was developed by the Electronics Industries Association. The parallel standard is based on the connection used on the commercially successful Centronics printer, which popularized this approach to data transfer. Parallel ports are typically used for connecting printers to a microcomputer and serial ports are commonly used to connect modems, mice, and serial printers to the microcomputer (see Exhibit 16.2).

Telecommunication

The preceding section explains data communication in stand-alone computer systems with local peripherals. But how can data be transmitted to and from remote computers located in different buildings or in other regions of the country? Telecommunication, the transmission of data over long distances, is needed for these tasks. Conceptually, telecommunication uses the same principles as local data communication. The cables used for local communication, however, are not effective for long distances.

There are two basic limitations to cables. First, there is a limit to the distance that data can be transferred over a cable, due to loss of signal strength. The electrons moving down the cable meet resistance, similar to friction, which causes the signal to diminish. In addition, there is background noise in the cable and its surrounding environment. The signal strength has to be loud enough to be differentiated from the noise. Just as in talking to someone in a noisy restaurant you have to talk more loudly to be heard above the din, for distances greater than several hundred feet *repeaters* are needed to amplify the electronic signal to overcome electrical resistance and background noise. The second problem is finding a physical place for all those cables as more computers are added to the system.

One way to avoid this tangle is to use the current primary means of remote voice communication—the telephone system. It is, after all, in place and working very well in North America. Since almost every workplace and home has a telephone, electronically connecting one location to another is as simple as dialing the appropriate phone number and connecting the appropriate type of interface unit to the telephone and the computer. However, there is one major problem with using this system. The telephone network, as invented and first built in the early 1900s, was designed for voice communication, not for data communication. It is, in fact, slow and inefficient for transmitting data. To overcome these disadvantages, telecommunication now uses microwave communication channels, either land-based or satellite.

Communication Hardware

The primary medium for telecommunication is the phone system. The telephone lines for the phone system serve as the cables connecting two devices. However, since the phone system is primarily designed to carry voice communication rather than data communication, special hardware is needed to adapt the signals sent and received by computers to travel over the phone lines. The signals transmitted over the phone system are primarily analog signals. **Analog signals** are continuous wave patterns that are varied in frequency or amplitude to convey information.

The human voice is made up of complex sound patterns that are combinations of sound waves of different frequencies. Like the music on a stereo, these patterns are composed of low frequency (bass) and high frequency (treble) sound waves. In addition to different frequencies, sound waves have varying amplitudes, or heights, which we hear as loud and soft sounds (see Exhibit 16.3).

In contrast to the analog networks that have been designed for transporting voice information, recent digital networks have been designed to transport computer data. To understand the need for these networks, recall that computers are binary machines that use either on/off or high/low states to process data and instructions. **Digital signals** use a pattern of discrete high or low amplitude pulses to convey information.

A special device called a **modem** is used to translate the digital signals of the computer into the analog signals transmitted over phone

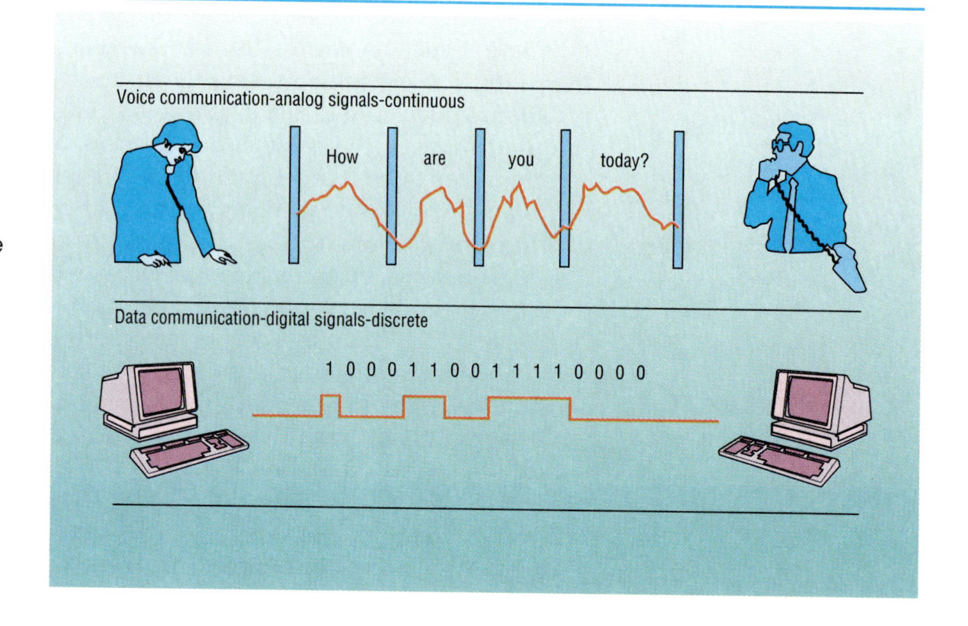

Exhibit 16.3

Voice and Data Communication Differences

Spoken words are continuous analog wave patterns. In contrast, computers communicate data by the user of discrete digital signals.

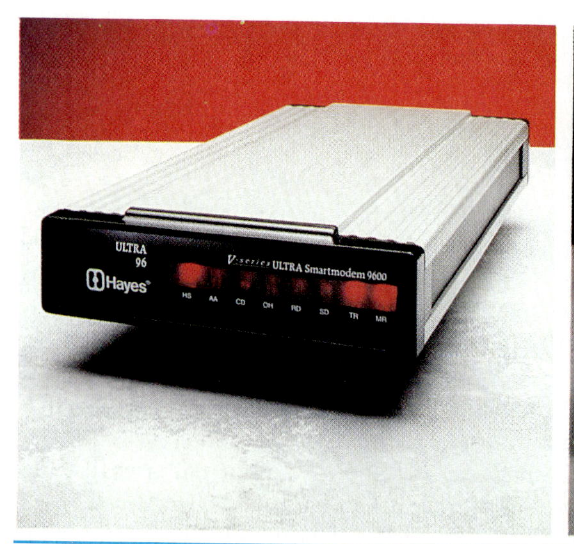

Exhibit 16.4

Types of Modems

An external modem connects to the computer via a cable (left). The internal modem (right) is placed directly inside the computer.

lines. At the other end of the phone line, another modem is used to convert the received analog signal back into the digital signal needed by the computer receiving the transmission (see Exhibit 16.4). The process of changing digital signals to analog is known as *modulation,* and changing analog back to digital is called *demodulation*. The term *modem* is an abbreviation for MOdulation/DEModulation.

When two computers communicate over phone lines, each computer must have a modem. The transmitting computer sends a digital signal to its modem, which converts the signal to analog and puts it out on the phone line. The modem attached to the receiving computer takes the analog signal from the phone line, converts it back to digital, and passes the signal on to the receiving computer (see Exhibit 16.5).

There are two basic types of modems: external and internal. An **external modem** is connected to the microcomputer via a cable attached to a serial port. An **internal modem** comes on a printed circuit board that is placed directly inside the microcomputer, thus eliminating the need for a cable between the computer and the modem. Both types of modems have modular phone jacks to attach the modem to the phone line the same way a phone is attached to the phone line. Internal modems create a much simpler connection to the phone line; external modems are more portable.

The performance of both internal and external modems is measured in terms of their speed of transmission. The amount of information, in bits per second (bps), that a modem can transmit is the most common measure of performance. In a way, this measure of capacity is similar to the capacity of a pipe carrying water. The capacity of a pipe is measured in the number of gallons of water than can flow through the pipe in a minute. Generally, pipes with a larger diameter can carry more water in a given period of time. The carrying capacity of a modem is measured in the number of bits a modem can pass in one second. For example, a speed of 300 bps means that 300 data bits could be transmitted each second. Most modems can transmit 1200 or 2400 bps. Newer modems can reach speeds of 9600 bps.

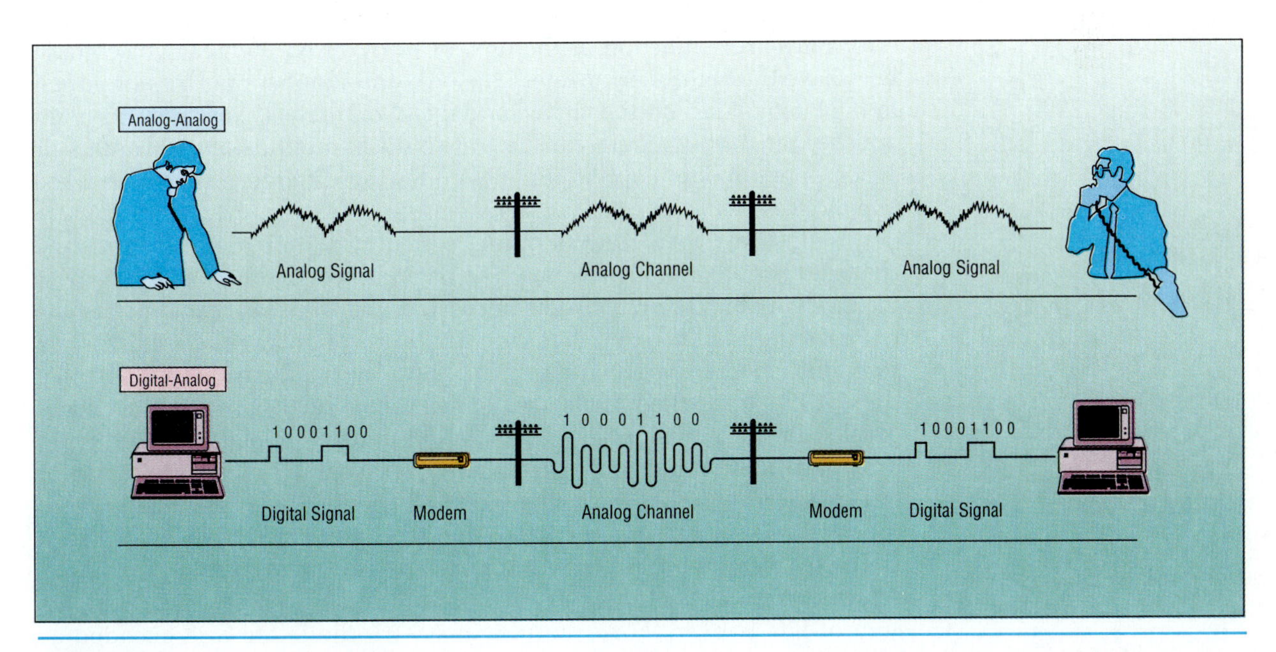

Exhibit 16.5

Voice and Data Communication

Communication Support Software

Now that the hardware considerations involved in data communication have been examined, let's look at the role communication support software plays. This section discusses three of the major functions that **communication support software (CSS)** must provide to accomplish the sending and receiving of information to remote computers: protocols, error detection and correction, and security.

The first function of the CSS is to handle a protocol. A **protocol** is a set of rules and procedures used for transmitting data between two computers. When computers communicate, characters are sent as a series of bits along the communication line. When this stream of bits is sent, there must be some way for the group of bits representing one character to be separated from the next group of bits. To accomplish this, the transmitting computer usually surrounds the group of bits with a start bit and a stop bit. A **start bit** is the bit at the beginning of the group that signals the start of the group. A **stop bit** is another bit, at the end of the group, that marks the end of the group.

In addition to start and stop bits, error check bits are also added to accomplish the second function of the CSS: error detection and correction. The start, stop, and error check bits, along with the bits that represent the character being transmitted, form a unit known as a **data packet.** It is these data packets that are sent between the computers during data communication. The use of error check bits for detecting errors in data transmission was discussed earlier. When the CSS detects an error using the error check bits, it responds with a signal to the sending computer to retransmit the complete message. This form of error control ensures a high accuracy rate, but can require a significant amount of retransmission. The error rates are a function of the type of media used. Regular voice-grade lines have the highest error rates. The type and number of extra bits added to the bits making up the character depend on the way in which the data will be transmitted. Data can be transmitted in either asynchronous or synchronous mode. Exhibit 16.6 illustrates the differences between these two modes.

In the **asynchronous mode,** sometimes abbreviated **async,** one character is transmitted at a time. The data packet contains a start bit to let the receiving unit know that a character is to follow; it also contains the bits representing the encoded character. The most popular code used in data communication is the seven-bit ASCII. Next comes an error check bit and a stop bit. The error check bit is used to make sure the data received were not garbled during transmission. The stop bit is used to signal the receiving unit that the complete character has been sent. This simple mode of transmission is used only for single-point-to-single-point transmission.

In asynchronous transmission, the commonly used error check method is a parity bit. A **parity bit** is an extra bit that makes the sum of bits representing a character either even or odd. In an even parity system, the sum of bits is even. For example, in ASCII, the letter *G* is encoded as 1000111. Since the number of 1s is already an even number (4), the eighth bit is a 0 to give 10001110. Although the parity bit scheme cannot catch all

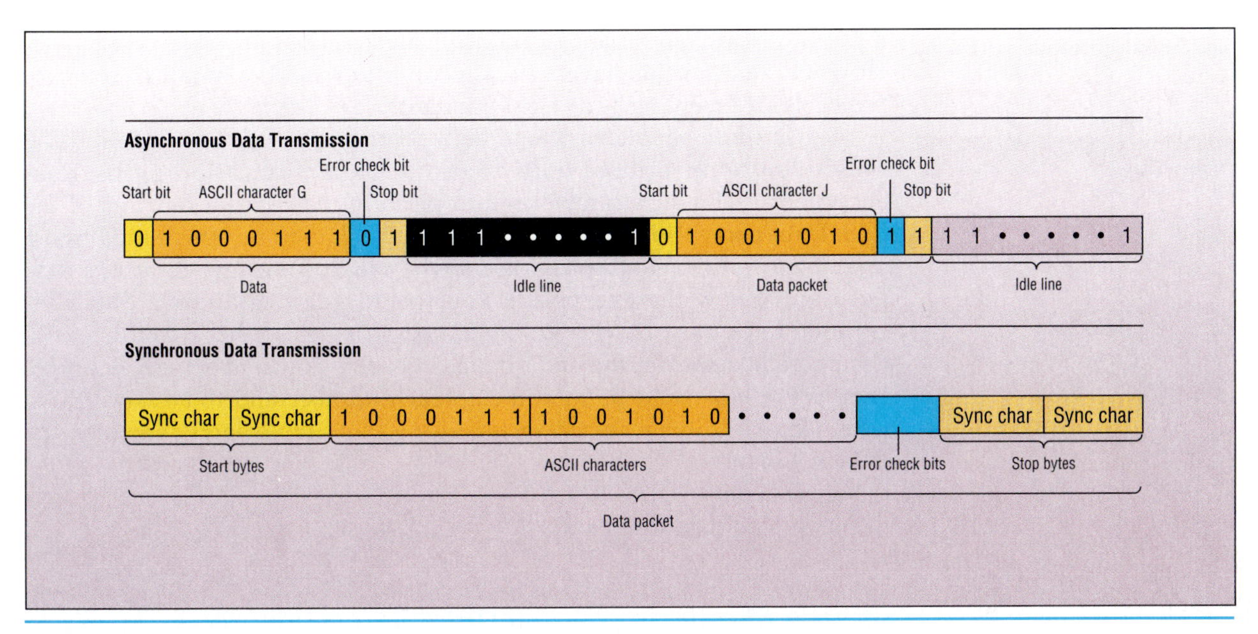

Exhibit 16.6

Asynchronous and Synchronous Data Transmission

In asynchronous data transmission, individual characters are sent. In synchronous data transmission, blocks of characters are sent.

errors, such as some double errors, its ability to catch most transmission errors has made it a standard feature.

The net result of adding start, stop, and error check bits is that each data packet contains ten bits to transmit a single character via asynchronous transmission. Thus, a 1200 bps modem would be able to send about 120 characters each second. Asynchronous transmission is especially appropriate for low-speed data communication, such as a person communicating with a microcomputer. When compared to a computer, most people are relatively slow to enter data and respond.

The **synchronous** or **sync mode** of data transmission is used when large volumes of data are to be sent and speeds of thousands of characters per second are needed. In the synchronous mode, a block of hundreds of characters is sent in the data packet rather than one character at a time. Each block is preceded by a sync byte or bytes to signal the start of the message, and is followed by an error check code and an ending sync byte or bytes. In synchronous transmission, a complex algorithm calculates a number by placing a different weight on each bit. This number is then compared before and after transmission. Through this method, almost all transmission errors can be detected.

The synchronous mode might be used when the contents of a file are to be sent from a central computing facility to a remote site for printing. The obvious advantage of this mode is its speed and the consequent reduced transmission costs. Its disadvantages are the complexity and expense of the timing devices needed to synchronize transmission.

In general, a protocol determines what format the data packet will take, how error check bits will be used to detect errors, and what must be done when errors are detected. Unfortunately, there are many different protocols in use today, with no universally accepted standard. Consequently, it is not always possible to communicate between any two computers. However, as in other facets of the computer field, a small number of protocols are emerging as de facto standards.

In those situations where high security is needed for transmitting sensitive organizational data across telecommunication paths, data encryption techniques can be used to perform the security function of the CSS. **Data encryption** techniques convert the data to be transmitted into a scrambled form. Unauthorized users who might somehow get to the data but don't know the encryption key would get meaningless data. Encryption keys must be very sophisticated schemes so they can't be easily deciphered. However, the underlying concept is not complicated. A simple encryption key could be to add 3 to each number and to advance three letters for each alphabetic character. Using this simple encryption key, the data would appear as shown:

the original data	5 A T	6 1 1
the encrypted data	8 D W	9 4 4

Using a Microcomputer in Data Communication

A major use of the microcomputer has been as a personal computer. That is, a person at home or at work does his or her computing tasks on a stand-alone machine. As users become more sophisticated in their use of personal computers, they sometimes want to connect their computers to larger computers for special applications or to other microcomputers to exchange data. To facilitate this, data communication equipment such as a modem and communication support software are added, allowing the microcomputer to communicate with other computers in addition to doing stand-alone computing. In this section three applications for microcomputers equipped for data communication are described: terminal emulation, file transfer, and accessing information utilities.

Terminal Emulation

A microcomputer can be used to access a remote mainframe computer and to act like a terminal of that mainframe computer. This process, called **terminal emulation**, involves altering the characteristics of the microcomputer so that it will mimic a terminal attached to the remote mainframe (often called the **host computer**). Terminals used with different host computers often have different keyboards and communicate with the host in different ways.

When a key is pressed on the keyboard of a terminal, a particular code is sent to the host computer, which then translates the code into the appropriate character. Different host computers use different coding schemes for their keyboards. Certain types of communication support software allow the user to alter the codes sent to the host when certain keys are pressed on the keyboard. When the microcomputer is altered to send the same codes normally sent by a terminal, the host computer cannot tell the difference between the microcomputer and a normal terminal. In addition, different host computers have specific communication protocols that are used by the terminals attached to them. The host computer expects its terminals to follow certain rules when sending data, such as the speed with which data can be sent (bps) and the type of parity used (odd, even, or none). Also important in terminal emulation is whether the direction of the communication is to be one-way or two-way. The possible directions include simplex, half-duplex, and full-duplex (see Exhibit 16.7).

A **simplex channel** can transmit data in only one direction. Although this is the cheapest mode, it has very limited use in data communication applications. However, it is now starting to be used in certain types of local-area networks, which are discussed later in this chapter.

A **half-duplex channel** can transmit data in either direction, but only one way at a time. This is the most common mode used for data communication between a user at a terminal and the CPU. The user types in data, which are transmitted over the communication channel to the CPU. The CPU processes the data and then uses the same channel to respond to the user at the terminal.

A **full-duplex channel** allows data to be transmitted in both directions simultaneously. This is analogous to trucks carrying goods in

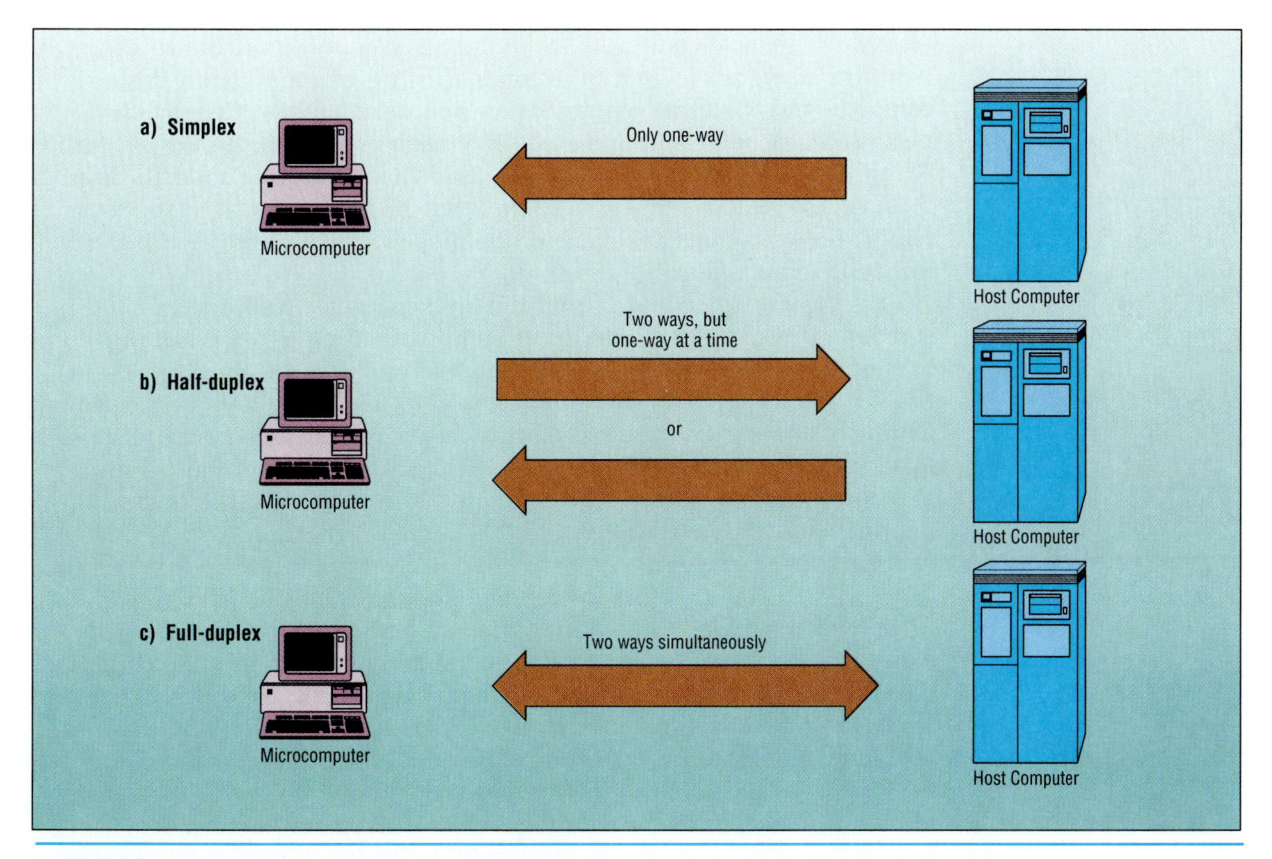

Exhibit 16.7

Three Common Types of Communication Channels

(a) Simplex; (b) Half-duplex; (c) Full-duplex

both directions on a two-lane highway. For high-speed communication between computers and peripherals or computers and computers, this communication method is necessary.

File Transfer

As end-user computing grows, more business professionals are finding they wish to manipulate more data. Often this data is already in electronic form but stored on another computer system. Rather than enter this data again, it would be much more efficient if the data could be transferred from one system to another. The solution to this need is communication support software that allows **file transfer**, the electronic transfer of data files from one computer to another across the phone lines.

When two computers exchange files, both computers must use communication support software that uses the same protocol. When the file transfer is performed between a microcomputer and a remote mainframe computer, the microcomputer is often referred to as the **local computer** and the mainframe is usually called the host computer. In this situation, the user begins by starting the communication support software on the microcomputer and using it to access the host computer. Once on the host computer, the user starts the communication support software located on the host computer. When the two computers are linked in this way, the user can switch between executing commands on the host computer and executing commands on the local computer. Commands are then used to send files from the local microcomputer to the host computer. This process is known as **uploading** a file. When uploading a file, the user must tell the local computer the name of the file to be transferred and must tell the host computer the name of the new file to be created to hold the incoming information.

When files are sent from the host computer to the local microcomputer, the process is referred to as **downloading** a file. When downloading a file, the user must tell the host computer what file is to be sent and tell the local microcomputer the name of the new file to be created. During a file transfer, the user instructs the computer (host or local) that is to send the file to begin transmitting the file. Then the user must instruct the other computer (local or host) to begin receiving the incoming information. Exhibit 16.8 illustrates this approach using the downloading of a file as an example.

Another important consideration that enters into the transfer of files is the type of file that is to be sent. Communication programs usually make a distinction between two types of files: text and binary. A text file contains data in the form of characters and can therefore be displayed directly on the screen or printed to a printer. Some word processors and the editors in most operating systems store data in this format. A binary file contains data in the form of 0s and 1s (binary). This data cannot be displayed on the screen or printed directly from the file. Most software programs are in binary form, so that they can be executed more quickly by the microcomputer. The arrangement of bits to form characters in these two file types is different. Text files typically use a parity bit, and binary files do not. Because of this difference, the data in these two types of files must be transmitted

Exhibit 16.8

Downloading a File with the KERMIT Communication Program

(a) After using the microcomputer version of KERMIT to access the host computer (in this case a VAX), the user starts the KERMIT software on the host computer. Once in KERMIT on the host computer, the user issues a SEND command, naming the file to be sent from the host computer.

```
VMS Kermit-32 version 3.3.111
Default terminal for transfers is: _LTA81:
Kermit-32>SEND REMOTE.FILE

Esc-chr: ^]  help: ^]?  port:1 speed: 1200 parity:none echo:rem  VT102 ....
```

(b) The user then issues a command to return to the copy of KERMIT running on the microcomputer. There the user issues a RECEIVE command naming the local file to be created to hold the file arriving from the host.

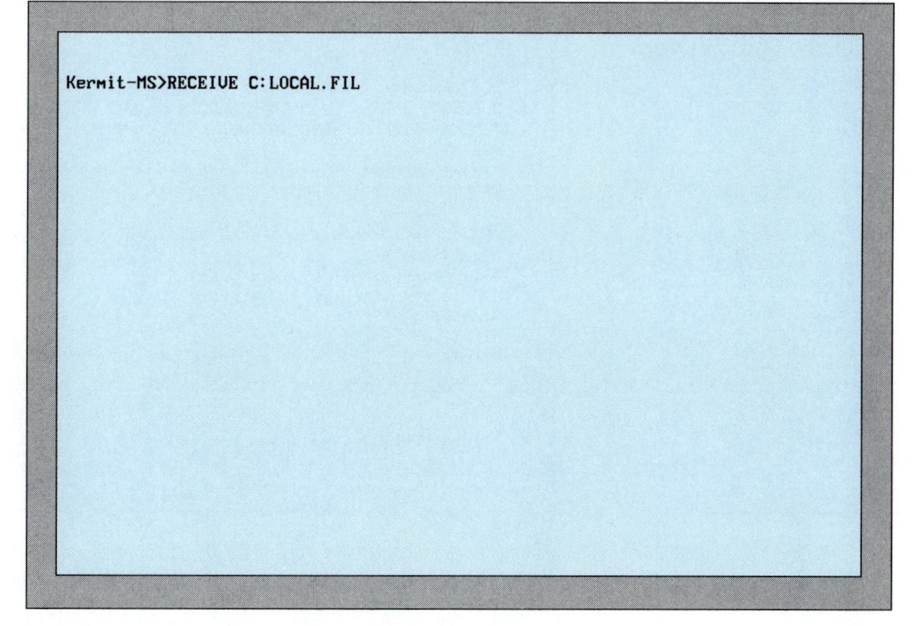

differently. Thus, to transmit a file properly, the communication program must be told which type of file is being transmitted.

Accessing Information Utilities

Increasingly, end-users are given the opportunity to communicate with other computer systems that provide information of various kinds. An **electronic bulletin board**, in which users can leave messages, information,

(c) Once the file transfer starts, the microcomputer screen displays the status of the transfer. As each packet arrives at the microcomputer, it is counted and its size is displayed.

```
        Kermit-MS: V2.30  8 Jan 1988

        File name: REMOTE.FILE  as  C:LOCAL.FIL
KBytes transferred: 2

        Receiving: Completed

Number of packets: 28
    Packet length: 4
Number of retries: 1
       Last error: None
     Last warning: None
```

Exhibit 16.9

A Bulletin Board System

```
PLEASE MAKE LIBERAL USE OF THE HELP OPTIONS AVAILABLE ON THIS
BULLETIN BOARD.  YOU CAN SELECT "H" FOR HELP AT VIRTUALLY ANY
TIME BY SIMPLY PRESSING THE "H" KEY AND THEN PRESSING THE RETURN
(OR ENTER) KEY.
****************************************************************
CHANNEL-ONE MAIN MENU

A ? at any prompt gives more HELP.
N) ews Center
M) essage system  ( 0 new ones)
F) ile transfer   ( 0 new ones)
P) rofile
O) ptions
S) ystem description & ordering
H) elp!  (or use H x, where x=letter)
G) OODBYE

Please [Enter] your selection :
```

and even useful programs for one another, is often established on a microcomputer running special software. The microcomputer is linked to a phone line with a modem and is capable of answering incoming calls automatically. A microcomputer with a communication program can call the microcomputer with the bulletin board. The user can read the messages and transfer the programs from the bulletin board's microcomputer to his or her own computer. The only cost for accessing a bulletin board is the charge for the phone call. Exhibit 16.9 shows a screen from a bulletin-board

Exhibit 16.10

The CompuServe Information Utility

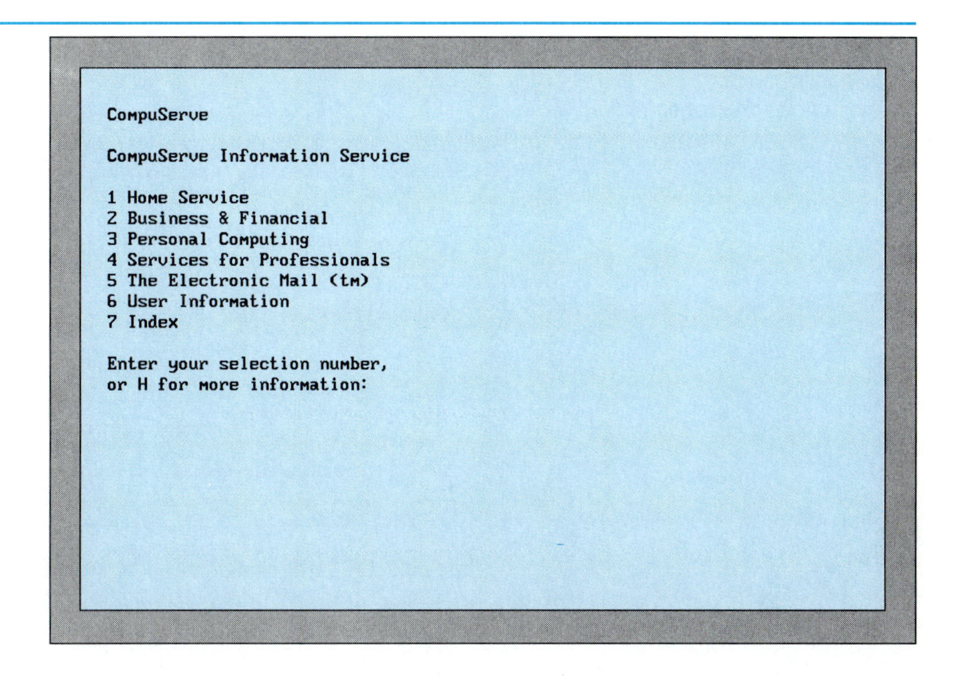

system from which instructors can get information about topics related to the teaching of computer information system courses.

Some specialized mainframe computers are operated by *information utility companies*. These companies sell access to information databases to users. Three of the largest information utilities are The Source, Dow Jones News/Retrieval Service, and CompuServe. Users are charged a fee to subscribe to the system and for the amount of time they are connected to the system over a communication line. These utilities provide users access to large databases containing information on such things as the stock market, encyclopedias, and abstracts from journals and magazines. Exhibit 16.10 shows a screen containing the services provided by CompuServe.

Choosing a Communication Program

In this section, some of the common features provided by communication programs available for microcomputers are discussed and a comparison of some of the current products available is presented.

Exhibit 16.11 shows screens from the PFS: First Choice and Crosstalk XVI communication programs. This exhibit illustrates the similarity of the type of features common in most communication programs. Typically, the program allows you to specify the telephone number you want the modem to dial in order to reach the computer you wish to communicate with. Many of the options discussed in this chapter (speed, stop bits, parity, and type of channel) can be controlled by the user. The automatic sign-on option in the exhibit refers to a common feature of most communication programs. A user can save a group of

Exhibit 16.11

Two Popular Communication Programs

(a) A screen from the PFS: First Choice communication program

```
Service Information

Service name: Dow Jones News
Phone number:
Create automatic sign-on (Y/N): N

Communication speed: 1200
Data bits (7 or 8): 8
Stop bits (1 or 2): 1
Parity (none,even,odd,mark,space): NONE
Full or half duplex (F/H): F
Use XON/XOFF (Y/N): Y
Terminal type (none,VT52,VT100): NONE

Esc to cancel                          ↵ to continue
```

(b) A screen from the Crosstalk XVI communication program

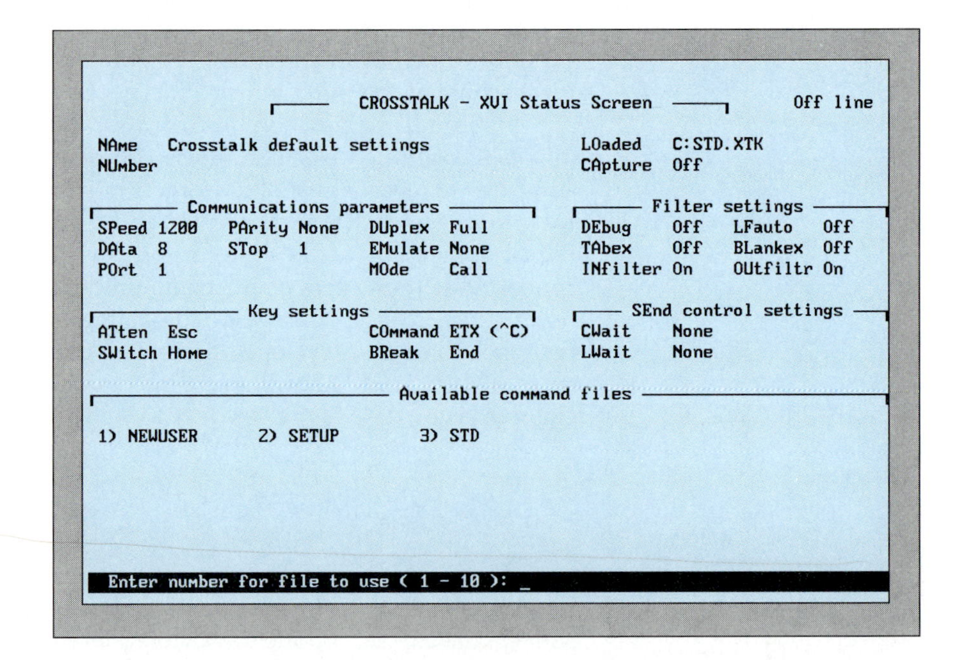

communications settings in a file and have the communication program use the contents of that file to dial the remote computer using the specified parameters. In this way, the user does not have to set all the options each time a connection with that remote computer is desired. Some communication programs also offer the capability to construct a listing of phone numbers so that a particular number can be simply highlighted and then called. There is sometimes the option to have the communication

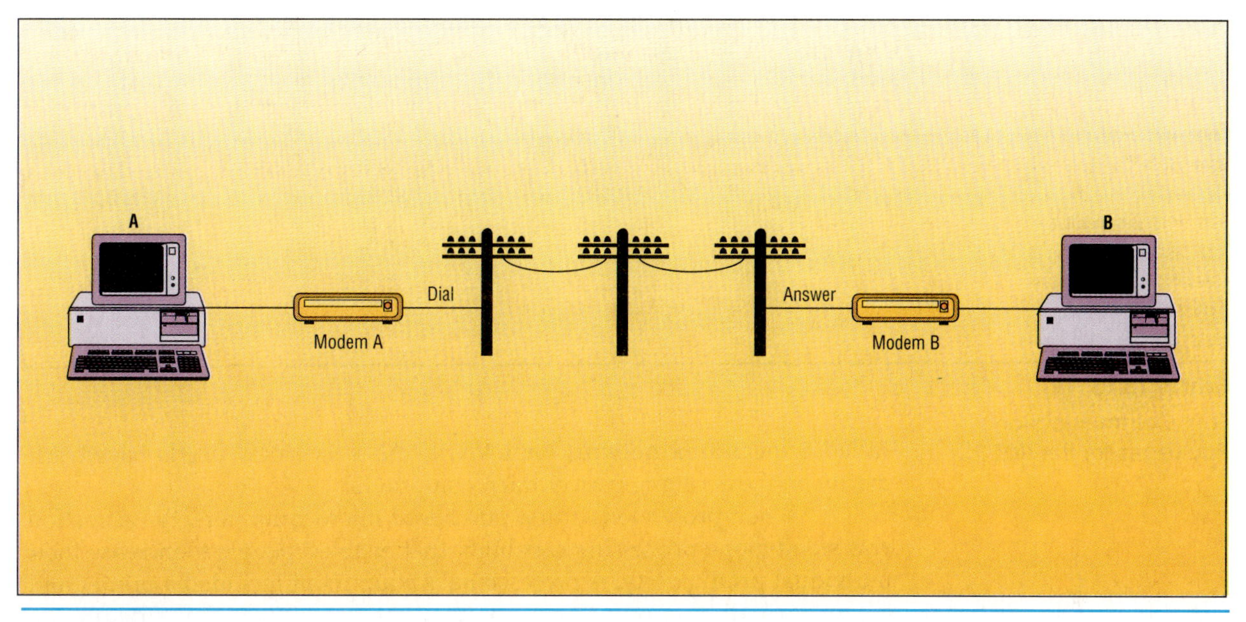

Exhibit 16.12

Transferring Files Between Microcomputers

If microcomputer A wishes to connect with microcomputer B, it must use a communication program to instruct its modem (A) to dial the number of microcomputer B. Microcomputer B's modem must be turned on and set up to answer the phone using a communication program running on microcomputer B.

program redial the number until a correction is made, in the event the number being dialed is busy. Communication programs also allow the user to set up the microcomputer to receive incoming calls. With this feature, the user leaves the microcomputer turned on, with the communication program waiting for a call. When another computer places an incoming call, the program causes the modem to answer the call and establish a connection with the calling computer. Exhibit 16.12 illustrates the use of a communication program to connect two microcomputers.

Now that you are familiar with some of the general functions and characteristics of communication programs, you have a basis for determining how well a particular communication program meets a user's needs. Exhibit 16.13 compares four of the programs currently available for microcomputers. There are also similar communication packages available for Macintosh computers. This exhibit shows the amount of primary memory required to run the communication software and the lowest and highest speed (in bits per second) the program can handle. The number of terminal emulations and protocols the communication package supports is also shown. In addition, the exhibit shows if the package supports a directory of phone numbers, automatic redialing of numbers, and a help facility.

Local-Area Networks

An emerging form of data communication that is bypassing the telephone network can be found within the business office itself. A system of electronic pathways that connects various communication devices is called a network. When a network is confined to a building or office complex, it is

	Crosstalk Mark 4	Freeway Advanced	Procomm	Smartcom III
Minimum RAM	256K	300K	130K	512K
Lowest BPS	110	75	300	110
Highest BPS	115200	115200	19200	115200
Terminal Emulations	13	3	11	3
Protocols Supported	8	6	8	4
Telephone Directory	Y	Y	Y	Y
Automatic Redial	Y	Y	Y	Y
Help Facility	Y	Y	Y	Y

Exhibit 16.13

Four Communication Packages for the IBM PC

called a **local-area network** or **LAN.** LANs serve new needs based primarily on the evolving uses of microcomputers.

When professionals first purchased microcomputers, the attraction was stand-alone processing capability that enabled people to increase their individual productivity. A professional's equipment included a printer and often hard disk capability as well. With more and more people in organizations wanting their own microcomputers, it became evident that it was too costly to equip each user with a printer and hard disk capability. Ways of sharing expensive peripherals were explored.

As more users got their own microcomputers, they wanted to share data and information electronically. Instead of using word processing software to write a memo on a microcomputer and a printer to produce hard copy output to send through office mail, why not just send a message electronically to the appropriate microcomputer? A co-worker could then read the memo and send a response electronically. This process is called **electronic mail (E-mail).**

In addition, users realized the advantages of allowing only authorized access to important data files stored on other microcomputers. For example, assume the company accountant had developed confidential earnings files and stored them in the hard disks of his or her microcomputer. They could be off-limits to others while still allowing the vice president of finance to electronically transfer a copy of that data to his or her microcomputer's hard disk. The data could then be used as input to an electronic spreadsheet for use in future planning.

Microcomputer users also realized they needed access to the database held in the company's main computer, which might be a mainframe computer. If those data could be downloaded to microcomputers, users could be sure they were using the latest information in preparing accurate reports and projections. Once this link was established, the next step in the process would be to provide the means for downloading software programs.

Another emerging objective in many organizations is the connection of computer equipment manufactured by different vendors. As organizations purchased microcomputer equipment during the late 1970s and 1980s, different departments often bought different kinds of computer systems. Department A got IBM PCs, Department B went with

Macintoshes, and Department C acquired Sun workstations. As long as microcomputers were used as stand-alone units, this wasn't a major problem. However, once organizations needed to share resources or information electronically, the realization that computers from different vendors weren't compatible caused significant problems. In theory, LANs can overcome these incompatibility problems. So far, though, there has been limited success in connecting highly different computer systems.

The future importance of LANs becomes clearer in light of studies that show 70 to 80 percent of an organization's communication takes place within a local area. Most of that communication now occurs through written correspondence (interoffice mail) or voice conversation (intercom telephone network or face-to-face meetings). The projection is that LANs will replace most written and voice communication within an organization and open exciting new ways of exchanging ideas.

Topology

The term **topology** refers to the patterns formed when hardware devices are connected to form a network. The three most common network topologies used with LANs are the star, the bus, and the ring. Exhibit 16.14 shows each of these topologies.

In the **star network topology,** each device is connected to a central unit. Any communication between one device and another goes through the central unit. The exhibit shows a typical configuration using microcomputers and peripherals. Each device is directly connected to the central communications controller, which is a microcomputer containing the interface cards and software to manage all data communication in this network. If a user at microcomputer PC 2 wants to print out a memo on the letter-quality printer, microcomputer PC 2 sends that request to the network controller. This central controller notifies microcomputer PC 2 when that task is complete.

In the **bus network topology,** each device is connected to a common cable. Each component must have its own interface device, usually a circuit board or card, which plugs into one of the expansion slots. The card contains the hardware and software necessary to access the network. All communication takes place on the common cable or bus. The data are sent down the bus and are available to all devices. Each message must contain information identifying the destination device.

In the **ring network topology,** each terminal is connected to two others, forming a circle or ring. All communication between terminals follows a clockwise or counterclockwise pattern. The message goes from terminal to terminal until the designated device is reached. The star network topology is the least costly, but also is limited in flexibility, capacity, and growth possibilities. The bus network gives the most flexibility, capacity, and growth possibilities, but is the most costly. The ring topology is a compromise solution, since it provides more flexibility, capacity, and growth than the star topology and is less expensive than a bus network.

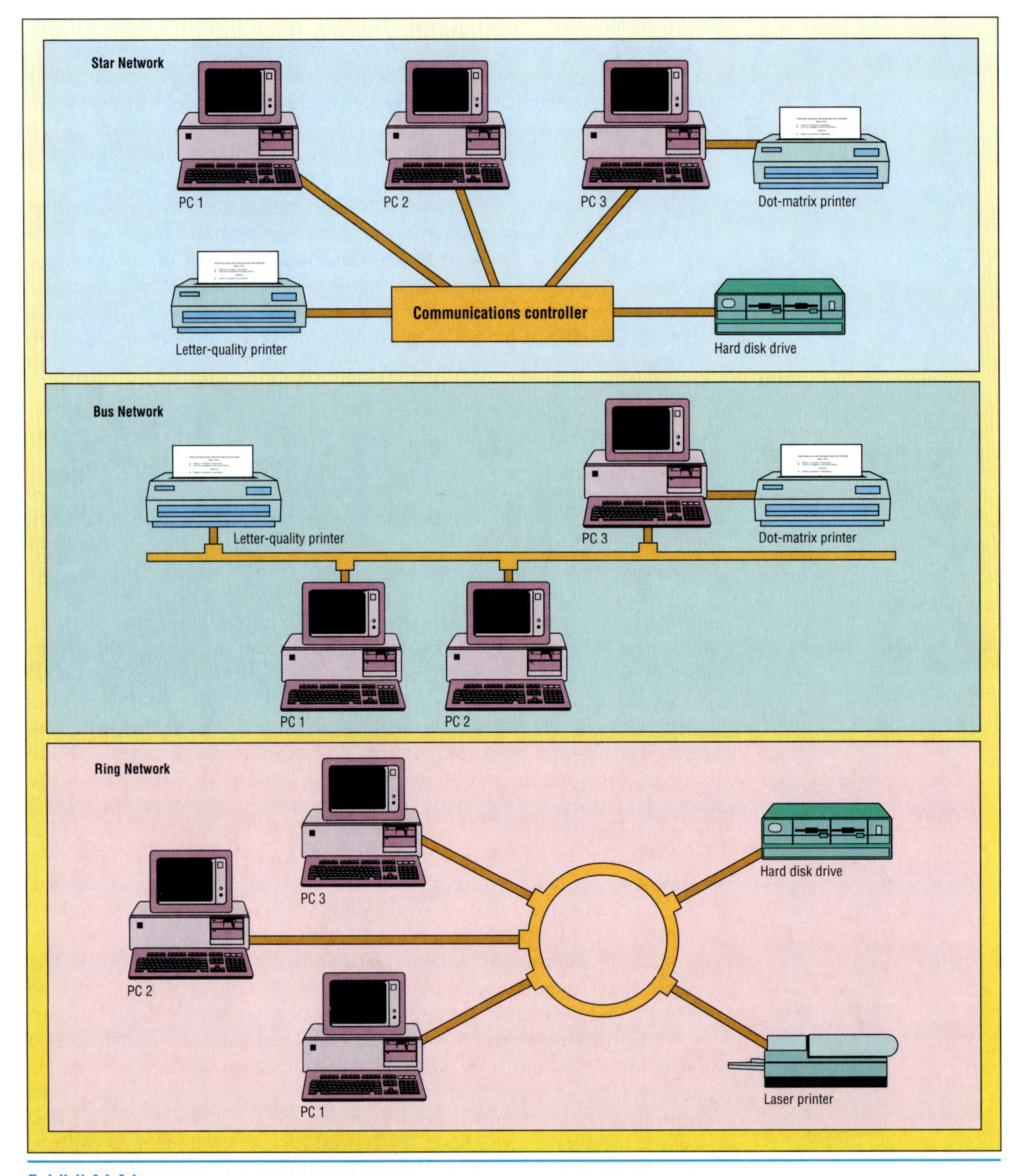

Exhibit 16.14

Three Common Network Topologies

Network Cables

Several different types of wires or cables can be used to connect devices in a network to form a data path. The most common are twisted pairs, coaxial cable, and coaxial for television (CATV) (see Exhibit 16.15).

Twisted pair wiring is the typical telephone cable used in your house. It is two individual copper wires twisted together to give the cable physical strength. It is relatively cheap and has low installation and maintenance costs. A major disadvantage of twisted pair wiring for LAN, however, is that it is highly susceptible to electrical interference from within and outside the network. For better immunity to interference, shielded twisted pair wiring is available at a slightly higher cost.

Coaxial cable is the most common transmission medium for LAN. Its major advantage is that it is sturdy enough to be laid in place as is. It doesn't require wiring conduits or mechanical support elements as does twisted pair wiring. Thus, coaxial cable saves on installation cost and gives greater configuration flexibility. Because of its inherent construction, it has greater shielding, which makes possible much lower error rates. It costs about twice as much as unshielded twisted pair wire.

A type of cable, **CATV**, used with cable television service has been designed to accommodate fifty television channels. It is an attractive transmission medium for LAN because it can easily accommodate not only data, but also voice, images, and video.

Exhibit 16.15

Transmission Cable Media

Wires or cables are used to connect devices in a network to form a data path. The most common types are shown here: shielded twisted pairs (top left); coaxial cable (top right); coaxial cable for CATV (bottom left); and shielded internal twisted pairs (bottom right).

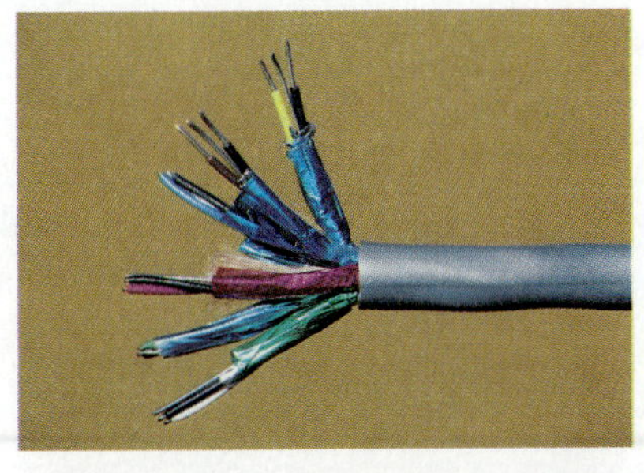

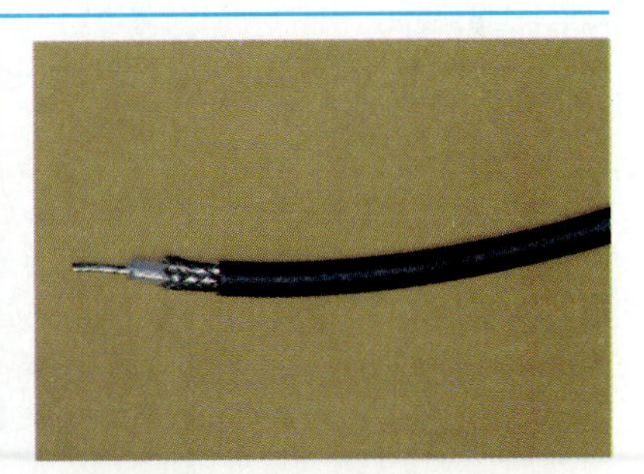

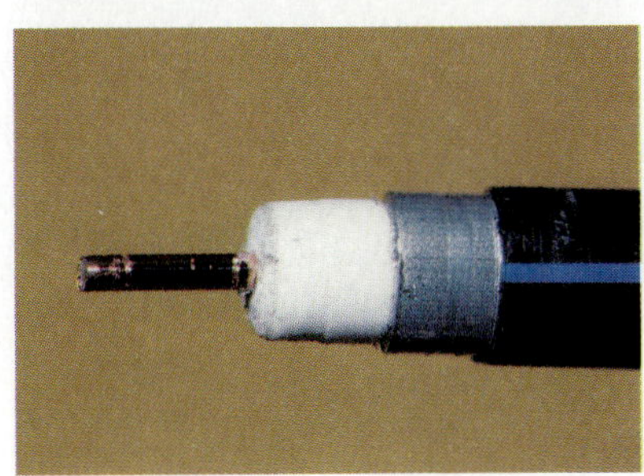

Network Management Software

In order to share peripheral devices and allow different computers on the network to communicate, network management software is required to oversee the network. Typically, the network management software runs on a special computer attached to the network, known as a **server**. A server provides various services to the members of the network. The network management software keeps track of the devices on the network by assigning an identifying address to each device. Data packets sent across the network are addressed to a specific device so that other devices will know the information is not for them to receive. The network management software also allows the user to have access to hard disk space and can divide up that space between private space assigned to only one device and public space accessible to a group of devices. When several devices send information to a common printer, the network management software controls the sequence of print requests. Many other functions are provided by network management software, including options that let a network manager monitor traffic on the network and adjust parameters to keep the traffic moving smoothly. Exhibit 16.16 shows a screen from the Novell Advanced Netware network operating system.

Exhibit 16.16

A Screen From the Novell NetWare System Configuration Utility

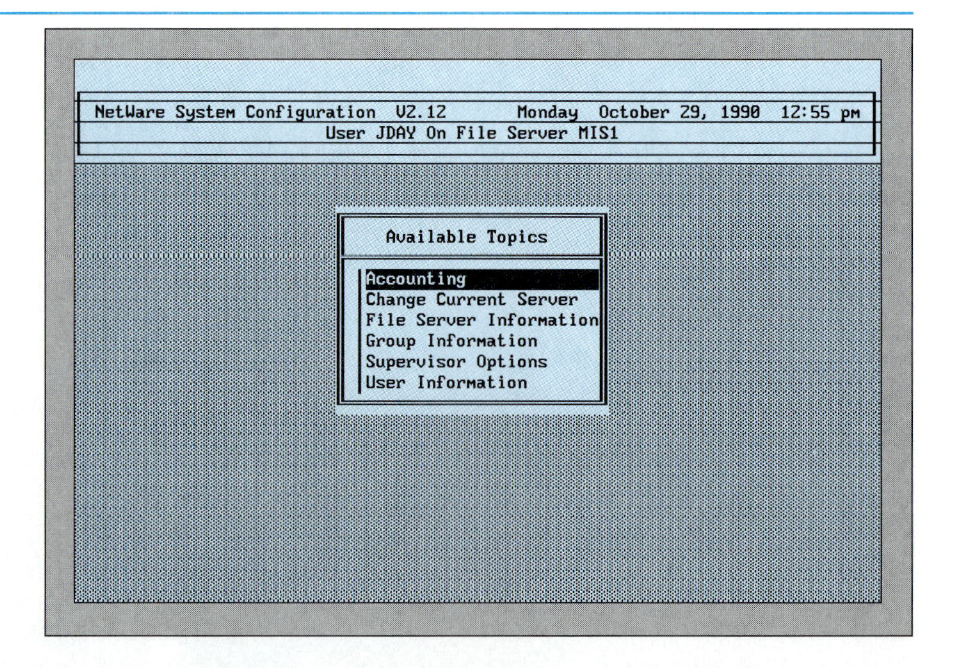

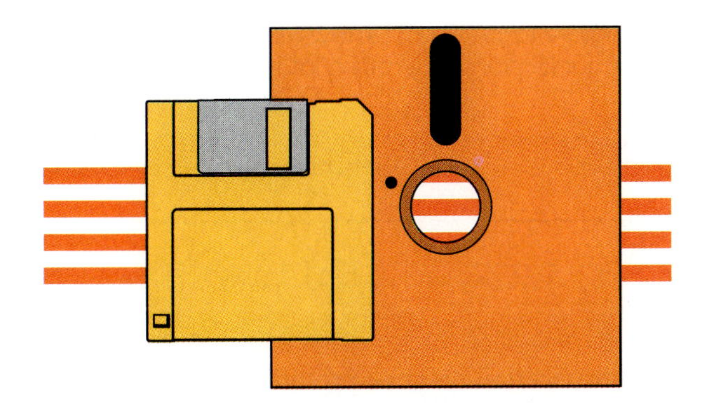

Computers at Work

Companies Improving Operations with Remote Software

A number of vendors have shipped products in the relatively new category of "remote communications software," or software that allows one PC to control another at a remote location. The first users of such software were technical support departments because it allowed users to demonstrate to support-personnel exactly what keystrokes they were typing and the system responses they were getting.

Although technical support remains an important function of remote communications software, some companies are gravitating toward such products for another reason—they hope to use them to improve customer service and internal operations.

The capacity to download files and access data from a host computer often takes a backseat to the more popular technical support functions of remote communications. In reality, file downloading and data access are often the primary features many firms use to help strengthen their lines of communication.

Before using remote communications software, Realty World Sterling, an Albuquerque, New Mexico, real estate firm, was dependent on the mail service or telephone lines to communicate with its bank. Questions relating to interest rates or a client's loan status could take days to answer.

Today telephone tag is a thing of the past. The bank downloads interest rate and qualification data to the company's PC every day. The company can also access the bank's computer for additional data. An employee can answer questions regarding loans quickly and with confidence. "I don't have to spend all of my time calling the bank," he said. "I see (remote communications software) as a necessity."

The door-to-door beauty and cosmetics company Avon Products Corporation of Rye, New York, also values remote communications. "We eventually want all of our district sales and division managers to be set up with systems running remote software," said Kevin Vessio, programmer analyst for Avon.

Avon will soon allow its managers to dial into headquarters to receive updated sales information. "Once set up, (remote communications) will definitely increase our efficiency," said Vessio.

Another company concerned with efficiency, as well as speed, is the Michelin Tire Co. of Greenville, South Carolina. Remote communications software is used to link the downtown headquarters and the aircraft division, stationed at the local airport, to organize the flight schedules of its five pilots.

"A common misconception is that corporate jets are royal barges," said Rob Traynham, aviation manager and pilot for Michelin. "(The planes) are having to be used as business tools now. Remote software helps me manage the business tools I'm responsible for."

Because pilots typically work unusual hours, it was often difficult to coordinate last-minute changes. "Before, I would end up having to call around at night," said Traynham. "Now, the person responsible for scheduling inputs the information at headquarters, and we get our own manifest at the airport. We don't have to come downtown or make phone calls."

Traynham, who also works unusual hours, likes the versatility of remote communications. On a Saturday morning he can go to his office and access all the information from headquarters. "It allows you so much freedom," he said. However, he noted that the program has had its share of glitches.

"In the last year (our system) has been in a constant development process," said Traynham. Michelin recently switched from a 1,200-bps modem to a 2,400-bps modem. "It makes all the difference in the world," said Traynham. Previously, it took about eight seconds after pressing the function key for the display to appear. Michelin has been able to cut that time in half with a 2,400-bps modem.

"The software is in a constant state of upgrade," Traynham said. "It's all part of the information explosion in the field. There are a lot of intangible factors, but I know (remote communications) is worth a lot to me."

Summary and Key Terms

The movement of data from one location to another is called **data communication.** The types of communication hardware and support software necessary to move those data differ, depending primarily on the distance involved.

The three main types of data communication involving microcomputers are communication with peripheral devices, telecommunication, and local-area networks.

When a microcomputer communicates with peripheral devices such as printers, the transmission medium is generally a cable. The cable hooks to the computer at an **input/output port.** The number of devices that can be connected to a computer is a function of the number of I/O ports. A **serial** port is used to send data sequentially along a single path, and a **parallel** port sends data along eight paths simultaneously.

In **telecommunication**, the distance between devices becomes too large for simple cables and a medium such as the phone system must be used. The primary difficulty with the existing phone system is that it was designed to carry voice communication, which consists of continuous frequency waves called **analog signals.** To convert the **digital signals** used in computers to the analog signals needed for the phone line, a device known as a modem is used. A **modem** converts digital signals to analog and analog signals to digital. The two most common types of modems are internal and external. An **external modem** is attached to an input/output port on the microcomputer with a cable. An **internal modem** is placed directly within the microcomputer. The speed of a modem is measured in terms of the number of bits it can transmit in a second (bps).

Communication support software performs three primary functions in the data communication process: protocol support, error detection and correction, and security. A **protocol** is a set of rules that govern the data transmission process. When data are transmitted a **data packet** is constructed, which contains a **start bit** followed by the bits that make up the character being transmitted. The end of the group of bits for the character is marked by a **stop bit.** Other bits are added to the packet to be used in error detection.

The type of bits added depend on whether the transmission mode is asynchronous or synchronous. In the **asynchronous** mode of data transmission, one character at a time is sent over the communication link. The **parity bit** method of error checking is used primarily with async. In the **synchronous** mode of data transmission, a block of characters is sent. Here, a more complex method of error-checking is used.

The error detection and control function of communication support software includes a method of detecting errors and a way for the receiving computer to request retransmission of the data containing the error. **Data encryption** provides security during the transmission of data by scrambling the data. The receiving computer must know how the data was scrambled so it can unscramble the data.

The three typical data communication applications for microcomputers are terminal emulation, file transfer, and accessing information utilities. **Terminal emulation** involves using a microcomputer to mimic a terminal on a **host computer.** Communication support software allows the user to alter the codes sent by a microcomputer keyboard to match those normally sent by a terminal. Communication characteristics can also be set to be the same as those for a normal terminal. One particularly important communication characteristic is the direction of transmission.

Transmission can be simplex, half-duplex, or full-duplex. A **simplex** communication channel allows data transmission in one direction only. **Half-duplex** channels allow communication in both directions but only in one direction at a time. **Full-duplex** channels allow transmission in both directions simultaneously.

File transfer applications involve the transmission of files between a **local computer** and a remote host computer. **Uploading** is the transfer of files from the local computer to the host. **Downloading** is the transfer of files from the host to the local computer. During a file transfer the user must distinguish between files that are text and binary.

A final application of data communication is the accessing of information. **Electronic bulletin boards** are typically established on microcomputers to allow users to share information. Larger computers are used to create information utilities, from which users can gain access to large databases of information.

Local-area networks are a group of computers and peripherals within a building or building complex that are interconnected so that the peripherals can be shared and the computers can communicate with one another.

Networks are often used to implement **electronic mail**, in which users can send electronic memos to one another rather than using memos on paper.

The **topology** of a network is the pattern in which the devices are interconnected. In a **star topology** all the devices are connected to a central hub through which all traffic must pass. A **bus topology** connects each device in series along a single cable. The **ring topology** connects each device in series but the two ends of the cable are joined to complete a circle or ring.

The three most common types of cable used in constructing local-area networks are **twisted pair, coaxial cable,** and **CATV** cable. Network management software is run on a computer designated as a **server** for the network. This software oversees the functions of the network and makes sure that the devices can communicate.

Review Questions

1. Explain the difference between serial and parallel transmission between a microcomputer and a peripheral device.
2. What is a modem? Why is it important in data communications?
3. What is a data packet?
4. Explain the difference between the asynchronous and synchronous modes of transmission.
5. Explain the difference between uploading and downloading a file.
6. What are some of the features provided by communication programs? Which do you think are the most important?
7. What are some communication applications in which you think data encryption would be needed?
8. What are the differences between the three most common network topologies?
9. What are some of the reasons for the emergence of local-area networks within organizations?
10. Explain what is meant by terminal emulation and how a microcomputer can be used to perform terminal emulation.

T F 11. A serial port is used to transmit data between a computer and a peripheral device across a single data path, one bit at a time.

T F 12. Analog signals use a pattern of discrete high and low amplitude pulses to convey information.

T F 13. A protocol is a device used to translate between analog and digital signals.

T F 14. A parity bit is used to indicate the beginning of a data packet.

T F **15.** In asynchronous mode one character is transmitted at a time.

T F **16.** Terminal emulation is the process of using software to make a microcomputer act like a terminal on a host computer.

T F **17.** A data packet is a series of start, stop, and parity bits along with bits that represent a character.

T F **18.** Uploading is the process of transferring a file from a remote host computer to a local microcomputer.

T F **19.** A half-duplex channel can transmit data in only one direction.

T F **20.** A topology is a pattern formed when hardware devices are connected to form a network.

21. _____ A device that translates between analog and digital signals is known as a:

a. LAN
b. modem
c. parallel port
d. coaxial cable

22. _____ A group of bits sent from one computer to another which often includes start, parity, and stop bits, in addition to the bits representing a character, is known as a:

a. protocol
b. modem
c. analog signal
d. data packet

23. _____ The process of sending a file from a local microcomputer to a remote host computer is known as:

a. downloading
b. terminal emulation
c. uploading
d. modulation

24. _____ Which of the following is not a common network topology?

a. star
b. ring
c. bus
d. spiral

25. _____ A device on a network that provides services to the network is a:

a. protocol
b. modem
c. server
d. host computer

26. _____ A type of signal that uses discrete high and low amplitudes to convey information is:

a. an analog signal
b. a duplex signal
c. a digital signal
d. a parallel signal

27. _____ A set of rules used to govern the transmission of data between two computers is known as a:

a. protocol
b. agenda
c. parity
d. modem

28. _____ A bit added to a data packet that helps detect errors is:

a. an error bit
b. a stop bit
c. a start bit
d. a parity bit

29. _____ The process of transmitting data across long distances is:

a. telecommunication
b. remote communication
c. data communication
d. peripheral transmission

30. _____ An input/output port that is capable of transmitting data along eight paths simultaneously is a:

a. serial port
b. parallel port
c. simplex port
d. synchronous port

CHAPTER 17

Decision Support and Expert Systems

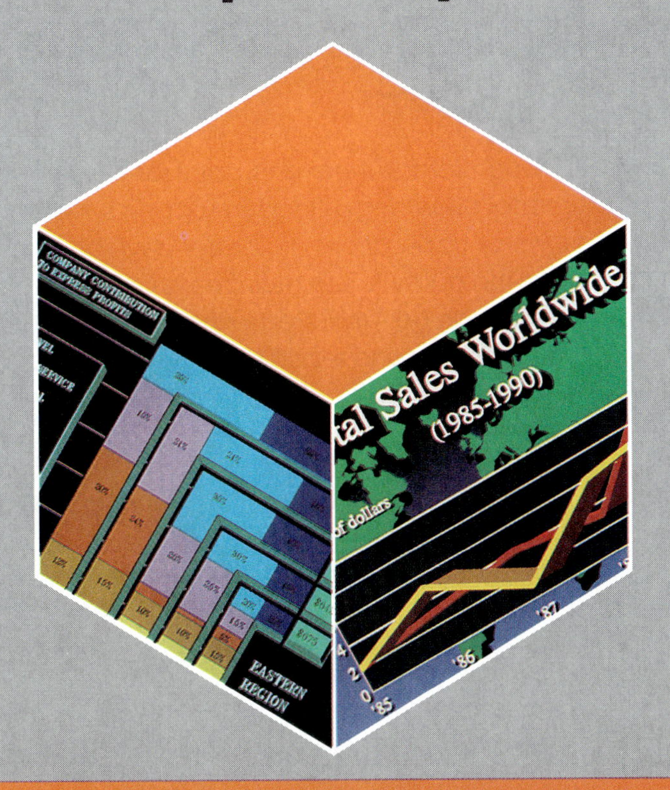

In earlier chapters, you learned about fundamental end-user software: word processing programs, spreadsheet programs, database management systems, graphics packages, and communication systems. The majority of business professionals routinely use one or more of these tools in support of everyday business functions. As users become more sophisticated in the use of computer software, however, they often need more than one of these tools and need to be able to easily exchange data between their software tools. One answer to this need is the development of integrated software.

Although spreadsheet and database management systems can be used for developing decision support systems (DSS), often more complex applications are better developed using specialized DSS tools. The ability to use mainframe data and develop ad hoc query systems can be facilitated with special application development tools for query and report generation. In addition, expert systems are being developed to offer artificial intelligence support for business problems.

In this chapter you will learn to do the following:

1. Describe two approaches by which software vendors are providing business professionals with multipurpose support tools
2. Explain what desktop organizers are
3. List and describe examples of specialized decision support tools
4. Describe some of the common application development tools
5. Explain what expert systems are and their role in business

Multipurpose Support Tools

Word processors, spreadsheets, graphics, databases, and communication programs are the most common microcomputer end-user tools in use today. A current trend involves providing a business professional with access to a number of these tools at the same time. The idea is to allow the business professional to process a set of data in a variety of ways without having to exit to the operating system and begin a new program.

Why might this be useful? Consider how nice it would be if you could build a spreadsheet model using data stored in a database, produce some charts from the spreadsheet results, and then embed the charts in a report you were preparing. Data would need to be entered only once. Even better, any changes that occurred to data items in the data file would automatically "percolate" through the information outputs you had created—the spreadsheet model, the charts, and the report.

Software vendors are using two basic approaches to provide such multipurpose tools: integrated software and a software integrator. Each of these is described in the following sections along with another multipurpose tool, the desktop organizer.

Integrated Software

Integrated software is a tightly interrelated set of tools in a single software product that allows the user to easily switch tools and exchange data among them. The intent of integrated software is to allow users to apply a very similar set of commands to several functions and to manipulate data without having to enter any data item more than once. The information processing functions most commonly included in integrated software packages are spreadsheets, word processors, business graphics, and data management. Each tool can be displayed in its own window on the screen, and data values can be moved from one window to another.

The first successful integrated software package was Lotus 1-2-3, which combined spreadsheet modeling, business graphics, and data management. As shown in Exhibit 17.1, Lotus 1-2-3 uses a master spreadsheet to organize data elements. Two additional examples of integrated packages are Symphony and Framework (see Exhibits 17.2 and 17.3). Symphony, which added word processing and communication capabilities to Lotus 1-2-3, is still organized around a master spreadsheet. Framework is organized around the concept of a "frame," which can hold an outline, a spreadsheet, a database, or other applications.

As all of the functions of integrated software must fit within the computer system's primary memory, these functions are generally slower and less capable than those provided with single-purpose software packages. Still, the ability to move data back and forth easily between different functions can more than make up for the lack of speed and "frills."

Some software vendors are taking another approach with integrated software. Rather than placing multiple functions within a package, they are developing "families" of single-function tools that can share data files (see Exhibit 17.4 on page 440). Although this approach does not produce a set of tools as tightly integrated as Lotus, Symphony, and Framework, the individual packages are often faster and more sophisticated.

These types of integrated software are exemplified by products like PFS: First Choice and Microsoft Works. PFS: First Choice lets the user run only one application tool at a time, but has a clipboard feature that allows data to be transferred from one application to another. A product such as Microsoft Works allows the user to have more than one application running at one time by providing several windows, each one able to run a separate application.

Since the individual tools must be integrated within one software package, the functionality of these packages still cannot compete with single-purpose software packages. For example, a word processor within

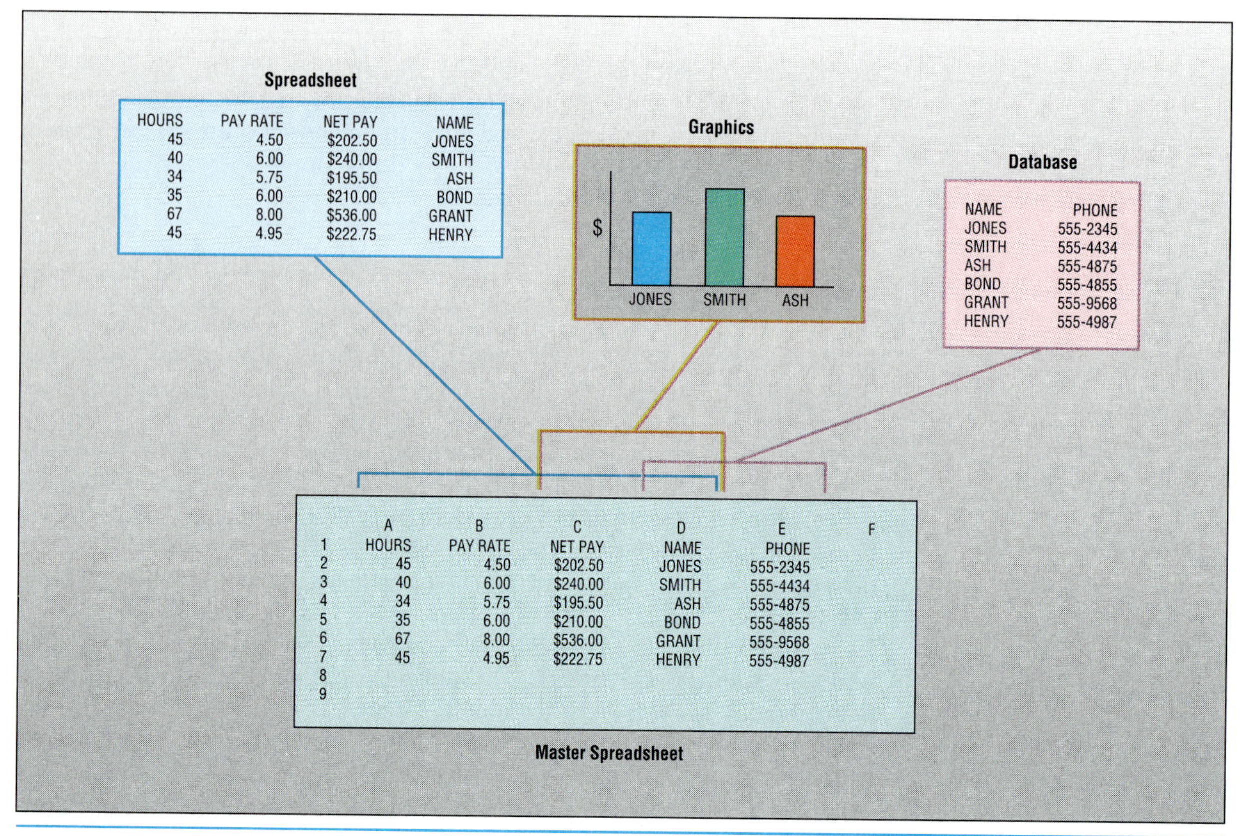

Exhibit 17.1

Master Spreadsheet in Lotus 1-2-3

In Lotus 1-2-3, spreadsheet, graphics, and data management functions all spring from an underlying master spreadsheet.

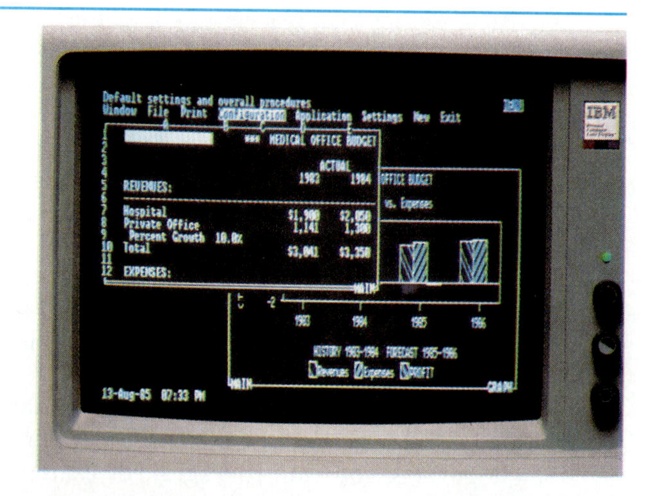

Exhibit 17.2

Symphony

A display screen from Symphony, an integrated software package.

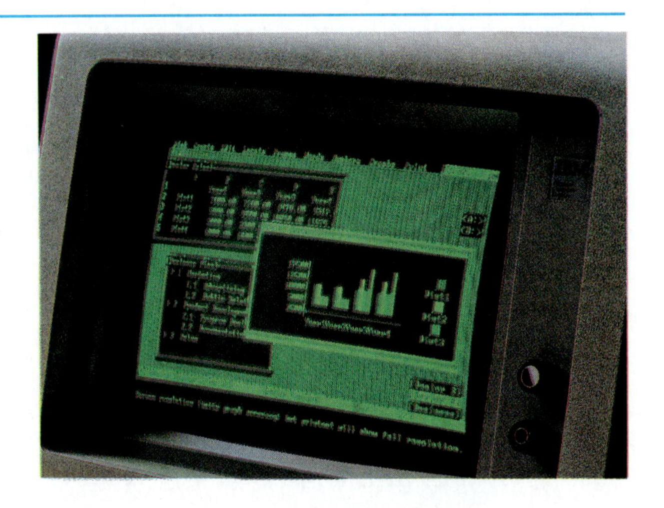

Exhibit 17.3

Framework

A display screen from Framework, integrated software organized in "frames" that can contain a spreadsheet, a graph, or an outline of these elements.

an integrated software package does not offer as many features as does WordPerfect.

Software Integrators

The second approach for providing business professionals with a set of multipurpose tools is through a **software integrator**, which is a specialized program that allows a user to run more than one application at the same time. A software integrator allows users to execute a number of applications at the same time, to view each application in its own window, to change the size of the windows, and to move data values from window to window.

What distinguishes these software integrators from integrated software is that they work with single-purpose tools. Thus, users have the best of both worlds—they can work with powerful single-purpose tools or a favorite tool and still integrate their end-user applications.

A few software integrators, such as Digital Research's GEM, require special versions of single-purpose tools that have been designed to run in their window environment. More recent software integrators such as Microsoft Windows and DESQview (Quarterdeck Office Systems) can work with any single-purpose tool, without the need for versions designed specifically to run in that software integrator.

Fitting applications into windows strains the speed and capacity of today's microcomputers. Software integrators require microcomputer systems with hard disks and at least 1–2 megabytes of primary memory and are still relatively slow. As the technology improves and microcomputers become even more powerful, window managers are likely to achieve the success that was initially predicted for them. The more recent Macintosh operating systems running on the Macintosh II and SE/30 computers have a windowing environment built in that allows for software integration. The new IBM Personal System/2 PCs announced in mid-1987 represented the first IBM compatible PCs with enough speed and power to

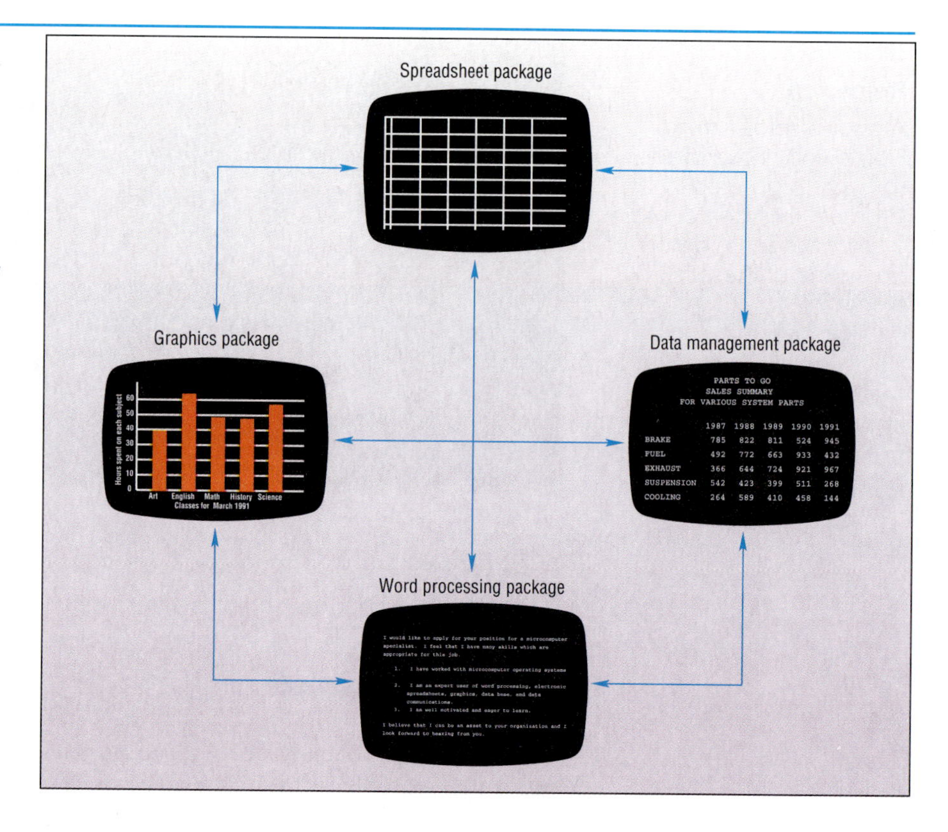

Exhibit 17.4

Software Integration

A family of single-purpose packages can provide a user with a loosely integrated set of end-user tools. Each package can read data files created by other family members.

make window managers a viable end-user tool. The OS/2 operating system for the newer PCs will include windowing capabilities directly in the operating system.

Desktop Organizers

When managers begin to spend a large portion of their time working with microcomputer end-user tools, interruptions that take them away from their microcomputers can be frustrating. Often the smaller the interruption, such as making a phone call or writing a memo, the greater the frustration. **Desktop organizers** are integrated packages that allow a business professional to juggle several tasks without having to leave the big jobs executing on their microcomputers.

These software packages share a number of traits (see Exhibit 17.5). First, they replace common office tools, such as Rolodex files, calendars, notepads, calculators, telephones, and alarm clocks. Second, they stay in the background of other applications, waiting to pop up in a window only when triggered by the user. Finally, they are inexpensive. Many are priced in the $50 to $100 range. On the down side, desktop organizers must be placed into the computer's memory (RAM) to be available at all times. When application programs are loaded into memory, they can sometimes conflict with the desktop organizer. Thus, certain organizers cannot be used.

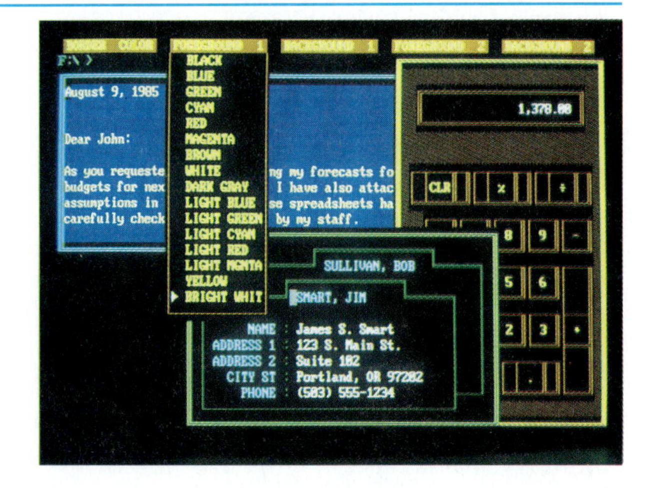

Exhibit 17.5

Desktop Organizer

Desktop organizers can execute a number of useful functions, such as performing calculations and retrieving addresses.

Still, desktop organizers have become popular. The main reason is that they fill a real need of many business professionals. Desktop organizers handle the little tasks that recur throughout a manager's workday, thus increasing on-the-job productivity. They also keep these tasks and the associated paperwork in one place, rather than scattered all over the desk and office.

Specialized DSS Tools

End-users, particularly business professionals, are often faced with the complex task of decision-making—and backing up their decisions. This *decision support* is not easily accomplished with typical end-user tools. This task often requires capabilities that are not commonly found in word processing, spreadsheet, graphics, database, and communication tools. This section examines a few of the most popular specialized end-user tools on the market today. The discussion includes specialized tools designed for financial modeling, statistical analysis, and project management.

Financial Modeling

Many applications require specialized end-user tools. One such application is **financial modeling,** which lets an end-user build models of financial situations that can be used to solve problems. IFPS (by Execucom Systems, Inc.) can handle more complex financial applications than spreadsheet programs such as Lotus 1-2-3. Exhibit 17.6a shows the statements a user enters to create the ratio analysis in Exhibit 17.6b. These statements define the relationships between variables involved in the model. IFPS lets a user perform a what-if analysis by specifying conditions rather than changing the base model, as would be required with a spreadsheet program. Exhibit

Exhibit 17.6

An Example of What-If Corporate Planning

(a) A user can build a model in a financial modeling language . .

```
==>| COLUMNS 1..6
  2| SALES = 100, PREVIOUS SALES * 1.25
  3| EXPENSES = 75, 100, 125, 150, 175
  4| NET INCOME = SALES - EXPENSES
  5| \
  6| \                                              RATIO ANALYSIS
  7| \ PERCENT OF SALES
  8| EXPENSE RATIO = EXPENSES / SALES
  $| NET INCOME RATIO = NET INCOME / SALES

 Menu                                   EDIT MODE      File: RATIO.MOD
Edit:  Append  Copy   Delete  Get     Include
       Locate  Move   Name    Replace Save      Undo    Visual
 File RATIO.MOD ready for edit.
```

(b) . . . to create a ratio analysis.

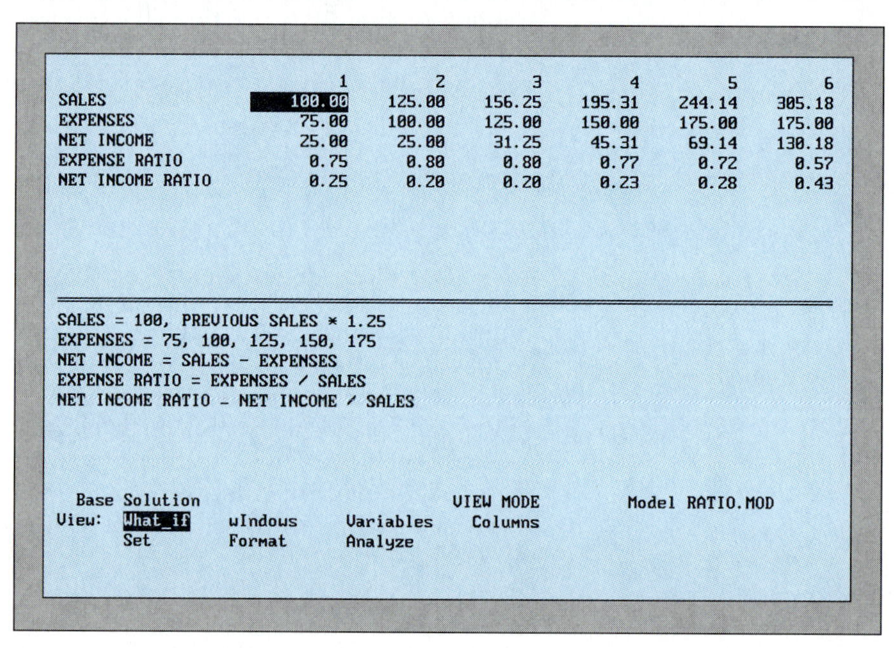

	1	2	3	4	5	6
SALES	100.00	125.00	156.25	195.31	244.14	305.18
EXPENSES	75.00	100.00	125.00	150.00	175.00	175.00
NET INCOME	25.00	25.00	31.25	45.31	69.14	130.18
EXPENSE RATIO	0.75	0.80	0.80	0.77	0.72	0.57
NET INCOME RATIO	0.25	0.20	0.20	0.23	0.28	0.43

```
SALES = 100, PREVIOUS SALES * 1.25
EXPENSES = 75, 100, 125, 150, 175
NET INCOME = SALES - EXPENSES
EXPENSE RATIO = EXPENSES / SALES
NET INCOME RATIO - NET INCOME / SALES

  Base Solution                         VIEW MODE          Model RATIO.MOD
View:  What_if    wIndows    Variables   Columns
       Set        Format     Analyze
```

17.6c shows how a what-if analysis can be performed by specifying a different assumption for the growth in sales. IFPS automatically answers this query by displaying the new model.

In addition, IFPS can specify goal-seeking situations in which, for example, the desired net income in a model can be stated at $100,800. The IFPS model will automatically modify the sales variable to determine what is required to generate that profit amount. IFPS can also generate management

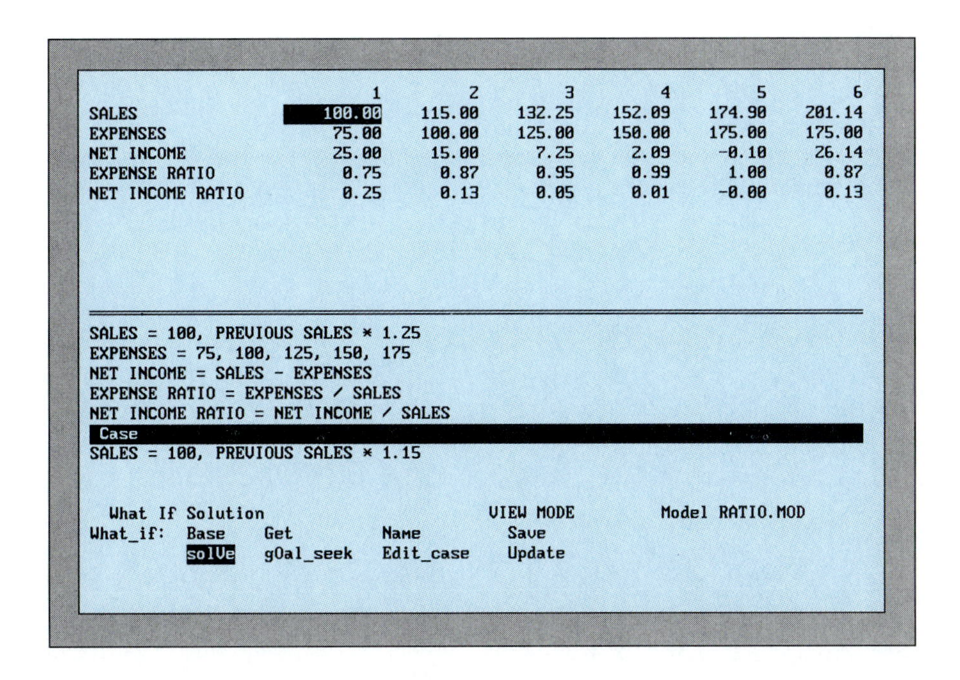

(c) The model can also be used to perform a what-if analysis.

report templates, which can be loaded with different sets of data. This is very useful for corporate financial officers who want a common way to compare accounting data from various divisions. IFPS applications include cash flow projections, lease versus purchase comparisons, risk analysis, budgeting, and return-on-investment decisions.

Statistical Analysis

Statistical analysis software tools are designed to allow an end-user to create applications that require **statistical analysis**. For example, SAS (by SAS Institute, Inc.) is a statistical analysis tool that lets the end-user perform complex statistical analyses such as regression analysis, analysis of variance, and discriminant analysis, using simple, English-like commands. These operations are incorporated into ready-to-use procedures so that the end-user doesn't have to be a statistician to produce the required analysis.

Results can be obtained and put into a report by issuing a few simple commands written in a nonprocedural language. SAS also has sophisticated graphics capabilities that display statistical results. The top three lines shown in Exhibit 17.7 shows the SAS commands needed to generate the results below in Exhibit 17.7.

Project Management

A final type of tool designed to perform a specialized type of application is the project manager. A **project manager** is used in step-by-step planning of

```
PROC    MEANS  MEAN  MIN  MAX;
        VAR AGE.  CLAIMS,  PREMIUM;
        BY DEPT;
```

K & G Supply Company
Medical Insurance Analysis
for Year Ending December 31, 1988

VARIABLE	MEAN	MINIMUM	MAXIMUM
		DEPT=Accounting	
AGE	45	18	72
CLAIMS	941	17	5025
PREMIUM	1175	864	1596
		DEPT=Marketing	
AGE	41	18	65
CLAIMS	1088	27	60310
PREMIUM	1128	864	1596
		DEPT=Customer Service	
AGE	44	18	72
CLAIMS	942	27	4484
PREMIUM	1144	864	1596
		DEPT=Production	
AGE	35	18	60
CLAIMS	943	31	38516
PREMIUM	1113	864	1596
		DEPT=Shipping	
AGE	37	18	61
CLAIMS	884	31	2479
PREMIUM	1097	864	1596
		DEPT=Human Resources	
AGE	42	18	72
CLAIMS	946	24	5334
PREMIUM	1215	864	1596

Exhibit 17.7

Performing a Statistical Analysis

The top three SAS statements produce the output shown below. The MEANS procedure determines the mean age in each department and the dollar amount of insurance premiums versus claims paid.

a project in which tasks must be scheduled and resources allocated to finish the entire job on schedule. This process includes identifying potential schedule problems, tracking progress, and optimizing cost/time/resource trade-offs. In the project manager, the job is divided into tasks of various durations, and these tasks' interdependence is diagrammed. The planned costs for each task are budgeted and compared to actual costs as the project progresses.

The Harvard Total Project Manager provides end-users with seven different tools for managing a project. The end-user can monitor cross-project resource allocation, perform cost and schedule tracking, create a "road map" of the project, set up a schedule with minimum time between tasks or negative time between tasks, and divide the project into sub-projects. Exhibit 17.8 shows an example of the type of graphical display used in the Harvard Total Project Manager.

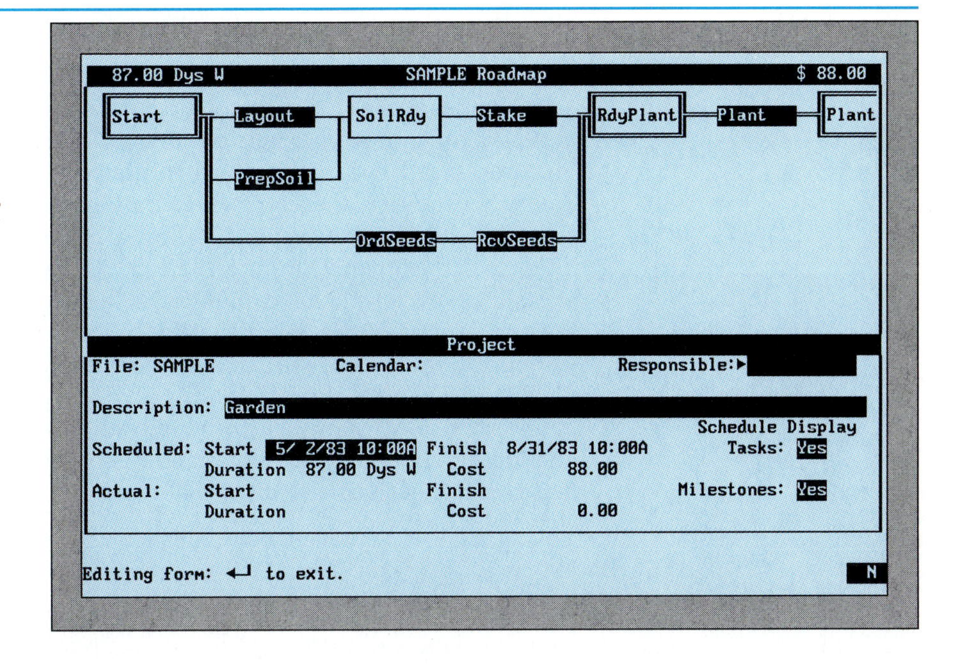

Exhibit 17.8

Project Management Software

The Roadmap is the one feature that no project manager can do without. It helps the project manager to keep the big picture in sight.

Application Development Tools

Some advanced tools make it possible for end-users to create applications based on data stored in large centralized computer systems. In addition to handling procedural statements as traditional programming languages do, these tools often include various productivity features that can further simplify the process of building an application to solve a problem. These tools include query facilities, report generators, and application generators. This section examines these tools and some of the current products that provide these capabilities to end-users.

Query Facilities

A **query facility** allows the end-user to make simple requests for data. Query facilities are most commonly found in end-user tools that work with data stored by a database management system (see Chapters 8 and 14). A query facility is useful for one-time requests to retrieve data from a database when no application exists that can retrieve that data in the way the user wants it. A query facility usually allows the user to use a *nonprocedural language,* in which the user specifies *what* data are to be retrieved rather than *how* they are to be retrieved. The query facility determines the necessary retrieval operations to obtain the data requested and then retrieves the requested data from the database. Some query facilities even allow users to enter and update data in the database in addition to simply doing retrievals.

Because query facilities use nonprocedural, English-like commands, users with little or no programming experience can retrieve data. There is, however, a great deal of variation in the ease with which inexperienced end-users can formulate queries. Exhibit 17.9a shows a query written for a query facility that is marketed as easy to use. Some query facilities have begun to allow users to enter queries in free-form English rather than requiring them to use specific key words to perform certain operations. This capability is implemented through the use of a natural language processor that translates the free-form English request submitted by the user into a series of retrieval commands. For example, INTELLECT (by Artificial Intelligence Corporation) can interpret commands written in English by matching words against its own internal dictionary. Exhibit 17.9b shows the query from 17.9a in INTELLECT and the data retrieved as a result of that query.

Report Generators

Query facilities typically give the user little control over the way data are displayed on a screen. If the user has special needs beyond the standard formatting, he or she can use a **report generator**—a facility that lets the user create printed reports by using nonprocedural statements to obtain summary information and format the printed output. A report generator is usually designed to handle the more formal formatting and other special needs of producing paper reports for use by managers. It includes features such as report headings and subheadings, page headings and subheadings,

Exhibit 17.9

Variability in the Way a Query Can Be Written

(a) A query written in a query language that is marketed as easy to use.

(b) The same query written in INTELLECT and the data resulting from that query.

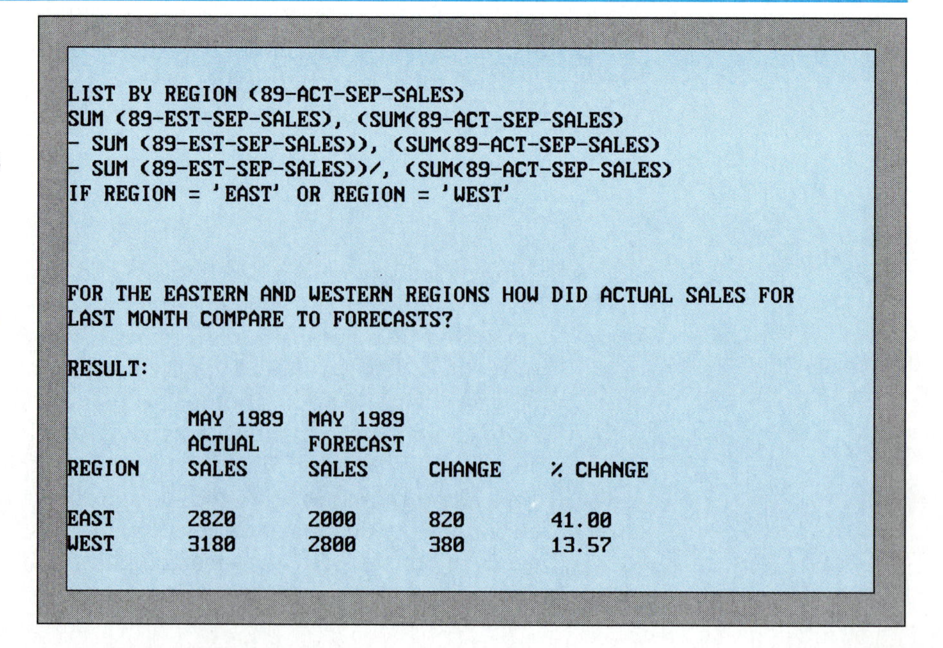

```
LIST BY REGION (89-ACT-SEP-SALES)
SUM (89-EST-SEP-SALES), (SUM(89-ACT-SEP-SALES)
- SUM (89-EST-SEP-SALES)), (SUM(89-ACT-SEP-SALES)
- SUM (89-EST-SEP-SALES))/, (SUM(89-ACT-SEP-SALES)
IF REGION = 'EAST' OR REGION = 'WEST'


FOR THE EASTERN AND WESTERN REGIONS HOW DID ACTUAL SALES FOR
LAST MONTH COMPARE TO FORECASTS?

RESULT:

          MAY 1989  MAY 1989
          ACTUAL    FORECAST
REGION    SALES     SALES     CHANGE    % CHANGE

EAST      2820      2000      820       41.00
WEST      3180      2800      380       13.57
```

Exhibit 17.10

An Example of Report Generation

The top two lines show the NOMAD2 LIST command with totals and subtotals. The bottom table shows subtotals produced by the NOMAD2 LIST command.

```
LIST BY MONTH SALES REP QUOTA SALES BONUS -
     SUBTOTAL ALL TOTAL ALL

PAGE 1

MONTH      SALES REP        QUOTA     SALES     BONUS
-----      ---------
_____      _________        _____    _______    _____
FEB        FOSTER             250     278.32     1.70
           JENKINS            450     455.18     0.31
           PORTER              75      81.20     0.37
                            -----    -------    -----
                              775     814.70     2.38

MAR        CRANDALL           600     610.44     0.63
           JENKINS            650     698.54     2.91
           WELLES              90      93.13     0.19
                            -----    -------    -----
                             1340    1402.11     3.73
                            =====    =======    =====
                             2115    2216.81     6.11
```

column positioning, automatic page numbering, and automatic totals and subtotals. Typically, the end-user can manipulate these formatting features by making choices in menus or by issuing commands. Exhibit 17.10 shows an example of the NOMAD2 LIST command at the top used to produce the table below with subtotals and totals.

Some report generators can produce graphs as well as tables for reports. Many types of graphs can be created, including pie charts, bar graphs, scatter diagrams, and line graphs. If a user does not specify the type of graph needed, the report generator will determine what graph type is most appropriate for displaying the data requested. As with the reports themselves, graphs can usually be created with a few simple commands.

Application Generators

Query facilities and report generators typically work best when data do not require a great deal of processing. They are primarily designed to deal with the output of desired information. More complex problems involving the input and processing of information cannot be solved by creating simple queries or generating reports; they require application programs written in a programming language. **Application generators** or *fourth-generation languages* are simplified programming languages that allow the user to concentrate on manipulating data to solve a problem rather than on describing the detailed steps the computer needs to perform in order to manipulate the data. The power and simplicity of these application generators allows an end-user to complete an application in a much shorter period of time and without the help of a professional programming staff.

One reason for this increased efficiency is that application generators often have their own data dictionaries (or use the data dictionary of a DBMS). The data dictionary stores descriptions of data and files. In traditional programming languages the description of the data has to be written in the program itself by the programmer; in an application generator the program simply makes a reference to the dictionary to obtain these data descriptions.

Another reason for the increased efficiency of application generators is that they can call on report generators to determine how formatting is done, instead of the programmer having to describe how data are to be produced as with traditional programming languages. One application generator, MANTIS, allows users to design and store screens that can later be used to format the data for output. Exhibits 17.11a and 17.11b show how a screen created by MANTIS functions. The program makes a reference to a screen stored in the MANTIS screen directory, and the data are generated according to the format associated with that screen.

There is a great deal of variation in the amount of training an end-user would need before being able to take advantage of an application generator. MANTIS is an example of an application generator that would require a fair amount of specialized training.

Role of Expert Systems in Business

For all its wonders, the computer is really just a machine that carries out instructions in a fast, accurate, and efficient way. The thoughts that direct the computer's actions belong to its programmers and users. But will we eventually build a computer that can think, reason, and learn like a human? This question is studied by a branch of computer science called artificial intelligence (AI).

Although the whole subject of AI is controversial, one area that is moving out of the laboratories and into the mainstream of business is expert systems. **Expert systems** are computer-based software designed to mimic the decision-making exhibited by human experts.

Expert systems currently in use include MYCIN, which diagnoses infectious diseases and recommends appropriate drugs, PROSPECTOR, which aids geologists in evaluating sites for potential mineral deposits, and XCON, which is used by Digital Equipment Corporation to configure minicomputers to meet customer processing requirements. TAD, a tax advisor system, is available at local offices of H&R Block. This expert system is used to search the myriad federal income tax regulations, advise the user on what income must be reported and which deductions are applicable, and even complete IRS tax forms.

How do expert systems work? They acquire their "intelligence" by mimicking the decision-making process of human experts. The two key people involved in building an expert system are the human expert and the knowledge engineer. The **human expert** is a person who has an in-depth knowledge of a specific problem area or domain. For example, this could be in infectious diseases, petroleum geology, microbiology, or child psychology. To capture the expertise of the human expert is the job of the **knowledge engineer.** This person is a systems analyst skilled in developing expert systems (see Exhibit 17.12).

By interviewing the human expert, the knowledge engineer discovers the expert's knowledge of the problem area. This is separated into a knowledge base and means of inference. The **knowledge base** is a collection of rules an expert might know about a particular type of problem. These facts and experience need to be stated as IF . . . THEN rules.

Exhibit 17.11

The MANTIS Approach to Formatting

(a) MANTIS lets an end-user create a screen with different variables associated with the various masks (indicated by the #s) on the screen.

```
                     DISPLAY OF PURCHASE ORDER
                             REQUESTED

     PURCHASE ORDER NUMBER: ######
     PURCHASE ORDER DATE:   ######

     SUPPLIER NUMBER:       ######
     SUPPLIER NAME:         ####################

 PRODUCT NUMBER   DESCRIPTION                      QUANTITY    COST

 #########        ##############################   #####    #######.##
 #########        ##############################   #####    #######.##
 #########        ##############################   #####    #######.##
 #########        ##############################   #####    #######.##
 #########        ##############################   #####    #######.##


#####################################################################
```

(b) This is the same MANTIS screen as it looks when it is used to display data.

```
                     DISPLAY OF PURCHASE ORDER
                             REQUESTED

     PURCHASE ORDER NUMBER: 000002
     PURCHASE ORDER DATE:   021290

     SUPPLIER NUMBER:       020202
     SUPPLIER NAME:         HERBST ELECTRIC

 PRODUCT NUMBER   DESCRIPTION                      QUANTITY    COST

 BC-123443        20 WATT STEREO                    1            150.00
 CC-584755        DISK DRIVE                        100          350.00
 DF-384744        TURNTABLE                         20           175.45
 ER-394755        RECEIVER                          45           125.87
 TR-384674        SPEAKER                           65            99.98


 RETURN = INSPECT ANOTHER ORDER,  CANCEL = EXIT PROGRAM
```

Exhibit 17.12
Building an Expert System

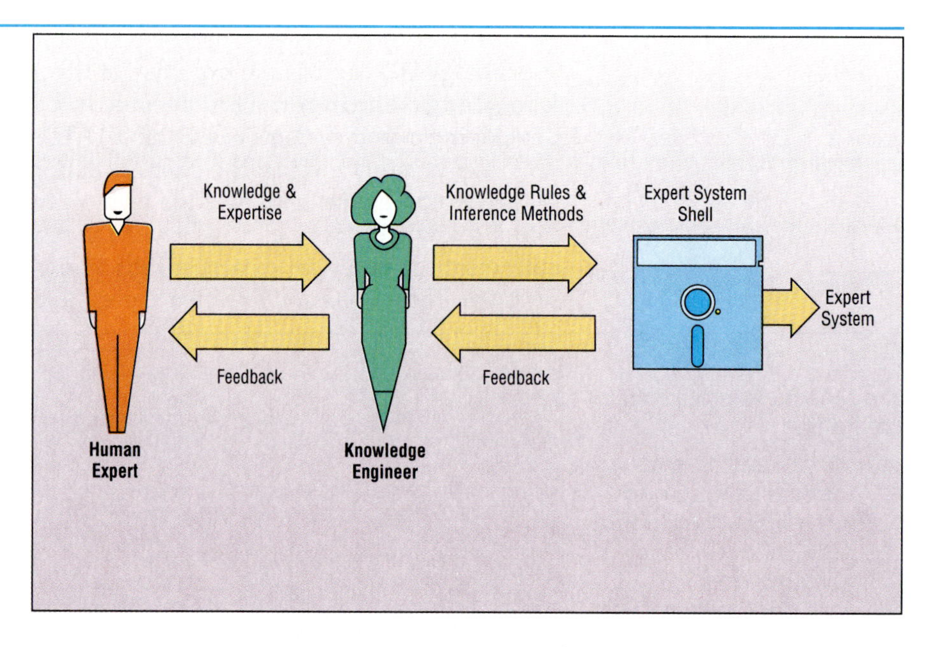

For example, a knowledge base for auto care would include such rules as, "IF a car has been driven more than 5000 miles since the last service, THEN lube and change the oil." For medical care, a knowledge base might include the rule, "IF the patient has a runny nose and a fever, THEN the patient is likely to have a cold." For the expert system to determine what is meant by the term *fever*, there would be another rule in the medical knowledge base which said, "IF the patient's temperature is over 102 degrees, THEN the person has a fever. " A third rule might be, "IF the patient has a cold, THEN prescribe two aspirin and bed rest."

An **inference method** is a reasoning strategy for solving problems using the knowledge base. It is a way of searching the knowledge base for the appropriate rules and determining how they should be linked to solve the problem posed. In the three-rule medical knowledge base example, assume a patient comes to the nurse and says he is sick. The first rule to apply is to see if the patient has a temperature over 102 degrees. If the patient has a fever and a running nose, then he has a cold. The solution for this sick patient is to give him two aspirin and prescribe rest.

Let's see how the inference method works with a more complex knowledge base. Exhibit 17.13 shows an advertising knowledge base that shows that certain media are best used to get across different messages to particular age groups. Look at rule 5. It states that IF the media that is going to be used is print (magazines, newspapers, and so on) AND you are trying to reach middle-income families, THEN the best place to advertise is *Time* magazine.

Let's pose a problem. What is the best medium to advertise that the local community is going to have a July Fourth parade. The two groups

Exhibit 17.13

Advertising Media Selection Knowledge Base

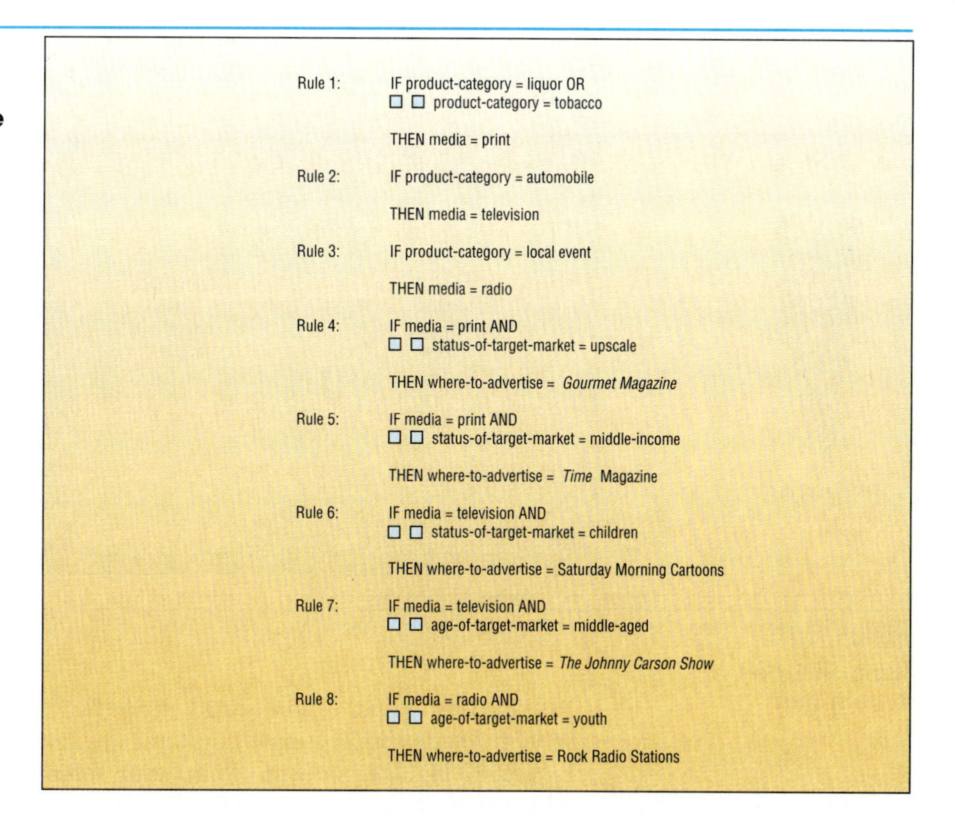

Rule 1: IF product-category = liquor OR
□ □ product-category = tobacco
THEN media = print

Rule 2: IF product-category = automobile
THEN media = television

Rule 3: IF product-category = local event
THEN media = radio

Rule 4: IF media = print AND
□ □ status-of-target-market = upscale
THEN where-to-advertise = *Gourmet Magazine*

Rule 5: IF media = print AND
□ □ status-of-target-market = middle-income
THEN where-to-advertise = *Time* Magazine

Rule 6: IF media = television AND
□ □ status-of-target-market = children
THEN where-to-advertise = Saturday Morning Cartoons

Rule 7: IF media = television AND
□ □ age-of-target-market = middle-aged
THEN where-to-advertise = *The Johnny Carson Show*

Rule 8: IF media = radio AND
□ □ age-of-target-market = youth
THEN where-to-advertise = Rock Radio Stations

that you are interested in reaching are the youth and the senior citizens of the community. To the expert system this would be stated as: The *product-category* is local event and the *age of the target market* is youth and senior citizens. The goal is to determine *where to advertise.*

The inference method would search the knowledge base for all rules that pertain to product-category. Rules 1 through 3 would then be checked to see which concerned local events. Rules 1 and 2 are not applicable. In rule 3 since the IF condition is true, then the media to use is radio. A search of the five media rules shows that only one is applicable to radio. Rule 8 states that *where to advertise* is rock radio stations.

But what about how best to reach the senior citizens for this local event? The inference system did not find a rule that covered the type of radio for senior citizens. It would then ask for more information. The knowledge engineer would pose the question to the human expert and then a new rule would be added to the knowledge base.

Rule 9: IF media = radio
AND age of target market = senior citizens
THEN where to advertise = Easy Listening Radio Stations

This shows that an important part of expert systems is their ability to be adapted to new situations without having to restructure the computer-

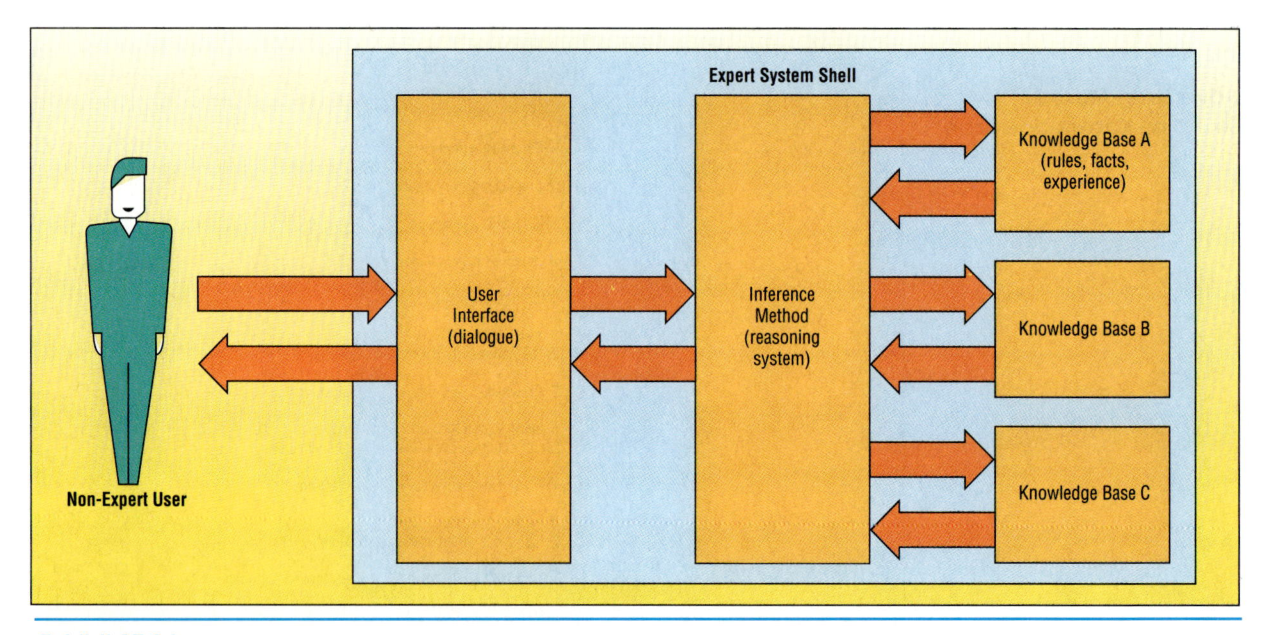

Exhibit 17.14

Using an Expert System Shell

based system. Rules can be added as needed. Specialized software packages written for developing expert systems are called **expert system shells** (see Exhibit 17.14). This software contains an inference method that can be used with a wide variety of knowledge bases. Through a user dialogue, the shell facilitates the entering of knowledge base rules. Many of the more popular expert system shells now available on personal computers include GURU, EXSYS, Personal Consultant, and VP-Expert.

The value of expert systems today stems from the increased complexity of business problems that need to be solved on a continuing basis and the shortage of experts to solve them. Although a business may have several experts, the demands on their time far exceeds what their schedules will allow. Further, these experts eventually retire or leave the firm. A major benefit of expert systems is that once they are built they can be used by nonexperts in handling difficult problems that previously could only be handled by the human experts.

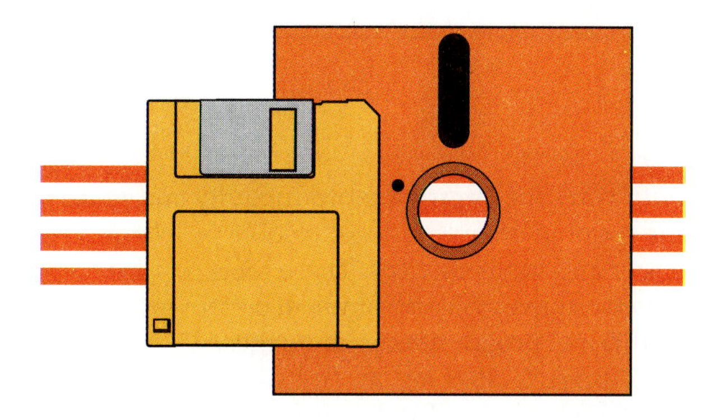

Computers at Work

Software Firms Sing the Praises of Integration

A number of companies promise an integrated software solution based on programs within their respective product lines.

Buy all your applications software from us, and integration will never be a problem.

That is the message a handful of software makers are trying to convey to PC users. Companies such as Lotus Development Corp. of Cambridge, Massachusetts; Migent Inc. of Incline Village, Nevada; WordPerfect Corp. of Orem, Utah; and The Santa Cruz Operation of Santa Cruz, California, promise an integrated-software solution based on programs within their respective product lines.

The foundation of Lotus's integration strategy is code-named LEAF (Lotus Extended Application Facility). "The initial release will be a run-time version of LEAF that lets users customize applications within 1-2-3," said James O'Donnell, a Lotus spokesman.

A later version of LEAF will create dynamic links among future Lotus products, including 1-2-3/G (the graphics-based spreadsheet that will run under OS/2's Presentation Manager) and the OS/2-based database, Lotus DBMS, Mr. O'Donnell said. LEAF will also provide ties to 1-2-3/M, Lotus's mainframe spreadsheet. "LEAF will allow you to develop a tight, seamless integration across those applications, not just within an application," Mr. O'Donnell said. "And in the future, you'll see more applications."

Migent also has its eye on the future, according to Nancy McSharry, a senior analyst with Market Researcher International Data Corp. in Framingham, Massachusetts. Scarcely on the market a week, Migent's Emerald Bay, a database "engine," lets networked users share data among different applications.

It's a common-sense-based, but innovative, approach to database management," Ms. McSharry said. "Information is pulled and pushed from a central database and read through the front end."

It is perhaps easiest to picture Emerald Bay as a set of three concentric circles, she explained. The center circle contains network "server engines"—programs that manipulate disk-based data. At the next level, memory-resident PC programs called "personal engines" act as messengers, moving database requests between users' applications and a network database.

On the outer tier are what Migent calls "surfaces"—end-user applications. When data is entered through an Emerald Bay surface, it is carried by a personal engine to the central repository: the server engine. Data on the server-engine level can be extracted through any surface, be it a database, a word processor or a spreadsheet.

Such applications have been integrated in yet another way by WordPerfect Corp., the maker of the best-selling word processor WordPerfect. The company is building a full set of applications with consistent user interfaces. Current members of the software family are WordPerfect, PlanPerfect (a spreadsheet), DataPerfect (a database), WordPerfect Executive (a low-end integrated product for corporate executives) and the WordPerfect Library.

The Library, a collection of software utilities, includes a menu shell for maintaining several applications in memory. Using the Library's shell, a portion of a screen in one program can be captured and pasted into a second program. Macros can be created to automate procedures between applications. The shell even accommodates non-WordPerfect applications.

Summary and Key Terms

A current trend with today's end-user tools is to provide a business professional with access to a number of tools at the same time. There are two basic approaches for providing multipurpose tools: integrated software and software integrators.

With **integrated software**, users apply similar sets of commands to manipulate data with a variety of end-user tools. No data item need be entered more than once. Each tool can be displayed in its window on the screen, and data values can be moved from one window to another. Although integrated software is very useful, the tools provided with these packages are generally slower and less powerful than those of single-purpose software packages.

Software integrators allow users to execute a number of applications at the same time, view each application in its own window, change the size of the windows, and move data values between the windows.

A **desktop organizer** is a software package that provides the business professional with a number of tools to handle the small tasks that occur throughout his or her workday; it can replace Rolodex files, calendars, notepads, calculators, telephones, and alarm clocks. One of the best features of desktop organizers is that they stay in the background of other applications, popping up only when triggered by the user.

Specialized decision support software allows the user to create applications that are generally too complex to develop with traditional end-user software. Some such specialized tools perform financial applications in which a **financial model** can be created and then used to perform what-if analyses. Other specialized tools are specifically designed to help end-users perform **statistical analysis. Project managers** let end-users create, and then track, complex scheduling applications by using menus and simple commands.

Application development tools provide users with ways for improving productivity and make the creation of applications to solve problems easier and more efficient. These tools require fewer commands to accomplish certain tasks than traditional programming languages.

A **query facility** lets an end-user retrieve data by using nonprocedural commands to describe *what* data is to be retrieved rather than *how* it is to be retrieved. Some query facilities allow users to write queries using English-like commands.

Report generators are designed to help users format data that is to appear on printed reports. Using simple commands, an end-user can create headings, number pages, and position columns easily and quickly. Some report generators also allow the end-user to present the data graphically.

Application generators allow users to create their own applications using simplified programming languages.

Expert systems are programs that mimic the decision-making of a human expert.

The development of expert systems requires a human expert, a knowledge engineer, and an expert systems shell. A **human expert** is a person who has in-depth knowledge of a specific problem area or domain. The job of capturing the expertise of the human expert belongs to a **knowledge engineer.** This is a person skilled in developing expert systems.

The expert's knowledge is divided into a knowledge base and a means for inference. A **knowledge base** is a collection of rules an expert might know about a particular class of problems. These are generally expressed in the IF . . . THEN rule format. The **inference method** is a reasoning strategy for solving problems using the knowledge base. **Expert system shells** are specialized software packages for developing expert systems. This shell includes a user interface and an inference method. Various knowledge bases can be developed for use by the shell.

Review Questions

1. Briefly describe the concept of integrated software. What advantages does such an approach offer?
2. What is a software integrator? How does its approach differ from that used in integrated software?
3. Briefly explain the concept of desktop organizers. Why have such programs become popular?
4. What is the purpose of financial modeling software?
5. Describe how specialized statistical analysis tools might be used.
6. What are project management tools used for?
7. Describe some of the features of a query facility.
8. How would a report generator be used?
9. What does an application generator do?
10. Why are expert systems being used in business?
11. What kind of skills should a knowledge engineer have?

T F **12.** Integrated software sits between applications and the operating system and allows the user to run several applications at the same time in separate windows.

T F **13.** A project manager allows a user to build complex financial models and set up what-if analyses with the models.

T F **14.** An expert system shell is a software package based on a particular inference method that aids in the development of expert systems.

T F **15.** An application generator is a simplified programming language that allows the user to concentrate on manipulating data to solve a problem.

T F **16.** A software integrator allows the user to run more than one application at a time.

T F **17.** Desktop organizers allow the user to schedule tasks and assign resources by task to design a project.

T F **18.** A report generator is a facility that provides a user with a set of nonprocedural commands that can be used to create and format printed reports.

T F **19.** A query facility is a software package that can be used to mimic the decision-making process of a human expert.

20. _____ This type of software contains an interrelated set of tools all in one software product that allows a user to easily switch between the tools and exchange data:

a. software integrator
b. integrated software
c. application generator
d. project manager

21. _____ This type of software usually includes items such as a calculator, calendar, and notepad, which sit in the background and can be triggered without the user having to leave the application he or she is using:

a. desktop organizer
b. window manager
c. project manager
d. software integrator

22. _____ This software helps an end-user schedule tasks and allocate resources by task:

a. desktop organizer
b. software integrator
c. window manager
d. project manager

23. _____ This type of software typically works with a database management system to allow the user to make simple requests for data using a nonprocedural language:

a. query facility
b. application generator
c. project manager
d. software integrator

24. _____ This type of software sits between application software and the operating system and allows the user to run several application programs simultaneously in separate windows:

a. software integrator
b. integrated software
c. project manager
d. application generator

25. _____ This type of software is designed to mimic the decision-making process of a human in a problem-solving task:

a. project manager
b. expert system
c. software integrator
d. window manager

26. _____ This person is responsible for capturing the expertise of a human expert during the design of an expert system:

a. system analyst
b. database administrator
c. knowledge engineer
d. knowledge worker

27. _____ This is a reasoning strategy for solving problems using a knowledge base:

a. algorithm
b. program
c. expert system
d. inference method

SPECIAL FEATURE

A Systems Approach to Selecting a Microcomputer System

Students in introductory computer courses often become convinced they could benefit from the purchase of their own personal computer. But choosing the right hardware and software can be difficult and confusing. Taking a lesson from systems developers can often help in making such a decision.

As described in Chapter 7, systems development takes place in four stages: systems analysis, systems design, systems acquisition, and systems implementation. The most important concept in systems development that applies to the purchase of a personal computer is matching the system to the situation. In other words, the first question to ask when deciding whether to purchase a microcomputer-based system should always be, "What kinds of problems do you think a microcomputer could solve for you?" This question is answered in the systems analysis stage.

Systems Analysis

In the systems analysis stage the user's needs are determined and the feasibility of the purchase of a microcomputer system assessed.

Typical needs of students considering the purchase of a microcomputer include word processing capabilities for papers and resumes, mathematical and accounting calculations, and storage and retrieval of lists of data. These needs apply to the majority of microcomputer users, which is why word processors, spreadsheets, and databases are the most popular microcomputer software packages on the market today. In addition the convenience of owning your own microcomputer rather than relying on the availability of computers in campus computer labs is often a major concern of student purchasers of microcomputers. When assessing needs it is also important to consider not only your current needs but future needs as well. Given the amount of money involved, it is important to purchase a system that will be useful for as long as possible.

Once an analysis of needs has been performed, the next step is to look at the financial feasibility of purchasing a microcomputer system. Some microcomputers cost a few hundred dollars, but many of those are limited in power and may not run the kind of software you need. Other microcomputers are as powerful as minicomputers, but they can cost thousands of dollars. Money may also be needed for peripherals like a printer or a modem. When looking at funding it is often useful to look for monthly purchase plans through schools and vendors. Schools often have discount offers, which apply to students as well as faculty.

After deciding that there is a need for a microcomputer system and that there are sufficient sources of funding for the purchase, the next step is to determine what the microcomputer system should be able. This is done by creating a list of user requirements.

A list of user requirements should include the functions the microcomputer system must perform. Remember, the software determines what the microcomputer can do for you. You have to determine the functions software can perform to meet your needs.

As mentioned previously, typical microcomputer users often need the functions provided by word processors, spreadsheets, and database management software, but there may also be other specialized software required to meet your needs. There are many good word processing, spreadsheet, and database packages available, each of which offers slightly different functions. You will need to decide which functions are more important to you.

One place you might start is this textbook. For example, Part IV, "End-User Software," describes the most popular types of microcomputer software packages used in business. The sections on classifying computers and choosing printers and so on might also help you when you begin your "systems design" and "systems acquisition." But you also need to check some other sources.

One good source of free advice is microcomputer owners. Another is your school. Even though the computing center is always busy, sometimes they offer seminars on choosing a microcomputer. If nothing else, the computing center gives you the chance to experiment with various brands of software and hardware. You will want to do this before you make a final decision.

You might get more relevant information from some of the computer magazines, especially the magazines written for owners of particular computers, such as *PC World* for the IBM-PC and PC-compatible owners, and *Macworld* for Macintosh owners. Read some of the product reviews in these magazines to get an idea of what professional computer reviewers look for. You might also look for the annual and quarterly buying guides some of these magazines offer. They list all possible types of products with information about features, requirements, and prices. The features are what you are interested in right now.

Popular Computer Magazines

It's a good idea to check the *Readers' Guide to Periodical Literature* in your library for articles that have appeared in general-interest magazines, such as *Consumer Reports.* Articles written for a general audience sometimes give you a better overview of available features than articles written for specialized audiences. Another source is the *Business Periodicals Index.*

After you do some reading, you need to talk to other people. Ask microcomputer owners what was important to them when they chose particular software. Or better yet, ask them what they don't like, and why. Most "micro" owners love to talk about that sort of thing. Microcomputer owners often form local user groups to exchange and discuss information. Ask your instructor for a list of user groups in your area.

Another strategy is to go to a computer store. Tell the sales representative you think you want to buy a microcomputer and see what kinds of questions you are asked. Sales representatives may be biased, but a good computer store will try to meet your needs. And if the personnel aren't helpful before you buy, they probably won't be helpful after you give them your money. Don't worry about asking the wrong questions, either. When you are making a large purchase, there are no wrong questions.

Systems Design

When you are ready to do your systems design, you will translate the functions you require into the capabilities offered by existing software. The type of software you need will determine the type of hardware you need to buy. For example, all software requires a minimum amount of primary memory, and some software requires two disk drives. These hardware requirements will play a major part in your choice of a microcomputer. Some functions will translate directly into hardware requirements. For example, the ability to print means you will need a printer. These general software and hardware requirements make up your systems design.

Once the systems design has been completed, you will be a lot more confident about the ways a microcomputer could help you. You will also be able to make a more realistic prediction of how much you will have to spend for a microcomputer—software and hardware—that will meet your needs.

This is a good time to review your feasibility study and needs analysis.

Systems Acquisition

In the systems acquisition stage, you'll be trying to choose among specific software packages and microcomputers. You will still have to do some research, but it will be more specific than before. In systems analysis, you went to your textbook, to magazines and buyer's guides, local microcomputer users' groups, and to computer stores to get an idea of what was available. Now that you have a sense of what is available and what you need, you're ready to narrow your options. You're ready to evaluate specific features and prices.

Excellent sources of information can be found in the campus library. For example, two services that rate hardware and software, Datapro Research and Auerbach, are often available. These services are expensive, but they publish books, newsletters, and updates regularly. During systems acquisition, always start with your software. A software checklist like the one below is often helpful.

Make out a separate sheet for each type of software package you are thinking about buying. One of the entries you need to pay special attention to is the brands and models of microcomputer the package is offered for. This fact will have a big effect on your choice of a microcomputer.

Perhaps the most important choice to be made when it comes to microcomputer brands and models comes down to a choice between IBM-compatible and Apple Macintosh. Although in the past IBM-compatible microcomputers dominated the market for business applications, Macintosh computers now offer the same types of software at competitive prices. This, coupled with the "friendly" user interface integrated throughout all Macintosh application software, has led to Apple out-selling IBM in the business microcomputer market in many cases.

The entry on the software checklist for operating system also requires a distinction between IBM compatible and Apple Macintosh computers. Many users prefer the friendly, graphic interface of the Macintosh over MS-DOS. You will need to determine which type of operating system you prefer. Many software packages today offer versions for both the Macintosh and IBM compatibles. These include products such as Microsoft Word, WordPerfect, and Microsoft Excel. Some products are only available for Macintosh computers, and others are available for only IBM-compatible computers. Thus, your choice of software can begin to limit some of your hardware choices and may force you into either the IBM compatible or the Macintosh models.

When listing specific models that software is designed for, you must also be aware of the different microprocessors used in various microcomputers. In the IBM-compatible market, models are based on the INTEL 8088, 80286, and 80386 microprocessors. Macintosh computers are based on the Motorola 68000, 68020, and 68030 microprocessors. Some software will run on only some of these microprocessors. For example the Lotus 1-2-3 spreadsheet package now comes in several versions, each designed for a different microprocessor and requiring different amounts of RAM and secondary storage. For example Lotus 1-2-3 Release 2.2 can run on all three INTEL processors and requires a minimum of 320K of RAM. Lotus 1-2-3 Release 3.0 requires at least an INTEL 80286 or 80386 microprocessor, 1Mbyte of RAM, and a hard disk. Lotus 1-2-3 Release 3.0/G is a version with a graphical user interface that requires at least an INTEL 80286 or 80386 microprocessor, a minimum of 4Mbytes of RAM, a hard disk, and can only be used with the OS/2 operating system. Again, as you can see, choosing a particular software product can directly determine the type of hardware you will need.

The checklist entry, "Ease of use: Reputation; Personal experience," will help you evaluate similar packages. You can judge a software package's reputation from reviews and from talking to users, but to decide if you like the software, you have to try it out. This means going to the campus computer center or back to the store to see if it has the software you are considering. You won't be able to take the software home or use it for an unlimited amount of time, but most stores will help you try out a particular software package.

To save time, you might narrow your choices down to two or three packages before you ask for any demonstrations. Once you get to that point, look over your user requirements to get an idea of the functions you will be using most often. Experiment with them. For example, for a given function, some software packages require that you hit several keys in sequence. Others require only one or two keystrokes. The difference may not seem significant until you spend several hours at your microcomputer.

Also, look at the way the software uses menus and commands. A menu saves you the labor of memorizing commands and options. Some software packages always show the menu. Others let you call the menu up only when you need it. Once you get used to using a package, you may prefer the directness of using commands rather than menus.

Also, be sure you look at the documentation when you take your "test drive." Is it clearly written; can you locate what you want to find out? Most software packages now also include tutorials with simple lessons to show you the basic functions. Others offer a telephone "hot line" with technical experts that will talk you through specific problems. Some stores include a free orientation lesson in the price of a microcomputer purchase, while other stores charge for the lesson.

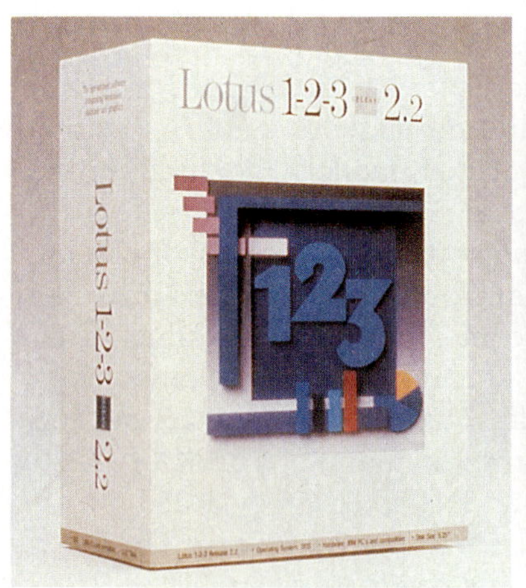

Lotus 1-2-3 Releases

Criteria	Software Packages A	B	C	D
Offered for which micros?				
Operating system?				
Primary memory requirements?				
Storage requirements Floppy disk drives Hard disk drive (size?)				
Display requirements Monochrome Hercules graphics Color (CGA, EGA, VGA?)				
Ease of use Reputation Personal experience				
Support Documentation Telephone hot line? Training? (free?)				
Special features				
Related packages				
Total price of software and support				

Software Package Comparison Sheet

Another entry on the software checklist concerns features. For example, some word processing packages can handle footnotes and others cannot. You will have to rate this particular feature as essential, preferable, or optional. If you want to, you can assign each feature a numerical value and compare the software packages' scores.

Make a checklist entry for each package and then compare them side by side. You could then arrange a test drive of just the packages that scored best. The checklist entry, "Related packages," is included because some software companies offer add-on packages. For example, add-on packages for the Lotus 1-2-3 spreadsheet include products that add built-in functions to Lotus, improve laser printer support, enhance spreadsheet graphs, and expand the spreadsheet's database capabilities.

When considering the price entry on the checklist, you may find mail-order houses that seem to offer lower prices, but is it a good idea to order from them? There are a couple of issues to consider. One is the kind of support you need versus the kind of support the software company offers. Mail-order houses don't charge as much as retail stores, but they don't offer the same kind of support either. Another issue to consider is the fact that some retail stores will offer you a lower price if you buy the software bundled with the hardware.

You might also want to look into *user-supported software* or *public domain software*. In the early days of microcomputers, almost everyone wrote and shared programs. Some software developers carry on that tradition. They will send you their program on a diskette and, if you like it, either ask you to send a modest sum or to buy their manual explaining how to use the program. These programs can often be found on electronic bulletin board systems or through local microcomputer user groups.

Once you've selected your software, you will know your hardware requirements. In most cases, the software you choose will limit your hardware options to machines that use a particular operating system.

When comparing hardware options, a checklist like the one below can be used to compare the price of a basic microcomputer plus the options. In some ways, buying a microcomputer is like buying a car. On some models, a certain feature may be standard. On other models, the same feature may mean an additional cost. And the little extras can add up fast.

When evaluating prices, it is helpful to know the manufacturer's suggested retail price. It might also be useful to check the advertisements that mail-order houses run in the computer magazines. In addition, some manufacturers and stores combine or bundle a microcomputer with certain software packages. If you happen on the right combination, you can save a lot of money this way.

Another thing to watch for is if the price of the monitor is included in the price of the microcomputer. The same is true of the keyboard.

In the process of determining prices, you will have to look at many individual components that go into a microcomputer. You will have to consider the microprocessor used, the amount of primary memory, the type of secondary storage, the resolution of the monitor, the type of input devices, and the type of printer that will make up your microcomputer system.

As you have already seen, the IBM-compatible computers can be based on several microprocessors. The software you choose will often narrow the possibilities, but there are still many options you need to consider. For example, microcomputers based on the INTEL 80386sx chip were recently introduced. This microprocessor is priced in the range of the 80286 processor, but can also run software designed for the 80386 processor. Computers based on the INTEL 80486 microprocessor are also appearing. To complicate matters even more, the speed of the microprocessors (measured in Megahertz) will also vary. For example, computers based on the 80386 microprocessor are available in 16, 20, 25, and 33 Mhz. In general, machines with a higher speed will cost more. The same complications exist in the Macintosh world. The hardware checklist has space for you to indicate both the type of processor and the speed of the processor as factors to be considered.

Most microcomputers today come with at least 640K of primary memory and many are moving to a standard of 1 to 2Mbytes of RAM. You can put as much as 16Mbytes of RAM in many of the newer microcomputers. Obviously, increased RAM adds to the price of the microcomputer, and there are variations in the amount of RAM that is standard in microcomputer models.

Macintosh Family of Computers

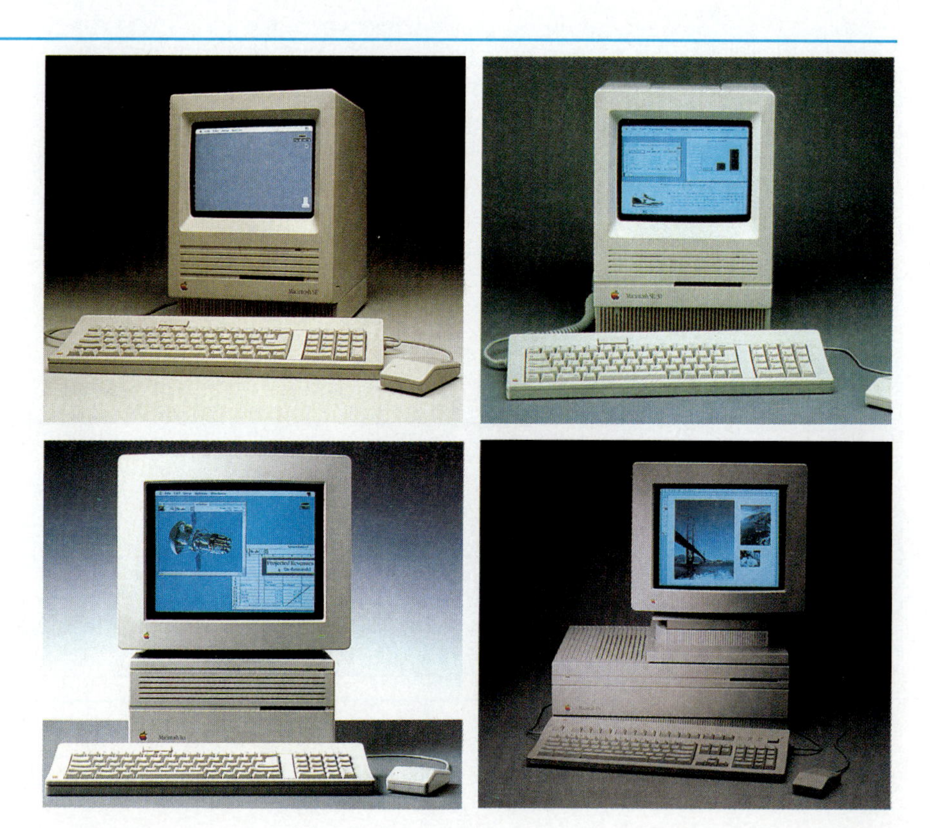

Criteria	Microcomputers A	B	C	D
Basic price Retail Discount				
Processor IBM (8088, 80286, 80368, or 80368sx) Macintosh (68000, 68020, or 68030) Speed (MHz)				
Primary memory (RAM)				
Input device Keyboard Extended keyboard (101 keys) Mouse				
Disk drives 3 1/2 Inch 5 1/4 inch Hard disk				
Monitor Monochrome Hercules graphics CGA, EGA, VGA				
Printer Dot matrix Ink-jet Laser				
Other items Modem Math coprocessor				
Total price of hardware configuration				

Microcomputer Comparison Sheet

Computer Disks

Most recent microcomputers offer a 3 1/2-inch floppy disk drive as standard. Both 3 1/2- and 5 1/4-inch drives are often available, as well as hard disk drives. With floppy disk drives, you must be alert to variations in storage capacity. Five and a quarter-inch drives are offered with 360K and 1.2Mbyte capacities and 3 1/2-inch drives are offered in 720K and 1.44Mbyte capacities. Each type of drive requires different diskettes. In general, the higher capacity drives can read diskettes from lower capacity drives, but not vice versa. With hard disk drives there is a large variety of sizes. Most hard disk drives have a capacity of 30 to 40Mbytes, but capacities of over 300Mbytes are also available. Naturally, higher capacity disk drives will be more expensive.

The main distinction in monitors is between monochrome and color. Monochrome monitors typically cannot display graphics unless a graphics card is added to the computer. Color monitors can display graphics and currently come in three resolutions: CGA, EGA, and VGA. The difference between the three is the *resolution*, or number of pixels (dots) that make up the screen. The more pixels, the clearer the image on the screen. CGA has the lowest resolution and VGA the highest. There is also variability within each category. For example, there are several different resolutions available within the VGA category. In general, a higher-resolution monitor will be less likely to cause eyestrain and will cost more.

There are two main types of keyboards. The older keyboards place the function keys to the left and have cursor movement keys included on the numeric keypad. Newer 101-key keyboards place function keys across the top (usually 12 function keys instead of 10) and offer separate cursor-movement keys in addition to those on the numeric keypad. Most newer microcomputers are standardizing on the 101-key keyboard.

For many users the "feel" of a keyboard can be very important. There are variations in the distances between keys, the size of keys, and the amount of pressure needed to press the key. The tilt of the keyboard is also important. Considering the amount of time you may spend at your microcomputer, attention to how the keyboard feels to you may be very important.

In addition, many microcomputers now come with a mouse pointing device as standard equipment—particularly Macintosh computers. Many newer software packages make extensive use of a mouse, so you will need to determine whether you will need one and what is the cost. Mice also come in different varieties. The two major types of mice are optical and mechanical. A mechanical mouse can be moved across the desktop; an optical mouse requires a pad on which it must be moved. Mice also come with different numbers of buttons.

Some miscellaneous items that may be required include a modem and a math coprocessor. You may need a modem if you plan to communicate with electronic bulletin boards or remote computers such as mainframes located in a computer center. The major factor to consider with a modem is the communication speed. A math coprocessor is helpful if you plan to use any software that performs a large number of calculations, such as a spreadsheet or a statistics program.

With printers the major distinction is in print quality and speed. At the low end are dot-matrix printers, which are inexpensive but are relatively slow and do not produce high-quality output. Newer dot-matrix printers achieve what is known as "near-letter" quality by using more pins to produce the dots. These printers produce higher quality output at faster speeds, but at a higher cost. Some newer printers use ink-jet technology to produce letter quality output. These printers often produce higher quality output, but require relatively expensive ink cartridges and sometimes require special paper. At the high end, laser printers produce the best quality output and cost the most.

Of course, you may be able to save some money by not buying a printer. If your equipment is compatible, you may be able to use a printer at your school's computing center.

Another purchase you need to plan for is supplies such as diskettes and fanfold paper. You need to have plenty of diskettes so that you can make backup copies of all your original software and important data files. You can save some money by purchasing some of these supplies by mail through discount houses.

Systems Implementation

Systems implementation consists of learning and starting to use your new system. You should research training while you are researching your possible purchase. If you have done so it should be easy to get your computer system operating.

You really should allow lots of time for familiarizing yourself with the software and the microcomputer before you need it. If you are hurrying or trying to meet a deadline, the chance you will make mistakes increases. And some mistakes can erase a lot of hard work.

In conclusion, although the purchase of a microcomputer can be difficult and confusing, the application of this systems approach should help you gather and organize the information you need to choose the software and hardware best suited to you. This process can make your transition into the information society as enjoyable and rewarding as possible.

PART V

Opportunities and Concerns

CHAPTER 18

The Information Age Society

Throughout this text you have seen the importance of information systems in the activities of the business world. Computerization is becoming common in offices, factories, and even in homes. This chapter explores these broad changes and why they are happening in our society. In this chapter, you will learn to do the following:

1. Give an overview of the computer technologies now available for use in the office
2. Discuss how computers are increasing the efficiency of modern factories through computer-aided manufacturing, design, and engineering
3. Explain the information services that are now or will soon be available in the home
4. Describe how, through telecommuting, the work place of the future for many may be the home

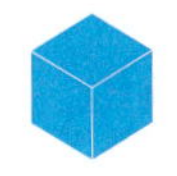

Electronic Office Systems

Since the advent of the early typewriters in the 1850s, machines have played an increasingly important role in the offices of business, industry, and government. In the 1900s the Morse telegraph, Edison's dictating machine, and the Bell telephone were added. Then came adding machines, copiers, tape recorders, and electric typewriters.

In the 1960s organizations began to use the newly developed large central computers, primarily for accounting. A decade later, the remote terminal allowed data to be entered and received from a large computer, which was often far away. In the late 1970s and early 1980s the microcomputer burst on the scene. It significantly changed the complexion of the office, both in the way work was done and in the social patterns of employees.

Why this increase in computerization? To understand, let's take a closer look at office work—people reading, thinking, writing, and communicating. Proposals are considered; money is collected and spent; organizations are managed. The key ingredient in these activities is *information*. More and more companies need and value any tool or technique that will increase their efficiency in gathering, storing, retrieving, manipulating, and distributing information. Increasingly, this is based on computers and electronic forms of information.

This is one aspect of the need for computerization. Another is the fact that information workers—primarily office workers—are becoming a large part of the work force. Today there are over 80 million white-collar workers: managers, professional and technical workers, as well as clerical personnel and salespeople. The majority of these knowledge workers are in the information sector, which as you have seen is over half of the total work force in the United States. Exhibit 18.1 shows the composition of this group throughout this century, including projection through the year 2000.

Exhibit 18.1

Information Workers Growth

The demand for information workers has increased dramatically since the 1950s.

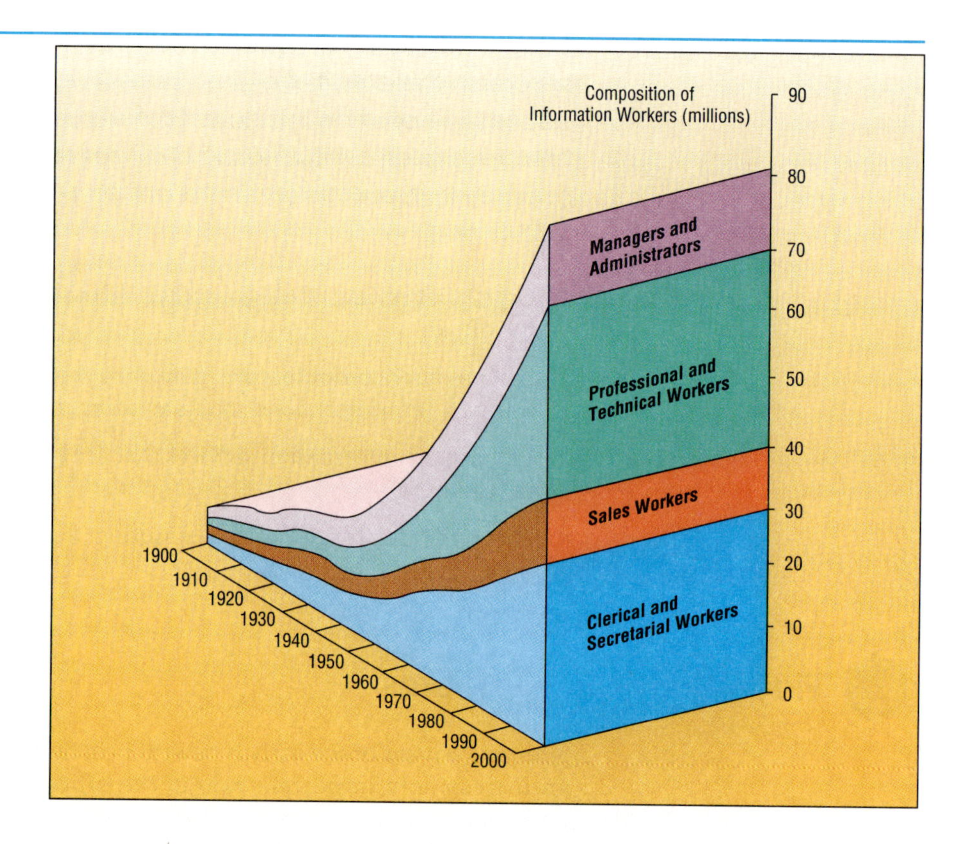

Supplying these workers with the tools and information they need to work efficiently is a crucial task for all successful organizations.

Major companies such as IBM, Apple, and Xerox have declared that their futures are based on the assumption that this move toward office automation, or more accurately, the electronic office, is only beginning. They predict that the "office of the future" will be the cornerstone of a large industry devoted to supplying increased computerization to a growing number of white-collar workers.

Electronic office systems consist of machines that utilize computer technology to simplify and streamline traditional office work by communicating various forms of information electronically. These systems include electronic mail, voice mail, facsimile, teleconferencing, and videotext. The modern office also routinely includes tools for end-user computing (see Exhibit 18.2). These tools allow workers to perform complex tasks that might not be attempted without computer support. Previous chapters discussed the computer-based tools of end-user computing. This section introduces the new electronic office systems.

Electronic Mail

The time saved by preparing a memo, letter, or other document with word processing can easily be lost while these documents snake their way

Exhibit 18.2
The Electronic Office

through interoffice mail. These delays are even more frustrating when most workers have microcomputers connected to a local-area network. These workers want the convenience of **electronic mail (E-mail),** which is the electronic exchange of text messages via personal computers.

It is estimated that 70 percent of all business phone calls are not completed. The other person is out of town, in a meeting, or on another line. The result is "phone tag," a series of short messages left with secretaries because the original message is too complex to easily explain. Much of this wasted effort could be replaced by electronic mail, in which detailed messages can be left in an electronic mailbox (see Exhibit 18.3).

When the other person has time to review the accumulated messages, he or she can bring them up on the screen and take appropriate action. This could include sending a reply by electronic mail. Electronic mail is particularly attractive to organizations with offices in different time zones—the offices may have few hours in common.

Voice Mail

An alternative to typing messages in a microcomputer and sending them by electronic mail is voice mail. **Voice mail** digitizes speech dictation, stores the message on disk, and can forward the voice output to other phones as requested. As with an answering machine, a message is created by the caller speaking into a phone terminal. Unlike an answering machine, however, which records a vocal message, voice mail uses a digitized form of the spoken message, which can then be stored on a disk. This digitized message is forwarded through a telecommunication system to one or more phones at a later time. On request, the digitized message is put through a speech synthesizer and is then heard as the original voice message.

Exhibit 18.3

Examples of Electronic Mail Facilities

(a) The Electronic messaging facility in Digital Equipment's All-in-one office automation product.

```
                    Electronic Messaging
                 ( 4 new mail messages )

SEL  Select message          Folder:  OUTBOX
                             Title:   Electronic Mail Use
C    Create                  Author:  John Day
E    Edit                    Date:    Modified on: 29-Oct-1990 03:44pm
D    Delete                  Number:  000013    Status:  SENT
P    Print
R    Read
I    Index
RI   Recall index                     II  Index - Inbox
                                      IR  Index - Read
RN   Read new mail                    IC  Index - Created
A    Answer                           IO  Index - Outbox
S    Send
F    Forward                          TR  Training

Enter option and press RETURN,
or press NEXT SCREEN for more options                        (more...)
```

(b) A screen from the mail facility in a WordPerfect office.

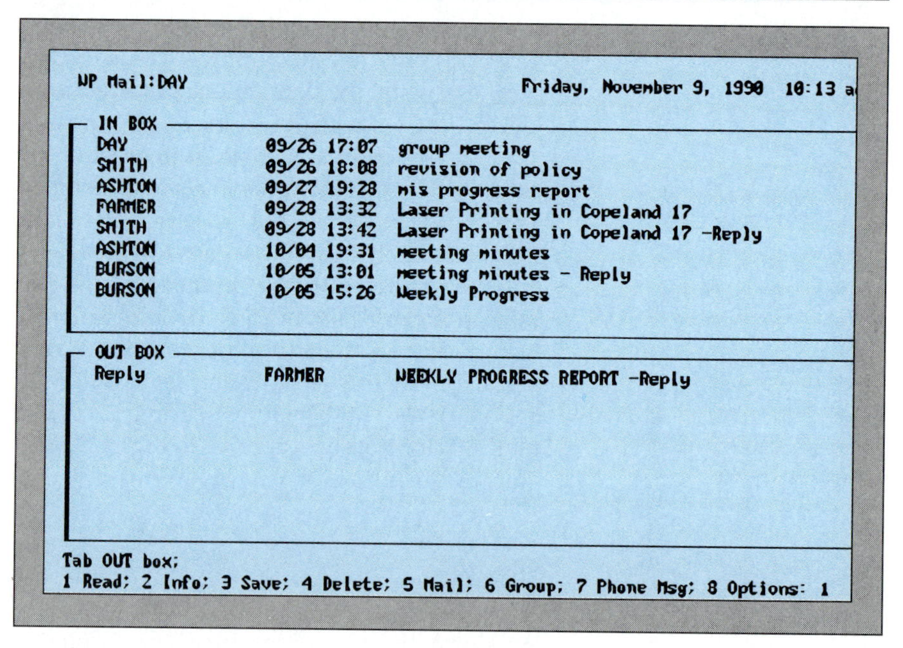

For example, you may want a message to be available to ten other parties at 2 P.M. local time, yet you want to leave the message at your convenience—at 9 A.M. This is made possible by a feature called store-and-forward. You record the message only once and then enter a distribution list of phone numbers. Voice mail does the rest.

One advanced feature is the ability to annotate a voice message. That is, assume you receive a message from someone who works for you. You can add a comment to the end of this message and send both messages to your boss, who is on vacation in Bermuda. Your boss can retrieve her voice mail at a convenient time and hear both the original message and your reaction. In addition, she can also retrieve voice mail from a different phone. Assume, for example, she decides to go to dinner and call the office for messages from there. A single call to the phone number at the office can forward the day's voice mail to the pay phone at the restaurant.

Both electronic and voice mail allow messages to be stamped for time and date of origin. In addition, these systems can verify that a party has received the message and will record the time the message was retrieved.

Facsimile

Facsimile (**FAX** machines) can be used to transmit and receive non-electronic documents electronically. Businesses increasingly are finding it necessary to quickly exchange documents between distant offices. FAX machines resemble office copiers. A document is fed into the machine, electronically encoded (digitized), and transmitted over ordinary telephone lines to another FAX machine. On the second machine, a replica of the original is printed on a thermal or high-quality laser printer (see Exhibit 18.4). FAX machines can be used to send charts and photographs as well as text or data. They can even be used to transmit signatures, which is especially useful when verified authorization is required. For high-volume operations, a letter-sized document can be sent in under twenty seconds, and the cost is approximately forty cents. In addition, FAX transmission permits certain security measures such as encryption, the "scrambling" of electronic data, to prevent "eavesdropping." Because of these advantages, FAX transmission is replacing regular and electronic mail for certain types of business communication. Today, FAX machines have become so useful

Exhibit 18.4
FAX Machines

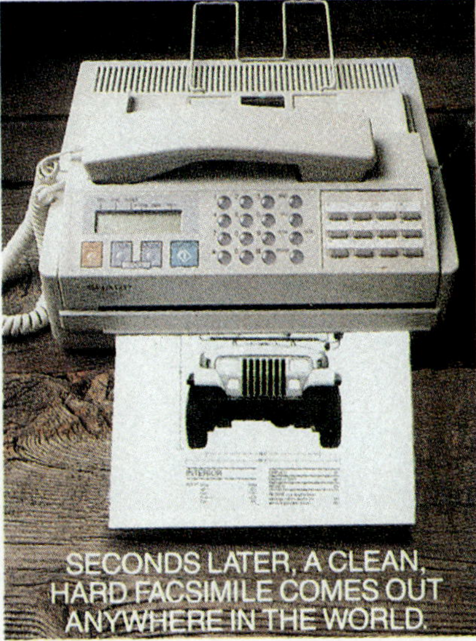

and affordable that it is difficult to find a small business without one. In addition, many retail businesses offer public FAX machines for anyone to use for a modest fee. Many businesspeople now even have personal FAX machines in their homes.

Teleconferencing

Electronic mail, voice mail, and facsimile are all methods of one-way communication between users separated by time or distance. These tools satisfy a surprisingly large percentage of white-collar workers' communication needs, but what about those occasions when individuals in widely separated locations need two-way communication?

A telephone conference call is one obvious solution. But when visual cues are also important, **teleconferencing,** sometimes called video conferencing, is a better solution. These are electronic meetings in which video images of the activities at each location are sent over telecommunication paths, along with verbal messages. Full video conferencing includes transmission of full-motion video images and audio of both parties in *real time*—as the events are happening. This closely simulates what would take place if all the parties were in the same room. Exhibit 18.5 shows a typical teleconferencing layout.

Videotext

Organizations are becoming more and more information intensive. Much of the communication of this information has been and will continue to exist in the form of paper documentation. So much so that a far greater number of

Exhibit 18.5

A Teleconferencing Facility

pages are produced for internal and external communication by corporations and government agencies than by all the traditional book, magazine, and newspaper publishers combined. A surprisingly large portion of this documentation can be produced more cost effectively using desktop publishing than with traditional printing methods.

Another corporate alternative to paper documents is videotext. **Videotext** is an interactive computer system that enables the retrieval of documents that contain text and graphics for display on a personal computer. Common applications using videotext include corporate policy manuals, price lists, parts and service catalogs, on-line expense forms, corporate phone directories, and company news bulletins. These documents are stored in electronic form on the organization's mainframe or minicomputer.

Authorized users use a menu selection procedure to search the videotext database for the desired document and have the appropriate pages displayed on their local personal computer. If it is desirable to have a hard copy output, the information can be printed on a local printer.

Videotext is gaining popularity in organizations because it allows the base document to be kept in one place, where it can easily be updated as required. This assures anyone accessing the document that it is the official and current version. A second advantage is the major reduction in the number of copies of corporate manuals, newsletters, telephone books, and so on, that have to be published and distributed throughout an organization.

Movement to the Information Age Office

The tools of word processing, electronic and voice mail, teleconferencing, and videotext, if implemented successfully, will change the office significantly. The office of the future will be heavily equipped with electronic machines, but even more importantly, the ways the office conducts its business of creating, storing, manipulating, and exchanging information will change.

As an example, let's take a look at an insurance company before electronic office systems. In this type of office, work focuses on processing transactions of new policies, sending out bills, collecting and crediting payments, and processing claims. For efficiency, these offices are generally set up as a production line (see Exhibit 18.6). Each desk handles a particular type of transaction or is involved in checking the accuracy of entries or calculations. These activities could be input logging, validation, journal updating, exceptions, reconciliation, posting, and output logging.

Tasks are fragmented and standardized. This assembly-line approach is quite efficient in processing large volumes of transactions in a routine fashion. A customer inquiry can, however, cause major disruptions. Trying to locate a particular customer file in the assembly line is often close to impossible. Another disadvantage is that the information is always less than up to date, because the file can only be updated after it has been through the entire process. Any type of reports generated by a management

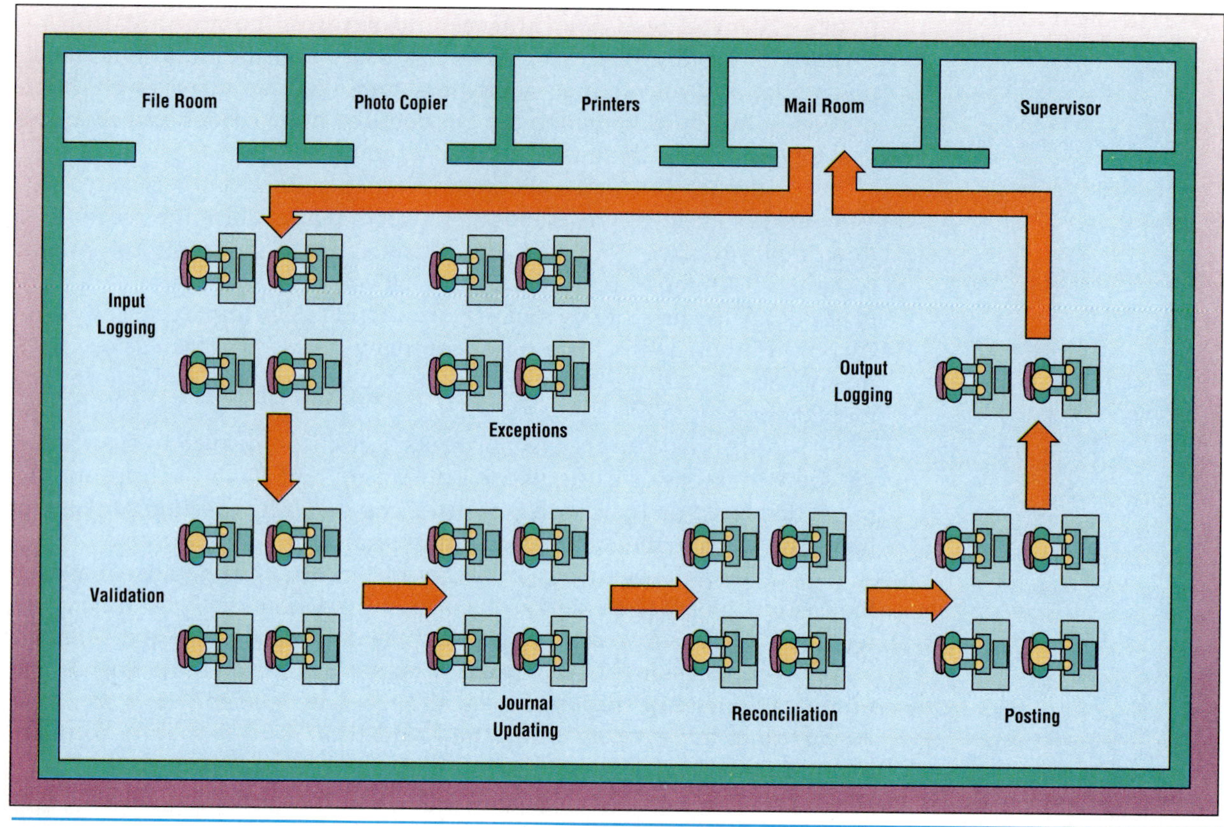

Exhibit 18.6

Industrial-Age Office

Documents are carried from the mail room to the beginning of the production line and eventually emerge at the other end; the flow is indicated by the orange arrows.

information system have to be compiled periodically rather than on demand. Too much effort is required to assemble data manually, and the data processing staff would need months to prepare programs to handle special requests.

Computerizing the office can result in an "information-age office" (see Exhibit 18.7). Each clerk has a computer workstation connected electronically to the host computer, which provides ready access to customer files. Alternatively, the workstations are personal microcomputers interconnected by a local-area network and also connected to a central host computer.

The important point here is that the clerk can process the claims of a few clients and update their records as necessary. The adjuster is responsible for all aspects of a few clients' records, as opposed to doing a few tasks on the records of many customers. In this way, client records are very timely—there is no work "in-progress."

Inquiries are handled quite easily, since the data are on-line electronically, and a database retrieval facility has been provided. *Ad hoc* queries by managers can draw upon the same database without any manual manipulation or rekeying of the basic data. Software routines can be used to extract the appropriate data from the database, which then can be used as input to various decision support systems.

Factory Automation

Office computerization has been closely paralleled by efforts to automate the factory. Particularly in the smokestack industries of steel, machine tool, textile, and tire production, advances in computer and machine technologies have been important in competing against companies that control costs by using the inexpensive and high-quality labor of third-world countries. Factory automation includes computer-aided manufacturing, computer-aided design, and computer-aided engineering.

Computer-Aided Manufacturing

Computer-aided manufacturing (CAM) uses computers to control the machines used in manufacturing. This results in a very flexible manufacturing system that can adjust to the changing demand for parts both quickly and efficiently. An example of CAM is shown in Exhibit 18.8.

In this exhibit, a set of machine tools is used to produce a variety of metal parts automatically. Each machine is driven by instructions from an individual microcomputer. In turn, each microcomputer is connected in a hierarchy to a minicomputer, which also controls the conveyor belt. The microcomputer determines the overall sequence of operations to be performed in tooling a particular piece. As the computer-controlled conveyor belt delivers each piece to a particular machine, the minicomputer downloads a program into the microcomputer that controls that tool. Ordering the machines to produce a different type of part is as simple as changing the programs downloaded into each microcomputer. Flexible manufacturing systems have been built that can run for hours without human intervention, manufacturing a wide variety of parts.

Another type of computer-programmable machine is called a robot. When the word *robot* is used, most people think of something like R2D2 in *Star Wars*. But real robots are much more primitive. In their simplest form, **robots** are any mechanical devices that can be programmed to perform useful tasks involving manipulation and/or mobility. The two major types of robots used in industry today are materials-handling machines and industrial robots.

In the 1970s, computer science technology was applied to materials-handling machines. Automatic storage and retrieval systems were programmed to transfer pallets of materials to or from storage racks or bins. For example, a part needed on the assembly line would be identified by part number. The computer would search its database to determine the part's location. A computer-generated command would then shuttle the materials-handling machine to the correct storage location, where it would retrieve the needed part and then deliver that part to the assembly line.

An industrial robot is a device that can be programmed to move a gripper or other tool through space to accomplish a useful industrial task. Human operators use a variety of methods to teach robots to perform certain repetitive tasks. These include leading the robot through the desired

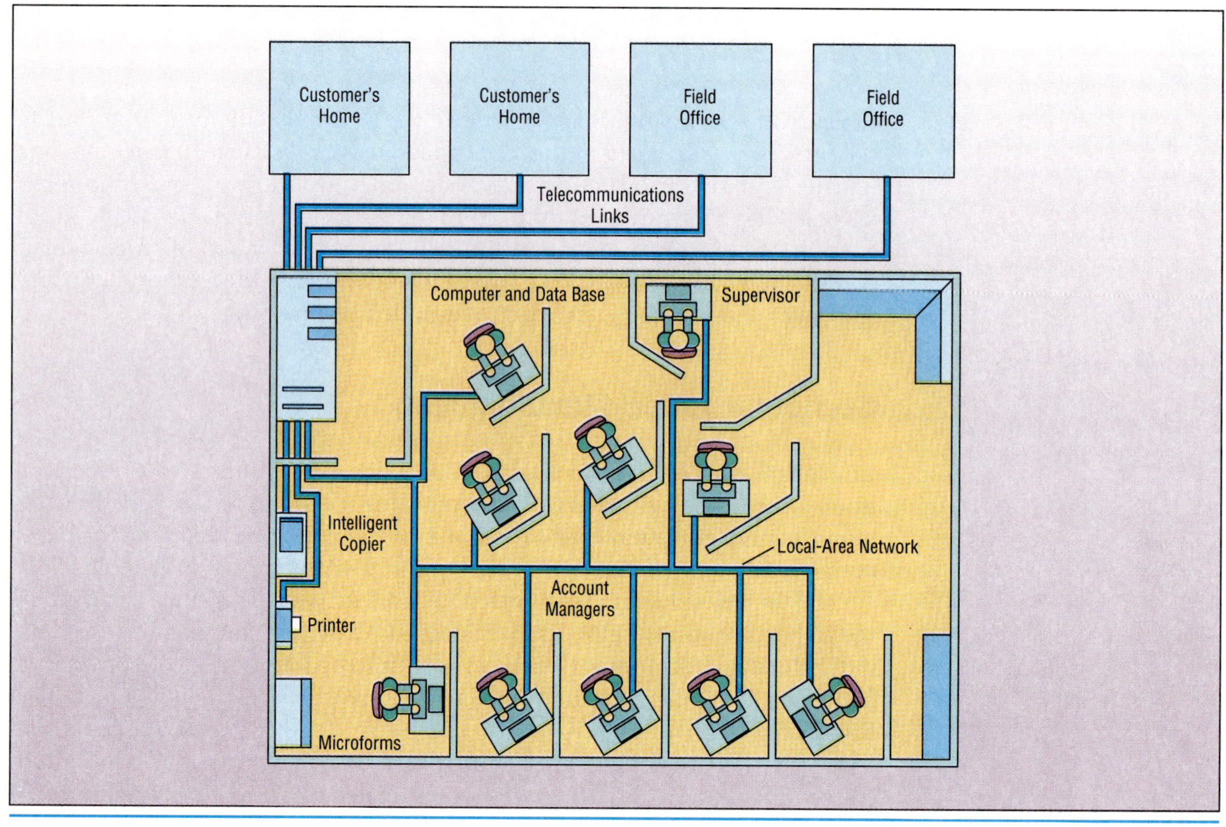

Exhibit 18.7

Information-Age Office

Each workstation is linked (color lines) to a computer that maintains and continuously updates all client records. Each adjuster operates as an account manager, handling all operations for a few clients rather than one repetitive operation for a large number of clients.

positions by using a teaching box, which is a control box used to move the robot and record the steps the robot went through, physically moving the robot's arm through the required motions, or designing software programs that control the robot's actions (see Exhibit 18.9).

An industrial robot is adequate for performing a surprising number of industrial tasks, such as spray painting, loading and unloading machine tools and presses, and performing a wide variety of materials-handling tasks. Robots have proved to be especially useful in simple, repetitive tasks such as arc welding automobile bodies. For human workers, arc welding is a hot, dirty, unpleasant job requiring heavy protective clothing as shelter from showers of hot sparks and choking smoke. Typically, a human welder cannot keep a torch on the work more than 30 percent of the time. But a robot welder can keep its torch on the work 90 percent of the time, with only brief breaks required to move materials into position. Thus, even though the robot cannot weld faster than a human, it can turn out about three times as much work.

The great majority of industrial tasks are still, however, beyond the capacities of current robot technology. Tasks are either too complex and unstructured or they depend on the ability to see, feel, and adapt to changing circumstances.

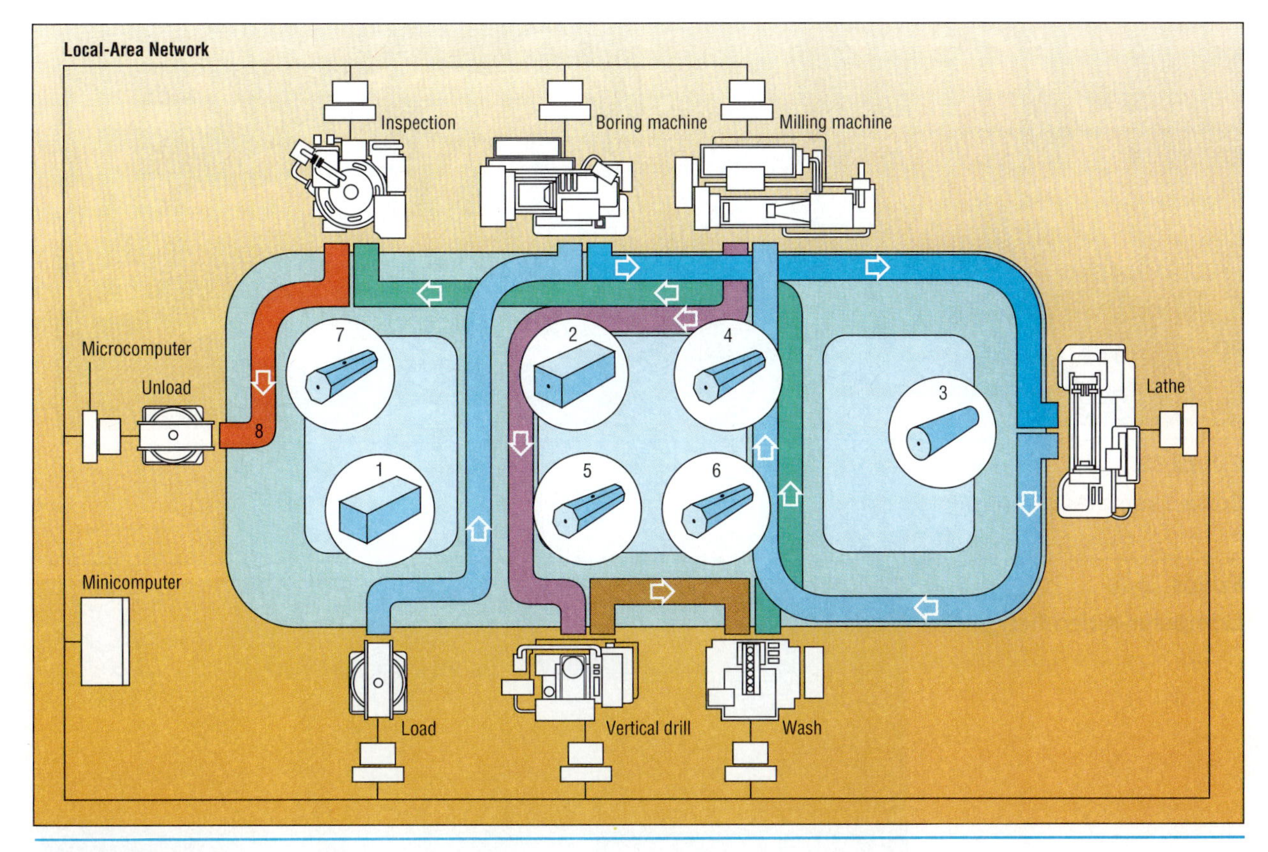

Exhibit 18.8

Computer-Aided Manufacturing

In this example of Computer-Aided manufacturing, eight machines are linked and coordinated in a metal-working process.

Computer-Aided Design

Computer-aided design (CAD) is simply the use of a computer graphics terminal and software in product design. Designers are no longer limited to drawings laboriously prepared with the manual tools of T-squares, compasses, pens, and pencils.

With a CAD system, the designer uses a combination of menus and pointing devices to generate drawings on a computer display screen. He or she can rotate the part design on the computer screen along any axis, zoom in close to see details, and back off to see the whole object. With a few keystrokes, the designer can quickly and effortlessly change the scale of any drawing; and a sequence of commands can divide the design into various segments or parts. If this overall design is to mesh with other parts to form a larger assemblage, those parts can be added to the design at the appropriate places. Each design image on the screen can be easily changed and then stored (see Exhibit 18.10). When needed, a perfect set of engineering drawings can be printed using a plotter.

These engineering drawings are essential to producing the detailed programs that control the machines in a flexible manufacturing system. Efficiency would improve if these instructions could be generated as a by-product of the computerized design process. In this way, once a design was

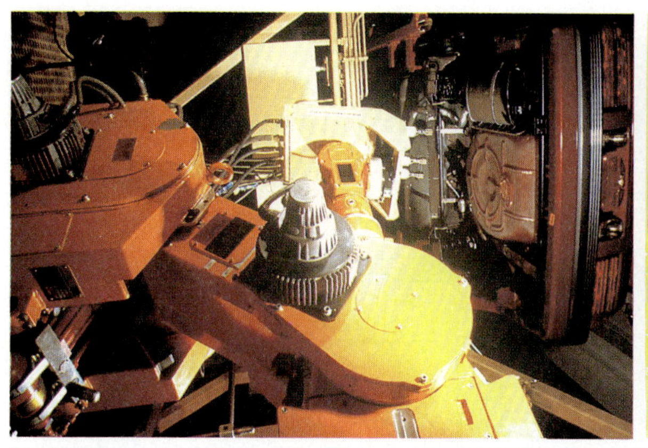

Exhibit 18.9

Some Examples of Industrial Robots

Exhibit 18.10

Computer-Aided Design

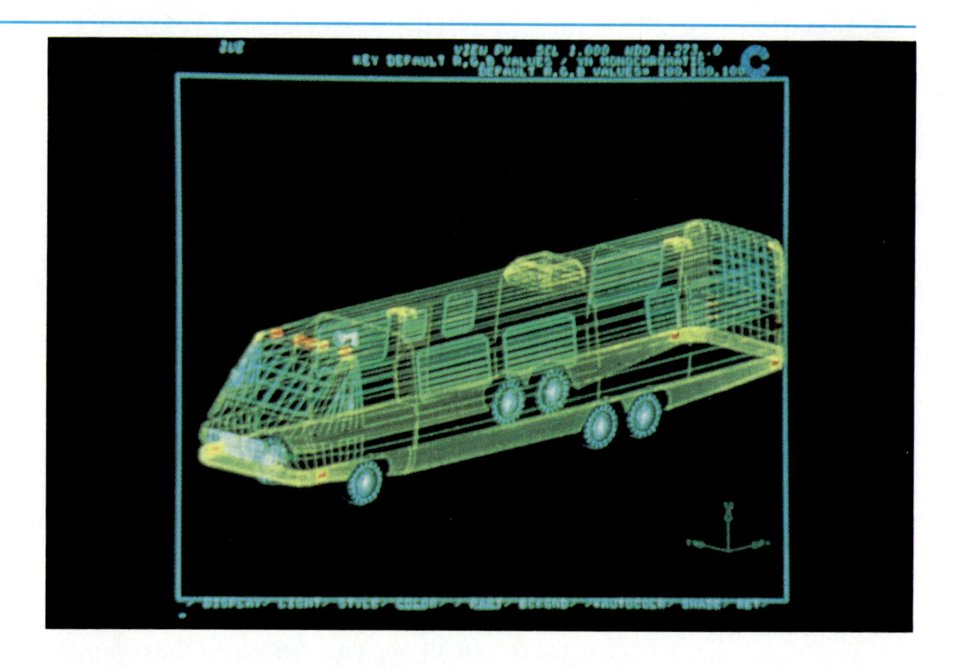

finalized, algorithms would translate the design into programming instructions for each of the machines needed to manufacture the newly designed product. This coordination of computer-aided design and manufacturing, called CAD/CAM, is currently being developed.

Computer-Aided Engineering

CAD/CAM provides a very sophisticated way of seeing various views of a design and then generating appropriate engineering drawings and machine instructions. **Computer-aided engineering (CAE)** allows designers and engineers to use computers to test their designs. For example, how will an airplane wing withstand the stress of flying at 600 miles per hour? How will the metal react to the variations in temperature found between the chill of 30,000 feet up and the heat of a desert runway?

Before CAE the primary method of testing designs was to build a prototype and subject it to the anticipated conditions. With CAE, the computer is used to simulate mechanical stress conditions, temperature fluctuations, and so on. General Motors has used CAE for many of its auto parts designs. It believes that the on-screen testing of a part has worked well and saved the company significant amounts of time and money. This computer process gives a good idea of how much a part is going to weigh, how strong and stiff it will be, and how well it will perform. As GM states, CAE lets it fix parts before the car is even built.

Movement to the Information Age Factory

Although individual robots can make some contribution to increasing the productivity of a manufacturing plant, significant gains can only come when the many activities of a factory can be coordinated to respond to continually changing product demand. This requires the development and maintenance of a factory information system.

Let's look first at a simple example of how this can be applied to the task of painting cars (see Exhibit 18.11). This assembly line uses a series of robots to paint the sides and roofs of a variety of car models. The management question becomes how to program these robots when the car models and corresponding colors change in an unpredictable pattern. Each of the robots has a machine controller (which can be a microcomputer) that uses software instructions to direct when the robot is to paint, what color is to be used, and what car model's paint routine to use.

At the start of the production line, a model-recognition sensor reads an identification code (for example, a bar code) on the car. This information is sent to the main computer, which checks the database to determine the car model and body style, such as two-door or convertible, to determine the painting routine. Information about car model and body style is then compared to the plant schedule showing how many cars of that model and body type are to be blue, green, red, and so on, and how many cars have already been painted in each color this day or week. Based on this comparison, the main computer sends instructions to the appropriate robots.

This integrated system, combined with local-area networks and other telecommunication links, allows the plant to remain very flexible. For example, assume market research has just received a study showing consumers' color preference for Model X has shifted from green to red. This information can be programmed into the plant schedule, and the paint assembly line can be modified quite easily.

Another major aspect of the modern factory is the overall production planning. This planning drives the master production schedule, which, in turn, establishes the conditions for materials requirement planning. This is a complex task, but an example may show why

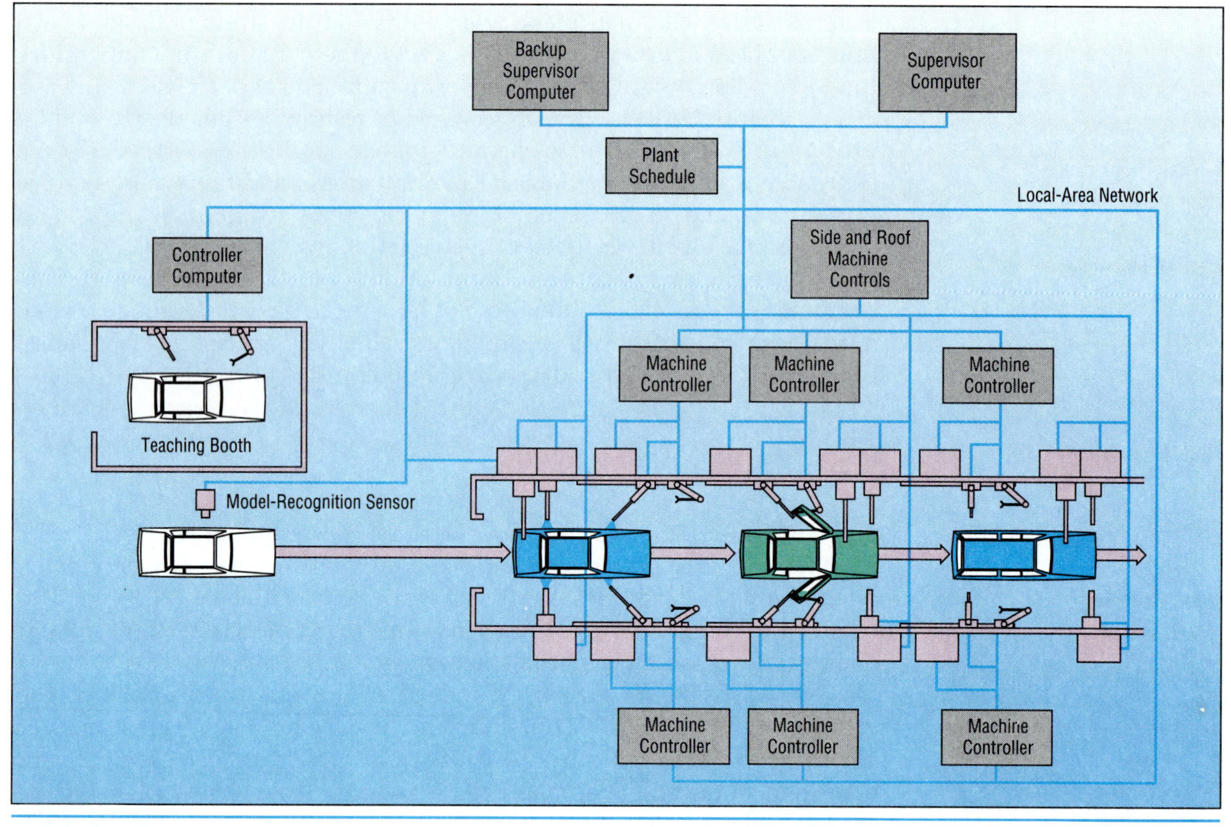

Exhibit 18.11

Robotic Automobile Painting System

This diagram shows the paint system developed by General Motors corporation; the system is at the GM assembly plant in Doraville, Georgia.

information in general, and the factory information system specifically, is the key to the factory of the future.

Materials requirement planning (MRP) uses a computer to schedule purchases and deliveries of the parts needed to meet the master production schedule. The goal is to make certain materials are available when needed without diverting company funds to excess inventory and warehousing costs. The back-scheduling algorithm is a relatively simple way of performing this task. The finished product is broken down into its component parts, such as six shelves, four vertical supports, twenty-four shelf supports, ninety-six bolts, and so on. These parts can be further divided into those that can be purchased from outside vendors and those that are to be produced in-house. A back schedule is projected for each subpart, and the appropriate purchase and shop orders are given.

While this calculation may seem straightforward for a simple product, imagine the nightmare of fast, accurate materials requirement planning for a product with 10,000 parts. Then imagine the complication of daily adjustments to the production schedule. If production needs to jump from 10,000 to 20,000 units overnight, can the right number of parts be made available? Without a computer, these calculations and adjustments are physically impossible. But this computerization also needs to be supported by a good factory information system, one that supplies accurate, timely information on inventory levels and required manufacturing lead times.

The factory of the future will be a computer- and information-intensive facility with a highly skilled work force. At the heart of the factory will be a **computer-integrated manufacturing (CIM)** system. CIM is the integration of CAD, CAM, and CAE, robotics, factory information systems, and telecommunication links to coordinate product design, planning, and manufacturing in a way that will maximize efficiency.

In this vision of the future, the factory will be made up of glass-enclosed, air-conditioned, sound-protected worker areas, and workers will spend much of their time at computer terminals. In many ways, the work environment will become more like that of today's office. There will still be noisy, dangerous processes, but these will be taken over by computer-controlled machines and robots. Factory workers will need fewer manual and craft skills and more technical and analytical skills. This shift in the nature of factory work will mean a further shift in the proportion of blue-collar and white-collar workers. As shown in Exhibit 18.12, the "factory of the future" already exists, and will become increasingly common in the future.

Home Information Services

As in the office and factory in the future, the computer will be used in a variety of ways in the home. Some home applications include:

- *Personal services.* By using a computer to gain access to an information utility, people will have the convenience of electronic mail, banking, and shopping, including travel and entertainment planning.
- *Computer-assisted education.* Students of any age will have access to electronic learning games with graphics of arcade-game quality.

Exhibit 18.12

The New Factory Worker

A technician monitors dishwasher production from a computer console at a refurbished General Electric plant in Louisville. The production line can easily be reprogrammed to make any of fifteen dishwasher models.

- *Control of home systems.* A computer can be programmed to monitor and adjust heating and air conditioning based on variations in temperature, time of day, and other variables. The same computer can be used to monitor and control major appliances.
- *Security.* Through a system of sensors, the computer can detect dangers and can respond by activating safety measures, such as a sprinkler system, and by activating various alarms at home or in the police or fire station.

Many of these applications are available today. Others can be seen in houses of the future, such as the Xanadu home (see Exhibit 18.13) located just outside Orlando, Florida. It is designed to showcase some of the options that the application of computer technology to the home will add to family life. These intelligent homes will have talking computers, an "electronic hearth," and various computer-activated sensors and control systems that regulate energy and lighting. These are all plausible extensions of existing technologies that can be purchased today. In the rest of this section, we will concentrate on the personal services information utilities offer.

Information Utilities

Some very resourceful companies have taken advantage of the recent advances in telecommunication, microcomputers, and databases to form information utilities. An **information utility,** like the electric or gas company, supplies its utility—information—to homes or offices in return for a fee. In many ways, these services integrate computer and telecommunications technology. Subscribers can use computer terminals to

Exhibit 18.13

The Intelligent Home

access information stored in the utility's database. This means that subscribers can perform extensive research quickly and easily from their homes or offices. The idea of using a computer for these personal services is not a futuristic notion. Many of these services have, in fact, been available since 1979.

Because they are changing so rapidly, it is hard to generalize about the charges for these services. Typically, subscribers must pay a one-time registration fee and then pay additional fees for *connect time*, the amount of time the user spends accessing the database. Usually the fees are higher for accessing the utility during business hours than at night or on weekends. In addition, subscribers must pay any telephone charges. In return, they gain access to a wealth of information.

Exhibit 18.14 shows a sampling of other information utilities. Home and business users equipped with a microcomputer, a modem, communication software, a telephone line, and a subscription to the appropriate utility can access any of these databases.

Travel and Entertainment Planning

The databases of the Official Airline Guide's (OAG) flight schedules, Cineman's Movie Reviews Database, and Mobil's Travel Guide can be used for travel and entertainment planning. These databases can be accessed through a variety of information utilities. For example, you could use CompuServe to get flight information and reservations for flights and rental cars. Exhibit 18.15 on page 491 shows the procedure for requesting flight information.

To determine what restaurants are available in Chicago or any of four thousand other cities in North America, you can call up the dining database. This component of the Mobil Travel Guide is an electronic guide that can be searched by city and by cuisine. For example, you can request and receive a printout of French restaurants in Chicago. Further, the Mobil Travel Guide provides an overall rating of the restaurants (one to five stars), along with helpful information on prices, hours, entertainment, and credit cards accepted. If you finish dinner early, you can get help in deciding which movie to see by consulting the Cineman Movie Reviews Database. This service reviews fifty current movies and is updated every Friday.

Teleshopping

Through information utilities such as CompuServe, you can use your personal computer to shop at home. Comp-U-Store offers price quotes for over 250,000 brand name products from over two hundred companies. Products such as major appliances, televisions, stereos, videocassette recorders, and cameras, with brand names such as General Electric, Canon, Maytag, Sony, and Zenith, are available through this service. When several dealers handle the same product, the computer searches for and displays the name of the merchant offering the lowest price. The subscriber can then

Producing Company	Product or Service	Product or Service Description
Dialog Information Services, Inc. Alto, California	Dialog	On-line access to databases Palo from many sources on a wide variety of subjects.
Mead Data Central New York, NY	Nexis	Collection of analyst's reports, government regulations and forecasts, and articles from business, trade, and news publications
Standard & Poor's Corp. Englewood, Colorado	CompuStat	On-line access to financial reports on U.S. and Canadian businesses and financial institutions
The Bureau of National Affairs, Inc. (BNA) Washington, D.C.	Laborlaw	On-line access to information on federal and state judicial and administrative decisions on labor and employment
Official Airlines Guides, Inc. Oak Brook, Illinois	OAG Electronic Edition	On-line access to North American and international airline schedules
Congressional Information Service, Inc. Bethesda, Maryland	American Statistics Index (ASI)	Citations and abstracts to U.S. government statistical documents available on-line and in print
Dow Jones & Co., Inc. Princeton, New Jersey	Dow Jones News	Up-to-the-minute news covering business and finance worldwide. On-line access to full text of the *Wall Street Journal* and other business news publications
CompuServe, Inc. Columbus, Ohio	CompuServe	On-line access to a variety of business and consumer-oriented databases and computer services
Nielsen Media Research Northbrook, Illinois	Nielsen Television Index	On-line ratings of television programs
Mobil Oil Corporation Fairfax, Virginia	Mobil Travel Guide	Information on 21,000 hotels and restaurants plus 16,000 points of interest in 4000 cities in the U.S. and Canada
Cineman Syndicates Middletown, New York	Movie Reviews Database	Reviews of movies made since 1920 with ratings for entertainment value

Exhibit 18.14

Representative Information Utilities Services

order the merchandise at the quoted price and charge it to a major credit card. The item is shipped directly to the purchaser.

Electronic Banking

CompuServe also gives you access to **electronic banking,** banking you perform by computer from the convenience of your home or office. For example, some participating banks let you use your CompuServe account to access your checking, savings, and credit card accounts. Through a series of menu choices you can instruct the bank to pay particular creditors a certain

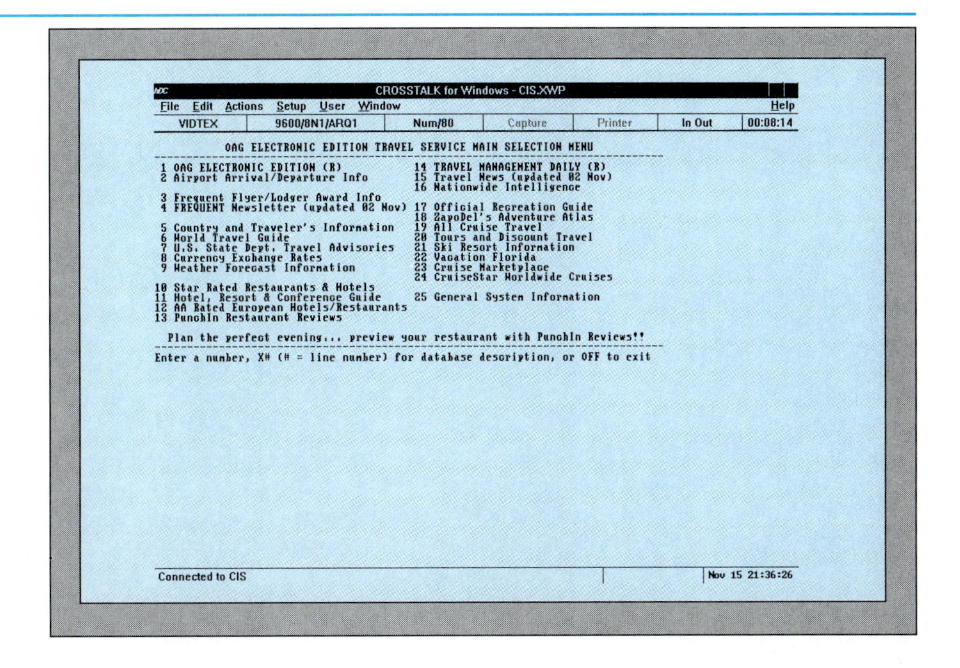

Exhibit 18.15

Electronically Booking a Flight

CompuServe provides flight information and makes reservations for travel world wide.

amount on a specific date. You can also create a standing order to pay recurring bills, such as a house or car payment. Anytime you desire, you can check the current status of your various accounts and move money electronically between them.

For more sophisticated investment decisions, you can subscribe to the Dow Jones News Service (DJNS). Through this service, you can get immediate on-line access to the complete text of the Dow Jones publications, *Wall Street Week,* and *Barrons.* This includes business and economic news, financial and investment services, and general information services.

The Dow Jones Real-Time Quotes service gives you current quotes as they are brought to the stock floor, as well as quotes for the last year and historical Dow Jones Averages. In addition, companies' detailed financial statements are available, including those registered with the Securities and Exchange Commission (SEC). With the appropriate software packages, this basic financial data can be entered into an electronic spreadsheet, such as Lotus 1-2-3. Then you could manipulate the data to explore the possible outcomes of various investment strategies (see Exhibit 18.16).

Correspondence

The major information utilities offer several methods of electronic correspondence, ranging from bulletin boards to electronic mail to computer conferencing.

Computer bulletin board systems, often referred to as "BBSs," allow users across the country to exchange announcements, comments,

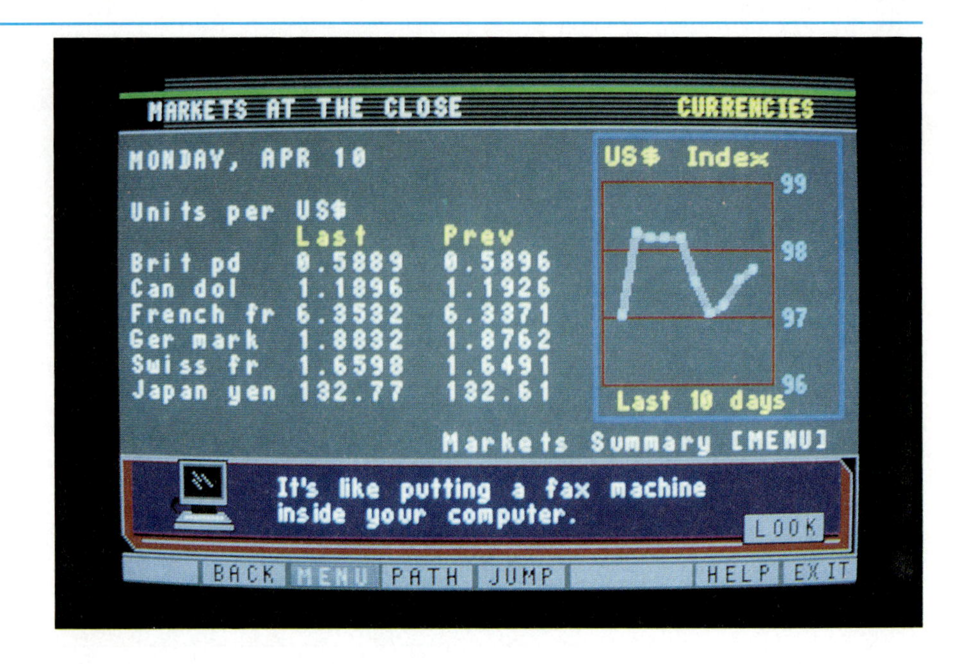

Exhibit 18.16

Financial Planning

A user can gather information and make financial decisions electronically.

computer programs, and other information. There may be over five hundred BBSs operating in North America. Some of the special interest BBSs are Genealogy Interest Group, Astronomy, Computer-Dial-a-Joke, and People's Message System. There is CompuServe's CB Simulator, where people chat via their keyboard using CB "handles" and lingo, while jumping from channel to channel meeting new people.

Most information utilities offer computer conferencing, a special form of teleconferencing, which allows several parties to conduct an ongoing on-screen dialogue about a subject of mutual interest. These "conversations" can be public or private. For example, several researchers around the country may want to exchange ideas on microcomputer software packages. Through a private computer conference, one person can present certain ideas. Anyone who is on the eligible list and finds the dialogue interesting can get a printout or add comments. Unlike a real-time conversation, each respondent can read the comments and provide a response when he or she sees fit—minutes, hours, or days later.

Research

Most of the information utilities are designed to provide information on a wide range of topics, but without much depth. Generally, this is adequate since most home researchers want only a specific fact or a capsule summary of an article. However, a term paper or extensive investment analysis requires in-depth research. For these occasions, there are information services such as Dialog, BRS, and Orbit.

Through Dialog, users can access over 175 encyclopedic databases and over fifty-five million units of information or records. Typical databases represented include the *Academic American Encyclopedia, Books in*

Print, Readers' Guide to Periodic Literature, International Software Directory, Medline, Claims, Federal Index, and the *Dissertation Index.*

Through other database services you can gain access to the full text of the *New York Times* newspaper and also magazines such as *Business Week, Harvard Business Review, Foreign Policy, Scientific American, Consumer Reports, Sports Illustrated, Time, U.S. News & World Report,* and *Variety,* as well as specialized newsletters drawn from nearly thirty different industry groups and interest areas.

Now, through the microcomputer and telecommunication, many of these research indexes once available only in libraries can be accessed from your home. The key differences are that the indexes are available on line and that the computer uses key words you specify to search the database. The advantages are speed and money. A typical search will take less than five minutes and cost less than $2.

Telecommuting

As you read the preceding descriptions of the office and home of the future, you may have wondered if the two could be combined. Why couldn't you just work at home and use your computer to send or receive information as needed? This concept is called **telecommuting.**

Through the use of a company's private data network and/or information utilities, the telecommuter can work at home using a microcomputer. When data are needed from the company's central database, a micro-to-mainframe link is used to extract the appropriate information and send it over the telecommunication link to the microcomputer.

Likewise, finished projects can be distributed to the appropriate people through the telecommunication network. Managers can send the telecommuter messages via electronic or voice mail service. A home equipped for telecommuting is often called "an electronic cottage" or "a virtual office."

This *virtual office* is ideal for jobs such as computer programmer, financial analyst, and professional writer. Furthermore, the combination of portable computers and telecommunications services can set up a virtual office anywhere—a client's office, a friend's home, a hotel room, or an airport. With mobile cellular phones and voice mail, you can even carry on business without taking your eyes off the road.

Experts predict that about 10 percent of the work force will become telecommuters by the year 2000. Most telecommuters will probably not work exclusively at home. Rather they will work at home two or three days a week. Studies have shown that some mixture of work at home and in the office seems necessary to meet the important psychological, social, and political requirements of today's work environment. Although some individuals thrive in the isolation of a home office, others find it personally unsatisfying. Also, only certain types of jobs lend themselves to the virtual office concept. In Computers at Work: "High-Tech Nomad," you can read about a writer who telecommuted while he toured the country on a specially equipped bicycle.

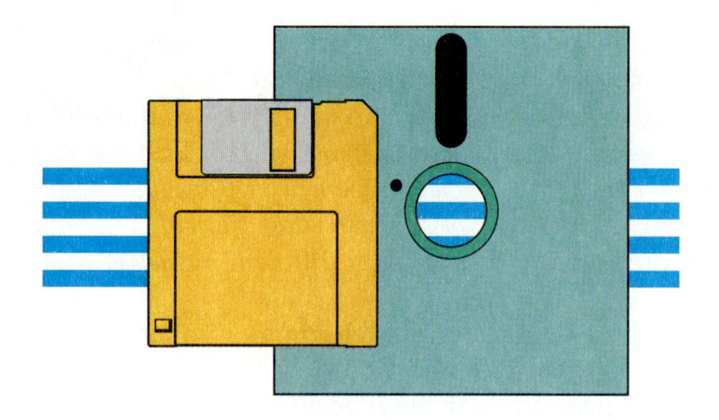

Computers at Work

High-Tech Nomad

I have been a high-tech nomad for six years. It's an odd career, I suppose . . . though it seems to contain all the essential elements: I have a home, a vehicle, and an office. I work on deadline, and get paid in approximate proportion to my effort. And, like most businesses these days, mine depends for its survival upon marketing, efficient information processing, and fast communication.

The thing that makes it odd is that I live full time on a bicycle.

Of course, the Winnebiko is no ordinary bicycle. It has a cellular phone with modem and FAX, solar panels, six computers, and an 8-key binary keyboard built into the under-seat handlebars. It carries a ham radio station and a navigation system. The 12-foot-long, 54-speed, 275-pound recumbent human-powered semi uses both disk and hydraulic brakes, gets about 40 miles per pizza, and has been my home and office since 1983. So what's my business? I'm a freelance writer and information consultant.

It may seem a bit crazy, this nomadness of mine, but it has so far yielded over 16,000 miles of wild adventure, two books (including *Computing Across America*), hundreds of magazine articles and online columns, a few consulting gigs, countless new friends, strong legs, and a lifetime of memories. This is a lifestyle constructed entirely of passions . . . with play at least as important as money in the "bottom line." But how can such a venture work in this age of high-stress career tracks and obsessive corporate yuppiedom?

Life in Dataspace

Computing Across America would be impossible without personal computer technology—and the complex web of communication networks that has evolved along with it. My home has become "Dataspace," a multilayered, shifting reality of nodes and mail servers, massive commercial systems and ham radio-linked bulletin boards. Because of my daily connection with these networks, it absolutely never matters where I am … as long as I can find a modular phone jack, pay phone, or cellular service area (and soon, direct satellite connection will make most of these efforts unnecessary).

The bike itself carries a network of six computers, one of which is a PC-compatible to allow use of commercial software packages. The other a 68000-based FORTH engine from Information Appliance, a pair of CMOS Z80s, a 68HC11, and an 80C85, all work together as needed to handle everything from solar charge management and security to speech synthesis and packet data communication. In addition, of course, there are dozens of dedicated controllers associated with various on-board subsystems, with somewhere around 6 megabytes of memory distributed throughout the machine.

Despite all this technology, I still depend heavily upon a human presence to hold the business together. I have an office near Louisville, staffed by a manager who takes care of "matter transfer" (the old-fashioned communications protocol that depends upon physical transportation of information-bearing objects). He also manages the bank accounts and the hardcopy end of the desktop publishing process, allowing me to maintain the illusion of stability with publishers and clients no matter where I happen to wander. We communicate daily through GEnie, exchanging the latest news, mail, financial matters, and other information related to the business.

It is occasionally surprising just how well this can work. From a sandy beach, I have done corporate intelligence work for a Fortune 500 client—inhaling raw data into my buffer from Dialog, editing it into a report, and transmitting the final copy through GEnie. I have worked as a columnist for a variety of national publications, making deadlines from various places and coloring my tales with the daily adventure of nomadic life. And even engineering consulting has become routine, for almost everything in that category—including circuit design—can be reduced to pure information if you think about it long enough.

And so, the trip goes on—six years and counting. At every layover, the tools improve: recent additions include a CD-ROM for maps and reference libraries, an extensive ham station (N4RVE here), a satellite navigation receiver, and a Createc digital oscilloscope for the mobile R&D lab. It must be working . . . and if anything, it demonstrates the liberating potential of all these information tools we have spent so many years creating.

See you in Dataspace, neighbor!

Summary and Key Terms

Office automation began in the 1850s with the introduction of the typewriter and continues today with the growing use of computers in the office. Office computerization will continue for two reasons. First, information is becoming increasingly important in business. Second, workers need efficient ways to communicate that information.

Electronic office systems are collections of machines that utilize computer technology. Such systems enable information workers to streamline traditional office work by communicating various forms of information electronically.

Electronic mail is the exchange of text messages electronically via a computer terminal or personal computer. Electronic mail saves time by letting workers exchange documents, memos, and letters electronically; it also provides access to electronic files.

Voice mail uses a digitized form of the spoken message, which can be stored on a disk and delivered electronically to one or more phones at a specified time. In addition, voice messages can be annotated, forwarded to other telephones, and verified as to time and date of delivery.

A **facsimile (FAX) machine** transforms a nonelectronic document into a digitized form that can be sent over telecommunication paths to another FAX machine, where a replica of the original is printed on paper. An added advantage of FAX transmission is that it enables certain security measures, like encryption.

Teleconferencing uses telecommunication paths to transmit real-time audio and full-motion video images. This technology allows workers in geographically dispersed locations to conduct meetings.

Videotext is an interactive computer system that enables the retrieval of documents containing both text and graphics for display on local terminals.

The factory of the future will use computer-aided manufacturing, design, and engineering. **Computer-aided manufacturing** (CAM) uses computers to control factory machines. A hierarchy of computers control factory machines and the movement of materials from machine to machine. **Robots** are any mechanical device that can be programmed to perform tasks involving manipulation or movement.

Computer-aided design (CAD), is the use of a computer graphics terminal in product design. CAD allows designers to quickly generate engineering drawings, which can be stored electronically and used to produce the programs that control each CAM machine. This process of integrating computer-aided design and manufacturing is called CAD/CAM.

Computer-aided engineering (CAE) allows designers and engineers to use computers to test their designs without building prototypes.

In the Information Age Factory, computers schedule purchases and deliveries of the parts needed to meet a master production schedule using a processed called **materials requirement planning (MRP).**

Computer-integrated manufacturing (CIM) is the integration of CAD, CAM, and CAE, robotics, factory information systems, and telecommunication links to coordinate product design, planning, and manufacturing in a way that will maximize efficiency.

Information utilities provide ready access to information for teleshopping, electronic banking, financial and travel planning, correspondence, and research that can be accessed from the office or from the home.

Computer bulletin board systems allow users across the country to exchange announcements, comments, computer programs, and other information.

Electronic banking is the process of conducting financial transactions electronically from a personal computer in the home or office.

In **telecommuting,** workers use their company's data network or information utilities to work at home several days a week. A home so equipped is often referred to as an electronic cottage, although portable computers and telecommunication services allow workers to set up virtual offices in almost any location.

Review Questions

1. Briefly discuss the major factors that account for the evolution of the electronic office.
2. What is meant by the term *electronic mail?* What advantages does it offer? How does it relate to FAX?
3. How might videotext lessen the cost and time associated with distributing corporate policy documents?
4. How is the office organized differently today from precomputer times?
5. How can computers aid in manufacturing? What role do robots play?
6. Briefly describe the benefits offered by CAD.
7. How might the task of testing new products by using prototypes be accomplished more economically and efficiently?
8. Briefly discuss the role of computerized material requirement planning in the modern firm.
9. Briefly summarize the major home information services that are available for use by owners of home computer systems.
10. What is telecommuting? How might it change work patterns in the future?

T F **11.** Electronic office systems are machines that simplify and streamline office work by communicating information electronically.

T F **12.** Electronic mail is sent with envelopes containing special computer chips inside.

T F **13.** Voice mail digitizes speech for storage and future output on telephones.

T F **14.** A facsimile machine is used to transmit nonelectronic documents electronically.

T F **15.** Teleconferencing is a way of displaying a conference on a television station.

T F **16.** A robot is any mechanical device that can be programmed to perform tasks involving manipulation and/or mobility.

T F **17.** Materials requirement planning is the process of determining how much a product will cost to produce.

T F **18.** An information utility supplies access to information in return for a fee.

T F **19.** Electronic banking refers to the way banks process checks based on the magnetic numbers encoded on them.

T F **20.** A computer bulletin board system allows users to exchange announcements, comments, computer programs, and other information.

21. _____ The use of computers to control machines used in the process of manufacturing a product is:

a. computer-aided design
b. computer-aided manufacturing
c. computer-aided engineering
d. computer-integrated manufacturing

22. _____ The use of a computer to test designs of products before they are even built is:

a. computer-aided design
b. computer-aided manufacturing
c. computer-aided engineering
d. computer-integrated manufacturing

23. _____ Which of the following is not a way that computers can be used in the home?

a. control of home systems
b. accessing information utilities
c. security control
d. all of the above

24. _____ The concept of working at home and sending and receiving information as needed is:

a. an information utility
b. videotext
c. FAX
d. telecommuting

25. _____ Which of the following is not an electronic office system?

a. electronic mail
b. facsimile
c. voice mail
d. robotics

CHAPTER 19

Issues and Concerns

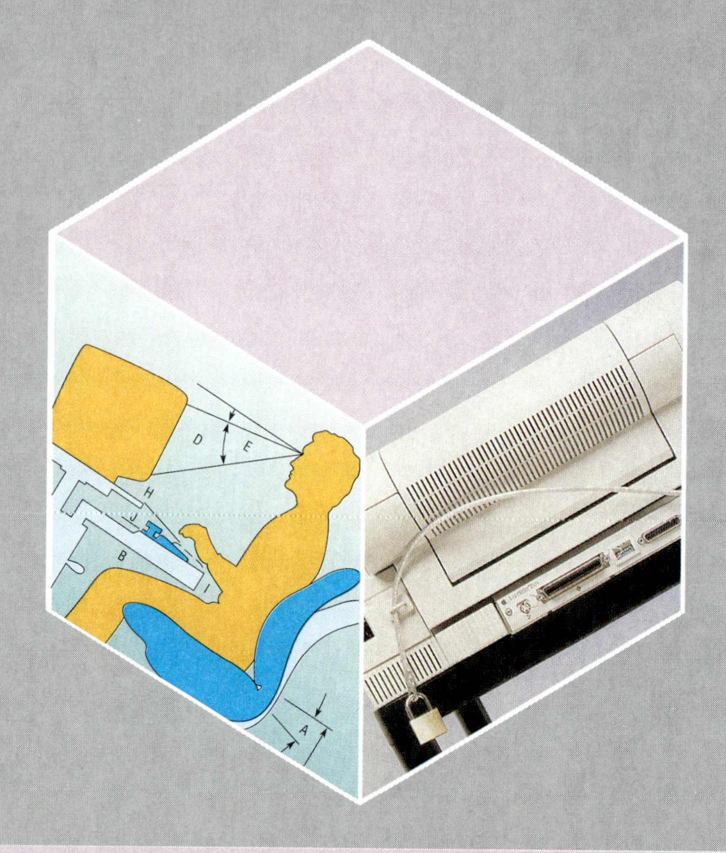

The Transition to the Information Society
The Problem: Displaced Workers
The Options

Worker Health
Potential Physical and Mental Problems
A Solution: Ergonomics

Privacy
Information Privacy
Concerns

Computer Crime
Theft or Damage to Computer Hardware and Software
Misuse of Computer Services
Theft of Money
Theft or Alteration of Data

Prevention and Protection Against Loss
Computer Security
Computer Crime Legislation
Ethics

Computers at Work
Judgment Day

Summary and Key Terms

Review Questions

The last chapter discussed some of the benefits we can look forward to in the information society. But some people are concerned that these benefits will have a cost. The benefit of the efficiency introduced by computers in the workplace, for example, may be offset by increased unemployment or unforeseen health hazards. Already we have learned that advanced computer-based information systems are open to electronic forms of old-fashioned crimes—bank robbery and forgery, for example. Some of these problems can be overcome by more technology, such as identification systems based on biometrics such as voice prints, retina scans, and fingerprints. Other problems involve ethical, not technological, issues. This chapter discusses some of the issues and concerns that will face the information society. Here, you will learn to do the following:

1. Discuss why the transition to the information society is having a major impact on people in the work force and how individuals can adapt
2. Explain the physical, mental, and social problems some computer users are experiencing and the proposed solutions
3. Discuss the ways technological advances used by private and government agencies affect our personal privacy
4. Describe the problem of computer crime and methods for protecting computer systems, programs, and data

The Transition to the Information Society

One of the most important themes of this text is the increasingly important roles information and computers are playing in our society. This trend has been noted by many social commentators. But what do these trends mean to today's workers, especially those in agricultural and industrial jobs? Although computerization is redefining the nature of work, it is also reducing the need for workers.

The Problem: Displaced Workers

In today's factory, more and more of the routine, well-structured tasks are being performed by robots. In some cases workers might welcome this trend, since robots are used for very monotonous or dangerous tasks, but the robots also replace workers.

In the electronic office, word processors, electronic mail, and end-user computing reduce the need for workers whose skills are limited to typing, filing, and mail delivery. The ready availability of effective software allows a smaller number of people to do the same amount of work.

As you go to the grocery store, fill your car with gasoline, and deposit and withdraw money from the bank, you see more and more computerization. The implications are clear. Gasoline stations with computerized pumps have fewer attendants. With the public acceptance of automatic teller machines (ATMs), banks are slowly reducing the number of tellers. Grocery stores check out shoppers more quickly and accurately with computerized scanners—and can use fewer clerks to do it (see Exhibit 19.1).

Is computerization having a good or bad impact on society? In many ways the answer depends on your perspective. If you are the bank clerk replaced by an automatic teller machine, you probably feel that computers are bad. If you use an ATM, you may be convinced that ATMs are great. Similarly, the factory worker who may be replaced by a robot often resents computers and fears permanent unemployment, but car buyers may feel the increased quality and reduced prices brought about by automation are long overdue. And if you are one of the people hired to repair or program the robots, this type of automation is good.

From a social viewpoint, does automation decrease or increase the total number of jobs? Obviously, new jobs will be created for robot and computer designers and repairers, as well as for programmers and those in related occupations, but will these new jobs offset the number of jobs lost to automation? The answer is not clear. What is clear is that a significant portion of the work force will be replaced by automation. What should we do?

The Options

One option is not to introduce any form of computerization into offices and factories. In this way, no jobs will be lost. Unfortunately, this is not a realistic option in a highly competitive world economy. The United States' auto industry, for example, has suffered in competition with highly automated foreign manufacturers. Foreign makes have, in essence, captured the market for small and medium-sized cars. Whereas American manufacturers have employed highly skilled workers in basically unautomated factories, the Japanese have proved that, using automation, they can produce high-quality, reliable products at generally lower prices. As James Baker, executive vice president of General Electric, has said, "We in America must either automate, emigrate, or evaporate."

A second option is to become more competitive by quickly automating offices and factories. At the same time, we must recognize the economic and social consequences for workers and local communities. Companies employing workers about to be replaced by automation can (1) allow workers to retire early, (2) share the cost savings of automation with workers so they can work fewer hours for the same pay, or (3) retrain workers.

Retrained workers can probably find employment. General Motors currently classifies just 16 percent of its work force as skilled tradespersons (technicians, inspectors, monitors), but, by the year 2000, GM predicts that number will swell to 50 percent. Surveys indicate the need for more highly trained personnel, such as engineers, technicians, computer specialists, and managers with basic technical skills.

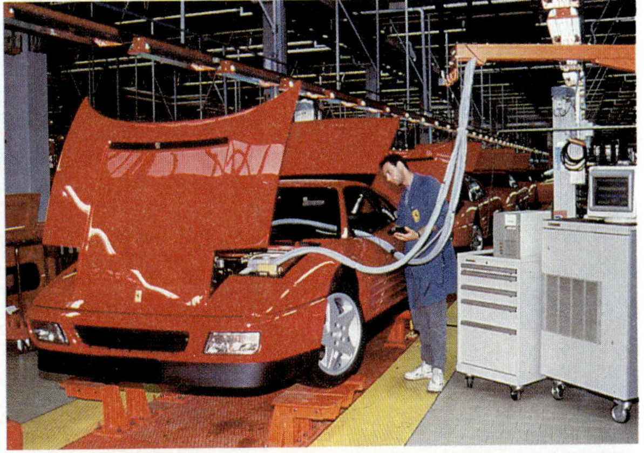

Exhibit 19.1

Workers Being Displaced by Computerization

The transition to the information society is causing blue- and white-collar workers and managers to be displaced by robots, users interacting with computerized systems, and professionals who use computers as productivity tools.

Clearly, educational programs for both children and adults will play an important part in creating a work force with computing literacy. Some of the techniques currently used in today's elementary and high schools may have to be adapted for adult education. For example, **computer-assisted instruction (CAI)**, now used for drill and practice in mathematics, English, and foreign languages, can be used to teach workers useful computer skills such as keyboarding and word processing. **Computer-based learning (CBL)**, which simulates or models actual situations, is another technique that can be adapted to retraining workers. One application of CBL in schools allows students to perform traditional laboratory experiments in chemistry without the risk or expense of combining and heating chemicals. This same technique can be used to retrain workers by modeling or simulating industrial applications of computer technology (see Exhibit 19.2).

Worker Health

Increased productivity is one of the positive side effects of the use of computers in offices and factories. Among the negative side effects are

Exhibit 19.2

Computer-Based Learning

concerns about health problems computer users may have either experienced or worried about. But although several computer-related health issues have been raised over the years, the facts are still inconclusive.

Potential Physical and Mental Problems

In the late 1970s, widely circulated rumors linked too many hours spent in front of a video display terminal with an increased risk of cataracts. Medical studies refuted these rumors. Then concern spread about the unusual number of birth defects occurring among babies born to women who had worked at one company's VDTs during their pregnancies. A report published by the U.S. National Institute of Occupational Safety and Health (NIOSH) showed no connection between the birth defects and the amount of radiation given off by computer terminals. Some labor groups have disagreed with this conclusion, based on other recent studies. However, everyone seems to agree with the NIOSH study conclusions that long hours at a computer were associated with eyestrain, headaches, nausea, lower and upper back pain, and stress.

What are the physical and psychological factors that might be responsible for these problems? In most cases they can be linked to poor working conditions, including badly designed worker-computer interfaces, the wrong type of lighting, and uncomfortable chairs.

But what about stress? For the most part, "computer-related" stress isn't directly caused by the computer itself. Often stress results from the type of job. A data-entry or order-processing clerk develops stress primarily due to the repetitive nature of the task, combined with pressure to perform at a high level of proficiency at an assembly-line pace. In some companies the computer is used as a watchdog to monitor workers' productivity, error rate, and hours worked. There is little chance for these workers to get away from the computer and reduce tension by socializing and talking with fellow workers about routine work matters.

A Solution: Ergonomics

What is being done to help users cope with these physical, mental, and social problems? **Ergonomics** is the science of adapting machines and the work environment to people. It determines how computers, the work itself, and the work environment can be better designed to accommodate workers' needs and concerns, while enabling them to attain high levels of productivity. Ergonomic studies have shown the best physical arrangement for people using computers for any length of time (see Exhibit 19.3). The

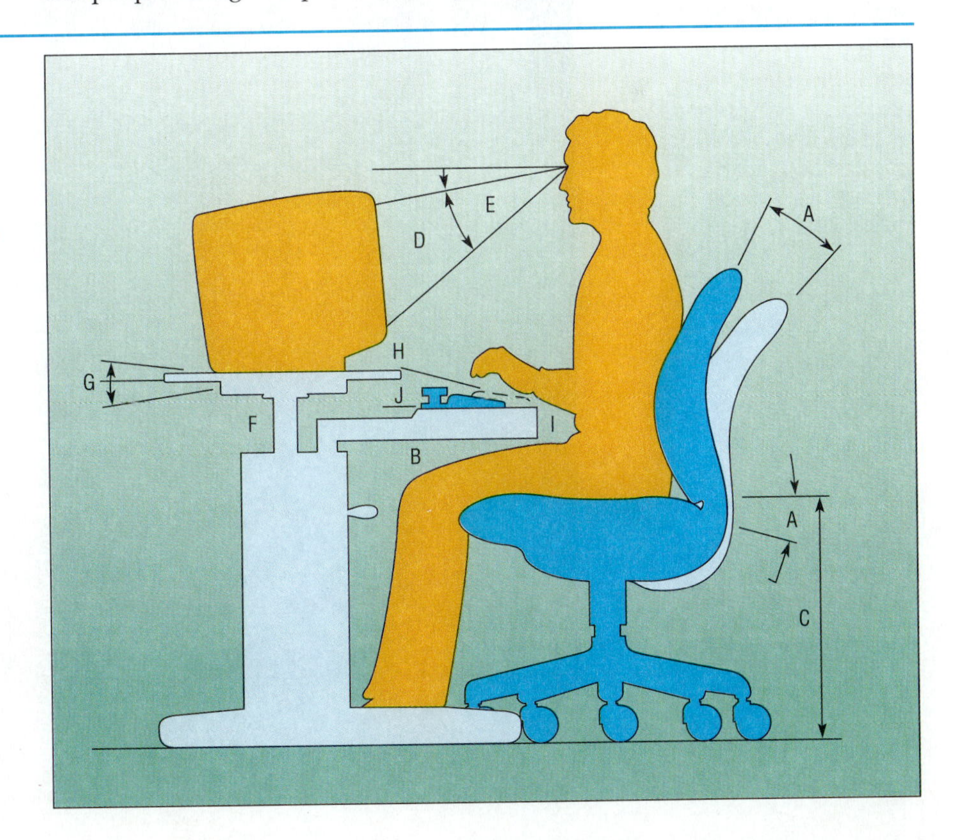

Exhibit 19.3

An Ergonomic Workstation

The letters A through J represent optimal angles and distances for working with a computer.

type of chair, the distance from the worker to the computer screen, and the ability to adjust all components can ease back pain and reduce fatigue.

Some users feel the eye fatigue associated with traditional black-and-white or green-and-black cathode ray tube displays can be eased by switching to amber-and-black screens. Others feel that flat-panel displays, which eliminate the flickering common to CRT significantly reduce eye fatigue.

Ergonomics also studies lighting. Because too much light from overhead or from windows causes glare on computer screens, computer workers are often more comfortable with light levels much lower than normal. Sometimes filters can be placed over computer screens to reduce glare and improve contrast.

Exhibit 19.4 shows a work area designed to give the computer professional a correct physical environment. In addition, it allows face-to-face meetings with other workers when needed. This exhibit also shows other aspects of office design considered by ergonomics.

Ergonomics is only now beginning to address the psychological problems of stress and overwork. Somebody has suggested that all personal computers should be sold with a warning sticker, "Computer use may be harmful to your personal and social life!" Alan J. Fridlund, a clinical

Exhibit 19.4

An Ergonomically Designed Office Work Area

The work area of a computer professional must be both quiet and comfortable, with easily accessible storage and indirect lighting.

psychophysiologist and avid personal computer user, suggests some more specific strategies. First, decide beforehand how much time you are going to spend on a task. When that time elapses, quit. Second, decide ahead of time the level of perfection you want to attain. Don't keep doing what-if scenarios because they are so easy to do. Third, after you accomplish small goals, reward yourself with "fun" activities not connected with the computer, such as going to the beach or gardening. And fourth, plan activities each day that have nothing to do with computers. If you do make computers a part of your life, these suggestions may help you keep your world in better balance.

Privacy

One of the keystones of an information society is the ability to collect and disseminate information efficiently. This, in turn, means that information will be stored in computer databases. The office, factory, and home information systems discussed in the last chapter depend on this. On-line encyclopedias should be a big help in searching for facts. Checking an inventory database for the location of parts and sending a robot to retrieve them is an important aspect of factory automation. But what about computerizing personnel files at the office? What about the information that is held in your medical records? What about your income and credit payment history? When does this pooling of personal information violate your privacy?

Although information in any computerized database should be accurate and secure against unauthorized use, personal information demands extra care. Its entry in a database opens the door to abuse of one of the fundamental protections offered by our Constitution, the right to personal privacy. Privacy might be loosely defined as the right to be left alone.

Several technological advances are being used in ways that may threaten our privacy. First, mass storage devices and data retrieval systems allow large databases to be stored on line relatively cheaply. This has created a tremendous increase in the number of computerized databases holding personal information. For example, financial institutions have records of the number and type of savings and checking accounts we have and the transactions in those accounts. Government agencies have data on the types of cars and real estate we own, where we live, and our current and past spouses. Schools have detailed information on the results of aptitude tests required for admission, courses taken, and grades received, as well as educational degrees granted. Exhibit 19.5 shows some of the types of databases that hold personal information. How many might contain personal data about you?

A second advance that affects us all are telecommunication networks, which allow the rapid exchange of data among computerized databases across the country and around the world. This has allowed the development of on-line information services such as credit bureaus, employment search services, and the FBI's National Crime Information Center.

Police
FBI
Security clearances
Police information systems

Regulatory
Tax
Licensing
Vehicles

Planning
Property owners
Vehicles
Economic data
Business information

Welfare
Medical
Educational
Veterans
Job openings and unemployment

Financial
Credit bureaus
Savings and loan associations
Banks

Market
Mailing lists
Customer data
Prospect data

Organizational
Personnel files
Membership lists
Professional bodies
Armed forces
Corporation employee dossiers recording intelligence, aptitude, and personality tests, and appraisals and attitudes

Social
Computerized dating
Marriage bureaus
Hobbyist data

Research
Medical case histories
Drug usage
Psychiatric and mental health records

Travel
Airline reservations with full passenger details
Hotel reservations
Car rentals

Service
Libraries
Information-retrieval profiles
Insurance records

Qualifications
Education records
Professional expertise
Membership of professional groups
Results of IQ and aptitude tests

Exhibit 19.5

Some Examples of Databases Containing Personal Information

Information Privacy

When applying for a loan, most people can see the necessity of allowing a credit check to verify their employment, income, and credit history. But what if their credit history contained information on their ethnic background and whether they were married or living with someone? Should an auto insurance company be able to purchase files listing names, addresses, type of cars owned, and car license expiration dates from the Department of Motor Vehicles? Should the police be able to question or arrest someone on the basis of information checks made against a file in the Police Information Bank? Would you feel differently if you knew that independent checks of these files have shown that up to 20 percent of these records contain some inaccuracies, including unfounded charges that should have been destroyed but were not?

There is a need for protection against these types of abuses. **Information privacy** concerns those computerized personnel data that can be collected, their accuracy, and their release. Only those data that are relevant and necessary to a decision should be collected. The records that are collected should be accurate and kept up to date. Individuals should have the opportunity to inspect any records and have inaccurate or misleading information corrected. *Confidentiality* means that people must consent to the release of information and that they have the right to know what information will be released to third parties.

What progress has been made in ensuring information privacy? In the private sector, retail credit bureaus maintain files on over 150 million Americans. The Fair Credit Reporting Act specifies the protection consumers have in terms of inspecting, questioning, and correcting their

The Military Selective Service Act., Selective Service Regulations, and the President's Proclamation on Registration require that you provide the indicated information, including your Social Security Account Number.

The principal purpose of the required information is to establish or verify your registration with the Selective Service System. This information may be furnished to the following agencies for the purposes stated:

Department of Defense—for exchange of information concerning registration, classification, enlistment, examination, and induction of individuals, and identification of prospects for recruiting.

Department of Transportation—for identification of recruiting prospects for the U.S. Coast Guard.

Alternative service employers—for exchange of information with employers regarding a registrant who is a conscientious objector for the purpose of placement and supervision of performance of alternative service in lieu of induction into military service.

Department of Justice—for review and processing violations of the Military Selective Service Act, or for perjury, and for defense of a civil action arising from administrative processing under such Act.

Federal Bureau of Investigation—for location of an individual when suspected of violation of the Military Selective Service Act.

Immigration and Naturalization Service—to provide information for use in determining an individual's compliance with the Immigration and Nationality Act.

Department of State—for determination of an alien's eligibility for possible entry into the United States and United States citizenship.

Office of Veterans' Reemployment Rights, United States Department of Labor—to assist veterans in need of information concerning reemployment rights.

Department of Health and Human Services—for location of parents pursuant to the Child Support Enforcement Act.

General Public—Registrant's Name, Selective Service Number, Date of Birth and Classification, Military Selective Service Act, Section 6, 50 U.S.C. App. 456.

Your failure to provide the required information may violate the Military Selective Service Act. Conviction of such violation may result in imprisonment for not more than five years or a fine of not more than $10,000 or both imprisonment and fine.

Exhibit 19.6

The Privacy Act Statement in the Selective Service Registration Regulations

own credit files. Many industries have also established their own codes of ethics. For credit reporting agencies, this means that only the individual's payment record on credit transactions is given. Evaluations such as "slow payer" or personal data such as religion, ethnic background, and life-style are not collected.

Record collection by federal agencies is covered by the Privacy Act of 1974. This legislation specifies the type of records that can be kept, who has access to the information, and the rules of conduct. Exhibit 19.6, The Privacy Act Statement in the Selective Service Registration, specifies why the information is being collected, who can use it, and for what purposes.

Concerns

As you read the last sentence of the Privacy Act Statement in Exhibit 19.6, you will note that the respondent has no choice but to provide the information requested. Similarly, if you apply for medical insurance, you must sign a waiver releasing information or you will be refused coverage. Government and private companies have managed to get the information they need and want without necessarily adhering to the spirit of the law.

Another threat to privacy comes from the telecommunication equivalent of "junk mail." Some businesses are now using telecommunications and computer voice synthesis to conduct "door-to-door" sales by telephone. These businesses begin by buying a mailing list of people who might be interested in their products. A common source of these lists is magazine publishers, who often survey readers on their ages, interests, and income. The companies then program a computer to match names on the mailing list with another computer file containing local telephone directories. When the computer finds a match, it dials the phone number periodically until the party answers. Then the computer proceeds to deliver a prerecorded sales pitch. If privacy is the right to be left alone, this application definitely has the potential for harassment.

A much broader concern involves Project Match. The federal government is using its extensive databases to match records held in various department's files in ways that were never intended. For example, the Selective Service System has cross-checked draft registration records with Social Security and motor-vehicle records to apprehend young men who have failed to register. In an effort to locate illegal aliens, the Federal Immigration and Naturalization Service sought access to the New York City Board of Education's computerized file of information on one million students with the goal of compiling a list of households with Spanish surnames. The Internal Revenue Service matches "lifestyle" data maintained by various business information services with its own internal files. Tax audits are triggered for those people reporting an income "too low" to support their actual lifestyles.

It has been argued that Project Match has a valid goal. Few people would question the value of catching people who are cheating on their income taxes, not registering for the draft, or collecting welfare benefits illegally. But many people are concerned that programs like Project Match may be the first steps toward establishing "Big Brother," the all-powerful surveillance system described in George Orwell's novel, *1984*. What if we allow Project Match to access data held by information utilities, the telephone company, magazine publishers, credit bureaus, and banks? It is certainly possible that through these records a fairly complete, if not always accurate, picture of our lifestyles, our friendships, and even our business associations could be gathered.

It is unlikely that Big Brother will be watching us in the near future. But the potential is there. Groups like the American Civil Liberties Union believe that the legal protection of the Privacy Act has become outmoded by new advances in computer technology. Democracy will continue to require a delicate balance between the benefits of providing information for reasoned decisions and the threat to individual privacy.

Computer Crime

As our society becomes more and more dependent on the computer, and information is recognized as a valuable resource, computers and the information stored in them become logical targets for theft and misuse. **Computer crime** is the generic term for all illegal acts that involve the computer in some way. Actually, not all computer crimes are new or exotic.

Exhibit 19.7

Major Types of Computer Crime

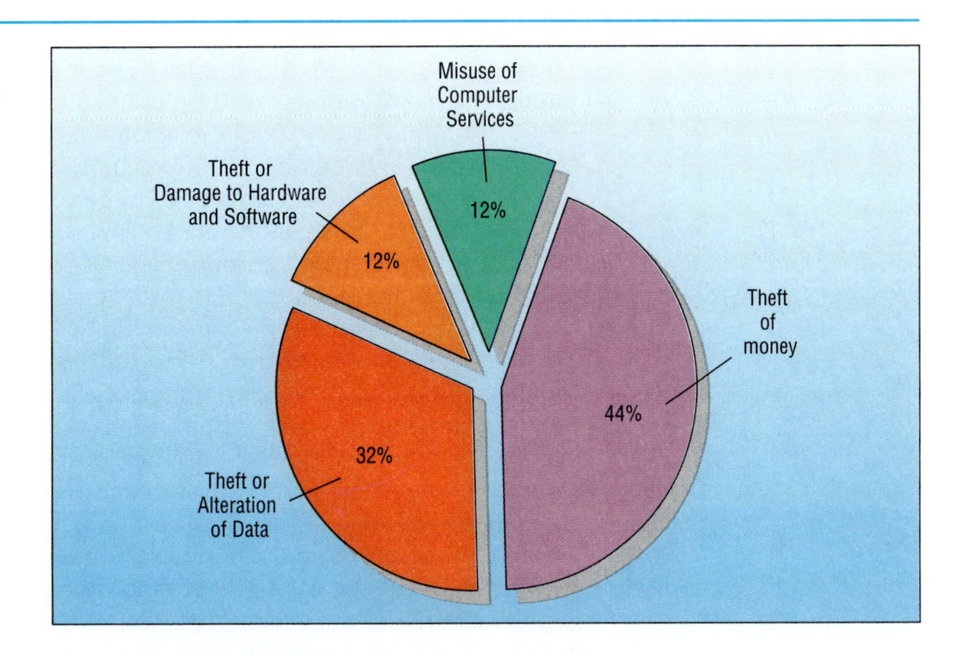

In some cases, hardware and software are simply new targets of thieves or vandals. In others, the computer replaces the bank robber's gun. In still other cases, the computer becomes an accomplice in white-collar crimes such as fraud.

Estimates of the financial loss caused by computer crime range as high as $5 billion per year. The estimated average loss per crime is over $400,000, compared to an average loss for a typical bank embezzlement of only $20,000. Even more alarming is the low rate of prosecution for computer criminals (about 6 percent according to the FBI). To avoid embarrassment and bad publicity, companies often do not prosecute computer criminals when they are caught. Even when prosecuted, computer criminals often receive very light sentences, partly due to the legal system's inexperience with this type of crime. For example, a recent invasion of the Internet network, which includes many government and academic computers, cost an estimated $90 million in machine downtime, lost access to the network, and recovery costs. The person responsible claimed his destruction was unintentional and he received three years' probation, four hundred hours of community service, and a $10,000 fine. The following sections give examples of the major types of computer crime (see Exhibit 19.7).

Theft or Damage to Computer Hardware and Software

Computer hardware, such as tape drives, printers, and even the CPU, have always been valuable items that individuals could steal and resell. However, the general security offered by centralized computer facilities housing mainframes or minicomputers meant that criminals had to be fairly ingenious to remove or damage the large and bulky computer equipment. The appearance of small, lightweight microcomputers on desktops throughout organizations greatly simplified this type of theft.

Computer software is also a valuable and vulnerable target of theft. Most proprietary software for microcomputers has been sold on highly portable and easily copied diskettes. Users have a legitimate need to protect valuable software by making backup copies, but it is just as easy to make extra copies to be shared among business associates, given to friends, or sold to other potential users.

When individuals illegally make copies for their own use or the use of a friend it is called **softlifting.** Most softlifters see themselves as helping a friend and do not realize a computer crime is being committed. Crime on a much larger scale occurs when organizations choose to consciously encourage or unconsciously allow employees to make and use illegal software copies. This practice is **software piracy.** This illegal copying of software has become a major concern of software companies. It has been estimated that, for the most popular software packages, one out of every two copies has been made illegally. Although the microcomputer has highlighted the software theft problem, software for larger computers is an equally attractive target for thieves. Some of these sophisticated programs can cost several hundred thousand dollars.

Software companies are taking major steps to prosecute organizations that are committing software piracy. Through the court system, Lotus Development Corporation has successfully stopped several major companies from illegally copying its software. Another approach software companies have taken is to remove the incentive for stealing. For large organizations with hundreds of potential users that need to standardize their operations by using a limited number of software packages, software companies have provided **site licensing.** This allows the organization to make copies of the software package and pay the software company a reduced fee for each copy made.

Misuse of Computer Services

Telecommunications offer the invaluable benefits of access to sophisticated computer systems. This technology can, however, be abused by unauthorized users. Several years ago newspapers headlined the story of the "Milwaukee Gang," a group of teenagers that was able to gain access to over sixty computer systems across the country. These included the computer systems of a bank, a cancer research lab, and the nuclear weapons facility in Los Alamos, New Mexico. Using home computers, they accessed time-share computers with phone numbers available through public electronic bulletin boards. Sometimes the bulletin boards had the appropriate passwords, but more often the Milwaukee Gang guessed at them or simply used the computer to cycle through randomly generated passwords.

Officials stated that the teenagers did not gain entry to confidential, classified, or critical data, but some people were reminded of the "prank" when the movie *WarGames* was released. *WarGames* is the story of a teenage computer whiz who gains access to a Defense Department computer and almost starts a nuclear war. Although computer experts rushed to poke holes in the plot, others feel that sophisticated computer installations take too little care in protecting against unauthorized telecommunication access.

Company computers can be directed to falsify records for the criminal's benefit. For example, a data entry clerk at a Social Security office changed the addresses of people who had died and had $100,000 in checks sent to herself. Another man broke into a computer and had $800,000 worth of telephone equipment sent to him.

In other cases of abuse of computer services, employees have sometimes used company computers for personal projects. For example, a computer programmer employed by a school board used the school's computer to develop a racehorse handicapping system. In other cases employees have developed computer games or applications software, which they can sell commercially for personal profit.

Theft of Money

The foremost type of computer crime involves money. Stanley Rifkin was a computer consultant retained by Security Pacific Bank of California. He used his position to eavesdrop on the electronic funds transfer wire room of the bank. This enabled him to obtain a code that would allow him to manipulate the bank's computerized electronic funds transfer system. He transferred $10 million from Security Pacific to a Swiss bank account. Later he converted the cash to diamonds. Rifkin was caught when he returned to this country and bragged about his exploits.

Computers have often been used in *fraud*, the use of deceit to gain valuables. The largest financial fraud to date has been the Equity Funding case, which involved several hundred million dollars. Equity Funding Corporation of America had subsidiary companies involved with investment programs, mutual funds, and insurance policies. Certain company officials used the computer to create false life insurance policies. Eventually, over fifty thousand fraudulent policies were issued. To give the picture of realism, the computer was programmed to fabricate the appropriate number of cancellations, lapses, and deaths that might be expected to occur among actual policies. To keep the "books in order" when outside audits were to be performed, the computer was used to shift assets from subsidiary to subsidiary as needed. This type of juggling went on for over ten years!

Theft or Alteration of Data

A company's computer-based information is often a valuable resource to the company itself, to its competitors, and to the individuals who might be profiled in the database. In Europe, Rodney Cox "kidnapped" both his company's financial tapes and disk files and their backup copies. He held about six hundred tapes and fifty disks for a ransom of $500,000. He was eventually caught when he went to pick up the money. Stolen data is often sold to competitors who wish to gain an advantage in the marketplace.

More subtle methods have also been used. An employee who had been fired erased valuable company records by walking through the data storage area with a powerful electromagnet. Software programming, in the form of "logic bombs," has also been used to disable or destroy valuable programs and data after an employee has left the company. For instance, an employee who had programmed most of a company's financial software anticipated being fired because of a personality conflict with the company owner. To ensure his revenge, he planted a query in the program code for duplicating disks. If this query was not answered correctly, it would trigger automatic erasure of the master disk. The first time someone tried to run the program, the company lost the master payroll file for the chain's 250 employees and the file containing postings to the general ledger.

TRW, one of the largest credit-rating companies in the United States, has also been a victim. The company collects and disseminates credit information on over fifty million individuals. Based on information in its database, TRW advises its clients about customers who may be bad credit risks. TRW's clients include banks, retail stores, several leasing establishments, and major concerns such as American Express, MasterCard, Visa, and Sears.

Six company employees, including a key TRW clerk in the consumer-relations department, decided they could sell good credit ratings for cash. People with bad credit ratings were identified by the computer. Selected people were then approached by the TRW employees, who offered a "clean bill of health" in return for a "management fee." The principal victims of this fraud were TRW's clients, who acted on false credit information. It is easy to see that manipulation of information records could be extended to school grades, aptitude test scores, and police files of arrests or warrants. How much of this goes on is unknown, but the potential for abuse is great.

A new threat to the data and programs stored on computers has come in the form of computer viruses. A **virus** is a program that attaches itself to other programs on the computer and instructs the computer to perform malicious operations (such as deleting files and formatting hard disks) when the host program is run. Another threat related to viruses is known as a **Trojan horse**. This is a program that looks like a useful utility or product but performs unexpected operations when it is run. Like its biological counterparts, a computer virus is designed to hide within a program and attempt to replicate itself and infect other computers. For example, the Pakistani Brain virus alters the boot track of the infected diskette and hides by marking the sectors it occupies as bad so that the DIR command cannot detect its presence. When a computer is booted with the infected diskette, the virus goes into the computer's RAM and then replicates itself onto any disk placed in the computer that is accessed (including the hard disk).

	Scores	Lehigh	Alameda
Computer	Macintosh	IBM PC & Compatible	IBM PC & Compatible
Area Infected	Application programs	DOS operating system	Disk boot track
Description	Infects any application Creates invisible files	Infects COMMAND.COM Activates after 4 accesses Destroys all system data	Replaces original boot track Infects through software reboot
Symptoms	System slows down Printing problems System crashes	COMMMAND.COM size changes Loss of all system data	Slow booting System crashes Lost data
	Pakistani Brain	**nVIR**	**Israeli**
Computer	IBM PC & Compatible	Macintosh	IBM PC & Compatible
Area Infected	Disk boot track	Application programs	Application programs
Description	Replaces original boot sector Adds seven bad sectors Replicates onto all bootable disks	Places nVIR resource in system file Places code resource in application Infects all applications executed	Infects any COM or EXE file Programs infected when executed Floppy or hard disk can be infected
Symptoms	BRAIN diskette label displayed Reboot slowed down Excessive floppy activity Program crashes	System crashes Beep when opening application Files disappear	General system slowdown Programs disappear on Friday the 13th EXE files grow until too large to execute

Exhibit 19.8

The Most Common Computer Viruses

In 1989, there were thirty-one known viruses for MS-DOS computers; by 1990 the number had grown to seventy-seven. Some experts estimate that viruses have cost users as much as $2 billion in lost time and recovery expenses. Exhibit 19.8 lists some of the more common computer viruses for both MS-DOS and Macintosh computers. The increase in viruses and their potential for destruction has lead to the development of anti-virus programs, which can be used to monitor your system for viruses. Most of these programs function by not allowing your programs to be altered by an incoming virus. Others detect viruses and inform you of an attack. In general, most experts recommend that you keep backups of all your data in case a virus strikes, write-protect all diskettes that don't need to be written to, always boot your computer with your own DOS disk (or your hard disk), and don't loan out your diskettes since they may come back infected.

Prevention and Protection Against Loss

How big a problem is computer crime? No one really knows because very few computer crimes are ever detected, let alone prosecuted. However, the Research Institute of America has estimated that billions of dollars are lost each year to white-collar computer-related crime. Most experts believe that the problem can only get worse, due to the significant increase in the number of computers sold, the growing automation of business activities, and the spread of computing literacy. So the problem is a serious one. Equally serious is the loss of data due to human error and natural disaster. What can be done to prevent, or at least minimize, these losses? The rest of this section discusses three solutions: computer security, computer crime legislation, and improved computer ethics.

Computer Security

Most organizations have sought protection through increased computer security. **Computer security** is defined as those safeguards taken to protect a computer system and data from unauthorized access or damage by either deliberate or accidental means.

During the last twenty years, most organizations have protected their large computers by controlling physical access to the main computer room and by controlling logical access to programs and data. For example, large computer systems are generally housed in a central location along with on-line disk drives and off-line disk and tape storage. Authorized personnel are granted physical access by security guards who match photo-identification badges to authorization lists or by computer identification systems that use fingerprints, voice recognition, or an access code (see Exhibit 19.9).

Access to programs and data storage from remote time-sharing terminals is controlled by passwords and account numbers. Operating systems allow valid users access to only certain programs and data records and limit the type of actions that can occur. This arrangement provides a reasonable level of protection, as long as authorized users don't share passwords, let unauthorized users see passwords, or use obvious passwords such as their initials or birth date. Password protection could have prevented many of the cases of unauthorized access reported in the press.

Additional protective mechanisms include a person being logged off the terminal after a specified number of invalid passwords have been entered. Alternatively, some telecommunication systems have a call-back feature. When the user logs on, the computer consults a software table that identifies the user and the phone number he or she is authorized to call from. The computer then breaks the connection and calls the user back at the authorized phone number. This prevents access from unauthorized phones. Its disadvantages are that it restricts the mobility of authorized users and forces the computer center to pay for the return calls.

The recent popularity of microcomputers has added to the security headaches of the data processing manager. Personal computers are generally found throughout a company's facilities, not located in one central location that can be locked and guarded. Burglary losses claim over $1 billion of business equipment annually. To minimize theft of these "transportable" microcomputers, corporations often use devices that lock the computer to the desk. Locks are also used to keep unauthorized users from turning on the computer. Sometimes alarms are installed on personal

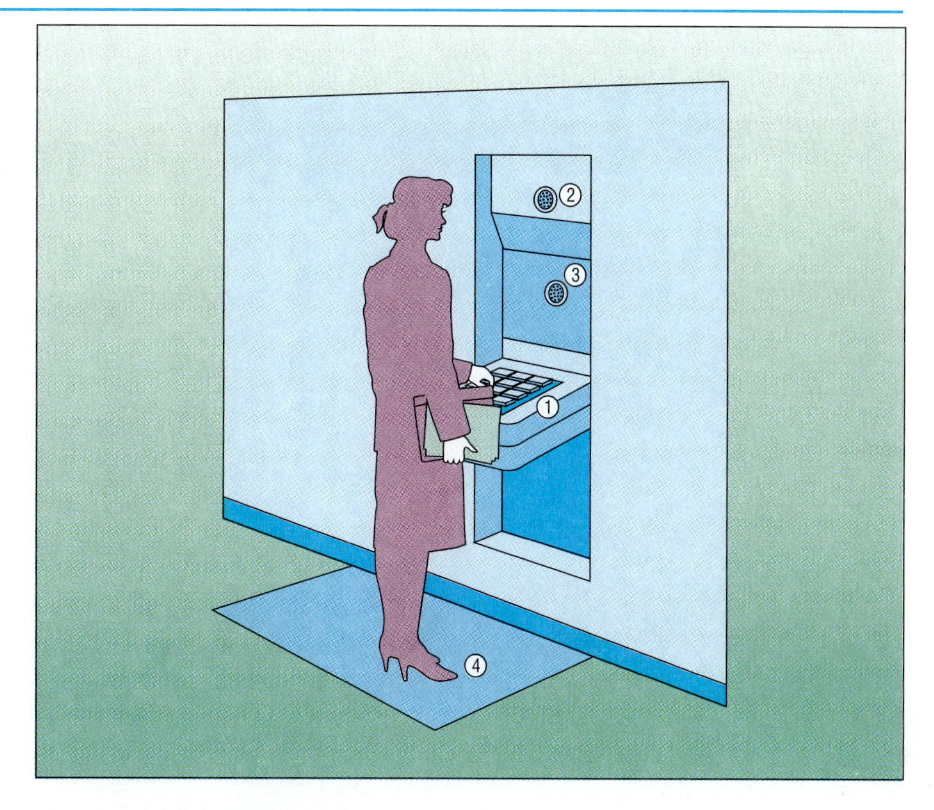

Exhibit 19.9

Controlling Facility Access With a Mantrap

(1) A user punches a pass number on a 12-button key pad, signaling the computer to retrieve the voice template and weight record registered by the person assigned that number.

(2) Through an overhead speaker, the computer broadcasts a 4-word phrase randomly selected from the 16 words previously registered.

(3) The user repeats the phrase into the microphone; the sounds are digitized for comparison with the record on file.

(4) If the voice patterns match and the weight on the floor scale is no more than 40 pounds over the weight on record, the exit door leading into the data-processing center will automatically unlock. If a user is not verified after several tries, a security officer investigates.

computers, so that any movement will immediately notify the police. With the appropriate key or combination, the computers can be unlocked and moved (see Exhibit 19.10).

The threat personal computers pose to confidential data may be a more serious problem for individual companies than is software piracy. The great attraction of the personal computer has been its availability, its ease of use, and, in many cases, its portability. Managers, the people using microcomputers in decision support systems, database queries, and electronic mail, often have access to highly confidential data. Think for a moment about all the diskettes executives use in their office microcomputers or in portable microcomputers in airports and hotel rooms. These diskettes often contain some of the company's most sensitive data. Electronic mail and word processing are useful because they allow fast delivery of important responses and sensitive data. But the messages they carry are not encoded and so would be very easy to read if they got into the wrong hands.

Many of these problems can be minimized if users are made aware of the potential seriousness of security problems. Protective measures can be taken. Diskettes can be locked up at the end of the workday. Workers can use shredders to destroy all preliminary printouts, instead of leaving them in wastebaskets where they could be retrieved by unauthorized personnel.

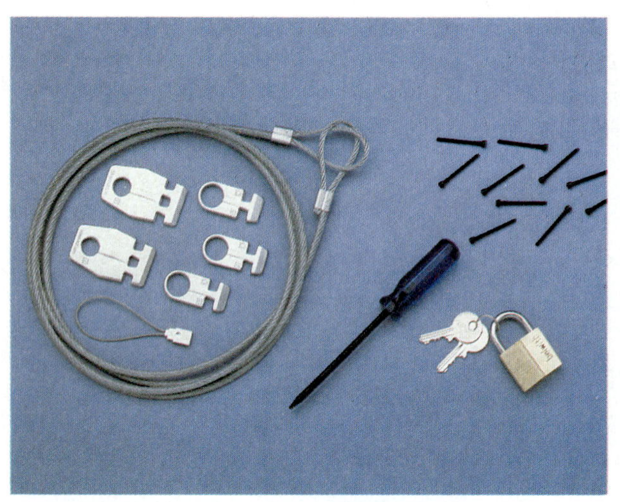

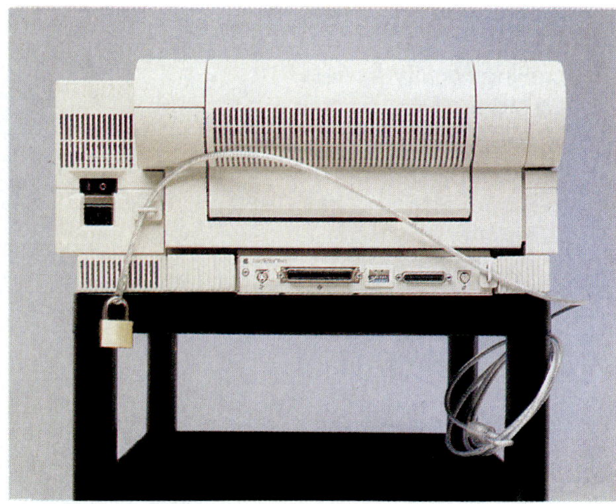

Exhibit 19.10

Personal Security Computer Devices

In addition, microcomputer database management systems now under development offer the password and access code protection of database management systems for large computers. Unauthorized personnel can be denied access by either a guard, various identification card readers, or closed-circuit television cameras.

Although deliberate acts receive much of the press coverage, accidental loss due to natural disasters or other uncontrollable situations is equally dangerous. "Acts of God," such as earthquakes, tornadoes, hurricanes, and floods, have caused significant losses to data processing installations. Electrical power and communication line failures due to brownouts or blackouts can cause problems. Also, *power surges*, sudden increases in voltage levels, can cause computer components to burn out. Lightning and thunderstorms can raise havoc with telecommunication links, but generally these cause temporary disruptions, as opposed to physical damage. Water pipes bursting, fires spreading from other buildings, even airplanes crashing into the center, and other more exotic chance happenings cause great loss to computer centers each year.

To protect against fire, companies can surround their computer rooms with fire walls and install automatic smoke, heat, and fire detection systems, plus some combination of handheld fire extinguishers and automatic dry and wet sprinkler systems. In the case of power outages, computer rooms can be equipped with the capability to switch from electricity from a public utility to an uninterruptible power supply (UPS) or a standby generator. In addition, audible alarm systems can signal danger to workers in the immediate area, and silent alarm systems can signal police or fire officials. No organization can afford to be fully protected against every possible eventuality. Instead, organizations must determine the probability some accident will happen, the potential loss, and the cost of protecting its computer and data from that accident.

In addition to providing a reasonable protection level, it is also very important to have a **disaster recovery plan.** Such a plan covers the actions to be taken by specific personnel after a disaster to resume running critical applications and move toward restoration of all data processing operations. These measures involve switching to an alternative computer system or retrieving backup programs and data from an offsite storage area.

Computer security has become such a concern to organizations that a special field has emerged to address these issues. **Electronic data processing (EDP) auditing** is concerned with the prevention, detection, and correction of deliberate and accidental loss to computer systems, programs, and data. Because computer crimes, especially financial fraud, are a special concern, EDP auditors have to have a solid background in financial accounting along with computer knowledge.

In addition, EDP auditors are trained in methods of physical security and disaster recovery. Special auditing software is available to detect deliberate and accidental actions against a company's programs and data, but more and more, EDP auditors are taking steps to prevent losses by becoming part of the systems development team. This ensures that proper security measures are incorporated into application programs as they are being developed.

Computer Crime Legislation

One of the problems of applying existing laws to computer crimes is shown by a 1981 Supreme Court case in which it was ruled that a person who steals a magnetic tape containing valuable programs or data can be prosecuted only for the cost of the tape itself. In the eyes of the law, the theft involved only a $20-tape, even though the magnetic tape contained a proprietary software program with a price of a million dollars. The law at that time recognized only tangible value, and electronic impulses were not considered property. It took three or four more years of court cases before a landmark decision was made recognizing data and programs as valuable resources, even in electronic form.

Many people have recommended that careful legislative action be taken to write laws that will deter and help prosecute criminals in the information age—laws focusing on information as well as on computer technology. In October of 1986 the federal government passed two major computer crime laws. The first is the Computer Fraud and Abuse Act. Its primary thrust is to make illegal unauthorized entry into computers of government agencies, committing computer fraud or theft across state lines either physically or electronically, and the posting of passwords to government computers on electronic bulletin boards. The second law is the Electronic Communications Privacy Act, which prohibits private citizens from intercepting data communications, such as electronic mail and electronic funds transfer, without authorization.

Legal protection for software developers is being established by several court decisions. The Apple Computer v. Franklin case confirmed that software either in the form of source code or in a ROM chip does have copyright protection. Franklin Computer Corporation developed an Apple Computer clone and copied the Apple operating system. The court ruled that this was illegal.

Although direct copying of software is now forbidden, what about developing software that is similar? The concept of software protection is being further extended by Lotus Development Corporation and other developers of popular packages who are trying to stop those writing software clones or twins. A lower court has ruled against a software vendor who developed a package that was not a direct copy but clearly had the **"look and feel"** of a popular spreadsheet package.

These federal laws, in addition to strengthened laws in almost all the states, should act as a strong deterrent. Furthermore, they give the computer security professional legal "teeth" to use as an adjunct to security policy.

Ethics

Although the movie *WarGames* and real-life examples of computer break-ins have focused attention on external threats to computer security, the truth is that company employees, who commit about 75 percent of computer crime, pose a greater threat to corporate data. Insiders who have

Exhibit 19.11

Company Policy Statement on Software Copying

I recognize that:

1. (Company, Organization) licenses the user of its computer software from a variety of outside companies. (Company, Organization) does not own this software or its related documentation and, unless authorized by the software developer, does not have the right to reproduce it.
2. With regard to use on local area networks or on multiple machines, (Company, Oraganization) employees shall use the software only in accordance with the license agreement.
3. (Company, Organization) employees learning of any misuse of software or related documentation within the company shall notify their department manager or (Company's, Organization's) legal counsel.
4. (Company, Organization) employees caught making, acquiring, or using unauthorized copies of computer software will be disciplined as appropriate under the circumstances.
5. According to the U.S. copyright law, illegal reproduction of software can be subject to civil damages of $50,000 or more, and criminal penalties including fines and imprisonment.

I am aware of the software protection policies of (Company, Organization).

____

Employee signature

____

Date

more access to a system than they really need and who know company procedures find it much easier to identify system vulnerabilities than people outside the company. For example, a dishonest programmer can bypass controls and surreptitiously enter information into the system, authorizing personal transactions.

This means that, in addition to computer security measures and crime legislation, employers need to carefully screen the people hired or trained as computer users. Further, it is important to educate company employees on proper computer usage and ethics. In recent years, the societies of computer professional as well as individual companies have moved to develop codes of ethics—agreements that guide the everyday conduct of computer and business professionals (see Exhibit 19.11).

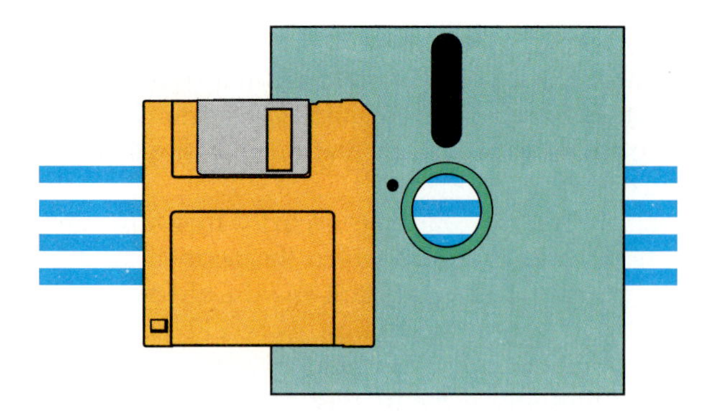

Computers at Work

Judgment Day

Robert Morris Jr. is sentenced to three years' probation and a $10,000 fine

Eighteen months after he unleashed a destructive worm program on the Internet network, disabling thousands of computers, Robert T. Morris Jr. was sentenced last week to three years' probation, 400 hours of community service, and a $10,000 fine. Morris must also pay the cost of his own supervision, about $91 per month, during his probation. Surprisingly, the sentence did not prohibit Morris from participating in the computer industry.

Although Robert Morris Sr. called the sentence a "reasonable end" to the case, Morris Jr.'s lawyer said the felony conviction would be appealed.

Standing before U.S. District Judge Howard Munson in federal court in Syracuse, N.Y., the Cornell University graduate student and son of one of the country's leading experts in computer security appeared upbeat before the judgment. His case fell into the pattern of light sentences for computer criminals. Judge Munson said he could find no analogies to other crimes to guide him in his deliberations, and added that he had received many letters about the case. "To a man, the people involved in the computer business did not feel Mr. Morris should be incarcerated," he said. This came as a great relief to the 10 members of the Morris family seated in the first row.

Morris achieved national notoriety in November 1988 when a program he had designed to take advantage of several security flaws in the Unix operating system worked better than he had intended—it slowed or completely stopped computer operations at university and governmental computers hooked into Internet.

While Morris was not "hacking" in the usual sense—that is, attempting to break into specific computers to steal specific information—his actions raised the fears of many corporate computer security experts. The Information Systems Security Association immediately contacted the United States Attorney General asking that the case be prosecuted to the fullest extent of the law.

Several users were hoping Morris would get a harsher sentence. Gerald Grindler, senior director of the ISSA and director of information security services at Ernst & Young in St. Louis, said before the sentencing that "we hope this won't be another light treatment that encourages more of this activity."

Sally Meglathery, current president of the ISSA and director of electronic data processing auditing for a major financial services organization, said prior to the sentencing that she would be dissatisfied with anything less than a prison term. "I think Morris should do jail time, six months to a year, to send a message about this sort of crime." And Rob Rosenberger, a board member of the Association of Shareware Publishers, said he thought Morris should be banned from government contracts "for life. I think to some extent he is to the computing world what Mike Milken is to the financial world."

Mary Jane Saunders, general counsel for the Software Publishers Association in Washington, says she believes there are grounds for an appeal. Regarding Morris's conviction in January on one count of violating the Computer Fraud and Abuse Act, "there was a question as to whether the judge correctly interpreted the language of the act. They're dealing with a law that's never been tried before." Morris, however, may have to contend with civil suits brought by some of the institutions that suffered because of his worm program.

Despite new and rewritten laws that address specific aspects of computer crime, such cases are likely to remain difficult to prosecute. Often corporations don't report them for fear of bad publicity. And the difficulty in assigning a dollar value to the damage done has a great impact on sentencing. In the Morris case, estimates of the cost of coping with the Internet worm ran from a few thousand dollars to $90 million. And law enforcement bodies still give computer crime low priority.

That suggests that most companies would do better to prevent such incidents from occurring rather than seek justice after the fact. While sales of anti-virus software and other computer security products are up, many experts say corporations do not take a sufficiently broad view of this issue. "Corporations tend to look at the Morris case and adopt an it-can't-happen-here mentality," according to Ernst & Young's Grindler. "They don't realize how connected most computers are."

Summary and Key Terms

The growing use of computers in factories, offices, and stores means that there are fewer and fewer jobs for workers without technical skills. New jobs will be created for robot designers and other information workers, but it is not clear whether these new jobs will offset the number of jobs lost to automation.

As a society, we have some options for dealing with the problem of displaced workers. One option is to stop introducing computers into our offices and factories. However, businesses that compete in the world economy need the efficiency that results from computerization.

A second option is to become more competitive by computerizing quickly. At the same time, employers can help displaced workers by allowing them to retire early, by sharing the cost savings of automation with workers, or by retraining workers. **Computer-assisted instruction (CAI)** and **computer-based learning (CBL)** may be helpful in training displaced workers.

Among the negative side effects of using computers in offices and factories are actual and potential health problems.

Ergonomics is the science of adapting machines and the work environment to people. It involves the design of office furniture, hardware, and office lighting. Ergonomics is only now beginning to address the psychological problems of stress and overwork.

The need to collect, store, and disseminate information can conflict with the right to privacy. Privacy might be loosely defined as the right to be left alone. Although information in any computerized database should be accurate and secure, personal information requires extra care.

Information privacy, protection from potential abuse, has three aspects: companies and agencies should collect only data that are relevant and necessary to a decision; they should keep records accurate and up to date; and individuals should be allowed the right to inspect, correct, and control the release of personal information. The value of data makes computers and the information stored in them logical targets for **computer crime,** a generic term for all illegal acts that involve the computer in some way.

Major types of **computer crimes** include theft or damage to hardware and software, misuse of computer services, theft of money, and theft or alteration of data. The illegal copying of software has become a major concern of software companies. When individuals illegally make copies of software for their own use or the use of a friend it is called **softlifting.** This occurs on a much larger scale when organizations choose to consciously encourage or unconsciously allow employees to make and use illegal software copies. This practice is called **software piracy.** An approach software companies are using to remove the incentive for stealing software in large organizations is **site licensing.** This practice allows organizations to make copies of the software packages and to pay the software company a reduced fee for each copy made.

A more recent threat to data and programs stored on computers is the invasion of a **virus**; a program that attaches itself to other programs and instructs the computer to perform malicious operations. Related to viruses are programs known as **Trojan horses**, which appear to be useful utilities, but perform unexpected operations when run.

Most organizations have sought protection through increased **computer security,** measures taken to protect a computer system and data from unauthorized access or damage by either deliberate or accidental means. Accidental loss is caused by natural disasters or other uncontrollable situations.

Electronic data processing (EDP) auditing is concerned with the prevention, detection, and correction of deliberate and accidental loss to computer systems, programs, and data. A **disaster recovery plan** covers the actions to be taken by specific personnel after a disaster to resume critical operations and move toward restoration of all data processing functions.

Stronger computer crime legislation at the federal and state level should act as a deterrent. Prosecution of those committing software piracy is actively being pursued. In addition, major software vendors are taking developers of packages that **"look and feel"** like their software products to court. Since about 75 percent of all computer crime is committed by company employees, professional organizations are educating employees about proper computer usage and establishing **codes of ethics.**

Review Questions

1. Name several professional careers that will be enhanced by computerization.
2. What is ergonomics? What role does it play in the computer age?
3. Briefly summarize the threats to personal privacy posed by technological advances.
4. What potential for technology abuse exists today? Does the government really provide protection?
5. What is computer crime? What forms may it take?
6. Briefly summarize the ways in which computer crime may be minimized or prevented.
7. What types of people are most likely to commit computer crime? What kinds of organizations are most often victimized?
8. Give some examples of "Acts of God" that can cause disruption of a business due to loss of computing services.
9. Do you think "look and feel" lawsuits help or hurt the software industry? Why?
10. Give five examples of how computer systems can be secured.

T F **11.** Ergonomics is the science of adapting machines and the work environment to people.

T F **12.** Information privacy concerns the collection, accuracy, and release of only noncomputerized forms of information.

T F **13.** Computer crime is a generic term for all illegal acts that involve the computer in some way.

T F **14.** Softlifting is the illegal copying of computer programs.

T F **15.** Site licensing refers to the protection of physical computer facilities and sites.

T F **16.** A computer virus is another name for a program that is badly written.

T F **17.** A Trojan horse is a program that looks like a useful utility or product but causes intentional damage when it is run.

T F **18.** Computer security refers to safeguards taken to protect a computer system and data from unauthorized access or damage.

T F **19.** EDP auditing is concerned with making sure users pay full price for the software they buy.

T F **20.** A code of ethics is an agreement between a company and an employee that governs the everyday conduct of the employee.

21. _____ Which of the following is not a category of computer crime?

a. theft or damage of hardware or software
b. misuse of computer services
c. theft or alteration of data
d. eliminating jobs by automating with computers

22. _____ Another word for a program that infects a computer by attaching itself to programs is:

a. an infector
b. an algorithm
c. a virus
d. a Trojan horse

23. _____ The field concerned with the prevention, detection, and correction of deliberate and accidental loss to computer systems, programs, and data is:

a. EDP auditing
b. computer security
c. antivirus programming
d. computer crime legislation

24. _____ Which is not one of the options for dealing with displacement of workers due to automation?

a. early retirement
b. let employees work fewer hours for the same pay
c. retrain workers
d. fire employees

25. _____ Which is not a physical or mental problem that is a concern with computerization?

a. stress
b. eyestrain
c. cataracts
d. headaches

SPECIAL
FEATURE
SPECIAL
FEATURE
SPECIAL
FEATURE
SPECIAL
FEATURE
SPECIAL
FEATURE
SPECIAL
FEATURE
SPECIAL
FEATURE
SPECIAL
FEATURE
SPECIAL
FEATURE
SPECIAL
FEATURE
SPECIAL
FEATURE

Careers in Computing

As you learn more about computers and their impact on our society, you may be considering a career in computing as a computer or business professional. This feature discusses professional positions, how they fit into organizations, some typical salary ranges, and where most of the jobs are geographically located. Using that background, you will then be able to evaluate the fields of study and courses that are available to you. An overview of these formal educational opportunities is presented at the end of this feature.

Types of Jobs for Computer Professionals

The types of jobs that are available within the computer field vary significantly with the size of the company and how far the company has progressed in its computing sophistication. The table of organization (below) shows a typical management information systems department of a larger organization. It supports both CIS computing and end-user computing.

The management information systems (MIS) department provides computer-based information systems that carry out the transactional processing requirements of the total organization. Further, it supports the development of information reporting systems and encourages the use of decision support systems for managers.

The traditional territory of data processing systems is assigned to the computer information systems director. The three main areas of responsibility are computer operations, technical support, and application development.

Computer operations is responsible for keeping the large mainframe and minicomputers and their peripherals operating. **Computer operators** are responsible for the operation of the large computer system for a particular work shift. Their responsibilities include starting and shutting down the computer each day, hanging magnetic tapes and mounting disk packs to meet program demands, and keeping the necessary supplies in order. **Maintenance technicians** do routine maintenance and make minor repairs. For more extensive work, service representatives of the computer manufacturer are called in. People within computer operations have had formal training in their specialty, but are not required to have a college degree.

The technical support group functions as the experts on the system software and details of operation of the computer hardware. Its responsibility is to ensure that the computer systems are running efficiently. Computer professionals within this group include system programmers, telecommunication analysts, and database specialists. The **system programmer** is responsible for creating or maintaining operating systems, database software, and language translators. The **telecommunication programmer** writes or modifies data communication software. **Telecommunication analysts** design and evaluate telecommunication or local-area networks. The **database administrator** designs and controls the use of an organization's common computerized data. This can include working with users to establish common data needs, interfacing with database management software, and ensuring there are effective security and control procedures.

People in the technical support group require at least a bachelor level degree in computer science. Often graduate education is required in a technical specialty that offers a master's degree. A solid mathematical background is a necessity for technical specialists.

The application development group is concerned with the development, enhancement, and maintenance of computer information systems.

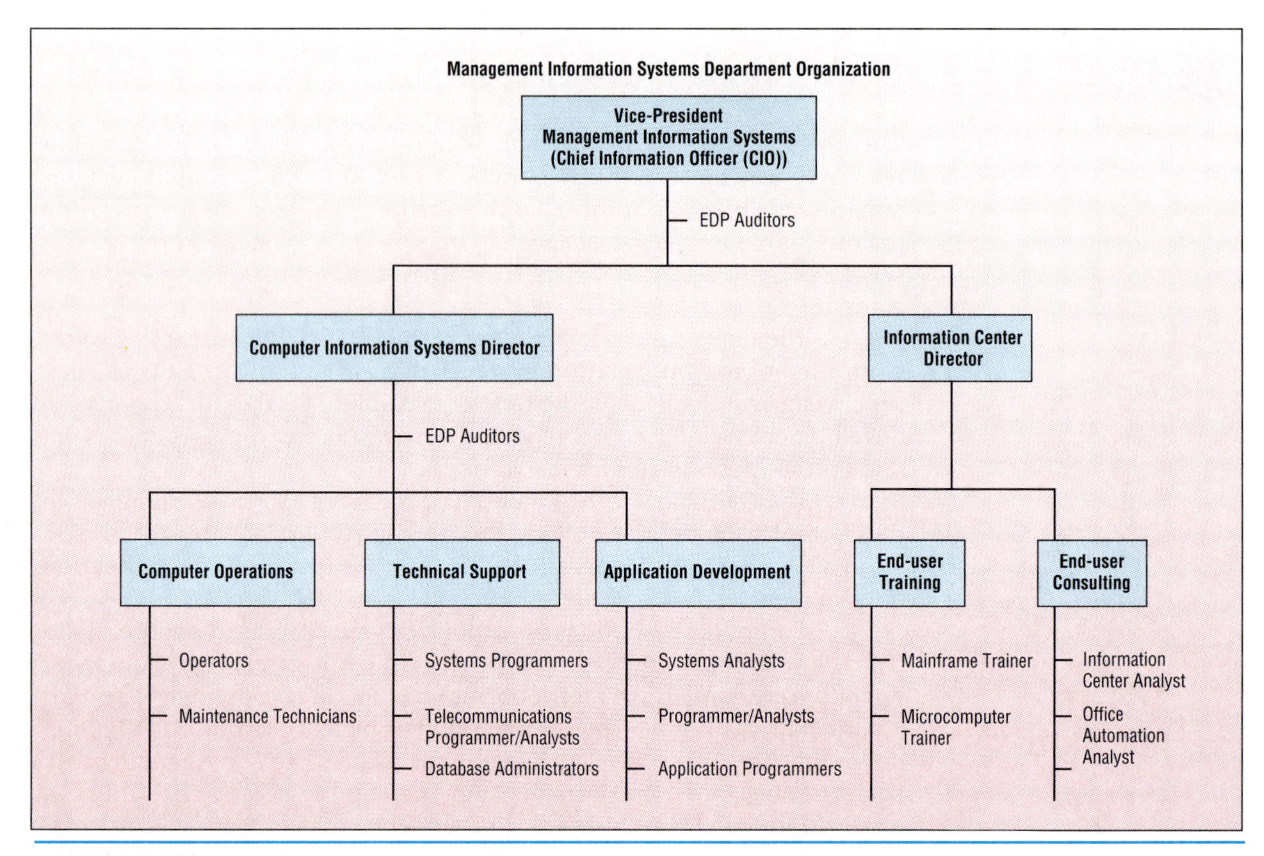

Management Information Systems Department Organization

The personnel that make up this group are programmers and systems analysts. **Systems analysts** work with the users to determine their business information needs. The analyst, a liaison between the user and the programming staff, translates the users' business needs into a set of programming specifications when computer solutions are appropriate. **Application programmers** design, code, and test computer programs to meet these specifications. In addition to new system development, programmers spend a large portion of their time maintaining and enhancing information systems that are already in operation.

Often people function as both programmers and analysts and thus the job title programmer/analyst is common. Application development people usually need a bachelor's degree in a business-oriented computer-science major. To work as an analyst, a strong set of communication skills is necessary, along with a good background in business concepts.

For the most part, the jobs described above are entry-level positions. As you gain experience, promotion opportunities are available in each of the functional areas. Moving from a junior to senior position generally requires assuming a leadership role. **Project leaders** accomplish project goals by organizing a group of users and technical specialists from each of the data processing areas.

More and more organizations are requiring the services of an electronic data processing **(EDP) auditor.** As discussed elsewhere, the needs for security and privacy are important factors in the operations of computer systems. EDP auditors need a solid background in accounting and data processing. At least a bachelor's degree is required, and some universities now offer graduate programs in this increasingly important field.

The highest position within the data processing department is the **computer information systems director.** This person has overall responsibility for data-center operations, technical support of computer information systems, development of new application software, and interfacing with end-users. This individual generally will have a technical degree and many years of data processing experience. In large companies, the director will also need a Master of Business Administration (MBA) degree or the equivalent. This degree will provide an overview of the functional areas of business and the information needs of managers.

A recent development in the computer profession is the emergence of a **vice president of management information systems,** sometimes referred to as chief information officer (CIO). This person is the senior executive responsible for all corporate information systems. He or she is responsible for long-range planning, budgeting, and data processing operations. This executive must have a broad understanding of how the organization functions and what makes it successful in its industry. A master's degree (MBA) is necessary, along with good strategic planning skills and a broad technical understanding of the computer and information fields.

Types of Jobs for Business Professionals in Computing

As we have seen, advancements in the microcomputer and end-user software industries have ushered in the age of end-user computing. This has resulted in most large organizations setting up an information center to support business professionals in their use of computers. Since managers and staff members are not computer professionals, they often want advice on the microcomputers and software that will best meet their needs and how to use it. The generic title of professionals that work in the information center is **consultant,** which conveys the focus of the position. This person acts as an advisor, performs liaison functions, and conducts training sessions for end-users.

In the more advanced information centers, the jobs have been divided into end-user training and end-user consulting. The **information center trainers** are people who train end-users in the use of specific hardware and software packages. Microcomputer trainers specialize in packages for word processing, spreadsheets, database management, graphics, and communication. In addition, these professionals will train users in more advanced software for decision support and expert systems. Mainframe trainers are needed to show end-users how to access data held in the mainframe databases and how to use fourth-generation languages for

Jobs Using Computers

query and report generation. To help the user become productive quickly, information center trainers may conduct group training sessions or select appropriate instructional videotapes or software tutorials.

In the advisor role, the **end-user analyst** works with end-users to determine how to best meet their business information needs. The information center analyst discusses which microcomputer and software packages would be best. If the user's needs are better served by a customized program, the consultant may act as a liaison between the application development group of the CIS department and the user.

An emerging role for end-user consulting is within organizations. As companies become more computerized, they move from stand-alone use of their personal computers to the need to share information electronically within the office and with other locations of the company. The office automation analyst is familiar with the work of an office and has the expertise to set up local-area networks and micro-mainframe telecommunication links.

There are two types of people needed in the information center. The first is a computer professional who understands both CIS computing and end-user computing. This knowledge is necessary since users' information needs become more substantial and they may best be handled by customized programs. In this case the consultant can act as a liaison between the application development group and the user. If an application requires setting up a local-area network, this consultant can arrange technical coordination with the telecommunication group.

Most computing needs of business professionals are not that sophisticated, however, and can be handled by the second type of information center personnel, those individuals who have a good understanding of end-user computing and enjoy working with people. These

Careers In Computing

information consultants are often individuals with degrees in business, education, or communication. They are often people who enjoyed using a personal computer in college and wanted to find a place where they could share their enthusiasm, help others to learn, and at the same time make a good salary.

The educational background for information center consultants is generally a bachelor's degree in business. Computing skills in end-user computing are necessary, along with the ability to work well with business professionals at all levels. For the more technical positions, CIS professionals need to supplement their traditional data-processing education with end-user computing courses. In addition, they need courses to improve their skills in communicating ideas, leading groups, and making people comfortable in learning new skills.

As we move toward an information society, all workers will need a basic understanding of end-user computing to function. With the current explosion in end-user computing, many business professionals in accounting, finance, marketing, production, and management departments are expected to use computers in the normal functions of their jobs. Thus, even business professionals in positions not directly related to the support of end-user computing are finding computer-related training beneficial to their careers. Workers in accounting and finance who know how to use spreadsheets have an advantage over co-workers that still use calculators. Managers who are able to work with a decision-support system are often able to make better decisions. A marketing analyst who understands the use of graphics and desktop publishing may be able to make a more convincing presentation. In general, any educational preparation for a business career can be enhanced by the inclusion of some end-user computing courses.

Salaries and Job Location

Computer professionals are one of the highest paid groups surveyed, according to private and government research. Only physicians and attorneys make substantially more money. The compensation for computing professionals differs significantly, depending on the type of industry in which they work. Communications, utilities, and aerospace are the highest-paying industries. Government, health care, financial services, and retail/wholesale organizations tend to pay less.

Within the computer profession, salaries for technical positions are a function of both specialty and years of experience. Sales representatives generally work on a base salary plus commission. Higher salaries are generally offered to those in some type of leadership position such as project leader, application development manager, or director of computer operations. The top salaries usually go to those in management positions such as computer information systems director, information center director, and vice president of MIS. Management salaries vary significantly depending on the computing power at the installation and the size of the professional computer staff.

Although there are jobs in almost all locations, some geographic areas clearly have greater demand for computer professionals. The computer job market is concentrated in cities such as San Francisco (Silicon Valley), Los Angeles, Dallas/Fort Worth, Miami, New York City, and Boston. Salaries in the computer field are a function of supply and demand. The forecast for the next ten years is that the demand for almost all the computer-professional jobs discussed here will outstrip the supply.

CORPORATE STAFF	Overall	Boston	Manhattan	Atlanta	Chicago	Denver	Dallas	San Francisco
Vice President	77,014	70,000	124,375	75,000	62,097	40,000	71,333	76,857
Director of DP/MIS	56,204	50,285	116,333	56,000	55,750	56,667	54,857	48,700
Information Center Director	45,417	39,000	87,500	44,000	54,167	36,000	48,833	67,500
Director of Security	55,875	NA	65,000	NA	35,000	NA	42,000	NA
SYSTEMS ANALYST								
Manager	50,666	43,500	63,333	40,000	51,388	NA	34,000	87,000
Senior Systems Analyst	44,299	35,730	50,000	35,000	66,500	NA	34,000	45,520
Junior Systems Analyst	30,316	27,000	NA	NA	30,000	NA	17,000	NA
APPLICATIONS PROGRAMMING								
Manager	49,164	41,625	NA	35,000	55,000	32,500	NA	71,687
Senior Application Programmer	36,669	39,000	NA	20,500	36,333	30,000	38,500	43,000
Junior Application Programmer	24,257	30,000	NA	NA	26,667	NA	21,000	26,000
SYSTEMS ANALYSIS/ PROGRAMMING								
Manager	50,547	48,500	76,000	43,750	45,833	44,000	47,333	65,000
Senior Systems Analyst	38,070	38,000	40,000	38,333	38,667	NA	36,500	41,200
Junior Systems Analyst	25,871	25,500	30,000	25,000	21,200	21,000	22,000	NA
OPERATING SYSTEMS PROGRAMMING								
Manager	50,156	47,667	NA	45,000	46,000	33,500	47,000	75,000
Senior Systems Programmer	46,315	40,000	59,000	45,000	37,900	29,250	39,333	56,500
Junior Systems Programmer	30,547	29,000	NA	25,000	NA	20,000	28,000	NA
DATABASE ADMINISTRATION								
Manager	52,409	NA	78,000	50,000	NA	NA	NA	70,000
Database Administrator	42,307	NA	NA	40,000	45,000	NA	37,000	44,333
TELECOMMUNICATIONS								
Manager	54,350	55,000	75,000	44,000	25,000	NA	67,500	64,750
Network Engineer	41,211	NA	39,000	38,000	NA	NA	35,000	49,500
Network Administrator	33,175	NA	29,000	30,000	NA	NA	32,500	41,500
COMPUTER OPERATIONS								
Manager	36,578	40,000	54,000	39,333	41,400	28,000	32,500	44,700
Shift Supervisor	32,074	27,859	31,000	33,500	32,725	NA	28,333	30,250
Computer Operator	20,716	21,400	22,000	21,500	21,129	17,267	19,667	25,667
Microcomputer Manager	30,053	18,000	NA	NA	NA	28,000	22,000	NA
DATA ENTRY								
Supervisor	24,005	21,000	NA	25,667	20,000	NA	33,000	22,000
Operator	17,431	17,580	18,500	18,000	18,425	13,000	20,467	23,400
OFFICE AUTOMATION								
Word-Processing Supervisor	29,980	20,000	NA	NA	NA	26,500	30,500	32,000
Word-Processing Operator	19,347	15,000	NA	NA	18,400	18,000	20,000	21,250
Microcomputer User Services	27,783	27,500	NA	18,000	NA	23,500	22,000	28,000
Consultant	49,433	80,000	NA	NA	65,000	10,000	41,000	45,000
PC Evaluator	33,438	23,000	NA	NA	NA	25,000	37,000	40,000

Salary Range by Region

	Overall	Consumer Mfg.	Industrial Mfg.	Banking	Financial	EDP Services	Govt.	Medical/ Legal
CORPORATE STAFF								
Vice President	77,014	114,000	88,000	77,207	69,833	68,750	61,400	85,000
Director of DP/MIS	56,204	60,976	54,222	91,600	54,167	67,500	47,404	51,800
Information Center Director	45,417	55,764	42,390	78,333	48,283	47,000	40,183	34,625
Director of Security	55,875	66,667	NA	61,500	42,000	NA	46,833	NA
SYSTEMS ANALYST								
Manager	50,666	52,429	48,682	59,450	51,000	44,000	46,000	55,000
Senior Systems Analyst	44,299	44,833	42,463	54,214	40,250	44,674	41,252	40,000
Junior Systems Analyst	30,316	31,000	31,750	35,000	24,000	28,000	28,667	NA
APPLICATIONS PROGRAMMING								
Manager	49,164	52,263	53,000	41,500	55,000	43,826	50,333	45,000
Senior Application Programmer	36,669	33,000	33,429	45,000	40,667	43,258	37,778	32,667
Junior Application Programmer	24,257	25,333	24,556	22,500	24,750	23,175	25,248	20,000
SYSTEMS ANALYSIS/ PROGRAMMING								
Manager	50,547	46,571	50,050	52,083	53,000	52,714	49,429	40,000
Senior Systems Analyst	38,070	32,660	36,333	40,000	34,250	37,594	39,333	35,000
Junior Systems Analyst	25,871	22,050	26,500	25,667	21,667	18,000	26,533	20,000
OPERATING SYSTEMS PROGRAMMING								
Manager	50,158	52,000	49,188	51,750	49,000	60,000	43,800	37,250
Senior Systems Programmer	46,315	46,607	42,462	54,667	38,000	NA	46,750	35,500
Junior Systems Programmer	30,547	24,333	26,500	25,350	29,000	24,000	38,000	25,000
DATABASE ADMINISTRATION								
Manager	52,409	52,333	56,400	55,000	57,500	NA	48,500	30,000
Database Administrator	42,307	44,667	42,625	29,000	NA	35,000	40,661	NA
TELECOMMUNICATIONS								
Manager	54,350	66,000	61,667	47,667	46,500	NA	40,250	NA
Network Engineer	41,211	54,000	40,000	37,250	28,500	NA	57,500	NA
Network Administrator	33,175	32,667	32,500	24,750	25,500	NA	39,951	NA
COMPUTER OPERATIONS								
Manager	36,578	39,136	37,733	35,278	25,529	42,000	31,933	31,000
Shift Supervisor	32,074	31,429	35,100	28,100	26,200	NA	32,127	NA
Computer Operator	20,716	20,231	20,223	18,789	17,527	22,667	22,019	19,857
Microcomputer Manager	30,053	22,000	30,000	28,000	NA	28,000	33,467	NA
DATA ENTRY								
Supervisor	24,005	22,000	22,412	21,167	24,000	19,650	35,875	NA
Operator	17,431	17,818	18,795	13,900	14,420	16,600	18,110	18,500
OFFICE AUTOMATION								
Word-Processing Supervisor	29,980	29,750	24,000	30,667	39,000	30,000	32,667	32,000
Word-Processing Operator	19,347	14,500	20,550	18,750	15,400	20,000	20,750	21,750
Microcomputer User Services	27,783	22,000	36,500	26,500	22,000	22,000	28,362	25,000
Consultant	49,433	35,000	45,000	80,000	NA	79,500	45,750	NA
PC Evaluator	33,438	32,333	NA	27,500	26,000	NA	35,000	NA

Average Salary by Industry for Computer Professionals

Formal Education

What avenues are available to people who want to become computer professionals? For people who want to become involved with computer operations, proprietary schools (vocational/technical) and community colleges often provide the required education. With continued education, computer operators may be able to become junior programmers.

The positions of programmer, analyst, and database specialist require a formal college education. Most community colleges now offer courses in computer education, and many have associate degree programs in the computer field. Many universities offer four-year degrees in computer science.

Although people outside the profession refer to these educational programs by the generic term *computer science,* three distinct fields have emerged. Becoming aware of these distinctions will help you prepare for the computer position you want. The three major educational program areas are computer information systems, computer science, and computer engineering. **Computer information systems** educational programs are generally located in the school of business and emphasize the programmer and analyst skills. A strong background in business core subjects such as accounting, finance, marketing, management science, and management are

How Compensation Compares by Profession

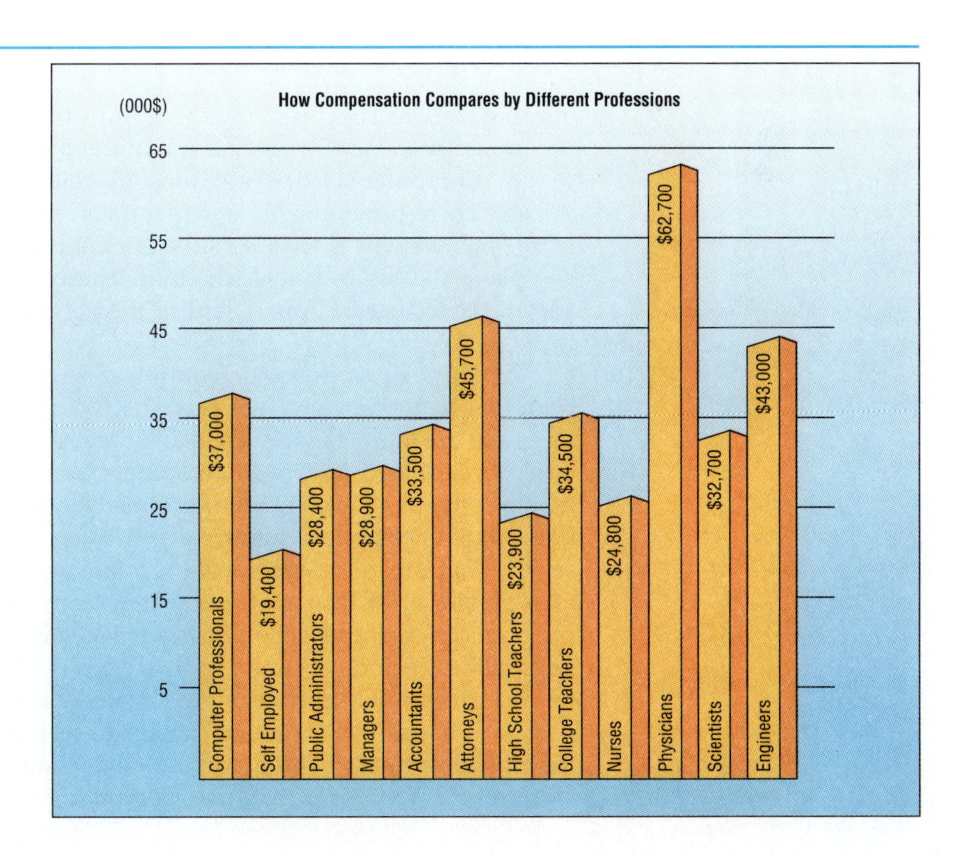

Major Computer Professions by State

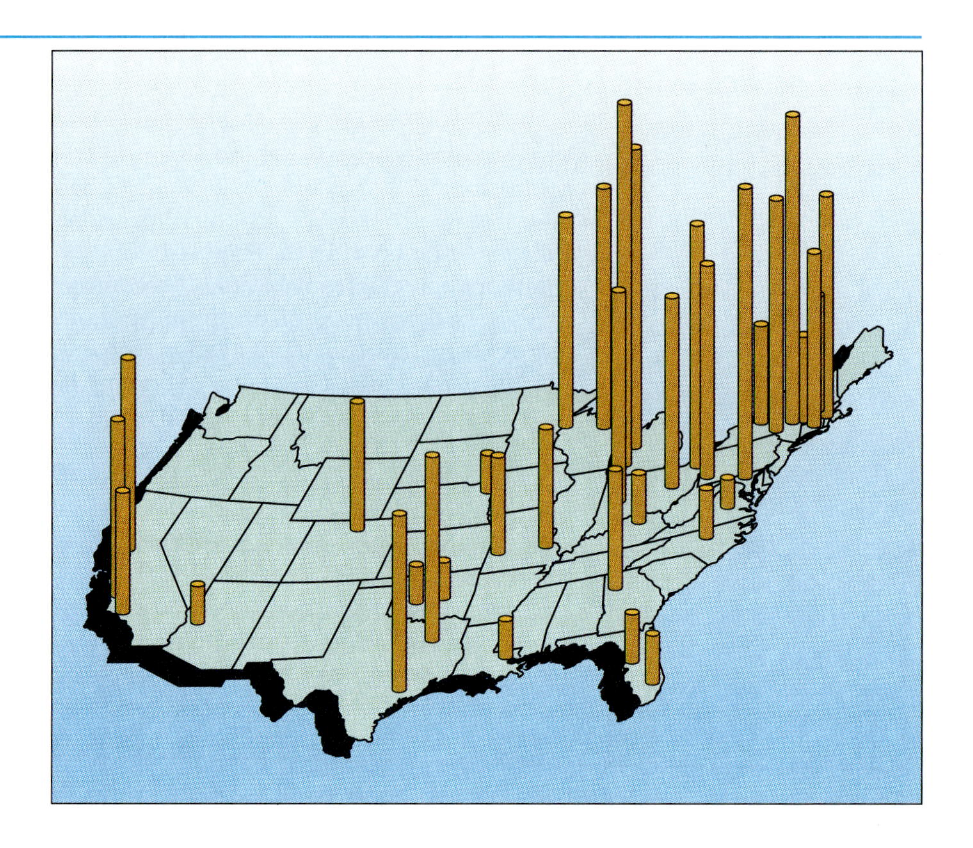

emphasized to complement the computer skills. People from these programs are trained for entry into applications development positions.

Computer science programs are generally located in the school of science. These programs place emphasis on programming, computer hardware, and systems software skills. A strong background in mathematics complements this technical program. These graduates primarily become part of the technical support staff or possibly the application development team.

Career positions for **computer engineers,** people who design computer hardware, have not been discussed here. Computer engineering programs are located in the school of engineering and emphasize the theory of electronics as it applies to computers. A strong background in mathematics, physics, and engineering is needed to supplement the technical knowledge of computer circuitry.

To prepare oneself for the position of computer center director or vice president of information systems, one can attend graduate-level programs offered under the title of Management Information Systems. The possibilities include a general MBA degree with an option in MIS, or a master's degree in MIS, now offered by many schools.

What is available for those interested in positions within the information centers? The following table shows the typical course work required for a minor in end-user computing. The assumption is that the

	Computer Information Systems (CIS)	Computer Science (CS)	Computer Engineering (CE)
Major	Introduction to CIS	Fundamentals of Computer Science	Introduction to Digital Systems
	COBOL Programming	Computer Logic	Network Theory
	Data Base Programming	Pascal Programming	Linear Active Circuit Design
	Systems Analysis	Data Structures	Communication Systems
	System Design	Assembly Language Programming	Analysis and Design of Computer Architecture
	Information Center Applications	Computer Organization	Analysis and Design of Microprocessors
	Systems Development Project	Programming Languages	Theory and Design of Operating Systems
	Information Resource Management	Operating Systems	Advanced Logic Design
Support	Accounting	Computer Electronics	General Chemistry
	Production Management	Advanced Computer Electronics	Analytic Geometry
	Statistics	Analytic Geometry	Calculus
	Organizational Behavior	Calculus	Calculus of Several Variables
	Economics	Linear Algebra	Differential Equations
	Marketing	Calculus of Several Variables	Vector Statics
	Business Finance	General Physics	Vector Dynamics
	Management Policies	Applied Probability Theory	Material Sciences

Typical College Curriculum for Computer Professionals

Typical Curriculum for End-User Computing Professionals

Business Major
Accounting
Finance
Management
Marketing
Quantitative Methods

End-User Computing Minor
End-User Software
Analysis and Design Methods
Software and Hardware Evaluation Methods
Query and Report Generation Software
Local Area Networks
Electronic Office
Decision Support and Expert Systems
Information Center Consulting

Typical Curriculum for End-User Computing Professionals

student's major is in one of the business fields. A specified number of courses from the list shown fulfill the requirements for the minor. The emphasis is on course work in advanced uses of end-user software; how to analyze, design, and evaluate microcomputer-based information solutions; telecommunication links within and external to the electronic office; and training and consulting business professionals.

CIS majors should take as many of these courses as can fit into their schedule. Additionally, CIS majors should take courses to improve all facets of their communication skills. Students who are not business majors but want to work in the information center will need, in addition to the end-user computing minor courses, a solid business background. At a minimum, these students should take core courses in accounting, finance, management, marketing, quantitative methods, and information systems.

PART VI

Appendixes

APPENDIX A

The History of the Computer

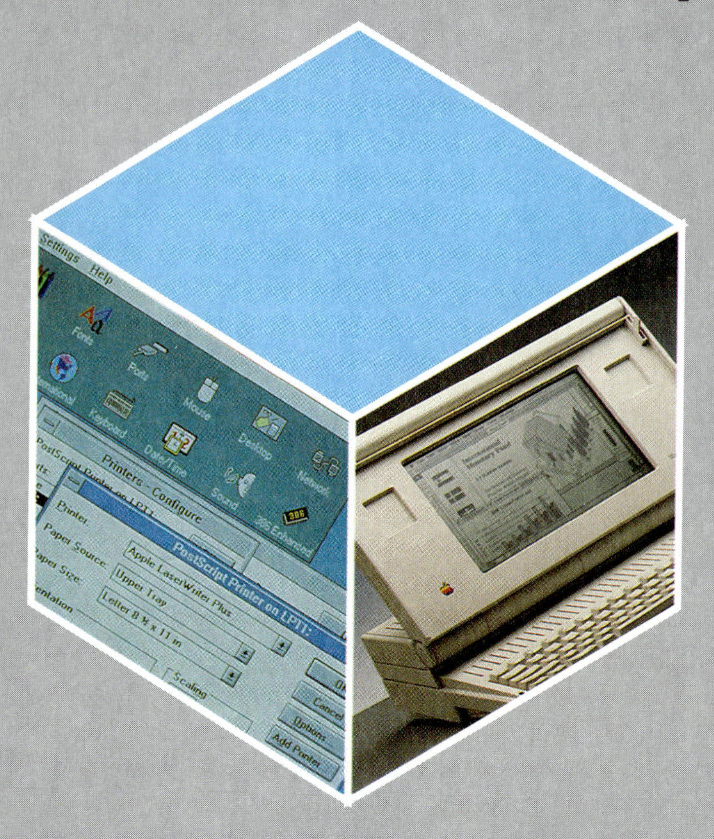

The Dawn of the Computer Age

The Beginning of Information Processing

500 BC	The abacus is invented.
100 AD	Paper is invented.
1458 AD	Johannes Gutenberg invents the printing press.

Calculating Machines Are Invented

1642	Blaise Pascal develops the mechanical calculator.
1676	Gottfried Leibniz improves Pascal's calculator.
1801	Joseph-Marie Jacquard invents an automated loom "programmed" by punched cards.
1822	Charles Babbage develops the Difference Engine.
1833	Babbage outlines plans for the Analytical Engine, a general-purpose computer.

Office Automation Begins

1837	Samuel Morse applies for a patent on his telegraph.
1844	Morse transmits the first telegraph message.
1867	Christopher Sholes begins his work on the typewriter.
1873	E. Remington and Sons acquires Sholes' typewriter and successfully markets it.
1876	Alexander Graham Bell invents the telephone.

Automated Data Processing Begins

1878	James Ritty develops the cash register.
1879	Thomas A. Edison invents the incandescent light bulb.
1885	Dorr E. Felt develops a key-driven calculating machine.
1890	Herman Hollerith develops an electromechanical tabulating machine to count the 1890 census.
1896	Hollerith leaves the Bureau of the Census to form his own company. This firm eventually becomes IBM. Guglielmo Marconi invents the radio.
1911	Hollerith's successor at the Bureau of the Census, James Powers, forms another company to sell punched-card equipment. This firm eventually merges with Remington Rand.
1914	James F. Smathers invents the electric typewriter.
1914	Thomas Watson, Sr., joins Hollerith's firm.
1915	Coast-to-coast telephone communication first takes place.
1930	The electric typewriter becomes a commercial success.

The General-Purpose Computer Is Developed

1930	Vannevar Bush develops a large-scale mechanical computer at MIT.
1937–38	George Stibitz and Samuel Williams at Bell Labs develop a small electronic computer using telephone relays as the basic electronic component.
1939	John Vincent Atansoff and Clifford Berry of Iowa State College develop a small special-purpose vacuum tube computer.
1941-45	Alan Turing and other British scientists develop the Collossus, a large special-purpose electronic computer.
1943-46	J. Presper Eckert, Jr., and John William Mauchly develop the ENIAC, the first large general-purpose computer, at the University of Pennsylvania.
1944	John von Neuman, working on the plans for the ENIAC's immediate successor, defines the basic computer architecture to be used for the next forty years.
1946	Eckert and Mauchly form their own company to build and market the UNIVAC computer.
1947	William Shockley, Walter Brattain, and John Bardeen invent the transistor at Bell Labs.
1950	The Whirlwind computer is built at MIT.

Today's computer technologies and uses reflect centuries of farfetched ideas and persistent hard work by many people. Often, these curious inventions were not immediately recognized as important or practical. For example, John Mauchly's plan to develop the first general-purpose electronic computer was not taken seriously—until a young army officer named Herman Goldstine saw this bizarre idea as a solution to a critical problem for the United States during World War II.

Tracing the history of the computer is useful for many reasons. First, it reveals the close connection between advances in computer technology and the real-world problems these advances solved. Second, it introduces the fascinating men and women who conceived and developed the computer's marvels. Third, it will increase your understanding of computer systems in use. Finally, this history illustrates a number of the issues and trends important to the productive use of computers in business today.

The Computer Age

Computer technology has gone through many changes since 1950. Exhibit A.1 shows the effects of these advances on business computing. Had automobile development paralleled that of the computer, today's luxury cars would cost $50, travel at 700 miles per hour, and get over 1000 miles per gallon. These changes are often divided into **computer generations,** based upon the main electronic component used. The first generation of computers (1951–58) used the vacuum tube; the second generation (1959–63) used the transistor. In the third generation (1964–70), integrated circuits or *chips* were introduced. In the fourth generation (1971–present), the chips have become smaller and more complex. The remainder of this appendix will discuss these computer generations.

The First Generation: 1951–58

The vacuum tube was the primary electronic element used in first-generation computers. These early computers, although useful, were still quite unreliable. Vacuum tubes generated so much heat that water cooling was necessary. Even with these cooling systems, computers were in constant need of repair. The bigger the computer, the more tubes it had, and the sooner it would fail.

Despite these technological obstacles, the computer industry was beginning to take shape. Remington Rand delivered the first UNIVAC 1 to the U.S. Bureau of the Census in 1951. This marked the first time an electronic computer had been built for a data processing application rather

Exhibit A.1

Computer Performance

This table shows performance differences for representative computers from each successive generation of computers. In each case, the computer system is handling the same data processing problem.

Computer Generation	Cost to Perform the Problem	Processing Time
1	$15.00	6 Hours
2	$ 2.50	45 Seconds
3	$ .50	30 Seconds
4	$ .20	5 Seconds
4 1/2	$ .05	1 Second

than a military one. By 1952, the Census Bureau had obtained three UNIVACs, which displaced much of the punched-card equipment that IBM had sold the bureau. IBM was forced to take a hard look at this new data processing technology. Thomas Watson, Jr., IBM's new president, directed IBM toward electronic computers and away from electromechanical punched-card equipment.

The use of the UNIVAC 1 by the Columbia Broadcasting System (CBS) to project the winner of the 1952 presidential election brought the electronic computer to the attention of the American public. On election eve, the UNIVAC projected that Eisenhower would win by a landslide. Because all the experts had predicted a close election, Remington Rand's staff thought there was an error in the computer program. They stalled CBS and began to make changes to the program. When they had "improved" the program to the point where Eisenhower would win by only a slim margin, the projection was released to CBS. By 11:00 P.M., voting results indicated an Eisenhower landslide! When this story spread, the computer's image as an electronic "brain" was formed.

1951-58

The First Generation

1951	The UNIVAC 1 is delivered to the U.S. Census Bureau.
1952	Thomas Watson, Jr., becomes president of IBM.
1953	J. Lyons and Sons company, a chain of British corner tea shops, builds its own electronic computer.
1954	General Electric Company becomes the first private firm in the U.S. to take delivery of a computer, a UNIVAC 1.
1954	John Backus of IBM begins designing Fortran, the first high-level programming language.
1955	IBM begins delivery of its 705 business computer.
1955	The SAGE air defense system is installed.
1956	Grace Hopper develops a business-oriented programming language, FLOW-MATIC.
1956	John McCarthy at MIT begins to design LISP, the first programming language aimed at artificial intelligence applications.
1956	AT&T is barred from competing in the computer industry.
1958	Jack Kilby at Texas Instruments builds the first integrated circuit.

Another important technical event took place in 1958. The leading electronic circuit technology at that time stacked components on top of one another, like dishes, with connecting wires running up through holes cut in the components. Jack Kilby at Texas Instruments wondered if it would be possible to build an entire circuit within a single piece of material rather than stacking the components. His research led to the development of the integrated circuit. A few months later, Robert Noyce at Fairchild Semiconductor also developed an integrated circuit, along with a greatly improved manufacturing method.

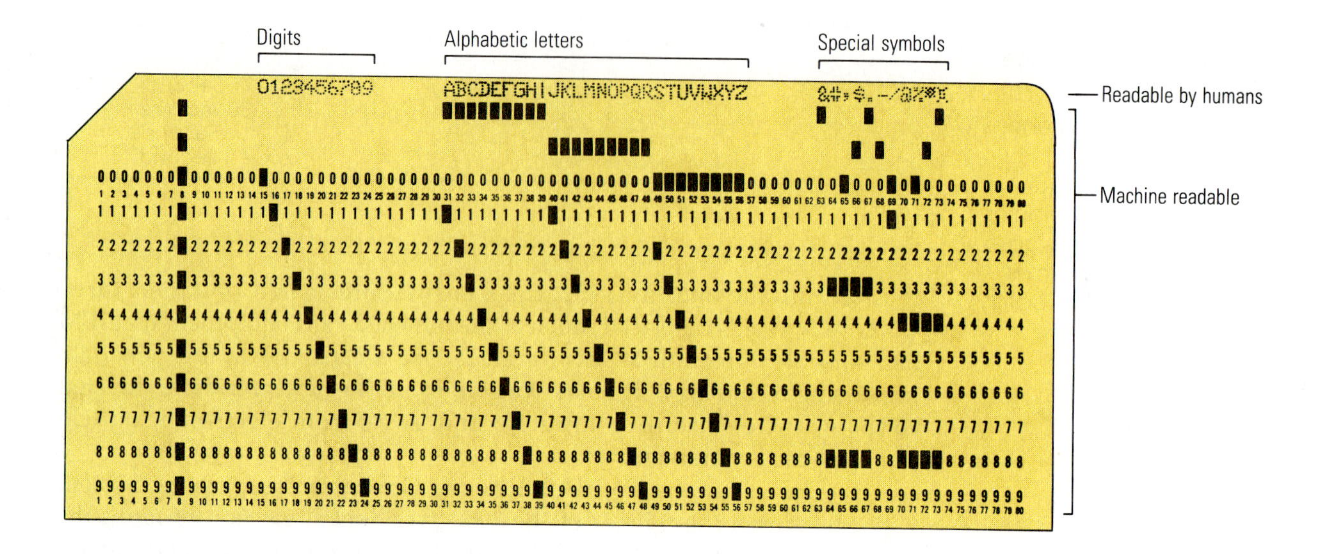

Exhibit A.2

Punched Cards

The punched card was the primary way of entering and storing data and programs during the first-generation computer era.

Another very important event of this period was an antitrust action by the U.S. Department of Justice against AT&T. In 1956, AT&T was barred from having anything to do with the computer market. However, this did not prevent the company from using or making computers for its own use.

Hardware

First-generation computers used vacuum tubes for data storage in ALU and CU circuits, as well as in primary memory. By the end of this era, the faster magnetic cores were being used for primary memory. Data and programs were entered most often by punched cards; computer output was produced either on cards or on paper. Cards were the primary form of secondary storage, but, by the end of this time period, magnetic tape was commonly used for secondary storage (see Exhibit A.2).

Work to improve the transistor continued throughout the 1950s. Much of this effort was funded by the U. S. government, which used electronics in the Cold War and in the space program. Transistor manufacturing was still more art than science, however, and engineers of the day, trained to use vacuum tubes, were slow to switch to transistors. After using the larger vacuum tube, working with transistors was rather like doing surgery on the head of a pin; but by 1958, advances in transistors were bringing the first computer generation to an end.

Software

First-generation computers had very skimpy operating systems—or none at all. Instead, a human operator loaded a stack of cards containing a program and data, which were processed as a batch. Military computers, such as the SAGE air defense system, led to systems software able to handle remote data entry and link computer systems together in networks.

Exhibit A.3

Differences in Language Levels

The task used to illustrate these different forms of programing is the addition of one variable to another variable.

LANGUAGE FORM				LANGUAGE TRANSLATION
Machine language				No translation needed.
011011	0110			
011100	0111			
110001	0110	100		
010101	0110			
Assembly language				These assembly language statements must be translated into machine language. Each assembly language statement will translate into one machine language statement.
FX		B		
FY		C		
ADA		X	Y	
STA		B		
High-level language				This BASIC statement must be translated into machine language. This one BASIC statement will translate into four machine language statements.
LET B = B + C				

The major software advances involved **programming languages**. As described in Chapter 3, all computers are directed by machine language instructions. Each instruction takes the form of a series of binary digits. The very first computers, such as the ENIAC, were actually directly programmed in machine language, which was very difficult and time consuming. By the early 1950s, though, most programming was being done in **assembly languages**, in which abbreviations replaced the binary digits of machine language. Assembly language programs are then translated to machine language instructions by systems software known as an *assembler*. Because these abbreviations are easier to remember and use than binary digits, programming is much easier. However, both machine and assembly languages require programmers to work at the level of a computer's electronic circuitry. Thus, programmers have to understand both the problem they are solving and details about computer hardware.

Prior to 1954, all programming was done in either machine or assembly language, and programmers rightly regarded their work as a complex, creative job. These programmers, in general, were convinced that programming could not be automated. Simply too many shortcomings in the hardware had to be overcome by programming skill. A result of this was that the cost of programming was usually as great as the cost of hardware.

In 1954, a group of IBM scientists led by John Backus began work on the design of a **high-level programming language** for scientific computing. This design was called **Fortran**, short for *for*mula *tran*slation. With high-level programming languages, program instructions are directed toward the problem being solved rather than the computer on which the program is run. As a result, a single program instruction may represent a series of machine language instructions. As you might expect, programming with a high-level language is not only easier, it is much faster. Exhibit A.3 illustrates some differences among machine, assembly, and high-level programming languages. The drawback of high-level languages is that they have to be translated into machine language. This is performed, as shown in Exhibit A.4, by a systems software program called a **compiler**.

Exhibit A.4

Program Translation to Machine Language

A systems software program called a compiler translates programming statements written in a high-level language to the instructions that will actually run on the computer system.

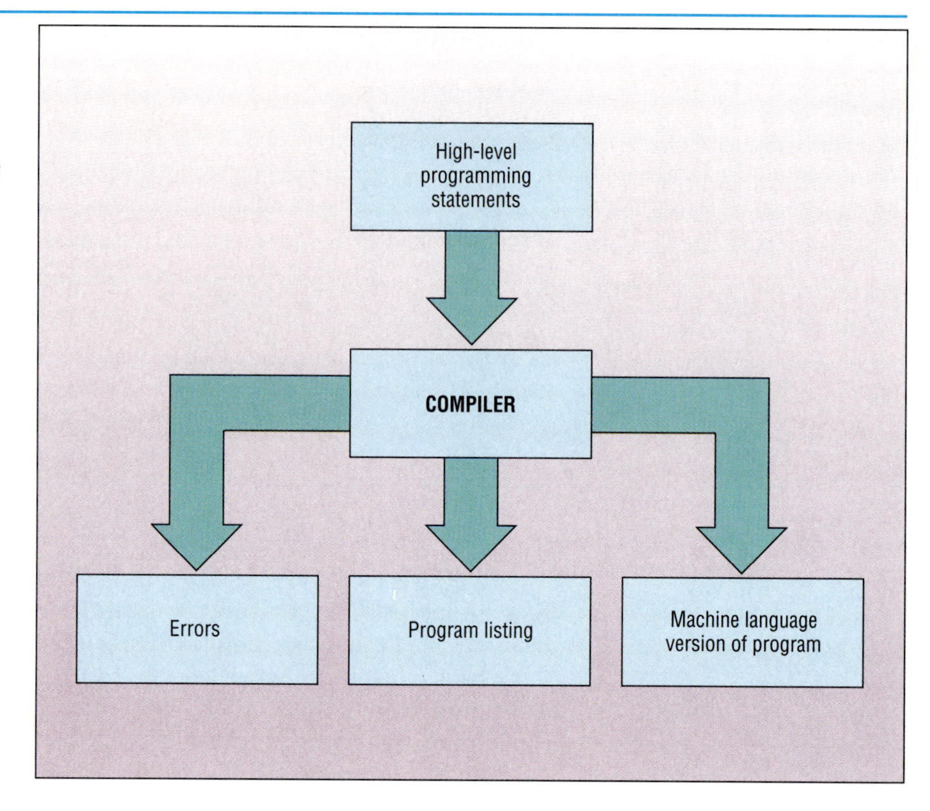

When Fortran first became available, many programmers refused to use it. They did not believe that a compiler could produce efficient machine language versions of their programs. Luckily, the Fortran designers had anticipated this reaction. Their primary goal in developing Fortran was to produce an efficient machine language translation. This early decision was a major factor in Fortran's success and aided the rapid acceptance of high-level programming languages in general. Fortran was available by 1956 and in general use by 1957. By the end of the 1950s, over two hundred other high-level programming languages had been developed.

Uses and Users

All earlier computing had involved scientific or large-scale computing. With this first generation of computers, however, business computing began. By the end of the 1950s, many large firms had begun to develop their own basic transaction processing systems, such as payroll, billing, and inventory control.

The first firm believed to have used an electronic computer for **business applications** was J. Lyons and Sons, a chain of British tea shops. Some of the employees actually built the firm's computer! The firm's computer group later broke away to become ICL, short for International Computers, Limited, which today is Europe's leading computer manufacturer. In the United States, General Electric was the first firm to purchase an electronic computer.

IBM's development in 1955 of the very successful 705 series of business computers proved to be an important milestone in the history of computers. IBM had finally caught up to, and even surpassed, Remington Rand's electronic computers.

First-generation computer users were not computer scientists—none then existed! These first users were scientists, engineers, and businesspeople who saw the advantage of using computers and taught themselves to write the necessary programs. End-user computing, in which computer users develop their own information systems, flourished out of necessity. However, the increasing complexity of computer systems soon discouraged this early end-user computing.

The Second Generation: 1959–63

The appearance in 1959 of the first transistorized computer systems launched the second generation of computers. The continuing trend toward smaller, faster, more reliable, and less expensive computers was started. One year later, Digital Equipment Corporation (DEC) introduced the first microcomputer, the PDP-1. The first minicomputers differed from regular computer systems in a number of ways. They were not only smaller, they were built to serve special purposes. They were very rugged, unlike their predecessors, and could function in harsh surroundings, with fewer climate controls needed. Also, they were less expensive. With these improvements, computer systems began to be used in new environments, such as laboratories and factories. Thus, the minicomputer not only opened up new markets for electronic computers, but it also introduced the computer to new uses and users.

Two other events in this era were to greatly affect the future of business computing. First, IBM began work on its **System/360 series** of computers, an immense project that would represent one of the most important events in the history of computing (see Exhibit A.5). Second was the launching of the **Telstar communications satellite** (see Exhibit A.6). This meant that business information processing was no longer tied to earth. Just as the telephone enabled firms to operate nationwide, communication satellites allowed firms to operate worldwide.

1959–63

The Second Generation

1959	IBM introduces a transistorized computer, the IBM 1401.
1960	Grace Hopper and others design the COBOL programming language.
1960	The Rand Corporation develops the first interactive computing system.
1961	IBM begins working on the System/360 family of computer systems.
1962	The Telstar communications satellite is launched.
1962	IBM and American Airlines develop the SABRE reservation system.
1963	John Kemeny and Thomas Kurtz develop the BASIC programming language.
1963	IBM begins to design the PL/1 programming language.

Exhibit A.5

The IBM System/360 Series family of computers.

Hardware

Although second-generation computers used transistors for most processing circuitry, magnetic cores were still used for primary memory. Most data and programs were entered into the computer from magnetic tape. Often, however, data would first be punched on cards and then copied onto tapes to speed data entry. Similarly, output was often directed to tape to be printed onto paper later. Whereas magnetic tapes were the most common secondary storage devices, magnetic disks did appear toward the end of this era.

Software

The first real operating systems appeared during this second generation of computer development. Besides improving computer system efficiency, these operating systems brought about new forms of data processing, such as interactive processing, real-time processing, and time-sharing. With **interactive processing**, users could carry on a dialogue with the computer. With real-time computing, events could be captured and processed as they occurred. With time-sharing, many people could use a computer system at the same time. For example, the SABRE reservation system, developed by IBM and American Airlines, allowed reservation clerks to interactively review or update a flight's data file as reservations were being made.

Exhibit A.6

The Telstar Satellite

Developments in programming languages also occurred. First, the U.S. Department of Defense sponsored a meeting to develop a business-oriented programming language that could be used by all its agencies on different computers. This resulted in the design of the *co*mmon *b*usiness-*o*riented *l*anguage, better known as COBOL. Second, two professors at Dartmouth College, John Kemeny and Thomas Kurtz, wanted to make computing available to all Dartmouth students. To achieve this, they needed an interactive programming language that was easy to learn and easy to use. Their work resulted in the *b*eginner's *a*ll-purpose *s*ymbolic *i*nstruction *c*ode, or BASIC. Finally, IBM began to develop a programming language able to handle both scientific and business data processing. At this time, scientific programs were written in Fortran, and business programs were written in COBOL. Few programmers knew both languages. This project resulted in the design of PL/1, or *p*rogramming *l*anguage *one*.

Uses and Users

All types of businesses were then using electronic computers for transaction processing. Some information reporting systems were being developed to provide managers with useful information from the growing databases being created by these transaction processing systems.

Even though information systems were now common in many firms, few employees actually came in contact with a computer. Data were usually recorded on paper and sent to the computer department for processing. Similarly, output was distributed by the computer department to users. Only computer specialists worked directly with the computer.

Computer systems had already become too complex for most users. Users explained their needs to programmers, who then developed application programs. Most programmers and other computer specialists obtained their computer skills from "on-the-job training," usually through the military. Colleges and universities had not yet begun to offer degrees, or even many courses, in computer science or information systems.

The Third Generation: 1964–70

In 1964 IBM introduced the six computers that made up the System/360 family of computer systems. These six computers used designs similar enough to allow a program written for one machine to run on another. The computers differed mainly in the size of their primary memory. At the same time, IBM introduced another 150 related products. The impact of these innovations on the computer industry was tremendous. First, the "life" of a computer system was extended, since a firm buying a System/360 computer could "grow" into larger models in the series as its information processing needs increased. More importantly, firms could make this move without rewriting their software—an enormous savings of both time and money. This was a powerful incentive to choose and continue to use IBM equipment. Second, the operating system became the key component of a computer system. With this software controlling all aspects of a computer's operation, efficiency improved and failures were less frequent. As a result, firms became more willing to depend on computer systems to handle all their information processing needs.

Three other events important to business computing occurred during this era. First, the development of the magnetic tape Selectric typewriter made it possible for typists to store and retrieve documents (see Exhibit A.7). This was a major step toward today's word processing systems, and it opened the office market to electronic computers. Second, DEC's success with its PDP-8 minicomputer spurred other firms to enter the minicomputer segment of the computer industry. Finally, responding to possible antitrust actions by the U.S. Department of Justice, IBM "unbundled" its software. IBM had previously charged customers a single price for its computer systems, which were made up of IBM hardware and IBM software. Other hardware vendors believed this unfair because they could not compete with IBM in developing both hardware and software. Joining the protest, software vendors, such as Computer Sciences

1964–70

The Third Generation

1964	IBM introduces the System/360 series of computer systems.
1964	IBM introduces the magnetic tape Selectric typewriter.
1964	IBM introduces the RPG programming language.
1965	DEC introduces the PDP-8 minicomputer.
1968	Computer Services Corporation becomes the first software company to be listed on the New York Stock Exchange.
1969	IBM "unbundles" its software from its hardware.
1970	Nicholas Wirth develops the Pascal programming language.

Exhibit A.7

The Magnetic Tape Selectric Typewriter

Corporation, argued that there were few incentives for IBM's customers to purchase non-IBM software. Perhaps the competing vendors' protests were justified, because after IBM unbundled its software, many new hardware and software products did appear.

Hardware

By 1964, some of the transistors and magnetic cores had been replaced by integrated circuits. In these solid-state devices, an entire circuit was fabricated within a single wafer, or chip, of a semiconducting material such as silicon. A semiconductor's ability to conduct electricity can be made to vary, depending on the chemicals added to it. With solid-state circuitry, computer systems were smaller, faster, more reliable, and less expensive. CRTs were being used for input and output, and the magnetic disk gained importance as a secondary storage medium. These changes reflected the continued growth of interactive business computing.

Software

Operating systems continued to grow in power. Both interactive and remote business computing were now common. More programming languages were also developed. For example, IBM developed RPG, or *r*eport *p*rogram *g*enerator, to aid small businesses switching from punched cards to electronic computers. With a minimum of training, a small firm's employees could duplicate the firm's existing data processing procedures on a small computer system. In 1971, Nicholas Wirth developed the Pascal language, named in honor of Blaise Pascal. This was the first programming language to use **structured programming concepts.**

Uses and Users

Data input and output were finally being performed by clerical employees rather than computer specialists, and the result was faster processing and fewer errors. It makes sense that a purchasing clerk entering a purchase order is more likely to catch an error than someone knowing little about the items being ordered. Also, information systems were being integrated, meaning that the outputs of some information systems became the inputs to other information systems. For example, an order entry system might have access to stock levels maintained by an inventory control system. A manufacturing scheduling system might have access to stock levels maintained by an inventory control system and equipment status as registered by a shop floor control system. Finally, a wide range of **information reporting systems** was being developed at this time to support firms' managers and other professional employees.

With interactive computing, users began to regain a more direct relationship with the computer, which had been lost during the second generation of computer development. However, the increased complexity of computer and information systems at that time limited direct user involvement to input and output tasks. Application design and development, along with computer management and operation, remained the responsibility of computer specialists.

It wasn't until this time that students could obtain college degrees in computer science and information systems. Computing literacy was beginning to take root, and computer education was not limited to colleges and universities. Elementary and high schools began to introduce students to computing. A new computer user/specialist was emerging. Many of the major events of the fourth generation of computers would be led by people who, having grown up with computers, found computing to be a natural and positive force in their lives.

The Fourth Generation: 1971–Present

Instead of a single, simple electronic circuit in a silicon chip, large-scale integration (LSI) technology places many circuits within a single chip. During the fourth generation of computing, LSI technology improved to where first hundreds, then thousands, and now hundreds of thousands of electronic components are manufactured as a single chip. The term *very large-scale integration* (VLSI) is used when referring to these very high chip densities. With LSI and VLSI technologies, computers have become even smaller, faster, more reliable, and less expensive.

A key achievement of this fourth generation of computers was the development in 1971 of the **microprocessor.** In the summer of 1969, Busicom, a now-defunct Japanese calculator manufacturer, approached Intel with a contract to design a set of chips for a new family of calculators. At least twelve chips were required in Busicom's initial plans. Ted Hoff, Jr., was assigned to the Busicom project. Hoff, who used a PDP-8 in this design work, wondered why the electronics for the calculator were more complex than those in the PDP-8.

Working with fellow engineers, Frederick Faggin and Stan Mazor, Hoff whittled the twelve chips down to four, one of which, the Intel 4004 microprocessor, contained all the logic and control circuits. By today's standards, the 4004 was very primitive. Its development, nonetheless, did reshape modern electronics and the computer industry. Intel's earliest microprocessors, the 4004 and 8008, were designed for special purposes. In

1971–Present

The Fourth Generation

1971	Ted Hoff of Intel develops the first microprocessor, the Intel 4004.
1971	Lexitron introduces a CRT-based word processor.
1973	Xerox develops Smalltalk, the first "user-friendly" software.
1975	MITS, Inc., develops Altair, the first commercially successful personal computer.
1976	Gary Kildall forms Digital Research to sell CP/M, the first commercially successful microcomputer operating system.
1977	Steve Jobs and Steve Wozniak form Apple Corporation.
1979	Dan Bricklin and Dan Fylstra develop VisiCalc, the first electronic spreadsheet.
1979	Seymour Rubenstein of MicroPro develops WordStar, the first commercially successful microcomputer word processing software.
1979	Tandy Corporation introduces the TRS-80 Model II, the first commercially successful business microcomputer.
1981	IBM introduces its personal computer, the IBM PC.
1981	Adam Osborne introduces the Osborne 1, the first portable microcomputer.
1982	The U.S. Department of Justice drops its antitrust suit against IBM.
1984	Apple introduces the Macintosh microcomputer.
1984	AT&T is broken up and the telecommunication industry becomes more competitive.
1985	Expert systems and other application software packages applying artificial intelligence concepts appear.
1985	Apple introduces desktop publishing using the Macintosh and a desktop laser printer.
1986	IBM computer dominance is challenged by DEC and PC clone manufacturers.
1987	Apple's Macintosh II and SE and the IBM PS/2 family of microcomputers are introduced.
1988	The erasable optical disk becomes commercially available.
1988	IBM's DB2 becomes the premier mainframe relational database management system.
1989	Steven Jobs introduces the NeXT computer.
1989	Robert Morris Jr. places a worm program in the Internet network.

1974, Intel developed the Intel 8080 (see Exhibit A.8), a microprocessor suited for general-purpose computing.

MITS, Inc., a small New Mexico instrument firm, soon developed the first commercially successful microcomputer, the Altair. Electronic computers suddenly became affordable. Although the price of a single Intel 8080 chip was close to $400, MITS bought them for less than $100 and was able to sell the Altair in kit form for as little as $439.

But the microcomputer did not become a household word until Steven Jobs and Steven Wozniak formed Apple Corporation in 1977 to build and sell Apple II computers. Apple microcomputers were used by many hobbyists and educators, but by relatively few business professionals. The world of business had not yet accepted the microcomputer.

Tandy Corporation's TRS-80 Model II opened the business world to the microcomputer in 1979. Two years later, the IBM PC met with overwhelming acceptance by business, and the microcomputer market exploded. The acceptance of the IBM PC by the business community resulted in its becoming the **de facto standard** for microcomputing for businesses.

Exhibit A.8

Microprocessors

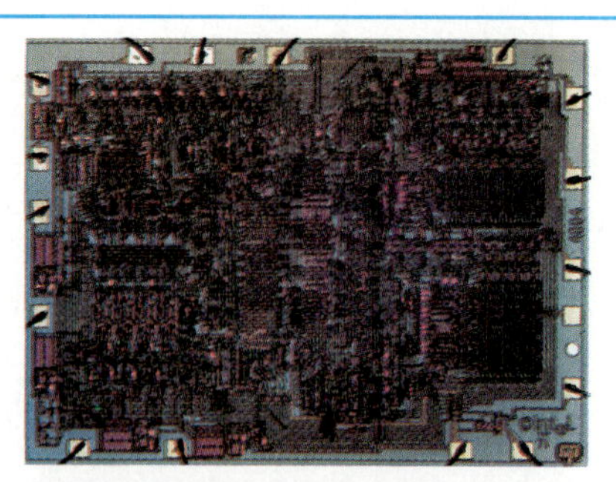

The Intel 4084 Microprocessor

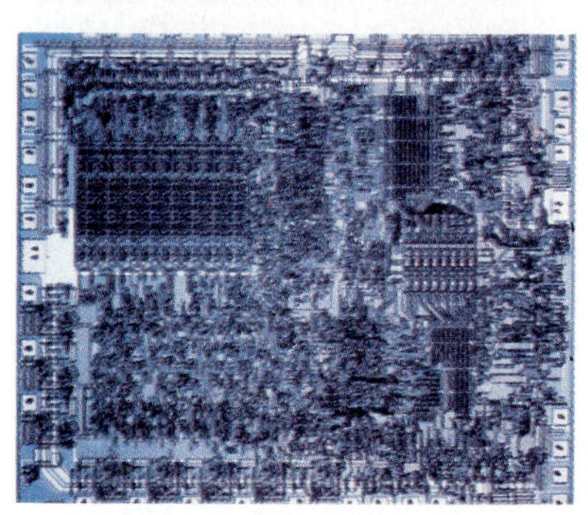

The Intel 8080 Microprocessor

The IBM PC

Managers and professionals are beginning to depend on microcomputers to the same degree that businesses rely on larger computer systems. Portable microcomputers, beginning with the Osborne I, and laptop computers, beginning with the Workslate, allow employees to take their computers along when attending meetings or visiting customers and clients. Very little if any computing power is "lost" when using a portable, such as the Compaq Portable III (see Exhibit A.9), or a laptop, such as the Toshiba 3100 computer (the first microcomputers to have a full-screen plasma display).

The appearance of microcomputers using 32-bit microprocessors, such as Motorola's 68020 and 68030 chips and Intel's 80386 and 80486 chips, are finally enabling microcomputers to operate software in a fashion similar to large computer systems. Among the first 32-bit microcomputers were Compaq's Deskpro 386, Apple's Macintosh II, and IBM's PS/2 Model 80. However, the main impact of IBM's PS/2 family of microcomputers, which spans the full range of Intel processors, will likely be the ease with which it can be integrated with a business's departmental and mainframe computer systems, thus truly "closing the loop" in business computing. Another impact, though not as significant, is the use of 3 1/2-inch disk drives in the PS/2 microcomputers, which should provide the momentum for finally moving the microcomputer industry to adopt this better (that is, smaller, more durable, greater capacity) technology.

Today, PCs continue to get faster and more powerful as new chips are introduced. The introduction of the 386SX chip has given users the

Exhibit A.9

Popular Microcomputers

The Apple Mac II

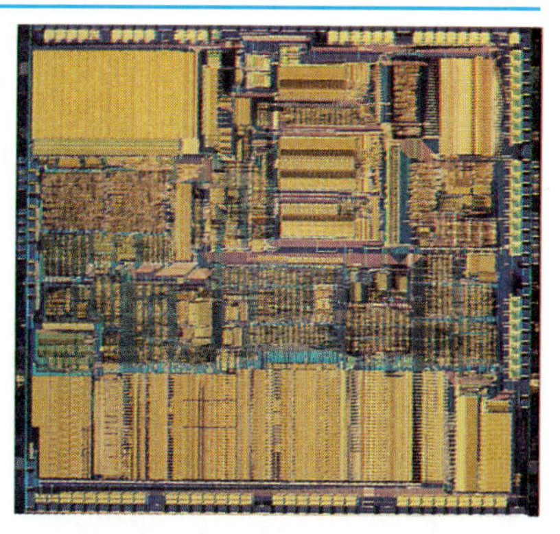

The Intel 80386 Microprocessor

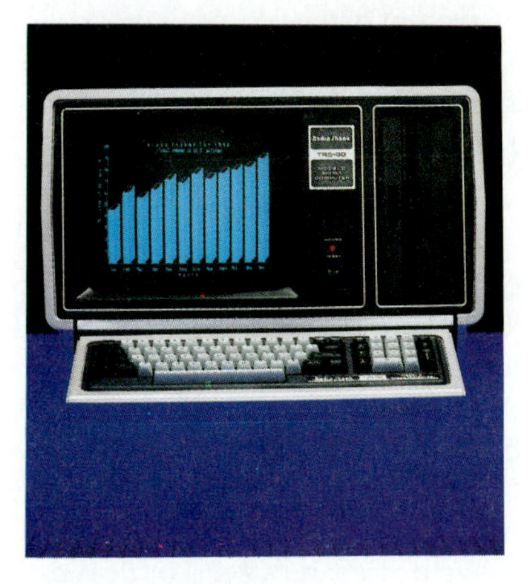

The TRS-80 Model II

The Compac Portable III

The Toshiba Laptop 3100

ability to run software designed for computers based on the 80386 chip but at prices comparable to computer using the 80286 chip. The recent introduction of the 80486 and 80586 chips will eventually displace the dominant 80386 computers.

In parallel with the development of more powerful microcomputers has been the development of local area networks. Users have realized that connecting powerful microcomputers together can produce a network system that rivals the power and performance of mainframe computers. The PC LAN marketplace is currently dominated by Novell's network operating system, which quickly captured over 50 percent of the market.

Although hardware advances brought about the microcomputer, the usefulness of its software was what eventually thrust the microcomputer into the business world. Electronic spreadsheet and word-processing software provided immediate and significant benefits to business users. As a result, VisiCalc was largely responsible for many Apple II sales to businesses. WordStar and Lotus 1-2-3 had much to do with the early success of the IBM PC.

Another key development in the computer industry relating to software was the merging of the office systems and computer systems industries. This merger moved slowly, as firms selling word processing systems added electronic components to their products. Many of the early office automation firms, such as Wang, now sell general-purpose computer systems, and a broad range of office automation software is available on computer systems of all sizes. This merging of related technologies continues today, with both desktop publishing and business graphics becoming increasingly common on microcomputers. If anything, this movement to place most office-related functions on microcomputer workstations will continue at an even faster rate with the 32-bit microcomputers.

A more recent extension of the marriage of graphics and text is seen in the area of multimedia. Multimedia is the use of a computer (such as the Macintosh IIfx) to control the presentation of text and graphics plus high-quality video images from laser disks.

Hardware

With VLSI technology, computer processor speeds and primary-memory capacities have greatly increased. Computers of all sizes are getting smaller and more powerful, enabling an increasing amount of business processing to be distributed to smaller computers located in offices, warehouses, plants, desks, and briefcases. Although a variety of input and output devices are used, CRT input and paper output still remain the major means of entering and receiving information. Magnetic disks are the most common secondary storage device; however, optical disks promise to gain increased usage as this technology continues to improve and as appropriate applications are identified.

IBM's dominance of all aspects of the computer industry has come under increasing challenge. In the mainframe area, DEC used its minicomputer success to propel itself into the larger computer systems. PC manufacturers built clones of the successful IBM PC and took over much of the microcomputer market by selling at a much lower price. More recently, computers based on the RISC (reduced instruction set computer) technology have regained attention as a way to increase computer performance.

Software

The operating systems on today's larger computers are extremely sophisticated. Microcomputer operating systems, such as Digital Research's CP/M and Microsoft's MS-DOS, are comparable to those on second-generation computers. With primary memory sizes and processor speeds increasing, more powerful microcomputer operating systems, such as AT&T's UNIX, have appeared. OS/2, the operating system announced by IBM as part of the PS/2 family of microcomputers, promises to move microcomputer operating systems into those available on third-generation computers, such as IBM's 360 family of mainframe computers.

Although microcomputer operating systems have lagged behind those available on larger computer systems, most advances in application software have been led by microcomputer software. Microcomputer software is much more user friendly than minicomputer software. The early research on Xerox's Smalltalk project, for example, was used by the designers of Apple's Macintosh microcomputers, but not by software designers for any of the larger computer systems. Microsoft's Windows system integrator software package, which has a user interface design similar to that of Apple's products, has been selected by IBM to serve as the "presentation manager" within the OS/2 operating environment. One possible outcome of this decision is that this user interface may become a standard across applications and operating environments for all of IBM's computer systems.

Another software issue of importance has been the development of the Ada programming language. Just as the U.S. Department of Defense sponsored the design of COBOL to reduce the costs of military data processing, the skyrocketing costs of weapons systems software motivated the Department of Defense to sponsor another design effort in 1975. This new language, named after Charles Babbage's friend and colleague, Ada Augusta Lovelace, is modeled after the Pascal programming language. It is too early to tell whether Ada will become as important to business computing as COBOL became.

Finally decades of academic research in the area of artificial intelligence began to bear fruit. Software packages that provided natural language input and output began to appear. Also appearing were software packages that provided **expert systems**, which mimicked the experience, knowledge, and insights of human experts by incorporating the rules used by them in solving problems. More recently, software vendors have moved towards the development of graphical user interfaces, similar to that used in Apple's Macintosh computers, and object-oriented programming as ways to design more powerful and easier to use software products.

Uses and Users

Computer-based information systems now handle all aspects of business activities. Many firms have become totally dependent on their computers. In these firms, business transactions are often automatically handled through information systems. The increasing use of **decision support systems** means that many key business decisions are also being made on the basis of computer output. It seems the computer has a place in a corporate boardroom, as well as in an accountant's office.

Improvements in both systems software and applications software have allowed users to become involved with all aspects of business computing. Employees are performing their day-to-day tasks with or through a computer system. Managers are buying hardware and software and then managing the computer operations in their own departments. Computer specialists today are becoming true experts who work only on the complex aspects of business computing.

Powerful microcomputers and spreadsheet, file management, and graphics software packages are allowing true **end-user computing**, in which managers and business professionals are designing and developing computer applications. IBM recognized the importance of end-user

Exhibit A.10

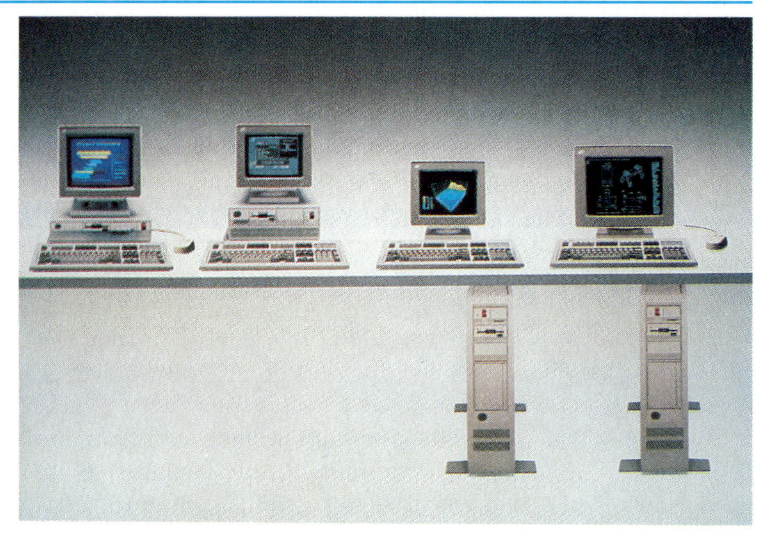

The IBM Personal System II Family

Desktop Publishing

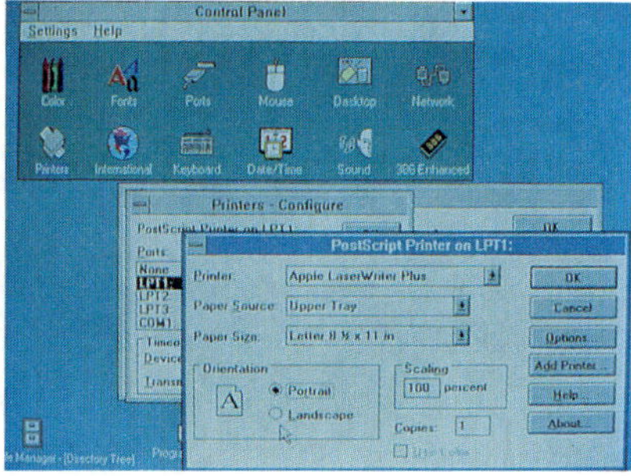

Microsoft's Windows 3.0

The NeXT Computer

The Macintosh Portable Computer

computing in the mainframe area and developed DB2, a relational database management system that has query capabilities and can also be used for production systems applications by computing professionals.

Recent threats to data and programs in the form of computer viruses have forced many organizations to take a more serious look at computer security, particularly with the wide access to computer systems created by networks.

Users have also begun demanding standards for products from different vendors, to allow integration of computer systems. In the database software environment, SQL is becoming a standard query language. An attempt to standardize the UNIX operating system is under way by members of the Open Systems Foundation (OSF), a group that includes many large computer vendors such as Digital, IBM, AT&T, and Sun Microsystems. The International Standards Organization (ISO) has developed the Open Systems Interconnect (OSI) standard for the networking of computers.

Computer Technology Trends

Three **technological trends** recur throughout the computer's history:

1. The time between the development of a new technology and its practical use is becoming shorter.
2. Computer systems are becoming more intelligent.
3. Computer technology is being made available to more people.

Each of these trends is important for a number of reasons.

As new computer technologies are constantly being developed and implemented, businesses and their employees face increased pressures. They must keep abreast of new technical developments, and they find themselves having to adjust to technical change on a fairly regular basis.

Intelligent computers are increasingly able to perform more and more of a business's information processing tasks. Many routine tasks can now be handled without human assistance, and more sophisticated tasks are also being trusted to the computer. Business policies on how best to use computers, including when to create human-computer information processing teams, need to be rethought more frequently.

As computer systems become less expensive and easier to use, a larger portion of a firm's employees are becoming computer users. This change affects hiring, promoting, and even career paths for employees. Personnel policies need to be revised to reflect this trend.

Summary and Key Terms

The major advances in computer technology are divided into **computer generations.** The first generation computers used vacuum tubes (1951–58), the second generation used transistors (1959-63), the third generation used chips (1964–70), and the fourth generation uses very large-scale integrated circuits (1971–present).

First-generation computers saw major advances in **programming languages** to include **assembly** and **high-level languages.** The use of a **compiler** allowed these different levels of languages to be translated into machine language. The primary use of these computer systems was scientific, but in the late 1950s **business applications** were being successfully automated.

The second-generation computers saw the development of the initial **IBM System/360** computers. The **Telstar communications satellite** allowed businesses to send data worldwide. The development of improved operating systems allowed **interactive processing**, in which users could carry on a dialogue with the computer system.

The third generation saw the full development of the IBM System/360 computers. These were the first computers to be built as a family; meaning that they could run the same software. Pressure from the federal government caused IBM to unbundle its offers so that firms could buy software, training, and maintenance from other vendors. This was also the generation that saw the successful introduction of a DEC minicomputer.

New high-level languages were introduced, including Pascal, the first language to use **structured programming concepts. Information reporting systems** were developed to answer users' needs. It was also around this time that schools started to offer college degrees in computer information systems.

Fourth-generation computers included the development of the **microprocessor**, which led to the personal computer revolution. In 1981 IBM introduced the IBM PC, which quickly became the **de facto standard.**

Software development in the form of microcomputer operating systems, such as CP/M and MS-DOS, helped forward the personal computer advancement. But it was VisiCalc, Lotus, and WordStar that enabled the microcomputer to become an end-user tool.

Software packages to facilitate the development of **expert systems** became available. There is **decision support system software** enabling true **end-user computing,** in which managers and business professionals design and develop computer applications.

The major **technological trends** recurring throughout the computer's history are shortened time between development and application of a technology, the increasing intelligence of computer systems, and the increased availability of computer technology.

Review Questions

1. Upon what are the various computer generations based? Briefly trace the first four computer generations.
2. Briefly trace the advances made in programming languages from the early use of machine languages to the present.
3. What major events occurred during the second generation of computers?
4. Briefly describe the most significant developments of the third generation of computers.
5. What development ushered in the fourth generation of computers? What was the significance of this development?
6. Why do applications for a new technology tend to lag behind its appearance? What characteristics mark its first successful use?
7. Briefly discuss the three trends that have recurred throughout the technological history of the computer.

APPENDIX B

Mainframe Operating System Concepts

When you are writing an application program, two simplifications are usually made: (1) the computer will be available exclusively for use by your program, and (2) you can specify logically what you want done.

In a multiuser environment, however, the computer is being shared. Thus, for the first assumption to be valid, the operating system (OS) must take responsibility for managing the flow of computer jobs and the assignment of computer resources. This is necessary not only to relieve users of any concern beyond their individual programs, but also to make effective use of expensive computer resources.

For the second assumption to be correct, the OS must provide an interface that allows you to concentrate more on what you want to accomplish than on the details of how it is done. For example, Chapter 5 explained how data was stored on a magnetic disk and how the read/write heads need to be positioned over the correct track to read data from a particular sector. Without an OS, you would have to know exactly where that data was stored on the disk and how to tell the read/write head to find the specific sector and track. This information is described as the *physical details.* An OS allows you to simply specify logically to retrieve the next employee pay record without concern for where that record is or how to find it.

Operating System Functions

As indicated above, one major function of an OS is to provide a useful interface that allows users to concentrate on what they want to accomplish—not on the details of how the computer internally carries out their instructions. Another important service of the OS is to make effective use of expensive computer resources in supporting a number of users. How does the OS accomplish these objectives? It does so through overall master control, resource management, and monitoring activities.

Master Control

A program called a **supervisor** (or executive or monitor) exercises overall master control of computer operations and coordinates work within the computer system. The way an OS exercises master control is, in many ways, similar to the way the office of a doctor with a large practice functions. The patients wait in the outer office, and when one of the examining rooms is free the nurse asks the next patient to enter it.

There are a number of examining rooms in which patients wait to be examined by the doctor. When the doctor completes the examination of one patient, he or she then goes into the examining room occupied by the next patient. The doctor starts that examination and (1) either completes it, after which the patient leaves the examining room, or (2) the doctor determines that more data are needed. If more data are necessary to complete the examination, the doctor calls in the technician to take the patient to X ray. When the X rays are ready, the doctor will pick up the exam at the point at which he or she left off. In the meantime, while waiting for the X ray results, the doctor goes into the examination room of the next patient and begins that examination.

The reason for this process is that, by sharing valuable resources in a controlled way, more patients can be diagnosed and treated each day. As the doctor is the most vital resource, it is important to keep him or her busy examining patients and diagnosing illnesses.

In computer systems, the control unit (CU) of the CPU is analogous to the doctor. In other words, the CPU is where the real work gets done. The CPU can process only one program at a time, just as a doctor can see only one patient at a time. The CPU works on one program until it is completed or there is a need for input/output (I/O) data (reading data from a computer terminal or sending data to the printer). Then the CU is directed by the OS to go on to the next scheduled program in primary memory.

In the doctor's office, the head nurse functions as the overall supervisor of what gets done, when, and by whom. For computers, the operating system performs this control function.

The patients in the outer-office waiting room are analogous to application programs waiting on disk to be read into primary memory and executed. The OS decides which of these programs should next be loaded into primary memory, using predefined rules. Primary memory, like the inner examining rooms at the doctor's office, is divided into areas that can hold different programs.

As you have seen, the supervisor plays a major role in deciding which programs are run and when. But the OS is not an autonomous unit. Rather, it carries out policies set by the data processing center management or programmers.

For example, the computer operator working at the console in Exhibit B.1 is directing the OS using a command language. At the beginning of the day, the computer operator starts the computer and uses the command language to set policy parameters such as priority rules, I/O device assignments, and prespecified or default memory allocations. Later, while the computer is processing jobs, the computer operator can check the status of jobs, change priorities for jobs that are awaiting processing, terminate jobs, and so on. At the end of the day, the operator gives commands to shut down the computer system.

Whereas the computer operator is in charge of monitoring the overall flow of work and making changes as needed, the programmer is responsible for writing the instructions that tell the computer how to process the program. The concept of a **job control language (JCL)** was introduced to allow the user to communicate to the operating system the special tasks associated with a particular program. Through a job control language, the programmer can specify the language in which the programming instructions are written (for example, COBOL) and the place

Exhibit B.1

Command Language Control

The operator can check the status of jobs, change priorities for jobs awaiting processing, and terminate jobs.

where the data can be found (for example, on a certain magnetic tape). In addition, the programmer can direct the output to a high-speed printer, which might be located in another building altogether.

A command language is also used by programmers using personal computers. Exhibit B.2 shows the DIRectory command, used to check the status of files on disk. There are many other common commands: TYPE is used to see what a particular file contains; COPY can be used to copy a file from one diskette to another, and ERASE is used to erase a single file or a collection of files.

Resource Management

The supervisor initiates and controls the execution of jobs. To accomplish this, it must allocate and schedule computer resources. This function is known as **resource management.** Computer resources include the CPU, primary memory, input/output devices, and support software.

CPU

One of the primary computer resources that needs to be shared is the CPU itself. The CPU can work only on one program at a time. But it can be shared by taking advantage of the fact that it is thousands of times faster than I/O devices or the users who are working interactively with the system. Two factors to be determined are the length of time a program should be able to use the CPU uninterrupted and which of the many programs in primary memory awaiting the use of the CPU should be chosen next.

Exhibit B.2

An Operating System Command

DIRectory is used to check the status of files on disk.

```
$ DIR

Directory VULCAN$DUA1:[PUBLIC]

4GL.DIR;1          COMMAND.DIR;1      DATABASE.DIR;1     BOND.WKS;23
HOLD.DIR;1         REUSME.TXT;1       HELP.COM;1         LOGIN.COM;33
LOGIN.JOU;1        MAIL.MAI;2         NETWORK.DIR;1      OFFICEAUTO.DIR;1
PC.DIR;1           PERSONAL.LGP;1     SECURITY.DIR;1     SYSTEMS.DIR;1
USER.COM;1

Total of 17 files.
$
```

Once a program is being run, the CPU continues to process the program's instructions until either some interrupting **event** occurs or a predetermined period of time elapses. For example, a convenient place to have the CPU switch to the next program is where there is a need to get data from or send data to an I/O device. This form of interrupt processing is based on events. Another means of redirecting the CPU is to allow it to process program instructions for a certain time period, typically several milliseconds. At the end of this time, the CPU is switched to the next program. This form of interrupt processing is based on **time slicing**.

Once it is determined that the CPU should be switched to another program, there are several scheduling schemes that may be used. The simplest is the **first-come first-serve** scheme. A list is kept of jobs in the order in which they arrive to be processed. When the CPU is available, the job at the head of the list is scheduled. Conceptually, this method is similar to the "take-a-number" approach at the local ice-cream store.

A second CPU scheduling method is the use of a **priority scheme**. Some programs are more important than others. A university administration running semester grade reports may need to have priority over students running instructional programs. Some computer systems allow users to set priority levels from 1 to 5. To keep everyone from designating his or her program as having top-priority level 5, many computer departments use a charge system. Top-priority programs cost much more to run than low-priority programs. This is analogous to a phone company charging more for a long-distance call placed during weekday business hours than it does for calls made on weekends.

Memory

In the early computer systems, only one application program at a time was loaded into memory. All primary memory was available for use by the program being run, regardless of whether that program needed 10 percent of the available space or 80 percent. If the program required 150 percent of the memory space, it would have to be rewritten to fit in the limited memory available.

As operating systems were developed, it was necessary to divide primary memory into a number of sections. One section contained the operating system itself, and the remaining portion of memory was made available for several different user programs. With the move to multiuser computer systems, there was a need to share user memory in more efficient ways. Allocation of memory is called **memory management**. Accommodating multiple programs in memory at one time required a way of allocating that space, as well as a means for moving programs in and out of memory.

One allocation method was that of **fixed partitions**. Primary memory for use by user programs was divided into sections of a predefined, fixed memory size. For example, with small minicomputers it is quite common to allocate a fixed partition of 16K to each CRT. This assures that, if the terminal is available, the user can process his or her program.

One of the problems with fixed partitions is **memory fragmentation**. That is, not every program will use all of the memory available to it, thus leaving memory locations unused. Another problem occurs when there are programs needing more than the fixed amount of memory available. One solution for accommodating programs of different sizes is to have fixed partitions of different sizes. However, this reduces, but doesn't eliminate, the fragmentation problem.

For larger computer systems that need to accommodate a greater variety of programs and efficiently use a large, expensive primary memory, the concept of **variable size partitions** or regions was introduced. Partition size is defined dynamically, depending on the needs of the program. Thus, if a program were to need just 20K, that is what would be assigned. Similarly, a very large program could be given 512K. The only restriction is that the memory locations must be contiguous, or assigned as a block. In other words, a program using 16K of memory must have all the locations next to each other. It wouldn't work to have 4K in one part of memory, another part of 8K in a second part of memory, and the remaining 4K located in a different area.

Although variable size partitions give flexibility and yield better memory utilization, there can still be memory fragmentation. Also, the number of programs that can be handled is limited to the number of complete programs that can be loaded into the primary memory partitions at any one time (see Exhibit B.3).

One way to accommodate more programs is for the OS to perform **swapping**, in which a program waiting on disk to be processed is exchanged with a program in primary memory. Exhibit B.4 shows a memory divided into four partitions, which could be fixed or variable, with the OS occupying its own memory space. Programs A, B, C, and D are being processed. Waiting to be processed is program E, which is held on the disk. At the end of a time slice, the intermediate processing results of program B in memory are copied and written back to the disk. The next waiting

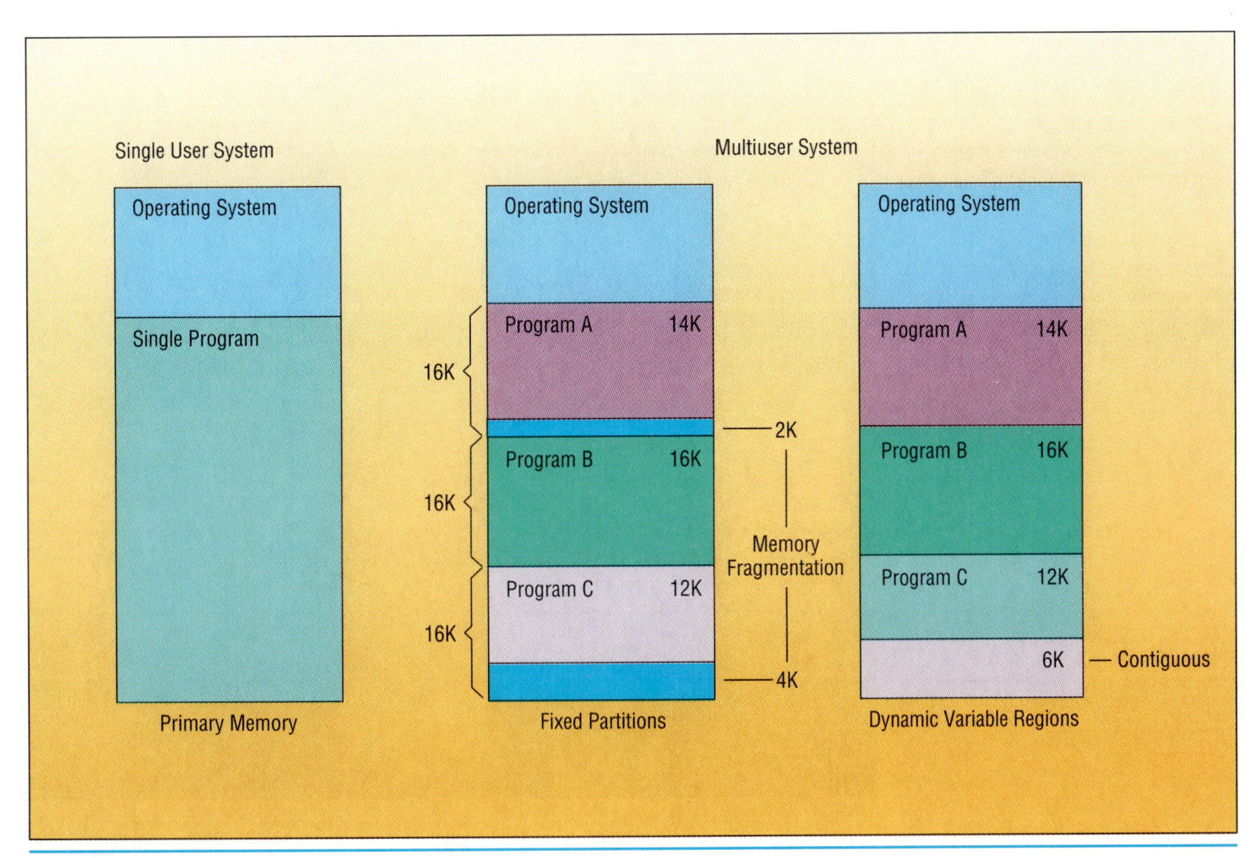

Exhibit B.3

Memory Management

Multiuser operating systems require more sophisticated management of primary memory than single-user systems. Fixed size partitions are sections of predefined, fixed memory size. Variable size partitions—partitions defined dynamically based upon the needs of the program—result in reduced memory fragmentation.

program, E, is read from the disk to the primary memory locations now available. At the next time slice, other programs could be swapped.

The next major advance in memory management is based on the concept that, even with large and complex programs, very few of the instructions need to be in primary memory at any one time. Therefore, it is a waste of resources to be swapping the complete program in and out of memory, or to have the total program in primary memory at one time. Why not bring in only those instructions that are relevant to the present state of processing for a particular program? This is the scheme implemented in virtual memory using demand paging.

To understand how demand paging works, consider the following analogy. When studying this textbook, you use, at any one time, only a few pages out of the total number available. You could be actively reading one page, on which a certain paragraph could refer you to a diagram on the next page. Later, you may need to turn to the glossary to look up the definition of a term introduced in a previous chapter. When you have finished studying (or processing) the page, you then turn to the next page.

In a similar way, programs can be subdivided into sections containing instructions. These sections are of a fixed length and are called **pages**. With previous memory-management schemes, the complete program had to reside in primary memory for processing to be

Exhibit B.4

Swapping Active Programs

Swapping allows the running of more programs than there are partitions. At the end of a time slice, the intermediate processing results of Program B in memory are copied and written back to disk. The next waiting program, Program E, is placed in the primary memory locations previously occupied by B.

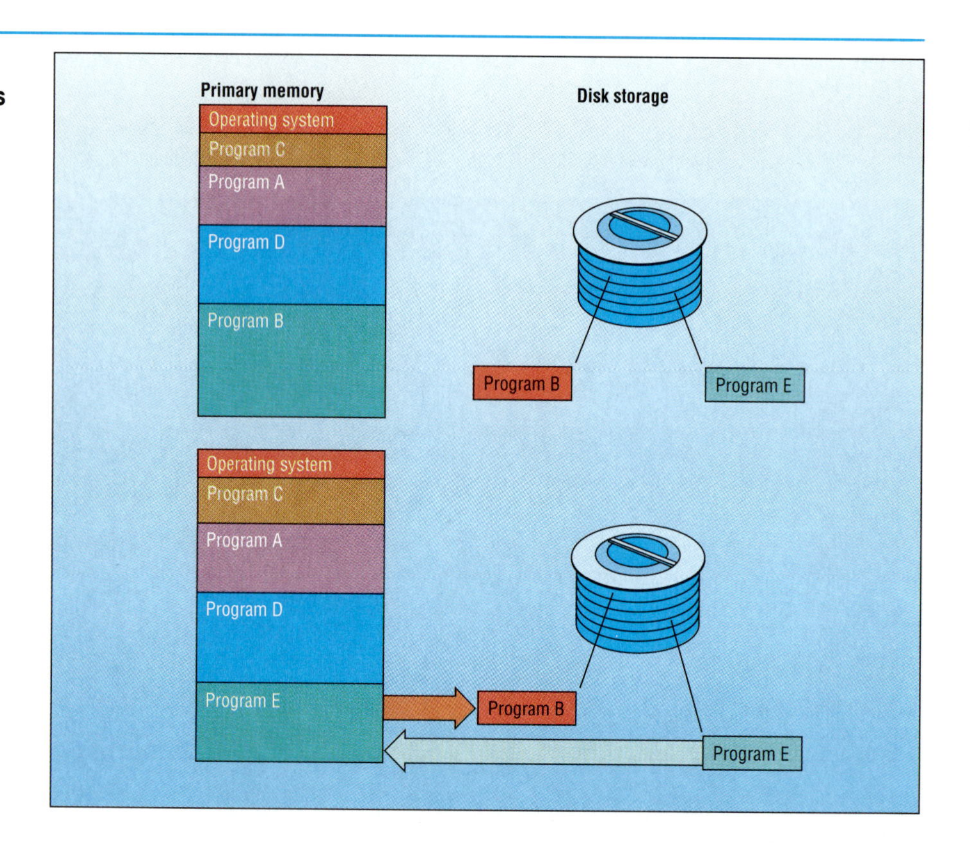

accomplished. The concept of **virtual memory** means that only relevant pages need to be in primary memory at any one time, and the remainder of the program is stored on disk, available on demand. In Exhibit B.5, program A has been divided into 10 pages, which are stored on disk. Pages A-1, A-7, and A-10 are actively being processed in primary memory. When, in processing the instructions of Program A, it becomes necessary to get a new page A-4, for example, it could be swapped for page A-10. But a problem comes about if page A-10 is later needed along with pages A-1, A-7, and A-4. Since all other memory locations are occupied by other programs, one of the A pages, which will be needed very soon, is swapped. When A-4 replaces A-10, and moments later page A-10 must be referred to for information, another swap will have to take place. When a large portion of CPU time is used shuffling pages back and forth from disk to primary memory, the system is said to be *thrashing*.

With the use of virtual memory, very large programs that can't fit in small fixed partitions or dominated dynamic partitions, can now be run efficiently. In general, more users can be accommodated in an interactive environment since each user's program takes up much less primary memory space. The major disadvantage is that virtual memory is a very complex undertaking for an OS. Because the OS is more complex, it takes more memory for the OS itself and requires more CPU resources to run the OS.

Exhibit B.5

Virtual Memory

Virtual memory makes it appear that primary memory is of unlimited size and can therefore readily accommodate very large programs.

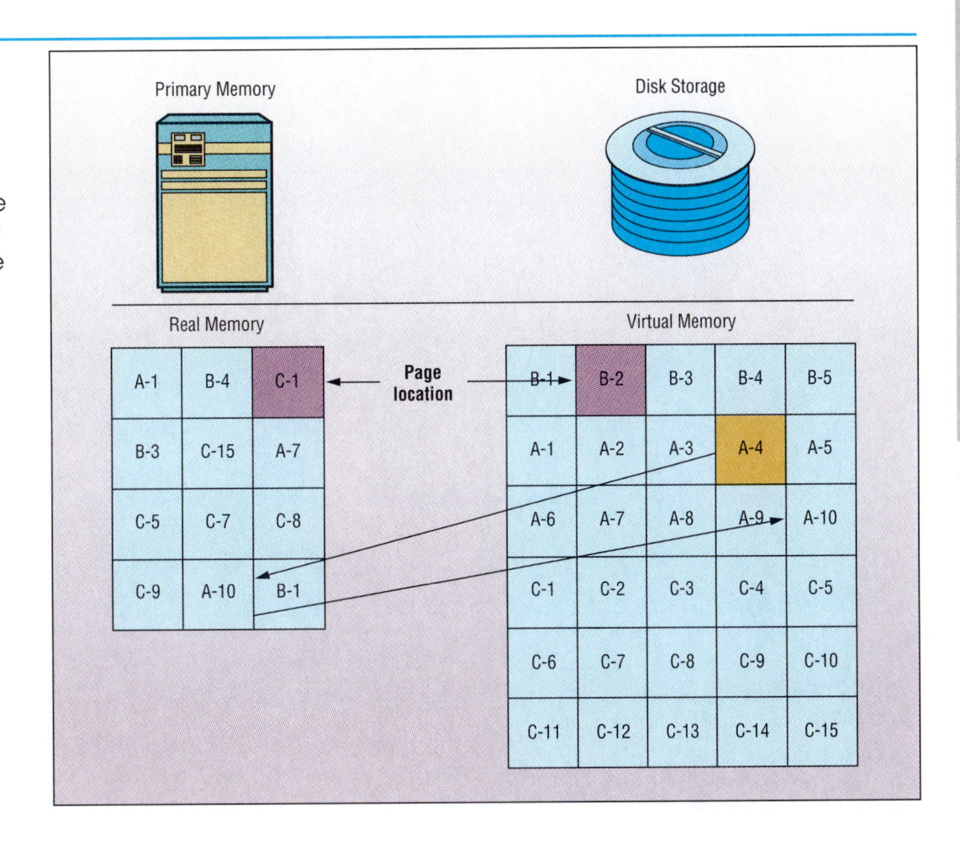

Input/Output Devices

Another key resource for any computer system involves input and output devices such as magnetic tapes, magnetic disks, and printers. Contention for the use of a limited number of these devices is inevitable, and some type of management is needed.

The way in which I/O devices are allocated or assigned varies with the type of device. Secondary storage devices such as magnetic tape and disk are assigned by the OS in response to the requirements of the application program being run. For a program that will require access to magnetic tape units, the OS assigns the required number of devices to only that program and only for the duration of its processing. This practice is somewhat wasteful of storage resources, since the tape units won't be continuously active for a program, but it does eliminate the problem of two different programs trying to write on the same tape unit.

Disk units, however, are not assigned to a particular program for the duration of its processing. Because disks are direct-access devices, they are shareable, and thus can be assigned and released as needed for an I/O operation. There are special precautions that need to be taken for controlling concurrent use, though, and these are discussed in Chapter 8, "File and Database Management."

In a multiuser environment, several programs can be backed up, waiting for the use of a printer. This can cause the CPU to become idle when all programs in memory are waiting on I/O operations. A concept called

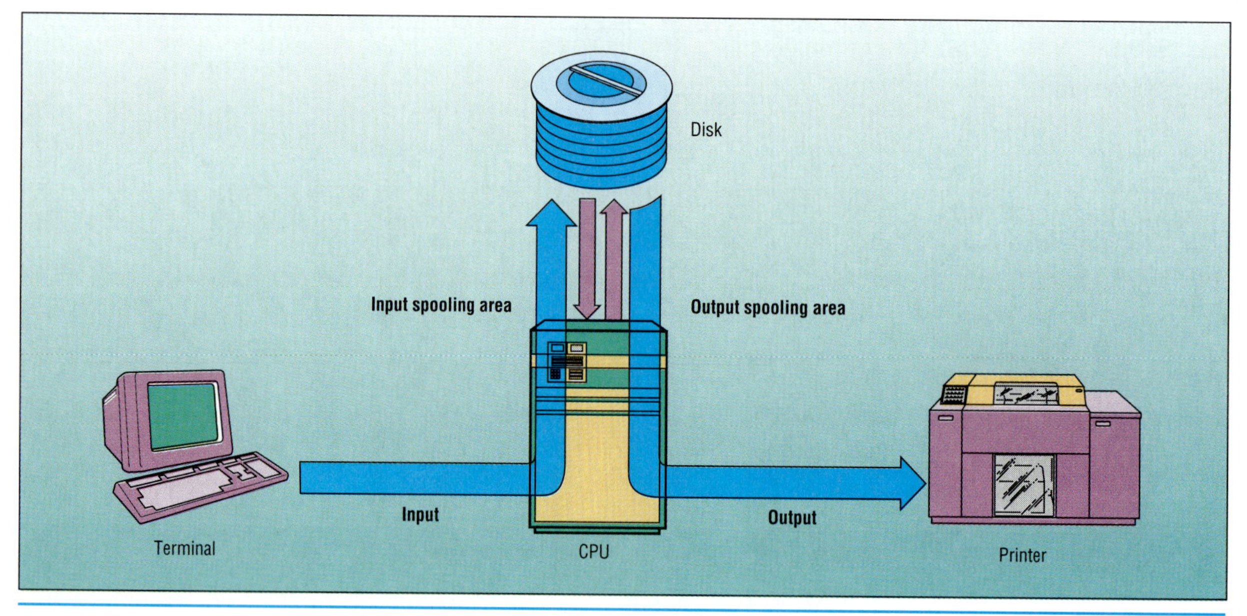

Exhibit B.6

Input and Output Spooling

Spooling allows programs and data to be read from input devices and placed in a job pool on disk to await processing. The spooling concept allows the CPU to be kept continuously active processing jobs.

spooling allows the output to be printed to be placed on disk, freeing the CPU to process other programs. When the current print job is finished and the printer is ready for another, the display data will be read from disk and printed on the high-speed printer (see Exhibit B.6). Spooling can also be used to read programs and data from input devices. Here, the information is stored on disk, forming a job pool. From the pool, the OS selects the next program to be sent to the CPU.

System Software

One of the functions of the OS is to manage the use of system support software, such as compilers, linkage editors, and utilities (see Exhibit B.7). To understand how these might be used, first consider how an application program written in the COBOL computer language is run.

The program is submitted in the English-like statements of the COBOL computer language. These source statements are translated into machine language. The OS calls on a system software module called a COBOL **compiler** to carry out this translation. The output of the compiler is called an **object module**. The COBOL program is called the **source module**.

Assume an accounts receivable COBOL program was written to produce a report that required company names to be sorted in alphabetical order. Instead of writing your own instructions for sorting, you could use a sort utility, which is stored on disk in machine language form. The OS now calls on another system software module, called a **linkage editor**, to link or combine your application program and the sort utility. The output is called a **load module**, which is in a form that can now be executed. When desired, it can be loaded into primary memory and processed, giving as output the accounts receivable report in alphabetical order.

Exhibit B.7

Phases in Running a Program

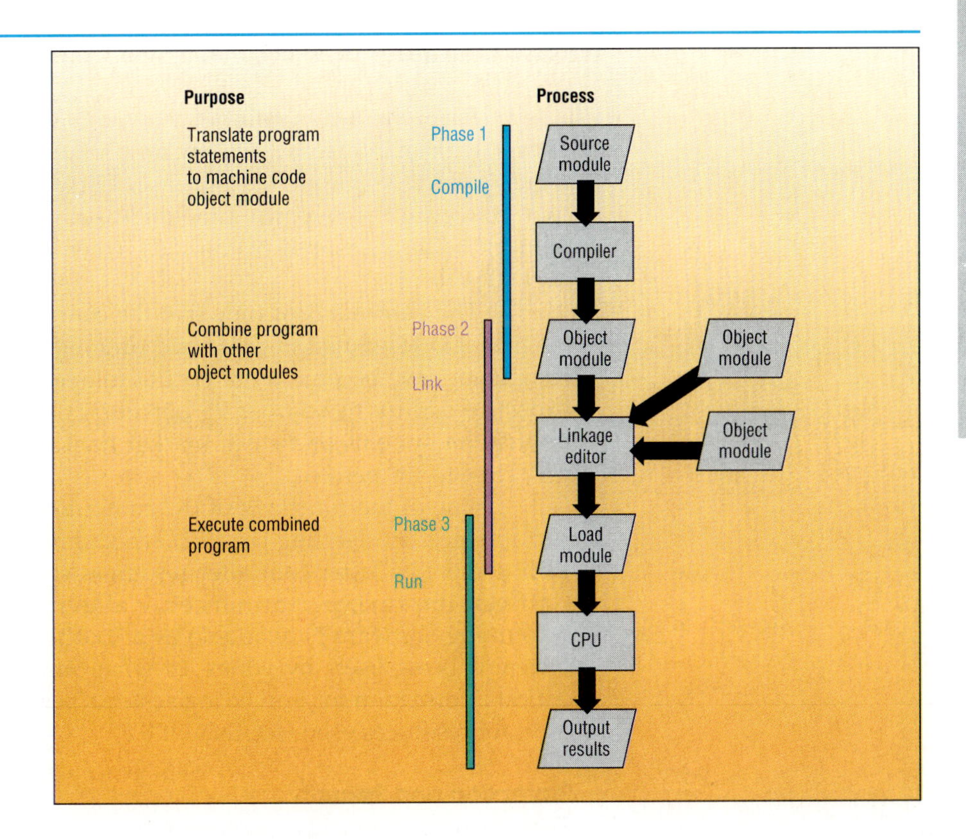

From this example you can see that the OS not only has to control the flow of a program through various job steps, but must also manage the use of system support software such as compilers and utilities.

Monitoring Activities

When large computer systems are being shared by many users and managed for efficiency, it is necessary to monitor system performance and protect the system from unauthorized users or system errors.

Performance

Four of the major criteria used to judge computer performance are CPU utilization, throughput, response time, and reliability. **CPU utilization** is the percentage of time that the CPU is actually working. For expensive computer systems, it is very important that the CPU be kept busy and not stand idle, awaiting tasks. A CPU utilization of 50 percent is considered lightly loaded; 80 to 90 percent is the target for a highly utilized system. Over 90 percent utilization causes significant reduction in response time because of contention for computer system resources.

A computer system's **throughput** is the number of programs completed per time period. In general, the higher the throughput, the greater the computer performance. However, this measure tends to be biased toward processing many small programs, rather than one long program.

From the user's point of view, a major criterion is **response time**. That is, with an interactive system, how long is the interval between a user's request and the computer's response? Often response time is a second or two. However, the response time increases significantly, sometimes to the point of being measured in minutes, when a system has CPU utilization over 90 percent.

The percentage of time that the computer is functioning relative to the time it is scheduled to be up and running is a measure of **reliability**. As computers have become more critical to operations, it is quite common to expect reliability to be over 95 percent. For applications such as airline reservation systems and stock market transactions, reliability needs to be very close to 100 percent.

One of the functions of the computer staff is to monitor computer performance. By selecting the CPU scheduling scheme, changing priorities, adding more or faster computer resources such as memory and disks, the staff can improve performance by alleviating bottlenecks. Resource accounting software is available as a tool to monitor how the computer system is being used, by whom, at what times, and for how long. This is critical information for improving systems performance and also for billing users for resources used (see Exhibit B.8).

Protection and Security

The increasing use of computers by multiple users and the shared use of primary memory and files, bring the problems of accidental and purposeful damage. A major function of the OS is to provide protection and security to minimize this damage.

Exhibit B.8

Monitoring Computer System Performance

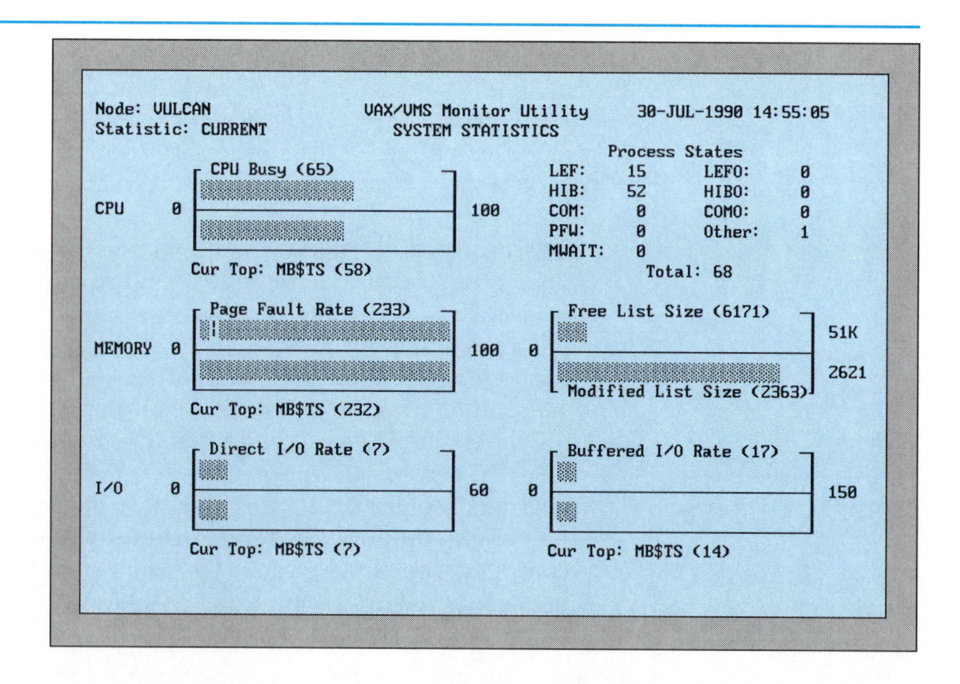

Protection is defined in terms of the way access to programs and data stored in the computer is controlled once the user is using the computer. One of the initial concerns in sharing memory was that a user could accidentally write over or destroy parts of the operating system. This was prevented by locating the OS in a specific part of memory and allowing no end-user programs to address these locations. If, perchance, an end-user program attempted to do so, the OS would abort that program. To keep anyone from using data stored in another user's files, an access code can be set up to specify which individuals are allowed to access specific data. Notation can also show whether the program can only read the file, or whether it can write to it as well.

Security is defined in terms of external threats from unauthorized users. One major problem here is authentication. That is, how does the operating system know that the user is who he or she purports to be? The most common approach is to use passwords. To sign on to a computer system, the user is required to supply a confidential sequence of alphanumeric characters, for example, T65RX2. If that password matches a valid password list stored in memory, the OS assumes the user is legitimate. The password can further be used to identify an access list, which specifies the rights the user has to view or change specific files.

Other possibilities include defining access rights by terminal. In other words, for a particular CRT located in a warehouse, the user, regardless of who it is, can only work on inventory records and would not be allowed access to payroll records. This technique is often combined with time and date restrictions. That is, payroll files can't be worked on after 5:00 P.M. nor anytime on weekends.

The protection and security of systems is becoming increasingly important as computers become more critical to the daily operations of organizations. Even with all the safeguards available, computer crime is, unfortunately, still on the rise.

Types of Operating Systems

The differences among various vendors' computer systems have led to the evolution of many types of operating systems. These types differ primarily in the way in which they handle multiple programs using the CPU concurrently.

Single Program

In the original operating systems, the complete computer system was made available to one program, which would be processed from start to finish. When the first program was completed, the computer was ready to process the next program. This serial type of operation is called a **batch-oriented** operating system.

The primary difficulty with this type of approach in the mainframe environment is that major portions of the computer system are idle most of the time. While the card reader is reading in the program, the CPU and the printer are idle. When the CPU is processing the program job, the card reader is idle. For a computer system costing millions of dollars, as the mainframes did in the 1960s, it wasn't cost effective to have such low utilization of expensive resources.

Multiprogramming

The concept of multiprogramming was developed to take advantage of the significantly faster speed of the CPU in relationship to input, storage, and output devices. **Multiprogramming** means that two or more programs are being run concurrently by the computer system. This approach dramatically improves computer utilization.

In **concurrent** operations, at any given point in time one program uses one computer resource while another program uses a different computer resource. For example, the computer could be doing an arithmetic calculation in the CPU for program 1, while data for program 2 were being read from magnetic tape. At the same time, the results of a third program could be printing out on the printer.

The basis for multiprogramming is **interrupt processing.** With event interrupts, the CPU processes a program until it requires an I/O operation. One possible multiprogramming sequence is as follows. The program being executed begins an I/O operation. While that I/O request is being handled by the card reader, disk, or output device, the CPU starts processing a second program. The CPU continues to process that second program until it needs to wait for an I/O event to occur. It then switches to processing a third program. Working in a round-robin fashion through the programs in process, the CPU will eventually get back to the first program. There, it will start processing where it left off, and processing will continue until the program is completed or another event interrupts the cycle.

Time-Sharing

Interactive systems were designed to allow direct communication between the user and the computer system. Combining the flexibility, for users, of the interactive approach with the computer efficiency of the multiprogramming concept led to **time-sharing** systems. These interactive, multiuser systems sequence tasks based on time slices, in contrast to the resource-based interruptions of batch-oriented systems.

Since each user's transaction tends to be short, time slices are typically allocated in milliseconds. Each user's program is put into a part of primary memory. The CPU works on one program for the allocated time slice, then switches to the next user's program. Because the CPU can execute millions of instructions per second, it can alternate among different programs so rapidly that it appears to the many users that each of them has exclusive use of the computer. Large computer systems can accommodate hundreds of interactive users at a time. However, when the number of users increases to the point that resources such as the CPU and I/O devices are heavily utilized, the response time will no longer be immediate. Instead of receiving responses within seconds, delays are noticeable, and the response time can stretch to minutes (see Exhibit B.9).

Most larger computer systems today offer both batch processing and time-sharing to serve the different needs of users. Batch processing is ideal for production jobs such as the weekly payroll, the monthly sales report, the quarterly income statement, and semester grades. In contrast, programs used for airline reservations, automatic teller machines, word processing, and decision support systems are inherently interactive. Continuous response is necessary to meet a range of fluctuating and varying user needs.

To handle both batch and interactive jobs and meet their very different response time requirements, computer systems utilize the concept of **foreground/background processing.** These terms simply refer respectively to high- and low-priority jobs. In general, when the CPU is available, the OS will assign it to a foreground (high-priority) job if one is waiting on the CPU. Only when no foreground job is waiting on the CPU will a background job be processed. The actual mix of interactive and batch jobs depends on the priority the users have set for each type. Thus, the high-priority interactive jobs are said to run in the foreground, and the low-priority batch jobs are said to run from the background.

Exhibit B.9

Time-Sharing

In a time-sharing system, it appears to the many users that each of them has exclusive use of the computer.

Multiprocessors

So far, this discussion has dealt with processing done by a computer system with a single CPU. But the tremendous demand for computing power, the need for increased reliability, and the decreasing price of hardware have led to the use of computer systems with multiple processors.

One of the early uses of multiple processors was in a "master/slave" relationship. Each slave processor was assigned a specific task, with one processor acting as the overall master control unit. This type of setup is used with remote job entry (RJE), where smaller processors aren't located next to the main computer, but rather are in a different building, or even in a distant city. RJE processors are used to run card readers and line printers and to transfer jobs to and from the main computer. Multiple processors are also used in time-sharing systems, where smaller processors are typically used to handle all input and output tasks. Thus, the main CPU is freed from having to perform so many "housekeeping" tasks, allowing it to concentrate more on processing programs.

With organizations becoming increasingly dependent on computers to carry out everyday tasks, a high degree of reliability has become paramount for certain industries. In the airline industry, for example, a major airline often uses two identical maxicomputers that are electrically connected. One computer will do interactive reservation processing, and the other is assigned batch administrative tasks. In the event that the first computer fails, the second computer will take over and assume the interactive tasks. Batch processing would then be suspended.

Tandem Corporation has commercially pioneered the concept of a single computer system designed for continuous operation—even if some components fail. This type of system is critical for organizations that have large on-line transaction processing needs, such as large international banks, stock market trading exchanges, point-of-sale networks for large retailers, and airline and hotel reservation systems. Tandem uses a system with up to sixteen processors, dual buses, shared memory, additional disks, multiple power supplies, and so on. If a hardware failure occurs, the OS senses this and automatically switches to an alternative electrical path and/or to a backup device. This action allows for continued operations. When repairs are necessary, removal and replacement of parts can be handled while the computer system continues to process work. Such a system is described as *fault-tolerant* (see Exhibit B.10).

During normal operations, the multiple processors all work concurrently. None stand idle for use as backup support. If one of the processors fails, the OS shifts its workload to an alternative working processor. This results in the overall computer system working at perhaps 90 percent of the normal rate, unlike most time-sharing systems, which have to shut down if they lose the host processor. *Fail-soft* is an industry term used to describe the system's ability to continue operation at a percentage of its normal rate, rather than shutting down altogether when a processor fails.

Exhibit B.10

Fault-tolerant Computer System

This fault-tolerant computer system is designed for continuous operation—even if some components fail.

Virtual Machines

Elsewhere in this book the limited portability of application programs written for a particular operating system on a specific computer has been discussed. In some of the more advanced computer systems, operating systems have been developed that are able to provide a **virtual machine** environment.

This means that, within limits, each user is given the illusion that he or she is working with the very computer and OS environment that is needed to run an application program or work with the computer interactively. This is done by running different guest operating systems in different areas of memory, with the virtual machine OS controlling the other operating systems.

IBM's OS/VM (virtual machine) is a good example of this type of operating system. It runs on the latest IBM maxicomputer systems. It allows some users to work interactively with the computer, under the virtual storage operating system, while other users run application programs designed for use with IBM operating systems from previous generations.

The advantage of a virtual machine approach is that one computer can be made to act as many different machines. Thus, the virtual machine can meet the specific needs of each user. It also helps eliminate the software compatibility problem, because it doesn't require that the older application software be rewritten or modified. Moreover, it enables management to take advantage of the latest computer technology and price/performance benefits.

Summary and Key Terms

Three of the major functions of an operating system are overall master control, resource management, and monitoring activities. A program called a **supervisor** exercises master control of computer operations and coordinates the work within the computer system. **Job control language (JCL)** is used to allow the user to communicate to the operating system the special tasks associated with a particular program.

The supervisor initiates and controls the execution of jobs. This requires allocating computer resources and scheduling when they are to be used, a function known as **resource management.** Computer resources include the CPU, memory, input/output devices, and support software.

One of the primary computer resources that is shared is the CPU itself. The CPU can work on only one program at a time. But, because it is thousands of times faster than I/O devices or users working interactively with the system, it can be shared in a couple of different ways. With **event** interrupts, the CPU works on a program until there is an I/O request. With **time slicing** interrupts, the CPU switches to the next program at the end of a fixed time period.

Once the CPU is to be switched, the CPU scheduling scheme is used to select the next program. The **first-come first-serve scheme** selects the job that has been waiting the longest. A **priority scheme** allows different programs to be selected, based on need.

With the move to multiuser computer systems came a need to share memory in more efficient ways. The allocation of memory is called **memory management.** One allocation method uses **fixed partitions,** in which primary memory is divided into sections of predefined size to accommodate user programs. Fixed partitions can lead to **memory fragmentation** caused when programs are of different sizes and don't use all the memory allocated to them. To better handle a variety of programs of different sizes, **variable size partitions** are used. With this allocation method, regions are defined dynamically, depending on the needs of a given program.

Swapping allows the OS to accommodate more programs at any one time than there are partitions or regions. This is accomplished by switching complete programs between primary memory and secondary storage. **Virtual memory** enables better memory management by keeping in primary memory only the active program instructions. Programs are divided into sections of fixed length known as **pages**. The remainder of the program is kept on disk, available on demand.

In the management of input/output devices, an operating system typically uses a concept called **spooling**, in which output to be printed is stored on disk while it is waiting to be printed, so that the CPU can continue to process other jobs.

An OS must also manage system support software, such as **compilers**, which take a **source module** written in a programming language and convert it to a machine code version called an **object module**. A **linkage editor** is then used to combine the object module with other operating system utilities to create a **load module**, which can then be executed by the OS.

CPU utilization, throughput, response time, and **reliability** are four major criteria used to judge computer performance.

Protection is how access to programs and data stored in the computer are controlled once the user is using the computer. **Security** is defined in terms of external threats from unauthorized users. One major problem is how the operating system authenticates that the user is who he or she purports to be. The most common approach is to use passwords.

There are many different types of operating systems. The early operating systems made the complete computer system available to one program, which would be processed from start to finish. This serial type of operation is called a **batch-oriented** operating system. **Multiprogramming** means that two or more programs are being run concurrently by the computer. In

concurrent operations, at any given point in time one program will be using one computer resource while another program uses a different computer resource.

The basis for multiprogramming is **interrupt processing**. These batch-oriented systems have the CPU process a program until it must wait for an I/O event to occur. **Time-sharing** systems allow direct communication between the user and the computer system. These interactive, multiuser systems sequence tasks based on time slices.

Foreground/background processing is used to deal with a mixture of batch and interactive jobs by assigning high and low priorities.

The tremendous demand for computing power, the need for increased reliability, and the decreasing price of hardware have led to operating systems designed for use with computer systems with multiple processors. In some of the more advanced computer systems, operating systems have been developed that are able to provide a **virtual machine** environment.

Review Questions

1. Briefly describe the functions of the operating system.
2. Briefly describe the master control function of the operating system.
3. What computer resources must be allocated and controlled by the resource management portion of the operating system?
4. Explain the concept of virtual memory. What advantages does it offer?
5. The Excell Corporation's new CPU is extremely fast. In fact, the firm's CPU frequently has to wait for its printer to catch up before it can process more data. How might this problem be corrected without replacing the current printer?
6. Briefly describe the four major criteria used to evaluate computer performance.
7. What is the role of the operating system in providing protection and security?
8. What is multiprogramming? What are some advantages and disadvantages to this approach?
9. What is a virtual machine? What are its advantages?

APPENDIX C

Introduction to MS-DOS 3.3

As you learned in Chapter 11, "Microcomputer Operating Systems," the primary function of the operating system is to provide an interface between application software and computer hardware. The operating system allows the user to concentrate on creating an application without having to worry about the details of how data are physically stored and moved among the various hardware components inside the computer. Since microcomputer hardware can be controlled by different operating systems, and each operating system has its own way of interacting with a user, it is the particular operating system used that determines how the microcomputer will behave and provides the microcomputer with its "personality."

In this appendix you will be introduced to the MS-DOS (MicroSoft Disk Operating System) operating system. Since IBM selected MS-DOS for its IBM PC family of computers in 1981, this operating system has become the standard operating system for 16-bit microcomputers. During its life span, MS-DOS has gone through four major versions.

Some of the more notable versions of MS-DOS include the original version, 1.0, which was designed primarily for PCs with two floppy disk drives. When hard disks became common, MS-DOS 2.0 was created, to allow the operating system to work with hard disks. As local area networks became established, MS-DOS 3.0 was created to support them. A further revision of the third version came in the form of MS-DOS 3.2, which added support for 3 1/2-inch floppy disks. Version 3.3 added additional commands to the operating system, and the current version, 4.0, includes menus, on-line help, and support for hard disks larger than 32MB.

Before You Start

To complete the exercises in this appendix you will need access to an IBM compatible microcomputer and a copy of MS-DOS. The microcomputer should have two floppy disk drives (or one floppy disk drive and a hard disk). You will need to become familiar with how to operate the microcomputer, including how to turn on all the necessary components and how to insert diskettes into the disk drives. When handling floppy diskettes, remember never to touch the exposed magnetic surfaces, and always follow instructions for protecting the diskettes from damage.

Components of MS-DOS

Like all operating systems, MS-DOS is simply a series of programs written to interact with the microcomputer CPU, primary memory, and secondary storage. The programs that make up MS-DOS are stored in files on a secondary storage device such as a floppy diskette or a hard disk. When the microcomputer is turned on, some of these files must be loaded into primary memory before the microcomputer can be used. The files for MS-DOS are divided into three general categories: the input/output handler, the command processor, and external utility programs.

The **input/output handler** function of the MS-DOS operating system is implemented using two special, hidden files called IBMBIO.COM and IBMDOS.COM. These files deal with the movement of data among the various hardware components of the microcomputer, including the keyboard, monitor, printer, and disk drives. Since the user would normally have no reason to interact with these files, they are hidden to prevent accidental erasure or alteration.

The **command processor** for MS-DOS is contained in a file called COMMAND.COM. This program provides the basic operating system functions, including erasing, renaming, copying, and listing files on disk. The command processor interprets instructions entered by the user at the keyboard and translates them into the appropriate actions. MS-DOS commands included in the command processor are known as **internal commands**. Unlike the files for the input/output handler, the COMMAND.COM file is not hidden from the user.

The **external utility programs** in MS-DOS provide additional operating system functions not included in the command processor. These utility programs deal with the preparation of floppy diskettes and hard disks, checking and comparing diskettes, and backing up disks. The programs providing each of these functions are stored in separate files. To keep the size of the MS-DOS operating system as small as possible, these commands are not included in the command processor. Since they are not part of the COMMAND.COM file these commands are known as **external commands**. Exhibit C.1 lists some of the internal and external commands in MS-DOS.

Booting a Microcomputer with MS-DOS

Before a microcomputer can be used, the operating system must be loaded into primary memory. The process of loading the operating system from secondary storage into primary memory is known as **booting** the microcomputer. Since the operating system is stored on a floppy diskette or a hard disk, the microcomputer always looks for an operating system on a secondary storage device when it is turned on.

For example, at the moment a microcomputer with two floppy disk drives is turned on, it looks for the operating system on drive A. Thus, the user must place a diskette containing the operating system files in drive A

Exhibit C.1

MS-DOS Internal and External Commands

Internal Commands	External Commands
DIR	FORMAT
ERASE	CHKDSK
RENAME	DISKCOPY
COPY	PRINT
TYPE	

prior to turning on the computer. When the microcomputer includes a hard disk drive, the operating system files are often placed on the hard disk. When a hard disk is present, the microcomputer will still look for the operating system on drive A, but if there is no diskette in drive A, it will move on to the hard disk to see if the operating system can be found there.

When a microcomputer is booted with MS-DOS, the diskette or hard disk must contain the two hidden input/output handler files (IBMBIO.COM and IBMDOS.COM) and the command processor (COMMAND.COM). It is these three programs that are loaded into primary memory. Once the COMMAND.COM file is loaded into memory, the diskette containing the COMMAND.COM file no longer has to remain in drive A. This allows the user to replace the MS-DOS diskette with other diskettes and still be able to execute any internal command since those commands have been loaded into memory.

The process of loading the operating system into primary memory at the moment the microcomputer is turned on is known as a **cold boot** since the PC was initially turned off (or cold). It is also possible to cause the operating system to be reloaded when the microcomputer is already turned on (or warm) using a process known as a **warm boot**. In a warm boot the user issues a certain key sequence (typically the simultaneous pressing of the CTRL, ALT, and DEL keys) to cause the primary memory of the microcomputer to be blanked out and force the microcomputer to go to drive A (the hard disk if present) and load the operating system again.

To summarize, the steps for booting a microcomputer with MS-DOS are illustrated in the following exercise.

Exercise 1: Booting a Microcomputer

1. If the computer has a hard disk containing MS-DOS, go to step 2; otherwise insert a diskette containing MS-DOS in drive A.

2. Turn on the computer (cold boot) or, if the computer is already on, hold down the CTRL and ALT keys and press the DEL key (warm boot).

3. MS-DOS will display a date and ask you to enter a new date if you desire. (**Note:** If your MS-DOS disk has not been set up to prompt you for the date, skip this step.)

```
Current date is Tue 1-01-1980
Enter new date (mm-dd-yy):
```

If you do not want to enter a date, press (RETURN). Otherwise, type in the date by entering the month, day, and year separated by hyphens and press (RETURN).

4. MS-DOS will display a time and ask you to enter a new time if you desire. (**Note:** If your MS-DOS disk has not been set up to prompt you for the time, skip this step.)

```
Current time is 0:01:28.43
Enter new time:
```

If you do not want to enter the time, press (RETURN). Otherwise, type in the time by entering the hour, minute, and seconds separated by colons and press (RETURN).

5. The version of the operating system will be displayed followed by the A> DOS prompt (or C> if you booted from a hard disk).

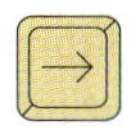

MS-DOS Files

Most MS-DOS commands are used to manipulate secondary storage media such as floppy diskettes and hard disks and the files stored on those disks. The basic unit of storage within an operating system is the file, and each operating system has its own conventions for naming files. In MS-DOS, all files have a two-part name, consisting of a file name and a file extension joined by a period. Both the file name and extension can be made up of a combination of letters, digits, and these special symbols:

```
! @ ? # $ % ^ & ( ) { } _ - ~ `
```

The file name cannot be more than eight characters long, and the extension is limited to just three characters. As indicated above, the file name is listed first, and the extension is added on the end, with a period separating the name and extension. The three-character extension is often used to indicate the type of file being stored. For example, MS-DOS command files often have a COM extension. This convention of using a common extension on files with a common purpose helps the user organize files on a disk. MS-DOS does not, however, require that files of a similar type have the same extension. Exhibit C.2 illustrates some valid and invalid MS-DOS file names.

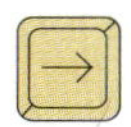

The MS-DOS Prompt

After the microcomputer is booted and the operating system is ready to receive instructions from the user, a prompt is displayed on the screen. Typically the MS-DOS prompt is A>. The user can type commands following this prompt (using (BACKSPACE) to correct errors when necessary) and press (RETURN) to have the operating system attempt to execute the

Exhibit C.2

Some Valid and Invalid MS-DOS File Names and Extensions

Valid	
PROGRAM.TXT	
REPORT.1	
JUNE25.RPT	
BIG_FILE.DAT	

Invalid	Reason
PROGRAMONE.TXT	File name is too long
REPORT.THREE	Extension is too long
JUNE/25.RPT	Slash (/) not allowed
BIG FILE.DAT	No blank spaces allowed

instruction. The prompt is displayed again after the operating system has finished the action that was requested. Thus, the user and the operating system are taking turns entering and executing instructions, and the prompt lets the user know when it is his or her turn.

In MS-DOS, the prompt also tells the user which disk drive is the current default drive (usually drive A). The concept of a default drive is particularly important when dealing with external commands. When the user attempts to execute an external command, the program for that command is not in primary memory since external commands are not part of the COMMAND.COM file. When MS-DOS cannot find the command issued by the user in primary memory, it will automatically look at the diskette in the default drive to see if the file for the command is located there. Thus, a user must often be aware of which drive is functioning as the default drive.

MS-DOS allows the user to determine which drive will be considered the default drive. In most PCs, drive A is automatically the default drive. In PCs with a hard disk the default drive is often drive C. To change the default drive, the user can type the letter of the new default drive, followed by a colon, at the prompt. For example, if the user wanted drive B to be the default, at the A> prompt the user would type

```
B:
```

and press (RETURN). The MS-DOS prompt would then automatically change to

```
B>
```

to indicate that the default drive is now drive B. To change the default drive back to A, the user could then type A: at the B> prompt, press (RETURN), and the prompt would change back to A>.

MS-DOS Commands for Manipulating Disks

Several MS-DOS commands can be used to work with an entire disk, including commands to prepare diskettes for use by the operating system, provide information on the amount of space on a disk that is in use, make copies of entire disks, and list the contents of a disk. With these commands the user must often supply the letter of the drive containing the diskette to be affected by the command. If the user omits the drive letter from the command, MS-DOS will assume that the command is to affect the diskette in the current default drive.

The FORMAT Command

Before information can be stored on a diskette by MS-DOS, the diskette must be **formatted**. The formatting process first initializes the diskette by writing to and reading information from the diskette to determine if there are any defective areas. This process destroys any data previously stored on the diskette. The diskette is also divided into regions known as **sectors** at this time.

Second, the diskette is organized into four areas: the boot record, the file allocation table (FAT), the root directory, and the data area. The **boot record** contains the boot code, along with some data about the characteristics of the diskette. The **root directory** is where MS-DOS records the names of the files stored on the diskette. A location in the **file allocation table** lists where each file is stored on the diskette. The file allocation table also contains a list of all the sectors on the diskette, including which sectors are available and which sectors are currently used by a file. Thus, before a diskette can be used to store files, it must be prepared using the FORMAT command.

The FORMAT command is an external command in MS-DOS and is actually a program contained in a file called FORMAT.COM. Thus, to use the FORMAT command, the FORMAT.COM file must, typically, be on the diskette in the default drive of the computer. The syntax for the FORMAT command is

FORMAT *d*:

where *d:* is the drive containing the blank diskette to be formatted. If the drive letter is omitted, MS-DOS will assume that the diskette to be formatted will be placed in the default drive. For example, when the user is preparing a new diskette, an MS-DOS disk containing the FORMAT.COM file is typically placed in drive A, the blank diskette to be formatted is placed in drive B, the command

```
FORMAT B:
```

is typed at the A> prompt, and RETURN is pressed. The operating system then responds with a prompt to insert the new diskette to be formatted into drive B, if it is not already there. When the user responds to this prompt by pressing RETURN, the formatting process begins.

A common option used on the format command is to add /V after the drive letter in the format command. In this case the FORMAT command would be

```
FORMAT  B:/V
```

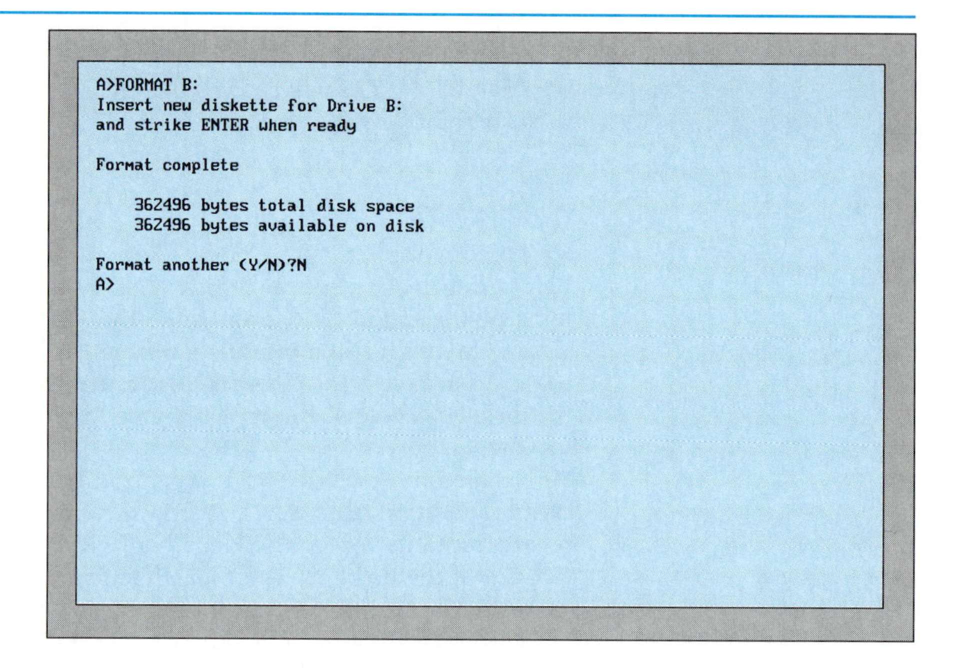

Exhibit C.3
The MS-DOS Format Command

This instructs MS-DOS to allow the user to enter a volume label for the disk. This volume label serves as an electronic label for the diskette. Exhibit C.3 illustrates what the screen will show during a FORMAT command.

Note that when the FORMAT command is completed, MS-DOS shows the user the amount of space on the diskette after formatting and the amount of space available for storing files. In this example 362,496 bytes of storage are available, which is the typical amount on a 360K diskette. A listing of **bad sectors** is also included when MS-DOS finds that part of the surface of the diskette was not reliable enough to be used. These sectors are marked by MS-DOS and will be skipped over when data is stored on the diskette.

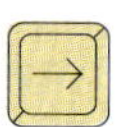

Formatting a System Disk

The formatting process described above creates a data diskette capable of storing files for the MS-DOS operating system, but that diskette cannot be used to boot the computer. A diskette capable of booting a PC with MS-DOS is typically called a **system disk**. To boot a computer, this system disk must contain the IBMBIO.COM and IBMDOS.COM hidden files and the COMMAND.COM command processor. In addition, these files must be positioned in the first sectors and tracks on the diskette so that they can be properly loaded into primary memory when the computer is booted.

The transfer of these operating system files to a new diskette is accomplished using the FORMAT command with an optional /S parameter. Assuming that the MS-DOS diskette containing the three operating system files and the FORMAT.COM file is in drive A and the blank diskette

Exhibit C.4

Using the Format Command to Create a System Disk

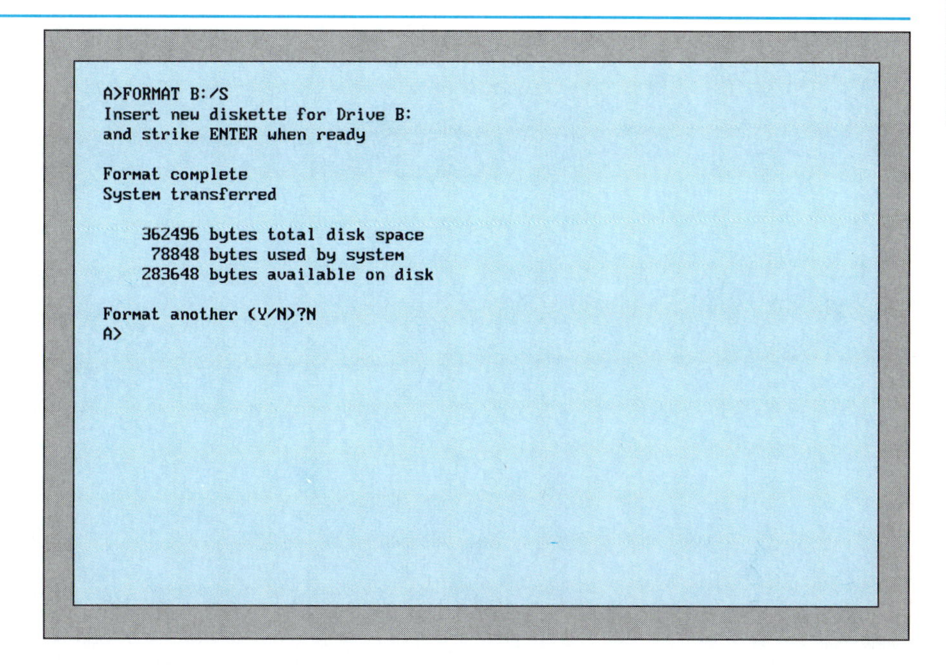

is in drive B, the command to make the new diskette a system disk would be

```
FORMAT B:/S
```

Exhibit C.4 shows the results of this command. This time the summary information also shows the amount of space taken up by the three system files on the disk.

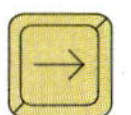

The CHKDSK Command

Another external command that deals with a diskette as a whole is the check disk (CHKDSK) command, which shows how disk space is allotted. The syntax for this command is

CHKDSK *d*:

where *d:* is the drive containing the diskette to be checked. Since CHKDSK is an external command, the CHKDSK.COM file must be on the diskette in the default drive. In addition, if the drive letter is omitted, MS-DOS will perform the CHKDSK operation on the diskette in the current default drive. For example, with the MS-DOS disk containing CHKDSK.COM in drive A, the user could perform a check disk operation on the diskette in drive B by typing

```
CHKDSK B:
```

Exhibit C.5

The CHKDSK Command

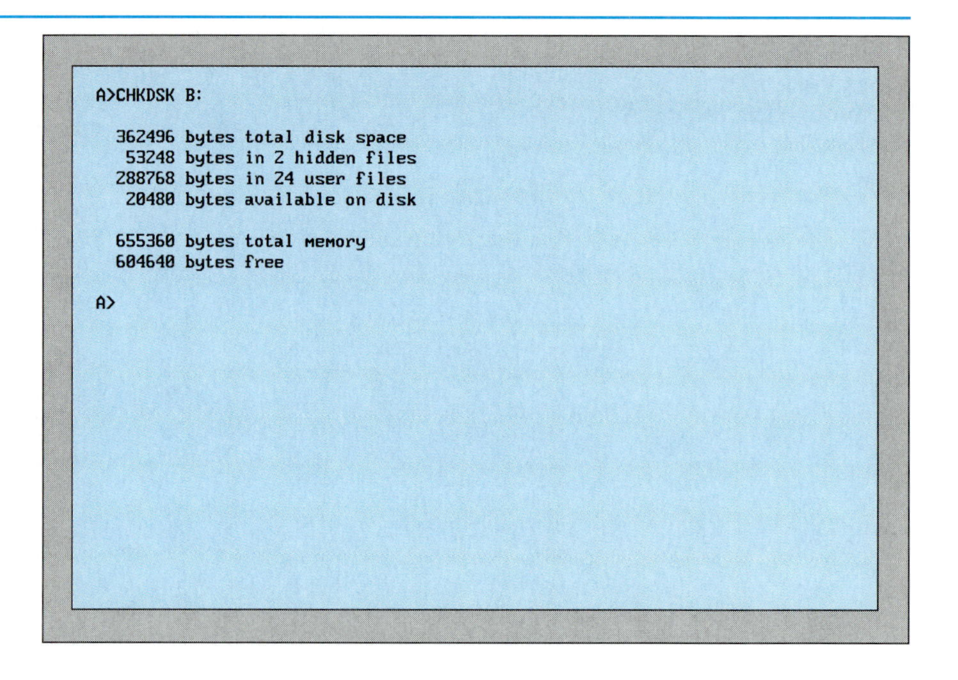
```
A>CHKDSK B:

  362496 bytes total disk space
   53248 bytes in 2 hidden files
  288768 bytes in 24 user files
   20480 bytes available on disk

  655360 bytes total memory
  604640 bytes free

A>
```

at the A> prompt and pressing (RETURN). The resulting display will look something like that in Exhibit C.5.

The result of the CHKDSK command is a list of the amount of space on the diskette, plus a breakdown of how much of that space is devoted to hidden files, user files, and the amount of free space. In addition, the two lines at the bottom show the size of the primary memory of the computer and the amount of primary memory still free.

A variation of the CHKDSK command includes the name of a file instead of a drive. For example, the user could enter the command

```
CHKDSK B:FILE1.TXT
```

to display information about the diskette in drive B and do a specific analysis of the file called FILE1.TXT on that disk. The analysis of the file will show whether the sectors in which the file are stored are adjacent to each other on the disk (contiguous) or are scattered across several nonadjacent sectors (noncontiguous). When a file is stored in adjacent sectors, it is very easy and efficient for the operating system to position the read/write heads of the disk drive over that location and read the file. When a file is scattered across non-contiguous sectors, the read/write heads must be repositioned several times during the reading of the file, which is much slower and less efficient. Exhibit C.6 illustrates this use of the CHKDSK command.

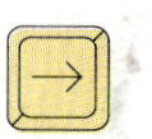

The DISKCOPY Command

An additional external command in MS-DOS that operates on diskettes is the DISKCOPY command. The DISKCOPY command (stored in the DISKCOPY.COM file) can be used to make a duplicate of an entire diskette.

Exhibit C.6

Using the CHKDSK Command to Check a File

```
A>CHKDSK B:FILE1.TXT

   362496 bytes total disk space
    53248 bytes in 2 hidden files
   288768 bytes in 24 user files
    20480 bytes available on disk

   655360 bytes total memory
   604640 bytes free

A:\FILE1.TXT
    Contains 3 non-contiguous blocks

A>
```

In the DISKCOPY command process, the diskette being copied is referred to as the **source diskette** and the copy being created is known as the **target diskette**. Since two diskettes are involved, they are typically placed in different drives.

Prior to inserting the source and target diskettes, the user must have placed a diskette containing the DISKCOPY.COM file in the default drive. He or she then issues the DISKCOPY command. For example, to make a copy of a diskette in drive A to a diskette in drive B, the user would type

```
DISKCOPY A: B:
```

at the A> prompt and press (RETURN). The first drive listed is the one to contain the source diskette and the second drive is the one to contain the target diskette. When this command is entered, the DISKCOPY command is loaded into memory and the user is prompted to put the source and target diskettes into the appropriate drives:

```
Insert source diskette in drive A
Insert target diskette in drive B
Strike any key when ready
```

Once the user presses a key, the contents of the diskette in drive A are copied to the diskette in drive B. It is not necessary for the target diskette to be formatted prior to the DISKCOPY. The DISKCOPY command will automatically format the target diskette. Thus, you must be careful with the DISKCOPY command since any files originally on the target diskette will be destroyed.

It is also possible to perform a DISKCOPY with only a single disk drive. For example, the user could enter

```
DISKCOPY A: A:
```

at the A> prompt and press RETURN. Since both the source diskette and the target diskette are to go in drive A, the DISKCOPY command will alternately prompt the user to insert the source and target diskettes in that drive. Initially, the source diskette will be placed in drive A. As much of the contents of that disk as possible will be copied to the primary memory of the computer. Then the user will be prompted to replace the source diskette with the target diskette. Once the target diskette is inserted in drive A, the information in primary memory is placed on the target disk. This process is repeated as many times as necessary, until all the information on the source diskette has been copied to the target diskette.

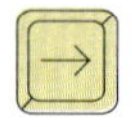

The DIR Command

MS-DOS can be instructed to display a list of the files stored on a diskette by using the directory (DIR) command. Unlike the commands discussed above, the DIR command is an internal command. Since the DIR command is loaded into primary memory, it is always available to MS-DOS, regardless of the current default drive setting. The general format for the DIR command is

```
DIR d:
```

where *d:* is the drive containing the diskette whose contents are to be listed. If the drive letter is omitted, the contents of the default drive will be listed. Exhibit C.7 shows the results of a DIR B: command.

The resulting display shows the file name and extension for each file, plus the size of each file in bytes and the date and time the file was last saved on the disk. At the bottom is a summary of the number of files listed and the current amount of free space on the diskette.

Occasionally, diskettes contain so many files that they cannot be listed on a single screen. In this case, when the DIR command is executed, the list of files scrolls off the top of the screen, and the user will not be able to see the information for some of the files. When this occurs, the user has two options. The display of files can be paused by adding a /P to the DIR command. For example,

```
DIR B:/P
```

instructs MS-DOS to begin listing the files on the diskette in drive B and pause when the screen becomes full. A prompt at the bottom of the screen instructs the user to press any key to continue listing files. When a key is pressed, files are again listed until the screen is full and the display pauses once more.

Exhibit C.7

The DIR Command

```
A>DIR B:

 Volume in drive B has no label
 Directory of B:\

COMMAND  COM    25308   2-02-88  12:00a
FILE1    TXT     6119   1-01-90   2:18a
FILE2    TXT     5432   1-05-89   2:20a
FILE3    TXT     6562   3-03-90  12:30a
FILE     TXT    18612   4-06-90   1:30p
FILELIST TXT     9833   1-01-90   4:34p
FILES    TXT    11029   3-09-90   3:56p
        7 file(s)    226050 bytes free

A>
```

Another option is the /W option, which instructs MS-DOS to display file names and extensions in five columns across the screen. This wide display can show more files per screen, but information about file sizes, dates, and times is omitted (see Exhibit C.8).

Like the CHKDSK command, the DIR command can also include file names and extensions to obtain information about a single file. For example,

```
DIR B:FILE1.TXT
```

would show the directory entry for the file FILE1.TXT on the diskette in drive B including the name, size, date, and time information for that file.

A more useful application of this feature is to use **wildcard characters** in the file name or extension to cause MS-DOS to list a group of files. The wildcard characters used in MS-DOS are the asterisk (*) and the question mark (?). Wildcard characters are used to represent one or more characters in the file name or extension. The question mark can be placed in a file name or extension to indicate that the DIR command is to list files with any character in that position in the file name or extension.

For example, suppose a diskette in drive B contained the following files:

```
FILE.TXT
FILE1.TXT
FILE2.TXT
FILE3.TXT
FILES.TXT
FILELIST.TXT
```

Exhibit C.8

The DIR/W Command

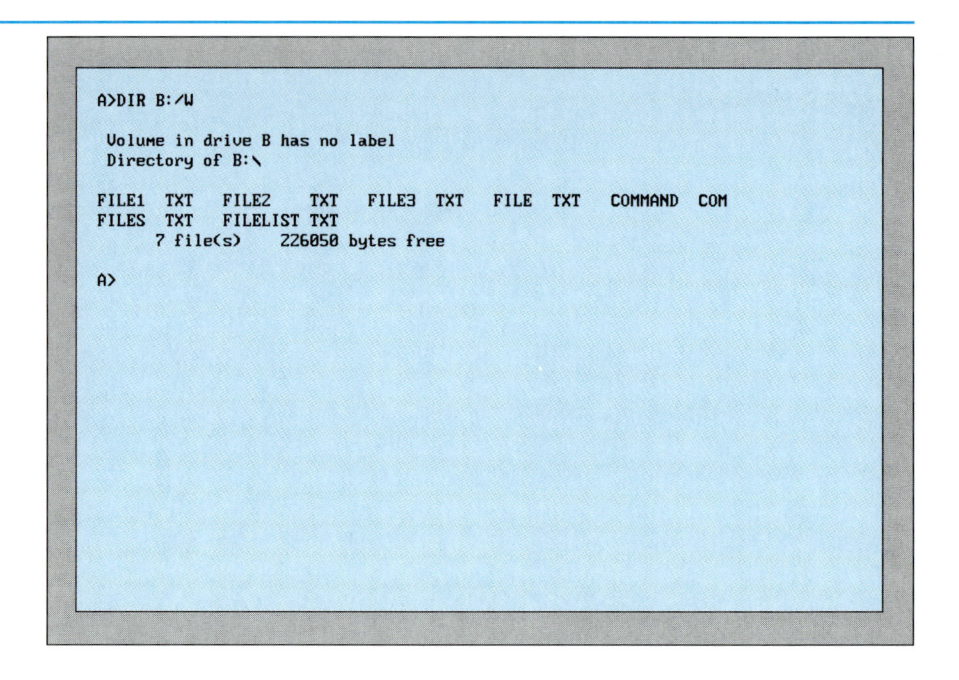

If the user wanted to list all the files that began with FILE followed by at most one character, the command

```
DIR B:FILE?.TXT
```

could be used. This would display a listing containing FILE1.TXT, FILE2.TXT, FILE3.TXT, and FILES.TXT. The FILELIST.TXT and FILE.TXT files would not be listed because the DIR command above instructs MS-DOS to list file names in which the first four characters are FILE and the fifth character is any character or no character. Thus, the question mark is used to mark a position in the file name or extension where a single character appears.

Another example of the use of the ? wildcard character would be

```
DIR B:F???.TXT
```

This would list only the FILE.TXT file since this command is asking for a list of files with a four-character file name in which the first character is F and the last four characters can be anything.

An asterisk can also be substituted in the file name or extension of a file listed in the DIR command. The asterisk wildcard is used to stand for any *group* of characters. For example,

```
DIR B:FILE*.TXT
```

would list all files that begin with the letters FILE and have the extension TXT. The asterisk indicates that any number of characters (including none) can appear at the end of the file name. Thus, this command would list

Exhibit C.9

Some Valid and Invalid Uses of the Asterisk Wildcard

Valid	Invalid
DIR *.*	DIR *ING.TXT
DIR *.TXT	DIR H*NG.TXT
DIR H*.COM	DIR FILE.*XT
DIR PROG.*	
DIR PROG.TX*	
DIR H*.H*	

FILE.TXT, FILE1.TXT, FILE2.TXT, FILE3.TXT, FILES.TXT, and FILELIST.TXT.

Another common use of the asterisk wildcard is to substitute an asterisk for the entire file name or extension. For example,

```
DIR C:*.TXT
```

would list all the files on drive C that had an extension of TXT.

```
DIR C:FILE.*
```

would list all files on drive C that had a file name of FILE and any extension.

```
DIR A:*.*
```

would list all the files on drive A, since the command is indicating that files with any file name and any extension are to be listed. This command would have the same effect as the command DIR A:.

In general, the question mark wildcard can appear anywhere in the file name or extension. The asterisk, however, can only appear at the end of a file name or extension or in place of the entire file name or extension. The asterisk cannot appear at the beginning or middle of the file name or extension. Exhibit C.9 illustrates some valid and invalid uses of the asterisk wildcard in the DIR command.

Exercise 2: Formatting and Copying Diskettes

Obtain an MS-DOS diskette containing the FORMAT.COM and DISKCOPY.COM files and two blank diskettes.

1. Put the MS-DOS diskette in drive A and boot the computer.
2. Type the command **FORMAT B:/S** at the A> prompt and press (RETURN).
3. When instructed to place a blank diskette in drive B, put one of the blank diskettes in drive B and press any key.
4. After the formatting is complete, answer **N** when asked if you want to format another diskette.

5. List the files on the newly formatted disk by entering the command **DIR B:** at the A> prompt. You should see only the COMMAND.COM file on this diskette. The IBMBIO.COM and IBMDOS.COM files are hidden and will not be listed by the DIR command.

6. Type the command **DISKCOPY A: B:** at the A> prompt and press (RETURN).

7. When prompted to do so, put the diskette you formatted in Step 3 in drive A as the source diskette and put the second blank diskette in drive B as the target diskette. Then press any key. This will format your second blank diskette and make it identical to the first diskette you formatted.

8. Issue the **DIR B:** command again to verify that the second diskette formatted with the DISKCOPY command also contains the COMMAND.COM file.

MS-DOS Commands for Manipulating Files

Other MS-DOS commands are designed to allow the user to perform specific operations on the files stored on diskettes, such as erasing, renaming, copying, displaying, and printing files. Like the DIR command, these commands can also be used to affect groups of files through the use of wildcard characters when specifying the names of the files to be affected.

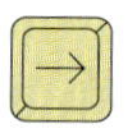

The ERASE Command

The ERASE command is an internal command that can be used to mark a file entry in the diskette directory to indicate that the file is no longer to be kept and that the locations on the diskette occupied by that file are free to be used for the storage of other files.

A common misconception about the ERASE command is that the information stored in the file is somehow blanked out. As indicated above, erasing a file simply tells MS-DOS that the locations occupied by the file can now be used for the storage of other files. The information contained in an erased file is only lost when other files are stored on the disk in the locations previously used by the erased file.

This procedure of only marking a file as erased rather than actually blanking out its contents has allowed the creation of utility programs that enable the user to restore files that were accidentally erased. When an unerase utility is run, it restores the file entries in the diskette directory and once again reserves the sectors occupied by the files so other files will not be stored there. Of course, the unerase utility must be run immediately after the accidental erasure of a file—before other files are stored in the locations occupied by the erased file.

```
ERASE d:filename.ext
```

The *d:* is the drive containing the diskette with the file to be erased. If the drive letter is omitted, it will be assumed that the file to be erased is on the default drive. The *filename.ext* is the name and extension of the file to be erased. By substituting wildcard characters in the file name or extension, groups of files could be erased with a single command. Some examples of ERASE commands include

```
ERASE A:FILE1.TXT
```

which would erase the file called FILE1.TXT from the diskette in drive A,

```
ERASE B:FILE*.TXT
```

which would erase all the files in drive B with file names beginning with FILE and having an extension of TXT, and

```
ERASE B:*.TXT
```

which would erase files on the diskette in drive B with any file name and an extension of TXT.

When an asterisk is substituted for both the file name and the extension MS-DOS will warn the user that all the files on the diskette will be erased by the command and ask the user if he or she is sure this is the desired action:

```
ERASE B:*.*
ARE YOU SURE (Y/N)?
```

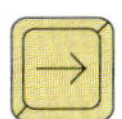

The RENAME Command

The RENAME command is an internal command that allows the file name and extension of files to be changed. The syntax for the rename command is

```
RENAME d:oldname.ext newname.ext
```

where *d:oldname.ext* is the designation of the drive containing the file to be renamed and the file name and extension of that file. The second part, *newname.ext*, is the new file name and extension for the file. If the drive letter is omitted in front of the original file name, MS-DOS will assume that the file is on the current default drive. During a renaming operation, a user can change either the file name or the extension or both. For example,

```
RENAME A:FILE1.TXT PART1.DAT
```

would change both the file name and the extension of the file.

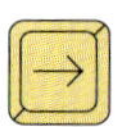

The COPY Command

The COPY command is an internal command that can be used to make copies of a file or a group of files. The copies are usually placed on a different diskette from the original files. If a copy is to be placed on the same disk as the original file, the name of the copy must be different from the original, since a diskette cannot contain two files with the same name. The same COPY command can be applied to both of these situations.

The general syntax for a copy command is

```
COPY d:original.fil d:copy.fil
```

where *d:original.fil* is the drive containing the file to be copied, the file name, and its extension, and *d:copy.fil* is the drive to contain the copy of the original file plus the file name and extension used to name the copy. As usual, if the drive letter is omitted in either part of the COPY command, MS-DOS will assume that the default drive is to be used. For example,

```
COPY B:FILE1.TXT A:FILE1.TXT
```

would put a copy of a file called FILE1.TXT on drive B onto drive A under the name of FILE1.TXT. If the copy to be placed on drive B needed to be stored under a different name, the user could have entered

```
COPY B:FILE1.TXT A:PART1.DAT
```

The two files resulting from this copy command would contain the same information, but on the diskette in drive B the file would be called FILE1.TXT and on the diskette in drive A the file would be called PART1.TXT.

When the user omits parts of the COPY command, MS-DOS will make certain assumptions. For example

```
COPY B:FILE1.TXT A:
```

would have the same effect as the command

```
COPY B:FILE1.TXT A:FILE1.TXT
```

Since the file name and extension were not specified for the copy, MS-DOS assumed that the user wanted to give the copy the same name as the original.

Wildcards can also be used in the COPY command to make copies of groups of files. For example,

```
COPY A:*.* B:
```

would copy all the files on drive A to drive B. When the files are copied, the files on drive B will all be named the same as the original files on drive A. This command basically accomplishes the same result as a DISKCOPY A: B:

command would, except that the diskette in drive B must already be formatted before the COPY command is used.

A disadvantage of the DISKCOPY command is that the files on the copy are stored in exactly the same sectors as they were on the original. Thus, any files scattered across non-contiguous sectors on the original diskette are scattered across non-contiguous sectors on the copy. When a COPY command copies all the files on one disk to another, the files on the copy do not have to be placed in the exact same sectors used to store them on the original diskette. Instead, each file is copied onto the first available sectors and thus each file can be placed in contiguous sectors. Consequently, the COPY command can be used to take a disk with many files stored in scattered sectors and make a copy of the disk in which all the files are brought back together in contiguous sectors. With all the file data in contiguous sectors, the files on the copy of the original diskette can be retrieved much more quickly and efficiently than on the original diskette.

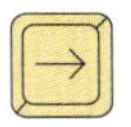

The TYPE Command

The TYPE command is an internal command that can be used to display the contents of a file on the screen. The general syntax for the TYPE command is

```
TYPE d:filename.ext
```

As usual, if the drive letter is omitted, the default drive will be used. One limitation of the TYPE command is that it is capable of displaying only the contents of files containing printable characters, such as letters and numbers. It is important to realize that not all files stored on diskettes contain printable characters. Files such as the COM files used in MS-DOS are actually stored in binary (1s and 0s). If a user attempts to use the TYPE command on one of these files, the results displayed on the screen will be unreadable. An example of the TYPE command would be

```
TYPE B:FILE1.TXT
```

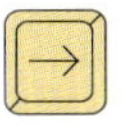

The PRINT Command

The PRINT command is an external command that is similar to the TYPE command, except that the results of a PRINT command are sent to a printer attached to the PC rather than to the screen. As with the TYPE command, the PRINT command can only be used to display files containing printable characters. The syntax for the PRINT command is

```
PRINT d:filename.ext
```

where *d:* is the drive containing the file named in the *filename.ext* part of the command. An example of the PRINT command would be

```
PRINT B:FILE1.TXT
```

Printing can also be accomplished with a variation of the copy command

```
COPY B:FILE1.TXT PRN:
```

where PRN: is the MS-DOS designation for the printer. This command essentially copies the file to the printer.

Exercise 3: Manipulating Files

1. Put an MS-DOS disk in drive A and a formatted diskette in drive B.
2. Boot the computer (if necessary).
3. Use the following COPY commands to copy the FORMAT.COM, CHKDSK.COM, and PRINT.COM files from the MS-DOS disk to your blank diskette:

```
A>COPY FORMAT.COM B:
A>COPY CHKDSK.COM B:
A>COPY PRINT.COM B:
```

4. Use this COPY command below to copy the DISKCOPY.COM file from the MS-DOS disk to your diskette:

```
A>COPY DISKCOPY.COM B:
```

5. Use the COPY command to make a copy of the PRINT.COM file called OUTPUT.COM on your disk:

```
A>COPY B:PRINT.COM B:OUTPUT.COM
```

6. Use the RENAME command to change the name of the OUTPUT.COM file on your disk to OUT.COM:

```
A>RENAME B:OUTPUT.COM OUT.COM
```

7. Use the DIR command to store the results of a directory command in a file called DIR.LST:

```
A>DIR B:>B:DIR.LST
```

The DIR.LST file will now contain the information that normally would go to your screen as a result of the DIR B: command.

8. Use the TYPE command to display the contents of the DIR.LST file on your screen:

```
A>TYPE B:DIR.LST
```

9. If you have a printer attached to your PC, use the PRINT command to print a copy of the DIR.LST file:

```
A>PRINT B:DIR.LST
```

APPENDIX D

Introduction to WordPerfect Version 5.1

Like all word processors, WordPerfect 5.1 allows users to create and edit documents electronically, save them on floppy diskettes or a hard disk, and print them out. WordPerfect 5.1 is one of the most advanced word processors on the market, providing features such as spell checking, a thesaurus, mail merge, table of contents generation, index generation, footnotes, and the ability to incorporate graphics.

In this appendix, you will be introduced to the word processing features of WordPerfect 5.1 and also use some of the more advanced features.

Before You Start

You will need a copy of the WordPerfect 5.1 program and a formatted data diskette to complete the exercises in this appendix.

WordPerfect 5.1 is often run from a hard disk because of the size of the program. It is possible, however, to run it using a dual-floppy system as long as both floppy drives are high-density. In either case, it is assumed here that your copy of WordPerfect 5.1 has been correctly installed for your computer and is configured for use with your printer. If it is not, consult your WordPerfect 5.1 documentation for instructions on how to install WordPerfect.

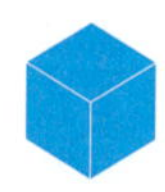

Starting WordPerfect 5.1

If you are using a hard disk, you should be able to boot your computer and type WP at the C> prompt to start WordPerfect 5.1, assuming that WordPerfect has been installed with the correct MS-DOS path. If you are using a dual-floppy system, you will need to boot your computer and then insert the WordPerfect 1 diskette in drive A, if it is not already there. Then type WP at the A> prompt. Once the necessary programs from this diskette have been loaded into memory, WordPerfect will prompt you to put the WordPerfect 2 disk in drive A. Replace the WordPerfect 1 diskette with the WordPerfect 2 diskette, and press any key as the prompt indicates. Once you are in WordPerfect the screen will look like Exhibit D.1. Insert your formatted data diskette in, drive B at this time (or drive A if you are using a hard disk).

At the top left corner of the screen is a blinking underscore. This is the cursor, which indicates your current position on the screen. The status line at the bottom of the screen always indicates your current position in your document. In WordPerfect 5.1 you can have two documents in memory at the same time and switch between them. The "Doc 1" at the bottom of the screen indicates that you are in the first document. The status line also shows which page, line, and character the cursor is on.

Exhibit D.1

The Document Screen in WordPerfect 5.1

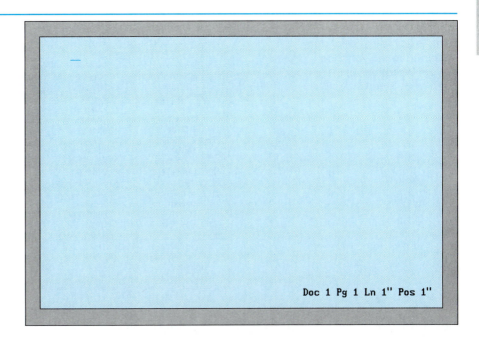

The Keyboard

Like most word processors, WordPerfect 5.1 assigns certain word processing functions to the various keys on the keyboard. Groups of keys are used to control movement within the document and editing of text in the document. In addition, WordPerfect 5.1 makes heavy use of the ten (or twelve) function keys on the keyboard, F1 through F10 (or F12), when implementing word processing functions. Exhibit D.2 shows the functions performed by the function keys in WordPerfect 5.1.

In the exhibit, there are four functions attached to each function key. The bottom function for each key is performed by pressing the function key by itself. The third function is accessed by holding down the ALT key on the keyboard and pressing the function key. The second function is obtained by holding down one of the SHIFT keys and pressing the function key. The top function is performed when you hold down the CTRL key and press the function key. Thus, each function key serves four different functions.

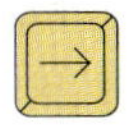

Keys for Cursor Movement

As with all word processors, only a portion of your document will be visible on screen at once. Portions of the document above or below the text currently displayed can be revealed simply by moving the cursor into those areas. When this is done, the display of the document will automatically shift or **scroll** to reveal the unseen portions of the document.

Exhibit D.2

Word Processing Functions Assigned to the Function Keys in WordPerfect 5.1

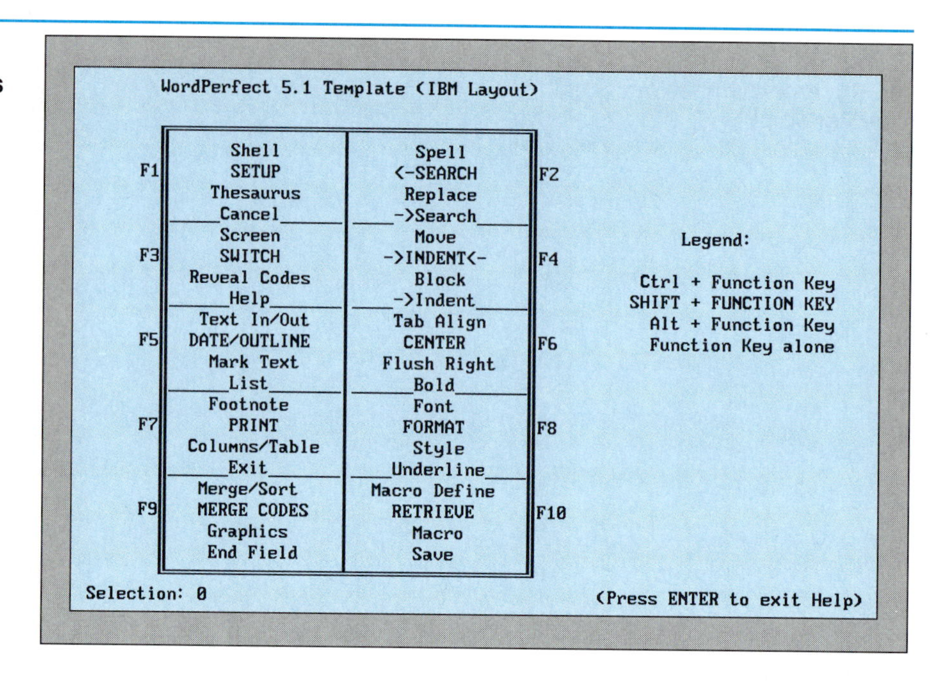

Movement within a document can be accomplished several ways. The arrow keys (located on the numeric keypad or in a separate area of the keyboard) can be used to move right or left one character at a time or up and down one line at a time. The PGUP and PGDN keys can be used to move up or down a page at a time. The plus (+) and minus (-) keys on the numeric keypad can be used to move up or down one screen (about twenty-four lines) at a time. Moving one word at a time can be accomplished by holding down the CTRL key and pressing the → or ← keys.

The HOME and END keys can be used in several combinations with other keys to accomplish more sophisticated movement functions. These functions and the others discussed above are summarized in Exhibit D.3.

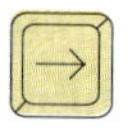

Keys for Editing

The DEL key can be used to delete the character the cursor currently rests on. The BACKSPACE key deletes characters to the left of the cursor and can be used to move the cursor to the left, deleting characters as you go. The INS key is used to move between insert and typeover mode. Normally, you will start out in **insert mode**, and the characters you type will be inserted in the document to the left of the cursor. Any characters under the cursor and to the right will be automatically pushed to the right to make room. In **typeover mode** characters that are entered will replace the characters under the cursor.

Other deletions can be accomplished with multiple keystrokes. For example, pressing the HOME key and then the DEL key will delete everything from the current cursor position to the end of the word. Pressing HOME and then BACKSPACE deletes characters to the left of the cursor to the

Exhibit D.3

Cursor Movement Functions in WordPerfect 5.1

Keystroke Sequence	Action
Up or Down Arrow	Up or down one line
Right or Left Arrow	Right or left one character
PgUp key	Up one page in document
PgDn key	Down one page in document
Plus key (+)	Up one screen (24 lines)
Minus key (-)	Down one screen (24 lines)
CTRL key + Left Arrow	Left one word
CTRL key + Right Arrow	Right one word
END key	End of current line
HOME, Right Arrow	Right edge of screen
HOME, Left Arrow	Left edge of screen
HOME, Up Arrow	Top of screen
HOME, Down Arrow	Bottom of screen
HOME, HOME, Up Arrow	Top of document
HOME, HOME, Down Arrow	Bottom of document
HOME, HOME, Left Arrow	Beginning of current line
HOME, HOME, Right Arrow	End of current line (same as END)
CTRL + HOME, Up Arrow	Top of current document page
CTRL + HOME, Down Arrow	Bottom of current document page

Keys joined with a + must be pressed simultaneously
Keys joined with a , are pressed one at a time in sequence

beginning of the word. Holding down the CTRL key and pressing END deletes characters from the cursor to the end of the line.

Function Keys

As Exhibit D.2 shows, each function key performs four different functions. Some of the more important functions to understand when you begin using WordPerfect 5.1 are described below.

Cancel. The Cancel function (F1) is used to cancel the current word processing function. Thus, if you accidentally pressed a function key to begin a word processing function, you could use F1 to cancel that function.

Exit. The Exit function (F7) is used to exit from a word processing function. You will often be directed to use Exit to indicate when you are finished with a task. Exit is also used when you are ready to exit from WordPerfect.

Help. The Help function (F3) is extremely important for both beginning and advanced users. When you press F3 you will be directed either to press a key on the keyboard to get a description of what that key can be used for or to press a letter on the keyboard to see a list of all the word processing features beginning with that letter. For example, pressing P would produce a list of all word processing functions that begin with the letter *P*, such as printing, page formatting, and so forth. If you select Help during a word processing function, WordPerfect will give you information related to that function.

Reveal Codes. The Reveal Codes key ((ALT)-(F3)) is invaluable for solving formatting problems and for understanding how WordPerfect works. Most of the commands you issue result in invisible codes being inserted into your document. These codes tell WordPerfect how to format the document. Since they are not normally displayed, it can sometimes be difficult to see why WordPerfect is formatting the document the way it is. When Reveal Codes is selected, the screen splits; the top half shows the document and the bottom half shows the same document with the codes exposed so that you can see why the document appears the way it does.

Exercise 1: Cover Letter

To learn the basic word processing features of WordPerfect 5.1, you will create a cover letter similar to the one used as an example in Chapter 12. This exercise will take you through the process of entering and editing text, formatting text, and saving and printing the document.

Entering Text

When entering text, the user simply begins typing. When the right margin is reached, the word that will go beyond the margin is automatically moved to the next line, along with the cursor. This **word wrap** feature is common in all word processors and allows the user to enter text without worrying about pressing (RETURN) at the end of each line. The only instance when (RETURN) should be pressed is when the user wants to end the line before the right margin, such as at the end of a paragraph.

Exhibit D.4 shows text for an example letter similar to the letter in Chapter 12; it will be used as an example in this appendix as well. Notice that there are some simple mistakes in the letter. Enter the text exactly as it is shown in Exhibit D.4; part of this exercise is learning how to correct the mistakes. Remember to press (RETURN) only when you have a line that ends before the right margin, such as the short lines at the top of the letter and the ends of paragraphs. The blank lines are created by pressing (RETURN) at the beginning of the line.

Revealing Codes

Use Reveal Codes ((ALT)-(F3)) to reveal the codes in the document at this point. You should see a code, either [Srt] or [Hrt], at the end of each line. While looking at the Reveal Codes display you can move the cursor to reveal parts of the document that are not displayed. Codes within the document are always enclosed in square brackets. The [Hrt] code stands for *hard return*, and is placed in the document when you press (RETURN). Thus, you should see a [Hrt] code at the end of each paragraph and short line and at the beginning of each blank line.

Exhibit D.4

The Example Letter Containing Some Mistakes

(Note: Margins in WordPerfect will be different from those shown here.)

Mr. William Williams
123 Charry Street
Appleton, OH 44444

Der Mr. Williams:

I have would like to appply for your position for a microcomputer specialist. I feel that I have many skills which are appropriate for this job.

1. I have worked with microcomputer operating systems.

2. I am well motivated and eager to learn.

3. I am an expert user of word processors, electronic spreadsheets, graphics, databases, and data communications.

I believe that I can be an asset to your organization and I look forward to hearing from you soon.

Sincerely,
Sincerely,

Sam Samuels

The [Srt] code stands for *soft return*. This represents places where WordPerfect has ended a line because a word wrap was needed. They are called soft returns because if enough text is deleted from a line that ends with a [Srt], WordPerfect will automatically shift words up from the lines below to fill out the line again. A line ending with a hard return will always end at that place, regardless of the deletion of text on that line. Thus, a soft return indicates where the line currently ends, but it is subject to change when necessary.

Once you are finished viewing these codes, press Reveal Codes ((ALT)-(F3)) again to return the display to normal.

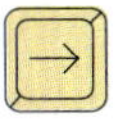

Editing Text

Now that the letter is entered with the mistakes, let's see how to fix them.

To fix the misspelling of *Cherry* as *Charry*, use the arrow keys to place the cursor on the *a* in *Charry*. Press the (INS) key. You should see the word *Typeover* in the bottom left corner of the screen; if not, press (INS) again. Now press *e* to replace the *a*.

In the greeting of the letter, the misspelling of the word *Dear* as *Der* can be fixed by positioning the cursor on the *r* in *Der* and pressing (INS) again to return to normal insert mode. Now the *a* can be typed. It will be inserted to the left of the cursor; the *r* and the rest of the line will automatically shift to the right to make room.

The next error is the extra word, *have*, in the first line of the first paragraph. Position the cursor at the beginning of this word and press (HOME) and then (DEL) to delete the word plus the blank space following it.

Next, move to the word *appply* in this same line and position the cursor on the first *p*. Press the (DEL) key to remove the letter the cursor is on.

Exhibit D.5

The Example Letter After Correcting the Mistakes

Mr. William Williams
123 Cherry Street
Appleton, OH 44444

Dear Mr. Williams:

I would like to apply for your position for a microcomputer specialist. I feel that I have many skills which are appropriate for this job.

1. I have worked with microcomputer operating systems.

2. I am well motivated and eager to learn.

3. I am an expert user of word processors, electronic spreadsheets, graphics, databases, and data communications.

I believe that I can be an asset to your organization and I look forward to hearing from you soon.

Sincerely,

Sam Samuels

Position the cursor at the beginning of the line containing the second *Sincerely*. Hold down CTRL and press END to delete the characters to the end of the line. This will not, however, delete the hard return at the end of the line. Press DEL to delete the invisible [Hrt], which is now at the beginning of the blank line under your cursor.

Your document should now look like Exhibit D.5.

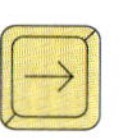

Formatting Text

Formatting options in WordPerfect can be broken into three major categories: character formatting, line formatting, and page formatting, which govern the appearance of individual characters, lines, and pages, respectively. Exhibit D.6 shows some of the more commonly used formatting options that fall into each category. You will need to use some character and line formatting options to complete the example letter.

Character Formatting

Below item 3 in the example letter you are going to add a fourth item that will demonstrate the use of two text appearance options, boldfacing and underlining. To begin, place your cursor on the blank line below item number 3, press RETURN, and enter the following text:

4. I have worked for

Now suppose you want the next word to be boldfaced for emphasis. One way to make words boldfaced is to press the Bold key (F6) to

Exhibit D.6

Some Character, Line, and Page Formats in WordPerfect 5.1

Character Formats

Character Size:

superscript/subscript
Fine, Small, Large, Very Large, and Extra Large

Character Appearance:

Bold, Underline, Italics, Outline, Shadow, etc.

Line Formats

Hyphenation
Justification
Line Spacing
Right/Left Margin
Tabs

Page Formats

Center Page (top to bottom)
Headers and Footers
Top/Bottom Margin
Page Numbering

turn boldfacing on before typing the word. Go ahead and press the Bold (F6) key.

When you do this the number in the bottom right corner of the screen that indicates your current cursor position should become brighter, indicating that boldfacing is now in effect. If your display does not show this, adjust the brightness and contrast controls until it does. Now type the word

four

and see how it is boldfaced. Press the Bold (F6) key again to stop boldfacing. The character position number in the bottom right corner of the screen should become dim again. Boldfacing is an example of a formatting option that must be turned both on and off. When text is to be boldfaced, you simply press the Bold key to turn it on, type the text, and then turn boldfacing off by pressing the Bold key again.

Continue typing the sentence as follows:

years as microcomputer consultant for CompuStore, Inc., with

Now suppose the next word to be typed needs to be underlined. Underlining is accomplished by using the Underline key (F8); it functions the same way as the Bold key.

Press the Underline key (F9) now and note how the position number in the bottom right corner of the screen is now underlined, indicating that underlining is now in effect. Now type the words

<u>sole responsibility</u>

Exhibit D.7

The Example Letter After the Addition of Item 4

Mr. William Williams
123 Cherry Street
Appleton, OH 44444

Dear Mr. Williams:

I would like to apply for your position for a microcomputer specialist. I feel that I have many skills which are appropriate for this job.

1. I have worked with microcomputer operating systems.

2. I am well motivated and eager to learn.

3. I am an expert user of word processors, electronic spreadsheets, graphics, databases, and data communications.

4. I have worked for **four** years as microcomputer consultant for CompuStore, Inc., with sole responsibility for all corporate clients.

I believe that I can be an asset to your organization and I look forward to hearing from you soon.

Sincerely,

Sam Samuels

and then press the Underline key ((F8)) again to turn off underlining. In general, all character formats are turned on and off as are boldfacing and underlining. Finish the sentence as follows:

for all corporate clients.

Exhibit D.7 shows the example letter after the addition of item 4.

Revealing Character Format Codes

Each time the Bold and Underline keys were pressed, a code was placed in your document. Press Reveal Codes ((ALT)-(F3)) and move the cursor so that the fourth item is visible on the screen. You should see a [BOLD] code in front of the word *four* and a [bold] code after the word. The capitalized code indicates where boldfacing is turned on and the lowercase code indicates where it is turned off. The underlined text should be surrounded by [UND] and [und] codes.

If you watch the bottom half of the Reveal Codes screen while you move the cursor, you will see that you can position the cursor on the codes that are displayed using the (→) and (←) keys. Once a code is highlighted, you can use (DEL) to delete it. Thus, if you want to cancel the boldfacing or underlining of text, the best method is to go to the Reveal Codes screen and delete one of the codes. With codes that occur in pairs, such as [BOLD][bold] and [UND][und], you can delete either code and the entire pair will be removed.

Line Formatting

As indicated in Exhibit D.6, line formatting options in WordPerfect 5.1 include options for setting tabs and performing indents. In the example letter, suppose that the four items in the letter need to be indented from the left margin by three spaces. Unless otherwise specified, indentation will use the normal tab settings, which in WordPerfect 5.1 are every five spaces. Thus, if you were to try an indent, you would get a five-space indent rather than the three-space indent desired.

To set tabs you will use a format command, which will insert a code in the document at your current location. Thus, when setting tabs, it is important to realize that the tab setting will affect only that part of the document below the Tab code and will not affect any part of the document above the code. To set up the tabs for the letter, follow these steps:

1. Position the cursor on the blank line above item 1.
2. Use Format ((SHIFT)-(F8)) to get the Format menu. This is a full-page menu that will temporarily replace your document on the screen (see Exhibit D.8). Once the formatting choices have been made from the menu, your document will be redisplayed exactly as it was.
3. As in all WordPerfect menus, choices can be made by entering a number or the first letter of a menu choice. A bold number and letter will appear on the screen for each choice. Type **1** or **L** to access the Line format options.
4. This selection will bring up another full-screen menu with Tab Set as choice number 8 (see Exhibit D.9). Enter an **8** or press **T** to select a tab setting.

Exhibit D.8

The Format Menu

```
Format

     1 - Line
              Hyphenation                        Line Spacing
              Justification                      Margins Left/Right
              Line Height                        Tab Set
              Line Numbering                     Widow/Orphan Protection

     2 - Page
              Center Page (top to bottom)        Page Numbering
              Force Odd/Even Page                Paper Size/Type
              Headers and Footers                Suppress
              Margins Top/Bottom

     3 - Document
              Display Pitch                      Redline Method
              Initial Codes/Font                 Summary

     4 - Other
              Advance                            Overstrike
              Conditional End of Page            Printer Functions
              Decimal Characters                 Underline Spaces/Tabs
              Language

Selection: 0
```

Exhibit D.9

The Line Format Menu

```
Format: Line

     1 - Hyphenation                     No

     2 - Hyphenation Zone - Left         10%
                            Right        4%

     3 - Justification                   Full

     4 - Line Height                     Auto

     5 - Line Numbering                  No

     6 - Line Spacing                    1

     7 - Margins - Left                  1"
                   Right                 1"

     8 - Tab Set                         Rel: -1", every 0.5"

     9 - Widow/Orphan Protection         No


Selection: 0
```

5. Your document will now be redisplayed with a ruler line at the bottom showing an L every five spaces. As the message at the bottom of the screen directs, hold down (CTRL) and press (END) to remove the L's.
6. Now put your cursor on the third dot after the +1″ marker (position 1.3″) and press **L** to put a left-aligned tab at that position. When text is tabbed to this position, the first character of the text will be aligned with this tab position. Other tab options include R for a right-justified tab, C for a centered tab, and D for a tab that aligns numbers' decimal points at that position.
7. Also add an L at position +5″. This will be used for placing the closing at the bottom of the letter later on.
8. Press the Exit ((F7)) key to finish the tab setting operation. Press (RETURN) twice to leave the format menus.

To indent the four items from the left margin, you will use the Indent key ((F4)). When this key is pressed, a code is inserted that will indent lines to the first tab stop. All lines will be indented until a line ending with a hard return is reached; there the indenting will stop.

To indent the four numbered items, position the cursor on the number that begins an item and press the Indent key ((F4)). Text will be indented three spaces and lines ending with soft returns will be reshuffled to fit between the new boundaries. Follow this procedure until all four numbered items are indented.

There is also an indenting option that allows text to be indented from both the left and right margins simultaneously. The double-indent key

Exhibit D.10

The Example Letter After the Line Formatting

Mr. William Williams
123 Cherry Street
Appleton, OH 44444

Dear Mr. Williams:

I would like to apply for your position for a microcomputer specialist. I feel that I have many skills which are appropriate for this job.

1. I have worked with microcomputer operating systems.

2. I am well motivated and eager to learn.

3. I am an expert user of word processors, electronic spreadsheets, graphics, databases, and data communications.

4. I have worked for **four** years as microcomputer consultant for CompuStore, Inc., with <u>sole responsibility</u> for all corporate clients.

I believe that I can be an asset to your organization and I look forward to hearing from you soon.

Sincerely,

Sam Samuels

(SHIFT-F4) indents text to the left using the first L tab stop and from the right margin an equal amount.

A final line format required in the example letter is to tab the two closing lines over to the 5" tab stop. Position your cursor at the beginning of each closing line and press TAB twice to move the text over. The letter should now look like Exhibit D.10.

After the tabs and indenting are finished, use Reveal Codes (ALT-F3) to look at the codes resulting from these operations.

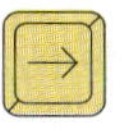

Block Moves

Another helpful feature of most word processors is the ability to pick up a part of the document (a **block**) and move it to another location within the document. This **block move** operation is accomplished in two steps in WordPerfect 5.1. First, the user must highlight the block using the Block key (ALT-F4), and he or she must then perform a move operation using the Move key (CTRL-F4). For example, suppose you want to move item 2 to below item 4. To do this follow these steps:

1. Position the cursor on the blank line above item 2.
2. Press Block (ALT-F4) to begin highlighting the text to be moved. When this key is pressed, a flashing "Block on" will appear in the bottom left corner of the screen.

3. Move the cursor down two lines to the blank line below item 2. Since you started on the blank line above item 2 and moved past item 2 to the blank line below, the [Hrt] on the blank line and the [Hrt] at the end of item 2 are also included in the block, although they won't be highlighted since they are hidden.

4. Press Move ((CTRL)-(F4)) to move the text. This will bring up this Line menu at the bottom of the screen:

   ```
   Move: 1 Block; 2 Tabular Column; 3 Rectangle: 0
   ```

   Press **1** or **B** to indicate that you want to move the currently highlighted block.

5. This selection causes another menu to appear:

   ```
   1 Move; 2 Copy; 3 Delete; 4 Append: 0
   ```

   This menu allows you to move the block, make a copy of the block, delete the block, or append the block to another file. Press **1** or **M** to indicate that you want to move the block.

6. The block of text seems to disappear from the document. In reality the block has been copied to a buffer in memory. The bottom of the screen tells you to move the cursor to the new location for the block and press (RETURN).

Exhibit D.11

The Example Letter After the Block Move

Mr. William Williams
123 Cherry Street
Appleton, OH 44444

Dear Mr. Williams:

I would like to apply for your position for a microcomputer specialist. I feel that I have many skills which are appropriate for this job.

1. I have worked with microcomputer operating systems.

2. I am an expert user of word processors, electronic spreadsheets, graphics, databases, and data communications.

3. I have worked for **four** years as microcomputer consultant for CompuStore, Inc. with sole responsibility for all corporate clients.

4. I am well motivated and eager to learn.

I believe that I can be an asset to your organization and I look forward to hearing from you soon.

Sincerely,

Sam Samuels

7. Position the cursor on the blank line below item 4 and press (RETURN). The blank line plus item 2 will be inserted above this blank line.

8. Now retype the numbers on the items so they read from 1 to 4 again (see Exhibit D.11).

Saving the Document

Now that the text in the letter has been entered, edited, and formatted, you are ready to save this letter in a document on your data diskette.

Press the Save key ((F10)) and a prompt will appear at the bottom of the screen asking you to indicate the name under which you want to save the file. The name must be a valid MS-DOS file name of no more that eight characters plus a three character extension. The extension is optional. In addition, you will need to indicate that the file is to go on your formatted data diskette in drive B (or drive A if you are using a hard disk).

Thus, at the "Document to be saved:" prompt type B:LETTER (A:LETTER for hard disk users) and press (RETURN). When you save a document for the first time, this is all that is needed to save the file. If you are saving a file for a second time you will be warned that a file under that name already exists on your diskette and you will be asked if you want to replace it.

To see how this works, press the Save ((F10)) key again. The file name should automatically reappear from the last Save operation. Press (RETURN) to save the file again. Now you should see a prompt asking

```
Replace B:\LETTER? No (Yes)
```

The default choice will be No, but to override this simply press **Y** to change it to Yes and the current document on your screen will be saved on the diskette under that name.

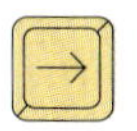

Printing the Document

Assuming that you have a printer attached to your computer, you can print a copy of the document by pressing the Print key ((SHIFT)-(F7)). This will produce the Print menu, shown in Exhibit D.12, in which you can press the **1** or **F** to print the full document. Option 2 can be used to print only the page the cursor is currently on. An extremely useful option in this menu is option 6, which can be used to view the document on the screen exactly as it will appear when printed. This preview option allows you to see the effect of formatting on your document and see how the margins will affect its final appearance.

Press the Print key ((SHIFT)-(F7)) and then choose the View Document option by typing **6** or **V**. The screen will show a representation of the current page of the document. The text on this page will be unreadable in this view, but you can see the overall appearance of your page. The menu at the bottom allows you to blow up this display to see letters at 100 percent (actual size) or even in closeup (200 percent). You can also view two pages together using the Facing Pages option.

Exhibit D.12

The Print Menu

```
Print

     1 - Full Document
     2 - Page
     3 - Document on Disk
     4 - Control Printer
     5 - Multiple Pages
     6 - View Document
     7 - Initialize Printer

Options

     S - Select Printer                    IBM Proprinter II
     B - Binding Offset                    0"
     N - Number of Copies                  1
     U - Multiple Copies Generated by      WordPerfect
     G - Graphics Quality                  Medium
     T - Text Quality                      High
     A - Banners                           No
     O - Form Number                       0

Selection: 0
```

Several formatting options, such as the justification of the right edge of the text, are not normally shown on the screen when you are editing the document. The preview option allows the user to see how these formatting options will be applied to the document when it printed.

To see how useful this feature is, use the following instructions to center the text of your letter from top to bottom and then view the result:

1. Cancel the current print operation by pressing the Cancel ((F1)) key twice.
2. Move to the top of your document using the (HOME), (HOME), (↑) sequence.
3. Press Format ((SHIFT)-(F8)), choose Page (press **P** or **2**), and then pick the Center Page option (press **1** or **C**). The No will automatically change to Yes.
4. Press (RETURN) twice to leave the formatting menus and then press Print ((SHIFT)-(F7)).
5. Choose the View Document option in the Print menu and make sure the display is showing the full page. The text on the screen will not be readable, but you should be able to see that the text has now been centered on the page.

Press the Cancel key ((F1)) to stop viewing the document. This will return you to the main Print menu. If you have a printer attached to your computer, make sure it is on and then pick the Full Document option (press **1** or **F**) to print your letter.

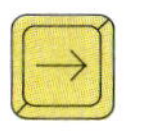

Exiting from WordPerfect

When you are finished with a document and want to leave WordPerfect or move on to another document, you must exit from the current editing session by pressing the Exit key (F7). When this key is pressed you will first be asked if you want to save the document you are working on. To be sure you have saved everything, accept the default answer of Yes by pressing RETURN. The previous name for the document, B:LETTER, will automatically appear as the name of the file. Press RETURN again to accept this default, and then **Y** to replace the old file.

Finally, you will be asked if you want to exit from WordPerfect. If you answer Yes, you will be returned to the MS-DOS prompt. If you answer No, the current document in memory will be cleared and you will remain in WordPerfect with the blank screen you began with. When you want to work on several documents in sequence, you must use this method to clear the current document before retrieving the next document.

If you plan to move on to the next exercise at this time, answer No when asked if you want to leave WordPerfect. If you want to stop working now make sure you answer Yes to this prompt so that WordPerfect will be properly closed down.

When WordPerfect is started, some temporary files are created on the default MS-DOS drive, and these files must be deleted when WordPerfect is exited. If you do not properly exit from WordPerfect, these files will be left on the disk, and the next time you start WordPerfect these files will be detected and WordPerfect will ask you if there are other copies of WordPerfect already running. At that point you must answer No to allow WordPerfect to delete those leftover files and recreate them for the current editing session.

Exercise 2: Departmental Report

This exercise will give you additional practice using the techniques you learned in the first exercise and introduce you to some additional formatting options including centering text, numbering pages, and working with margins. You will also be introduced to the spelling checker and thesaurus of WordPerfect 5.1. Exhibit D.13 shows a two-page report consisting of a cover memo and the minutes of a meeting.

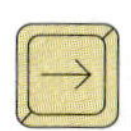

Entering the Memo

If you are not already in WordPerfect, start the program so you can get to the blank editing screen.

INTEROFFICE COMMUNICATION

To: Marketing Department Employees

From: J.P. Sells, Director of Marketing

Date: March 1, 1990

Subject: Next Meeting

The next meeting for the Marketing Department will be on March 15th at 3 pm in the conference room. The minutes from the February 15th meeting are on the attached page. The tentative agenda for the upcoming meeting is shown below:

1. Report from departmental budget committee.
2. Discussion of revised travel policy.
3. Discussion of ideas for marketing the new line of cosmetics products.
4. Report on progress on the new computer system and its application to marketing research needs.
5. Presentation of results of recent survey of public opinion of the proposed line of household cleaners.

If anyone has further items to be added to this agenda, please notify my secretary no later than the 10th of March.

TYREL CORPORATION
Marketing Department

Minutes of February 15, 1990 Meeting #2

The second monthly meeting of 1990 for the Marketing Department of Tyrel Corporation was held on February 15th. J.P. Sells, Director of the Marketing Department, called the meeting to order at 9:00 a.m. in the conference room.

PRESENT Ashton, Beck, Burson, Clark, Coleman, Hartley, Hostetler, Stamler, and Sells were present. Walchli was excused. A sufficient number of the department employees were present to constitute a quorum.

MINUTES Minutes from the January 15th meeting were read and approved.

DIRECTOR Mr. Sells updated the staff on the status of the new computer system, which is due to be installed on the 24th of February. The new system will be used in the analysis of market research survey results and should hopefully be available by the beginning of March.

TRAVEL Beck moved to have the travel policy revised because the allowances for plane fare were too low for flights to Europe and more staff members will need to fly there when the new European marketing campaign gets underway. Ashton seconded the motion and Sells agreed to revise the policy and bring the new policy to a vote at the next meeting.

COSMETICS Mr. Sells announced that the marketing department has been asked to come up with a campaign for marketing a new line of cosmetics to European women. He requested that staff members begin developing ideas to be presented at the next meeting.

RESEARCH Mr. Sells asked for volunteers to conduct a survey of city residents to obtain a sampling of public opinion about a new line of biodegradable household cleaners designed to be safer for the environment. Stamler and Burson volunteered and will present their results at the next meeting.

Exhibit D.13

An Example Memo for Exercise 2

Some of the formatting for the memo needs to be done at the very top of the page in order for it to affect the memo. As a rule, any page formats that are to affect the current page must be placed at the very top of the page, before any text appears. If you enter any page formatting options after the first text on the page, those formatting options will not take effect until the next page in the document. Thus, before entering the text for the memo, you will set up page formatting options for margins and tabs.

The example memo uses margins of 1.5 inches on the top, bottom, left, and right margins. The top and bottom margins are a page formatting option and therefore must be set at the top of the page. Settings for the left and right margins and tabs are line formatting options and thus would not have to be at the very top of the page. Set up margins and tabs as follows:

1. Make sure you are at the top of the document by using the key sequence (HOME), (HOME), (HOME), (↑). This sequence is similar to the (HOME), (HOME), (↑) sequence used to move to the top of the document, but it instead moves the cursor to the top of the document, *before* any codes or text already in the document.
2. Press Format ((SHIFT)-(F8)) and select the Page option by pressing **2** or **P**. Under Page, choose Margins - Top/Bottom by pressing **5** or **M**.
3. Enter **1.5** for both the top and bottom margins, pressing (RETURN) after each entry.
4. Press (RETURN) again after entering the margins to back up to the main Format menu. Then select the Line format option by pressing **1** or **L**.
5. Under Line formats, select the Margins - Left/Right option by pressing **7** or **M**.
6. Enter **1.5** for the right and left margins.
7. While in the Line format menu, also select the Tab Set option by pressing **8** or **T**. Delete all the current tabs by moving the cursor to the beginning of the ruler, holding down (CTRL), and pressing (END).
8. Move to positions 1.8, 2.1, and 2.5 and type an **L** at each location.
9. Press the Exit key ((F7)) to leave the ruler, then press (RETURN) twice to exit from the Format menus.
10. Press Reveal Codes ((ALT)-(F3)) and look at the codes that have been placed in the document as a result of the formatting you have done. If you have made a mistake in any of the formatting, you can delete the unwanted codes on this screen. Once you have finished viewing and changing any codes, press the Reveal Codes key again to return the document display to normal.

Now that the line and page formats are set up, you are ready to begin entering text. The first line of the memo needs to be centered. Press the Center key ((SHIFT)-(F6)) and the cursor will move to the center of the screen. Then type the line to be centered and press (RETURN). As you type the text, WordPerfect will keep it centered on the line. Lines can also be centered by first typing the text at the left margin, and then going back and pressing Center ((SHIFT)-(F6)). This will move the text to the center of the line.

Type the beginning of the memo, tabbing the next four lines over to position 25 using the (TAB) key. Then enter the text for the first paragraph.

The numbered agenda items need to be entered using a combination of a tab and an indent. Press (TAB) to move to position 1.8 and type the number and period for the first item. Then press the Indent key ((F4)) to indent the rest of the text to position 2.1. This will cause the text following the number to line up. Follow this same procedure for the other four agenda items. Finally, type the text of the concluding paragraph.

The next page of the document is to show the minutes from the last meeting. You could create two separate documents that would be printed separately and then put together. In this case, however, you will put both pages in the same document.

Normally, as you create a long document, WordPerfect will automatically break the document into pages based on settings for the size of the pages and the top and bottom margins. Using a process similar to word wrap, a page break is automatically placed in the document when text reaches beyond the bottom of the page. A dashed line is shown on the screen to indicate the page break and the next line of text is automatically placed below the line. This line is actually a **soft page break**, meaning that if text is deleted on the page above, text on the current page will move up to the previous page automatically to fill in the gap.

In the example memo and meeting minutes, the memo is not long enough to fill the entire first page. Before typing the minutes you must force WordPerfect to move to a new page by putting in a **hard page break**. A hard page break is inserted in the document by holding down (CTRL) and pressing (RETURN). This will place a double line across your screen. With a hard page break between the memo and the minutes, the text on the minutes page will not move to the memo page if text is removed from the memo.

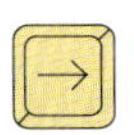

Entering the Minutes

Immediately after creating the hard page break, you need to set up the formatting for that page so that it will be at the top. Set the options as follows:

1. Press Format ((SHIFT)-(F8)) and choose the Page option by pressing **2** or **P**.
2. The minutes page of the document will return to one-inch margins on all sides of the page, set up a header, and start the numbering of pages. All of these options except the right and left margins are controlled under Page formatting. Under Page formatting, reset the top and bottom margins to one inch.
3. To set up the left and right margins, press (RETURN) to leave the Page format menu and then choose the Line option by pressing **1** or **L**. In the Line format menu, choose the Margin option and set the right and left margin to one inch.

4. Leave the Line format menu by pressing (RETURN) and then go back into the Page format menu (press **2** or **P**). In the Page format menu, choose the Header option (press **3** or **H**). The following line menu will appear:

```
1 Header A; 2 Header B: 0
```

5. Press **1** or **A** to set up the first header (Header A). A second line menu will appear:

```
1 Discontinue; 2 Every Page; 3 Odd Pages;
4 Even Pages; 5 Edit: 0
```

6. Select the Every Page option (**2** or **E**). This will bring up a blank screen where you can type the text for the header.

7. The text for the header needs to be aligned with the right margin, which is why the right and left margins were set before the header. To cause the text in the header to be lined up with the right margin, press the Flush Right key ((ALT)-(F6)).

8. The cursor will move to the right margin and, as you type the text for the header (Marketing #2), it will flow to the left so that the 2 is lined up with the right margin.

9. As the prompt at the bottom of the screen indicates, press the Exit key ((F7)) when you are finished with the header. This will return you to the Page format menu.

10. Now select the Page number option (press **6** or **N**). This will bring up a second menu from which you will select the Page Number Position (**4** or **P**) option. This displays a template showing page numbers in various positions. In the minutes, page numbers will be centered at the bottom of the page. Select the number on the template that appears centered at the bottom of the example page, in this case **6**.

11. After selecting the page number position, press (RETURN) to leave the Page Numbering menu. You will be returned to the Page format menu. From this menu, select the New page number option (press **6** or **N**) and change the **2** to **1.** The page number initially shows a 2 since you are actually on the second page of the document, but the minutes should be numbered beginning with page 1.

12. Formatting options such as headers and page numbers do not actually appear on screen when you are working on a document. To see if the header and page numbers are correct, press Print ((SHIFT)-(F7)) and choose the View option (6 or V) to see what your document will look like when it printed. This display will show any headers and page numbers. When you are finished, press the Exit key ((F7)) twice to leave the print menu.

13. Once all the formatting is finished, use Reveal Codes ((ALT)-(F3)) to display the codes so you can correct any mistakes you may have made. Then press Reveal Codes ((ALT)-(F3)) again to return the display to normal.

Now that the formatting options are set, you are ready to begin entering text. The first line of the title of the minutes needs to be centered and bold. Press the Bold key (F6), then press Center (SHIFT-F6) and type the text. At the end of the line, press the Bold key (F6) again to stop boldfacing and then press RETURN.

The second line of the title simply needs to be centered. Press Center (SHIFT-F6), type the second line of the title, and then press RETURN. Press RETURN again to put a blank line in after the title.

The third line of text in the document needs to be underlined but you will not underline it at this time. First, enter the first section of text located at the left margin:

Minutes of February 15, 1990

Then press the Flush Right key (ALT-F6) and type the text that is aligned with the right margin:

Meeting #2

For purposes of illustration, the underlining will be applied to this text after it has been entered. You apply character formatting to text after it has been entered by highlighting the text to be formatted and then issuing the command(s) to change the appearance of the text.

To underline the third line of the minutes, position the cursor at the beginning of the line and press the Block key (ALT-F4). Then press the END key to move to the end of the line. With the entire line highlighted, press the Underline key (F8). The highlighted text will automatically be underlined.

To set up the indenting for the paragraphs, you need to set a tab position at 2.5 inches. Press the Format (SHIFT-F8) key and then select the Line option (**1** or **L**). From the Line format menu select the Tab Set option (**8** or **T**). When the ruler line appears at the bottom of the screen, hold down the CTRL key and press END to clear the current tab settings. Move the cursor to the 2.5 inch position and press the **L** key to put a left-justified tab at this position. Then press the Exit key (F7) to leave the ruler. Press RETURN twice to leave the format menus.

To enter the text for the first paragraph, press Indent (F4) and type the text. Press RETURN to finish the paragraph and press it a second time to put a blank line below the paragraph.

The remaining paragraphs can be entered by typing the capitalized heading first and then pressing Indent (F4) to begin the paragraph.

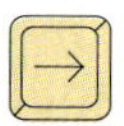

Search and Replace

Now that the memo and the minutes have been entered and formatted, the two-page document will be used to illustrate the search and replace functions in WordPerfect 5.1. First, position your cursor at the beginning of the document by pressing HOME, HOME, ↑.

WordPerfect has both a forward search and a backward search capability. The forward search key is the F2 key. The backward search key is SHIFT-F2. In this example, you will be performing a forward search, which is why you moved your cursor to the beginning of the document. A forward search always takes place from the current cursor position to the end of the document.

To illustrate the Search function, suppose that you wanted to locate a reference in the document to an employee named Walchli. To perform the forward search, press the Search key ((F2)). A "Srch ->:" prompt will appear at the bottom of the screen, along with a cursor. Type *Walchli* at this prompt and press the Search key ((F2)) again. The cursor should move to the first occurrence of that word in your document.

Since a search always locates the first occurrence of the text you specify, it is helpful if you can think of a relatively unique series of characters to search for. For example, searching for a series of characters such as *the* would probably not help you locate the text you wanted since that sequence of characters probably appears in many words in a document.

In addition to simply searching for a string of text in your document, you can also use the Replace option to replace the text each time it is found with another string of text. The Replace key ((ALT)-(F2)) functions like Search, except that, in addition to specifying a string to search for, you also specify a string to replace the string you are searching for. To get a feel for the Replace function follow these steps:

1. Suppose that you realize you have misspelled the director's name. Instead of *Sells*, it should have been *Sales*. Return to the top of the document by pressing (HOME), (HOME), (↑). Then press Replace ((ALT)-(F2)).
2. You will see a "w/Confirm? No (Yes)" prompt. This option allows you to indicate if you want WordPerfect to pause each time it finds the text being searched for and ask you to confirm that it should replace the text. If you accept the default answer of No, WordPerfect will automatically replace all occurrences of the text being searched for with the replacement string.
3. Unless you are certain the text you are searching for is unique, you will want to respond Y to this prompt. For example, if you are replacing every occurrence of *Sells* with *Sales*, and you had a company name such as Sellstate in the document, the replace function would also change *Sellstate* to *Salestate*. Thus, you must be very careful if you are replacing without the confirm option.
4. After answering the confirm prompt, you will be shown the "Srch ->:" prompt to specify the text to be searched for. At this prompt, type Sells. Note that the capitalization is important since WordPerfect will search for the exact text you have entered.
5. After typing the text after the "Srch ->:" prompt, press the Search key ((F2)) again.
6. The prompt "Replace with:" will appear. This is where you type the text that is to replace the text being searched for. At the prompt, type *Sales* and press Search ((F2)) again.

7. Now the searching process begins. WordPerfect will pause each time it locates *Sells* and show a "Confirm No (Yes)" prompt at the bottom of the screen. Press **Y** to have *Sells* replaced with *Sales*. WordPerfect will immediately locate the next occurrence of *Sells*.

8. Continue the replacement operation until all occurrences of *Sells* have been replaced.

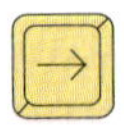

Spell Checker and Thesaurus

WordPerfect 5.1 also has a built in spelling checker and a thesaurus. If you are using a dual-floppy computer, you will need copies of the Spelling and Thesaurus diskettes. You will be prompted to insert these diskettes when using these parts of WordPerfect. To check the spelling in your two-page doc-ument, follow the steps below:

1. If you are not operating from a hard disk, remove your data diskette from drive B and replace it with the Spelling diskette.

2. Press the Spell key ((CTRL)-(F2)).

3. The line menu that follows will appear at the bottom of the screen, asking you if you want to check the word the cursor is on, the page the cursor is on, or the entire document.

```
Check: 1 Word; 2 Page; 3 Document;
4 New Sup. Dictionary; 5 Look up; 6 Count: 0
```

   This menu also lets you work with a supplemental dictionary and/or look up the spelling of a word by typing it and seeing what resembles that spelling in the dictionary. Choose the third option (press **3** or **D**) to check the entire document.

4. WordPerfect will stop on the word *TYREL* at the top of the minutes page. This name of the corporation is not in WordPerfect's spelling dictionary. On the bottom of the screen will be any words WordPerfect thinks are close to the misspelled word.

5. In this case the only word it will find is *twirl*. Each word that is suggested will have a letter in front of it. If you want to replace the word in the document with a word from the list, simply press the letter corres-ponding to the word you want.

6. If you do not want to replace the word, there are several options offered in the form of a line menu at the bottom of the screen. This menu lets you skip the word you are on (Skip Once), skip the word you are on and all future occurrences of the word in that document (Skip), add the word to the user dictionary so it will be recognized as spelled correctly in the future (Add), or go into the document to change the spelling of the word and return to spell checking (Edit).

7. Since TYREL is properly spelled and you don't want WordPerfect to stop on this word again, pick the Skip option by pressing **2**.
8. WordPerfect will automatically jump to the next word it cannot match to a word in the dictionary and again display a list of suggested words.
9. In the minutes, WordPerfect will stop on many of the employee names since those are not commonly in a spelling dictionary. Skip past these names, but if you find any spelling errors of your own, go ahead and correct them.

To see how the thesaurus works, position the cursor on the word *next* in the first paragraph of the memo.

If you are using a dual-floppy computer, you will need to remove the Spelling diskette and replace it with the Thesaurus diskette. Then tell WordPerfect that the disk is in drive B. Press the Thesaurus key ((ALT)-(F1)). A display similar to Exhibit D.14 will appear, showing words with a meaning similar to the *next* and also some words that have the opposite meaning.

The line menu at the bottom allows you to replace the word in the document by selecting option 1 and then typing the letter of the word you want to replace the word in the document. In addition, if you press the letter of a word without selecting option 1 first, WordPerfect will display synonyms and antonyms of that word. To practice using the thesaurus, try the following steps:

1. Put the cursor on the word *upcoming* near the end of the first paragraph of the memo.

Exhibit D.14

The Thesuarus Function in WordPerfect 5.1

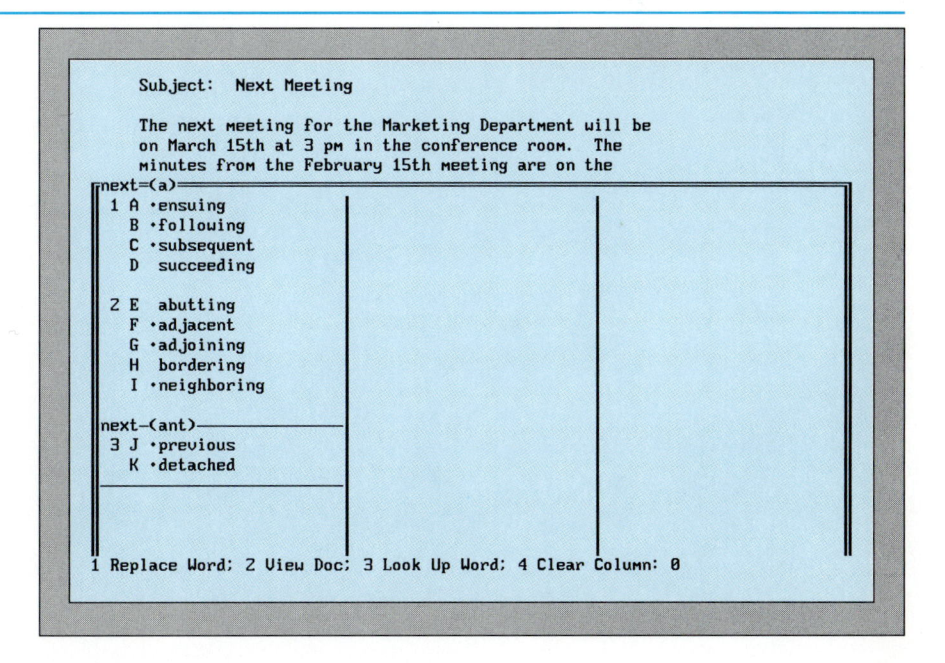

2. Press the Thesaurus key ((ALT)-(F1)).
3. The resulting list of synonyms will include *approaching* as choice A. Press **1** to replace the word and then **A** to pick *approaching*.

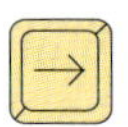

Printing the Document

To check your work before printing, press the Print key ((SHIFT)-(F7)) and choose the View option. Look at the resulting display and see if everything looks good.

Stop viewing the document by pressing the Exit ((F7)) key. If you have a printer attached to your computer, print the Full document by using option 1.

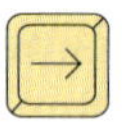

Saving the Document and Exiting WordPerfect

Now that you have finished editing the memo and minutes, save the entire document on your data diskette following these steps:

1. Put your data diskette in drive B.
2. Press the Exit key ((F7)).
3. When asked if you want to save the document, answer **Y** for Yes and enter a name of **MINUTES** for the file.

APPENDIX E

Introduction to Lotus 1-2-3 Release 2.2

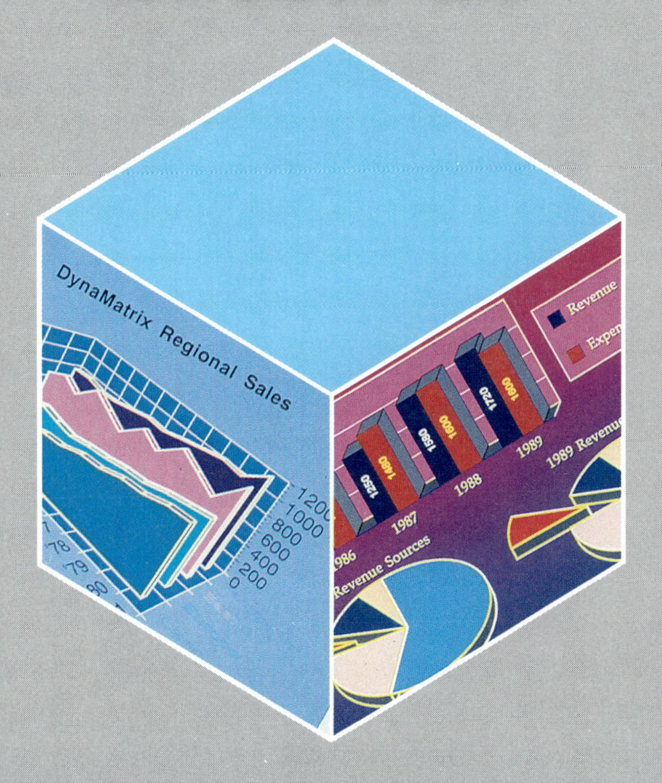

This appendix will introduce you to the features of Lotus 1-2-3 release 2.2. Earlier releases of Lotus include version 1A and 2.0; there is also release 3.0, which is designed for microcomputers that use an 80286 or 80386 processor. Although this appendix is written for release 2.2, the exercises can be completed using any version of the program.

You should be familiar with the general features of electronic spreadsheets from Chapter 13, "Electronic Spreadsheets." This appendix illustrates the specific features of Lotus 1-2-3 and demonstrates how this software package can be applied to some simple business applications.

Before You Start

You will need a copy of the Lotus 1-2-3 release 2.2 program and a formatted data diskette to complete the exercises in this appendix.

Lotus 1-2-3 is often run from a hard disk because of the size of the program. It is possible, however, to run it using a dual-floppy system. In either case, it is assumed that your copy of Lotus 1-2-3 has been correctly installed for your computer and is configured to use your printer. If it is not, consult your Lotus 1-2-3 documentation for installation instructions.

Starting Lotus 1-2-3

If you are using a hard disk, you should be able to boot your computer and type **LOTUS** at the C> prompt to start Lotus 1-2-3, assuming that Lotus has been installed with the correct MS-DOS path. If you are using a dual-floppy system, you will need to boot your computer and then insert the Lotus System disk in drive A if it is not already there. Then type **LOTUS** at the A> prompt. Once in Lotus 1-2-3, the screen will look like Exhibit E.1. Insert your formatted data diskette in drive B at this time (or drive A if you are using a hard disk).

The screen currently displays the Lotus 1-2-3 Access system, which is a menu that allows you to work with various parts of Lotus. Choosing 1-2-3 puts you into the spreadsheet itself. The other choices in this menu allow you to run the various utility programs that come with Lotus.

You interact with the menu in the Access system and all menus in Lotus 1-2-3 in the same way. The first choice in the menu is always highlighted, and the → and ← keys can be used to move the cursor to the other choices. When the highlight is moved past one side of the screen, it automatically wraps around to the other side of the screen.

As each choice in the menu is highlighted, the line below the menu provides additional information about what would happen if that option

Exhibit E.1
The Lotus Access System

```
1-2-3  PrintGraph  Translate  Install  Exit
Use 1-2-3

                         1-2-3 Access System
                        Copyright  1986, 1989
                    Lotus Development Corporation
                         All Rights Reserved
                             Release 2.2

 The Access system lets you choose 1-2-3, PrintGraph, the Translate utility,
 and the Install program, from the menu at the top of this screen.  If
 you're using a two-diskette system, the Access system may prompt you to
 change disks.  Follow the instructions below to start a program.

 o  Use → or ← to move the menu pointer (the highlighted rectangle
    at the top of the screen) to the program you want to use.

 o  Press ENTER to start the program.

 You can also start a program by typing the first character of its name.

 Press HELP (F1) for more information.
                           Press NUM LOCK
```

were selected. Thus, the line below the menu choices provides additional information to the user about each of the menu choices. All Lotus 1-2-3 menus have this feature.

To select from the menu, simply move the highlight to your choice and press (RETURN). An alternative method of selecting a menu choice is simply to press the first letter of the option you want. In Lotus 1-2-3 menus, each choice in the menu will always begin with a unique letter. When using this second method of selecting a menu choice, it is not necessary to move the highlight to the menu choice before selecting it.

To begin using the Lotus 1-2-3 spreadsheet, use one of the two methods described above to select the 1-2-3 choice from the Access system menu.

The Lotus 1-2-3 Spreadsheet

Once you have selected the 1-2-3 option from the Access system menu, the Lotus 1-2-3 spreadsheet will appear (see Exhibit E.2). The columns are labeled with letters of the alphabet. After the 26th column, two-letter column labels such as AA, AB, AC, and so on are used until the 256th column (IV) is reached. Rows are labeled with numerals, 1 through 8192. Each cell on the spreadsheet grid is identified by the combination of its column letters and row numbers. Examples of cell addresses would include A1, BA56, IV8192, and so on.

When the spreadsheet first appears, you see the upper left corner of the spreadsheet. The current cell pointer is highlighting cell A1.

Exhibit E.2

Lotus 1-2-3 Spreadsheet

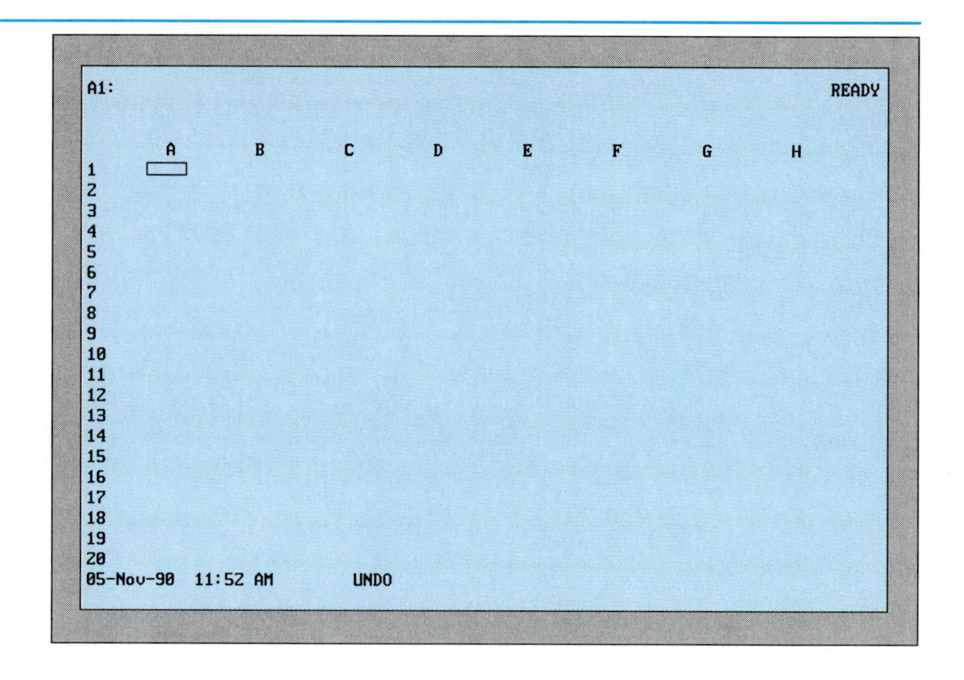

The Status Line

At the bottom of the screen is a single line known as the **status line**. This status line usually shows the current date and time in the bottom left corner. In addition, several highlighted words may appear on the status line while you are using Lotus 1-2-3. A complete list of status indicators can be found in your Lotus 1-2-3 manual. Some of these status indicators are shown in Exhibit E.3.

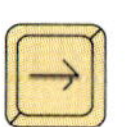

The Control Panel

The three lines at the top of the screen represent the control panel. The **control panel** is the area where the user interacts with the spreadsheet.

The first line of the control panel always displays information about the cell highlighted with the current cell pointer. In the top left corner, the

Exhibit E.3

Some of the Status Indicators used in Lotus 1-2-3

UNDO	Indicates that you can press the UNDO key to reverse the action you performed.
CAPS	Indicates that the caps lock key is on and letters will be in uppercase.
SCROLL	Indicates that the Scroll Lock key has been pressed and the use of movement keys will now shift the screen rather than the current cell pointer.
NUM	Indicates that the Num Lock key has been pressed and the numeric keypad can now be used to enter numbers rather than be used to move the current pointer.

address of the current cell is displayed along with information indicating any special format associated with the cell, the current protection status of the cell, any special display width attached to the cells in that column, and the current contents of the cell.

In addition to information about the current cell, the first line of the control panel also displays a **mode indicator** in the right corner, which indicates the current state of Lotus. A complete list of all mode indicators can be found in the Lotus 1-2-3 manual. Some examples are shown in Exhibit E.4.

The second line of the control panel is where information typed by the user appears before it is entered into the current cell on the spreadsheet. The second line is also where menus are displayed when the user begins entering a command.

The third line of the control panel is used only when menus are displayed on the second line. The third line displays additional information about the choice currently highlighted in the menu.

The Keyboard

Lotus 1-2-3 makes use of many of the special keys on a microcomputer keyboard to allow the user to move around the spreadsheet and to accomplish common functions. Perhaps one of the most useful keys in Lotus 1-2-3 is the ESC key. Many menus in Lotus 1-2-3 have submenus and you may pick an incorrect menu option occasionally. The ESC key is used to "back out" of a menu choice and return to the previously displayed menu. ESC is also used to exit from the Help facility in Lotus.

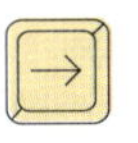

Moving Around

The current cell pointer can be moved one cell in any direction using the arrow keys on the keyboard. The user can move up and down one screen (20 rows) at a time using the PGUP and PGDN keys. TAB and SHIFT-TAB are used to move right and left one screen (about eight columns). In addition, the HOME key will always move the current cell pointer to cell A1.

Exhibit E.4

Some of the Mode Indicators used in Lotus 1-2-3

READY	Indicates that Lotus 1-2-3 is ready to receive an instruction from the user.
MENU	Indicates that a menu is displayed and Lotus is currently waiting for a choice to be made from that menu.
HELP	Indicates that the user has entered the Help facility and Lotus is currently displaying help information.
WAIT	Indicates that Lotus is currently busy executing an instruction and cannot accept any input from the user at this time.
ERROR	Indicates that an error has occurred while executing an instruction and the instruction could not be completed.

The F5 (GoTo) key can be used to position the current cell pointer on a specific cell on the spreadsheet. When this key is pressed, the user is asked to supply the address of a cell. After typing the address and pressing RETURN, the current cell pointer is moved to that cell and the screen is shifted to display that cell, if necessary.

More complex movement functions can be accomplished with combinations of keys such as END and the arrow keys. A complete list of all movement keys can be found in your Lotus 1-2-3 manual.

Function Keys

As you have already seen with the F5 (GoTo) key, the function keys on the keyboard can be used to accomplish special functions in Lotus 1-2-3. The features associated with some of the function keys are shown in Exhibit E.5.

In addition, some function keys can be pressed while holding down the ALT key, to achieve other functions. One important function activated in that way is the Undo ((ALT-F4)) function. Undo reverses the effect of the last command, changing the spreadsheet back to the way it was when last in the Ready mode. Pressing Undo a second time reverses the first Undo.

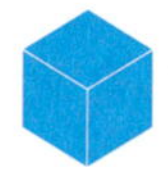

Exercise 1: Break-Even Analysis

Exhibit E.6 shows a break-even analysis that will be used to demonstrate the basic features of the Lotus 1-2-3 spreadsheet. On the example spreadsheet, several cells contain labels and others display values. Cells displaying values may contain a simple number or a formula that makes a calculation and displays the resulting number.

This spreadsheet introduces you to the basic skills of entering data, creating formulas, and formatting, saving, and printing the spreadsheet.

Entering Data

In Lotus 1-2-3, cells can contain one of three types of entries: labels, numbers, or formulas. Lotus 1-2-3 refers to numbers and formulas as **values**. The procedure for making an entry in a cell is similar for all three

Exhibit E.5

Some of the Function Keys Used in Lotus 1-2-3

F1 HELP	Enters the Lotus 1-2-3 Help facility. Information displayed will be related to the task you are currently performing or the error currently being displayed.
F2 EDIT	Brings the contents of the current cell to be second line of the control panel and enters the EDIT mode.
F5 GOTO	Allows the user to position the current cell pointer on a cell.
F9 CALC	Recalculates all the formulas on the spreadsheet. This is primarily used when the automatic recalculation feature has been turned off.

Exhibit E.6

Break-even Analysis Spreadsheet

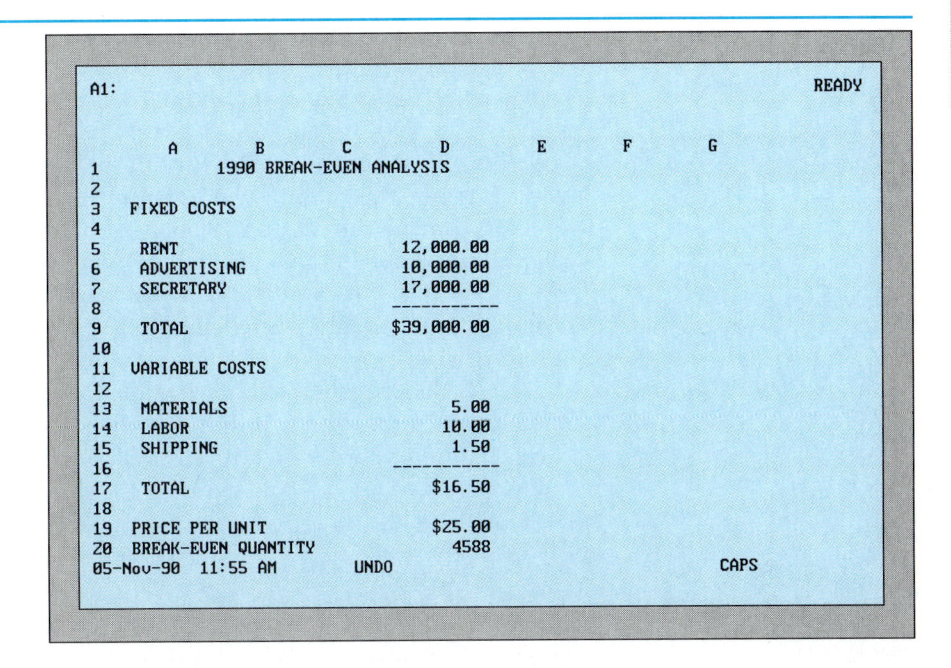

```
A1:                                                          READY

        A        B        C          D         E        F        G
1            1990 BREAK-EVEN ANALYSIS
2
3    FIXED COSTS
4
5     RENT                       12,000.00
6     ADVERTISING                10,000.00
7     SECRETARY                  17,000.00
8                               -----------
9     TOTAL                     $39,000.00
10
11   VARIABLE COSTS
12
13    MATERIALS                       5.00
14    LABOR                          10.00
15    SHIPPING                        1.50
16                               -----------
17    TOTAL                          $16.50
18
19   PRICE PER UNIT                  $25.00
20   BREAK-EVEN QUANTITY               4588
05-Nov-90   11:55 AM        UNDO                          CAPS
```

types. First, the current cell pointer must be moved to the cell that is to receive the entry. The user then begins typing the entry, and the characters automatically appear on the second line of the control panel. Once the entry is complete, the user presses (RETURN) to have the entry placed in the current cell on the spreadsheet.

Labels

Labels are entries that do not need to be treated as a number to be used in calculations. Lotus determines whether an entry is a label or a value based on the first character of the entry. If the entry begins with a digit (0 to 9), a plus sign (+), a minus sign (-), a pound sign (#), a dollar sign ($), a period (.), an @, or a left parenthesis, Lotus assumes that the entry is to be treated as a value. If it begins with any other character, the entry is treated as a label. The decision Lotus makes about your entry is reflected in the mode indicator on the first line of the control panel. This indicator will change to "VALUE" or "LABEL" after you have typed the first character, indicating how Lotus will treat your entry.

Labels may consist of any characters, including spaces, and have a maximum length of 240 characters. The capitalization used will be reflected on the spreadsheet and used when the spreadsheet is printed. Thus, use capital letters where you want capital letters to appear. To practice entering labels, enter the following labels for the break-even spreadsheet:

Cell	Label
A3	FIXED COSTS
A11	VARIABLE COSTS
A19	PRICE PER UNIT
A20	BREAK-EVEN QUANTITY

As you made the entries you may have noticed they were too long to fit in column A. The entire label, however, was still displayed because the cells to the right were empty. Lotus will always allow a long label to be displayed across the cells to the right as long as those cells are empty. Problems arise, however, when you need to make an entry in the cell immediately to the right, which would then prevent the long label from spilling over. In this case, the display of the long label is chopped off. The only alternative then is to change the width of the column containing the long label so that it can display the entire label. In the break-even spreadsheet, columns B and C were left empty to allow any long labels in column A to spill over.

To indent labels slightly within a cell, simply begin the entry with one or two blank spaces. In the following cells on the break-even spreadsheet, begin the entry with a single space and then type the label indicated:

Cell	Label
A5	RENT
A6	ADVERTISING
A7	SECRETARY
A9	TOTAL
A13	MATERIALS
A14	LABOR
A15	SHIPPING
A17	TOTAL

When making entries, use (BACKSPACE) to correct any mistakes while the entry is in the control panel. If you notice an error after making the entry in a cell, simply make the entry again. The new entry will replace the one currently in the cell.

Label Prefixes

Occasionally, you will want to begin a label with a character that Lotus will interpret as indicating that your entry is to be a value. For example, go to cell B1 and try entering the following label:

```
1990 BREAK-EVEN ANALYSIS
```

When you type the **1** in 1990, the mode indicator on the first line of the control panel changes to "VALUE." Because your entry begins with a number, Lotus assumes you are entering a value. Once you finish typing the entry and press (RETURN), Lotus will beep and the mode indicator will change to "EDIT." Lotus is rejecting your entry because it assumed you were entering a value and you are not permitted to have letters in a value entry. The cursor on the second line of the control panel rests under the space after 1990, which is where the characters start that Lotus believes are incorrect.

The problem in this case is that Lotus has decided that your entry is a value because it starts with a number. To override this feature, Lotus allows you to begin an entry with a special label-prefix character, which signals to Lotus that your entry is to be treated as a label. The label-prefix character is also used to specify label placement in the cell as left-justified, centered, or right-justified, assuming that the label is not wider than the column. The label prefixes in Lotus are shown in Exhibit E.7.

To fix the entry you are working on for cell B1, press the (HOME) key to move to the beginning of the entry on the second line of the control panel. Then type the single quote label prefix ('). Now press (RETURN); Lotus will now allow the entry to go into the cell since a label is allowed to contain both digits and letters.

Repeating Labels

An additional label prefix character used to produce a special effect is the repeating text prefix character (\). When an entry begins with a backslash (\), Lotus will repeat any characters following the backslash until the entire cell is filled. For example, using the backslash followed by a hyphen is a good way to draw a line across a cell. A backslash followed by an equal sign (=) makes a double line. The advantage to using this method rather than entering a series of minus signs or equal signs is that the repeating text label prefix will keep the cell filled even if the width of the cell changes.

To see the use of repeating text, enter a backslash (\) followed by a hyphen (-) in cells D8 and D16.

Numbers

Some of the values displayed on the break-even spreadsheet are numbers. Others are the results of calculations based on formulas. Entering formulas will be discussed later, but numbers can be entered in the same way as labels.

A number can contain only digits and a single period and may be up to 240 characters long. When entering numbers, dollar signs and commas are not part of the entry itself. These are added later using the Lotus numeric formatting options (see "Formatting").

To practice entering numbers, make the following entries on your break-even spreadsheet:

Cell	Number
D5	12000
D6	10000
D7	17000
D13	5
D14	10
D15	1.5
D19	25

Exhibit E.7

Lotus Label Prefixes

"	right justify	Lines the last character in the label up with the right edge of the cell.
'	left-justify	Lines the first character in the label up with the left edge of the cell.
^	centererd	Centers the label left to right within the cell.

When making these entries, remember to use the (BACKSPACE) key to correct any mistakes while the entry is in the control panel. If an incorrect entry is made in a cell, simply type the entry again. The new entry will replace the one currently in the cell. Exhibit E.8 shows the break-even spreadsheet after the labels and numbers have been entered.

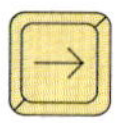

Editing Data

As indicated above, editing can be done on an entry while it is still in the control panel. When the user presses the Edit key ((F2)) to begin editing an entry or enters an invalid entry, Lotus will go into Edit mode. In Edit mode, certain keys on the keyboard can be used to edit the entry. Those keys include:

Key	Action
(HOME)	Move to the beginning of the entry
(END)	Move to the end of the entry
(INS)	Change between insert and overtype
(BACKSPACE)	Move the cursor left, deleting characters as it moves
(DEL)	Delete the character the cursor is on

In addition to being able to edit an entry while it is in the control panel, entries already stored in cells can be brought back to the control panel by placing the current cell pointer on the cell containing the entry and pressing the Edit key ((F2)). This brings the entry to the second line of the control panel and places Lotus into Edit mode.

Exhibit E.8

Break-even after Labels and Numbers Have Been Added

```
A1:                                                        READY

       A        B        C        D        E        F        G
1          1990 BREAK-EVEN ANALYSIS
2
3   FIXED COSTS
4
5    RENT                             12000
6    ADVERTISING                      10000
7    SECRETARY                        17000
8                                ----------
9    TOTAL
10
11  VARIABLE COSTS
12
13   MATERIALS                            5
14   LABOR                               10
15   SHIPPING                           1.5
16                               ----------
17   TOTAL
18
19  PRICE PER UNIT                       25
20  BREAK-EVEN QUANTITY
05-Nov-90  11:56 AM      UNDO                          CAPS
```

Another simple way of changing the contents of a cell is to make a second entry for the same cell. In this case the second entry will replace the first.

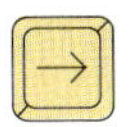

Ranges

Formulas and commands often affect a group of cells. Lotus 1-2-3 uses the concept of a **range** to allow the user to specify a group of cells to be operated on. A valid range is any continuous group of cells that can be referenced by a beginning cell address and an ending cell address. When specifying a range to Lotus the user separates the two cell addresses with a period.

Valid ranges could be a single cell (A1..A1), part of a row (A1..D1), part of a column (A1..A10), or a block of cells (A1..C4). Notice that the beginning cell address in the block is one corner of the block and the ending cell address is the cell in the opposite corner.

The concept of a range will be used below in entering formulas and when you use Lotus commands to format and print your spreadsheet.

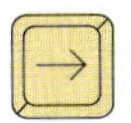

Entering Formulas

The numbers on the break-even spreadsheet for the two totals and the break-even quantity are the results of formulas. Formulas are entered in the same way as labels and numbers. Put the current cell pointer on the cell to contain the formula, type the formula on the second line of the control panel, and press (RETURN) to enter the formula in the current cell.

For the total of fixed costs in cell D9, you will need a formula that adds the numbers in cells D5, D6, and D7. You could enter the formula 12000+10000+17000 in cell D9, and the result of that calculation (39000) would be displayed. This illustrates that the contents of a cell are not always the same as what is displayed on the screen.

However, since the numbers for the fixed expenses are already entered in cells D5, D6, and D7, it would be inefficient to enter those numbers again in the formula. Like most spreadsheets, Lotus allows you to use cell addresses in formulas to add numbers that are stored in other cells on the spreadsheet. Thus, the formula for cell D9 might be D5+D6+D7. To enter this formula:

1. Move the current cell pointer to cell D9
2. Type **D5+D6+D7** on the second line of the control panel

Before pressing (RETURN), look at the mode indicator on the first line of the control panel. It says "LABEL," but it should say "VALUE" since numbers and formulas should be treated as values by Lotus. The indicator says "LABEL" because the first letter of your entry is a letter (the letter *D* in the cell address D5). To prevent Lotus from treating this formula as a label, you must begin the formula with a character that is allowed in values.

Typically, all formulas that start with a cell address begin with a plus sign (+). Thus, to fix your formula:

1. Press the Edit key (F2)
2. Press HOME to move to the beginning of your formula
3. Type a plus sign (+)
4. Press RETURN to enter the formula
5. You should see 39000 displayed in cell D9

Using Functions

Lotus also has numerous built-in functions to accomplish common tasks such as adding numbers, averaging numbers, and performing statistical, mathematical, and financial calculations.

To illustrate these functions, consider the formula in cell D17. Like the formula in D9, this formula needs to add the contents of three cells: D13, D14, and D15. Notice that the cells being added are a valid range, D13..D15. Lotus provides an @SUM function that can be used to add the contents of all the cells in a specified range. The general format for the @SUM function is

@SUM(*range*)

The benefit of this method is that the range can be any size. When using the method of entering all the cell addresses separated by plus signs, as was done in cell D9, the formula could quickly become too complex as the number of cells to be added increases. To complete the entry in cell D17:

1. Place the current cell pointer on cell D17
2. Type the formula **@SUM(D13.D15)**
3. Press RETURN
4. The number 16.5 should be displayed in cell D17

Order of Operations

In complex formulas involving combinations of addition, subtraction, multiplication, and division, it is important to understand the order in which Lotus will perform these operations. As a rule, Lotus will perform any exponentiation first, then all multiplication and division, and finally, any additions and subtractions. The formula for cell D20 will illustrate this concept.

To calculate the break-even quantity, the total fixed cost must be divided by the difference between the price per unit and the total variable cost per unit. Translating this into a formula, you might write

+D9/D19-D17

Following the normal rules for the order of operations, Lotus will perform the division first and then the subtraction. In this instance, this is wrong. The subtraction should be performed first and the fixed cost should be divided by the result of that subtraction.

The normal order of operations can be altered by using parentheses to indicate which operations are to be performed first. The formula should be

```
+D9/(D19-D17)
```

Enter this formula into cell D20 and verify that the correct break-even quantity of 4588.235 is displayed on the screen.

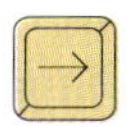

Formatting

At the present time, the display of numbers on your break-even spreadsheet is inconsistent. Some numbers are displayed with no decimal places, others with one, and still others with three. Lotus allows you to determine the formatting of numbers by specifying the number of decimal places and display of dollar signs and commas. In the break-even spreadsheet displayed in Exhibit E.6, three different formats are shown.

The numbers in cells D5 through D7 and D13 through D15 are displayed with two decimal places and commas between thousands. The totals in D9 and D17 are formatted with two decimal places, commas between thousands, and a dollar sign. The break-even quantity is formatted with no decimal places and no commas between thousands. These formats can be attached to the cells using a Lotus command. Any number entered into a formatted cell takes on that format.

All Lotus commands are found in the menus that are accessed by pressing the slash key (/). The slash causes Lotus to enter Command mode, in which a series of menus are shown that enable you to specify what you want Lotus to do. These menus function the same way as the Access menu you saw when you first loaded Lotus. The steps below show you how to use a command to apply formats to the cells in the break-even spreadsheet.

To apply the format to the break-even quantity, follow these steps:

1. Place the current cell pointer on D20.
2. Press the slash (/) to enter Command mode.
3. Select the Range option.
4. Select the Format option in the next menu.
5. From the next menu, select the Fixed option.
6. Press (RETURN) to accept the two–decimal place default (2).
7. The range D20..D20 will appear.
8. Press (RETURN) to format this range.

To apply the format to the fixed costs, follow these steps:

1. Place the current cell pointer on cell D5.
2. Press the slash (/) to enter the Command mode.
3. Select the Range option.

4. Select the Format option in the next menu.
5. From the next menu, select the comma option (,).
6. Press (RETURN) to accept the two–decimal place default (2).
7. The range D5..D5 will appear, but it should be D5..D7. Press (↓) twice.
8. The range should now appear as D5..D7; press (RETURN).

The entries in cells D5 through D7 will change to asterisks because the numbers are now too long to be displayed in the normal display width of nine characters, due to the additional decimal places and comma. Unlike labels, numbers that are too long to be displayed will not spill over into the cells to the right. When a number is too long to be displayed in a column, you must widen the column.

Column Widths

The display width of columns on the spreadsheet is normally nine characters. This can be altered for any column on the spreadsheet by using a command. To alter the width of column D follow these steps:

1. Place the current cell pointer on any cell in column D.
2. Press the slash (/) to enter Command mode.
3. Select the Worksheet option.
4. Select the Column option in the next menu.
5. Select the Set-width option in the next menu.
6. A prompt will appear showing the current width of nine.
7. Type **12** to set the width to twelve characters; then press (RETURN).

In the Set-width command, you have the option of typing a new column width, as was done above, or you can use the (→) and (←) keys to expand and shrink the column one character at a time and see the effect of the changes on the spreadsheet as you do this. Then once the desired width has been obtained, you can press (RETURN) to set the width.

Formatting the Remaining Numbers

To continue the formatting process, give the variable costs the same format as the fixed costs, as follows:

1. Place the current cell pointer on cell D13.
2. Press the slash (/) to enter the command mode.
3. Select the Range option.
4. Select the Format option in the next menu.
5. From the next menu, select the comma option (,).
6. Press (RETURN) to accept the two–decimal place default (2).

7. The range D13..D13 will appear, but it should be D13..D15. Press (↓) twice.
8. The range should now be D13..D15. Press (RETURN).

To complete the formatting process, use the steps below to format the totals for the fixed costs and variable costs:

1. Place the current cell pointer on cell D9.
2. Press the slash (/) to enter Command mode.
3. Select the Range option.
4. Select the Format option in the next menu.
5. From the next menu, select the Currency option.
6. Press (RETURN) to accept the two–decimal place default (2).
7. The range D9..D9 will appear; press (RETURN) to format this range.

Use the same process to apply the current format with two decimals to cells D17 and D19. The spreadsheet should now look like Exhibit E.6.

Saving the Spreadsheet

The break-even spreadsheet is now complete, and you are ready to save it on your data diskette. To save files on the diskette in drive B you can either enter B: in front of the file name, or you can specify in Lotus the default drive to be used when saving and retrieving all files. To see how the second method works, use the following steps to set up your copy of Lotus 1-2-3 to always work with files on drive B:

1. Press the slash (/) to enter the Command mode.
2. Select the Worksheet option.
3. Select the Global option.
4. Select the Default option.
5. Select the Directory option.
6. At the prompt type **B:** and press (RETURN).
7. Select the Update option to store this new default setting.

To save your spreadsheet, you will also use a command:

1. Press the slash (/) to enter Command mode.
2. Select the File option.

3. Select the Save option.
4. At the prompt, enter the file name of **BRKEVEN**.
5. Press (RETURN).

This will save the entire spreadsheet in a file called BRKEVEN.WK1. If you already have a file called BRKEVEN.WK1 on your disk, Lotus will give you an additional menu that allows you to cancel the current save operation, replace the original file on the disk with the spreadsheet you are currently saving, or do a backup, which renames the original file on the disk with a BAK extension and saves the current spreadsheet under the WK1 extension.

Printing the Spreadsheet

If your microcomputer has a printer attached to it, you can print all or part of the spreadsheet you are currently working on. Use the following steps to print your spreadsheet:

1. Type a slash (/) to enter the command mode.
2. Select the Print option.
3. Select the Printer option.
4. The Print Settings screen appears (see Exhibit E.9).

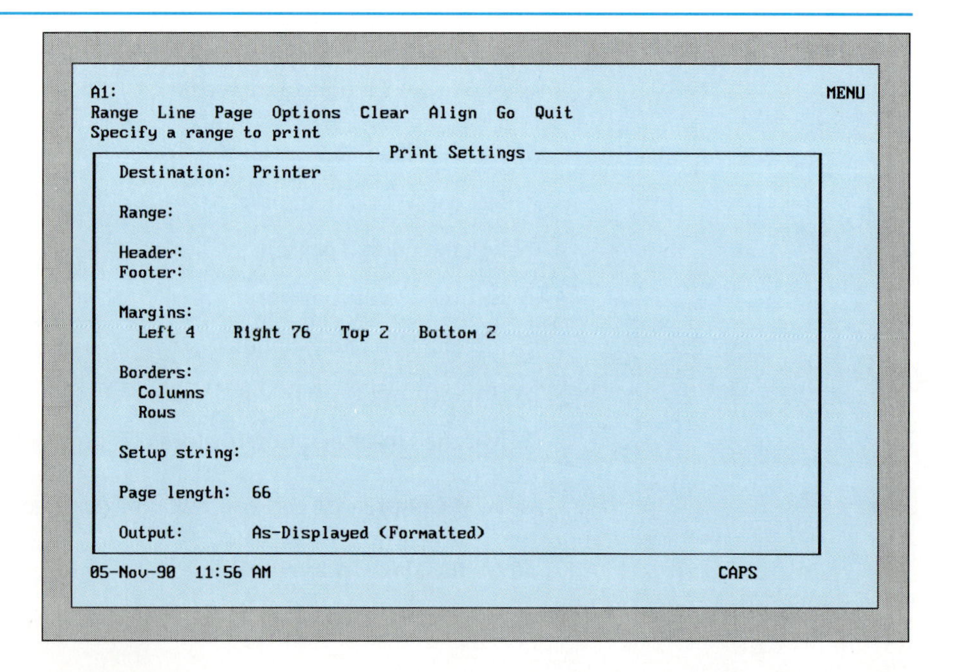

Exhibit E.9

Print Settings Screen

This screen shows the current settings in effect for printing the current spreadsheet. The menu at the top of the screen allows you to change the current print settings on the screen.

Select the Range option from this menu and the Print Settings screen is replaced by your spreadsheet. A prompt to enter a range appears in the control panel with the current cell address as the first address in the range.

Specifying a Range by Pointing

The first address in a range is known as the **anchor cell**. When the anchor cell address appears by itself (as it does here) without a period or a second address, moving the current cell pointer on the spreadsheet will change the address that appears in the range specification.

To see this, press (HOME) and note how the anchor cell address after the prompt in the control panel has changed to A1.

Now type the period that will separate the anchor cell address from the ending cell address (known as the **free cell**). When you type the period, Lotus displays two periods and a second cell address that is the address of the cell the current cell pointer is on. Thus, the range after the prompt will be A1..A1.

When a second address appears in a range, the movement of the current cell pointer will cause the second cell address, rather than the anchor cell address, to change. As you move the current cell pointer to change the second address, a highlight that follows your movement and highlights the range will appear.

To see how this works, move the current cell pointer over and down to cell D20. Notice how a highlight extends from the anchor cell (A1) and currently highlights all the cells in the range A1..D20. You should have witnessed the same effect when formatting groups of cells with the Range Format command.

This method of moving to establish the position of the anchor cell, locking it in with a period, and moving to expand the highlight to cover the range desired is known in Lotus as **pointing**. During the pointing operation, the mode indicator will display the word "POINT."

Some commands automatically start you with a range containing only the anchor cell, as the print command does. Other commands, such as the Range Format command, give you a range containing both cell addresses. In the latter case, the anchor cell cannot be changed by moving the current cell pointer. The anchor cell is locked in, and only the second address is altered by the movement of the cursor. This is why the instructions for formatting, above, had you place your cursor on the beginning cell of the range before issuing the command.

After the anchor cell is locked in with the period and the second address appears, it is still possible to change the anchor cell address by pressing (ESC) to unlock it. When you press (ESC), the second address and the period disappear and the anchor cell can once again be changed by moving the current cell pointer on the screen.

Printing the Break-Even Spreadsheet

On your spreadsheet you should now have the range from A1 to D20 highlighted. Press (RETURN) to enter this range and the Print Settings menu should once again appear. On this screen the currently selected range of A1..D20 should now appear after the "Range:" heading.

To print the spreadsheet, make sure your printer is turned on and ready to receive the printout. Then choose the Align option from the menu. This option tells Lotus that it is at the top of the page so that it knows where to begin the second page, if necessary.

Finally, to print the currently selected range, choose the Go option; the printer will begin printing the spreadsheet. The printer should pause after the last line of the range is printed. To get the printer to eject the page, choose the Page option in the Print menu. If you had a second page to print, this would cause printing to begin at the top of the next page. A common error in printing with Lotus is to use the Form Feed button on the printer itself to eject the page. The problem with this method is that Lotus does not know it is at the top of a new page. So when the next print command is issued, Lotus thinks it is still in the middle of the previous page.

Automatic Recalculation

Now that the original break-even spreadsheet has been saved, you can experiment with the automatic recalculation feature of Lotus, which is what makes it ideal for performing a what-if analysis. To see this feature at work, position the current cell pointer on cell D5 and type a new entry of **10000.** Take note of the original values in cells D9 and D20; then press (RETURN) to replace the contents of cell D5. After the new entry is placed in cell D5, the values displayed in cells D9 and D20 will be automatically recalculated since they are based on the number that appears in cell D5.

Anytime the contents of a cell are changed, Lotus makes sure any formula that is directly or indirectly based on that cell is automatically updated. In this example, when the rent was changed from 12000 to 10000, the total fixed costs dropped from 39000 to 37000 and the break-even quantity dropped from 4588 to 4353.

Use the procedure described in "Saving the Spreadsheet," to save this new version of the break-even spreadsheet in a file called **BRKEVEN2.WK1.** Then print a copy of the spreadsheet.

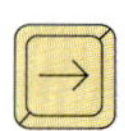

Exiting Lotus

When you are finished with Lotus you can execute the Quit command by typing a slash, selecting the Quit option, and selecting the Yes option in the next menu. This will return you to the Access System menu, where you can select the Exit option to return to the MS-DOS prompt.

Exhibit E.10

Personnel Spreadsheet

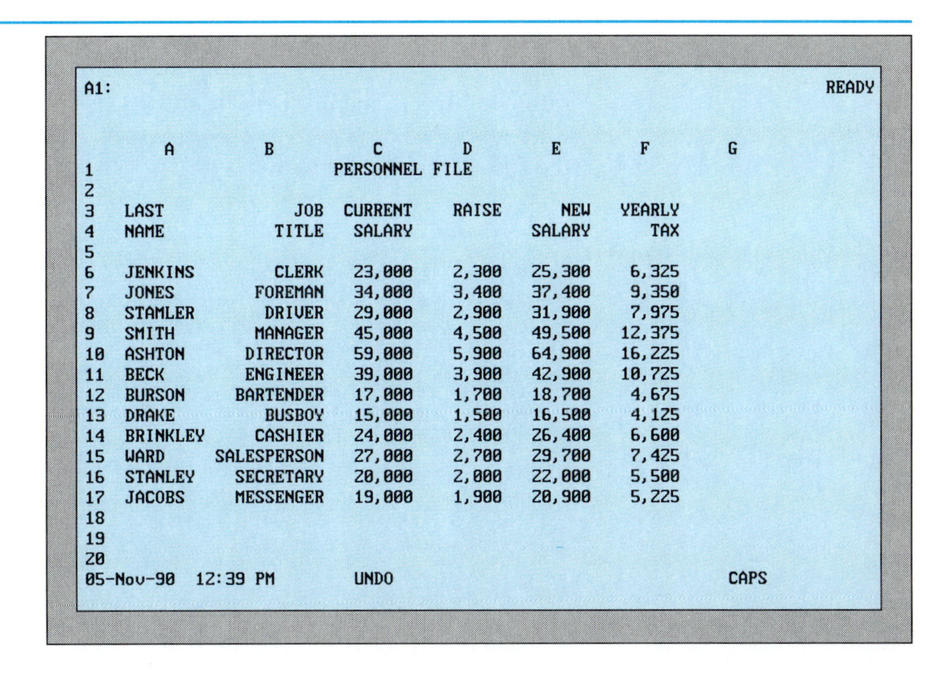

A1: READY

	A	B	C	D	E	F	G
1			PERSONNEL FILE				
2							
3	LAST	JOB	CURRENT	RAISE	NEW	YEARLY	
4	NAME	TITLE	SALARY		SALARY	TAX	
5							
6	JENKINS	CLERK	23,000	2,300	25,300	6,325	
7	JONES	FOREMAN	34,000	3,400	37,400	9,350	
8	STAMLER	DRIVER	29,000	2,900	31,900	7,975	
9	SMITH	MANAGER	45,000	4,500	49,500	12,375	
10	ASHTON	DIRECTOR	59,000	5,900	64,900	16,225	
11	BECK	ENGINEER	39,000	3,900	42,900	10,725	
12	BURSON	BARTENDER	17,000	1,700	18,700	4,675	
13	DRAKE	BUSBOY	15,000	1,500	16,500	4,125	
14	BRINKLEY	CASHIER	24,000	2,400	26,400	6,600	
15	WARD	SALESPERSON	27,000	2,700	29,700	7,425	
16	STANLEY	SECRETARY	20,000	2,000	22,000	5,500	
17	JACOBS	MESSENGER	19,000	1,900	20,900	5,225	
18							
19							
20							

05-Nov-90 12:39 PM UNDO CAPS

Exercise 2: Personnel File

Exhibit E.10 shows a spreadsheet used to maintain a personnel file containing employee information. This exercise will allow you to practice the skills you learned in the first exercise and introduce you to one of the most useful Lotus commands, the Copy command.

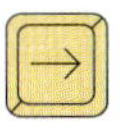

Entering the Personnel Data

Follow the steps below to enter the labels and numbers required to construct the personnel spreadsheet:

1. Enter the title in cell C1.
2. Enter the column headings in rows 3 and 4. When you are entering these labels, they will not line up exactly as they appear in Exhibit E.10. Do not attempt to correct this at this time. Simply type the label and enter it into the cell.
3. Enter the names in cells A6 through A17.
4. Enter the job titles in cells B6 through B17. As with the column headings, these labels will not line up exactly as they are shown in the exhibit. This will be corrected later.
5. Enter the current salaries in cells C6 through C17. Remember that you cannot enter the comma when you type your entries. That will be added later when you format the numbers. You may also notice that the job title

SALESPERSON is chopped off when you enter the corresponding salary. This is because the label was too long for its column width and spilled over into column C. Then, when an entry was made in column C, the SALESPERSON label could no longer spill over. This will also be fixed later, when the spreadsheet is formatted.

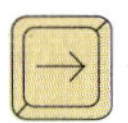

Entering Formulas

The personnel spreadsheet requires formulas in columns D, E, and F to calculate the raises, new salaries, and yearly tax for each employee.

The RAISE Column Formulas

In the RAISE column, a formula will be used to calculate a 10 percent raise for each employee. For example, the formula for cell D6 would be

```
+C6*.1
```

Note how this formula begins with a plus sign to ensure Lotus will treat this entry as a value rather than a label. The asterisk is used to indicate multiplication. To calculate a 10 percent raise for the first employee, the current salary cell for that employee (C6) is multiplied by .1. Enter the formula in cell D6.

Let's take a closer look at the formulas required to calculate the raises for some of the other employees. Do not enter these formulas at this time.

Cell	Formula
D7	+C7*.1
D8	+C8*.1
D9	+C9*.1
etc.	

From the three example formulas given above, you should be able to see a pattern developing. In each formula, Lotus is being told to take the value in the cell to the left of the cell containing the formula and multiply it by .1. In fact, Lotus sees all these formulas as exactly the same since it interprets cell addresses as distances relative to the location of the formula. Thus, each formula in the RAISE column would have the same description: *Take the value in the cell to the left of the cell containing the formula and multiply it by .1.*

Since all the formulas in the RAISE column have the same structure, Lotus allows you to make copies of the formula rather then having to type it twelve times. To use the Copy command, you must first enter the formula to be copied, *once*. Then the formula in that cell can be copied to other cells requiring the same formula. You should have already entered the raise formula in cell D6, so you are ready to copy that formula into cells D7 through D17.

Exhibit E.11

Copying the Raise Formula

```
D6: (T) +C6*0.1                                                        READY

        A          B          C         D         E         F         G
1                        PERSONNEL FILE
2
3   LAST             JOB  CURRENT    RAISE      NEW    YEARLY
4   NAME           TITLE   SALARY             SALARY      TAX
5
6   JENKINS        CLERK   23,000 +C6*0.1
7   JONES        FOREMAN   34,000
8   STAMLER       DRIVER   29,000
9   SMITH        MANAGER   45,000
10  ASHTON      DIRECTOR   59,000
11  BECK        ENGINEER   39,000
12  BURSON     BARTENDER   17,000
13  DRAKE         BUSBOY   15,000
14  BRINKLEY     CASHIER   24,000
15  WARD     SALESPERSON   27,000
16  STANLEY    SECRETARY   20,000
17  JACOBS     MESSENGER   19,000
18
19
20
05-Nov-90  12:41 PM        UNDO                                    CAPS
```

The Copy Command

The Copy command requires the specification of two ranges: a range indicating the location of the cell (or cells) containing the formula to be copied and a range indicating the cells where the copies are to be placed. In this instance, the range for the location of the formula to be copied is D6..D6 and the range for the location of the copies is D7..D17 (see Exhibit E.11).

To see how the Copy command can be used to fill in the rest of the formulas in the RAISE column, follow these steps:

1. Place the current cell pointer on cell D6.
2. Press the slash (/) to enter the Command mode.
3. Select the Copy option.

A range will appear with the current cell address already filled in as the range—D6..D6. This first range is the location of the cell containing the formula to be copied, which is why you placed the current cell pointer on cell D6 in the first step. Since D6 is the cell containing the formula to be copied, you can simply press (RETURN) to accept this default range. If you had not placed the current cell pointer on D6 to start with, you would have had to press (ESC) to unlock the anchor cell in this range and then move to the cell containing the formula. Thus, it is always easier to place the current cell pointer on the cell containing the formula to be copied before beginning the Copy command.

After you press (RETURN) to accept the D6..D6 range as the cell to copy from, a second range appears where you will specify the range the formula is to be copied to. This time the range is a single address, which indicates that you have an unlocked anchor cell that can be changed by moving the current cell pointer. Initially, the address in this range will also be D6. The range that is to receive copies of the formula is D7..D17.

Press the ↓ key; the anchor cell address in the range should change to D7. Lock this in by typing a period and the range becomes D7..D7. Now you can move the current cell pointer to change the second address in the range. Press the ↓ key ten times, until the range reads D7..D17. Finally, press RETURN to accept this range.

Once you press RETURN the entire RAISE column should be filled in with the numbers shown in Exhibit E.10. To verify that the formulas are in the cells, place the current cell pointer on cell D7 and look at the entry that appears on the first line of the control panel. The formula should be +C7*.1. Move the current cell pointer to cell D8 and see that the formula is +C8*.1. Lotus has placed the correct cell addresses in each formula because, as the formula is copied, the cell address in the formula is automatically filled in with the address of the cell to the left since Lotus always interprets the formula as *Cell to the left, times .1.*

The NEW SALARY Column Formulas

In the NEW SALARY column, there is a situation similar to that of the RAISE column. In this column, the formula needs to add the raise to the current salary for each employee. Thus, in cell E6 you should enter the formula

```
+C6+D6
```

Lotus will interpret this formula as *take the cell to the left of the cell containing the formula and add its value to the cell that is two columns to the left of the formula cell.* This interpretation of the formula would apply to all the cells in the NEW SALARY column. You can take advantage of that fact by copying the formula you just entered into cell E6 to the remaining eleven cells in the NEW SALARY column. Use the following steps to copy the formula:

1. Place the current cell pointer on cell E6.
2. Press the slash (/) to enter Command mode.
3. Select the Copy option.
4. The address E6..E6 appears as the range to copy from. Press RETURN.
5. The address E6 appears as the range to copy to. Press the ↓ key to change E6 to E7.
6. Press a period (.) to lock in the anchor cell address.
7. The range becomes E7..E7. Press the ↓ key ten times.
8. When the range reads E7..E17, press RETURN.

The NEW SALARY column should now be filled in and you can verify that the formula is correct by placing the current cell pointer on some of the cells in the NEW SALARY column and checking to make sure that each formula adds the cell to the left and the cell that is two columns to the left of the cell containing the formula.

The YEARLY TAX Column

The YEARLY TAX column requires a formula very similar to the one in the RAISE column. In this case, the yearly tax is computed by taking the new salary for each employee and multiplying it by .25. Each cell in the YEARLY TAX column can therefore take the cell to the left and multiply that value by .25. Use the following steps to fill in this column:

1. Move to cell F6.
2. Type the formula **+E6*.25** and press (RETURN).
3. The current cell pointer should still be on cell F6. Press the slash **(/)** to enter Command mode.
4. Select the Copy option.
5. The address F6..F6 appears as the range to copy from. Press (RETURN).
6. The address F6 appears as the range to copy to. Press the (↓) key to change F6 to F7.
7. Press a period to lock in the anchor cell address. The range becomes F7..F7.
8. Press the (↓) key ten times.
9. When the range reads F7..F17, press (RETURN).

Once the YEARLY TAX column is filled in, you have completed all the formulas for the personnel spreadsheet. Now you are ready to do some formatting to improve the spreadsheet's appearance.

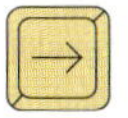

Formatting the Personnel Spreadsheet

To complete the personnel spreadsheet, you need to improve the alignment of the labels and format the numbers.

Aligning Labels

To align the column headings with the numbers below them, you could have used label prefixes when you entered each label. With a large number of labels, however, it is easier to use a command to change the alignment of a whole group of labels. The labels in cells B3 through F4 and those in cells B6 through B17 need to be right-justified within their cells. To accomplish this you will use a Range, Label-prefix command to align all the labels at once. Follow these steps:

1. Place the current cell pointer on cell B3.
2. Press the slash (/) to enter Command mode.

3. Select the Range option.
4. Select the Label-prefix option from the next menu.
5. Select the Right option for right-justified.
6. A range of B3..B3 should appear. Press the (END) key and then the (HOME) key.
7. The range should change to B3..F17. Press (RETURN) to accept this range.

After you press (RETURN) all the labels in the range will be right-justified. This procedure illustrates several shortcuts. First, you will notice that the range used included the cells to be right-justified (B3..F4 and B6..B17) but also included many cells that did need to be right-justified. The extra cells in this range, however, do not contain labels. The entries in these cells are all values. When a label prefix command is applied to a range of cells in this way, only the cells containing labels are affected by the command. Another shortcut used in this procedure is the use of the (END), (HOME) key sequence to move the current cell pointer to the bottom right corner of the spreadsheet. The bottom right corner of the spreadsheet is the cell at the intersection of the last column containing an entry and the last row containing an entry.

The final formatting step required for the labels is to widen column B to accommodate the SALESPERSON job title, which is currently truncated. Use the following procedure to accomplish this:

1. Place the current cell pointer on any cell in column B.
2. Press the slash (/) to enter Command mode.
3. Select the Worksheet option.
4. Select the Column option.
5. Select the Set-Width option.
6. Type **12** and press (RETURN) to set the width to twelve characters.

Column B should now be wide enough to display the SALESPERSON job title that was previously chopped off.

Formatting the Numbers

All the numbers on the personnel spreadsheet require a numeric format with no decimal places and commas between thousands. This formatting can be accomplished by following these steps:

1. Place the current cell pointer on cell C6.
2. Press the slash (/) to enter Command mode.
3. Select the Range option.
4. Select the Format option.
5. Select the comma format (,).

6. Type **0** to replace the default of two decimal places (2).
7. Press (RETURN) to enter the decimal places setting.
8. The range C6..C6 appears. Press (END) and then (HOME).
9. The range changes to C6..F17. Press (RETURN) to enter the range.

Notice how the cursor was placed in the upper left corner of the range to be formatted before the command was issued. Also note the use of (END), (HOME) to jump to the bottom right corner of the spreadsheet. Now the formatting of the personnel spreadsheet is complete and you are ready to save and print the results.

Saving the Personnel Spreadsheet

Save this spreadsheet in a file called PRSNNEL.WK1 by following these steps:

1. Press the slash (/) to enter Command mode.
2. Select the File option.
3. Select the Save option.
4. Type the file name: **PRSNNEL**.
5. Press (RETURN).

This will save a copy of the spreadsheet on your data diskette in drive B, assuming that you correctly set up drive B as the default drive in the first exercise.

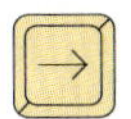

Printing the Personnel Spreadsheet

If you have a printer attached to your computer, follow these instructions to print a copy of the spreadsheet:

1. Press the slash (/) to enter Command mode.
2. Select the Print option.
3. Select the Printer option.
4. Select the Range option.
5. An unlocked anchor cell should appear as the range. Press (HOME) to change the anchor cell to A1.
6. Type a period (.) to lock the anchor cell in.

7. The range should read A1..A1. Press (END) and then press (HOME).
8. The range should expand to A1..F17. Press (RETURN) to enter the range.
9. Make sure the printer is on and will begin printing at the top of the paper.
10. Select the Align option to set the top of the page.
11. Select the Go option to print the range.
12. Select the Page option to eject the paper.

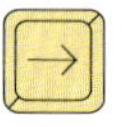

Retrieving a Spreadsheet

To illustrate how spreadsheets are retrieved and to reinforce your understanding of the automatic recalculation feature, you will retrieve the personnel spreadsheet from your disk and change some of the salaries.

First use the following procedure to erase the personnel spreadsheet from memory:

1. Press the slash (/) to enter Command mode.
2. Select the Worksheet option.
3. Select the Erase option.
4. Select the Yes option.

The personnel spreadsheet disappears and you have a blank spreadsheet. Now, to retrieve the personnel spreadsheet from your diskette, use this procedure:

1. Press the slash (/) to enter Command mode.
2. Select the File option.
3. Select the Retrieve option.
4. The third line of the control panel shows a list of files. Highlight the PRSNNEL.WK1 entry and press (RETURN).

The personnel spreadsheet then returns to the screen. You could have retrieved the personnel spreadsheet without going through the first step of erasing the spreadsheet; since both the spreadsheet in memory and the spreadsheet being retrieved are the same you would not have noticed the retrieval.

An important concept to realize about the retrieval of a spreadsheet is that the spreadsheet being retrieved will normally *replace* the current spreadsheet in memory. Thus, you must be careful to save the spreadsheet in memory before retrieving another spreadsheet. If you mistakenly retrieve a spreadsheet and destroy the spreadsheet in memory, you can reverse this operation by using the Undo feature immediately after the retrieval.

To see once again the power of the Lotus automatic recalculation feature, go to cell C6 and change the salary of the first employee from 23000 to 25000 by entering **25000** in cell C6. When you make this change you should see the raise, new salary, and yearly tax for the employee change automatically.

Save this new version of the personnel spreadsheet in a file called **PRSNNEL2.WK1** and print a copy if you have a printer attached to your computer.

You are now finished with the second exercise and can use the Quit command to leave Lotus, followed by the Exit option to leave the Access system.

APPENDIX F

Introduction to dBASE IV

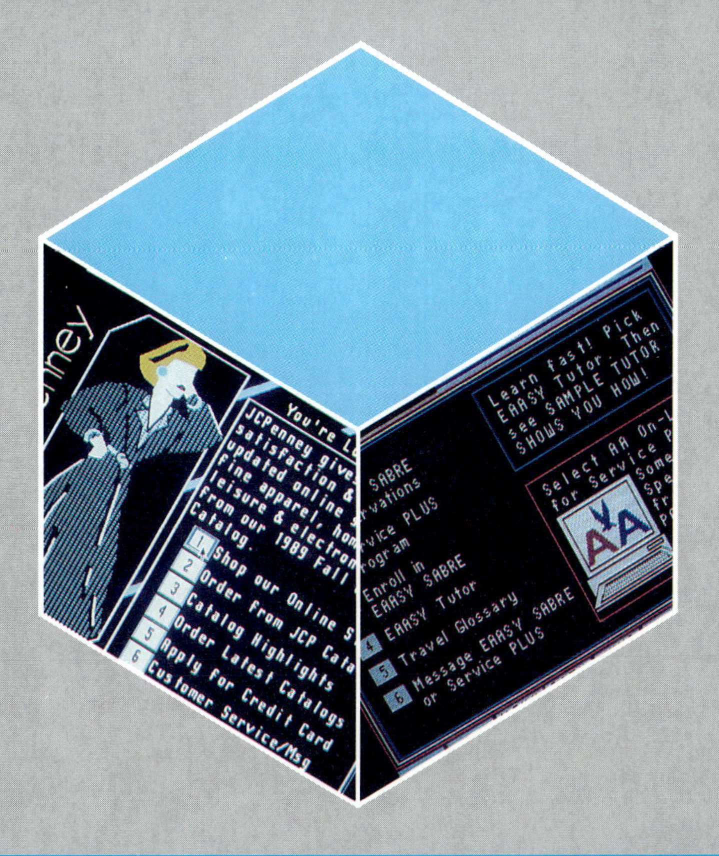

dBASE IV is the most recent release of the popular relational database software from Ashton Tate. In this appendix you will learn how to create a database with two tables, enter data into the tables, organize data using indexes and sorts, construct queries (views), design forms, and create reports.

Before You Start

It is assumed that you will have access to the dBASE IV software, and you should also have a formatted data disk to store your work. The dBASE IV software requires a computer with a hard disk drive, therefore it is assumed that you have a microcomputer with a hard disk (labeled drive C) and that the dBASE IV software has already been correctly installed for your computer and printer.

Starting dBASE IV

Boot your microcomputer from the hard disk to obtain the C> prompt. Then place your formatted data disk in drive A. To begin using dBASE IV, make the subdirectory containing the dBASE software your current directory. Most likely, the software will be in a subdirectory labeled DBASE. If this is the case, you can type

```
CHDIR C:\DBASE
```

at the C> prompt to make this subdirectory your current directory. To run dBASE, type **DBASE** at the DOS prompt and press RETURN.

You should see a logo screen, which after a moment is replaced by the copyright screen. Press RETURN to acknowledge the copyright agreement. You will now see the main screen for dBASE IV, known as the **Control Center** (see Exhibit F.1).

The Control Center is a new feature added in dBASE IV. It is the replacement for the Assist menu system used in previous versions of dBASE. In the dBASE environment, you have two general interfaces for interacting with dBASE: the menu-oriented Control Center and the command-oriented Dot prompt. In the Dot prompt interface, you type dBASE commands to accomplish various functions and press RETURN to have them executed.

In contrast, the Control Center allows the user to pick tasks from a series of menus to accomplish the same functions as can be performed from the Dot prompt. With the menus, the user does not need to know the syntax for each command. In this appendix, you will be using the Control Center rather than the Dot prompt. Once you are familiar with dBASE, you might want to learn the commands and use them at the Dot prompt, since that method is a little faster.

Exhibit F.1

dBase Control Center

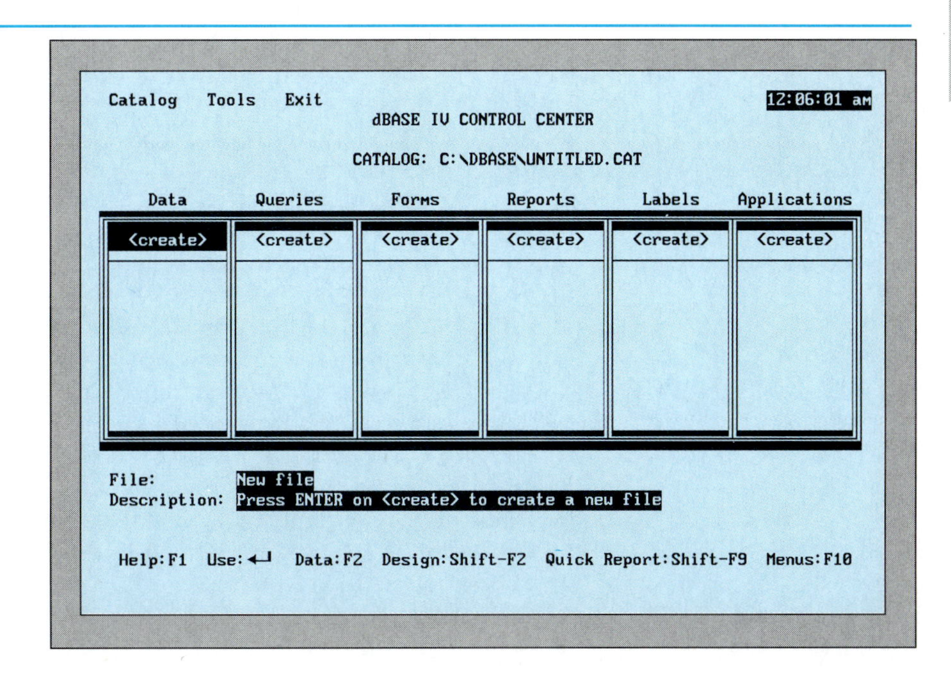

The Control Center

The panels in the middle of the Control Center screen summarize all the major parts of a dBASE database: Data files, Queries, Forms, Reports, Labels, and Applications. The Data files include the structure for the files in your database, indexes for organizing data, and the data itself. Queries (or views) represent instructions for retrieving data by specifying filtering and sorting of data from one or more files. The Forms are screen layouts that can be used for displaying and editing data, using data files or queries as the basis for the data to be displayed. Reports are layouts for printed reports based on data files or queries. Labels are a specific type of report designed for creating mailing labels. Applications are programs that link various forms, reports, queries, and files to produce an entire system. In this appendix, you will be introduced to the Files, Queries, Forms, and Reports panels of the Control Center.

At the top of the Control Center screen is a group of words that represent pull-down menus containing commands for working with the Control Center. The Catalog menu allows you to determine which catalog (or database) you want to work with. The Exit menu allows you to leave the Control Panel and go to the Dot prompt interface of dBASE or go to DOS. Choosing the Go to DOS option in the Exit menu is the way you leave dBASE when you are finished.

All pull-down menus in dBASE IV work in the same way. To see the pull-down menus, press the Menus key F10. The pull-down menu for the first word at the top of the screen will appear. If you had already used a pull-down menu on the screen, the last menu you accessed would be highlighted instead. You can also hold down the ALT key and press the first letter of one of the pull-down menus to access that menu directly instead of using the Menus key F10.

To access the menus for the other words at the top of the screen, simply use the → and ← keys to highlight the word you want; its menu will automatically pull down. Within a menu, the ↑ and ↓ keys can be used to highlight a specific option. Pressing RETURN selects the high-lighted option.

In many circumstances, some of the options in a menu will be bright and others will be dim. When this happens it indicates that only the bright choices can currently be selected; the dim ones do not apply under the current circumstances. In this case, the highlight cannot be positioned on a dim choice and so those choices cannot be selected. To leave the pull-down menus without selecting any options, the ESC key can be used.

Some additional information on the Control Center screen includes the name of the current catalog at the top (this should currently read C:\DBASE\UNTITLED.CAT); information about the current active file and its description; and the navigation line at the bottom, which indicates the functions that are currently available for use with this screen and the keys used to accomplish those functions. All dBASE screens contain a navigation line at the bottom indicating the effects of pressing certain keys. Below the navigation line is a message line where dBASE will occasionally display messages to the user.

The Keyboard

dBASE IV uses many different keys on the keyboard to accomplish tasks. To move a cursor around on the various screens, the arrow keys can be used. To move through lists of items, the PGUP and PGDN keys can be used to move up and down. The TAB and SHIFT-TAB keys can be used to move left and right across screens and through fields in a line. The HOME and END keys are used to move to the beginning and end of the item you are working on, such as a screen, a record, or a field.

For editing text, the DEL key will delete the character currently highlighted by the cursor. The BACKSPACE key allows you to move to the left, deleting characters as you go. The INS key toggles between typeover and insert modes.

When you are working on a task, the ESC key allows you to abandon the task without saving what you have done. Holding down the CTRL key and pressing END allows you to leave the task and save what you have done. Holding down the CTRL key and pressing RETURN allows you to save what you have done but remain in the task.

The function keys are associated with numerous functions. A complete list of all the function key assignments can be found in the dBASE IV documentation. Some of the function keys you will be using in this appendix are shown in Exhibit F.2.

Exhibit F.2

Some of the Function Key Assignments in dBASE IV

F1 (HELP)	Enter the help facility
F2 (DATA)	Switch between Browse and Edit
F3 (PREVIOUS)	Move to the previous field, object, or page
F4 (NEXT)	Move to the next field, object, or page
F5 (FIELD)	Place a field in a query, form, or report layout
F6 (SELECT)	Select a block of text and fields
F7 (MOVE)	Reposition the selected text and fields
F10 (MENUS)	Activate the pull-down menus
SHIFT+F1 (PICK)	Display a list of items
SHIFT+F2 (DESIGN)	Display design screens
SHIFT+F9 (QUICK REPORT)	Print a quick report

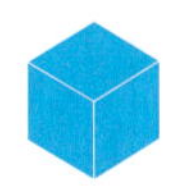

Exercise 1: Creating a Database

In this first exercise, you will learn how to create a catalog (database), set up the structure for files in the catalog, and enter data.

On the Control Center screen, press F10 (Menus) to bring up the Catalog pull-down menu. In this menu, choose the Use a different catalog option by highlighting it and pressing RETURN. A box will appear on the screen with two choices in the list: <create> and UNTITLED.CAT. UNTITLED.CAT is the current catalog listed at the top of the Control Center screen. To create the database for this exercise, highlight the <create> option and press RETURN to create a new catalog.

You will then be asked to enter a name for the new catalog. Catalog names can be up to eight characters. Type **A:PURCHASE** and press RETURN. This creates a file called PURCHASE.CAT on your disk in drive A. The information at the top of the Control Center reflecting the current catalog should be updated to show your new catalog as the current catalog.

Creating Files

dBASE refers to the tables of your database as **data files**. All data files in the current catalog are listed in the Data panel area of the Control Center. Since you have just created the PURCHASE catalog, there are no files listed in the data panel at this time. The panels in the Control Center will always list all the elements available for the current catalog. Since you have not created any data, queries, forms, reports, labels, or applications yet, all the panels in the Control Center are empty.

Also note that each panel is divided by a line with a <create> option above the line. This line always divides each panel into items that are active (above the line) and items that are not active (below the line). The <create> option is always active in each panel.

To create a new data file, move the highlight to the <create> option in the Data panel and press (RETURN). This will bring up the file design screen (see Exhibit F.3). This screen is an example of what dBASE IV refers to as a **work surface**. All work surfaces in dBASE have certain common characteristics. Pull-down menus always appear at the top, and below the work surface are a status, a navigation, and a message line. The navigation and message lines were described above. The status line is the highlighted bar that indicates what the current screen is ("Database"), the current file being used, the current cursor position, the data file or query that is active (if any), and any current toggle keys activated ((CAPS LOCK), (NUM LOCK), or (INS)).

On this database work surface are shown six columns that represent the information needed to create the structure for a data file. On this screen you will define the fields in the data file and specify the type of data they are to hold. You can also set up an index for each field if you want one. The Num column automatically numbers the fields as you enter them.

For the first data file in the PURCHASE catalog, you will create a PRODUCT file with the following fields:

Num	Field Name	Field Type	Width	Dec	Index
1	PROD_CODE	Character	6		N
2	PROD_DESC	Character	20		N
3	PROD_GROUP	Character	10		N
4	STOCK_QNTY	Numeric	4	0	N
5	PROD_PRICE	Numeric	7	2	N
6	PROD_SUPP	Character	3		N

When entering this information, simply type the name of the field and press (RETURN) to move to the field type. Character will always appear as the

Exhibit F.3

File Design Workplace

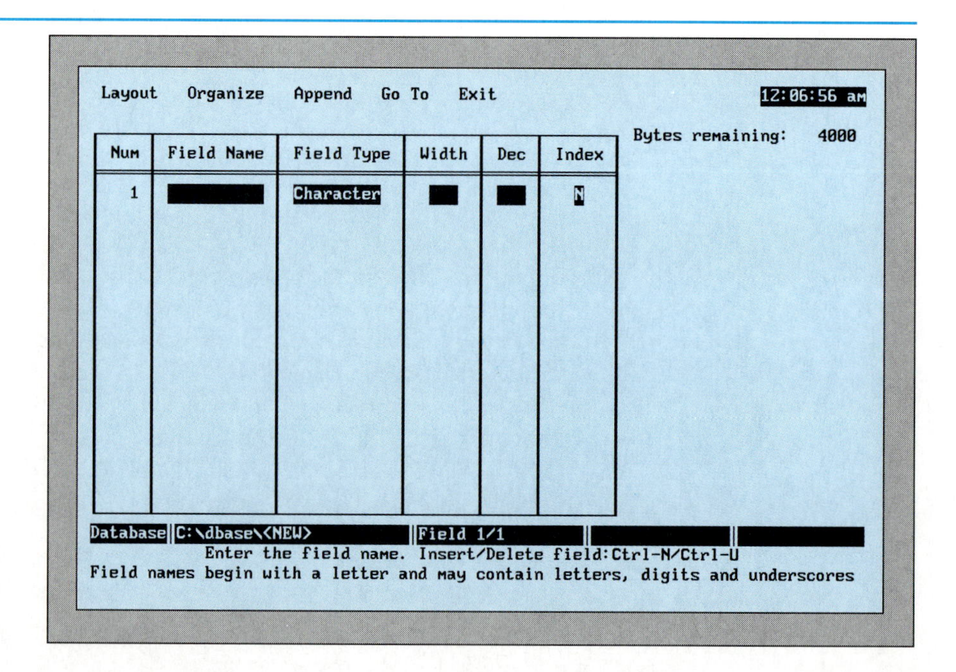

default type. Press RETURN to accept the Character default type or press SPACEBAR to change to other types. Press RETURN when you have the type you want. As you press the SPACEBAR, the types you will see are Character, Numeric, Float, Date, Logical, and Memo, in that order.

After pressing RETURN to enter the data type, you can type the width for the field and press RETURN. If the field type is Character, the Dec (decimal) column will automatically be skipped. If the field is Numeric or Float, you will be able to enter the number of decimal places, if you desired. In the Index column you can enter **Y** or **N** to indicate whether you want an index created for the field. At this time you will not set up any indexes.

As you finish entering a field, dBASE will automatically move you to the next line and add the next number in the Num column. Go ahead and enter the fields for the PRODUCT file now. If you make a mistake, use the arrow keys and the DEL key to make any necessary changes.

To finish the file design, make sure you have pressed RETURN after entering the sixth field so that dBASE moves to the Field Name column for the seventh field. Then press RETURN again without entering a field name; dBASE prompts you to indicate the name of the file. Enter **A:PRODUCT;** dBASE will save the file on your disk under the name PRODUCT.DBF.

After you have saved the file structure, the message line will display a message asking if you want to input data into this file at this time. Respond **N** to this prompt; you will be returned to the Control Center.

Now the Data panel in the Control Center will include PRODUCT as well as <create> in the active area above the dividing line. Highlight the <create> item in the Data panel and press RETURN to create a second file. On the design screen create the following fields:

Num	Field Name	Field Type	Width	Dec	Index
1	SUPP_ID	Character	3		N
2	SUPP_NAME	Character	15		N
3	SUPP_PHONE	Character	8		N

Press RETURN after entering the third field and then press RETURN again when the cursor is on the Field Name column of the fourth field. After the prompt "Save as:", type **A:SUPPLIER** and press RETURN; and your file will be saved on your disk as SUPPLIER.DBF. When the message line displays the prompt asking you if you want to insert data records, answer **Y.** A default form like that shown in Exhibit F.4 will appear.

Entering Data

The status bar at the bottom of the screen indicates that you are viewing the Edit screen. In Edit mode, you can work on one record in a table at a time. On your screen, the area after each field name is blank since your file currently does not contain any data. After you enter data in a field, you can press TAB or RETURN to move to the next field. While a record is on the screen, you can use the arrow keys or TAB and SHIFT-TAB to move around and fix any mistakes. When the last field is filled in and you press RETURN,

Exhibit F.4

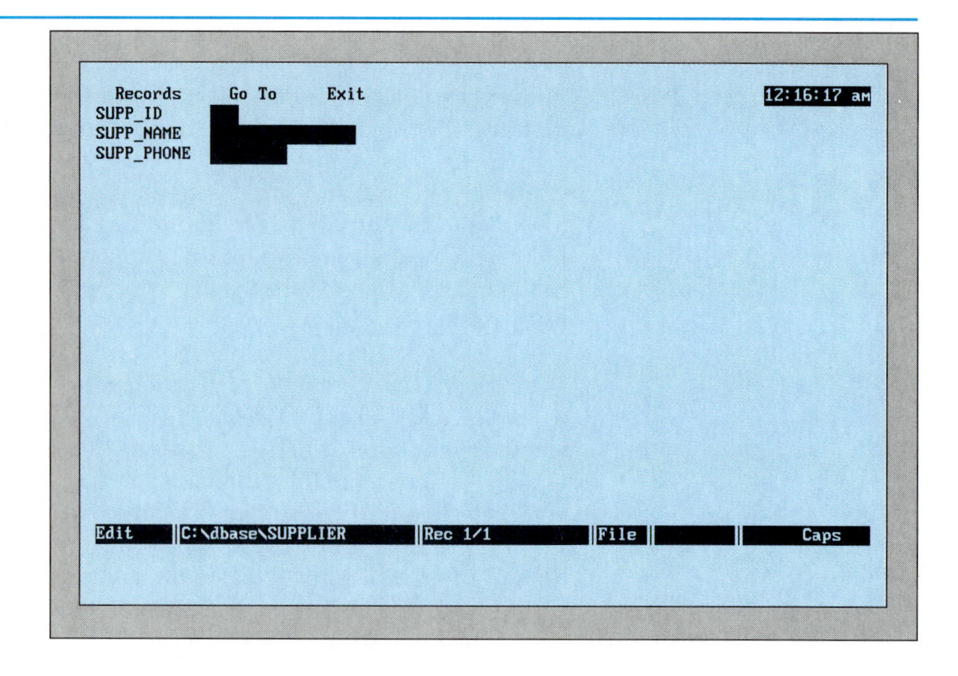

the final record is placed in the file and the fields are blanked out so that you can enter the next record.

Enter the following records in your SUPPLIER file:

SUPP_ID	SUPP_NAME	SUPP_PHONE
111	HERBST ELEC.	555-2343
222	P & W ELEC.	555-4389
333	HIGH VOLTAGE	555-5489
444	IMACO	555-4783

Make sure you use the same capitalization that appears above. As you enter these records, you will notice that if you completely fill a field, dBASE will beep and automatically move to the next field. This will occur on the SUPP_ID and SUPP_PHONE fields. When you fill in the phone number, dBASE will automatically move to the next record as you type the last digit since that is the last field in the record.

To see records that are already entered, you can activate the Go To pull-down menu, which gives you options for going to the top or bottom record in the file or going to a specific record number. Records are always stored in your file in the order they were entered. This is the order in which the records will appear in Edit mode unless you set up an index (see Exercise 2). Even without using the Go To menu, you can move through the records in the file with the PGUP and PGDN keys.

In addition to Edit mode, dBASE IV includes a Browse mode to show several records at a time. Now that you have entered the Supplier records, press the F2 key (Data) and dBASE will automatically switch to Browse mode. Press the ↑ key three times to see all the records you have entered (see Exhibit F.5). On this screen you can use the arrow keys and TAB to move around. At this time, look over your data and fix any mistakes you may find. When you are finished, hold down the ALT key and press **E** to get the Exit menu. Choose the Exit option to return to the Control Center.

Now the Data panel will show SUPPLIER as the active file since it is above the dividing line along with the <create> item. The PRODUCT file appears below the dividing line, indicating that it is not currently active. To enter data into the PRODUCT table, move the highlight to the word PRODUCT in the Data panel. Press the F2 key (Data) to access the Edit screen for the PRODUCT data file. On this screen, enter the following records, making sure you use the same capitalization:

CODE	DESCRIPTION	GROUP	QNTY	PRICE	SUPPLIER
12111	KEYBOARD	COMPUTER	200	125.00	111
12222	TURNTABLE	STEREO	45	175.95	222
12333	HARD DISK	COMPUTER	320	350.00	111
12444	SPEAKER	STEREO	345	59.90	333
12555	RECEIVER	STEREO	100	150.00	222
12666	ANTENNA	TELEVISION	35	15.89	444
12777	COLOR TV	TELEVISION	10	259.00	444
12888	DISK DRIVE	COMPUTER	125	204.00	222
12999	MONITOR	COMPUTER	36	235.00	111
12112	NEEDLE	STEREO	340	7.95	333
12113	B & W TV	TELEVISION	359	175.00	333

Once you have entered the last record, press the F2 key (Data) to switch to Browse mode. Press ↑ ten times to reveal all the records you have

Exhibit F.5
dBase Browse Screen

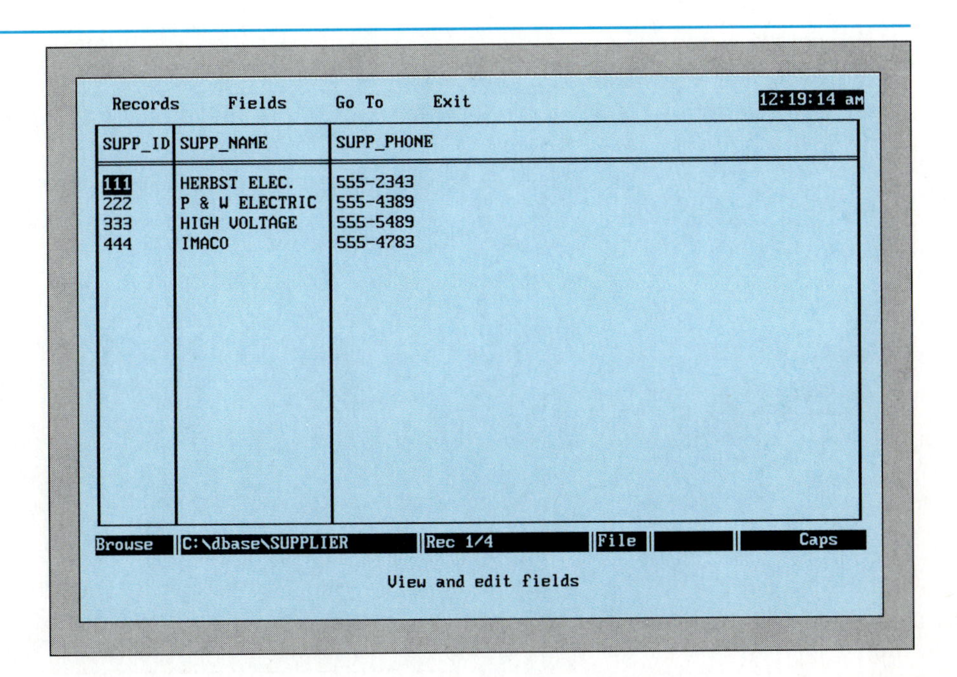

entered. On the Browse screen, check your data and correct any errors you may have made. Then hold down the CTRL key and press END. This has the same effect as selecting the Exit option in the Exit pull-down menu; it will return you to the Control Center once again.

Printing File Structures and Data

To print a copy of the data in your PRODUCT file, highlight the PRODUCT item in the Data panel and press SHIFT-F9 (Quick Report) to get a default report showing the data in the file. Make sure your printer is ready and then select the Begin printing option from the menu that appears. The resulting report will look like Exhibit F.6.

To print the structure of the PRODUCT file, press SHIFT-F2 key (Design) while the PRODUCT item is highlighted in the Data panel. On the Design screen the Organize pull-down menu should already be activated (if not, hold down ALT and press **O**). Use the ← key to move to the Layout menu and choose the Print database structure option. Make sure the printer is ready and then select the Begin printing option.

To leave the design screen, press ESC and select **Y** to abandon the design task since you weren't really altering the design.

Use the same procedure to print the data for the SUPPLIER file and the structure for the SUPPLIER file. This finishes the first exercise. To leave dBASE, press F10 (Menus) and move to the Exit menu. Highlight the Quit to DOS choice and press RETURN to leave dBASE.

Exhibit F.6

dBase Quick Report

Page No. 1
01/01/80

PROD_CODE	PROD_DESC	PROD_GROUP	STOCK_QNTY	PROD_PRICE	PROD_SUPP
12111	KEYBOARD	COMPUTER	200	125.00	111
12222	TURNTABLE	STEREO	45	175.95	222
12333	HARD DISK	COMPUTER	320	350.00	111
12444	SPEAKER	STEREO	345	59.90	333
12555	RECEIVER	STEREO	100	150.00	222
12666	ANTENNA	TELEVISION	35	15.89	444
12777	COLOR TV	TELEVISION	10	259.00	444
12888	DISK DRIVE	COMPUTER	125	204.00	222
12999	MONITOR	COMPUTER	36	235.00	111
12112	NEEDLE	STEREO	340	7.95	333
12113	B & W TV	TELEVISION	359	175.00	333
			1915	1757.69	

Cancel viewing: ESC, Continue viewing: SPACEBAR

Exercise 2: Organizing and Displaying Data

To begin Exercise 2, get back into dBASE IV and make the PURCHASE catalog the current catalog by selecting the Use a different catalog option in the Catalog pull-down menu, if necessary.

As mentioned in Exercise 1, the records in your data files are in the order in which they were entered into the file. This is the order in which the records will appear when you edit or browse the records and when you display the records on queries and reports. There are two methods of changing the order in which records are displayed: indexing and sorting.

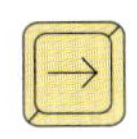

File Organization

A file can have indexes created for any field. Several indexes can be created for a single file, but only one index can be active at a time. An index alters the order of the records when you are editing or browsing the data and when the data are displayed on queries and reports. The actual order in which the records are stored in the file, however, is unchanged.

In contrast, sorting actually changes the order in which records are stored in the file. Sorting creates a second file into which the records from the current data file are copied in the order specified. After such a sort, you have two data files with the exact same structure and data; the only difference is the order of the records.

Creating Indexes

To see how indexing works, you will set up two indexes on the PRODUCT file and see how they affect the display of data.

Follow these steps to set up an index on the PROD_GROUP field:

1. Highlight the PRODUCT file in the Control Center Data panel.
2. Press (RETURN); a box will appear with three choices.
3. Highlight the Modify structure/order option and press (RETURN).
4. The Design screen should appear; the Organize pull-down menu should automatically be activated; and the Create new index option should be highlighted. Press (RETURN).
5. The Index box should appear (see Exhibit F.7). The Name of index option is highlighted; press (RETURN).
6. Type **GROUPS** and press (RETURN).
7. The Index expression option is highlighted; press (RETURN).
8. Press (SHIFT)-(F1) (Pick).
9. A list of the fields in the file appears. Highlight the PROD_GROUP field and press (RETURN).
10. Press (RETURN) to finish the expression field.
11. Press (CTRL)-(END) to save your index settings.

Exhibit F.7
Index Box

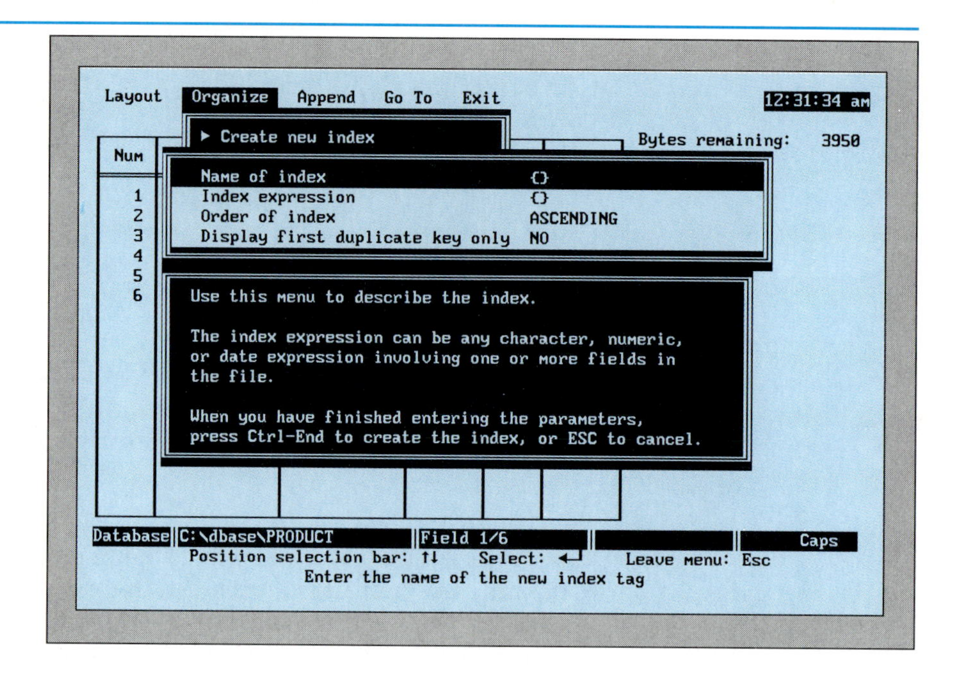

Follow these steps to set up an index on the PROD_CODE field:

1. Press ALT-**O** to bring back the Organize menu.
2. The Create new index option should be highlighted; press RETURN.
3. The Name of index option is highlighted, press RETURN.
4. Type **CODES** and press RETURN.
5. The Index expression option is highlighted; press RETURN.
6. Press SHIFT-F1 (Pick).
7. A list of the fields in the file appears. Highlight the PROD_CODE field and press RETURN.
8. Press RETURN again to finish the expression field.
9. Press CTRL-END to save your index settings.

To see a display using the GROUPS index, use the following steps:

1. Press ALT-**O** to bring the Organize menu back again.
2. Highlight the Order records by index option and press RETURN.
3. Highlight the GROUPS index from the resulting list and press RETURN.
4. Press F2 (Data). The Browse screen is displayed; note how the records are in order by groups.
5. Press ESC to return to the Control Center.

To display the file using the CODES index, follow these steps:

1. The PRODUCT file in the Data panel should still be highlighted. Press (SHIFT)-(F2) (Design).
2. The Design screen appears, and then the Organize menu automatically appears.
3. Highlight the Order records by index option and press (RETURN).
4. Highlight the CODES index from the resulting list and press (RETURN).
5. Press the (F2) (Data) key. The Browse screen is displayed; note how the records are in order by codes.
6. Press (ESC) to return to the Control Center.

Sorting Files

The following steps illustrate the sorting process. You will create a second file called SUPPSORT containing the records in the PRODUCT file sorted by the PROD_SUPP field.

1. The PRODUCT item in the Data panel should still be highlighted. Press (SHIFT)-(F2) (Design) to get the Design screen.
2. The Organize menu automatically appears. Highlight the Sort database on field list option and press (RETURN).
3. A box with two columns will appear. With the cursor in the left column, press (SHIFT)-(F1) (Pick).
4. Highlight the PROD_SUPP field from the resulting list and press (RETURN) to select PROD_SUPP.
5. Press (RETURN) again to finish the sort field.
6. In the right-hand column, a default sort of Ascending appears. Press (RETURN) to accept the default sort type.
7. The highlight will move to the next line, ready for another field. Press (RETURN) to finish entering fields.
8. Enter **A:SUPPSORT** as the name for the sorted file.
9. Press (CTRL)-(END) to indicate you are finished.
10. Answer **N** to the prompt asking if you want to Input records.

To look at the data in the sorted file, highlight the SUPPSORT entry in the Data panel on the Control Center screen. Press (F2) (Data) to look at the data. The Browse screen will appear, showing the records in the SUPPSORT file in order by the value in the PROD_SUPP field. Press (ESC) to leave the Browse screen and return to the Control Center.

Since you don't need the SUPPSORT file to be kept permanently, use the steps on the next page to delete this file from the PURCHASE catalog.

1. Highlight the SUPPSORT entry in the Data panel and press (RETURN).
2. In the resulting box, the Close file option is highlighted; press (RETURN).
3. Highlight the SUPPSORT entry in the Data panel again. Then press the (DEL) key.
4. At the confirmation prompt, press **Y** to acknowledge the delete.
5. A second prompt appears, asking to delete the SUPPSORT disk file. Press **Y** again to delete the SUPPSORT.DBF file from your disk. Now the sorted version of the PRODUCT file is gone.

Displaying Data

This section will introduce you to dBASE queries. In general, a dBASE **query** is a template layout that indicates what data is to be displayed from one or more files in the database. The user can indicate which fields are to be displayed and set up a condition specifying that only some of the records are to be displayed. As the data are displayed, the user can have the records sorted and can set up fields that represent calculations.

The instructions for a query are stored in a file. All the queries created using the tables of the database are displayed in the Queries panel of the Control Center. These queries can then be used to print data and can be used as the basis for forms and reports.

Filtering Fields

The steps below will guide you through the process of creating a query that will display data from some of the fields in a file. Before beginning with the first query, make sure that no files are active in the Data panel. If any file besides the <create> item appears above the dividing line in the Data panel, highlight that item, press (RETURN), and use the Close file option to make the file inactive. Once this is done, follow these steps to create a query:

1. Move the cursor to the <create> item in the Queries panel and press (RETURN).
2. The Query screen appears. The Layout menu automatically appears with the Add a file to query option highlighted. Press (RETURN) to pick this option.
3. In the list that appears, the PRODUCT.DBF entry is highlighted; press (RETURN).

At this point dBASE will read the structure of the PRODUCT file and display a File skeleton at the top of the screen (see Exhibit F.8). This screen uses a query-by-example (QBE) interface to allow the user to build a prototype of the information to be displayed by the query.

The File skeleton represents an outline of the PRODUCT file. The first column heading is the file itself (PRODUCT.DBF), then there are headings for each field in the file. A highlight appears in the row below the

Exhibit F.8

File Selection and Query Screen

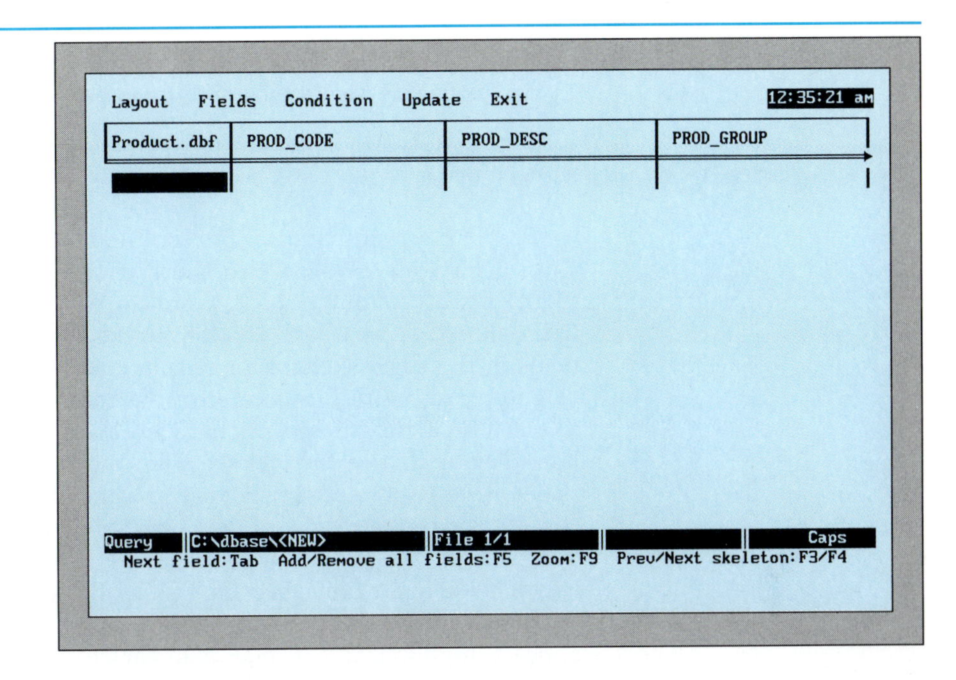

headings and can be moved left and right along the row using (TAB) and (SHIFT)-(TAB). Note that not all of the columns in the PRODUCT file are displayed. If you move to the right, the screen will scroll to reveal additional columns that did not fit on the screen.

In the File skeleton, you will indicate which fields are to be included in the query (also called a view), set up conditions to indicate which records are to be displayed, indicate sorting, and produce summary statistics. In the current query, you will only be concerned with indicating which fields are to be included in the query. The other options will be illustrated later.

To include a field in the query, in the file skeleton move the highlight under the column heading corresponding to the field you want to include and press (F5) (Field).

When (F5) (Field) is pressed, a downward pointing arrow appears in front of the column heading in the file skeleton and a box appears at the bottom of the screen for each column. This area at the bottom of the screen is known as the View skeleton.

The View skeleton is a representation of what the query will look like. The first box will eventually contain the name of the query, but since you have not yet named it, the word NEW appears here.

The second box represents the column that has been selected as the first field in the query. To see how this works follow these steps:

1. Use (TAB) to position the highlight under the PROD_CODE column.
2. Press (F5) (Field). The View skeleton appears with PROD_CODE in the second box.
3. Use (TAB) to put the highlight under the PROD_PRICE column.

4. Press F5 (Field). A third box appears for the PROD_PRICE field.
5. Use SHIFT-TAB to put the highlight under the STOCK_QNTY column.
6. Press F5 (Field). A fourth box appears, indicating STOCK_QNTY is the next field.

The screen should now look like Exhibit F.9. The File skeleton should have arrows next to the PROD_CODE, STOCK_QNTY, and PROD_PRICE column headings, and corresponding boxes for each of those fields should appear at the bottom in the View skeleton. The order of the fields in the View skeleton represents the order in which the fields were selected from the File skeleton. Note how the STOCK_QNTY and PROD_PRICE fields appear in the View skeleton in the opposite order from how they appear in the File skeleton. When selecting fields for the View skeleton, you can select any fields you want, in any order you want.

To see the results of the query, press CTRL-END to save the query design. Enter **A:QUERY1** after the Save as: prompt. This will save your query layout in a file called QUERY1.QBE. In the Control Center Query panel, highlight the QUERY1 entry and press RETURN. In the box that appears, highlight the Display data choice and press RETURN. Exhibit F.10 shows the resulting display.

Press ESC when you are finished viewing the data. If you would like a hard copy of the results of the query, highlight the QUERY1 entry in the Queries panel and press SHIFT-F9 (Quick Report). After making sure the printer is ready, select the Begin printing option from the menu.

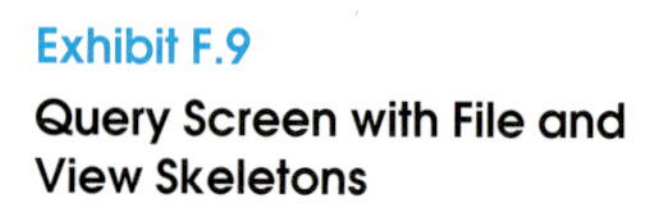

Exhibit F.9

Query Screen with File and View Skeletons

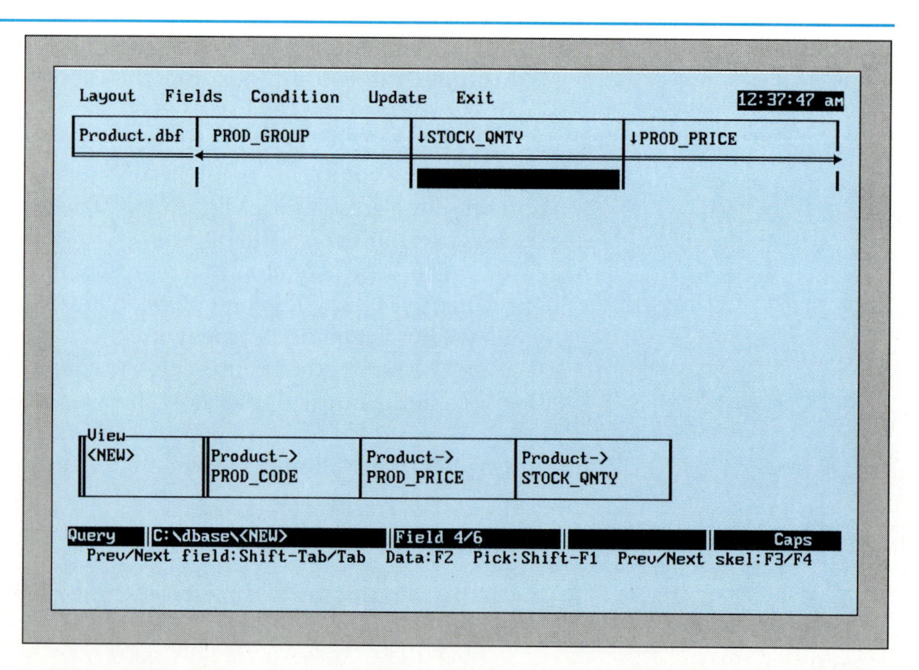

Exhibit F.10

Browse Screen—Results of Query

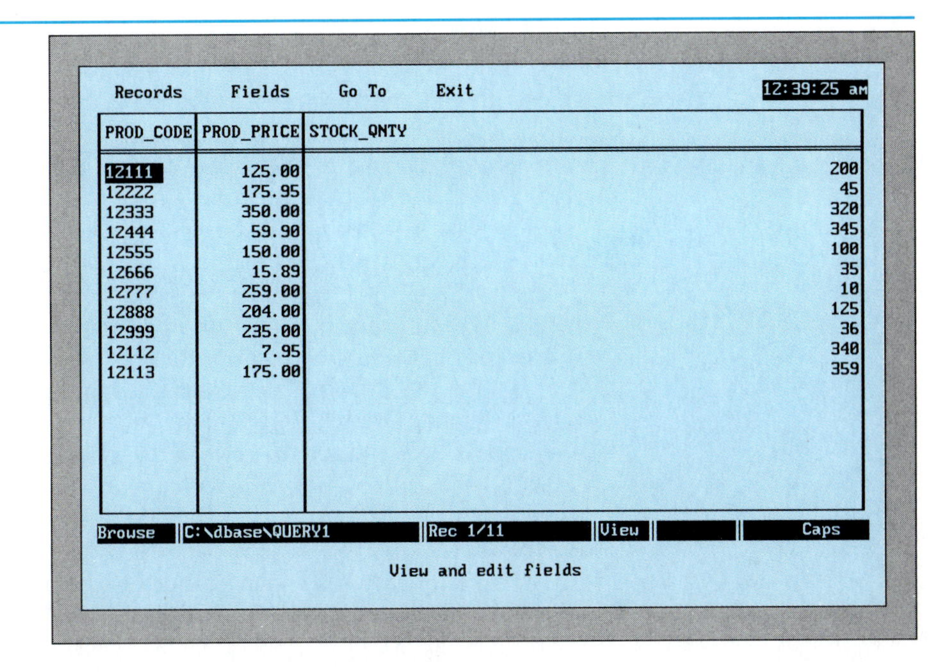

PROD_CODE	PROD_PRICE	STOCK_QNTY
12111	125.00	200
12222	175.95	45
12333	350.00	320
12444	59.90	345
12555	150.00	100
12666	15.89	35
12777	259.00	10
12888	204.00	125
12999	235.00	36
12112	7.95	340
12113	175.00	359

Filtering Records

The query described below will introduce you to the construction of queries that result in the display of a subset of the records in a file. Before beginning, make sure that no files are active (above the dividing line) in the Data panel of the Control Center. Follow these steps to create the query:

1. Highlight the <create> option in the Queries panel and press (RETURN).
2. The Layout menu will automatically appear with the Add a file to query option highlighted. Press (RETURN).
3. PRODUCT.DBF is highlighted; press (RETURN).
4. Use (TAB) to move the highlight under the PROD_CODE field.
5. Press (F5) (Field) to include the field in the View skeleton.
6. Use (TAB) to move the highlight under the PROD_DESC field.
7. Press (F5) (Field) to include the field in the View skeleton.
8. Use (TAB) to move the highlight under the PROD_PRICE field.
9. Press (F5) (Field) to include the field in the View skeleton.
10. Use (SHIFT)-(TAB) to move the highlight under the STOCK_QNTY field.
11. Press (F5) (Field) to include the field in the View skeleton.
12. Use (SHIFT)-(TAB) to move the highlight under the PROD_GROUP field.
13. Press (F5) (Field) to include the field in the View skeleton.
14. Use (TAB) to move the highlight under the STOCK_QNTY field again.
15. Type **>100** and press (RETURN).

The last step is the key to filtering records. To filter records, the user must set up a true/false condition that can be applied to the records in the file to determine which records will be displayed. The condition will always involve one or more of the fields in the file. Thus, conditions are represented by placing an example of the condition under the column heading for the field used to determine which records will be displayed. In the current query, records will be printed if the value in the STOCK_QNTY field is greater than 100.

Press (CTRL)-(END) to save your query design and enter the name **A:QUERY2** after the Save as: prompt. This will save your query layout in a file called QUERY2.QBE on your disk.

On the Control Center screen, highlight the QUERY2 entry in the Queries panel, press (RETURN), highlight the Display data option, and press (RETURN). You should see the code, description, price, quantity, and group for all products with a quantity greater than 100. Press (ESC) after viewing the data. If you want a printout, use (SHIFT)-(F9) (Quick Print) as you did with QUERY1.

To illustrate a filtering condition that involves a character field, use the steps following to produce a query that displays only products in the COMPUTER group:

1. Highlight the <create> option in the Queries panel and press (RETURN).
2. The Layout menu will automatically appear with the Add a file to query option highlighted. Press (RETURN).
3. PRODUCT.DBF is highlighted; press (RETURN).
4. Use (TAB) to move the highlight under the PROD_CODE field.
5. Press (F5) (Field) to include the field in the View skeleton.
6. Use (TAB) to move the highlight under the PROD_DESC field.
7. Press (F5) (Field) to include the field in the View skeleton.
8. Use (TAB) to move the highlight under the PROD_PRICE field.
9. Press (F5) (Field) to include the field in the View skeleton.
10. Use (SHIFT)-(TAB) to move the highlight under the STOCK_QNTY field.
11. Press (F5) (Field) to include the field in the View skeleton.
12. Use (SHIFT)-(TAB) to move the highlight under the PROD_GROUP field.
13. Press (F5) (Field) to include the field in the View skeleton.
14. The highlight will still be under the PROD_GROUP field. Type **"COMPUTER"** (with the quotation marks) and press (RETURN).

In the condition below the PROD_GROUP field, you must place quotation marks around the example entry, and you must capitalize the word COMPUTER so that it matches the data in the file. In a character field, a condition is created by entering the text that you want dBASE to match when selecting records to display. In this case, records that contain the word COMPUTER in the PROD_GROUP field will be displayed.

After entering the condition, press CTRL-END to save the query. Type **A:QUERY3** after the Save as: prompt and press RETURN.

Highlight the QUERY3 entry in Queries panel of the Control Center and press RETURN. Highlight the Display data option and press RETURN to verify that the query is displaying only the four products in the COMPUTER group. Press ESC when you are finished viewing the data. If you want a printout of the data, use SHIFT-F9 (Quick Report) as described in the first query.

Conditions Involving More Than One Field

In the File skeleton on the Query Design screen, it is possible to enter conditions under more than one field for the same query. When this is done, the user can decide if the multiple conditions must all be simultaneously true for a record to be selected (a logical AND relationship) or if records are to be selected if any one of the conditions is true (a logical OR relationship). The two queries below will illustrate the use of multiple conditions in a single query.

To illustrate a multiple condition in which all conditions must simultaneously be true for a record to be selected, follow these steps:

1. Highlight the <create> option in the Queries panel and press RETURN.
2. The Layout menu will automatically appear with the Add a file to query option highlighted. Press RETURN.
3. PRODUCT.DBF is highlighted; press RETURN. The highlight appears under the first column—PRODUCT.DBF.

This column in the File skeleton represents the entire file rather than one of the fields. Pressing F5 (Field) under this column will select all the fields for printing in the order they appear in the file. Follow these steps to complete the query:

4. Press F5 (Field) to select all the fields for the query.
5. Use TAB to move below the STOCK_QNTY field and enter **>100.**
6. Use SHIFT-TAB to move below the PROD_GROUP field and enter **"COMPUTER"**.
7. Press CTRL-END.
8. Enter **A:QUERY4** after the Save as: prompt and press RETURN.

To see the results of this query, highlight the QUERY4 entry in the Queries panel and press RETURN. Then select the Display data option. The resulting screen should show the three products in the COMPUTER group that also have a STOCK_QNTY greater than 100. Since both of the conditions in the File skeleton appear on the same row below the column headings, dBASE assumes that both conditions must simultaneously be true for the record to be displayed. Thus, the PROD_GROUP field must contain the word COMPUTER and the STOCK_QNTY field must contain a value greater than 100 for a record to be selected for display. Press ESC when you are finished.

To create a multiple condition in which a true result in any condition will cause a record to be selected for display, follow these steps:

1. Highlight the <create> option in the Queries panel and press (RETURN).
2. The Layout menu will automatically appear with the Add a file to query option highlighted. Press (RETURN).
3. PRODUCT.DBF is highlighted; press (RETURN).
4. Place the highlight under the PRODUCT.DBF column (the first column).
5. Use (F5) (Field) to include all the fields in the query.
6. Use (TAB) to move below the STOCK_QNTY column and enter **>100**.
7. Use (SHIFT)-(TAB) to move the highlight below the PROD_GROUP column.
8. Press the (↓) key to move to the second row.
9. Enter **"COMPUTER"** on this second line.
10. Press (CTRL)-(END).
11. Enter **A:QUERY5** after the Save as: prompt and press (RETURN).

To see the results of this query, highlight the QUERY5 entry in the Queries panel and press (RETURN). Then highlight the Display data option and press (RETURN). The resulting screen should show seven products: any product in the COMPUTER group and any product with a quantity greater than 100. Since the conditions in the File skeleton appear on the different rows below the column headings, dBASE applies each condition to the records separately. This results in the display of any records meeting the first condition *or* any records meeting the second condition. Press (ESC) when you are finished viewing the data.

If you want a printout of the data from QUERY4 or QUERY5 use (SHIFT)-(F9) (Quick Report), as described previously.

Queries Involving More Than One File

It is also possible to produce a query that displays fields from more than one file. This type of query requires files to have a common field that can be used to match or join records from the two files. In the PURCHASE database, the PRODUCT file contains a PROD_SUPP field that contains the same supplier numbers found in the SUPP_ID field of the SUPPLIER file. Thus, it is possible to display data from both files simultaneously by matching records that have the same supplier number.

As an example, suppose you wanted to display the code, description, and price for products in the PRODUCT file and also display the number, name, and phone number in the SUPPLIER file for the supplier of each product. To produce this query, follow these steps:

1. Highlight the <create> option in the Queries panel and press (RETURN).

2. The Layout menu will automatically appear with the Add a file to query option highlighted. Press (RETURN).
3. PRODUCT.DBF is highlighted; press (RETURN).
4. Use (F5) (Field) to select the PROD_CODE, PROD_DESC, and PROD_PRICE fields, in that order.
5. This completes the fields needed from the PRODUCT File skeleton. Press (F10) (Menus) key.
6. In the Layout menu, highlight the Add a file to query option again and press (RETURN).
7. This time, highlight the SUPPLIER.DBF file and press (RETURN).
8. A Supplier File skeleton appears below the PRODUCT File skeleton. Use (F5) (Field) to select the SUPP_ID, SUPP_NAME, and SUPP_PHONE fields, in that order.

Now that all the fields for the query have been selected, you must tell dBASE how to link the records in the two files together. This is done by placing the same entry below the matching field in each File skeleton. Placing the same entry in both File skeletons tells dBASE to match records that have the same value in those two fields. The entry made in the columns can be anything; the key is that the entry must be the same in both File skeletons.

In this example query, the PROD_SUPP field in the PRODUCT file needs to be matched with the SUPP_ID field in the SUPPLIER file. To link the two files and complete the query, use the following steps:

1. Use (TAB) to move the highlight under the SUPP_ID field.
2. Type **SUPPLIER**.
3. Press (F3) (Previous) to move to the PRODUCT File skeleton.
4. Use (TAB) to move the highlight under the PROD_SUPP field.
5. Type **SUPPLIER.**
6. Press (CTRL)-(END) and type **A:QUERY6** after the Save as: prompt.

Note how the linking entry is the same under the common field in the two files. Also note that this entry is not in quotes since it is not to be considered as part of a condition for filtering records. Highlight the QUERY6 entry in the Queries panel and press (RETURN). Then select the Display data option. The resulting screen should show all the products and the matching supplier information for the supplier of each product. Press (ESC) when you are finished. As before, use (SHIFT)-(F9) (Quick Report) to get a printout, if you want one.

Sorting Records in a Query

All the previous queries have displayed the records from the file in the order in which they are normally displayed in the file itself. Since the order of the records in your PRODUCT file is determined by the index that is currently in effect, the order of the records displayed in all your queries has also been governed by the same current index. Thus, one way of ordering records in queries is to set up an index and make that the current index. Of course, that would mean that you must be certain that index is always the current index whenever you execute a query needing that particular order. In addition, an index can only order the records on the basis of one field at a time.

To overcome these limitations, dBASE allows a sort to be specified in the query itself. To experiment with sorting and to see how an existing query can be changed, follow these steps:

1. Highlight the QUERY1 entry in the Queries panel and press (RETURN).
2. Highlight the Modify query option and press (RETURN).
3. Put the highlight under the PROD_GROUP field and press (F5) (Field) to add this field to the query.
4. Type **ASC1** under the PROD_GROUP field.
5. Press (CTRL)-(END) to save the query.

Since you are modifying an existing query, you will not be asked to give a name for the query. The ASC1 you placed below the PROD_GROUP field in the File skeleton stands for an ascending sort. Since this entry is not enclosed in quotes, dBASE will interpret it as an instruction to sort. The number 1 after the ASC indicates that the sorting on this field is to be the first (or primary) sort for records displayed by the query. Also note how the PROD_GROUP field has been added to the View skeleton so that you will be able to see the effects of this sort. In general, this is not necessary when sorting. You can sort the records on a field that will not be displayed in the results.

To see the results of the sort, highlight the QUERY1 entry in the Queries panel and press (RETURN). Then highlight the Display data option and press (RETURN). Verify that the records are sorted by product group and press (ESC) when you are finished viewing the data. As before, use (SHIFT)-(F9) (Quick Report) if you want a printout of the data using the query.

Multiple Sorts

It is possible to sort on more than one field in a single query. With a multiple sort, you establish a primary sort field and then set up a secondary sort field, which is used to determine the order of records that have the same value in the primary sort field. You can continue to add additional sort fields beyond the secondary sort field as well. Use the following steps to modify the first query for a multiple sort:

1. Highlight the QUERY1 entry in the Queries panel and press (RETURN).
2. Highlight the Modify query option and press (RETURN).
3. Put the highlight under the PROD_PRICE field.
4. Type **DSC2** under the PROD_PRICE field.
5. Press (CTRL)-(END) to save the query.

The DSC indicates a descending sort (highest to lowest) and the 2 indicates that this is to be the secondary sort since there is already an ASC1 under the PROD_GROUP field. This query will sort the records by the PROD_GROUP field in ascending order, and then any records in the same product group will be sorted by product price in descending order. In a multiple sort with primary and secondary sort fields, both fields can be in ascending or descending order, or the fields can be sorted in different orders, as illustrated here.

To see the results of the sort, highlight the QUERY1 entry in the Queries panel and press (RETURN). Then select the Display data option. Verify that the records are sorted by product group and then by product price. Press (ESC) when you are finished viewing the data. As before, use (SHIFT)-(F9) (Quick Report) if you want a printout of the data using the query.

Calculated Fields in Queries

In addition to displaying data from database files, a query can also create new fields from calculations based on other fields in the file. For example, suppose a user wants to determine the value of all the products in the PRODUCT file by multiplying the price of each product by the number of that product in stock. To do this, the user could create a new field containing the result of that multiplication and have the values displayed in that field along with the rest of the fields in the query. The following steps illustrate this process:

1. Highlight the QUERY2 entry in the Queries panel and press (RETURN).
2. Highlight the Modify query option and press (RETURN).
3. Press (F10) (Menus).
4. Move to the Fields menu and highlight the Create calculated fields option. Press (RETURN).
5. A Calculated Fields skeleton will appear with the highlight in the column heading area. Type **STOCK_QNTY*PROD_PRICE** as the column heading.
6. Press the (↓) key to move the highlight below the heading.
7. Press (F5) (Field) to include the calculated field in the query.
8. A box appears asking for a field name. Type **INVENTORY** and press (RETURN).
9. Press (CTRL)-(END) to save the query.

To see the results of the query, highlight the QUERY2 entry in the Queries panel and press (RETURN). Then select the Display data option. Verify that the calculated field is now included in the query and that it contains the result of the multiplication of the product price and stock quantity. You will have to tab over to the INVENTORY column to see the values displayed there. Press (ESC) when you are finished. As before, use (SHIFT)-(F9) (Quick Report) if you want a printout of the data using the query.

This concludes the example queries. If you wish to stop, you can leave dBASE by using the Exit menu in the Control Center, or you can stay in dBASE and continue with the third exercise.

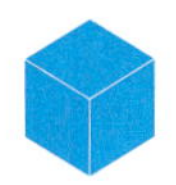

Exercise 3: Forms and Reports

Now that you have learned how to set up data files and queries, you can learn to create forms and reports based on those files and queries. A **form** is basically a microcomputer screen that is used to display text and values from fields in a file or query to the user. A **report** accomplishes the same thing but its output is sent to a printer.

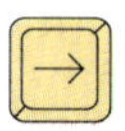

Creating a Simple Form

In this part of the exercise you will learn to create a simple form to display data from a single file. Forms can be simple forms like this one or complex forms based on queries, which show data from several files.

Forms, like data files and queries, have their own panel in the Control Center listing all the forms associated with the current catalog. To begin this exercise, get back into dBASE, if necessary.

First, make sure that no files or queries are currently active in the Control Center. To determine which files or queries are active, look above the line dividing the Data and Queries panels. If any entries appear above the line along with the <create> entry, those entries are considered active. Highlight any active entries, press (RETURN), and use the Close option to make them inactive. (If any files or queries are left active, the form you create will be automatically attached to that file or query. This may or may not be the file or query you want to attach to the form.) Once there are no active files or queries, create a simple form to display the data in the PRODUCT file by following these steps:

1. Highlight the <create> item in the Forms panel and press (RETURN).
2. The Layout menu will automatically appear with the Use different file or view option highlighted. Press (RETURN).
3. Highlight PRODUCT.DBF as the file to attach to the form and press (RETURN). You will see a Forms Design screen similar to Exhibit F.11.

On the Forms Design screen, the ruler at the top indicates your current column position. A cursor appears in the area below this ruler. You can position the cursor anywhere in the area below the ruler and enter text or place fields on the form. To enter text, simply position the cursor and begin typing. The normal dBASE editing keys can be used to alter the text to correct errors. In addition, (F6) (Select) can be used to mark a block of text and the (F7) (Move) can be used to reposition the marked block. Fields are placed on the form by putting the cursor where the field is to begin and then using (F5) (Field) to access a field. Exhibit F.12 shows the completed form for the PRODUCT data.

Exhibit F.11

Form Design Screen

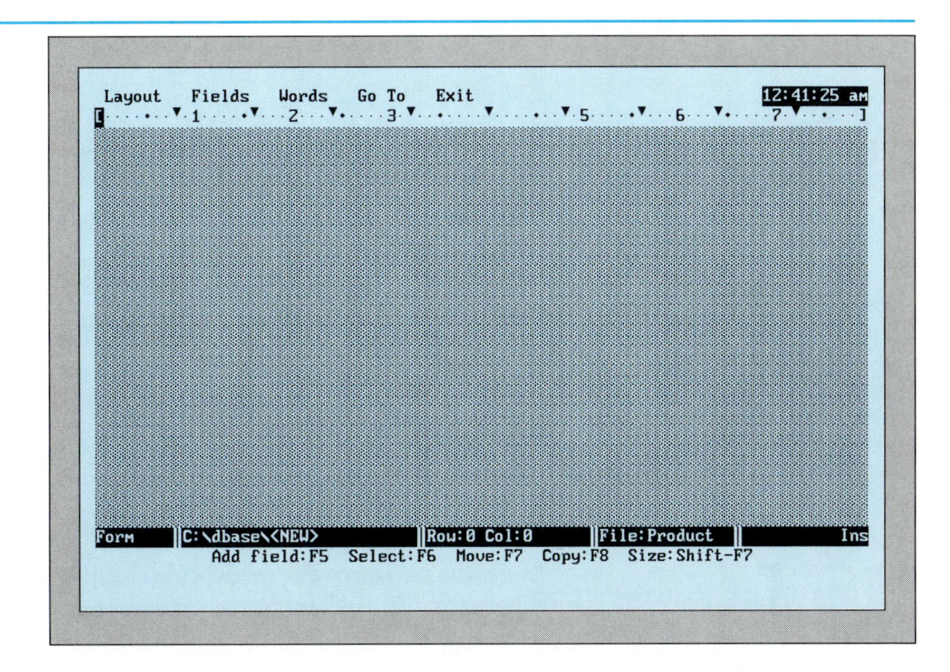

Exhibit F.12

Completed Form

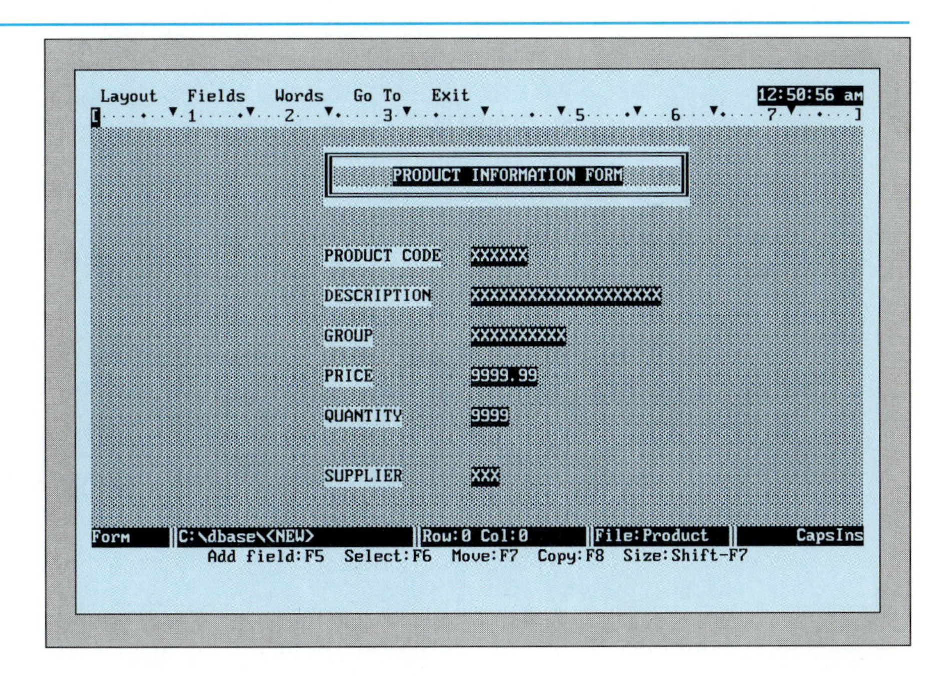

Place the text in the positions shown by positioning the cursor and typing the text. Fix any mistakes as indicated above. Do not attempt to create the box around the title yet.

The X's and 9s are templates where fields have been placed. The X's show the locations for data from character fields and the 9s indicate where data from numeric fields will appear. Place the fields on the form as shown on the next page.

1. Position the cursor where you want the field to begin.
2. Press F5 (Field). A list of fields from the file will appear.
3. Select the field you want and press RETURN. The Display Attributes and Editing Options box appears.
4. The template entry shows the default template for the field. Press CTRL-END to accept the default template. The field is placed on the form.

To create the box around the title, follow this procedure:

1. Press F10 (Menus).
2. In the Layout menu, select the Box option.
3. Choose the Double line option in the submenu.
4. Put the cursor where you want the top left corner and press RETURN.
5. Move the cursor over and down to locate the bottom right corner. A box will expand out as you move the cursor.
6. Press RETURN. The box is now finished.

Use CTRL-END to save your form design; enter **A:PRODFORM** as the name of your form. This will create three files on your disk for the form: PRODFORM.FMT, PRODFORM.FMO, and PRODFORM.SCR.

To see if your form works, highlight the PRODFORM entry in the Forms panel of the Control Center and press RETURN. Then highlight the Display data option and press RETURN. This will produce an Edit screen, but this time the product data will be displayed with your form rather than the default Edit form. The data from the product file should automatically be displayed on the form. You can use the PGUP and PGDN keys to move through the records.

To see how the form can be used to enter data, press F10 (Menus), highlight the Add new records option, and press RETURN. The form will blank out and you can enter the new record. For your new record, use a product code of **12114** and then make up the rest of the product information. Press CTRL-END when you are finished.

Creating a Simple Report

Reports, like forms, can be used to display data from a file or from a query. Since the form above used a file, this report will illustrate the use of a query. Specifically, the report will be based on QUERY2, which was the query containing the INVENTORY calculated field. Calculated fields can also be created within reports and forms.

The reports associated with the current catalog are always listed in the Reports panel of the Control Center. Before beginning the report, you should always look in the Data and Queries panels to determine which entry is currently active. You just finished a form based on the PRODUCT data file, so the PRODUCT entry should be active (above the dividing line) in the Data panel. Since the report is going to be based on the QUERY2 query, highlight the PRODUCT entry in the Data panel, press (RETURN), then highlight the Close file option, and press (RETURN) again. Then highlight the QUERY2 entry in the Queries panel, press (RETURN), highlight the Use view option to make QUERY2 active, and press (RETURN) again. Now you are ready to create the report, as follows:

1. Highlight the <create> entry in the Reports panel and press (RETURN).
2. A Reports Design screen appears (see Exhibit F.13). Press (ESC) to leave the Layout menu that automatically appears.

The Reports Design screen is divided into areas called **bands**. Each band is used to print information at a different place in the report. The first band is the Page Header band. Information placed in this band will appear at the top of each page in the report. The last band is a matching Page Footer band, in which you can place information that is to appear at the bottom of each page. The Report Intro and Report Summary bands contain information that appears at the beginning and end of the report itself. The Detail band represents the records being displayed from the file or query attached to the report.

For more complex reports, you can also add Group bands, which can be used to group the data on the basis of a field in the file or query. For this simple report, you will not be concerned with Group bands.

Exhibit F.14 shows the completed design for this report. Fill in the bands on your Report Design screen as follows:

1. Position your cursor in the Page Header band using the (↓) key.

Exhibit F.13
Report Design Screen

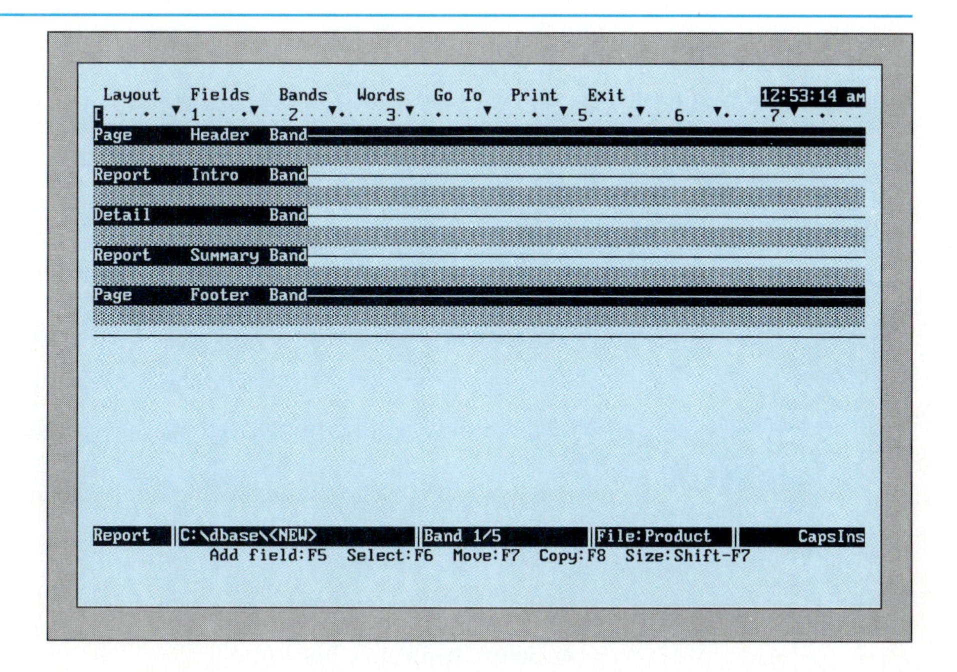

Exhibit F.14

Completed Report Design

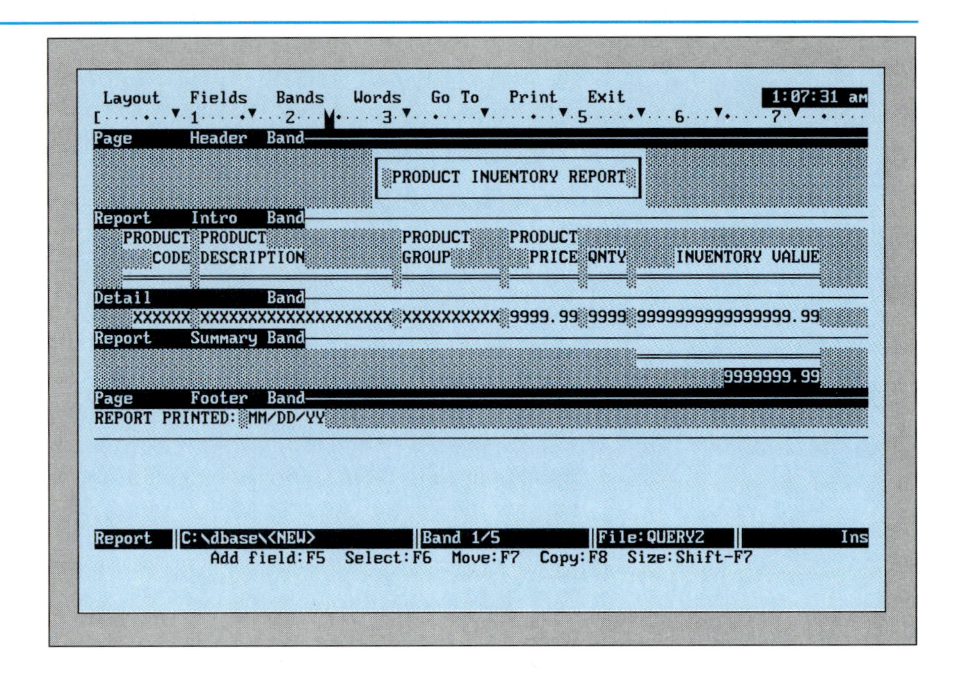

2. Press RETURN twice to expand the band.
3. In position 30 of the middle line of the band, type the title.

Use these steps to create the box:

1. Press F10 (Menus).
2. In the Layout menu, select the Box option.
3. Select the Single line option in the submenu.
4. Position the cursor where you want the box's top left corner and press RETURN.
5. Move the cursor to locate the bottom right corner. The box should expand as you move.
6. Press RETURN when you reach the bottom right corner.

To create the Report Intro perform the following steps:

1. Press ↓ key to move into the Report Intro band.
2. Press RETURN twice to expand the band to three lines.
3. Enter the headings on the first two lines, as shown in the Exhibit F.14.

Follow these steps to create the lines in the Report Intro band:

1. Press F10 (Menus).
2. Select the Line option in the Layout menu.
3. Select the Double line option.

4. Place the cursor where the line begins and press (RETURN).
5. Move the cursor to locate the end of the line and press (RETURN).

Use this same procedure to draw all the lines in the Report Intro band.

To create the Detail band follow these steps:

1. Press the (↓) key to move into the Detail band.
2. Position the cursor where you want a field to begin.
3. Press (F5) (Field) and select the field you want to place from the resulting list. The field definition menu appears.
4. Press (CTRL)-(END) to accept the default template. Use this procedure to place each field in the Detail band.

To create the Report Summary band perform the following procedure:

1. Press the (↓) key to move into the Report Summary band.
2. Press (RETURN) to expand the band to two lines.
3. Put the cursor on the first line. Press (F10) (Menus) and select the Line option in the Layout menu.
4. Select a double line.
5. Move the cursor to location of the line and press (RETURN).
6. Position the cursor at the end of the line and press (RETURN).
7. Move to the second line in the Report Summary band.
8. Move to the location of the field.
9. Press (F5) (Field).
10. Move to the Summary column.
11. Highlight the Sum entry and press (RETURN).
12. The Name entry will be highlighted; press (RETURN).
13. Enter **INVENSUM** as the name of the summary field and press (RETURN).
14. The Field to Summarize entry is highlighted; press (RETURN).
15. Highlight INVENTORY as the field to summarize on and press (RETURN).
16. Press (CTRL)-(END) to finish the summary field.

Use the following steps to create the Page Footer band:

1. Press the (↓) key to move to the Page Footer band.
2. Enter the text at the beginning of the band.
3. Move to the right of the text to the field location and press (F5) (Field).

4. Move to the Predefined fields in the third column.
5. Highlight the Date entry and press (RETURN).
6. Press (CTRL)-(END) to accept the MM/DD/YY default format.

Follow these steps to save the report:

1. Press (CTRL)-(END).
2. Enter **A:INVENREP** as the name of the report.

This report will display the report title at the beginning of each page and the date the report is printed at the bottom of each page. Column headings will appear at the beginning of the report, and a total of the INVENTORY calculated field will be displayed at the end. The detail band will display all the records resulting from the QUERY2 query on which this report is based. To get a copy of your report, highlight the INVENREP entry in the Reports panel of the Control Center, press (RETURN), and select the Print report option. Make sure the printer is ready and then select the Begin printing option.

APPENDIX G

The BASIC Programming Language

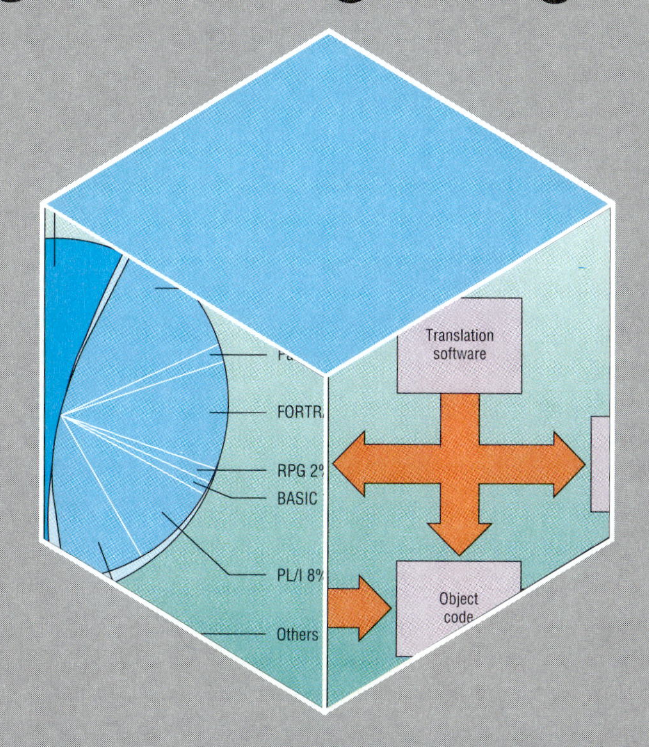

This appendix is a general introduction to structured programming using the BASIC programming language. BASIC, which stands for Beginner's All-purpose Symbolic Instruction Code, was developed by John Kemeny and Thomas Kurtz of Dartmouth College. BASIC first became available for general use in 1964. There are currently many versions of BASIC available. This appendix is designed for use with Microsoft BASIC (commonly known as BASICA or GWBASIC), which runs on IBM and IBM-compatible personal computers.

The programs presented in this appendix are designed to introduce you to the fundamental control structures of programming languages in general, while emphasizing structured programming techniques. This appendix is not designed to be an exhaustive coverage of the BASIC programming language. Many advanced programming concepts, such as arrays, string manipulation, and file handling, are not covered. For more complete information, refer to a comprehensive text for BASIC or the reference manual accompanying your BASIC software.

In this appendix, the various features of BASIC will be introduced gradually, in the context of an example payroll program designed to illustrate structured programming techniques. Instead of being presented in many different program applications, new features are added to the same application. This approach will enable you to concentrate on learning how BASIC commands are used to accomplish certain tasks without having to understand new background information for each application.

To create and execute the payroll program in this appendix, you will need a copy of BASIC compatible with the microcomputer you will be using. It is assumed that you already know how to boot the microcomputer and that you have a basic understanding of the MS-DOS operating system.

The BASIC Environment

BASIC is an **interactive programming language**. With an interactive programming language, the programmer is able to "converse" directly with the computer to build, test, and run programs. This interactive capability allows the programmer to discover programming errors quickly so that he or she can easily change and rerun the program as many times as necessary.

Before you begin working with the BASIC interpreter, the microcomputer must first be booted with the MS-DOS operating system. Once the MS-DOS prompt is reached, the diskette containing the BASIC programming language must be placed in the default drive. The BASIC interpreter is started by typing **BASICA** (or **GWBASIC** when using an IBM-compatible machine) at the MS-DOS prompt and pressing (RETURN).

The BASIC interpreter will be loaded into memory, and following some initial information, the prompt "Ok" will be displayed. Similar to the MS-DOS prompt, the Ok prompt is a signal from the BASIC interpreter that it is waiting for an instruction to be entered. This instruction can be either direct or indirect. A **direct** instruction or command is an instruction that the interpreter will execute immediately after (RETURN) is pressed. An **indirect** instruction or statement is an instruction that is stored by BASIC as part of a program to be executed later.

To differentiate between the two types of instructions, a line number is placed in front of all program statements to tell BASIC that the instruction is part of a program. The line number also indicates to BASIC the relative position of the instruction within the program since all program statements are stored in numerical order by line number.

Like many microcomputer software packages, BASIC is only able to work actively with one program at a time. Thus, as indirect statements are entered, they are combined to form the current program in primary memory. Since the contents of primary memory are temporary, BASIC provides **commands** (direct instructions) that are used to move programs between primary memory and secondary storage diskettes (see Exhibit G.1). These commands allow you to work on different programs by moving one program at a time from disk into primary memory. The program is then saved back on the disk before you move on to the next program.

In general, BASIC commands are direct instructions used to manage the program in primary memory and stored programs on disk.

Exhibit G.1

Working with Programs in Primary Memory

In BASIC, only one program can be active in primary memory. Additional programs must be moved to and from secondary storage.

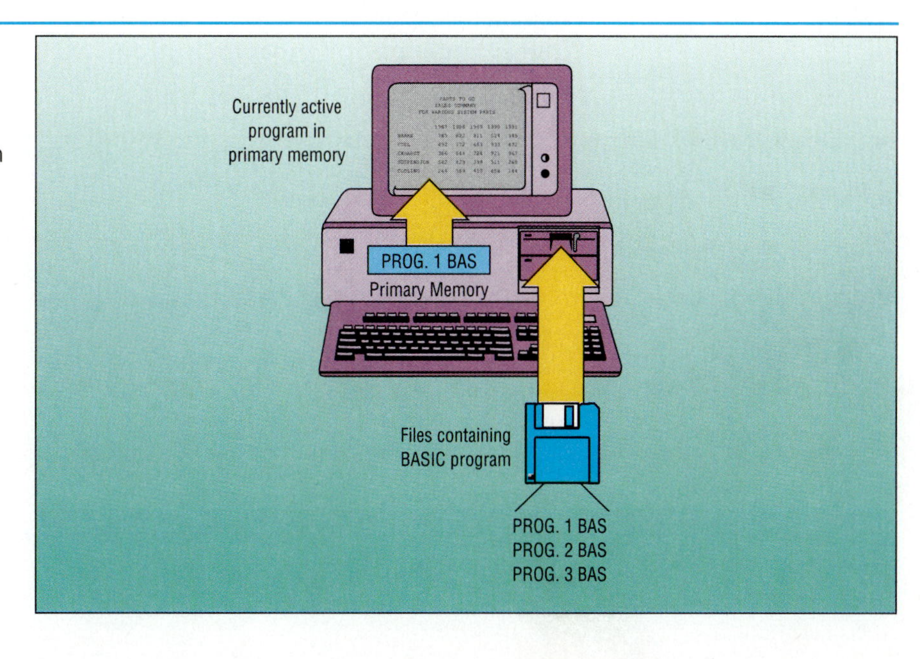

BASIC **statements** are indirect instructions that are stored as part of a program. They are executed as a group whenever the program is run.

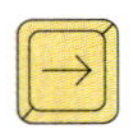

Program Elements

To begin writing BASIC programs, it is necessary to understand the fundamental elements of a BASIC program. These elements include the statements, each containing a keyword from the BASIC language, and variables, which are used to hold data to be processed.

BASIC Statements

As indicated above, the statements that make up a BASIC program begin with a line number that is used to position the statement within the program (see Exhibit G.2). BASIC will automatically arrange the statements in primary memory in ascending order by line number. In BASIC, a line number can be any whole number from 0 to 65529, with no two statements having the same line number.

The line number in each statement is followed by a keyword that indicates the type of processing BASIC is to perform. Examples of keywords in Exhibit G.2 include REM, INPUT, LET, PRINT, and END. When writing statements, keywords must be spelled correctly and must have at least one space before and after.

A statement within a program is created in the interpreter simply by typing a line number followed by the statement that is to be entered. When (RETURN) is pressed, the statement is stored in primary memory as part of the current program. The order in which the program statements are typed is not important. The statements will be automatically sorted by BASIC according to line number.

You can number your program statements with any numbers within the 0 to 65529 range. You do not have to begin with the number 1. As the example payroll program in Exhibit G.2 illustrates, it is common to

```
 10   REM      VERSION 1
 20   REM
 30   REM      THIS PROGRAM CALCULATES THE TOTAL PAY FOR AN EMPLOYEE
 40   REM      GIVEN THE PAY RATE FOR THE EMPLOYEE AND THE HOURS WORKED
 50   REM
 60   REM      RATE     - PAY RATE FOR THE EMPLOYEE
 70   REM      HOURS    - HOURS WORKED
 80   REM      PAY      - TOTAL PAY
 90   REM
100   INPUT RATE
110   INPUT HOURS
120   LET PAY = RATE*HOURS
130   PRINT PAY
140   END
```

Exhibit G.2

An Example BASIC Program

number program statements in increments of ten (10, 20, 30, 40, and so on). This allows additional statements to be inserted in the program later by simply entering the new statement with a number between two existing line numbers. For example, if a new statement was required between statements 100 and 110, it could be entered as line number 105. BASIC would automatically place the new statement between statements 100 and 110. If you number your program statements in increments of one (1, 2, 3, 4 . . .), it is not possible to enter additional statements between existing ones without renumbering the existing lines in the program.

Constants, Variables, and Expressions

The purpose of all programs is to manipulate data. Most of the keywords in BASIC statements are designed to input data, perform computations with data, or display data. Data within a program can be one of two basic forms: constant or variable. These two basic forms can also be combined to produce more complex expressions.

A **variable** is the name of a location in primary memory where a piece of data is stored while the program is using it. The actual data stored in that location can change (or vary) each time the program is executed. The example payroll program in Exhibit G.2 contains three variables: RATE, HOURS, and PAY. RATE and HOURS represent a pay rate for and number of hours worked by an employee, respectively. When this program is executed, the user will type the pay rate and the hours worked, and BASIC will store those two pieces of data in storage locations RATE and HOURS. The data in these two locations are then multiplied to get the total pay, which is stored in the PAY variable. The next time the program is executed, the user may enter a different pay rate and hours worked.

Variables are used because BASIC can directly interact only with data stored in primary memory. Thus, data must be placed in the primary memory location represented by the variable name so that BASIC can perform additional operations with that data. Once the data are processed, new data can be moved into those primary memory locations to replace the data already processed. Thus, variables represent the data that are currently being processed by the program (see Exhibit G.3).

In addition to variables, BASIC can also work with constants. A **constant** is a piece of data whose value remains the same every time the program is run. For example, if the program contained the statement

```
120 LET PAY = RATE*40
```

the 40 would be considered a constant since it can never change. Each time the program executes, the contents of the variable RATE will be multiplied by the constant 40.

Statement 120 in the example payroll program (Exhibit G.2) illustrates the concept of an expression. An **expression** is a combination of constants and variables connected with mathematical symbols representing multiplication (*), division (/), addition (+), or subtraction (-). Thus, RATE*HOURS in statement 120 is an expression that represents the multiplication of the contents of the RATE and HOURS variables.

Exhibit G.3

The Use of Variables in a BASIC Program

a) The first time the program is executed, the variables contain one set of values.

b) The next time the program is executed, the same variables are used to store completely different values.

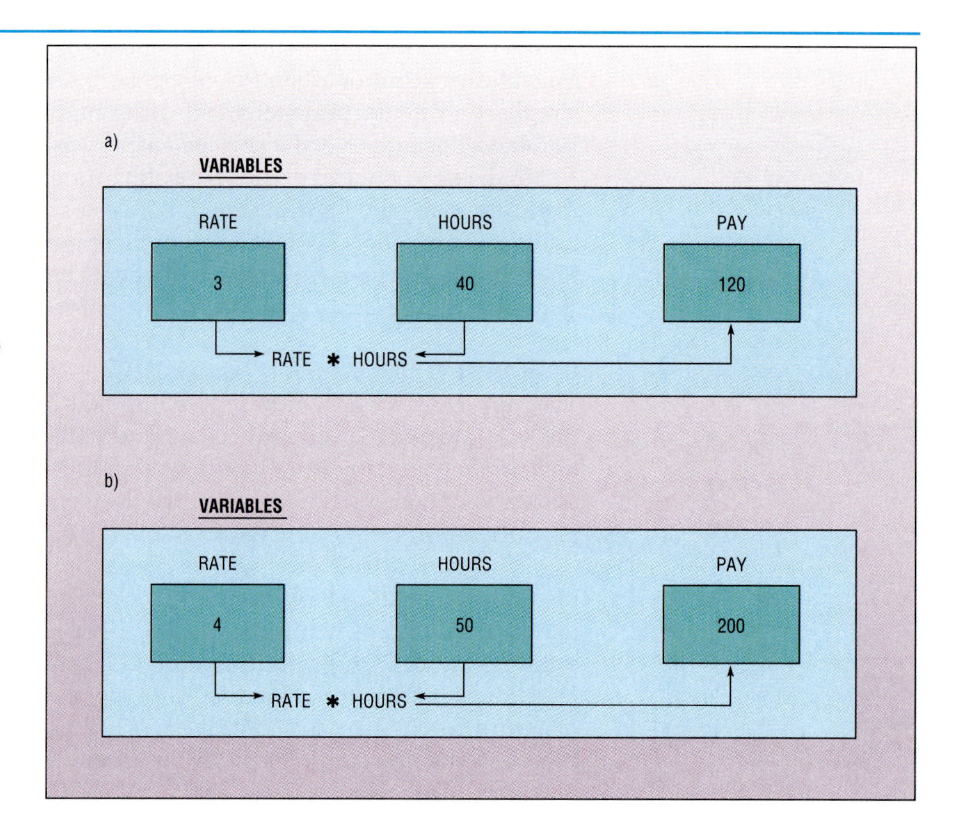

Understanding BASIC Programs

On a general level, all programs are series of instructions designed to manipulate data to produce desired information. This process is usually divided into three steps: input, processing, and output. Before a program can process data, the data must be placed into variables in primary memory. This would be considered the input stage. The contents of these variables can then be manipulated or processed by the program during the processing stage. Once the desired data are obtained, results can be displayed or printed during the output stage.

BASIC includes several **keywords** that can be used in each of these stages of processing. When reading a program, it is often helpful to look for the statements corresponding to the input, processing, and output tasks. In many programs, statements involved with the three stages will appear in sequence, with input statements occurring first, followed by statements involved with processing, and ending with statements accomplishing the output task. In more complex programs, statements involving input, processing, and output will be intermixed, and some of the stages may be repeated.

Exhibit G.4 shows the example payroll program again with the input, processing, and output statements identified. You should now know enough about BASIC to begin to understand how this program works. The specific BASIC keywords used in this program are described below.

```
10    REM VERSION 1
20    REM
30    REM THIS PROGRAM CALCULATES THE TOTAL PAY FOR AN EMPLOYEE
40    REM GIVEN THE PAY RATE FOR THE EMPLOYEE AND THE HOURS WORKED
50    REM
60    REM RATE   - PAY RATE FOR THE EMPLOYEE
70    REM HOURS  - HOURS WORKED
80    REM PAY    - TOTAL PAY
90    REM
100   INPUT RATE
110   INPUT HOURS                                          Input
120   LET PAY = RATE*HOURS                                 Processing
130   PRINT PAY                                            Output
140   END
```

Exhibit G.4

Input, Processing, and Output Steps in the Example Payroll Program

The REM Keyword

The first nine statements in the program (lines 10 through 90) use the REM keyword. This BASIC keyword is used to create **remarks** in the program, to make the program more readable. When BASIC encounters the REM keyword, everything following the REM in the statement is ignored. Thus, a programmer will use the REM statement to document the program for other users so that they can understand the intent of the program. In the payroll program, the programmer has included information about the overall function of the program and an indication of what data are being stored in the variables used in the program. Although information in statements containing the REM keyword serves no function in the program itself, it is very helpful to readers of the program since it makes the purpose of the program clear.

The INPUT Keyword

Statements 100 and 110 in the payroll program use the INPUT keyword to accomplish the input stage of the program. The INPUT statement is used to place a piece of data in a variable. Following the INPUT keyword, the programmer writes the name of a variable to be created in primary memory to store the data being input. When BASIC processes an INPUT statement, it pauses in the execution of the program and displays a question mark on the screen. It then waits for the user to type data at the keyboard and press (RETURN). When (RETURN) is pressed, the letters or numbers typed are placed in the variable referenced in the INPUT statement.

The LET Keyword

The LET keyword in the payroll program represents the processing step of the program. The purpose of the program is to determine the total pay for an employee, given an hourly pay rate and the number of hours worked. A statement containing a LET keyword always includes a single variable to the left of the equal sign and another variable, constant, or expression to the right. The variable to the left of the equal sign is the **receiving** variable. When this statement is executed, BASIC determines the value represented by the variable, constant, or expression to the right of the equal sign and then stores that value in the receiving variable.

For example, suppose the user entered a pay rate of 3 in the RATE variable during the first INPUT statement and 40 hours in the HOURS variable during the second INPUT statement. When the LET statement is processed, the expression RATE*HOURS would be 3*40, which is 120. As a result of the LET statement, the variable called PAY will contain the value 120.

The PRINT Keyword

Statement 130 contains the PRINT keyword, which represents the output step in the program. The PRINT keyword is used to display information on the screen. In this case, the PRINT keyword is being used to display the contents of the PAY variable. As you will see later, the PRINT keyword can be used to display both the contents of variables and the text messages that can be used to label data.

The END Keyword

The END keyword is used to indicate where BASIC is to stop the program. When this statement is processed, the program stops and control of the computer is returned to the BASIC interpreter, causing the Ok prompt to reappear.

Putting It All Together

Exhibit G.5 illustrates the interaction between the user and the BASIC payroll program. When the payroll program is executed with the RUN command, the first nine statements will be ignored by BASIC. Then a question mark will appear as the first INPUT statement is executed. The user types 3 as the pay rate and then presses (RETURN). BASIC then continues with the next INPUT statement, which again causes the program to pause with a question mark displayed on the screen. The user then types 40 as the hours for the employee and presses (RETURN). BASIC then executes the LET statement, which multiplies the pay rate by the hours to determine the total pay. The amount of the total pay is placed in the PAY variable. The contents of the PAY variable are then displayed on the screen with the PRINT statement. Finally, the END statement causes the program to stop, and the Ok prompt reappears as control is returned to the BASIC interpreter.

Note how the general flow of the program starts at the top and works through the statements in order. Also note that this program is designed to process one employee and then stop. If the user wanted to calculate the pay for another employee, the program would have to be executed again.

```
RUN
?       3
?       40
        120
Ok
```

Exhibit G.5

The Interaction Between the User and the Example Payroll Program

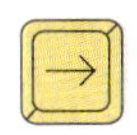

BASIC Commands

To begin entering and executing programs, you need to learn the BASIC interpreter commands used to store, retrieve, edit, and execute programs. As mentioned earlier, BASIC commands are direct instructions that are executed immediately after pressing (RETURN). BASIC commands are not part of a program but rather are general housekeeping tools to help you work with your programs. Exhibit G.6 summarizes some of the common BASIC commands, which will be described below. To help you become familiar with the BASIC environment and programming language, try the commands described below using the payroll program in Exhibit G.2.

Entering and Editing Programs

There are several BASIC commands that are useful when creating and modifying a program in primary memory. Once you are in the BASIC interpreter, a program can be entered in primary memory by simply typing BASIC statements preceded by a line number.

Get into the BASIC interpreter following the instructions earlier in this appendix and type the statements in the payroll program. The NEW command is commonly used when first beginning to enter a new program. This command will clear any program statements currently in memory to make sure they will not accidentally become part of your program.

Once a program is entered into primary memory, the statements can be displayed on the screen by typing the LIST command and pressing (RETURN). BASIC also makes use of the function keys on the keyboard as shortcuts to commonly used commands. Pressing (F1) has the same effect as typing LIST. After pressing (F1), however, you still must press (RETURN). The listing of the program can also be limited by specifying a range of line numbers in the LIST command. For example,

```
LIST 20-40
```

would list only lines 20 through 40 in the program. A listing of the program can also be sent to a printer attached to your microcomputer by using the LLIST command instead of the normal LIST.

Command	Function Performed
NEW	Clears primary memory of all BASIC statements. Used when beginning a new program.
LIST	Displays the BASIC statements contained in the program currently in primary memory.
LLIST	Prints the BASIC statements contained in the program currently in primary memory on a printer.
RENUM	Renumbers the statements of the program in primary memory beginning with 10 and increasing in increments of 10.
RUN	Executes the instructions in the program currently in primary memory.
SAVE	Places a copy of the program currently in primary memory into a file on disk.
FILES	Lists the files on a disk.
LOAD	Places a copy of a program contained in a file on disk into primary memory.
KILL	Deletes a file from disk.
SYSTEM	Leaves BASIC and returns the user to DOS.

Exhibit G.6

Some Common BASIC Commands

The contents of the program in primary memory can be altered in several ways. To add a new line to the program, you simply enter the new statement using a line number not already used in the program. The new line number should correspond to the position in the program where the new statement is to be placed. To alter an existing statement in the program, simply retype the statement using the same line number. When a second statement is entered using the line number of an existing statement, the second statement replaces the existing statement. Thus, when entering a new statement, you must be careful to use a new line number so that you will not inadvertently destroy an existing line in the program.

Another helpful command related to line numbers is RENUM. When this command is entered, the lines of the program are renumbered beginning with 10 and increasing in increments of ten. To delete a line from the program, simply type the line number and then press (RETURN) immediately after the last digit of the line number. Throughout the process of inserting, altering, and deleting lines in the program, BASIC will always maintain the statements in order by line number.

When a statement contains only a minor error, the method of retyping the entire line to replace the old statement with a new one becomes rather inefficient. A more advanced method of editing existing lines in a program can be accomplished using the screen editing capability of BASIC. The arrow keys on the keyboard can be used to position the cursor on any statement that appears on the screen. New characters can be typed to replace the original ones, or the (INS) key can be used to toggle between the default typeover mode and insert mode when new characters need to be squeezed into the line. The (DEL) key can be used to delete characters at the cursor location. Once the statement has been altered, the user *must* press (RETURN) while the cursor is still on the BASIC statement to make the altered version of the statement replace the original one in the program.

Thus, to use the screen editing capability, the statement to be changed must be displayed on the screen using the LIST command. If the desired line scrolls off the screen because the program listing is too long, the user must limit the amount of the program listed so the desired line will remain on the screen. Changes may be made to any line on the screen, but the user must be careful to press (RETURN) after changing each line. If the cursor is moved off the line before pressing (RETURN), the change will not be made.

Program Execution and Syntax Errors

One of the main advantages of an interpreter like BASIC is that once a program has been entered in primary memory, the programmer can execute the program to see if it will work. To execute the program in primary memory, simply type RUN and press (RETURN). BASIC will then attempt to execute the statements in the program. The (F2) key can also be used to execute a program. Pressing (F2) has the same effect as typing RUN and pressing (RETURN).

When typing in the statements for the program, anything you type following the line number will become stored in primary memory as part of the program. In other words, BASIC does not check to make sure you have typed valid BASIC statements. Thus, if you misspelled a BASIC keyword or made any other mistake while typing the statement, it will be discovered only when the program is executed.

Any mistakes made in the spelling or punctuation required in a BASIC statement are known as **syntax errors**. When BASIC executes a statement containing a syntax error, it will be unable to understand the instruction and execution will halt. When the program stops because of a syntax error, BASIC displays the message "Syntax error in ##," where ## is the line number of the statement containing the error. In addition, the line containing the syntax error is displayed and the cursor is placed at the location in the statement where BASIC began having problems. You can move the cursor along this line and make any change you like. When you press (RETURN), the new version of the statement will replace the old one. This process is known as **debugging** your program.

You may at times have several syntax errors in the same program. In this case, BASIC will stop the program on the first line it cannot process. The remaining lines in the program will not be processed. Thus, after fixing the first syntax error, you may encounter other syntax errors farther down in the program when you run the program again. The general debugging process of running the program, discovering a syntax error, and fixing the error may need to be repeated several times.

Working with Program Files

Since the BASIC interpreter works with one program at a time in primary memory, the programs you create must be saved on disk and retrieved when you need them again. BASIC provides several commands for working with the files containing your programs. In general, BASIC program files must follow MS-DOS naming conventions and should have an extension of BAS to make them more easily identifiable to BASIC.

Once a program is created in primary memory, it must be saved on disk using BASIC's SAVE command. With the SAVE command, the word *SAVE* must be followed by a double quotation mark and the name of the file. The file extension is optional. If it is omitted, BASIC will automatically assign an extension of BAS. The closing quotation mark after the file name is also optional. Thus, after you have entered and executed the payroll program, you could save it using the command

```
SAVE "PROG1"
```

The (F4) key can be used as a shortcut; it will type SAVE " on the screen. Then you only have to type the file name and press (RETURN).

If you want to save a program on a disk other than the one in the current MS-DOS default drive, you can enter the drive designation in front of the file name. Thus, if you wanted the payroll program to be saved in a file on the diskette in drive B you could use

```
SAVE "B:PROG1"
```

Another important point to remember with the SAVE command is that if there is already a file on the disk with the name you supply in the SAVE command, the program being saved will replace the previous contents of the file. Thus, you must be careful when saving programs to only use the name of an existing file when you actually want to replace the old version of a program with the version currently in primary memory.

To help you remember the names of files on your disk, the FILES command can be used to list the file names and file extensions much the way the DIR command lists files in MS-DOS. As with the DIR command, you specify which drive to list and can use wildcards to produce filtered lists of files. For example, to list the files on the diskette in drive B that have a BAS extension, you would use the command

```
FILES "B:*.BAS"
```

Note how the file specification must be in quotes, as it was in the SAVE command.

Previously created programs can be brought back into the interpreter using the LOAD command. LOAD is complementary to the SAVE command. When a LOAD command is executed, the retrieved program replaces any statements already in primary memory. Thus, if you have not saved the program currently in memory at the time of the LOAD, it will be lost when the new program is brought into primary memory.

To see how the LOAD command works with the payroll program, first make sure the program is saved and then use the NEW command to clear the program from primary memory. To verify that primary memory is empty, use the LIST command. Notice that no lines are displayed. Now, type the command

```
LOAD "PROG1"
```

and press (RETURN). Use LIST again to verify that the lines of the payroll program are now back in primary memory. The syntax for the LOAD command is similar to that of the SAVE command. The file name must be enclosed in quotation marks. If the file is on a drive other than the current MS-DOS default drive, the drive letter must be included in front of the file name. The BAS extension is assumed by BASIC, and the second quotation mark is optional. The (F3) key can be used to type LOAD " on the screen, following which you can simply type the file specification and press (RETURN).

A final useful command for working with your files is the KILL command, which can be used to delete a disk file containing a program. As in the other commands designed for working with files, the file name (with the drive specification, if necessary) must be enclosed in quotation marks or at least preceded by a quotation mark. The only difference with the KILL command is that the file extension *is* required. Thus, since your program files will usually be created with a BAS extension, you must include that BAS extension after the file name when using KILL.

Exiting BASIC

The final BASIC command you will need to know is the SYSTEM command, which is used to leave the BASIC interpreter. When the SYSTEM command is executed, the contents of primary memory are cleared. Thus, if there is a program in memory that you wish to keep, you should use the SAVE command to place a copy of the program in a file on disk before using the SYSTEM command to leave the BASIC interpreter.

Exhibit G.7 shows an example of a session within the BASIC interpreter. In this exhibit, the information typed by the user is shown in blue and the responses from BASIC are shown in black. In this example, the NEW command is used to make sure that primary memory contains no statements before entering the program. The payroll program is then entered with an error in statement 120 (there is a + where the = should be). When the program is executed, with the RUN command, the two INPUT statements are processed correctly. When statement 120 is reached, a syntax error is generated, and BASIC displays the statement with the cursor under the plus sign. The user then replaces the + with an = and presses (RETURN). The LIST command is used to view the program; you can see that statement 120 is now correct. The program is executed a second time and the user enters a pay rate of 3 dollars per hour and 40 as the number of hours worked. The program displays the resulting pay of 120. The user then saves the program and exits from BASIC.

Programming Exercises

1. Write a BASIC program that would allow a user to enter the price of a product and the quantity ordered. Have the program compute a total by multiplying the price by the quantity. Print the total. Use the program to determine the total of an order using a price of $5.95 and a quantity of 16.

2. Create a program that would permit the input of a beginning mileage, an ending mileage, and the number of gallons of gasoline. The program should compute total miles by subtracting the beginning mileage from the ending mileage. The total mileage should then be divided by the number of gallons used to determine miles per gallon. Print the miles per gallon. Use the program to compute the miles per gallon for a trip where the beginning mileage was 12,340, the ending mileage was 12,783, and the number of gallons used was 16.4.

3. Create a program to compute the average of three test scores. The user should be asked to input three test scores. The program should then compute the total score by adding the three scores. This total score should then be divided by three to determine the average. Print the average. Use the program to compute the average for test scores of 93, 89, and 86.

4. Create a program to calculate a student's tuition bill based on the number of hours for which the student is enrolled. The user should input the number of hours and the tuition per hour. The program should then compute the tuition by multiplying the number of hours times the tuition per hour. The resulting tuition should be printed. Use the program to determine the tuition for a student enrolled for 17 hours when the tuition per hour is $355.

```
NEW
Ok
10  REM  VERSION 1
20  REM
30  REM  THIS PROGRAM CALCULATES THE TOTAL PAY FOR AN EMPLOYEE
40  REM  GIVEN THE PAY RATE FOR THE EMPLOYEE AND THE HOURS WORKED
50  REM
60  REM  RATE  - PAY RATE FOR THE EMPLOYEE
70  REM  HOURS - HOURS WORKED
80  REM  PAY   - TOTAL PAY
90  REM
100 INPUT RATE
110 INPUT HOURS
120 LET PAY + RATE*HOURS
130 PRINT PAY
140 END
RUN
? 3
? 40
Syntax error in 120
Ok
120 LET PAY ± RATE*HOURS
LIST
10  REM  VERSION 1
20  REM
30  REM  THIS PROGRAM CALCULATES THE TOTAL PAY FOR AN EMPLOYEE
40  REM  GIVEN THE PAY RATE FOR THE EMPLOYEE AND THE HOURS WORKED
50  REM
60  REM  RATE  - PAY RATE FOR THE EMPLOYEE
70  REM  HOURS - HOURS WORKED
80  REM  PAY   - TOTAL PAY
90  REM
100 INPUT RATE
110 INPUT HOURS
120 LET PAY = RATE*HOURS
130 PRINT PAY
140 END
Ok
RUN
? 3
? 40
120
Ok
SAVE "PROG1
Ok
SYSTEM

A:\>
```

Exhibit G.7

An Example Session in BASIC

Writing BASIC Programs

The first part of this appendix presented a general overview of programming in BASIC. This part is designed to provide a more detailed understanding of how data is stored and manipulated by BASIC and to serve as an introduction to the overall program design process.

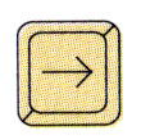

Working with Data

This section discusses further the interaction between a BASIC program and the data it processes. Variables used to store different types of data are described, rules followed by BASIC when performing calculations are introduced, and more sophisticated ways of inputting and outputting data are covered.

Storing Data in Variables

Earlier in this appendix, you were introduced to the use of variables to represent locations in primary memory where data are stored. Here, a more detailed discussion of the rules for creating variables in BASIC will be presented. BASIC distinguishes between two types of data: numeric and string. For numeric data, there are three types of variables, which vary in the precision with which they store numeric data. Rules differ for naming and storing data in these two types of variables.

All variables in BASIC are named using letters, numbers, and a period. Special symbols, such as !, @, #, %, ^, &, *, and so on, are not allowed in variable names. Variable names cannot be reserved words such as PRINT, INPUT, REM, and END since these words have special meanings as BASIC commands. A keyword you might be tempted to use as a variable name is NAME. NAME cannot be used by itself as a valid variable name since it is a keyword. The maximum length of a BASIC variable name is 40 characters. Periods can be used as separators to make long variable names easier to read. For example, a variable name of AVERAGEPAYRATE is not as readable as AVERAGE.PAY.RATE.

In well-structured programs, it is good practice to make variable names as meaningful as possible. This allows readers of the program to understand the functioning of the program more quickly. For example, using a variable name of A to represent the variable to hold the average pay of an employee is not as understandable as using a variable name of AVERAGE.PAY.

String Variables

As mentioned above, BASIC allows the creation of variables to store string data. **String data** are characters, numbers, and special symbols that are to be stored in primary memory and will not be used in arithmetic calculations. A BASIC program can be used to input, store, and output string data. Variables designed to hold string data are identified to BASIC by placing a dollar sign ($) at the end of the variable name. String variables can hold up to 255 characters. Some examples of valid string variable names include

```
FIRST.NAME$
ADDRESS$
CITY$
STATE$
```

Numeric Variables

Numeric data can consist of numbers, a period, and a plus or a minus sign. Dollars signs and commas cannot be stored as part of numeric data. When creating a variable to hold numeric data, there are three choices that determine the precision, or number of digits, that are stored: integer, single-precision, and double-precision.

Integer variables are designed to hold whole numbers. Thus, data entered into an integer variable are rounded to the nearest whole number. Single-precision variables are designed to store numbers with seven significant digits, and double-precision variables can hold up to seventeen significant digits. As an example, suppose the number 55.9834745 is to be stored in a BASIC variable. Here is how that number would be stored in the three types of numeric variables:

```
Original data       55.9834745
Double-precision    55.9834745
Single-precision    55.98347
Integer             56
```

A special character is used at the end of the variable name to indicate the precision of a numeric variable, similar to the way a dollar sign is used to identify string variables to BASIC. The symbols for numeric variables are

```
% Integer
! Single-precision
# Double-precision
```

If a variable name does not end with any of the four special symbols, BASIC assumes the variable is a single-precision numeric variable. This technique for naming variables was used in the example payroll program in the first part of this appendix.

Here are some examples of valid variable names along with the type of data they will be able to store:

```
SALARY!            Single-precision
MILEAGE#           Double-precision
AGE%               Integer
TOTAL.PAY          Single-precision
CUSTOMER.NAME$     String
```

Manipulating Data

One of the main functions of any program is to manipulate data in some way to produce meaningful information. Often this involves the storage of some initial data in variables, followed by the manipulation of that data to produce other data. As indicated earlier, all data manipulated by BASIC must be stored in variables.

Expressions

The main mechanism for manipulating data in BASIC is the LET keyword, which is used to place the results of an expression into a variable. Thus, the key to understanding data manipulation in BASIC is to understand how complex expressions are evaluated by BASIC. As you learned earlier in this appendix, an expression is a group of variables and constants joined by symbols representing mathematical operations. In BASIC, the numeric operators include

```
+ addition
- subtraction
* multiplication
/ division
^ exponentiation (raise to a power)
```

The simplest expression would be a single variable or constant preceded by a plus or minus sign. If there is no symbol preceding the variable or constant, the plus is assumed. Thus, the following examples would be considered simple expressions:

```
-3
-BALANCE
+450
+AGE
```

The more common structure for an expression is the joining of two variables or constants with a numeric operator, as illustrated in these examples:

```
RATE*HOURS
SALARY/12
8+4
100-AGE
SPEED.OF.LIGHT^2
```

Complex Expressions

When using more than one numeric operator in an expression, it becomes important to understand the order in which BASIC will process the various operations that make up such a complex expression. When several numeric operations appear in the same expression BASIC performs the operations in the following order:

1. Perform exponentiations in left to right order
2. Perform multiplication and division in left to right order
3. Perform addition and subtraction in left to right order

To see the importance of the order of operations, consider an expression that is to average three people's ages which are stored in the variables AGE1, AGE2 and AGE3:

```
LET AGE1 = 40
LET AGE2 = 50
LET AGE3 = 60
LET AVERAGE.AGE = AGE1+AGE2+AGE3/3
```

Doing the calculation by hand would produce 50 as the average of the three ages. The order of operations, however, says that the division operation should be performed before any addition. Thus, BASIC would first divide AGE3 by 3, producing a result of 20, which would then be added to 40 and 50 to produce a final answer of 110!

Thus, when writing expressions you must be aware of the order in which BASIC will perform the operations within the expression. When the normal order of operations is inappropriate for an expression such as the one above, parentheses can be used to force BASIC to perform certain calculations first. Thus, the example expression above would have to be written as

```
LET AVERAGE.AGE = (AGE1+AGE2+AGE3)/3
```

Any calculations inside parentheses are performed first. Thus, the addition of the three ages would be performed first, producing a sum of 150, which is then divided by 3 to produce the correct answer of 50.

String Expressions

When the LET keyword is used to place data in a string variable, the string data must be enclosed in quotation marks to indicate to BASIC that the data is not to be treated as a number. Some examples of LET statements involving string data would be

```
LET FIRST.NAME$ = "Joe"
LET MIDDLE.INITIAL$ = " C."
LET LAST.NAME$ = " Public"
LET FULL.NAME$ = FIRST.NAME$ + MIDDLE.INITIAL$ +
  LAST.NAME$
```

Notice how the string data placed into the MIDDLE.INITIAL$ and LAST.NAME$ variables begin with a blank space. The fourth expression illustrates the only manipulation allowed with variables containing string data, which is the joining of two strings through the operation of **concatenation**. In concatenation, the plus sign is used to attach one string to the end of another string. In this example, the three parts of the name are joined together to produce

```
Joe C. Public
```

which was stored in the FULL.NAME$ variable. The blank spaces in front of the middle initial and last name were used to space apart the three parts of the name when they were concatenated.

Expressions in the Example Program

Exhibit G.8 illustrates the use of string and numeric variables in expressions. In this exhibit, several new variables are added to the payroll program introduced in the first part of this appendix.

The FIRST.NAME$ and LAST.NAME$ variables have been added in INPUT statements that ask the user to give the name of the employee. These two names are then concatenated in statement 100.

The result of the RATE*HOURS expression is now stored in a variable called GROSS.PAY. Notice that none of the numeric variables in this program end with special symbols, which means they will default to single-precision numeric variables. The FEDERAL.TAX, STATE.TAX, and RETIREMENT variables are filled in with calculations that take a percentage of the gross pay. The expression in line 150 subtracts all the deductions for federal tax, state tax, and retirement from the gross pay and puts the result in the NET.PAY variable. Finally, both the full name of the employee and the net pay are displayed to the user on screen.

When this program is executed, the user will see a question mark appear for each of the four initial INPUT statements in the program. When

```
10    REM   VERSION 2
20    REM
30    REM   THIS PROGRAM CALCULATES THE NET PAY AND DEDUCTIONS FOR
40    REM   AN EMPLOYEE GIVEN THE PAY RATE AND THE HOURS WORKED
50    REM
60    INPUT FIRST.NAME$
70    INPUT LAST.NAME$
80    INPUT RATE
90    INPUT HOURS
100   LET FULL.NAME$ = FIRST.NAME$ + LAST.NAME$
110   LET GROSS.PAY = RATE*HOURS
120   LET FEDERAL.TAX = GROSS.PAY * .15
130   LET STATE.TAX = GROSS.PAY * .1
140   LET RETIREMENT = GROSS.PAY * .06
150   LET NET.PAY = GROSS.PAY - (FEDERAL.TAX + STATE.TAX + RETIREMENT)
160   PRINT FULL.NAME$
170   PRINT NET.PAY
180   END
```

Exhibit G.8

The Payroll Program with String and Numeric Variables

entering string data with the INPUT statement, the data must be enclosed in quotation marks if it contains a comma or blank spaces at the beginning or end of the data. Thus, to get the concatenation in line 100 to work, the user must enter the employee's last name in quotation marks with a space as the first character. When the data does not contain a leading blank, as is the case with the first name, the quotation marks are optional.

Improving the Input Stage

So far the payroll program has used the INPUT keyword in its simplest form: INPUT followed by a single variable. When the program is run, a question mark is displayed to the user indicating that the program has paused and is waiting for data. With four INPUT statements now in the payroll program, there will be a series of four question marks displayed to the user. The problem with this approach is the user must know which piece of data is to be entered after each question mark. In this case, the question marks are of no help to the user in distinguishing which piece of data the program is waiting for.

The full version of the INPUT statement is

```
INPUT "prompt"; variable or list of variables
```

The *"prompt"* is an informational message that is displayed on the screen when the program pauses for input. For example, consider the following four statements as replacements for the lines in the payroll program using the INPUT keyword:

```
60 INPUT "Enter first name ", FIRST.NAME$
70 INPUT "Enter last name ", LAST.NAME$
80 INPUT "Pay rate "; RATE
90 INPUT "Hours worked "; HOURS
```

Following the INPUT keyword, the programmer can type a text string enclosed in quotation marks. When the program pauses for input, this message will be displayed on the screen the same way the question mark was displayed before. Following the prompt is a comma in lines 60 and 70, but in lines 80 and 90 a semicolon was used. The comma after the prompt indicates to BASIC that the normal display of a question mark is to be suppressed when the INPUT statement is processed. When the semicolon is used after the prompt, the question mark will appear. When constructing the prompt message, a blank space is usually included at the end of the prompt to separate the prompt from the characters the user types.

With the INPUT statement, it is also possible to fill in more than one variable with a single INPUT statement. For example,

```
INPUT "Enter first and last name ", FIRST.NAME$,
  LAST.NAME$
```

could be used in place of lines 60 and 70 above. When more than one variable is listed in the INPUT statement, the user must enter a comma to separate the data for the two variables when entering the data. The interaction between this INPUT statement and the user would look like this:

```
Enter first and last name "Joe", " Public"
```

The characters in boldface represent the characters the user would type. As mentioned earlier, the last name would have to be entered in quotation marks to get the leading blank to be stored as part of the last name. The quotation marks around the first name would be optional.

Improving the Output Stage

Just as the input stage of the payroll program was improved by providing the user with more information, the output stage can also be improved. Currently the payroll program simply prints the name of the employee and a number representing the net pay for the employee. Like INPUT statements, PRINT statements have many options, which let the programmer control the way information is displayed to the user. Suppose the user of the payroll program wanted the following information to be displayed by the program:

```
PAYROLL INFORMATION FOR <full.name>

PAY RATE         <rate>
HOURS WORKED     <hours>
GROSS PAY        <gross.pay>

                 DEDUCTIONS

FEDERAL          STATE            RETIREMENT
<federal.tax>    <state.tax>      <retirement>

NET PAY          <net.pay>
```

This information includes all the data input by the user plus all the data calculated by the program. The information enclosed in angle brackets (<rate>, <hours>, and so on) are indications of where the contents of variables are to appear. The words in uppercase indicate actual words the user wants to appear on the screen. Exhibit G.9 shows the payroll program containing the PRINT statements necessary to generate the screen shown above. In general, each line that appears on the screen is the result of a print statement. Since the screen proposed by the user contains twelve lines (including the blank lines), the program requires twelve PRINT statements to generate the screen. These PRINT statements exemplify several different options available with the PRINT statement.

```
 10   REM  VERSION 3
 20   REM
 30   REM  THIS PROGRAM CALCULATES THE NET PAY AND DEDUCTIONS FOR
 40   REM  AN EMPLOYEE GIVEN THE PAY RATE AND THE HOURS WORKED
 50   REM
 60   INPUT "Enter first name ", FIRST.NAME$
 70   INPUT "Enter last name ", LAST.NAME$
 80   INPUT "Pay rate "; RATE
 90   INPUT "Hours worked "; HOURS
100   LET FULL.NAME$ = FIRST.NAME$ + LAST.NAME$
110   LET GROSS.PAY = RATE*HOURS
120   LET FEDERAL.TAX = GROSS.PAY * .15
130   LET STATE.TAX = GROSS.PAY * .1
140   LET RETIREMENT = GROSS.PAY * .06
150   LET NET.PAY = GROSS.PAY - (FEDERAL.TAX + STATE.TAX + RETIREMENT)
160   PRINT "PAYROLL INFORMATION FOR "; FULL.NAME$
170   PRINT
180   PRINT "PAY RATE          ";RATE
190   PRINT "HOURS WORKED      ";HOURS
200   PRINT "GROSS PAY         ";GROSS.PAY
210   PRINT
220   PRINT TAB(14);"DEDUCTIONS"
230   PRINT
240   PRINT "FEDERAL","STATE","RETIREMENT"
250   PRINT FEDERAL.TAX,STATE.TAX,RETIREMENT
260   PRINT
270   PRINT "NET PAY           ";NET.PAY
280   END
```

Exhibit G.9

The Payroll Program with More Complex INPUT and PRINT Statements

Literals

Just as the INPUT statement can contain a string of text enclosed in quotation marks to be displayed on the screen, a PRINT statement can also contain a string of text to be printed on the screen. A **literal** is a string of text included in a PRINT statement. The term *literal* comes from the fact that the string is printed by BASIC literally as it appears inside the quotation marks. Thus, BASIC does not alter or process the text inside the quotes. It prints the text exactly as it appears, including all spaces and special characters. Thus, all the words appearing on the example screen proposed by the user appear in PRINT statements as literals.

Semicolons

When several literals and variables are combined in the same PRINT statement, BASIC requires that each literal and variable be separated from the others by a semicolon or comma. Semicolons and commas not only serve to separate the literals and variables within the PRINT statement, but also tell BASIC how to space the various items being printed. The semicolon is a signal to BASIC that the two elements on either side are to be printed immediately next to each other on the screen. Thus,

```
160 PRINT "PAYROLL INFORMATION FOR "; FULL.NAME$
```

tells BASIC that the full name of the employee is to be printed immediately after the literal. Note the use of a blank space at the end of the literal. This is to provide a space between the last word in the literal and the first character

```
240   PRINT "FEDERAL"          , "STATE"        ,     "RETIREMENT"
250   PRINT FEDERAL.TAX        , STATE.TAX      ,     RETIREMENT

      FEDERAL                  STATE          RETIREMENT
      18                       12             7.2
```

Exhibit G.10

Formatting in PRINT Statements

The comma can be used in a PRINT statement to print data in columns.

of data in the FULL.NAME$ variable. Thus, if FULL.NAME$ contained "Joe Public," the result of the PRINT statement would be

```
PAYROLL INFORMATION FOR Joe Public
```

Without the blank space at the end of the literal the result would be

```
PAYROLL INFORMATION FORJoe Public
```

Thus, blanks spaces are common within literals, particularly when a semicolon is used. This use of blank spaces within literals is also shown in lines 180, 190, 200, and 270 of the program in Exhibit G.9. Notice how various numbers of blank spaces appear at the ends of the literals in these statements. This causes the data printed in the variables following the literals to line up.

Commas

Commas can also be used to separate various elements within a PRINT statement. The comma causes the elements being printed to be placed in columns or print zones. In BASIC, the print zones or columns are fourteen characters wide. In the processing of a PRINT statement, a comma causes BASIC to move along the PRINT line to the beginning of the next print zone before printing the literal or variable following the comma. Exhibit G.10 illustrates how lines 240 and 250 take advantage of print zones to line up information in columns.

The TAB Function

Information can be more precisely positioned on the screen using the TAB function. The TAB function causes BASIC to move to a particular position on the PRINT line before printing the element following the TAB in the PRINT statement. The TAB function is treated as another element within the PRINT statement and therefore must be separated from other elements by a semicolon. Line 220 in the program in Exhibit G.9 illustrates a TAB function followed with a position on the PRINT line that precedes the information to be positioned at that location. Thus, line 220 tells BASIC to move to position 14 on the print line and print the word DEDUCTIONS.

Printing Blank Lines

Lines 170, 210, 230, and 260 illustrate the use of the PRINT statement to generate blank lines on the screen. The screen proposed by the user included several blank lines to space the output. In BASIC, a PRINT statement with nothing following it tells BASIC to print a blank line.

Program Development with BASIC

As you learned in Chapter 9, the program development process consists of three stages: design, coding, and testing. As with most other programming languages, this general process should be applied when writing BASIC programs.

Program Design

Prior to the program design stage, program specifications should be developed. These specifications should indicate the goals of the program, including its major functions and a description of the required input and output data. These guidelines are usually produced during the process of systems development.

For simple programs such as the payroll program in this appendix, the program specifications would include a statement of the purpose of the program, a description of what data are to be input, and a sample showing how the data are to be displayed to the user. Exhibit G.11 shows a layout for the input and output for the payroll program.

During the program design stage, the tasks that need to be performed by the program to accomplish the general goals would be specified in more detail. Commonly, a tool such as a flowchart or pseudocode would be used to plan the logic required in the program. Exhibit G.12 shows a flowchart for the payroll program. Refer to Chapter 9 for more information on the meaning of the symbols in a flowchart.

Exhibit G.11

An Example Input and Output Layout for Designing the Payroll Program

```
Enter first name "XXXX"
Enter last name " YYYY"
Pay rate ? #
Hours worked ? ##


PAYROLL INFORMATION FOR XXXX YYYY

PAY RATE            #
HOURS WORKED        ##
GROSS PAY           ###

                DEDUCTIONS

FEDERAL         STATE          RETIREMENT
 #####           #####            #####

NET PAY         #####
```

Exhibit G.12

A Flowchart of the Payroll Program

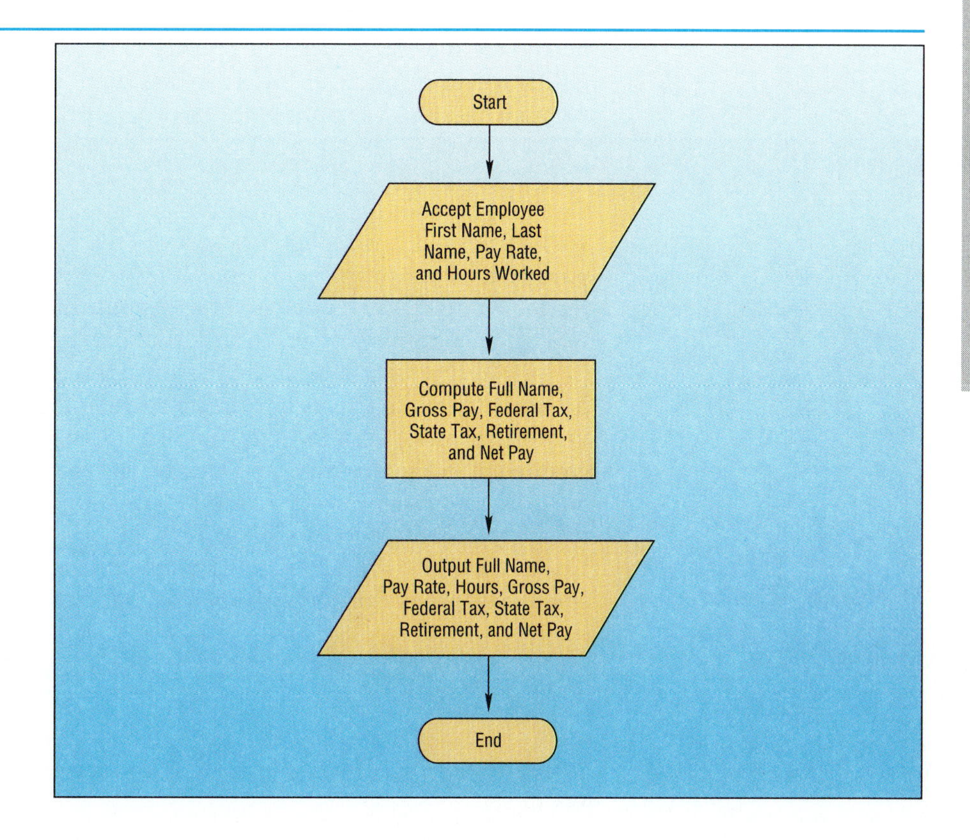

Program Coding

Program coding involves the translation of the flowchart or pseudocode representation of the program into actual BASIC programming statements. The input step in the flowchart is translated into INPUT statements, the computation step is translated into LET statements, and the output step is translated into PRINT statements.

Program Testing

After the program is coded, the testing stage begins. Initially, the program must be executed to discover any syntax errors that result from incorrect coding of BASIC statements. All syntax errors, or "bugs," must be discovered and corrected through the process of debugging the program.

Once the program is free from syntax errors, test data are run through the program to determine if there are any logic errors in the program. The program can be syntactically correct, but still may produce the wrong answer. Thus, several example sets of data similar to the data that will eventually be processed by the program should be used as input data. The output generated by the program for each set of data should also be compared to the expected output.

In addition, it is sometimes helpful to process nonrepresentative test data with the program to see if it is processed correctly. For example, the payroll program could be given a pay rate of 100 and hours of 3000 to make sure the correct answer of 300,000 is generated. Extreme sets of data will sometimes uncover an error that would otherwise be missed when running "normal" data through the program.

Program Style

One of the major goals in program development should be the creation of well-structured, readable programs. A little extra care and attention on the part of a programmer can go a long way to making a program more readable and understandable. Throughout this appendix, special attention will be given to the structure and readability of the programs.

In the payroll program there are three important elements that can be used to make the program more readable: comments, meaningful variable names, and indentation. The use of REM statements to place comments in the program and the use of meaningful variable names have already been introduced. Exhibit G.13 shows the payroll program with REM statements used to label the input, processing, and output steps. Under each of these labels, the statements are indented to indicate which statements are performing part of the same function.

```
 10   REM    VERSION 4
 20   REM
 30   REM    THIS PROGRAM CALCULATES THE NET PAY AND DEDUCTIONS FOR
 40   REM    AN EMPLOYEE GIVEN THE PAY RATE AND THE HOURS WORKED
 50   REM
 60   REM INPUT PAYROLL DATA
 70     INPUT "Enter first name ", FIRST.NAME$
 80     INPUT "Enter last name ", LAST.NAME$
 90     INPUT "Pay rate "; RATE
100     INPUT "Hours worked "; HOURS
110   REM PROCESS PAYROLL DATA
120     LET FULL.NAME$ = FIRST.NAME$ + LAST.NAME$
130     LET GROSS.PAY = RATE*HOURS
140     LET FEDERAL.TAX = GROSS.PAY * .15
150     LET STATE.TAX = GROSS.PAY * .1
160     LET RETIREMENT = GROSS.PAY * .06
170     LET NET.PAY = GROSS.PAY - (FEDERAL.TAX + STATE.TAX + RETIREMENT)
180   REM OUTPUT PAYROLL DATA
190     PRINT "PAYROLL INFORMATION FOR "; FULL.NAME$
200     PRINT
210     PRINT "PAY RATE          ";RATE
220     PRINT "HOURS WORKED      ";HOURS
230     PRINT "GROSS PAY         ";GROSS.PAY
240     PRINT
250     PRINT TAB(14);"DEDUCTIONS"
260     PRINT
270     PRINT "FEDERAL","STATE","RETIREMENT"
280     PRINT FEDERAL.TAX,STATE.TAX,RETIREMENT
290     PRINT
300     PRINT "NET PAY           ";NET.PAY
310   END
```

Exhibit G.13

The Payroll Program with REM Statements and Indentation for Readability

Programming Exercises

1. Modify the product order program (Exercise 1 in the first set of exercises) by expanding the input section to include a product description in addition to price and quantity. Include prompts within the INPUT statements to tell the user what to enter. Calculate a subtotal by multiplying the price by the quantity. Then calculate tax as 6 percent of the subtotal. Add the tax to the subtotal to determine the total for the order. The output should look something like this:

```
ORDER INFORMATION

PRODUCT:    XXXXXXXX
PRICE:      #####
QUANTITY:   #####

SUBTOTAL    TAX        TOTAL
  ######    #####      ######
```

   Use the program to produce an order for a product with a description of WIDGET, a price of $5.95, and a quantity of 16.

2. Modify the mileage program (Exercise 2 in the first set) by including prompts in the INPUT statements used to get the beginning mileage, ending mileage, and number of gallons. Rather than computing total miles and miles per gallon separately, use one statement to compute miles per gallon by subtracting the beginning mileage from the ending mileage and dividing the result by the number of gallons. The output should look like this:

```
BEGINNING   ENDING      NUMBER OF   MILES PER
MILEAGE     MILEAGE     GALLONS     GALLON
########    ########    #########   #########
```

   Use the program to compute the miles per gallon for a trip where the beginning mileage was 12,340, the ending mileage was 12,783, and the number of gallons used was 16.4.

3. Modify the test averaging program (Exercise 3) by adding prompts to the INPUT statements used to get the user to enter the three test scores. Also create a new INPUT statement to allow the user to enter a student name along with the three test scores. Rather than computing the total score and the average separately, use one statement to compute the average by adding the three test scores and dividing by three. The output should look like this:

```
NAME        TEST 1    TEST 2    TEST 3   AVERAGE
XXXXXXXX    ######    ######    ######   ######
```

   Use the program to calculate the average for a student named BILL FARMER with test scores of 93, 89, and 86.

4. Modify the tuition program (Exercise 4) by adding prompts to the INPUT statements used to obtain the total hours for which a student is enrolled and the tuition per hour. Also create a new INPUT statement to allow the user to enter a student name along with the number of hours and tuition per hour. Calculate tuition as the number of hours times the tuition per hour. The output should look like this:

```
NAME:       XXXXXXX
HOURS       TUITION
ENROLLED    PER HOUR      TUITION
#######     #######       #######
```

Use the program to calculate the tuition for a student named RUTH STAMLER enrolled for 17 hours with tuition of $355 per hour.

Control Structures in BASIC

The example payroll program developed at this point exemplifies the basic **sequence control structure** of programming languages. The sequence control structure is represented by the general beginning-to-end flow of a program. In the payroll program, statements are processed once from beginning to end, with the program stopping when the END statement is reached.

Selection Control Structures for Decision Making

In many problem-solving tasks, however, it is also common to have more than one alternative set of steps to perform, depending on the presence or absence of certain conditions. For example, suppose that the calculation of gross pay in the payroll program depended on whether the employee worked more than forty hours. If the person works forty hours or less, the gross pay is simply the pay rate times the number of hours worked. On the other hand, employees who work more than forty hours should be paid 1.5 times the normal pay rate (time and a half) for any hours worked over 40 and the normal pay rate for the 40 regular hours they worked.

In effect, there are two alternative ways to compute an employee's gross pay, depending on whether the hours worked are over forty. In programming languages this is accomplished using the selection control structure described in Chapter 9, "Program Development." In a selection control structure, a group of statements may be executed, depending on whether the result of a logical condition is true or false. A logical condition is simply a logical comparison of two variables or constants. The logical condition can be greater than, less than, equal to, or not equal to.

The IF-THEN Statement

In BASIC, the selection control structure is provided by the IF keyword. The general form for an IF statement is

```
IF logical condition THEN clause
```

The clause is any valid BASIC statement without the line number, and the logical condition is a comparison of two variables, constants or expressions, using one of the following relational operators:

Operator	Relationship
=	equal to
<> or ><	not equal to
<	less than
>	greater than
<= or =<	less than or equal to
>= or =>	greater than or equal to

Some examples of valid logical conditions in BASIC would be

```
TAXABLE.INCOME > 5000
AGE/2 >= 30
TEMP > AVERAGE.TEMP
UNITS*PRICE <> TOTAL.SALE
2<>3
```

If the logical condition in the IF statement is true, the clause in the IF statement is executed and BASIC continues with the next line of the program. When the logical condition is false, BASIC goes on to the next line of the program without executing the clause in the IF statement.

In the payroll program, the logical condition to test if an employee has worked more than forty hours would be

```
IF HOURS > 40
```

If this logical condition is false, then the gross pay for the employee should simply be the number of hours worked times the pay rate for the employee.

When this logical condition is true, the gross pay is the normal pay rate for the initial forty hours the employee worked, plus 1.5 times the normal pay rate for the hours worked beyond forty. To calculate the gross pay for employees working overtime, the following two lines could be added to the payroll program:

```
LET OT.HOURS = HOURS - 40
IF HOURS > 40 THEN GROSS.PAY=(40*RATE)+
  (OT.HOURS*1.5*RATE)
```

To calculate the gross pay for overtime hours, a variable called OT.HOURS has been added to hold the number of overtime hours the employee has worked. Exhibit G.14 shows the payroll program with these statements added to it.

```
 10   REM   VERSION 5
 20   REM
 30   REM   THIS PROGRAM CALCULATES THE NET PAY AND DEDUCTIONS FOR
 40   REM   AN EMPLOYEE GIVEN THE PAY RATE AND THE HOURS WORKED
 50   REM
 60   REM INPUT PAYROLL DATA
 70      INPUT "Enter first name ", FIRST.NAME$
 80      INPUT "Enter last name ", LAST.NAME$
 90      INPUT "Pay rate "; RATE
100      INPUT "Hours worked "; HOURS
110   REM PROCESS PAYROLL DATA
120      LET FULL.NAME$ = FIRST.NAME$ + LAST.NAME$
130      LET GROSS.PAY = RATE*HOURS
140      LET OT.HOURS = HOURS - 40
150      IF HOURS > 40 THEN LET GROSS.PAY=(40*RATE)+(OT.HOURS*1.5*RATE)
160      LET FEDERAL.TAX = GROSS.PAY * .15
170      LET STATE.TAX = GROSS.PAY * .1
180      LET RETIREMENT = GROSS.PAY * .06
190      LET NET.PAY = GROSS.PAY - (FEDERAL.TAX + STATE.TAX + RETIREMENT)
200   REM OUTPUT PAYROLL DATA
210      PRINT "PAYROLL INFORMATION FOR "; FULL.NAME$
220      PRINT
230      PRINT "PAY RATE      ";RATE
240      PRINT "HOURS WORKED ";HOURS
250      PRINT "GROSS PAY     ";GROSS.PAY
260      PRINT
270      PRINT TAB(14);"DEDUCTIONS"
280      PRINT
290      PRINT "FEDERAL","STATE","RETIREMENT"
300      PRINT FEDERAL.TAX,STATE.TAX,RETIREMENT
310      PRINT
320      PRINT "NET PAY       ";NET.PAY
330   END
```

Exhibit G.14

The Payroll Program with an IF-THEN Statement

Note that gross pay is computed as it was in the previous payroll program, in line 130. For employees working forty hours or less, this will be the correct computation for gross pay. For employees working more than forty hours, this will produce an incorrect gross pay since this formula doesn't take overtime into account. In line 140, overtime hours are computed by subtracting forty from the number of hours the employee worked. For employees working forty hours or less, this will produce zero or a negative number of overtime hours. The IF statement in line 150, however, will only use the overtime hours when the employee has worked more than forty hours. In line 150, the IF statement recalculates the gross pay for employees who have worked overtime. Thus, for employees working more than forty hours, the IF statement replaces the incorrect gross pay calculated in line 130 with the correct gross pay. Regardless of whether the logical condition in the IF statement is true or false, BASIC always continues with the line following the IF statement (see Exhibit G.15).

The IF-THEN-ELSE Statement

The calculation of gross pay in line 130 of the payroll program (Exhibit G.14) should really only be performed for employees who have not worked any overtime hours. For employees working overtime hours, the calculation

```
130    LET GROSS.PAY = RATE*HOURS
140    LET OT.HOURS = HOURS - 40
             True
150    IF HOURS > 40 THEN LET GROSS.PAY=(40*RATE)+(OT.HOURS*1.5*RATE)
             False
160    LET FEDERAL.TAX = GROSS.PAY * .15
170    LET STATE.TAX = GROSS.PAY * .1
180    LET RETIREMENT = GROSS.PAY * .06
190    LET NET.PAY = GROSS.PAY - (FEDERAL.TAX + STATE.TAX + RETIREMENT)
```

Exhibit G.15

Processing of an IF Statement in BASIC

```
                              HOURS > 40

                         True                          False
GROSS.PAY=(40*RATE)+(OT.HOURS*1.5*RATE)         GROSS.PAY = RATE*HOURS
```

Exhibit G.16

Selection Structure Containing Two Alternative Ways of Calculating Gross Pay

of gross pay in line 130 was incorrect but the IF statement recalculated the gross pay correctly for those employees. A better selection structure for this calculation would be to separate the two methods of calculating the gross pay so that only the correct computation is used for each group of employees (see Exhibit G.16).

This change in the structure of the program requires the use of a more complex version of the IF-THEN statement—the IF-THEN-ELSE statement. The general form for an IF-THEN-ELSE statement is

```
IF logical condition THEN clause ELSE clause
```

In this statement, the clause following the THEN is executed when the logical condition is true and the clause following the ELSE is executed when the condition is false. After executing one of the two clauses, BASIC continues with the next line of the program. Thus, for the calculation of gross pay, the IF statement would be

```
IF HOURS > 40 THEN GROSS.PAY=(40*RATE)+
  (OT.HOURS*1.5*RATE)
ELSE     GROSS.PAY=HOURS*RATE
```

When this statement is executed, BASIC first determines if the logical condition is true or false. When the logical condition is true, the clause after the word THEN is executed. When the condition is false, the clause following the word ELSE is executed. Exhibit G.17 shows the payroll

```
 10    REM  VERSION 6
 20    REM
 30    REM  THIS PROGRAM CALCULATES THE NET PAY AND DEDUCTIONS FOR
 40    REM  AN EMPLOYEE GIVEN THE PAY RATE AND THE HOURS WORKED
 50    REM
 60    REM INPUT PAYROLL DATA
 70      INPUT "Enter first name ", FIRST.NAME$
 80      INPUT "Enter last name ", LAST.NAME$
 90      INPUT "Pay rate "; RATE
100      INPUT "Hours worked "; HOURS
110    REM PROCESS PAYROLL DATA
120      LET FULL.NAME$ = FIRST.NAME$ + LAST.NAME$
130      LET OT.HOURS = HOURS - 40
140      IF HOURS > 40 THEN LET GROSS.PAY=(40*RATE)+(OT.HOURS*1.5*RATE)
                          ELSE LET GROSS.PAY=HOURS*RATE
150      LET FEDERAL.TAX = GROSS.PAY * .15
160      LET STATE.TAX = GROSS.PAY * .1
170      LET RETIREMENT = GROSS.PAY * .06
180      LET NET.PAY = GROSS.PAY - (FEDERAL.TAX + STATE.TAX + RETIREMENT)
190    REM OUTPUT PAYROLL DATA
200      PRINT "PAYROLL INFORMATION FOR "; FULL.NAME$
210      PRINT
220      PRINT "PAY RATE              ";RATE
230      PRINT "HOURS WORKED          ";HOURS
240      PRINT "GROSS PAY             ";GROSS.PAY
250      PRINT
260      PRINT TAB(14);"DEDUCTIONS"
270      PRINT
280      PRINT "FEDERAL","STATE","RETIREMENT"
290      PRINT FEDERAL.TAX,STATE.TAX,RETIREMENT
300      PRINT
310      PRINT "NET PAY               ";NET.PAY
320    END
```

Exhibit G.17

The Payroll Program Using an IF-THEN-ELSE to Calculate Gross Pay

program with the IF-THEN-ELSE statement used to calculate the gross pay for an employee. Note how the old statement for calculating gross pay (GROSS.PAY = HOURS*RATE) has now been dropped and the lines of the program have been renumbered.

Also note the way line 140 of the payroll program now appears to occupy two separate lines on the program listing. This is typed as one line with a large number of blank spaces (entered with space bar) in front of the ELSE part of the statement. In BASIC, statements can be up to 255 characters in length, with the 255th character being the return character entered at the end of the line.

Since microcomputer screens display only eighty characters, BASIC will automatically wrap the eighty-first character to the next line and allow you to continue typing. Thus, when line 140 was entered, SPACEBAR was pressed until the cursor was lined up under the word THEN in the line above before the word ELSE was typed. This is not required by BASIC, but notice how much more readable the statement is with this indentation. As noted earlier, indentation can be a powerful tool for making programs more readable. Exhibit G.18 shows a flowchart for the version of the payroll program containing the IF-THEN-ELSE selection control structure.

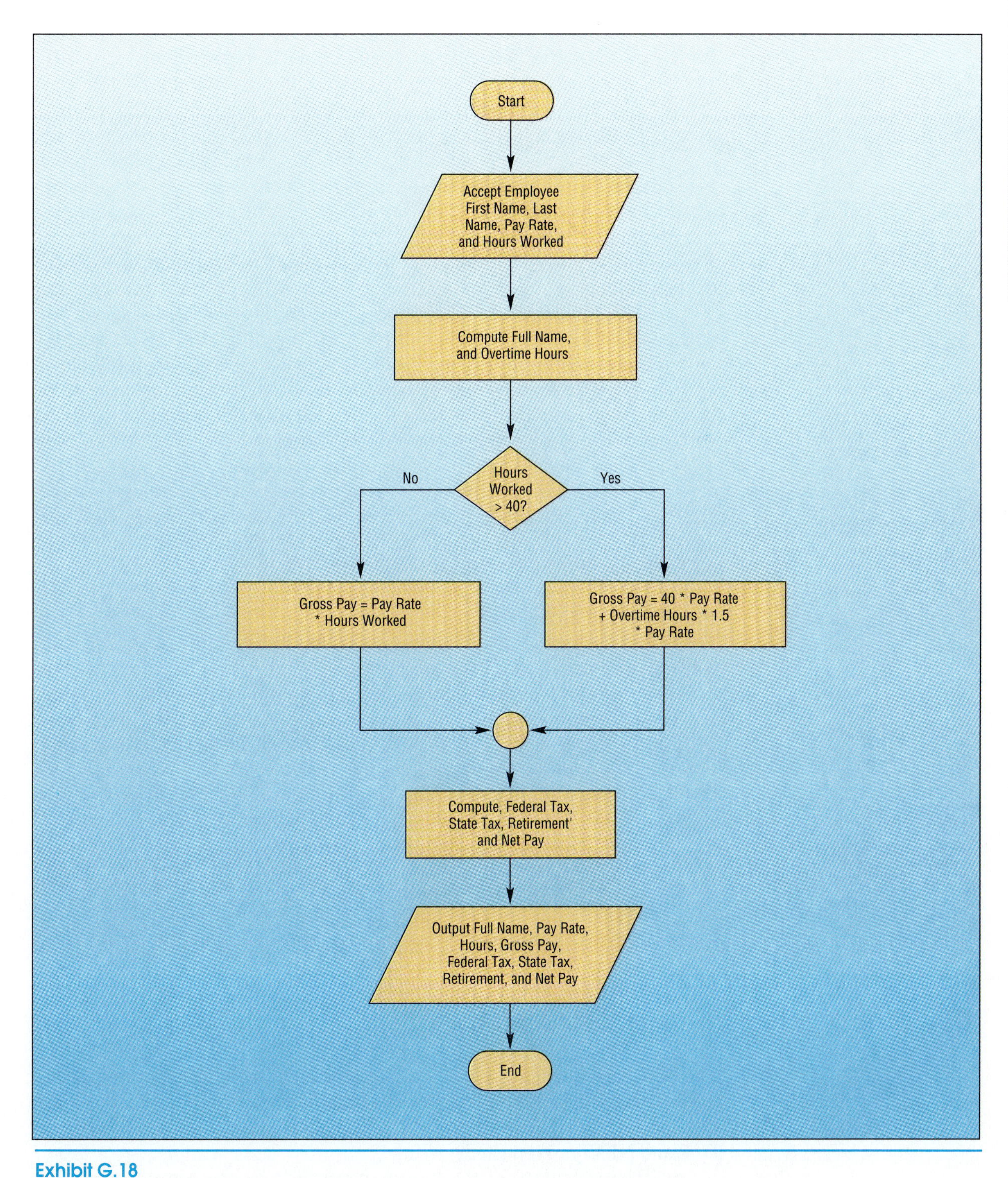

Exhibit G.18

A Flowchart for the Version of the Payroll Program Using the IF-THEN-ELSE Selection Structure

Iterative Control Structures for Program Repetition

One of the major shortcomings of the current version of the payroll program is that it is limited to processing the payroll information for only one employee. When the payroll for additional employees is to be processed, the program must be run again for each employee. A better design would be to have the program repeat the execution of the statements involved with the input, processing, and output of data for each employee. This would require the incorporation of an **iterative control structure** into the program.

As you learned in Chapter 9, "Program Development," loops can be controlled by either a pretest or post-test condition. In BASIC, the two most common statements for creating loops are the FOR-NEXT and WHILE-WEND statements. Both of these use pretest conditions, meaning that a logical condition is tested prior to each execution of the statements within the loop to determine if the loop will be executed.

In the payroll program, the input, processing, and output statements should be repeated within a loop to allow several employees to be processed during a single execution of the program. The creation of this loop in the payroll program will be illustrated below, first using a FOR-NEXT loop and then a WHILE-WEND loop.

The FOR-NEXT Statement

The FOR-NEXT statement is commonly used when there are a specific and constant number of times the loop is to executed within the program. For example, suppose the company using the payroll program has five employees, and every time the payroll program is executed, all five employees need to be processed. A FOR-NEXT loop could be set up to have the program perform the input, processing, and output steps five times and then allow the program to end. The syntax for the FOR-NEXT loop is

```
FOR counter variable = start TO stop STEP
  increment
    .
    .
    (statements within the loop)
    .
    .
NEXT counter variable
```

The FOR-NEXT statement is a two-part statement with the beginning of the loop marked by the FOR part of the statement and the end of the loop marked with the NEXT part of the statement. All the statements between FOR and NEXT are repeated.

The execution of the loop is controlled by the counter variable. Following the equal sign, the programmer indicates a starting value for the counter variable and an ending value for the counter variable. When BASIC executes the FOR statement, the starting value is placed in the counter variable. The statements up to the NEXT statement are then executed. The NEXT statement references the same counter variable appearing in the FOR statement. FOR and NEXT statements must always appear in pairs. There can never be a FOR without a matching NEXT.

When the NEXT statement is executed, BASIC will increase the value in the counter variable by the increment specified in the FOR statement. The increment is optional in the FOR statement; if left off, the increment is assumed to be 1. After increasing the value in the counter variable by 1 (or whatever the increment is set to) BASIC returns to the FOR statement and tries to execute the loop again.

Before executing the loop a second time, BASIC checks the value in the counter variable to see if it is *less than or equal* to the end value specified after the word TO. If the counter value is still *less than or equal* to the end value after the incrementation caused by the NEXT statement, the loop will be executed again. If the counter value is *greater than* the end value after incrementation, the loop will not be executed again and BASIC will move on to the statement following the NEXT statement at the end of the loop.

Exhibit G.19a shows the payroll program flowchart with a FOR-NEXT loop added. Exhibit G.19b shows the code for the program. In the program, note the construction of the FOR statement with a counter variable called COUNTER, which starts at a value of 1 and ends when the value exceeds 5. The STEP part of the FOR statement was omitted, which means an increment of 1 will be used.

As the program is executed the counter will begin at 1 and the loop will continue for five repetitions. At the end of the fifth execution of the loop, the NEXT statement will increment the counter variable to 6. BASIC will then go back to the FOR statement and test the value of the counter against the end value of 5. This time the counter value exceeds the end value, and the loop will not be executed the sixth time. Instead, BASIC will skip to line 350, which is the statement after the NEXT statement in the loop.

Another addition to this new version of the payroll program is the PRINT statement in line 330, which generates a blank line. This was added because after the output information is displayed, the loop will cause the INPUT statements to be executed again, which will display the prompts associated with them. Without the PRINT in line 330, the prompts from the INPUT statements would be displayed immediately after the last line of payroll information displaying the net pay for the first employee. The PRINT statement in line 330 provides a blank line between the end of the output information and the beginning of the prompt for input of information for the next employee.

A More Flexible FOR-NEXT Loop

The FOR-NEXT loop presented in the previous section is useful when a loop is always executed a specific number of times. Suppose, however, that the number of employees to be processed by the payroll program was unknown or was constantly changing. Under these circumstances it would not be possible to predetermine the end value for the counter. A possible solution to this problem would be to modify the FOR statement to contain a variable where the end value normally appears.

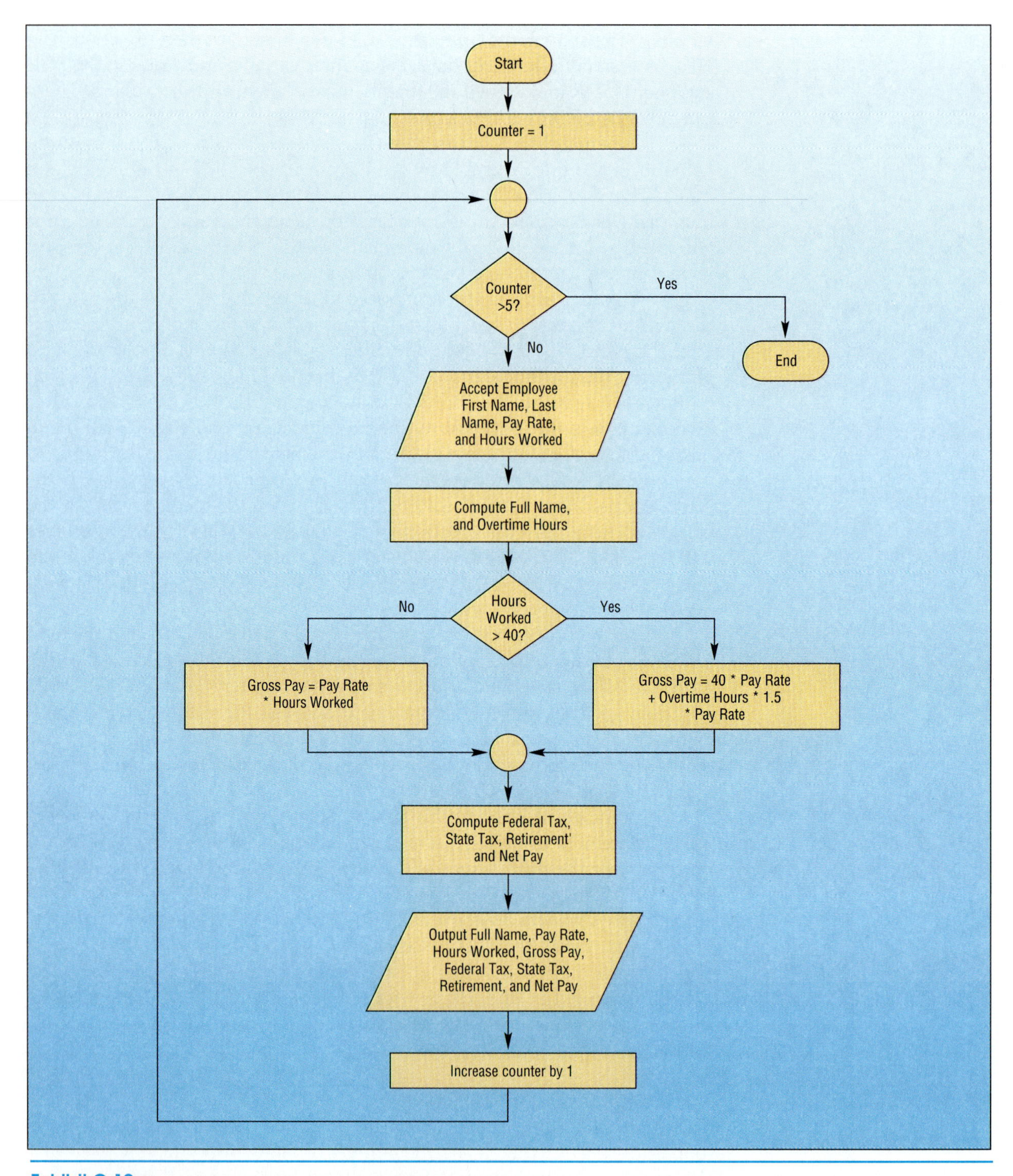

Exhibit G.19a

Flowchart for the Payroll Program with a FOR-NEXT Loop

```
 10   REM  VERSION 7
 20   REM
 30   REM  THIS PROGRAM CALCULATES THE NET PAY AND DEDUCTIONS FOR
 40   REM  AN EMPLOYEE GIVEN THE PAY RATE AND THE HOURS WORKED
 50   REM
 60   FOR COUNTER = 1 TO 5
 70     REM INPUT PAYROLL DATA
 80      INPUT "Enter first name ", FIRST.NAME$
 90      INPUT "Enter last name ", LAST.NAME$
100      INPUT "Pay rate "; RATE
110      INPUT "Hours worked "; HOURS
120     REM PROCESS PAYROLL DATA
130      LET FULL.NAME$ = FIRST.NAME$ + LAST.NAME$
140      LET OT.HOURS = HOURS - 40
150      IF HOURS > 40 THEN LET GROSS.PAY=(40*RATE)+(OT.HOURS*1.5*RATE)
                       ELSE LET GROSS.PAY=HOURS*RATE
160      LET FEDERAL.TAX = GROSS.PAY * .15
170      LET STATE.TAX = GROSS.PAY * .1
180      LET RETIREMENT = GROSS.PAY * .06
190      LET NET.PAY = GROSS.PAY - (FEDERAL.TAX + STATE.TAX + RETIREMENT)
200   REM OUTPUT PAYROLL DATA
210     PRINT "PAYROLL INFORMATION FOR "; FULL.NAME$
220     PRINT
230     PRINT "PAY RATE      ";RATE
240     PRINT "HOURS WORKED  ";HOURS
250     PRINT "GROSS PAY     ";GROSS.PAY
260     PRINT
270     PRINT TAB(14);"DEDUCTIONS"
280     PRINT
290     PRINT "FEDERAL","STATE","RETIREMENT"
300     PRINT FEDERAL.TAX,STATE.TAX,RETIREMENT
310     PRINT
320     PRINT "NET PAY       ";NET.PAY
330     PRINT
340   NEXT COUNTER
350   END
```

Exhibit G.19b

Code for the Version of the Payroll Program Using a FOR-NEXT Loop

As the program begins, the user could be asked how many employees were to be processed using an INPUT statement. This INPUT statement could then fill in the variable representing the end value for the loop, and the program would process the loop the correct number of times. Exhibit G.20 shows the payroll program set up to use this type of loop.

The WHILE-WEND Statement

An alternative to the FOR-NEXT loop is the WHILE-WEND loop. Like the FOR-NEXT loop, the WHILE-WEND loop is a pretest loop that consists of two parts that must appear as a pair within the program. The general syntax for the WHILE-WEND statement is

```
WHILE logical condition
    .
    .
    (statements within the loop)
    .
    .
WEND
```

```
 10     REM  VERSION 8
 20     REM
 30     REM  THIS PROGRAM CALCULATES THE NET PAY AND DEDUCTIONS FOR
 40     REM  AN EMPLOYEE GIVEN THE PAY RATE AND THE HOURS WORKED
 50     REM
 60     REM OBTAIN NUMBER OF EMPLOYEES TO BE PROCESSED
 70       INPUT "Enter the number of employees to process ", END.VALUE
 80     FOR COUNTER = 1 TO END.VALUE
 90       REM INPUT PAYROLL DATA
100        INPUT "Enter first name ", FIRST.NAME$
110        INPUT "Enter last name ", LAST.NAME$
120        INPUT "Pay rate "; RATE
130        INPUT "Hours worked "; HOURS
140       REM PROCESS PAYROLL DATA
150        LET FULL.NAME$ = FIRST.NAME$ + LAST.NAME$
160        LET OT.HOURS = HOURS - 40
170        IF HOURS > 40 THEN LET GROSS.PAY=(40*RATE)+(OT.HOURS*1.5*RATE)
           ELSE LET GROSS.PAY=HOURS*RATE
180        LET FEDERAL.TAX = GROSS.PAY * .15
190        LET STATE.TAX = GROSS.PAY * .1
200        LET RETIREMENT = GROSS.PAY * .06
210        LET NET.PAY = GROSS.PAY - (FEDERAL.TAX + STATE.TAX + RETIREMENT)
220       REM OUTPUT PAYROLL DATA
230        PRINT "PAYROLL INFORMATION FOR "; FULL.NAME$
240        PRINT
250        PRINT "PAY RATE      ";RATE
260        PRINT "HOURS WORKED  ";HOURS
270        PRINT "GROSS PAY     ";GROSS.PAY
280        PRINT
290        PRINT TAB(14);"DEDUCTIONS"
300        PRINT
310        PRINT "FEDERAL","STATE","RETIREMENT"
320        PRINT FEDERAL.TAX,STATE.TAX,RETIREMENT
330        PRINT
340        PRINT "NET PAY       ";NET.PAY
350        PRINT
360     NEXT COUNTER
370     END
```

Exhibit G.20

The Payroll Program with a FOR-NEXT Loop Using a Variable to Determine the End Value

Repetition of the statements between the WHILE and WEND is controlled by the logical condition in the WHILE statement. Prior to each execution of the loop, BASIC evaluates the logical condition to see if it is true or false. When the condition is true, the statements within the loop are executed. When the WEND statement is executed, BASIC returns to the WHILE statement to evaluate the logical condition again. When the condition is false, the statements within the loop are skipped and BASIC continues processing statements following the WEND (see Exhibit G.21).

Unlike the NEXT in a FOR-NEXT loop, the WEND in a WHILE-WEND loop does not change the value in any variable. Therefore, somewhere within the loop a statement (or statements) must be capable of altering the contents of one or more variables that will cause the logical condition to become false. Thus, the condition for the WHILE-WEND loop must be carefully constructed to ensure that it can eventually become false so that the loop can stop. If the condition controlling the WHILE-WEND loop can never become false, the program will enter the loop and never be able to leave, causing what is known as an **infinite loop**.

A loop similar to the FOR-NEXT loop in Exhibit G.20 is shown in Exhibit G.22. Within the WHILE-WEND loop, the logical condition uses a

Exhibit G.21

The Flow of a WHILE-WEND Loop

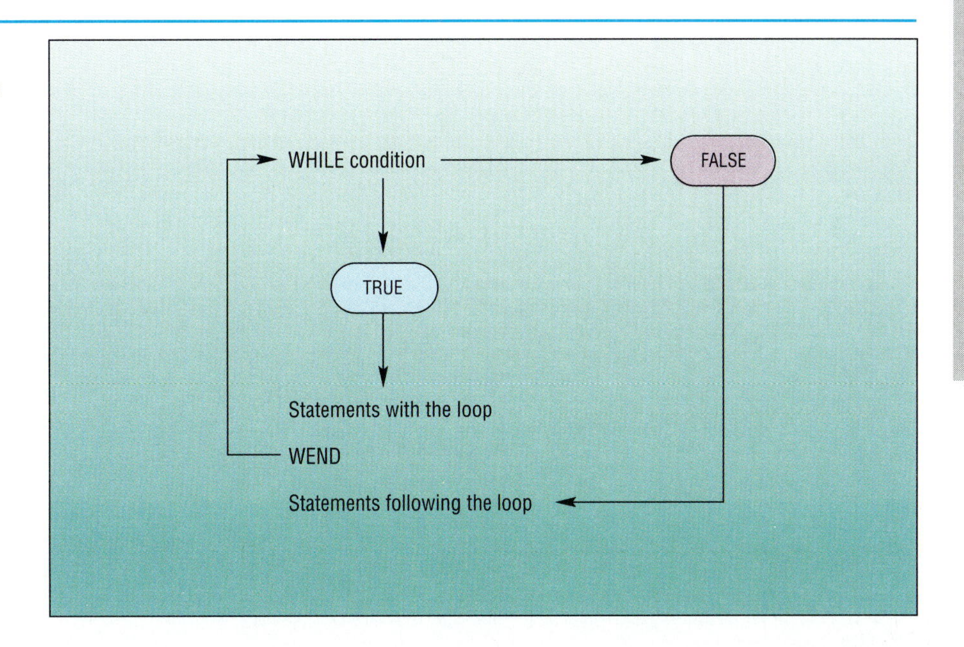

variable called EMPLOYEE.COUNT to keep track of the number of the employees that have been processed. At the beginning of the program the user is asked to indicate the number of employees to be processed. That number is stored in a variable called END.VALUE. This represents the number of times the loop should be processed within the program to input, process, and output the payroll information. The condition checks the EMPLOYEE.COUNT variable against the END.VALUE variable to determine if all the employees have been processed.

The key to having the loop count the number of employees that have been processed is line 370. This is an example of an **accumulator** variable in BASIC. Notice how this statement takes the value in the EMPLOYEE.COUNT variable, adds 1 to it, and stores the result of that addition back in the EMPLOYEE.COUNT variable. In effect, this statement has increased the value in the EMPLOYEE.COUNT variable by 1. Each time through the loop, the EMPLOYEE.COUNT variable increases by 1 to count how many times the loop has been executed, similar to the way a variable controls a FOR-NEXT loop.

Another critical addition to the program related to the use of a WHILE-WEND loop, is the assignment statement located in line 80. This starts the EMPLOYEE.COUNT variable at 1 before entering the loop for the first time. This is known as **initializing** the loop. Typically the initialization of a WHILE-WEND loop ensures that the logical condition controlling the loop will be true the first time the WHILE is executed.

Putting all these components together, the program begins by obtaining the END.VALUE from the user and starting EMPLOYEE.COUNT at 1. The WHILE statement will then begin the loop the first time (assuming the user has not entered 0 or a negative number as the END.VALUE). After the first pass through the loop, the assignment statement in line 370 changes the EMPLOYEE.COUNT to 2 by adding 1 to

```
 10    REM  VERSION 9
 20    REM
 30    REM  THIS PROGRAM CALCULATES THE NET PAY FOR AN EMPLOYEE
 40    REM  GIVEN THE PAY RATE AND THE HOURS WORKED
 50    REM
 60    REM OBTAIN NUMBER OF EMPLOYEES TO BE PROCESSED
 70     INPUT "Enter the number of employees to process ", END.VALUE
 80     LET EMPLOYEE.COUNT = 1
 90     WHILE EMPLOYEE.COUNT <= END.VALUE
100       REM INPUT PAYROLL DATA
110       INPUT "Enter first name ", FIRST.NAME$
120       INPUT "Enter last name ", LAST.NAME$
130       INPUT "Pay rate "; RATE
140       INPUT "Hours worked "; HOURS
150       REM PROCESS PAYROLL DATA
160       LET FULL.NAME$ = FIRST.NAME$ + LAST.NAME$
170       LET OT.HOURS = HOURS - 40
180       IF HOURS > 40 THEN LET GROSS.PAY=(40*RATE)+(OT.HOURS*1.5*RATE)
                       ELSE LET GROSS.PAY=HOURS*RATE
190       LET FEDERAL.TAX = GROSS.PAY * .15
200       LET STATE.TAX = GROSS.PAY * .1
210       LET RETIREMENT = GROSS.PAY * .06
220       LET NET.PAY = GROSS.PAY - (FEDERAL.TAX + STATE.TAX + RETIREMENT)
230     REM OUTPUT PAYROLL DATA
240       PRINT "PAYROLL INFORMATION FOR "; FULL.NAME$
250       PRINT
260       PRINT "PAY RATE     ";RATE
270       PRINT "HOURS WORKED ";HOURS
280       PRINT "GROSS PAY    ";GROSS.PAY
290       PRINT
300       PRINT TAB(14);"DEDUCTIONS"
310       PRINT
320       PRINT "FEDERAL","STATE","RETIREMENT"
330       PRINT FEDERAL.TAX,STATE.TAX,RETIREMENT
340       PRINT
350       PRINT "NET PAY      ";NET.PAY
360       PRINT
370     LET EMPLOYEE.COUNT = EMPLOYEE.COUNT + 1
380    WEND
390    END
```

Exhibit G.22

The Payroll Program with a WHILE-WEND Loop

the initial value of 1. Control then passes back to the WHILE statement, where the logical condition is evaluated to see if the loop should be executed again. The logical condition ensures that as long as the count remains less than or equal to the end value, the loop will continue to be executed.

Suppose that the user has entered 2 as the END.VALUE for the loop. After the first pass through the loop the count is 2, and the logical condition allows the loop to execute a second time since the count and end values are equal. At the end of the second pass through the loop, the count becomes 3. Control again passes back to the WHILE statement which tests the logical condition again. This time the count is greater than the end value, which means the logical condition is now false. This causes BASIC to skip the loop before the third pass is made and continue with the statement following the WEND, which in this case is an END statement that stops the entire program.

```
 10    REM  VERSION 10
 20    REM
 30    REM  THIS PROGRAM CALCULATES THE NET PAY FOR AN EMPLOYEE
 40    REM  GIVEN THE PAY RATE AND THE HOURS WORKED
 50    REM
 60    REM OBTAIN NUMBER OF EMPLOYEES TO BE PROCESSED
 80     LET ANSWER$ = "Y"
 90     WHILE ANSWER$ = "Y"
100       REM INPUT PAYROLL DATA
110       INPUT "Enter first name ", FIRST.NAME$
120       INPUT "Enter last name ", LAST.NAME$
130       INPUT "Pay rate "; RATE
140       INPUT "Hours worked "; HOURS
150      REM PROCESS PAYROLL DATA
160       LET FULL.NAME$ = FIRST.NAME$ + LAST.NAME$
170       LET OT.HOURS = HOURS - 40
180       IF HOURS > 40 THEN LET GROSS.PAY=(40*RATE)+(OT.HOURS*1.5*RATE)
                     ELSE LET GROSS.PAY=HOURS*RATE
190       LET FEDERAL.TAX = GROSS.PAY * .15
200       LET STATE.TAX = GROSS.PAY * .1
210       LET RETIREMENT = GROSS.PAY * .06
220       LET NET.PAY = GROSS.PAY - (FEDERAL.TAX + STATE.TAX + RETIREMENT)
230     REM OUTPUT PAYROLL DATA
240       PRINT "PAYROLL INFORMATION FOR "; FULL.NAME$
250       PRINT
260       PRINT "PAY RATE         ";RATE
270       PRINT "HOURS WORKED     ";HOURS
280       PRINT "GROSS PAY        ";GROSS.PAY
290       PRINT
300       PRINT TAB(14);"DEDUCTIONS"
310       PRINT
320       PRINT "FEDERAL","STATE","RETIREMENT"
330       PRINT FEDERAL.TAX,STATE.TAX,RETIREMENT
340       PRINT
350       PRINT "NET PAY          ";NET.PAY
360       PRINT
370     INPUT "Process another employee (Y/N)"; ANSWER$
380    WEND
390    END
```

Exhibit G.23

The Payroll Program with a WHILE-WEND Loop Controlled by an ANSWER$ Variable

Another WHILE-WEND Loop

In the preceding program, the WHILE-WEND loop was controlled by asking the user to specify the number of times the loop was to be executed. Suppose, however, that the user doesn't know or doesn't want to specify how many employees are to be processed. Rather than controlling the execution of the loop by counting the number of times it is executed, the user could be asked after each execution of the loop to indicate whether the loop is to be executed again. The program shown in Exhibit G.23 illustrates this approach.

In this loop, the variable ANSWER$ is used to control the WHILE-WEND loop. The INPUT statement in line 370 is used to ask the user for permission to execute the loop another time and stores the user's response in a string variable called ANSWER$. As the prompt in the INPUT statement indicates, the user is supposed to enter an uppercase *Y* if the loop is to be executed again and an *N* if the loop is not to be executed again. The WHILE statement looks at the contents of the ANSWER$ variable to determine if the loop is to be executed. As long as the user responds with Y, the logical condition controlling the loop remains true. Note that anything

```
10    REM  VERSION 10
20    REM
30    REM  THIS PROGRAM CALCULATES THE NET PAY FOR AN EMPLOYEE
40    REM  GIVEN THE PAY RATE AND THE HOURS WORKED
50    REM
60    REM OBTAIN NUMBER OF EMPLOYEES TO BE PROCESSED
80      LET ANSWER$ = "Y"
90      WHILE ANSWER$ = "Y"
100   REM INPUT PAYROLL DATA                                         Input
110      INPUT "Enter first name ", FIRST.NAME$
120      INPUT "Enter last name ", LAST.NAME$
130      INPUT "Pay rate "; RATE
140      INPUT "Hours worked "; HOURS
150   REM PROCESS PAYROLL DATA
160      LET FULL.NAME$ = FIRST.NAME$ + LAST.NAME$                   Processing
170      LET OT.HOURS = HOURS - 40
180      IF HOURS > 40 THEN LET GROSS.PAY=(40*RATE)+(OT.HOURS*1.5*RATE)
         ELSE LET GROSS.PAY=HOURS*RATE
190      LET FEDERAL.TAX = GROSS.PAY * .15
200      LET STATE.TAX = GROSS.PAY * .1
210      LET RETIREMENT = GROSS.PAY * .06
220      LET NET.PAY = GROSS.PAY - (FEDERAL.TAX + STATE.TAX + RETIREMENT)
230   REM OUTPUT PAYROLL DATA
240      PRINT "PAYROLL INFORMATION FOR "; FULL.NAME$                Output
310      PRINT
250      PRINT
260      PRINT "PAY RATE        ";RATE
270      PRINT "HOURS WORKED    ";HOURS
280      PRINT "GROSS PAY       ";GROSS.PAY
290      PRINT
300      PRINT TAB(14);"DEDUCTIONS"
320      PRINT "FEDERAL","STATE","RETIREMENT"
330      PRINT FEDERAL.TAX,STATE.TAX,RETIREMENT
340      PRINT
350      PRINT "NET PAY         ";NET.PAY
360      PRINT
370     INPUT "Process another employee (Y/N)"; ANSWER$
380   WEND
390   END
```

Exhibit G.24

The Input, Processing, and Output Stages of the Payroll Program

other than an uppercase *Y* (including a lowercase *y*) entered into the ANSWER$ variable will cause the logical condition to become false, which causes the loop to stop.

As with the WHILE-WEND loop in the previous program, the logical condition controlling the loop must be initialized prior to the first execution of the loop to ensure that the loop will be executed the first time. Thus, the assignment statement in line 80 sets the ANSWER$ variable equal to Y to make sure the logical condition will be true as the WHILE statement is executed for the first time.

Structuring Programs with Subroutines

Exhibit G.24 shows the version of the payroll program using a WHILE-END loop, with the input, processing, and output stages of the program highlighted. Since statements have been added to the first payroll program

Exhibit G.25

The General Layout of Tasks for the Payroll Program

```
Begin loop to process many employees
       Obtain input data from user
       Perform payroll calculations
       Display payroll information
       Determine if process is to be repeated
End of loop
```

to improve printing, and incorporate decision-making capabilities, and create a loop, the size of each of the three sections has grown. With these additions, the program has become more complex and more difficult to read. Complex programs such as this can be broken into many individual tasks in addition to the general tasks of input, processing, and output.

In general terms, the payroll program could be broken into four basic tasks: obtain input from the user, process the payroll data, display the payroll information to the user, and determine if the process is to be repeated. Furthermore, these four tasks would be within a loop, which allows them to be executed as many times as necessary. Exhibit G.25 shows a general layout for these tasks.

This general layout represents a summary of the payroll program that is logical and easy to understand. In BASIC, it is possible to break a complex program into individual tasks using **subroutines**. A subroutine is generally a group of statements that perform some distinct task. Thus, the statements in the payroll program could be broken into four groups of statements organized around the four identified tasks required for the payroll application. These groups of statements (or subroutines) could then be executed in series within a loop to process the payroll information. In BASIC, the modularization of a program by creating subroutines is accomplished using the GOSUB-RETURN statement.

The GOSUB-RETURN Statement

GOSUB-RETURN is another example of a two-part statement that requires a pairing of a GOSUB statement with a matching RETURN statement. The syntax of the GOSUB statement is

```
GOSUB line-number
```

where *line-number* is the number of another statement in the program. When the GOSUB statement is executed, BASIC goes to the line indicated and continues processing statements at that location. The statement at the line referenced in the GOSUB is the first statement in the block of statements representing the subroutine. The last statement in the block of statements for the subroutine is always a RETURN statement. The syntax for a RETURN statement is simply

```
RETURN
```

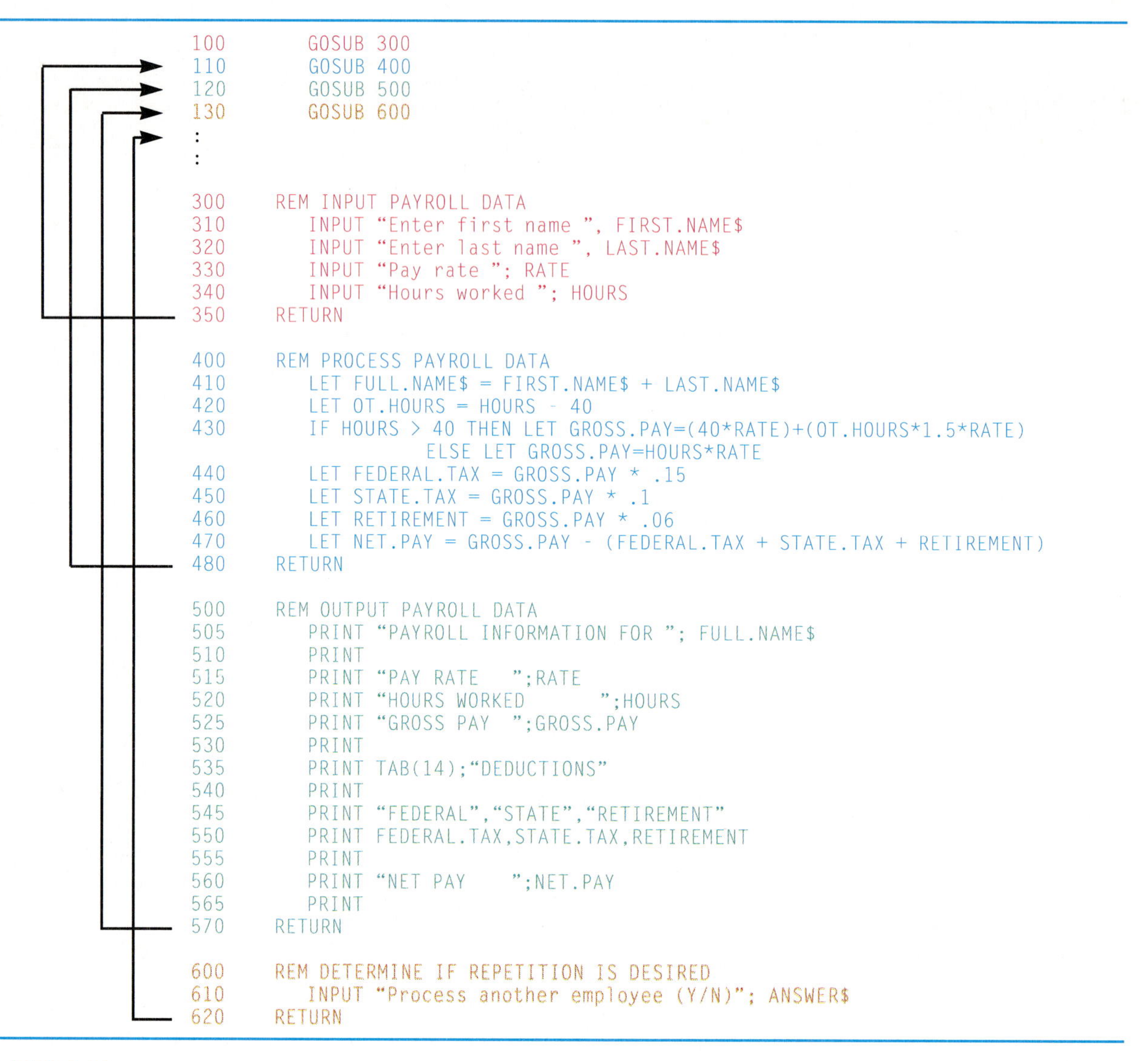

```
100      GOSUB 300
110      GOSUB 400
120      GOSUB 500
130      GOSUB 600
 :
 :

300    REM INPUT PAYROLL DATA
310      INPUT "Enter first name ", FIRST.NAME$
320      INPUT "Enter last name ", LAST.NAME$
330      INPUT "Pay rate "; RATE
340      INPUT "Hours worked "; HOURS
350    RETURN

400    REM PROCESS PAYROLL DATA
410      LET FULL.NAME$ = FIRST.NAME$ + LAST.NAME$
420      LET OT.HOURS = HOURS - 40
430      IF HOURS > 40 THEN LET GROSS.PAY=(40*RATE)+(OT.HOURS*1.5*RATE)
                 ELSE LET GROSS.PAY=HOURS*RATE
440      LET FEDERAL.TAX = GROSS.PAY * .15
450      LET STATE.TAX = GROSS.PAY * .1
460      LET RETIREMENT = GROSS.PAY * .06
470      LET NET.PAY = GROSS.PAY - (FEDERAL.TAX + STATE.TAX + RETIREMENT)
480    RETURN

500    REM OUTPUT PAYROLL DATA
505      PRINT "PAYROLL INFORMATION FOR "; FULL.NAME$
510      PRINT
515      PRINT "PAY RATE    ";RATE
520      PRINT "HOURS WORKED        ";HOURS
525      PRINT "GROSS PAY   ";GROSS.PAY
530      PRINT
535      PRINT TAB(14);"DEDUCTIONS"
540      PRINT
545      PRINT "FEDERAL","STATE","RETIREMENT"
550      PRINT FEDERAL.TAX,STATE.TAX,RETIREMENT
555      PRINT
560      PRINT "NET PAY     ";NET.PAY
565      PRINT
570    RETURN

600    REM DETERMINE IF REPETITION IS DESIRED
610      INPUT "Process another employee (Y/N)"; ANSWER$
620    RETURN
```

Exhibit G.26

Subroutines for the Payroll Program

This RETURN statement serves two functions. First, it marks the end of the subroutine. Second, it causes BASIC to return to the statement following the GOSUB that caused BASIC to begin processing the subroutine. Thus, a GOSUB is like a temporary detour from the normal top-to-bottom processing of the program. When the GOSUB is executed, BASIC temporarily transfers execution to another part of the program. But when the RETURN statement is reached, BASIC takes up where it left off when the GOSUB was encountered.

In the payroll program, a separate subroutine could be constructed for each of the four tasks required in the program. Four GOSUB statements could then be used to execute each part in the sequence required. Exhibit G.26 shows the four subroutines that would be required in the payroll

```
10    REM  VERSION 11
20    REM
30    REM  THIS PROGRAM CALCULATES THE NET PAY FOR AN EMPLOYEE
40    REM  GIVEN THE PAY RATE AND THE HOURS WORKED
50    REM
60      LET ANSWER$ = "Y"
70      WHILE ANSWER$ = "Y"
80       GOSUB 300
90       GOSUB 400
100      GOSUB 500
110      GOSUB 600
120     WEND
130     END
300     REM INPUT PAYROLL DATA
310      INPUT "Enter first name ", FIRST.NAME$
320      INPUT "Enter last name ", LAST.NAME$
330      INPUT "Pay rate "; RATE
340      INPUT "Hours worked "; HOURS
350     RETURN
400     REM PROCESS PAYROLL DATA
410      LET FULL.NAME$ = FIRST.NAME$ + LAST.NAME$
420      LET OT.HOURS = HOURS - 40
430      IF HOURS > 40 THEN LET GROSS.PAY=(40*RATE)+(OT.HOURS*1.5*RATE)
                       ELSE LET GROSS.PAY=HOURS*RATE
440      LET FEDERAL.TAX = GROSS.PAY * .15
450      LET STATE.TAX = GROSS.PAY * .1
460      LET RETIREMENT = GROSS.PAY * .06
470      LET NET.PAY = GROSS.PAY - (FEDERAL.TAX + STATE.TAX + RETIREMENT)
480     RETURN
500     REM OUTPUT PAYROLL DATA
505      PRINT "PAYROLL INFORMATION FOR "; FULL.NAME$
510      PRINT
515      PRINT "PAY RATE            ";RATE
520      PRINT "HOURS WORKED        ";HOURS
525      PRINT "GROSS PAY           ";GROSS.PAY
530      PRINT
535      PRINT TAB(14);"DEDUCTIONS"
540      PRINT
545      PRINT "FEDERAL","STATE","RETIREMENT"
550      PRINT FEDERAL.TAX,STATE.TAX,RETIREMENT
555      PRINT
560      PRINT "NET PAY             ";NET.PAY
565      PRINT
570     RETURN
600     REM DETERMINE IF REPETITION IS DESIRED
610      INPUT "Process another employee (Y/N)"; ANSWER$
620     RETURN
```

Exhibit G.27

The Payroll Program with a Main Module and Subroutines

program and their interaction with corresponding GOSUB-RETURN statements. Note how the line numbers and indentation for the subroutines helps make the program more readable.

Creating a Main Module

By breaking the tasks of the payroll program into subroutines, a main module can be created, with a structure similar to the general layout for the payroll program should in Exhibit G.24. The **main module** controls the execution of the various tasks within the program. When a user reads the program, the main module serves as a summary of the general sequence of steps the program is performing. Exhibit G.27 shows the complete payroll program with a main module and subroutines.

When looking at the main module for the payroll program, you can see that the program basically contains four tasks within a single loop. With more complex programs, the main module will also be more complex, but will still serve as a basic summary of the tasks to be performed.

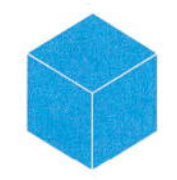

Programming Exercises

1. Reorganize the product order program to include a main module that uses a loop to allow the user to process as many orders as desired. After each order is processed, the user should be asked if another order is to be processed. The variable containing the user's answer to this question should be used to control the loop in the main module. Use an IF statement to apply a discount of 10 percent to any order with a subtotal greater than $50. Create a new variable for the discount and use the IF statement to compute the value for this variable as either 10 percent of the subtotal or zero, depending whether the subtotal is greater than $50. When computing the tax, subtract the discount from the subtotal and calculate the tax as 6 percent of the result of this subtraction. When displaying the output, include an additional column between the subtotal and tax to show the amount of the discount. Use the program to process the following three orders:

Description	Price	Quantity
WIDGET	5.95	16
GADGET	6.00	5
TRINKET	7.95	12

2. Reorganize the mileage program to include a main module that uses a FOR-NEXT loop to allow the user to process four mileage calculations each time the program is run. Add an IF statement to determine if the miles per gallon for a car is below 20. If miles per gallon is below 20, place the word YES in a string variable that holds the maintenance status of the car. If miles per gallon is 20 or above, place the word NO in this variable. Print the contents of this maintenance status variable with the rest of the output for this program. Use the program to compute miles per gallon for the following four trips:

Beginning Mileage	Ending Mileage	Number of Gallons
12,340	12,783	16.4
14,590	14,999	15.6
11,789	12,100	19.5
9,567	10,000	18.9

3. Reorganize the test averaging program to include a main module that uses a loop to allow the user to process as many students as desired. After each student is processed, the user should be asked if another student is to be processed. The variable containing the user's answer to this question should be used to control the loop in the main module. Use an IF statement to determine if a student passes or fails. If the average of the three test scores is 60 or above, place the word PASS in a string variable representing the student's grade for the course. If the average is below 60, place the word FAIL in this variable. Include this variable on the output in a column following the column for the student's average. Use this program to process the following students:

Name	Test 1	Test 2	Test 3
BILL FARMER	93	89	86
TIM HOWER	75	49	52
MARK BURSON	69	79	89
DIRK ASHTON	96	96	88

4. Reorganize the tuition program to include a main module that uses a loop to allow the user to process as many students as desired. After each student is processed, the user should be asked if another student is to be processed. The variable containing the user's answer to this question should be used to control the loop in the main module. Add a string variable for the status of the student to determine if the student is a resident of the state where the university is located. In the INPUT section of the program, ask the user to enter the word YES if the student is a resident of the state and NO if the student is not. When calculating the tuition, if the student is not a resident of the state, calculate tuition as the tuition per hour multiplied by 1.25 times the number of hours. If the student is a resident, then tuition should simply be the hours times the tuition per hour. On the output, add a heading of RESIDENT below the NAME heading and print the contents of the new variable (YES or NO) next to this heading. Use the program to process the following students:

Name	Resident	Hours Enrolled	Tuition Per Hour
RUTH STAMLER	YES	17	355
TOM SCHULTZ	NO	18	360
HANK COLEMAN	YES	16	345

Advanced Topics

In the earlier parts of this appendix you were introduced to the BASIC environment, learned how data is handled in BASIC, and became familiar with some of the control structures used in BASIC. In this section, some of the more advanced options of the BASIC statements you have been learning will be introduced. The intention is to provide an introduction to advanced options that allow the construction of more complex BASIC programs.

Complex Logical Conditions

As you know from earlier parts of this appendix, logical conditions can be used as the basis for IF statements and to control WHILE-WEND loops. The conditions introduced so far have always involved the comparison of two elements with a logical operator to produce an expression that can be true or false.

With more complex programming tasks, simple logical conditions must sometimes be joined to form more complex conditions involving multiple true/false expressions. This combination of simple conditions to create complex multiple conditions is accomplished using **logical operators**.

Logical Operators

The logical operators available in BASIC include AND, OR, and NOT. The AND operator is used to join two simple conditions to create a multiple condition that is true only when both simple conditions are true. For example, suppose overtime pay is to be given only to employees with pay rates over $5 an hour. To identify these employees, two conditions are required. First, the pay rate in the RATE variable would have to be greater than $5 an hour. This could be evaluated using the condition

```
RATE>5
```

In addition, the hours worked by the employee must also be greater than 40. This could be evaluated using the condition

```
HOURS>40
```

To identify employees that have a pay rate greater than $5 an hour and have worked overtime hours, a multiple condition could be created as follows:

```
RATE>5 AND HOURS>40
```

This multiple condition is true only if RATE>5 is true *and* HOURS>40 is also true. If either of the two simple conditions is false, or both are false, then the multiple condition is also false (see Exhibit G.28).

	RATE>5	HOURS>40	RATE>5 AND HOURS>40
RATE=1 HOURS=35	False	False	False
RATE=9 HOURS=35	True	False	False
RATE=1 HOURS=45	False	True	False
RATE=9 HOURS=45	True	True	True

Exhibit G.28

Evaluating a Multiple Condition Containing an AND

	RATE<3	HOURS<30	RATE<3 OR HOURS<30
RATE=5 HOURS=40	False	False	False
RATE=2 HOURS=40	True	False	True
RATE=5 HOURS=20	False	True	True
RATE=2 HOURS=20	True	True	True

Exhibit G.29

Evaluating a Multiple Condition Containing an OR

The OR operator is used to join two simple conditions to create a multiple condition that is true if either of the simple conditions is true. For example, suppose employees with a pay rate less than $3 an hour or working less than thirty hours a week needed to be identified for a special training program. This could be accomplished with the multiple condition

```
RATE<3 OR HOURS<30
```

This multiple condition would be true for employees that satisfy either the pay rate cutoff of less than $3 an hour, or worked less than thirty hours a week, or both. Thus, if either of the simple conditions is true, the entire multiple condition is also true (see Exhibit G.29).

The NOT logical operator is used to test for the opposite of a condition. For example, the normal condition for determining if an employee has worked overtime hours is

```
HOURS>40
```

When the HOURS variable contains a number greater than 40 this condition is true. Adding a NOT to the condition,

```
NOT HOURS>40
```

would create a condition that is false if the HOURS variable contains a number greater than 40. The same thing could be accomplished using a different relational operator in the expression itself. Thus, the condition HOURS<=40 would produce the same effect.

Using Multiple Conditions

As indicated above, multiple conditions can be used in IF statements and to control WHILE-WEND loops. Exhibit G.30 shows the payroll program with a multiple condition that gives overtime pay only to employees with pay rates greater than $5 an hour.

A multiple condition controlling a WHILE-WEND loop could be used with the WHILE-WEND loop controlled by the ANSWER$ variable. In the previous versions of the payroll program using this WHILE-WEND loop, the user had to type an uppercase *Y* when asked if another employee was to be processed. If the user accidentally typed a lowercase *y* the loop would not be executed again since the condition controlling the WHILE-WEND loop tests for Y. To improve this, a multiple condition could be created that allows the loop to be executed if the ANSWER$ variable contains either an uppercase or a lowercase *y*. This would require a multiple condition that used an OR to join a simple condition testing for an uppercase *Y* with a simple condition testing for a lowercase *y*:

```
ANSWER$ = "Y" OR ANSWER$ = "y"
```

Exhibit G.31 shows the payroll program with this multiple condition included to control the WHILE-WEND loop.

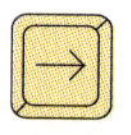

Complex IFs and Loops

As programming problems become more complex, simple IF statements and loops must sometimes be combined to produce the desired effect. IF statements must sometimes contain other IF statements, and loops must sometimes be within other loops. This multiple grouping of statements is known as **nesting**, which refers to the placing of one control structure within another. In this section, the payroll program will be modified to include nested IF statements and nested loops.

Nested IF Statements

To illustrate the concept of nested IF statements, suppose the payroll program needed to differentiate between employees in three different

```
 10     REM  VERSION 12
 20     REM
 30     REM  THIS PROGRAM CALCULATES THE NET PAY FOR AN EMPLOYEE
 40     REM  GIVEN THE PAY RATE AND THE HOURS WORKED
 50     REM
 60       LET ANSWER$ = "Y"
 70       WHILE ANSWER$ = "Y"
 80        GOSUB 300
 90        GOSUB 400
100        GOSUB 500
110        GOSUB 600
120       WEND
130       END
300       REM INPUT PAYROLL DATA
310        INPUT "Enter first name ", FIRST.NAME$
320        INPUT "Enter last name ", LAST.NAME$
330        INPUT "Pay rate "; RATE
340        INPUT "Hours worked "; HOURS
350       RETURN
400       REM PROCESS PAYROLL DATA
410        LET FULL.NAME$ = FIRST.NAME$ + LAST.NAME$
420        LET OT.HOURS = HOURS-40
430        IF RATE>5 AND HOURS>40 THEN LET GROSS.PAY=(40*RATE)+(OT.HOURS*1.5*RATE)
                                  ELSE LET GROSS.PAY=HOURS*RATE
440        LET FEDERAL.TAX = GROSS.PAY * .15
450        LET STATE.TAX = GROSS.PAY * .1
460        LET RETIREMENT = GROSS.PAY * .06
470        LET NET.PAY = GROSS.PAY - (FEDERAL.TAX + STATE.TAX + RETIREMENT)
480       RETURN
500       REM OUTPUT PAYROLL DATA
505        PRINT "PAYROLL INFORMATION FOR "; FULL.NAME$
510        PRINT
515        PRINT "PAY RATE          ";RATE
520        PRINT "HOURS WORKED      ";HOURS
525        PRINT "GROSS PAY         ";GROSS.PAY
530        PRINT
535        PRINT TAB(14);"DEDUCTIONS"
540        PRINT
545        PRINT "FEDERAL","STATE","RETIREMENT"
550        PRINT FEDERAL.TAX,STATE.TAX,RETIREMENT
555        PRINT
560        PRINT "NET PAY           ";NET.PAY
565        PRINT
570       RETURN
600       REM DETERMINE IF REPETITION IS DESIRED
610        INPUT "Process another employee (Y/N)";ANSWER$
620       RETURN
```

Exhibit G.30

The Payroll Program Using a Multiple Condition in the IF Statement

departments and include a new deduction for insurance that depended on which department the employee was in. Assume that employees work for either the Information Systems, Accounting, or Marketing department. Furthermore, employees in Information Systems must have $5 deducted from their pay each week for insurance. The deduction for employees in Accounting is $7 and for Marketing employees the deduction is $3.

```
10      REM  VERSION 13
20      REM
30      REM  THIS PROGRAM CALCULATES THE NET PAY FOR AN EMPLOYEE
40      REM  GIVEN THE PAY RATE AND THE HOURS WORKED
50      REM
60        LET ANSWER$ = "Y"
70        WHILE ANSWER$ = "Y" OR ANSWER$ = "y"
80         GOSUB 300
90         GOSUB 400
100        GOSUB 500
110        GOSUB 600
120       WEND
130       END
300       REM INPUT PAYROLL DATA
310        INPUT "Enter first name ", FIRST.NAME$
320        INPUT "Enter last name ", LAST.NAME$
330        INPUT "Pay rate "; RATE
340        INPUT "Hours worked "; HOURS
350       RETURN
400       REM PROCESS PAYROLL DATA
410        LET FULL.NAME$ = FIRST.NAME$ + LAST.NAME$
420        LET OT.HOURS = HOURS- 40
430        IF RATE>5 AND HOURS>40 THEN LET GROSS.PAY=(40*RATE)+(OT.HOURS*1.5*RATE)
                                  ELSE LET GROSS.PAY=HOURS*RATE
440        LET FEDERAL.TAX = GROSS.PAY * .15
450        LET STATE.TAX = GROSS.PAY * .1
460        LET RETIREMENT = GROSS.PAY * .06
470        LET NET.PAY = GROSS.PAY - (FEDERAL.TAX + STATE.TAX + RETIREMENT)
480       RETURN
500       REM OUTPUT PAYROLL DATA
505        PRINT "PAYROLL INFORMATION FOR "; FULL.NAME$
510        PRINT
515        PRINT "PAY RATE        ";RATE
520        PRINT "HOURS WORKED    ";HOURS
525        PRINT "GROSS PAY       ";GROSS.PAY
530        PRINT
535        PRINT TAB(14);"DEDUCTIONS"
540        PRINT
545        PRINT "FEDERAL","STATE","RETIREMENT"
550        PRINT FEDERAL.TAX,STATE.TAX,RETIREMENT
555        PRINT
560        PRINT "NET PAY         ";NET.PAY
565        PRINT
570       RETURN
600       REM DETERMINE IF REPETITION IS DESIRED
610        INPUT "Process another employee (Y/N)";ANSWER$
620       RETURN
```

Exhibit G.31

The Payroll Program with a Multiple Condition in the WHILE Statement

Incorporating this new function into the payroll program will require the user to enter a department along with the name, pay rate, and hours worked that are currently entered. To simplify this process, assume that codes will be used to identify the departments, as follows:

Code	Department
MIS	Information Systems
ACT	Accounting
MKT	Marketing

When the user is asked to enter the department for the employee, one of these codes will be entered. The input subroutine for the payroll program would become

```
REM INPUT PAYROLL DATA
    INPUT "Enter first name ", FIRST.NAME$
    INPUT "Enter last name ", LAST.NAME$
    INPUT "Pay rate "; RATE
    INPUT "Hours worked "; HOURS
    INPUT "Enter Department (MIS, ACT, or MKT) ",
      DEPARTMENT$
RETURN
```

The employee's department is stored in the DEPARTMENT$ variable. The amount of insurance deducted from the employee's gross pay can be calculated by setting up a series of IF statements with conditions that determine which code the DEPARTMENT$ variable contains. First, an IF statement can be constructed to determine whether the department code is MIS:

```
IF DEPARTMENT$="MIS" THEN LET INSURANCE=5
```

If the department code is MIS, a variable called INSURANCE is set to the insurance deduction for the Information Systems department. If the department code is not MIS, it could be either ACT or MKT. To determine which of the remaining two departments the employee works in requires another IF statement in the ELSE part of the first IF statement

```
IF DEPARTMENT$="MIS" THEN LET INSURANCE=5
    ELSE IF DEPARTMENT$="ACT" THEN LET INSURANCE=7
       ELSE LET INSURANCE=3
```

The second IF statement is executed only if the first IF statement is false. When the first IF statement is true, the insurance variable is set to 5 and the program skips to the statement beyond this nested IF structure. The second IF statement checks to see if the department code is ACT. When the condition in the second IF statement is true, the insurance deduction for the Accounting department is placed in the INSURANCE variable. When the condition of the second IF statement is false, it is assumed the department is Marketing and the Marketing insurance deduction is placed in the INSURANCE variable.

To understand how this nested IF statement works, let's look at how employees from the three departments will be processed by this statement. When the department code is MIS, the first IF is true and the INSURANCE variable is set to 5. BASIC then skips to the statement following the nested IF without processing the second IF. When the department code is ACT, the first IF is false, so the ELSE part of that IF is processed. The second IF is then true, and the INSURANCE variable is set to 7. BASIC then skips past the second ELSE clause and goes on with the statement following the nested IF. When the department code is MKT, the first IF is false, so processing goes to the ELSE clause for the first IF. The second IF is also false, which causes BASIC to go to the ELSE clause of the second IF and set the INSURANCE variable to 3. Note that this nested IF structure assumes that when the code is neither MIS nor ACT then it must be MKT.

A problem will occur, however, if the user of the program does not type a valid department code for an employee. For example, if the user entered mis as the department code, this lowercase code will not match the MIS code the first IF is looking for. This lowercase mis will not match MIS or ACT and the INSURANCE variable will be set to 3 because it was assumed that the code was MKT.

A safer approach to the calculation of the insurance deduction would be to set up a third IF to test for the MKT code and have an ELSE clause on that IF that will handle the possibility of a department code that doesn't match any of the three valid codes. A possible nested IF structure to handle invalid department codes would be

```
IF DEPARTMENT$="MIS" THEN LET INSURANCE=5
  ELSE IF DEPARTMENT$="ACT" THEN LET INSURANCE=7
  ELSE IF DEPARTMENT$="MKT" THEN LET INSURANCE=3
  ELSE LET INSURANCE=0
```

In this nested IF structure, the INSURANCE variable is set to zero if the department code is not recognized as one of the three valid department codes. Exhibit G.32 shows the payroll program with the insurance deduction incorporated. In this version of the payroll program the nested IF is used to determine the appropriate insurance deduction based on the department for the employee. This insurance deduction is also included in the calculation of the net pay for the employee and is printed with the rest of the payroll information.

Using GOSUB with IF Statements

One of the restrictions with the BASIC programming language is the limitation of 255 characters per statement. The nested IF statement introduced above is very close to exceeding that limit. In addition, the nested IF used above only needed to determine the value for one variable based on the department. If more operations need to be performed differentially for each department, it might not be possible to include them all in a single nested IF structure and still remain under the 255-character-per-statement limitation. For example, suppose both the retirement and insurance deductions depend on the department in which the employee works. The table below lists the deductions that are to be made differently depending on the employee's department

Code	Retirement	Insurance
MIS	.055%	5
ACT	.065%	7
MKT	.060%	3

```
 10     REM  VERSION 14
 20     REM
 30     REM  THIS PROGRAM CALCULATES THE NET PAY FOR AN EMPLOYEE
 40     REM  GIVEN THE PAY RATE AND THE HOURS WORKED
 50     REM
 60       LET ANSWER$ = "Y"
 70       WHILE ANSWER$ = "Y"
 80        GOSUB 300
 90        GOSUB 400
100        GOSUB 500
110        GOSUB 600
120       WEND
130       END
300       REM INPUT PAYROLL DATA
310        INPUT "Enter first name ", FIRST.NAME$
320        INPUT "Enter last name ", LAST.NAME$
330        INPUT "Pay rate "; RATE
340        INPUT "Hours worked "; HOURS
345        INPUT "Enter Department (MIS, ACT, or MKT)", DEPARTMENT$
350       RETURN
400       REM PROCESS PAYROLL DATA
410        LET FULL.NAME$ = FIRST.NAME$ + LAST.NAME$
420        LET OT.HOURS = HOURS-40
430        IF RATE>5 AND HOURS>40 THEN LET GROSS.PAY=(40*RATE)+(OT.HOURS*1.5*RATE)
                                   ELSE LET GROSS.PAY=HOURS*RATE
440        LET FEDERAL.TAX = GROSS.PAY * .15
450        LET STATE.TAX = GROSS.PAY * .1
460        LET RETIREMENT = GROSS.PAY * .06
465        IF DEPARTMENT$="MIS" THEN LET INSURANCE=5
                                 ELSE IF DEPARTMENT$="ACT" THEN LET INSURANCE=7
                                 ELSE IF DEPARTMENT$="MKT" THEN LET INSURANCE=3 ELSE LET
                                  INSURANCE=0
470        LET NET.PAY=GROSS.PAY-(FEDERAL.TAX+STATE.TAX+RETIREMENT+INSURANCE)
480       RETURN
500       REM OUTPUT PAYROLL DATA
505        PRINT "PAYROLL INFORMATION FOR "; FULL.NAME$
510        PRINT
515        PRINT "PAY RATE     ";RATE
520        PRINT "HOURS WORKED ";HOURS
525        PRINT "GROSS PAY    ";GROSS.PAY
530        PRINT
535        PRINT TAB(14);"DEDUCTIONS"
540        PRINT
550        PRINT FEDERAL.TAX,STATE.TAX,RETIREMENT,INSURANCE
555        PRINT
560        PRINT "NET PAY      ";NET.PAY
565        PRINT
570       RETURN
600       REM DETERMINE IF REPETITION IS DESIRED
610        INPUT "Process another employee (Y/N)";ANSWER$
```

Exhibit G.32

The Payroll Program Using a Nested IF to Process Insurance Deductions Based on Employee Department

To filter through all three department codes and set two variables equal to the correct amounts would require a very long IF statement.

By combining a GOSUB with the nested IF, however, it is possible to separate the filtering aspect of the IF statement from the assignment of values to variables. Exhibit G.33 shows the payroll program with a nested IF containing GOSUBs to call on subroutines to do the processing for each department. Using this method allows the IF statement to execute the block of statements in the subroutine, rather than trying to perform all the operations within the IF statement itself. The number of operations that can

```
 10    REM  VERSION 15
 20    REM
 30    REM  THIS PROGRAM CALCULATES THE NET PAY FOR AN EMPLOYEE
 40    REM  GIVEN THE PAY RATE AND THE HOURS WORKED
 50    REM
 60      LET ANSWER$ = "Y"
 70      WHILE ANSWER$ = "Y"
 80       GOSUB 300
 90       GOSUB 400
100       GOSUB 500
110       GOSUB 600
120      WEND
130      END
300      REM INPUT PAYROLL DATA
310       INPUT "Enter first name ", FIRST.NAME$
320       INPUT "Enter last name ", LAST.NAME$
330       INPUT "Pay rate "; RATE
340       INPUT "Hours worked "; HOURS
350       INPUT "Enter Department (MIS, ACT, or MKT) ", DEPARTMENT$
360      RETURN
400      REM PROCESS PAYROLL DATA
405       LET FULL.NAME$ = FIRST.NAME$ + LAST.NAME$
410       LET OT.HOURS = HOURS-40
415       IF RATE>5 AND HOURS>40 THEN LET GROSS.PAY=(40*RATE)+(OT.HOURS*1.5*RATE)
                                 ELSE LET GROSS.PAY=HOURS*RATE
420       LET FEDERAL.TAX = GROSS.PAY * .15
425       LET STATE.TAX = GROSS.PAY * .1
430       LET INSURANCE = 0
435       LET RETIREMENT = 0
440       IF DEPARTMENT$="MIS" THEN GOSUB 700
                               ELSE IF DEPARTMENT$="ACT" THEN GOSUB 800
                               ELSE IF DEPARTMENT$="MKT" THEN GOSUB 900
445       LET NET.PAY=GROSS.PAY-(FEDERAL.TAX+STATE.TAX+RETIREMENT+INSURANCE)
450      RETURN
500      REM OUTPUT PAYROLL DATA
505       PRINT "PAYROLL INFORMATION FOR "; FULL.NAME$
510       PRINT
515       PRINT "PAY RATE      ";RATE
520       PRINT "HOURS WORKED  ";HOURS
525       PRINT "GROSS PAY     ";GROSS.PAY
530       PRINT
535       PRINT TAB(14);"DEDUCTIONS"
540       PRINT
545       PRINT "FEDERAL","STATE","RETIREMENT","INSURANCE"
550       PRINT FEDERAL.TAX,STATE.TAX,RETIREMENT,INSURANCE
555       PRINT
560       PRINT "NET PAY       ";NET.PAY
565       PRINT
570      RETURN
600      REM DETERMINE IF REPETITION IS DESIRED
610       INPUT "Process another employee (Y/N)";ANSWER$
620      RETURN
700      REM PROCESS DEDUCTIONS FOR MIS DEPARTMENT
710       LET INSURANCE = 5
720       LET RETIREMENT = GROSS.PAY* .055
730      RETURN
800      REM PROCESS DEDUCTIONS FOR ACT DEPARTMENT
810       LET INSURANCE = 7
820       LET RETIREMENT = GROSS.PAY * .065
830      RETURN
```

Exhibit G.33

The Payroll Program Using GOSUBs Within a Nested IF Statement

be performed differentially based on the IF statement is thus no longer constrained by the length of the IF statement itself.

In Exhibit G.33, the nested IF in line 440 directs BASIC to one of the three subroutines beginning in line 700, 800, or 900. The problem of an invalid department code is handled this time by starting the INSURANCE and RETIREMENT variables at 0 in lines 430 and 435. The nested IF in line 440 will then change the values in these two variables only if one of the valid department codes is found. If the code is invalid, these two deductions are left at 0 and are printed that way.

Nested Loops

Just as it is possible to nest one IF statement within another, it is also possible to nest one loop within another. In the payroll application, suppose that the hours an employee works need to be entered as five separate hours per day rather than the total for the week. Each time an employee is processed, the entry of hours must be repeated five times. The loop that allows for the repetition of the payroll process for multiple employees would contain another loop for the repetition of the entry of the number of hours worked per day. Exhibit G.34 illustrates this nested loop structure.

In this version of the payroll program, the input stage is now broken into two subroutines. The first subroutine, beginning in line 300, is used to obtain data about the employee that is not repeated, such as the name, pay rate, and department. The second subroutine is used to ask the user to enter the number of hours worked on a particular day, which is placed in a variable called DAY.HOURS. This value is then added to the HOURS variable. This subroutine is repeated five times using a FOR-NEXT loop. This loop asks the user for a daily hour number five times and adds the daily hour number to the HOURS variable each time. After the fifth execution of the loop, the HOURS variable will have accumulated the hours for all five days, which represents the number of hours the employee has worked during the week.

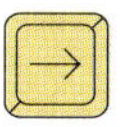

More Complex PRINT Statements

This final advanced topic deals with ways of improving the interaction between a program and the user. The three areas discussed include the use of PRINT statements to make INPUT statements more understandable, the use of PRINT USING statements to improve the formatting of output information, and the use of LPRINT and LPRINT USING statements to direct output to a printer rather than the screen.

Using PRINT with INPUT Statements

The length of the prompt included in an INPUT statement is restricted by the 255-character limit on the length of statements in BASIC. PRINT statements can be used before INPUT statements when more explanatory text needs to be displayed on the screen to help the user understand what

```
 10     REM  VERSION 16
 20     REM
 30     REM  THIS PROGRAM CALCULATES THE NET PAY FOR AN EMPLOYEE
 40     REM  GIVEN THE PAY RATE AND THE HOURS WORKED
 50     REM
 60       LET ANSWER$ = "Y"
 70       WHILE ANSWER$ = "Y"
 80        GOSUB 300
 90          LET HOURS=0
100        FOR WORKDAY = 1 TO 5       inner loop      outer loop
110          GOSUB 350
120        NEXT WORKDAY
130        GOSUB 400
140        GOSUB 500
150        GOSUB 600
160       WEND
170       END
300       REM INPUT PAYROLL DATA
305        INPUT "Enter first name ", FIRST.NAME$
310        INPUT "Enter last name ", LAST.NAME$
315        INPUT "Pay rate "; RATE
320        INPUT "Enter Department (MIS, ACT, or MKT) ", DEPARTMENT$
325       RETURN
350       REM ENTER HOURS WORKED
355        INPUT "Enter hours worked for next day ",DAY.HOURS
360        HOURS = HOURS + DAY.HOURS
365       RETURN
400       REM PROCESS PAYROLL DATA
405        LET FULL.NAME$ = FIRST.NAME$ + LAST.NAME$
410        LET OT.HOURS = HOURS-40
415        IF RATE>5 AND HOURS>40 THEN LET GROSS.PAY=(40*RATE)+(OT.HOURS*1.5*RATE)
                                   ELSE LET GROSS.PAY=HOURS*RATE
420        LET FEDERAL.TAX = GROSS.PAY * .15
425        LET STATE.TAX = GROSS.PAY * .1
430        LET INSURANCE = 0
435        LET RETIREMENT = 0
440        IF DEPARTMENT$="MIS" THEN GOSUB 700
                                ELSE IF DEPARTMENT$="ACT" THEN GOSUB 800
                                ELSE IF DEPARTMENT$="MKT" THEN GOSUB 900
445        LET NET.PAY=GROSS.PAY-(FEDERAL.TAX+STATE.TAX+RETIREMENT+INSURANCE)
450       RETURN
500       REM OUTPUT PAYROLL DATA
505        PRINT "PAYROLL INFORMATION FOR "; FULL.NAME$
510        PRINT
515        PRINT "PAY RATE      ";RATE
520        PRINT "HOURS WORKED ";HOURS
525        PRINT "GROSS PAY     ";GROSS.PAY
530        PRINT
535        PRINT TAB(14);"DEDUCTIONS"
540        PRINT
545        PRINT "FEDERAL","STATE","RETIREMENT","INSURANCE"
550        PRINT FEDERAL.TAX,STATE.TAX,RETIREMENT,INSURANCE
555        PRINT
560        PRINT "NET PAY       ";NET.PAY
565        PRINT
570       RETURN
600       REM DETERMINE IF REPETITION IS DESIRED
610        INPUT "Process another employee (Y/N)";ANSWER$
620       RETURN
700       REM PROCESS DEDUCTIONS FOR MIS DEPARTMENT
710        LET INSURANCE = 5
720        LET RETIREMENT = GROSS.PAY * .055
730       RETURN
800       REM PROCESS DEDUCTIONS FOR ACT DEPARTMENT
810        LET INSURANCE = 7
820        LET RETIREMENT = GROSS.PAY * .065
830       RETURN
900       REM PROCESS DEDUCTIONS FOR MKT DEPARTMENT
910        LET INSURANCE = 3
920        LET RETIREMENT = GROSS.PAY * .06
930       RETURN
```

Exhibit G.34

A Nested Loop Structure to Process Multiple Employees, Each Working Multiple Days

```
REM INPUT PAYROLL DATA
      PRINT "Enter the name of the employee below"
      PRINT
      INPUT "        First name: ", FIRST.NAME$
      INPUT "        Last name : ", LAST.NAME$
      PRINT
      PRINT "        Enter the pay rate below"
      PRINT "Rates greater than 5 qualify for overtime"
      PRINT
      INPUT "        Enter pay rate ", RATE
      PRINT
      PRINT "Enter the employee's department below"
      PRINT " Valid codes are MIS, ACT, or MKT "
      PRINT
      INPUT "        Enter Department ",DEPARTMENT$
      PRINT
      PRINT "You will now be asked to enter the"
      PRINT "        hours for five work days"
      PRINT
RETURN
REM ENTER HOURS WORKED
      PRINT "Entering the hours for day #";WORKDAY
      INPUT "Hours = ",DAY.HOURS
      PRINT
      HOURS = HOURS + DAY.HOURS
RETURN
```

Exhibit G.35

The Input Stage of the Payroll Program with PRINT Statements Added

needs to be entered. Since both PRINT statements and INPUT statement prompts are displayed on the screen, the user will simply see a series of messages without being aware that they are originating from different types of statements. Exhibit G.35 shows the input subroutines from the payroll program, with additional PRINT statements added to help clarify the input process.

Note how the text within the PRINT and INPUT statements has been spaced to improve the appearance of the messages displayed to the user. The PRINT statement in the subroutine controlling the entry of the daily hours uses the variable WORKDAY from the FOR-NEXT loop to tell the user the number of the day of the week for which hours are being entered.

The PRINT USING Statement

When numeric data are displayed with a PRINT statement, BASIC does not use consistent formatting. The number of decimal places used in the number will vary depending on whether there are decimal values to display. The exact placement of the numbers on the screen is also left to BASIC to determine. Exhibit G.36 shows the output generated by the payroll program at this point.

When numeric output needs to be more precisely positioned and formatted, the PRINT USING statement can be used in place of the normal PRINT statement. In a PRINT USING statement, a format string is included to instruct BASIC how to print the number. For example, the PRINT statement

```
PRINT NET.PAY
```

Exhibit G.36

An Example of the Output Displayed by the Payroll Program

```
PAYROLL INFORMATION FOR James Jones

PAY RATE            6
HOURS WORKED        45
GROSS PAY           285

                    DEDUCTIONS

FEDERAL       STATE       RETIREMENT       INSURANCE
42.75         28.5        17.1             5

NET PAY       191.65
```

would print the value in the NET.PAY variable. An equivalent PRINT USING statement might be

```
PRINT USING "####"; NET.PAY
```

This statement displays the contents of the NET.PAY variable using the format string to determine how the number will be displayed on the screen. The format string is enclosed in quotes and uses the # symbol to represent a position for a digit. This format string would display the value in the NET.PAY variable as long as it was four digits or less. When the number is less than four digits, blanks will be placed in front of the number to right-justify the number within the four-digit area specified in the format string. If the number is larger than four digits, the number would still be printed, but a % sign will be added in front of the number to warn you that it is too large to be displayed in the format string you specified.

To control the display of decimal places, a decimal point can be added to the format string along with # symbols to represent the number of digits to be displayed to the right of the decimal place. An example would be

```
PRINT USING "####.##"; NET.PAY
```

Commas can also be included in the format string to indicate where commas are to be placed within the number when it is displayed. For example:

```
PRINT USING "###,###.##"; NET.PAY
```

Dollar signs can also be added to a number by placing two dollar signs at the front of the format string. For example:

```
PRINT USING "$$##,###.##"; NET.PAY
```

The first dollar sign reserves a position in the format string for the dollar sign itself. The second dollar sign also serves as a place marker. In this case a number as big as 999,999.99 could be printed with this format string.

The double dollar sign causes the dollar sign to float to the position immediately in front of the first digit of the number. Blank spaces are added in front of the dollar sign to cause the number to be right-justified within the format area. Thus, when the number is smaller than the format string, the dollar sign will float to the right until it is immediately in front of the number. Some examples of output possible with this format string are

```
    $5.00
   $55.00
  $555.00
$5,555.00
```

Spaces can also be added to the format to more precisely position a number on the screen when it is printed. For example,

```
PRINT USING "    ###.##    ";NET.PAY
```

would print the number in the NET.PAY variable with four spaces before and four spaces after the number. This is particularly useful when printing more than one number with a single format string. For example, the print statement

```
PRINT FEDERAL.TAX,STATE.TAX
```

could be replaced with the PRINT USING statement

```
PRINT USING "    ####.##          ####.##";
  FEDERAL.TAX,STATE.TAX
```

In this PRINT statement, the comma between the variables is not used to space the numbers into columns. Instead, the numbers are formatted according to the spacing specified in the format string.

Text strings can also be included with the PRINT USING statement as part of the format string. For example,

```
PRINT USING "NET PAY   $###.##"; NET.PAY
```

could be used in the payroll program when the net pay is to be displayed. Exhibit G.37 shows the payroll program with PRINT USING statements added.

```
10        REM  PROGRAM Version 17
20        REM
30        REM  THIS PROGRAM CALCULATES THE NET PAY FOR AN EMPLOYEE
40        REM  GIVEN THE PAY RATE AND THE HOURS WORKED
50        REM
60          LET ANSWER$ = "Y"
70          WHILE ANSWER$ = "Y"
80           GOSUB 200
81            LET HOURS=0
82           FOR WORKDAY = 1 TO 5
83            GOSUB 300
84           NEXT WORKDAY
90           GOSUB 400
100          GOSUB 500
110          GOSUB 600
120         WEND
130         END
200         REM INPUT PAYROLL DATA
205          PRINT "Enter the name of the employee below"
210          PRINT
215          INPUT "        First name: ", FIRST.NAME$
220          INPUT "        Last name : ", LAST.NAME$
225          PRINT
230          PRINT "                     Enter the pay rate below"
235          PRINT "Rates greater than 5 qualify for overtime"
240          PRINT
245          INPUT "        Enter pay rate ",RATE
250          PRINT
255          PRINT "Enter the employee's department below"
260          PRINT " Valid codes are MIS, ACT, or, MKT"
265          PRINT
270          INPUT "        Enter Department ",DEPARTMENT$
275          PRINT
280          PRINT "You will now be asked to enter the"
285          PRINT "        hours for five work days"
290          PRINT
295         RETURN
300         REM ENTER HOURS WORKED
305          PRINT "Entering the hours for day #";WORKDAY
310          INPUT "Hours= ";DAY.HOURS
315          LET HOURS = HOURS + DAY.HOURS
320         RETURN
400         REM PROCESS PAYROLL DATA
410          LET FULL.NAME$ = FIRST.NAME$ + LAST.NAME$
420          LET OT.HOURS = HOURS-40
430          IF RATE>5 AND HOURS>40 THEN LET GROSS.PAY=(40*RATE)+(OT.HOURS*1.5*RATE)
                                    ELSE LET GROSS.PAY=HOURS*RATE
440          LET FEDERAL.TAX = GROSS.PAY * .15
450          LET STATE.TAX = GROSS.PAY * .1
460          LET INSURANCE = 0
461          LET RETIREMENT = 0
465          IF DEPARTMENT$="MIS" THEN GOSUB 700
                   ELSE IF DEPARTMENT$="ACT" THEN GOSUB 800
                                 ELSE IF DEPARTMENT$="MKT" THEN GOSUB 900
470          LET NET.PAY=GROSS.PAY-(FEDERAL.TAX+STATE.TAX+RETIREMENT+INSURANCE)
480         RETURN
500                              REM OUTPUT PAYROLL DATA
505          PRINT "PAYROLL INFORMATION FOR"; FULL.NAME$
510          PRINT
515          PRINT USING "PAY RATE       $$#,###.##"   ;RATE
520          PRINT USING "HOURS WORKED ###.##"         ;HOURS
525          PRINT USING "GROSS PAY      $$#,###.##"   ;GROSS.PAY
530          PRINT
535          PRINT TAB(20);"DEDUCTIONS"
540          PRINT
545          PRINT " FEDERAL            STATE          RETIREMENT       INSURANCE"
550          PRINT USING "$$###.##      $$###.##        $$###.##        $$###.##";
                                 FEDERAL.TAX, STATE.TAX, RETIREMENT, INSURANCE
555          PRINT
560          PRINT USING "NET PAY           $$#,###.##";NET.PAY
565          PRINT
570         RETURN
570         RETURN
```

Exhibit G.37 *(continued on page G-63)*

```
600     REM DETERMINE IF REPETITION IS DESIRED
610      INPUT "Process another employee (Y/N)";ANSWER$
620     RETURN
700     REM PROCESS DEDUCTIONS FOR MIS DEPARTMENT
710      LET INSURANCE = 5
720      LET RETIREMENT = GROSS.PAY * .055
730     RETURN
800     REM PROCESS DEDUCTIONS FOR ACT DEPARTMENT
810      LET INSURANCE = 7
820      LET RETIREMENT = GROSS.PAY * .065
830     RETURN
900     REM PROCESS DEDUCTIONS FOR MKT DEPARTMENT
910      LET INSURANCE = 3
920      LET RETIREMENT = GROSS.PAY + .06
930     RETURN
```

Exhibit G.37 *(continued from page G-62)*

The Payroll Program with PRINT USING Statements

Exhibit G.38

The Output Resulting from the LPRINT and LPRINT USING Commands

```
PAYROLL INFORMATION FOR Jim Jones

PAY RATE                $7.00
HOURS WORKED            45.00
GROSS PAY             $332.50

                      DEDUCTIONS

 FEDERAL     STATE       RETIREMENT      INSURANCE
  $49.88    $33.25           $18.29          $5.00

NET PAY               $226.09
```

Sending Output to a Printer

The PRINT and PRINT USING statements send output to the microcomputer screen. When printed output is desired, LPRINT statements can be used in place of PRINT statements and LPRINT USING statements can be used in place of PRINT USING statements. The syntax for LPRINT and LPRINT USING is exactly the same as with PRINT and PRINT USING. The only difference is the addition of the L in front of the word PRINT. Exhibit G.38 shows the output generated by the payroll program with LPRINT and LPRINT USING statements used in the output subroutine of the payroll program.

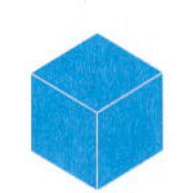

Programming Exercises

1. In the product order program, modify the condition controlling the loop in the main module to allow the user to enter either an uppercase or a lowercase *y* to continue the loop. Display some additional text on the screen during the input process using PRINT statements in addition to the INPUT statements. Improve the output by incorporating PRINT USING statements for printing the numeric data. Add an additional loop in the main module to allow three quantities to be entered. These three quantities should be accumulated to produce a final quantity, which is then multiplied by the price to determine the subtotal for the order. Use the program to process the following orders:

Description	Price	Quantity 1	Quantity 2	Quantity 3
WIDGET	5.95	4	5	7
GADGET	6.00	1	3	4
TRINKET	7.95	3	5	4

2. In the mileage program, display some additional text on the screen during the input process using PRINT statements in addition to the INPUT statements. Improve the output by incorporating PRINT USING statements for printing the numeric data. Add an additional loop in the main module to allow the number of gallons to be entered as four separate amounts. These four amounts should be accumulated to produce a final number of gallons, which is then used in the miles-per-gallon calculation. Use the program to calculate miles per gallon for the following trips:

Beginning	Ending		Gallons		
Mileage	Mileage	1	2	3	4
12,340	12,783	3	4	3	6
14,590	14,999	5	4	3	4
11,789	12,100	5	6	6	3
9,567	10,000	4	3	7	5

3. In the test averaging program, modify the condition controlling the loop in the main module to allow the user to enter either an uppercase or a lowercase *y* to continue the loop. Display some additional text on the screen during the input process using PRINT statements in addition to the INPUT statements. Improve the output by incorporating PRINT USING statements for printing the numeric data. Instead of assigning a pass or fail grade to the student, create a nested IF structure to assign one of three grades: GOOD, AVERAGE, or POOR. If the average is above 80, the grade variable should contain GOOD. If the average is between 60 and 80, the grade should be AVERAGE. If the average is below 60, the grade should be POOR. Process the data on the next page with the program.

Name	Test 1	Test 2	Test 3
BILL FARMER	93	89	86
TIM HOWER	75	49	52
MARK BURSON	69	79	89
DIRK ASHTON	96	96	88

4. In the tuition program, modify the condition controlling the loop in the main module to allow the user to enter either an uppercase or a lowercase *y* to continue the loop. Display some additional text on the screen during the input process using PRINT statements in addition to the INPUT statements. Improve the output by incorporating PRINT USING statements for printing the numeric data. Add a room charge to the tuition, based on whether the student lives in a single or double dorm room. Add an INPUT statement to allow the user to enter the type of room for a student. The user should enter either SINGLE, DOUBLE, or NONE for this variable. Using a nested IF, place a value of $400 in a room-charge variable when the student has a single room, $350 when the student has a double room, and 0 when the type of room is NONE. Display the room charge in a column following the column that displays the tuition. Use the program to process the following students:

Name	Resident	Hours Enrolled	Tuition Per Hours
RUTH STAMLER	YES	17	355
TOM SCHULTZ	NO	18	360
HANK COLEMAN	YES	16	345

References

Acknowledgments

22 From "A Margin for the Electronic Broker", by R.D.R. Hoffman, *Personal Computing*, Special October 1989 Issue. **48** From "A Copy Writer's Journey Into the Age of PCs", by Marlene C. Piturro, *Personal Computing*, Special October 1989 Issue. **75** From "How Steve Jobs Linked Up with IBM", by Brenton R. Schlender, *Fortune*, October 9, 1989. **105** From "The Ultimate Interface", by Scott Leibs, *InformationWeek*, June 25, 1990. **128** From "Multimedia Gets Down to Business", by Rachel Parker, *InfoWorld*, August 14, 1989. **157** From "Quaker Oats Builds Decision-Support System to Gain Marketing Edge", by George Briggs, *MIS Week*, June 18, 1990, Vol. 11, No. 25. **185** From "The Software Prototype", *.EXE*, Vol. 4, No. 4, September 1989. **199** From "Managing the Data Base Environment", James Martin, Prentice-Hall, 1983. Adapted by permission of Prentice-Hall, Inc., Englewood Cliffs, New Jersey. **210** From "United Technologies Puts Insurance Costs On-line", by Michael Puttre, *MIS Week*, April 30, 1990. **234** From "A Master Programmer: Charles Simonyi", by Susan Lammers, *Programmers at Work*, 1986. **262** From "A Different Orientation", by John Sloat and Will McClatchy, *InformationWeek*, February 12, 1990. **290** "A Computer Jock's $550-Million Jackpot", by Bro Uttal, *Fortune*, January 5, 1987. **316** From *InfoWorld*, January 23, 1989, p. 58. **317** From *Macworld*, September 1989, p. 184-185. **318** From "Programs Help Corporate Writers in Matter of Style", by Kathleen Doler, *PC Week*, April 19, 1988. **346** From *Macworld*, November 1989, p. 184. **347** From "Where 1-2-3 Makes Deals in a Hurry", by Chris Brown, *Lotus Magazine*, June 1989. **376** From *Infoworld*, January 30, 1989, p. 49. **378** From "Smile — You're on Corporate Camera", by Meghan O'Leary, *PC Week*, March 29, 1988. **404** From "The Package Puzzle: Work-Processor or Page-Layout Software?", by Dale Lewallen, *PC Week*, Supplement: Desktop Publishing, August 21, 1989. **431** From "Companies Improved with Remote Software" by Julie Webber, *InfoWorld*, January 18, 1988. **453** From "Software Firms Sing the Praises of Integration", by Marilyn Stoll, *PC Week*, April 26, 1988. **494** From "High Tech Nomad", by Steven K. Roberts, *Popular Computing*, August 1984. **506** From "Telemetic Society: A Challenge for Tomorrow, James Martin, © 1981, pp. 200-201. Reprinted by permission of Prentice-Hall, Inc., Englewood Cliffs, N.J. **520** From "Judgement Day: Robert Morris Jr. Is Sentenced to Three Years' Probation and a $10,000 Fine," by Scott Liebs, *InformationWeek*, May 7, 1990.

Photo Credits

5L Courtesy of Xerox Corporation **5TR** Courtesy of Compaq Computer Corporation **5BR** Courtesy of Apple Computer, Inc. **7TL,BL** Courtesy of IBM **7TR** Courtesy of Hewlett-Packard Company **7BR** Courtesy of Motorola Corporation **11TL, TC, TR, ML, BR** Courtesy of IBM **11MC** Courtesy of Data General Corporation **11MR** Courtesy of Houston Instruments **11BL** Courtesy of Maxell Corporation of America **12TL** Courtesy of NASA **12TL** Courtesy of the New York Stock Exchange **12BL** Courtesy of GTE Corporation **12BR** Courtesy of IBM **13** Courtesy of Hewlett-Packard Company **32** Courtesy of Federal Express Corporation. All rights reserved. **35** Courtesy of IBM **36L** "Smokers #4", John Stamos/Courtesy of ACM SIGGRAPH **36R** "The Magic Revealed", Herbert Paston/Courtesy of ACM SIGGRAPH **37** Courtesy of Hewlett-Packard Company **38** Courtesy of Prodigy Services **66** Courtesy of IBM **67** Courtesy of AST Corporation **69** Courtesy of INTEL Corporation **72TL** Courtesy of Hewlett-Packard Company **72TR** Courtesy of Cray Research Inc. **72BL** Courtesy of Digital Equipment Corporation **72BR** Courtesy of UNISYS Corporation **81** Courtesy of NCR Corporation **85** Courtesy of IBM **86** Courtesy of Apple Computer Inc. **88TL** Courtesy of Caere Corporation **88TR** Courtesy of Radio Shack, A Division of Tandy Corporation **88BL,BR** Courtesy of NCR Corporation **89** Courtesy of Hewlett-Packard Company **93** Mark Alsop **94T** Courtesy of Apple Computer, Inc. **94BL** Courtesy of Microsoft Corporation **94BR** Courtesy of IBM **95** Courtesy of Toshiba American Information Systems **96** Courtesy of Toshiba American Information Systems **102** Courtesy of Hewlett-Packard Company **103** Courtesy of Houston Instruments **115T** Courtesy of UNISYS Corporation **115ML** Courtesy of Toshiba American Information Systems **115MR** Courtesy of IBM **115B** Courtesy of Seagate Technology **117L** Courtesy of IBM **117R** Courtesy Hewlett-Packard Company **121** Courtesy of Iomega Corporation **122L** Courtesy of IBM **122R** Courtesy of NeXT Computer **126T** Courtesy of Xerox Corporation **126B** Courtesy of IBM **127** Courtesy of UNISYS Corporation **182** Courtesy of IBM **270L** Courtesy of Hewlett-Packard Company **270R** Courtesy of Compaq Computer Corporation **271** Courtesy Digital Corporation **272** Courtesy of IBM **273** Courtesy of Apple Computer Inc. **274TL** Courtesy of IBM **274TR** Courtesy of Compaq Computer Corporation **274B** Courtesy of Tandon Corporation **277** Courtesy of Apple Computer Inc. **278** Courtesy of IBM **394TL** Courtesy of Polaroid Corporation **394TR,BL** Courtesy of Computer Associates **394BR** Courtesy of Software Publishing **401T** Courtesy Aldus Corporation **401B** Courtesy of IBM **411** Gus Schonefeld/Berg & Associates **414** Courtesy of Hayes Microcomputer Products, Inc. **429** Milt and Joan Mann/Cameramann International, Ltd. **438** Courtesy of Lotus Development Corporation **439** Milt and Joan Mann/Cameramann International, Ltd. **441** Courtesy of Polytron Corporation **462** Courtesy of Lotus Development Corporation **465** Courtesy of Apple Computer Inc. **467** Courtesy of Seagate Technology **475** Courtesy of IBM **477L,R** Copyright © 1987 Sharp Electronics Corporation **478** Courtesy of NEC America, Inc. **484T** Courtesy of General Motors **484B** Courtesy of CADAM Inc. **487** William Strode/Hillstrom stock photo **488** Courtesy Intellisys **491** Courtesy of CompuServe **492** Courtesy of Prodigy Services **501TL** Courtesy of IBM **501TR** Courtesy of Hewlett-Packard Company **501BL** Courtesy of General Motors **501BR** Courtesy of Apple Computer Inc. **502** Ed Kashi **504** Courtesy Westinghouse Furniture Systems **528** Courtesy of General Motors **529TL** Courtesy of IBM **529TR,BR** Courtesy of IBM **529BL** Courtesy of Hewlett-Packard Company **A-10** Courtesy of IBM **A-11** Courtesy of AT & T Bell Laboratories **A-13** Courtesy of IBM **A-16TL** Courtesy of INTEL Corporation **A-16C** Courtesy of INTEL Corporation **A-16B** Courtesy of Chemical Bank **A-17TL** Courtesy of Apple Computer, Inc. **A-17TR** Courtesy of INTEL Corporation **A-17RC** Compaq Computer Corporation **A-17BR** Courtesy Toshiba America, Inc. **A-17BL** Radio Shack, a division of TANDY Corporation **A-20T** Courtesy of IBM **A-20ML** Courtesy of CompuScan, Inc. **A-20MR** Courtesy of Microsoft Corporation **A-20BL** Courtesy of NeXT Computer **A-20BR** Courtesy of Apple Computer Inc. **B-15** Courtesy of Data General Corporation **B-17** Courtesy of Tandem Computers

Glossary

Absolute cell address: Cell address used in a spreadsheet formula which is marked to prevent it from being changed when the formula is copied.

Acceptance test: Tests that check on key performance factors.

Access time: Amount of time it takes from the point of requesting data until the data are retrieved.

Accounting: Financial transactions involved with business activities.

Ada: Programming language designed to facilitate development of embedded computer systems.

Adjustment: An electronic spreadsheet feature in which cell addresses in formulas are adjusted during a copy command.

Algorithm: A series of steps when taken will accomplish the specific task of a module.

Alphanumeric: Information presented in the form of letters, digits, and special characters.

Analog signals: Type of continuous wave pattern.

Application generators: Prototyping tool that covers the total range of systems development activities.

Application software: Programs that have been written, usually by computing professionals, to perform specific user-oriented tasks.

Arithmetic-logic unit (ALU): Unit that contains the electronic circuits that actually perform the data processing operations.

Arithmetic operations: Operations such as addition, subtraction, multiplication, and division.

Arrow keys: Special keys on a computer keyboard used to move the cursor up, down, left, and right.

Artificial test data: Data developed to ensure that each path of the program is exercised and later to see how the program handles unusual conditions.

Ascending sort: Sort that goes from lowest to highest.

ASCII: Abbreviation for American Standard Code for Information Interchange. A standard binary code for representing data and/or program instructions.

Assembler: Software that translates assembly programs into machine language instructions.

Assembly languages: Computer languages that replace the binary digits of machine language with abbreviations to indicate processing operations.

Asychronous (async) mode: Means of transmitting data one character at a time.

Audit log: File where data on all operations performed by users of the database are chronologically recorded.

Authorization rules: Specifically state who is allowed to do what with various data records.

Automatic recalculation: A feature of electronic spreadsheets in which formulas within the spreadsheet are recalculated automatically when values in the spreadsheet are changed.

Background task: The task that is not currently interacting with the user.

Backup: Duplicate set of computer-readable data or equipment that is used only when the original data or equipment are damaged, lost, or destroyed.

Bar code: Numbers and letters encoded by different combinations of bar widths and different widths of space between bars.

Bar graph: Type of graph used to show how data differ across one or more category.

BASIC: Beginner's All-Purpose Symbolic Instruction Code. Interactive programming language that is easy to learn and use.

Batch-oriented operating system: Operating system that facilitates the running of a series of programs, one after another.

Batch processing: The processing of transactions as a group.

Bernoulli box: Technology which offers the removability and convenience of floppy diskettes but with the much greater storage capacities typical of hard disks.

Bit: Smallest piece of data.

Bit density: Measurement of storage capacity in terms of the number of bits per inch.

Block: A group of characters or a group of statements in a program.

Block move: The process of moving a block within a document.

Booting: Process of loading the operating system into primary memory from diskette or hard disk.

Buses: Electronic highways inside a computer used to send signals between functional units.

Business computing: The use of computers and information systems to handle or support business activities.

Bus network topology: Network pattern formed when each hardware device is connected to a common cable.

Buying: The determination of which goods are needed and from which suppliers they should be purchased.

Byte: Combination of bits that may be used to represent a character.

Cable TV (CATV): Type of cable used in local area networks which is broadband and can accommodate data, voice, images, and video.

Call: The passing of program execution from the main program to a subprogram.

Cathode-ray tube (CRT): Terminal screen using cathode-ray tube technology to display a visual image.

CDROM: Version of optical disks used with microcomputers.

Central processing unit (CPU): Computer hardware that interprets and executes program instructions. It consists of the control unit and the arithmetic-logic unit.

Centralized MIS architecture: MIS architecture in which all computing resources are at one site.

Character-addressable display: Type of monitor in which only blocks of pixels can be addressed or manipulated.

Characters: Letters, numbers, and special symbols.

Character formation: Printer feature that refers to whether characters are fully-formed, dot-matrix, or image.

Character transfer: Printer feature that refers to how ink is transferred to the paper.

C language: Programming language for use in building systems software.

Coaxial cable: Transmission cable often used in a local area network.

COBOL (Common Business-Oriented Language): Business-oriented programming language.

Code of ethics: Guide for everyday conduct of computer and business professionals.

Color monitor: Monitor that uses a triad to red, green, and blue phosphor dots to display various colors, RGB monitors use three electronic guns-one for each color.

Command dialogue style: User-interface mode whereby users direct information system activities through special instructions or commands.

Command-line interface: Operating system interface in which instructions to the computer must be typed and entered for processing.

Communication software: Software that electronically links a personal computer to another computer system.

Compiler: Program that translates program language statements into object code. Each language has a different compiler.

Computer: A set of electromechanical and electronic devices designed to process information signals.

Computer-aided design (CAD): The use of computer graphics terminals to aid designers in product design.

Computer-aided engineering (CAE): Use of a computer in testing engineering designs.

Computer-aided instruction (CAI): Training method in which a program is developed that instructs users through an interactive dialogue.

Computer-aided manufacturing (CAM): The use of a computer to control the factory machines used in manufacturing products.

Computer-aided software engineering (CASE): Automation of the software development process.

Computer-assisted instruction (CAI): Interaction between computer and student whereby the computer serves as the instructor.

Computer-based learning (CBL): Instruction that simulates or models actual situations.

Computer bulletin board: Software systems that allow users from across the country to exchange announcements, comments, computer programs, and other information electronically.

Computer crime: Generic term for the illegal acts that involve the computer.

Computer generations. Eras in time representing particular stages in the development of computer technology.

Computer hardware: The physical devices that can be used to enter, process, store and retrieve, and deliver data and information.

Computer information system: A computer system that serves a practical use in a business.

CIS computing: The development of computer information systems in which the user role is assumed by the CIS professional.

Computer-integrated manufacturing (CIM): The integration of CAD/CAM/ CAE, robotics, factory information systems, and telecommunication lines.

Computer literacy: An understanding of what computers are, how computers work, and what computers do.

Computer operators: Responsible for the operation of the large computer system for a particular work shift.

Computer output microform (COM): Technique in which a microphotographic copy of information is recorded on a microform such as a microfilm reel or a microfiche card.

Computer or CIS professionals: Individuals who have the technical understanding of computer systems and knowledge of business functions.

Computer-readable form: Form with data that can be captured quickly and accurately.

Computer science education programs: College education programs located in the science school that teach skills needed by systems support and database programmers.

Computer security: Safeguards taken to protect a computer system and data from unauthorized access or damage.

Computer-specific: Operating system that is tailored to the specific hardware characteristics of a particular computer.

Computer system: Composed of computer hardware and software.

Computing literacy: Ability to use the computer as a tool to enrich personal and professional life.

Concurrent operations: At a given point in time, the use of one computer resource by one program while another program uses a different resource.

Consultant: Generic term for professionals who work in the information center.

Control panel: Area of an electronic spreadsheet where the user interacts with the spreadsheet program.

Control structure: A method for controlling the order of execution of the programming statements within a program described as a block.

Control unit: Unit that contains the electronic circuits that direct and coordinate the Processing activities.

Correct Program: Completely and accurately performs the information processing activities stated in the program specification.

CPU: *See* Central processing unit.

CPU utilization: Percentage of time that the CPU is actually working.

Creator role: Involves those people who develop computer-based information systems.

Criterion: A comparison of values in records of a database that is used as the basis for a selection of records.

CRT: *See* Cathode ray tube.

Current cell pointer: Cursor indicating a user's position in an electronic spreadsheet.

Cursor: Word processing symbol that shows where the next entered character will appear.

Cylinder method: A method of organizing data on a multi-platter disk by grouping data in the same track on all the platters into a cylinder.

Data: Letters and/or digits that are used singularly or in combination to represent events or facts.

Database: Integrated collection of data items that can be retrieved in any combination necessary to produce needed information.

Database Administrator (DBA): Person that acts as the keeper of the database.

Database management system (DBMS): Software for creating and managing a database that divides the accessing of data into logical and physical concerns.

Data communication: Movement of data from one device to another.

Data currentness: The degree to which stored data represent a business's current activities.

Data dictionary: Complete description of the characteristics of a database.

Data encryption: Provides security during the transmission of data by scrambling the data.

Data entry design: Refers to the manner in which data are initially entered into the information system.

Data file: Organized set of related data items.

Data flow diagram: A graphic view of the flow of data between processes, data files, and external organizations.

Data labels: Identify values in computer graphics.

Data organization: The way in which data are arranged.

Data packet: The means of sending data in a telecommunication network. Start and stop information, origin and destination information, and error check bits are added to the encoded data.

Data redundancy: Abundance of files that contain many of the same data items.

Debugging: The overall process of finding errors in a program and correcting them.

Decimal field: Classification of numeric data that allows decimal places in the data.

Decision support system: System that allows managers to produce management reports in an ad hoc fashion.

Decision support system generators: Software packages used to develop decision support systems.

Dedicated charting programs: Programs that are designed to do only charts and graphs.

De facto standard: Standard informally accepted by vendors, generally because it has come to dominate a market segment of the business.

Demand reports: Reports that are distributed only when requested by a manager.

Demodulation: Action performed by a modem in which data signals are converted from analog to digital form.

Descending sort: Arranges records from largest to smallest.

Desktop organizers: Integrated software that allows a business professional to juggle several small tasks simultaneously with a large task.

Desktop publishing: Involves the combination of graphics into text to create professional-quality publications using a microcomputer, laser printer, and page-layout software.

Dialogues: Interactive "conversations" between an information system and a user.

Digital scanner: Device used to capture digital images of paper documents.

Digital signals: Discrete pattern of impulses that is generated by on/off or high/low electrical signals to represent 1s and 0s.

Direct access: Method in which data can be assessed directly.

Direct conversion: An immediate switch from an old system to the new system.

Disaster recovery plan: Covers the actions to be taken by specific personnel to resume running critical applications and restore all data processing applications.

Disk cartridge: Single-platter removable disk.

Diskette: A small, flexible mylar plastic disk coated with magnetic oxide. Diskettes are available in a variety of physical sizes, all of which are designed to be removable.

Disk pack: Multiplatter hard disk, which can be loaded onto, and later removed from, a disk drive.

Distributed MIS architecture: System in which multiple computer systems, connected in a computer network, are located throughout a firm.

Documentation: Permanent description of the work performed during a systems development project.

Dot-addressable display: Display in which each individual pixel is addressable.

Dot-matrix printer: Printer that uses rows and columns of small dots to form characters on the paper.

Download: Transfer of data from a larger computer to a smaller computer.

Drawing program: Software that lets a user create graphics using elements such as lines, boxes, circles, and curves.

Dumping: Means of moving all files, intact, and from one location to another.

Easy-to-use language: A programming language whose syntax is easy to learn and use.

EBCDIC: Abbreviation for Extended Binary Coded Decimal Interchange Code, which is a popular code for representing data in a computer.

Edit checking: Process in which the computer can be used to test the accuracy of the data being entered.

Editor: A program used to create and edit files that are not associated with any particular software product.

EDP auditor: Professionally trained individual capable of verifying the accuracy of information processed by a computer system such as financial records and reports.

Electronic banking: Financial transactions you perform by computer from the convenience of your home or office.

Electronic data processing (EDP) auditing: Prevention, detection, and correction of deliberate and accidental loss to computer systems, programs, and data.

Electronic mail: Process of sending messages electronically from one microcomputer to another.

Electronic office systems: Collections of machines that utilize computer technology to enable workers to streamline traditional office work by communicating various forms of information electronically.

Electronic spreadsheet: Software that divides a microcomputer screen into a table of rows and columns.

Embedded command: Message to the word processor telling it how to format a document.

Embedded computer: A special-purpose computer that is part of a larger device like a microwave oven or an automobile.

End-user computing: The development of computer information systems in which both the user and creator roles are assumed by the business professional.

End-user software: Prebuilt programs, called packages, which are available to help information workers design their own computer-based applications.

End-user tools: Software packages used in end-user computing.

Erasable optical disks: Use a combination of light energy and magnetic fields to store data and to provide read/ write and erase capabilities.

Ergonomics: The science of adapting machines and the work environment to people.

Evaluation matrix: Used to select the best of several vendor alternatives.

Event interrupts: Method used to execute several programs by processing a program until an input/output request is made.

Exception reports: Management reports which identify abnormal situations.

Expansion slots; Built-in brackets for holding additional circuit boards.

Expert systems: Computer-based software that offers solutions to particular types of problems comparable to what a human expert would give.

Expert system shells: Specialized software packages for developing expert systems. This shell includes a user interface and inference methods. Various knowledge bases can be developed for use by the shell.

Exploding pie chart: Graphs in which one or more slices of the pie can be pulled away from the rest to emphasize the data represented by that slice.

External modem: Attached to an input/ output port on the microcomputer via a cable.

Facsimile (FAX) machines: Machine used to transmit nonelectronic documents electronically.

Family of computers: Series of computer models based on the same computer architecture.

Field: Group of related characters treated as a unit.

File: Collection of similar type records.

File manager: Database programs that deal with only single tables at a time.

File transfer: The electronic transfer of data files from one computer to another across the phone lines.

Financial modeling system: End-user tool that can perform financial analyses that are far too complicated for an electronic spreadsheet.

Firmware: Permanently coded instructions within ROM.

First-come-first-serve scheme: Scheduling scheme in which a list is kept of the order in which jobs arrive. Jobs are processed in that sequence.

Fixed media: Media that cannot be touched or removed by the user.

Fixed partitions: Allocation method in which primary memory for use by user programs is divided into sections of a fixed memory size,

Flat-panel displays: Create a screen image by illuminating discrete dots to display alphanumeric data, graphics, and video images.

Flowcharts: Visually portray a program's processing flow by showing the operations to be performed, the order in which they are performed, and the conditions that affect their order.

Foreground/background processing: Means of running both batch and interactive jobs to meet their very different response time requirements.

Foreground task: The task that the user is currently operating in.

Formatting commands: Commands used to change the appearance of a document or spreadsheet.

Formula: Combination of cell addresses and numbers joined together by mathematical symbols.

FORTRAN (FORmula TRANslation): Program language often used for writing scientific and engineering programs.

Fourth generation language: Very high level programming language.

Full-duplex channel: Communication channel that allows transmission in both directions simultaneously.

Functions: Instructions used to specify an action for the computer system to take.

Function keys: Keys used to provide means of executing common tasks in one step.

General ledger: Computer system used to produce financial statements.

General-purpose programming language: Provide a set of processing capabilities that can be applied to most information processing problems.

General-purpose computer systems: Flexible computer systems that can be programmed in different ways to perform significantly different tasks.

Global commands: Spreadsheet commands which affect all the cells in the spreadsheet.

Global search and replace: Word processor feature which allows a user to find all occurrences of a piece of text in a document and have them replaced with another piece of text.

Graphical interface: Operating system interface in which the user interacts with the computer using a mouse to manipulate icons and pull-down menus.

Graphics: Pictures or graphs depicting information.

Hackers: People who see the computer as a combination of tool, toy, and lover.

Half-duplex channel: Communications path that can transmit data in two directions, but only one way at a time.

Hard copy: Permanent form of the information being displayed on a computer screen.

Hard disks: Rigid aluminum platters coated with a magnetic oxide: they come in different physical sizes and have significantly different storage capacities.

Hardware: Devices that physically enter, process, store, and retrieve, and that deliver data and information.

Hardware control: Commands that operate directly on primary memory.

Hierarchical database model: Structure of database in which the relationship among records is always "one-to-many."

High-level programming language: Have more powerful commands that are "problem-oriented" rather than "machine-oriented" and that translate into multiple machine language instructions.

Host computer: Large computer to which other smaller computers or terminals are connected.

Human expert: A person who has indepth knowledge of a specific problem area or domain.

Human-computer interface: Refers to the means of interaction between a human being and the machine.

Icons: Graphic symbols of functions that can be performed on the computer.

Index: A sorted list of all values that appear in a field of the database.

Indexed file organization: File organization in which records are organized logically in sequence by key. There is an index to specify the correspondence between the key value and the disk location of the record.

Inference method: A reasoning strategy for solving problems using the knowledge base.

Information: Meaning given to a set of data.

Information center: Facility with end-user tools that is staffed by end-user computing specialists who first train and then support business users.

Information center trainer: Person who trains end-users in the use of specific hardware and software package.

Information privacy: Protection from potential abuse of information.

Information processing cycle: Stages of input, processing, storage, retrieval, and output.

Information reporting systems: Use raw data to produce summary reports that are useful to managers.

Information society: Society in which the collection, processing, and distribution of information is the primary source of wealth and work.

Information utility: Supplies information to homes or offices in return for a fee.

Information workers: Professional employees that collect and process data which is combined with their experience, knowledge, judgment, and creativity to create and communicate information.

Input design: Specifications for data entry formats and procedures.

Input/Output port: Connectors on the back of a microcomputer to which peripheral devices can be attached.

Insert mode: Word processing feature in which new characters are inserted in front of the cursor and old characters are pushed to the right.

Integer field: Numeric field that does not allow decimal places in the data.

Integrated software: Software that combines a number of personal computing tools into one software package.

Interactive-oriented operating system: Operating system designed to handle conversational or immediate responses with a programmer or end-user.

Interactive processing: A computer user has direct connection to the computer system and is able to carry on a dialogue with the executing software.

Interactive programming language: A programming language allowing a programmer to interactively create and debug a program.

Interface devices: Devices used to coordinate the flow of electrical signals between two hardware units.

Internal modem: Modem that plugs directly into expansion slots inside the computer.

Interpreter: A systems software program that translates a high-level programming language one statement at a time and then immediately executes each statement.

Inventory: Supply of goods held in reserve.

Iterative control structure: A block of statements that are repeated a number of times depending on certain conditions.

Job control language (JCL): Language developed to allow the user to communicate with the operating system.

Join: A command used to combine tables in a database during retrieval.

Justification: Word processing feature which causes the first and last characters of each line to align.

Keyboard macros: Cells on a spreadsheet that contain commands to be executed.

Key entry: The entry of data or functions into the computer system by means of pressing keys of a keypad or keyboard.

Keyless entry: The entry of data into the computer system or the selection of functions by means other than keying.

Knowledge base: A collection of rules an expert might know about a particular class of problems. These are generally expressed in the IF.. THEN rule format.

Knowledge engineer: A person skilled in developing expert systems.

Language Translator: Part of the operating system responsible for translating the commands written in a programming language into machine code.

Legend: Key to a graph that indicates the type of bar or line associated with each series of data being graphed.

Linkage editor: System software module for linking or combining application program and other object modules.

Line graph: Type of graph similar to bar graphs, except that data are graphed as a group of points joined by a line.

Load module: Software module that is in a form (object code) that be processed.

Local area networks (LAN): Communication network for transferring data between microcomputers and shared peripherals within a building complex, such as an office or factory.

Local computer: Microcomputer.

Logic errors: Those actions that cause a program to give incorrect results.

Logical operations: Complex relational operations.

Logic errors: Errors that indicate that the program design is incorrect.

Look and feel software: Packages that have been developed by vendors to look and feel similar to the most popular software.

Machine language: Lowest level of computer language. It consists of binary digits.

Macro: Set of commands that are often used together.

Magnetic Ink Character Recognition (MICR): Means of character recognition often used by the banking industry as a standard method for processing checks.

Magnetic strip: Strip used on bank cards as a means of account identification.

Mail-merge programs: Software that links documents with address lists to "mass mail" letters.

Maintainable program: Can be easily changed at some future time by the same or another programmer.

Maintenance technicians: Do routine maintenance and minor repairs.

Management information system (MIS): Information system that provides managers with information enabling them to make better decisions and improve job performance.

Management reports: Information presented to managers to aid them in planning and controlling work activities.

Manufacturing: The making and assembling of parts into finished goods.

Many-to-many data model: Data model in which each higher level or parent record can be associated with one or more lower level child records. Further, each child record can be associated with one or more parent records.

Mark-sense reader: Optical reader programmed to read data from specific locations on a mark-sense document.

Materials requirement planning (MRP): Use of a computer to schedule purchases and deliveries.

Memory fragmentation: Locations in primary memory that are available for use by programs that go unused.

Memory management: Allocation of memory.

Menu dialogue style: Design in which the information system lists a series of actions and the user selects an action from this list.

Microprocessor: Miniature integrated circuits on a silicon chip.

Middle manager: Manager responsible for ensuring that business objectives are achieved.

MIS: *See* Management information system.

MIS architecture: Location where data entry, processing, storage, and retrieval and release actually occur.

Modem: A communication device that enables computer equipment to send and receive digital data over the analog telephone network, by using modulation and demodulation techniques.

Modula-2: Programming language that builds on Pascal.

Modulation: Conversion of digital signals to analog signals by a modem in order to communicate data over a telephone line.

Module: A single purpose function shown as a box on a structure chart.

Monochrome monitor: Monitor that can display only one color, such as green or amber, on a black background.

Motherboard: Large circuit board containing a collection of chips. This would generally include the CPU chip and RAM and ROM chips.

Mouse: Hand-sized box that is used to control the cursor and select functions by moving it around the desk top.

Multiprogramming: Two or more programs can be run concurrently by the computer system.

Multitasking: Operating system that allows for concurrent tasks.

Network database model: database structure that allows for "many-to-many" relationships among parent and child records.

Nonprocedural commands: Commands that allow the programmer to describe what processing is to occur.

Nonvolatile storage: Storage that retains the stored information if the power supply is turned off.

Normalization: Process used to group data into tables in which the data within a table are closely related.

Number system: Method of representing numbers.

Numeric keypad: Set of keys similar to those on a calculator.

Object code: Machine code version of a program.

Office: Business location which most clerical and administrative activities are handled.

One-on-one training: Training method in which the training can be personalized to each user.

One-to-many: Data model in which each parent record can be related to more than one child, but each child can be related to only one parent.

Operating manager: Manager responsible for seeing that a business's day-to-day activities are performed.

Operating systems software: A set of programs that have been written by computer specialists to ease the task of working with the computer system itself.

Optical character recognition (OCR): Device that uses light images to read data.

Optical disk system: Uses light energy rather than magnetic fields to store data.

Optical recognition (OR) machine: Devices that use light images to read data.

Output design: Specifications for the format and procedures used in presenting data or information.

Page: Means for dividing programs or memory into fixed-length blocks.

Painting programs: Software that lets a user create graphics using a screen that is made up of thousands of dots that can be made either black or white.

Parallel conversion: Conversion process in which the old and the new information systems are run together for a period of time.

Parallel port: Peripheral port that sends data along eight paths simultaneously.

Parity bit: Extra bit that makes the sum of bits representing a character either even or odd. It is a means of checking for errors that may have occurred during data transmission.

Pascal: Programming language developed for teaching structured programming concepts.

Periodic reports: Information system reports that occur at regular intervals such as weekly, monthly, or quarterly.

Peripherals: Devices added to the computer and used for input, storage, or the display of information.

Personal computer support center: Facility with end-user tools that is directed toward microcomputer end users.

Pie charts: Type of graph used to compare values across one category as percentages of the whole.

Pilot study: A controlled test of the new information system.

Pixels: Picture elements on a visual display device that can be illuminated.

Plotter: Output device that is specialized to produce graphics.

Precedence: Order in which computers perform mathematical operations when a calculation is made.

Presentation manager: Software that lets a user display a group of previously create graphic images on the screen in any order desired.

Prespecified reports: Carefully designed and programmed reports that can be produced very efficiently.

Primary key: Field that uniquely identifies a record.

Primary memory: Device that provides temporary storage for all the data and information being processed as well as the software directing the processing.

Primary sort order: The initial or main sort order in a multiple sort.

Printer: Device, similar to a typewriter, that uses papers as its output medium.

Priority scheme: Allows different programs to be selected for execution, based on need.

Program coding: The translation of the overall program design and specific module logic into a particular programming language.

Program data dependence: Situation in which subsequent changes in either the programs or data will have a significant effect on the other.

Program data independence: Situation in which changes in either programs or data can be made without significantly affecting the other.

Program design: Activity for producing a clear, logical flow for a program's information processing operations.

Program development: Developing correct step-by-step procedures which will enable a computer system to produce the desired results and be easily modified to accommodate future changes in specifications.

Program development process: Involves the three distinct activities of program design, coding, and testing.

Program documentation: Statements in a program used to guide the reader of the program listing by explaining the purpose of a particular block of code.

Program maintenance: Modification of programs to reflect change in business needs.

Program testing: An activity undertaken to ensure that the program meets the program specifications and performs as expected.

Programmer: Individual who designs and develops computer programs.

Project definition: A statement of the overall purpose of the project and the scope of this activity.

Project development team: A group of CIS professionals and users who are charged with analyzing, designing, acquiring, and implementing an information system.

Project management tools: Used to measure how the project is going.

Projection: Retrieval of a subset of the fields in a database.

Prompts: Simple instructions displayed on the computer screen that tell the user what to do next.

Protection: Method of controlling programs and data stored in the computer once a user is using the computer.

Protocol: Set of rules and procedures used for transmitting data between two hardware devices in a network.

Prototyping: Building a "quick and dirty" information system and then continuing to refine the design.

Pseudocode: English-like key words used to describe the logic of a program using control structures.

Purchasing: Term for business function of buying and selling.

Query-By-Example: A method of retrieving information from a database by building an example of the records to be retrieved.

Query facility: Facility of the DBMS that can be used to create database structures, perform data manipulation, and ensure data integrity.

QWERTY keyboard: Keyboard arrangement of a standard typewriter.

RAM (Random Access Memory): Memory in which instructions or data can be written into or data read out of and transferred to the CPU for processing as needed.

Random access memory. *See* RAM.

Range: Continuous group of cells on a spreadsheet.

Range commands: Spreadsheet commands that affect only the cells in a specified range.

Raster scan: Process of moving a beam of electrons across the screen to create brighter (on) or darker (off) points.

Read only memory. *See* ROM.

Read/write memory: *See* RAM (Random Access Memory).

Record: A collection of all related data items.

Relational database model: Database structure that shows relationships among records by grouping tables together as needed.

Relational database program: Microcomputer database program that allows data to be related and processed across more than one table.

Relative file organization: File organization by which records are arranged by using the key value to directly calculate the relative location on disk.

Reliability: Percentage of time that the computer is up relative to the time it is scheduled to be up and running.

Removable media: Media such as magnetic tape and diskettes that allow the user to physically swap one set of data for another.

Report generator: Very high level programming language used by an end-user to prepare management reports.

Representative test data: Data normally expected to be processed when the program is operational.

Request for a Proposal (RFP): Formal statement that describes selection criteria.

Resolution: Quality of the image on a video monitor.

Resource management: The allocation and scheduling of computer resources.

Response time: The length of time between a user's request and the computer's response.

Ring network topology: Pattern used to connect hardware devices in which each terminal is connected to two others.

Robots: Mechanical devices that can be programmed to perform useful tasks.

ROM (Read Only Memory): Memory that can be used only to read data or written instructions that have been permanently loaded onto the chip.

Root directory: The top or main directory in a directory tree structure.

Row: A collection data in the columns of a database table similar to a record in a file.

RPG (Report Program Generator): Programming language developed to duplicate punched card processing procedures.

Ruler: A line in the document on which margins and tabs can be specified.

Run-time errors: Occur when the program processes data causing the program to crash.

Sales: Business activity that covers the selling and delivering of goods.

Scaling: Graphics program feature that allows the user to manually set the points on each axis of a graph.

Schema: Logical description of the organization of a complete database.

Scrolling: Process of moving the window of a spreadsheet to reveal additional cells not currently shown on the screen.

Search and replace: Function with which the user specifies a string to search for and a string to replace it once it is located,

Secondary sort order: Second sort order in a multiple sort used to order records with the same value in the field used as a basis for the primary sort.

Secondary storage devices: Used to provide permanent storage of data and information that is kept in computer-readable form.

Sector method: Method of organizing data on the disk in which the disk surface is logically divided into sectors.

Security: External threats from unauthorized users.

Selection: Database retrieval operation in which a subset of the rows of a table are displayed using a criterion.

Selection control structure: A block of statements that are executed differently depending on whether a decision statement is true or false.

Self-documenting: Term used to describe the use of meaningful variable names and labels to make a program easier to understand.

Semiconductor: Device that can be made to serve as a conductor or as an insulator, depending on conditions.

Senior manager: Manager responsible for making sure that business will, over time, be successful.

Sequence control structure: A series of statements in a block which are executed in order from top to bottom.

Sequential access: Method in which data must be accessed in sequential order.

Sequential file organization: File organization by which records are sequenced by primary key values.

Serial port: Peripheral port used to send data sequentially along a single path.

Simplex channel: Can transmit data in only one direction.

Single-entry, single-exit processing flow: Processing flow in which a single path exists into and from program modules.

Site license: Process in which a firm pays a flat fee and can then copy software and run it on a large number of microcomputers.

Soft copy: Temporary copy of the output, such as a visual display or computer voice output.

Softlifting: When individuals illegally make copies of software for their own use.

Software: A correction of instructions written in a computing language, called a program, used to direct the computer to accomplish specific tasks.

Software integrator: Software package that integrates multiple independent application packages.

Software piracy: Unauthorized copying of software programs for distribution for profit or for associates' use.

Sophisticated control structures: Programming language characteristic of facilitating a programmer's use of the structured programming techniques.

Sophisticated data structures: Programming language characteristic facilitating a programmer's use of many data structures.

Sort: To arrange data or information on the basis of a predetermined sequence.

Sort/merge: Method of combining selected data items from several files to produce needed information.

Sort utility: Prewritten instructions stored in machine language on disk that can be linked to a program to sort data.

Source code: The initial version of a program written in a high-level language.

Source data automation: A form of keyless data entry that captures the data from its original source.

Source documents: Source of data.

Source module: Initial form in which a program is entered into a computer system, prior to being translated into machine language or object code.

Spaghetti code: Program written where the flow of the program goes any which way and individual blocks have multiple entry and exit points.

Special-purpose programming language: Programming language that focuses on a particular type of information processing problem.

Speech synthesizers: Devices enabling computers to transform electronic data into voice output.

Spelling checker: Software that makes use of online dictionaries to locate and correct spelling errors.

Spooling: Concept that allows input or output to be placed onto disk to await processing, thus freeing the CPU to process other programs.

Spreadsheet charting program: A charting program that is incorporated into spreadsheet programs.

Standardized: Programming language characteristic in which versions of the language written for different computer systems are the same.

Star network topology: Pattern used in which each device is connected to a central unit.

Start bit: A bit at the beginning of the group that signals the start of a group.

Start-up file: Special file containing instructions for the operating system to perform when the computer is booted.

Statistical analysis software: Specialized software designed to allow the user to set up a complex statistical analysis with a few non-procedural commands.

Steering committee: Gives overall guidance to the project development team concerning the business purpose of the project, assists in providing resources such as personnel and financial support, and ensures that actions are taken to keep the project proceeding on schedule and within budget.

Step-wise refinement: The breaking down of a general statement into lower level specifics.

Stop bit: Signals the end of a group.

Structure charts: Used to visually show the overall organization of a program design as a hierarchical structure of program modules.

Structured programming: The use of particular design methods when developing solutions to programming problems.

Structured Query Language (SQL): Standard relational database query language developed by the American National Standards Institute.

Structured walkthrough: Design technique that help a systems analysts to recognize errors in the software designs.

Subdirectory: A directory located below the root directory used to break the files on a disk into logical groupings.

Subprograms: Single purpose functions corresponding to modules on a structure chart, that have been written into a programming language.

Subschema: Logical description of a particular subset of the total data that is useful in answering a user's specific question.

Subsystem: Part of a system that can itself be modeled as a system.

Supervisor: Set of programs that handle the overall management of the jobs and tasks that are being conducted by the computer system.

Swapping: Process in which a program that is waiting on a disk to be processed can be exchanged with a program in Primary memory.

Synchronous (sync) mode: Means of data transmission used when large volumes of data are to be sent.

Syntax: Set of rules, similar to rules of grammar, that the programmer follows in coding the commands.

Syntax errors: Violations of the grammatical rules of the programming language that generally cause the program not to run.

Systems acquisition: Stage at which hardware and software are purchased and the programs are written.

Systems analysis: Analysis of a business activity to assess the feasibility of a proposed information system and to determine how it should function.

Systems analyst: Individual who defines the information processing needs of a business, department, or person.

Systems design: Specification of appropriate hardware and software components required to implement an information system.

Systems designer: Individual who devises a hardware/software design to meet the information processing needs of a business, a department, or a person.

Systems development: Consists of analyzing, designing, acquiring, and implementing a computer information system.

Systems implementation: Stage at which the information system is introduced into the business.

Systems life cycle: The complete set of activities that produce, enhance, and later phase out a computer information system.

Systems maintenance: Covers the efforts taken to ensure that an existing information system continues to meet business needs or is phased out.

Systems software: Programs written to act as an interface between the application programmer and the computer itself.

Table: Group of related information in the relational data model similar to a file.

Telecommunication(s): Transmission of data over long distances.

Telecommunication analyst: Designs and evaluates telecommunication or local-area networks.

Telecommunication programmer: Writes or modifies data-communication software.

Telecommuting: Using terminals and telephone lines to allow user working at home to communicate with a computer at the office.

Teleconferencing: Using electronic equipment to communicate, thereby eliminating the need to travel to a conference.

Template: A partially completed spreadsheet which can be completed by an inexperienced user to create an application.

Terminal: Generic term for various input and output devices.

Terminal emulation: Use of software by a microcomputer to take on the characteristics of a certain type of terminal.

Test data: Used to determine where the program behaves according to program specifications and where it doesn't.

Thesaurus program: Advanced word processing feature that permit the electronic lookup of synonyms and antonyms of words in a document.

Throughput: Number of programs completed per time period.

Time-sharing: Use of a computer system by many people at the same time.

Time slicing: Procedure in which the CPU processes one set of program instructions for several milliseconds and then switches to the next program as a means of sharing the computer.

Topology: Patterns formed when hardware devices are connected to form a network.

Tracks: Series of invisible concentric circles on a disk that are used to record data.

Transaction: Single business event.

Transaction processing: The processing of a single event immediately after it is recorded.

Transaction processing systems: Systems used to record, process, and manage data about everyday business activities.

Transistor: Electronic components that function as semiconductors.

Trojan horse: Type of computer virus that appears to be a useful utility, but performs unexpected operations when run.

Twisted pair wiring: Telephone cable in which two individual copper wires are twisted to give it physical strength.

Typeover mode: Word processing feature in which characters can be replaced by typing new characters over them.

Upload: Transferring data from a smaller to a larger computer.

User role: Involves people that use computer-based information systems to aid them in carrying out their jobs.

User's view: Subset of the information from a database needed by a user performing a particular task. Same a subschema.

Utilities: Programs that have been written to accomplish common tasks such as sorting records or copying disk files to magnetic tape for backup.

Variable size partitions/ regions: Allocation method in which partition size is defined depending on the needs of the program.

Very high-level language: Consists of powerful commands that allow a programmer to concentrate on what the processing tasks are to be performed, rather than on how the tasks are to be performed.

Videotext: Service that combines graphics and text.

Virtual machine: An environment in which the computer simulated different operating system environment in memory using guest operating systems.

Virtual memory: Concept in which only relevant instructions need to be in primary memory at any one time, while the remainder of the program is stored on disk, available on demand.

Virus: A program that attaches itself to other programs and instructs the computer to perform malicious operations.

Voice mail: Digitized form of the spoken method that is stored on a disk and can be delivered at a later time to one or more phones.

Voice recognition: System in winch the spoken word is converted into electrical signal patterns that are compared to a voice template.

Volatile storage: Any type of storage that loses its data if the power supply is turned off.

Von Neumann architecture: When digital computers use program instructions stored in primary memory to sequence computer actions.

Winchester technology: Technology that seals the hard disk inside a hermetic (airtight) container.

Window: Function that allows the computer's disk display screen to be divided into separate areas or boxes.

Word wrap: Feature of word processors which moves words to the next line automatically as the user reaches the right margin.

Workshops: Training method that uses a classroom setting for training groups of users.

X-axis: A line across the bottom of a graph displaying the values for one of the variables being graphed.

XY graph: Type of graph used to show the relationship between two variables.

Y-axis: A line along the left side of a graph displaying values representing the data being graphed.

Index